ACCOUNTANT'S HANDBOOK OF FORMULAS AND TABLES

Third Edition

Lawrence Lipkin, M.B.A., C.P.A.

Irwin K. Feinstein, Ph.D.

Professor of Mathematics, Statistics
and Computer Science, Emeritus
The University of Illinois at Chicago

Lucile Derrick, Ph.D.

Professor of Information and Decision Sciences, Emeritus
The University of Illinois at Chicago

PRENTICE HALL
Englewood Cliffs, New Jersey 07632

Prentice-Hall International (UK) Limited, *London*
Prentice-Hall of Australia Pty. Limited, *Sydney*
Prentice-Hall Canada, Inc., *Toronto*
Prentice-Hall Hispanoamericana, S.A., *Mexico*
Prentice-Hall of India Private Limited, *New Delhi*
Prentice-Hall of Japan, Inc., *Tokyo*
Simon & Schuster Asia Pte. Ltd., *Singapore*
Editora Prentice-Hall do Brasil, Ltda., *Rio de Janeiro*

10 9 8 7 6 5 4 3 2 1

Printed in the United States of America

Library of Congress Cataloging-in-Publication Data

Lipkin, Lawrence.
Accountant's handbook of formulas and tables / Lawrence Lipkin, Irwin K. Feinstein, Lucile Derrick. — 3rd ed.
p. cm.
Includes index.
ISBN 0-13-002957-2
1. Business mathematics—Tables. 2. Interest—Tables.
I. Feinstein, Irwin K. II. Derrick, Lucile. III. Title.
HF5699.L56 1988
657'.076—dc19 88–19837
CIP

ISBN 0-13-002957-2

PRENTICE HALL
BUSINESS & PROFESSIONAL DIVISION
A division of Simon & Schuster
Englewood Cliffs, New Jersey 07632

Acknowledgments

The authors wish to express their gratitude to the following authors and publishers for granting permission to use the various tables included in this book.

Professors Simpson, Pirenian, and Crenshaw, and their publishers, Prentice-Hall, Inc., for Tables VI and VII, which were taken from their book *Mathematics of Finance*, 3rd ed.

Professors Croxton and Cowden and their publishers, Prentice-Hall, Inc., for Tables VIII, IX, X, XI, and XII, taken from their book *Applied General Statistics*, 2nd ed.

The Interstate Commerce Commission for Table XIV, taken from their publication "105,000 Random Decimal Digits."

Dr. Norman Hamilton, Associate Director, and Mr. George Yanus, Data Processing Analyst, both of the Computer Center, University of Illinois at Chicago, who programmed Tables I, II, III, IV, and V for the second edition.

The Authors' Comments on the Third Edition

The rapid advancement of computer technology in recent years has had a profound influence on accountants, auditors, and statisticians. No longer can individuals associated with numerical measurement state that they cannot do a particular mathematical computation because it is too complex or too time consuming. On the other hand, the same technological revolution has created some difficult problems for the accountant and auditor engaged in the verification of data.

For many years in the past, computer printouts of complex mathematical problems have been accepted by users as being correct simply because a computer was assumed to be perfect. For the most part, this may have been true in the past when the users of computers were highly skilled professionals. Today, with the advent of the microcomputer, many less-skilled persons are programming and operating these computers. Thus, the auditor must verify more carefully than ever before the results obtained from this medium.

The formulas and tables included in this edition will aid the accountant, auditor, statistician, and other users of computer information in two ways:

1. These materials will aid in programming a particular computer application.
2. These materials will aid in test checking and verifying computer printouts of complex mathematical problems.

The third edition has been expanded in the following areas:

1. New tables have been added to use with non-normal distributions:
   "t" Table
   Sample number, 99% confidence, discovery sampling
   Sample number, 95% confidence, discovery sampling
2. Two new formulas to deal with the present value of an annuity have been added to Chapter 3.

3. A new Chapter 4 has been inserted, which presents a convenient method for computing the number of days between dates and elapsed full months between dates. Chapter 4 also deals with the basic approaches to factorials, permutations, combinations, expected values, probability, and arithmetic and geometric progressions. In addition, applications illustrating uses of these basic formulas are included as well.
4. The materials on universe averages and dispersion have been completely rewritten and are presented in Chapter 5.
5. In order to meet the present needs of the auditor, in particular, the materials on sampling, in Chapter 6, have been expanded to include the relationships of samples to the universe, with a description of the various types of samples and their uses. Also included in Chapter 6 are additional examples illustrating the computations of sample values and the estimation of universe values from them. Also added are new materials on sampling from non-normal universes, a condition that the auditor frequently must handle. In order to facilitate sample selection, two new tables of necessary sample sizes under differing conditions have been included for use when dealing with exploratory or discovery sampling.
6. A problem involving regression and discriminant analysis has been inserted in Chapter 7 to illustrate the use of E. Altman's "Z score."
7. Chapter 12, Finance, has been expanded to include venture capital investment, capital asset pricing, and adjustable rate mortgages.
8. A new chapter, Chapter 13, has been added to deal with capitalized values.
9. The recent trend toward personal involvement in planning for pension and retirement coverage is the focus of the new Chapter 19, Pensions.
10. There are other problems that the auditor faces but which do not fall logically into other chapters. These have been added to Chapter 20, Other Applications.

How to Use This Handbook

This new edition of formulas and tables has been compiled for the professional accountant as a reference work. No person is expected to commit to memory all of the many mathematical formulas learned in professional preparation. However, the accountant is supposed to know where to look for a particular formula should the need arise. The first place to look now will be in this handbook.

Since this handbook is intended especially for the professional accountant, it is assumed that the reader has a sufficient knowledge of accounting theory, mathematics, and statistics to be able to recognize a problem and know how to use the proper formula in order to solve it. This handbook is not a substitute for a textbook but is merely a tool to aid in problem solving. To aid you in solving problems and recalling theories, every formula is illustrated with a simple problem and its solution. In many cases the pending problem can be solved by merely substituting the actual data in the formula and performing the indicated operations.

If you are seeking a specific formula, you need only turn to the index to see if the formula is included in the handbook. When you locate the page on which the formula is presented, a rapid glance over the formula and the illustrative problem will be sufficient to ascertain if the formula is the one you are seeking. The illustrated problem and solution that is considerably like your problem will be of great help in reaching an answer.

The next step is to familiarize yourself with the symbols used in the formula, for many writers use different symbols to represent the same item. After you are familiar with the symbols, you can then assemble all of the facts for your particular problem. You must be sure that your facts are complete, for in many cases a missing fact makes it impossible to use the given formula.

Next, substitute your data in the formula and perform the indicated computations, preferably on a calculator. It is wise, however, to validate the answer by checking it through the use of some other technique. This is particularly important if the computations were performed manually.

EXAMPLE

Here is an example of one of the problems that the professional accountant encounters. It illustrates how this new handbook can help solve this problem. Suppose that you are examining the books of a client and wish to verify independently the computation of depreciation by the sum of the years' digit method. The following facts have been ascertained: Asset cost $100,000, 20-year estimated life, salvage value $10,000. What should be the correct amount of depreciation for the fourteenth year?

Referring to the index under the heading Depreciation balance, you find the formula for "Depreciation by the Sum of the Years' Digit Method," on pages 143–144.

The formula is

$$D_j = \frac{Y - D}{\Sigma Y} \times (C - S)$$

where

D_j = Depreciation for particular year
Y = Estimated life of asset
D = Number of years of prior depreciation
ΣY = Sum of the years
C = Cost of asset
S = Salvage value of asset

The facts show the following:

D_{14} = Unknown
$Y = 20$
$D = 13$
$\Sigma Y_{20} = 210$ (Table VIII, Column 1)
$C = \$100{,}000$
$S = \$10{,}000$

Substituting in formula:

$$D_{14} = \frac{20 - 13}{210} \times (\$100{,}000 - \$10{,}000)$$
$$= \frac{7}{210} \times \$90{,}000$$
$$= \$3000$$

Sometimes a problem arises that you do not know how to solve. If this is the case, it is suggested that you browse through the various formulas and problems under the topic concerned. You may find a problem illustrated that is exactly like the one that you are working on, or a similar problem may give you further insight into your particular problem. Suppose, for example, that you want to prepare supplemental financial statements that reflect the changing price level. A review of Chapter 14, "Price Level Adjustments," will give you an excellent insight into the problems you will probably encounter. Further, it will suggest the data that will have to be obtained in order to prepare the supplementary financial statements.

USE OF TABLES

It is hardly necessary to explain the use and convenience of the various mathematical tables included in this new edition. An example of the use of the tables was demonstrated in the illustration regarding "Depreciation by the Sum of the Years' Digits." What is the sum of 1 through 20? Merely by referring to the appropriate table, you can determine that the sum of 1 through 20 is 210. Most of the tables included in this handbook are most likely quite familiar to you. The convenience of having them in one place will prove to be very worthwhile.

USE OF FORMULAS

You may wonder, why bother to express accounting methods in formula form? A mathematician uses a formula because it expresses very simply relationships that would take many pages of complex prose to explain. After spending some time reading the explanation of relationships when language is used, the reader may still not comprehend the explanation due to inept writing. However, formulas with the use of mathematical notations make the expression of complex relationships easy to comprehend. If one understands the formula, there is little left to do but substitute the known facts in the formula and perform the indicated operations, mostly simple arithmetic.

USE OF SYMBOLS

Symbols are the mathematicians' shorthand. Everyone knows that x represents an unknown quantity. Descartes, when designing his mathematical system, decided that the latter part of the alphabet, $\cdots x, y, z$, should denote variable quantities and the

beginning part of the alphabet, $a, b, c \cdots$, should denote constant quan
However, in working with applied mathematics, in many cases the symbols used are
first letter in the word describing the term. Thus, interest is usually expressed by th
symbol "i"; time by the symbol "t."

In the formulas pertaining to accounting, this method of notation has been followed; for instance, "inventory" is usually denoted by the symbol I, "accounts receivable" by the symbol A/R, "accounts payable" by the symbol A/P. Subscripts further identify the term, for instance:

A/R_1 = Accounts *r*eceivable at the beginning of the period

A/R_2 = Accounts *r*eceivable at the end of the period

---

[1] Herbert Western Turnbull, "The Great Mathematician," James R. Newman. *The World Book of Mathematics,* Vol. I, Simon and Schuster, New York, 1950, p. 131.

Contents

1

Simple Interest

SIMPLE INTEREST

Formula:

$$I = P \times R \times T$$

where

I = Interest
P = Principal
R = Rate of interest
T = Time

Example:

What is the amount of simple interest on $1500 for 90 days at 6% interest?

Solution:

$$I = P \times R \times T$$

$$I = 1500 \times .06 \times \frac{90}{360*}$$

$$I = \$22.50$$

***Note:** In most business transactions, 360 days is used for the number of days in the year. This type of computation is called ordinary simple interest. Exact simple interest is computed by using 365 days in the year.

TIME REQUIRED TO YIELD AN AMOUNT OF INTEREST

Formula:

$$T = \frac{I}{P \times R}$$

where

T = Time
I = Interest
P = Principal
R = Rate of interest

Example:

What is the amount of time in years required for \$5000 to yield \$575 at simple interest at 5%?

Solution:

$$T = \frac{I}{P \times R}$$

$$T = \frac{575}{5000 \times .05}$$

$$T = \frac{575}{250}$$

$$T = 2.3 \text{ years}$$

PRINCIPAL OF A LOAN TO OBTAIN SPECIFIC AMOUNT OF CASH

Formula:

$$P = \frac{C}{1 - RT}$$

where

P = Principal of loan
C = Cash required
R = Rate of discount
T = Time

Example:

If \$3000 net cash is required and the bank will discount a note for 90 days at 6%, what is the principal amount of the note?

Solution:

$$P = \frac{C}{1 - RT}$$

$$P = \frac{3000}{1 - \left(.06 \times \dfrac{90}{360}\right)}$$

$$P = \frac{3000}{1 - .015}$$

$$P = \frac{3000}{.985}$$

$$P = \$3045.69$$

PRESENT VALUE OF AN INTEREST-BEARING NOTE (simple interest)

Formulas:

$$(1)\ Mv = P(1 + R_1T_1)$$

$$(2)\ Pv = \frac{Mv}{1 + R_2T_2}$$

where

Mv = Maturity value
P = Principal of note
R_1 = Rate of interest on note
T_1 = Time on note
Pv = Present value of note
R_2 = Rate of interest on maturity value (current rate of interest)
T_2 = Time remaining on note at valuation dates

Example:

Mr. Jones died on September 14, 19X1. In his estate was a note for \$1500 from Mr. Smith, dated August 15, 19X1, with interest at 6% for

60 days. What valuation should the executor place on the note, if money cost 7% on September 14, 19X1?

Solution:

$$(1)\quad Mv = P(1 + R_1T_1)$$

$$Mv = 1500\left(1 + .06 \times \frac{60}{360}\right)$$

$$Mv = 1500 + 15$$

$$Mv = \$1515.00$$

$$(2)\quad Pv = \frac{Mv}{1 + R_2T_2}$$

$$Pv = \frac{1515.00}{1 + \left(.07 \times \frac{30}{360}\right)}$$

$$Pv = \frac{1515.00}{1.00583}$$

$$Pv = 1506.22$$

PROCEEDS FROM DISCOUNTING AN INTEREST-BEARING NOTE

Formulas:

$$(1)\quad Mv = P(1 + R_1T_1)$$

$$(2)\quad C = Mv(1 - R_2T_2)$$

where

Mv = Maturity value of note
P = Principal of note
R_1 = Rate of interest on note
T_1 = Time on note
C = Cash proceeds
R_2 = Rate of discount by purchaser of note
T_2 = Time remaining on note at discount date

Example:

Able received from Baker a $1500, 6%, 60-day note dated August 15, 19X1. On September 14, 19X1, Able discounted the note at his bank at 7%. How much cash did Able receive from the bank?

Solution:

$$(1)\quad Mv = P(1 + R_1T_1)$$

$$Mv = \$1500\left(1 + .06 \times \frac{60}{360}\right)$$

$$Mv = \$1515.00$$

$$(2)\quad C = Mv(1 - R_2T_2)$$

$$C = 1515.00\left(1 - .07 \times \frac{30}{360}\right)$$

$$C = 1515.00 - 8.84$$

$$C = 1506.16$$

RATE OF INTEREST CORRESPONDING TO DISCOUNT RATE

Formula:

$$i = \frac{D}{1 - TD}$$

where

i = Interest rate
D = Discount rate
T = Time

Example:

A bank discounts a 90-day note at 6%. What is the actual rate of interest that the borrower must pay?

Solution:

$$i = \frac{D}{1 - TD}$$

$$i = \frac{.06}{1 - \left(\frac{90}{360} \times .06\right)}$$

$$i = \frac{.06}{1 - .015}$$

$$i = \frac{.06}{.985}$$

$$i = .0609 \quad \text{or} \quad 6.09\%$$

EFFECTIVE RATE OF INTEREST ON ACCOUNTS RECEIVABLE FINANCING

Formula:

$$i = \frac{R \times 360}{a}$$

where

i = Effective rate of interest
R = Daily rate of interest charged on the face amount of the invoice financed
a = The percent of the face amount of the invoice

Example:

The XYZ Commercial Finance Company will loan 75% of the face amount of an invoice which is assigned to it. The charge for the financing is 1/30th of 1% per day computed on the face amount of the invoice. What is the effective rate of interest?

Solution:

$$i = \frac{R \times 360}{a}$$

$$i = \frac{\frac{.01}{30} \times 360}{.75}$$

$$i = \frac{.12}{.75}$$

$$i = .16 \quad \text{or} \quad 16\%$$

RATE OF INTEREST EQUIVALENT TO CASH DISCOUNT RATE

Formula:

$$i = D \times \frac{360}{N - n}$$

where

i = Effective rate of interest

D = Percent of cash discount
N = Number of days credit
n = Number of days in discount period

Example:

If the terms of an invoice are $2/10$, $N/30$, what is the effective rate of interest equivalent to the cash discount?

Solution:

$$i = D \times \frac{360}{N - n}$$

$$i = .02 \times \frac{360}{30 - 10}$$

$$i = .02 \times \frac{360}{20}$$

$$i = .36 \text{ or } 36\%$$

2

Compound Interest

COMPOUND AMOUNT—USING INTEREST TABLES

Formula:

$$S = P(1 + R)^n$$

where

S = Compound amount or future value
P = Principal
R = Interest rate per period
n = Number of conversion periods

Example:

How much will \$3000 accumulate over 20 years at 6% per year if interest is compounded semiannually?

Solution:

$$\begin{aligned} S &= P(1 + R)^n \\ &= 3000(1 + .03)^{40} = 3000(1.03)^{40} \\ &= 3000(3.26203779) \qquad \text{(Table I)} \\ &= \$9786.11 \end{aligned}$$

Example:

What will be the compound amount at the end of 4 years if \$500 is invested at 8% compounded quarterly?

Solution:

$$S = P(1 + R)^n$$
$$= 500(1 + .02)^{16} = 500(1.02)^{16} \quad \text{(Table I)}$$
$$= 500(1.37278571) = \$686.39$$

COMPOUND AMOUNT—USING LOGARITHMS

Formula:

$$S = P(1 + R)^n$$

Example:

What will be the compound amount at the end of 4 years if \$500 is invested at 8% compounded quarterly? (This is the same example as in the previous section.)

Solution:

$$S = 500(1.02)^{16}$$

Solving for $(1.02)^{16}$ by means of logarithms

$$\log 1.02 = .0086002 \quad \text{(Table VII)}$$
$$16 \log 1.02 = .1376032$$
$$\text{Therefore } (1.02)^{16} = 1.3728 \quad \text{(Table VI)}$$
$$S = 500(1.3728) = \$686.40$$

Example:

How much will \$3000 accumulate over 20 years at 6% interest if interest is compounded semiannually?

Solution:

$$S = P(1 + R)^n$$
$$= 3000(1 + .03)^{40} = 3000(1.03)^{40}$$

Solving for $(1.03)^{40}$ by means of logarithms

$$\log 1.03 = .0128372$$
$$40 \log 1.03 = .513488 \quad \text{(Table VII)}$$
$$\text{Therefore } (1.03)^{40} = 3.2621 \quad \text{(Table VI)}$$
$$S = 3000(3.2621) = \$9786.30$$

PRESENT VALUE—INTEREST-BEARING NOTE (from tables)

Formulas:

1. $S = P(1 + R)^n$
2. $P_v = S(1 + R)^{-n}$

where

S = Future value
P = Principal
R = Rate of interest per period
P_v = Present value
n = Number of conversion periods

Example:

The XYZ Company acquired a \$300,000 10-year note with interest at 6% compounded semiannually. The company decides to sell the note immediately for a yield of 7%. How much money should the XYZ Company receive for the note?

Solution:

$$\begin{aligned} S &= P(1 + R)^n \\ &= 300{,}000(1 + .03)^{20} = 300{,}000(1.03)^{20} \\ &= 300{,}000(1.806111) \qquad \text{(Table I)} \\ &= 541{,}833.30 \\ P_v &= S(1 + R)^{-n} \\ &= 541{,}833.30(1 + .07)^{-10} = 541{,}833.30(1.07)^{-10} \\ &= 541{,}833.30(.508349) \qquad \text{(Table II)} \\ P_v &= \$275{,}440.42 \end{aligned}$$

PRESENT VALUE—NONINTEREST-BEARING NOTE (using logarithms)

Formula:

$P_v = S(1 + R)^{-n}$
(See symbols given previously.)

Example:

A boy is to receive \$10,000 10 years from now to help finance his college education. How much should be invested for him if money is worth 8% compounded semiannually?

Solution:

$$P_v = S(1 + R)^{-n}$$
$$= 10{,}000(1 + .04)^{-20} = 10{,}000(1.04)^{-20}$$

Using logarithms, we compute $(1.04)^{-20}$.

$$\log 1.04 = .0170333 \qquad \text{(Table VII)}$$
$$-20 \log 1.04 = -.340666 \text{ or } 9.659334 - 10$$
$$(1.04)^{-20} = .456387$$
$$P_v = 10{,}000(.456387)$$
$$P_v = \$4563.87$$

PRESENT VALUE—NONINTEREST-BEARING NOTE (from tables)

Formula:

$$P_v = S(1 + R)^{-n}$$

where

P_v = Present value
S = Future value
R = Rate of interest per period
n = Number of conversion periods

Example:

What is the present value of a \$5000 10-year noninterest-bearing note if money is worth 5%?

Solution:

$$P_v = S(1 + R)^{-n}$$
$$= 5000(1 + .05)^{-10}$$
$$= 5000(1.05)^{-10}$$

$$(1.05)^{-10} = .613913 \qquad \text{(Table II)}$$

$$P_v = 5000(.613913)$$

$$= \$3069.57$$

DETERMINING THE TIME (USING LOGARITHMS) GIVEN *S, P,* AND *R*

Formula:

$$n = \frac{\log S - \log P}{\log (1 + R)}$$

where

n = Number of conversion periods
S = Future value or compound amount
R = Rate of interest per period
P = Principal

Example:

How long will it take \$50,000 to amount to \$80,000 if the principal is invested at 8%?

Solution:

$S = 80{,}000$
$P = 50{,}000$
$R = 8\%$
$\log 80{,}000 = 4.903090$
$\log 50{,}000 = 4.698970$
$\log 1.08 = 0.033424$

$$n = \frac{\log S - \log P}{\log (1 + R)}$$

$$= \frac{4.903090 - 4.698970}{.033424}$$

$$= \frac{.204120}{.033424}$$

= 6.11 or 6 years, one month approximately

DETERMINING THE TIME (USING TABLES) GIVEN *S, P* AND *R*

Formula:

$$(1 + R)^n = \frac{S}{P}$$

Example:

How long will it take $1000 to amount to $1373 if the principal is invested at 8% compounded quarterly?

Solution:

$$n \log 1.02 = \log 1.373$$

$$n = \frac{\log 1.373}{\log 1.02}$$

$$= \frac{.137671}{.008600} = 16.00789 \text{ conversion periods}$$

NOMINAL RATE WHEN PRESENT VALUE AND FUTURE VALUE ARE KNOWN (USING LOGARITHMS) CASE A

Formula (1):

$$R = \left(\frac{S}{P}\right)^{1/n} - 1$$

where

R = Rate of interest per period
S = Future amount
P = Principal
n = Number of conversion periods

Example:

If $480 is invested for a period of 4 years after which time $544 is returned, what is the annual rate?

$$R = \left(\frac{S}{P}\right)^{1/n} - 1$$

$$R = \left(\frac{544}{480}\right)^{1/4} - 1 = \left(\frac{17}{15}\right)^{1/4} - 1$$

Let us compute $\left(\frac{17}{15}\right)^{1/4}$ by means of logarithms.

$$\log\left(\frac{17}{15}\right)^{1/4} = \frac{1}{4}(\log 17 - \log 15)$$

$$= \frac{1}{4}(1.230449 - 1.176091)$$

$$= \frac{1}{4}(.054358) = .0135895$$

Thus $\left(\frac{17}{15}\right)^{1/4} = 1.03179$ (Table VI)

$$R = 1.03179 - 1$$

$$R = .03179 \text{ or } 3.18\%$$

NOMINAL RATE WHEN PRESENT VALUE AND FUTURE AMOUNT ARE KNOWN (USING LOGARITHMS) CASE B

Formula (2):

$$(1 + R)^n = \frac{S}{P}$$

where

R = Rate of interest per period (nominal rate)
n = Number of conversion periods
S = Future amount
P = Principal

Example:

What is the required nominal rate of interest compounded annually for \$10,000 to double itself in 20 years?

Solution:

$$(1 + R)^{20} = \frac{20{,}000}{10{,}000}$$

$$20 \log (1 + R) = \log 2$$

$$\log(1 + R) = \frac{1}{20}\log 2$$

$$= .05\,(.301030) = .0150515 \qquad \text{(Table VI)}$$

$$1 + R = 1.035265$$

$$R = .03527 \text{ or } 3.53\%$$

RATE OF SIMPLE INTEREST EQUIVALENT TO A COMPOUND INTEREST RATE ON A PER YEAR BASIS USING INTEREST TABLES

Formula:

$$R_e = (1 + R)^m - 1$$

where

R_e = Effective rate of interest
R = Nominal rate of interest per period
m = Number of conversion periods per year

Example:

What is the effective rate of interest on a note for 1 year that bears interest at the rate of 7% compounded semiannually?

Solution:

$$R_e = (1 + R)^m - 1$$

$$= (1 + .035)^2 - 1 = (1.035)^2 - 1$$

$$(1.035)^2 = 1.071225 \qquad \text{(Table I)}$$

$$R_e = 1.071225 - 1 = .071225 \text{ or } 7.12\%$$

RATE OF COMPOUND INTEREST ON A PER YEAR BASIS EQUIVALENT TO A SIMPLE INTEREST RATE USING LOGARITHMS

Formula:

$$R = m[(1 + R_e)^{\frac{1}{m}} - 1]$$

where

R = Nominal rate of interest

R_e = Effective rate of interest
m = Number of conversion periods per year

Example:

What is the nominal rate of interest on a note for 1 year compounded quarterly that will give an effective rate of 6%?

Solution:

$$R = 4[(1 + .06)^{1/4} - 1]$$
$$= 4[(1.06)^{1/4} - 1]$$

Using logarithms, we compute $(1.06)^{1/4}$

$$\log 1.06 = .0253059 \qquad \text{(Table VII)}$$
$$\frac{1}{4}\log 1.06 = .006327$$
$$(1.06)^{1/4} = 1.01467 \qquad \text{(Table VI)}$$
$$R = 4(1.01467) - 4$$
$$= 4.05868 - 4 = .05868$$
$$R = 5.87\%$$

FORCE OF INTEREST (NOMINAL RATE KNOWN)

Formula:

$$i = e^R - 1$$

where

i = Force of interest
$e \doteq 2.7182818$
R = Nominal rate of interest

Example:

What is the force of interest if the nominal rate of 6% is continuously compounded?

Solution:

$$i = e^R - 1$$
$$i = 2.7182818^{.06} - 1$$

$$i = 1.061837 - 1$$
$$i = .061837$$

FORCE OF INTEREST (EFFECTIVE RATE KNOWN)

Formula:

$$i = \frac{\log (1 + R_e)}{\log e}$$

where

i = Force of interest
R_e = Effective rate of interest
$e \doteqdot 2.7182818$

Example:

If the effective rate of interest R_e is 6%, what is the force of interest?

Solution:

$$i = \frac{\log (1 + R_e)}{\log e} = \frac{0.0253059}{0.4342945}$$
$$i = .058269$$

3

Annuities

AMOUNT OF AN ORDINARY ANNUITY (tables)

Formula:

$$S = R \cdot s_{\overline{n}|i} = R \cdot \frac{(1 + i)^n - 1}{i}$$

where

S = Amount after a fixed number of years
R = Amount per period
i = Interest rate per period
n = Number of conversion periods
$s_{\overline{n}|i}$ = Amount of annuity of \$1 per period for n interest periods at a rate of i per period

Example:

Find the amount of an annuity in which a payment of \$1000 is made at the end of each year for 10 years if money is worth 4% compounded annually.

Solution:

$$S = R \cdot s_{\overline{n}|i} = R \cdot \frac{(1 + i)^n - 1}{i}$$

$$= \$1000\, s_{\overline{10}|.04} = 1000 \cdot \frac{(1 + .04)^{10} - 1}{.04}$$

$$= 1000\ (12.00610712) \qquad \text{(Table III)}$$
$$= \$12{,}006.11$$

AMOUNT OF AN ORDINARY ANNUITY (logarithms)

Formula:

$$S = R \cdot s_{\overline{n|}i} = R \cdot \frac{(1 + i)^n - 1}{i}$$

(See above for symbols.)

Example:

Mr. Able deposited \$300 in a bank on January 1 and July 1 of each year to provide for his son's education. Interest is 7% compounded semiannually. At the end of 10 years, what will be the balance in the account?

Solution:

$$S = \$300\ s_{\overline{20|}.035} = 300 \cdot \frac{(1 + .035)^{20} - 1}{.035}$$

We will use logarithms to compute $(1.035)^{20}$ and then do the rest of the example with ordinary arithmetic.

$$\text{Let} \qquad N = (1.035)^{20}$$
$$\text{Then } \log N = 20 \log 1.035$$
$$= 20(.0149403) = 0.298806 \qquad \text{(Table VII)}$$
$$N = 1.9898$$
$$S = 300\frac{1.9898 - 1}{.035}$$
$$= 300\frac{.9898}{.035}$$
$$= 300(28.280) = \$8484.00$$

PRESENT VALUE OF AN ORDINARY ANNUITY (tables)

Formula:

$$A = R \cdot a_{\overline{n|}i} = R \cdot \frac{1 - (1 + i)^{-n}}{i}$$

where

A = Present value
R = Amount per period
i = Interest rate per period
n = Number of conversion periods
$a_{\overline{n}|i}$ = Present value of annuity of \$1 per period for n periods at a rate of i per period

Example:

Find the present value of an annuity in which a payment of \$2000 is made at the end of each year for 10 years if money is worth 4% compounded annually?

Solution:

$$A = \$2000\, a_{\overline{10}|.04} = \$2000 \frac{1 - (1 + .04)^{-10}}{.04}$$

$$= \$2000\,(8.11089578) \qquad \text{(Table IV)}$$

$$= \$16{,}221.79$$

PRESENT VALUE OF AN ORDINARY ANNUITY (logarithms)

Formula:

$$A = R \cdot a_{\overline{n}|i} = R \cdot \frac{1 - (1 + i)^{-n}}{i}$$

(See page 18 for symbols.)

Example:

Mr. C. C. Smith in his will devised to his grandson \$10,000 per year for 10 years or an equivalent amount in one lump sum payment. If money is worth 5%, how much would the grandson receive if he elected the lump sum settlement?

Solution:

$$A = \$10{,}000 \cdot a_{\overline{10}|.05} = \$10{,}000 \frac{1 - (1 + .05)^{-10}}{.05}$$

$$= \$10{,}000 \frac{1 - 1.05^{-10}}{.05}$$

We will use logarithms to compute $(1.05)^{-10}$ and then do the rest of the example with ordinary arithmetic.

$$
\begin{aligned}
\text{Let} \qquad N &= (1.05)^{-10} \\
\text{Then } \log N &= -10 \log 1.05 \\
&= -10\,(0.0211893) = -0.211893 \qquad \text{(Table VII)} \\
&= 10.000000 - 0.211893 - 10.000000 \\
&= 9.788107 - 10 \\
N &= 0.61391 \\
A &= \$10{,}000\frac{1 - 0.61391}{.05} = \$10{,}000\frac{0.38609}{.05} \\
&= \$10{,}000\,(7.7218) = \$77{,}218.00
\end{aligned}
$$

FINDING THE PERIODIC RENT OF ANNUITY (tables)

Formula:

$$R = \frac{1}{a_{\overline{n}|i}} = S \cdot \frac{i}{1 - (1 + i)^{-n}}$$

where

R = Amount per period
i = Interest rate per period
n = Number of conversion periods
S = Total amount

Example:

With money worth 10% compounded annually, what equal payments should be made at the end of each year for 20 years to pay off a mortgage on a house amounting to \$80,000, not including taxes and insurance?

Solution:

$$
\begin{aligned}
R &= S \cdot \frac{.10}{1 - (1 + .10)^{-20}} \\
&= \$80{,}000\,(.11745962) \qquad \text{(Table V)} \\
&= \$9396.77
\end{aligned}
$$

FINDING THE PERIODIC RENT OF ANNUITY (logarithms)

Formula:

$$R = \frac{1}{a_{\overline{n}|i}} = S \cdot \frac{i}{1 - (1 + i)^{-n}}$$

(See symbols at top of page 18.)

Example:

The XYZ Bank financed a mortgage of \$50,000 at 8% compounded quarterly for 20 years payable in equal quarterly installments including interest. How much is the quarterly payment?

Solution:

$$R = \$50{,}000 \frac{0.02}{1 - (1 + 0.02)^{-80}}$$

We will use logarithms to compute $(1 + .02)^{-80}$ and then do the rest by ordinary arithmetic.

Let $N = (1.02)^{-80}$

Then $\log N = -80(0.0086002)$ (Table VII)

$= -0.688016$

$= 9.311984 - 10$

$N = 0.20511$ (tabular value is .20510853) (Table VI)

$$R = \$50{,}000 \frac{0.02}{.79489}$$

$= \$50{,}000\ (.025161)$

$= \$1258.04$

FINDING THE PERIODIC RENT OF ANNUITY WHERE PAYMENT INTERVAL DOES NOT COINCIDE WITH INTEREST PERIOD

Formula:

$$R = \frac{1}{a_{\overline{n}|i}} = S \cdot \frac{i}{1 - (1 + i)^{-n}}$$

(See page 21 for symbols.)

Example:

The XYZ Bank financed a mortgage of $100,000 at 10% interest per annum for 20 years, payable in quarterly installments including interest. How much is the quarterly payment?

Solution:

Since the payment interval does not coincide with the interest period, we need to compute the equivalent rate.

$$r = (1 + i)^m - 1 = (1 + .10)^{\frac{1}{4}} - 1$$

$$\text{Let} \qquad N = (1.10)^{\frac{1}{4}}$$

$$\text{Then } \log N = \tfrac{1}{4} \log 1.10 = \tfrac{1}{4}(0.041393) \qquad \text{(Table VI)}$$

$$= 0.010349$$

$$N = 1.02412$$

$$\text{So} \qquad r = 2.412\% \text{ quarterly}$$

$$R = \$100{,}000 \cdot \frac{0.02412}{1 - (1.02412)^{-80}}$$

$$\text{Let} \qquad M = (1.02412)^{-80}$$

$$\text{Then } \log M = -80 \log 1.02412$$

$$= -80\,(0.0103424) \qquad \text{(Table VII)}$$

$$= -0.827392 = 9.172608 - 10$$

$$M = 0.14880$$

$$R = \$100{,}000 \frac{0.02412}{1 - 0.14880} = \$100{,}000 \frac{0.02412}{0.85120}$$

$$= \$100{,}000\,(0.028337) = \$2833.70$$

Note: Had the interest and payment period been annually, the problem could have easily been solved by tables. From Table V, we see that the rent would be $11,745.96 per year. This compares with the results obtained in this example: 4 × $2833.70 = $11,334.80. Thus the results obtained from quarterly payments with interest computed annually vary $411.10 from the results obtained with the interest computed for the period coinciding with the payment period.

FINDING THE TERM OF AN ANNUITY (logarithms)

Formula:

$$n = \frac{\log\left(1 + \frac{S}{R}i\right)}{\log(1 + i)}$$

where

n = Number of conversion periods
R = Rent
S = Amount of the annuity
i = Interest rate per period

Example:

The controller of the XYZ Company wishes to set up a fund to accumulate \$750,000 for future plant expansion. The controller has budgeted \$10,000 per month to be invested for this purpose. The controller has been advised that the funds could be safely invested at a rate of 8% per year. How many months will be required to accumulate the necessary funds?

Solution:

$$n = \frac{\log\left[1 + \frac{750{,}000}{10{,}000} \cdot \frac{.08}{12}\right]}{\log\left(1 + \frac{.08}{12}\right)}$$

$$= \frac{\log[1 + 75(0.0067)]}{\log\left(1 + \frac{.08}{12}\right)} = \frac{\log(1 + .50)}{\log(1 + .00667)}$$

$$= \frac{0.176091}{0.003029} \qquad \text{(Table VI)}$$

$$= 58.135$$

Five years should be adequate.

FINDING THE INTEREST RATE OF AN ANNUITY USING TABLES

Formula:

$$\frac{S}{R} = \frac{(1 + i)^n - 1}{i}$$

where

S = Amount of the annuity
R = Rent
n = Number of conversion periods
i = Interest rate per period

Example:

The XYZ Corporation desires to accumulate $450,000 by the end of 11 years for a proposed expansion program. If the company can set aside $25,000 at the end of each year, what rate of yearly interest will the fund have to earn?

Solution:

$$\frac{450{,}000}{25{,}000} = \frac{(1 + i)^{11} - 1}{i}$$

or

$$18 = \frac{(1 + i)^{11} - 1}{i}$$

From Table III, we see that $\frac{(1 + .09)^{11} - 1}{.09} = 17.56029339$ and $\frac{(1 + .095)^{11} - 1}{.095} = 18.03851828.$

We conclude that the interest rate per annum must be in excess of 9%, but less than 9.5%. Interpolation yields 9.46%.

FINDING THE INTEREST RATE OF AN ANNUITY

Formula:

$$\frac{S}{R} = \frac{(1 + i)^n - 1}{i}$$

(See top of page for symbols.)

Example:

The Able Manufacturing Company desires to accumulate \$300,000 by the end of 5 years. The company can set aside \$12,000 quarterly. What yearly rate of interest must the money earn?

Solution:

We first find the quarterly rate:

$$\frac{300{,}000}{12{,}000} = \frac{(1 + i)^{20} - 1}{i}$$

$$25 = \frac{(1 + i)^{60} - 1}{i}$$

From Table III, we see that $\frac{(1 + .0225)^{20} - 1}{.0225} = 24.91$.

The money must earn just in excess of $2\frac{1}{4}\%$ per quarter.

To find the yearly rate, r, we solve

$$\begin{aligned} r &= (1 + i)^m - 1 \\ &= (1.0225)^4 \end{aligned}$$

From Table I, we see that $1.0225^4 = 1.0930$. Thus $r = 9.3\%$. Hence the money must earn about 9.3% per annum.

QUANTITY INCREASING OR DECREASING AT A CONSTANT RATE

Formula:

$$Q_t = Q_o e^{rt}$$

where

Q_t = Quantity at time (t)
Q_o = Quantity at time (o)
$e \doteqdot 2.7182818$
r = Rate of increase or decrease
t = Time period

Example:

If 300,000 pounds of various chemicals are mixed in Department 1, immediately a catalytic reaction takes place causing the product to decrease at a constant rate of 4% per hour. The product is then sent to Department 2, where it is immediately stabilized. The product is processed for 10 hours in Department 1. How many pounds will Department 2 receive?

Solution:

$$Q_t = Q_o e^{rt}$$
$$rt = (-.04)(10) = -.4$$
$$Q_{10} = 300{,}000 \times 2.7182818^{-.4}$$
$$Q_{10} = 300{,}000 \times .67032$$
$$Q_{10} = 201{,}096 \text{ lbs.}$$

PRESENT VALUE OF AN ANNUITY
Increasing arithmetically (immediate)

Formula:

$$A = R_1 \cdot a_{\overline{n}|i} + D \cdot \frac{a_{\overline{n}|i} - nV^n}{i}$$

where

A = The present value
R_1 = The first payment
D = The dollar amount of the increase in each successive payment
n = number of payments

$$a_{\overline{n}|i} = \frac{1 - (1 + i)^{-n}}{i}$$
$$V^n = (1 + i)^{-n}$$

Example:

What is the present value of a series of five payments, the first payment being $115.00, made at the end of year 1, and each subsequent payment increases by $15.00, with interest at 6% per year?

Solution:

$$A = R_1 \cdot a_{\overline{n}|i} + D \cdot \frac{a_{\overline{n}|i} - nV^n}{i}$$

$$A = 115\, a_{\overline{5}|.06} + 15\left(\frac{a_{\overline{5}|.06} - 5V^5}{.06}\right)$$

$$A = 484.42 + 15\left(\frac{4.21236 - 3.73629}{.06}\right)$$

$$A = 484.42 + (15 \times 7.93450)$$

$$A = \$603.44$$

PRESENT VALUE OF AN ANNUITY
Increasing geometrically (immediate)

Formula:

$$A = R_1 \cdot \frac{1 - \left(\dfrac{1+k}{1+i}\right)^n}{i-k}$$

where

A = The present value
R_1 = The first payment
i = The original rate of interest
k = The constant rate of increase of interest
n = The number of payments

Example:

A contract between Smith and Wesson requires the payment of \$1000 one year hence with interest at 7.5% for 20 years. As an inflation hedge, the interest rate is to increase 5.9% with each succeeding payment. What is the present value of the contract?

Solution:

$$A = R_1 \cdot \frac{1 - \left(\dfrac{1+k}{1+i}\right)^n}{i-k}$$

$$A = 1000 \cdot \frac{1 - \left(\dfrac{1.059}{1.075}\right)^{20}}{.075 - .059}$$

$$A = 1000 \cdot \frac{1 - (.98512)^{20}}{.016} = 1000\left(\frac{1 - .74088}{.016}\right)$$

$$A = 1000\left(\frac{.25912}{.016}\right) = 1000(16.195)$$

$$A = \$16,195.00$$

4

Basic Computing

NUMBER OF DAYS BETWEEN DATES

TABLE 1
NUMBER OF DAYS IN EACH MONTH AND CUMULATED DAYS FOR YEAR

Month	No. Days	Cumulated Days
January	31	31
February	28*	59*
March	31	90*
April	30	120*
May	31	151*
June	30	181*
July	31	212*
August	31	243*
September	30	273*
October	31	304*
November	30	334*
December	31	365*

* +1 day for leap years

Formula:

$$D = C_y + (C_2 + D_2) - (C_1 + D_1)$$

where

D = Elapsed days
C_1 = Cumulative days of month prior to commencement date
C_2 = Cumulative days of terminal month prior to termination
C_y = 365 or 366 (use if time span crosses year)
D_1 = Number of days in commencement month
D_2 = Number of days in terminal month

Example:

(1) How many days have elapsed between May 17, 19X1, and November 12, 19X1, not a leap year?
(2) How many days have elapsed between June 30, 19X1, and April 15, 19X2, not a leap year?

Solution:

(1) $D = C_y + (C_2 + D_2) - (C_1 + D_1)$
$D = 0 + (304 + 12) - (120 + 17)$
$D = 179$

(2) $D = C_y + (C_2 + D_2) - (C_1 + D_1)$
$D = 365 + (90 + 15) - (151 + 30)$
$D = 289$

ELAPSED FULL MONTHS BETWEEN DATES

Formula:

$$M = 12(Y_2 - Y_1 + 1) + M_1 + M_2$$

where

M = Number of full months
Y_1 = The first full year
Y_2 = The last full year
M_1 = Number of full months in commencement year following commencement month
M_2 = Number of full months in terminal year preceding terminal month

Example:

What is the number of full months between May 17, 1940, and December 12, 1986?

Solution:

$$M = 12(Y_2 - Y_1 + 1) + M_1 + M_2$$
$$M = 12(1985 - 1941 + 1) + 7 + 11$$
$$M = 12(45) + 18$$
$$M = 558$$

ARITHMETIC SERIES

Formulas:

(1) $t_n = t_1 + (n - 1)d$

(2) $S_n = \frac{n}{2}(t_1 + t_n)$

where

t_n = Last term of the series
t_1 = First term of the series
d = Difference between a term and its succeeding term
S_n = Sum of n terms

Example:

What is the sum of a series of 12 payments starting with \$50 and decreasing by \$3 with each payment?

Solution:

(1) $t_n = t_1 + (n - 1)d$
$t_n = 50 + (12 - 1)(-3)$
$t_n = 50 - 33$
$t_n = \$17$

(2) $S_n = \frac{N}{2}(t_1 + t_n)$

$S_n = \frac{12}{2}(50 + 17)$

$S_n = \$402$

GEOMETRIC SERIES

Formulas:

(1) $t_n = t_1 r^{n-1}$

(2) $S_n = \dfrac{t_1(1 - r^n)}{1 - r}$

where

t_n = The last term of the series
t_1 = The first term of the series
r = Rate of change
n = The number of terms
S_n = The sum of the first n terms

Example:

The production of an oil well has been decreasing at a constant rate of 20% per year. The production of the well after 5 years will be insufficient to be worth recovering and the well will be abandoned. The well will produce 24,000 barrels of oil this year. How many barrels of oil will be produced in year 5? How many barrels of oil will be recovered over the next 5 years?

Solution:

(1)
$$t_n = t_1 r^{n-1}$$
$$t_n = 24{,}000 \cdot .80^{(5-1)}$$
$$t_n = 9830$$

(2)
$$S_n = \frac{t_1(1 - r^n)}{1 - r}$$
$$S_n = \frac{24{,}000\,(1 - .80^5)}{1 - .80} = \frac{24{,}000 \cdot (.17232)}{.2}$$
$$S_n = 80{,}678$$

FACTORIAL

Formula:

$$n! = n(n - 1)(n - 2) \cdots (2)(1)$$

where

n is any positive integer

Example:

(1) $5! = 5 \cdot 4 \cdot 3 \cdot 2 \cdot 1$

Solution:

(1) $5! = 120$

(2) $0! = 1$ (by definition)

(3) $\frac{5!}{0!} = \frac{120}{1} = 120$

PROBABILITY

Formula:

$$P(E) = \frac{n(E)}{n(S)}$$

where

$P(E)$ = Probability of the event's occurring
$n(E)$ = Number of total elements having characteristic E
$n(S)$ = Total number of elements in S

Example:

An inventory of report covers consists of 1000 boxes of which 600 are blue, 100 are red, 200 are white, 50 are green, and 50 are purple. Because of poor inventory management, the boxes are all mixed up. Your usual procedure is to take a box on the top of the pile. Your preference for report covers is either blue or purple. What is the probability of satisfying your preference?

Solution:

$$P(E) = \frac{n(E)}{n(S)}$$

$$P(E) = \frac{600 + 50}{1000} = \frac{650}{1000}$$

$$P(E) = .65$$

PERMUTATIONS—WITH AND WITHOUT REPLACEMENT

Formula:

$$x = N_1 \cdot N_2 \cdot N_3 \cdot \cdot \cdot N_n$$

where

x = The answer
N_1 = The first number
N_2 = The second number
N_3 = The third number
. . .
N_n = The last number

Example:

How many ways can 3 letters of the alphabet be used in a row:

1. If no letter is repeated (without replacement).
2. If letters can be repeated (with replacement).
3. If adjacent letters cannot be used (with the restriction that the first letter chosen is an *a* or a *z*).

Solution:

(1) $x = N_1 \cdot N_2 \cdot N_3$
$x = 26 \cdot 25 \cdot 24$
$x = 15{,}600$

(2) $x = N_1 \cdot N_2 \cdot N_3$
$x = 26 \cdot 26 \cdot 26$
$x = 17{,}576$

(3) $x = N_1 \cdot N_2 \cdot N_3$
$x = 26 \cdot 25 \cdot 25$
$x = 16{,}250$

PERMUTATIONS—GENERAL

Formula:

$${}_nP_r = \frac{n!}{(n - r)!}$$

where

$_nP_r$ = Number of permutations
n = Number in set
r = Number in each permutation

Example:

How many permutations can be found from 26 letters of the alphabet using 3 letters at a time, without replacement?

Solution:

$$_nP_r = \frac{n!}{(n - r)!}$$

$$_{26}P_3 = \frac{26 \cdot 25 \cdot 24 \cdot 23 \cdot 22 \cdots 1}{23 \cdot 22 \cdots 1}$$

$$= 26 \cdot 25 \cdot 24 = 15{,}600$$

COMBINATIONS

Formula:

$$_nC_r = \frac{n!}{r!\,(n - r)!}$$

where

$_nC_r$ = Number of combinations
n = Number in set
r = Number in each combination

Example:

How many different quarters (3 months each) can be made from a set of 1 year (12 months)?

Solution:

$$_nC_r = \frac{n!}{r!(n - r)!}$$

$$_{12}C_3 = \frac{12!}{3!\,(9)\,!}$$

$${}_{12}C_3 = \frac{12 \cdot 11 \cdot 10 \cdot 9 \cdot 8 \cdots 1}{3 \cdot 2 \cdot 9 \cdot 8 \cdots 1}$$

$${}_{12}C_3 = 220$$

EMPIRICAL PROBABILITY APPROXIMATION

Formula:

$$P = \frac{E_1 + E_2 + E_3 + \cdots + E_n}{n}$$

where

P = Probability
E_1 = Number of times event No. 1 occurred
E_2 = Number of times event No. 2 occurred
E_3 = Number of times event No. 3 occurred
n = Total number of events

Example:

In order to determine a sample size, the auditor is required to determine an expected error rate. He is examining cancelled checks and determines that there are five possible places an error can be made on a check:

1. The date is not correct.
2. The dollar amount is not correct.
3. The written dollar amount is not correct.
4. The payee is not correct.
5. The check is not signed or the signature is not authorized.

A tabulation of the errors from the prior year's audit, from a universe of 10,000, reveals the following:

Error Type	Number Times Occurred
Error No. 1	50
Error No. 2	70
Error No. 3	100
Error No. 4	30
Error No. 5	10

1. What is the expected error rate that a check is incorrect?
2. What error rate should be used if you are designing a sample to detect error No. 5?

Solution:

$$(1)\ P = \frac{E_1 + E_2 + E_3 + E_4 + E_5}{n}$$

$$P = \frac{50 + 70 + 100 + 30 + 10}{10{,}000} = \frac{260}{10{,}000}$$

$$P = .026$$

$$(2)\ P = \frac{E_5}{n}$$

$$P = \frac{10}{10{,}000}$$

$$P = .001$$

EXPECTED VALUE*

Formula:

$$E(x) = X_1P_1 + X_2P_2 + X_3P_3 + \cdots + X_nP_n$$

where

$E(x)$ = Expected value
X_i = The net value of the event
P_i = The probability of the event's occurring

Example:

You are considering starting a business that will require a $300,000 investment. The present value of the estimated cash flow of the business over the next 5 years is $1,000,000, with a success probability of .80. If the venture fails, you lose $300,000. What, if any, is the expected value?

*The expected value is an arithmetic mean where relative frequencies $\left(\frac{f_i}{n_i}\right)$ or probabilities (P_i) are used as weights for the values (X_i).

Solution:

$$E(x) = X_1P_1 + X_2P_2$$
$$E(x) = (700{,}000 \cdot .80) + (-300{,}000 \cdot .20)$$
$$E(x) = 560{,}000 - 60{,}000$$
$$E(x) = \$500{,}000$$

5

Statistics: Universe

INTRODUCTION

The auditor's concern is often concentrated on information from samples of data. However, since every sample is drawn from some universe and the characteristics of a sample reflect universe characteristics from which it came, it is necessary to understand universes in order to comprehend samples and sampling techniques. Therefore, a summary discussion of universes precedes the discussion on sampling.

When *all* the members of a group under study are included, the group is referred to as a *population* or *universe,* and each member is a *universe item.* A count of these items may be made, or some measurement taken of a common characteristic of each item. For example: 1. All the people in the United States may form a universe. A total count including every person might be taken. This universe is commonly referred to as a census. 2. Using the same universe, a measurement of the common characteristic "height" might be obtained for every person in order to calculate the average height for the whole group.

A statistical measure computed from the items in a universe is called a *parameter.* A parameter for a stated universe is a single fixed value which may or may not be known. For example: The amount of sales as listed on each sales slip over a stated amount of time may be a universe for which the average sale may have been computed and found to be a stated amount, say $22.28, and is therefore known. However, if this average had not been computed, it would still exist but be unknown.

Universe notation: X = One universe value
N = Total number of items in universe

Parameter notation: μ = Universe arithmetic mean (variables)
π = Universe arithmetic mean (attributes)
σ = Standard deviation

The X values may arise from *variables*.

This occurs when they arise from universe items with values that can vary from other values of universe items in any degree. Example: Inventory values for stated time periods, where values may vary by any number of dollars and cents from one time period to another.

The X values may arise from *attributes*.

This occurs when they arise from universe items by counting the number of times a characteristic occurs in a stated group of these items. Example: The number of errors made by a cashier is counted for a given time period. This count may be compared with the counted number of errors made by the same cashier over a preceding like time period. These values can differ only in whole numbers.

Values arising from attributes may be expressed in number form or they may be expressed as a percent when the number found is divided by the total number of that group.

FREQUENCY DISTRIBUTIONS

In order to expedite the handling of large amounts of data, they are frequently grouped. The universe values are often arranged to show the X values in groups or intervals, in ascending order of size, and

FREQUENCY DISTRIBUTION OF WAGES OF PART-TIME WORKERS IN A SMALL FIRM

Wages (X) (in dollars)	Number Workers frequency (f)
100–124	15
125–149	21
150–174	35
175–199	20
200–224	9
	100

A graph of a frequency distribution has X values on the horizontal axis and f values on the vertical axis.

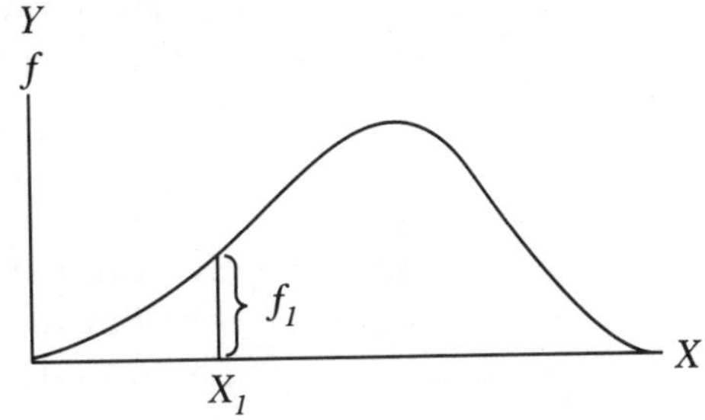

the frequency of occurrence for each of these intervals shown to the right of the interval. This arrangement is called a *frequency distribution*.

Frequency distributions may be symmetrical, skewed to the right, or skewed to the left, depending upon the nature of the data.

SYMMETRICAL

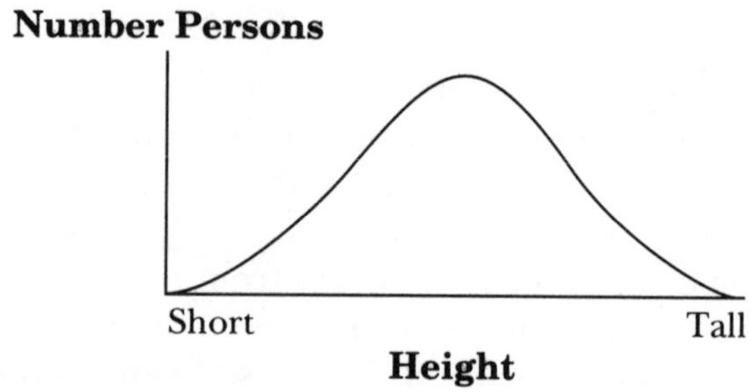

RIGHT SKEWED

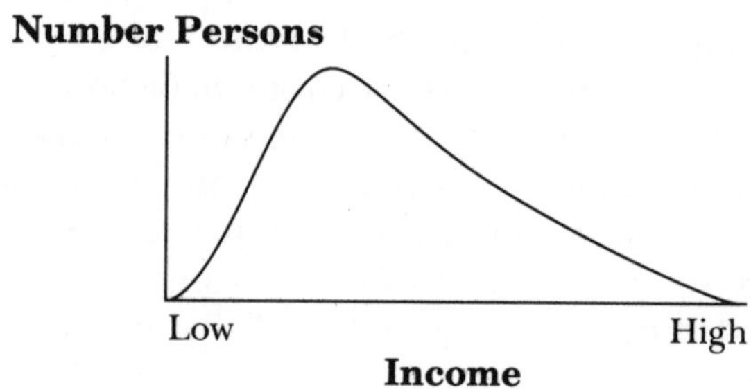

LEFT SKEWED

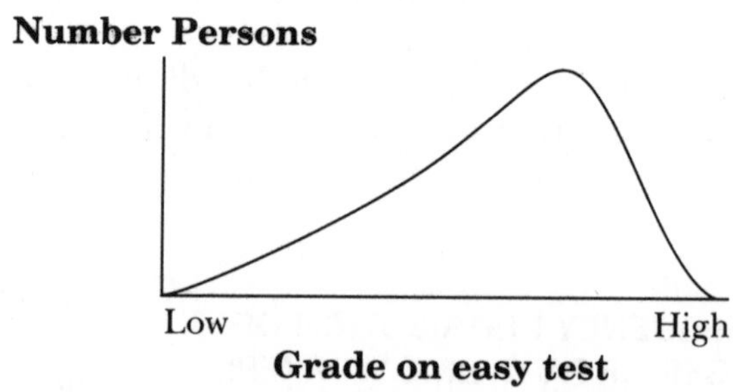

The auditor is ordinarily concerned about the average, the variation, and the skewness of the data with which he or she is working.

AVERAGES

An *average* is one number that is computed from a group of values to represent each member of the group for which it is computed. The size of the average computed is affected by the distribution of the values and by the type of average computed. It is important to select the average that most fairly represents the whole group. Types of averages and their computations follow.

MEANS

Every mean is the result obtained from computing the sum of all the observed X values, or some transformation of these X values, and dividing that sum by the total number of observations in the group.

Sometimes the observed X values are transformed in a manner that makes a right-skewed distribution become more symmetrical, and the average therefore more representative of the group.

When the observed X values are transformed by using logarithm X for X, the mean derived is called a *geometric mean*. When the observed X values are transformed by using reciprocal X for X, the mean derived is called a *harmonic mean*.

If all three means were computed for the same set of data, they would relate to each other: Arithmetic mean larger than geometric mean larger than harmonic mean, or: $M_A > M_G > M_H$. Hereafter μ will be used for arithmetic mean (more frequently used notation).

ARITHMETIC MEAN

The arithmetic mean is the amount each member in the group would receive if the sum of all the values were distributed equally to each member. In computing the arithmetic mean, each value (X) is weighted by the number of times it occurs (f). In a symmetrical distribution, the arithmetic mean has high and low X values equally weighted and is therefore centrally located between the high and low values. The arithmetic mean is pulled toward the low values in a right-skewed distribution by the greater concentration of weights for the low values. It is pulled toward the high values in a left-skewed distribution by the greater concentration of weights for the high values. The grouped data used to compute the arithmetic mean following is right skewed.

ARITHMETIC MEAN—VARIABLES
(ungrouped data)

Formula:

$$\mu = \frac{\sum_{1}^{N} fX}{N}$$

where

μ = Arithmetic mean

$\sum_{1}^{N}$ = Add all observations from first through last

f = Frequency or number of times an observation occurs

X = Magnitude of any one observation

N = Total number of observations $= \sum_{1}^{N} f$

Example:

What is the average (arithmetic mean) amount outstanding from the following amounts on statements being mailed to customers?

$20.00, $15.20, $43.80, $5.70, $20.00,
$31.20, $43.80, $10.30, $4.20, $43.80

Solution:

X	f	fX
$20.00	2	$40.00
15.20	1	15.20
43.80	3	131.40
5.70	1	5.70
31.20	1	31.20
10.30	1	10.30
4.20	1	4.20
	10	$238.00

$$\sum_{1}^{N} fX = \$238.00$$

$$N = 10$$

$$\mu = \frac{\$238.00}{10} = \$23.80$$

ARITHMETIC MEAN, SHORTCUT METHOD—VARIABLES (grouped data)

Formula:

$$\mu = \mu' + \frac{\left(\sum_{1}^{K} f \frac{x'}{i}\right) i}{N}$$

where

μ = Arithmetic mean

μ' = Assumed arithmetic mean

K = Number of classes

f = Frequency or number of observations in a class

x' = Deviation = difference between midpoint of a class and assumed mean

i = Class range

$\frac{x'}{i}$ = Deviation divided by class range

$\sum_{1}^{K}$ = Add for all K classes

N = Total number of observations = $\sum_{1}^{K} f$

Example and Solution:

What is the average (arithmetic mean) weekly wage of 100 part-time workers when computed from the following frequency distribution:

Wage Class (In Dollars)	Number of Workers f	$\frac{x'}{i}$	$f\frac{x'}{i}$
60.00–64.99	4	−4	−16
65.00–69.99	8	−3	−24
70.00–74.99	12	−2	−24
75.00–79.99	15	−1	−15
80.00–84.99	23	0	0
85.00–89.99	18	1	18
90.00–94.99	10	2	20
95.00–99.99	5	3	15
100.00–104.99	3	4	12
105.00–109.99	2	5	10
	100		−4

μ' = midpoint of class to left of 0 in x'/i column = \$82.50

$$\sum_{1}^{K} f\frac{x'}{i} = -4 \qquad N = 100 \qquad i = \$5.00$$

$$\mu = \$82.50 + \frac{(-4)(\$5)}{100} = \$82.50 - \frac{\$20}{100} = \$82.30$$

GEOMETRIC MEAN

The geometric mean is the antilog of the amount each member in the group would receive if the sum of all the logarithms of the values were distributed equally to each member.

GEOMETRIC MEAN—VARIABLES (grouped data)

Formula:

$$M_G = \text{Antilog} \sum_{1}^{N} \frac{f \log X}{N}$$

where

M_G = Geometric mean

$\sum_{1}^{N}$ = Add all $f \log X$ values from first through last

f = The frequency of occurrence in each class

Log X = Logarithm of each observation X (or log of each class midpoint)

N = Total number of observations = Σf

Example and Solution:

What is the geometric mean (average) weekly wage for 100 part-time workers when computed from the following set of grouped data?

Wage Class (In Dollars)	f (Number Workers)	X (Midpoint)	log X	f log X
60.00–64.99	4	62.50	1.795880	7.183520
65.00–69.99	8	67.50	1.829304	14.634432
70.00–74.99	12	72.50	1.860338	22.324056
75.00–79.99	15	77.50	1.889302	28.339530
80.00–84.99	23	82.50	1.916454	44.078442
85.00–89.99	18	87.50	1.942008	34.956144
90.00–94.99	10	92.50	1.966142	19.661420
95.00–99.99	5	97.50	1.989005	9.945025
100.00–104.99	3	102.50	2.010724	6.032172
105.00–109.99	2	107.50	2.031408	4.062816
	100			191.217557

$$M_G = \text{Antilog}\,\frac{191.217557}{100} = \text{Antilog}\ 1.91217557$$

$$M_G = \$81.69$$

HARMONIC MEAN

The harmonic mean is the reciprocal of the amount each member in the group would receive if the sum of all the reciprocals of the values were distributed equally to each member.

HARMONIC MEAN—VARIABLES (grouped data)

Formula:

$$M_H = \text{Reciprocal}\,\frac{\sum_{1}^{N} f\left(\frac{1}{X}\right)}{N}$$

where

M = Harmonic mean

$\sum_{1}^{N}$ = Add all f reciprocal X values from first through last

f = The frequency of occurrence in each class

Reciprocal X = Reciprocal of each class midpoint $= \frac{1}{X}$

N = Total number of observations $= \Sigma f$

Example and Solution:

What is the harmonic mean (average) weekly wage for 100 part-time workers when computed from the following set of data?

Wage Class (In Dollars)	f (Number Workers)	X (Midpoint)	$\frac{1}{X}$	$f\left(\frac{1}{X}\right)$
60.00–64.99	4	62.50	.01600	.06400
65.00–69.99	8	67.50	.01481	.11848
70.00–74.99	12	72.50	.01379	.17772
75.00–79.99	15	77.50	.01290	.19350
80.00–84.99	23	82.50	.01212	.27876
85.00–89.99	18	87.50	.01143	.20574

Wage Class (In Dollars)	f (Number Workers)	X (Midpoint)	$\frac{1}{X}$	$f\left(\frac{1}{X}\right)$
90.00–94.99	10	92.50	.01081	.10810
95.00–99.99	5	97.50	.01026	.05513
100.00–104.99	3	102.50	.00975	.02925
105.00–109.00	2	107.50	.00930	.01860
	100			1.24928

$$M_H = \text{Reciprocal } \frac{1.24928}{100} = \text{reciprocal } .0124928$$

$$M_H = \$80.05$$

d_1 ARITHMETIC MEAN—Attributes—NUMBER OF SUCCESSES

This mean is one of counts showing "how many." Since only a success or a failure can occur, a success is indicated by "1," a failure or nonoccurrence is indicated by "0."

Formula:

$$\pi_{\text{number}} = \sum_{1}^{N} fS$$

where

f = Number of occurrences
S = A success (or lack of success)
N = Total number items examined
$\sum_{1}^{N}$ = Sum of fS

Example:

A check was made to determine the accuracy of computations of overtime for 1000 days of work by one worker. The magnitude of the error was not considered, only that an error did or did not occur. A statement found with at least one error was called a "success."

Solution:

S (Success)	f (Frequency of Occurrence)	fS
0 (no error)	950	0
1 (1 or more errors)	50	50
	1000	50

$\pi_{\text{number}} = 50$

d_2 ARITHMETIC MEAN—Attributes—PERCENT OF SUCCESSES

Formula:

$$\pi_{\%} = \frac{\sum_{1}^{N} fS}{N}$$

where

f = Number of occurrences
S = A success (or lack of success)
N = Total number of items examined
$\sum_{1}^{N}$ = Sum of fS

Example:

Same as for d_1 above.

Solution:

$$\pi_{\%} = \frac{\sum_{1}^{N} fS}{N} = \frac{50}{1000} = .05 \text{ or } 5\%$$

MEDIAN

When a median is selected as the average to represent the members of a group, it is the value of the item belonging to the center position when values are arranged in order of magnitude. The magnitudes of the values above or below the center do not affect the magnitude of the median. Thus, the median is free of the influence of unusual extreme values above and below it.

MEDIAN (ungrouped data)

Example (odd number of observations):

What is the median average amount of assets of the 11 firms having the following assets (expressed in thousands of dollars)?

150, 220, 180, 502, 307, 142, 678, 996, 810, 760, 910

Solution:

Arrange observations in order of magnitude and eliminate the 5 lowest. The observation in the sixth position (middle position) is the median.

$$\underbrace{142,\ 150,\ 180,\ 220,\ 307}_{\text{5 lowest observations}},\ \underset{\text{Median}}{\boxed{502}},\ \underbrace{678,\ 760,\ 810,\ 910,\ 996}_{\text{5 highest observations}}$$

Median = \$502,000

Example (even number of observations):

What is the median average amount of assets of the 10 firms having the following assets (expressed in thousands of dollars)?

150, 508, 673, 810, 270, 816, 513, 278, 680, 627

Solution:

Arrange observations in order of magnitude and compute the value midway between the 2 center position observations. This value is the median.

150, 270, 278, 508, 513, 627, 673, 680, 810, 816

→←

570

Median

Median = \$570,000

MEDIAN (grouped data)

Formula:

$$Md. = l_{Md.} + \frac{\left(\frac{N}{2} - \sum_{1}^{\text{Md. class}} f\right) i}{f_{Md.}}$$

where

$Md.$ = Median

$l_{Md.}$ = Lower limit of median class

N = Total number of observations = Σf

f = Frequency = number of observations in a class

$\sum_{1}^{\text{Md. class}} f$ = Add frequencies in classes beginning with smallest class and continuing to median class. (Median class is class containing observation in center position.)

i = Median class range

$f_{Md.}$ = Number of observations in median class

Example:

What is the number of miles traveled daily that has half of the salesmen traveling more and half traveling less? The miles traveled daily were obtained from the expense records and were then classified into the following groups:

Class (Miles Traveled Daily)	f (Number of Salesmen's Daily Reports)
Under 10	9
10.00–13.99	12
14.00–17.99	20
18.00–21.99	25
22.00–25.99	12
26.00–29.99	9
30.00–33.99	6
34.00–37.99	3
38.00–41.99	3
42.00–45.99	2
46 and over	1
	102

$N = 102$ $\qquad f_{Md.} = 25$

$N/2 = 51$ $\qquad$ Median class = 18.00 − 21.99

$\sum_{1}^{\text{Md. class}} f = 9 + 12 + 20 = 41$ $\qquad l_{Md.} = 18.00 \qquad i = 4$

$$Md. = 18.00 \text{ miles} + \left(\frac{51 - 41}{25}\right) 4 \text{ miles} = 18.00 + 1.6 = 19.6 \text{ miles}$$

MODE

When a mode is selected as the average to represent the members of a group, the value of the item that occurs most frequently is selected.

The magnitudes of the other items or their frequencies of occurrence do not affect the magnitude of the mode.

MODE (ungrouped data)

Method:

Find the observation that occurs most frequently in the set of observations.

Example:

The following errors were reported representing those made in registering sales on the cash registers (expressed in number of cents):

50, 83, 52, 93, 50, 63, 50, 83, 48, 50, 15, 50, 91, 37, 29

50 cents occurs 5 times
83 cents occurs 2 times
52, 93, 63, 48, 15, 91, 37, 29 cents each occurs 1 time

Therefore the mode was 50 cents.

MODE (grouped data)

Formula:

$$Mo. = l_{Mo.} + \left(\frac{\Delta_1}{\Delta_1 + \Delta_2}\right) i$$

where

$Mo.$ = Mode
$l_{Mo.}$ = Lower limit of modal class
Δ_1 = Difference between number of observations falling in modal class and number of observations falling in class *preceding* modal class
Δ_2 = Difference between number of observations falling in modal class and number of observations falling in class *following* modal class
i = Range of modal class

Example and Solution:

What is the most frequently occurring amount of a sale when the amounts classified are as follows:

Class (Amount of Sale in Dollars)	*f* (Number of Sales Transactions)
Under 1.00	3
1.00–1.99	4
2.00–2.99	10
3.00–3.99	25
4.00–4.99	15
5.00–5.99	8
6.00–6.99	4
7.00–7.99	4
8.00–8.99	3
9.00–9.99	2
10.00 and over	1
	79

Modal class = class having highest f = \$3–\$3.99

$$l_{Mo.} = \$3$$
$$\Delta_1 = 25 - 10 = 15$$
$$\Delta_2 = 25 - 15 = 10$$
$$i = \$1$$
$$Mo. = \$3 + \left(\frac{15}{15 + 10}\right) \$1 = \$3 + \$0.60 = \$3.60$$

RELATIONSHIPS AMONG AVERAGES

Shown below are

1. Three frequency distributions of daily sales for 100 days of one item sold in one department of a drug store for which the 5 averages have been computed
2. The relative sizes of the averages
3. The graph (histogram) of each of these distributions

x Sales (in dollars)	Symmetrical *f* (Number Days)	Right Skewed *f* (Number Days)	Left Skewed *f* (Number Days)
0.00– 9.99	5	10	2
10.00–19.99	10	20	9
20.00–29.99	20	35	14
30.00–39.99	30	13	20
40.00–49.99	20	11	34
50.00–59.99	10	8	17
60.00–69.99	5	3	4
	100	100	100

	Symmetrical	Right Skewed	Left Skewed
μ =	\$35.00	\$34.31	\$39.20
M_G =	30.95	23.47	35.88
M_H =	24.83	18.05	30.70
M_d =	35.00	25.71	41.47
M_o =	35.00	24.05	44.52

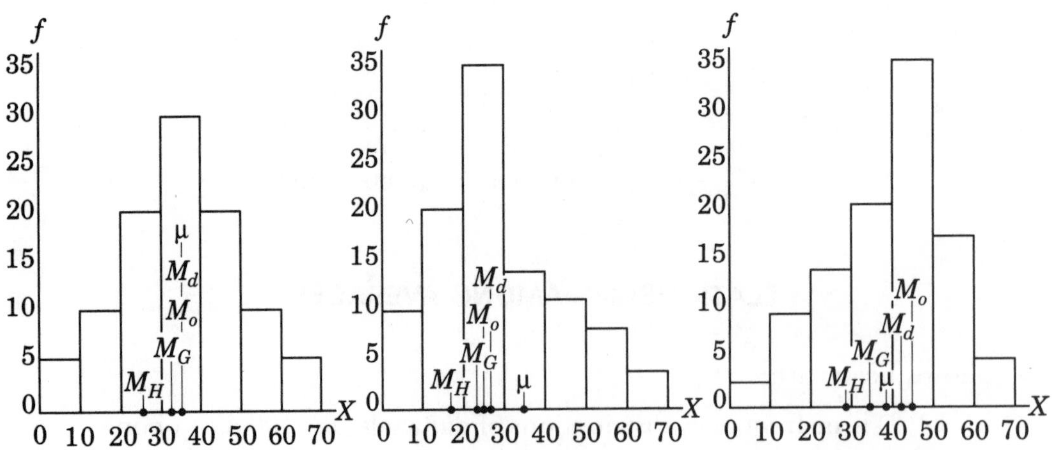

$\mu = M_d = M_o$
$\mu > M_G > M_H$

$\mu > M_d > M_o$
$\mu > M_G > M_H$

$\mu < M_d < M_o$
$\mu > M_H > M_G$

VARIATION

In order to understand the measurements or counts being used, it is often important not only to know the average (central tendency) but also the dispersion (variation) about the average. These measures are discussed following.

Detailed computations are included with each illustration for the understanding of the process and the measure which they impart. However, a calculator can reduce greatly the necessary number of calculations to arrive at the same results. A computer can streamline the whole process even more.

STANDARD DEVIATION—VARIABLES (ungrouped data)

Formula:

$$\sigma = \sqrt{\frac{\sum_{1}^{N} f x^2}{N}}$$

where

σ = Standard deviation

f = Frequency = number of times an observation occurs

x^2 = Squared deviation = squared difference between observation and arithmetic mean

$\sum_{1}^{N} fx^2$ = Add all products of fx^2 from first through last

N = Total number of observations

Example:

What is the standard deviation of the following numbers of days absent during a work year for 20 employees of a unit?

X (Days Absent)	f (Number Workers)	x $(X - \mu)$*	fx*	fx^2
1	1	−9	−9	81
3	1	−7	−7	49
3	1	−7	−7	49
4	1	−6	−6	36
6	1	−4	−4	16
7	1	−3	−3	9
7	1	−3	−3	9
9	1	−1	−1	1
10	1	0	0	0
11	1	1	1	1
11	1	1	1	1
11	1	1	1	1
12	1	2	2	4
14	1	4	4	16
14	1	4	4	16
14	1	4	4	16
15	1	5	5	25
15	1	5	5	25
16	1	6	6	36
17	1	7	7	49
200	20			440

Solution:

$$\sum_{1}^{20} fx^2 = 440 \qquad M = 200/20 = 10$$

$$N = 20$$

$$\sigma = \sqrt{\frac{440}{20}} = \sqrt{22} = 4.7$$

*These two columns have been included for clarity. They can be omitted when computations are made.

STANDARD DEVIATION—VARIABLES (grouped data)

Formula:

$$\sigma = i\sqrt{\frac{\sum_{1}^{k} f\left(\frac{x'}{i}\right)^2}{N} - \left(\frac{\sum_{1}^{k} f\frac{x'}{i}}{N}\right)^2}$$

where

σ = Standard deviation

i = Class size

f = Class frequency (number of observations in a class)

x' = deviation = difference between class midpoint and assumed mean (Assumed mean is midpoint of class opposite x'/i column value of 0.)

k = Total number of classes

N = Total number of observations

$\sum_{1}^{k}$ = Add from first through kth class

Example:

What is the range of wages paid to approximately the middle two thirds of the 100 part-time workers having the following wage distribution?

Class ($ Weekly Wage)	f (Number Workers)	$\frac{x'}{i}$	$f\frac{x'}{i}$	$f\left(\frac{x'}{i}\right)^2$
60.00–64.99	4	−4	−16	64
65.00–69.99	8	−3	−24	72
70.00–74.99	12	−2	−24	48
75.00–79.99	15	−1	−15	15
80.00–84.99	23	0	0	0
85.00–89.99	18	1	18	18
90.00–94.99	10	2	20	40
95.00–99.99	5	3	15	45
100.00–104.99	3	4	12	48
105.00–109.99	2	5	10	50
	100		−4	400

Solution:

$$N = 100 \qquad \sum_{1}^{k} f\left(\frac{x'}{i}\right)^2 = 400$$

$$\sum_{1}^{k} f\frac{x'}{i} = -4 \qquad i = 5$$

$$\sigma = 5\sqrt{\frac{400}{100} - \left(\frac{-4}{100}\right)^2} = 5\sqrt{4.00 - .0016} = 5\sqrt{4.00} = 10$$

$\sigma = \$10 \qquad \mu = \$82.30$ (see p. 48 for the computation of mean)

Range of middle 2/3 = \$82.30 ± \$10 = range from \$72.30 to \$92.30.

Note: In a normal distribution:

$\mu \pm 1\sigma$ includes about the middle 68% of the observations

$\mu \pm 2\sigma$ includes about the middle 95% of the observations

$\mu \pm 3\sigma$ includes about the middle 99.7% of the observations.

The preceding distribution is not normal. For that distribution $M \pm \sigma$ includes the middle 66%, or the middle 66% of the workers received wages between \$82.30 + \$10.00 and \$83.20 − \$10.00.

VARIATION: ESTIMATION OF STANDARD DEVIATION FROM TOTAL RANGE

The total range can be obtained quickly. It is the difference between the highest observation and the lowest observation. Its reliability as an adequate measure of variation is questioned, however, when the low or high items seem abnormally extreme to represent the group.

If the population distribution can be assumed to be approximately normal, then the range can be assumed to be about six times the standard deviation in size. Dividing the range by 6 can furnish a quick first approximation to the standard deviation but in many cases cannot be relied upon for precision results.*

RELATIVE VARIATION—COEFFICIENT OF VARIATION

When it is impossible to compare the variation of two distributions by using the absolute values of their σ's, a measure called *coefficient of variation* can be applied. This situation can arise when the distributions

*The divisor 5 instead of 6 is sometimes used to in part compensate for unusual extreme measures.

have measurements in different units or the arithmetic means are not equal.

Formula:

$$V = \frac{\sigma}{\mu}$$

where

V = Coefficient of variation
μ = Arithmetic mean
σ = Standard deviation

Example:

The variation between the productivity and wages paid a group of workers was to be compared. The data showed the following:

	Productivity (Units per Hour)	Wages (Dollars per Hour)
μ	200	\$12.50
σ	10	1.25
V	10/200 = 5%	1.25/12.50 = 10%

Solution:

Wages paid to this group of workers varied on the average 2 times as much as their productivity.

PROBABLE ERROR—VARIABLES

Formula:

$$P.E._{\cdot i} = 0.6745\sigma$$

where

$P.E.$ = Probable error based on standard deviation (σ)
σ = Standard deviation

Example:

It is known that the arithmetic mean size of sale for all sales is \$7 and the standard deviation is \$2. What are the lowest and highest points of sales that have equal probabilities of having sales fall in this range as having sales fall outside this range?

Solution:

$$PE_\sigma = 0.6745\ (\$2) = \$1.35$$
$$\$7 \pm \$1.35 = \$5.65 \text{ to } \$8.35.$$

Therefore one might expect (if the sales were normally distributed) to find 50 percent of the sales falling between \$5.65 and \$8.35, and the other 50 percent of the sales less than \$5.65 or larger than \$8.35.

QUARTILE DEVIATION—VARIABLES (grouped data)

Formula:

$$Q.D. = \frac{Q_3 - Q_1}{2}$$

where

$Q.D.$ = Quartile deviation

Q_1 = First quartile point (With respect to magnitude, 25% of observations are below this point and 75% are above it.)

Q_3 = Third quartile point (With respect to magnitude, 75% of observations are below this point and 25% are above it.)

Example:

What was the range of the middle 50% of the workers' intelligence scores which were grouped into the following classes? (Scores are in whole numbers only.)

Class (Intelligence Score)	f Number of Workers
65–69	1
70–74	3
75–79	8
80–84	18
85–89	20
90–94	18
95–99	8
100–104	3
105–109	1
	80

Solution:

Note: Q_1 and Q_3 are positional points comparable to the median, which is Q_2. The computation therefore is very similar.

$$Q_1 = 80 + \left(\frac{80/4 - 12}{18}\right)4 = 80 + \left(\frac{8}{18}\right)4 = 82 \text{ (rounded to whole number)}$$

$$Q_3 = 90 + \left(\frac{3/4(80) - 50}{18}\right)4 = 90 + \left(\frac{10}{18}\right)4 = 92 \text{ (rounded to whole number)}$$

$$Q.D. = \frac{92 - 82}{2} = 5 \qquad \text{Median} = 87$$

Middle 50% of workers, according to scores, fell between $Md. \pm Q.D.$ or 87 ± 5 or between 82 and 92.

Note: This answer was known when Q_1 and Q_3 were computed because this distribution is a symmetrical one. This would not have been true if the distribution had been skewed (not symmetrical). In this latter case, the median plus and minus the quartile deviation usually includes more than the middle 50%—the excess over 50% depending upon the amount of the skewness.

6

Statistics: Samples

INTRODUCTION

A *sample* contains a portion of the items from the universe. When it is not practical or feasible because of excessive time consumption or cost, or it is impossible to use the entire universe, sampling is used to reflect the characteristics of the universe.

A statistical measure computed from the items in a sample is called a *statistic*. Unlike the parameter in the universe, a statistic can vary from sample to sample, drawn from the same universe, depending upon which particular values from the universe fell in the given sample.

Sample notation:

X = One sample value (comes from universe)
n = Total number of values in one sample
k = Total number of samples

Statistic notation:

$\bar{X}$ = Sample arithmetic mean (average)
$\bar{\bar{X}}$ = Arithmetic mean of all sample arithmetic means
s = Sample standard deviation

Since the X values in a sample come directly from the universe, they will appear in the sample either as variables or attributes, depending upon the type of data in the universe from which they were drawn.

SAMPLING DISTRIBUTIONS

Although practically only one sample is ordinarily taken, theoretically it is possible to envision the number of samples taken approaching infinity. If the same statistic were computed for each of these samples, then a frequency distribution of that statistic could be constructed. This distribution would be a *sampling distribution* and would form the basis for prediction of universe parameters.

These sampling distributions are also referred to as *probability distributions*. If the items in the samples occur due to a purely random selection, the laws of probability apply. This makes possible the expression of results arrived at objectively for which the risks can be stated numerically.

The difference between any sample statistic and its corresponding fixed universe parameter arises because of *sampling error*. Sampling error is not a mistake of calculation or a bias in measurement. It arises because the whole universe is not reflected in any one sample. The sampling distribution is therefore determined by the variation of each sample statistic away from its parent universe parameter. The sampling distribution is therefore sometimes called a "curve of error," and its measure of variation comparable to the universe standard deviation is called a *standard error*.

Central Tendency

Like universe frequency distributions, sampling distributions have central tendency measured by an average. While any average discussed under "universe" can be computed for a sampling distribution, the arithmetic mean is generally employed because of its moment properties, which makes it compatible mathematically with the higher moments used to measure other properties of the distribution. For example, second moment measures variation and third moment skewness. For variables, the mean of sample means $\bar{\bar{X}}$ can be a good predictor of the universe mean μ, and for attributes, the proportion p from a sample can be used to predict the universe proportion π.

SAMPLE ARITHMETIC MEAN (variables)

Formula:

$$\overline{X} = \frac{\sum_{1}^{n} X}{n}$$

where

$\overline{X}$ = Arithmetic mean of sample

$\sum_{1}^{n} X$ = Sum of all values in sample

n = Number of items in sample

Example:

The sum of the amounts of sales on a sample of 10 sales slips was \$510. What is the arithmetic mean of the sample?

Solution:

$$\overline{X} = \frac{\$510}{10} = \$51$$

SAMPLE ARITHMETIC MEAN (attributes)

Formula:

$$p = \frac{\sum_{1}^{n} \text{successes}}{n}$$

where

p = Proportion of successes in total sample

$\sum_{1}^{n}\text{successes}$ = Number (count) of successes in sample

n = Number in sample (total)

Example:

1000 sales slips were examined to see if any of them contained errors. An error was found on 2 of them (2 successes). What is the proportion of sales slips with error in this sample?

Solution:

$$p = \frac{2}{1000} = .005 = .5\%$$

VARIATION

The variation of the sampling distribution is measured by the standard error s, so called because it measures the extent of sampling error around the average of the sampling distribution. If the sampling distribution is one of arithmetic means $\overline{X}$, its variation is measured by the standard error $s_{\bar{x}}$ of the sample means. The size of $s_{\bar{x}}$ which measures the variation of the sampling distribution of means, understates the size of σ which measures the variation of the universe from which the samples were taken. This relationship is due to the fact that the magnitude of the standard error of the means depends upon the sizes of the sample means $\overline{X}$ while the magnitude of the standard deviation of the universe depends upon the sizes of values X. The $\overline{X}$'s, being averages, do not have as wide a range in values as the X's.

STANDARD ERROR OF THE MEAN—VARIABLES

Sample small relative to universe. Standard deviation of universe known.

Formula:

$$s_{\bar{x}} = \frac{\sigma}{\sqrt{n}}$$

where

$s_{\bar{x}}$ = Standard error of mean
σ = Standard deviation of the universe
n = Number of items in sample

Example:

It is known that the standard deviation of the universe price changes on a given item over a stated time period was 3 cents. A sample of 9 items was taken from this universe and its arithmetic mean price change calculated. What would the standard error of all such means from like samples be expected to be?

Solution:

$$s_{\bar{x}} = \frac{\sigma}{\sqrt{n}}$$

$$s_{\bar{x}} = \frac{3}{\sqrt{9}} = 1$$

STANDARD ERROR OF THE MEAN—VARIABLES

Sample size small relative to size of universe. Standard deviation of universe not known.

Formula:

$$\sigma_{\bar{x}} = \frac{s}{\sqrt{n-1}} \quad \text{or} \quad \sigma_{\bar{x}} = \frac{s}{\sqrt{n}}$$

if "s" is computed using "$n - 1$"

where

$\sigma_{\bar{x}}$ = Standard error of mean
s = Standard deviation for items in sample
n = Number of items in sample

Example:

Book inventories have been compared to physical inventories and the size of the discrepancies noted. There are too many figures to use all of them. A random sample of 101 is selected. The standard deviation for these 101 is then computed and found to be $2000. What is the standard error for a sampling distribution of means for all samples like the one taken? (Thus a measure of the variation among the discrepancies could be obtained.)

Solution:

$$\sigma_{\bar{x}} = \frac{s}{\sqrt{n-1}} = \frac{2000}{\sqrt{101-1}} = 200$$

Therefore the standard error of the mean discrepancy is $200.

STANDARD ERROR OF THE MEAN—VARIABLES

Sample size large relative to size of universe. Standard deviation of universe known.

Formula:

$$\sigma_{\bar{x}} = \frac{\sigma}{\sqrt{n}} \sqrt{\frac{N - n}{N - 1}}$$

where

$\sigma_{\bar{x}}$ = Standard error of the mean
σ = Standard deviation of the universe
n = Number in sample
N = Number in universe

Example:

What is the standard error for the sampling distribution of means for samples of petty cash amounts if there are a total of 101 such accounts and a random sample of 36 of the 101 have been studied? It is known that the standard deviation of the 101 accounts is $12.

Solution:

$$\sigma_{\bar{x}} = \frac{\$12}{\sqrt{36}} \sqrt{\frac{101 - 36}{101 - 1}} = \$2 \sqrt{\frac{65}{100}} = \$2(.8) = \$1.60$$

Therefore the standard error of the mean is $1.60.

STANDARD ERROR OF A PROPORTION

Attributes. Universe large relative to sample. Arithmetic mean of universe (π) known.

Formula:

$$\sigma_p = \sqrt{\frac{\pi(1 - \pi)}{n}}$$

where

σ_p = Standard error of a proportion

π = Proportion of "successes" in universe (success is a favorable event happening)

$1 - \pi$ = Proportion of "failures" in universe (failure is unfavorable event happening)

n = Number in the sample

Example:

It is believed that in a universe of workers, there is an even split (50% for and 50% against) changing the lunch period from one-half hour to one hour. A sample of 100 workers is taken and their preferences recorded. It is desired to know the standard error for the proportion in all like samples to the one that was taken.

Solution:

$$\sigma_p = \sqrt{\frac{50(1 - 50)}{100}} = \sqrt{\frac{2500}{100}} = 5$$

$$= 5 \text{ percent}$$

STANDARD ERROR OF A PROPORTION

Sample size large relative to size of universe. Arithmetic mean of universe (π) known.

Formula:

$$\sigma_p = \sqrt{\frac{\pi(1 - \pi)}{n}} \sqrt{\frac{N - n}{N - 1}}$$

where

σ_p = Standard error of a proportion

π = Proportion of "successes" in universe (A success is the occurrence of a favorable event.)

$1 - \pi$ = Proportion of "failures" in universe (A failure is the occurrence of an unfavorable event.)

n = Number of items in the sample

N = Number of items in the universe

Example:

Suppose that in the previous example there are 1000 workers and from this 1000 a sample of 100 workers is taken. What is the standard error of the proportion (assumed 50% as above)?

Solution:

$$\sigma_p = \sqrt{\frac{50 \times 50}{100}}\sqrt{\frac{1000 - 100}{1000 - 1}} = (5)\left(\frac{30}{31.6}\right) = 4.75$$

$$= 4.75\%$$

STANDARD ERROR OF DIFFERENCES BETWEEN ARITHMETIC MEANS

Variables. Assuming independence. Universe standard deviation (σ) known.

Formula:

$$\sigma_{\bar{x}_1 - \bar{x}_2} = \sqrt{\sigma_{\bar{x}_1}{}^2 + \sigma_{\bar{x}_2}{}^2}$$

where

$\sigma_{\bar{x} - \bar{x}_2}$ = Standard error of difference between arithmetic means

$\sigma_{\bar{x}_1}{}^2$ = Standard error squared of mean 1 (See pages 65–68 for method of computation of this standard error.)

$\sigma_{\bar{x}_2}{}^2$ = Standard error squared for mean 2 (See pages 65–68 for method of computation of this standard error.)

Example:

The average working capital requirement per week this year, based on a sample of 16 representative weeks, was $200,000, and last year based on the sample of the same number of weeks, it was $195,000. The standard deviation for all weeks is known to be $10,000. What is the standard error of the difference between the arithmetic means?

Solution:

$$\sigma_{\bar{x}_1}{}^2 = \left(\frac{10{,}000}{\sqrt{16}}\right)^2 = \left(\frac{10{,}000}{4}\right)^2 = (2500)^2 = 6{,}250{,}000$$
$$= \$6{,}250{,}000$$
$$\sigma_{\bar{x}_2}{}^2 = \$6{,}250{,}000 \text{ also}$$
$$\sigma_{\bar{x}_1-\bar{x}_2} = \sqrt{6{,}250{,}000 + 6{,}250{,}000} = \sqrt{12{,}500{,}000}$$
$$= \$3{,}536$$

STANDARD ERROR OF DIFFERENCE BETWEEN PROPORTIONS

Assuming independence.

Formula:

$$\sigma_{p_1-p_2} = \sqrt{\sigma_{p_1}{}^2 + \sigma_{p_2}{}^2}$$

where

$\sigma_{p_1-p_2}$ = Standard error of difference between proportions
$\sigma_{p_1}{}^2$ = Standard error squared of proportion 1 (See pages 65–68 for method of computation.)
$\sigma_{p_2}{}^2$ = Standard error squared of proportion 2 (See pages 65–68 for method of computation.)

Example:

The proportion of 100 overdue accounts receivable, which were overdue for as much or more than 3 months, selected at random from this year's list, was 5%. The comparable proportion from last year's list was 3%. What is the standard error of the difference between the proportions?

Solution:

$$\sigma_{p_1}{}^2 = \frac{p(1-p)}{n} = \frac{(5)(95)}{100} = 4.75$$
$$= 4.75\%$$
$$\sigma_{p_2}{}^2 = \frac{p(1-p)}{n} = \frac{(3)(97)}{100} = 2.91$$
$$= 2.91\%$$

$$\sigma_{p_1-p_2} = \sqrt{4.75 + 2.91} = 2.77$$
$$= 2.77\%$$

STANDARD ERROR OF MEDIAN

Formula:

$$\sigma_{Md.} = 1.25\ \sigma_{\bar{x}}$$

where

$\sigma_{Md.}$ = Standard error of median
$\sigma_{\bar{x}}$ = Standard error of arithmetic mean

Example:

A random sample of 121 persons having expense accounts was selected. The vouchers belonging to each of these 121 persons were then classified under the appropriate name. The median amounts of the expenses and the arithmetic mean amounts were then computed for each of the 121 individuals. The standard error of the arithmetic mean amounts was then computed and found to be \$2.20. What was the standard error of the median amounts?

Solution:

$$\sigma_{Md.} = 1.25\ \sigma_{\bar{x}}$$
$$= 1.25\,(\$2.20)$$
$$= \$2.75$$

Therefore the standard error of the median amounts in this case is \$2.75.

SKEWNESS

If the universe is symmetrical, the sampling distribution of sample x's or p's from that universe will also be symmetrical. If the universe is not radically skewed, the sampling distribution of $\overline{X}$ or p will tend to approach symmetry as the number of samples is increased.

SAMPLE TYPES

Selecting a proper sample type can often yield results that reveal the necessary information while using a smaller sample with corresponding reduction of time and cost expenditures.

Random Sampling

A random sample is one so selected that each item in the group has an equal chance of being chosen for the sample. The basic method for selection of every sample, regardless of type, must be a random process. Random selection makes possible objectivity and the application of the laws of probability. See page XX for a description of this process and examples of its use.

Systematic Sampling

A systematic sample is one that has the first item indicated by a random starting point and then moving a distance of "k" items for the next sample item where $k = N/n$. For example, if the group contains 4000 items and a sample of 100 is to be taken, then $k = 4000/100 = 40$. If the random start falls on 15, then the next sample item is at location 55.* In order to avoid biased results with systematic sampling, the group must be a uniform, random mix of the item being sampled. If this is not true, a periodic random restart may help in avoiding the periodic bias.

Stratified Sampling

When using this process, the group is divided into sub groups, or strata, and a random sampling process applied separately to each stratum. Sampling error can be reduced if variation within strata is reduced by putting items of like or similar size into a given stratum. This process also provides for more intensive sampling in those strata of greater importance for the business operations or for auditing.

Cluster Sampling

In this sampling process, the number of sample items taken at one location (a cluster) is no longer one, as in simple random sampling, but is increased to reflect the variability at that location, thus reducing the number of points at which sampling is done. Cluster sampling can be an efficient process if the variation of the items within a cluster is great while the variation between clusters is small. In instances where the cost of locating individual sample items by simple random sampling is very

---

* When N is extremely large, careful measurement instead of count to determine the distance "k" from the previous item sampled may be used.

high relative to the cost of examining these items, cluster sampling, even with larger total sample size, may result in a saving in time and cost, to offset the loss in sampling reliability through use of the cluster process.

Multistage Sampling

Multistage sampling consists of a random selection of primary units, then a subsequent random selection of secondary within the primary units; for example, a selection of store locations in a chain store business (primary units) followed by selection of items to be sampled within each store (secondary units). In order to avoid the possibility that multistage sampling might fail to include locations of special concern, multistage sampling may be combined with stratified sampling to ensure that these special locations will be included.

Exploratory Sampling

When the auditor is sampling to find the presence or absence of an event that may be a very small proportion of the total group, he may explore by deciding the upper tolerance limit for this event and the risk he is willing to take in failing to locate the event, if it does not exist, and let these decisions dictate the necessary sample size. Lowering the tolerance limit or the failure risk will have the effect of increasing the sample size. Such a situation may arise when fraud or negligence is suspected.

Judgment Sampling

If the sample selection is made merely on the basis of judgment, it is at once robbed of its two major reasons for using sampling: objectivity and numerical expression of precision and risk. This does not imply that the auditor's judgment and experience do not play an important role in other areas, such as selecting the sample type and evaluating the results.

ESTIMATION, HYPOTHESIS TESTING, EXPLORATORY SAMPLING, SAMPLE SIZE

Estimation (normal curve)

With proper sampling procedures, the auditor may:

(1) Estimate, using a sample statistic, the confidence interval for its corresponding universe parameter, and

(2) State numerically the degree of confidence to be associated with the estimate.

Formula:

Confidence interval = statistic ± Z (standard error of statistic)

Example 1. Estimating a universe mean, using variables, sample small relative to size of universe, standard deviation of universe known.

$$\text{Confidence interval} = \bar{X} \pm Z\sigma_{\bar{X}}$$

where

Confidence interval = range within which fixed universe parameter value is expected to fall with stated risk
$\bar{X}$ = Sample mean
Z = Distance on X axis of normal curve, expressed in $\sigma_{\bar{X}}$ units
$\sigma_{\bar{X}}$ = Standard error of the mean

The price changes on a given item is under study. Over a long period of time, it is known that standard deviation of all these price changes on this item is 3 cents. A sample of 9 observations was taken and the standard error of the mean computed and found to be 1 cent. (See page 65 for this computation.)

What is the 95% confidence interval within which the universe mean, one fixed value μ, lies if the sample mean $\bar{X}$ drawn from it has a value of 4.5 cents?

Solution:

$$\begin{aligned}
95\% \text{ confidence interval} &= 4.5 \text{ cents} \pm 1.96 \frac{3 \text{ cents}}{\sqrt{9}} \\
&= 4.5 \text{ cents} \pm 1.96 \text{ (1 cent)} \\
&= 4.5 \text{ cents} \pm 1.96 \text{ cents} \\
&= 6.46 \text{ cents to } 2.54 \text{ cents}
\end{aligned}$$

Therefore, given the same conditions, if this experiment were repeated 100 times, the fixed universe mean (μ) should fall within this range of 6.46 cents to 2.54 cents 95 times out of the 100 and fall outside the range only 5 times out of the 100.

Example 2. Estimating a universe mean, using variables, sample small relative to size of universe, standard deviation of universe not known.

Follow same procedure as in Example 1 above, except use to compute the standard error of the mean:

$$\sigma_{\bar{x}} = \frac{s}{\sqrt{n - 1}}$$

Example 3. Estimating a universe mean, using variables, sample size large relative to size of universe, standard deviation of universe known.

Follow same procedure as in Example 1 above, except use to compute the standard error of the mean:

$$\sigma_{\bar{x}} = \frac{\sigma}{\sqrt{n}} \sqrt{\frac{N - n}{N - 1}}$$

Example 4. Estimating a universe proportion from sample proportion. Arithmetic mean of universe (π) known.

Formula:

$$\text{Confidence interval} = p \pm Z\sigma_p$$

where

Confidence interval = Range within which fixed universe parameter value is expected to fall with stated risk

p = Sample proportion

Z = Distance on X axis of normal curve, expressed in σ_p units

σ_p = Standard error of the proportion

Example:

Can a sample of 100 having a 60% preference of office workers for a 30-minute lunch hour come from a universe of 1000 workers where these workers are evenly divided (50% for, 50% against) for a 30-minute vs. a 1-hour lunch period if one is willing to be off in his decision 1 time in 100?

Solution:

$$\begin{aligned} 99\% \text{ confidence interval} &= 60\% \pm 2.33 \sqrt{\frac{50\% \,(1 - 50\%)}{100}} \\ &= 60\% \pm 2.33\,(5\%) \\ &= 60\% \pm 11.65\% \\ &= 71.65\% \text{ to } 48.35\% \end{aligned}$$

Therefore, if this experiment were repeated many times, 99 out of every 100 times the universe proportion of preference (π, a single fixed value) would fall in the range 48.35% to 71.65%. It is possible that π does equal 50% and the sample with $p = 60\%$ was a sample produced by this universe.

Example 5. Estimating a universe proportion from a sample proportion, sample considered large relative to universe, π known.

The same procedure followed in Example 4 above would be followed, except the σ_p would be adjusted for sample size by multiplying the 5% derived from

$$\sqrt{\frac{50\%(1-50\%)}{100}}$$ by a factor to adjust for sample size, or 5%

$$\sqrt{\frac{1000-100}{1000-1}} = 4.75\%$$

$$60\% \pm 2.33(4.75\%) = 60\% \pm 11.07\% = 71.07\% \text{ to } 48.93\%$$

Since the 50% could still fall in the range 48.93% to 71.07%, the statement can still be made that the sample with proportion of 60% could be drawn from this universe with a risk of being wrong 1 time in 100.

Confidence Levels and Significance Levels

The relationship existing between "Confidence Level" and "Significance Level" is illustrated in the diagram that follows for 95% confidence and 5% significance. (If 99% confidence were used, significance would be 1% with .5% in each end of the curve.)

A sample value ($\overline{X}$ or p) falling on the X axis within the 95% confidence band can be accepted with 95% *confidence* that it belongs to

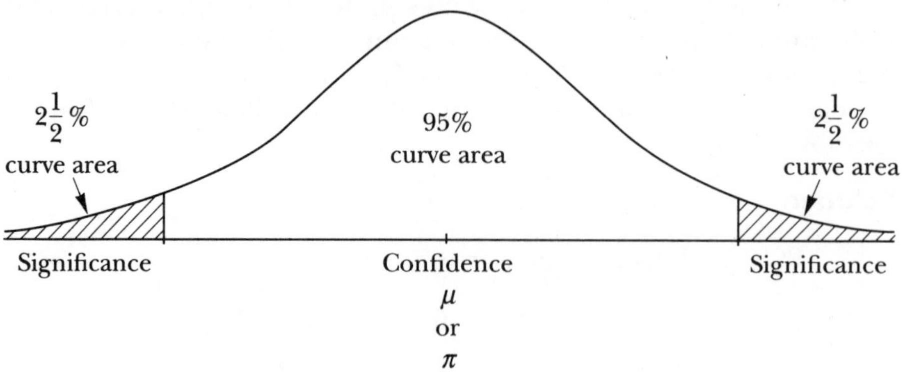

that universe. It can also be said that the sample value is not *significantly* different from the universe value because it does not fall on the X axis in the significance zone.

The following examples, using differences in means, will illustrate the use of significance levels.

Example 6. Differences between arithmetic means. Variates. Assuming independence.

Formula:

$$Z = \frac{(\overline{X}_1 - \overline{X}_2) - 0}{\sigma_{\bar{x}_1 - \bar{x}_2}}$$

where

Z = Distance on X axis of normal curve expressed in standard error units

$(\overline{X}_1 - \overline{X}_2)$ = Difference between two sample means

0 = Assumed difference in universe between means

$\sigma_{\bar{x}_1 - \bar{x}_2}$ = Standard error difference between arithmetic means

Example:

If the average working capital requirement per week this year, based on a sample of 16 representative weeks, was \$200,000, and last year based on the sample of the same number of weeks it was \$195,000, was this a significant difference this year from last based on the 95 percent confidence level? This is the 5% significancy level. The standard deviation for all weeks is known to be \$10,000.

Solution:

$$\begin{aligned}
\sigma_{\bar{x}_1}{}^2 &= \left(\frac{10{,}000}{\sqrt{16}}\right)^2 = \left(\frac{10{,}000}{4}\right)^2 = (2500)^2 = 6{,}250{,}000 \\
&= \$6{,}250{,}000 \\
\sigma_{\bar{x}_2}{}^2 &= \$6{,}250{,}000 \text{ also} \\
\sigma_{\bar{x}_1 - \bar{x}_2} &= \sqrt{6{,}250{,}000 + 6{,}250{,}000} = \sqrt{12{,}500{,}000} \\
&= \$3536 \\
Z &= \frac{(\$200{,}000 - \$195{,}000) - 0}{\$3536} = \frac{5000}{3536} = 1.41
\end{aligned}$$

Therefore, the difference could be attributed to sampling error and is not significant. Z equals 1.41. It would have to be 1.96 or greater to show significance at the 95% level, where the decision was to be made. The 1.96 standard errors is arrived at by consulting the value to the extreme left in the row, and the value at the top of the column, in which .4750 appears in Table XI, "Areas Under the Normal Curve." The .4750 is 50% minus one half of the 5% significance level (95% confidence level).

Example 7. Difference between sample proportions. Assuming independence.

Formula:

$$Z = \frac{(p_1 - p_2) - 0}{\sigma_{p_1 - p_2}}$$

where

Z = Distance on X axis of normal curve expressed in standard error units

$(p_1 - p_2)$ = Difference between two sample proportions

0 = Assumed difference in universe between proportions

$\sigma_{p_1 - p_2}$ = Standard error difference between sample proportions

Example:

The proportion of 100 overdue accounts receivable, which were overdue for as much or more than 3 months, selected at random from this year's list, was 5%. The comparable proportion from last year's list was 3%. Is this a significant increase over last year at the 5% level of significance?

Solution:

$$\sigma_{p_1}^{\ 2} = \frac{p(1-p)}{n} = \frac{(5)(95)}{100} = 4.75$$

$$= 4.75\%$$

$$\sigma_{p_2}^{\ 2} = \frac{p(1-p)}{n} = \frac{(3)(97)}{100} = 2.91$$

$$= 2.91\%$$

$$\sigma_{p_1-p_2} = \sqrt{4.75 + 2.91} = \sqrt{7.66} = 2.77$$
$$= 2.77\%$$
$$Z = \frac{(5\% - 3\%) - 0}{2.77\%} = \frac{2}{2.77} = .72$$

It is therefore not a significant difference at the 5% level of significance. The difference could be attributed to errors of sampling. (The Z value of .72 is less than 1.96, which is necessary at the 95% confidence level.) The 1.96 standard errors is arrived at by consulting the value to the extreme left in the row, and the value at the top of the column, in which .4750 appears in Table XI "Areas Under the Normal Curve." The .4750 is 50% minus one half of the 5% significance level (95% confidence level).

HYPOTHESIS TESTING (normal curve)

Hypothesis testing is in some ways another approach to estimation. Hypothesis testing involves a null hypothesis, H_0, with a probability of occurring of β and an alternate hypothesis, H_1, with its probability of occurring α.

Formula:

$$Z = \frac{H_1 \text{ value} - H_0 \text{ value}}{\sigma_{\bar{X}}}$$

where

H_1 = Sample $\bar{X}$ value

H_0 = Assumed universe μ value

$$\sigma_{\bar{X}} = \frac{\sigma}{\sqrt{n}}$$

where σ = Standard deviation of universe

where n = Number in the sample

Z = Distance on X axis of normal curve measured in standard error units

Example:

The inventory of a given item has been found over a long period of time to have an average value of \$1000 and a standard deviation of \$250. A sample of 100 items was taken and the $\bar{X}$ found to equal \$1035.

Does this difference indicate that the true average value of the inventory is not \$1000, or does sampling error account for the difference at the 5% level of significance?

Solution:

$$Z = \frac{1035 - 1000}{\sqrt{\frac{250}{100}}} = \frac{35}{25} = 1.4$$

Z value of 1.4 for a normal curve has a probability value of 8.08%. This means that there are about 8 chances in 100 that a sample value as large or larger than \$1035 could occur due to sampling error. Since 8% > 5% (the probability value set for rejection of H_0), H_0 is accepted and the difference of \$35 attributed to sampling error.

It is often preferable in hypothesis testing to determine the critical value, that is, the value where acceptance of H_0 stops and rejection of H_0 begins (or acceptance of H_1 begins). This approach is illustrated in the following example.

Formula:

$$\text{Critical value} = \frac{\overline{X} - \mu}{\frac{\sigma}{\sqrt{n}}} = Z$$

where

H_0 = The null hypothesis
H_1 = The alternate hypothesis
$\overline{X}$ = Mean of sample
μ = Value of null hypothesis
σ = Standard deviation of universe
n = Number in sample

Example:

A new method is being tried to produce a certain audit. Under the previous method, it took an average of 10 hours to produce the audit with a standard deviation of 2 hours. By how many hours will the new method have to reduce the average time used for a sample of 100 trials in order to reject the null hypothesis (H_0) of 10 hours if α is 5%?

Solution:

$$\text{Critical value} = \frac{\overline{X} - 10}{\frac{2}{\sqrt{100}}} = -1.64$$

$$\overline{X} = .2(-1.64) + 10 = -3.28 + 10 = 6.72$$

Therefore, any reduction in the time equal to or less than 6.72 hours would indicate a rejection of the null hypothesis of 10 hours. Suppose that the new method actually averaged only 6 hours. Graphically, this is illustrated below:

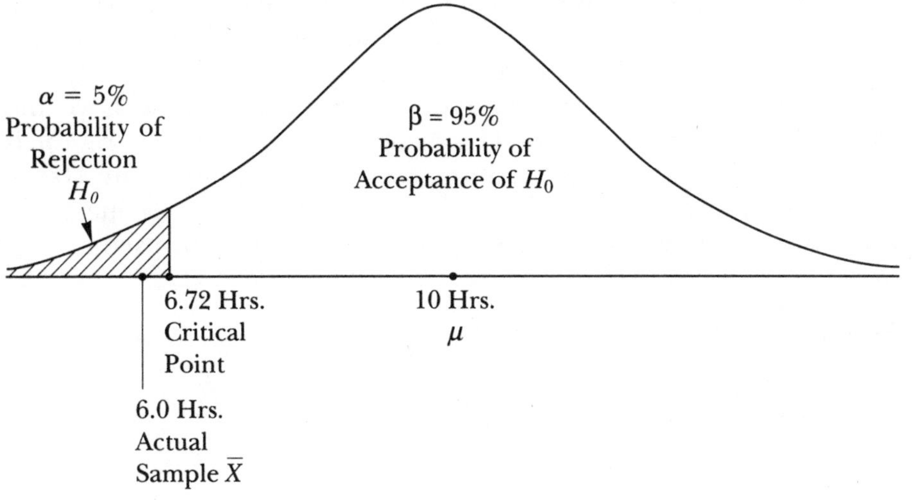

Since the 6 hours falls in the rejection area, to the left of the critical point, the answer would be: reject H_0 and accept H_1. This can raise questions, however, about this decision. These questions involve the types of errors that might be made. They are:

Type I error: H_0 is rejected when it should be accepted.

Type II error: H_0 is accepted when it should be rejected.

Type I can occur if a very improbable sample has happened to be selected. Type II can occur when our assumption about H_0 did not fit the universe as that universe actually exists.

The final decision in this case will depend upon our confidence in our controls and our experience and other information available to substantiate or refute the confidence. Lacking this confidence, another sample might be taken. This would be equivalent to increasing the sample size.

ESTIMATION (*t* curve)

When very small samples are drawn from a normal population of which the standard deviation is not known, the statistic "t," instead of the normal curve "Z," is used in the confidence interval or significance level process. For most universes, sample size of 25 or less would be considered small. In some cases, it is advisable to use "t" even for samples as large as 50. While there is one standard normal curve, there are many t curves depending upon the significance level and degrees of freedom. "Degrees of freedom" is the expression used for the sample size (n) corrected for loss of freedom in the determination of the numerical size of any item or items in the sample. For example, if we find $\Sigma(X_j - \overline{X})$, this sum must be 0. This means that $n - 1$ of these residuals are free but the last one is fixed by the sum $= 0$ requirement. Hence the degrees of freedom here is "$n - 1$." As the sample size (n) increases, the t curve approaches the normal curve and "Z" may be used instead of "t."

Formula:

$$\text{Confidence interval} = \overline{X} \mp t \frac{s}{\sqrt{n}}$$

where

Confidence interval is the range within which the fixed μ universe value is expected to fall with a stated risk

$\overline{X}$ = Sample mean
t = Distance along x axis of t curve
s = Sample standard deviation
n = Sample size

Example:

A retailer who had stocked a new item for only 4 months wished to order the optimum number of items for future sales without investing too much in inventory. Sales for the past 4 months had averaged

\$560 per month with a standard deviation of \$9. What is the largest monthly sale he might expect at the 5% level of significance (or confidence interval of 95%)?

Solution:

$$\begin{aligned} \text{95\% confidence interval} &= \$560 \pm 3.18\left(\frac{\$9}{\sqrt{4}}\right) \\ &= \$560 \pm 3.18\ (\$4.50) \\ &= \$560 \pm \$14.31 \\ &= \$574.31 \text{ to } \$545.69 \end{aligned}$$

Therefore, if he decides his monthly average could be as high as \$574.31, he would be correct 95 times out of 100.

Note: The 3.18 used above was read from the tabled "t" values in the column headed $t_{.025}$ ($\frac{1}{2}$ of 5%) and opposite "degrees of freedom" line $3 \cdot (n - 1) = 4 - 1 = 3$.

HYPOTHESIS TESTING (*t* curve)

As in estimation, "t" should be used instead of "Z" if (1) the sample is small (usually with samples as large or larger than 50, "Z" may be used), and (2) the sample standard deviation (s) must be used in place of the universe standard deviation (σ).

ESTIMATING A DOLLAR VALUE

Formulas:

(1) $\sigma = \frac{1}{5}(R_2 - R_1)$

(2) $n = \dfrac{Z^2\sigma^2}{E^2}$

(3) $\bar{X} = \dfrac{\sum_1^n x_i}{n}$

(4) $I = N\left(\bar{X} \pm 1.96\dfrac{\sigma}{\sqrt{n}}\right)^*$

---

* 1.96 for 95% confidence

where

σ = Standard deviation
R_1 = Low inventory value
R_2 = High inventory value
n = Sample size
Z^2 = Square of confidence level in standard error units
E^2 = Square of maximum allowance for sampling error
$\bar{X}$ = Average of sample values
I = Estimated inventory
N = Number in universe

Example:

During the course of your audit of the XYC Company, you wish to gain some insight as to the validity of the inventory value the company has recorded on the books as the closing inventory. The amount recorded is \$350,641. The inventory consists of 2000 items. Since this is only one of several audit tests of the inventory, you are willing to accept the following risks: (1) a 10% error rate not in excess of \$5, and (2) a 95% confidence level. By reviewing the inventory records, you have determined that the range of the inventory values is \$120 to \$276.70. You are required to determine:

1. the sample size
2. the estimated standard deviation
3. the range of inventory values

You are also required to:

4. form an opinion regarding the recorded inventory value
5. determine if any further audit procedures are required

Solution:

(1) $\sigma = \frac{1}{5}(R_2 - R_1)$
$\sigma = \frac{1}{5}(\$276.70 - \$120)$
$\sigma = \$31.34$

(2) $$n = \frac{Z^2\sigma^2}{E^2}$$

$$n = \frac{1.96^2 \times \$31.34^2}{\$5^2}$$

$$n = \frac{\$3773}{\$25}$$

$$n = 151$$

(3) $\bar{X} = \dfrac{\sum_{1}^{n} X_i}{n}$ (mean average of sample values)

we assume $\bar{X} = \$176.34$ (value to be computed from sample values)

(4) $I = N\left(\bar{X} \pm 1.96 \dfrac{6}{\sqrt{n}}\right)$

$$I = 2000\left(\$176.34 \pm 1.96 \frac{\$31.34}{\sqrt{151}}\right)$$

$$I = 2000\left[\$176.34 \pm 1.96\left(\frac{\$31.34}{12.288}\right)\right]$$

$$I = 2000[\$176.34 \pm 1.96(\$2.550)]$$

$$I = 2000(\$176.34 \pm \$4.998)$$

$$I = \$352,680 \pm \$9996$$

$$= \text{Range from } \$342,684 \text{ to } \$362,676$$

The amount recorded does not seem to be out of line with the results obtained.

DISCOVERY SAMPLING

Formula:

$$P = 1 - \frac{C_n^d \, C_n^{N-d}}{C_n^N}$$

where

P = Probability of finding at least one discrepancy

d = Number of discrepancies in universe

n = Sample size

N = Universe size

$$C_n^N = \frac{N!}{n!\,(N-n)!}$$

Example:

An auditor wishes to determine if there are any nonexistent employees on the payroll. The company has 500 employees who are paid weekly. The universe is 26,000.

Solution:

For audit risk purposes and considering the amount of the average payroll check, $200, the auditor is willing to initially accept a 1% error rate or 10 per 1000 which is 260 discrepancies in the universe of 26,000 as not being material. He is also willing to accept a 5% risk of missing the discrepancies due to sample error.

By considering Table XV he obtains a sample size of 298. He applies his audit procedures to the 298 randomly selected checks and finds no discrepancies. He can probably conclude that there are 260 or less discrepancies with a 95% confidence level.

If the auditor still feels uncomfortable, and in this case he should, he can increase his sample size to 372 (298 + 74). If he finds no discrepancies, he can conclude there are 208 or less discrepancies in the universe of 26,000 at a 95% confidence level.

The procedure could be extended to a sample size of 1458 (298 + 1160) and if 52 discrepancies existed, the auditor would expect to find at least one at the 95% confidence level. If the auditor finds one or more discrepancies, he would examine the nature of the discrepancies and decide what additional audit procedures are required.

SAMPLE SIZE

Variables. Sample small in proportion to size of universe. Standard deviation of universe can be determined.

Formula:

$$n = \frac{Z^2\sigma^2}{E^2}$$

where

n = Number of items in sample

Z^2 = Square of confidence level in standard error units

σ^2 = Square of standard deviation of universe

E^2 = Square of maximum difference between true mean and sample mean—the allowance for sampling error

Example:

A random sample is to be taken from 4000 statements to verify the amounts on the statements. The allowable sampling error is \$5. The sample size is to be large enough that this error is not exceeded more than 1 time in 100. What size should the sample be?

Solution:

$$Z^2 = (2.58)^2$$

$$\sigma^2 = (31.34)^2$$

(This was obtained from the knowledge that the total range in the statements was from \$120 to \$276.70 or \$156.70. The standard deviation could be estimated to be 1/5 of \$156.70 or \$31.34.)

$$E^2 = (\$5)^2$$

$$n = \frac{(2.58)^2(31.34)^2}{(5)^2} = \frac{6.6564 \times 982.20}{25} = \frac{6538}{25}$$

$$= 262$$

Therefore the required sample size would be 262.

SAMPLE SIZE
Proportions. Sample small in relation to size of universe.

Formula:

$$n = \frac{Z^2\pi(1 - \pi)}{E^2}$$

where

n = Number of items in sample

Z^2 = Square of confidence level in standard error units

π = Proportion of "successes" in universe (A success is the occurrence of a favorable event.)

$1 - \pi$ = Proportion of "failures" in universe (A failure is the occurrence of an unfavorable event.)

E^2 = Square of maximum difference between true proportion and sample proportion—the allowance for sampling error

Example:

From 10,000 items, a random sample is to be taken for verification purposes. It is believed that 90% of the totals on the forms to be studied are correct. The sample size is to be large enough that an observed difference in the sample proportion from the true proportion would not vary more than 3% five times out of 100.

Solution:

$$Z^2 = (1.96)^2$$
$$\pi = .90$$
$$1 - \pi = .10$$
$$E^2 = (.03)^2$$
$$n = \frac{(1.96)^2(.90)(.10)}{(.03)^2} = \frac{(3.84)(.09)}{.0009} = \frac{.3456}{.0009}$$
$$= 384, \text{ sample size}$$

SAMPLE SIZE
Variables. Finite universe.

Formula:

$$n = \frac{N}{\dfrac{(N-1)E^2}{Z^2\sigma^2} + 1}$$

where

n = Number of items in sample
N = Number of items in universe
Z^2 = Square of confidence level in standard error units
σ^2 = Square of standard deviation of universe
E^2 = Square of maximum allowance for sampling error

Example:

A sample is to be taken from a universe of 2000 items for verification. The universe standard deviation was estimated from a pilot study to be $50. The error is not to exceed $10, two times out of 100. How many should be selected for the sample to be verified?

Solution:

$$n = ?$$
$$N = 2000$$
$$Z^2 = (2.33)^2$$
$$\sigma^2 = (50)^2$$
$$E^2 = (10)^2$$

$$n = \frac{2000}{\dfrac{(1999)(100)}{(2.33)^2(50)^2} + 1} = \frac{2000}{\dfrac{199900}{13572} + 1} = \frac{2000}{15.7288}$$

$$= 127, \text{ sample size}$$

SAMPLE SIZE
Proportions. Finite universe.

Formula:

$$n = \frac{N}{\dfrac{(N-1)E^2}{Z^2\pi(1-\pi)} + 1}$$

where

n = Number in sample
N = Number in universe
E^2 = Square of maximum allowance for sampling error
Z^2 = Square of confidence level in standard error units
π = Proportion of successes in universe (A success is the occurrence of a favorable event.)
$1 - \pi$ = Proportion of failures in universe (A failure is the occurrence of an unfavorable event.)

Example:

A sample is to be taken from a total of 2000 items for verification. It is estimated that the universe proportion of error is 10 percent. An allowance of .05 is to be made for sampling error. *Z* is to be 2.33. What size random sample should be selected?

Solution:

$$N = 2000$$
$$E^2 = (.05)^2$$
$$Z^2 = (2.33)^2$$
$$\pi = .90 \qquad 1 - \pi = .10$$

$$\text{Therefore } n = \frac{2000}{\dfrac{(2000 - 1)(.05)^2}{(2.33)^2(.90)(.10)} + 1} = \frac{2000}{\dfrac{4.9975}{.4886} + 1}$$
$$= \frac{2000}{11.228}$$
$$= 178, \text{ sample size}$$

Sample size, instead of being computed from the formulas on the pages preceding, may be read directly from Table XIV.

SAMPLE SIZE
Variables. Sample small relative to size of universe.

Example:

Suppose the sample number is to be obtained from Table XIV for the data given on page 87 where

n = Number of items in sample
$Z = 2.58$
$\sigma = 31.34$
$E = 5$

Solution:

$$\text{Table XIV entries: column: } \frac{\sigma}{E} = \frac{31.34}{5} = 6.27 \quad \text{row: } Z = 2.58$$

n for column 6.0 = 240
n for column 6.5 = 282
n for 6.27 = 262

SAMPLE SIZE
Proportions. Sample small relative to size of universe.

Example:

Suppose the sample number is to be obtained from Table XIV for the data given on page 88, where

n = Number of items in sample
$Z = 1.96$
$\pi = .90$
$1 - \pi = .10$
$E = .03$

Table XIII entries: column: $\dfrac{\sqrt{\pi(1-\pi)}}{E} = \dfrac{\sqrt{(.90)(.10)}}{.03} = 10$

row: $Z = 1.96$

n for column 10.0, row 1.96 = 384

Where the sample is large relative to the universe size, the sample size may be read from Table XIII and then a finite universe correction multiplier applied to that sample size.

SAMPLE SIZE
Variables. Sample large relative to size of universe.

Formula:

$$n_f = \left[\frac{N}{N + (n-1)}\right] n$$

where

n_f = Sample number with finite correction
N = Universe or population size
n = Sample number without finite correction

Example:

Referring to the previous example on pages 88 and 89, where
$N = 2000$
$Z = 2.33$

$\sigma = 50$
$E = 10$
n_f = sample number with finite correction

Solution:

Table XIV entries: column: $\frac{\sigma}{E} = 5$ row: $Z = 2.33$ $n = 137$

$$n_f = \left[\frac{2000}{2000 + (137 - 1)}\right](137) = (.936)(137) = 127$$

Where the sample is large relative to the universe size, the sample size may be read from Table XIII and then a finite universe correction multiplier applied to that sample size.

SAMPLE SIZE
Proportions. Sample large relative to size of universe.

Formula:

$$n_f = \left[\frac{N}{N + (n - 1)}\right]n$$

where

n_f = Sample number with finite correction
N = Universe or population size
n = Sample number without finite correction

Example:

Referring to the previous example on pages 88 and 89, where

$N = 2000$
$E = .05$
$Z = 2.33$
$\pi = .90$
$1 - \pi = .10$
n_f = sample number with finite correction

Solution:

Table XIV entries: column: $\frac{\sqrt{\pi(1 - \pi)}}{E} = \frac{\sqrt{(.09)(.10)}}{.05} = 6$

$$\text{Row: } Z = 2.33$$
$$n = 196$$
$$n_f = \frac{2000}{2000 + (196 - 1)}(196) = (.911)(196) = 179$$

RANDOM NUMBERS

After the sample size has been determined, the specific sample items may be chosen randomly. Table XVII, a table of 35,000 random digits, may be used to designate these items. The random digits in Table XVII are a part, with slight modifications, of the set originally compiled by the United States Interstate Commerce Commission.

Steps in Use of Table XVII

1. Assign the items in the universe, or subsection of the universe to be sampled, consecutive numbers of 0 through N, where N is the highest number assigned.
2. Obtain a random start position on any page of the pages of random numbers.
3. Determine the column or columns, or other number sets, to be used.
4. Follow down the numbers in the column, or columns, selected until a number falls within the range of the numbers assigned in step 1. The item belonging to this number belongs in the sample. Continue down the same columns, letting a second number determine a second sample item, and so on, until all n items needed for the sample have been indicated.

Example 1:

Suppose a day's billing consists of 1000 separate invoices. It is decided to audit the entire invoice when one falls into the sample. From previous experience of the accuracy of the process, it is known that a 2 percent sample will fail only five times out of a hundred on the average to detect an invoice in error. Therefore, a sample of twenty invoices is to be audited. The sample items are to be selected at random.

Solution:

1. Number the completed invoices 0 through 999. (If the invoices carry consecutive numbers, these may be used also. The range

in these numbers might be, for example, 3003 to 4003, where 3003 would become 0, or the assigned number on each invoice would equal the invoice number minus 3003.)

2. Obtain a random start on a page of random numbers by placing a pencil above the random numbers; then without looking at it, move the hand and bring the pencil point down on the page. The number on which the pencil point falls, or the one closest to it, forms the left-hand digit of the first random number. Suppose the pencil is above page 294 and its point lands on the number 7, the second digit from the left side of line 24, column (3). This 7 and the two numbers immediately to the right of it, namely 6 and 3, will form the three-digit number. Three digits, representing three columns, will have to be used since the maximum number on the invoices, 999, (universe) contains three digits. This three-digit number from the table is 763. Therefore, invoice 763 from step 1 above falls in the sample and is the first one to be audited.
3. Continue down the same three columns of figures to determine the other invoices in the sample. By reference to this table, it can be noted that the invoices having the following numbers fall in the sample: 763, 883, 483, 808, 906, 566, 411, 791, 279, 587, 988, 357, 795, 99, 884, 482, 560, 336, 872, 947.
4. If the bottom of the page is reached with the three columns being used, continue from the top of the page to the bottom with the next three columns. This should continue the random process since a random start was used. If at any time the place is lost, take another random start. Avoid overlapping the same way since this could lead to a repeat bias.

Example 2:

Suppose that only 800 invoices are in the universe. The same numbering process as in Example 1 can be used to assign consecutive numbers. Also, a three-digit random number is used and the sample size is 16. As in Example 1 above, invoice 763 is the first one in the sample. The second number, reading down the columns, 883, however, is too large and is skipped. The next number encountered, 483, is used. Going on down the columns, 808 and 906 are skipped, while 566, 411, 791, 279, 587 are used, 988 skipped, and 357, 795, 99, (884 skipped), 482, 560, 536 (872, 947 skipped), and 699, 98, 397 are used, making the total of 16 to be audited.

Production of the Random Set Compiled by the United States Interstate Commerce Commission

In producing this particular set of random decimal digits, it was calculated that addition modulo 10 of 10 decimal digits from the original set would yield a set with probabilities in the range $1/10 \pm 10^{-7}$. This derived set was produced by tabulating 75,000 machine cards that had been punched from waybills received during three months in the regular course of the commission's work. Fourteen columns, which apparently were independent, were selected from these cards. These included positions from such fields as the shipment weight, revenue, serial number of the car, and so on. Each of these columns was then tabulated by wiring into counters with no carryover and so controlled that the total in the units position of the counter would be cut in a summary card at the end of each 10 cards. The totals (mod 10) of the 14 columns for each block of ten cards were cut in the first 14 columns of the summary cards until 1500 summary cards had been completed from the first 15,000 cards of the original set. The 1500 summary cards were then replaced in the summary punch, which was wired to punch in the next 14 columns, using totals from the second 15,000 cards of the original set. This operation was repeated until 70 columns of the summary cards had been punched. The random numbers in Table XVII are a part of this set.

Tests for Randomness

The set of random numbers compiled by the United States Interstate Commerce Commission, of which this is a part, was subjected to three tests for randomness. On the first of these, the frequency test in which the actual frequencies of the digits were compared to the expected frequencies, χ^2 was equal to 1.938 with a P of .99. The serial test was next applied, where the frequencies of digits following any specified digit were tabulated. Here χ^2 was equal to 75.461 with a P of .96. The gap test, checking the number of nonzero digits appearing between successive zeros, had a χ^2 of 3.072 and P of .69.

The digits appearing in Table XVII have been tabulated and further checked for randomness since they form only a part of the original set.

Use of Machine Methods of Selection

In many sampling problems it is desirable to have sets of random numbers in a form suitable for machine use. In most such cases machines and sources of numerical data are available from which sets of any size can be constructed. Random selection of machine cards may also be accomplished without the use of recorded random numbers. Data recorded on the cards themselves can be used to generate random digits by addition modulo 10, and these digits may be used to make the selection as the cards pass through the machine. For example, a listing of a 10 percent random sample from a deck of cards could be obtained without disturbing the order of the cards. Several columns in the cards would be selected for independence and irregularity and the digits in these columns added into separate counters. The counters would not be cleared, so that at any time the digit in the units position of each counter would be the result of addition modulo 10 of the digits in the column wired to it. The units digits read successively from the counters would form a random sequence which could be used to control the listing. Extensions of this principle to other problems and for other types of equipment will suggest themselves.

Other Distributions of Random Numbers

It is possible by the use of suitable transformations to obtain from the 35,000 random digits in Table XVII other sets of random numbers which will follow any given distribution function.

Let

$$y = \int_{-\infty}^{x} \phi(z)\,dz$$

If y is distributed between 0 and 1 with uniform probability, x will be distributed according to $\phi(x)$, where ϕ is any probability density function.

SAMPLING FROM DISTRIBUTIONS THAT ARE NOT NORMAL

Many problems with which the auditor deals will involve distributions that are not normal, not even symmetrical. These distributions involving business transactions are most often right skewed. Several characteristics found in the business world contribute to this right-skewed tendency:

1. There is a lower limit but not an upper limit. Example: debt, accounts receivable, errors, and so on have a lower limit of zero but no upper limit.

2. Geometric rather than arithmetic accumulation of capital. Example: Compounding of income on capital.
3. Nonlinear attributes. Example: value (price times number).
4. Uneven distribution of human capacities and resources available. Example: distribution of personal income.

Right-skewed curves present special problems. The following example illustrates one way of dealing with this problem.

Formula:

Total universe average: $\mu = \dfrac{N_1\overline{X}_1 + N_2\overline{X}_2}{N_1 + N_2}$

Total universe amount: $N\mu$

where

μ = Mean of universe

N = Number in universe

N_1 and N_2 = Number in Group 1 and in Group 2, respectively

$\overline{X}_1$ and $\overline{X}_2$ = Mean for Group 1 and mean for Group 2, respectively

Example:

The auditor has reason to verify the total accounts payable figure of $302,500. He knows the distribution of the amounts is right skewed like the following diagram.

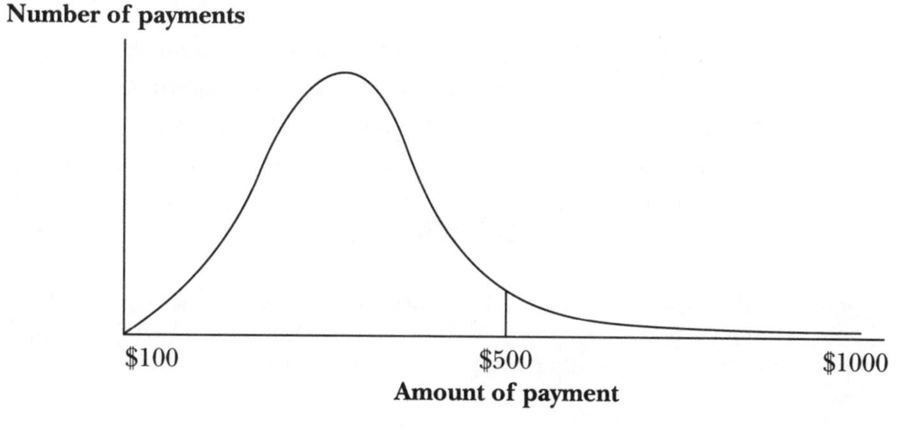

He divides the total into 2 groups. Group 1 are the 900 (N_i) accounts, ranging from \$100 to \$500. He tests this group to find $\bar{X}_1$. In this group at the lower range of values, he is willing to allow \$12 for sampling error and to use the 95% confidence level. He has estimated the standard deviation to be \$80. What size sample should he take to test Group 1?

$$n = \frac{Z^2\sigma^2}{E^2} \qquad n = \frac{(1.96)^2(80)^2}{(12)^2} = \frac{24586.24}{144} = 171$$

He checked the 171 sample items and found their mean ($\bar{X}_1$) to be \$210. Group 2, the 120 (N_2) amounts, vary from \$500 to \$1000. He tests each one of these and finds their mean ($\bar{X}_2$) to be \$690.

Solution:

$$\mu = \frac{900(\$210) + 120(\$690)}{210 + 690} = \frac{\$189{,}000 + \$82{,}800}{900}$$

$$= \$302$$

$$N\mu = 900(\$302) = \$271{,}800$$

Conclusion:

The test figure of \$271,800 is to be considered with the reported figure of \$302,500. Unless the testing has already uncovered a source of error, further checking is advised.

Other Approaches to Right Skewness

For some right-skewed distributions, symmetry can be achieved by a transformation on the universe values. The two most common transformations are

1. Geometric—the logarithm of each value involved is used and the geometric mean instead of the arithmetic mean is obtained.
2. Harmonic—the reciprocal of each value involved is used and the harmonic mean instead of the arithmetic mean is obtained.

REFERENCES

1. Kendall, M. G., and Smith, B. Babington, Randomness and random sampling numbers, *Jour. Roy., Stat. Soc.*, Vol. 101 (1938), pp. 147–166; Kendall, M. G., and Smith, B. Babington, Second paper on random sampling numbers, *Jour. Roy., Stat. Soc. Supp.*, Vol. 6 (1939), pp. 51–61.

2. Tippett, L. H. C., Random sampling numbers, *Tracts for Computers,* No. 15 (1927), Cambridge; Kendall, M. G., and Smith, B. Babington, Tables of random sampling numbers, *Tracts for Computers,* No. 24 (1939), Cambridge.
3. H. Burke Horton and R. Tynes Smith, III, A direct method for producing random digits in any number system, *Annals of Math. Stat.,* Vol. 20 (1949), pp. 82–90; H. Burke Horton, A method for obtaining random numbers, *Annals of Math. Stat.,* Vol. 19 (1948), pp. 81–85.

7

Statistical Correlation

REGRESSION

Linear. One independent variable.

Formula:

$$Y' = b_{11} + b_{12}X$$

where

Y' = Any value of the dependent variable on the regression line

b_{11} = Y intercept of regression line (value of Y' where $X = 0$)

b_{12} = Slope of regression line (ratio of the change in Y for a given change in X)

X = Any value of the independent variable

Example:

a. What is the average relationship between total cost and units produced on a given job?

b. What is the fixed cost, the average variable cost?

DATA

Job Lot Number	Number Units Produced X	Total Cost (dollars) Y	XY	X^2	Y^2
1	5	9	45	25	81
2	4	8	32	16	64
3	3	6	18	9	36
4	8	12	96	64	144
5	9	14	126	81	196
6	6	12	72	36	144
7	10	14	140	100	196
8	3	8	24	9	64
9	2	7	14	4	49
10	2	6	12	4	36
11	3	10	30	9	100
12	6	10	60	36	100
13	9	15	135	81	225
14	7	14	98	49	196
15	5	11	55	25	121
16	7	13	91	49	169
17	6	11	66	36	121
18	6	13	78	36	169
19	7	10	70	49	100
20	5	10	50	25	100
21	5	12	60	25	144
22	6	14	84	36	196
23	4	9	36	16	81
24	8	14	112	64	196
25	9	13	117	81	169
	145	275	1721	965	3197
	ΣX	ΣY	ΣXY	ΣX^2	ΣY^2

Solution (least squares method):

I $\quad \Sigma Y = b_{11}N + B_{12}\Sigma X$ (with summations over all values of variables indicated)

II $\quad \Sigma XY = b_{11}\Sigma X + b_{12}\Sigma X^2$

I $\quad 275 = 25\, b_{11} + 145\, b_{12}$

II $\quad 1721 = 145\, b_{11} + 965\, b_{12}$

I (5.8)	$1595 = 145\ b_{11} + 841\ b_{12}$	(multiply each side of Equation I by 5.8 to cancel out b_{11})
II-I (5.8)	$126 = \qquad 124\ b_{12}$	(Equation II minus Equation I)

$$b_{12} = \frac{126}{124} = 1.02$$

Substituting 1.02 for b_{12} in Equation I:

$$b_{11} = \frac{275 - 145\ (1.02)}{25} = 5.08$$

(a) Therefore the average line of relationship is

$$Y' = 5.08 + 1.02\ X$$

(b) Average fixed cost: \$5.08
Average variable cost: for each additional unit produced, total cost increased \$1.02

STANDARD ERROR OF ESTIMATE
Linear regression, one independent variable.

Formula:

$$S_{yx} = \sqrt{\frac{\Sigma Y^2 - b_{11}\Sigma Y - b_{12}\Sigma XY}{N - 2}}$$

where

S_{yx} = Standard error of estimate
ΣY^2 = Sum of all squared values of dependent variable
b_{11} = Y intercept of regression line (Y value where $X = 0$)
ΣY = Sum of all values of dependent variable
b_{12} = Slope of regression line
ΣXY = Sum of all individual products formed by multiplying each X value by its corresponding Y value
N = Total number of paired observations

Example:

Using the data given on page 101 and assuming a normal distribution of Y values for each X, what would be the expected total cost of 20 units? What statement could be made concerning the reliability of this result?

Solution:

Expected total cost for 20 units:

$$Y' = \$5.08 + \$1.02(20) = \$5.08 + \$20.40 = \$25.48$$

Statement concerning reliability of the \$25.48:

$$S_{yx} = \sqrt{\frac{3197 - 5.08(275) - 1.02(1721)}{23}} = \sqrt{\frac{44.58}{23}}$$
$$= \sqrt{1.9386} = 1.39$$

If the statement is made that the cost of producing 20 units will average \$25.48 but that the cost may be anywhere in the range of \$25.48 ± \$1.39 (between \$24.09 and \$26.87), that statement would hold in approximately 2/3 (68%) of the cases like this but would be expected to be outside this range of \$24.09 to \$26.87 in the other 1/3 of the cases like this. Therefore, \$25.48 ± (1.96)(\$1.39) would give a 95% confidence interval, and \$25.48 ± (2.58)(\$1.39) would give a 99% confidence interval, when the stated assumptions hold.

COEFFICIENT OF DETERMINATION
Linear regression, one independent variable.

Formula:

$$r^2 = 1 - \frac{S_{yx}^2}{S_y^2}$$

where

r^2 = Coefficient of determination
S_{yx}^2 = Standard error of estimate squared (See page 102.)
S_y^2 = Standard deviation of Y variable squared

Example:

What is the percent of variation in cost of producing which is associated with the number of pieces produced? (See data on page 101, and computation of $S_{yx} = 1.39$ on page 102.)

Solution:

$$r^2 = 1 - \frac{(1.39)^2}{S_y^2} \text{ where } S_y^2 = \frac{\Sigma Y^2}{N} - \frac{(\Sigma Y)^2}{N^2} = \frac{3197}{25} - \frac{(275)^2}{(25)^2}$$

$$r^2 = 127.88 - 121 = 6.88$$

$$r^2 = 1 - \frac{(1.39)^2}{6.88} = 1 - \frac{1.93}{6.88} = 1 - .28 = .72$$

Therefore 72 percent of the variance in cost of producing is associated with the variation in the number of pieces produced. This leaves 28 percent of the variation in cost which is *not* related to variation in number of units produced. This 28 percent might be due to any of several other factors, one of which might be variation in materials quality.

COEFFICIENT OF CORRELATION
Linear regression, one independent variable.

1. Where coefficient of determination, r^2, is known:

Formula:

$$r = \pm\sqrt{r^2}$$

where

r = Coefficient of correlation
r^2 = Coefficient of determination

Example:

What is the coefficient of correlation for the data given on page 00 where r^2, or coefficient of determination, is .72?

Solution:

$$r = \pm\sqrt{.72} = \pm.85$$

Note: The sign given to r depends on the sign of b_{12}, which for this example is plus. (See page 102.) Therefore the result would be plus .85.

2. Where coefficient of determination, r^2, is not known:

Formula:

$$r = \frac{N\Sigma XY - (\Sigma X)(\Sigma Y)}{\sqrt{[N\Sigma X^2 - (\Sigma X)^2][N\Sigma Y^2 - (\Sigma Y)^2]}}$$

where

r = Coefficient of correlation

$N\Sigma XY$ = Multiply each X by each corresponding Y. Add these products. Then multiply this sum by N, the total number of paired observations.

$(\Sigma X)(\Sigma Y)$ = Add all X values. Add all Y values. Multiply sum of X values by sum of Y values.

$N\Sigma X^2$ = Square each X value. Add squared X values. Multiply this sum by N, the total number of paired observations.

$(\Sigma X)^2$ = Add all X values. Square this sum.

$N\Sigma Y^2$ = Square each Y value. Add squares. Multiply sum by N.

$(\Sigma Y)^2$ = Add all Y values. Square sum.

Example:

What is the coefficient of correlation for the data given on pages 100 and 101 where:

$$N = 25 \qquad \Sigma X = 145$$
$$\Sigma XY = 1721 \qquad \Sigma Y = 275$$
$$\Sigma X^2 = 965 \qquad \Sigma Y^2 = 3197$$

Solution:

$$r = \frac{(25)(1721) - (145)(275)}{\sqrt{[(25)(965) - (145)^2][(25)(3197) - (275)^2]}}$$
$$= \frac{43025 - 39875}{\sqrt{(24125 - 21025)(79925 - 75625)}}$$
$$= \frac{3150}{\sqrt{(3100)(4300)}} = \frac{3150}{3651} = .86$$

Note: The difference in the .86 obtained here and the .85 obtained in 1 preceding is due to rounding.

REGRESSION

Linear relationships, more than one independent variable.

Formula:

$$X_1 = b_{11} + b_{12}X_2 + b_{13}X_3$$

where

X_1 = Any value of dependent variable on the net regression line (same as Y' used on page 102)
b_{11} = Point of intersection of the regression lines of the planes
b_{12} = Rate of change in X_1 as X_2 changes
X_2 = Any value of first independent variable
b_{13} = Rate of change in X_1 as X_3 changes
X_3 = Any value of second independent variable

Example:

(1) What is the average relationship between total cost (X_1), units produced (X_2), and thickness of materials (X_3)?
(2) What total cost would be expected if 10 units were produced and the material thickness were $\frac{5}{1000}$ of an inch?
(3) What is the change in cost if pieces produced changed from 10 to 11, while material thickness did not change?
(4) What is the change in cost if materials thickness changed from $\frac{4}{1000}$ to $\frac{5}{1000}$ of an inch, while pieces produced did not change?

Data

Job Lot Number	Total cost ($) X_1	Number Units Produced X_2	Material Thickness (thous. inch) X_3	X_1^2	X_2^2	X_3^2	X_1X_2	X_1X_3	X_2X_3
1	9	5	4	81	25	16	45	36	20
2	8	4	3	64	16	9	32	34	12
3	6	3	2	36	9	4	18	12	6
4	12	8	5	144	64	25	96	60	40
5	12	6	4	144	36	16	72	48	24
6	14	9	6	196	81	36	126	84	54
7	14	10	6	196	100	36	140	84	60
8	8	3	4	64	9	16	24	32	12
9	7	2	3	49	4	9	14	21	6
10	6	2	2	36	4	4	12	12	4
11	10	3	6	100	9	36	30	60	18
12	10	6	5	100	36	25	60	50	30
13	15	9	9	225	81	81	135	135	81
14	14	7	7	196	49	49	98	98	49
15	11	5	6	121	25	36	55	66	30

Job Lot Number	Total cost ($) X_1	Number Units Produced X_2	Material Thickness (thous. inch) X_3	X_1^2	X_2^2	X_3^2	X_1X_2	X_1X_3	X_2X_3
16	13	7	7	169	49	49	91	91	49
17	11	6	5	121	36	25	66	55	30
18	13	6	8	169	36	64	78	104	48
19	10	7	6	100	49	36	70	60	42
20	10	5	5	100	25	25	50	50	25
21	12	5	7	144	25	49	60	84	35
22	14	6	9	196	36	81	84	126	54
23	9	4	4	81	16	16	36	36	16
24	14	8	9	196	64	81	112	126	72
25	13	9	8	169	81	64	117	104	72
	275	145	140	3197	965	888	1721	1658	889
	ΣX_1	ΣX_2	ΣX_3	ΣX_1^2	ΣX_2^2	ΣX_3^2	ΣX_1X_2	ΣX_1X_3	ΣX_2X_3

Solution: (least squares method)

$$\begin{array}{rrcl}
\text{I} & \Sigma X_1 & = & b_{11}N + b_{12}\Sigma X_2 + b_{13}\Sigma X_3 \\
\text{II} & \Sigma X_1X_2 & = & b_{11}\Sigma X_2 + b_{12}\Sigma X_2^2 + b_{13}\Sigma X_2X_3 \\
\text{III} & \Sigma X_1X_3 & = & b_{11}\Sigma X_3 + b_{12}\Sigma X_2X_3 + b_{13}\Sigma X_3^2 \\
\text{I} & 275 & = & 25b_{11} + 145b_{12} + 140b_{13} \\
\text{II} & 1721 & = & 145b_{11} + 965b_{12} + 889b_{13} \\
\text{III} & 1658 & = & 140b_{11} + 889b_{12} + 888b_{13} \\
\text{II} & 1721 & = & 145b_{11} + 965b_{12} + 889b_{13} \\
\text{I}' = (\text{I})(5.8) & 1595 & = & 145b_{11} + 841b_{12} + 812b_{13} \\
\hline
\text{IV} = \text{II} - \text{I}' & 126 & = & 124b_{12} + 77b_{13} \\
\text{III} & 1658 & = & 140b_{11} + 889b_{12} + 888b_{13} \\
\text{I}'' = \text{I}(5.6) & 1540 & = & 140b_{11} + 812b_{12} + 784b_{13} \\
\hline
\text{V} = \text{III} - \text{I}(5.6) & 118 & = & 77b_{12} + 104b_{13} \\
\text{IV} & 126 & = & 124b_{12} + 77b_{13} \\
\text{V}' = \text{V}(1.61) & 190 & = & 124b_{12} + 167b_{13} \\
\hline
\text{V}' - \text{IV} & 64 & = & 90b_{13} \qquad b_{13} = .71
\end{array}$$

Substituting in V: $b_{12} = \dfrac{118 - 104b_{13}}{77} = \dfrac{118 - (104)(.71)}{77}$

$$b_{12} = .57$$

Substituting in I: $b_{11} = \dfrac{275 - 145b_{12} - 140b_{13}}{25}$

$$= \frac{275 - 145(.57) - 140(.71)}{25} = \frac{93}{25}$$

$$b_{11} = 3.72$$

a. Therefore the average relationship is:
$X_1 = 3.72 + .57X_2 + .71X_3$

b. If 10 units were produced and material thickness were $\frac{5}{1000}$ of an inch, a total cost of $12.97 would be expected:

$$X_1 = 3.72 + .57(10) + .71(5) = 12.97$$

c. If pieces produced is increased one piece, say from 10 to 11, while materials thickness does not change, the expected change in total cost would be $0.57.

d. If materials thickness changed $\frac{1}{1000}$ of an inch, say from $\frac{4}{1000}$ to $\frac{5}{1000}$ of an inch, while number of pieces produced remained constant, the total cost would be expected to change $0.71 (the value of b_{13}).

MULTIPLE COEFFICIENT OF DETERMINATION
Linear regression. More than one independent variable.

Formula:

$$R^2_{1.23} = 1 - \frac{S^2_{1.23}}{S^2_1}$$

where

$R^2_{1.23}$ = The coefficient of determination for variable 1 (the dependent variable) with variables 2 and 3 (the two independent variables)

$S^2_{1.23}$ = Standard error of estimate squared for variable 1 as the dependent and variables 2 and 3 as independent

S^2_1 = Standard deviation squared for variable 1 (dependent variable)

Example:

What is the percent of variation in cost of producing dependent upon the number of pieces produced and the thickness of the materials used? (See data on pages 106 and 107. See $S^2_1 = 6.88$ used on page 104 and there indicated as S^2_y). (See pages 106 and 107 for values of data needed for $S^2_{1.23}$).

Solution:

$$R^2_{1.23} = 1 - \frac{S^2_{1.23}}{S^2_1} = 1 - \frac{S^2_{1.23}}{6.88}$$

where

$$S^2_{1.23} = \frac{\Sigma X_1^2 - b_{11}\Sigma X_1 - b_{12}\Sigma X_1 X_2 - b_{13}\Sigma X_1 X_3}{n - 3}$$

$$= \frac{3197 - (3.72)(275) - (.57)(1721) - (.71)(1658)}{22} = .72$$

$$R^2_{1.23} = 1 - \frac{.72}{6.88} = 1 - .11 = .89$$

Therefore 89 percent of the variation in cost of producing is dependent upon number of pieces produced and thickness of material. By referring to pages 103 and 104, it can be noted that the coefficient of determination is increased from 72 percent to 89 percent by adding a second independent variable.

PARTIAL CORRELATION

Linear relationship, two independent variables.

Formula:

$$r_{12.3} = \frac{r_{12} - (r_{13})(r_{23})}{\sqrt{(1 - r^2_{13})(1 - r^2_{23})}}$$

where

$r_{12.3}$ = The partial correlation coefficient, i.e., the relationship between variables 1 and 2 with the effects of variable 3 taken out

r_{12} = Zero order correlation coefficient for variables 1 and 2

r_{13} = Zero order correlation coefficient for variables 1 and 3

r_{23} = Zero order correlation coefficient for variables 2 and 3

r^2_{13} = The zero order correlation coefficient squared for variables 1 and 3

r^2_{23} = The zero order correlation coefficient squared for variables 2 and 3

Example:

It can be seen by reference to page 105 that the correlation between total cost of producing and number of pieces produced is .86. This is a gross relationship. How much would this relationship be reduced if the effect on either one or both of the given variables of the thickness of material used were to be taken out?

Solution:

$$r_{12} = .86 \text{ (see page 105 for computations.)}$$

$$r_{13} = \frac{(25)(1658) - (275)(140)}{\sqrt{[(25)(3197) - (275)^2][(25)(888) - (140)^2]}}$$

$$= \frac{41450 - 38500}{\sqrt{(79925 - 75625)(22200 - 19600)}} = \frac{2950}{\sqrt{11{,}180{,}000}}$$

$$= .88$$

$$r_{23} = \frac{25(889) - (145)(140)}{\sqrt{[25(965) - (145)^2][25(888) - (140)^2]}}$$

$$= \frac{22225 - 20300}{\sqrt{(24125 - 21025)(22200 - 19600)}}$$

$$= \frac{1925}{\sqrt{8{,}060{,}00}} = .68$$

Therefore

$$r_{12.3} = \frac{.86 - (.88)(.68)}{\sqrt{[1 - (.88)^2][1 - (.68)^2]}} = \frac{.86 - .60}{\sqrt{(1 - .77)(1 - .46)}}$$

$$= \frac{.26}{\sqrt{(.23)(.54)}} = \frac{.26}{\sqrt{.1242}} = \frac{.26}{.35} \doteq .74$$

Partialling out the effects of material thickness reduced the gross relationship between total cost and number of units produced from .86 to .74.

RANK ORDER COEFFICIENT OF CORRELATION

Formula:

$$\rho = 1 - \frac{6\,\Sigma d^2}{N(N^2 - 1)}$$

where

ρ = Rank order correlation coefficient
Σd^2 = Sum of squared differences between each pair of corresponding ranks
N = Total number of pairs of ranks

Example:

For 20 jobs, it was possible to know their relative positions with respect to time spent and cost but not possible to measure either variable precisely enough to have confidence in its exact size. The time spent and costs were therefore ranked as to their relative position among the 20 jobs as follows:

Job Number	Rank in Amount of Time Spent on Job	Rank in Cost of Job	Difference in Ranks	Difference Squared
1	3	1	2	4
2	7	9	2	4
3	13	15	2	4
4	17	16	1	1
5	20	18	2	4
6	1	2	1	1
7	8	8	0	0
8	2	4	2	4
9	14	12	2	4
10	10	7	3	9
11	16	19	3	9
12	4	5	1	1
13	19	20	1	1
14	11	10	1	1
15	5	6	1	1
16	18	14	4	16
17	15	13	2	4
18	12	17	5	25
19	6	3	3	9
20	9	11	2	4
				$106 = \Sigma d^2$

$$\rho = 1 - \frac{6(106)}{20(20^2 - 1)} = 1 - \frac{636}{7980} = 1 - .08 = .92$$

The rank order correlation coefficient is .92.

RELIABILITY OF CORRELATION COEFFICIENTS
Linear relationships.

Formula:

$$\sigma_r = \frac{1 - r^2}{\sqrt{N - 2}}$$

where

σ_r = Standard error of the correlation coefficient, r
r^2 = Coefficient of correlation, squared
N = Number of pairs of observations used to compute r

Example:

A correlation coefficient of .40 was found from a sample of 51 clerical workers when the total number of minutes reporting late for work each morning for a month was matched against the total job production for that month for each of the 51. How reliable was this .40? Could the .40 have arisen due to sampling error while in reality there was no real basis for believing that there was a relationship between reporting on time for work in the morning and production?

Solution:

The hypothesis to be tested is that there is no correlation in this type of universe.

Therefore $$\sigma_r = \frac{1 - 0}{\sqrt{51 - 2}} = \frac{1}{7} = .14$$

If one wishes to maintain his confidence at the 95 percent level, he will have to reject the above hypothesis and say there does seem to exist a relationship between the two variables since .40 is outside the limits of $0 \pm 1.96\sigma_r$, outside the range of $\pm .2744$.

RELIABILITY OF CORRELATION COEFFICIENTS

Formula:

$$Z = \frac{1}{2} \log_e \frac{1 + r}{1 - r} = 1.15129 \log_{10} \frac{1 + r}{1 - r}$$

where

Z = A transformation of r and a statistic whose sampling distribution is approximately normal
r = Zero order coefficient of correlation between two variables

Formula:

$$\sigma_z = \frac{1}{\sqrt{N - m - 1}}$$

where

σ_z = Standard error of Z
N = Number of pairs of observations used to compute r
m = Number of variables used to compute r

Example:

A correlation coefficient of .40 was found from a sample of 52 clerical workers when the total number of minutes reporting late for work each morning for a month was matched against the total job production for that month for each of the 52. What is the probable range within which the true value of the universe relationship probably falls if one accepts a 95 percent confidence interval?

Solution:

$$Z = 1.15129 \log_{10}\frac{1 + .40}{1 - .40} = 1.15129 \log_{10}\frac{1.40}{.60}$$
$$= (1.15129)(0.367915) = .42$$
$$\sigma_z = \frac{1}{\sqrt{52 - 2 - 1}} = \frac{1}{7} = .14$$

Therefore, a 95 percent confidence interval = (1.96)(.14) = .27 on each side of the mean.

$$Z \pm 1.96\sigma_Z = .42 \pm .27 = .15 \text{ to } .69$$

The true correlation would therefore have a Z value range of .15 to .69.

E. ALTMAN'S *Z* SCORE*

Formula:

$$Z = 1.2(WCTA) + 1.4(RETA) + 3.3(EBIT) + 0.6(MEBD) + 1.0(SLTA)$$

where

$WCTA$ = Working capital total assets
$RETA$ = Retained earnings/total assets
$EBIT$ = Earnings before interest and taxes/total assets
$MEBD$ = Market value of equity/bank value of total debt
$SLTA$ = Sales/total assets

Example:

The following data were obtained concerning an operating firm in 198X. What is its *Z* Score?

Working capital	$2,073,656
Total assets	5,052,601
Retained earnings	1,575,060
Earnings before interest and taxes	879,109
Market value of common stock	2,708,468
Book value of total debt	2,000,000
Sales	9,112,908

Solution:

$$Z = 1.2\left(\frac{2{,}073{,}656}{5{,}052{,}601}\right) + 1.4\left(\frac{1{,}575{,}060}{5{,}052{,}601}\right) + 3.3\left(\frac{879{,}109}{5{,}052{,}601}\right) + 0.6\left(\frac{2{,}708{,}468}{2{,}000{,}000}\right) + 1.0\left(\frac{9{,}112{,}908}{5{,}052{,}601}\right)$$

$$Z = 1.2(.4104) + 1.4(.3117) + 3.3(.1740) + 0.6(1.3542) + 1.0(1.8036)$$

$$Z = .49 + .44 + .57 + .81 + 1.80$$

$$Z = 4.11$$

---

* From E. Altman et al., *Contemporary Studies in Economics and Financial Analysis*, Vol. 3, page 265.

Conclusion:

With a *Z* Score of 4.11, the firm is in the positive *Z* Range and does not appear to have financial difficulties. However, the auditor explained that the *Z* Score is "descriptive" of the last 12 months' performance and not necessarily "predictive" of the future performance. He called the firm's attention to the pending labor problems and the litigation that was on hold, both of which could affect the firm's financial condition and be reflected in its 198X+1 *Z* Score.

8

Statistics: Index Numbers

INDEX NUMBERS

Aggregative of prices weighted with fixed weights.

Formula:

$$I = \frac{\Sigma\, p_n q_o}{\Sigma\, p_o q_o}$$

where

p_n = Price of item in period for which index is being computed

p_o = Price of item in base year

q_o = Fixed weight

$\Sigma\, p_n q_o$ = Sum of products formed by multiplying each present period price by its corresponding fixed weight

$\Sigma\, p_o q_o$ = Sum of products formed by multiplying each base year price by its corresponding fixed weight

Example:

If data are as given following, what are the aggregative price indexes for 1986 and 1987, using 1985 weights and 1985 as base?

	Prices (p)			Quantities (q)		
Item	**1985**	**1986**	**1987**	**1985**	**1986**	**1987**
1	20	22	30	103	106	99
2	18	15	18	43	46	45
3	15	15	19	71	70	80

Solution:

$$I_{1986} = \frac{(22)(103) + (15)(43) + (15)(71)}{(20)(103) + (18)(43) + (15)(71)} = \frac{3976}{3899}$$

$$= 102, \text{ price index for 1986}$$

$$I_{1987} = \frac{(30)(103) + (18)(43) + (19)(71)}{(20)(103) + (18)(43) + (15)(71)} = \frac{5213}{3899}$$

$$= 134, \text{ price index for 1987}$$

INDEX NUMBERS
Aggregative price index weighted with variable weights.

Formula:

$$I = \frac{\Sigma\, p_n q_n}{\Sigma\, p_o q_n}$$

where

p_n = Price of item in period for which I is being constructed

p_o = Price of item in base period

q_n = Variable weight

$\Sigma\, p_n q_n$ = Sum of products formed by multiplying the price of each item in the present period by its corresponding weight for the same period

$\Sigma\, p_o q_n$ = Sum of products formed by multiplying the price of each item in the base period by its corresponding weight in the present period

Example:

If data are as given following, what are the aggregative price indexes for 1986 and 1987, using variable weights and 1985 as base?

	Prices (p)			Quantities (q)		
Item	**1985**	**1986**	**1987**	**1985**	**1986**	**1987**
1	20	22	30	103	106	99
2	18	15	18	43	46	45
3	15	15	19	71	70	80

Solution:

$$I_{1986} = \frac{(22)(106) + (15)(46) + (15)(70)}{(20)(106) + (18)(46) + (15)(70)} = \frac{4072}{3998}$$

$$= 102, \text{ price index for 1986}$$

$$I_{1987} = \frac{(30)(99) + (18)(45) + (19)(80)}{(20)(99) + (18)(45) + (15)(80)} = \frac{5300}{3990}$$

$$= 133, \text{ price index for 1987}$$

INDEX NUMBERS

Arithmetic mean of price relatives with fixed weights.

Formula:

$$I = \frac{\Sigma\left(\frac{p_n}{p_o} \times p_o q_o\right)}{\Sigma\, p_o q_o}$$

where

p_n = Price of an item in present period

p_o = Price of an item in base period

$p_o q_o$ = Fixed weight (product of base period price and fixed quantity)

$\frac{p_n}{p_o}$ = Price of an item in the present period relative to price of the same item in base period

$\Sigma\left(\frac{p_n}{p_o} \times p_o q_o\right)$ = Sum of weighted price relatives

$\Sigma\, p_o q_o$ = Sum of fixed weights

Example:

What is the arithmetic mean of the price relatives for 1987 if 1986 is the base year and fixed weights (from 1986) are used for the following data?

Item	Prices (p) 1986	1987	Quantities (q) 1986	1987
1	20	22	103	105
2	18	19	98	100
3	15	14	70	60

Solution:

$$I_{1987} = \frac{\left[\frac{22}{20} \times (20)(103)\right] + \left[\frac{19}{18} \times (18)(98)\right] + \left[\frac{14}{15} \times (15)(70)\right]}{(20)(103) + (18)(98) + (15)(70)}$$

$$= \frac{5108}{4874} = 105,$$ arithmetic mean of price relatives weighted by fixed weights

INDEX NUMBERS
Arithmetic mean of price relatives with variable weights.

Formula:

$$I = \frac{\Sigma\left(\frac{p_n}{p_o} \times p_n q_n\right)}{\Sigma\, p_n q_n}$$

where

p_n = Price of an item in present period
p_o = Price of an item in base period
q_n = Variable quantity
$p_n q_n$ = Variable weight
$\Sigma\left(\frac{p_n}{p_o} \times p_n q_n\right)$ = Sum of price relatives weighted by variable weights
$\Sigma\, p_n q_n$ = Sum of variable weights

Example:

What is the arithmetic mean of the price relatives for 1987 if 1986 is the base year and variable weights are employed for the following data?

Item	Prices (p) 1986	1987	Quantities (q) 1986	1987
1	20	22	103	105
2	18	19	98	100
3	15	14	70	60

Solution:

$$I_{1987} = \frac{\left[\frac{22}{20} \times (22)(105)\right] + \left[\frac{19}{18} \times (19)(100)\right] + \left[\frac{14}{15} \times (14)(60)\right]}{(22)(105) + (19)(100) + (14)(60)}$$

$$= \frac{5330}{5050} = 106, \text{ the arithmetic mean of price relatives weighted by variable weights}$$

Note: For a discussion of indexing, see Chapter 14, "Price Level Adjustments."

9

Statistics: Time Series

SECULAR TREND—LINEAR

Least squares method. Odd number of time periods.

Formula:

$$Y' = a + bX \qquad a = \frac{\Sigma Y}{N} \qquad b = \frac{\Sigma XY}{\Sigma X^2}$$

where

Y' = Trend value
a = Average (arithmetic mean) trend value
b = Rate of change in trend
X = Any time value
ΣY = Sum of values of variable
N = Number of time periods for which there are observations
ΣXY = Sum of products formed by multiplying the value of each Y by each corresponding X
ΣX^2 = Sum of all X's after they have been squared

Example:

(1) What is the secular trend in sales for the following data?

(2) With this formula, what level of secular trend in sales might be estimated for 1990?

Time Period		Sales (thous. $)		
X	X	Y	XY	X^2
1930	−5	6	−30	25
1935	−4	9	−36	16
1940	−3	15	−45	9
1945	−2	20	−40	4
1950	−1	21	−21	1
1955	0	22	0	0
1960	1	25	25	1
1965	2	36	72	4
1970	3	45	135	9
1975	4	48	192	16
1980	5	50	250	25
	0	297	502	110
	ΣX	ΣY	ΣXY	ΣX^2

Solution:

$$a = \frac{\Sigma Y}{N} = \frac{297}{11} = 27 \qquad b = \frac{\Sigma XY}{\Sigma X^2} = \frac{502}{110} = 4.56$$

(1) $Y' = 27 + 4.56X$ (with origin at 1955)

(2) 1990 is time period number 7. Therefore $Y' = 27 + 4.56(7) = 58.92$, or approximately $59,000 in 1990 if the straight line trend continues.

SECULAR TREND—LINEAR

Least squares method. Even number of time periods.

Formula:

$$Y' = a + bX \qquad a = \frac{\Sigma Y}{N} \qquad b = \frac{\Sigma XY}{\Sigma X^2}$$

where

Y' = Trend value
a = Average (arithmetic mean) trend value
b = Rate of change in trend
X = Any time value
ΣY = Sum of values of variable
N = Number of time periods for which there are observations

ΣXY = Sum of products formed by multiplying the value of each Y by its corresponding X

ΣX^2 = Sum of all X's after they have been squared

Example:

(1) What is the secular trend for the following sales data?

(2) With this formula, what would the estimate of secular trend in sales be for 1995?

Time Period		Sales (thous. $)		
X	X	Y	XY	X^2
1935	−9	9	−81	81
1940	−7	15	−105	49
1945	−5	20	−100	25
1950	−3	21	−63	9
1955	−1	22	−22	1
	0			
1960	1	25	25	1
1965	3	36	108	9
1970	5	45	225	25
1975	7	48	336	49
1980	9	59	531	81
	0	300	854	330
	ΣX	ΣY	ΣXY	ΣX^2

Solution:

$$a = \frac{\Sigma Y}{N} = \frac{300}{10} = 30 \qquad b = \frac{\Sigma XY}{\Sigma X^2} = \frac{854}{330} = 2.59$$

(1) $Y' = 30 + 2.59X$ (with origin at June 30, 1957)

(2) 1995 is time period number 15 in this problem. Therefore $Y' = 30 + 2.59(15) = 30 + 38.85 = 68.85$, or approximately $68,850 if the straight line secular trend continues.

SECULAR TREND
Moving average method. Odd number of periods averaged.

Formula:

$$A = \frac{V_1 + V_2 + \cdots + V_n}{n}$$

where

A = Moving average
V_1 = Value belonging to first time period in average
V_n = Value belonging to nth or last time period in average
n = Number of time periods in average

Example:

What is the secular trend for the following production values which show a three-year cyclical fluctuation on the average?

Year	Production (in thousands of tons)	3-Year Moving Average
1975	30	
1976	35	31
1977	28	30
1978	27	29
1979	32	29
1980	28	29
1981	27	29
1982	35	
...	...	
...	...	
...	...	

Solution:

For the 31, the first moving average shown above:

$$V_1 = 30 \qquad V_2 = 35 \qquad V_3 = 28$$

$$A = \frac{V_1 + V_2 + V_3}{3} = \frac{30 + 35 + 28}{3} = 31$$

The same method would be followed to obtain the moving averages for all the data. The data would then be plotted. Then points would be placed on the graph showing the location of the moving averages. These points would form the guide points for drawing in the secular trend line. The trend line would not necessarily pass through all of these points. For the data just given, it appears that although the level of production fluctuates from year to year, it does so because of cycle. The secular trend appears so far to be moving almost horizontally.

SECULAR TREND
Moving average method. Even number of periods averaged and centered.

Formula:

$$A = \frac{V_1 + 2V_2 + 2V_3 + \cdots + V_n}{2n}$$

where

A = Moving average
V_1 = Value belonging to first time period in average
$2V_2$ = 2 times value belonging to second time period in average
V_n = Value belonging to nth or last time period in average
n = Number of time periods in average

Example:

Year	Production (in thousands of tons)	4-Year Moving (centered) Sum	Average
1975	15		
1976	20		
1977	22	144	18
1978	14	152	19
1979	17	164	20.5
1980	26	...	...
1981	28	...	...
1982	15	...	...
...	...	...	...
...	...		
...	...		

Solution:

An even number moving average centered is equivalent to an odd number moving average weighted, where the end values are weighted by 1 and each of the nonend values weighted by 2. Hence for the 4-year centered moving average in the previous table with the first result of 18:

$$A = \frac{V_1 + 2V_2 + 2V_3 + 2V_4 + V_5}{2n}$$

$$= \frac{15 + 2(20) + 2(22) + 2(14) + 17}{8} = 18$$

Computations can be speeded if the method just indicated is followed where the moving centered sums are obtained first, then multiplication of each of these sums by the reciprocal of "$2n$" (in this case 8) is performed to obtain the averages. After the averages are obtained, they would be plotted on the graph showing the original time series data. These averages would then form the guides for drawing in the secular trend line. All the averages will not necessarily fall on the smooth secular trend line.

SEASONAL

Ratio to moving average method. Data assumed to contain seasonal, cycle, and secular trend, related to each other as multiplied factors.

Formula:

$$S = \frac{T \times C \times S}{T \times C}$$

where

S = Seasonal value
T = Secular trend value
C = Cycle value
$T \times C \times S$ = Original data
$T \times C$ = Measurement of trend and cycle

Example:

(1) What is the seasonal index for sales of the second quarter?

(2) What is the seasonal pattern for sales for each of the four quarters?

(3) What would be the estimated sales level for the fourth quarter, 1978, if the seasonal effects were eliminated?

Year	Quarter	Sales (in thousands of $) $T \times C \times S$	4-quarter moving (centered) Sum	Average $T \times C$	Seasonal $(T \times C \times S) \div (T \times C)$ (in percent)
1974	1	2			
	2	5			
	3	6	36	4.500	133
	4	5	37	4.625	108
1975	1	2	40	5.000	40
	2	6	44	5.500	109
	3	8	47	5.875	136
	4	7	48	6.000	117
1976	1	3	49	6.125	49
	2	6	51	6.375	94
	3	9	52	6.500	138
	4	8	54	6.750	119
1977	1	3	57	7.125	42
	2	8	59	7.375	108
	3	10	61	7.625	131
	4	9	62	7.750	116
1978	1	4	63	7.875	51
	2	8	65	8.125	98
	3	11			
	4	10			

Solution:

Quarterly averages, in percents (seasonal)

	Quarter 1	Quarter 2	Quarter 3	Quarter 4
	40	109	133	108
	49	94	136	117
	42	108	138	118
	51	98	131	116
Total	182	409	538	459
Average (seasonal index)	46	102	135	115

(1) Seasonal index for the second quarter, from above, is 102. This indicates that seasonal effects tended to push sales up about 2 percent on the average in the second quarter.

(2) Seasonal pattern:

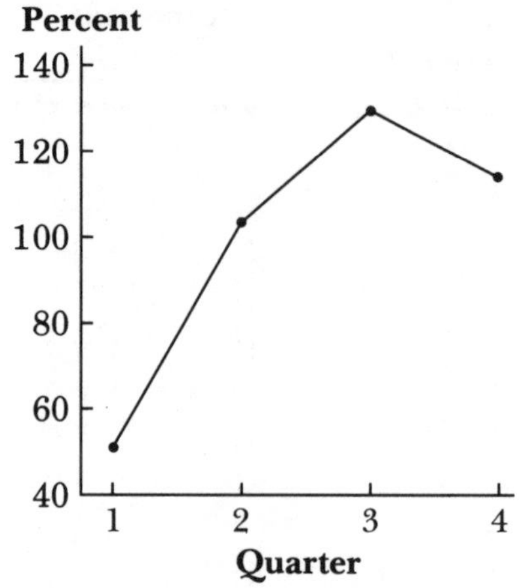

(3) Sales for fourth quarter = \$10,000 (1978)
Seasonal index for fourth quarter = 115%
Sales adjusted for seasonal effect: $\frac{\$10{,}000}{1.15} = \$8696$

CYCLE

Assuming data contain secular trend, cycle, seasonal and random elements, related to each other as multiplied factors.

Formula:

$$C \times R = \frac{T \times C \times S \times R}{T \times S}$$

where

T = Secular trend value
C = Cycle value
S = Seasonal index
R = Value of random element

Example:

What is the cyclical pattern for the following sales data:

Year	Quarter	Sales (in thousands of $) $T \times C \times S \times R$	Secular Trend[a] T	Seasonal Index[b] S (in %)	$S \times T$	Cycle X Random $\frac{T \times C \times S \times R}{S \times T} = C \times R$
1974	1	8	15.00	70	10.500	76
	2	21	16.25	110	17.875	117
	3	31	17.50	120	21.000	148
	4	34	18.75	100	18.750	181
1975	1	27	20.00	70	14.000	193
	2	47	21.25	110	23.375	201
	3	55	22.50	120	27.000	204
	4	47	23.75	100	23.750	198
1976	1	32	25.00	70	17.500	183
	2	44	26.25	110	28.875	152
	3	40	27.50	120	33.000	121
	4	24	28.75	100	28.750	83
1977	1	15	30.00	70	21.000	71
	2	22	31.25	110	34.375	64
	3	23	32.50	120	39.000	59
	4	25	33.75	100	33.750	74
1978	1	16	35.00	70	24.500	65
	2	27	36.25	110	39.875	68
	3	36	37.50	120	45.000	80
	4	36	38.75	100	38.750	93
1979	1	30	40.00	70	28.000	107
	2	58	41.25	110	45.375	128
	3	80	42.50	120	51.000	157
	4	77	43.75	100	43.750	176

[a] See pp. 121–125 for a method of obtaining secular trend values.
[b] See pp. 126–128 for a method of obtaining seasonal indexes.

10

Inventory

ESTIMATING INVENTORY—GROSS PROFIT METHOD

Formula:

$$I_2 = (I_1 + P + T) - [S(1 - R)]$$

where

I_2 = Ending inventory
I_1 = Beginning inventory
P = Purchases
S = Sales
R = Estimated gross profit percentage of sales
T = Transportation—in

Example:

It is desired to prepare interim financial statements for the month ended March 31, 19XI. However, it is not considered practicable to take a physical inventory, and the company does not maintain a perpetual inventory. The following data are obtained from the firm's books and other records, sales for the period $100,000, purchases for the period $58,000. Transportation—in, $2000. Inventory: Jan. 1, 19XI $20,000. For the prior year, the profit and loss statement showed a gross profit ratio of 38%. However, management has indicated that the costs have risen but the selling price has remained more or less constant, and they believe that a 35% gross profit ratio is probably being maintained. Compute the ending inventory.

Solution:

$$I_2 = (I_1 + P + T) - [S(1 - R)]$$
$$I_2 = (20{,}000 + 58{,}000 + 2000) - [100{,}000(1 - .35)]$$
$$I_2 = 80{,}000 - [100{,}000(.65)]$$
$$I_2 = 80{,}000 - 65{,}000$$
$$I_2 = \$15{,}000$$

ESTIMATING INVENTORY—RETAIL INVENTORY METHOD

Formula:

$$I_{r2} = (I_{r1} + P_r + M_u) - (S + M_j + E + W_r)$$
$$I_{c2} = I_{r2} \times \frac{I_{c1} + P_c + T}{I_{r1} + P_r + M_u}$$

where

I_{c2} = Ending inventory at cost (approximate lower of cost or market)
I_{r2} = Ending inventory at retail
I_{r1} = Beginning inventory at retail
P_r = Purchases at retail
M_u = Net additional markups (additional markup minus markup cancellation)
S = Sales
M_j = Net markdowns (markdowns minus markdown cancellation)
E = Employee discounts (if not recorded on books)
W_r = Worthless inventory at retail—due to breakage, spoilage, etc., or possibly known theft
I_{c1} = Beginning inventory at cost
P_c = Purchases at cost
T = Transportation—in

Example:

The Downtown Department Store uses the retail inventory method of accounting. At the end of the first quarter of operations it is necessary to evaluate the inventories of the various departments in order to prepare financial statements. An actual physical inventory is taken only at the end of the fiscal year. From the data obtained from the books and other records, estimate the inventory for the Junior Miss Department at the end of the first quarter.

Information obtained from the General Ledger:

	Retail	**Dr.**	**Cr.**
Sales			\$36,625
Purchases	\$80,000	\$52,000	
Transportation—in		3,666	
Inventory	30,000	20,000	

The buyer's records on markups and markdowns are summarized as follows:

Additional markups	\$4000	
Markup cancellations	500	\$3500
Markdowns	\$3500	
Markdown cancellations	2000	\$1500

Two suits damaged—shopworn and completely unsaleable or returnable to manufacturer, price at retail \$100 each or \$200.

Employee discounts totaled \$175.

Solution:

$$I_{r2} = (I_{r1} + P_r + M_u) - (S + M_j + E + W_r)$$

$$I_{c2} = I_{r2} \times \frac{I_{c1} + P_c + T}{I_{r1} + P_r + M_u}$$

$$I_{r2} = (30{,}000 + 80{,}000 + 3500) - (36{,}625 + 1500 + 175 + 200)$$

$$I_{r2} = 113{,}500 - 38{,}500$$

$$I_{r2} = \$75{,}000$$

$$I_{c2} = 75{,}000 \times \frac{20{,}000 + 52{,}000 + 3666}{30{,}000 + 80{,}000 + 3500}$$

$$I_{c2} = 75{,}000 \times \frac{75{,}666}{113{,}500}$$

$$I_{c2} = 75{,}000 \times .6667$$

$$I_{c2} = \$50{,}000$$

MAXIMUM INVENTORY LIMIT

Formula:

$$I_2 = O + P$$

where

I_2 = Maximum inventory
O = Standard order
P = Order point

Example:

From the following information, determine what the maximum amount of inventory of part X532 could be. When the inventory reaches 4050 units, an order is automatically placed for 5000 units.

Solution:

$$I_2 = O + P$$
$$I_2 = 5000 + 4050$$
$$I_2 = 9050$$

MINIMUM INVENTORY LIMIT

Formula:

$$I_1 = D \times U$$

where

I_1 = Minimum inventory
D = Number of days inventory desired on hand
U = Maximum daily inventory usage

Example:

Determine the minimum inventory from the following information. The inventory control manager has ascertained that the stock for item X532 should never fall below an 8-day supply. The company uses this part in several products, and for the past 2 years the number of parts placed into production for the various products averaged 150 units per day. However, it is possible if all product lines are producing at capacity that 225 units per day would be required. What should be established as the minimum inventory?

Solution:

$$I_1 = D \times U$$
$$I_1 = 8 \times 225$$
$$I_1 = 1800$$

DETERMINING THE ORDER POINT

Formula:

$$P = (T \times U) + I_1$$

where

P = Order point
T = Number of days required to fill order
U = Maximum usage
I_1 = Minimum inventory

Example:

From the following information, determine the order point for item X532. The purchasing agent has informed you that on the average it takes 10 working days from the time the order is initiated from inventory control until it is received and placed in stock by the company. The maximum possible usage is 225 units per day and the minimum inventory is 1800 units.

Solution:

$$P = (T \times U) + I_1$$
$$P = (10 \times 225) + I_1$$
$$P = 2250 + 1800$$
$$P = 4050$$

OPTIMUM ORDER SIZE

Formula:

$$Q = \sqrt{\frac{2(CN)}{UI + A}}$$

where

Q = Optimum order size
C = Cost of placing an order
N = Number of units consumed in one year
U = Unit price of material
I = Assumed rate of interest
A = Annual carrying cost per unit

Example:

A purchasing agent desires to know the optimum order size for material #X53. A study of the inventory records for the past several years indicated the average annual consumption per year is 2500 units. Cost studies showed that the average cost to prepare a purchase order and handle the invoices and other paper work amounted to $20 per order. The standard price of the material obtained from the cost accounting department is $10 per unit. A review of the financial pages of a leading business paper revealed that the current market for a relatively "risk free" investment is yielding 6%. Statistical studies prepared for the warehouse operations revealed that, on the average, annual carrying costs amounted to 5% of the inventory cost. Determine the optimum order size.

Solution:

$$Q = \sqrt{\frac{2(CN)}{UI + A}}$$

$$Q = \sqrt{\frac{2(20 \times 2500)}{10 \times .06 + .50}}$$

$$Q = \sqrt{\frac{100{,}000}{1.10}} = \sqrt{90{,}909}$$

$$Q = 302 \text{ units}$$

Note: A equals $10 times 5% or $.50.

11

Depreciation

DEPRECIATION—STRAIGHT LINE

Formula:

$$D_j = \frac{C - S}{L}$$

where

D_j = Depreciation for particular year
C = Cost
S = Salvage value
L = Estimated life of asset

Example:

An asset cost $70,000 and has an estimated salvage value of $10,000. It is estimated that the life of the asset will be 15 years. What is the annual charge for depreciation?

Solution:

$$D_j = \frac{C - S}{L}$$

$$D_j = \frac{70{,}000 - 10{,}000}{15}$$

$$D_j = \frac{60{,}000}{15}$$

$$D_j = \$4000$$

DEPRECIATION—UNITS OF PRODUCTION

Formula:

$$D_j = (C - S)\frac{U_x}{U_n}$$

where

D_j = Depreciation for particular year
C = Cost
S = Salvage value
U_x = Units produced in particular year
U_n = Estimated number of units that asset will produce during its life

Example:

The XYZ Company purchased a machine that cost $100,000. From past experience and future projections it is estimated that the asset will have a salvage value of $20,000 at the end of its useful life. Engineering estimates indicate that with adequate maintenance the machine will probably produce 500,000 units during its efficient life. During the eighth year of its life the machine produced 30,000 units. What is the annual charge for depreciation by the units of production method of depreciation?

Solution:

$$D_j = (C - S)\frac{U_x}{U_n}$$

$$D_8 = (100{,}000 - 20{,}000)\frac{30{,}000}{500{,}000}$$

$$D_8 = 80{,}000 \times .06$$

$$D_8 = \$4800$$

Note: Units may be interpreted to be units, labor hours, machine hours, etc.

DEPRECIATION—SUM OF THE YEARS' DIGITS METHOD

Formula:

$$D_j = \frac{Y - D}{\Sigma Y} \times (C - S)$$

where

D_j = Depreciation for particular year
Y = Estimated life of asset
D = Number of years of prior depreciation ($D = j - 1$)
ΣY = Sum of the years
C = Cost of the asset
S = Estimated salvage value

Example:

An asset cost $100,000 and has an estimated life of 20 years. The expected salvage value is $10,000. What is the amount of depreciation for the fourteenth year?

Solution:

$$D_j = \frac{Y - D}{\Sigma Y} \times (C - S)$$

$$D_{14} = \frac{20 - 13}{210} \times (100{,}000 - 10{,}000)$$

$$D_{14} = \frac{7}{210} \times 90{,}000$$

$$D_{14} = \$3000$$

Note: If the ΣY is not included in the tables, it may be calculated by the following formula:

$$\Sigma Y = \frac{Y + 1}{2} \times Y$$

$$\Sigma Y = \frac{20 + 1}{2} \times 20$$

$$\Sigma Y = 210$$

DEPRECIATION—DECLINING BALANCE (real)

Formulas:

(1) $R = 1 - \sqrt[L]{\frac{S}{C}}$

(2) $D_j = R(C - A)$

where

R = Constant rate
L = Estimated life of asset
D_j = Depreciation for particular year
C = Cost of asset
S = Salvage value
A = Accumulated depreciation balance at beginning of year

Example:

What is the amount of depreciation for the third year if an asset cost $20,000, has a salvage value of $5000, and an estimated life of 10 years? The accumulated depreciation per books on the first day of the fiscal year is $4844.60

Solution:

(1) $R = 1 - \sqrt[L]{\frac{S}{C}}$

$R = 1 - \sqrt[10]{\frac{5000}{20{,}000}}$

$R = 1 - \sqrt[10]{.25}$ (See note for solving.)

$R = 1 - .8705$

$R = .1295$ or 12.95%

(2) $D_j = R(C - A)$

$D_3 = .1295(20{,}000.00 - 4844.60)$

$D_3 = .1295(15{,}155.40)$

$D_3 = 1962.62$

Note: solution for $\sqrt[10]{.25}$.

Log .25 = 9.397940 − 10
Divide by 10 = .939794 − 1
Antilog closest = 8705
Place decimal point .8705
$\sqrt[10]{.25} = .8705$

DEPRECIATION—200% DECLINING BALANCE

Formula:

$$D_j = 2\left[\frac{(C - S) - A}{L}\right]$$

where

D_j = Depreciation for particular year
C = Cost of asset
S = Salvage value of asset
A = Balance in reserve at beginning of year
L = Estimated life of asset

Example:

What is the amount of depreciation in year 2 of an asset that cost \$11,000, has a 10-year life and an estimated salvage value of \$1000, and the balance in the reserve account at the beginning of the fiscal year is \$2000?

Solution:

$$D_j \text{ or } D_2 = 2\left[\frac{(C - S) - A}{L}\right]$$

$$D_2 = 2\left[\frac{(\$11{,}000 - \$1000) - \$2000}{10}\right]$$

$$D_2 = 2\left[\frac{8000}{10}\right]$$

$$D_2 = 2(800)$$

$$D_2 = \$1600$$

Note: For tax purposes salvage value is not a factor.

DEPRECIATION—COMPOSITE RATE

Formulas:

$$(1)\ R = \frac{\dfrac{(C - S)_1}{L_1} + \dfrac{(C - S)_2}{L_2} + \dfrac{(C - S)_3}{L_3} + \cdots + \dfrac{(C - S)_n}{L_n}}{\Sigma C}$$

$$(2)\ D_j = \Sigma C_x \times R$$

where

R = Composite rate of depreciation
C = Cost
S = Salvage value
ΣC = Sum of the cost
ΣC_x = Sum of the asset costs at end of particular accounting period
D_j = Depreciation for a particular year
$L_1 - L_2 - L_3$ = Estimated life of assets

Example:

At the end of the year 19A a composite rate of depreciation was computed for the office equipment of a small firm from the following facts:

Item	Cost	Salvage	Estimated Life (in years)
Typewriter	300	50	5
Calculator	600	100	10
Computer	4000	400	9
Desks & chairs	1500	0	15
Total	6400		

(1) What is the composite rate of depreciation?

(2) If at the end of the fiscal year 19C the total assets in the group amounted to $8000, what amount should be charged to depreciation expense for that year?

Solution:

$$(1)\quad R = \frac{\dfrac{(C-S)_1}{L_1} + \dfrac{(C-S)_2}{L_2} + \dfrac{(C-S)_3}{L_3} + \dfrac{(C-S)_4}{L_4}}{\Sigma C}$$

$$R = \frac{\dfrac{300-50}{5} + \dfrac{600-100}{10} + \dfrac{4000-400}{9} + \dfrac{1500-0}{15}}{6400}$$

$$R = \frac{50 + 50 + 400 + 100}{6400}$$

$$R = \frac{600}{6400}$$

$$R = .09375 \text{ or } 9.375\%$$

(2) $D_j = \Sigma C_x \times R$
$D_j = 8000 \times .09375$
$D_j = \$750$

DETERMINING ACCUMULATED DEPRECIATION BALANCE— DECLINING BALANCE METHOD OF DEPRECIATION (real)

Formula:

$$A_n = C[1 - (1 - R)^n]$$

where

A_n = Accumulated depreciation at the end of a series of accounting periods
C = Cost of asset
R = Constant rate of depreciation
n = The number of years

Example:

What should be the balance in the reserve account at the end of year 2 if an asset cost \$20,000 and has a scrap value of \$5000 and the constant rate is 12.95%?

Solution:

$$A_n = C[1 - (1 - R)^n]$$
$$A_2 = 20{,}000[1 - (1 - .1295)^2]$$
$$A_2 = 20{,}000[1 - (.8705)^2]$$
$$A_2 = 20{,}000[1 - .75777025]$$
$$A_2 = 20{,}000 \times .24222975$$
$$A_2 = \$4844.60$$

DETERMINING ACCUMULATED DEPRECIATION BALANCE— DECLINING BALANCE METHOD OF DEPRECIATION (200% method)

Formula:

$$A_n = C - S\left[1 - \left(1 - \frac{2}{L}\right)^n\right]$$

where

A_n = Accumulated depreciation at the end of a series of accounting periods
C = Cost of asset
S = Salvage value (if used)
L = Estimated life of the asset
n = Number of years of life expired

Example:

An asset cost \$11,000, has a salvage value of \$1000, and an estimated life of 10 years. If 200% declining balance method is used, what is the balance in the accumulated depreciation account at the end of the second year?

Solution:

$$A_n = (C - S)\left[1 - \left(1 - \frac{2}{L}\right)^n\right]$$
$$A_2 = (11{,}000 - 1000)\left[1 - \left(1 - \frac{2}{10}\right)^2\right]$$
$$A_2 = 10{,}000[1 - (1 - .20)^2]$$
$$A_2 = 10{,}000[1 - .80^2]$$
$$A_2 = 10{,}000[1 - .64]$$
$$A_2 = 10{,}000 \times .36$$
$$A_2 = \$3600$$

DETERMINING ACCUMULATED DEPRECIATION BALANCE—SUM OF THE YEARS' DIGIT METHOD OF DEPRECIATION

Formula:

$$A_n = (C - S)\left[1 - \frac{R(R + 1)}{2\Sigma Y}\right]$$

where

A_n = Accumulated depreciation at the end of a series of accounting periods
C = Cost of the asset

S = Salvage value of the asset
Y = Estimated life of the asset
ΣY = Sum of the years
R = Remaining life of the asset ($R = Y - n$)
n = Number of years of life expired

Example:

An asset cost $7000, has an estimated useful life of 8 years, and the salvage value is estimated to be $2000. What should be the balance in the accumulated depreciation account at the end of the fifth year?

Solution:

$$A_n = (C - S)\left[1 - \frac{R(R + 1)}{2\,\Sigma Y}\right]$$

$$A_5 = (7000 - 2000)\left[1 - \frac{3(3 + 1)}{2 \times 36}\right]$$

$$A_5 = 5000\left[1 - \frac{12}{72}\right]$$

$$A_5 = 5000(.8333)$$

$$A_5 = \$4166.50$$

12

Finance

VALUE OF A BOND (approximate yield to maturity)

Note: Bonds are generally valued on a yield basis.

Formulas:

	Discount		Premium
(1)	$\bar{I} = I + \dfrac{d}{n}$	or	$\bar{I} = I - \dfrac{p}{n}$

(2) $\overline{C} = \dfrac{C + M}{2}$

(3) $Y = \dfrac{\bar{I}}{\overline{C}}$

where

$\bar{I}$ = Average income
$\overline{C}$ = Average cost
Y = Yield (approximate)
I = Annual coupon interest
M = Maturity value
d = Discount
p = Premium
n = Number of years to maturity
C = Cost of bond

Example:

A 20-year, 10%, $1000 bond is purchased at $1020. What is the approximate yield to maturity?

Solution:

$$(1)\quad \bar{I} = I - \frac{p}{n} = 100 - \frac{20}{20} = \$99$$

$$(2)\quad \overline{C} = \frac{C + M}{2} = \frac{1020 + 1000}{2} = \$1010$$

$$(3)\quad Y = \frac{\bar{I}}{\overline{C}} = \frac{99}{1010}$$

$$Y = .098 = 9.8\%$$

VALUE OF A BOND (known yield)

Formulas:

$$(1)\quad A = S(1 + r_e)^{-n}$$

$$(2)\quad A_{\overline{n}|r} = RS\,\frac{1 - (1 + r_e)^{-n}}{r_e}$$

$$(3)\quad V = A + A_{\overline{n}|r}$$

where

A = Present value of the face value of the bond
S = Sum (face value, or maturity value)
r_e = Effective rate of interest
R = Nominal rate of interest
$A_{\overline{n}|r}$ = Present value of the series of interest payments
V = Value of the bond
n = Number of periods

Example:

On January 1, 19XI, the XYZ Company issued $100,000, 6%, 20-year bonds, interest payable semiannually. The bonds were issued to yield 4%. How much did the XYZ Company receive for each $1000 bond?

Solution:

(1)
$$A = S(1 + r_e)^{-n}$$
$$A = 1000(1 + .02)^{-40}$$
$$A = 1000(.45289042) \qquad \text{(Table II)}$$
$$A = \$452.89$$

(2)
$$A_{\overline{n}|r} = RS\frac{1 - (1 + r_e)^{-n}}{r_e}$$

$$A_{\overline{n}|r} = .03 \times 1000\frac{1 - (1 + .02)^{-40}}{.02}$$
$$A_{\overline{n}|r} = 30(27.35547924) \qquad \text{(Table IV)}$$
$$A_{\overline{n}|r} = \$820.66$$

(3)
$$V = A + A_{\overline{n}|r}$$
$$V = 452.89 + 820.66$$
$$V = \$1273.55$$

THEORETICAL VALUE OF A STOCKRIGHT

Formula:

$$V = \frac{M - S}{n + 1}$$

where

V = Theoretical value of a stockright
M = Market value of the stock
S = Subscription price of the stock
n = Number of rights required to subscribe to one share of stock

Example:

Mr. Smith owns 10 shares of AT&P Company $100 par value common stock. He received 40 rights in the mail along with a notice stating that he could purchase one share of additional stock of the AT&P Company for $170 plus 4 rights. The market value of the stock on the date the rights were received was $200. What is the theoretical value of the rights?

Solution:

$$V = \frac{M - S}{n + 1}$$

$$V = \frac{200 - 170}{4 + 1} = \frac{30}{5}$$

$$V = \$6$$

ALLOCATION OF COST TO RIGHTS

Formula:

$$V.R. = \frac{M.V.R.}{M.V.S. + M.V.R.} \times C$$

where

$V.R.$ = Value allocated to rights
$M.V.R.$ = Market value of rights on date of issuance
$M.V.S.$ = Market value of the stock ex rights
C = Cost

Example:

Mr. Smith owns 10 shares of AT&P Company $100 par value common stock which cost him $120 per share, or $1200. He received 40 rights. On the date the rights were issued, the stock was quoted ex rights at $195 per share and the rights were quoted separately at $5 per right. What cost should be assigned to each right?

Solution:

$$V.R. = \frac{M.V.R.}{M.V.S. + M.V.R.} \times C$$

$$V.R. = \frac{5}{195 + 5} \times 120 = \frac{1}{40} \times 120$$

$$V.R. = \$3$$

COMPUTING GOODWILL

Formula:

$$G = \frac{E_t - (A \times r)}{R}$$

where

G = Goodwill
E_t = Estimated annual future earnings
A = Fair market value or appraised value of the net assets exclusive of goodwill
r = Normal industry rate of return
R = Capitalization rate of excess earnings

Example:

The president of the XYZ Company requests that you advise him as to the possible value of the goodwill, if any, of the A.B.C. Company which the president is investigating as a possible new subsidiary company.

After analyzing the income statements for the past 5 years and eliminating unusual and nonrecurring items, you have determined that the average normal operating income is $622,000 per year. You have concluded from various studies that it would be reasonable to expect that if your firm took over, the annual future earnings for the next 5 years would be in the vicinity of $600,000 per year.

The A.B.C. Company's tangible assets have been appraised by a reputable firm of appraisers at approximately $10,000,000. The most recent balance sheet of the A.B.C. Company reveals that approximately $2,000,000 of liabilities would be involved in the purchase.

From statistics obtained from the industry trade association, it appears that the average industry rate of return on net assets for the past 5 years is 7%. You have also learned from sources active in the industry that goodwill is generally valued at 5 years' annual earnings in excess of normal.

Solution:

$$G = \frac{E_t - (A \times r)}{R}$$

$$G = \frac{600{,}000 - (8{,}000{,}000 \times .07)}{.20}$$

$$G = \frac{40{,}000}{.20}$$

$$G = \$200{,}000$$

AMORTIZATION OF BOND DISCOUNT OR PREMIUM BY BONDS OUTSTANDING METHOD

Formula:

$$A_j = \frac{B/O_n}{\Sigma B/O} \times D \text{ or } P$$

where

A_j = Amortization for a particular year

B/O_n = Face value of the bonds outstanding at the end of a particular year

$\Sigma B/O$ = Sum of the bonds outstanding at the end of each year ($\Sigma B/O = B/O_1 + B/O_2 + B/O_3 + \cdots + B/O_n$)

D = Discount

P = Premium

Example:

On January 1, 19X1, the A.B.C. Company issued \$500,000, 6% serial bonds, interest payable annually. The bonds sold for \$490,000. The bonds are to be retired in the amount of \$100,000 at the end of each year. What amount of discount should be amortized for the year 19X3 using the bonds outstanding method?

Solution:

$$A_j = \frac{B/O_n}{\Sigma B/O} \times D$$

$$A_3 = \frac{300{,}000}{1{,}500{,}000} \times 10{,}000$$

$$A_3 = \frac{1}{5} \times 10{,}000$$

$$A_3 = 2000$$

VENTURE CAPITAL INVESTMENT, % OF COMPANY SOLD

Formula:

$$\% = \frac{A}{B(1 + i)^{-n}}$$

where

$\%$ = Percent of company given to venture capitalist
A = The amount of capital required
B = The estimated total value of the company n years hence
i = The rate of return required by the venture capitalist
n = The number of years required to obtain the future value

Example:

The founders of HITECH Corporation need \$1,500,000 in order to expand the business. The only source for the funds are venture capitalists. At the present time, venture capitalists require a 50% annual rate of return for an investment of this type. With the additional capital, it is estimated that at the end of 5 years the company will be worth \$25,000,000. What percent of the company's common stock should be sold to the venture capitalist?

Solution:

$$\% = \frac{A}{B(1+i)^{-n}}$$

$$\% = \frac{1{,}500{,}000}{25{,}000{,}000 \cdot \dfrac{1}{(1+.50)^5}}$$

$$\% = \frac{1{,}500{,}000}{3{,}292{,}181}$$

$$\% = 45.6\%$$

Verification:

$\$1{,}500{,}000 \cdot S_{\overline{5|}.50} = \$11{,}390{,}625$
Future value = \$25,000,000
% to investor = 45.6%

ESOP—DILUTED VALUE PER SHARE—NUMBER OF SHARES TO BE CONTRIBUTED

Formulas:

$$(1)\ V_d = \frac{(V \cdot O_1) - C}{O_1}$$

$$(2)\ N = \frac{C}{V_d}$$

where

V_d = Diluted value
V = Value per share prior to dilution
C = Dollar value of contribution made to ESOP
O_1 = Number of primary shares outstanding
O_2 = Number of shares outstanding after contribution
N = Number of new shares to be issued

Example:

The XYZ Company intends to contribute $200,000 to the company's ESOP in the form of newly issued stock. The appraised value of the shares based upon the number of shares presently outstanding is $22 per share. There are presently 100,000 shares of stock outstanding. What is the diluted value per share? How many new shares should be issued?

Solution:

$$(1)\ V_d = \frac{(V \cdot O_1) - C}{O_1}$$

$$V_d = \frac{(22.00 \cdot 100{,}000) - 200{,}000}{100{,}000} = \frac{2{,}000{,}000}{100{,}000}$$

$$V_d = \$20$$

$$(2)\ N = \frac{C}{V_d}$$

$$N = \frac{200{,}000}{20}$$

$$N = 10{,}000 \text{ shares}$$

Verification:

$$O_1 \cdot V = 100{,}000 \cdot 22 = \underline{\underline{\$2{,}200{,}000}}$$

$$O_2 \cdot V_d = 110{,}000 \cdot 20 = \underline{\underline{\$2{,}200{,}000}}$$

INVESTMENT DECISION (capital asset pricing)

Formulas:

(1) $R_i = R_f + (R_m - R_f)\,\beta$

(2) $$V_d = d \cdot \frac{1 - \left(\dfrac{1 + k}{1 + R_i}\right)^n}{R_i - k}$$

(3) $V_2 = V_t \cdot V^n$

(4) $V = V_d + V_2$

where

R_i = Expected rate of return
R_f = Interest free rate of return
R_m = Market rate or portfolio rate of return
V_d = Present value of dividend stream
k = Rate of dividend increase
d = Current dividend
V_2 = Present value of future market price
V_t = Future market price
β = Volatility of stock in relation to either overall market or portfolio

$$V^n = (1 + i)^{-n} = \frac{1}{(1 + i)^n}$$

Example:

The XYZ shares are selling for $75 per share. The current dividend rate is $3, with an anticipated growth rate of 10% per year. The market rate of return is 9% and the interest free rate is 5%. The Beta (β) of the XYZ shares is 1.5. The investment strategy is to hold a security for 5 years. At the end of the 5 years, it is estimated that the market value of the XYZ shares will be $95. Does the security meet your investment requirements?

Solution:

(1) $R_i = R_f + (R_m - R_f)\beta$
$= 5 + (9 - 5)1.5 = 5 + 4(1.5)$

$$= 5 + 6$$
$$= 11\%$$

$$(2)\quad V_d = d \cdot \frac{1 - \left(\frac{1 + k}{1 + R_i}\right)^n}{R_i - k}$$

$$= \$3 \cdot \frac{1 - \left(\frac{1 + .10}{1 + .11}\right)^5}{.11 - .10}$$

$$= \$3 \cdot \frac{1 - \left(\frac{1.10}{1.11}\right)^5}{.01} = 3 \cdot \frac{1 - .955759}{.01}$$

$$= \$3 \cdot 4.42407 = \$13.27$$

$$(3)\quad V_2 = V_t \cdot V^n$$
$$= \$95 \cdot \frac{1}{(1 + .11)^5} = \$95 \cdot 0.593451$$
$$= \$56.38$$

$$(4)\quad V = V_d + V_2$$
$$= \$13.27 + \$56.38 = \$69.65$$

The investment does not meet your criteria. However, remember the formula inputs are estimates. You might buy on a market pullback or correction.

ADJUSTABLE RATE MORTGAGES (new monthly payment)

Formulas:

$$(1)\quad i_2 = I + S$$

$$(2)\quad A_2 = R_1 \cdot a_{\overline{n}|i_1}$$

$$(3)\quad R_2 = A_n \cdot \frac{1}{a_{\overline{n}|i_2}}$$

where

i = Current rate of interest
i_2 = New rate of interest

I = Interest index
S = Bank spread
A_n = Principal balance of mortgage at start of new interest period
R_1 = Monthly payment of principal and interest of current year
n = Remaining number of periodic payments
R_2 = New monthly payment

$$a_{\overline{n}|i} = \frac{1 - (1 + i)^{-n}}{i}$$

Example:

On December 1, 19X0, Mr. & Mrs. Able purchased a home, financing it with a \$75,000, 9%, 30-year adjustable rate mortgage, with the first monthly payment due on January 1, 19X1. The monthly payments based on the original interest rate of 9% amounted to \$603.47. The mortgage provided that on December 1 of each subsequent year, the interest rate would be adjusted by using the one-year Treasury Constant Maturity Index plus a spread of 2.75 points. The rate could not increase or decrease by more than 2 points for any one year. Further, the rate could not increase by more than 5 points during the life of the mortgage, nor could the rate fall below 8%. On December 1, 19X1, the index was 7.87%.

(1) What is the new annual rate of interest?
(2) What is the principal balance on December 1, 19X1, after the December payment?
(3) What is the new monthly payment?

Solution:

(1) $i_2 = I + S$
$i_2 = 7.87 + 2.75$
$i_2 = 10.62\%$

Subject to:

Maximum annual increase	9.0 + 2.0 =	11.0%
Maximum cap rate	9.0 + 5.0 =	14.0%
Minimum rate		8.0%

$i_2 = 10.62\%$

$$(2)\ A_n = R_1 \cdot a_{\overline{n}|i_1}$$

$$A_{348} = 603.47 \cdot a_{\overline{348}|\frac{.09}{12}} = (603.47)(123.43278)$$

$$A_{348} = \$74{,}487.98$$

$$(3)\quad R_2 = A_n \cdot \frac{1}{a_{\overline{n}|i}}$$

$$R_2 = \$74{,}487.98 \cdot \frac{1}{a_{\overline{348}|\frac{.1062}{12}}}$$

$$R_2 = \$691.44$$

INTERNAL RATE OF RETURN—DECISION TO REPLACE EQUIPMENT

Formula:

$$(1)\ V_1 - V^n \cdot V_2 = R \cdot a_{\overline{n}|i} \text{ (equal annual savings)}$$

$$(2)\ V_1 - V^n \cdot V_2 = \sum_{1}^{n} R(1+i)^{-n} \text{ (unequal annual savings)}$$

where

V_1 = Cost or investment in asset
V_2 = Residual value
n = Number of periods
i = Interest rate
R = Periodic payment or annual savings
$V^n = (1+i)^{-n}$

$$a_{\overline{n}|i} = \frac{1-(1+i)^{-n}}{i}$$

Example:

The controller and plant manager of the XYZ Corporation are considering a \$100,000 expenditure for a new machine of advanced design and technology to replace the current machine. The new machine has an expected economic life of 10 years and an estimated residual value of \$15,000. It is also estimated that the direct cash flow savings using the new equipment will be \$25,000 per year over the life of the new equipment as compared to the present equipment. At the present time, corporate policy requires a 20% internal rate of return, *IRR*, before income taxes.

Solution:

(1) Equal annual savings—use formula (1)

(2) Calculate the present value of the residual value $V^n \cdot V_2$
$i = 20\%, n = 10 \qquad V^n \cdot \$15{,}000 = \$2423$

(3) Net present value $= V_1 - V^n \cdot V_2$
$\$100{,}000 - \$2423 = \$97{,}577$

(4) Using a calculator or computer determine (i)
$PV = \$97{,}577$
$n = 10$
$PMT = \$25{,}000$
$IRR = i = 22.16\%$

(5) Go back to step 1 and discount residual value at 22.16% and repeat steps 2–4

(6) Repeat step 5 using 22.03%
$IRR = 22.04\%$

(7) Repeat process until it repeats the same answer

Note: Since many of the inputs into the formula are estimates, it may not be necessary to obtain the accuracy of steps 5 through 7. The decision can be made after step 4.

COST OF CAPITAL (real estate)

Formula:

$$COC = i_1 \frac{M}{M + E} + i_2 \frac{E}{M + E}$$

where

COC = Cost of capital (real estate people call this the CAP RATE)

i_1 = Interest rate on mortgage
i_2 = Return on equity investment
M = Mortgage
E = Equity investment

Example:

An income-producing property is offered for sale for $5,000,000. An insurance company will give a mortgage loan of $4,000,000 for 30 years at 9% interest. The investors will be required to make a down payment of $1,000,000. Equity investors require a 12% return on investment for an investment of this type. What is the cost of capital?

Solution:

$$COC = i_1\frac{M}{M+E} + i_2\frac{E}{M+E}$$

$$COC = .09\frac{4{,}000{,}000}{4{,}000{,}000 + 1{,}000{,}000} + .12\frac{1{,}000{,}000}{4{,}000{,}000 + 1{,}000{,}000}$$

$$COC = .09 \times .80 + .12 \times .20$$

$$COC = .072 + .024$$

$$COC = .096 = 9.6\%$$

Note: Usually real estate investors compute the CAP RATE before taxes, as each individual investor's tax situation is different.

COST OF CAPITAL (weighted average after tax)

Formula:

$$COC = \frac{I(1-t) + D}{L+V} + G\frac{V}{L+V}$$

where

COC = Weighted average cost of capital after tax
I = Interest expense on long-term debt
D = Dividends paid on common stock
L = Long-term liabilities
V = Total market value of outstanding common stock
t = Corporate income tax rate
G = Compound growth rate of share value

Example:

The following information was extracted from the XYZ Company's financial statements:

Interest expense on long-term debt	\$ 450,000
Dividends paid on common stock	\$ 320,000
Long-term liabilities	\$3,000,000
Corporate income tax rate	34%

The company has 1,000,000 outstanding shares of common stock which are traded on an exchange. The average price of the shares for the year was \$8 per share. For the last 10 years the value of the shares had a compound growth rate of 9%. What is the weighted average cost of capital?

Solution:

$$COC = \frac{I(1 - t) + D}{L + V} + G\frac{V}{L + V}$$

$$COC = \frac{450{,}000(1 - .34) + 320{,}000}{3{,}000{,}000 + 8{,}000{,}000} + .09\frac{8{,}000{,}000}{3{,}000{,}000 + 8{,}000{,}000}$$

$$COC = .056 + .065$$

$$COC = .121 = 12.1\%$$

ANNUALIZED YIELD

Formula:

$$AY = \left(1 + \frac{D}{V}\right)^m - 1$$

where

AY = Annualized yield
D = Periodic dividend
V = Market value of investment
m = Number of dividend periods in year

Example:

You have \$10,000 invested in a money market account. Your dividend for the last month was \$50, which was reinvested in the account. What is the annualized yield?

Solution:

$$AY = \left(1 + \frac{D}{V}\right)^m - 1$$
$$AY = \left(1 + \frac{50}{10{,}000}\right)^{12} - 1$$
$$AY = (1.005)^{12} - 1$$
$$AY = 1.0617 - 1$$
$$AY = .0617 = 6.17\%$$

TAXABLE EQUIVALENT YIELD

Formula:

$$TEY = \frac{i}{1 - t}$$

where

TEY = Taxable equivalent yield
i = Tax-free yield
t = Tax rate

Example:

A municipal bond exempt from federal income tax is presently yielding 6%. If you are in a 35% tax bracket, what is the taxable equivalent yield?

Solution:

$$TEY = \frac{i}{1 - t}$$
$$TEY = \frac{.06}{1 - .35} = \frac{.06}{.65}$$
$$TEY = .0923 = 9.23\%$$

13

Capitalized Values

CAPITALIZED VALUE OF A LEASE
(calculator or tables)

Formula:

$$V = R \cdot \ddot{a}_{\overline{n}|i} + O \cdot V^n$$

where

V = Capitalized value of the lease
R = Monthly lease payments
n = Number of lease payments
O = Option price
i = Interest rate
$V^n = (1 + i)^{-n}$
$\ddot{a}_{\overline{n}|i} = a_{\overline{n-1}|i} + 1 = a_{\overline{n}|i}(1 + i)$

Example:

The XYZ Company entered into a lease for a factory building. The lease was for a period of 10 years, with monthly payments of \$1000 per month payable at the beginning of each month and including an option to purchase the building at the termination of the lease period for \$100,000. At the time the lease was executed, mortgage interest rates for factory buildings were 15% per year. What is the capitalized value of the lease?

Solution:

$$V = R \cdot \ddot{a}_{\overline{n}|i} + O \cdot V^n$$

$$V = \left(1000 \cdot \ddot{a}_{\overline{120}|.0125}\right) + 100{,}000\,(1 + .0125)^{-120}$$

$$V = 1000\,(61.75763284 + 1)^{*} + 100{,}000\,(.22521441)^{**}$$

$$V = 62{,}757.63 + 22{,}521.44$$

$$V = \$85{,}279.07$$

DETERMINATION OF EFFECTIVE RATE OF INTEREST FOR A LEASE (using interest tables)

Formula:

$$\frac{A}{R} = a_{\overline{n}|i}$$

where

A = The balance to be financed

R = The monthly lease payments

n = The number of lease payments

$$a_{\overline{n}|i} = \frac{1 - (1 + i)^{-n}}{i}$$

Example:

A microcomputer is offered by a manufacturer through a third-party lease under the following terms: cost \$18,380.00 with a down payment of \$496.26 and 60 monthly payments of \$496.26, beginning one month after date of purchase. At the termination of the lease, the lessee may purchase the equipment for the sum of \$1.00. What is the effective rate of interest?

Solution:

$$\frac{A}{R} = a_{\overline{n}|i}$$

---

* See Table IV

** See Table II

$$\frac{17{,}883.74}{496.26} = a_{\overline{60}|i}$$

$$36.0370 = a_{\overline{60}|i}$$

Interpolate (using Table IV)

$$
\begin{array}{lcr}
 & \underline{a_{\overline{60}|i}} & \underline{\qquad i \qquad} \\
1.1268\left[\begin{array}{l} .9270\left[\begin{array}{l}36.9640\\36.0370\end{array}\right. \\ \qquad\quad 35.8372\end{array}\right. & & \left.\begin{array}{c}\left.\begin{array}{c}.01750\\x\end{array}\right]\\ .01875\end{array}\right].00125
\end{array}
$$

$$.9270 : 1.1268 = x : .00125$$

$$x = .00103$$

and

$$i = .01750 + .00103 = .01853 = 1.853\%$$

Annual rate: (business convention multiply by 12)

$$1.853\%(12) = 22.24\%$$

A more exact annual rate would be determined as follows:

$$R_e = (1 + i)^m - 1$$

$$R_e = (1 + .01853)^{12} - 1$$

$$R_e = 24.65\%$$

DETERMINATION OF EFFECTIVE RATE OF INTEREST FOR A LEASE (using a calculator)

Formula:

$$V = R \cdot \ddot{a}_{\overline{n}|i} + S \cdot V^n$$

where

V = Present value of the lease (cost of asset)

R = The monthly lease payments

n = The number of lease payments

S = The salvage or residual value of the asset

$V^n = (1 + i)^{-n}$

$\ddot{a}_{\overline{n}|i} = a_{\overline{n-1}|i} + 1 = a_{\overline{n}|i}(1 + i)$

Example:

The ABC Leasing Company proposes to lease a piece of equipment that it will purchase for $300,000. The terms negotiated with the lessee are $4300 monthly payments for 120 months, payable at the beginning of each month. The leasing company's appraiser is of the opinion that the residual value of the asset 10 years hence will be $50,000. What is the annual rate of return?

Solution:

A solution to a problem of this type is only practical with the aid of a computer or a calculator programmed for compound interest problems. The solution is by a trial-and-error method using iterative techniques.

Step 1. The minimum monthly interest rate would probably be an annuity due ($\ddot{a}_{\overline{n}|}$) of $4300 with 120 payments whose present value is $300,000, which equals .010190. This was determined by finding the periodic interest rate for 119 periods (n − 1) on the principal of $295,700 ($300,000 − $4300).

Step 2. Using the interest rate determined in step 1, find the present value of the salvage value of $50,000. $\$50{,}000(1 + .010190)^{-120}$ equals $14,811.

Step 3. A possible maximum monthly interest rate might be for an annuity due of $4300 with 120 payments whose present value is the cost of the asset less the present value of the salvage value, which is $300,000 − $14,811 = $285,189, which equals .01128. This was determined by finding the periodic rate for 119 periods (n − 1) on the principal of $280,889 ($285,189 − $4300).

Step 4. Set up the following table:

$4300 Periodic payment	$a_{\overline{119}|i}$	+ First payment +	V^{120}	= V
Trial No. 1:				
Using 1.019%	$295,704 +	$4300	+ $14,811	= $314,815
Trial No. 2:				
Using 1.128%	$280,869 +	$4300	+ $13,014	= $298,183

Since Trial No. 2 is getting pretty close, take a third trial about halfway between Trial No. 1 and No. 2, say 1.0750%.

Trial No. 3:

Using 1.075% $287,939 + $4300 + $13,859 = $306,098

Step 5. Interpolate between Trial No. 2 and Trial No. 3.

$$7915\left[\begin{array}{l} 6098\left[\begin{array}{l}306{,}098\\300{,}000\end{array}\right.\\ \quad\quad 298{,}183\end{array}\right. \qquad \left.\begin{array}{r}\left.\begin{array}{r}.01075\\x\end{array}\right]\\.01128\end{array}\right].00053$$

$6098 : 7915 = x : .00053$

$x = .000408$

$i = .01075 + .000408 = .011158 = 1.1158\%$

Proof:

$$V = R \cdot \ddot{a}_{\overline{n}|i} + S \cdot V^n$$
$$V = 4300 \cdot \ddot{a}_{\overline{120}|.011158} + 50{,}000\ V^{120}$$
$$V = 286{,}773 + 13{,}203$$
$$V = \$299{,}976 \text{ (close enough)}$$

The annual rate of interest is approximately:

$1.1158 \times 12 = 13.39\%$

or more exact

$$R_e = (1 + i)^m - 1$$
$$R_e = 14.24\%$$

BOND YIELD (using a calculator)

Formula:

$$V = R \cdot a_{\overline{n}|i} + F \cdot V^n$$

where

V = Price of the bond

R = Periodic interest income

F = Face value of bond

$V^n = (1 + i)^{-n}$

$$a_{\overline{n}|i} = \frac{1 - (1 + i)^{-n}}{i}$$

Example:

A 20-year, 5% bond is purchased at 102. What is the yield to maturity?

Solution:

By trial and error:

Step 1. The maximum yield would be the nominal rate of 5%. The value of the bond would be \$623.11 + \$376.89 = \$1000.

Step 2. A guess for the minimum yield might be $4\frac{3}{4}$%. The value of the bond would be \$636.53 + 395.29 = \$1031.82.

Step 3. Interpolate:

$$.0025\left[\begin{array}{l}\left[\begin{array}{l}.0475 \\ x\end{array}\right. \\ .0500\end{array}\right. \qquad \left.\begin{array}{r}\left.\begin{array}{r}1031.82 \\ 1020.00\end{array}\right]11.82 \\ 1000.00\end{array}\right]31.82$$

$$x : .0025 = 11.82 : 31.82$$

$$x = .0009$$

$$i = .0475 + .0009 = .0484 = 4.84\%$$

Proof:

$$V = R \cdot a_{\overline{n|}i} + F \cdot V^n$$

$$V = 50 \cdot a_{\overline{20|}.0484} + 1000V^{20}$$

$$V = 631.65 + 388.56$$

$$V = 1020.21 \text{ (close enough)}$$

Note: Compare this method with approximate method on page 145.

VALUATION OF A WASTING ASSET (using a calculator)

$$V = \frac{R}{i + \dfrac{1}{s_{\overline{n|}r}}}$$

where

V = Value

i = Rate of return on investment

r = Rate of return on income reinvested

R = Net income produced by the wasting asset
n = Number of periods

Example:

The XYZ Mining Company has a cash flow of $525,000 per year that is expected to continue for 20 years, at which time the mine will be depleted. The rate of return for an investment of this type is estimated to be 10%, and it is also estimated that a sinking fund established to recover the cost of the investment would probably earn an average of 8% over the next 20 years. What is the value of the mine?

Solution:

$$V = \frac{R}{i + \frac{1}{S_{\overline{n|}r}}}$$

$$V = \frac{525{,}000}{.10 + \frac{1}{S_{\overline{20|}.08}}} = \frac{525{,}000}{.10 + .0218522} = \frac{525{,}000}{.1218522}$$

$$V = \$4{,}308{,}498$$

Proof:

Cash flow =	$ 525,000.00
Less return on investment	
.10($4,308,498)	430,849.80
Available for sinking	
fund investment	$ 94,150.20
$S_{\overline{20|}.08} \times \$94{,}150.20$	= $4,308,498.00

DISCOUNTED CASH FLOW
CAPITALIZED VALUE
(using calculator or tables)

Formula:

$$\text{V} = \sum_{1}^{n} \text{R}_n \cdot \text{V}^n + \text{S}_n \cdot \text{V}^n$$

where

V = Capitalized value
Σ = Sum
n = Number of periods
R_n = Cash flow for period n
S_n = Residual value at end of nth period
$V^n = (1 + i)^{-n}$

Example:

The ABC Company is considering the acquisition of the XYZ Company, a small but growing company. You are requested to give the management of the ABC Company some guidance as to a possible purchase price for negotiation purposes. Your analysis of the situation leads you to the following conclusions regarding the probable cash flows if the ABC Company made the acquisition. The cash flow for the next five years would be as follows:

n Year	R_n Cash Flow
1	\$100,000
2	\$125,000
3	\$175,000
4	\$250,000
5	\$300,000

At the end of the fifth year, the cash flow will stabilize, as the market would be fully penetrated. You have also determined that a discount rate of 15% is a satisfactory measure of the inherent business risk.

Solution:

$$V = \sum_{1}^{n} R_n \cdot V^n + S_n \cdot V^n$$

$$R_1 \cdot V^n = 100{,}000 \cdot V^1 = \$\ 86{,}957$$
$$R_2 \cdot V^n = 125{,}000 \cdot V^2 = 94{,}518$$
$$R_3 \cdot V^n = 175{,}000 \cdot V^3 = 115{,}065$$
$$R_4 \cdot V^n = 250{,}000 \cdot V^4 = 142{,}938$$
$$R_5 \cdot V^n = 300{,}000 \cdot V^5 = \underline{149{,}153}$$
$$\sum_{1}^{5} R_n \cdot V^n = \underline{\underline{\$588{,}631}}$$

The residual value (S_n) at the end of the fifth year is \$300,000 ÷ .15 = \$2,000,000.

$$S_n \cdot V^n = 2{,}000{,}000 \cdot V^5 = \$994{,}353$$
$$V = 588{,}631 + 994{,}353$$
$$V = \$1{,}582{,}984$$

CAPITALIZED VALUE OF AN ENDOWMENT FUND (using calculator or tables)

Formula:

$$V = C_1 + \frac{M}{i} + \left(\frac{C_2}{i} \cdot \frac{1}{S_{\overline{n|}i}}\right)$$

where

V = Capitalized value
C_1 = Original cost
M = Annual maintenance expense
C_2 = Renewal cost
i = Assumed rate of interest
n = Renewal time period

$$\frac{1}{S_{\overline{n|}i}} = \frac{1}{a_{\overline{n|}i}} - i$$

Example:

A philanthropist wishes to endow a building for his alma mater. Under the terms of the endowment the building is to cost \$1,000,000. The endowment provides \$20,000 for annual maintenance, and the building is to be renovated at the end of each 25-year period at an estimated cost of \$300,000. It will take one year to construct the building. Interest is assumed at the rate of 8%. How much money is required to fund the endowment?

Solution:

$$V = C_1 + \frac{M}{i} + \left(\frac{C_2}{i} \cdot \frac{1}{S_{\overline{n|}i}}\right)$$

$$V = 1{,}000{,}000 + \frac{20{,}000}{.08} + \left(\frac{300{,}000}{.08} \cdot \frac{1}{S_{\overline{25|}.08}}\right)$$

$$V = 1{,}000{,}000 + 250{,}000 + (3{,}750{,}000 \times .01367878)$$

$$V = 1{,}000{,}000 + 250{,}000 + 51{,}295.43$$

$$V = \$1{,}301{,}295.43$$

Proof:

Initial contribution	\$1,301,295.43
Less building cost	1,000,000.00
Fund balance	\$ 301,295.43
Annual fund earnings	
(8% × 301,295.43) =	\$ 24,103.63
Required for annual maintenance	20,000.00
Balance to renovation fund	\$ 4,103.63
Renovating fund balance 25 years hence:	
$\$4{,}103.63 \times S_{\overline{25|}.08}$	= \$ 299,999.73

$$\frac{1}{S_{\overline{25|}.08}} = \frac{1}{a_{\overline{25|}.08}} - i$$

$$.01367878 = .09367878 - .08$$

CAPITALIZED VALUE OF A WASTING ASSET VARIABLE INCOME STREAM (using calculator or tables)

Formula:

$$V = \sum_{1}^{n} R_n \cdot V^n$$

where

V = Present value

R_n = Income of a particular year

$V^n = (1 + i)^{-n}$

Σ = Sum

Example:

An oil field has been producing for several years. As the pressure declines, the flow of oil decreases. The production of the field has been decreasing at the constant rate of 20% per year. Geologists estimate that the field will probably produce for the next 5 years, after which the flow of oil will be insufficient to be worth recovering, and the field will be abandoned. The field produced 30,000 barrels of oil last year. The current price of oil at the well head net of expense is $20 per barrel. The price of oil is expected to escalate at the rate of 7% per year. Income is received at the end of each year; 12% is considered a fair return on the investment. What is the proved reserve of the oil field? What is the present value of the oil field?

Solution:

Proved reserve:

$$S_n = \frac{t_1(1 - r^n)}{1 - r}$$

where

S_n = Proved reserve

t_1 = First year's production*

r = Common ratio = (1 − constant decline rate)

$$S_n = \frac{24{,}000(1 - .80^5)}{1 - .80}$$

$$S_n = \frac{16{,}135.68}{.20}$$

S_n = 80,678 barrels

Present value of the field:

Year	Annual Production	Net Selling Price Per bbl.	R_n	$R_n \times V^n$
1	24,000	$20.00	$480,000	$ 428,571
2	19,200	21.40	410,880	327,551
3	15,360	22.90	351,744	250,364
4	12,288	24.50	301,056	191,327
5	9,830	26.22	257,743	146,250
Total	80,678			$1,334,063

V = $1,334,063

*t_1 = 30,000 × 80% = 24,000 barrels

LEVERAGE BUY-OUT VALUE

Formula:

$$V = \frac{E}{d \cdot r + (1 - d)\frac{1}{a_{\overline{n}|i}}}$$

where

V = The value of the company
E = Earnings or cash flow
d = Down payment in percent
r = Rate of return on equity investment

$$a_{\overline{n}|i} = \frac{1 - (1 + i)^{-n}}{i}$$

Example:

The management employees of the XYZ Corporation are contemplating the purchase of the company. You have been retained to give them an indication of value as a basis for negotiations and obtaining financing. A down payment of 25% will be required. Financing from a local bank can be obtained for a 5-year period at 2 points over prime (prime is presently 8%), payable in 5 annual installments of principal and interest. The rate of return required on an equity investment of this type is 20%. The cash flow for the prior year was \$750,000. The management is optimistic and believes that they can increase the cash flow over the next few years to \$1,000,000. However, you are going to base your value on demonstrated earnings rather than projections. What value should be placed on the company?

Solution:

$$V = \frac{E}{d \cdot r + (1 - d)\frac{1}{a_{\overline{n}|i}}}$$

$$V = \frac{750{,}000}{(.25 \cdot .20) + (1 - .25)\frac{1}{a_{\overline{5}|.10}}}$$

$$V = \frac{750{,}000}{.05 + .75(.26380)}$$

$$V = \frac{750{,}000}{.05 + .19785}$$

$$V = \frac{750{,}000}{.24785}$$

$$V = \$3{,}026{,}024$$

Verification:

Value	$3,026,024
Less down payment of 25%	$ 756,506
Balance to finance	$2,269,518
Periodic payment @ 10% for 5 years	$ 598,693
Cash flow	$ 750,000
Less return on investment:	
Down payment $ 756,506	
Rate of return × .20	151,301
Available for debt service	$ 598,699
(Difference $6 due to rounding off)	

14

Price Level Adjustments

CONVERTING DEPRECIATION EXPENSE TO COMMON DOLLARS

Formula:

$$D_2 = D_1 \times \frac{P_2}{P_1}$$

where

D_2 = Adjusted depreciation expense
D_1 = Depreciation expense based on historical cost
P_1 = Index of general price level (or special index) on date asset was acquired
P_2 = Index of general price level (or special index) at the end of the current year

Example:

A building was purchased on January 1, 1970 at a cost of \$550,000. The estimated economic life of the building is 50 years. The index of the general price level on the date of acquisition was 60, and the index of the general price level at the end of the current year, December 31, 1986 was 240. Determine the economic depreciation for the current year.

Solution:

Historical depreciation based on cost and straight line method:

$\$550{,}000 \div 50 = \$11{,}000$

$$D_2 = D_1 \times \frac{P_2}{P_1}$$

$$D_2 = 11{,}000 \times \frac{240}{60}$$

$$D_2 = \$44{,}000$$

Note: For simplicity purposes salvage value is ignored.

CONVERTING ASSET VALUES TO COMMON DOLLARS

Formula:

$$C_2 = C_1 \times \frac{P_2}{P_1}$$

where

C_2 = Adjusted cost
C_1 = Original historical cost
P_2 = Index of general price level (or special index) at the end of the current year
P_1 = Index of general price level (or special index) on date asset was acquired

Example:

See example for converting depreciation expense to common dollars, page 174.

Solution:

$$C_2 = C_1 \times \frac{P_2}{P_1}$$

$$C_2 = 550{,}000 \times \frac{240}{60}$$

$$C_2 = \$2{,}200{,}000$$

CONVERTING THE ALLOWANCE FOR DEPRECIATION TO COMMON DOLLARS

Formula:

$$A_2 = A_1 \times \frac{P_2}{P_1}$$

where

A_2 = Adjusted allowance
A_1 = Allowance based on historical cost
P_1 = Index of general price level (or special index) on date asset was acquired
P_2 = Index of general price level (or special index) at the end of the current year

Example:

See example for converting depreciation expense to common dollars, page 174.

Solution:

Allowance per books:

$11,000 annual depreciation on cost times years elapsed (15) equals $165,000

$$A_2 = A_1 \times \frac{P_2}{P_1}$$

$$A_2 = 165{,}000 \times \frac{240}{60}$$

$$A_2 = \$660{,}000$$

CONVERTING LONG-TERM DEBT TO COMMON DOLLARS

Formula:

$$L_2 = L_1 \times \frac{P_2}{P_1}$$

where

L_2 = Adjusted liability
L_1 = Liability based on historical cost
P_2 = Index of general price level (or special index) at the end of the current year
P_1 = Index of general price level (or special index) on the date liability was acquired

Example:

On January 1, 19X1, the XYZ Company issued $600,000, 6%, 30-year bonds, which were sold at par. The index of the general price level on the date the bonds were sold was 60. Ten years later the index of the general price level was 240. What amount should be shown as the liability for Bonds Payable at the later date?

Solution:

$$L_2 = L_1 \times \frac{P_2}{P_1}$$

$$L_2 = 600{,}000 \times \frac{240}{60}$$

$$L_2 = \$2{,}400{,}000$$

CURRENT COST/CURRENT DOLLARS

Formula:

$$CCD = RC \times \frac{\overline{CPI}}{CPI_t}$$

where

CCD = Current cost/current dollar
RC = Replacement cost
$\overline{CPI}$ = Average CPI index for year
CPI_t = CPI at transaction date

Example:

From the following data restate the plant and equipment account of the XYZ Company as of December 31, 19X2, and 19X1.

	December 31,	
	19X2	19X1
Plant & equipment (cost)	\$100,000	\$ 85,000
Replacement cost as determined by management	\$220,000	\$170,000
CPI at year end	243	213
Average CPI for year	221	(not required)

Additional equipment, which cost \$15,000, was acquired on March 31, 19X2, when the CPI was 215.

Solution:

$$CCD = RC \times \frac{\overline{CPI}}{CPI_t}$$

CCD (19X1) =	$170{,}000 \times \dfrac{221}{213} =$	176,385
Add:		
19X2 additions	$15{,}000 \times \dfrac{221}{215} =$	15,419
CCD (19X2)		191,804

and would be presented as follows:

	December 31,	
	19X2	19X1
Plant & equipment (*CC/CD*)	\$191,804	\$176,385

15

Marketing

CALCULATING THE SELLING PRICE (markup based on cost)

Formula:

$$S = C(1 + R)$$

where

S = Selling price
C = Cost
R = Markup % based on cost

Example:

The buyer of the men's shoe department is charged with the responsibility of setting the selling price for the merchandise that he purchases for his department. It has been his policy to mark up new merchandise at 66 2/3% of cost. Determine the selling price of a pair of shoes that cost $30.

Solution:

$$S = C(1 + R)$$
$$S = 30(1 + .6667)$$
$$S = 30 + 20$$
$$S = \$50$$

CALCULATING THE SELLING PRICE
(markup based on selling price)

Formula:

$$S = \frac{C}{1 - R}$$

where

S = Selling price
C = Cost
R = Markup % based on selling price

Example:

The cost accounting department has estimated that the standard manufacturing cost of a proposed new product will be $240. Determine the selling price of the product if the gross profit margin is 40% based on selling price.

Solution:

$$S = \frac{C}{1 - R}$$

$$S = \frac{240}{1 - .40}$$

$$S = \frac{240}{.60}$$

$$S = \$400$$

LOADING THE SELLING PRICE
(markup based on selling price)

Formula:

$$S = \frac{C}{1 - (R + r)}$$

where

S = Selling price

C = Cost
R = Markup % based on selling price
r = Load factor % based on selling price (for instance, sales commissions)

Example:

The General Manufacturing Company desires to establish the selling price of its product so as to yield a 40% gross profit rate, computed after paying a 10% sales commission to its sales agents. The standard manufacturing cost of the product is \$240. Determine the selling price.

Solution:

$$S = \frac{C}{1 - (R + r)}$$

$$S = \frac{240}{1 - (.40 + .10)}$$

$$S = \frac{240}{1 - .50}$$

$$S = \frac{240}{.50}$$

$$S = \$480$$

LOADING THE SELLING PRICE (markup based on cost)

Formula:

$$S = \frac{C(1 + R)}{1 - r}$$

where

S = Selling price
C = Cost
R = Markup % based on cost
r = Load factor % based on selling price (for instance, sales commissions)

Example:

The buyer of the men's shoe department desires to allow a 10% sales commission to his salespeople and still maintain the same profit on his sales. If a pair of shoes cost $30 and the usual markup based on cost is 66 2/3%, determine the selling price of the pair of shoes.

Solution:

$$S = \frac{C(1 + R)}{1 - r}$$

$$S = \frac{30(1 + .66\ 2/3)}{1 - .10}$$

$$S = \frac{30 + 20}{.90}$$

$$S = \frac{50}{.90} = 55.55$$

$$S = \$56$$

AFTER TAX BREAKEVEN POINT

Formula:

$$BE_{pt} = \frac{FE + \dfrac{P}{1 - t}}{1 - \dfrac{V}{S}}$$

where

BE_{pt} = Required sales volume with profit after taxes
FE = Total fixed expenses
P = After tax profit
t = Effective tax rate
V = Total variable expenses
S = Normal budget, or capacity sales volume

Example:

A company has fixed expenses of $375,000, total variable expenses of $1,200,000, and a budget sales volume of $1,800,000. The company desires to make a profit after taxes (bottom line) of \$500,000. The effective tax rate including state and federal income taxes is 37%. What is the required sales volume?

Solution:

$$BE_{pt} = \frac{375{,}000 + \dfrac{500{,}000}{1 - .37}}{1 - \dfrac{1{,}200{,}000}{1{,}800{,}000}}$$

$$BE_{pt} = \frac{1{,}168{,}651}{1 - .6667} = \frac{1{,}168{,}651}{.3333}$$

$$BE_{pt} = \$3{,}506{,}304$$

BREAKEVEN POINT WITH PROFIT

Formula:

$$BE_P = \frac{FE + P}{1 - \dfrac{V}{S}}$$

where

BE_P = Breakeven point with profit
FE = Total fixed expenses
P = Profit before taxes
V = Total variable expenses
S = Normal budget, or capacity sales volume

Example:

A company has fixed expenses of \$375,000 and total variable expenses of \$1,200,000. The budget sales volume for this company is \$1,800,000. What is the required sales volume to make a profit before taxes of \$500,000?

Solution:

$$BE_P = \frac{375{,}000 + 500{,}000}{1 - \dfrac{1{,}200{,}000}{1{,}800{,}000}}$$

$$BE_P = \frac{875{,}000}{1 - .6667} = \frac{875{,}000}{.3333}$$

$$BE_P = \$2{,}625{,}263$$

CASH FLOW—BREAKEVEN POINT

Formula:

$$BE_c = \frac{FE - D}{1 - \frac{V}{S}}$$

where

BE_c = Breakeven point, cash flow
D = Depreciation, included in expenses
(See Breakeven Point problem (p. 182) for other symbols.)

Example:

Refer to the breakeven problem on page 182. Included in the various categories of expenses is depreciation, that is a total of \$10,000. What is the cash flow breakeven point?

Solution:

$$BE_c = \frac{375{,}000 - 10{,}000}{1 - \frac{1{,}200{,}000}{1{,}800{,}000}}$$

$$BE_c = \frac{365{,}000}{1 - .6667} = \frac{365{,}000}{.3333}$$

$$BE_c = \$1{,}095{,}110$$

EFFECT OF A PRICE CUT ON PROFIT

Formulas:

Profit before price cut: $PB_{\%} = \frac{PB}{V(SP_1)}$

Profit after price cut: $PA_{\%} = \frac{PA}{V(SP_2)}$

$$\text{Percentage cut in profit: } PC_{\%} = \frac{PB_{\%} - PA_{\%}}{PB_{\%}}$$

where

$PB_{\%}$ = Total profit before price cut (in percent)
PB = Total profit before price cut (in dollars)
V = Sales volume
SP_1 = Selling price before price cut
$PA_{\%}$ = Total profit after price cut (in percent)
PA = Total profit after price cut (in dollars)
SP_2 = Selling price after price cut
$PC_{\%}$ = Percentage cut in profit

Example:

In 1985, the ABC Manufacturing Company sold 9000 units of a particular product to one firm at a per unit price of $2.54. At the end of the year, it was necessary in order to meet competition to lower the per unit price in the 1986 contract to $2.49.

The total profit on the item in 1985 (before the price cut) was $2286, and in 1986 (after the price cut) was $1792.80. What percentage cut in profit occurred on this item in 1986, assuming no change in variable and fixed expenses?

Solution:

$$\text{Percentage profit before price cut: } \frac{2286}{9000(2.54)} = \frac{2286}{22{,}860} = 10\%$$

$$\text{Percentage profit after price cut: } \frac{1792.80}{9000(2.49)} = \frac{1792.80}{22{,}410} = 8\%$$

$$\text{Percentage cut in profit: } \frac{10\% - 8\%}{10\%} = \frac{2\%}{10\%} = 20$$

RESTORING PROFIT MARGINS WITH SALES VOLUME INCREASE

Formula:

$$X = \frac{LP}{\frac{PB}{V}}$$

where

X = Volume of sales to customer (2) necessary to cover profit loss

LP = Profit loss (in dollars) from customer (1)

PB = Profit from sales to customer (1) before price cut

V = Sales volume to customer (1)

Example:

The ABC Company had to lower its price from $2.54 to $2.49 per unit to retain customer (1) to whom it was selling annually 9000 items of a product at a total profit of $2286. When the price was lowered, the total profit fell to $1792.80, giving a loss in total profit of $493.20.

A new customer (2) has been found who will pay the original price of $2.54. How many units will ABC Company have to sell to customer (2) to restore the lost profit, assuming he was able to do this by increasing production efficiencies, thus not increasing his expenses?

Solution:

$$X = \frac{493.20}{\frac{2286}{9000}} = \frac{493.20}{.254} = 1942$$

GROSS PROFIT VARIATION

Formulas:

(1) $V_{sq} = P_1(Q_2 - Q_1)$

(2) $V_{sp} = Q_2(P_2 - P_1)$

(3) $V_{cq} = C_1(Q_1 - Q_2)$

(4) $V_{cp} = Q_2(C_1 - C_2)$

where

V_{sq} = Selling volume variation due to change in number of units sold

V_{sp} = Selling price variation due to change in unit selling price

V_{cq} = Cost volume variation due to change in number of units sold
V_{cp} = Cost price variation due to change in unit cost
P_1 = Average selling price of base period
P_2 = Average selling price of current period
Q_1 = Quantity sold in base year
Q_2 = Quantity sold in current period
C_1 = Average cost per unit, base year
C_2 = Average cost per unit, current period

Example:

As part of your analytical review of the financial statements of the XYZ Company for the year ended June 30, 19X2, you wish to determine the causes of the variation in gross profit as compared to the prior year. You have obtained the following data from the company's financial statements and statistical records:

	Base year—19X1		Current year—19X2	
Sales	\$2,575,000		\$3,525,000	
Cost of sales	1,493,000		2,325,000	
Gross profit	\$1,082,000		\$1,200,000	
Number pounds sold	1,000,000		1,500,000	
Average selling price		\$2.575		\$2.350
Average cost		\$1.493		\$1.550

Solution:

Gross profit—current year	\$1,200,000
Gross profit—prior year	1,082,000
Variation	\$ 118,000

(1) $V_{sq} = P_1(Q_2 - Q_1) = \$2.575(1{,}500{,}000 - 1{,}000{,}000)$
$= \$1{,}287{,}500$

(2) $V_{sp} = Q_2(P_2 - P_1) = 1{,}500{,}000(\$2.350 - 2.575)$
$= 1{,}500{,}000(-\$.225)$
$= -\$337{,}500$

(3) $V_{cq} = C_1(Q_1 - Q_2) = \$1.493(1{,}000{,}000 - 1{,}500{,}000)$
$= \$1.493(-500{,}000)$
$= -\$746{,}500$

$$
\begin{aligned}
(4)\ V_{cp} = Q_2(C_1 - C_2) &= 1{,}500{,}000(\$1.493 - \$1.550) \\
&= 1{,}500{,}000(-.057) \\
&= -\$85{,}500
\end{aligned}
$$

Summary:

Gross profit variation:		+$118,000
Caused by		
Selling function:		
Increase in volume	+$1,287,500	
Decrease in selling price	− 337,500	+ $950,000
Cost function:		
Increase in volume	−$746,500	
Increase in unit cost	− 85,500	− 832,000
Total variation		$118,000

16

Cost and Production

EQUIVALENT UNITS OF PRODUCTION

Formula:

$$E.U. = T - \%_1(W/P_1) + \%_2(W/P_2)$$

where

$E.U.$ = Equivalent units of production
T = Number of units transferred to next department
$\%_1$ = Percentage of completion of beginning work in process
$\%_2$ = Percentage of completion of ending work in process
W/P_1 = Number of units in beginning work in process
W/P_2 = Number of units in ending work in process

Example:

From the following information compute the equivalent number of units for Department 10 of the General Manufacturing Company. The production records of the department showed that 200,000 units were actually transferred to Department 11. The physical inventory at the end of the year revealed that there were 15,000 units of production still in process. The department foreman estimated that these units were on the average 80% completed. Reference to prior records revealed that at the beginning of the accounting period there were 45,000 units in process, which were estimated to be on the average 20% completed.

Solution:

$$E.U. = T - \%_1(W/P_1) + \%_2(W/P_2)$$
$$E.U. = 200{,}000 - .20(45{,}000) + .80(15{,}000)$$
$$E.U. = 200{,}000 - 9000 + 12{,}000$$
$$E.U. = 203{,}000$$

BREAKEVEN POINT

Formula:

$$B/E = \frac{F/E}{1 - \frac{V}{S}}$$

where

B/E = Breakeven point
F/E = Total fixed expenses
V = Total variable expenses
S = Normal, budget, or capacity sales volume

Example:

The following data were assembled from the company's flexible budget:

Budget sales volume $1,800,000

Item	Amount	Fixed	Variable
Materials	$ 400,000		$ 400,000
Labor	175,000		175,000
Manufacturing expenses	600,000	$100,000	500,000
Selling expenses	100,000	30,000	70,000
General expenses	300,000	245,000	55,000
Totals	$1,575,000	$375,000	$1,200,000

Determine the estimated breakeven point.

Solution:

$$B/E = \frac{F/E}{1 - \frac{V}{S}}$$

$$B/E = \frac{375{,}000}{1 - \dfrac{1{,}200{,}000}{1{,}800{,}000}}$$

$$B/E = \frac{375{,}000}{1 - .6667} = \frac{375{,}000}{.3333}$$

$$B/E = \$1{,}125{,}000$$

POINT OF PROFITABILITY—BREAKEVEN POINT

Formula:

$$PP = \frac{FC}{1 - \dfrac{V}{S}}$$

where

PP = Point of profitability
FC = Total fixed costs
V = Total variable costs
S = Total sales

Example:

The Good Company, a small business, wishes to determine the point at which its sales volume will cover costs and begin to show a profit. Its total sales volume in 1985 was $906,000. Its total fixed costs were $140,000 and total variable costs, $702,150. At what sales level does it begin to show a profit?

Solution:

$$PP = \frac{140{,}000}{1 - \dfrac{702{,}150}{906{,}000}} = \frac{140{,}000}{1 - .775} = \frac{140{,}000}{.225}$$

$$PP = \$622{,}222$$

Conclusion:

The Good Company has a breakeven point, where sales reach a volume to begin showing a profit, of $622,222. If the sales volume in 1986 was below this point, they were operating in the negative profit (loss) range.

NORMAL BURDEN RATE
(job order cost)

Formula:

$$N.B.R. = \frac{M/E}{B}$$

where

$N.B.R.$ = Normal burden rate
M/E = Estimated manufacturing expenses at normal capacity
B = Base at normal capacity (direct labor cost, direct labor hours, machine hours, etc.)

Example:

Determine the normal burden rate from the following data gathered from the books and records of the General Manufacturing Company for Department 3.

Estimates of the departmental capacity:

Engineering estimate	100,000 units	(theoretical)
Foreman's estimate	80,000 units	(practical)
Controller's estimate	60,000 units	(normal)

The controller's staff made the following estimate of manufacturing expenses based on normal capacity:

Fixed expenses	$ 80,000
Variable expenses	$ 40,000
Total	$120,000

Solution:

$$N.B.R. = \frac{M/E}{B}$$

$$N.B.R. = \frac{120{,}000}{60{,}000}$$

$$N.B.R. = \$2$$

VOLUME VARIATION
(job order cost)

Formula:

$$V_v = A\left(\frac{V/E}{B}\right) + F/E - A(N.B.R.)$$

where

V_v = Volume variance
A = Attained capacity
V/E = Variable expenses at normal capacity
B = Base at normal capacity
F/E = Fixed expenses at normal capacity
$N.B.R.$ = Normal burden rate

Example:

From the following data determine the volume variation for Department 3 of the General Manufacturing Company.

Manufacturing expense per general ledger: $115,000
Normal burden rate: $2 per direct labor hour
Normal capacity: 60,000 direct labor hours
Attained capacity per production records: 50,000 hours
Budgeted expenses at normal capacity:

Fixed expenses	$80,000
Variable expenses	40,000

Solution:

$$V_v = A\left(\frac{V/E}{B}\right) + F/E - A(N.B.R.)$$

$$V_v = 50{,}000\left(\frac{40{,}000}{60{,}000}\right) + 80{,}000 - 50{,}000(2.00)$$

$$V_v = 33{,}333.33 + 80{,}000 - 100{,}000$$

$$V_v = \$13{,}333.33$$

BUDGET VARIATION
(job order cost)

Formula:

$$V_b = M/E - A\left(\frac{V/E}{B}\right) - F/E$$

where

V_b = Budget variation
M/E = Actual manufacturing expenses for the period
A = Attained capacity
V/E = Variable expenses at normal capacity
B = Base at normal capacity
F/E = Fixed expenses at normal capacity

Example:

See example for volume variation, page 193.

Solution:

$$V_b = M/E - A\left(\frac{V/E}{B}\right) - F/E$$

$$V_b = 115{,}000 - 50{,}000\left(\frac{40{,}000}{60{,}000}\right) - 80{,}000$$

$$V_b = 115{,}000 - 33{,}333.33 - 80{,}000$$

$$V_b = \$1666.67$$

Proof of Variations:

Actual manufacturing expenses	$115,000.00
Less applied manufacturing expenses ($2 × 50,000)	100,000.00
Total variation	$ 15,000.00
Represented by:	
Volume variation	$ 13,333.33
Budget variation	1,666.67
Total variation	$ 15,000.00

QUANTITY VARIATION
(standard cost)

Formula:

$$V_q = P_s(Q_a - Q_s)$$

where

V_q = Quantity variation
P_s = Standard price
Q_a = Actual quantity
Q_s = Standard quantity

Example:

The bill of materials for assembly No. 56 shows that 2 units of part No. 137 are required for each assembly. The standard price for part No. 137 is 30¢ each. The production records indicate that 3000 assemblies were produced during the period. The material requisition register shows that 6100 units of part No. 137 were consumed.

Determine the quantity variation.

Solution:

$$V_q = P_s(Q_a - Q_s)$$
$$V_q = .30(6100 - 6000)$$
$$V_q = .30 \times 100$$
$$V_q = \$30$$

PRICE VARIATION
(standard cost)

Formula:

$$V_p = Q_a(P_a - P_s)$$

where

V_p = Price variation
Q_a = Actual quantity
P_a = Actual price
P_s = Standard price

Example:

The General Manufacturing Company has established that the standard price for part No. 137 should be 30¢ per unit. The accounting department received an invoice for 5000 units at 33¢ per unit.

Determine the price variation.

Solution:

$$V_p = Q_a(P_a - P_s)$$
$$V_p = 5000(.33 - .30)$$
$$V_p = 5000 \times .03$$
$$V_p = \$150$$

LABOR WAGE RATE VARIATION (standard cost)

Formula:

$$V_w = T_a(w_a - w_s)$$

where

V_w = Wage rate variation
T_a = Actual time
W_a = Actual wage rate
W_s = Standard wage rate

Example:

From the following data taken from the records of Department 15 of the General Manufacturing Company, determine the labor wage rate variation.

Data

Standard	Actual
Wage rate $12.00 per hour	$14.00 per hour
Direct labor hours 250	260

Solution:

$$V_w = T_a(W_a - W_s)$$
$$V_w = 260(\$14 - \$12)$$

$$V_w = 260 \times \$2$$
$$V_w = \$520$$

LABOR EFFICIENCY VARIATION
(standard cost)

Formula:

$$V_E = W_s(T_a - T_s)$$

where

V_E = Labor efficiency variation
W_s = Standard wage rate
T_a = Actual time
T_s = Standard time

Example:

See example for labor wage rate variation, page 196.

Solution:

$$V_E = W_s(T_a - T_s)$$
$$V_E = \$12(260 - 250)$$
$$V_E = \$12(10)$$
$$V_E = \$120$$

VOLUME VARIATION
(standard cost—3-factor analysis)

Formula:

$$V_v = F/E + A\left(\frac{V/E}{B} - S.B.R.\right)$$

where

V_v = Volume variation
F/E = Fixed expenses at normal capacity
A = Attained capacity
V/E = Variable expenses at normal capacity

B = Base at normal capacity
$S.B.R.$ = Standard overhead rate

Example:

From the following data pertaining to manufacturing expenses under a standard cost system, analyze the variation by the following factors: volume, budget, efficiency.

	Data	
	Standard	**Actual**
Capacity	Normal 100%	80%
Fixed expenses	\$ 30,000	\$ 32,000
Variable expenses	70,000	56,000
Total	\$100,000	\$ 88,000
Direct labor hours (base)	200,000	170,000
Standard overhead rate	\$.50	. . .

Solution:

$$V_v = F/E + A\left(\frac{V/E}{B} - S.B.R.\right)$$

$$V_v = 30{,}000 + 170{,}000\left(\frac{70{,}000}{200{,}000} - .50\right)$$

$$V_v = 30{,}000 + 59{,}500 - 85{,}000$$

$$V_v = 89{,}500 - 85{,}000$$

$$V_v = \$4500$$

BUDGET VARIATION
(standard cost—3-factor analysis)

Formula:

$$V_b = M/E_a - A\left(\frac{V/E}{B}\right) - F/E$$

where

V_b = Budget variation
M/E_a = Actual manufacturing expenses
A = Attained capacity
V/E = Variable expenses at normal capacity

F/E = Fixed expenses at normal capacity
B = Base at normal capacity

Example:

See example for volume variation above.

Solution:

$$V_b = M/E_a - A\left(\frac{V/E}{B}\right) - F/E$$
$$V_b = 88{,}000 - 170{,}000\left(\frac{70{,}000}{200{,}000}\right) - 30{,}000$$
$$V_b = 88{,}000 - 59{,}500 - 30{,}000$$
$$V_b = -\$1500$$

EFFICIENCY VARIATION (standard cost—3-factor analysis)

Formula:

$$V_e = S.B.R.[A - C(B)]$$

where

V_e = Efficiency variation
$S.B.R.$ = Standard burden rate
A = Attained capacity
C = Percentage of normal capacity attained
B = Base at normal capacity

Example:

See example for volume variation, page 197.

Solution:

$$V_e = S.B.R.[A - C(B)]$$
$$V_e = .50[170{,}000 - .80(200{,}000)]$$
$$V_e = .50(170{,}000 - 160{,}000)$$
$$V_e = .50(10{,}000)$$
$$V_e = \$5000$$

CONTROLLABLE VARIATION
(standard cost—2-factor analysis)

Formula:

$$V_c = M/E_a - F/E - C(V/E)$$

where

V_c = Controllable variation
M/E_a = Actual manufacturing expenses
F/E = Fixed expenses at normal capacity
C = Percentage of normal capacity attained
V/E = Variable expenses at normal capacity

Example:

See example for volume variation, page 197.

Solution:

$$V_c = M/E_a - F/E - C(V/E)$$
$$V_c = 88{,}000 - 30{,}000 - .80(70{,}000)$$
$$V_c = 88{,}000 - 30{,}000 - 56{,}000$$
$$V_c = \$2000$$

VOLUME VARIATION
(standard cost—2-factor analysis)

Formula:

$$V_v = F/E + C[V/E - S.B.R.(B)]$$

where

V_v = Volume variation
F/E = Fixed expenses at normal capacity
C = Percentage of normal capacity attained
V/E = Variable expenses at normal capacity
$S.B.R.$ = Standard burden rate
B = Base at normal capacity

Example:

See example for volume variation, page 197.

Solution:

$$V_v = F/E + C[V/E - S.B.R.(B)]$$
$$V_v = 30{,}000 + .80[70{,}000 - .50(200{,}000)]$$
$$V_v = 30{,}000 + .80(70{,}000 - 100{,}000)$$
$$V_v = 30{,}000 + .80(-30{,}000)$$
$$V_v = 30{,}000 - 24{,}000$$
$$V_v = \$6000$$

17

Ratio Analysis

CURRENT RATIO

Formula:

$$C.R. = \frac{C/A}{C/L}$$

where

$C.R.$ = Current ratio
C/A = Current assets
C/L = Current liabilities

Example:

From the following data extracted from the balance sheet compute the current ratio.

Current Assets		**Current Liabilities**	
Cash	$ 2,000	Accounts Payable	$15,000
Accounts Receivable	18,000	Notes Payable	5,000
Inventories	25,000	Withholding taxes	2,000
Prepaid Expenses	5,000	Accrued Expenses	3,000
Total	$50,000		$25,000

Solution:

$$C.R. = \frac{C/A}{C/L}$$

$$C.R. = \frac{50,000}{25,000}$$

$$C.R. = \frac{2}{1}$$

$$C.R. = 2 : 1$$

ACID TEST RATIO

Formula:

$$A.T.R. = \frac{C/A - I}{C/L}$$

where

$$A.T.R. = \text{Acid test ratio}$$
$$C/A = \text{Current assets}$$
$$I = \text{Inventories}$$
$$C/L = \text{Current liabilities}$$

Example:

See data given for example for current ratio, page 202.

Solution:

$$A.T.R. = \frac{C/A - I}{C/L}$$

$$A.T.R. = \frac{50,000 - 25,000}{25,000}$$

$$A.T.R. = \frac{1}{1}$$

$$A.T.R. = 1 : 1$$

Note: Since the purpose of the acid test ratio is to determine the degree of absolute liquidity, prepaid expenses (P/P) should be excluded from current assets if material in amount. Therefore, the correct formula should be:

$$A.T.R. = \frac{C/A - I - P/P}{C/L}$$

INVENTORY TURNOVER

Formula:

$$T_i = \frac{C}{\frac{I_1 + I_2}{2}}$$

where

T_i = Inventory turnover
C = Cost of goods sold
I_1 = Beginning inventory
I_2 = Ending inventory

Example:

From the following Cost of Goods Sold section of a statement of income, compute the inventory turnover.

Cost of Goods Sold:

Beginning inventory	$ 17,000	
Purchases	56,000	
Total goods available for sale	73,000	
Less ending inventory	13.000	
Cost of goods sold		$ 60,000

Solution:

$$T_i = \frac{C}{\frac{I_1 + I_2}{2}}$$

$$T_i = \frac{60{,}000}{\frac{17{,}000 + 13{,}000}{2}} = \frac{60{,}000}{\frac{30{,}000}{2}}$$

$$T_i = \frac{60{,}000}{15{,}000}$$

$$T_i = 4$$

Note: For a manufacturing firm, the inventory turnover refers to the finished goods inventory only and is computed by the same formula.

RAW MATERIAL INVENTORY TURNOVER

Formula:

$$T_{r/m} = \frac{C}{\frac{I_{r_1} + I_{r_2}}{2}}$$

where

$T_{r/m}$ = Raw material inventory turnover
C = Raw material consumed
I_{r1} = Beginning inventory of raw materials
I_{r2} = Ending inventory of raw materials

Example:

From the following data abstracted from a manufacturing statement compute the raw material inventory turnover.

Materials Consumed:

Beginning inventory	$ 15,000	
Purchases	78,000	
Total available	93,000	
Less ending inventory	9,000	
Materials consumed		$84,000

Solution:

$$T_{r/m} = \frac{C}{\frac{I_{r_1} + I_{r_2}}{2}}$$

$$T_{r/m} = \frac{84{,}000}{\frac{15{,}000 + 9000}{2}}$$

$$T_{r/m} = \frac{84{,}000}{\frac{24{,}000}{2}}$$

$$T_{r/m} = \frac{84{,}000}{12{,}000}$$

$$T_{r/m} = 7$$

ACCOUNTS RECEIVABLE TURNOVER

Formula:

$$T_{a/r} = \frac{S}{\frac{A/R_1 + A/R_2}{2}}$$

where

$T_{a/r}$ = Accounts receivable turnover
S = Sales on account
A/R_1 = Accounts receivable at beginning of period
A/R_2 = Accounts receivable at end of period

Example:

From the following data abstracted from a firm's financial statements compute the accounts receivable turnover for the current year.

	Current Year	Prior Year
Cash	$ 20,000	$10,000
Accounts receivable	50,000	30,000
Inventory	45,000	35,000
Sales on account	400,000	300,000
Usual terms of sale	2/10, *n*/30	2/10, *n*/30

Solution:

$$T_{a/r} = \frac{S}{\frac{A/R_1 + A/R_2}{2}}$$

$$T_{a/r} = \frac{400{,}000}{\frac{30{,}000 + 50{,}000}{2}}$$

$$T_{a/r} = \frac{400{,}000}{\frac{80{,}000}{2}}$$

$$T_{a/r} = \frac{400{,}000}{40{,}000}$$

$$T_{a/r} = 10$$

COLLECTION PERIOD FOR ACCOUNTS RECEIVABLE

Formula:

$$C.P. = \frac{360}{T_{a/r}}$$

where

$C.P.$ = Collection period
$T_{a/r}$ = Accounts receivable turnover
360 = Number of days in year

Example:

See example for accounts receivable turnover, page 206.

Solution:

$$C.P. = \frac{360^*}{T_{a/r}}$$

$$C.P. = \frac{360}{10}$$

$$C.P. = 36 \text{ days}$$

ACCOUNTS PAYABLE TURNOVER

Formula:

$$T_{a/p} = \frac{P}{\frac{A/P_1 + A/P_2}{2}}$$

where

$T_{a/p}$ = Accounts payable turnover
A/P_1 = Accounts payable at beginning of period
A/P_2 = Accounts payable at end of period
P = Purchases on account

---

*365 days, instead of 360 days may be used.

Example:

From the following data extracted from a firm's financial statements compute the accounts payable turnover for the current year.

	Current Year	Prior Year
Accounts payable	\$ 10,000	\$ 5,000
Purchases on account	300,000	250,000
Terms of purchase	mostly 2/10, *n*/30	

Solution:

$$T_{a/p} = \frac{P}{\dfrac{A/P_1 + A/P_2}{2}}$$

$$T_{a/p} = \frac{300{,}000}{\dfrac{5000 + 10{,}000}{2}}$$

$$T_{a/p} = \frac{300{,}000}{\dfrac{15{,}000}{2}} = \frac{300{,}000}{7500}$$

$$T_{a/p} = 40$$

PAYMENT PERIOD FOR ACCOUNTS PAYABLE

Formula:

$$P.\ P. = \frac{360}{T_{a/p}}$$

where

$P.\ P.$ = Payment period
$T_{a/p}$ = Accounts payable turnover
360 = Number of days in year

Example:

See example for accounts payable turnover, page 207.

Solution:

$$P.\ P. = \frac{360}{T_{a/p}}$$

$$P.\,P. = \frac{360}{40}$$

$$P.\,P. = 9 \text{ days}$$

RETURN ON INVESTMENT—NET WORTH

Formula:

$$R.I._{n/w} = \frac{N/I}{\frac{N/W_1 + N/W_2}{2}}$$

where

$R.I._{n/w}$ = Return on investment based on net worth
N/I = Net income for the period
N/W_1 = Net worth at beginning of period
N/W_2 = Net worth at end of period

Example:

From the following tabulated data compute the return on investment as measured by the net worth or total capital per books.

	Current year	**Prior Year**
Assets	\$300,000	\$200,000
Liabilities	120,000	60,000
Net worth	\$180,000	\$140,000
Sales	\$400,000	\$350,000
Expenses	360,000	330,000
Net income	\$ 40,000	\$ 20,000

Solution:

$$R.I._{n/w} = \frac{N/I}{\frac{N/W_1 + N/W_2}{2}}$$

$$R.I._{n/w} = \frac{40{,}000}{\frac{140{,}000 + 180{,}000}{2}} = \frac{40{,}000}{\frac{320{,}000}{2}}$$

$$R.I._{n/w} = \frac{40{,}000}{160{,}000}$$

$$R.I._{n/w} = .25 \text{ or } 25\%$$

RETURN ON INVESTMENT—TOTAL ASSETS

Formula:

$$R.I._a = \frac{N/I}{\frac{A_1 + A_2}{2}}$$

where

$R.I._a$ = Return on investment based on total assets
N/I = Net income for the period
A_1 = Total assets at beginning of period
A_2 = Total assets at end of period

Example:

See example for return on investment—net worth, page 209.

Solution:

$$R.I._a = \frac{N/I}{\frac{A_1 + A_2}{2}}$$

$$R.I._a = \frac{40{,}000}{\frac{200{,}000 + 300{,}000}{2}}$$

$$R.I._a = \frac{40{,}000}{\frac{500{,}000}{2}} = \frac{40{,}000}{250{,}000}$$

$$R.I._a = .16 \text{ or } 16\%$$

ASSET TURNOVER

Formula:

$$A_t = \frac{S}{\frac{A_1 + A_2}{2}}$$

where

A_t = Asset turnover
S = Net sales
A_1 = Total assets at beginning of year
A_2 = Total assets at end of year

Example:

See example for return on investment—net worth, page 209.

Solution:

$$A_t = \frac{S}{\frac{A_1 + A_2}{2}}$$

$$A_t = \frac{400{,}000}{\frac{200{,}000 + 300{,}000}{2}}$$

$$A_t = \frac{400{,}000}{250{,}000}$$

$$A_t = 1.6$$

TIMES BOND INTEREST EARNED

Formula:

$$X_{i/e} = \frac{N/I + i}{i}$$

where

$X_{i/e}$ = Times bond interest earned
N/I = Net income
i = Bond interest expense

Example:

From the following condensed statement of income compute the number of times the bond interest was earned.

Condensed Statement of Income

Sales	$1,400,000
Operating expenses	860,000
Net income before bond Interest and federal income taxes	540,000
Bond interest	60,000
Net income before federal income taxes	480,000
Federal income taxes	240,000
Net Income	$ 240,000

Solution:

$$X_{i/e} = \frac{N/I + i}{i}$$

$$X_{i/e} = \frac{240{,}000 + 60{,}000}{60{,}000}$$

$$X_{i/e} = \frac{300{,}000}{60{,}000}$$

$$X_{i/e} = 5$$

BOOK VALUE PER SHARE OF COMMON STOCK

Formula:

$$B.V._{c/s} = \frac{T/C - P/C}{n}$$

where

$B.V._{c/s}$ = Book value per share of common stock
T/C = Total capital
P/C = Capital assigned to preferred shares
n = Number of shares of common stock outstanding

Example:

The stockholders' equity section of the General Manufacturing Company is presented below. From this and the other additional data given, determine the book value per share of common stock.

Stockholders' Equity

Preferred stock, 5%, cumulative, $50 par	
Authorized 10,000 shares	
Issued 7,000 shares	$ 350,000
Common stock, $100 par	
Authorized 3,000 shares	
Issued 2,500 shares	250,000
Capital in excess of par	75,000
Retained income	525,000
Total stockholders' equity	$1,200,000

The preferred stock dividend is 2 years in arrears, including the current year.

Solution:

$$B.V._{c/s} = \frac{T/C - P/C}{n}$$

$$B.V._{c/s} = \frac{1{,}200{,}000 - 385{,}000}{2500}$$

$$B.V._{c/s} = \frac{815{,}000}{2500}$$

$$B.V._{c/s} = \$326$$

Note: A suitable general formula for P/C is difficult to formulate because of the various rights and privileges of individual preferred stock issues.

P/C in this example is computed as follows:

Par value of preferred stock outstanding	$350,000
Dividend arrearage 2($350,000 × .05)	35,000
Capital assigned to preferred stock	$385,000

EARNINGS PER SHARE OF COMMON STOCK

Formula:

$$E.P.S. = \frac{N/I - P/D}{n}$$

where

$E.P.S.$ = Earnings per share of common stock
N/I = Net income
P/D = Preferred dividends due
n = Number of common shares outstanding

Example:

From the following data abstracted from a firm's financial statements determine the earnings per share of common stock.

Net income		$125,600
Preferred stock, 8%, $100 par		
Authorized	1000 shares	
Issued	700 shares	$ 70,000
Common stock, $10 par		
Authorized	50,000 shares	
Issued	30,000 shares	$300,000

Solution:

$$E.P.S. = \frac{N/I - P/D}{n}$$

$$E.P.S. = \frac{125{,}600 - 5600}{30{,}000}$$

$$E.P.S. = \frac{120{,}000}{30{,}000}$$

$$E.P.S. = \$4$$

WEIGHTED AVERAGE NUMBER OF SHARES OUTSTANDING

Formula:

$$WASO = O + I_1 \frac{n_1}{365} + I_2 \frac{n_2}{365} + \cdots + I_n \frac{n_n}{365}$$

where

$WASO$ = Weighted average number of shares outstanding
O = Number of outstanding shares at beginning of year

I_1 = Number of first additional shares issued
I_2 = Number of second additional shares issued
I_n = Number of nth additional shares issued
n_1 = Number of days in year the first issue was outstanding
n_2 = Number of days in year the second issue was outstanding
n_n = Number of days in year the nth issue was outstanding

Example:

The XYZ Company had 500,000 shares of stock outstanding on January 1, 19X1. On November 10, 19X1, the company issued 200,000 additional shares. What is the weighted average number of shares outstanding for the year ended December 31, 19X1?

Solution:

$$WASO = O + I_1 \frac{n_1}{365}$$

$$WASO = 500{,}000 + (200{,}000) \frac{51}{365}$$

$$WASO = 500{,}000 + 27{,}945$$

$$WASO = 527{,}945$$

TIMES PREFERRED DIVIDENDS EARNED

Formula:

$$x_{D/e} = \frac{N/I}{P/D}$$

where

$x_{D/e}$ = Times preferred dividends earned
N/I = Net income
P/D = Preferred dividend requirement

Example:

See example for earnings per share of common stock, page 213.

Solution:

$$x_{D/e} = \frac{N/I}{P/D}$$

$$x_{D/e} = \frac{125{,}600}{5600}$$

$$x_{D/e} = 22.4 \text{ times}$$

18

Single Entry

DETERMINING SALES

Formula:

$$S = C + A/R_2 - A/R_1$$

where

S = Net sales
C = Cash collected
A/R_1 = Accounts receivable at beginning of year
A/R_2 = Accounts receivable at end of year

Example:

You are required to determine the net sales of the XYZ Company from an incomplete set of records. An examination of the bank statement reveals that \$50,000 was collected from customers. A schedule of accounts receivable at the beginning of the year totaled \$32,000, and a similar schedule at the end of the year totaled \$24,000.

Solution:

$$S = C + A/R_2 - A/R_1$$
$$S = 50{,}000 + 24{,}000 - 32{,}000$$
$$S = \$42{,}000$$

Note: In the absence of adequate accounting records, the determination of sales discounts and gross sales is generally not practicable.

DETERMINING PURCHASES

Formula:

$$P = D + A/P_2 - A/P_1$$

where

P = Purchases (net)
D = Payments made to suppliers
A/P_1 = Accounts payable at beginning of year
A/P_2 = Accounts payable at end of year

Example:

From the following incomplete data determine the net purchases of the XYZ Company. An analysis of the check stubs for the year revealed that \$63,000 was paid to suppliers of merchandise. Unpaid invoices for merchandise at the end of the year were determined to be \$12,000. Analysis of payments made during the year indicated that invoices in the amount of \$27,000 were applicable to the prior year.

Solution:

$$P = D + A/P_2 - A/P_1$$
$$P = 63{,}000 + 12{,}000 - 27{,}000$$
$$P = \$48{,}000$$

Note: In the absence of adequate records, the determination of purchase discounts and gross purchases is generally not practicable.

DETERMINING AN EXPENSE (simple case)

Formula:

$$E = E_d + E_{a2} - E_{a1}$$

where

E = Expense
E_d = Expense paid in cash during year
E_{a1} = Accrual at beginning of year
E_{a2} = Accrual at end of year

Example:

During the course of your review of incomplete records, you have determined the following facts. Wages paid during the year as determined from examination of payroll records amounted to $15,000. Your computations of accrued wages at the beginning and end of the year are $400 and $700, respectively. What should be the proper expense for wages shown on the income statement?

Solution:

$$E = E_d + E_{a2} - E_{a1}$$
$$E = 15{,}000 + 700 - 400$$
$$E = \$15{,}300$$

DETERMINING AN EXPENSE (complex case)

Formula:

$$E = E_d + (E_{a2} - E_{a1}) + (P/P_1 - P/P_2)$$

where

E = Expense
E_d = Expense paid in cash during year
E_{a1} = Accrual at beginning of year
E_{a2} = Accrual at end of year
P/P_1 = Prepaid expense at beginning of year
P/P_2 = Prepaid expense at end of year

Example:

The following facts were determined during a review of advertising accounts. Examination of cancelled checks revealed that $1500 was paid for advertising, of which $200 represented payment for an advertisement that will be run in the next year. An inventory of advertising suppliers, circulars, etc., at the end of the year aggregated $400. From the balance sheet at the end of the prior year, it was learned that $150 of supplies were on hand and that there was accrued advertising expense of $63. Unpaid bills at the end of the year for advertising amounted to $150.

Solution:

$$E = E_d + (E_{a2} - E_{a1}) + (P/P_1 - P/P_2)$$
$$E = 1500 + (150 - 63) + (150 - 600)$$
$$E = 1500 + 87 - 450$$
$$E = \$1137$$

DETERMINING EXPENSE (prepaid expenses)

Formula:

$$E = E_d + P/P_1 - P/P_2$$

where

E = Expense for year
P/P_1 = Prepaid amount at beginning of period
P/P_2 = Prepaid amount at end of period
E_d = Expenses actually paid during the period

Example:

Examination of insurance transactions revealed the following facts. The amount of $600 was paid out during the year. Prepaid insurance at the beginning of the year amounted to $175, and analysis of the insurance policies revealed that $215 was unexpired as of the end of the current year. What is the amount of insurance expense for the year?

Solution:

$$E = E_d + P/P_1 - P/P_2$$
$$E = \$600 + \$175 - \$215$$
$$E = \$560$$

DETERMINING INVENTORY

See Gross Profit Method in Chapter 10, page 130.

19

Pension Plans

The pension problems illustrated in this chapter are based upon practical applications and require the use of two decrement tables. The first decrement table is a mortality table that is used to determine the present value of a life annuity payable in monthly installments at the beginning of each month commencing at retirement age 65. The second decrement table is a termination table that gives the termination experience from all causes; for example, mortality, disability, resignation, discharge. This table is used to calculate the normal cost and the accrued liability.

The tables used in the examples are for illustrative purposes only. For actual solutions to a particular problem, appropriate tables will need to be secured or constructed. This book shows how to construct a commutation table. See page 222.

The mortality tables and the resulting actuarial functions are the PBGC tables for healthy males and females, and use 6% interest. The termination table is a unisex table, also using 6% interest. However, it is not unusual to use different rates of interest for each table.

PROBABILITY SYMBOLS

$l_x^{(T)}$	number employed at age x	=	$l_{x+1} - l_{x-d_x}$
$d_x^{(T)}$	number of employees terminating between age x and age $x + 1$	=	$l_x^{(T)} - l_{x+1}^{(T)}$

$q_x^{(T)}$	the probability that an employee aged x will terminate within 1 year	=	$\frac{d_x^{(T)}}{l_x^{(T)}}$
$_nq_x^{(T)}$	the probability that an employee aged x will terminate within n years	=	$\frac{l_x^{(T)} - l_{x+n}^{(T)}}{l_x^{(T)}}$
$_{n\vert}q_x^{(T)}$	the probability that an employee aged x will terminate within the year after attaining age $x + n + 1$	=	$\frac{l_x^{(T)} - l_{x+n+1}^{(T)}}{l_x^{(T)}}$
$p_x^{(T)}$	the probability that an employee aged x will survive 1 year	=	$\frac{l_{x+1}^{(T)}}{l_x^{(T)}}$
$_np_x^{(T)}$	the probability that an employee aged x will survive n years	=	$\frac{l_{x+n}^{(T)}}{l_x^{(T)}}$

COMMUTATION SYMBOLS

(Superscript $^{(T)}$ omitted for simplicity)

$$V^x = (1 + i)^{-x}$$
$$D_x = V^x \cdot l_x$$
$$C_x = V^{x+1} \cdot d_x$$
$$N_x = D_x + D_{x+1} + D_{x+2} + \cdots + D_w$$
$$N_x^{(12)} = N_x - \left(\frac{11}{24} \cdot D_x\right)$$
$$M_x = C_x + C_{x+1} + C_{x+2} + \cdots + C_w$$
$$S_x = N_x + N_{x+1} + N_{x+2} + \cdots + N_w$$
$$R_x = M_x + M_{x+1} + M_{x+2} + \cdots + M_w$$
$\ddot{a}_x$ = present value of a life annuity due

CONSTRUCTION OF A TERMINATION COMMUTATION TABLE

Formulas:

See probability symbols and commutation symbols on pages 221 and 222.

Example:

A large professional firm has 10,000 employees, most of whom are covered by a pension plan. You are required to construct a termination commutation table to facilitate your actuarial computations. The plan assumptions for active employees are interest rate 6%, no salary scale, decrements from all causes; that is, mortality, disability, resignation, discharge, and so on are determined by studies of actual experience and the rates of decrement have been smoothed and are shown as $q_x^{(T)}$ in the solution to the problem. The normal entry age is 22 and the normal retirement age is 65.

Solution:

1. Determine the radix, usually any large round number, such as: 10,000 or 100,000.
2. At age 22 in the $l_x^{(T)}$ column enter the radix, say 10,000.
3. In the $q_x^{(T)}$ column enter the results of your termination studies.
4. $d_x^{(T)}$ is equal to $l_x^{(T)} \cdot q_x^{(T)}$
5. $D_x^{(T)}$ is equal to $l_x^{(T)} \cdot v^x$
6. At the end of the table, age 65, enter the value of $D_x^{(T)}$ in the $N_x^{(T)}$ column.
7. $N_x^{(T)}$ is equal to $N_{x+1}^{(T)} + D_x^{(T)}$
8. The first $l_x^{(T)}$ after the radix is $l_x^{(T)} = l_{x-1}^{(T)} - d_{x-1}^{(T)}$

Let us go to age 23 and compute the rest of the line values on the table (superscripts omitted).

$$l_{23} = l_{22} - d_{22} = 10{,}000 - 2500 = 7500$$
$$d_{23} = l_{23} \times q_{23} = 7500 \times .236 = 1770$$
$$D_{23} = l_{23} \times (1.06)^{-23} = 7500(1.06)^{-23} = 1963.479$$
$$N_{23} = N_{24} + D_{23} = 6175.560 + 1963.479 = 8139.039$$ (See note below.)
$$\ddot{a}_{23} = N_{23}/D_{23} = 8139.039/1963.479 = 4.145$$

It is very difficult to make a commutation table manually, with a pc it is easy, but always test check a number of values manually.

Note: The N_x column is computed from the bottom of the table and worked up; compute N_{64} and work up to N_{22}.

The table was computer-generated; and the computer carried out the computations to more than 3 places; therefore, the additions in some of the columns may be off by 1 in the last decimal place.

TERMINATION TABLE
$i = .06$

Age: x	$l_x^{(T)}$	$q_x^{(T)}$	$d_x^{(T)}$	$D_x^{(T)}$	$N_x^{(T)}$	$\ddot{a}_x^{(T)}$
22	10,000.000	0.250	2,500.000	2,775.051	10,914.090	3.933
23	7,500.000	0.236	1,770.000	1,963.479	8,139.039	4.145
24	5,730.000	0.223	1,277.790	1,415.187	6,175.560	4.364
25	4,452.210	0.211	939.416	1,037.359	4,760.373	4.589
26	3,512.794	0.199	699.046	772.147	3,723.014	4.822
27	2,813.748	0.188	528.985	583.481	2,950.866	5.057
28	2,284.763	0.178	406.688	446.969	2,367.385	5.297
29	1,878.075	0.168	315.517	346.611	1,920.417	5.541
30	1,562.559	0.159	248.447	272.057	1,573.805	5.785
31	1,314.112	0.150	197.117	215.849	1,301.748	6.031
32	1,116.995	0.142	158.613	173.087	1,085.899	6.274
33	958.382	0.134	128.423	140.102	912.812	6.515
34	829.959	0.127	105.405	114.461	772.710	6.751
35	724.554	0.120	86.946	94.268	658.249	6.983
36	637.607	0.113	72.050	78.260	563.981	7.206
37	565.558	0.107	60.515	65.488	485.720	7.417
38	505.043	0.101	51.009	55.170	420.233	7.617
39	454.034	0.096	43.587	46.791	365.062	7.802
40	410.446	0.090	36.940	39.905	318.272	7.976
41	373.506	0.085	31.748	34.258	278.367	8.126
42	341.758	0.081	27.682	29.571	244.110	8.255
43	314.076	0.076	23.870	25.638	214.538	8.368
44	290.206	0.072	20.895	22.349	188.900	8.452
45	269.311	0.068	18.313	19.565	166.552	8.513
46	250.998	0.064	16.064	17.203	146.986	8.544
47	234.934	0.061	14.331	15.190	129.783	8.544
48	220.603	0.057	12.574	13.456	114.593	8.516
49	208.029	0.054	11.234	11.971	101.137	8.448
50	196.795	0.051	10.037	10.684	89.165	8.346
51	186.759	0.048	8.964	9.565	78.482	8.205
52	177.794	0.046	8.179	8.590	68.917	8.023
53	169.616	0.043	7.293	7.731	60.326	7.803

TERMINATION TABLE

$i = .06$

Age: x	$l_x^{(T)}$	$q_x^{(T)}$	$d_x^{(T)}$	$D_x^{(T)}$	$N_x^{(T)}$	$\ddot{a}_x^{(T)}$
54	162.322	0.041	6.655	6.980	52.595	7.535
55	155.667	0.039	6.071	6.315	45.615	7.223
56	149.596	0.037	5.535	5.725	39.300	6.864
57	144.061	0.035	5.042	5.201	33.575	6.455
58	139.019	0.033	4.588	4.735	28.373	5.992
59	134.431	0.031	4.167	4.320	23.638	5.472
60	130.264	0.029	3.778	3.949	19.319	4.892
61	126.486	0.028	3.542	3.617	15.370	4.249
62	122.945	0.026	3.197	3.317	11.752	3.543
63	119.748	0.025	2.994	3.048	8.435	2.768
64	116.754	0.023	2.685	2.803	5.387	1.922
65	114.069	0.022	2.510	2.584	2.584	1.000

PROBABILITY OF TERMINATION AND SURVIVAL

Formulas:

See probability symbols on pages 221 and 222.

Example:

Using the $d_x^{(T)}$ and the $l_x^{(T)}$ columns of the termination table on pages 224 and 225, what is the probability of an employee aged 30:

1. terminating in one year?
2. terminating in five years?
3. being employed to age 65?

Solution:

(1) $$q_x^{(T)} = \frac{d_x^{(T)}}{l_x^{(T)}}$$

$$q_{30}^{(T)} = \frac{d_{30}^{(T)}}{l_{30}^{(T)}} = \frac{248.447}{1562.559}$$

$$q_{30}^{(T)} = .159$$

(2) $${}_nq_x^{(T)} = \frac{l_x^{(T)} - l_{x+n}^{(T)}}{l_x^{(T)}}$$

$$_5q_{30}^{(T)} = \frac{l_{30}^{(T)} - l_{35}^{(T)}}{l_{30}^{(T)}}$$

$$_5q_{30}^{(T)} = \frac{1562.559 - 724.554}{1562.559} = \frac{838.005}{1562.559}$$

$$_5q_{30}^{(T)} = .536$$

(3) $$_np_x^{(T)} = \frac{l_{x+n}^{(T)}}{l_x^{(T)}}$$

$$_{35}p_{30}^{(T)} = \frac{l_{65}^{(T)}}{l_{30}^{(T)}} = \frac{114.069}{1562.559}$$

$$_{35}p_{30}^{(T)} = .073$$

PRESENT VALUE OF A LIFE ANNUITY

Formula:

$$\ddot{a}_x^{(m)} = B_x\left(\frac{N_x^{(m)}}{D_x}\right)$$

where

$\ddot{a}_x^{(m)}$ = The present value of a life annuity made more frequently than once a year and payable at the beginning of each period

B_x = Annual benefit payable in "*m*" installments

$N_x^{(m)}$ = Commutation factor

D_x = Commutation factor

x = Age

Example:

The pension plan of the XYZ Company provides for a 30% of salary pension at retirement age 65, which is payable in monthly installments at the beginning of each month. The salary of employee *A*, a female, is $24,000 per year. The projected pension is $7200. The plan uses the PBGC Actuarial Tables for Healthy Males and Females. What is the present value of the benefits at retirement age?

Solution:

$$\ddot{a}_x^{(m)} = B_x\left(\frac{N_x^{(m)}}{D_x}\right)$$

$$\ddot{a}_{65}^{(12)} = B_{65}\left(\frac{N_{65}^{(12)}}{D_{65}}\right)$$

$$\ddot{a}_{65}^{(12)} = 7200\left(\frac{1980.0228}{191.2656}\right)$$

$$\ddot{a}_{65}^{(12)} = 7200(10.3522)$$

$$\ddot{a}_{65}^{(12)} = \$74{,}535.84$$

FOREBORN ANNUITY

Formula:

$$\ddot{S}_{x:\overline{n}|}^{(T)} = R\left(\frac{N_x^{(T)} - N_{x+n}^{(T)}}{D_{x+n}^{(T)}}\right)$$

where

$\ddot{S}_{x:\overline{n}|}^{(T)}$ = The accumulation of a periodic payment at the beginning of each period with interest and decrements according to the termination table

R = Periodic payment

$N_x^{(T)}$ = Commutation factor

$D_x^{(T)}$ = Commutation factor

n = Accumulation period

Example:

A payment of \$17.65 is made at the beginning of each year for a period of 43 years commencing at age 22. What amount will be accumulated at age 65? Use the termination table on pages 224 and 225.

Solution:

$$\ddot{S}_{x:\overline{n}|}^{(T)} = R\left(\frac{N_x^{(T)} - N_{x+n}^{(T)}}{D_{x+n}^{(T)}}\right)$$

$$\ddot{S}_{22:\overline{43}|}^{(T)} = R\left(\frac{N_{22}^{(T)} - N_{65}^{(T)}}{D_{65}^{(T)}}\right)$$

$$\ddot{S}_{22:\overline{43}|}^{(T)} = 17.65\left(\frac{10{,}914.090 - 2.584}{2.584}\right)$$

$$\ddot{S}_{22:\overline{43}|}^{(T)} = 17.65\left(\frac{10{,}911.506}{2.584}\right)$$

$$\ddot{S}_{22:\overline{43}|}^{(T)} = 17.65(4{,}222.71904)$$

$$\ddot{S}_{22:\overline{43}|}^{(T)} = \$74{,}530.99$$

UNIT CREDIT COST METHOD

Formulas:

$$(1)\quad FSC = FB_r[\ddot{a}_r^{(12)}]\left[\frac{N_r^{(T)}}{D_x^{(T)}}\right]$$

$$(2)\quad \text{AL} = \Sigma FB[\ddot{a}_r^{(12)}]\left[\frac{N_r^{(T)}}{D_x^{(T)}}\right]$$

where

FSC = Future service cost or normal cost
FB_r = Future benefit at retirement age (r)
$\ddot{a}_r^{(12)}$ = Present value of a life annuity at retirement age payable at the beginning of each month
$N_x^{(T)}$ = Commutation factor
$D_x^{(T)}$ = Commutation factor
AL = Accrued liability
x = Attained age
r = Retirement age

Example:

During the course of the examination of the XYZ Company's pension accounts, it is desired to test the computations for pension cost and the accrued liability. A review of the plan documents reveals the following information:

1. The plan uses the unit credit cost method.
2. Normal retirement is age 65.
3. For each year of credited service an employee will receive $600 per year payable in monthly installments on the first of each month.
4. Interest is assumed at 6% for both active and retired employees.
5. For retired employees the plan uses the PBGC Actuarial Functions for Healthy Males and Females.
6. For active employees the plan uses the unisex termination table shown on pages 224 and 225.

What is the FSC or normal cost and the accrued liability for a male employee aged 55 with 7 years of credited service?

Solution:

$$(1)\quad FSC = FB_r[\ddot{a}_r^{(12)}]\left[\frac{N_r^{(T)}}{D_x^{(T)}}\right]$$

$$FSC = FB_{65}[\ddot{a}_{65}^{(12)}]\left[\frac{N_{65}^{(T)}}{D_{55}^{(T)}}\right]$$

$$FSC = 600(9.0888)\left(\frac{2.584}{6.315}\right)$$

$$FSC = 5453.28(.40918)$$

$$FSC = \$2231.37$$

$$(2)\quad AL = \Sigma \mathrm{FB}[\ddot{a}_r^{(12)}]\left[\frac{N_r^{(T)}}{D_x^{(T)}}\right]$$

$$AL = (7)(600)[\ddot{a}_{65}^{(12)}]\left[\frac{N_{65}^{(T)}}{D_{55}^{(T)}}\right]$$

$$AL = (4200)(9.0888)\left(\frac{2.584}{6.315}\right)$$

$$AL = (38{,}172.96)(.40918)$$

$$AL = \$15{,}619.61$$

ENTRY AGE NORMAL

Formulas:

$$(1)\quad NC = (PB)_r[\ddot{a}_r^{(12)}]\left[\frac{N_r^{(T)}}{N_e^{(T)} - N_r^{(T)}}\right]$$

$$(2)\quad AL = NC\left[\frac{N_e^{(T)} - N_x^{(T)}}{D_x^{(T)}}\right]$$

where

NC = Normal cost

$(PB)_r$ = Projected benefit at retirement age r

$\ddot{a}_r^{(12)}$ = Present value of a life annuity at retirement age payable at the beginning of each month

AL = Accrued liability

$N_x^{(T)}$ = Commutation factor

$D_x^{(T)}$ = Commutation factor

r = Retirement age

e = Normal entry age
x = Attained age

Example:

A female employee aged 36 has a projected pension of $7200 per year at age 65 payable in monthly installments at the beginning of each month. The plan provisions are

1. The plan uses the entry age normal method.
2. The normal entry is age 22.
3. Normal retirement age is 65.
4. Interest is assumed at 6% for both active and retired employees.
5. For retired employees the plan uses the PBGC Actuarial Functions for Healthy Males and Females.
6. For active employees the plan uses the unisex termination table shown on pages 224 and 225.

What is the normal cost and the accrued liability for this employee?

Solution:

$$(1)\quad NC = (PB)_r[\ddot{a}_r^{(12)}]\left[\frac{N_r^{(T)}}{N_e^{(T)} - N_r^{(T)}}\right]$$

$$NC = (PB)_{65}[\ddot{a}_{65}^{(12)}]\left[\frac{N_{65}^{(T)}}{N_{22}^{(T)} - N_{65}^{(T)}}\right]$$

$$NC = 7200(10.3522)\left(\frac{2.584}{10{,}914.090 - 2.584}\right)$$

$$NC = 74{,}535.84\left(\frac{2.584}{10{,}911.506}\right)$$

$$NC = 74{,}535.84(.0002368)$$

$$NC = \$17.65$$

$$(2)\quad AL = NC\left[\frac{N_e^{(T)} - N_x^{(T)}}{D_x^{(T)}}\right]$$

$$AL = 17.65\left[\frac{N_{22}^{(T)} - N_{36}^{(T)}}{D_{36}^{(T)}}\right]$$

$$AL = 17.65\left(\frac{10{,}914.090 - 563.981}{78.260}\right)$$

$$AL = 17.65\left(\frac{10{,}350.109}{78.260}\right)$$

$$AL = 17.65(132.25286)$$
$$AL = \$2334.26$$

ATTAINED AGE NORMAL

Formulas:

$$(1)\ NC = (PB)_r[\ddot{a}_r^{(12)}]\left[\frac{N_r^{(T)}}{N_a^{(T)} - N_r^{(T)}}\right]$$

$$(2)\ AL = NC\left[\frac{N_a^{(T)} - N_x^{(T)}}{D_x^{(T)}}\right]$$

where

a = Attained age at start of employment or plan inception, whichever is later

See entry age normal, pages 229 and 230, for other symbols.

Example:

See example for entry age normal, page 230. Employee commenced employment at age 32.

Solution:

$$(1)\ NC = (PB)_r[\ddot{a}_r^{(12)}]\left[\frac{N_r^{(T)}}{N_a^{(T)} - N_r^{(T)}}\right]$$
$$NC = (PB)_{65}[\ddot{a}_{65}^{(12)}]\left[\frac{N_{65}^{(T)}}{N_{32}^{(T)} - N_{65}^{(T)}}\right]$$
$$NC = 7200(10.3522)\left(\frac{2.584}{1085.899 - 2.584}\right)$$
$$NC = 74{,}535.84\left(\frac{2.584}{1083.315}\right)$$
$$NC = (74{,}535.84)(.002385)$$
$$NC = \$177.77$$

$$(2)\ AL = NC\left[\frac{N_a^{(T)} - N_x^{(T)}}{D_x^{(T)}}\right]$$
$$AL = 177.77\left[\frac{N_{32}^{(T)} - N_{36}^{(T)}}{D_{36}^{(T)}}\right]$$

$$AL = 177.77\left(\frac{1085.899 - 563.981}{78.260}\right)$$

$$AL = 177.77\left(\frac{521.918}{78.260}\right)$$

$$AL = 177.77(6.69026)$$

$$AL = \$1189.33$$

AGGREGATE COST METHOD

Formula:

$$NC = \frac{\text{Present Value of Total Projected Benefits} - \text{Assets}}{\text{Present Value of Total Future Salaries}}$$

or

$$NC = CP\left\{\frac{[\Sigma(PB)_r \cdot \ddot{a}_r^{(12)} \cdot {}_{r-x}\backslash\ddot{a}_r^{(T)}] - A}{\Sigma(S) \cdot \ddot{a}_{\overline{r-x}|}^{(T)}}\right\}$$

where

NC = Normal cost
CP = Current payroll
Σ = Sum of
$(PB)_r$ = Projected benefit at retirement age = $\ddot{a}_r^{(12)}$
S = Salaries
A = Assets

Example:

The XYZ Company has a pension plan that uses the aggregate cost method. During the course of your examination, you wish to test the contribution for the current year, which is recorded on the books as \$4000. The current eligible payroll is \$200,000. From the most recent actuarial report, you obtain the following data:

1. The total present value of the projected future benefits is \$1,200,000.
2. The present value of the total future salaries is \$20,000,000.
3. The plan has assets valued at \$500,000.

What is the correct amount that should be recorded as pension expense?

Solution:

$$NC = CP\left\{\frac{[\Sigma(PB)_r \cdot \ddot{a}_{65}^{12} \cdot {}_{r-x}\backslash\ddot{a}_r^{(T)}] - A}{\Sigma(S)\ddot{a}_{\overline{r-x|}}^{(T)}}\right\}$$

$$NC = 200{,}000\left(\frac{1{,}200{,}000 - 500{,}000}{20{,}000{,}000}\right)$$

$$NC = 200{,}000\left(\frac{700{,}000}{20{,}000{,}000}\right)$$

$$NC = 200{,}000(.035)$$

$$NC = \$7000$$

UNFUNDED LIABILITY

Formula:

$$UL = \Sigma AL - A$$

where

UL = Unfunded liability
ΣAL = The sum of the accrued liabilities
A = Value of plan assets

Example:

The sum of the accrued liabilities for all the participants in a pension plan is \$157,750. The value of the plan assets is \$145,000. What is the unfunded liability?

Solution:

$$UL = AL - A$$

$$UL = 157{,}750 - 145{,}000$$

$$UL = \$12{,}750$$

PAST SERVICE LIABILITY (entry age normal)

Formula:

$$PSL = NC\left[\frac{N_e^{(T)} - N_a^{(T)}}{D_a^{(T)}}\right]$$

where

PSL = Past service liability
NC = Normal cost
$N_e^{(T)}$ = Commutation factor
$N_a^{(T)}$ = Commutation factor
$D_a^{(T)}$ = Commutation factor
e = Normal entry age
a = Attained age at plan inception or date of employment, whichever is later

Example:

Refer to the problem for entry age normal on pages 229 and 230. The plan was put into effect 4 years ago, at which time the employee was aged 32.

Solution:

$$PSL = NC\left[\frac{N_e^{(T)} - N_a^{(T)}}{D_a^{(T)}}\right]$$

$$PSL = 17.65\left[\frac{N_{22}^{(T)} - N_{32}^{(T)}}{D_{32}^{(T)}}\right]$$

$$PSL = 17.65\left(\frac{10{,}914.090 - 1085.899}{173.087}\right)$$

$$PSL = 17.65(56.782)$$

$$PSL = \$1002.20$$

AMORTIZING THE PAST SERVICE LIABILITY (entry age normal)

Formula:

$$AAC = PSL\left[\frac{D_{a+t}^{(T)}}{N_a^{(T)} - N_{a+t}^{(T)}}\right]$$

where

AAC = Amortized annual cost
PSL = Past service liability
$D_a^{(T)}$ = Commutation factor
$N_a^{(T)}$ = Commutation factor

a = Attained age at plan inception or date of employment, whichever is later

t = Amortization period, which cannot be more than (r-a)

Example:

Refer to the example for past service liability on pages 233 and 234. The amortization period is 15 years. What amount should be amortized each year?

Solution:

$$AAC = PSL\left[\frac{D_{a+t}^{(T)}}{N_a^{(T)} - N_{a+t}^{(T)}}\right]$$

$$AAC = 1002.20\left[\frac{D_{47}^{(T)}}{N_{32}^{(T)} - N_{47}^{(T)}}\right]$$

$$AAC = 1002.20\left(\frac{15.190}{1085.899 - 129.783}\right)$$

$$AAC = 1002.20\left(\frac{15.190}{956.116}\right)$$

$$AAC = 1002.20(.01589)$$

$$AAC = \$15.92$$

ACTUARIAL GAIN OR LOSS (immediate gain or loss)

Formulas:

(1) $LG = [(NC_o + AL_o)(1 + i) - {}^iBP] - AL_1$

(2) $IG = A_1 - [A_o(1 + i) + {}^iC - {}^iBP]$

(3) $AG = LG + IG$

(4) $AG = [(UL_o + NC_o)(1 + i) - {}^iC] - UL_1$

where

LG = Liability gain from all plan assumptions except investment gain or loss

NC_o = Normal cost at beginning of plan year

AL_o = Accrued liability at beginning of plan year

${}^iBP$ = Benefits paid during plan year with interest for approximately one-half year. Use (13/24)

AL_1 = Accrued liability at end of plan year
i = Assumed rate of interest per plan
IG = Investment gain or loss
${}^{i}C$ = Company contribution with interest from date of contribution
AG = Actuarial gain or loss from all causes
UL_o = Unfunded liability at beginning of plan year
UL_1 = Unfunded liability at end of plan year
A_o = Net assets at beginning of plan year
A_1 = Net assets at end of plan year

Example:

You are engaged to audit the pension plan of the XYZ Company. One of the objectives of your audit procedures is to determine if the plan assumptions are reasonable for the current year under examination. The following data are available:

	Beginning of Plan Year	End of Plan Year
Accrued liability	$600,000	$650,000
Net assets	500,000	540,000
Unfunded liability	100,000	110,000
Normal cost	30,000	
Company contribution	$25,000 made on April 15, 19X1	
Benefits paid	$20,000 paid in monthly installments	
Plan rate of interest	6%	

(1) Compute the liability gain or loss.
(2) Compute the investment gain or loss.
(3) Compute the actuarial gain or loss.
(4) Check your computations.
(5) Form an opinion as to the reasonableness of the plan assumptions for the current year.

Solution:

$$(1)\ LG = [(NC_o + AL_o)(1 + i) - {}^{i}BP] - AL_1$$

$$LG = \left\{(30{,}000 + 600{,}000)(1.06) - \left[20{,}000 + (20{,}000)(.06)\frac{13}{24}\right]\right\} - 650{,}000$$

$$LG = (667{,}800 - 20{,}650) - 650{,}000$$
$$LG = 647{,}150 - 650{,}000$$
$$LG = -\$2850 \quad (\textit{loss})$$

(2) $$IG = A_1 - [A_o(1 + i) + {}^iC - {}^iBP]$$
$$IG = 540{,}000 - \left\{[500{,}000(1.06)] + \left[25{,}000 + (25{,}000)(.06)\frac{260}{365}\right] - 20{,}650\right\}$$
$$IG = 540{,}000 - (530{,}000 + 26{,}068 - 20{,}650)$$
$$IG = 540{,}000 - 535{,}418$$
$$IG = \$4582 \quad \textit{gain}$$

(3) $$AG = LG + IG$$
$$AG = -2850 + 4582$$
$$AG = \$1732$$

(4) $$AG = [(UL_o + NC_o)(1 + i) - {}^iC] - UL_1$$
$$AG = [(100{,}000 + 30{,}000)(1.06) - 26{,}068] - 110{,}000$$
$$AG = (137{,}800 - 26{,}068) - 110{,}000$$
$$AG = 111{,}732 - 110{,}000$$
$$AG = \$1732 \text{ (same as formula 3)}$$

Opinion:

- The actuarial gain is \$1732, which amounts to .3% of the beginning accrued liability.
- The liability loss is \$2850, which amounts to .5% of the beginning net assets.
- The investment gain is \$4582, which amounts to .9% of the beginning net assets.
- **Conclusion:** Considering the long-range nature of plan assumptions, we would consider the current year's results to be in accordance with plan assumptions. However, a better opinion could be formed if the previous analysis were done for at least the 5 prior years.

PRESENT VALUE OF VESTED BENEFIT

Formula:

$$PVB = AL \times V\%$$

where

PVB = Present value of vested benefit
AL = Accrued liability
$V\%$ = Cumulative % vested

Example:

Employee A of the XYZ Company pension plan has an accrued liability of $15,619.61. The employee has 7 years of credited service. The plan vests 10% for each year of credited service. What is the present value of the vested benefit?

Solution:

$$PVB = AL \times V\%$$
$$PVB = 15{,}619.61 \times .70$$
$$PVB = \$10{,}933.73$$

SMALL PENSION PLAN
(interest only and life insurance death benefit)

FORMULAS:

$$(1)\quad SFC = \frac{[(PB)_r(\ddot{a}_r^{12})] - CV}{\ddot{S}_{\overline{r-a}|i}}$$

$$(2)\quad NC = SFC + LP$$

where

SFC = Side fund contribution
$(PB)_r$ = Projected retirement benefit at retirement age (r)
$\ddot{a}_r^{12}$ = Present value of life annuity at retirement age
$\ddot{S}_{\overline{n}|i}$ = Amount of an annuity due or $S_{\overline{n}|i}(1 + i)$
CV = Cash value of life insurance policy at retirement age
LP = Annual life insurance premium
a = Attained age at time of eligibility

Example:

A small company has a pension plan that is funded by a side fund and an ordinary life insurance policy. The plan provides for a pension of 30% of salary payable in monthly installments at the beginning of each month at retirement age 65. The plan also provides for a death benefit of 100 times the monthly benefit. Interest is assumed at 6% and there are no other actuarial assumptions. Mr. Able, a male employee, aged 55, a nonsmoker, just became eligible for the plan. He earns $60,000 per year. His death benefit would be $150,000, computed as follows: (60,000 × .30 ÷ 12) × 100. The life insurance premium is $4940 and the cash value of the policy at age 65 is $34,551. The plan uses the PBGC Actuarial Functions for Healthy Males and Females to determine the life annuity without loading it. What is the side fund contribution? What is the normal cost?

Solution:

(1) $$SFC = \frac{(PB)_r(\ddot{a}_r^{12}) - CV}{\ddot{S}_{\overline{r-a}|i}}$$

$$SFC = \frac{(18{,}000)(9.0888) - 34{,}551}{\ddot{S}_{\overline{65-55}|.06}}$$

$$SFC = \frac{163{,}598.40 - 34{,}551}{13.971643}$$

$$SFC = \frac{129{,}047.40}{13.971643}$$

$$SFC = \$9236.38$$

(2) $$NC = SFC + LP$$

$$NC = 9236.38 + 4940$$

$$NC = \$14{,}176.38$$

PBGC ACTUARIAL FUNCTIONS FOR HEALTHY MALES

AGE x	D_x	$N_x^{(12)}$	$\ddot{a}_x^{(12)}$	AGE x	D_x	$N_x^{(12)}$	$\ddot{a}_x^{(12)}$
16	3,930.8061	63,752.9726	16.2188	41	884.8809	12,487.3150	14.1119
17	3,703.0641	59,926.5482	16.1830	42	832.6595	11,626.3689	13.9629
18	3,488.6183	56,321.7717	16.1444	43	783.3143	10,816.3259	13.8084
19	3,286.7030	52,925.6980	16.1030	44	736.6886	10,054.3818	13.6481
20	3,096.5982	49,726.1263	16.0583	45	692.6193	9,337.8916	13.4820
21	2,917.6178	46,711.5608	16.0102	46	650.9517	8,664.3699	13.3103
22	2,749.1143	43,871.1738	15.9583	47	611.5384	8,031.4826	13.1332
23	2,590.4775	41,194.7680	15.9024	48	574.2490	7,437.0352	12.9509
24	2,441.0387	38,672.7833	15.8428	49	538.9798	6,878.9512	12.7629
25	2,300.2668	36,296.2650	15.7792	50	505.6160	6,355.2631	12.5693
26	2,167.6607	34,056.7760	15.7113	51	474.0407	5,864.1191	12.3705
27	2,042.7483	31,946.3669	15.6389	52	444.1435	5,403.7813	12.1667
28	1,925.0821	29,957.5489	15.5617	53	415.8428	4,972.6090	11.9579
29	1,814.1483	28,083.3115	15.4802	54	389.0570	4,569.0430	11.7439
30	1,709.5593	26,317.0998	15.3941	55	363.7195	4,191.5990	11.5243
31	1,610.9516	24,652.7357	15.3032	56	339.7432	3,838.8687	11.2993
32	1,517.9829	23,084.3948	15.2073	57	317.0464	3,509.5282	11.0694
33	1,430.3294	21,606.5864	15.1060	58	295.5521	3,202.3333	10.8351
34	1,347.6173	20,214.1667	14.9999	59	275.2115	2,916.1040	10.5959
35	1,269.5597	18,902.3258	14.8889	60	255.9565	2,649.7177	10.3522
36	1,195.8857	17,666.5333	14.7728	61	237.7235	2,402.1180	10.1047
37	1,126.3405	16,502.5225	14.6515	62	220.4527	2,172.3103	9.8539
38	1,060.6812	15,406.2759	14.5249	63	204.0882	1,959.3580	9.6005
39	998.6934	14,374.0057	14.3928	64	188.5858	1,762.3751	9.3452
40	940.1615	13,402.1395	14.2551	65	173.8971	1,580.5216	9.0888

PBGC ACTUARIAL FUNCTIONS FOR HEALTHY MALES

AGE x	D_x	$N_x^{(12)}$	$\ddot{a}_x^{(12)}$	AGE x	D_x	$N_x^{(12)}$	$\ddot{a}_x^{(12)}$
66	159.9776	1413.0043	8.8325	91	3.5954	10.3757	2.8858
67	146.8124	1259.0608	8.5760	92	2.6625	7.2079	2.7072
68	134.3978	1117.9384	8.3181	93	1.9266	4.8826	2.5343
69	122.7239	988.8911	8.0579	94	1.3585	3.2164	2.3675
70	111.7548	871.1947	7.7956	95	0.9306	2.0540	2.2071
71	101.4579	764.1594	7.5318	96	0.6171	1.2671	2.0534
72	91.8030	667.1267	7.2669	97	0.3944	0.7521	1.9071
73	82.7523	579.4719	7.0025	98	0.2420	0.4275	1.7666
74	74.2815	500.6021	6.7393	99	0.1418	0.2315	1.6321
75	66.3689	429.9471	6.4781	100	0.0788	0.1185	1.5037
76	58.9948	366.9580	6.2202	101	0.0412	0.0569	1.3816
77	52.1413	311.1044	5.9666	102	0.0201	0.0254	1.2665
78	45.8141	261.8631	5.7158	103	0.0090	0.0104	1.1569
79	39.9945	218.7164	5.4687	104	0.0037	0.0039	1.0527
80	34.6648	181.1646	5.2262	105	0.0013	0.0013	0.9536
81	29.8079	148.7259	4.9895	106	0.0004	0.0004	0.8599
82	25.4149	120.9315	4.7583	107	0.0001	0.0001	0.7726
83	21.4754	97.3222	4.5318	108	0.0000	0.0000	0.6863
84	17.9742	77.4516	4.3091	109	0.0000	0.0000	0.5972
85	14.8867	60.8925	4.0904	110	0.0000	0.0000	0.5417
86	12.1878	47.2428	3.8762				
87	9.8517	36.1258	3.6670				
88	7.8521	27.1906	3.4629				
89	6.1616	20.1133	3.2643				
90	4.7522	14.5977	3.0718				

PBGC ACTUARIAL FUNCTIONS FOR HEALTHY FEMALES

AGE x	D_x	$N_x^{(12)}$	$\ddot{a}_x^{(12)}$	AGE x	D_x	$N_x^{(12)}$	$\ddot{a}_x^{(12)}$
16	3,936.4628	64,758.7145	16.4510	41	893.6354	13,201.4610	14.7728
17	3,713.6442	60,924.3768	16.4056	42	841.6671	12,331.6444	14.6515
18	3,503.4379	57,307.0772	16.3574	43	792.6027	11,512.4651	14.5249
19	3,305.1301	53,894.5304	16.3063	44	746.2818	10,741.0929	14.3928
20	3,118.0473	50,675.1466	16.2522	45	702.5433	10,014.8579	14.2551
21	2,937.3270	47,639.9294	16.2188	46	661.2345	9,331.2478	14.1119
22	2,767.1449	44,780.6025	16.1830	47	622.2116	8,687.8987	13.9629
23	2,606.8985	42,086.9038	16.1444	48	585.3380	8,082.5875	13.8084
24	2,456.0157	39,549.1600	16.1030	49	550.4966	7,513.2185	13.6481
25	2,313.9583	37,158.2539	16.0583	50	517.5654	6,977.8154	13.4820
26	2,180.2137	34,905.5952	16.0102	51	486.4290	6,474.5208	13.3103
27	2,054.2982	32,783.0928	15.9583	52	456.9771	6,001.5906	13.1332
28	1,935.7555	30,783.1267	15.9024	53	429.1123	5,557.3849	12.9509
29	1,824.0861	28,898.5530	15.8428	54	402.7571	5,140.3521	12.7629
30	1,718.8931	27,122.6803	15.7792	55	377.8257	4,749.0219	12.5693
31	1,619.8022	25,449.2038	15.7113	56	354.2308	4,382.0106	12.3705
32	1,526.4603	23,872.1833	15.6389	57	331.8899	4,038.0193	12.1667
33	1,438.5333	22,386.0229	15.5617	58	310.7419	3,715.8223	11.9579
34	1,355.6372	20,985.4836	15.4802	59	290.7260	3,414.2543	11.7439
35	1,277.4821	19,665.6675	15.3941	60	271.7924	3,132.2062	11.5243
36	1,203.7967	18,421.9578	15.3032	61	253.8759	2,868.6256	11.2993
37	1,134.3251	17,250.0023	15.2073	62	236.9155	2,622.5232	11.0694
38	1,068.8254	16,145.6978	15.1060	63	220.8538	2,392.9694	10.8351
39	1,007.0180	15,105.2008	14.9999	64	205.6540	2,179.0821	10.5959
40	948.6889	14,124.9170	14.8889	65	191.2656	1,980.0228	10.3522

PBGC ACTUARIAL FUNCTIONS FOR HEALTHY FEMALES

AGE x	D_x	$N_x^{(12)}$	$\ddot{a}_x^{(12)}$	AGE x	D_x	$N_x^{(12)}$	$\ddot{a}_x^{(12)}$
66	177.6408	1795.0019	10.1047	91	9.1074	35.3022	3.8762
67	164.7351	1623.2762	9.8539	92	7.3617	26.9949	3.6669
68	152.5066	1464.1459	9.6005	93	5.8675	20.3180	3.4628
69	140.9223	1316.9488	9.3452	94	4.6043	15.0294	3.2642
70	129.9460	1181.0573	9.0888	95	3.5511	10.9078	3.0717
71	119.5446	1055.8786	8.8325	96	2.6867	7.7529	2.8857
72	109.7067	940.8430	8.5760	97	1.9896	5.3857	2.7070
73	100.4299	835.3882	8.3181	98	1.4397	3.6482	2.5340
74	91.7064	738.9565	8.0578	99	1.0152	2.4031	2.3671
75	83.5097	651.0070	7.7956	100	0.6954	1.5344	2.2065
76	75.8152	571.0239	7.5318	101	0.4611	0.9464	2.0525
77	68.6005	498.5154	7.2669	102	0.2947	0.5616	1.9057
78	61.8373	433.0147	7.0025	103	0.1808	0.3191	1.7644
79	55.5075	374.0786	6.7392	104	0.1060	0.1725	1.6283
80	49.5947	321.2811	6.4781	105	0.0589	0.0882	1.4968
81	44.0843	274.2120	6.2202	106	0.0308	0.0421	1.3683
82	38.9630	232.4749	5.9666	107	0.0150	0.0186	1.2393
83	34.2349	195.6789	5.7158	108	0.0067	0.0074	1.0962
84	29.8862	163.4372	5.4687	109	0.0027	0.0025	0.9036
85	25.9036	135.3764	5.2282	110	0.0010	0.0005	0.5417
86	22.2742	111.1363	4.9895				
87	18.9915	90.3667	4.7583				
88	16.0476	72.7244	4.5318				
89	13.4313	57.8759	4.3090				
90	11.1242	45.5020	4.0904				

MORTALITY TABLE FOR HEALTHY MALE PARTICIPANTS
SEPTEMBER 2, 1974

Age x	l_x	d_x	$1000_{q}x$	Age x	l_x	d_x	$1000_{q}x$
15	10,000.0000	14.3700	1.437	40	9,670.2357	22.5026	2.327
16	9,985.6300	14.1197	1.414	41	9,647.7331	24.6596	2.556
17	9,971.5103	13.8105	1.385	42	9,623.0735	27.1178	2.818
18	9,957.6998	13.4529	1.351	43	9,595.9557	29.6995	3.095
19	9,944.2469	13.0369	1.311	44	9,566.2562	32.6209	3.410
20	9,931.2100	12.5828	1.267	45	9,533.6353	35.9323	3.769
21	9,918.6272	12.0908	1.219	46	9,497.7030	39.7004	4.180
22	9,906.5364	11.5609	1.167	47	9,458.0026	43.8378	4.635
23	9,894.9755	11.3693	1.149	48	9,414.1648	48.0405	5.103
24	9,883.6062	11.1586	1.129	49	9,366.1243	52.6002	5.616
25	9,872.4476	10.9288	1.107	50	9,313.5241	57.7066	6.196
26	9,861.5188	10.6800	1.083	51	9,255.8175	63.4301	6.853
27	9,850.8388	10.4222	1.058	52	9,192.3874	69.3382	7.543
28	9,840.4166	10.6572	1.083	53	9,123.0492	75.5206	8.278
29	9,829.7594	10.9209	1.111	54	9,047.5286	81.7263	9.033
30	9,818.8385	11.2033	1.141	55	8,965.8023	88.5373	9.875
31	9,807.6352	11.5044	1.173	56	8,877.2650	95.9987	10.814
32	9,796.1308	11.8337	1.208	57	8,781.2663	104.1722	11.863
33	9,784.2971	12.6902	1.297	58	8,677.0941	112.3857	12.952
34	9,771.6069	13.6607	1.398	59	8,564.7084	121.2934	14.162
35	9,757.9462	14.7638	1.513	60	8,443.4150	130.9489	15.509
36	9,743.1824	16.0080	1.643	61	8,312.4661	141.3950	17.010
37	9,727.1744	17.4311	1.792	62	8,171.0711	152.6765	18.685
38	9,709.7433	18.9146	1.948	63	8,018.3946	164.5134	20.517
39	9,690.8287	20.5930	2.125	64	7,853.8812	177.1993	22.562

MORTALITY TABLE FOR HEALTHY MALE PARTICIPANTS SEPTEMBER 2, 1974

Age x	l_x	d_x	$1000q_x$	Age x	l_x	d_x	$1000q_x$
65	7,676.6819	190.7425	24.847	90	900.3755	178.3014	198.030
66	7,485.9394	203.8571	27.232	91	722.0741	155.2712	215.035
67	7,282.0823	215.7972	29.634	92	566.8029	132.0554	232.983
68	7,066.2851	226.6370	32.073	93	434.7475	109.7933	252.545
69	6,839.6481	237.6299	34.743	94	324.9542	88.9978	273.878
70	6,602.0182	248.6782	37.667	95	235.9564	70.1149	297.152
71	6,353.3400	259.6674	40.871	96	165.8415	53.4927	322.553
72	6,093.6726	271.1928	44.504	97	112.3488	39.2665	349.505
73	5,822.4798	282.4136	48.504	98	73.0823	27.6883	378.865
74	5,540.0662	293.1415	52.913	99	45.3940	18.6513	410.875
75	5,246.9247	303.1411	57.775	100	26.7427	11.9210	445.768
76	4,943.7836	312.1604	63.142	101	14.8217	7.1712	483.830
77	4,631.6232	317.8590	68.628	102	7.6505	4.0112	524.301
78	4,313.7642	322.0139	74.648	103	3.6393	2.0685	568.365
79	3,991.7503	324.3537	81.256	104	1.5708	0.9682	616.382
80	3,667.3966	324.6306	88.518	105	0.6026	0.4030	668.696
81	3,342.7660	321.6343	96.218	106	0.1996	0.1449	725.745
82	3,021.1317	315.1342	104.310	107	0.0547	0.0430	786.495
83	2,705.9975	305.2798	112.816	108	0.0117	0.0100	852.659
84	2,400.7177	293.0772	122.079	109	0.0017	0.0016	924.666
85	2,107.6405	278.5753	132.174	110	0.0001	0.0001	1000.000
86	1,829.0652	261.8837	143.179				
87	1,567.1815	243.1435	155.147				
88	1,324.0380	222.7138	168.208				
89	1,101.3242	200.9487	182.461				

MORTALITY TABLE FOR HEALTHY FEMALE PARTICIPANTS
SEPTEMBER 2, 1974

Age x	l_x	d_x	$1000q_x$	Age x	l_x	d_x	$1000q_x$
15	10,000.0000	00.0000	0.000	40	9,757.9462	14.7638	1.513
16	10,000.0000	00.0000	0.000	41	9,743.1824	16.0080	1.643
17	10,000.0000	00.0000	0.000	42	9,727.1744	17.4311	1.792
18	10,000.0000	00.0000	0.000	43	9,709.7433	18.9146	1.948
19	10,000.0000	00.0000	0.000	44	9,690.8287	20.5930	2.125
20	10,000.0000	14.3700	1.437	45	9,670.2357	22.5026	2.327
21	9,985.6300	14.1197	1.414	46	9,647.7331	24.6596	2.556
22	9,971.5103	13.8105	1.385	47	9,623.0735	27.1178	2.818
23	9,957.6998	13.4529	1.351	48	9,595.9557	29.6995	3.095
24	9,944.2469	13.0369	1.311	49	9,566.2562	32.6209	3.410
25	9,931.2100	12.5828	1.267	50	9,533.6353	35.9323	3.769
26	9,918.6272	12.0908	1.219	51	9,497.7030	39.7004	4.180
27	9,906.5364	11.5609	1.167	52	9,458.0026	43.8378	4.635
28	9,894.9755	11.3693	1.149	53	9,414.1648	48.0405	5.103
29	9,883.6062	11.1586	1.129	54	9,366.1243	52.6002	5.616
30	9,872.4476	10.9288	1.107	55	9,313.5241	57.7066	6.196
31	9,861.5188	10.6800	1.083	56	9,255.8175	63.4301	6.853
32	9,850.8388	10.4222	1.058	57	9,192.3874	69.3382	7.543
33	9,840.4166	10.6572	1.083	58	9,123.0492	75.5206	8.278
34	9,829.7594	10.9209	1.111	59	9,047.5286	81.7263	9.033
35	9,818.8385	11.2033	1.141	60	8,965.8023	88.5373	9.875
36	9,807.6352	11.5044	1.173	61	8,877.2650	95.9987	10.814
37	9,796.1308	11.8337	1.208	62	8,781.2663	104.1722	11.863
38	9,784.2971	12.6902	1.297	63	8,677.0941	112.3857	12.952
39	9,771.6069	13.6607	1.398	64	8,564.7084	121.2934	14.162

MORTALITY TABLE FOR HEALTHY FEMALE PARTICIPANTS SEPTEMBER 2, 1974

Age x	l_x	d_x	1000_{qX}	Age x	l_x	d_x	1000_{qX}
65	8,443.4150	130.9489	15.509	90	2,107.6405	278.5753	132.174
66	8,312.4661	141.3950	17.010	91	1,829.0652	261.8837	143.179
67	8,171.0711	152.6765	18.685	92	1,567.1815	243.1435	155.147
68	8,018.3946	164.5134	20.517	93	1,324.0380	222.7138	168.208
69	7,853.8812	177.1993	22.562	94	1,101.3242	200.9487	182.461
70	7,676.6819	190.7425	24.847	95	900.3755	178.3014	198.030
71	7,485.9394	203.8571	27.232	96	722.0741	155.2712	215.035
72	7,282.0823	215.7972	29.634	97	566.8029	132.0554	232.983
73	7,066.2851	226.6370	32.073	98	434.7475	109.7933	252.545
74	6,839.6481	237.6299	34.743	99	324.9542	88.9978	273.878
75	6,602.0182	248.6782	37.667	100	235.9564	70.1149	297.152
76	6,353.3400	259.6674	40.871	101	165.8415	53.4927	322.553
77	6,093.6726	271.1928	44.504	102	112.3488	39.2665	349.505
78	5,822.4798	282.4136	48.504	103	73.0823	27.6883	378.865
79	5,540.0662	293.1415	52.913	104	45.3940	18.6513	410.875
80	5,246.9247	303.1411	57.775	105	26.7427	11.9210	445.768
81	4,943.7836	312.1604	63.142	106	14.8217	7.1712	483.830
82	4,631.6232	317.8590	68.628	107	7.6505	4.0112	524.301
83	4,313.7642	322.0139	74.648	108	3.6393	2.0685	568.365
84	3,991.7503	324.3537	81.256	109	1.5708	0.9682	616.382
85	3,667.3966	324.6306	88.518	110	0.6026	0.6026	1000.000
86	3,342.7660	321.6343	96.218				
87	3,021.1317	315.1342	104.310				
88	2,705.9975	305.2798	112.816				
89	2,400.7177	293.0772	122.079				

20

Other Applications

BONUS AFTER FEDERAL INCOME TAXES (single tax rate)

Formulas:

$$(1) \quad B = r(NI_1 - B - T)$$

$$(2) \quad T = R(NI_1 - B)$$

where

B = Bonus
T = Federal income tax
r = Rate of bonus
NI_1 = Net income before bonus and taxes
R = Rate of tax

Example:

The General Manufacturing Company has an agreement with its president whereby he is to receive a bonus of 15% of the net income calculated after deducting the bonus and income taxes. The net income before bonus and taxes amounted to $500,000. The single federal income tax rate is 34%. What is the amount of the bonus?

Solution:

$$(1) \quad B = r(NI_1 - B - T)$$

$$
\begin{aligned}
(2)\quad T &= R(NI_1 - B)\\
B &= .15(500{,}000 - B - T)\\
T &= .34(500{,}000 - B) = 170{,}000 - .34B
\end{aligned}
$$

Substituting T in Formula (1) and solving for B:

$$
\begin{aligned}
B &= .15[500{,}000 - B - (170{,}000 - .34B)]\\
B &= .15(500{,}000 - B - 170{,}000 + .34B)\\
B &= 75{,}000 - .15B - 25{,}500 + .051B\\
B &= 49{,}500 - .099B\\
1.099B &= 49{,}500\\
B &= \$45{,}041
\end{aligned}
$$

BONUS AFTER FEDERAL INCOME TAXES (double tax rate)

Formulas:

$$(1)\quad B = r(NI_1 - B - T)$$

$$(2)\quad T = R_1 G_1 + R_2(NI_1 - G_1 - B)$$

where

B = Bonus
T = Federal income tax
NI_1 = Net income before bonus and taxes
R_1 = Tax rate on first tax base
R_2 = Tax rate on second tax base
G_1 = First tax base
r = Rate of bonus

Example:

The General Manufacturing Company has an agreement with its president whereby he is to receive a bonus of 10% of the net income after deducting the bonus and taxes. The net income before bonus and taxes amounted to $72,000. The tax rates are 15% on the first $50,000 of taxable income and 25% on taxable income in excess of $50,000. What is the amount of the bonus?

Solution:

$$(1) \quad B = r(NI_1 - B - T)$$

$$(2) \quad T = R_1 G_1 + R_2(NI_1 - G_1 - B)$$

$$B = .10(72{,}000 - B - T)$$
$$T = .15(50{,}000) + .25(72{,}000 - 50{,}000 - B)$$
$$T = 7500 + .25(22{,}000 - B)$$
$$T = 7500 + 5500 - .25B$$
$$T = 13{,}000 - .25B$$

Substituting T in formula (1) and solving for B:

$$B = .10[72{,}000 - B - (13{,}000 - .25B)]$$
$$B = .10(72{,}000 - B - 13{,}000 + .25B)$$
$$B = 7200 - .10B - 1300 + .025B$$
$$B = 5900 - .075B$$
$$1.075B = 5900$$
$$B = \$5488$$

BONUS AFTER FEDERAL INCOME TAXES (triple tax rate plus a phased out surtax)

Formulas:

$$(1) \quad B = r(NI_1 - B - T)$$

$$(2) \quad T = R_3(NI_1 - B) - (R_{3-1}b_1 + R_{3-2}b_2) + R_4(NI_1^* - E - B)$$

*where NI is equal to or less than the limit M

$$(3) \quad R_3 M = R_1 b_1 + R_2 b_2 + R_3(M - b_3) + R_4(M - E)$$

where

B = Bonus
r = Rate of bonus
NI_1 = Net income before bonus and taxes
T = Tax

R_1 = Tax rate on first tax base
R_2 = Tax rate on second tax base
R_3 = Tax rate on third tax base
R_4 = Surtax rate
b_1 = First tax base
b_2 = Second tax base
b_3 = Third tax base
E = Exemption from surtax
M = Maximum taxable income subject to surtax

Example:

The General Manufacturing Company has an agreement with its president whereby he is to receive a bonus of 10% of the net income after deducting the bonus and taxes. The net income before bonus and taxes is \$300,000. The tax structure is 15% on the first \$50,000 of taxable income, 25% on the next \$25,000 of taxable income, and 34% on taxable income in excess of \$75,000. The surtax is 5% on taxable income in excess of \$100,000 and phases out when the effective tax rate on all taxable income is equal to the maximum regular tax rate, that is, 34%. What is the amount of the bonus?

Solution:

(1) $B = r(NI_1 - B - T)$

(2) $T = R_3(NI_1 - B) - (R_{3-1}b_1 + R_{3-2}b_2) + R_4(NI_1^* - E - B)$
*where NI is equal to or less than the limit M

(3) $R_3 M = R_1 b_1 + R_2 b_2 + R_3(M - b_3) + R_4(M - E - B)$

Solve Formula (3) to find the limit M:

$$.34M = .15(50{,}000) + .25(25{,}000) + .34(M - 75{,}000) + .05(M - 100{,}000)$$
$$.34M = 7500 + 6250 + .34M - 25{,}500 + .05M - 5000$$
$$.34M = -16{,}750 + .39M$$
$$-.39M + .34M = -16{,}750$$
$$-.05M = -16{,}750$$
$$M = \$335{,}000$$

If Net Taxable Income is equal to or greater than M, use single-rate tax formula.

Returning to Formulas (1) and (2):

$$(1)\ B = .10(300{,}000 - B - T)$$

$$(2)\ T = .34(300{,}000 - B) - [.19(50{,}000) + .09(25{,}000)]$$

335,000
limit

$$+ .05(300{,}000 - 100{,}000 - B)$$

$$T = 102{,}000 - .34B - (9500 + 2250) + 10{,}000 - .05B$$

$$T = 100{,}250 - .39B$$

Substituting T in Formula (1) and solving for B:

$$B = .10(300{,}000 - B - (100{,}250 - .39B))$$

$$B = .10(300{,}000 - B - 100{,}250 + .39B)$$

$$B = 30{,}000 - .10B - 10{,}025 + .039B)$$

$$B = 19{,}975 - .061B$$

$$1.061B = 19{,}975$$

$$B = \$18{,}827$$

Verification:

Net income before tax and bonus				$300,000
Less bonus				18,827
Taxable income				$281,173
Tax:				
Regular 1st	$50,000 @ 15%	= $ 7,500		
2nd	$25,000 @ 25%	= $ 6,250		
Balance	$206,173 @ 34%	= $70,009		
	$281,173	$83,849		
Surtax:				
Taxable income	$281,173			
Exemption	100,000			
Balance	$181,173			
Rate	5%	$ 9,059		
Total Tax				92,908
Net income				$188,265
Bonus 10% of $188,265				$18,827

ANNUALIZED TAX FOR THE *n*th MONTH PERIOD OF A YEAR

Formulas:

(1) $TI_{12} = TI_n \cdot \frac{12}{n}$

(2) Calculate the tax to TI_{12} as if for a full year. Call it T

(3) $AT = T \cdot \frac{n}{12}$

where

TI_n = Taxable income for the nth month period
TI_{12} = Annualized taxable income
T = The annual tax on TI_{12}
AT = The annualized tax for the nth month period of the year

Example:

The XYZ Company, a calendar-year taxpayer, has taxable income for the 8 months ending August 31, 19X1, of $56,667. The tax rates are 15% on the first $50,000; 25% on the second $25,000; and 34% on taxable income in excess of $75,000. What is the annualized tax for the 8 months ended August 31, 19X1?

Solution:

(1) $TI_{12} = TI_n \cdot \frac{12}{n}$

(2) T = Tax on TI_{12} using applicable tax rates

(3) $AT = T \cdot \frac{n}{12}$

$$TI_{12} = 56{,}667 \cdot \frac{12}{8}$$

$$TI_{12} = \$85{,}001$$

$$T = .15(50{,}000) + .25(25{,}000) + .34(85{,}001 - 75{,}000)$$

$$T = \$17{,}150$$

$$AT = \$17{,}150 \cdot \frac{8}{12} = \$11{,}433$$

DETERMINING NET SALES WHEN SALES TAX COLLECTIONS ARE NOT RECORDED

Formula:

$$S = \frac{T}{1 + R}$$

where

S = Net sales
T = Total receipts (sales plus tax)
R = Rate of sales tax

Example:

The cash receipts of the XYZ retail store amounted to $20,600 for the month of October, 19A. There is a 3% sales tax in effect. The sales tax is added to the sale and rung up on the cash register as one amount. What amount should be shown as Sales for the month of October, 19A?

Solution:

$$S = \frac{T}{1 + R}$$

$$S = \frac{20{,}600}{1 + .03}$$

$$S = \frac{20{,}600}{1.03}$$

$$S = \$20{,}000$$

DETERMINING GROSS AMOUNT WHEN PARTIAL DISCOUNTS ARE ALLOWED

Formula:

$$G = \frac{A}{1 - R}$$

where

G = Gross amount
A = Amount of partial payment
R = Rate of discount

Example:

On February 1, 19A, Jones Manufacturing Company purchased materials from the Able Supply Company. The amount of the invoice was \$1000 and the terms stated were 2/10, *n*/30. On February 8, 19A, the bookkeeper of the Jones Manufacturing Company was instructed to send a check in the amount of \$400 to the Able Supply Company to apply on account. Assuming that partial discounts will be allowed, what is the amount that should be debited to accounts payable?

Solution:

$$G = \frac{A}{1 - R}$$

$$G = \frac{400}{1 - .02}$$

$$G = \frac{400}{.98}$$

$$G = \$408.16$$

DETERMINING GROSS WAGES WHEN NET WAGES ARE GIVEN

Formula:

$$G = N + \left[R_1\left(G - D\frac{E}{n}\right) - A\right] + R_2\left(G - D\frac{E}{n}\right) + R_3 G$$

where

G = Gross wages
N = Net wages
R_1 = Federal withholding percentage
R_2 = State withholding percentage
R_3 = FICA tax rate imposed on employee
D = Number of dependents claimed on W-4
n = Number of pay periods in year
E = Statutory exemption from tax
A = Fixed amount per optional percentage method

Example:

Smith agrees to work for Jones & Company. Smith wants $350 per week take-home pay regardless of deductions required by law for withholding and FICA taxes. Mr. Smith, single, claims 3 exemptions on his W-4 form. The current FICA tax rate imposed on employees is 7.15%. The alternative optional percentage method for federal withholding in the applicable wage bracket is 28% applied to the gross wages after deducting an appropriate amount for each exemption, the exemption is $1900 per year, and the table indicates that you are to subtract $46.75 from the product of the taxable wages multiplied by the rate (28%). The state tax rate is 3% and the annual exemption for each dependent is $1000. What is the gross amount of wages that should be recorded in the payroll records?

Solution:

$$G = N + \left[R_1\left(G - D \cdot \frac{E}{n}\right) - A\right] + R_2\left(G - D \cdot \frac{E}{n}\right) + R_3 G$$

$$G = 350 + \left[.28\left(G - 3 \cdot \frac{1900}{52}\right) - 46.75\right] + .03\left(G - 3 \cdot \frac{1000}{52}\right) + .0715G$$

$$G = 350 + [.28(G - 109.62) - 46.75] + .03(G - 57.69) + .0715G$$

$$G = 350 + .28G - 30.69 - 46.75 + .03G - 1.73 + .0715G$$

$$G = 270.83 + .3815G$$

$$.6185G = 270.83$$

$$G = \$437.88$$

DETERMINING CONSOLIDATED RETAINED INCOME

Formula:

$$R_c = R_{p2} + \%_s (R_{s2} - R_{s1})$$

where

R_c = Consolidated retained income

R_{p2} = Parent company's retained income at balance sheet data

R_{s1} = Retained income of subsidiary company on date control was obtained

R_{s2} = Retained income of subsidiary company at balance sheet date

$\%_s$ = Percentage of subsidiary company's outstanding stock owned by the parent company

Example:

P Company purchased 800 shares of S Company on January 1, 19A, for $250,000. The retained income on S Company's books on the date of purchase was $150,000. On December 31, 19C, the following information is obtained from the trial balances and books of Company P and Company S:

	Company P	Company S
Retained income	$500,000	$290,000
Common stock Co. P $100 par value authorized & issued 1000 shares	100,000	
Common Stock Co. S $10 par value authorized & issued 1000 shares		10,000

Determine the consolidated retained income that will appear on the consolidated balance sheet at December 31, 19C.

Solution:

$$R_c = R_{p2} + \%_s(R_{s2} - R_{s1})$$
$$R_c = 500{,}000 + .80(290{,}000 - 150{,}000)$$
$$R_c = 500{,}000 + .80(140{,}000)$$
$$R_c = 500{,}000 + 112{,}000$$
$$R_c = \$612{,}000$$

DETERMINING THE MINORITY INTEREST

Formula:

$$M = \%_m(C_s + R_{s2})$$

where

M = Minority interest
$\%_m$ = Percentage of subsidiary common stock outstanding owned by minority shareholders
C_s = Value assigned to subsidiary outstanding common stock
R_{s2} = Retained income of subsidiary company on balance sheet date

Example:

See example for consolidated retained income on pages 256 and 257.

Solution:

$$M = \%_m(C_s + R_{s2})$$
$$M = .20(10{,}000 + 290{,}000)$$
$$M = .20(300{,}000)$$
$$M = \$60{,}000$$

DETERMINING CONSOLIDATED RETAINED INCOME (mutual stock holdings)

Formulas:

(1) $\theta_p = R_{p2} + \%_s(\theta_s - R_{s1})$

(2) $\theta_s = R_{s2} + \%_p(\theta_p - R_{p1})$

(3) $R_c = \theta_p(1 - \%_p)$

where

R_c = Consolidated retained income
θ_p = True retained income of the parent company
θ_s = True retained income of the subsidiary company
R_{p2} = Retained income on the books of the parent company at the consolidated balance sheet date
R_{s2} = Retained income on the books of the subsidiary company at the consolidated balance sheet date
R_{p1} = Retained income on the books of the parent company

on the date the subsidiary company acquired its interest in the parent company

R_{s1} = Retained income on the books of the subsidiary company on the date the parent company achieved control of the subsidiary company

$\%_s$ = Percentage of the outstanding common stock of the subsidiary company owned by the parent company

$\%_p$ = Percentage of the outstanding common stock of the parent company owned by the subsidiary company

Example:

On January 2, 19A, Company P purchased 800 of the 1000 outstanding shares of Company S at a cost of $150,000. On the date of this acquisition, the capital stock account of Company S was $100,000 and the retained income account was $25,000. On the same date, Company S acquired 200 shares of the 2000 outstanding shares of Company P at a cost of $30,000. On the date of this purchase, the capital stock account of Company P was $200,000 and the retained income account was $70,000.

The condensed balance sheets of companies P & S as of December 31, 19C, are presented below:

Assets	**Co. P**	**Co. S**
All other assets	$269,600	$160,000
Investment in Co. S (cost)	150,000	
Investment in Co. P (cost)		30,000
Total assets	$419,600	$190,000
Equities		
Liabilities	$ 50,000	$ 40,000
Capital stock, $100 par	200,000	100,000
Retained income	169,600	50,000
Total equities	$419,600	$190,000

From the foregoing data determine the consolidated retained income that will appear on the consolidated balance sheet as of December 31, 19C.

Solution:

(1) $\theta_p = R_{p2} + \%_s(\theta_s - R_{s1})$

$$(2) \qquad \theta_s = R_{s2} + \%_p(\theta_p - R_{p1})$$

$$(3) \qquad R_c = \theta_p(1 - \%_p)$$

$$\theta_p = 169{,}600 + .80(\theta_s - 25{,}000)$$
$$\theta_s = 50{,}000 + .10(\theta_p - 70{,}000)$$

Substitute equation (2) in equation (1) and solve for θ_p:

$$\theta_p = 169{,}600 + .80[50{,}000 + .10(\theta_p - 70{,}000) - 25{,}000]$$
$$\theta_p = 169{,}600 - .80(50{,}000 + .10\theta_p - 7000 - 25{,}000)$$
$$\theta_p = 169{,}600 + 40{,}000 + .08\theta_p - 5600 - 20{,}000$$
$$\theta_p = 184{,}000 + .08\theta_p$$
$$\theta_p - .08\theta_p = 184{,}000$$
$$.92\theta_p = 184{,}000$$
$$\theta_p = \$200{,}000$$

$$R_c = 200{,}000(1 - .10)$$
$$R_c = 200{,}000(.90)$$
$$R_c = \$180{,}000$$

CO-INSURANCE

Formula:

$$R = \frac{C}{\%(FV)} \times L$$

where

R = Recovery from insurance company
$\%$ = Co-insurance requirement
FV = Fair value or sound value of property at date of disaster
L = Loss due to peril insured against
C = The coverage or face value of the policy

Example:

The XYZ Company had a fire insurance policy on its building for a face value of \$1,000,000. The policy contained an 80% co-insurance requirement. On February 17, 19XI, a fire occurred that caused damage in the amount of \$600,000. Several days later, insurance appraisers estimated the fair value of the building before the fire to be \$1,500,000. What amount is recoverable from the insurance company?

Solution:

$$R = \frac{C}{\%(FV)} \times L$$

$$R = \frac{1{,}000{,}000}{.80(1{,}500{,}000)} \times 600{,}000$$

$$R = \frac{1{,}000{,}000}{1{,}200{,}000} \times 600{,}000$$

$$R = \$500{,}000$$

Note (1): Insurer will never pay more than the face value of the policy.

Note (2): Fair value for insurance purposes is sometimes called sound value. Sound value is the replacement cost minus accrued depreciation. For instance, if in the previous example the replacement cost is \$3,000,000 for the building new and it would have a 50-year life and the old building is 25 years old, the sound value would be (3,000,000 − 1,500,000) = \$1,500,000.

NET SAVINGS ON REFINANCING A MORTGAGE

Formula:

$$S = \left[\frac{P}{a_{\overline{n_1}|i_1}} - \frac{P}{a_{\overline{n_2}|i_2}}\right] a_{\overline{n_2}|i_3} - F$$

where

S = Net savings
P = Principal balance
n_1 = Number of periods remaining on current mortgage
n_2 = Number of periods on new mortgage
i_1 = Interest rate on current mortgage
i_2 = Interest rate on new mortgage
i_3 = Interest rate on invested funds
F = Total refinancing costs

$$a_{\overline{n}|i} = \frac{1 - (1 + i)^{-n}}{i}$$

Example:

Your present mortgage has a balance of \$150,000 with 324 remaining payments at 12% interest. You are considering refinancing the \$150,000 balance at 10% for 20 years. The total of the refinancing costs, \$3000, are currently in a savings account earning 5% interest. Should you refinance? What are your savings, if any?

Solution:

$$S = \left[\frac{P}{a_{\overline{n_1}|i_1}} - \frac{P}{a_{\overline{n_2}|i_2}}\right] a_{\overline{n_2}|i_3} - F$$

$$S = \left[\frac{P}{a_{\overline{324}|\frac{.12}{12}}} - \frac{P}{a_{\overline{240}|\frac{.10}{12}}}\right] a_{\overline{240}|\frac{.05}{12}} - 3000$$

$$S = (1562.17 - 1447.53)(151.525) - 3000$$
$$S = (114.64)(151.525) - 3000$$
$$S = \$14{,}370.82$$

Refinancing would result in a net savings of \$14,370.82.

RULE OF 78's—INTEREST REBATE

Formulas:

(1) $TC = (N)(PMT)$

(2) $TFC = TC - L$

(3) $$R = \frac{(N - K)(N - K + 1)}{N(N + 1)} \cdot TFC$$

(4) $POB = (TC - R) - (K \cdot PMT)$

where

TC = Total cost (Loan plus finance charges)
L = Amount of loan
TFC = Total finance charges
PMT = Periodic payments
N = Number of periodic payments
R = Rebate of finance charges

POB = Pay-off balance
K = Number of payments made

Example:

On January 1, 19X1, Mr. Able purchased an automobile and financed \$15,000 of the purchase price for a period of 36 months at 8% interest. The periodic monthly payments are \$470.05 per month and commenced on February 1, 19X1. The loan agreement contained the following clause:

> REBATE FOR REPAYMENT: In the event of the prepayment of the contract in full at any time before maturity of the final installment, buyer shall receive a rebate of unearned finance charges computed on the Rule of 78's. (Sometimes there will also be an additional fee of \$10.00, which will reduce the amount of the rebate.)

After the 20th payment but before the 21st payment, Mr. Able traded in the automobile for a new automobile.

1. What is the amount of the rebate of finance charges?
2. What is the pay-off balance?

Solution:

(1)
$$TC = (N)(PMT)$$
$$TC = (36)(470.05)$$
$$TC = \$16{,}921.80$$

(2)
$$TFC = TC - L$$
$$TFC = 16{,}921.80 - 15{,}000.00$$
$$TFC = \$1921.80$$

(3)
$$R = \frac{(N - K)(N - K + 1)}{N(N + 1)} TFC$$
$$R = \frac{(36 - 20)(36 - 20 + 1)}{36(36 + 1)} 1921.80$$
$$R = \frac{(16)(17)}{(36)(37)} 1921.80$$
$$R = \frac{272}{1332} 1921.80$$
$$R = \$392.44$$

(4) $POB = (TC - R) - (K \cdot PMT)$
$POB = (16{,}921.80 - 392.44) - 20(470.05)$
$POB = 16{,}529.36 - 9401.00$
$POB = \$7128.36$

PURCHASE—FINANCE—LEASE

Formulas:

(1) Purchase $PV = C - V^n S - T$

$$T = (D \cdot t)a_{\overline{n|}i}$$

or

$$T = \sum_{1}^{n} D(1 + i)^{-n}$$

(2) Finance $PV = C \cdot d + R \cdot a_{\overline{n|}i} - V^n \cdot S - T$

(3) Lease $PV = Ra_{\overline{n|}i} - (R \cdot 12 \cdot t)a_{\overline{n|}i}$

where

PV = Present value
C = Cost of asset
S = Residual value of asset
T = Tax benefits
D = Annual depreciation of asset for tax purposes
t = Marginal or average tax rate
i = Internal rate of return or opportunity cost of money
d = Down payment percentage
R = Periodic payments
$V^n = (1 + i)^{-n}$

$$a_{\overline{n|}i} = \frac{1 - (1 + i)^{-n}}{i}$$

Example:

A truck costs \$15,000. You can purchase it for cash. Or you can finance it with a 20% down payment, with the balance at 10% interest payable over 60 months in the amount of \$254.96 per month. Or you can lease it for \$400 a month with *no* option to buy. The residual value of the truck is \$3000. Your internal rate of return is 20%. The truck will be depreciated for tax purposes over 5 years using straight line depreciation. Your marginal tax rate is 40%. Which option is best?

Solution:

Purchase:

$$PV = C - V^nS - T$$
$$T = (D \cdot t)a_{\overline{n}|i}$$
$$PV = 15{,}000 - V^n(3{,}000) - T$$
$$T = (2400)(.40)a_{\overline{5}|.20}$$
$$T = 960\, a_{\overline{5}|.20}$$
$$T = 2871$$
$$V^n \cdot S = \frac{1}{(1+i)^n}(3000) = \frac{1}{(1+.20)^5}(3000)$$
$$V^nS = 1206$$
$$PV = 15{,}000 - 1206 - 2871$$
$$PV = \$10{,}923$$

Finance:

$$PV = (C)(d) + (R)a_{\overline{n}|i} - V^n(S) - T$$
$$PV = 15{,}000(.20) + (254.96)a_{\overline{60}|\frac{.20}{12}} - 1206 - 2871$$
$$PV = 3000 + 9623 - 1206 - 2871$$
$$PV = \$8546$$

Lease:

$$PV = Ra_{\overline{n}|i} - (R \cdot 12 \cdot t)a_{\overline{n}|i}$$
$$PV = 400a_{\overline{60}|\frac{.20}{12}} - (400 \cdot 12 \cdot .40)a_{\overline{5}|.20}$$
$$PV = 15{,}098 - 1920a_{\overline{5}|.20}$$
$$PV = 15{,}098 - 5742$$
$$PV = \$9356$$

The best course of action is to finance.

Appendix

I. FUNDAMENTALS OF ALGEBRA

The Language of Algebra

An *algebraic expression* is composed of symbols (numbers, letters, and so on) that are combined by one or more of the operations of algebra (addition, subtraction, multiplication, division, roots, and so on).

Illustrations:

$$xy^2, \frac{3}{x^3} - y^2 + 6, \quad 4\sqrt{x} + \frac{a^3}{3}, \quad (a^2 - 3nx^3)^4$$

A *term* is composed of a single symbol or several symbols, combined by any of the operations of algebra except addition or subtraction.

Illustrations:

$\frac{5}{4}, 3x^2y^3, \sqrt{x-3}, \frac{\sqrt{5}}{a^2b^2}$ are all terms

$\sqrt{x} - \sqrt{3}$ two terms

When a term is composed of the product of two or more symbols, any one of these is a *factor,* or divisor, of the term. Likewise, the product of two or more of these factors is also a factor of the term. For example, in the term $6xy^2$, 6, x, and y^2 are factors or divisors of the term. Any of the symbols 2, 3, x, y, or the product of two or more of these would be a factor or divisor of $6xy^2$.

Any factor of a term is the *coefficient* of the remaining factor, or of the product of the remaining factors of the term. For example, in the term $2xy$, 2 is the coefficient of xy, x is the coefficient of $2y$, and y is the coefficient of $2x$. Most frequently, we are interested in the numerical coefficient; that is, the factor that is an explicit number, sometimes referred to as the *coefficient of the term.*

Some Basic Assumptions

Expressions are often referred to by more specific names describing the number of terms in the particular expression. Thus an expression of one term is called a *monomial;* an expression of two terms, a *binomial;* an expression of three terms, a *trinomial;* and so on. An expression of two or more terms is often referred to by the name *multinomial*.

Illustrations:

$3x,\ \sqrt{7}\,x^3,\ 5y^2z^3$	monomials
$4x + 6,\ 3z^2 - 5y^3,\ 2y^3 + 2y^2$	binomials
$3x^2 - 7x + 4,\ \sqrt{2}\,y^3 - 5y + 2$	trinomials

If an algebraic expression can be written so that a particular symbol has only integral (whole number) exponents wherever it appears in the expression and does not appear under a radical sign, the expression is called *rational* with respect to that symbol; otherwise, *irrational.*

Illustrations:

$\sqrt{x^2 + 4}$	irrational with respect to x
$\sqrt[3]{s^2 + 2ts}$	irrational with respect to s and t
$\sqrt{2}\,x^2 - \sqrt[3]{3}\,x$	rational with respect to x
$\sqrt{s}\,y^2 - 2\,y^3 + 6$	rational with respect to y but irrational with respect to s

A *polynomial* in a particular symbol (or symbols) is an algebraic expression each of whose terms is the product of an explicit number and the symbol (or symbols) with nonnegative integral exponents.

Illustrations:

$3x^3 - 6x^2 + 7x - 3$	polynomial in x
$\frac{1}{3}y^3 - \frac{3}{7}y + \sqrt{2}$	polynomial in y
$\frac{1}{4}x - \sqrt{3}\,y + xy$	polynomial in x and y

In a polynomial, the degree of a term in a certain letter is the exponent of that letter. The degree of a term in certain letters is the sum of the exponents of those letters. For example, the term $8x^3y^2$ is of third degree in x, second degree in y, and fifth degree in x and y. The degree of a polynomial in a certain letter or letters is the degree of the term having the highest degree in that letter or letters.

Illustrations:

$5x^3 - 6x + 5$	a polynomial of degree three in x
$s^3 - s^2t^2 + t^2$	a polynomial of third degree in s, second degree in t, and fourth degree in s and t

Symbols of Grouping

Parentheses ( ), brackets [ ], braces { }, and the vinculum $\overline{}$ are the four commonly used symbols for grouping terms. These symbols may be thought of as the punctuation marks which, along with the order of operations, comprise the grammatical structure of the language of algebra.

There are three important principles of grouping.

1. We may remove parentheses (or insert terms within parentheses) or any other symbols of grouping preceded by a plus sign by simply rewriting the enclosed terms (or the terms to be enclosed) each with its original sign. What this amounts to is multiplying each term within the parentheses by $+1$.

Illustration:
Remove the symbols of grouping:

$$(r + s) + (3x - y)$$

Solution:

$$(r + s) + (3x - y) = r + s + 3x - y$$

Illustration:
Enclose the terms $4s - 3t$ within parentheses preceded by a plus sign:

Solution:

$$4s - 3t = +(4s - 3t) = (4s - 3t)$$

If no sign precedes the parentheses, the sign is taken as positive.

2. We may remove parentheses (or insert terms within parentheses) or any other symbols of grouping preceded by a minus sign by rewriting the enclosed terms (or the terms to be enclosed) each with its own sign changed. What this amounts to is multiplying each term within the parentheses by -1.

Illustration:
Remove the symbols of grouping and simplify:

$$-(3 + 4a - 5b) - (-2 - a + 3b)$$

Solution:

$$\begin{aligned} -(3 + 4a - 5b) - (-2 - a + 3b) &= -3 - 4a + 5b + 2 \\ &\quad + a - 3b \\ &= -1 - 3a + 2b \end{aligned}$$

Illustration:
Enclose the terms $3z - 4w^2 + x^3$ within parentheses preceded by a minus sign:

Solution:

$$3z - 4w^2 + x^3 = -(-3z + 4w^2 - x^3)$$

3. We may remove parentheses or any other symbols of grouping preceded by a multiplier or factor, by multiplying every term within the parentheses by the multiplier or factor.

Illustration:
Remove the symbols of grouping:

$$-5(3c - 2de + 5f^3)$$

Solution:

$$-5(3c - 2de + 5f^3) = -15c + 10de - 25f^3$$

Illustration:
Remove the symbols of grouping and simplify:

$$3x - \{-4 - [8x^2 + x(5 - x)] + 6\}$$

Solution:

$$3x - \{-4 - [8x^2 + x(5 - x)] + 6\} =$$
$$3x - \{-4 - [8x^2 + 5x - x^2] + 6\} =$$
$$3x - \{-4 - 8x^2 - 5x + x^2 + 6\} =$$
$$3x + 4 + 8x^2 + 5x - x^2 - 6 = 7x^2 + 8x - 2$$

Order of Operations

An apparently clear expression such as $150 - 10 \div 2$ could be interpreted in two distinct ways:

$$150 - 10 \div 2 = 140 \div 2 = 70$$
$$150 - 10 \div 2 = 150 - 5 = 145$$

To avoid any possible duplication of meaning of algebraic expressions, mathematicians have agreed that powers and roots shall take priority over multiplications and divisions (which are to be performed left to right), which in turn shall take priority over additions and subtractions (except where some symbols of grouping indicate otherwise).

Illustrations:

$$8 - 4 \div 2 = 8 - 2 = 6$$
$$(8 - 4) \div 2 = 4 \div 2 = 2$$
$$4 \cdot 3 - 1 = 12 - 1 = 11$$
$$4(3 - 1) = 4 \cdot 2 = 8$$
$$\sqrt{5^2 + 12^2} = \sqrt{25 + 144} = \sqrt{169} = 13$$

Number Systems

The numbers represented by the symbols $\{0, 1, 2, 3, \cdots\}$ are called whole numbers. If to each whole number, say a, we assign its opposite for addition (sometimes called its *negative*), say $-a$, then we have the set of integers: $\{\cdots, -3, -2, -1, 0, 1, 2, 3, \cdots\}$. Note that the opposite of 4 is -4 since $4 + (-4) = 0$; the opposite of -5 is $-(-5)$ or 5, since $-5 + 5 = 0$.

Those numbers which may be expressed as the ratio of a to b or in the form of $\frac{a}{b}$, where a and b are integers and $b \neq 0$ are called *rational numbers*. Numbers of the form $\frac{3}{4}$, $\frac{-7}{8}$, $\frac{6}{-7}$, and $\frac{6}{1}$ are examples of rational numbers.

Numbers like π, $\sqrt{2}$, $\sqrt[3]{-5}$ are examples of irrational numbers. The irrational number π cannot be expressed precisely as a rational form. If you were to write $\pi = \frac{22}{7}$ you would be approximating π by the rational number $\frac{22}{7}$.

The rational numbers joined to the irrational numbers form the real numbers. All the properties that hold for the whole numbers also hold for the real numbers.

Structural Properties

If we add any two whole numbers, say $12 + 27 = 39$ and $5 + 1 = 6$, we see that the sum in each case is also a whole number.

These are illustrations of the *closure property for addition*—the sum of any two whole numbers is always a whole number.

Notice that $12 + 27 = 27 + 12$, $5 + 1 = 1 + 5$, $368 + 453 = 453 + 368$. If a and b are any two whole numbers, then $a + b = b + a$. This property is known as the *commutative property for addition.*

Furthermore, observe that

$$\begin{aligned} (3 + 9) + 21 &= 3 + (9 + 21) \\ 12 + 21 &= 3 + 30 \\ 33 &= 33 \end{aligned}$$

If a, b, and c are any three whole numbers, then $a + (b + c) = (a + b) + c$. This property is called the *associative property for addition.*

Similarly $11 \times 34 = 374$ illustrates the *closure property for multiplication* of whole numbers.

Furthermore, $14 \times 10 = 10 \times 14$ and $25 \times 12 = 12 \times 25$ are examples of the commutative property for multiplication. If a and b are any two whole numbers, then $a \times b = b \times a$.

Also note that

$$\begin{aligned} 6 \times (25 \times 4) &= (6 \times 25) \times 4 \\ 6 \times 100 &= 150 \times 4 \\ 600 &= 600 \end{aligned}$$

If a, b, and c are any three whole numbers, then

$$a \times (b \times c) = (a \times b) \times c.$$

This equation illustrates the *associative property for multiplication.*

The next property we wish to represent connects multiplication and addition. Study these equations:

$$\begin{aligned} 16 \times (7 + 3) &= (16 \times 7) + (16 \times 3) = 112 + 48 = 160; \quad 16 \times 10 = 160 \\ 4 \times (20 + 5) &= (4 \times 20) + (4 \times 5) = 80 + 20 = 100; \quad 4 \times 25 = 100 \\ 12 \times (3 + 9) &= (12 \times 3) + (12 \times 9) = 36 + 108 = 144; \quad 12 \times 12 = 144 \end{aligned}$$

These statements illustrate the *distributive law for multiplication over addition*. If a, b, and c are any whole numbers, then

$$a \times (b + c) = (a \times b) + (a \times c)$$

When zero is added to any whole number, a, the sum is that number; that is, $a + 0 = 0 + a = a$. Zero is the *additive identity for addition.*

When any whole number, b, is multiplied by one, the product is that number; that is, $b \cdot 1 = 1 \cdot b = b$. One is the *identity for multiplication.*

Addition of Polynomials

Like terms or similar terms are terms whose literal factors are identical.

Illustrations:

$$6y^2z, \quad -y^2z, \quad \frac{9}{2}y^2z, \quad \sqrt[3]{3}\,y^2z \qquad \text{are similar terms}$$

The sum of two similar terms is a similar term whose coefficient is the sum of the coefficients of the terms added.

Illustrations:

$$3y^2z^3 + 7y^2z^3 = (3 + 7)y^2z^3 = 10y^2z^3$$

$$-4aBC^2d + 4aBC^2d - 11aBC^2d = (-4 + 4 - 11)aBC^2d = -11aBC^2d$$

The sum of two polynomials is found by adding the terms of one polynomial to the terms of the other.

Illustration:

Add $7x - 11y + 13$ and $7x - 13y - 14$

Solution:

$$(7x - 11y + 13) + (7x - 13y - 14) = 7x - 11y + 13 + 7x - 13y - 14 = 14x - 24y - 1$$

We may sometimes prefer to write one polynomial under the other, with similar terms in the same column.

Illustration:

Add $7x - 11y + 13$ and $7x - 13y - 14$

Solution:

$$\begin{array}{r} 7x - 11y + 13 \\ 7x - 13y - 14 \\ \hline 14x - 24y - 1 \end{array}$$

Illustration:

Add $5z^3 - 7z + 3$ and $-z^3 + 2z^2 - 7$

Solution:

$$\begin{array}{r} 5z^3 + 0z^2 - 7z + 3 \\ \underline{-z^3 + 2z^2 + 0z - 7} \\ 4z^3 + 2z^2 - 7z - 4 \end{array}$$

Subtraction of Polynomials

The difference of two similar terms is a similar term whose coefficient is the difference of the coefficients of the terms subtracted.

Illustration:

Subtract $6x^2y^3$ from $13x^2y^3$

Solution:

$$13x^2y^3 - 6x^2y^3 = (13 - 6)x^2y^3 = 7x^2y^3$$

Illustration:

Subtract $4a^2 - 3ab + 3b^2$ from $2a^2 - 5b^2 + 2ba$

Solution:

$$(2a^2 + 2ab - 5b^2) - (4a^2 - 3ab + 3b^2) =$$
$$2a^2 + 2ab - 5b^2 - 4a^2 + 3ab - 3b^2 = -2a^2 + 5ab - 8b^2$$

We may prefer to write the subtrahend under the minuend, with like terms in the same column, and then subtract.

Illustration:

Subtract $4a^2 - 3ab + 3b^2$ from $2a^2 - 5b^2 + 2ba$

$$\begin{array}{rl} 2a^2 + 2ab - 5b^3 & \text{minuend} \\ \underline{4a^2 - 3ab + 3b^2} & \text{subtrahend} \\ -2a^2 + 5ab - 8b^2 & \text{difference} \end{array}$$

Multiplication of Polynomials

The product of two monomials can be found by utilizing the commutative and associative properties of real numbers.

Illustrations:

$$-3x^2 \cdot 4y^3 = -3 \cdot 4 \cdot x^2 \cdot y^3 = -12x^2y^3$$
$$-8x^2yz^3 \cdot 2x^3yz = -8 \cdot 2 \cdot x^2 \cdot x^3 \cdot y \cdot y \cdot z^3 \cdot z = -16x^5y^2z^4$$

To multiply a polynomial by a monomial, we merely apply the distributive law.

Illustrations:

$$-2xy(x^2y - xy^2 + y^3) = -2x^3y^2 + 2x^2y^3 - 2xy^4$$
$$xyz(xy - yz + xz) = x^2y^2z - xy^2z^2 + x^2yz^2$$

To multiply two polynomials, we multiply each term in one polynomial by each term in the other. This can be justified by applying the distributive law as follows:

$$\begin{aligned}(ax + by)(cx - dy) &= ax(cx - dy) + by(cx - dy)\\ &= ax \cdot cx - ax \cdot dy + by \cdot cx - by \cdot dy\\ &= acx^2 - adxy + bcxy - bdy^2\end{aligned}$$

Illustration:

Multiply $2x^2 - x + 7$ by $3x - 2$

Solution:

$$\begin{array}{rrrr} & 2x^2 & - x & + 7 \\ & & 3x & - 2 \\ \hline & -4x^2 & + 2x & - 14 \\ 6x^3 & - 3x^2 & + 21x & \\ \hline 6x^3 & - 7x^2 & + 23x & - 14 \end{array}$$

Division of Polynomials

When we divide a polynomial by a monomial, we divide each term of the polynomial by the monomial.

Illustration:

Divide $14x^4y - 21x^2y^3 + 7xy^4$ by $-7xy$

Solution 1:

$$\begin{aligned}\frac{14x^4y - 21x^2y^3 + 7xy^4}{-7xy} &= \frac{14x^4y}{-7xy} + \frac{-21x^2y^3}{-7xy} + \frac{7xy^4}{-7xy}\\ &= -2x^3 + 3xy^2 - y^3\end{aligned}$$

Solution 2:

$$
\begin{array}{r l}
 & -2x^3 + 3xy^2 - y^3 \\
-7xy \,\big) & 14x^4y - 21x^2y^3 + 7xy^4 \\
 & \underline{14x^4y} \\
 & \quad - 21x^2y^3 \\
 & \quad \underline{- 21x^2y^3} \\
 & \qquad + 7xy^4 \\
 & \qquad \underline{+ 7xy^4}
\end{array}
$$

The division of a polynomial by a polynomial is illustrated by the following:

Illustration:

Divide $x^4 - y^4$ by $x - y$

Solution:

$$
\begin{array}{r l}
 & x^3 + x^2y + xy^2 + y^3 \\
x - y \,\big) & x^4 \qquad\qquad\qquad - y^4 \\
 & \underline{x^4 - x^3y} \\
 & \quad + x^3y \\
 & \quad \underline{+ x^3y - x^2y^2} \\
 & \qquad + x^2y^2 \\
 & \qquad \underline{+ x^2y^2 - xy^3} \\
 & \qquad\quad + xy^3 - y^4 \\
 & \qquad\quad \underline{+ xy^3 - y^4}
\end{array}
$$

Factoring

Certain types of products of two polynomials occur so frequently that it is expedient to utilize special techniques that will facilitate and shorten the work of multiplication and assist in the work of factoring.

The type products are

(1) $a(x + y) = ax + ay$

(2) $(x + y)(x - y) = x^2 - y^2$

(3) $(x + y)^2 = x^2 + 2xy + y^2; (x - y)^2 = x^2 - 2xy + y^2$

(4) $(x + a)(x + b) = x^2 + (a + b)x + ab$

(5) $(ax + b)(cx + d) = acx^2 + (bc + ad)x + bd$

$$(6) \qquad (x + y - z)^2 = x^2 + y^2 + z^2 + 2xy - 2xz - 2yz$$
$$(7) \qquad (x + y)^3 = x^3 + 3x^2y + 3xy^2 + y^3$$
$$(8) \qquad (x - y)^3 = x^3 - 3x^2y + 3xy^2 - y^3$$

Illustrations:

$$\begin{aligned}
4s^3t - 6s^2t^2 + 12st^3 &= 2st(2s^2 - 3st + 6t^2) \\
3x(z - 8) - 4w(z - 8) &= (z - 8)(3x - 4w) \\
x^2 - (3y + 2z)^2 &= [x - (3y + 2z)][x + (3y + 2z)] \\
&= (x - 3y - 2z)(x + 3y + 2z) \\
-4xz^2 + 8xzw - 4xw^2 &= -4x(z^2 - 2zw + w^2) = -4x(z - w)^2 \\
(a - c)^2 - (a - c) - 20 &= [(a - c) - 5][(a - c) + 4] \\
&= (a - c - 5)(a - c + 4) \\
10s^2 - 7st - 12t^2 &= (5s + 4t)(2s - 3t) \\
27x^3 - 8y^3 &= (3x - 2y)(9x^2 + 6xy + 4y^2) \\
1 + 64a^6 &= (1 + 4a^2)(1 - 4a^2 + 16a^4) \\
a^2 - b^2 - a + b &= (a - b)(a + b) - 1(a - b) \\
&= (a - b)[(a + b) - 1] \\
&= (a - b)(a + b - 1) \\
x^4 + 64 &= x^4 + 16x^2 + 64 - 16x^2 \\
&= (x^2 + 8)^2 - (4x)^2 \\
&= [(x^2 + 8) - 4x][(x^2 + 8) + 4x] \\
&= (x^2 - 4x + 8)(x^2 + 4x + 8)
\end{aligned}$$

Multiplication and Division of Fractions

The product of two fractions is a fraction whose numerator is the product of the two numerators and whose denominator is the product of the two denominators.

$$\frac{a}{b}\cdot\frac{c}{d} = \frac{ac}{bd} \qquad b, d \neq O$$

Illustration:

$$\begin{aligned}
\frac{2x + 2y}{x + y}\cdot\frac{x^2 - y^2}{x^2 + 2xy + y^2} &= \frac{2(x + y)}{(x + y)}\cdot\frac{(x - y)(x + y)}{(x + y)(x + y)} \\
&= \frac{2(x - y)}{x + y}
\end{aligned}$$

The quotient of a fraction $\frac{a}{b}$ divided by a fraction $\frac{c}{d}$, that is, $\frac{a}{b} \div \frac{c}{d}$, is the product of $\frac{a}{b}$ and the reciprocal of $\frac{c}{d}$. In symbols

$$\frac{a}{b} \div \frac{c}{d} = \frac{a}{b} \cdot \frac{d}{c} \qquad b, d \neq O$$

Illustration:

$$\begin{aligned} \frac{x^2 - x - 30}{x - 4} \div \frac{x - 6}{x^2 - 5x + 4} &= \frac{(x - 6)(x + 5)}{x - 4} \div \frac{x - 6}{(x - 4)(x - 1)} \\ &= \frac{(x - 6)(x + 5)(x - 4)(x - 1)}{(x - 4)(x - 6)} \\ &= (x + 5)(x - 1) \end{aligned}$$

Oftentimes exercises involve combinations of multiplication and division. However, no new difficulties are introduced.

Illustration:

$$\begin{aligned} \frac{3x^2 + x - 10}{x^2 - 16} \cdot \frac{x^2 - 3x - 4}{3x - 5} \div \frac{x^2 - 1}{x + 4} &= \frac{(3x - 5)(x + 2)}{(x + 4)(x - 4)} \\ &\quad \cdot \frac{(x - 4)(x + 1)}{3x - 5} \cdot \frac{x + 4}{(x - 1)(x + 1)} \\ &= \frac{x + 2}{x - 1} \end{aligned}$$

Addition and Subtraction of Fractions

The algebraic sum of two or more fractions having the same denominators is a fraction having the same denominator whose numerator is the algebraic sum of the numerators of the fractions being added.

$$\frac{a}{d} + \frac{b}{d} + \frac{c}{d} = \frac{a + b + c}{d} \qquad d \neq O$$

Illustration:

$$\frac{7}{3ax^2} - \frac{2y}{3ax^2} + \frac{6x}{3ax^2} = \frac{7 - 2y + 6x}{3ax^2}$$

To add two or more fractions not having the same denominator, we transform each fraction into an equivalent fraction whose denominator is the L.C.D. of the given fractions. Then we add, as in the case of fractions whose denominators are alike.

Illustration:

$$m + \frac{1}{2m - 1} = \frac{m(2m - 1)}{2m - 1} + \frac{1}{2m - 1}$$
$$= \frac{2m^2 - m + 1}{2m - 1}$$

Illustration:

$$\frac{3x - 1}{x + 1} - \frac{3x + 1}{x - 1} + \frac{8}{x^2 - 1}$$
$$= \frac{(3x - 1)(x - 1) - (3x + 1)(x + 1) + 8}{(x + 1)(x - 1)}$$
$$= \frac{3x^2 - 4x + 1 - 3x^2 - 4x - 1 + 8}{(x + 1)(x - 1)}$$
$$= \frac{-8x + 8}{(x + 1)(x - 1)}$$
$$= \frac{-8(x - 1)}{(x + 1)(x - 1)} = \frac{-8}{(x + 1)}$$

Complex Fractions

If the numerator or denominator (or both) of a fraction is also a fraction, we call the entire fraction a *complex fraction*. There are several suitable techniques for simplifying such a fraction. We illustrate two of them:

Illustration:

$$\frac{s + \frac{t^2}{s + 2t}}{s - \frac{3t^2}{s - 2t}} = \frac{\frac{s(s + 2t)}{s + 2t} + \frac{t^2}{s + 2t}}{\frac{s(s - 2t)}{s - 2t} - \frac{3t^2}{s - 2t}} = \frac{\frac{s^2 + 2st + t^2}{s + 2t}}{\frac{s^2 - 2st - 3t^2}{s - 2t}}$$

$$= \frac{(s + t)(s + t)}{(s + 2t)} \cdot \frac{(s - 2t)}{(s - 3t)(s + t)}$$
$$= \frac{(s + t)(s - 2t)}{(s + 2t)(s - 3t)}$$

Illustration:

$$\frac{m+n-\dfrac{n^2}{m+n}}{m-n-\dfrac{n^2}{m+n}} = \frac{m+n-\dfrac{n^2}{m+n}}{m-n-\dfrac{n^2}{m+n}}\cdot\frac{m+n}{m+n}$$

$$= \frac{m^2+2mn+n^2-n^2}{m^2-n^2-n^2}$$

$$= \frac{m^2+2mn}{m^2-2n^2}$$

Laws of Exponents

The symbol $a \cdot a \cdot a \cdots a$ to x factors a means a taken x times as a factor in a product, and is denoted by a^x. Therefore, a^x is referred to as a power; x is called the exponent; and a is called the base. We define

$$a^1 = a$$
$$a^n a^1 = a^{n+1}$$

Exponents obey five basic laws. We state them without proof.*

In the following laws, x and y are positive integers, and a and b are any positive numbers.

I. $a^x \cdot a^y = a^{x+y}$

II. $(a^x)^y = a^{xy}$

IIIa. $\dfrac{a^x}{a^y} = a^{x-y}, x > y$

IIIb. $\dfrac{a^x}{a^y} = \dfrac{1}{a^{y-x}}, x < y$

IV. $(ab)^x = a^x b^x$

V. $\left(\dfrac{a}{b}\right)^x = \dfrac{a^x}{b^x}$

Illustrations:

$s^4 \cdot s^5 = s^{4+5} = s^9$ Law I

---

* For a detailed proof of the laws see: Feinstein, I. K. and Murphy, K. H., *College Algebra,* Ames, Iowa: Littlefield, Adams & Co., 1982.

$$\frac{t^{12}}{t^3} = t^{12-3} = t^9 \qquad \text{IIIa}$$

$$(r^2)^3 = r^6 \qquad \text{II}$$

$$\frac{y^7}{y^4} = y^{7-4} = y^3 \qquad \text{IIIa}$$

$$\frac{w^4}{w^8} = \frac{1}{w^{8-4}} = \frac{1}{w^4} \qquad \text{IIIb}$$

$$(-2z)^3 = (-2)^3 z^3 = -8z^3 \qquad \text{IV}$$

$$\left(\frac{3x}{2y}\right)^2 = \frac{(3x)^2}{(2y)^2} = \frac{3^2x^2}{2^2y^2} = \frac{9x^2}{4y^2} \qquad \text{V}$$

$$\left(\frac{c^3}{d^2}\right)^m = \frac{(c^3)^m}{(d^2)^m} = \frac{c^{3m}}{d^{2m}} \qquad \text{II and V}$$

$$\left(\frac{ab^2}{2m^3n}\right)^3 = \frac{a^3b^6}{8m^9n^3} \qquad \text{II, IV and V}$$

Zero, Negative, and Fractional Exponents

It is desirable to use zero as an exponent of a power and to so define the power as to be consistent with the laws of exponents. It is easy to show that to do this we must define

$$a^0 = 1, \qquad a \neq 0$$

Illustrations:

$$(3x^2)^0 = 1; \quad (2x^3 - 3x^2 + 7)^0 = 1; \quad (1 + .03)^0 = 1$$

What meaning can we give to a negative exponent that would be consistent with the properties or laws of exponents previously stated? We must define

$$a^{-y} = \frac{1}{a^y} \qquad a \neq 0, y > 0$$

Illustrations:

$$y^{-4} = \frac{1}{y^4}; \qquad -3^{-2} = -\frac{1}{3^2} = -\frac{1}{9}; \qquad \frac{3a}{b^{-2}} = 3ab^2$$

If p and q are integers and if $\frac{p}{q}$ is expressed with a positive denominator, we define

$$a^{\frac{p}{q}} = \sqrt[q]{a^p}$$

Illustrations:

$$(8)^{\frac{2}{3}} = \sqrt[3]{8^2} = (\sqrt[3]{8})^2 = 4$$

$$(25)^{-\frac{3}{2}} = (5^2)^{-\frac{3}{2}} = 5^{-3} = \frac{1}{5^3} = \frac{1}{125}$$

$$\left(\frac{a^{-5}b^3}{a^2b^{-3}}\right)^2 = \frac{a^{-10}b^6}{a^4b^{-6}} = \frac{b^{6-(-6)}}{a^{4-(-10)}} = \frac{b^{12}}{a^{14}}$$

$$a^{-1} + b^{-1} = \frac{1}{a} + \frac{1}{b} = \frac{b}{ab} + \frac{a}{ab} = \frac{b+a}{ab}$$

$$\frac{9 - a^{-4}}{3a^{-1} + a^{-3}} = \frac{(3 - a^{-2})(3 + a^{-2})}{a^{-1}(3 + a^{-2})} = \frac{3 - a^{-2}}{a^{-1}}\cdot\frac{a^2}{a^2}$$

$$= \frac{3a^2 - 1}{a}$$

Radicals

An indicated root of some number or expression, such as $\sqrt[n]{a}$, is called a *radical; n* is the index or order of the radical; the symbol $\sqrt{\ }$ is the radical sign; the number or expression, a, of which the root is taken is called the *radicand*. In $k\sqrt[n]{a}$, k is the coefficient of the radical.

A number x is an nth root of a if the nth power of x equals a. In symbols

x is an nth root of a, if $x^n = a$

There are n distinct nth roots of a real number a. Some of these may be complex numbers. Mathematicians have agreed that the symbol $\sqrt[n]{a}$ will stand for the principal nth root of a, unless otherwise specified. The principal nth root of a real number a is the positive real nth root if a is positive; and is the negative real nth root if a is negative and n is odd.

Illustration:

In $x^4 = 16$, the solutions, x, are the fourth roots of 16; $x = 2$ is the principal fourth root; $\sqrt[4]{16} = 2$.

In $x^3 = -27$, the solutions, x, are the cube roots of -27; $x = -3$ is the principal cube root; $\sqrt[3]{-27} = -3$.

The laws of exponents, together with the relation between a power with a rational exponent and a root, enable us to formulate several useful properties for operations on radicals. (In the following laws, consider n, p, q, and r positive integers and assume $a, b > 0$.)

Law I	$\sqrt[q]{a^p} = (\sqrt[q]{a})^p$
Law II	$\sqrt[q]{a} \cdot \sqrt[q]{b} = \sqrt[q]{ab}$
Law III	$\dfrac{\sqrt[q]{a}}{\sqrt[q]{b}} = \sqrt[q]{\dfrac{a}{b}}$
Law IV	$\sqrt[qr]{a^{pr}} = \sqrt[q]{a^p}$
Law V	$k\sqrt[n]{a} = \sqrt[n]{k^n a}$

Illustrations:

$$\sqrt[3]{3^3} = 3; \; \sqrt{4^2} = 4$$

$$\sqrt[3]{27} \cdot \sqrt[3]{8} = \sqrt[3]{27 \cdot 8} = \sqrt[3]{216} = 6$$

$$\sqrt[3]{-64s^6t^{-3}} = \sqrt[3]{-64} \cdot \sqrt[3]{s^6t^{-3}} = -4s^2t^{-1}$$

$$\frac{\sqrt[3]{8t^6}}{\sqrt[3]{27s^3}} = \sqrt[3]{\frac{8t^6}{27s^3}} = \frac{2t^2}{3s}$$

$$\sqrt[6]{16x^4} = \sqrt[6]{2^4 \cdot x^4} = \sqrt[3]{2^2 \cdot x^2} = \sqrt[3]{4x^2}$$

$$\sqrt[8]{64z^6} = \sqrt[8]{2^6z^6} = \sqrt[4]{2^3z^3} = \sqrt[4]{8z^3}$$

$$2\sqrt[3]{3} = \sqrt[3]{2^3 \cdot 3} = \sqrt[3]{24}$$

$$\sqrt[3]{\frac{128z}{9x^2y}} = \sqrt[3]{\frac{128z}{9x^2y} \cdot \frac{3xy^2}{3xy^2}} =$$

$$\sqrt[3]{\frac{64 \cdot 2 \cdot 3xy^2z}{27x^3y^3}} = \frac{4}{3xy}\sqrt[3]{6xy^2z}$$

II. LOGARITHMS

Definition

If

$$b^x = N \quad \text{then} \quad x = \log_b N$$

where

b = Base (positive number different from 1)
x = Logarithm of N, base b
N = Number (positive)

The *logarithm* of a positive number N to a positive number b ($b \neq 1$) is that exponent x which must be applied to b so that $b^x = N$. This definition implies that the following two forms are equivalent:

$$b^x = N \quad \text{and} \quad x = \log_b N$$

Illustrations:

Base	Number	Logarithm	Exponential Form	Logarithmic Form
3	81	4	$3^4 = 81$	$\log_3 81 = 4$
$\frac{1}{4}$	64	-3	$\left(\frac{1}{4}\right)^{-3} = 64$	$\log_{\frac{1}{4}} 64 = -3$
3	1	0	$3^0 = 1$	$\log_3 1 = 0$
2	2	1	$2^1 = 2$	$\log_2 2 = 1$

Remember:

$$\text{If } b^x = N \quad \text{then} \quad x = \log_b N \qquad (b > 0, b \neq 1)$$

Some Properties of Logarithms

Property 1:

The logarithm of a *product* is equal to the sum of the logarithms of its factors. In symbols

$$\log_b MN = \log_b M + \log_b N$$

Property 2:

The logarithm of a *quotient* equals the logarithm of the numerator minus the logarithm of the denominator. In symbols

$$\log_b \frac{M}{N} = \log_b M - \log_b N$$

Property 3:

The logarithm of the kth *power of a number* equals k times the logarithm of the number. In symbols

$$\log_b M^k = k \log_b M$$

Illustration 1:

$$\log_b 81 = \log_b 3^4 = 4 \log_b 3$$

Illustration 2:

$$\log_5 125 = \log_5 5^3 = 3 \log_5 5 = 3$$

Illustration 3:

$$\log_{10} 16 + \log_{10} 5 = \log_{10}(16 \cdot 5) = \log_{10}(10 \cdot 8)$$
$$= \log_{10} 10 + \log_{10} 8$$
$$= 1 + \log_{10} 8$$

Illustration 4:

$$\log_{10} 14 - \log_{10} 7 = \log_{10}\frac{14}{7} = \log_{10} 2$$

Illustration 5:

Show that

$$\log_{10}\frac{24}{7} - \log_{10}\frac{18}{21} = 2 \log_{10} 3$$

Solution:

$$\log_{10}\frac{24}{7} - \log_{10}\frac{8}{21} = \log_{10}\left(\frac{24}{7} \cdot \frac{21}{8}\right) = \log_{10} 9$$
$$= \log_{10} 3^2 = 2 \log_{10} 3$$

Common Logarithms:

Common logarithms use the base 10 and are the most convenient for computation in our decimal numeration system. Let us examine the following table:

$\log 10{,}000 = 4$	$10^4 = 10{,}000$
$\log 1{,}000 = 3$	$10^3 = 1{,}000$
$\log 100 = 2$	$10^2 = 100$
$\log 10 = 1$	$10^1 = 10$
$\log 1 = 0$	$10^0 = 1$
$\log 0.1 = -1$	$10^{-1} = 0.1$
$\log 0.01 = -2$	$10^{-2} = 0.01$
$\log 0.001 = -3$	$10^{-3} = 0.001$
$\log 0.0001 = -4$	$10^{-4} = 0.0001$

We see that numbers that are integral powers of 10 will have integral logarithms; all other numbers will not. We assert that the larger of two positive numbers will have the larger logarithm, and conversely. We expect the log 368 to be between 2 and 3 since it must be greater than log 100 = 2 and less than log 1000 = 3. It would be composed of the integer 2 and some decimal fraction. The log 0.04 would be between −2 and −1 since it would be greater than log 0.01 = −2 and less than log 0.10 = −1. We may think of it as being composed of the integer -2 and a positive decimal fraction. The integer or the whole number part of the logarithm of a number is called the *characteristic;* the decimal fraction part is called the *mantissa.*

The logarithms of all numbers with the same digit sequence have the same mantissa. In actual computation the mantissa of the log of a number will be found in a table prepared for that purpose. The mantissas will usually be irrational and will be approximated to five places, six places, and so on, according to the particular table used. The technique of using the table will be explained presently.

The characteristic of the log of any positive number depends on the position of the decimal point and is independent of the digit sequence of the number. The log of a number is found by determining the characteristic by inspection and calculating the mantissa from a table.

The simplest way to find the characteristic of the logarithm of a number is to observe the number of places the decimal point in the number would have to be moved—and whether to the right or left—to give a number between 1 and 10. If the decimal point must be moved to the right, the characteristic is negative; to the left, positive.

Illustrations:

Find the characteristic of the log 148.49; of log 0.000053; of log 0.00852; of log 88.295; of log 1.8632.

Solutions:

The characteristic of

$\log 148.49 = 2$ because the decimal point would have to be moved 2 places to the left to get a number between 1 and 10

$\log 0.000053 = -5$ because the decimal point would have to be moved 5 places to the right to get a number between 1 and 10

$\log 0.00852 = -3$ because the decimal point would have to be moved 3 places to the right to get a number between 1 and 10

$\log 88.295 = 1$ because the decimal point would have to be moved 1 place to the left to get a number between 1 and 10

$\log 1.8632 = 0$ because the number already is between 1 and 10

Suppose the characteristic of log 33.254 is 1 and the mantissa is .520536. Then log 33.254 = 1.520536. Suppose the log of .33254 is required to be found. The characteristic is -1; the mantissa again will be .520536. Then log .33254 = $-1 + .520536$. The characteristic here is negative yet the mantissa is positive. It would be incorrect to write log 0.33254 = -1.520536 since this is not equivalent to $-1 + .520536$. We may write log 0.33254 = $\bar{1}.530536$, the bar above the characteristic indicating that it is negative. However, it is more useful to subtract the characteristic from a suitable multiple of 10, append the mantissa to this, and write minus that multiple of 10 following the mantissa. Then log 0.33254 = 9.520536 − 10.

Illustrations:

log 0.003951 = 7.596707 − 10;
log 0.000009342 = 4.970440 − 10

Tables of Logarithms

The logarithms of numbers between 1 and 10 are found in tables. For any 4-digit numbers we shall use in this treatment 6-place mantissas (Table VI), which will enable us to obtain directly mantissas correct to 6 significant figures for any 4-digit numbers. By the process of interpolation, these tables will yield mantissas for 5-digit numbers as well. Table VII will yield directly mantissas correct to 7 significant figures for any 5-digit number between 1 and 1.1, and by interpolation for any 6-digit number between 1 and 1.1.

Illustration 1:
Find the mantissa of the logarithm of 33.267.

Solution:
The mantissas of 33260 and 33270 can be found directly from Table VI. Since 33267 lies $\frac{7}{10}$ of the way from 33260 to 33270, we calculate a mantissa which is $\frac{7}{10}$ of the way from the mantissa of 33260 to the mantissa of 33270. We have structured the problem following.

$$\begin{array}{ll} \textbf{Number} & \textbf{Mantissa} \end{array}$$

$$10\left\{\begin{array}{l} \phantom{7\{}33270 \\ 7\left\{\begin{array}{l} 33267 \\ 33260 \end{array}\right. \end{array}\right. \quad \left.\begin{array}{r} 522053 \\ \left.\begin{array}{r} N \\ 521922 \end{array}\right\} d \end{array}\right\} 131$$

Then

$$\frac{d}{131} = \frac{7}{10} \quad \text{or} \quad d = 91.7$$

This correction 92 when added to 521922 produces 522014. The logarithm of 33.267 = 1.522014.

Illustration 2:
Find the mantissa for the logarithm of .103556.

Solution:

Since this number lies between 1 and 1.1, Table VII may be used. Since 103556 lies $\frac{6}{10}$ of the way between 103550 and 103560, we calculate a mantissa which is $\frac{6}{10}$ of the way from the mantissa of 103550 to the mantissa of 103560. We have structured the problem following.

$$\begin{array}{cc} \textbf{Number} & \textbf{Mantissa} \\ 10\left\{\begin{array}{l} \;\;103560 \\ 6\left\{\begin{array}{l} 103556 \\ 103550 \end{array}\right. \end{array}\right. & \left.\begin{array}{r} 0151920 \\ \left.\begin{array}{r} N \\ 0151501 \end{array}\right\}d \end{array}\right\}419 \end{array}$$

Then

$$\frac{d}{419} = \frac{6}{10} \quad \text{or} \quad d = 251.4$$

This correction, 251, when added to 0151501 produces 0151752. The logarithm of .103556 = 9.0151752 − 10.

Illustration 3:
Find N if $\log N = 7.966339 - 10$.

Solution:

The mantissa of the number N we are seeking is $\frac{10}{47}$ of the way from the mantissa of 92540 to the mantissa of 92550. We therefore calculate N to be $\frac{10}{47}$ of the way from 92540 to 92550. Thus the first four digits of

N will be 9254. The fifth digit will then be found by solving the proportion $\frac{x}{10} = \frac{10}{47}$. We have structured the problem below.

$$\begin{array}{c c c}
 & \textbf{Number} & \textbf{Mantissa} \\
10\left\{\begin{array}{l} \\ x\left\{\begin{array}{c} \\ \\ \end{array}\right. \end{array}\right. & \begin{array}{c} 92550 \\ N \\ 92540 \end{array} & \left.\begin{array}{c} 966376 \\ \left.\begin{array}{c} 966339 \\ 966329 \end{array}\right\}10 \end{array}\right\}47
\end{array}$$

Then

$$\frac{x}{10} = \frac{10}{47} \quad \text{or} \quad x = 2.1$$

The digit sequence of N is consequently 92542. The characteristic $7 - 10$ indicates that the decimal point in N will have to be moved 3 places to the right to yield a number between 1 and 10. Therefore if log $N = 7.966339 - 10$, then $N = 0.0092542$.

Logarithmic Computation

Logarithms serve as an excellent means of (or aid to) computation. They are especially adaptable to problems where multiplication, division, powers, and roots are the sole or principal operations involved.

Illustration 1:
By means of logarithms, find x if

$$x = 1000\ (1.045)^{20}$$

Solution:

$$\begin{aligned} \log x &= \log\,[1000\ (1.045)^{20}] = \log 1000 + 20 \log 1.045 \\ &= 3 + 20 \log 1.045 \end{aligned}$$

We are now ready to structure the problem.

$$\begin{aligned} \log 1.045 &= 0.019116 \qquad \text{(Table VI)} \\ 20 \log 1.045 &= 0.382320 \\ \log x &= 3 + 0.382320 = 3.382320 \\ x &= 2411.70 \end{aligned}$$

As a check on our work, from Table I we find that

$$(1.045)^{20} = 2.41171 \text{ so } 1000\ (2.41171) = 2411.71$$

Illustration 2:

By means of logarithms, find x if

$$x = (1.035)^{-12}$$

Solution:

$$\begin{aligned} \log x &= -12 \log 1.035 && \text{(Table VI)} \\ \log 1.035 &= 0.014940 \\ -12 \log 1.035 &= -.179280 \\ \log x &= -.179280 = 10.000000 - 10 - .179280 \\ &= 9.820720 - 10 \\ x &= 0.66179 \end{aligned}$$

As a check on our work, from Table II, we find that

$$(1.035)^{-12} = 0.66178330$$

Illustration 3:

Evaluate r given

$$(1 - r)^{20} = \frac{185}{1775}$$

Solution:

$$\begin{aligned} \log (1 - r)^{20} &= \log 185 - \log 1775 \\ 20 \log (1 - r) &= \log 185 - \log 1775 \\ \log (1 - r) &= \frac{1}{20} (\log 185 - \log 1775) \\ &= \frac{1}{20} (2.267172 - 3.249198) \\ &= \frac{1}{20} (19.017974 - 20) \\ &= 0.9508987 - 1 \\ &= 9.950899 - 10 && \text{(Table VI)} \\ 1 - r &= 0.8931 \\ r &= 0.1069 \text{ or } 10.7\% \end{aligned}$$

Illustration 4:

Evaluate

$$\sqrt[10]{\frac{4797}{23{,}546}}$$

Solution:

$$\text{Let } N = \sqrt[10]{\frac{4797}{23{,}546}}$$

$$\log N = \log\left(\frac{4797}{23{,}546}\right)^{\frac{1}{10}}$$

$$= \frac{1}{10}[\log 4797 - \log 23{,}546]$$

$$= \frac{1}{10}[3.680970 - 4.371917] \qquad \text{(Table VI)}$$

$$= \frac{1}{10}[33.680970 - 4.371917 - 30]$$

$$= \frac{1}{10}[29.309053 - 30]$$

$$= \frac{1}{10}[99.309053 - 100]$$

$$= 9.930905 - 10$$

$$N = 0.85291$$

Illustration 5:

Evaluate x given $x = \dfrac{1500 \times (1.06)^{25}}{29}$

Solution:

The chief difficulty here is to evaluate $(1.06)^{25}$, assuming that tables are not available. Once this has been done, then the rest of the example can be performed by ordinary arithmetic.

$$\text{Let } N = (1.06)^{25}$$

$$\text{Then } \log N = 25 \log 1.06$$

$$= 25 \times (.0253059) = 0.6326475 \qquad \text{(Table VII)}$$

$$N = 4.2919 \qquad \text{(Tabular value is 4.29187072)}$$

$$x = \frac{1500 \times 4.2919}{29} = \frac{6437.85}{29}$$

$$= 221.995$$

Tables

TABLE I
AMOUNT OF 1 AT COMPOUND INTEREST
$(1 + i)^n$

TABLE I

N	1/6	5/24	1/4	7/24	1/3	N
1	1.0016 6667	1.0020 8333	1.0025 0000	1.0029 1667	1.0033 3333	1
2	1.0033 3611	1.0041 7101	1.0050 0625	1.0058 4184	1.0066 7778	2
3	1.0050 0834	1.0062 6303	1.0075 1877	1.0087 7555	1.0100 3337	3
4	1.0066 8335	1.0083 5941	1.0100 3756	1.0117 1781	1.0134 0015	4
5	1.0083 6116	1.0104 6016	1.0125 6266	1.0146 6865	1.0167 7815	5
6	1.0100 4176	1.0125 6529	1.0150 9406	1.0176 2810	1.0201 6741	6
7	1.0117 2516	1.0146 7480	1.0176 3180	1.0205 9618	1.0235 6797	7
8	1.0134 1137	1.0167 8870	1.0201 7588	1.0235 7292	1.0269 7986	8
9	1.0151 0039	1.0189 0701	1.0227 2632	1.0265 5834	1.0304 0313	9
10	1.0167 9222	1.0210 2973	1.0252 8313	1.0295 5247	1.0338 3780	10
11	1.0184 8688	1.0231 5688	1.0278 4634	1.0325 5533	1.0372 8393	11
12	1.0201 8436	1.0252 8846	1.0304 1596	1.0355 6695	1.0407 4154	12
13	1.0218 8466	1.0274 2447	1.0329 9200	1.0385 8736	1.0442 1068	13
14	1.0235 8780	1.0295 6494	1.0355 7448	1.0416 1657	1.0476 9138	14
15	1.0252 9378	1.0317 0987	1.0381 6341	1.0446 5462	1.0511 8369	15
16	1.0270 0261	1.0338 5926	1.0407 5882	1.0477 0153	1.0546 8763	16
17	1.0287 1428	1.0360 1314	1.0433 6072	1.0507 5732	1.0582 0326	17
18	1.0304 2880	1.0381 7150	1.0459 6912	1.0538 2203	1.0617 3060	18
19	1.0321 4618	1.0403 3436	1.0485 8404	1.0568 9568	1.0652 6971	19
20	1.0338 6643	1.0425 0172	1.0512 0550	1.0599 7829	1.0688 2060	20
21	1.0355 8954	1.0446 7360	1.0538 3352	1.0630 6990	1.0723 8334	21
22	1.0373 1552	1.0468 5000	1.0564 6810	1.0661 7052	1.0759 5795	22
23	1.0390 4438	1.0490 3094	1.0591 0927	1.0692 8018	1.0795 4448	23
24	1.0407 7612	1.0512 1642	1.0617 5704	1.0723 9891	1.0831 4296	24
25	1.0425 1075	1.0534 0645	1.0644 1144	1.0755 2674	1.0867 5344	25
26	1.0442 4826	1.0556 0105	1.0670 7247	1.0786 6370	1.0903 7595	26
27	1.0459 8868	1.0578 0022	1.0697 4015	1.0818 0980	1.0940 1053	27
28	1.0477 3199	1.0600 0397	1.0724 1450	1.0849 6508	1.0976 5724	28
29	1.0494 7821	1.0622 1231	1.0750 9553	1.0881 2956	1.1013 1609	29
30	1.0512 2734	1.0644 2525	1.0777 8327	1.0913 0327	1.1049 8715	30
31	1.0529 7939	1.0666 4281	1.0804 7773	1.0944 8624	1.1086 7044	31
32	1.0547 3435	1.0688 6498	1.0831 7892	1.0976 7849	1.1123 6601	32
33	1.0564 9224	1.0710 9178	1.0858 8687	1.1008 8005	1.1160 7389	33
34	1.0582 5307	1.0733 2322	1.0886 0159	1.1040 9095	1.1197 9414	34
35	1.0600 1682	1.0755 5931	1.0913 2309	1.1073 1122	1.1235 2679	35
36	1.0617 8351	1.0778 0006	1.0940 5140	1.1105 4088	1.1272 7187	36
37	1.0635 5315	1.0800 4548	1.0967 8653	1.1137 7995	1.1310 2945	37
38	1.0653 2574	1.0822 9557	1.0995 2850	1.1170 2848	1.1347 9955	38
39	1.0671 0129	1.0845 5036	1.1022 7732	1.1202 8648	1.1385 8221	39
40	1.0688 7979	1.0868 0984	1.1050 3301	1.1235 5398	1.1423 7748	40
41	1.0706 6125	1.0890 7402	1.1077 9559	1.1268 3101	1.1461 8541	41
42	1.0724 4569	1.0913 4293	1.1105 6508	1.1301 1760	1.1500 0603	42
43	1.0742 3310	1.0936 1656	1.1133 4149	1.1334 1378	1.1538 3938	43
44	1.0760 2349	1.0958 9493	1.1161 2485	1.1367 1957	1.1576 8551	44
45	1.0778 1686	1.0981 7804	1.1189 1516	1.1400 3500	1.1615 4446	45
46	1.0796 1322	1.1004 6591	1.1217 1245	1.1433 6010	1.1654 1628	46
47	1.0814 1258	1.1027 5855	1.1245 1673	1.1466 9490	1.1693 0100	47
48	1.0832 1493	1.1050 5596	1.1273 2802	1.1500 3943	1.1731 9867	48
49	1.0850 2029	1.1073 5816	1.1301 4634	1.1533 9371	1.1771 0933	49
50	1.0868 2866	1.1096 6516	1.1329 7171	1.1567 5778	1.1810 3303	50
51	1.0886 4004	1.1119 7696	1.1358 0414	1.1601 3165	1.1849 6981	51
52	1.0904 5444	1.1142 9358	1.1386 4365	1.1635 1537	1.1889 1971	52
53	1.0922 7186	1.1166 1502	1.1414 9026	1.1669 0896	1.1928 8277	53
54	1.0940 9231	1.1189 4131	1.1443 4398	1.1703 1244	1.1968 5905	54
55	1.0959 1580	1.1212 7243	1.1472 0484	1.1737 2585	1.2008 4858	55
56	1.0977 4233	1.1236 0842	1.1500 7285	1.1771 4922	1.2048 5141	56
57	1.0995 7190	1.1259 4927	1.1529 4804	1.1805 8257	1.2088 6758	57
58	1.1014 0452	1.1282 9500	1.1558 3041	1.1840 2594	1.2128 9714	58
59	1.1032 4019	1.1306 4561	1.1587 1998	1.1874 7935	1.2169 4013	59
60	1.1050 7893	1.1330 0112	1.1616 1678	1.1909 4283	1.2209 9659	60

TABLE I

N	1/6	5/24	1/4	7/24	1/3	N
61	1.1069 2072	1.1353 6154	1.1645 2082	1.1944 1641	1.2250 6658	61
62	1.1087 6559	1.1377 2688	1.1674 3213	1.1979 0013	1.2291 5014	62
63	1.1106 1354	1.1400 9714	1.1703 5071	1.2013 9400	1.2332 4730	63
64	1.1124 6456	1.1424 7234	1.1732 7658	1.2048 9807	1.2373 5813	64
65	1.1143 1867	1.1448 5249	1.1762 0977	1.2084 1235	1.2414 8266	65
66	1.1161 7586	1.1472 3760	1.1791 5030	1.2119 3689	1.2456 2093	66
67	1.1180 3616	1.1496 2768	1.1820 9817	1.2154 7171	1.2497 7300	67
68	1.1198 9955	1.1520 2274	1.1850 5342	1.2190 1683	1.2539 3891	68
69	1.1217 6605	1.1544 2279	1.1880 1605	1.2225 7230	1.2581 1871	69
70	1.1236 3566	1.1568 2784	1.1909 8609	1.2261 3813	1.2623 1244	70
71	1.1255 0839	1.1592 3789	1.1939 6356	1.2297 1437	1.2665 2015	71
72	1.1273 8423	1.1616 5297	1.1969 4847	1.2333 0104	1.2707 4188	72
73	1.1292 6321	1.1640 7308	1.1999 4084	1.2368 9816	1.2749 7769	73
74	1.1311 4531	1.1664 9823	1.2029 4069	1.2405 0578	1.2792 2761	74
75	1.1330 3055	1.1689 2844	1.2059 4804	1.2441 2393	1.2834 9170	75
76	1.1349 1894	1.1713 6371	1.2089 6291	1.2477 5262	1.2877 7001	76
77	1.1368 1047	1.1738 0405	1.2119 8532	1.2513 9190	1.2920 6258	77
78	1.1387 0515	1.1762 4947	1.2150 1528	1.2550 4179	1.2963 6945	78
79	1.1406 0300	1.1786 9999	1.2180 5282	1.2587 0233	1.3006 9068	79
80	1.1425 0400	1.1811 5562	1.2210 9795	1.2623 7355	1.3050 2632	80
81	1.1444 0817	1.1836 1636	1.2241 5070	1.2660 5547	1.3093 7641	81
82	1.1463 1552	1.1860 8223	1.2272 1108	1.2697 4813	1.3137 4099	82
83	1.1482 2605	1.1885 5323	1.2302 7910	1.2734 5156	1.3181 2013	83
84	1.1501 3976	1.1910 2938	1.2333 5480	1.2771 6580	1.3225 1386	84
85	1.1520 5666	1.1935 1069	1.2364 3819	1.2808 9086	1.3269 2224	85
86	1.1539 7675	1.1959 9718	1.2395 2928	1.2846 2680	1.3313 4532	86
87	1.1559 0005	1.1984 8884	1.2426 2811	1.2883 7362	1.3357 8314	87
88	1.1578 2655	1.2009 8569	1.2457 3468	1.2921 3138	1.3402 3575	88
89	1.1597 5626	1.2034 8774	1.2488 4901	1.2959 0010	1.3447 0320	89
90	1.1616 8918	1.2059 9501	1.2519 7114	1.2996 7980	1.3491 8554	90
91	1.1636 2533	1.2085 0750	1.2551 0106	1.3034 7054	1.3536 8283	91
92	1.1655 6471	1.2110 2522	1.2582 3882	1.3072 7233	1.3581 9510	92
93	1.1675 0732	1.2135 4819	1.2613 8441	1.3110 8520	1.3627 2242	93
94	1.1694 5316	1.2160 7642	1.2645 3787	1.3149 0920	1.3672 6483	94
95	1.1714 0225	1.2186 0991	1.2676 9922	1.3187 4435	1.3718 2238	95
96	1.1733 5459	1.2211 4868	1.2708 6847	1.3225 9069	1.3763 9512	96
97	1.1753 1018	1.2236 9274	1.2740 4564	1.3264 4825	1.3809 8310	97
98	1.1772 6903	1.2262 4210	1.2772 3075	1.3303 1706	1.3855 8638	98
99	1.1792 3114	1.2287 9677	1.2804 2383	1.3341 9715	1.3902 0500	99
100	1.1811 9653	1.2313 5676	1.2836 2489	1.3380 8856	1.3948 3902	100
101	1.1831 6519	1.2339 2209	1.2868 3395	1.3419 9131	1.3994 8848	101
102	1.1851 3713	1.2364 9276	1.2900 5104	1.3459 0546	1.4041 5344	102
103	1.1871 1236	1.2390 6879	1.2932 7616	1.3498 3101	1.4088 3395	103
104	1.1890 9088	1.2416 5018	1.2965 0935	1.3537 6802	1.4135 3007	104
105	1.1910 7270	1.2442 3695	1.2997 5063	1.3577 1651	1.4182 4183	105
106	1.1930 5782	1.2468 2911	1.3030 0000	1.3616 7652	1.4229 6931	106
107	1.1950 4625	1.2494 2667	1.3062 5750	1.3656 4807	1.4277 1254	107
108	1.1970 3799	1.2520 2964	1.3095 2315	1.3696 3121	1.4324 7158	108
109	1.1990 3306	1.2546 3804	1.3127 9696	1.3736 2597	1.4372 4649	109
110	1.2010 3144	1.2572 5187	1.3160 7895	1.3776 3238	1.4420 3731	110
111	1.2030 3316	1.2598 7114	1.3193 6915	1.3816 5047	1.4468 4410	111
112	1.2050 3822	1.2624 9587	1.3226 6757	1.3856 8029	1.4516 6691	112
113	1.2070 4662	1.2651 2607	1.3259 7424	1.3897 2186	1.4565 0580	113
114	1.2090 5836	1.2677 6175	1.3292 8917	1.3937 7521	1.4613 6082	114
115	1.2110 7346	1.2704 0292	1.3326 1240	1.3978 4039	1.4662 3202	115
116	1.2130 9191	1.2730 4960	1.3359 4393	1.4019 1742	1.4711 1946	116
117	1.2151 1373	1.2757 0178	1.3392 8379	1.4060 0635	1.4760 2320	117
118	1.2171 3892	1.2783 5950	1.3426 3200	1.4101 0720	1.4809 4327	118
119	1.2191 6749	1.2810 2274	1.3459 8858	1.4142 2001	1.4858 7975	119
120	1.2211 9943	1.2836 9154	1.3493 5355	1.4183 4482	1.4908 3268	120

TABLE I

N	1/6	5/24	1/4	7/24	1/3	N
121	1.2232 3477	1.2863 6590	1.3527 2693	1.4224 8166	1.4958 0212	121
122	1.2252 7349	1.2890 4583	1.3561 0875	1.4266 3057	1.5007 8813	122
123	1.2273 1561	1.2917 3134	1.3594 9902	1.4307 9157	1.5057 9076	123
124	1.2293 6114	1.2944 2245	1.3628 9777	1.4349 6471	1.5108 1006	124
125	1.2314 1007	1.2971 1916	1.3663 0501	1.4391 5003	1.5158 4609	125
126	1.2334 6242	1.2998 2149	1.3697 2077	1.4433 4755	1.5208 9892	126
127	1.2355 1820	1.3025 2945	1.3731 4508	1.4475 5731	1.5259 6858	127
128	1.2375 7739	1.3052 4306	1.3765 7794	1.4517 7935	1.5310 5514	128
129	1.2396 4002	1.3079 6231	1.3800 1938	1.4560 1371	1.5361 5866	129
130	1.2417 0609	1.3106 8723	1.3834 6943	1.4602 6042	1.5412 7919	130
131	1.2437 7560	1.3134 1783	1.3869 2811	1.4645 1951	1.5464 1678	131
132	1.2458 4856	1.3161 5412	1.3903 9543	1.4687 9103	1.5515 7151	132
133	1.2479 2497	1.3188 9611	1.3938 7142	1.4730 7500	1.5567 4341	133
134	1.2500 0485	1.3216 4381	1.3973 5609	1.4773 7147	1.5619 3256	134
135	1.2520 8819	1.3243 9723	1.4008 4948	1.4816 8047	1.5671 3900	135
136	1.2541 7500	1.3271 5639	1.4043 5161	1.4860 0204	1.5723 6279	136
137	1.2562 6529	1.3299 2130	1.4078 6249	1.4903 3621	1.5776 0400	137
138	1.2583 5907	1.3326 9197	1.4113 8214	1.4946 8302	1.5828 6268	138
139	1.2604 5633	1.3354 6841	1.4149 1060	1.4990 4252	1.5881 3889	139
140	1.2625 5709	1.3382 5064	1.4184 4787	1.5034 1472	1.5934 3269	140
141	1.2646 6136	1.3410 3866	1.4219 9399	1.5077 9968	1.5987 4413	141
142	1.2667 6913	1.3438 3249	1.4255 4898	1.5121 9743	1.6040 7328	142
143	1.2688 8041	1.3466 3214	1.4291 1285	1.5166 0801	1.6094 2019	143
144	1.2709 9521	1.3494 3763	1.4326 8563	1.5210 3145	1.6147 8492	144
145	1.2731 1353	1.3522 4896	1.4362 6735	1.5254 6779	1.6201 6754	145
146	1.2752 3539	1.3550 6614	1.4398 5802	1.5299 1707	1.6255 6810	146
147	1.2773 6078	1.3578 8920	1.4434 5766	1.5343 7933	1.6309 8666	147
148	1.2794 8972	1.3607 1813	1.4470 6631	1.5388 5460	1.6364 2328	148
149	1.2816 2220	1.3635 5296	1.4506 8397	1.5433 4293	1.6418 7802	149
150	1.2837 5824	1.3663 9370	1.4543 1068	1.5478 4434	1.6473 5095	150
151	1.2858 9783	1.3692 4035	1.4579 4646	1.5523 5889	1.6528 4212	151
152	1.2880 4100	1.3720 9293	1.4615 9132	1.5568 8660	1.6583 5160	152
153	1.2901 8773	1.3749 5146	1.4652 4530	1.5614 2752	1.6638 7943	153
154	1.2923 3804	1.3778 1594	1.4689 0842	1.5659 8169	1.6694 2570	154
155	1.2944 9194	1.3806 8639	1.4725 8069	1.5705 4913	1.6749 9045	155
156	1.2966 4943	1.3835 6282	1.4762 6214	1.5751 2990	1.6805 7375	156
157	1.2988 1051	1.3864 4525	1.4799 5279	1.5797 2403	1.6861 7567	157
158	1.3009 7519	1.3893 3367	1.4836 5268	1.5843 3156	1.6917 9625	158
159	1.3031 4349	1.3922 2812	1.4873 6181	1.5889 5253	1.6974 3557	159
160	1.3053 1539	1.3951 2859	1.4910 8021	1.5935 8697	1.7030 9369	160
161	1.3074 9092	1.3980 3511	1.4948 0791	1.5982 3493	1.7087 7067	161
162	1.3096 7007	1.4009 4768	1.4985 4493	1.6028 9645	1.7144 6657	162
163	1.3118 5285	1.4038 6633	1.5022 9129	1.6075 7157	1.7201 8146	163
164	1.3140 3927	1.4067 9105	1.5060 4702	1.6122 6032	1.7259 1540	164
165	1.3162 2934	1.4097 2186	1.5098 1214	1.6169 6274	1.7316 6845	165
166	1.3184 2305	1.4126 5878	1.5135 8667	1.6216 7888	1.7374 4068	166
167	1.3206 2043	1.4156 0182	1.5173 7064	1.6264 0878	1.7432 3215	167
168	1.3228 2146	1.4185 5099	1.5211 6406	1.6311 5247	1.7490 4292	168
169	1.3250 2616	1.4215 0631	1.5249 6697	1.6359 1000	1.7548 7306	169
170	1.3272 3454	1.4244 6778	1.5287 7939	1.6406 8140	1.7607 2264	170
171	1.3294 4660	1.4274 3542	1.5326 0134	1.6454 6673	1.7665 9172	171
172	1.3316 6234	1.4304 0924	1.5364 3284	1.6502 6600	1.7724 8035	172
173	1.3338 8178	1.4333 8926	1.5402 7393	1.6550 7928	1.7783 8862	173
174	1.3361 0492	1.4363 7549	1.5441 2461	1.6599 0659	1.7843 1658	174
175	1.3383 3176	1.4393 6794	1.5479 8492	1.6647 4799	1.7902 6431	175
176	1.3405 6231	1.4423 6662	1.5518 5488	1.6696 0350	1.7962 3185	176
177	1.3427 9658	1.4453 7155	1.5557 3452	1.6744 7318	1.8022 1929	177
178	1.3450 3457	1.4483 8274	1.5596 2386	1.6793 5706	1.8082 2669	178
179	1.3472 7630	1.4514 0021	1.5635 2292	1.6842 5518	1.8142 5411	179
180	1.3495 2176	1.4544 2396	1.5674 3172	1.6891 6760	1.8203 0163	180

TABLE I

N	1/6	5/24	1/4	7/24	1/3	N
181	1.3517 7096	1.4574 5401	1.5713 5030	1.6940 9433	1.8263 6930	181
182	1.3540 2391	1.4604 9037	1.5752 7868	1.6990 3544	1.8324 5720	182
183	1.3562 8062	1.4635 3306	1.5792 1688	1.7039 9096	1.8385 6539	183
184	1.3585 4109	1.4665 8209	1.5831 6492	1.7089 6094	1.8446 9394	184
185	1.3608 0532	1.4696 3746	1.5871 2283	1.7139 4541	1.8508 4292	185
186	1.3630 7333	1.4726 9921	1.5910 9064	1.7189 4441	1.8570 1240	186
187	1.3653 4512	1.4757 6733	1.5950 6836	1.7239 5800	1.8632 0244	187
188	1.3676 2070	1.4788 4185	1.5990 5604	1.7289 8621	1.8694 1311	188
189	1.3699 0006	1.4819 2277	1.6030 5368	1.7340 2909	1.8756 4449	189
190	1.3721 8323	1.4850 1011	1.6070 6131	1.7390 8667	1.8818 9664	190
191	1.3744 7020	1.4881 0388	1.6110 7896	1.7441 5901	1.8881 6963	191
192	1.3767 6099	1.4912 0410	1.6151 0666	1.7492 4614	1.8944 6352	192
193	1.3790 5559	1.4943 1077	1.6191 4443	1.7543 4811	1.9007 7840	193
194	1.3813 5401	1.4974 2392	1.6231 9229	1.7594 6496	1.9071 1433	194
195	1.3836 5627	1.5005 4355	1.6272 5027	1.7645 9673	1.9134 7138	195
196	1.3859 6236	1.5036 6968	1.6313 1839	1.7697 4347	1.9198 4962	196
197	1.3882 7230	1.5068 0233	1.6353 9669	1.7749 0522	1.9262 4912	197
198	1.3905 8609	1.5099 4150	1.6394 8518	1.7800 8203	1.9326 6995	198
199	1.3929 0373	1.5130 8721	1.6435 8390	1.7852 7393	1.9391 1218	199
200	1.3952 2524	1.5162 3948	1.6476 9285	1.7904 8098	1.9455 7589	200
201	1.3975 5061	1.5193 9831	1.6518 1209	1.7957 0322	1.9520 6114	201
202	1.3998 7987	1.5225 6372	1.6559 4162	1.8009 4069	1.9585 6801	202
203	1.4022 1300	1.5257 3573	1.6600 8147	1.8061 9343	1.9650 9657	203
204	1.4045 5002	1.5289 1435	1.6642 3168	1.8114 6149	1.9716 4689	204
205	1.4068 9094	1.5320 9958	1.6683 9225	1.8167 4492	1.9782 1905	205
206	1.4092 3576	1.5352 9146	1.6725 6323	1.8220 4376	1.9848 1311	206
207	1.4115 8448	1.5384 8998	1.6767 4464	1.8273 5806	1.9914 2915	207
208	1.4139 3712	1.5416 9517	1.6809 3650	1.8326 8785	1.9980 6725	208
209	1.4162 9368	1.5449 0703	1.6851 3885	1.8380 3319	2.0047 2748	209
210	1.4186 5417	1.5481 2559	1.6893 5169	1.8433 9412	2.0114 0990	210
211	1.4210 1860	1.5513 5085	1.6935 7507	1.8487 7069	2.0181 1460	211
212	1.4233 8696	1.5545 8283	1.6978 0901	1.8541 6294	2.0248 4165	212
213	1.4257 5927	1.5578 2155	1.7020 5353	1.8595 7091	2.0315 9112	213
214	1.4281 3554	1.5610 6701	1.7063 0867	1.8649 9466	2.0383 6309	214
215	1.4305 1576	1.5643 1923	1.7105 7444	1.8704 3423	2.0451 5764	215
216	1.4328 9996	1.5675 7823	1.7148 5087	1.8758 8966	2.0519 7483	216
217	1.4352 8812	1.5708 4402	1.7191 3800	1.8813 6101	2.0588 1474	217
218	1.4376 8027	1.5741 1661	1.7234 3585	1.8868 4831	2.0656 7746	218
219	1.4400 7640	1.5773 9602	1.7277 4444	1.8923 5162	2.0725 6305	219
220	1.4424 7653	1.5806 8226	1.7320 6380	1.8978 7097	2.0794 7159	220
221	1.4448 8066	1.5839 7535	1.7363 9396	1.9034 0643	2.0864 0317	221
222	1.4472 8879	1.5872 7530	1.7407 3494	1.9089 5803	2.0933 5784	222
223	1.4497 0094	1.5905 8212	1.7450 8678	1.9145 2583	2.1003 3570	223
224	1.4521 1711	1.5938 9583	1.7494 4950	1.9201 0986	2.1073 3682	224
225	1.4545 3731	1.5972 1645	1.7538 2312	1.9257 1018	2.1143 6128	225
226	1.4569 6153	1.6005 4398	1.7582 0768	1.9313 2684	2.1214 0915	226
227	1.4593 8980	1.6038 7845	1.7626 0320	1.9369 5987	2.1284 8051	227
228	1.4618 2212	1.6072 1987	1.7670 0970	1.9426 0934	2.1355 7545	228
229	1.4642 5849	1.6105 6824	1.7714 2723	1.9482 7528	2.1426 9403	229
230	1.4666 9892	1.6139 2359	1.7758 5580	1.9539 5775	2.1498 3635	230
231	1.4691 4342	1.6172 8593	1.7802 9544	1.9596 5680	2.1570 0247	231
232	1.4715 9199	1.6206 5528	1.7847 4617	1.9653 7246	2.1641 9248	232
233	1.4740 4464	1.6240 3164	1.7892 0804	1.9711 0480	2.1714 0645	233
234	1.4765 0139	1.6274 1504	1.7936 8106	1.9768 5385	2.1786 4447	234
235	1.4789 6222	1.6308 0549	1.7981 6526	1.9826 1968	2.1859 0662	235
236	1.4814 2716	1.6342 0300	1.8026 6068	1.9884 0232	2.1931 9298	236
237	1.4838 9620	1.6376 0759	1.8071 6733	1.9942 0183	2.2005 0362	237
238	1.4863 6936	1.6410 1927	1.8116 8525	2.0000 1825	2.2078 3863	238
239	1.4888 4665	1.6444 3806	1.8162 1446	2.0058 5163	2.2151 9809	239
240	1.4913 2806	1.6478 6398	1.8207 5500	2.0117 0203	2.2225 8209	240

TABLE I

N	1/6	5/24	1/4	7/24	1/3	N
241	1.4938 1360	1.6512 9703	1.8253 0688	2.0175 6950	2.2299 9069	241
242	1.4963 0329	1.6547 3723	1.8298 7015	2.0234 5408	2.2374 2400	242
243	1.4987 9713	1.6581 8460	1.8344 4483	2.0293 5582	2.2448 8208	243
244	1.5012 9513	1.6616 3915	1.8390 3094	2.0352 7477	2.2523 6502	244
245	1.5037 9729	1.6651 0090	1.8436 2851	2.0412 1099	2.2598 7290	245
246	1.5063 0361	1.6685 6986	1.8482 3759	2.0471 6452	2.2674 0581	246
247	1.5088 1412	1.6720 4604	1.8528 5818	2.0531 3542	2.2749 6383	247
248	1.5113 2881	1.6755 2947	1.8574 9033	2.0591 2373	2.2825 4704	248
249	1.5138 4769	1.6790 2016	1.8621 3405	2.0651 2951	2.2901 5553	249
250	1.5163 7077	1.6825 1812	1.8667 8939	2.0711 5280	2.2977 8938	250
251	1.5188 9806	1.6860 2336	1.8714 5636	2.0771 9367	2.3054 4868	251
252	1.5214 2955	1.6895 3591	1.8761 3500	2.0832 5215	2.3131 3351	252
253	1.5239 6527	1.6930 5578	1.8808 2534	2.0893 2830	2.3208 4396	253
254	1.5265 0521	1.6965 8298	1.8855 2740	2.0954 2217	2.3285 8010	254
255	1.5290 4939	1.7001 1753	1.8902 4122	2.1015 3382	2.3363 4204	255
256	1.5315 9780	1.7036 5944	1.8949 6682	2.1076 6329	2.3441 2984	256
257	1.5341 5047	1.7072 0873	1.8997 0424	2.1138 1065	2.3519 4361	257
258	1.5367 0738	1.7107 6541	1.9044 5350	2.1199 7593	2.3597 8342	258
259	1.5392 6856	1.7143 2951	1.9092 1463	2.1261 5919	2.3676 4937	259
260	1.5418 3401	1.7179 0103	1.9139 8767	2.1323 6049	2.3755 4153	260
261	1.5444 0373	1.7214 7999	1.9187 7264	2.1385 7987	2.3834 6000	261
262	1.5469 7774	1.7250 6641	1.9235 6957	2.1448 1740	2.3914 0487	262
263	1.5495 5604	1.7286 6029	1.9283 7850	2.1510 7311	2.3993 7622	263
264	1.5521 3863	1.7322 6167	1.9331 9944	2.1573 4708	2.4073 7414	264
265	1.5547 2553	1.7358 7055	1.9380 3244	2.1636 3934	2.4153 9872	265
266	1.5573 1674	1.7394 8694	1.9428 7752	2.1699 4995	2.4234 5005	266
267	1.5599 1226	1.7431 1088	1.9477 3472	2.1762 7898	2.4315 2822	267
268	1.5625 1212	1.7467 4236	1.9526 0405	2.1826 2646	2.4396 3331	268
269	1.5651 1630	1.7503 8140	1.9574 8556	2.1889 9245	2.4477 6542	269
270	1.5677 2483	1.7540 2803	1.9623 7928	2.1953 7701	2.4559 2464	270
271	1.5703 3771	1.7576 8226	1.9672 8522	2.2017 8019	2.4641 1105	271
272	1.5729 5494	1.7613 4409	1.9722 0344	2.2082 0205	2.4723 2476	272
273	1.5755 7653	1.7650 1356	1.9771 3395	2.2146 4264	2.4805 6584	273
274	1.5782 0249	1.7686 9067	1.9820 7678	2.2211 0202	2.4888 3439	274
275	1.5808 3283	1.7723 7544	1.9870 3197	2.2275 8023	2.4971 3051	275
276	1.5834 6755	1.7760 6789	1.9919 9955	2.2340 7734	2.5054 5428	276
277	1.5861 0666	1.7797 6804	1.9969 7955	2.2405 9340	2.5138 0579	277
278	1.5887 5017	1.7834 7589	2.0019 7200	2.2471 2846	2.5221 8514	278
279	1.5913 9809	1.7871 9146	2.0069 7693	2.2536 8259	2.5305 9243	279
280	1.5940 5042	1.7909 1478	2.0119 9437	2.2602 5583	2.5390 2773	280
281	1.5967 0717	1.7946 4585	2.0170 2436	2.2668 4824	2.5474 9116	281
282	1.5993 6835	1.7983 8469	2.0220 6692	2.2734 5988	2.5559 8280	282
283	1.6020 3396	1.8021 3133	2.0271 2209	2.2800 9081	2.5645 0274	283
284	1.6047 0402	1.8058 8577	2.0321 8989	2.2867 4107	2.5730 5108	284
285	1.6073 7852	1.8096 4803	2.0372 7037	2.2934 1073	2.5816 2792	285
286	1.6100 5749	1.8134 1813	2.0423 6354	2.3000 9985	2.5902 3335	286
287	1.6127 4092	1.8171 9609	2.0474 6945	2.3068 0847	2.5988 6746	287
288	1.6154 2882	1.8209 8191	2.0525 8813	2.3135 3666	2.6075 3035	288
289	1.6181 2120	1.8247 7562	2.0577 1960	2.3202 8448	2.6162 2212	289
290	1.6208 1807	1.8285 7724	2.0628 6389	2.3270 5197	2.6249 4286	290
291	1.6235 1943	1.8323 8677	2.0680 2105	2.3338 3921	2.6336 9267	291
292	1.6262 2530	1.8362 0425	2.0731 9111	2.3406 4624	2.6424 7164	292
293	1.6289 3567	1.8400 2967	2.0783 7409	2.3474 7313	2.6512 7988	293
294	1.6316 5057	1.8438 6307	2.0835 7002	2.3543 1992	2.6601 1748	294
295	1.6343 6998	1.8477 0445	2.0887 7895	2.3611 8669	2.6689 8454	295
296	1.6370 9393	1.8515 5383	2.0940 0089	2.3680 7348	2.6778 8115	296
297	1.6398 2242	1.8554 1124	2.0992 3589	2.3749 8036	2.6868 0742	297
298	1.6425 5546	1.8592 7668	2.1044 8398	2.3819 0739	2.6957 6345	298
299	1.6452 9305	1.8631 5017	2.1097 4519	2.3888 5462	2.7047 4933	299
300	1.6480 3521	1.8670 3173	2.1150 1956	2.3958 2211	2.7137 6516	300

TABLE I

N	1/6	5/24	1/4	7/24	1/3	N
301	1.6507 8193	1.8709 2138	2.1203 0711	2.4028 0993	2.7228 1104	301
302	1.6535 3324	1.8748 1914	2.1256 0787	2.4098 1812	2.7318 8708	302
303	1.6562 8513	1.8787 2501	2.1309 2189	2.4168 4676	2.7409 9337	303
304	1.6590 4961	1.8826 3902	2.1362 4920	2.4238 9590	2.7501 3001	304
305	1.6618 1469	1.8865 6118	2.1415 8982	2.4309 6559	2.7592 9711	305
306	1.6645 8438	1.8904 9152	2.1469 4380	2.4380 5591	2.7684 9477	306
307	1.6673 5869	1.8944 3004	2.1523 1116	2.4451 6690	2.7777 2309	307
308	1.6701 3762	1.8983 7677	2.1576 9193	2.4522 9864	2.7869 8216	308
309	1.6729 2118	1.9023 3172	2.1630 8616	2.4594 5118	2.7962 7210	309
310	1.6757 0938	1.9062 9492	2.1684 9388	2.4666 2458	2.8055 9301	310
311	1.6785 0223	1.9102 6636	2.1739 1511	2.4738 1890	2.8149 4499	311
312	1.6812 9974	1.9142 4608	2.1793 4990	2.4810 3421	2.8243 2814	312
313	1.6841 0190	1.9182 3410	2.1847 9828	2.4882 7055	2.8337 4256	313
314	1.6869 0874	1.9222 3042	2.1902 6027	2.4955 2801	2.8431 8837	314
315	1.6897 2025	1.9262 3506	2.1957 3592	2.5028 0663	2.8526 6567	315
316	1.6925 3646	1.9302 4805	2.2012 2526	2.5101 0649	2.8621 7455	316
317	1.6953 5735	1.9342 6940	2.2067 2833	2.5174 2763	2.8717 1514	317
318	1.6981 8294	1.9382 9913	2.2122 4515	2.5247 7013	2.8812 8752	318
319	1.7010 1325	1.9423 3726	2.2177 7576	2.5321 3404	2.8908 9181	319
320	1.7038 4827	1.9463 8379	2.2233 2020	2.5395 1943	2.9005 2812	320
321	1.7066 8802	1.9504 3876	2.2288 7850	2.5469 2636	2.9101 9654	321
322	1.7095 3250	1.9545 0217	2.2344 5070	2.5543 5490	2.9198 9720	322
323	1.7123 8172	1.9585 7405	2.2400 3682	2.5618 0510	2.9296 3019	323
324	1.7152 3569	1.9626 5441	2.2456 3691	2.5692 7703	2.9393 9562	324
325	1.7180 9442	1.9667 4328	2.2512 5101	2.5767 7076	2.9491 9361	325
326	1.7209 5791	1.9708 4066	2.2568 7913	2.5842 8634	2.9590 2425	326
327	1.7238 2617	1.9749 4658	2.2625 2133	2.5918 2384	2.9688 8767	327
328	1.7266 9921	1.9790 6105	2.2681 7764	2.5993 8333	2.9787 8396	328
329	1.7295 7705	1.9831 8409	2.2738 4808	2.6069 6486	2.9887 1324	329
330	1.7324 5967	1.9873 1573	2.2795 3270	2.6145 6851	2.9986 7562	330
331	1.7353 4711	1.9914 5597	2.2852 3153	2.6221 9433	3.0086 7120	331
332	1.7382 3935	1.9956 0483	2.2909 4461	2.6298 4240	3.0187 0011	332
333	1.7411 3642	1.9997 6234	2.2966 7197	2.6375 1277	3.0287 6244	333
334	1.7440 3831	2.0039 2852	2.3024 1365	2.6452 0552	3.0388 5832	334
335	1.7469 4504	2.0081 0337	2.3081 6969	2.6529 2070	3.0489 8784	335
336	1.7498 5662	2.0122 8692	2.3139 4011	2.6606 5839	3.0591 5114	336
337	1.7527 7304	2.0164 7918	2.3197 2496	2.6684 1864	3.0693 4831	337
338	1.7556 9433	2.0206 8018	2.3255 2427	2.6762 0153	3.0795 7947	338
339	1.7586 2049	2.0248 8993	2.3313 3808	2.6840 0712	3.0898 4473	339
340	1.7615 5152	2.0291 0845	2.3371 6643	2.6918 3547	3.1001 4422	340
341	1.7644 8744	2.0333 3576	2.3430 0934	2.6996 8666	3.1104 7803	341
342	1.7674 2826	2.0375 7188	2.3488 6687	2.7075 6074	3.1208 4629	342
343	1.7703 7397	2.0418 1682	2.3547 3903	2.7154 5780	3.1312 4911	343
344	1.7733 2459	2.0460 7060	2.3606 2588	2.7233 7788	3.1416 8661	344
345	1.7762 8013	2.0503 3325	2.3665 2745	2.7313 2107	3.1521 5890	345
346	1.7792 4060	2.0546 0478	2.3724 4377	2.7392 8742	3.1626 6609	346
347	1.7822 0600	2.0588 8520	2.3783 7488	2.7472 7701	3.1732 0831	347
348	1.7851 7634	2.0631 7455	2.3843 2081	2.7552 8990	3.1837 8567	348
349	1.7881 5164	2.0674 7283	2.3902 8161	2.7633 2616	3.1943 9829	349
350	1.7911 3189	2.0717 8006	2.3962 5732	2.7713 8586	3.2050 4629	350
351	1.7941 1711	2.0760 9627	2.4022 4796	2.7794 6907	3.2157 2977	351
352	1.7971 0731	2.0804 2147	2.4082 5358	2.7875 7586	3.2264 4887	352
353	1.8001 0249	2.0847 5568	2.4142 7422	2.7957 0629	3.2372 0370	353
354	1.8031 0266	2.0890 9892	2.4203 0990	2.8038 6043	3.2479 9438	354
355	1.8061 0783	2.0934 5121	2.4263 6068	2.8120 3836	3.2588 2103	355
356	1.8091 1801	2.0978 1257	2.4324 2658	2.8202 4013	3.2696 8377	356
357	1.8121 3320	2.1021 8301	2.4385 0764	2.8284 6583	3.2805 8271	357
358	1.8151 5343	2.1065 6256	2.4446 0391	2.8367 1553	3.2915 1799	358
359	1.8181 7868	2.1109 5123	2.4507 1542	2.8449 8928	3.3024 8972	359
360	1.8212 0898	2.1153 4905	2.4568 4221	2.8532 8717	3.3134 9801	360

TABLE I

N	3/8	5/12	11/24	1/2	13/24	N
1	1.0037 5000	1.0041 6667	1.0045 8333	1.0050 0000	1.0054 1667	1
2	1.0075 1406	1.0083 5069	1.0091 8767	1.0100 2500	1.0108 6267	2
3	1.0112 9224	1.0125 5216	1.0138 1312	1.0150 7512	1.0163 3818	3
4	1.0150 8459	1.0167 7112	1.0184 5976	1.0201 5050	1.0218 4334	4
5	1.0188 9115	1.0210 0767	1.0231 2770	1.0252 5125	1.0273 7833	5
6	1.0227 1200	1.0252 6187	1.0278 1704	1.0303 7751	1.0329 4330	6
7	1.0265 4717	1.0295 3379	1.0325 2786	1.0355 2940	1.0385 3841	7
8	1.0303 9672	1.0338 2352	1.0372 6028	1.0407 0704	1.0441 6382	8
9	1.0342 6070	1.0381 3111	1.0420 1439	1.0459 1058	1.0498 1971	9
10	1.0381 3918	1.0424 5666	1.0467 9029	1.0511 4013	1.0555 0623	10
11	1.0420 3220	1.0468 0023	1.0515 8808	1.0563 9583	1.0612 2356	11
12	1.0459 3983	1.0511 6190	1.0564 0786	1.0616 7781	1.0669 7185	12
13	1.0498 6210	1.0555 4174	1.0612 4973	1.0669 8620	1.0727 5128	13
14	1.0537 9908	1.0599 3983	1.0661 1379	1.0723 2113	1.0785 6202	14
15	1.0577 5083	1.0643 5625	1.0710 0015	1.0776 8274	1.0844 0423	15
16	1.0617 1739	1.0687 9106	1.0759 0890	1.0830 7115	1.0902 7809	16
17	1.0656 9883	1.0732 4436	1.0808 4015	1.0884 8651	1.0961 8376	17
18	1.0696 9521	1.0777 1621	1.0857 9400	1.0939 2894	1.1021 2142	18
19	1.0737 0656	1.0822 0670	1.0907 7055	1.0993 9858	1.1080 9125	19
20	1.0777 3296	1.0867 1589	1.0957 6992	1.1048 9558	1.1140 9341	20
21	1.0817 7446	1.0912 4387	1.1007 9220	1.1104 2006	1.1201 2808	21
22	1.0858 3111	1.0957 9072	1.1058 3749	1.1159 7216	1.1261 9544	22
23	1.0899 0298	1.1003 5652	1.1109 0592	1.1215 5202	1.1322 9566	23
24	1.0939 9012	1.1049 4134	1.1159 9757	1.1271 5978	1.1384 2893	24
25	1.0980 9258	1.1095 4526	1.1211 1256	1.1327 9558	1.1445 9542	25
26	1.1022 1043	1.1141 6836	1.1262 5099	1.1384 5955	1.1507 9531	26
27	1.1063 4372	1.1188 1073	1.1314 1297	1.1441 5185	1.1570 2879	27
28	1.1104 9251	1.1234 7244	1.1365 9862	1.1498 7261	1.1632 9603	28
29	1.1146 5685	1.1281 5358	1.1418 0803	1.1556 2197	1.1695 9722	29
30	1.1188 3682	1.1328 5422	1.1470 4131	1.1614 0008	1.1759 3253	30
31	1.1230 3245	1.1375 7444	1.1522 9859	1.1672 0708	1.1823 0217	31
32	1.1272 4383	1.1423 1434	1.1575 7995	1.1730 4312	1.1887 0631	32
33	1.1314 7099	1.1470 7398	1.1628 8553	1.1789 0833	1.1951 4513	33
34	1.1357 1401	1.1518 5346	1.1682 1542	1.1848 0288	1.2016 1883	34
35	1.1399 7293	1.1566 5284	1.1735 6974	1.1907 2689	1.2081 2760	35
36	1.1442 4783	1.1614 7223	1.1789 4860	1.1966 8052	1.2146 7163	36
37	1.1485 3876	1.1663 1170	1.1843 5212	1.2026 6393	1.2212 5110	37
38	1.1528 4578	1.1711 7133	1.1897 8040	1.2086 7725	1.2278 6621	38
39	1.1571 6895	1.1760 5121	1.1952 3356	1.2147 2063	1.2345 1715	39
40	1.1615 0834	1.1809 5142	1.2007 1171	1.2207 9424	1.2412 0412	40
41	1.1658 6399	1.1858 7206	1.2062 1497	1.2268 9821	1.2479 2731	41
42	1.1702 3598	1.1908 1319	1.2117 4346	1.2330 3270	1.2546 8691	42
43	1.1746 2437	1.1957 7491	1.2172 9728	1.2391 9786	1.2614 8313	43
44	1.1790 2921	1.2007 5731	1.2228 7656	1.2453 9385	1.2683 1617	44
45	1.1834 5057	1.2057 6046	1.2284 8141	1.2516 2082	1.2751 8621	45
46	1.1878 8851	1.2107 8446	1.2341 1195	1.2578 7892	1.2820 9347	46
47	1.1923 4309	1.2158 2940	1.2397 6830	1.2641 6832	1.2890 3815	47
48	1.1968 1438	1.2208 9536	1.2454 5057	1.2704 8916	1.2960 2044	48
49	1.2013 0243	1.2259 8242	1.2511 5889	1.2768 4161	1.3030 4055	49
50	1.2058 0732	1.2310 9068	1.2568 9336	1.2832 2581	1.3100 9868	50
51	1.2103 2909	1.2362 2022	1.2626 5413	1.2896 4194	1.3171 9505	51
52	1.2148 6783	1.2413 7114	1.2684 4129	1.2960 9015	1.3243 2986	52
53	1.2194 2358	1.2465 4352	1.2742 5498	1.3025 7060	1.3315 0331	53
54	1.2239 9642	1.2517 3745	1.2800 9531	1.3090 8346	1.3387 1562	54
55	1.2285 8641	1.2569 5302	1.2859 6242	1.3156 2887	1.3459 6700	55
56	1.2331 9361	1.2621 9033	1.2918 5641	1.3222 0702	1.3532 5765	56
57	1.2378 1808	1.2674 4946	1.2977 7742	1.3288 1805	1.3605 8780	57
58	1.2424 5990	1.2727 3050	1.3037 2557	1.3354 6214	1.3679 5765	58
59	1.2471 1912	1.2780 3354	1.3097 0098	1.3421 3946	1.3753 6742	59
60	1.2517 9582	1.2833 5868	1.3157 0377	1.3488 5015	1.3828 1732	60

TABLE I

N	3/8	5/12	11/24	1/2	13/24	N
61	1.2564 9005	1.2887 0601	1.3217 3408	1.3555 9440	1.3903 0758	61
62	1.2612 0189	1.2940 7561	1.3277 9203	1.3623 7238	1.3978 3842	62
63	1.2659 3140	1.2994 6760	1.3338 7774	1.3691 8424	1.4054 1004	63
64	1.2706 7864	1.3048 8204	1.3399 9135	1.3760 3016	1.4130 2268	64
65	1.2754 4369	1.3103 1905	1.3461 3298	1.3829 1031	1.4206 7655	65
66	1.2802 2660	1.3157 7872	1.3523 0275	1.3898 2486	1.4283 7188	66
67	1.2850 2745	1.3212 6113	1.3585 0081	1.3967 7399	1.4361 0890	67
68	1.2898 4630	1.3267 6638	1.3647 2727	1.4037 5785	1.4438 8782	68
69	1.2946 8323	1.3322 9458	1.3709 8227	1.4107 7664	1.4517 0888	69
70	1.2995 3829	1.3378 4580	1.3772 6594	1.4178 3053	1.4595 7230	70
71	1.3044 1156	1.3434 2016	1.3835 7841	1.4249 1968	1.4674 7832	71
72	1.3093 0310	1.3490 1774	1.3899 1981	1.4320 4428	1.4754 2716	72
73	1.3142 1299	1.3546 3865	1.3962 9027	1.4392 0450	1.4834 1906	73
74	1.3191 4129	1.3602 8298	1.4026 8994	1.4464 0052	1.4914 5425	74
75	1.3240 8807	1.3659 5082	1.4091 1893	1.4536 3252	1.4995 3296	75
76	1.3290 5340	1.3716 4229	1.4155 7739	1.4609 0069	1.5076 5543	76
77	1.3340 3735	1.3773 5746	1.4220 6546	1.4682 0519	1.5158 2189	77
78	1.3390 3999	1.3830 9645	1.4285 8326	1.4755 4622	1.5240 3259	78
79	1.3440 6139	1.3888 5935	1.4351 3093	1.4829 2395	1.5322 8777	79
80	1.3491 0162	1.3946 4627	1.4417 0861	1.4903 3857	1.5405 8766	80
81	1.3541 6075	1.4004 5729	1.4483 1645	1.4977 9026	1.5489 3251	81
82	1.3592 3885	1.4062 9253	1.4549 5456	1.5052 7921	1.5573 2256	82
83	1.3643 3600	1.4121 5209	1.4616 2310	1.5128 0561	1.5657 5806	83
84	1.3694 5226	1.4180 3605	1.4683 2221	1.5203 6964	1.5742 3925	84
85	1.3745 8770	1.4239 4454	1.4750 5202	1.5279 7148	1.5827 6638	85
86	1.3797 4241	1.4298 7764	1.4818 1267	1.5356 1134	1.5913 3970	86
87	1.3849 1644	1.4358 3546	1.4886 0432	1.5432 8940	1.5999 5945	87
88	1.3901 0988	1.4418 1811	1.4954 2709	1.5510 0585	1.6086 2590	88
89	1.3953 2279	1.4478 2568	1.5022 8113	1.5587 6087	1.6173 3929	89
90	1.4005 5525	1.4538 5829	1.5091 6658	1.5665 5468	1.6260 9988	90
91	1.4058 0733	1.4599 1603	1.5160 8360	1.5743 8745	1.6349 0792	91
92	1.4110 7911	1.4659 9902	1.5230 3231	1.5822 5939	1.6437 6367	92
93	1.4163 7066	1.4721 0735	1.5300 1288	1.5901 7069	1.6526 6739	93
94	1.4216 8205	1.4782 4113	1.5370 2544	1.5981 2154	1.6616 1934	94
95	1.4270 1335	1.4844 0047	1.5440 7014	1.6061 1215	1.6706 1978	95
96	1.4323 6465	1.4905 8547	1.5511 4712	1.6141 4271	1.6796 6897	96
97	1.4377 3602	1.4967 9624	1.5582 5655	1.6222 1342	1.6887 6718	97
98	1.4431 2753	1.5030 3289	1.5653 9856	1.6303 2449	1.6979 1466	98
99	1.4485 3926	1.5092 9553	1.5725 7330	1.6384 7611	1.7071 1170	99
100	1.4539 7128	1.5155 8426	1.5797 8093	1.6466 6849	1.7163 5856	100
101	1.4594 2367	1.5218 9919	1.5870 2159	1.6549 0183	1.7256 5550	101
102	1.4648 9651	1.5282 4044	1.5942 9544	1.6631 7634	1.7350 0280	102
103	1.4703 8988	1.5346 0811	1.6016 0263	1.6714 9223	1.7444 0073	103
104	1.4759 0384	1.5410 0231	1.6089 4331	1.6798 4969	1.7538 4957	104
105	1.4814 3848	1.5474 2315	1.6163 1763	1.6882 4894	1.7633 4959	105
106	1.4869 9387	1.5538 7075	1.6237 2575	1.6966 9018	1.7729 0107	106
107	1.4925 7010	1.5603 4521	1.6311 6783	1.7051 7363	1.7825 0428	107
108	1.4981 6724	1.5668 4665	1.6386 4401	1.7136 9950	1.7921 5951	108
109	1.5037 8536	1.5733 7518	1.6461 5447	1.7222 6800	1.8018 6704	109
110	1.5094 2456	1.5799 3091	1.6536 9934	1.7308 7934	1.8116 2715	110
111	1.5150 8490	1.5865 1395	1.6612 7880	1.7395 3373	1.8214 4013	111
112	1.5207 6647	1.5931 2443	1.6688 9299	1.7482 3140	1.8313 0627	112
113	1.5264 6934	1.5997 6245	1.6765 4208	1.7569 7256	1.8412 2584	113
114	1.5321 9360	1.6064 2812	1.6842 2623	1.7657 5742	1.8511 9915	114
115	1.5379 3933	1.6131 2157	1.6919 4560	1.7745 8621	1.8612 2648	115
116	1.5437 0660	1.6198 4291	1.6997 0036	1.7834 5914	1.8713 0812	116
117	1.5494 9550	1.6265 9226	1.7074 9065	1.7923 7644	1.8814 4438	117
118	1.5553 0611	1.6333 6973	1.7153 1665	1.8013 3832	1.8916 3553	118
119	1.5611 3851	1.6401 7543	1.7231 7852	1.8103 4501	1.9018 8189	119
120	1.5669 9278	1.6470 0950	1.7310 7642	1.8193 9673	1.9121 8375	120

TABLE I

N	3/8	5/12	11/24	1/2	13/24	N
121	1.5728 6900	1.6538 7204	1.7390 1052	1.8284 9372	1.9225 4141	121
122	1.5787 6726	1.6607 6317	1.7469 8098	1.8376 3619	1.9329 5518	122
123	1.5846 8764	1.6676 8302	1.7549 8798	1.8468 2437	1.9434 2535	123
124	1.5906 3021	1.6746 3170	1.7630 3167	1.8560 5849	1.9539 5224	124
125	1.5965 9508	1.6816 0933	1.7711 1224	1.8653 3878	1.9645 3615	125
126	1.6025 8231	1.6886 1603	1.7792 2983	1.8746 6548	1.9751 7739	126
127	1.6085 9199	1.6956 5193	1.7873 8464	1.8840 3880	1.9858 7626	127
128	1.6146 2421	1.7027 1715	1.7955 7682	1.8934 5900	1.9966 3309	128
129	1.6206 7905	1.7098 1181	1.8038 0654	1.9029 2629	2.0074 4819	129
130	1.6267 5660	1.7169 3602	1.8120 7399	1.9124 4092	2.0183 2187	130
131	1.6328 5694	1.7240 8992	1.8203 7933	1.9220 0313	2.0292 5444	131
132	1.6389 8015	1.7312 7363	1.8287 2273	1.9316 1314	2.0402 4624	132
133	1.6451 2633	1.7384 8727	1.8371 0438	1.9412 7121	2.0512 9757	133
134	1.6512 9555	1.7457 3097	1.8455 2444	1.9509 7757	2.0624 0877	134
135	1.6574 8791	1.7530 0485	1.8539 8310	1.9607 3245	2.0735 8015	135
136	1.6637 0349	1.7603 0903	1.8624 8052	1.9705 3612	2.0848 1204	136
137	1.6699 4238	1.7676 4365	1.8710 1689	1.9803 8880	2.0961 0477	137
138	1.6762 0466	1.7750 0884	1.8795 9238	1.9902 9074	2.1074 5867	138
139	1.6824 9043	1.7824 0471	1.8882 0718	2.0002 4219	2.1188 7408	139
140	1.6887 9977	1.7898 3139	1.8968 6146	2.0102 4340	2.1303 5131	140
141	1.6951 3277	1.7972 8902	1.9055 5541	2.0202 9462	2.1418 9071	141
142	1.7014 8951	1.8047 7773	1.9142 8921	2.0303 9609	2.1534 9262	142
143	1.7078 7010	1.8122 9763	1.9230 6303	2.0405 4808	2.1651 5737	143
144	1.7142 7461	1.8198 4887	1.9318 7707	2.0507 5082	2.1768 8531	144
145	1.7207 0314	1.8274 3158	1.9407 3151	2.0610 0457	2.1886 7677	145
146	1.7271 5578	1.8350 4588	1.9496 2653	2.0713 0959	2.2005 3210	146
147	1.7336 3261	1.8426 9190	1.9585 6231	2.0816 6614	2.2124 5165	147
148	1.7401 3373	1.8503 6978	1.9675 3906	2.0920 7447	2.2244 3577	148
149	1.7466 5924	1.8580 7966	1.9765 5695	2.1025 3484	2.2364 8479	149
150	1.7532 0921	1.8658 2166	1.9856 1617	2.1130 4752	2.2485 9908	150
151	1.7597 8374	1.8735 9591	1.9947 1691	2.1236 1276	2.2607 7900	151
152	1.7663 8293	1.8814 0256	2.0038 5936	2.1342 3082	2.2730 2488	152
153	1.7730 0687	1.8892 4174	2.0130 4371	2.1449 0197	2.2853 3710	153
154	1.7796 5564	1.8971 1358	2.0222 7016	2.1556 2648	2.2977 1601	154
155	1.7863 2935	1.9050 1822	2.0315 3890	2.1664 0462	2.3101 6197	155
156	1.7930 2809	1.9129 5580	2.0408 5012	2.1772 3664	2.3226 7535	156
157	1.7997 5194	1.9209 2645	2.0502 0402	2.1881 2282	2.3352 5651	157
158	1.8065 0101	1.9289 3031	2.0596 0079	2.1990 6344	2.3479 0581	158
159	1.8132 7539	1.9369 6752	2.0690 4062	2.2100 5875	2.3606 2364	159
160	1.8200 7517	1.9450 3821	2.0785 2373	2.2211 0905	2.3734 1035	160
161	1.8269 0046	1.9531 4254	2.0880 5029	2.2322 1459	2.3862 6632	161
162	1.8337 5133	1.9612 8063	2.0976 2052	2.2433 7566	2.3991 9193	162
163	1.8406 2790	1.9694 5264	2.1072 3462	2.2545 9254	2.4121 8755	163
164	1.8475 3025	1.9776 5869	2.1168 9278	2.2658 6551	2.4252 5357	164
165	1.8544 5849	1.9858 9893	2.1265 9520	2.2771 9483	2.4383 9036	165
166	1.8614 1271	1.9941 7351	2.1363 4210	2.2885 8081	2.4515 9831	166
167	1.8683 9301	2.0024 8257	2.1461 3367	2.3000 2371	2.4648 7780	167
168	1.8753 9948	2.0108 2625	2.1559 7011	2.3115 2383	2.4782 2922	168
169	1.8824 3223	2.0192 0469	2.1658 5164	2.3230 8145	2.4916 5296	169
170	1.8894 9135	2.0276 1804	2.1757 7846	2.3346 9686	2.5051 4941	170
171	1.8965 7695	2.0360 6645	2.1857 5078	2.3463 7034	2.5187 1897	171
172	1.9036 8911	2.0445 5006	2.1957 6880	2.3581 0219	2.5323 6203	172
173	1.9108 2794	2.0530 6902	2.2058 3274	2.3698 9270	2.5460 7900	173
174	1.9179 9355	2.0616 2347	2.2159 4281	2.3817 4217	2.5598 7026	174
175	1.9251 8602	2.0702 1357	2.2260 9922	2.3936 5088	2.5737 3622	175
176	1.9324 0547	2.0788 3946	2.2363 0217	2.4056 1913	2.5876 7729	176
177	1.9396 5199	2.0875 0129	2.2465 5189	2.4176 4723	2.6016 9388	177
178	1.9469 2569	2.0961 9921	2.2568 4858	2.4297 3546	2.6157 8639	178
179	1.9542 2666	2.1049 3338	2.2671 9247	2.4418 8414	2.6299 5523	179
180	1.9615 5501	2.1137 0393	2.2775 8377	2.4540 9356	2.6442 0082	180

TABLE I

N	3/8	5/12	11/24	1/2	13/24	N
181	1.9689 1084	2.1225 1103	2.2880 2270	2.4663 6403	2.6585 2357	181
182	1.9762 9426	2.1313 5483	2.2985 0947	2.4786 9585	2.6729 2391	182
183	1.9837 0536	2.1402 3547	2.3090 4430	2.4910 8933	2.6874 0225	183
184	1.9911 4425	2.1491 5312	2.3196 2742	2.5035 4478	2.7019 5901	184
185	1.9986 1104	2.1581 0793	2.3302 5905	2.5160 6250	2.7165 9462	185
186	2.0061 0584	2.1671 0004	2.3409 3940	2.5286 4281	2.7313 0951	186
187	2.0136 2873	2.1761 2963	2.3516 6871	2.5412 8603	2.7461 0410	187
188	2.0211 7984	2.1851 9683	2.3624 4719	2.5539 9246	2.7609 7883	188
189	2.0287 5927	2.1943 0182	2.3732 7507	2.5667 6242	2.7759 3413	189
190	2.0363 6711	2.2034 4474	2.3841 5258	2.5795 9623	2.7909 7044	190
191	2.0440 0349	2.2126 2576	2.3950 7995	2.5924 9421	2.8060 8820	191
192	2.0516 6850	2.2218 4504	2.4060 5740	2.6054 5668	2.8212 8785	192
193	2.0593 6226	2.2311 0272	2.4170 8516	2.6184 8397	2.8365 6982	193
194	2.0670 8487	2.2403 9899	2.4281 6347	2.6315 7639	2.8519 3457	194
195	2.0748 3644	2.2497 3398	2.4392 9255	2.6447 3427	2.8673 8255	195
196	2.0826 1707	2.2591 0787	2.4504 7264	2.6579 5794	2.8829 1421	196
197	2.0904 2689	2.2685 2082	2.4617 0398	2.6712 4773	2.8985 2999	197
198	2.0982 6599	2.2779 7299	2.4729 8679	2.6846 0397	2.9142 3037	198
199	2.1061 3448	2.2874 6455	2.4843 2131	2.6980 2699	2.9300 1578	199
200	2.1140 3249	2.2969 9565	2.4957 0778	2.7115 1712	2.9458 8670	200
201	2.1219 6011	2.3065 6646	2.5071 4644	2.7250 7471	2.9618 4358	201
202	2.1299 1746	2.3161 7716	2.5186 3753	2.7387 0008	2.9778 8690	202
203	2.1379 0465	2.3258 2790	2.5301 8129	2.7523 9358	2.9940 1712	203
204	2.1459 2179	2.3355 1885	2.5417 7795	2.7661 5555	3.0102 3472	204
205	2.1539 6900	2.3452 5017	2.5534 2777	2.7799 8633	3.0265 4016	205
206	2.1620 4638	2.3550 2205	2.5651 3098	2.7938 8626	3.0429 3391	206
207	2.1701 5406	2.3648 3464	2.5768 8783	2.8078 5569	3.0594 1647	207
208	2.1782 9214	2.3746 8812	2.5886 9856	2.8218 9497	3.0759 8831	208
209	2.1864 6073	2.3845 8265	2.6005 6343	2.8360 0444	3.0926 4992	209
210	2.1946 5996	2.3945 1841	2.6124 8268	2.8501 8447	3.1094 0177	210
211	2.2028 8993	2.4044 9557	2.6244 5656	2.8644 3539	3.1262 4436	211
212	2.2111 5077	2.4145 1431	2.6364 8532	2.8787 5757	3.1431 7819	212
213	2.2194 4259	2.4245 7478	2.6485 6921	2.8931 5135	3.1602 0373	213
214	2.2277 6550	2.4346 7718	2.6607 0848	2.9076 1711	3.1773 2151	214
215	2.2361 1962	2.4448 2167	2.6729 0340	2.9221 5520	3.1945 3200	215
216	2.2445 0507	2.4550 0842	2.6851 5421	2.9367 6597	3.2118 3571	216
217	2.2529 2196	2.4652 3762	2.6974 6116	2.9514 4980	3.2292 3315	217
218	2.2613 7042	2.4755 0945	2.7098 2453	2.9662 0705	3.2467 2483	218
219	2.2698 5056	2.4858 2407	2.7222 4456	2.9810 3809	3.2643 1126	219
220	2.2783 6250	2.4961 8167	2.7347 2151	2.9959 4328	3.2819 9295	220
221	2.2869 0636	2.5065 8243	2.7472 5565	3.0109 2299	3.2997 7041	221
222	2.2954 8225	2.5170 2652	2.7598 4724	3.0259 7761	3.3176 4416	222
223	2.3040 9031	2.5275 1413	2.7724 9654	3.0411 0750	3.3356 1474	223
224	2.3127 3065	2.5380 4544	2.7852 0381	3.0563 1303	3.3536 8265	224
225	2.3214 0339	2.5486 2063	2.7979 6933	3.0715 9460	3.3718 4843	225
226	2.3301 0865	2.5592 3988	2.8107 9336	3.0869 5257	3.3901 1261	226
227	2.3388 4656	2.5699 0338	2.8236 7616	3.1023 8733	3.4084 7572	227
228	2.3476 1724	2.5806 1131	2.8366 1801	3.1178 9927	3.4269 3830	228
229	2.3564 2080	2.5913 6386	2.8496 1917	3.1334 8877	3.4455 0088	229
230	2.3652 5738	2.6021 6121	2.8626 7993	3.1491 5621	3.4641 6401	230
231	2.3741 2709	2.6130 0355	2.8758 0055	3.1649 0199	3.4829 2823	231
232	2.3830 3007	2.6238 9106	2.8889 8130	3.1807 2650	3.5017 9409	232
233	2.3919 6643	2.6348 2394	2.9022 2246	3.1966 3013	3.5207 6214	233
234	2.4009 3631	2.6458 0238	2.9155 2432	3.2126 1329	3.5398 3294	234
235	2.4099 3982	2.6568 2655	2.9288 8714	3.2286 7635	3.5590 0703	235
236	2.4189 7709	2.6678 9666	2.9423 1120	3.2448 1973	3.5782 8499	236
237	2.4280 4826	2.6790 1290	2.9557 9679	3.2610 4383	3.5976 6737	237
238	2.4371 5344	2.6901 7545	2.9693 4420	3.2773 4905	3.6171 5473	238
239	2.4462 9276	2.7013 8452	2.9829 5369	3.2937 3580	3.6367 4765	239
240	2.4554 6636	2.7126 4029	2.9966 2556	3.3102 0448	3.6564 4670	240

TABLE I

N	3/8	5/12	11/24	1/2	13/24	N
241	2.4646 7436	2.7239 4295	3.0103 6010	3.3267 5550	3.6762 5245	241
242	2.4739 1689	2.7352 9272	3.0241 5758	3.3433 8928	3.6961 6549	242
243	2.4831 9408	2.7466 8977	3.0380 1830	3.3601 0622	3.7161 8639	243
244	2.4925 0605	2.7581 3431	3.0519 4255	3.3769 0675	3.7363 1573	244
245	2.5018 5295	2.7696 2654	3.0659 3062	3.3937 9129	3.7565 5411	245
246	2.5112 3490	2.7811 6665	3.0799 8280	3.4107 6024	3.7769 0211	246
247	2.5206 5203	2.7927 5484	3.0940 9939	3.4278 1404	3.7973 6033	247
248	2.5301 0448	2.8043 9132	3.1082 8068	3.4449 5311	3.8179 2936	248
249	2.5395 9237	2.8160 7628	3.1225 2697	3.4621 7788	3.8386 0981	249
250	2.5491 1584	2.8278 0993	3.1368 3855	3.4794 8877	3.8594 0228	250
251	2.5586 7502	2.8395 9248	3.1512 1573	3.4968 8621	3.8803 0738	251
252	2.5682 7006	2.8514 2411	3.1656 5880	3.5143 7064	3.9013 2571	252
253	2.5779 0107	2.8633 0504	3.1801 6807	3.5319 4250	3.9224 5789	253
254	2.5875 6820	2.8752 3548	3.1947 4384	3.5496 0221	3.9437 0454	254
255	2.5972 7158	2.8872 1563	3.2093 8641	3.5673 5022	3.9650 6627	255
256	2.6070 1135	2.8992 4570	3.2240 9610	3.5851 8697	3.9865 4371	256
257	2.6167 8764	2.9113 2589	3.2388 7321	3.6031 1291	4.0081 3749	257
258	2.6266 0059	2.9234 5641	3.2537 1804	3.6211 2847	4.0298 4824	258
259	2.6364 5035	2.9356 3748	3.2686 3092	3.6392 3411	4.0516 7658	259
260	2.6463 3703	2.9478 6930	3.2836 1214	3.6574 3028	4.0736 2316	260
261	2.6562 6080	2.9601 5209	3.2986 6203	3.6757 1744	4.0956 8862	261
262	2.6662 2178	2.9724 8606	3.3137 8090	3.6940 9602	4.1178 7360	262
263	2.6762 2011	2.9848 7142	3.3289 6906	3.7125 6650	4.1401 7875	263
264	2.6862 5593	2.9973 0838	3.3442 2684	3.7311 2934	4.1626 0472	264
265	2.6963 2939	3.0097 9716	3.3595 5454	3.7497 8498	4.1851 5216	265
266	2.7064 4063	3.0223 3799	3.3749 5250	3.7685 3391	4.2078 2173	266
267	2.7165 8978	3.0349 3106	3.3904 2103	3.7873 7658	4.2306 1410	267
268	2.7267 7699	3.0475 7661	3.4059 6046	3.8063 1346	4.2535 2993	268
269	2.7370 0241	3.0602 7484	3.4215 7112	3.8253 4503	4.2765 6988	269
270	2.7472 6616	3.0730 2599	3.4372 5332	3.8444 7175	4.2997 3464	270
271	2.7575 6841	3.0858 3026	3.4530 0740	3.8636 9411	4.3230 2486	271
272	2.7679 0929	3.0986 8789	3.4688 3368	3.8830 1258	4.3464 4125	272
273	2.7782 8895	3.1115 9909	3.4847 3250	3.9024 2764	4.3699 8447	273
274	2.7887 0754	3.1245 6409	3.5007 0419	3.9219 3978	4.3936 5522	274
275	2.7991 6519	3.1375 8310	3.5167 4908	3.9415 4948	4.4174 5419	275
276	2.8096 6206	3.1506 5637	3.5328 6752	3.9612 5723	4.4413 8206	276
277	2.8201 9829	3.1637 8410	3.5490 5983	3.9810 6352	4.4654 3955	277
278	2.8307 7404	3.1769 6653	3.5653 2635	4.0009 6883	4.4896 2735	278
279	2.8413 8944	3.1902 0389	3.5816 6743	4.0209 7368	4.5139 4616	279
280	2.8520 4465	3.2034 9641	3.5980 8341	4.0410 7855	4.5383 9670	280
281	2.8627 3982	3.2168 4431	3.6145 7462	4.0612 8394	4.5629 7969	281
282	2.8734 7509	3.2302 4783	3.6311 4142	4.0815 9036	4.5876 9583	282
283	2.8842 5062	3.2437 0720	3.6477 8415	4.1019 9831	4.6125 4585	283
284	2.8950 6656	3.2572 2264	3.6645 0316	4.1225 0830	4.6375 3047	284
285	2.9059 2306	3.2707 9440	3.6812 9880	4.1431 2084	4.6626 5043	285
286	2.9168 2027	3.2844 2271	3.6981 7142	4.1638 3645	4.6879 0645	286
287	2.9277 5835	3.2981 0781	3.7151 2138	4.1846 5563	4.7132 9928	287
288	2.9387 3744	3.3118 4992	3.7321 4902	4.2055 7891	4.7388 2965	288
289	2.9497 5771	3.3256 4930	3.7492 5470	4.2266 0680	4.7644 9831	289
290	2.9608 1930	3.3395 0617	3.7664 3878	4.2477 3984	4.7903 0601	290
291	2.9719 2237	3.3534 2078	3.7837 0163	4.2689 7854	4.8162 5350	291
292	2.9830 6708	3.3673 9337	3.8010 4359	4.2903 2343	4.8423 4154	292
293	2.9942 5358	3.3814 2417	3.8184 6504	4.3117 7505	4.8685 7089	293
294	3.0054 8203	3.3955 1344	3.8359 6634	4.3333 3392	4.8949 4231	294
295	3.0167 5259	3.4096 6141	3.8535 4785	4.3550 0059	4.9214 5658	295
296	3.0280 6541	3.4238 6834	3.8712 0995	4.3767 7559	4.9481 1447	296
297	3.0394 2066	3.4381 3445	3.8889 5299	4.3986 5947	4.9749 1676	297
298	3.0508 1849	3.4524 6001	3.9067 7736	4.4206 5277	5.0018 6423	298
299	3.0622 5906	3.4668 4526	3.9246 8342	4.4427 5603	5.0289 5766	299
300	3.0737 4253	3.4812 9045	3.9426 7156	4.4649 6981	5.0561 9784	300

TABLE I

N	3/8	5/12	11/24	1/2	13/24	N
301	3.0852 6906	3.4957 9583	3.9607 4213	4.4872 9466	5.0835 8558	301
302	3.0968 3882	3.5103 6164	3.9788 9554	4.5097 3113	5.1111 2167	302
303	3.1084 5197	3.5249 8815	3.9971 3214	4.5322 7979	5.1388 0691	303
304	3.1201 0866	3.5396 7560	4.0154 5233	4.5549 4119	5.1666 4212	304
305	3.1318 0907	3.5544 2425	4.0338 5649	4.5777 1590	5.1946 2810	305
306	3.1435 5335	3.5692 3435	4.0523 4499	4.6006 0447	5.2227 6566	306
307	3.1553 4168	3.5841 0616	4.0709 1824	4.6236 0750	5.2510 5565	307
308	3.1671 7421	3.5990 3994	4.0895 7662	4.6467 2553	5.2794 9886	308
309	3.1790 5111	3.6140 3594	4.1083 2051	4.6699 5916	5.3080 9615	309
310	3.1909 7255	3.6290 9442	4.1271 5031	4.6933 0896	5.3368 4834	310
311	3.2029 3870	3.6442 1565	4.1460 6642	4.7167 7550	5.3657 5627	311
312	3.2149 4972	3.6593 9988	4.1650 6922	4.7403 5938	5.3948 2078	312
313	3.2270 0578	3.6746 4738	4.1841 5912	4.7640 6118	5.4240 4272	313
314	3.2391 0706	3.6899 5841	4.2033 3652	4.7878 8148	5.4534 2296	314
315	3.2512 5371	3.7053 3324	4.2226 0181	4.8118 2089	5.4829 6233	315
316	3.2634 4591	3.7207 7212	4.2419 5540	4.8358 7999	5.5126 6171	316
317	3.2756 8383	3.7362 7534	4.2613 9770	4.8600 5939	5.5425 2196	317
318	3.2879 6764	3.7518 4316	4.2809 2911	4.8843 5969	5.5725 4395	318
319	3.3002 9752	3.7674 7583	4.3005 5003	4.9087 8149	5.6027 2857	319
320	3.3126 7364	3.7831 7365	4.3202 6088	4.9333 2540	5.6330 7668	320
321	3.3250 9617	3.7989 3687	4.3400 6208	4.9579 9202	5.6635 8918	321
322	3.3375 6528	3.8147 6578	4.3599 5403	4.9827 8198	5.6942 6695	322
323	3.3500 8115	3.8306 6064	4.3799 3715	5.0076 9589	5.7251 1090	323
324	3.3626 4395	3.8466 2172	4.4000 1187	5.0327 3437	5.7561 2192	324
325	3.3752 5386	3.8626 4931	4.4201 7859	5.0578 9805	5.7873 0091	325
326	3.3879 1107	3.8787 4368	4.4404 3774	5.0831 8754	5.8186 4879	326
327	3.4006 1573	3.8949 0512	4.4607 8975	5.1086 0347	5.8501 6647	327
328	3.4133 6804	3.9111 3389	4.4812 3503	5.1341 4649	5.8818 5487	328
329	3.4261 6817	3.9274 3028	4.5017 7403	5.1598 1722	5.9137 1492	329
330	3.4390 1630	3.9437 9457	4.5224 0716	5.1856 1631	5.9457 4754	330
331	3.4519 1261	3.9602 2705	4.5431 3486	5.2115 4439	5.9779 5368	331
332	3.4648 5729	3.9767 2799	4.5639 5756	5.2376 0211	6.0103 3426	332
333	3.4778 5050	3.9932 9769	4.5848 7570	5.2637 9012	6.0428 9024	333
334	3.4908 9244	4.0099 3644	4.6058 8971	5.2901 0907	6.0756 2256	334
335	3.5039 8329	4.0266 4450	4.6270 0004	5.3165 5962	6.1085 3218	335
336	3.5171 2322	4.0434 2219	4.6482 0712	5.3431 4242	6.1416 2006	336
337	3.5303 1244	4.0602 6978	4.6695 1140	5.3698 5813	6.1748 8717	337
338	3.5435 5111	4.0771 8757	4.6909 1333	5.3967 0742	6.2083 3448	338
339	3.5568 3942	4.0941 7585	4.7124 1335	5.4236 9096	6.2419 6295	339
340	3.5701 7757	4.1112 3492	4.7340 1191	5.4508 0941	6.2757 7359	340
341	3.5835 6574	4.1283 6507	4.7557 0947	5.4780 6346	6.3097 6736	341
342	3.5970 0411	4.1455 6659	4.7775 0647	5.5054 5378	6.3439 4527	342
343	3.6104 9288	4.1628 3978	4.7994 0337	5.5329 8105	6.3783 0830	343
344	3.6240 3222	4.1801 8495	4.8214 0064	5.5606 4595	6.4128 5747	344
345	3.6376 2234	4.1976 0238	4.8434 9872	5.5884 4918	6.4475 9379	345
346	3.6512 6343	4.2150 9239	4.8656 9809	5.6163 9143	6.4825 1825	346
347	3.6649 5567	4.2326 5528	4.8879 9921	5.6444 7338	6.5176 3189	347
348	3.6786 9925	4.2502 9134	4.9104 0254	5.6726 9575	6.5529 3573	348
349	3.6924 9437	4.2680 0089	4.9329 0855	5.7010 5923	6.5884 3080	349
350	3.7063 4123	4.2857 8423	4.9555 1772	5.7295 6453	6.6241 1813	350
351	3.7202 4001	4.3036 4166	4.9782 3051	5.7582 1235	6.6599 9877	351
352	3.7341 9091	4.3215 7350	5.0010 4739	5.7870 0341	6.6960 7377	352
353	3.7481 9412	4.3395 8006	5.0239 6886	5.8159 3843	6.7323 4417	353
354	3.7622 4985	4.3576 6164	5.0469 9539	5.8450 1812	6.7688 1103	354
355	3.7763 5829	4.3758 1856	5.0701 2745	5.8742 4321	6.8054 7542	355
356	3.7905 1963	4.3940 5114	5.0933 6553	5.9036 1443	6.8423 3842	356
357	3.8047 3408	4.4123 5969	5.1167 1012	5.9331 3250	6.8794 0108	357
358	3.8190 0183	4.4307 4452	5.1401 6171	5.9627 9816	6.9166 6450	358
359	3.8333 2309	4.4492 0596	5.1637 2079	5.9926 1215	6.9541 2977	359
360	3.8476 9805	4.4677 4431	5.1873 8784	6.0225 7521	6.9917 9797	360

TABLE I

N	7/12	5/8	2/3	17/24	3/4	N
1	1.0058 3333	1.0062 5000	1.0066 6667	1.0070 8333	1.0075 0000	1
2	1.0117 0069	1.0125 3906	1.0133 7778	1.0142 1684	1.0150 5625	2
3	1.0176 0228	1.0188 6743	1.0201 3363	1.0214 0088	1.0226 6917	3
4	1.0235 3830	1.0252 3535	1.0269 3452	1.0286 3580	1.0303 3919	4
5	1.0295 0894	1.0316 4307	1.0337 8075	1.0359 2197	1.0380 6673	5
6	1.0355 1440	1.0380 9084	1.0406 7262	1.0432 5975	1.0458 5224	6
7	1.0415 5490	1.0445 7891	1.0476 1044	1.0506 4951	1.0536 9613	7
8	1.0476 3064	1.0511 0753	1.0545 9451	1.0580 9161	1.0615 9885	8
9	1.0537 4182	1.0576 7695	1.0616 2514	1.0655 8642	1.0695 6084	9
10	1.0598 8865	1.0642 8743	1.0687 0264	1.0731 3433	1.0775 8255	10
11	1.0660 7133	1.0709 3923	1.0758 2732	1.0807 3569	1.0856 6441	11
12	1.0722 9008	1.0776 3260	1.0829 9951	1.0883 9091	1.0938 0690	12
13	1.0785 4511	1.0843 6780	1.0902 1950	1.0961 0034	1.1020 1045	13
14	1.0848 3662	1.0911 4510	1.0974 8763	1.1038 6439	1.1102 7553	14
15	1.0911 6483	1.0979 6476	1.1048 0422	1.1116 8342	1.1186 0259	15
16	1.0975 2996	1.1048 2704	1.1121 6958	1.1195 5785	1.1269 9211	16
17	1.1039 3222	1.1117 3221	1.1195 8404	1.1274 8805	1.1354 4455	17
18	1.1103 7182	1.1186 8053	1.1270 4794	1.1354 7442	1.1439 6039	18
19	1.1168 4899	1.1256 7229	1.1345 6159	1.1435 1737	1.1525 4009	19
20	1.1233 6395	1.1327 0774	1.1421 2533	1.1516 1728	1.1611 8414	20
21	1.1299 1690	1.1397 8716	1.1497 3950	1.1597 7457	1.1698 9302	21
22	1.1365 0808	1.1469 1083	1.1574 0443	1.1679 8964	1.1786 6722	22
23	1.1431 3771	1.1540 7902	1.1651 2046	1.1762 6290	1.1875 0723	23
24	1.1498 0602	1.1612 9202	1.1728 8793	1.1845 9476	1.1964 1353	24
25	1.1565 1322	1.1685 5009	1.1807 0718	1.1929 8564	1.2053 8663	25
26	1.1632 5955	1.1758 5353	1.1885 7857	1.2014 3596	1.2144 2703	26
27	1.1700 4523	1.1832 0262	1.1965 0242	1.2099 4613	1.2235 3523	27
28	1.1768 7049	1.1905 9763	1.2044 7911	1.2185 1658	1.2327 1175	28
29	1.1837 3557	1.1980 3887	1.2125 0897	1.2271 4774	1.2419 5709	29
30	1.1906 4069	1.2055 2661	1.2205 9236	1.2358 4004	1.2512 7176	30
31	1.1975 8610	1.2130 6115	1.2287 2964	1.2445 9390	1.2606 5630	31
32	1.2045 7202	1.2206 4278	1.2369 2117	1.2534 0978	1.2701 1122	32
33	1.2115 9869	1.2282 7180	1.2451 6731	1.2622 8810	1.2796 3706	33
34	1.2186 6634	1.2359 4850	1.2534 6843	1.2712 2930	1.2892 3434	34
35	1.2257 7523	1.2436 7318	1.2618 2489	1.2802 3385	1.2989 0359	35
36	1.2329 2559	1.2514 4614	1.2702 3705	1.2893 0217	1.3086 4537	36
37	1.2401 1765	1.2592 6767	1.2787 0530	1.2984 3473	1.3184 6021	37
38	1.2473 5167	1.2671 3810	1.2872 3000	1.3076 3197	1.3283 4866	38
39	1.2546 2789	1.2750 5771	1.2958 1153	1.3168 9436	1.3383 1128	39
40	1.2619 4655	1.2830 2682	1.3044 5028	1.3262 2237	1.3483 4861	40
41	1.2693 0791	1.2910 4574	1.3131 4661	1.3356 1644	1.3584 6123	41
42	1.2767 1220	1.2991 1477	1.3219 0092	1.3450 7706	1.3686 4969	42
43	1.2841 5969	1.3072 3424	1.3307 1360	1.3546 0469	1.3789 1456	43
44	1.2916 5062	1.3154 0446	1.3395 8502	1.3641 9980	1.3892 5642	44
45	1.2991 8525	1.3236 2573	1.3485 1559	1.3738 6289	1.3996 7584	45
46	1.3067 6383	1.3318 9839	1.3575 0569	1.3835 9441	1.4101 7341	46
47	1.3143 8662	1.3402 2276	1.3665 5573	1.3933 9487	1.4207 4971	47
48	1.3220 5388	1.3485 9915	1.3756 6610	1.4032 6475	1.4314 0533	48
49	1.3297 6586	1.3570 2790	1.3848 3721	1.4132 0455	1.4421 4087	49
50	1.3375 2283	1.3655 0932	1.3940 6946	1.4232 1475	1.4529 5693	50
51	1.3453 2504	1.3740 4375	1.4033 6325	1.4332 9585	1.4638 5411	51
52	1.3531 7277	1.3826 3153	1.4127 1901	1.4434 4836	1.4748 3301	52
53	1.3610 6628	1.3912 7297	1.4221 3713	1.4536 7279	1.4858 9426	53
54	1.3690 0583	1.3999 6843	1.4316 1805	1.4639 6964	1.4970 3847	54
55	1.3769 9170	1.4087 1823	1.4411 6217	1.4743 3942	1.5082 6626	55
56	1.3850 2415	1.4175 2272	1.4507 6992	1.4847 8266	1.5195 7825	56
57	1.3931 0346	1.4263 8224	1.4604 4172	1.4952 9987	1.5309 7509	57
58	1.4012 2990	1.4352 9713	1.4701 7799	1.5058 9158	1.5424 5740	58
59	1.4094 0374	1.4442 6773	1.4799 7918	1.5165 5831	1.5540 2583	59
60	1.4176 2526	1.4532 9441	1.4898 4571	1.5273 0060	1.5656 8103	60

TABLE I

N	7/12	5/8	2/3	17/24	3/4	N
61	1.4258 9474	1.4623 7750	1.4997 7801	1.5381 1898	1.5774 2363	61
62	1.4342 1246	1.4715 1736	1.5097 7653	1.5490 1399	1.5892 5431	62
63	1.4425 7870	1.4807 1434	1.5198 4171	1.5599 8617	1.6011 7372	63
64	1.4509 9374	1.4899 6881	1.5299 7399	1.5710 3607	1.6131 8252	64
65	1.4594 5787	1.4992 8111	1.5401 7381	1.5821 6424	1.6252 8139	65
66	1.4679 7138	1.5086 5162	1.5504 4164	1.5933 7124	1.6374 7100	66
67	1.4765 3454	1.5180 8069	1.5607 7792	1.6046 5762	1.6497 5203	67
68	1.4851 4766	1.5275 6869	1.5711 8310	1.6160 2394	1.6621 2517	68
69	1.4938 1102	1.5371 1600	1.5816 5766	1.6274 7078	1.6745 9111	69
70	1.5025 2492	1.5467 2297	1.5922 0204	1.6389 9870	1.6871 5055	70
71	1.5112 8965	1.5563 8999	1.6028 1672	1.6506 0827	1.6998 0418	71
72	1.5201 0550	1.5661 1743	1.6135 0217	1.6623 0008	1.7125 5271	72
73	1.5289 7279	1.5759 0566	1.6242 5885	1.6740 7471	1.7253 9685	73
74	1.5378 9179	1.5857 5507	1.6350 8724	1.6859 3274	1.7383 3733	74
75	1.5468 6283	1.5956 6604	1.6459 8782	1.6978 7476	1.7513 7486	75
76	1.5558 8620	1.6056 3896	1.6569 6107	1.7099 0137	1.7645 1017	76
77	1.5649 6220	1.6156 7420	1.6680 0748	1.7220 1317	1.7777 4400	77
78	1.5740 9115	1.6257 7216	1.6791 2753	1.7342 1077	1.7910 7708	78
79	1.5832 7334	1.6359 3324	1.6903 2172	1.7464 9476	1.8045 1015	79
80	1.5925 0910	1.6461 5782	1.7015 9053	1.7588 6576	1.8180 4398	80
81	1.6017 9874	1.6564 4631	1.7129 3446	1.7713 2440	1.8316 7931	81
82	1.6111 4257	1.6667 9910	1.7243 5403	1.7838 7128	1.8454 1691	82
83	1.6205 4090	1.6772 1659	1.7358 4972	1.7965 0703	1.8592 5753	83
84	1.6299 9405	1.6876 9920	1.7474 2205	1.8092 3229	1.8732 0196	84
85	1.6395 0235	1.6982 4732	1.7590 7153	1.8220 4769	1.8872 5098	85
86	1.6490 6612	1.7088 6136	1.7707 9868	1.8349 5386	1.9014 0536	86
87	1.6586 8567	1.7195 4175	1.7826 0400	1.8479 5145	1.9156 6590	87
88	1.6683 6134	1.7302 8888	1.7944 8803	1.8610 4110	1.9300 3339	88
89	1.6780 9344	1.7411 0319	1.8064 5128	1.8742 2348	1.9445 0865	89
90	1.6878 8232	1.7519 8508	1.8184 9429	1.8874 9923	1.9590 9246	90
91	1.6977 2830	1.7629 3499	1.8306 1758	1.9008 6901	1.9737 8565	91
92	1.7076 3172	1.7739 5333	1.8428 2170	1.9143 3350	1.9885 8905	92
93	1.7175 9290	1.7850 4054	1.8551 0718	1.9278 9337	2.0035 0346	93
94	1.7276 1219	1.7961 9704	1.8674 7456	1.9415 4928	2.0185 2974	94
95	1.7376 8993	1.8074 2328	1.8799 2439	1.9553 0192	2.0336 6871	95
96	1.7478 2646	1.8187 1967	1.8924 5722	1.9691 5197	2.0489 2123	96
97	1.7580 2211	1.8300 8667	1.9050 7360	1.9831 0013	2.0642 8814	97
98	1.7682 7724	1.8415 2471	1.9177 7409	1.9971 4709	2.0797 7030	98
99	1.7785 9219	1.8530 3424	1.9305 5925	2.0112 9355	2.0953 6858	99
100	1.7889 6731	1.8646 1570	1.9434 2965	2.0255 4021	2.1110 8384	100
101	1.7994 0295	1.8762 6955	1.9563 8585	2.0398 8779	2.1269 1697	101
102	1.8098 9947	1.8879 9624	1.9694 2842	2.0543 3699	2.1428 6885	102
103	1.8204 5722	1.8997 9621	1.9825 5794	2.0688 8855	2.1589 4036	103
104	1.8310 7655	1.9116 6994	1.9957 7499	2.0835 4318	2.1751 3242	104
105	1.8417 5783	1.9236 1788	2.0090 8016	2.0983 0161	2.1914 4591	105
106	1.8525 0142	1.9356 4049	2.0224 7403	2.1131 6458	2.2078 8175	106
107	1.8633 0768	1.9477 3824	2.0359 5719	2.1281 3283	2.2244 4087	107
108	1.8741 7697	1.9599 1161	2.0495 3024	2.1432 0710	2.2411 2417	108
109	1.8851 0967	1.9721 6105	2.0631 9377	2.1583 8815	2.2579 3260	109
110	1.8961 0614	1.9844 8706	2.0769 4840	2.1736 7673	2.2748 6710	110
111	1.9071 6676	1.9968 9010	2.0907 9472	2.1890 7361	2.2919 2860	111
112	1.9182 9190	2.0093 7067	2.1047 3335	2.2045 7955	2.3091 1807	112
113	1.9294 8194	2.0219 2923	2.1187 6491	2.2201 9532	2.3264 3645	113
114	1.9407 3725	2.0345 6629	2.1328 9000	2.2359 2170	2.3438 8472	114
115	1.9520 5822	2.0472 8233	2.1471 0927	2.2517 5948	2.3614 6386	115
116	1.9634 4522	2.0600 7785	2.1614 2333	2.2677 0944	2.3791 7484	116
117	1.9748 9865	2.0729 5333	2.1758 3282	2.2837 7239	2.3970 1865	117
118	1.9864 1890	2.0859 0929	2.1903 3837	2.2999 4911	2.4149 9629	118
119	1.9980 0634	2.0989 4622	2.2049 4063	2.3162 4041	2.4331 0876	119
120	2.0096 6138	2.1120 6464	2.2196 4023	2.3326 4712	2.4513 5708	120

TABLE I

N	7/12	5/8	2/3	17/24	3/4	N
121	2.0213 8440	2.1252 6504	2.2344 3784	2.3491 7003	2.4697 4226	121
122	2.0331 7581	2.1385 4795	2.2493 3409	2.3658 0999	2.4882 6532	122
123	2.0450 3600	2.1519 1387	2.2643 2965	2.3825 6781	2.5069 2731	123
124	2.0569 6538	2.1653 6333	2.2794 2518	2.3994 4433	2.5257 2927	124
125	2.0689 6434	2.1788 9685	2.2946 2135	2.4164 4039	2.5446 7224	125
126	2.0810 3330	2.1925 1496	2.3099 1882	2.4335 5685	2.5637 5728	126
127	2.0931 7266	2.2062 1818	2.3253 1828	2.4507 9454	2.5829 8546	127
128	2.1053 8284	2.2200 0704	2.3408 2040	2.4681 5434	2.6023 5785	128
129	2.1176 6424	2.2338 8209	2.3564 2587	2.4856 3710	2.6218 7553	129
130	2.1300 1728	2.2478 4385	2.3721 3538	2.5032 4369	2.6415 3960	130
131	2.1424 4238	2.2618 9287	2.3879 4962	2.5209 7500	2.6613 5115	131
132	2.1549 3996	2.2760 2970	2.4038 6928	2.5388 3191	2.6813 1128	132
133	2.1675 1044	2.2902 5489	2.4198 9507	2.5568 1530	2.7014 2112	133
134	2.1801 5425	2.3045 6898	2.4360 2771	2.5749 2608	2.7216 8177	134
135	2.1928 7182	2.3189 7254	2.4522 6789	2.5931 6514	2.7420 9439	135
136	2.2056 6357	2.3334 6612	2.4686 1635	2.6115 3339	2.7626 6009	136
137	2.2185 2994	2.3480 5028	2.4850 7379	2.6300 3175	2.7833 8005	137
138	2.2314 7137	2.3627 2559	2.5016 4095	2.6486 6114	2.8042 5540	138
139	2.2444 8828	2.3774 9263	2.5183 1855	2.6674 2249	2.8252 8731	139
140	2.2575 8113	2.3923 5196	2.5351 0734	2.6863 1673	2.8464 7697	140
141	2.2707 5036	2.4073 0416	2.5520 0806	2.7053 4481	2.8678 2554	141
142	2.2839 9640	2.4223 4981	2.5690 2145	2.7245 0767	2.8893 3424	142
143	2.2973 1971	2.4374 8950	2.5861 4826	2.7438 0627	2.9110 0424	143
144	2.3107 2074	2.4527 2380	2.6033 8924	2.7632 4156	2.9328 3677	144
145	2.3241 9995	2.4680 5333	2.6207 4517	2.7828 1452	2.9548 3305	145
146	2.3377 5778	2.4834 7866	2.6382 1681	2.8025 2612	2.9769 9430	146
147	2.3513 9470	2.4990 0040	2.6558 0492	2.8223 7735	2.9993 2175	147
148	2.3651 1117	2.5146 1916	2.6735 1028	2.8423 6919	3.0218 1667	148
149	2.3789 0765	2.5303 3553	2.6913 3369	2.8625 0264	3.0444 8029	149
150	2.3927 8461	2.5461 5012	2.7092 7591	2.8827 7870	3.0673 1389	150
151	2.4067 4252	2.5620 6356	2.7273 3775	2.9031 9838	3.0903 1875	151
152	2.4207 8186	2.5780 7646	2.7455 2000	2.9237 6270	3.1134 9614	152
153	2.4349 0308	2.5941 8944	2.7638 2347	2.9444 7269	3.1368 4736	153
154	2.4491 0668	2.6104 0312	2.7822 4896	2.9653 2937	3.1603 7372	154
155	2.4633 9314	2.6267 1814	2.8007 9729	2.9863 3379	3.1840 7652	155
156	2.4777 6293	2.6431 3513	2.8194 6927	3.0074 8698	3.2079 5709	156
157	2.4922 1655	2.6596 5472	2.8382 6573	3.0287 9002	3.2320 1677	157
158	2.5067 5448	2.6762 7756	2.8571 8750	3.0502 4395	3.2562 5690	158
159	2.5213 7721	2.6930 0430	2.8762 3542	3.0718 4984	3.2806 7882	159
160	2.5360 8525	2.7098 3558	2.8954 1032	3.0936 0878	3.3052 8391	160
161	2.5508 7908	2.7267 7205	2.9147 1306	3.1155 2184	3.3300 7354	161
162	2.5657 5921	2.7438 1437	2.9341 4448	3.1375 9012	3.3550 4910	162
163	2.5807 2614	2.7609 6321	2.9537 0544	3.1598 1472	3.3802 1196	163
164	2.5957 8037	2.7782 1923	2.9733 9681	3.1821 9674	3.4055 6355	164
165	2.6109 2242	2.7955 8310	2.9932 1945	3.2047 3730	3.4311 0528	165
166	2.6261 5280	2.8130 5550	3.0131 7425	3.2274 3752	3.4568 3857	166
167	2.6414 7203	2.8306 3710	3.0332 6208	3.2502 9854	3.4827 6486	167
168	2.6568 8062	2.8483 2858	3.0534 8383	3.2733 2148	3.5088 8560	168
169	2.6723 7909	2.8661 3063	3.0738 4038	3.2965 0751	3.5352 0224	169
170	2.6879 6796	2.8840 4395	3.0943 3265	3.3198 5777	3.5617 1625	170
171	2.7036 4778	2.9020 6922	3.1149 6154	3.3433 7343	3.5884 2913	171
172	2.7194 1906	2.9202 0715	3.1357 2795	3.3670 5566	3.6153 4234	172
173	2.7352 8233	2.9384 5845	3.1566 3280	3.3909 0564	3.6424 5741	173
174	2.7512 3815	2.9568 2381	3.1776 7702	3.4149 2455	3.6697 7584	174
175	2.7672 8704	2.9753 0396	3.1988 6153	3.4391 1360	3.6972 9916	175
176	2.7834 2954	2.9938 9961	3.2201 8728	3.4634 7399	3.7250 2891	176
177	2.7996 6622	3.0126 1149	3.2416 5519	3.4880 0693	3.7529 6662	177
178	2.8159 9760	3.0314 4031	3.2632 6623	3.5127 1365	3.7811 1387	178
179	2.8324 2426	3.0503 8681	3.2850 2134	3.5375 9537	3.8094 7223	179
180	2.8489 4673	3.0694 5173	3.3069 2148	3.5626 5334	3.8380 4327	180

TABLE I

N	7/12	5/8	2/3	17/24	3/4	N
181	2.8655 6559	3.0886 3580	3.3289 6762	3.5878 8880	3.8668 2859	181
182	2.8822 8139	3.1079 3977	3.3511 6074	3.6133 0301	3.8958 2981	182
183	2.8990 9469	3.1273 6440	3.3735 0181	3.6388 9724	3.9250 4853	183
184	2.9160 0608	3.1469 1043	3.3959 9182	3.6646 7276	3.9544 8639	184
185	2.9330 1612	3.1665 7862	3.4186 3177	3.6906 3086	3.9841 4504	185
186	2.9501 2538	3.1863 6973	3.4414 2265	3.7167 7283	4.0140 2613	186
187	2.9673 3444	3.2062 8454	3.4643 6546	3.7430 9997	4.0441 3133	187
188	2.9846 4389	3.2263 2382	3.4874 6123	3.7696 1359	4.0744 6231	188
189	3.0020 5431	3.2464 8834	3.5107 1097	3.7963 1502	4.1050 2078	189
190	3.0195 6630	3.2667 7890	3.5341 1571	3.8232 0559	4.1358 0843	190
191	3.0371 8043	3.2871 9627	3.5576 7649	3.8502 8663	4.1668 2700	191
192	3.0548 9732	3.3077 4124	3.5813 9433	3.8775 5949	4.1980 7820	192
193	3.0727 1755	3.3284 1462	3.6052 7029	3.9050 2554	4.2295 6379	193
194	3.0906 4174	3.3492 1722	3.6293 0543	3.9326 8613	4.2612 8551	194
195	3.1086 7048	3.3701 4982	3.6535 0080	3.9605 4266	4.2932 4516	195
196	3.1268 0440	3.3912 1326	3.6778 5747	3.9885 9651	4.3254 4449	196
197	3.1450 4409	3.4124 0834	3.7023 7652	4.0168 4906	4.3578 8533	197
198	3.1633 9018	3.4337 3589	3.7270 5903	4.0453 0174	4.3905 6947	198
199	3.1818 4329	3.4551 9674	3.7519 0609	4.0739 5597	4.4234 9874	199
200	3.2004 0404	3.4767 9172	3.7769 1880	4.1028 1315	4.4566 7498	200
201	3.2190 7306	3.4985 2167	3.8020 9825	4.1318 7475	4.4901 0004	201
202	3.2378 5099	3.5203 8743	3.8274 4558	4.1611 4219	4.5237 7579	202
203	3.2567 3845	3.5423 8985	3.8529 6188	4.1906 1695	4.5577 0411	203
204	3.2757 3609	3.5645 2979	3.8786 4829	4.2203 0049	4.5918 8689	204
205	3.2948 4456	3.5868 0810	3.9045 0595	4.2501 9428	4.6263 2604	205
206	3.3140 6448	3.6092 2565	3.9305 3599	4.2802 9982	4.6610 2349	206
207	3.3333 9652	3.6317 8331	3.9567 3956	4.3106 1862	4.6959 8116	207
208	3.3528 4134	3.6544 8196	3.9831 1782	4.3411 5216	4.7312 0102	208
209	3.3723 9958	3.6773 2247	4.0096 7194	4.3719 0199	4.7666 8503	209
210	3.3920 7191	3.7003 0574	4.0364 0309	4.4028 6963	4.8024 3517	210
211	3.4118 5900	3.7234 3265	4.0633 1244	4.4340 5662	4.8384 5343	211
212	3.4317 6151	3.7467 0410	4.0904 0119	4.4654 6453	4.8747 4183	212
213	3.4517 8012	3.7701 2100	4.1176 7053	4.4970 9490	4.9113 0240	213
214	3.4719 1550	3.7936 8426	4.1451 2167	4.5289 4932	4.9481 3717	214
215	3.4921 6834	3.8173 9478	4.1727 5582	4.5610 2938	4.9852 4819	215
216	3.5125 3932	3.8412 5350	4.2005 7419	4.5933 3667	5.0226 3756	216
217	3.5330 2913	3.8652 6134	4.2285 7802	4.6258 7280	5.0603 0734	217
218	3.5536 3847	3.8894 1922	4.2567 6854	4.6586 3940	5.0982 5964	218
219	3.5743 6803	3.9137 2809	4.2851 4699	4.6916 3810	5.1364 9659	219
220	3.5952 1851	3.9381 8889	4.3137 1464	4.7248 7054	5.1750 2031	220
221	3.6161 9062	3.9628 0257	4.3424 7274	4.7583 3837	5.2138 3297	221
222	3.6372 8506	3.9875 7009	4.3714 2255	4.7920 4327	5.2529 3671	222
223	3.6585 0256	4.0124 9240	4.4005 6537	4.8259 8691	5.2923 3374	223
224	3.6798 4382	4.0375 7048	4.4299 0247	4.8601 7098	5.3320 2624	224
225	3.7013 0958	4.0628 0529	4.4594 3516	4.8945 9719	5.3720 1644	225
226	3.7229 0055	4.0881 9783	4.4891 6473	4.9292 6725	5.4123 0656	226
227	3.7446 1747	4.1137 4906	4.5190 9249	4.9641 8290	5.4528 9886	227
228	3.7664 6107	4.1394 5999	4.5492 1977	4.9993 4586	5.4937 9560	228
229	3.7884 3210	4.1653 3162	4.5795 4791	5.0347 5789	5.5349 9907	229
230	3.8105 3128	4.1913 6494	4.6100 7822	5.0704 2076	5.5765 1156	230
231	3.8327 5938	4.2175 6097	4.6408 1208	5.1063 3624	5.6183 3540	231
232	3.8551 1715	4.2439 2073	4.6717 5083	5.1425 0612	5.6604 7291	232
233	3.8776 0533	4.2704 4523	4.7028 9583	5.1789 3221	5.7029 2646	233
234	3.9002 2469	4.2971 3552	4.7342 4847	5.2156 1631	5.7456 9841	234
235	3.9229 7600	4.3239 9261	4.7658 1013	5.2525 6026	5.7887 9115	235
236	3.9458 6003	4.3510 1757	4.7975 8219	5.2897 6590	5.8322 0708	236
237	3.9688 7755	4.3782 1143	4.8295 6608	5.3272 3507	5.8759 4863	237
238	3.9920 2933	4.4055 7525	4.8617 6318	5.3649 6965	5.9200 1825	238
239	4.0153 1617	4.4331 1009	4.8941 7494	5.4029 7152	5.9644 1839	239
240	4.0387 3885	4.4608 1703	4.9268 0277	5.4412 4257	6.0091 5152	240

TABLE I

N	7/12	5/8	2/3	17/24	3/4	N
241	4.0622 9816	4.4886 9714	4.9596 4812	5.4797 8470	6.0542 2016	241
242	4.0859 9490	4.5167 5149	4.9927 1244	5.5185 9985	6.0996 2681	242
243	4.1098 2987	4.5449 8119	5.0259 9719	5.5576 8993	6.1453 7401	243
244	4.1338 0388	4.5733 8732	5.0595 0384	5.5970 5690	6.1914 6432	244
245	4.1579 1773	4.6019 7100	5.0932 3387	5.6367 0272	6.2379 0030	245
246	4.1821 7225	4.6307 3331	5.1271 8876	5.6766 2936	6.2846 8455	246
247	4.2065 6826	4.6596 7540	5.1613 7002	5.7168 3882	6.3318 1969	247
248	4.2311 0657	4.6887 9837	5.1957 7915	5.7573 3309	6.3793 0833	248
249	4.2557 8803	4.7181 0336	5.2304 1768	5.7981 1420	6.4271 5315	249
250	4.2806 1346	4.7475 9150	5.2652 8713	5.8391 8418	6.4753 5680	250
251	4.3055 8370	4.7772 6395	5.3003 8904	5.8805 4507	6.5239 2197	251
252	4.3306 9961	4.8071 2185	5.3357 2497	5.9221 9893	6.5728 5139	252
253	4.3559 6202	4.8371 6636	5.3712 9647	5.9641 4784	6.6221 4777	253
254	4.3813 7180	4.8673 9865	5.4071 0511	6.0063 9389	6.6718 1388	254
255	4.4069 2980	4.8978 1989	5.4431 5248	6.0489 3918	6.7218 5248	255
256	4.4326 3689	4.9284 3127	5.4794 4016	6.0917 8583	6.7722 6638	256
257	4.4584 9394	4.9592 3396	5.5159 6977	6.1349 3598	6.8230 5838	257
258	4.4845 0182	4.9902 2918	5.5527 4290	6.1783 9177	6.8742 3131	258
259	4.5106 6142	5.0214 1811	5.5897 6118	6.2221 5538	6.9257 8805	259
260	4.5369 7361	5.0528 0197	5.6270 2626	6.2662 2898	6.9777 3146	260
261	4.5634 3929	5.0843 8198	5.6645 3977	6.3106 1477	7.0300 6444	261
262	4.5900 5935	5.1161 5937	5.7023 0336	6.3553 1496	7.0827 8993	262
263	4.6168 3470	5.1481 3537	5.7403 1872	6.4003 3177	7.1359 1085	263
264	4.6437 6623	5.1803 1121	5.7785 8751	6.4456 6746	7.1894 3018	264
265	4.6708 5487	5.2126 8816	5.8171 1143	6.4913 2427	7.2433 5091	265
266	4.6981 0152	5.2452 6746	5.8558 9217	6.5373 0448	7.2976 7604	266
267	4.7255 0711	5.2780 5038	5.8949 3145	6.5836 1039	7.3524 0861	267
268	4.7530 7257	5.3110 3820	5.9342 3100	6.6302 4430	7.4075 5168	268
269	4.7807 9883	5.3442 3218	5.9737 9254	6.6772 0853	7.4631 0831	269
270	4.8086 8682	5.3776 3364	6.0136 1782	6.7245 0542	7.5190 8163	270
271	4.8367 3749	5.4112 4385	6.0537 0860	6.7721 3733	7.5754 7474	271
272	4.8649 5180	5.4450 6412	6.0940 6666	6.8201 0664	7.6322 9080	272
273	4.8933 3068	5.4790 9577	6.1346 9377	6.8684 1573	7.6895 3298	273
274	4.9218 7511	5.5133 4012	6.1755 9173	6.9170 6701	7.7472 0448	274
275	4.9505 8605	5.5477 9849	6.2167 6234	6.9660 6290	7.8053 0851	275
276	4.9794 6447	5.5824 7224	6.2582 0743	7.0154 0584	7.8638 4833	276
277	5.0085 1134	5.6173 6269	6.2999 2881	7.0650 9830	7.9228 2719	277
278	5.0377 2766	5.6524 7120	6.3419 2833	7.1151 4275	7.9822 4839	278
279	5.0671 1440	5.6877 9915	6.3842 0786	7.1655 4167	8.0421 1525	279
280	5.0966 7257	5.7233 4789	6.4267 6924	7.2162 9759	8.1024 3112	280
281	5.1264 0316	5.7591 1882	6.4696 1437	7.2674 1304	8.1631 9935	281
282	5.1563 0718	5.7951 1331	6.5127 4513	7.3188 9055	8.2244 2335	282
283	5.1863 8564	5.8313 3277	6.5561 6343	7.3707 3269	8.2861 0652	283
284	5.2166 3956	5.8677 7860	6.5998 7119	7.4229 4204	8.3482 5232	284
285	5.2470 6995	5.9044 5221	6.6438 7033	7.4755 2122	8.4108 6421	285
286	5.2776 7786	5.9413 5504	6.6881 6280	7.5284 7282	8.4739 4570	286
287	5.3084 6432	5.9784 8851	6.7327 5055	7.5817 9951	8.5375 0029	287
288	5.3394 3036	6.0158 5406	6.7776 3556	7.6355 0392	8.6015 3154	288
289	5.3705 7703	6.0534 5315	6.8228 1979	7.6895 8874	8.6660 4303	289
290	5.4019 0540	6.0912 8723	6.8683 0526	7.7440 5666	8.7310 3835	290
291	5.4334 1652	6.1293 5778	6.9140 9396	7.7989 1039	8.7965 2114	291
292	5.4651 1144	6.1676 6626	6.9601 8792	7.8541 5268	8.8624 9505	292
293	5.4969 9126	6.2062 1418	7.0065 8917	7.9097 8626	8.9289 6376	293
294	5.5290 5704	6.2450 0302	7.0532 9977	7.9658 1391	8.9959 3099	294
295	5.5613 0988	6.2840 3429	7.1003 2176	8.0222 3843	9.0634 0047	295
296	5.5937 5085	6.3233 0950	7.1476 5724	8.0790 6261	9.1313 7597	296
297	5.6263 8106	6.3628 3018	7.1953 0829	8.1362 8931	9.1998 6129	297
298	5.6592 0162	6.4025 9787	7.2432 7701	8.1939 2136	9.2688 6025	298
299	5.6922 1363	6.4426 1411	7.2915 6553	8.2519 6163	9.3383 7670	299
300	5.7254 1821	6.4828 8045	7.3401 7596	8.3104 1303	9.4084 1453	300

TABLE I

N	7/12	5/8	2/3	17/24	3/4	N
301	5.7588 1648	6.5233 9845	7.3891 1047	8.3692 7845	9.4789 7764	301
302	5.7924 0958	6.5641 6969	7.4383 7121	8.4285 6084	9.5500 6997	302
303	5.8261 9863	6.6051 9575	7.4879 6035	8.4882 6315	9.6216 9550	303
304	5.8601 8479	6.6464 7823	7.5378 8008	8.5483 8835	9.6938 5821	304
305	5.8943 6920	6.6880 1871	7.5881 3262	8.6089 3943	9.7665 6215	305
306	5.9287 5302	6.7298 1883	7.6387 2017	8.6699 1942	9.8398 1136	306
307	5.9633 3742	6.7718 8020	7.6896 4497	8.7313 3135	9.9136 0995	307
308	5.9981 2355	6.8142 0445	7.7409 0927	8.7931 7828	9.9879 6202	308
309	6.0331 1261	6.8567 9323	7.7925 1533	8.8554 6329	10.0628 7174	309
310	6.0683 0576	6.8996 4819	7.8444 6543	8.9181 8949	10.1383 4328	310
311	6.1037 0421	6.9427 7099	7.8967 6187	8.9813 6000	10.2143 8085	311
312	6.1393 0915	6.9861 6331	7.9494 0695	9.0449 7796	10.2909 8871	312
313	6.1751 2179	7.0298 2683	8.0024 0299	9.1090 4656	10.3681 7112	313
314	6.2111 4334	7.0737 6324	8.0557 5235	9.1735 6897	10.4459 3241	314
315	6.2473 7500	7.1179 7426	8.1094 5736	9.2385 4842	10.5242 7690	315
316	6.2838 1803	7.1624 6160	8.1635 2041	9.3039 8814	10.6032 0898	316
317	6.3204 7363	7.2072 2699	8.2179 4388	9.3698 9139	10.6827 3304	317
318	6.3573 4306	7.2522 7216	8.2727 3017	9.4362 6145	10.7628 5354	318
319	6.3944 2756	7.2975 9886	8.3278 8171	9.5031 0163	10.8435 7494	319
320	6.4317 2839	7.3432 0885	8.3834 0092	9.5704 1527	10.9249 0176	320
321	6.4692 4680	7.3891 0391	8.4392 9026	9.6382 0571	11.0068 3852	321
322	6.5069 8408	7.4352 8581	8.4955 5220	9.7064 7634	11.0893 8981	322
323	6.5449 4148	7.4817 5634	8.5521 8921	9.7752 3054	11.1725 6023	323
324	6.5831 2031	7.5285 1732	8.6092 0380	9.8444 7176	11.2563 5443	324
325	6.6215 2184	7.5755 7055	8.6665 9850	9.9142 0344	11.3407 7709	325
326	6.6601 4739	7.6229 1787	8.7243 7582	9.9844 2904	11.4258 3292	326
327	6.6989 9825	7.6705 6110	8.7825 3833	10.0551 5208	11.5115 2667	327
328	6.7380 7574	7.7185 0211	8.8410 8858	10.1263 7608	11.5978 6312	328
329	6.7773 8118	7.7667 4275	8.9000 2917	10.1981 0457	11.6848 4709	329
330	6.8169 1590	7.8152 8489	8.9593 6270	10.2703 4115	11.7724 8344	330
331	6.8566 8125	7.8641 3042	9.0190 9178	10.3430 8940	11.8607 7707	331
332	6.8966 7855	7.9132 8124	9.0792 1906	10.4163 5295	11.9497 3290	332
333	6.9369 0918	7.9627 3925	9.1397 4719	10.4901 3545	12.0393 5589	333
334	6.9773 7448	8.0125 0637	9.2006 7884	10.5644 4057	12.1296 5106	334
335	7.0180 7583	8.0625 8453	9.2620 1670	10.6392 7203	12.2206 2345	335
336	7.0590 1461	8.1129 7568	9.3237 6347	10.7146 3354	12.3122 7812	336
337	7.1001 9219	8.1636 8178	9.3859 2190	10.7905 2886	12.4046 2021	337
338	7.1416 0998	8.2147 0479	9.4484 9471	10.8669 6177	12.4976 5486	338
339	7.1832 6937	8.2660 4670	9.5114 8468	10.9439 3608	12.5913 8727	339
340	7.2251 7178	8.3177 0949	9.5748 9457	11.0214 5563	12.6858 2268	340
341	7.2673 1861	8.3696 9517	9.6387 2720	11.0995 2428	12.7809 6635	341
342	7.3097 1131	8.4220 0577	9.7029 8538	11.1781 4591	12.8768 2359	342
343	7.3523 5129	8.4746 4330	9.7676 7195	11.2573 2444	12.9733 9977	343
344	7.3952 4000	8.5276 0983	9.8327 8977	11.3370 6382	13.0707 0027	344
345	7.4383 7890	8.5809 0739	9.8983 4170	11.4173 6802	13.1687 3052	345
346	7.4817 6945	8.6345 3806	9.9643 3064	11.4982 4105	13.2674 9600	346
347	7.5254 1310	8.6885 0392	10.0307 5951	11.5796 8692	13.3670 0222	347
348	7.5693 1135	8.7428 0707	10.0976 3124	11.6617 0970	13.4672 5474	348
349	7.6134 6566	8.7974 4961	10.1649 4879	11.7443 1348	13.5682 5915	349
350	7.6578 7755	8.8524 3367	10.2327 1511	11.8275 0237	13.6700 2109	350
351	7.7025 4850	8.9077 6139	10.3009 3321	11.9112 8051	13.7725 4625	351
352	7.7474 8003	8.9634 3489	10.3696 0610	11.9956 5208	13.8758 4035	352
353	7.7926 7366	9.0194 5636	10.4387 3681	12.0806 2128	13.9799 0915	353
354	7.8381 3093	9.0758 2796	10.5083 2839	12.1661 9235	14.0847 5847	354
355	7.8838 5336	9.1325 5189	10.5783 8391	12.2523 6954	14.1903 9415	355
356	7.9298 4250	9.1896 3034	10.6489 0647	12.3391 5716	14.2968 2211	356
357	7.9760 9992	9.2470 6553	10.7198 9918	12.4265 5952	14.4040 4828	357
358	8.0226 2717	9.3048 5969	10.7913 6517	12.5145 8099	14.5120 7864	358
359	8.0694 2582	9.3630 1506	10.8633 0761	12.6032 2594	14.6209 1923	359
360	8.1164 9748	9.4215 3390	10.9357 2966	12.6924 9879	14.7305 7612	360

TABLE I

N	19/24	5/6	7/8	11/12	23/24	N
1	1.0079 1667	1.0083 3333	1.0087 5000	1.0091 6667	1.0095 8333	1
2	1.0158 9601	1.0167 3611	1.0175 7656	1.0184 1736	1.0192 5851	2
3	1.0239 3852	1.0252 0891	1.0264 8036	1.0277 5285	1.0290 2640	3
4	1.0320 4470	1.0337 5232	1.0354 6206	1.0371 7392	1.0388 8790	4
5	1.0402 1505	1.0423 6692	1.0445 2235	1.0466 8135	1.0488 4391	5
6	1.0484 5009	1.0510 5331	1.0536 6192	1.0562 7593	1.0588 9533	6
7	1.0567 5032	1.0598 1209	1.0628 8147	1.0659 5846	1.0690 4308	7
8	1.0651 1626	1.0686 4386	1.0721 8168	1.0757 2974	1.0792 8808	8
9	1.0735 4843	1.0775 4922	1.0815 6327	1.0855 9060	1.0896 3125	9
10	1.0820 4735	1.0865 2880	1.0910 2695	1.0955 4185	1.1000 7355	10
11	1.0906 1356	1.0955 8321	1.1005 7343	1.1055 8431	1.1106 1593	11
12	1.0992 4758	1.1047 1307	1.1102 0345	1.1157 1884	1.1212 5933	12
13	1.1079 4996	1.1139 1901	1.1199 1773	1.1259 4626	1.1320 0473	13
14	1.1167 2123	1.1232 0167	1.1297 1701	1.1362 6743	1.1428 5311	14
15	1.1255 6194	1.1325 6168	1.1396 0203	1.1466 8322	1.1538 0545	15
16	1.1344 7264	1.1419 9970	1.1495 7355	1.1571 9448	1.1648 6275	16
17	1.1434 5388	1.1515 1636	1.1596 3232	1.1678 0210	1.1760 2602	17
18	1.1525 0622	1.1611 1233	1.1697 7910	1.1785 0695	1.1872 9627	18
19	1.1616 3023	1.1707 8827	1.1800 1467	1.1893 0993	1.1986 7453	19
20	1.1708 2647	1.1805 4483	1.1903 3980	1.2002 1194	1.2101 6182	20
21	1.1800 9551	1.1903 8271	1.2007 5527	1.2112 1388	1.2217 5921	21
22	1.1894 3794	1.2003 0256	1.2112 6188	1.2223 1667	1.2334 6773	22
23	1.1988 5432	1.2103 0509	1.2218 6042	1.2335 2124	1.2452 8847	23
24	1.2083 4525	1.2203 9096	1.2325 5170	1.2448 2852	1.2572 2248	24
25	1.2179 1132	1.2305 6089	1.2433 3653	1.2562 3945	1.2692 7086	25
26	1.2275 5312	1.2408 1556	1.2542 1572	1.2677 5498	1.2814 3471	26
27	1.2372 7124	1.2511 5569	1.2651 9011	1.2793 7607	1.2937 1512	27
28	1.2470 6631	1.2615 8199	1.2762 6052	1.2911 0368	1.3061 1323	28
29	1.2569 3892	1.2720 9517	1.2874 2780	1.3029 3880	1.3186 3015	29
30	1.2668 8968	1.2826 9596	1.2986 9280	1.3148 8240	1.3312 6702	30
31	1.2769 1923	1.2933 8510	1.3100 5636	1.3269 3549	1.3440 2499	31
32	1.2870 2817	1.3041 6331	1.3215 1935	1.3390 9907	1.3569 0523	32
33	1.2972 1714	1.3150 3133	1.3330 8265	1.3513 7414	1.3699 0891	33
34	1.3074 8678	1.3259 8993	1.3447 4712	1.3637 6174	1.3830 3720	34
35	1.3178 3772	1.3370 3984	1.3565 1366	1.3762 6289	1.3962 9131	35
36	1.3282 7060	1.3481 8184	1.3683 8315	1.3888 7863	1.4096 7243	36
37	1.3387 8607	1.3594 1669	1.3803 5650	1.4016 1002	1.4231 8180	37
38	1.3493 8480	1.3707 4516	1.3924 3462	1.4144 5811	1.4368 2062	38
39	1.3600 6743	1.3821 6804	1.4046 1843	1.4274 2397	1.4505 9015	39
40	1.3708 3463	1.3936 8611	1.4169 0884	1.4405 0869	1.4644 9164	40
41	1.3816 8707	1.4053 0016	1.4293 0679	1.4537 1336	1.4785 2635	41
42	1.3926 2542	1.4170 1099	1.4418 1322	1.4670 3906	1.4926 9556	42
43	1.4036 5037	1.4288 1942	1.4544 2909	1.4804 8692	1.5070 0056	43
44	1.4147 6261	1.4407 2625	1.4671 5534	1.4940 5805	1.5214 4265	44
45	1.4259 6281	1.4527 3230	1.4799 9295	1.5077 5358	1.5360 2314	45
46	1.4372 5168	1.4648 3840	1.4929 4289	1.5215 7466	1.5507 4336	46
47	1.4486 2993	1.4770 4539	1.5060 0614	1.5355 2243	1.5656 0466	47
48	1.4600 9825	1.4893 5410	1.5191 8370	1.5495 9805	1.5806 0837	48
49	1.4716 5736	1.5017 6538	1.5324 7655	1.5638 0270	1.5957 5586	49
50	1.4833 0798	1.5142 8009	1.5458 8572	1.5781 3755	1.6110 4852	50
51	1.4950 5083	1.5268 9910	1.5594 1222	1.5926 0382	1.6264 8774	51
52	1.5068 8665	1.5396 2325	1.5730 5708	1.6072 0268	1.6420 7491	52
53	1.5188 1617	1.5524 5345	1.5868 2133	1.6219 3538	1.6578 1146	53
54	1.5308 4013	1.5653 9056	1.6007 0602	1.6368 0312	1.6736 9882	54
55	1.5429 5928	1.5784 3548	1.6147 1219	1.6518 0714	1.6897 3844	55
56	1.5551 7438	1.5915 8911	1.6288 4093	1.6669 4871	1.7059 3176	56
57	1.5674 8617	1.6048 5235	1.6430 9328	1.6822 2907	1.7222 8028	57
58	1.5798 9544	1.6182 2612	1.6574 7035	1.6976 4951	1.7387 8546	58
59	1.5924 0295	1.6317 1134	1.6719 7322	1.7132 1129	1.7554 4882	59
60	1.6050 0947	1.6453 0893	1.6866 0298	1.7289 1573	1.7722 7188	60

TABLE I

N	19/24	5/6	7/8	11/12	23/24	N
61	1.6177 1579	1.6590 1984	1.7013 6076	1.7447 6412	1.7892 5615	61
62	1.6305 2271	1.6728 4501	1.7162 4766	1.7607 5780	1.8064 0319	62
63	1.6434 3102	1.6867 8538	1.7312 6483	1.7768 9808	1.8237 1455	63
64	1.6564 4151	1.7008 4193	1.7464 1340	1.7931 8631	1.8411 9181	64
65	1.6695 5501	1.7150 1561	1.7616 9452	1.8096 2385	1.8588 3657	65
66	1.6827 7232	1.7293 0741	1.7771 0934	1.8262 1207	1.8766 5042	66
67	1.6960 9426	1.7437 1830	1.7926 5905	1.8429 5235	1.8946 3499	67
68	1.7095 2168	1.7582 4929	1.8083 4482	1.8598 4607	1.9127 9190	68
69	1.7230 5539	1.7729 0137	1.8241 6783	1.8768 9466	1.9311 2283	69
70	1.7366 9625	1.7876 7554	1.8401 2930	1.8940 9953	1.9496 2942	70
71	1.7504 4509	1.8025 7284	1.8562 3043	1.9114 6211	1.9683 1337	71
72	1.7643 0278	1.8175 9428	1.8724 7245	1.9289 8385	1.9871 7637	72
73	1.7782 7018	1.8327 4090	1.8888 5658	1.9466 6620	2.0062 2015	73
74	1.7923 4815	1.8480 1374	1.9053 8408	1.9645 1064	2.0254 4642	74
75	1.8065 3757	1.8634 1385	1.9220 5619	1.9825 1865	2.0448 5695	75
76	1.8208 3933	1.8789 4230	1.9388 7418	2.0006 9174	2.0644 5350	76
77	1.8352 5431	1.8946 0016	1.9558 3933	2.0190 3141	2.0842 3784	77
78	1.8497 8340	1.9103 8849	1.9729 5292	2.0375 3920	2.1042 1179	78
79	1.8644 2752	1.9263 0839	1.9902 1626	2.0562 1665	2.1243 7715	79
80	1.8791 8757	1.9423 6096	2.0076 3066	2.0750 6530	2.1447 3577	80
81	1.8940 6448	1.9585 4731	2.0251 9742	2.0940 8673	2.1652 8948	81
82	1.9090 5915	1.9748 6853	2.0429 1790	2.1132 8253	2.1860 4017	82
83	1.9241 7254	1.9913 2577	2.0607 9343	2.1326 5428	2.2069 8973	83
84	1.9394 0557	2.0079 2015	2.0788 2537	2.1522 0361	2.2281 4004	84
85	1.9547 5920	2.0246 5282	2.0970 1510	2.1719 3215	2.2494 9305	85
86	1.9702 3437	2.0415 2493	2.1153 6398	2.1918 4152	2.2710 5069	86
87	1.9858 3206	2.0585 3764	2.1338 7341	2.2119 3340	2.2928 1493	87
88	2.0015 5323	2.0756 9212	2.1525 4481	2.2322 0946	2.3147 8774	88
89	2.0173 9886	2.0929 8955	2.1713 7957	2.2526 7138	2.3369 7112	89
90	2.0333 6994	2.1104 3113	2.1903 7914	2.2733 2087	2.3593 6710	90
91	2.0494 6745	2.1280 1806	2.2095 4496	2.2941 5964	2.3819 7770	91
92	2.0656 9240	2.1457 5154	2.2288 7848	2.3151 8944	2.4048 0498	92
93	2.0820 4580	2.1636 3280	2.2483 8117	2.3364 1201	2.4278 5103	93
94	2.0985 2866	2.1816 6308	2.2680 5450	2.3578 2912	2.4511 1794	94
95	2.1151 4201	2.1998 4360	2.2878 9998	2.3794 4255	2.4746 0782	95
96	2.1318 8689	2.2181 7563	2.3079 1910	2.4012 5411	2.4983 2281	96
97	2.1487 6433	2.2366 6043	2.3281 1340	2.4232 6561	2.5222 6507	97
98	2.1657 7538	2.2552 9926	2.3484 8439	2.4454 7887	2.5464 3678	98
99	2.1829 2110	2.2740 9343	2.3690 3363	2.4678 9576	2.5708 4013	99
100	2.2002 0256	2.2930 4420	2.3897 6267	2.4905 1814	2.5954 7735	100
101	2.2176 2083	2.3121 5291	2.4106 7309	2.5133 4789	2.6203 5067	101
102	2.2351 7699	2.3314 2085	2.4317 6648	2.5363 8691	2.6454 6236	102
103	2.2528 7214	2.3508 4935	2.4530 4444	2.5596 3713	2.6708 1471	103
104	2.2707 0738	2.3704 3976	2.4745 0858	2.5831 0047	2.6964 1002	104
105	2.2886 8381	2.3901 9343	2.4961 6053	2.6067 7889	2.7222 5062	105
106	2.3068 0256	2.4101 1171	2.5180 0193	2.6306 7436	2.7483 3885	106
107	2.3250 6475	2.4301 9597	2.5400 3445	2.6547 8888	2.7746 7710	107
108	2.3434 7151	2.4504 4761	2.5622 5975	2.6791 2444	2.8012 6775	108
109	2.3620 2399	2.4708 6800	2.5846 7953	2.7036 8308	2.8281 1324	109
110	2.3807 2335	2.4914 5857	2.6072 9547	2.7284 6684	2.8552 1599	110
111	2.3995 7074	2.5122 2072	2.6301 0931	2.7534 7779	2.8825 7847	111
112	2.4185 6735	2.5331 5590	2.6531 2276	2.7787 1800	2.9102 0319	112
113	2.4377 1434	2.5542 6553	2.6763 3759	2.8041 8958	2.9380 9263	113
114	2.4570 1291	2.5755 5107	2.6997 5554	2.8298 9465	2.9662 4935	114
115	2.4764 6426	2.5970 1400	2.7233 7840	2.8558 3536	2.9946 7591	115
116	2.4960 6960	2.6186 5578	2.7472 0796	2.8820 1385	3.0233 7489	116
117	2.5158 3015	2.6404 7792	2.7712 4603	2.9084 3231	3.0523 4890	117
118	2.5357 4714	2.6624 8190	2.7954 9444	2.9350 9294	3.0816 0057	118
119	2.5558 2181	2.6846 6925	2.8199 5501	2.9619 9796	3.1111 3258	119
120	2.5760 5540	2.7070 4149	2.8446 2962	2.9891 4960	3.1409 4760	120

TABLE I

N	19/24	5/6	7/8	11/12	23/24	N
121	2.5964 4917	2.7296 0017	2.8695 2013	3.0165 5014	3.1710 4835	121
122	2.6170 0439	2.7523 4684	2.8946 2843	3.0442 0185	3.2014 3756	122
123	2.6377 2234	2.7752 8306	2.9199 5643	3.0721 0703	3.2321 1800	123
124	2.6586 0431	2.7984 1042	2.9455 0605	3.1002 6802	3.2630 9247	124
125	2.6796 5160	2.8217 3051	2.9712 7922	3.1286 8714	3.2943 6377	125
126	2.7008 6550	2.8452 4493	2.9972 7792	3.1573 6677	3.3259 3476	126
127	2.7222 4736	2.8689 5530	3.0235 0410	3.1863 0930	3.3578 0830	127
128	2.7437 9848	2.8928 6326	3.0499 5976	3.2155 1714	3.3899 8729	128
129	2.7655 2022	2.9169 7046	3.0766 4691	3.2449 9271	3.4224 7467	129
130	2.7874 1392	2.9412 7854	3.1035 6757	3.2747 3848	3.4552 7339	130
131	2.8094 8095	2.9657 8920	3.1307 2378	3.3047 5691	3.4883 8643	131
132	2.8317 2267	2.9905 0411	3.1581 1762	3.3350 5052	3.5218 1680	132
133	2.8541 4048	3.0154 2498	3.1857 5115	3.3656 2181	3.5555 6754	133
134	2.8767 3575	3.0405 5352	3.2136 2647	3.3964 7335	3.5896 4173	134
135	2.8995 0991	3.0658 9146	3.2417 4570	3.4276 0768	3.6240 4246	135
136	2.9224 6437	3.0914 4056	3.2701 1098	3.4590 2742	3.6587 7287	136
137	2.9456 0054	3.1172 0256	3.2987 2445	3.4907 3517	3.6938 3611	137
138	2.9689 1988	3.1431 7925	3.3275 8829	3.5227 3358	3.7292 3537	138
139	2.9924 2383	3.1693 7241	3.3567 0468	3.5550 2530	3.7649 7388	139
140	3.0161 1385	3.1957 8385	3.3860 7585	3.5876 1304	3.8010 5488	140
141	3.0399 9142	3.2224 1538	3.4157 0401	3.6204 9949	3.8374 8165	141
142	3.0640 5802	3.2492 6884	3.4455 9142	3.6536 8740	3.8742 5752	142
143	3.0883 1514	3.2763 4608	3.4757 4035	3.6871 7953	3.9113 8582	143
144	3.1127 6430	3.3036 4897	3.5061 5308	3.7209 7868	3.9488 6993	144
145	3.1374 0702	3.3311 7938	3.5368 3192	3.7550 8765	3.9867 1327	145
146	3.1622 4483	3.3589 3920	3.5677 7919	3.7895 0929	4.0249 1927	146
147	3.1872 7927	3.3869 3036	3.5989 9726	3.8242 4646	4.0634 9142	147
148	3.2125 1189	3.4151 5478	3.6304 8849	3.8593 0205	4.1024 3321	148
149	3.2379 4428	3.4436 1441	3.6622 5526	3.8946 7899	4.1417 4819	149
150	3.2635 7801	3.4723 1119	3.6943 0000	3.9303 8021	4.1814 3995	150
151	3.2894 1466	3.5012 4712	3.7266 2512	3.9664 0869	4.2215 1208	151
152	3.3154 5586	3.5304 2418	3.7592 3309	4.0027 6744	4.2619 6824	152
153	3.3417 0322	3.5598 4438	3.7921 2638	4.0394 5948	4.3028 1210	153
154	3.3681 5837	3.5895 0975	3.8253 0749	4.0764 8785	4.3440 4738	154
155	3.3948 2296	3.6194 2233	3.8587 7893	4.1138 5566	4.3856 7784	155
156	3.4216 9864	3.6495 8418	3.8925 4324	4.1515 6600	4.4277 0725	156
157	3.4487 8709	3.6799 9739	3.9266 0300	4.1896 2202	4.4701 3944	157
158	3.4760 8999	3.7106 6403	3.9609 6077	4.2280 2689	4.5129 7828	158
159	3.5036 0903	3.7415 8623	3.9956 1918	4.2667 8381	4.5562 2765	159
160	3.5313 4594	3.7727 6612	4.0305 8085	4.3058 9599	4.5998 9150	160
161	3.5593 0243	3.8042 0583	4.0658 4843	4.3453 6670	4.6439 7380	161
162	3.5874 8024	3.8359 0755	4.1014 2460	4.3851 9923	4.6884 7855	162
163	3.6158 8112	3.8678 7345	4.1373 1207	4.4253 9689	4.7334 0980	163
164	3.6445 0685	3.9001 0572	4.1735 1355	4.4659 6303	4.7787 7164	164
165	3.6733 5919	3.9326 0661	4.2100 3179	4.5069 0103	4.8245 6820	165
166	3.7024 3995	3.9653 7833	4.2468 6957	4.5482 1428	4.8708 0365	166
167	3.7317 5094	3.9984 2315	4.2840 2968	4.5899 0625	4.9174 8218	167
168	3.7612 9397	4.0317 4334	4.3215 1494	4.6319 8039	4.9646 0805	168
169	3.7910 7088	4.0653 4120	4.3593 2819	4.6744 4021	5.0121 8555	169
170	3.8210 8352	4.0992 1904	4.3974 7232	4.7172 8924	5.0602 1899	170
171	3.8513 3377	4.1333 7920	4.4359 5020	4.7605 3106	5.1087 1276	171
172	3.8818 2349	4.1678 2403	4.4747 6476	4.8041 6926	5.1576 7126	172
173	3.9125 5459	4.2025 5590	4.5139 1896	4.8482 0748	5.2070 9894	173
174	3.9435 2898	4.2375 7720	4.5534 1575	4.8926 4938	5.2570 0030	174
175	3.9747 4859	4.2728 9034	4.5932 5813	4.9374 9867	5.3073 7989	175
176	4.0062 1535	4.3084 9776	4.6334 4914	4.9827 5908	5.3582 4228	176
177	4.0379 3122	4.3444 0191	4.6739 9182	5.0284 3437	5.4095 9210	177
178	4.0698 9818	4.3806 0526	4.7148 8925	5.0745 2835	5.4614 3403	178
179	4.1021 1820	4.4171 1030	4.7561 4453	5.1210 4486	5.5137 7277	179
180	4.1345 9330	4.4539 1955	4.7977 6080	5.1679 8777	5.5666 1309	180

TABLE I

N	19/24	5/6	7/8	11/12	23/24	N
181	4.1673 2550	4.4910 3555	4.8397 4120	5.2153 6099	5.6199 5980	181
182	4.2003 1683	4.5284 6084	4.8820 8894	5.2631 6847	5.6738 1775	182
183	4.2335 6934	4.5661 9802	4.9248 0722	5.3114 1418	5.7281 9184	183
184	4.2670 8509	4.6042 4967	4.9678 9928	5.3601 0214	5.7830 8701	184
185	4.3008 6618	4.6426 1842	5.0113 6840	5.4092 3641	5.8385 0826	185
186	4.3349 1471	4.6813 0690	5.0552 1787	5.4588 2108	5.8944 6063	186
187	4.3692 3278	4.7203 1779	5.0994 5103	5.5088 6027	5.9509 4921	187
188	4.4038 2254	4.7596 5377	5.1440 7123	5.5593 5816	6.0079 7914	188
189	4.4386 8614	4.7993 1756	5.1890 8185	5.6103 1894	6.0655 5561	189
190	4.4738 2574	4.8393 1187	5.2344 8631	5.6617 4686	6.1236 8385	190
191	4.5092 4352	4.8796 3947	5.2802 8807	5.7136 4621	6.1823 6915	191
192	4.5449 4170	4.9203 0313	5.3264 9059	5.7660 2130	6.2416 1686	192
193	4.5809 2249	4.9613 0566	5.3730 9738	5.8188 7649	6.3014 3235	193
194	4.6171 8813	5.0026 4987	5.4201 1199	5.8722 1620	6.3618 2108	194
195	4.6537 4087	5.0443 3862	5.4675 3797	5.9260 4484	6.4227 8853	195
196	4.6905 8298	5.0863 7477	5.5153 7892	5.9803 6692	6.4843 4025	196
197	4.7277 1676	5.1287 6123	5.5636 3849	6.0351 8695	6.5464 8185	197
198	4.7651 4452	5.1715 0091	5.6123 2033	6.0905 0950	6.6092 1896	198
199	4.8028 6858	5.2145 9675	5.6614 2813	6.1463 3917	6.6725 5731	199
200	4.8408 9129	5.2580 5172	5.7109 6562	6.2026 8061	6.7365 0265	200
201	4.8792 1501	5.3018 6882	5.7609 3657	6.2595 3852	6.8010 6080	201
202	4.9178 4213	5.3460 5106	5.8113 4477	6.3169 1762	6.8662 3764	202
203	4.9567 7505	5.3906 0148	5.8621 9403	6.3748 2270	6.9320 3908	203
204	4.9960 1619	5.4355 2316	5.9134 8823	6.4332 5857	6.9984 7112	204
205	5.0355 6798	5.4808 1919	5.9652 3125	6.4922 3011	7.0655 3980	205
206	5.0754 3289	5.5264 9268	6.0174 2703	6.5517 4222	7.1332 5123	206
207	5.1156 1340	5.5725 4679	6.0700 7951	6.6117 9986	7.2016 1155	207
208	5.1561 1201	5.6189 8468	6.1231 9271	6.6724 0802	7.2706 2699	208
209	5.1969 3123	5.6658 0955	6.1767 7065	6.7335 7176	7.3403 0384	209
210	5.2380 7360	5.7130 2463	6.2308 1739	6.7952 9617	7.4106 4842	210
211	5.2795 4168	5.7606 3317	6.2853 3704	6.8575 8639	7.4816 6713	211
212	5.3213 3806	5.8086 3845	6.3403 3374	6.9204 4759	7.5533 6644	212
213	5.3634 6532	5.8570 4377	6.3958 1166	6.9838 8503	7.6257 5287	213
214	5.4059 2608	5.9058 5246	6.4517 7501	7.0479 0398	7.6988 3300	214
215	5.4487 2300	5.9550 6790	6.5082 2804	7.1125 0976	7.7726 1348	215
216	5.4918 5872	6.0046 9347	6.5651 7504	7.1777 0777	7.8471 0103	216
217	5.5353 3594	6.0547 3258	6.6226 2032	7.2435 0342	7.9223 0241	217
218	5.5791 5735	6.1051 8868	6.6805 6825	7.3099 0220	7.9982 2448	218
219	5.6233 2567	6.1560 6526	6.7390 2322	7.3769 0964	8.0748 7413	219
220	5.6678 4367	6.2073 6580	6.7979 8968	7.4445 3131	8.1522 5834	220
221	5.7127 1410	6.2590 9385	6.8574 7208	7.5127 7285	8.2303 8415	221
222	5.7579 3975	6.3112 5296	6.9174 7497	7.5816 3993	8.3092 5866	222
223	5.8035 2344	6.3638 4674	6.9780 0287	7.6511 3830	8.3888 8906	223
224	5.8494 6800	6.4168 7880	7.0390 6040	7.7212 7374	8.4692 8258	224
225	5.8957 7629	6.4703 5279	7.1006 5217	7.7920 5208	8.5504 4654	225
226	5.9424 5119	6.5242 7239	7.1627 8288	7.8634 7922	8.6323 8832	226
227	5.9894 9559	6.5786 4133	7.2254 5723	7.9355 6111	8.7151 1537	227
228	6.0369 1243	6.6334 6334	7.2886 7998	8.0083 0376	8.7986 3523	228
229	6.0847 0466	6.6887 4220	7.3524 5593	8.0817 1321	8.8829 5548	229
230	6.1328 7523	6.7444 8172	7.4167 8992	8.1557 9558	8.9680 8380	230
231	6.1814 2716	6.8006 8573	7.4816 8683	8.2305 5704	9.0540 2794	231
232	6.2303 6346	6.8573 5811	7.5471 5159	8.3060 0381	9.1407 9571	232
233	6.2796 8717	6.9145 0277	7.6131 8917	8.3821 4218	9.2283 9500	233
234	6.3294 0136	6.9721 2362	7.6798 0458	8.4589 7848	9.3168 3379	234
235	6.3795 0912	7.0302 2465	7.7470 0287	8.5365 1912	9.4061 2011	235
236	6.4300 1357	7.0888 0986	7.8147 8914	8.6147 7055	9.4962 6209	236
237	6.4809 1784	7.1478 8327	7.8831 6855	8.6937 3928	9.5872 6794	237
238	6.5322 2511	7.2074 4897	7.9521 4627	8.7734 3189	9.6791 4592	238
239	6.5839 3856	7.2675 1104	8.0217 2755	8.8538 5501	9.7719 0441	239
240	6.6360 6141	7.3280 7363	8.0919 1767	8.9350 1535	9.8655 5182	240

TABLE I

N	19/24	5/6	7/8	11/12	23/24	N
241	6.6885 9689	7.3891 4091	8.1627 2195	9.0169 1966	9.9600 9669	241
242	6.7415 4828	7.4507 1709	8.2341 4576	9.0995 7475	10.0555 4762	242
243	6.7949 1887	7.5128 0640	8.3061 9454	9.1829 8752	10.1519 1329	243
244	6.8487 1198	7.5754 1312	8.3788 7374	9.2671 6491	10.2492 0245	244
245	6.9029 3095	7.6385 4156	8.4521 8889	9.3521 1392	10.3474 2398	245
246	6.9575 7916	7.7021 9607	8.5261 4554	9.4378 4163	10.4465 8679	246
247	7.0126 5999	7.7663 8104	8.6007 4931	9.5243 5518	10.5466 9991	247
248	7.0681 7688	7.8311 0088	8.6760 0587	9.6116 6177	10.6477 7246	248
249	7.1241 3328	7.8963 6006	8.7519 2092	9.6997 6867	10.7498 1361	249
250	7.1805 3267	7.9621 6306	8.8285 0023	9.7886 8321	10.8528 3266	250
251	7.2373 7855	8.0285 1442	8.9057 4960	9.8784 1281	10.9568 3897	251
252	7.2946 7447	8.0954 1870	8.9836 7491	9.9689 6493	11.0618 4201	252
253	7.3524 2397	8.1628 8052	9.0622 8207	10.0603 4711	11.1678 5133	253
254	7.4106 3066	8.2309 0453	9.1415 7704	10.1525 6695	11.2748 7657	254
255	7.4692 9816	8.2994 9540	9.2215 6584	10.2456 3215	11.3829 2747	255
256	7.5284 3010	8.3686 5786	9.3022 5454	10.3395 5045	11.4920 1386	256
257	7.5880 3017	8.4383 9668	9.3836 4926	10.4343 2966	11.6021 4566	257
258	7.6481 0208	8.5087 1665	9.4657 5620	10.5299 7768	11.7133 3289	258
259	7.7086 4955	8.5796 2262	9.5485 8156	10.6265 0248	11.8255 8566	259
260	7.7696 7636	8.6511 1948	9.6321 3165	10.7239 1208	11.9389 1419	260
261	7.8311 8630	8.7232 1214	9.7164 1280	10.8222 1461	12.0533 2878	261
262	7.8931 8319	8.7959 0557	9.8014 3141	10.9214 1824	12.1688 3985	262
263	7.9556 7089	8.8692 0479	9.8871 9394	11.0215 3124	12.2854 5790	263
264	8.0186 5329	8.9431 1483	9.9737 0689	11.1225 6195	12.4031 9354	264
265	8.0821 3429	9.0176 4078	10.0609 7682	11.2245 1876	12.5220 5748	265
266	8.1461 1785	9.0927 8779	10.1490 1037	11.3274 1019	12.6420 6053	266
267	8.2106 0795	9.1685 6102	10.2378 1421	11.4312 4478	12.7632 1361	267
268	8.2756 0860	9.2449 6570	10.3273 9508	11.5360 3119	12.8855 2774	268
269	8.3411 2384	9.3220 0708	10.4177 5979	11.6417 7814	13.0090 1404	269
270	8.4071 5773	9.3996 9047	10.5089 1519	11.7484 9444	13.1336 8376	270
271	8.4737 1440	9.4780 2122	10.6008 6820	11.8561 8897	13.2595 4823	271
272	8.5407 9797	9.5570 0473	10.6936 2579	11.9648 7071	13.3866 1890	272
273	8.6084 1262	9.6366 4644	10.7871 9502	12.0745 4869	13.5149 0733	273
274	8.6765 6255	9.7169 5183	10.8815 8298	12.1852 3205	13.6444 2520	274
275	8.7452 5201	9.7979 2643	10.9767 9683	12.2969 3001	13.7751 8427	275
276	8.8144 8525	9.8795 7581	11.0728 4380	12.4096 5187	13.9071 9645	276
277	8.8842 6659	9.9619 0561	11.1697 3118	12.5234 0701	14.0404 7375	277
278	8.9546 0037	10.0449 2149	11.2674 6633	12.6382 0491	14.1750 2829	278
279	9.0254 9096	10.1286 2917	11.3660 5666	12.7540 5512	14.3108 7231	279
280	9.0969 4276	10.2130 3441	11.4655 0966	12.8709 6729	14.4480 1817	280
281	9.1689 6022	10.2981 4303	11.5658 3287	12.9889 5116	14.5864 7835	281
282	9.2415 4783	10.3839 6089	11.6670 3390	13.1080 1655	14.7262 6543	282
283	9.3147 1008	10.4704 9390	11.7691 2045	13.2281 7336	14.8673 9214	283
284	9.3884 5153	10.5577 4801	11.8721 0025	13.3494 3162	15.0098 7132	284
285	9.4627 7678	10.6457 2925	11.9759 8113	13.4718 0141	15.1537 1592	285
286	9.5376 9043	10.7344 4366	12.0807 7097	13.5952 9292	15.2989 3903	286
287	9.6131 9714	10.8238 9736	12.1864 7771	13.7199 1644	15.4455 5386	287
288	9.6893 0162	10.9140 9650	12.2931 0939	13.8456 8234	15.5935 7375	288
289	9.7660 0859	11.0050 4730	12.4006 7410	13.9726 0110	15.7430 1217	289
290	9.8433 2282	11.0967 5603	12.5091 8000	14.1006 8327	15.8938 8270	290
291	9.9212 4913	11.1892 2900	12.6186 3532	14.2299 3954	16.0461 9908	291
292	9.9997 9235	11.2824 7257	12.7290 4838	14.3603 8065	16.1999 7515	292
293	10.0789 5738	11.3764 9318	12.8404 2756	14.4920 1747	16.3552 2491	293
294	10.1587 4912	11.4712 9729	12.9527 8130	14.6248 6097	16.5119 6248	294
295	10.2391 7255	11.5668 9143	13.0661 1813	14.7589 2219	16.6702 0212	295
296	10.3202 3267	11.6632 8219	13.1804 4667	14.8942 1231	16.8299 5823	296
297	10.4019 3451	11.7604 7621	13.2957 7557	15.0307 4259	16.9912 4533	297
298	10.4842 8316	11.8584 8018	13.4121 1361	15.1685 2440	17.1540 7810	298
299	10.5672 8373	11.9573 0085	13.5294 6960	15.3075 6920	17.3184 7134	299
300	10.6509 4140	12.0569 4502	13.6478 5246	15.4478 8859	17.4844 4003	300

TABLE I

N	19/24	5/6	7/8	11/12	23/24	N
301	10.7352 6135	12.1574 1957	13.7672 7117	15.5894 9423	17.6519 9924	301
302	10.8202 4883	12.2587 3140	13.8877 3480	15.7323 9793	17.8211 6424	302
303	10.9059 0914	12.3608 8749	14.0092 5248	15.8766 1158	17.9919 5039	303
304	10.9922 4758	12.4638 9489	14.1318 3343	16.0221 4719	18.1643 7325	304
305	11.0792 6954	12.5677 6068	14.2554 8698	16.1690 1687	18.3384 4850	305
306	11.1669 8043	12.6724 9202	14.3802 2249	16.3172 3286	18.5141 9196	306
307	11.2553 8569	12.7780 9612	14.5060 4943	16.4668 0749	18.6916 1963	307
308	11.3444 9083	12.8845 8025	14.6329 7737	16.6177 5323	18.8707 4766	308
309	11.4343 0138	12.9919 5175	14.7610 1592	16.7700 8263	19.0515 9232	309
310	11.5248 2293	13.1002 1802	14.8901 7481	16.9238 0839	19.2341 7008	310
311	11.6160 6111	13.2093 8650	15.0204 6384	17.0789 4330	19.4184 9754	311
312	11.7080 2160	13.3194 6472	15.1518 9290	17.2355 0028	19.6045 9148	312
313	11.8007 1010	13.4304 6026	15.2844 7196	17.3934 9236	19.7924 6881	313
314	11.8941 3239	13.5423 8076	15.4182 1109	17.5529 3271	19.9821 4664	314
315	11.9882 9427	13.6552 3394	15.5531 2044	17.7138 3459	20.1736 4221	315
316	12.0832 0160	13.7690 2755	15.6892 1024	17.8762 1141	20.3669 7295	316
317	12.1788 6028	13.8837 6945	15.8264 9083	18.0400 7668	20.5621 5644	317
318	12.2752 7626	13.9994 6753	15.9649 7262	18.2054 4405	20.7592 1044	318
319	12.3724 5553	14.1161 2976	16.1046 6613	18.3723 2729	20.9581 5287	319
320	12.4704 0413	14.2337 6417	16.2455 8196	18.5407 4029	21.1590 0184	320
321	12.5691 2817	14.3523 7887	16.3877 3081	18.7106 9708	21.3617 7561	321
322	12.6686 3376	14.4719 8203	16.5311 2345	18.8822 1180	21.5664 9262	322
323	12.7689 2712	14.5925 8188	16.6757 7078	19.0552 9874	21.7731 7151	323
324	12.8700 1446	14.7141 8673	16.8216 8377	19.2299 7231	21.9818 3107	324
325	12.9719 0207	14.8368 0495	16.9688 7351	19.4062 4706	22.1924 9028	325
326	13.0745 9629	14.9604 4499	17.1173 5115	19.5841 3766	22.4051 6832	326
327	13.1781 0351	15.0851 1537	17.2671 2797	19.7636 5892	22.6198 8451	327
328	13.2824 3017	15.2108 2466	17.4182 1534	19.9448 2579	22.8366 5841	328
329	13.3875 8274	15.3375 8153	17.5706 2473	20.1276 5336	23.0555 0972	329
330	13.4935 6777	15.4653 9471	17.7243 6769	20.3121 5685	23.2764 5835	330
331	13.6003 9185	15.5942 7300	17.8794 5591	20.4983 5162	23.4995 2441	331
332	13.7080 6162	15.7242 2528	18.0359 0115	20.6862 5318	23.7247 2818	332
333	13.8165 8377	15.8552 6049	18.1937 1529	20.8758 7717	23.9520 9016	333
334	13.9259 6506	15.9873 8766	18.3529 1029	21.0672 3937	24.1816 3103	334
335	14.0362 1228	16.1206 1589	18.5134 9826	21.2603 5573	24.4133 7166	335
336	14.1473 3230	16.2549 5436	18.6754 9137	21.4552 4233	24.6473 3314	336
337	14.2593 3201	16.3904 1231	18.8389 0192	21.6519 1538	24.8835 3675	337
338	14.3722 1839	16.5269 9908	19.0037 4231	21.8503 9127	25.1220 0397	338
339	14.4859 9845	16.6647 2407	19.1700 2506	22.0506 8653	25.3627 5651	339
340	14.6006 7927	16.8035 9677	19.3377 6277	22.2528 1782	25.6058 1626	340
341	14.7162 6798	16.9436 2674	19.5069 6820	22.4568 0198	25.8512 0533	341
342	14.8327 7177	17.0848 2363	19.6776 5417	22.6626 5600	26.0989 4605	342
343	14.9501 9788	17.2271 9716	19.8498 3364	22.8703 9701	26.3490 6095	343
344	15.0685 5361	17.3707 5714	20.0235 1969	23.0800 4232	26.6015 7278	344
345	15.1878 4633	17.5155 1345	20.1987 2549	23.2916 0938	26.8565 0452	345
346	15.3080 8345	17.6614 7606	20.3754 6433	23.5051 1579	27.1138 7936	346
347	15.4292 7244	17.8086 5503	20.5537 4965	23.7205 7936	27.3737 2070	347
348	15.5514 2085	17.9570 6049	20.7335 9496	23.9380 1800	27.6360 5219	348
349	15.6745 3626	18.1067 0266	20.9150 1391	24.1574 4983	27.9008 9769	349
350	15.7986 2634	18.2575 9185	21.0980 2028	24.3788 9312	28.1682 8130	350
351	15.9236 9880	18.4097 3845	21.2826 2796	24.6023 6631	28.4382 2733	351
352	16.0497 6142	18.5631 5293	21.4688 5096	24.8278 8800	28.7107 6034	352
353	16.1768 2203	18.7178 4587	21.6567 0340	25.0554 7697	28.9859 0512	353
354	16.3048 8854	18.8738 2792	21.8461 9956	25.2851 5218	29.2636 8671	354
355	16.4339 6890	19.0311 0982	22.0373 5380	25.5169 3274	29.5441 3038	355
356	16.5640 7116	19.1897 0240	22.2301 8065	25.7508 3796	29.8272 6163	356
357	16.6952 0339	19.3496 1659	22.4246 9473	25.9868 8731	30.1131 0622	357
358	16.8273 7375	19.5108 6340	22.6209 1081	26.2251 0044	30.4016 9015	358
359	16.9605 9046	19.6734 5392	22.8188 4378	26.4654 9719	30.6930 3968	359
360	17.0948 6180	19.8373 9937	23.0185 0866	26.7080 9758	30.9871 8131	360

TABLE I

N	1	1 1/8	1 1/4	1 3/8	1 1/2	N
1	1.0100 0000	1.0112 5000	1.0125 0000	1.0137 5000	1.0150 0000	1
2	1.0201 0000	1.0226 2656	1.0251 5625	1.0276 8906	1.0302 2500	2
3	1.0303 0100	1.0341 3111	1.0379 7070	1.0418 1979	1.0456 7837	3
4	1.0406 0401	1.0457 6509	1.0509 4534	1.0561 4481	1.0613 6355	4
5	1.0510 1005	1.0575 2994	1.0640 8215	1.0706 6680	1.0772 8400	5
6	1.0615 2015	1.0694 2716	1.0773 8318	1.0853 8847	1.0934 4326	6
7	1.0721 3535	1.0814 5821	1.0908 5047	1.1003 1256	1.1098 4491	7
8	1.0828 5671	1.0936 2462	1.1044 8610	1.1154 4186	1.1264 9259	8
9	1.0936 8527	1.1059 2789	1.1182 9218	1.1307 7918	1.1433 8998	9
10	1.1046 2213	1.1183 6958	1.1322 7083	1.1463 2740	1.1605 4083	10
11	1.1156 6835	1.1309 5124	1.1464 2422	1.1620 8940	1.1779 4894	11
12	1.1268 2503	1.1436 7444	1.1607 5452	1.1780 6813	1.1956 1817	12
13	1.1380 9328	1.1565 4078	1.1752 6395	1.1942 6656	1.2135 5244	13
14	1.1494 7421	1.1695 5186	1.1899 5475	1.2106 8773	1.2317 5573	14
15	1.1609 6896	1.1827 0932	1.2048 2918	1.2273 3469	1.2502 3207	15
16	1.1725 7864	1.1960 1480	1.2198 8955	1.2442 1054	1.2689 8555	16
17	1.1843 0443	1.2094 6997	1.2351 3817	1.2613 1843	1.2880 2033	17
18	1.1961 4748	1.2230 7650	1.2505 7739	1.2786 6156	1.3073 4064	18
19	1.2081 0895	1.2368 3611	1.2662 0961	1.2962 4316	1.3269 5075	19
20	1.2201 9004	1.2507 5052	1.2820 3723	1.3140 6650	1.3468 5501	20
21	1.2323 9194	1.2648 2146	1.2980 6270	1.3321 3492	1.3670 5783	21
22	1.2447 1586	1.2790 5071	1.3142 8848	1.3504 5177	1.3875 6370	22
23	1.2571 6302	1.2934 4003	1.3307 1709	1.3690 2048	1.4083 7715	23
24	1.2697 3465	1.3079 9123	1.3473 5105	1.3878 4451	1.4295 0281	24
25	1.2824 3200	1.3227 0613	1.3641 9294	1.4069 2738	1.4509 4535	25
26	1.2952 5631	1.3375 8657	1.3812 4535	1.4262 7263	1.4727 0953	26
27	1.3082 0888	1.3526 3442	1.3985 1092	1.4458 8388	1.4948 0018	27
28	1.3212 9097	1.3678 5156	1.4159 9230	1.4657 6478	1.5172 2218	28
29	1.3345 0388	1.3832 3989	1.4336 9221	1.4859 1905	1.5399 8051	29
30	1.3478 4892	1.3988 0134	1.4516 1336	1.5063 5043	1.5630 8022	30
31	1.3613 2740	1.4145 3785	1.4697 5853	1.5270 6275	1.5865 2642	31
32	1.3749 4068	1.4304 5140	1.4881 3051	1.5480 5986	1.6103 2432	32
33	1.3886 9009	1.4465 4398	1.5067 3214	1.5693 4569	1.6344 7918	33
34	1.4025 7699	1.4628 1760	1.5255 6629	1.5909 2419	1.6589 9637	34
35	1.4166 0276	1.4792 7430	1.5446 3587	1.6127 9940	1.6838 8132	35
36	1.4307 6878	1.4959 1613	1.5639 4382	1.6349 7539	1.7091 3954	36
37	1.4450 7647	1.5127 4519	1.5834 9312	1.6574 5630	1.7347 7663	37
38	1.4595 2724	1.5297 6357	1.6032 8678	1.6802 4633	1.7607 9828	38
39	1.4741 2251	1.5469 7341	1.6233 2787	1.7033 4971	1.7872 1025	39
40	1.4888 6373	1.5643 7687	1.6436 1946	1.7267 7077	1.8140 1841	40
41	1.5037 5237	1.5819 7611	1.6641 6471	1.7505 1387	1.8412 2868	41
42	1.5187 8989	1.5997 7334	1.6849 6677	1.7745 8343	1.8688 4712	42
43	1.5339 7779	1.6177 7079	1.7060 2885	1.7989 8396	1.8968 7982	43
44	1.5493 1757	1.6359 7071	1.7273 5421	1.8237 1999	1.9253 3302	44
45	1.5648 1075	1.6543 7538	1.7489 4614	1.8487 9614	1.9542 1301	45
46	1.5804 5885	1.6729 8710	1.7708 0797	1.8742 1708	1.9835 2621	46
47	1.5962 6344	1.6918 0821	1.7929 4306	1.8999 8757	2.0132 7910	47
48	1.6122 2608	1.7108 4105	1.8153 5485	1.9261 1240	2.0434 7829	48
49	1.6283 4834	1.7300 8801	1.8380 4679	1.9525 9644	2.0741 3046	49
50	1.6446 3182	1.7495 5150	1.8610 2237	1.9794 4464	2.1052 4242	50
51	1.6610 7814	1.7692 3395	1.8842 8515	2.0066 6201	2.1368 2106	51
52	1.6776 8892	1.7891 3784	1.9078 3872	2.0342 5361	2.1688 7337	52
53	1.6944 6581	1.8092 6564	1.9316 8670	2.0622 2460	2.2014 0647	53
54	1.7114 1047	1.8296 1988	1.9558 3279	2.0905 8019	2.2344 2757	54
55	1.7285 2457	1.8502 0310	1.9802 8070	2.1193 2566	2.2679 4398	55
56	1.7458 0982	1.8710 1788	2.0050 3420	2.1484 6639	2.3019 6314	56
57	1.7632 6792	1.8920 6684	2.0300 9713	2.1780 0780	2.3364 9259	57
58	1.7809 0060	1.9133 5259	2.0554 7335	2.2079 5541	2.3715 3998	58
59	1.7987 0960	1.9348 7780	2.0811 6676	2.2383 1480	2.4071 1308	59
60	1.8166 9670	1.9566 4518	2.1071 8135	2.2690 9163	2.4432 1978	60

TABLE I

N	1	1 1/8	1 1/4	1 3/8	1 1/2	N
61	1.8348 6367	1.9786 5744	2.1335 2111	2.3002 9164	2.4798 6807	61
62	1.8532 1230	2.0009 1733	2.1601 9013	2.3319 2065	2.5170 6609	62
63	1.8717 4443	2.0234 2765	2.1871 9250	2.3639 8456	2.5548 2208	63
64	1.8904 6187	2.0461 9121	2.2145 3241	2.3964 8934	2.5931 4442	64
65	1.9093 6649	2.0692 1087	2.2422 1407	2.4294 4107	2.6320 4158	65
66	1.9284 6015	2.0924 8949	2.2702 4174	2.4628 4589	2.6715 2221	66
67	1.9477 4475	2.1160 2999	2.2986 1976	2.4967 1002	2.7115 9504	67
68	1.9672 2220	2.1398 3533	2.3273 5251	2.5310 3978	2.7522 6896	68
69	1.9868 9442	2.1639 0848	2.3564 4442	2.5658 4158	2.7935 5300	69
70	2.0067 6337	2.1882 5245	2.3858 9997	2.6011 2190	2.8354 5629	70
71	2.0268 3100	2.2128 7029	2.4157 2372	2.6368 8732	2.8779 8814	71
72	2.0470 9931	2.2377 6508	2.4459 2027	2.6731 4453	2.9211 5796	72
73	2.0675 7031	2.2629 3994	2.4764 9427	2.7099 0026	2.9649 7533	73
74	2.0882 4601	2.2883 9801	2.5074 5045	2.7471 6139	3.0094 4996	74
75	2.1091 2847	2.3141 4249	2.5387 9358	2.7849 3486	3.0545 9171	75
76	2.1302 1975	2.3401 7659	2.5705 2850	2.8232 2771	3.1004 1059	76
77	2.1515 2195	2.3665 0358	2.6026 6011	2.8620 4710	3.1469 1674	77
78	2.1730 3717	2.3931 2675	2.6351 9336	2.9014 0024	3.1941 2050	78
79	2.1947 6754	2.4200 4942	2.6681 3327	2.9412 9450	3.2420 3230	79
80	2.2167 1522	2.4472 7498	2.7014 8494	2.9817 3730	3.2906 6279	80
81	2.2388 8237	2.4748 0682	2.7352 5350	3.0227 3618	3.3400 2273	81
82	2.2612 7119	2.5026 4840	2.7694 4417	3.0642 9881	3.3901 2307	82
83	2.2838 8390	2.5308 0319	2.8040 6222	3.1064 3291	3.4409 7492	83
84	2.3067 2274	2.5592 7473	2.8391 1300	3.1491 4637	3.4925 8954	84
85	2.3297 8997	2.5880 6657	2.8746 0191	3.1924 4713	3.5449 7838	85
86	2.3530 8787	2.6171 8232	2.9105 3444	3.2363 4328	3.5981 5306	86
87	2.3766 1875	2.6466 2562	2.9469 1612	3.2808 4300	3.6521 2535	87
88	2.4003 8494	2.6764 0016	2.9837 5257	3.3259 5459	3.7069 0723	88
89	2.4243 8879	2.7065 0966	3.0210 4948	3.3716 8646	3.7625 1084	89
90	2.4486 3267	2.7369 5789	3.0588 1260	3.4180 4715	3.8189 4851	90
91	2.4731 1900	2.7677 4867	3.0970 4775	3.4650 4530	3.8762 3273	91
92	2.4978 5019	2.7988 8584	3.1357 6085	3.5126 8967	3.9343 7622	92
93	2.5228 2869	2.8303 7331	3.1749 5786	3.5609 8916	3.9933 9187	93
94	2.5480 5698	2.8622 1501	3.2146 4483	3.6099 5276	4.0532 9275	94
95	2.5735 3755	2.8944 1492	3.2548 2789	3.6595 8961	4.1140 9214	95
96	2.5992 7293	2.9269 7709	3.2955 1324	3.7099 0897	4.1758 0352	96
97	2.6252 6565	2.9599 0559	3.3367 0716	3.7609 2021	4.2384 4057	97
98	2.6515 1831	2.9932 0452	3.3784 1600	3.8126 3287	4.3020 1718	98
99	2.6780 3349	3.0268 7807	3.4206 4620	3.8650 5657	4.3665 4744	99
100	2.7048 1383	3.0609 3045	3.4634 0427	3.9182 0110	4.4320 4565	100
101	2.7318 6197	3.0953 6592	3.5066 9683	3.9720 7636	4.4985 2633	101
102	2.7591 8059	3.1301 8879	3.5505 3054	4.0266 9241	4.5660 0423	102
103	2.7867 7239	3.1654 0341	3.5949 1217	4.0820 5943	4.6344 9429	103
104	2.8146 4012	3.2010 1420	3.6398 4857	4.1381 8775	4.7040 1171	104
105	2.8427 8652	3.2370 2561	3.6853 4668	4.1950 8783	4.7745 7188	105
106	2.8712 1438	3.2734 4215	3.7314 1351	4.2527 7029	4.8461 9046	106
107	2.8999 2653	3.3102 6837	3.7780 5618	4.3112 4588	4.9188 8332	107
108	2.9289 2579	3.3475 0889	3.8252 8188	4.3705 2551	4.9926 6657	108
109	2.9582 1505	3.3851 6836	3.8730 9791	4.4306 2024	5.0675 5657	109
110	2.9877 9720	3.4232 5151	3.9215 1163	4.4915 4127	5.1435 6991	110
111	3.0176 7517	3.4617 6309	3.9705 3053	4.5532 9996	5.2207 2346	111
112	3.0478 5192	3.5007 0792	4.0201 6216	4.6159 0783	5.2990 3432	112
113	3.0783 3044	3.5400 9089	4.0704 1419	4.6793 7657	5.3785 1983	113
114	3.1091 1375	3.5799 1691	4.1212 9436	4.7437 1799	5.4591 9763	114
115	3.1402 0489	3.6201 9097	4.1728 1054	4.8089 4412	5.5410 8559	115
116	3.1716 0693	3.6609 1812	4.2249 7067	4.8750 6710	5.6242 0188	116
117	3.2033 2300	3.7021 0345	4.2777 8281	4.9420 9927	5.7085 6490	117
118	3.2353 5623	3.7437 5212	4.3312 5509	5.0100 5313	5.7941 9338	118
119	3.2677 0980	3.7858 6933	4.3853 9578	5.0789 4137	5.8811 0628	119
120	3.3003 8689	3.8284 6036	4.4402 1323	5.1487 7681	5.9693 2287	120

TABLE I

N	1	1 1/8	1 1/4	1 3/8	1 1/2	N
121	3.3333 9076	3.8715 3054	4.4957 1589	5.2195 7249	6.0588 6272	121
122	3.3667 2467	3.9150 8525	4.5519 1234	5.2913 4161	6.1497 4566	122
123	3.4003 9192	3.9591 2996	4.6088 1125	5.3640 9756	6.2419 9184	123
124	3.4343 9584	4.0036 7018	4.6664 2139	5.4378 5390	6.3356 2172	124
125	3.4687 3980	4.0487 1147	4.7247 5166	5.5126 2439	6.4306 5604	125
126	3.5034 2719	4.0942 5947	4.7838 1105	5.5884 2298	6.5271 1589	126
127	3.5384 6147	4.1403 1989	4.8436 0869	5.6652 6379	6.6250 2262	127
128	3.5738 4608	4.1868 9849	4.9041 5380	5.7431 6117	6.7243 9796	128
129	3.6095 8454	4.2340 0110	4.9654 5572	5.8221 2964	6.8252 6393	129
130	3.6456 8039	4.2816 3361	5.0275 2392	5.9021 8392	6.9276 4289	130
131	3.6821 3719	4.3298 0199	5.0903 6797	5.9833 3895	7.0315 5753	131
132	3.7189 5856	4.3785 1226	5.1539 9757	6.0656 0986	7.1370 3090	132
133	3.7561 4815	4.4277 7052	5.2184 2253	6.1490 1199	7.2440 8636	133
134	3.7937 0963	4.4775 8294	5.2836 5282	6.2335 6091	7.3527 4766	134
135	3.8316 4673	4.5279 5575	5.3496 9848	6.3192 7237	7.4630 3887	135
136	3.8699 6319	4.5788 9525	5.4165 6971	6.4061 6237	7.5749 8445	136
137	3.9086 6282	4.6304 0782	5.4842 7683	6.4942 4710	7.6886 0922	137
138	3.9477 4945	4.6824 9991	5.5528 3029	6.5835 4300	7.8039 3836	138
139	3.9872 2695	4.7351 7803	5.6222 4067	6.6740 6671	7.9209 9743	139
140	4.0270 9922	4.7884 4879	5.6925 1868	6.7658 3513	8.0398 1240	140
141	4.0673 7021	4.8423 1883	5.7636 7516	6.8588 6536	8.1604 0958	141
142	4.1080 4391	4.8967 9492	5.8357 2110	6.9531 7476	8.2828 1573	142
143	4.1491 2435	4.9518 8386	5.9086 6761	7.0487 8091	8.4070 5796	143
144	4.1906 1559	5.0075 9256	5.9825 2596	7.1457 0165	8.5331 6383	144
145	4.2325 2175	5.0639 2797	6.0573 0753	7.2439 5505	8.6611 6129	145
146	4.2748 4697	5.1208 9716	6.1330 2388	7.3435 5943	8.7910 7871	146
147	4.3175 9544	5.1785 0726	6.2096 8668	7.4445 3337	8.9229 4489	147
148	4.3607 7139	5.2367 6546	6.2873 0776	7.5468 9571	9.0567 8906	148
149	4.4043 7910	5.2956 7908	6.3658 9911	7.6506 6552	9.1926 4090	149
150	4.4484 2290	5.3552 5546	6.4454 7284	7.7558 6218	9.3305 3051	150
151	4.4929 0712	5.4155 0209	6.5260 4125	7.8625 0528	9.4704 8847	151
152	4.5378 3620	5.4764 2649	6.6076 1677	7.9706 1473	9.6125 4580	152
153	4.5832 1456	5.5380 3629	6.6902 1198	8.0802 1068	9.7567 3398	153
154	4.6290 4670	5.6003 3919	6.7738 3963	8.1913 1358	9.9030 8499	154
155	4.6753 3717	5.6633 4301	6.8585 1263	8.3039 4414	10.0516 3127	155
156	4.7220 9054	5.7270 5562	6.9442 4403	8.4181 2337	10.2024 0574	156
157	4.7693 1145	5.7914 8499	7.0310 4708	8.5338 7257	10.3554 4182	157
158	4.8170 0456	5.8566 3920	7.1189 3517	8.6512 1331	10.5107 7345	158
159	4.8651 7461	5.9225 2639	7.2079 2186	8.7701 6750	10.6684 3505	159
160	4.9138 2635	5.9891 5481	7.2980 2089	8.8907 5730	10.8284 6158	160
161	4.9629 6462	6.0565 3280	7.3892 4615	9.0130 0521	10.9908 8850	161
162	5.0125 9426	6.1246 6880	7.4816 1172	9.1369 3404	11.1557 5183	162
163	5.0627 2021	6.1935 7132	7.5751 3187	9.2625 6688	11.3230 8811	163
164	5.1133 4741	6.2632 4900	7.6698 2102	9.3899 2717	11.4929 3443	164
165	5.1644 8088	6.3337 1055	7.7656 9378	9.5190 3867	11.6653 2844	165
166	5.2161 2569	6.4049 6479	7.8627 6495	9.6499 2545	11.8403 0837	166
167	5.2682 8695	6.4770 2065	7.9610 4951	9.7826 1193	12.0179 1300	167
168	5.3209 6982	6.5498 8713	8.0605 6263	9.9171 2284	12.1981 8169	168
169	5.3741 7952	6.6235 7336	8.1613 1967	10.0534 8328	12.3811 5442	169
170	5.4279 2131	6.6980 8856	8.2633 3616	10.1917 1868	12.5668 7173	170
171	5.4822 0052	6.7734 4206	8.3666 2786	10.3318 5481	12.7553 7481	171
172	5.5370 2253	6.8496 4328	8.4712 1071	10.4739 1781	12.9467 0543	172
173	5.5923 9275	6.9267 0177	8.5771 0085	10.6179 3418	13.1409 0601	173
174	5.6483 1668	7.0046 2716	8.6843 1461	10.7639 3078	13.3380 1960	174
175	5.7047 9985	7.0834 2922	8.7928 6854	10.9119 3483	13.5380 8990	175
176	5.7618 4785	7.1631 1780	8.9027 7940	11.0619 7393	13.7411 6125	176
177	5.8194 6633	7.2437 0287	9.0140 6414	11.2140 7607	13.9472 7866	177
178	5.8776 6099	7.3251 9453	9.1267 3994	11.3682 6962	14.1564 8784	178
179	5.9364 3760	7.4076 0297	9.2408 2419	11.5245 8332	14.3688 3516	179
180	5.9958 0198	7.4909 3850	9.3563 3449	11.6830 4634	14.5843 6769	180

TABLE I

N	1	1 1/8	1 1/4	1 3/8	1 1/2	N
181	6.0557 6000	7.5752 1156	9.4732 8867	11.8436 8823	14.8031 3320	181
182	6.1163 1760	7.6604 3269	9.5917 0478	12.0065 3894	15.0251 8020	182
183	6.1774 8077	7.7466 1256	9.7116 0109	12.1716 2886	15.2505 5791	183
184	6.2392 5558	7.8337 6195	9.8329 9611	12.3389 8875	15.4793 1627	184
185	6.3016 4813	7.9218 9177	9.9559 0856	12.5086 4985	15.7115 0602	185
186	6.3646 6462	8.0110 1305	10.0803 5741	12.6806 4378	15.9471 7861	186
187	6.4283 1126	8.1011 3695	10.2063 6188	12.8550 0263	16.1863 8629	187
188	6.4925 9437	8.1922 7474	10.3339 4140	13.0317 5892	16.4291 8208	188
189	6.5575 2032	8.2844 3783	10.4631 1567	13.2109 4561	16.6756 1981	189
190	6.6230 9552	8.3776 3776	10.5939 0462	13.3925 9611	16.9257 5411	190
191	6.6893 2648	8.4718 8618	10.7263 2843	13.5767 4430	17.1796 4042	191
192	6.7562 1974	8.5671 9490	10.8604 0753	13.7634 2454	17.4373 3503	192
193	6.8237 8194	8.6635 7584	10.9961 6263	13.9526 7163	17.6988 9505	193
194	6.8920 1976	8.7610 4107	11.1336 1466	14.1445 2086	17.9643 7848	194
195	6.9609 3996	8.8596 0278	11.2727 8484	14.3390 0802	18.2338 4416	195
196	7.0305 4936	8.9592 7332	11.4136 9465	14.5361 6938	18.5073 5182	196
197	7.1008 5485	9.0600 6514	11.5563 6584	14.7360 4171	18.7849 6210	197
198	7.1718 6340	9.1619 9087	11.7008 2041	14.9386 6229	19.0667 3653	198
199	7.2435 8203	9.2650 6327	11.8470 8066	15.1440 6889	19.3527 3758	199
200	7.3160 1785	9.3692 9523	11.9951 6917	15.3522 9984	19.6430 2864	200
201	7.3891 7803	9.4746 9980	12.1451 0879	15.5633 9396	19.9376 7407	201
202	7.4630 6981	9.5812 9018	12.2969 2265	15.7773 9063	20.2367 3918	202
203	7.5377 0051	9.6890 7969	12.4506 3418	15.9943 2975	20.5402 9027	203
204	7.6130 7751	9.7980 8184	12.6062 6711	16.2142 5178	20.8483 9462	204
205	7.6892 0829	9.9083 1026	12.7638 4545	16.4371 9775	21.1611 2054	205
206	7.7661 0037	10.0197 7875	12.9233 9351	16.6632 0922	21.4785 3735	206
207	7.8437 6138	10.1325 0126	13.0849 3593	16.8923 2834	21.8007 1541	207
208	7.9221 9899	10.2464 9190	13.2484 9763	17.1245 9786	22.1277 2614	208
209	8.0014 2098	10.3617 6493	13.4141 0385	17.3600 6108	22.4596 4203	209
210	8.0814 3519	10.4783 3479	13.5817 8015	17.5987 6192	22.7965 3666	210
211	8.1622 4954	10.5962 1605	13.7515 5240	17.8407 4489	23.1384 8471	211
212	8.2438 7204	10.7154 2349	13.9234 4681	18.0860 5514	23.4855 6198	212
213	8.3263 1076	10.8359 7200	14.0974 8989	18.3347 3839	23.8378 4541	213
214	8.4095 7386	10.9578 7668	14.2737 0852	18.5868 4105	24.1954 1309	214
215	8.4936 6960	11.0811 5280	14.4521 2987	18.8424 1011	24.5583 4429	215
216	8.5786 0630	11.2058 1577	14.6327 8150	19.1014 9325	24.9267 1946	216
217	8.6643 9236	11.3318 8119	14.8156 9126	19.3641 3878	25.3006 2025	217
218	8.7510 3629	11.4593 6486	15.0008 8740	19.6303 9569	25.6801 2955	218
219	8.8385 4665	11.5882 8271	15.1883 9850	19.9003 1363	26.0653 3149	219
220	8.9269 3211	11.7186 5089	15.3782 5348	20.1739 4294	26.4563 1147	220
221	9.0162 0144	11.8504 8571	15.5704 8165	20.4513 3466	26.8531 5614	221
222	9.1063 6345	11.9838 0368	15.7651 1267	20.7325 4051	27.2559 5348	222
223	9.1974 2708	12.1186 2147	15.9621 7658	21.0176 1294	27.6647 9278	223
224	9.2894 0136	12.2549 5596	16.1617 0378	21.3066 0512	28.0797 6467	224
225	9.3822 9537	12.3928 2422	16.3637 2508	21.5995 7094	28.5009 6115	225
226	9.4761 1832	12.5322 4349	16.5682 7164	21.8965 6504	28.9284 7556	226
227	9.5708 7951	12.6732 3123	16.7753 7504	22.1976 4281	29.3624 0270	227
228	9.6665 8830	12.8158 0508	16.9850 6723	22.5028 6040	29.8028 3874	228
229	9.7632 5418	12.9599 8289	17.1973 8057	22.8122 7473	30.2498 8132	229
230	9.8608 8673	13.1057 8269	17.4123 4783	23.1259 4351	30.7036 2954	230
231	9.9594 9559	13.2532 2275	17.6300 0217	23.4439 2523	31.1641 8398	231
232	10.0590 9055	13.4023 2151	17.8503 7720	23.7662 7920	31.6316 4674	232
233	10.1596 8145	13.5530 9762	18.0735 0692	24.0930 6554	32.1061 2144	233
234	10.2612 7827	13.7055 6997	18.2994 2575	24.4243 4519	32.5877 1326	234
235	10.3638 9105	13.8597 5763	18.5281 6857	24.7601 7994	33.0765 2896	235
236	10.4675 2996	14.0156 7991	18.7597 7068	25.1006 3241	33.5726 7690	236
237	10.5722 0526	14.1733 5630	18.9942 6781	25.4457 6611	34.0762 6705	237
238	10.6779 2731	14.3328 0656	19.2316 9616	25.7956 4539	34.5874 1105	238
239	10.7847 0659	14.4940 5064	19.4720 9236	26.1503 3552	35.1062 2222	239
240	10.8925 5365	14.6571 0871	19.7154 9352	26.5099 0263	35.6328 1555	240

TABLE I

N	1	1 1/8	1 1/4	1 3/8	1 1/2	N
241	11.0014 7919	14.8220 0118	19.9619 3719	26.8744 1379	36.1673 0779	241
242	11.1114 9398	14.9887 4869	20.2114 6140	27.2439 3698	36.7098 1740	242
243	11.2226 0892	15.1573 7212	20.4641 0467	27.6185 4112	37.2604 6467	243
244	11.3348 3501	15.3278 9255	20.7199 0598	27.9982 9606	37.8193 7164	244
245	11.4481 8336	15.5003 3134	20.9789 0480	28.3832 7263	38.3866 6221	245
246	11.5626 6520	15.6747 1007	21.2411 4111	28.7735 4263	38.9624 6214	246
247	11.6782 9185	15.8510 5056	21.5066 5538	29.1691 7884	39.5468 9907	247
248	11.7950 7477	16.0293 7488	21.7754 8857	29.5702 5505	40.1401 0256	248
249	11.9130 2551	16.2097 0535	22.0476 8218	29.9768 4605	40.7422 0410	249
250	12.0321 5577	16.3920 6453	22.3232 7820	30.3890 2769	41.3533 3716	250
251	12.1524 7733	16.5764 7526	22.6023 1918	30.8068 7682	41.9736 3722	251
252	12.2740 0210	16.7629 6060	22.8848 4817	31.2304 7137	42.6032 4178	252
253	12.3967 4212	16.9515 4391	23.1709 0877	31.6598 9035	43.2422 9040	253
254	12.5207 0954	17.1422 4878	23.4605 4513	32.0952 1385	43.8909 2476	254
255	12.6459 1664	17.3350 9908	23.7538 0195	32.5365 2304	44.5492 8863	255
256	12.7723 7580	17.5301 1894	24.0507 2447	32.9839 0023	45.2175 2796	256
257	12.9000 9956	17.7273 3278	24.3513 5853	33.4374 2886	45.8957 9088	257
258	13.0291 0056	17.9267 6527	24.6557 5051	33.8971 9350	46.5842 2774	258
259	13.1593 9156	18.1284 4138	24.9639 4739	34.3632 7991	47.2829 9116	259
260	13.2909 8548	18.3323 8635	25.2759 9673	34.8357 7501	47.9922 3603	260
261	13.4238 9533	18.5386 2570	25.5919 4669	35.3147 6692	48.7121 1957	261
262	13.5581 3429	18.7471 8523	25.9118 4602	35.8003 4496	49.4428 0136	262
263	13.6937 1563	18.9580 9107	26.2357 4410	36.2925 9971	50.1844 4338	263
264	13.8306 5279	19.1713 6959	26.5636 9090	36.7916 2295	50.9372 1003	264
265	13.9689 5931	19.3870 4750	26.8957 3704	37.2975 0777	51.7012 6818	265
266	14.1086 4891	19.6051 5179	27.2319 3375	37.8103 4850	52.4767 8720	266
267	14.2497 3540	19.8257 0974	27.5723 3292	38.3302 4079	53.2639 3901	267
268	14.3922 3275	20.0487 4898	27.9169 8708	38.8572 8160	54.0628 9810	268
269	14.5361 5508	20.2742 9740	28.2659 4942	39.3915 6923	54.8738 4157	269
270	14.6815 1663	20.5023 8325	28.6192 7379	39.9332 0330	55.6969 4919	270
271	14.8283 3179	20.7330 3506	28.9770 1471	40.4822 8485	56.5324 0343	271
272	14.9766 1511	20.9662 8171	29.3392 2740	41.0389 1627	57.3803 8948	272
273	15.1263 8126	21.2021 5237	29.7059 6774	41.6032 0136	58.2410 9532	273
274	15.2776 4508	21.4406 7659	30.0772 9234	42.1752 4538	59.1147 1175	274
275	15.4304 2153	21.6818 8420	30.4532 5849	42.7551 5501	60.0014 3243	275
276	15.5847 2574	21.9258 0540	30.8339 2422	43.3430 3839	60.9014 5392	276
277	15.7405 7300	22.1724 7071	31.2193 4827	43.9390 0517	61.8149 7573	277
278	15.8979 7873	22.4219 1100	31.6095 9013	44.5431 6649	62.7422 0036	278
279	16.0569 5852	22.6741 5750	32.0047 1000	45.1556 3503	63.6833 3337	279
280	16.2175 2810	22.9292 4177	32.4047 6888	45.7765 2501	64.6385 8337	280
281	16.3797 0338	23.1871 9574	32.8098 2849	46.4059 5223	65.6081 6212	281
282	16.5435 0042	23.4480 5170	33.2199 5135	47.0440 3407	66.5922 8455	282
283	16.7089 3542	23.7118 4228	33.6352 0074	47.6908 8954	67.5911 6882	283
284	16.8760 2477	23.9786 0050	34.0556 4075	48.3466 3927	68.6050 3635	284
285	17.0447 8502	24.2483 5976	34.4813 3626	49.0114 0556	69.6341 1190	285
286	17.2152 3287	24.5211 5381	34.9123 5296	49.6853 1239	70.6786 2357	286
287	17.3873 8520	24.7970 1679	35.3487 5737	50.3684 8543	71.7388 0293	287
288	17.5612 5905	25.0759 8323	35.7906 1684	51.0610 5211	72.8148 8497	288
289	17.7368 7164	25.3580 8804	36.2379 9955	51.7631 4157	73.9071 0825	289
290	17.9142 4036	25.6433 6653	36.6909 7454	52.4748 8477	75.0157 1487	290
291	18.0933 8276	25.9318 5440	37.1496 1173	53.1964 1443	76.1409 5059	291
292	18.2743 1659	26.2235 8776	37.6139 8187	53.9278 6513	77.2830 6485	292
293	18.4570 5976	26.5186 0313	38.0841 5665	54.6693 7328	78.4423 1082	293
294	18.6416 3036	26.8169 3741	38.5602 0860	55.4210 7716	79.6189 4549	294
295	18.8280 4666	27.1186 2796	39.0422 1121	56.1831 1697	80.8132 2967	295
296	19.0163 2713	27.4237 1252	39.5302 3885	56.9556 3483	82.0254 2811	296
297	19.2064 9040	27.7322 2929	40.0243 6684	57.7387 7481	83.2558 0954	297
298	19.3985 5530	28.0442 1687	40.5246 7142	58.5326 8296	84.5046 4668	298
299	19.5925 4085	28.3597 1431	41.0312 2982	59.3375 0735	85.7722 1638	299
300	19.7884 6626	28.6787 6109	41.5441 2019	60.1533 9808	87.0587 9963	300

TABLE I

N	1	1 1/8	1 1/4	1 3/8	1 1/2	N
301	19.9863 5092	29.0013 9715	42.0634 2169	60.9805 0730	88.3646 8162	301
302	20.1862 1443	29.3276 6287	42.5892 1446	61.8189 8928	89.6901 5184	302
303	20.3880 7658	29.6575 9908	43.1215 7964	62.6690 0038	91.0355 0412	303
304	20.5919 5734	29.9912 4707	43.6605 9939	63.5306 9914	92.4010 3668	304
305	20.7978 7692	30.3286 4860	44.2063 5688	64.4042 4625	93.7870 5223	305
306	21.0058 5569	30.6698 4590	44.7589 3634	65.2898 0464	95.1938 5802	306
307	21.2159 1424	31.0148 8166	45.3184 2305	66.1875 3945	96.6217 6589	307
308	21.4280 7339	31.3637 9908	45.8849 0333	67.0976 1812	98.0710 9238	308
309	21.6423 5412	31.7166 4182	46.4584 6463	68.0202 1037	99.5421 5876	309
310	21.8587 7766	32.0734 5404	47.0391 9543	68.9554 8826	101.0352 9114	310
311	22.0773 6544	32.4342 8040	47.6271 8538	69.9036 2622	102.5508 2051	311
312	22.2981 3909	32.7991 6605	48.2225 2519	70.8648 0108	104.0890 8282	312
313	22.5211 2048	33.1681 5667	48.8253 0676	71.8391 9210	105.6504 1906	313
314	22.7463 3169	33.5412 9843	49.4356 2309	72.8269 8099	107.2351 7535	314
315	22.9737 9500	33.9186 3804	50.0535 6838	73.8283 5198	108.8437 0298	315
316	23.2035 3295	34.3002 2272	50.6792 3799	74.8434 9182	110.4763 5852	316
317	23.4355 6828	34.6861 0022	51.3127 2846	75.8725 8983	112.1335 0390	317
318	23.6699 2397	35.0763 1885	51.9541 3757	76.9158 3794	113.8155 0646	318
319	23.9066 2321	35.4709 2744	52.6035 6429	77.9734 3071	115.5227 3905	319
320	24.1456 8944	35.8699 7537	53.2611 0884	79.0455 6538	117.2555 8014	320
321	24.3871 4633	36.2735 1260	53.9268 7270	80.1324 4191	119.0144 1384	321
322	24.6310 1780	36.6815 8961	54.6009 5861	81.2342 6298	120.7996 3005	322
323	24.8773 2797	37.0942 5750	55.2834 7059	82.3512 3410	122.6116 2450	323
324	25.1261 0125	37.5115 6789	55.9745 1397	83.4835 6357	124.4507 9887	324
325	25.3773 6227	37.9335 7303	56.6741 9540	84.6314 6257	126.3175 6085	325
326	25.6311 3589	38.3603 2573	57.3826 2284	85.7951 4518	128.2123 2426	326
327	25.8874 4725	38.7918 7939	58.0999 0563	86.9748 2842	130.1355 0913	327
328	26.1463 2172	39.2282 8804	58.8261 5445	88.1707 3231	132.0875 4176	328
329	26.4077 8494	39.6696 0628	59.5614 8138	89.3830 7988	134.0688 5489	329
330	26.6718 6279	40.1158 8935	60.3059 9989	90.6120 9723	136.0798 8771	330
331	26.9385 8142	40.5671 9310	61.0598 2489	91.8580 1357	138.1210 8603	331
332	27.2079 6723	41.0235 7402	61.8230 7270	93.1210 6126	140.1929 0232	332
333	27.4800 4690	41.4850 8923	62.5958 6111	94.4014 7585	142.2957 9585	333
334	27.7548 4737	41.9517 9649	63.3783 0938	95.6994 9614	144.4302 3279	334
335	28.0323 9584	42.4237 5420	64.1705 3824	97.0153 6421	146.5966 8628	335
336	28.3127 1980	42.9010 2143	64.9726 6997	98.3493 2547	148.7956 3658	336
337	28.5958 4700	43.3836 5792	65.7848 2835	99.7016 2870	151.0275 7113	337
338	28.8818 0547	43.8717 2407	66.6071 3870	101.0725 2609	153.2929 8469	338
339	29.1706 2353	44.3652 8097	67.4397 2794	102.4622 7332	155.5923 7946	339
340	29.4623 2976	44.8643 9038	68.2827 2453	103.8711 2958	157.9262 6516	340
341	29.7569 5306	45.3691 1477	69.1362 5859	105.2993 5761	160.2951 5913	341
342	30.0545 2259	45.8795 1731	70.0004 6182	106.7472 2378	162.6995 8652	342
343	30.3550 6781	46.3956 6188	70.8754 6760	108.2149 9811	165.1400 8032	343
344	30.6586 1849	46.9176 1308	71.7614 1094	109.7029 5433	167.6171 8152	344
345	30.9652 0468	47.4454 3623	72.6584 2858	111.2113 6995	170.1314 3925	345
346	31.2748 5672	47.9791 9738	73.5666 5894	112.7405 2629	172.6834 1084	346
347	31.5876 0529	48.5189 6335	74.4862 4217	114.2907 0853	175.2736 6200	347
348	31.9034 8134	49.0648 0169	75.4173 2020	115.8622 0577	177.9027 6693	348
349	32.2225 1616	49.6167 8071	76.3600 3670	117.4553 1110	180.5713 0843	349
350	32.5447 4132	50.1749 6949	77.3145 3716	119.0703 2163	183.2798 7806	350
351	32.8701 8873	50.7394 3790	78.2809 6887	120.7075 3855	186.0290 7623	351
352	33.1988 9062	51.3102 5658	79.2594 8099	122.3672 6720	188.8195 1237	352
353	33.5308 7953	51.8874 9696	80.2502 2450	124.0498 1713	191.6518 0506	353
354	33.8661 8832	52.4712 3130	81.2533 5230	125.7555 0211	194.5265 8213	354
355	34.2048 5021	53.0615 3266	82.2690 1921	127.4846 4027	197.4444 8087	355
356	34.5468 9871	53.6584 7490	83.2973 8195	129.2375 5407	200.4061 4808	356
357	34.8923 6769	54.2621 3274	84.3385 9922	131.0145 7044	203.4122 4030	357
358	35.2412 9137	54.8725 8174	85.3928 3171	132.8160 2078	206.4634 2390	358
359	35.5937 0428	55.4898 9828	86.4602 4211	134.6422 4107	209.5603 7526	359
360	35.9496 4133	56.1141 5964	87.5409 9514	136.4935 7188	212.7037 8089	360

TABLE I

N	1 5/8	1 3/4	1 7/8	2	2 1/8	N
1	1.0162 5000	1.0175 0000	1.0187 5000	1.0200 0000	1.0212 5000	1
2	1.0327 6406	1.0353 0625	1.0378 5156	1.0404 0000	1.0429 5156	2
3	1.0495 4648	1.0534 2411	1.0573 1128	1.0612 0800	1.0651 1428	3
4	1.0666 0161	1.0718 5903	1.0771 3587	1.0824 3216	1.0877 4796	4
5	1.0839 3388	1.0906 1656	1.0973 3216	1.1040 8080	1.1108 6261	5
6	1.1015 4781	1.1097 0235	1.1179 0714	1.1261 6242	1.1344 6844	6
7	1.1194 4796	1.1291 2215	1.1388 6790	1.1486 8567	1.1585 7589	7
8	1.1376 3899	1.1488 8178	1.1602 2167	1.1716 5938	1.1831 9563	8
9	1.1561 2563	1.1689 8721	1.1819 7583	1.1950 9257	1.2083 3854	9
10	1.1749 1267	1.1894 4449	1.2041 3788	1.2189 9442	1.2340 1573	10
11	1.1940 0500	1.2102 5977	1.2267 1546	1.2433 7431	1.2602 3856	11
12	1.2134 0758	1.2314 3931	1.2497 1638	1.2682 4179	1.2870 1863	12
13	1.2331 2545	1.2529 8950	1.2731 4856	1.2936 0663	1.3143 6778	13
14	1.2531 6374	1.2749 1682	1.2970 2009	1.3194 7876	1.3422 9809	14
15	1.2735 2765	1.2972 2786	1.3213 3922	1.3458 6834	1.3708 2193	15
16	1.2942 2248	1.3199 2935	1.3461 1433	1.3727 8571	1.3999 5189	16
17	1.3152 5359	1.3430 2811	1.3713 5398	1.4002 4142	1.4297 0087	17
18	1.3366 2646	1.3665 3111	1.3970 6686	1.4282 4625	1.4600 8202	18
19	1.3583 4664	1.3904 4540	1.4232 6187	1.4568 1117	1.4911 0876	19
20	1.3804 1977	1.4147 7820	1.4499 4803	1.4859 4740	1.5227 9482	20
21	1.4028 5160	1.4395 3681	1.4771 3455	1.5156 6634	1.5551 5421	21
22	1.4256 4793	1.4647 2871	1.5048 3082	1.5459 7967	1.5882 0124	22
23	1.4488 1471	1.4903 6146	1.5330 4640	1.5768 9926	1.6219 5051	23
24	1.4723 5795	1.5164 4279	1.5617 9102	1.6084 3725	1.6564 1696	24
25	1.4962 8377	1.5429 8054	1.5910 7460	1.6406 0599	1.6916 1582	25
26	1.5205 9838	1.5699 8269	1.6209 0725	1.6734 1811	1.7275 6266	26
27	1.5453 0810	1.5974 5739	1.6512 9926	1.7068 8648	1.7642 7336	27
28	1.5704 1936	1.6254 1290	1.6822 6112	1.7410 2421	1.8017 6417	28
29	1.5959 3868	1.6538 5762	1.7138 0352	1.7758 4469	1.8400 5166	29
30	1.6218 7268	1.6828 0013	1.7459 3734	1.8113 6158	1.8791 5276	30
31	1.6482 2811	1.7122 4913	1.7786 7366	1.8475 8882	1.9190 8476	31
32	1.6750 1182	1.7422 1349	1.8120 2379	1.8845 4059	1.9598 6531	32
33	1.7022 3076	1.7727 0223	1.8459 9924	1.9222 3140	2.0015 1245	33
34	1.7298 9201	1.8037 2452	1.8806 1172	1.9606 7603	2.0440 4458	34
35	1.7580 0275	1.8352 8970	1.9158 7319	1.9998 8955	2.0874 8053	35
36	1.7865 7030	1.8674 0727	1.9517 9582	2.0398 8734	2.1318 3949	36
37	1.8156 0207	1.9000 8689	1.9883 9199	2.0806 8509	2.1771 4108	37
38	1.8451 0560	1.9333 3841	2.0256 7434	2.1222 9879	2.2234 0533	38
39	1.8750 8857	1.9671 7184	2.0636 5573	2.1647 4477	2.2706 5269	39
40	1.9055 5875	2.0015 9734	2.1023 4928	2.2080 3966	2.3189 0406	40
41	1.9365 2408	2.0366 2530	2.1417 6833	2.2522 0046	2.3681 8077	41
42	1.9679 9260	2.0722 6624	2.1819 2648	2.2972 4447	2.4185 0462	42
43	1.9999 7248	2.1085 3090	2.2228 3760	2.3431 8936	2.4698 5784	43
44	2.0324 7203	2.1454 3019	2.2645 1581	2.3900 5314	2.5223 8317	44
45	2.0654 9970	2.1829 7522	2.3069 7548	2.4378 5421	2.5759 8381	45
46	2.0990 6407	2.2211 7728	2.3502 3127	2.4866 1129	2.6307 2347	46
47	2.1331 7387	2.2600 4789	2.3942 9811	2.5363 4352	2.6866 2634	47
48	2.1678 3794	2.2995 9872	2.4391 9120	2.5870 7039	2.7437 1715	48
49	2.2030 6531	2.3398 4170	2.4849 2603	2.6388 1179	2.8020 2114	49
50	2.2388 6512	2.3807 8893	2.5315 1839	2.6915 8803	2.8615 6409	50
51	2.2752 4668	2.4224 5274	2.5789 8436	2.7454 1979	2.9223 7233	51
52	2.3122 1944	2.4648 4566	2.6273 4032	2.8003 2819	2.9844 7274	52
53	2.3497 9300	2.5079 8046	2.6766 0295	2.8563 3475	3.0478 9278	53
54	2.3879 7714	2.5518 7012	2.7267 8926	2.9134 6144	3.1126 6051	54
55	2.4267 8177	2.5965 2785	2.7779 1656	2.9717 3067	3.1788 0454	55
56	2.4662 1697	2.6419 6708	2.8300 0249	3.0311 6529	3.2463 5414	56
57	2.5062 9300	2.6882 0151	2.8830 6504	3.0917 8859	3.3153 3916	57
58	2.5470 2026	2.7352 4503	2.9371 2251	3.1536 2436	3.3857 9012	58
59	2.5884 0934	2.7831 1182	2.9921 9355	3.2166 9685	3.4577 3816	59
60	2.6304 7099	2.8318 1628	3.0482 9718	3.2810 3079	3.5312 1510	60

TABLE I

N	1 5/8	1 3/4	1 7/8	2	2 1/8	N
61	2.6732 1614	2.8813 7306	3.1054 5276	3.3466 5140	3.6062 5342	61
62	2.7166 5590	2.9317 9709	3.1636 8000	3.4135 8443	3.6828 8630	62
63	2.7608 0156	2.9831 0354	3.2229 9900	3.4818 5612	3.7611 4764	63
64	2.8056 6459	3.0353 0785	3.2834 3023	3.5514 9324	3.8410 7202	64
65	2.8512 5664	3.0884 2574	3.3449 9454	3.6225 2311	3.9226 9480	65
66	2.8975 8956	3.1424 7319	3.4077 1319	3.6949 7357	4.0060 5207	66
67	2.9446 7539	3.1974 6647	3.4716 0781	3.7688 7304	4.0911 8067	67
68	2.9925 2636	3.2534 2213	3.5367 0046	3.8442 5050	4.1781 1826	68
69	3.0411 5492	3.3103 5702	3.6030 1359	3.9211 3551	4.2669 0328	69
70	3.0905 7368	3.3682 8827	3.6705 7010	3.9995 5822	4.3575 7497	70
71	3.1407 9551	3.4272 3331	3.7393 9329	4.0795 4939	4.4501 7344	71
72	3.1918 3343	3.4872 0990	3.8095 0691	4.1611 4038	4.5447 3963	72
73	3.2437 0073	3.5482 3607	3.8809 3517	4.2443 6318	4.6413 1534	73
74	3.2964 1086	3.6103 3020	3.9537 0270	4.3292 5045	4.7399 4329	74
75	3.3499 7754	3.6735 1098	4.0278 3463	4.4158 3546	4.8406 6709	75
76	3.4044 1467	3.7377 9742	4.1033 5653	4.5041 5216	4.9435 3126	76
77	3.4597 3641	3.8032 0888	4.1802 9446	4.5942 3521	5.0485 8130	77
78	3.5159 5713	3.8697 6503	4.2586 7498	4.6861 1991	5.1558 6366	78
79	3.5730 9143	3.9374 8592	4.3385 2514	4.7798 4231	5.2654 2576	79
80	3.6311 5417	4.0063 9192	4.4198 7248	4.8754 3916	5.3773 1606	80
81	3.6901 6042	4.0765 0378	4.5027 4509	4.9729 4794	5.4915 8402	81
82	3.7501 2553	4.1478 4260	4.5871 7156	5.0724 0690	5.6082 8018	82
83	3.8110 6507	4.2204 2984	4.6731 8103	5.1738 5504	5.7274 5614	83
84	3.8729 9488	4.2942 8737	4.7608 0317	5.2773 3214	5.8491 6458	84
85	3.9359 3104	4.3694 3740	4.8500 6823	5.3828 7878	5.9734 5933	85
86	3.9998 8992	4.4459 0255	4.9410 0701	5.4905 3636	6.1003 9534	86
87	4.0648 8813	4.5237 0584	5.0336 5089	5.6003 4708	6.2300 2874	87
88	4.1309 4257	4.6028 7070	5.1280 3185	5.7123 5402	6.3624 1685	88
89	4.1980 7038	4.6834 2093	5.2241 8245	5.8266 0110	6.4976 1821	89
90	4.2662 8903	4.7653 8080	5.3221 3587	5.9431 3313	6.6356 9259	90
91	4.3356 1622	4.8487 7496	5.4219 2591	6.0619 9579	6.7767 0106	91
92	4.4060 6999	4.9336 2853	5.5235 8703	6.1832 3570	6.9207 0596	92
93	4.4776 6863	5.0199 6703	5.6271 5428	6.3069 0042	7.0677 7096	93
94	4.5504 3074	5.1078 1645	5.7326 6343	6.4330 3843	7.2179 6109	94
95	4.6243 7524	5.1972 0324	5.8401 5086	6.5616 9920	7.3713 4277	95
96	4.6995 2134	5.2881 5429	5.9496 5369	6.6929 3318	7.5279 8380	96
97	4.7758 8856	5.3806 9699	6.0612 0970	6.8267 9184	7.6879 5346	97
98	4.8534 9675	5.4748 5919	6.1748 5738	6.9633 2768	7.8513 2247	98
99	4.9323 6607	5.5706 6923	6.2906 3596	7.1025 9423	8.0181 6307	99
100	5.0125 1702	5.6681 5594	6.4085 8538	7.2446 4612	8.1885 4904	100
101	5.0939 7042	5.7673 4867	6.5287 4636	7.3895 3904	8.3625 5570	101
102	5.1767 4744	5.8682 7727	6.6511 6035	7.5373 2982	8.5402 6001	102
103	5.2608 6959	5.9709 7212	6.7758 6961	7.6880 7642	8.7217 4054	103
104	5.3463 5872	6.0754 6413	6.9029 1716	7.8418 3795	8.9070 7752	104
105	5.4332 3705	6.1817 8476	7.0323 4686	7.9986 7471	9.0963 5292	105
106	5.5215 2715	6.2899 6599	7.1642 0336	8.1586 4820	9.2896 5042	106
107	5.6112 5196	6.4000 4039	7.2985 3218	8.3218 2116	9.4870 5549	107
108	5.7024 3481	6.5120 4110	7.4353 7966	8.4882 5759	9.6886 5542	108
109	5.7950 9937	6.6260 0182	7.5747 9302	8.6580 2274	9.8945 3935	109
110	5.8892 6974	6.7419 5685	7.7168 2039	8.8311 8319	10.1047 9831	110
111	5.9849 7037	6.8599 4110	7.8615 1078	9.0078 0686	10.3195 2527	111
112	6.0822 2614	6.9799 9007	8.0089 1410	9.1879 6299	10.5388 1519	112
113	6.1810 6232	7.1021 3989	8.1590 8124	9.3717 2225	10.7627 6501	113
114	6.2815 0458	7.2264 2734	8.3120 6402	9.5591 5670	10.9914 7376	114
115	6.3835 7903	7.3528 8982	8.4679 1522	9.7503 3983	11.2250 4258	115
116	6.4873 1219	7.4815 6539	8.6266 8863	9.9453 4663	11.4635 7474	116
117	6.5927 3101	7.6124 9278	8.7884 3904	10.1442 5356	11.7071 7570	117
118	6.6998 6289	7.7457 1141	8.9532 2227	10.3471 3863	11.9559 5318	118
119	6.8087 3566	7.8812 6136	9.1210 9519	10.5540 8141	12.2100 1719	119
120	6.9193 7762	8.0191 8343	9.2921 1572	10.7651 6303	12.4694 8005	120

TABLE I

N	1 5/8	1 3/4	1 7/8	2	2 1/8	N
121	7.0318 1750	8.1595 1914	9.4663 4289	10.9804 6629	12.7344 5650	121
122	7.1460 8454	8.3023 1073	9.6438 3682	11.2000 7562	13.0050 6371	122
123	7.2622 0841	8.4476 0116	9.8246 5876	11.4240 7713	13.2814 2131	123
124	7.3802 1930	8.5954 3418	10.0088 7111	11.6525 5868	13.5636 5151	124
125	7.5001 4786	8.7458 5428	10.1965 3745	11.8856 0985	13.8518 7911	125
126	7.6220 2526	8.8989 0673	10.3877 2252	12.1233 2205	14.1462 3154	126
127	7.7458 8317	9.0546 3760	10.5824 9232	12.3657 8849	14.4468 3896	127
128	7.8717 5377	9.2130 9376	10.7809 1405	12.6131 0426	14.7538 3429	128
129	7.9996 6977	9.3743 2290	10.9830 5619	12.8653 6634	15.0673 5326	129
130	8.1296 6441	9.5383 7355	11.1889 8849	13.1226 7367	15.3875 3452	130
131	8.2617 7145	9.7052 9509	11.3987 8203	13.3851 2714	15.7145 1963	131
132	8.3960 2524	9.8751 3775	11.6125 0919	13.6528 2969	16.0484 5317	132
133	8.5324 6065	10.0479 5266	11.8302 4374	13.9258 8628	16.3894 8280	133
134	8.6711 1314	10.2237 9183	12.0520 6081	14.2044 0400	16.7377 5931	134
135	8.8120 1872	10.4027 0819	12.2780 3695	14.4884 9208	17.0934 3670	135
136	8.9552 1403	10.5847 5558	12.5082 5014	14.7782 6193	17.4566 7223	136
137	9.1007 3626	10.7699 8881	12.7427 7983	15.0738 2716	17.8276 2651	137
138	9.2486 2322	10.9584 6361	12.9817 0695	15.3753 0371	18.2064 6357	138
139	9.3989 1335	11.1502 3672	13.2251 1396	15.6828 0978	18.5933 5093	139
140	9.5516 4569	11.3453 6587	13.4730 8485	15.9964 6598	18.9884 5963	140
141	9.7068 5993	11.5439 0977	13.7257 0519	16.3163 9530	19.3919 6440	141
142	9.8645 9641	11.7459 2819	13.9830 6216	16.6427 2320	19.8040 4364	142
143	10.0248 9610	11.9514 8193	14.2452 4457	16.9755 7767	20.2248 7957	143
144	10.1878 0066	12.1606 3287	14.5123 4291	17.3150 8922	20.6546 5826	144
145	10.3533 5242	12.3734 4394	14.7844 4934	17.6613 9101	21.0935 6975	145
146	10.5215 9440	12.5899 7921	15.0616 5776	18.0146 1883	21.5418 0811	146
147	10.6925 7031	12.8103 0385	15.3440 6385	18.3749 1120	21.9995 7153	147
148	10.8663 2457	13.0344 8416	15.6317 6504	18.7424 0943	22.4670 6242	148
149	11.0429 0235	13.2625 8764	15.9248 6064	19.1172 5761	22.9444 8750	149
150	11.2223 4951	13.4946 8292	16.2234 5178	19.4996 0277	23.4320 5786	150
151	11.4047 1269	13.7308 3987	16.5276 4150	19.8895 9482	23.9299 8909	151
152	11.5900 3927	13.9711 2957	16.8375 3478	20.2873 8672	24.4385 0136	152
153	11.7783 7741	14.2156 2434	17.1532 3855	20.6931 3445	24.9578 1951	153
154	11.9697 7604	14.4643 9776	17.4748 6178	21.1069 9714	25.4881 7318	154
155	12.1642 8490	14.7175 2472	17.8025 1543	21.5291 3708	26.0297 9686	155
156	12.3619 5453	14.9750 8141	18.1363 1260	21.9597 1983	26.5829 3004	156
157	12.5628 3629	15.2371 4533	18.4763 6846	22.3989 1422	27.1478 1730	157
158	12.7669 8238	15.5037 9538	18.8228 0037	22.8468 9251	27.7247 0842	158
159	12.9744 4585	15.7751 1179	19.1757 2787	23.3038 3036	28.3138 5847	159
160	13.1852 8059	16.0511 7625	19.5352 7277	23.7699 0696	28.9155 2797	160
161	13.3995 4140	16.3320 7184	19.9015 5914	24.2453 0510	29.5299 8294	161
162	13.6172 8395	16.6178 8309	20.2747 1337	24.7302 1121	30.1574 9507	162
163	13.8385 6481	16.9086 9605	20.6548 6425	25.2248 1543	30.7983 4184	163
164	14.0634 4149	17.2045 9823	21.0421 4295	25.7293 1174	31.4528 0661	164
165	14.2919 7242	17.5056 7870	21.4366 8313	26.2438 9797	32.1211 7875	165
166	14.5242 1697	17.8120 2807	21.8386 2094	26.7687 7593	32.8037 5380	166
167	14.7602 3549	18.1237 3856	22.2480 9508	27.3041 5145	33.5008 3357	167
168	15.0000 8932	18.4409 0399	22.6652 4687	27.8502 3448	34.2127 2628	168
169	15.2438 4077	18.7636 1981	23.0902 2024	28.4072 3917	34.9397 4671	169
170	15.4915 5319	19.0919 8316	23.5231 6187	28.9753 8395	35.6822 1633	170
171	15.7432 9092	19.4260 9286	23.9642 2116	29.5548 9163	36.4404 6343	171
172	15.9991 1940	19.7660 4949	24.4135 5031	30.1459 8947	37.2148 2327	172
173	16.2591 0509	20.1119 5535	24.8713 0437	30.7489 0925	38.0056 3827	173
174	16.5233 1555	20.4639 1457	25.3376 4133	31.3638 8744	38.8132 5808	174
175	16.7918 1943	20.8220 3308	25.8127 2211	31.9911 6519	39.6380 3982	175
176	17.0646 8649	21.1864 1865	26.2967 1065	32.6309 8849	40.4803 4816	176
177	17.3419 8765	21.5571 8098	26.7897 7397	33.2836 0826	41.3405 5556	177
178	17.6237 9495	21.9344 3165	27.2920 8223	33.9492 8043	42.2190 4237	178
179	17.9101 8162	22.3182 8420	27.8038 0877	34.6282 6604	43.1161 9702	179
180	18.2012 2207	22.7088 5418	28.3251 3019	35.3208 3136	44.0324 1620	180

TABLE I

N	1 5/8	1 3/4	1 7/8	2	2 1/8	N
181	18.4969 9193	23.1062 5912	28.8562 2638	36.0272 4798	44.9681 0505	181
182	18.7975 6804	23.5106 1866	29.3972 8062	36.7477 9294	45.9236 7728	182
183	19.1030 2853	23.9220 5448	29.9484 7964	37.4827 4880	46.8995 5542	183
184	19.4134 5274	24.3406 9044	30.5100 1363	38.2324 0378	47.8961 7098	184
185	19.7289 2135	24.7666 5252	31.0820 7638	38.9970 5185	48.9139 6461	185
186	20.0495 1632	25.2000 6894	31.6648 6532	39.7769 9289	49.9533 8636	186
187	20.3753 2096	25.6410 7015	32.2585 8154	40.5725 3275	51.0148 9582	187
188	20.7064 1992	26.0897 8887	32.8634 2994	41.3839 8340	52.0989 6235	188
189	21.0428 9925	26.5463 6018	33.4796 1926	42.2116 6307	53.2060 6530	189
190	21.3848 4636	27.0109 2148	34.1073 6212	43.0558 9633	54.3366 9419	190
191	21.7323 5011	27.4836 1261	34.7468 7516	43.9170 1426	55.4913 4894	191
192	22.0855 0080	27.9645 7583	35.3983 7907	44.7953 5455	56.6705 4011	192
193	22.4443 9019	28.4539 5591	36.0620 9867	45.6912 6164	57.8747 8908	193
194	22.8091 1153	28.9519 0013	36.7382 6302	46.6050 8687	59.1046 2835	194
195	23.1797 5959	29.4585 5839	37.4271 0546	47.5371 8861	60.3606 0170	195
196	23.5564 3069	29.9740 8316	38.1288 6368	48.4879 3238	61.6432 6449	196
197	23.9392 2269	30.4986 2961	38.8437 7988	49.4576 9103	62.9531 8386	197
198	24.3282 3505	31.0323 5563	39.5721 0075	50.4468 4485	64.2909 3902	198
199	24.7235 6887	31.5754 2186	40.3140 7764	51.4557 8174	65.6571 2147	199
200	25.1253 2687	32.1279 9174	41.0699 6659	52.4848 9738	67.0523 3530	200
201	25.5336 1343	32.6902 3159	41.8400 2847	53.5345 9533	68.4771 9743	201
202	25.9485 3465	33.2623 1065	42.6245 2900	54.6052 8723	69.9323 3787	202
203	26.3701 9834	33.8444 0108	43.4237 3892	55.6973 9298	71.4184 0005	203
204	26.7987 1406	34.4366 7810	44.2379 3403	56.8113 4084	72.9360 4106	204
205	27.2341 9316	35.0393 1997	45.0673 9529	57.9475 6765	74.4859 3193	205
206	27.6767 4880	35.6525 0807	45.9124 0895	59.1065 1901	76.0687 5798	206
207	28.1264 9597	36.2764 2696	46.7732 6662	60.2886 4939	77.6852 1909	207
208	28.5835 5153	36.9112 6443	47.6502 6537	61.4944 2237	79.3360 2999	208
209	29.0480 3424	37.5572 1156	48.5437 0784	62.7243 1082	81.0219 2063	209
210	29.5200 6480	38.2144 6276	49.4539 0236	63.9787 9704	82.7436 3645	210
211	29.9997 6585	38.8832 1586	50.3811 6303	65.2583 7298	84.5019 3872	211
212	30.4872 6205	39.5636 7214	51.3258 0984	66.5635 4044	86.2976 0492	212
213	30.9826 8005	40.2560 3640	52.2881 6878	67.8948 1125	88.1314 2902	213
214	31.4861 4860	40.9605 1704	53.2685 7194	69.2527 0747	90.0042 2189	214
215	31.9977 9852	41.6773 2608	54.2673 5766	70.6377 6162	91.9168 1160	215
216	32.5177 6275	42.4066 7929	55.2848 7062	72.0505 1685	93.8700 4385	216
217	33.0461 7639	43.1487 9618	56.3214 6194	73.4915 2719	95.8647 8228	217
218	33.5831 7676	43.9039 0011	57.3774 8936	74.9613 5774	97.9019 0891	218
219	34.1289 0338	44.6722 1836	58.4533 1728	76.4605 8489	99.9823 2447	219
220	34.6834 9806	45.4539 8218	59.5493 1698	77.9897 9659	102.1069 4886	220
221	35.2471 0490	46.2494 2687	60.6658 6667	79.5495 9252	104.2767 2153	221
222	35.8198 7036	47.0587 9184	61.8033 5167	81.1405 8437	106.4926 0186	222
223	36.4019 4325	47.8823 2070	62.9621 6452	82.7633 9606	108.7555 6965	223
224	36.9934 7483	48.7202 6131	64.1427 0510	84.4186 6398	111.0666 2551	224
225	37.5946 1879	49.5728 6589	65.3453 8082	86.1070 3726	113.4267 9130	225
226	38.2055 3135	50.4403 9104	66.5706 0671	87.8291 7800	115.8371 1061	226
227	38.8263 7123	51.3230 9788	67.8188 0559	89.5857 6156	118.2986 4921	227
228	39.4572 9977	52.2212 5210	69.0904 0819	91.3774 7679	120.8124 9551	228
229	40.0984 8089	53.1351 2401	70.3858 5335	93.2050 2633	123.3797 6104	229
230	40.7500 8120	54.0649 8868	71.7055 8810	95.0691 2686	126.0015 8096	230
231	41.4122 7002	55.0111 2598	73.0500 6787	96.9705 0939	128.6791 1456	231
232	42.0852 1941	55.9738 2068	74.4197 5665	98.9099 1958	131.4135 4574	232
233	42.7691 0422	56.9533 6255	75.8151 2708	100.8881 1797	134.2060 8359	233
234	43.4641 0217	57.9500 4639	77.2366 6072	102.9058 8033	137.0579 6286	234
235	44.1703 9383	58.9641 7220	78.6848 4811	104.9639 9794	139.9704 4457	235
236	44.8881 6273	59.9960 4522	80.1601 8901	107.0632 7790	142.9448 1652	236
237	45.6175 9537	61.0459 7601	81.6631 9255	109.2045 4346	145.9823 9387	237
238	46.3588 8130	62.1142 8059	83.1943 7741	111.3886 3433	149.0845 1974	238
239	47.1122 1312	63.2012 8050	84.7542 7199	113.6164 0701	152.2525 6579	239
240	47.8777 8658	64.3073 0291	86.3434 1459	115.8887 3515	155.4879 3281	240

TABLE I

N	1 5/8	1 3/4	1 7/8	2	2 1/8	N
241	48.6558 0061	65.4326 8071	87.9623 5361	118.2065 0986	158.7920 5138	241
242	49.4464 5737	66.5777 5262	89.6116 4774	120.5706 4005	162.1663 8247	242
243	50.2499 6231	67.7428 6329	91.2918 6614	122.9820 5285	165.6124 1810	243
244	51.0665 2419	68.9283 6340	93.0035 8863	125.4416 9391	169.1316 8199	244
245	51.8963 5521	70.1346 0976	94.7474 0591	127.9505 2779	172.7257 3023	245
246	52.7396 7098	71.3619 6543	96.5239 1977	130.5095 3835	176.3961 5200	246
247	53.5966 9064	72.6107 9982	98.3337 4327	133.1197 2911	180.1445 7023	247
248	54.4676 3686	73.8814 8882	100.1775 0096	135.7821 2369	183.9726 4234	248
249	55.3527 3596	75.1744 1487	102.0558 2910	138.4977 6617	187.8820 6099	249
250	56.2522 1792	76.4899 6713	103.9693 7590	141.2677 2149	191.8745 5479	250
251	57.1663 1646	77.8285 4156	105.9188 0169	144.0930 7592	195.9518 8908	251
252	58.0952 6910	79.1905 4104	107.9047 7923	146.9749 3744	200.1158 6672	252
253	59.0393 1723	80.5763 7550	109.9279 9384	149.9144 3619	204.3683 2889	253
254	59.9987 0613	81.9864 6208	111.9891 4372	152.9127 2491	208.7111 5588	254
255	60.9736 8510	83.4212 2516	114.0889 4016	155.9709 7941	213.1462 6794	255
256	61.9645 0749	84.8810 9660	116.2281 0779	159.0903 9900	217.6756 2613	256
257	62.9714 3073	86.3665 1579	118.4073 8481	162.2722 0698	222.3012 3319	257
258	63.9947 1648	87.8779 2982	120.6275 2328	165.5176 5112	227.0251 3439	258
259	65.0346 3063	89.4157 9359	122.8892 8934	168.8280 0414	231.8494 1850	259
260	66.0914 4337	90.9805 6998	125.1934 6352	172.2045 6422	236.7762 1864	260
261	67.1654 2933	92.5727 2995	127.5408 4096	175.6486 5551	241.8077 1329	261
262	68.2568 6756	94.1927 5273	129.9322 3172	179.1616 2862	246.9461 2720	262
263	69.3660 4165	95.8411 2590	132.3684 6107	182.7448 6119	252.1937 3240	263
264	70.4932 3983	97.5183 4560	134.8503 6971	186.3997 5841	257.5528 4921	264
265	71.6387 5498	99.2249 1665	137.3788 1415	190.1277 5358	263.0258 4726	265
266	72.8028 8475	100.9613 5269	139.9546 6691	193.9303 0865	268.6151 4651	266
267	73.9859 3162	102.7281 7636	142.5788 1692	197.8089 1483	274.3232 1838	267
268	75.1882 0301	104.5259 1945	145.2521 6973	201.7650 9312	280.1525 8677	268
269	76.4100 1131	106.3551 2304	147.9756 4792	205.8003 9499	286.1058 2924	269
270	77.6516 7399	108.2163 3769	150.7501 9131	209.9164 0289	292.1855 7811	270
271	78.9135 1370	110.1101 2360	153.5767 5740	214.1147 3094	298.3945 2164	271
272	80.1958 5829	112.0370 5077	156.4563 2160	218.3970 2556	304.7354 0523	272
273	81.4990 4099	113.9976 9916	159.3898 7763	222.7649 6607	311.2110 3259	273
274	82.8234 0041	115.9926 5889	162.3784 3784	227.2202 6540	317.8242 6703	274
275	84.1692 8066	118.0225 3042	165.4230 3355	231.7646 7070	324.5780 3270	275
276	85.5370 3148	120.0879 2470	168.5247 1543	236.3999 6412	331.4753 1590	276
277	86.9270 0824	122.1894 6339	171.6845 5384	241.1279 6340	338.5191 6636	277
278	88.3395 7212	124.3277 7900	174.9036 3923	245.9505 2267	345.7126 9865	278
279	89.7750 9017	126.5035 1513	178.1830 8246	250.8695 3312	353.0590 9349	279
280	91.2339 3538	128.7173 2664	181.5240 1526	255.8869 2378	360.5615 9923	280
281	92.7164 8683	130.9698 7986	184.9275 9054	261.0046 6226	368.2235 3321	281
282	94.2231 2974	133.2618 5276	188.3949 8287	266.2247 5550	376.0482 8330	282
283	95.7542 5560	135.5939 3518	191.9273 8880	271.5492 5061	384.0393 0932	283
284	97.3102 6226	137.9668 2905	195.5260 2734	276.9802 3563	392.2001 4464	284
285	98.8915 5402	140.3812 4855	199.1921 4035	282.5198 4034	400.5343 9771	285
286	100.4985 4177	142.8379 2040	202.9269 9298	288.1702 3715	409.0457 5366	286
287	102.1316 4307	145.3375 8401	206.7318 7410	293.9336 4189	417.7379 7593	287
288	103.7912 8227	147.8809 9173	210.6080 9674	299.8123 1473	426.6149 0792	288
289	105.4778 9061	150.4689 0909	214.5569 9855	305.8085 6102	435.6804 7471	289
290	107.1919 0633	153.1021 1500	218.5799 4227	311.9247 3224	444.9386 8480	290
291	108.9337 7481	155.7814 0201	222.6783 1619	318.1632 2689	454.3936 3185	291
292	110.7039 4865	158.5075 7654	226.8535 3462	324.5264 9142	464.0494 9653	292
293	112.5028 8782	161.2814 5913	231.1070 3839	331.0170 2125	473.9105 4833	293
294	114.3310 5974	164.1038 8467	235.4402 9536	337.6373 6168	483.9811 4748	294
295	116.1889 3947	166.9757 0265	239.8548 0090	344.3901 0891	494.2657 4686	295
296	118.0770 0973	169.8977 7745	244.3520 7842	351.2779 1109	504.7688 9398	296
297	119.9957 6114	172.8709 8855	248.9336 7989	358.3034 6931	515.4952 3298	297
298	121.9456 9226	175.8962 3085	253.6011 8639	365.4695 3870	526.4495 0668	298
299	123.9273 0976	178.9744 1489	258.3562 0863	372.7789 2947	537.6365 5870	299
300	125.9411 2854	182.1064 6715	263.2003 8754	380.2345 0806	549.0613 3557	300

TABLE I

N	1 5/8	1 3/4	1 7/8	2	2 1/8	N
301	127.9876 7188	185.2933 3033	268.1353 9481	387.8391 9822	560.7288 8895	301
302	130.0674 7155	188.5359 6361	273.1629 3346	395.5959 8219	572.6443 7784	302
303	132.1810 6796	191.8353 4297	278.2847 3847	403.5079 0183	584.8130 7087	303
304	134.3290 1032	195.1924 6147	283.5025 7731	411.5780 5987	597.2403 4863	304
305	136.5118 5673	198.6083 2955	288.8182 5064	419.8096 2106	609.9317 0604	305
306	138.7301 7440	202.0839 7531	294.2335 9284	428.2058 1349	622.8927 5479	306
307	140.9845 3974	205.6204 4488	299.7504 7270	436.7699 2976	636.1292 2583	307
308	143.2755 3851	209.2188 0267	305.3707 9406	445.5053 2835	649.6469 7188	308
309	145.6037 6601	212.8801 3171	311.0964 9645	454.4154 3492	663.4519 7003	309
310	147.9698 2721	216.6055 3402	316.9295 5576	463.5037 4362	677.5503 2439	310
311	150.3743 3690	220.3961 3086	322.8719 8493	472.7738 1849	691.9482 6879	311
312	152.8179 1987	224.2530 6315	328.9258 3465	482.2292 9486	706.6521 6950	312
313	155.3012 1107	228.1774 9176	335.0931 9405	491.8738 8076	721.6685 2810	313
314	157.8248 5575	232.1705 9787	341.3761 9144	501.7113 5837	737.0039 8432	314
315	160.3895 0966	236.2335 8333	347.7769 9503	511.7455 8554	752.6653 1899	315
316	162.9958 3919	240.3676 7104	354.2978 1368	521.9804 9725	768.6594 5702	316
317	165.6445 2158	244.5741 0528	360.9408 9769	532.4201 0719	784.9934 7048	317
318	168.3362 4505	248.8541 5212	367.7085 3952	543.0685 0934	801.6745 8173	318
319	171.0717 0904	253.2090 9978	374.6030 7464	553.9298 7952	818.7101 6659	319
320	173.8516 2431	257.6402 5903	381.6268 8229	565.0084 7712	836.1077 5763	320
321	176.6767 1320	262.1489 6356	388.7823 8633	576.3086 4666	853.8750 4748	321
322	179.5477 0979	266.7365 7043	396.0720 5607	587.8348 1959	872.0198 9224	322
323	182.4653 6008	271.4044 6041	403.4984 0713	599.5915 1598	890.5503 1495	323
324	185.4304 2218	276.1540 3847	411.0640 0226	611.5833 4630	909.4745 0914	324
325	188.4436 6654	280.9867 3414	418.7714 5230	623.8150 1323	928.8008 4246	325
326	191.5058 7612	285.9040 0199	426.6234 1703	636.2913 1349	948.5378 6036	326
327	194.6178 4661	290.9073 2202	434.6226 0610	649.0171 3976	968.6942 8989	327
328	197.7803 8661	295.9982 0016	442.7717 7997	661.9974 8256	989.2790 4356	328
329	200.9943 1790	301.1781 6866	451.0737 5084	675.2374 3221	1010.3012 2323	329
330	204.2604 7556	306.4487 8661	459.5313 8367	688.7421 8085	1031.7701 2422	330
331	207.5797 0829	311.8116 4038	468.1475 9711	702.5170 2447	1053.6952 3936	331
332	210.9528 7855	317.2683 4408	476.9253 6456	716.5673 6496	1076.0862 6320	332
333	214.3808 6283	322.8205 4010	485.8677 1514	730.8987 1226	1098.9530 9629	333
334	217.8645 5185	328.4698 9956	494.9777 3480	745.5166 8650	1122.3058 4959	334
335	221.4048 5081	334.2181 2280	504.2585 6733	760.4270 2023	1146.1548 4889	335
336	225.0026 7964	340.0669 3995	513.7134 1547	775.6355 6064	1170.5106 3943	336
337	228.6589 7318	346.0181 1140	523.3455 4201	791.1482 7185	1195.3839 9052	337
338	232.3746 8150	352.0734 2835	533.1582 7092	806.9712 3729	1220.7859 0032	338
339	236.1507 7007	358.2347 1334	543.1549 8850	823.1106 6203	1246.7276 0070	339
340	239.9882 2009	364.5038 2083	553.3391 4453	839.5728 7527	1273.2205 6222	340
341	243.8880 2866	370.8826 3769	563.7142 5349	856.3643 3278	1300.2764 9916	341
342	247.8512 0913	377.3730 8385	574.2838 9575	873.4916 1944	1327.9073 7477	342
343	251.8787 9128	383.9771 1282	585.0517 1879	890.9614 5182	1356.1254 0648	343
344	255.9718 2163	390.6967 1229	596.0214 3852	908.7806 8086	1384.9430 7137	344
345	260.1313 6374	397.5339 0476	607.1968 4049	926.9562 9448	1414.3731 1164	345
346	264.3584 9840	404.4907 4809	618.5817 8125	945.4954 2037	1444.4285 4026	346
347	268.6543 2400	411.5693 3618	630.1801 8965	964.4053 2878	1475.1226 4674	347
348	273.0199 5676	418.7717 9956	641.9960 6821	983.6934 3535	1506.4690 0298	348
349	277.4565 3106	426.1003 0606	654.0334 9448	1003.3673 0406	1538.4814 6930	349
350	281.9651 9969	433.5570 6141	666.2966 2251	1023.4346 5014	1571.1742 0052	350
351	286.5471 3418	441.1443 0999	678.7896 8418	1043.9033 4314	1604.5616 5228	351
352	291.2035 2511	448.8643 3541	691.5169 9076	1064.7814 1000	1638.6585 8739	352
353	295.9355 8240	456.7194 6128	704.4829 3433	1086.0770 3820	1673.4800 8237	353
354	300.7445 3561	464.7120 5185	717.6919 8935	1107.7985 7897	1709.0415 3413	354
355	305.6316 3431	472.8445 1276	731.1487 1415	1129.9545 5055	1745.3586 6673	355
356	310.5981 4837	481.1192 9174	744.8577 5254	1152.5536 4156	1782.4475 3839	356
357	315.6453 6828	489.5388 7934	758.8238 3540	1175.6047 1439	1820.3245 4858	357
358	320.7746 0552	498.1058 0973	773.0517 8232	1199.1168 0868	1859.0064 4524	358
359	325.9871 9286	506.8226 6140	787.5465 0324	1223.0991 4485	1898.5103 3220	359
360	331.2844 8474	515.6920 5797	802.3130 0017	1247.5611 2775	1938.8536 7676	360

TABLE I

N	2 1/4	2 3/8	2 1/2	2 5/8	2 3/4	N
1	1.0225 0000	1.0237 5000	1.0250 0000	1.0262 5000	1.0275 0000	1
2	1.0455 0625	1.0480 6406	1.0506 2500	1.0531 8906	1.0557 5625	2
3	1.0690 3014	1.0729 5558	1.0768 9062	1.0808 3528	1.0847 8955	3
4	1.0930 8332	1.0984 3828	1.1038 1289	1.1092 0720	1.1146 2126	4
5	1.1176 7769	1.1245 2619	1.1314 0821	1.1383 2389	1.1452 7334	5
6	1.1428 2544	1.1512 3369	1.1596 9342	1.1682 0489	1.1767 6836	6
7	1.1685 3901	1.1785 7549	1.1886 8575	1.1988 7027	1.2091 2949	7
8	1.1948 3114	1.2065 6665	1.2184 0290	1.2303 4062	1.2423 8055	8
9	1.2217 1484	1.2352 2261	1.2488 6297	1.2626 3706	1.2765 4602	9
10	1.2492 0343	1.2645 5915	1.2800 8454	1.2957 8128	1.3116 5103	10
11	1.2773 1050	1.2945 9243	1.3120 8666	1.3297 9554	1.3477 2144	11
12	1.3060 4999	1.3253 3900	1.3448 8882	1.3647 0267	1.3847 8378	12
13	1.3354 3611	1.3568 1580	1.3785 1104	1.4005 2612	1.4228 6533	13
14	1.3654 8343	1.3890 4017	1.4129 7382	1.4372 8993	1.4619 9413	14
15	1.3962 0680	1.4220 2988	1.4482 9817	1.4750 1879	1.5021 9896	15
16	1.4276 2146	1.4558 0309	1.4845 0562	1.5137 3803	1.5435 0944	16
17	1.4597 4294	1.4903 7841	1.5216 1826	1.5534 7365	1.5859 5595	17
18	1.4925 8716	1.5257 7490	1.5596 5872	1.5942 5234	1.6295 6973	18
19	1.5261 7037	1.5620 1205	1.5986 5019	1.6361 0146	1.6743 8290	19
20	1.5605 0920	1.5991 0984	1.6386 1644	1.6790 4912	1.7204 2843	20
21	1.5956 2066	1.6370 8870	1.6795 8185	1.7231 2416	1.7677 4021	21
22	1.6315 2212	1.6759 6955	1.7215 7140	1.7683 5617	1.8163 5307	22
23	1.6682 3137	1.7157 7383	1.7646 1068	1.8147 7552	1.8663 0278	23
24	1.7057 6658	1.7565 2346	1.8087 2595	1.8624 1338	1.9176 2610	24
25	1.7441 4632	1.7982 4089	1.8539 4410	1.9113 0173	1.9703 6082	25
26	1.7833 8962	1.8409 4911	1.9002 9270	1.9614 7340	2.0245 4575	26
27	1.8235 1588	1.8846 7165	1.9478 0002	2.0129 6208	2.0802 2075	27
28	1.8645 4499	1.9294 3261	1.9964 9502	2.0658 0233	2.1374 2682	28
29	1.9064 9725	1.9752 5663	2.0464 0739	2.1200 2964	2.1962 0606	29
30	1.9493 9344	2.0221 6898	2.0975 6758	2.1756 8042	2.2566 0173	30
31	1.9932 5479	2.0701 9549	2.1500 0677	2.2327 9203	2.3186 5828	31
32	2.0381 0303	2.1193 6263	2.2037 5694	2.2914 0282	2.3824 2138	32
33	2.0839 6034	2.1696 9749	2.2588 5086	2.3515 5215	2.4479 3797	33
34	2.1308 4945	2.2212 2781	2.3153 2213	2.4132 8039	2.5152 5626	34
35	2.1787 9356	2.2739 8197	2.3732 0519	2.4766 2900	2.5844 2581	35
36	2.2278 1642	2.3279 8904	2.4325 3532	2.5416 4051	2.6554 9752	36
37	2.2779 4229	2.3832 7878	2.4933 4870	2.6083 5858	2.7285 2370	37
38	2.3291 9599	2.4398 8165	2.5556 8242	2.6768 2799	2.8035 5810	38
39	2.3816 0290	2.4978 2884	2.6195 7448	2.7470 9473	2.8806 5595	39
40	2.4351 8897	2.5571 5228	2.6850 6384	2.8192 0596	2.9598 7399	40
41	2.4899 8072	2.6178 8464	2.7521 9043	2.8932 1012	3.0412 7052	41
42	2.5460 0528	2.6800 5940	2.8209 9520	2.9691 5688	3.1249 0546	42
43	2.6032 9040	2.7437 1081	2.8915 2008	3.0470 9725	3.2108 4036	43
44	2.6618 6444	2.8088 7395	2.9638 0808	3.1270 8355	3.2991 3847	44
45	2.7217 5639	2.8755 8470	3.0379 0328	3.2091 6950	3.3898 6478	45
46	2.7829 9590	2.9438 7984	3.1138 5086	3.2934 1020	3.4830 8606	46
47	2.8456 1331	3.0137 9699	3.1916 9713	3.3798 6222	3.5788 7093	47
48	2.9096 3961	3.0853 7466	3.2714 8956	3.4685 8360	3.6772 8988	48
49	2.9751 0650	3.1586 5231	3.3532 7680	3.5596 3392	3.7784 1535	49
50	3.0420 4640	3.2336 7030	3.4371 0872	3.6530 7431	3.8823 2177	50
51	3.1104 9244	3.3104 6997	3.5230 3644	3.7489 6751	3.9890 8562	51
52	3.1804 7852	3.3890 9364	3.6111 1235	3.8473 7791	4.0987 8547	52
53	3.2520 3929	3.4695 8461	3.7013 9016	3.9483 7158	4.2115 0208	53
54	3.3252 1017	3.5519 8724	3.7939 2491	4.0520 1633	4.3273 1838	54
55	3.4000 2740	3.6363 4694	3.8887 7303	4.1583 8176	4.4463 1964	55
56	3.4765 2802	3.7227 1018	3.9859 9236	4.2675 3928	4.5685 9343	56
57	3.5547 4990	3.8111 2455	4.0856 4217	4.3795 6219	4.6942 2975	57
58	3.6347 3177	3.9016 3876	4.1877 8322	4.4945 2569	4.8233 2107	58
59	3.7165 1324	3.9943 0268	4.2924 7780	4.6125 0699	4.9559 6239	59
60	3.8001 3479	4.0891 6737	4.3997 8975	4.7335 8530	5.0922 5136	60

TABLE I

N	2 1/4	2 3/8	2 1/2	2 5/8	2 3/4	N
61	3.8856 3782	4.1862 8509	4.5097 8449	4.8578 4191	5.2322 8827	61
62	3.9730 6467	4.2857 0936	4.6225 2910	4.9853 6027	5.3761 7620	62
63	4.0624 5862	4.3874 9496	4.7380 9233	5.1162 2597	5.5240 2105	63
64	4.1538 6394	4.4916 9796	4.8565 4464	5.2505 2690	5.6759 3162	64
65	4.2473 2588	4.5983 7579	4.9779 5826	5.3883 5324	5.8320 1974	65
66	4.3428 9071	4.7075 8722	5.1024 0721	5.5297 9751	5.9924 0029	66
67	4.4406 0576	4.8193 9241	5.2299 6739	5.6749 5469	6.1571 9130	67
68	4.5405 1939	4.9338 5298	5.3607 1658	5.8239 2225	6.3265 1406	68
69	4.6426 8107	5.0510 3199	5.4947 3449	5.9768 0021	6.5004 9319	69
70	4.7471 4140	5.1709 9400	5.6321 0286	6.1336 9122	6.6792 5676	70
71	4.8539 5208	5.2938 0511	5.7729 0543	6.2947 0061	6.8629 3632	71
72	4.9631 6600	5.4195 3298	5.9172 2806	6.4599 3650	7.0516 6706	72
73	5.0748 3723	5.5482 4689	6.0651 5876	6.6295 0984	7.2455 8791	73
74	5.1890 2107	5.6800 1775	6.2167 8773	6.8035 3447	7.4448 4158	74
75	5.3057 7405	5.8149 1817	6.3722 0743	6.9821 2725	7.6495 7472	75
76	5.4251 5396	5.9530 2248	6.5315 1261	7.1654 0809	7.8599 3802	76
77	5.5472 1993	6.0944 0676	6.6948 0043	7.3535 0005	8.0760 8632	77
78	5.6720 3237	6.2391 4892	6.8621 7044	7.5465 2943	8.2981 7869	78
79	5.7996 5310	6.3873 2871	7.0337 2470	7.7446 2583	8.5263 7861	79
80	5.9301 4530	6.5390 2777	7.2095 6782	7.9479 2225	8.7608 5402	80
81	6.0635 7357	6.6943 2968	7.3898 0701	8.1565 5521	9.0017 7751	81
82	6.2000 0397	6.8533 2001	7.5745 5219	8.3706 6479	9.2493 2639	82
83	6.3395 0406	7.0160 8636	7.7639 1599	8.5903 9474	9.5036 8286	83
84	6.4821 4290	7.1827 1841	7.9580 1389	8.8158 9260	9.7650 3414	84
85	6.6279 9112	7.3533 0797	8.1569 6424	9.0473 0978	10.0335 7258	85
86	6.7771 2092	7.5279 4903	8.3608 8834	9.2848 0166	10.3094 9583	86
87	6.9296 0614	7.7067 3782	8.5699 1055	9.5285 2771	10.5930 0696	87
88	7.0855 2228	7.8897 7285	8.7841 5832	9.7786 5156	10.8843 1465	88
89	7.2449 4653	8.0771 5495	9.0037 6228	10.0353 4116	11.1836 3331	89
90	7.4079 5782	8.2689 8738	9.2288 5633	10.2987 6887	11.4911 8322	90
91	7.5746 3688	8.4653 7583	9.4595 7774	10.5691 1155	11.8071 9076	91
92	7.7450 6621	8.6664 2851	9.6960 6718	10.8465 5073	12.1318 8851	92
93	7.9193 3020	8.8722 5618	9.9384 6886	11.1312 7268	12.4655 1544	93
94	8.0975 1512	9.0829 7227	10.1869 3058	11.4234 6859	12.8083 1711	94
95	8.2797 0921	9.2986 9286	10.4416 0385	11.7233 3464	13.1605 4584	95
96	8.4660 0267	9.5195 3682	10.7026 4395	12.0310 7218	13.5224 6085	96
97	8.6564 8773	9.7456 2581	10.9702 1004	12.3468 8782	13.8943 2852	97
98	8.8512 5871	9.9770 8443	11.2444 6530	12.6709 9363	14.2764 2255	98
99	9.0504 1203	10.2140 4018	11.5255 7693	13.0036 0721	14.6690 2417	99
100	9.2540 4630	10.4566 2364	11.8137 1635	13.3449 5190	15.0724 2234	100
101	9.4622 6234	10.7049 6845	12.1090 5926	13.6952 5689	15.4869 1395	101
102	9.6751 6324	10.9592 1145	12.4117 8574	14.0547 5738	15.9128 0409	102
103	9.8928 5442	11.2194 9272	12.7220 8038	14.4236 9476	16.3504 0620	103
104	10.1154 4364	11.4859 5567	13.0401 3239	14.8023 1675	16.8000 4237	104
105	10.3430 4112	11.7587 4712	13.3661 3570	15.1908 7756	17.2620 4353	105
106	10.5757 5955	12.0380 1736	13.7002 8910	15.5896 3810	17.7367 4973	106
107	10.8137 1414	12.3239 2028	14.0427 9632	15.9988 6610	18.2245 1035	107
108	11.0570 2270	12.6166 1338	14.3938 6623	16.4188 3633	18.7256 8438	108
109	11.3058 0572	12.9162 5795	14.7537 1289	16.8498 3079	19.2406 4070	109
110	11.5601 8634	13.2230 1908	15.1225 5571	17.2921 3885	19.7697 5832	110
111	11.8202 9054	13.5370 6578	15.5006 1960	17.7460 5749	20.3134 2668	111
112	12.0862 4707	13.8585 7109	15.8881 3509	18.2118 9150	20.8720 4591	112
113	12.3581 8763	14.1877 1216	16.2853 3847	18.6899 5365	21.4460 2717	113
114	12.6362 4685	14.5246 7032	16.6924 7193	19.1805 6494	22.0357 9292	114
115	12.9205 6241	14.8696 3124	17.1097 8373	19.6840 5477	22.6417 7723	115
116	13.2112 7506	15.2227 8498	17.5375 2832	20.2007 6120	23.2644 2610	116
117	13.5085 2875	15.5843 2613	17.9759 6653	20.7310 3118	23.9041 9782	117
118	13.8124 7065	15.9544 5387	18.4253 6570	21.2752 2075	24.5615 6326	118
119	14.1232 5124	16.3333 7215	18.8859 9984	21.8336 9530	25.2370 0625	119
120	14.4410 2439	16.7212 8974	19.3581 4983	22.4068 2980	25.9310 2392	120

TABLE I

N	2 1/4	2 3/8	2 1/2	2 5/8	2 3/4	N
121	14.7659 4744	17.1184 2037	19.8421 0358	22.9950 0908	26.6441 2708	121
122	15.0981 8126	17.5249 8285	20.3381 5617	23.5986 2807	27.3768 4057	122
123	15.4378 9034	17.9412 0120	20.8466 1007	24.2180 9206	28.1297 0369	123
124	15.7852 4287	18.3673 0473	21.3677 7533	24.8538 1697	28.9032 7054	124
125	16.1404 1083	18.8035 2821	21.9019 6971	25.5062 2967	29.6981 1048	125
126	16.5035 7008	19.2501 1201	22.4495 1895	26.1757 6820	30.5148 0852	126
127	16.8749 0040	19.7073 0217	23.0107 5692	26.8628 8211	31.3539 6575	127
128	17.2545 8566	20.1753 5059	23.5860 2585	27.5680 3277	32.2161 9981	128
129	17.6428 1384	20.6545 1517	24.1756 7649	28.2916 9363	33.1021 4530	129
130	18.0397 7715	21.1450 5991	24.7800 6841	29.0343 5059	34.0124 5430	130
131	18.4456 7214	21.6472 5508	25.3995 7012	29.7965 0229	34.9477 9679	131
132	18.8606 9976	22.1613 7739	26.0345 5937	30.5786 6047	35.9088 6120	132
133	19.2850 6550	22.6877 1010	26.6854 2335	31.3813 5031	36.8963 5489	133
134	19.7189 7948	23.2265 4322	27.3525 5894	32.2051 1076	37.9110 0465	134
135	20.1626 5652	23.7781 7362	28.0363 7291	33.0504 9491	38.9535 5727	135
136	20.6163 1629	24.3429 0524	28.7372 8223	33.9180 7041	40.0247 8010	136
137	21.0801 8341	24.9210 4924	29.4557 1429	34.8084 1975	41.1254 6155	137
138	21.5544 8753	25.5129 2416	30.1921 0715	35.7221 4077	42.2564 1175	138
139	22.0394 6350	26.1188 5611	30.9469 0983	36.6598 4697	43.4184 6307	139
140	22.5353 5143	26.7391 7894	31.7205 8257	37.6221 6795	44.6124 7080	140
141	23.0423 9684	27.3742 3444	32.5135 9714	38.6097 4986	45.8393 1375	141
142	23.5608 5077	28.0243 7251	33.3264 3706	39.6232 5579	47.0998 9488	142
143	24.0909 6991	28.6899 5136	34.1595 9799	40.6633 6626	48.3951 4199	143
144	24.6330 1673	29.3713 3770	35.0135 8794	41.7307 7962	49.7260 0839	144
145	25.1872 5961	30.0689 0697	35.8889 2764	42.8262 1259	51.0934 7362	145
146	25.7539 7295	30.7830 4351	36.7861 5083	43.9504 0067	52.4985 4415	146
147	26.3334 3734	31.5141 4079	37.7058 0460	45.1040 9869	53.9422 5411	147
148	26.9259 3968	32.2626 0164	38.6484 4972	46.2880 8128	55.4256 6610	148
149	27.5317 7332	33.0288 3843	39.6146 6096	47.5031 4341	56.9498 7192	149
150	28.1512 3822	33.8132 7334	40.6050 2748	48.7501 0092	58.5159 9339	150
151	28.7846 4108	34.6163 3858	41.6201 5317	50.0297 9107	60.1251 8321	151
152	29.4322 9551	35.4384 7662	42.6606 5700	51.3430 7309	61.7786 2575	152
153	30.0945 2216	36.2801 4044	43.7271 7342	52.6908 2876	63.4775 3796	153
154	30.7716 4890	37.1417 9378	44.8203 5276	54.0739 6301	65.2231 7025	154
155	31.4640 1101	38.0239 1138	45.9408 6158	55.4934 0454	67.0168 0744	155
156	32.1719 5125	38.9269 7928	47.0893 8312	56.9501 0641	68.8597 6964	156
157	32.8958 2016	39.8514 9503	48.2666 1770	58.4450 4670	70.7534 1331	157
158	33.6359 7611	40.7979 6804	49.4732 8314	59.9792 2918	72.6991 3217	158
159	34.3927 8557	41.7669 1978	50.7101 1522	61.5536 8395	74.6983 5831	159
160	35.1666 2325	42.7588 8413	51.9778 6810	63.1694 6815	76.7525 6316	160
161	35.9578 7227	43.7744 0762	53.2773 1480	64.8276 6669	78.8632 5865	161
162	36.7669 2440	44.8140 4981	54.6092 4767	66.5293 9294	81.0319 9826	162
163	37.5941 8020	45.8783 8349	55.9744 7886	68.2757 8950	83.2603 7821	163
164	38.4400 4925	46.9679 9510	57.3738 4083	70.0680 2898	85.5500 3861	164
165	39.3049 5036	48.0834 8498	58.8081 8685	71.9073 1474	87.9026 6467	165
166	40.1893 1174	49.2254 6775	60.2783 9152	73.7948 8175	90.3199 8795	166
167	41.0935 7126	50.3945 7261	61.7853 5131	75.7319 9740	92.8037 8762	167
168	42.0181 7661	51.5914 4371	63.3299 8510	77.7199 6233	95.3558 9178	168
169	42.9635 8558	52.8167 4049	64.9132 3472	79.7601 1134	97.9781 7880	169
170	43.9302 6626	54.0711 3808	66.5360 6559	81.8538 1426	100.6725 7872	170
171	44.9186 9725	55.3553 2761	68.1994 6723	84.0024 7689	103.4410 7464	171
172	45.9293 6794	56.6700 1664	69.9044 5391	86.2075 4190	106.2857 0419	172
173	46.9627 7871	58.0159 2954	71.6520 6526	88.4704 8988	109.2085 6105	173
174	48.0194 4124	59.3938 0786	73.4433 6689	90.7928 4024	112.2117 9648	174
175	49.0998 7866	60.8044 1080	75.2794 5106	93.1761 5230	115.2976 2089	175
176	50.2046 2593	62.2485 1556	77.1614 3734	95.6220 2629	118.4683 0546	176
177	51.3342 3002	63.7269 1780	79.0904 7327	98.1321 0448	121.7261 8386	177
178	52.4892 5019	65.2404 3210	81.0677 3510	100.7080 7223	125.0736 5392	178
179	53.6702 5832	66.7898 9236	83.0944 2848	103.3516 5912	128.5131 7940	179
180	54.8778 3913	68.3761 5231	85.1717 8919	106.0646 4017	132.0472 9183	180

TABLE I

N	2 1/4	2 3/8	2 1/2	2 5/8	2 3/4	N
181	56.1125 9051	70.0000 8592	87.3010 8392	108.8488 3698	135.6785 9236	181
182	57.3751 2380	71.6625 8796	89.4836 1102	111.7061 1895	139.4097 5365	182
183	58.6660 6409	73.3645 7443	91.7207 0130	114.6384 0457	143.2435 2187	183
184	59.9860 5053	75.1069 8307	94.0137 1883	117.6476 6269	147.1827 1873	184
185	61.3357 3667	76.8907 7392	96.3640 6180	120.7359 1384	151.2302 4349	185
186	62.7157 9074	78.7169 2980	98.7731 6335	123.9052 3158	155.3890 7519	186
187	64.1268 9603	80.5864 5688	101.2424 9243	127.1577 4390	159.6622 7475	187
188	65.5697 5119	82.5003 8523	103.7735 5474	130.4956 3468	164.0529 8731	188
189	67.0450 7060	84.4597 6938	106.3678 9361	133.9211 4509	168.5644 4446	189
190	68.5535 8468	86.4656 8890	109.0270 9095	137.4365 7515	173.1999 6668	190
191	70.0960 4034	88.5192 4902	111.7527 6822	141.0442 8525	177.9629 6577	191
192	71.6732 0125	90.6215 8118	114.5465 8743	144.7466 9774	182.8569 4733	192
193	73.2858 4827	92.7738 4373	117.4102 5211	148.5462 9855	187.8855 1338	193
194	74.9347 7986	94.9772 2252	120.3455 0842	152.4456 3889	193.0523 6499	194
195	76.6208 1241	97.2329 3156	123.3541 4613	156.4473 3691	198.3613 0503	195
196	78.3447 8069	99.5422 1368	126.4379 9978	160.5540 7950	203.8162 4092	196
197	80.1075 3825	101.9063 4126	129.5989 4978	164.7686 2409	209.4211 8755	197
198	81.9099 5786	104.3266 1686	132.8389 2352	169.0938 0047	215.1802 7020	198
199	83.7529 3191	106.8043 7401	136.1598 9661	173.5325 1273	221.0977 2763	199
200	85.6373 7288	109.3409 7789	139.5638 9402	178.0877 4119	227.1779 1514	200
201	87.5642 1377	111.9378 2612	143.0529 9137	182.7625 4440	233.4253 0781	201
202	89.5344 0858	114.5963 4949	146.6293 1616	187.5600 6119	239.8445 0378	202
203	91.5489 3278	117.3180 1279	150.2950 4906	192.4835 1280	246.4402 2763	203
204	93.6087 8376	120.1043 1559	154.0524 2529	197.5362 0501	253.2173 3389	204
205	95.7149 8140	122.9567 9309	157.9037 3592	202.7215 3039	260.1808 1057	205
206	97.8685 6848	125.8770 1692	161.8513 2932	208.0429 7056	267.3357 8286	206
207	100.0706 1127	128.8665 9608	165.8976 1255	213.5040 9854	274.6875 1689	207
208	102.3222 0002	131.9271 7773	170.0450 5287	219.1085 8113	282.2414 2360	208
209	104.6244 4952	135.0604 4820	174.2961 7919	224.8601 8138	290.0030 6275	209
210	106.9784 9964	138.2681 3385	178.6535 8367	230.7627 6114	297.9781 4698	210
211	109.3855 1588	141.5520 0203	183.1199 2326	236.8202 8362	306.1725 4602	211
212	111.8466 8999	144.9138 6208	187.6979 2134	243.0368 1607	314.5922 9104	212
213	114.3632 4051	148.3555 6630	192.3903 6937	249.4165 3249	323.2435 7904	213
214	116.9364 1342	151.8790 1100	197.2001 2861	255.9637 1647	332.1327 7746	214
215	119.5674 8273	155.4861 3751	202.1301 3182	262.6827 6402	341.2664 2884	215
216	122.2577 5109	159.1789 3328	207.1833 8512	269.5781 8658	350.6512 5564	216
217	125.0085 5049	162.9594 3294	212.3629 6975	276.6546 1398	360.2941 6517	217
218	127.8212 4287	166.8297 1947	217.6720 4399	283.9167 9759	370.2022 5471	218
219	130.6972 2084	170.7919 2531	223.1138 4509	291.3696 1353	380.3828 1671	219
220	133.6379 0831	174.8482 3354	228.6916 9122	299.0180 6589	390.8433 4417	220
221	136.6447 6124	179.0008 7908	234.4089 8350	306.8672 9012	401.5915 3614	221
222	139.7192 6837	183.2521 4996	240.2692 0809	314.9225 5648	412.6353 0338	222
223	142.8629 5191	187.6043 8852	246.2759 3829	323.1892 7359	423.9827 7423	223
224	146.0773 6833	192.0599 9275	252.4328 3674	331.6729 9202	435.6423 0052	224
225	149.3641 0911	196.6214 1758	258.7436 5766	340.3794 0806	447.6224 6378	225
226	152.7248 0157	201.2911 7625	265.2122 4911	349.3143 6752	459.9320 8154	226
227	156.1611 0960	206.0718 4168	271.8425 5533	358.4838 6967	472.5802 1378	227
228	159.6747 3457	210.9660 4792	278.6386 1922	367.8940 7125	485.5761 6966	228
229	163.2674 1610	215.9764 9156	285.6045 8470	377.5512 9062	498.9295 1432	229
230	166.9409 3296	221.1059 3324	292.7446 9931	387.4620 1200	512.6500 7597	230
231	170.6971 0395	226.3571 9915	300.0633 1680	397.6328 8981	526.7479 5305	231
232	174.5377 8879	231.7331 8263	307.5648 9972	408.0707 5317	541.2335 2176	232
233	178.4648 8904	237.2368 4572	315.2540 2221	418.7826 1044	556.1174 4361	233
234	182.4803 4904	242.8712 2080	323.1353 7276	429.7756 5397	571.4106 7331	234
235	186.5861 5690	248.6394 1230	331.2137 5708	441.0572 6488	587.1244 6683	235
236	190.7843 4543	254.5445 9834	339.4941 0101	452.6350 1809	603.2703 8967	236
237	195.0769 9320	260.5900 3255	347.9814 5354	464.5166 8731	619.8603 2538	237
238	199.4662 2555	266.7790 4582	356.6809 8987	476.7102 5035	636.9064 8433	238
239	203.9542 1562	273.1150 4816	365.5980 1462	489.2238 9442	654.4214 1265	239
240	208.5431 8547	279.6015 3056	374.7379 6499	502.0660 2165	672.4180 0150	240

TABLE I

N	2 1/4	2 3/8	2 1/2	2 5/8	2 3/4	N
241	213.2354 0714	286.2420 6691	384.1064 1411	515.2452 5472	690.9094 9654	241
242	218.0332 0381	293.0403 1600	393.7090 7446	528.7704 4266	709.9095 0769	242
243	222.9389 5089	300.0000 2350	403.5518 0133	542.6506 6678	729.4320 1915	243
244	227.9550 7729	307.1250 2406	413.6405 9636	556.8952 4678	749.4913 9968	244
245	233.0840 6653	314.4192 4338	423.9816 1127	571.5137 4701	770.1024 1317	245
246	238.3284 5802	321.8867 0041	434.5811 5155	586.5159 8287	791.2802 2953	246
247	243.6908 4833	329.5315 0954	445.4456 8034	601.9120 2742	813.0404 3585	247
248	249.1738 9242	337.3578 8290	456.5818 2235	617.7122 1814	835.3990 4783	248
249	254.7803 0499	345.3701 3261	467.9963 6791	633.9271 6386	858.3725 2165	249
250	260.5128 6186	353.5726 7326	479.6962 7710	650.5677 5191	881.9777 6599	250
251	266.3744 0125	361.9700 2425	491.6886 8403	667.6451 5540	906.2321 5456	251
252	272.3678 2528	370.5668 1233	503.9809 0113	685.1708 4073	931.1535 3881	252
253	278.4961 0135	379.3677 7412	516.5804 2366	703.1565 7530	956.7602 6112	253
254	284.7622 6363	388.3777 5876	529.4949 3425	721.6144 3540	983.0711 6831	254
255	291.1694 1456	397.6017 3053	542.7323 0761	740.5568 1433	1010.1056 2543	255
256	297.7207 2638	407.0447 7163	556.3006 1530	759.9964 3071	1037.8835 3013	256
257	304.4194 4273	416.7120 8496	570.2081 3068	779.9463 3701	1066.4253 2721	257
258	311.2688 8019	426.6089 9697	584.4633 3395	800.4199 2836	1095.7520 2371	258
259	318.2724 2999	436.7409 6065	599.0749 1730	821.4309 5148	1125.8852 0436	259
260	325.4335 5967	447.1135 5847	614.0517 9023	842.9935 1396	1156.8470 4748	260
261	332.7558 1476	457.7325 0548	629.4030 8498	865.1220 9370	1188.6603 4129	261
262	340.2428 2059	468.6036 5249	645.1381 6211	887.8315 4866	1221.3485 0067	262
263	347.8982 8406	479.7329 8923	661.2666 1616	911.1371 2681	1254.9355 8444	263
264	355.7259 9545	491.1266 4773	677.7982 8157	935.0544 7639	1289.4463 1301	264
265	363.7298 3035	502.7909 0561	694.7432 3860	959.5996 5639	1324.9060 8662	265
266	371.9137 5153	514.7321 8962	712.1118 1957	984.7891 4737	1361.3410 0400	266
267	380.2818 1094	526.9570 7912	729.9146 1506	1010.6398 6249	1398.7778 8161	267
268	388.8381 5168	539.4723 0975	748.1624 8044	1037.1691 5888	1437.2442 7336	268
269	397.5870 1010	552.2847 7711	766.8665 4245	1064.3948 4930	1476.7684 9088	269
270	406.5327 1782	565.4015 4056	786.0382 0601	1092.3352 1410	1517.3796 2437	270
271	415.6797 0398	578.8298 2715	805.6891 6116	1121.0090 1347	1559.1075 6404	271
272	425.0324 9731	592.5770 3555	825.8313 9019	1150.4355 0007	1601.9830 2206	272
273	434.5957 2850	606.6507 4014	846.4771 7494	1180.6344 3195	1646.0375 5516	273
274	444.3741 3240	621.0586 9522	867.6391 0432	1211.6260 8579	1691.3035 8793	274
275	454.3725 5037	635.8088 3923	889.3300 8192	1243.4312 7054	1737.8144 3660	275
276	464.5959 3276	650.9092 9916	911.5633 3397	1276.0713 4139	1785.6043 3360	276
277	475.0493 4124	666.3683 9502	934.3524 1732	1309.5682 1410	1834.7084 5278	277
278	485.7379 5142	682.1946 4440	957.7112 2775	1343.9443 7972	1885.1629 3523	278
279	496.6670 5533	698.3967 6720	981.6540 0845	1379.2229 1969	1937.0049 1595	279
280	507.8420 6407	714.9836 9043	1006.1953 5866	1415.4275 2133	1990.2725 5114	280
281	519.2685 1052	731.9645 5307	1031.3502 4262	1452.5824 9377	2045.0050 4629	281
282	530.9520 5200	749.3487 1121	1057.1339 9869	1490.7127 8423	2101.2426 8507	282
283	542.8984 7317	767.1457 4310	1083.5623 4866	1529.8439 9481	2159.0268 5891	283
284	555.1136 8882	785.3654 5450	1110.6514 0737	1570.0023 9968	2218.4000 9753	284
285	567.6037 4682	804.0178 8404	1138.4176 9256	1611.2149 6267	2279.4061 0021	285
286	580.3748 3112	823.1133 0879	1166.8781 3487	1653.5093 5544	2342.0897 6796	286
287	593.4332 6482	842.6622 4987	1196.0500 8824	1696.9139 7602	2406.4972 3658	287
288	606.7855 1328	862.6754 7831	1225.9513 4045	1741.4579 6789	2472.6759 1059	288
289	620.4381 8733	883.1640 2092	1256.6001 2396	1787.1712 3955	2540.6744 9813	289
290	634.3980 4654	904.1391 6641	1288.0151 2706	1834.0844 8459	2610.5430 4683	290
291	648.6720 0259	925.6124 7162	1320.2155 0524	1882.2292 0231	2682.3329 8062	291
292	663.2671 2265	947.5957 6782	1353.2208 9287	1931.6377 1887	2756.0971 3758	292
293	678.1906 3291	970.1011 6730	1387.0514 1519	1982.3432 0899	2831.8898 0887	293
294	693.4499 2215	993.1410 7003	1421.7277 0057	2034.3797 1822	2909.7667 7861	294
295	709.0525 4540	1016.7281 7044	1457.2708 9308	2087.7821 8583	2989.7853 6502	295
296	725.0062 2767	1040.8754 6449	1493.7026 6541	2142.5864 6820	3072.0044 6256	296
297	741.3188 6779	1065.5962 5677	1531.0452 3205	2198.8293 6299	3156.4845 8528	297
298	757.9985 4232	1090.9041 6787	1569.3213 6285	2256.5486 3377	3243.2879 1138	298
299	775.0535 0952	1116.8131 4185	1608.5543 9692	2315.7830 3541	3332.4783 2894	299
300	792.4922 1348	1143.3374 5397	1648.7682 5684	2376.5723 4009	3424.1214 8298	300

TABLE I

N	2 1/4	2 3/8	2 1/2	2 5/8	2 3/4	N
301	810.3232 8829	1170.4917 1850	1689.9874 6326	2438.9573 6402	3518.2848 2377	301
302	828.5555 6227	1198.2908 9682	1732.2371 4984	2502.9799 9482	3615.0376 5642	302
303	847.1980 6242	1226.7503 0562	1775.5430 7859	2568.6832 1969	3714.4511 9197	303
304	866.2600 1883	1255.8856 2538	1819.9316 5556	2636.1111 5420	3816.5985 9975	304
305	885.7508 6925	1285.7129 0898	1865.4299 4694	2705.3090 7200	3921.5550 6124	305
306	905.6802 6381	1316.2485 9057	1912.0656 9562	2776.3234 3514	4029.3978 2543	306
307	926.0580 6975	1347.5094 9459	1959.8673 3801	2849.2019 2531	4140.2062 6563	307
308	946.8943 7632	1379.5128 4509	2008.8640 2146	2923.9934 7585	4254.0619 3793	308
309	968.1994 9978	1412.2762 7516	2059.0856 2199	3000.7483 0459	4371.0486 4122	309
310	989.9839 8853	1445.8178 3670	2110.5627 6254	3079.5179 4759	4491.2524 7886	310
311	1012.2586 2827	1480.1560 1032	2163.3268 3161	3160.3552 9371	4614.7619 2203	311
312	1035.0344 4741	1515.3097 1556	2217.4100 0240	3243.3146 2017	4741.6678 7488	312
313	1058.3227 2247	1551.2983 2131	2272.8452 5246	3328.4516 2895	4872.0637 4144	313
314	1082.1349 8373	1588.1416 5644	2329.6663 8377	3415.8234 8421	5006.0454 9433	314
315	1106.4830 2086	1625.8600 2078	2387.9080 4336	3505.4888 5067	5143.7117 4543	315
316	1131.3788 8883	1664.4741 9627	2447.6057 4445	3597.5079 3300	5285.1638 1843	316
317	1156.8349 1383	1704.0054 5843	2508.7958 8806	3691.9425 1624	5430.5058 2343	317
318	1182.8636 9939	1744.4755 8807	2571.5157 8526	3788.8560 0730	5579.8447 3358	318
319	1209.4781 3263	1785.9068 8329	2635.8036 7989	3888.3134 7749	5733.2904 6375	319
320	1236.6913 9061	1828.3221 7177	2701.6987 7189	3990.3817 0627	5890.9559 5150	320
321	1264.5169 4690	1871.7448 2335	2769.2412 4119	4095.1292 2606	6052.9572 4017	321
322	1292.9685 7821	1916.1987 6290	2838.4722 7222	4202.6263 6824	6219.4135 6427	322
323	1322.0603 7122	1961.7084 8352	2909.4340 7902	4312.9453 1041	6390.4474 3729	323
324	1351.8067 2957	2008.2990 6000	2982.1699 3100	4426.1601 2481	6566.1847 4182	324
325	1382.2223 8098	2055.9961 6268	3056.7241 7927	4542.3468 2809	6746.7548 2222	325
326	1413.3223 8456	2104.8260 7154	3133.1422 8375	4661.5834 3232	6932.2905 7983	326
327	1445.1221 3821	2154.8156 9074	3211.4708 4085	4783.9499 9742	7122.9285 7077	327
328	1477.6373 8632	2205.9925 6339	3291.7576 1187	4909.5286 8485	7318.8091 0647	328
329	1510.8842 2751	2258.3848 8678	3374.0515 5217	5038.4038 1283	7520.0763 5690	329
330	1544.8791 2263	2312.0215 2784	3458.4028 4097	5170.6619 1292	7726.8784 5671	330
331	1579.6389 0289	2366.9320 3912	3544.8629 1199	5306.3917 8813	7939.3676 1427	331
332	1615.1807 7820	2423.1466 7505	3633.4844 8479	5445.6845 7257	8157.7002 2366	332
333	1651.5223 4571	2480.6564 0858	3724.3215 9691	5588.6337 9260	8382.0369 7981	333
334	1688.6815 9849	2539.6129 4829	3817.4296 3684	5735.3354 2966	8612.5429 9676	334
335	1726.6769 3446	2599.9287 5581	3912.8653 7776	5885.8879 8468	8849.3879 2917	335
336	1765.5271 6548	2661.6770 6376	4010.6870 1220	6040.3925 4428	9092.7460 9722	336
337	1805.2515 2671	2724.8918 9402	4110.9541 8751	6198.9528 4857	9342.7966 1490	337
338	1845.8696 8606	2789.6080 7651	4213.7280 4219	6361.6753 6084	9599.7235 2181	338
339	1887.4017 5399	2855.8612 6832	4319.0712 4325	6528.6693 3907	9863.7159 1866	339
340	1929.8682 9346	2923.6879 7345	4427.0480 2433	6700.0469 0922	10134.9681 0642	340
341	1973.2903 3006	2993.1255 6282	4537.7242 2494	6875.9231 4058	10413.6797 2935	341
342	2017.6893 6249	3064.2122 9493	4651.1673 3056	7056.4161 2302	10700.0559 2190	342
343	2063.0873 7314	3136.9873 3694	4767.4465 1383	7241.6470 4625	10994.3074 5975	343
344	2109.5068 3904	3211.4907 8619	4886.6326 7667	7431.7402 8122	11296.6509 1490	344
345	2156.9707 4292	3287.7636 9236	5008.7984 9359	7626.8234 6360	11607.3088 1506	345
346	2205.5025 8463	3365.8480 8006	5134.0184 5593	7827.0275 7952	11926.5098 0747	346
347	2255.1263 9279	3445.7869 7196	5262.3689 1733	8032.4870 5348	12254.4888 2718	347
348	2305.8667 3662	3527.6244 1254	5393.9281 4026	8243.3398 3864	12591.4872 6992	348
349	2357.7487 3820	3611.4054 9234	5528.7763 4377	8459.7275 0940	12937.7531 6985	349
350	2410.7980 8481	3697.1763 7278	5666.9957 5236	8681.7953 5652	13293.5413 8202	350
351	2465.0410 4172	3784.9843 1164	5808.6706 4617	8909.6924 8463	13659.1137 7002	351
352	2520.5044 6516	3874.8776 8904	5953.8874 1232	9143.5719 1235	14034.7393 9870	352
353	2577.2158 1562	3966.9060 3415	6102.7345 9763	9383.5906 7505	14420.6947 3216	353
354	2635.2031 7147	4061.1200 5246	6255.3029 6257	9629.9099 3027	14817.2638 3730	354
355	2694.4952 4283	4157.5716 5371	6411.6855 3664	9882.6950 6594	15224.7385 9282	355
356	2755.1213 8579	4256.3139 8049	6571.9776 7505	10142.1158 1142	15643.4189 0413	356
357	2817.1116 1697	4357.4014 3752	6736.2771 1693	10408.3463 5147	16073.6129 2399	357
358	2880.4966 2836	4460.8897 2166	6904.6840 4485	10681.5654 4320	16515.6372 7940	358
359	2945.3078 0249	4566.8358 5255	7077.3011 4597	10961.9565 3608	16969.8173 0458	359
360	3011.5772 2805	4675.2982 0405	7254.2336 7462	11249.7078 9515	17436.4872 8046	360

TABLE I

N	3	3 1/2	4	4 1/2	5	N
1	1.0300 0000	1.0350 0000	1.0400 0000	1.0450 0000	1.0500 0000	1
2	1.0609 0000	1.0712 2500	1.0816 0000	1.0920 2500	1.1025 0000	2
3	1.0927 2700	1.1087 1787	1.1248 6400	1.1411 6612	1.1576 2500	3
4	1.1255 0881	1.1475 2300	1.1698 5856	1.1925 1860	1.2155 0625	4
5	1.1592 7407	1.1876 8631	1.2166 5290	1.2461 8194	1.2762 8156	5
6	1.1940 5230	1.2292 5533	1.2653 1902	1.3022 6012	1.3400 9564	6
7	1.2298 7387	1.2722 7926	1.3159 3178	1.3608 6183	1.4071 0042	7
8	1.2667 7008	1.3168 0904	1.3685 6905	1.4221 0061	1.4774 5544	8
9	1.3047 7318	1.3628 9735	1.4233 1181	1.4860 9514	1.5513 2822	9
10	1.3439 1638	1.4105 9876	1.4802 4428	1.5529 6942	1.6288 9463	10
11	1.3842 3387	1.4599 6972	1.5394 5406	1.6228 5305	1.7103 3936	11
12	1.4257 6089	1.5110 6866	1.6010 3222	1.6958 8143	1.7958 5633	12
13	1.4685 3371	1.5639 5606	1.6650 7351	1.7721 9610	1.8856 4914	13
14	1.5125 8972	1.6186 9452	1.7316 7645	1.8519 4492	1.9799 3160	14
15	1.5579 6742	1.6753 4883	1.8009 4351	1.9352 8244	2.0789 2818	15
16	1.6047 0644	1.7339 8604	1.8729 8125	2.0223 7015	2.1828 7459	16
17	1.6528 4763	1.7946 7555	1.9479 0050	2.1133 7681	2.2920 1832	17
18	1.7024 3306	1.8574 8920	2.0258 1652	2.2084 7877	2.4066 1923	18
19	1.7535 0605	1.9225 0132	2.1068 4918	2.3078 6031	2.5269 5020	19
20	1.8061 1123	1.9897 8886	2.1911 2314	2.4117 1402	2.6532 9771	20
21	1.8602 9457	2.0594 3147	2.2787 6807	2.5202 4116	2.7859 6259	21
22	1.9161 0341	2.1315 1158	2.3699 1879	2.6336 5201	2.9252 6072	22
23	1.9735 8651	2.2061 1448	2.4647 1554	2.7521 6635	3.0715 2376	23
24	2.0327 9411	2.2833 2849	2.5633 0416	2.8760 1383	3.2250 9994	24
25	2.0937 7793	2.3632 4498	2.6658 3633	3.0054 3446	3.3863 5494	25
26	2.1565 9127	2.4459 5856	2.7724 6978	3.1406 7901	3.5556 7269	26
27	2.2212 8901	2.5315 6711	2.8833 6858	3.2820 0956	3.7334 5632	27
28	2.2879 2768	2.6201 7196	2.9987 0332	3.4296 9999	3.9201 2914	28
29	2.3565 6551	2.7118 7798	3.1186 5145	3.5840 3649	4.1161 3560	29
30	2.4272 6247	2.8067 9370	3.2433 9751	3.7453 1813	4.3219 4238	30
31	2.5000 8035	2.9050 3148	3.3731 3341	3.9138 5745	4.5380 3949	31
32	2.5750 8276	3.0067 0759	3.5080 5875	4.0899 8104	4.7649 4147	32
33	2.6523 3524	3.1119 4235	3.6483 8110	4.2740 3018	5.0031 8854	33
34	2.7319 0530	3.2208 6033	3.7943 1634	4.4663 6154	5.2533 4797	34
35	2.8138 6245	3.3335 9045	3.9460 8899	4.6673 4781	5.5160 1537	35
36	2.8982 7833	3.4502 6611	4.1039 3255	4.8773 7846	5.7918 1614	36
37	2.9852 2668	3.5710 2543	4.2680 8986	5.0968 6049	6.0814 0694	37
38	3.0747 8348	3.6960 1132	4.4388 1345	5.3262 1921	6.3854 7729	38
39	3.1670 2698	3.8253 7171	4.6163 6599	5.5658 9908	6.7047 5115	39
40	3.2620 3779	3.9592 5972	4.8010 2063	5.8163 6454	7.0399 8871	40
41	3.3598 9893	4.0978 3381	4.9930 6145	6.0781 0094	7.3919 8815	41
42	3.4606 9589	4.2412 5799	5.1927 8391	6.3516 1548	7.7615 8756	42
43	3.5645 1677	4.3897 0202	5.4004 9527	6.6374 3818	8.1496 6693	43
44	3.6714 5227	4.5433 4160	5.6165 1508	6.9361 2290	8.5571 5028	44
45	3.7815 9584	4.7023 5855	5.8411 7568	7.2482 4843	8.9850 0779	45
46	3.8950 4372	4.8669 4110	6.0748 2271	7.5744 1961	9.4342 5818	46
47	4.0118 9503	5.0372 8404	6.3178 1562	7.9152 6849	9.9059 7109	47
48	4.1322 5188	5.2135 8898	6.5705 2824	8.2714 5557	10.4012 6965	48
49	4.2562 1944	5.3960 6459	6.8333 4937	8.6436 7107	10.9213 3313	49
50	4.3839 0602	5.5849 2686	7.1066 8335	9.0326 3627	11.4673 9979	50
51	4.5154 2320	5.7803 9930	7.3909 5068	9.4391 0490	12.0407 6978	51
52	4.6508 8590	5.9827 1327	7.6865 8871	9.8638 6463	12.6428 0826	52
53	4.7904 1247	6.1921 0824	7.9940 5226	10.3077 3853	13.2749 4868	53
54	4.9341 2485	6.4088 3202	8.3138 1435	10.7715 8677	13.9386 9611	54
55	5.0821 4859	6.6331 4114	8.6463 6692	11.2563 0817	14.6356 3092	55
56	5.2346 1305	6.8653 0108	8.9922 2160	11.7628 4204	15.3674 1246	56
57	5.3916 5144	7.1055 8662	9.3519 1046	12.2921 6993	16.1357 8309	57
58	5.5534 0098	7.3542 8215	9.7259 8688	12.8453 1758	16.9425 7224	58
59	5.7200 0301	7.6116 8203	10.1150 2635	13.4233 5687	17.7897 0085	59
60	5.8916 0310	7.8780 9090	10.5196 2741	14.0274 0793	18.6791 8589	60

TABLE I

N	3	3 1/2	4	4 1/2	5	N
61	6.0683 5120	8.1538 2408	10.9404 1250	14.6586 4129	19.6131 4519	61
62	6.2504 0173	8.4392 0793	11.3780 2900	15.3182 8014	20.5938 0245	62
63	6.4379 1379	8.7345 8020	11.8331 5016	16.0076 0275	21.6234 9257	63
64	6.6310 5120	9.0402 9051	12.3064 7617	16.7279 4487	22.7046 6720	64
65	6.8299 8273	9.3567 0068	12.7987 3522	17.4807 0239	23.8399 0056	65
66	7.0348 8222	9.6841 8520	13.3106 8463	18.2673 3400	25.0318 9559	66
67	7.2459 2868	10.0231 3168	13.8431 1201	19.0893 6403	26.2834 9037	67
68	7.4633 0654	10.3739 4129	14.3968 3649	19.9483 8541	27.5976 6488	68
69	7.6872 0574	10.7370 2924	14.9727 0995	20.8460 6276	28.9775 4813	69
70	7.9178 2191	11.1128 2526	15.5716 1835	21.7841 3558	30.4264 2554	70
71	8.1553 5657	11.5017 7414	16.1944 8308	22.7644 2168	31.9477 4681	71
72	8.4000 1727	11.9043 3624	16.8422 6241	23.7888 2066	33.5451 3415	72
73	8.6520 1778	12.3209 8801	17.5159 5290	24.8593 1759	35.2223 9086	73
74	8.9115 7832	12.7522 2259	18.2165 9102	25.9779 8688	36.9835 1040	74
75	9.1789 2567	13.1985 5038	18.9452 5466	27.1469 9629	38.8326 8592	75
76	9.4542 9344	13.6604 9964	19.7030 6485	28.3686 1112	40.7743 2022	76
77	9.7379 2224	14.1386 1713	20.4911 8744	29.6451 9862	42.8130 3623	77
78	10.0300 5991	14.6334 6873	21.3108 3494	30.9792 3256	44.9536 8804	78
79	10.3309 6171	15.1456 4013	22.1632 6834	32.3732 9802	47.2013 7244	79
80	10.6408 9056	15.6757 3754	23.0497 9907	33.8300 9643	49.5614 4107	80
81	10.9601 1727	16.2243 8835	23.9717 9103	35.3524 5077	52.0395 1312	81
82	11.2889 2079	16.7922 4195	24.9306 6267	36.9433 1106	54.6414 8878	82
83	11.6275 8842	17.3799 7041	25.9278 8918	38.6057 6006	57.3735 6322	83
84	11.9764 1607	17.9882 6938	26.9650 0475	40.3430 1926	60.2422 4138	84
85	12.3357 0855	18.6178 5881	28.0436 0494	42.1584 5513	63.2543 5344	85
86	12.7057 7981	19.2694 8387	29.1653 4914	44.0555 8561	66.4170 7112	86
87	13.0869 5320	19.9439 1580	30.3319 6310	46.0380 8696	69.7379 2467	87
88	13.4795 6180	20.6419 5285	31.5452 4163	48.1098 0087	73.2248 2091	88
89	13.8839 4865	21.3644 2120	32.8070 5129	50.2747 4191	76.8860 6195	89
90	14.3004 6711	22.1121 7595	34.1193 3334	52.5371 0530	80.7303 6505	90
91	14.7294 8112	22.8861 0210	35.4841 0668	54.9012 7503	84.7668 8330	91
92	15.1713 6556	23.6871 1568	36.9034 7094	57.3718 3241	89.0052 2747	92
93	15.6265 0652	24.5161 6473	38.3796 0978	59.9535 6487	93.4554 8884	93
94	16.0953 0172	25.3742 3049	39.9147 9417	62.6514 7529	98.1282 6328	94
95	16.5781 6077	26.2623 2856	41.5113 8594	65.4707 9168	103.0346 7645	95
96	17.0755 0559	27.1815 1006	43.1718 4138	68.4169 7730	108.1864 1027	96
97	17.5877 7076	28.1328 6291	44.8987 1503	71.4957 4128	113.5957 3078	97
98	18.1154 0388	29.1175 1311	46.6946 6363	74.7130 4964	119.2755 1732	98
99	18.6588 6600	30.1366 2607	48.5624 5018	78.0751 3687	125.2392 9319	99
100	19.2186 3198	31.1914 0798	50.5049 4818	81.5885 1803	131.5012 5785	100
101	19.7951 9094	32.2831 0726	52.5251 4611	85.2600 0134	138.0763 2074	101
102	20.3890 4667	33.4130 1602	54.6261 5196	89.0967 0140	144.9801 3678	102
103	21.0007 1807	34.5824 7158	56.8111 9803	93.1060 5297	152.2291 4361	103
104	21.6307 3961	35.7928 5808	59.0836 4596	97.2958 2535	159.8406 0080	104
105	22.2796 6180	37.0456 0812	61.4469 9179	101.6741 3749	167.8326 3083	105
106	22.9480 5165	38.3422 0440	63.9048 7147	106.2494 7368	176.2242 6238	106
107	23.6364 9320	39.6841 8155	66.4610 6632	111.0306 9999	185.0354 7550	107
108	24.3455 8800	41.0731 2791	69.1195 0898	116.0270 8149	194.2872 4927	108
109	25.0759 5564	42.5106 8738	71.8842 8934	121.2483 0016	204.0016 1173	109
110	25.8282 3431	43.9985 6144	74.7596 6091	126.7044 7367	214.2016 9232	110
111	26.6030 8134	45.5385 1109	77.7500 4735	132.4061 7498	224.9117 7694	111
112	27.4011 7378	47.1323 5898	80.8600 4924	138.3644 5286	236.1573 6578	112
113	28.2232 0899	48.7819 9155	84.0944 5121	144.5908 5324	247.9652 3407	113
114	29.0699 0526	50.4893 6125	87.4582 2926	151.0974 4163	260.3634 9578	114
115	29.9420 0242	52.2564 8889	90.9565 5843	157.8968 2651	273.3816 7056	115
116	30.8402 6249	54.0854 6601	94.5948 2077	165.0021 8370	287.0507 5409	116
117	31.7654 7037	55.9784 5732	98.3786 1360	172.4272 8196	301.4032 9180	117
118	32.7184 3448	57.9377 0332	102.3137 5814	180.1865 0965	316.4734 5639	118
119	33.6999 8751	59.9655 2294	106.4063 0847	188.2949 0259	332.2971 2921	119
120	34.7109 8714	62.0643 1624	110.6625 6080	196.7681 7320	348.9119 8567	120

TABLE I

N	5 1/2	6	6 1/2	7	7 1/2	N
1	1.0550 0000	1.0600 0000	1.0650 0000	1.0700 0000	1.0750 0000	1
2	1.1130 2500	1.1236 0000	1.1342 2500	1.1449 0000	1.1556 2500	2
3	1.1742 4137	1.1910 1600	1.2079 4962	1.2250 4300	1.2422 9687	3
4	1.2388 2465	1.2624 7696	1.2864 6635	1.3107 9601	1.3354 6914	4
5	1.3069 6001	1.3382 2558	1.3700 8666	1.4025 5173	1.4356 2933	5
6	1.3788 4281	1.4185 1911	1.4591 4230	1.5007 3035	1.5433 0153	6
7	1.4546 7916	1.5036 3026	1.5539 8655	1.6057 8148	1.6590 4914	7
8	1.5346 8651	1.5938 4807	1.6549 9567	1.7181 8618	1.7834 7783	8
9	1.6190 9427	1.6894 7896	1.7625 7039	1.8384 5921	1.9172 3866	9
10	1.7081 4446	1.7908 4770	1.8771 3747	1.9671 5136	2.0610 3156	10
11	1.8020 9240	1.8982 9856	1.9991 5140	2.1048 5195	2.2156 0893	11
12	1.9012 0749	2.0121 9647	2.1290 9624	2.2521 9159	2.3817 7960	12
13	2.0057 7390	2.1329 2826	2.2674 8750	2.4098 4500	2.5604 1307	13
14	2.1160 9146	2.2609 0396	2.4148 7418	2.5785 3415	2.7524 4405	14
15	2.2324 7649	2.3965 5819	2.5718 4101	2.7590 3154	2.9588 7735	15
16	2.3552 6270	2.5403 5168	2.7390 1067	2.9521 6375	3.1807 9315	16
17	2.4848 0215	2.6927 7279	2.9170 4637	3.1588 1521	3.4193 5264	17
18	2.6214 6627	2.8543 3915	3.1066 5438	3.3799 3228	3.6758 0409	18
19	2.7656 4691	3.0255 9950	3.3085 8691	3.6165 2754	3.9514 8940	19
20	2.9177 5749	3.2071 3547	3.5236 4506	3.8696 8446	4.2478 5110	20
21	3.0782 3415	3.3995 6360	3.7526 8199	4.1405 6237	4.5664 3993	21
22	3.2475 3703	3.6035 3742	3.9966 0632	4.4304 0174	4.9089 2293	22
23	3.4261 5157	3.8197 4966	4.2563 8573	4.7405 2986	5.2770 9215	23
24	3.6145 8990	4.0489 3464	4.5330 5081	5.0723 6695	5.6728 7406	24
25	3.8133 9235	4.2918 7072	4.8276 9911	5.4274 3264	6.0983 3961	25
26	4.0231 2893	4.5493 8296	5.1414 9955	5.8073 5292	6.5557 1508	26
27	4.2444 0102	4.8223 4594	5.4756 9702	6.2138 6763	7.0473 9371	27
28	4.4778 4307	5.1116 8670	5.8316 1733	6.6488 3836	7.5759 4824	28
29	4.7241 2444	5.4183 8790	6.2106 7245	7.1142 5705	8.1441 4436	29
30	4.9839 5129	5.7434 9117	6.6143 6616	7.6122 5504	8.7549 5519	30
31	5.2580 6861	6.0881 0064	7.0442 9996	8.1451 1290	9.4115 7683	31
32	5.5472 6238	6.4533 8668	7.5021 7946	8.7152 7080	10.1174 4509	32
33	5.8523 6181	6.8405 8988	7.9898 2113	9.3253 3975	10.8762 5347	33
34	6.1742 4171	7.2510 2528	8.5091 5950	9.9781 1354	11.6919 7248	34
35	6.5138 2501	7.6860 8679	9.0622 5487	10.6765 8148	12.5688 7042	35
36	6.8720 8538	8.1472 5200	9.6513 0143	11.4239 4219	13.5115 3570	36
37	7.2500 5008	8.6360 8712	10.2786 3603	12.2236 1814	14.5249 0088	37
38	7.6488 0283	9.1542 5235	10.9467 4737	13.0792 7141	15.6142 6844	38
39	8.0694 8699	9.7035 0749	11.6582 8595	13.9948 2041	16.7853 3858	39
40	8.5133 0877	10.2857 1794	12.4160 7453	14.9744 5784	18.0442 3897	40
41	8.9815 4076	10.9028 6101	13.2231 1938	16.0226 6989	19.3975 5689	41
42	9.4755 2550	11.5570 3267	14.0826 2214	17.1442 5678	20.8523 7366	42
43	9.9966 7940	12.2504 5463	14.9979 9258	18.3443 5475	22.4163 0168	43
44	10.5464 9677	12.9854 8191	15.9728 6209	19.6284 5959	24.0975 2431	44
45	11.1265 5409	13.7646 1083	17.0110 9813	21.0024 5176	25.9048 3863	45
46	11.7385 1456	14.5904 8748	18.1168 1951	22.4726 2338	27.8477 0153	46
47	12.3841 3287	15.4659 1673	19.2944 1278	24.0457 0702	29.9362 7915	47
48	13.0652 6017	16.3938 7173	20.5485 4961	25.7289 0651	32.1815 0008	48
49	13.7838 4948	17.3775 0403	21.8842 0533	27.5299 2997	34.5951 1259	49
50	14.5419 6120	18.4201 5427	23.3066 7868	29.4570 2506	37.1897 4603	50
51	15.3417 6907	19.5253 6353	24.8216 1279	31.5190 1682	39.9789 7698	51
52	16.1855 6637	20.6968 8534	26.4350 1762	33.7253 4799	42.9774 0026	52
53	17.0757 7252	21.9386 9846	28.1532 9377	36.0861 2235	46.2007 0528	53
54	18.0149 4001	23.2550 2037	29.9832 5786	38.6121 5092	49.6657 5817	54
55	19.0057 6171	24.6503 2159	31.9321 6963	41.3150 0148	53.3906 9004	55
56	20.0510 7860	26.1293 4089	34.0077 6065	44.2070 5159	57.3949 9179	56
57	21.1538 8793	27.6971 0134	36.2182 6509	47.3015 4520	61.6996 1617	57
58	22.3173 5176	29.3589 2742	38.5724 5233	50.6126 5336	66.3270 8739	58
59	23.5448 0611	31.1204 6307	41.0796 6173	54.1555 3910	71.3016 1894	59
60	24.8397 7045	32.9876 9085	43.7498 3974	57.9464 2683	76.6492 4036	60

TABLE I

N	5 1/2	6	6 1/2	7	7 1/2	N
61	26.2059 5782	34.9669 5230	46.5935 7932	62.0026 7671	82.3979 3339	61
62	27.6472 8550	37.0649 6944	49.6221 6198	66.3428 6408	88.5777 7839	62
63	29.1678 8620	39.2888 6761	52.8476 0251	70.9868 6457	95.2211 1177	63
64	30.7721 1994	41.6461 9967	56.2826 9667	75.9559 4509	102.3626 9515	64
65	32.4645 8654	44.1449 7165	59.9410 7195	81.2728 6124	110.0398 9729	65
66	34.2501 3880	46.7936 6994	63.8372 4163	86.9619 6153	118.2928 8959	66
67	36.1338 9643	49.6012 9014	67.9866 6234	93.0492 9884	127.1648 5631	67
68	38.1212 6074	52.5773 6755	72.4057 9539	99.5627 4976	136.7022 2053	68
69	40.2179 3008	55.7320 0960	77.1121 7209	106.5321 4224	146.9548 8707	69
70	42.4299 1623	59.0759 3018	82.1244 6327	113.9893 9220	157.9765 0360	70
71	44.7635 6163	62.6204 8599	87.4625 5339	121.9686 4965	169.8247 4137	71
72	47.2255 5751	66.3777 1515	93.1476 1936	130.5064 5513	182.5615 9697	72
73	49.8229 6318	70.3603 7806	99.2022 1461	139.6419 0699	196.2537 1675	73
74	52.5632 2615	74.5820 0074	105.6503 5856	149.4168 4047	210.9727 4550	74
75	55.4542 0359	79.0569 2079	112.5176 3187	159.8760 1931	226.7957 0141	75
76	58.5041 8479	83.8003 3603	119.8312 7794	171.0673 4066	243.8053 7902	76
77	61.7219 1495	88.8283 5620	127.6203 1101	183.0420 5451	262.0907 8245	77
78	65.1166 2027	94.1580 5757	135.9156 3122	195.8549 9832	281.7475 9113	78
79	68.6980 3439	99.8075 4102	144.7501 4725	209.5648 4820	302.8786 6046	79
80	72.4764 2628	105.7959 9348	154.1589 0683	224.2343 8758	325.5945 6000	80
81	76.4626 2973	112.1437 5309	164.1792 3577	239.9307 9471	350.0141 5200	81
82	80.6680 7436	118.8723 7828	174.8508 8609	256.7259 5034	376.2652 1340	82
83	85.1048 1845	126.0047 2097	186.2161 9369	274.6967 6686	404.4851 0440	83
84	89.7855 8347	133.5650 0423	198.3202 4628	293.9255 4054	434.8214 8723	84
85	94.7237 9056	141.5789 0449	211.2110 6229	314.5003 2838	467.4330 9878	85
86	99.9335 9904	150.0736 3875	224.9397 8134	336.5153 5137	502.4905 8119	86
87	105.4299 4698	159.0780 5708	239.5608 6712	360.0714 2596	540.1773 7477	87
88	111.2285 9407	168.6227 4050	255.1323 2349	385.2764 2578	580.6906 7788	88
89	117.3461 6674	178.7401 0493	271.7159 2451	412.2457 7558	624.2424 7872	89
90	123.8002 0591	189.4645 1123	289.3774 5961	441.1029 7988	671.0606 6463	90
91	130.6092 1724	200.8323 8190	308.1869 9448	471.9801 8847	721.3902 1447	91
92	137.7927 2419	212.8823 2482	328.2191 4912	505.0188 0166	775.4944 8056	92
93	145.3713 2402	225.6552 6431	349.5533 9382	540.3701 1778	833.6565 6660	93
94	153.3667 4684	239.1945 8017	372.2743 6441	578.1960 2602	896.1808 0910	94
95	161.8019 1791	253.5462 5498	396.4721 9810	618.6697 4784	963.3943 6978	95
96	170.7010 2340	268.7590 3028	422.2428 9098	661.9766 3019	1035.6489 4751	96
97	180.0895 7969	284.8845 7209	449.6886 7889	708.3149 9430	1113.3226 1858	97
98	189.9945 0657	301.9776 4642	478.9184 4302	757.8970 4390	1196.8218 1497	98
99	200.4442 0443	320.0963 0520	510.0481 4181	810.9498 3698	1286.5834 5109	99
100	211.4686 3567	339.3020 8351	543.2012 7103	867.7163 2557	1383.0772 0993	100
101	223.0994 1064	359.6602 0853	578.5093 5365	928.4564 6836	1486.8080 0067	101
102	235.3698 7822	381.2398 2104	616.1124 6164	993.4484 2114	1598.3186 0072	102
103	248.3152 2152	404.1142 1030	656.1597 7164	1062.9898 1062	1718.1924 9577	103
104	261.9725 5871	428.3610 6292	698.8101 5680	1137.3990 9736	1847.0569 3296	104
105	276.3810 4944	454.0627 2669	744.2328 1699	1217.0170 3418	1985.5862 0293	105
106	291.5820 0715	481.3064 9029	792.6079 5010	1302.2082 2657	2134.5051 6815	106
107	307.6190 1755	510.1848 7971	844.1274 6685	1393.3628 0243	2294.5930 5576	107
108	324.5380 6351	540.7959 7249	898.9957 5220	1490.8981 9860	2466.6875 3494	108
109	342.3876 5701	573.2437 3084	957.4304 7609	1595.2610 7250	2651.6891 0006	109
110	361.2189 7814	607.6383 5469	1019.6634 5704	1706.9293 4758	2850.5657 8257	110
111	381.0860 2194	644.0966 5598	1085.9415 8174	1826.4144 0191	3064.3582 1626	111
112	402.0457 5315	682.7424 5533	1156.5277 8456	1954.2634 1004	3294.1850 8248	112
113	424.1582 6957	723.7070 0265	1231.7020 9055	2091.0618 4875	3541.2489 6366	113
114	447.4869 7440	767.1294 2281	1311.7627 2644	2237.4361 7816	3806.8426 3594	114
115	472.0987 5799	813.1571 8818	1397.0273 0366	2394.0567 1063	4092.3558 3363	115
116	498.0641 8968	861.9466 1947	1487.8340 7840	2561.6406 8038	4399.2825 2116	116
117	525.4577 2011	913.6634 1664	1584.5432 9349	2740.9555 2800	4729.2287 1024	117
118	554.3578 9471	968.4832 2164	1687.5386 0757	2932.8224 1496	5083.9208 6351	118
119	584.8475 7892	1026.5922 1494	1797.2286 1706	3138.1199 8401	5465.2149 2828	119
120	617.0141 9576	1088.1877 4784	1914.0484 7717	3357.7883 8289	5875.1060 4790	120

TABLE I

N	8	8 1/2	9	9 1/2	10	N
1	1.0800 0000	1.0850 0000	1.0900 0000	1.0950 0000	1.1000 0000	1
2	1.1664 0000	1.1772 2500	1.1881 0000	1.1990 2500	1.2100 0000	2
3	1.2597 1200	1.2772 8912	1.2950 2900	1.3129 3237	1.3310 0000	3
4	1.3604 8896	1.3858 5870	1.4115 8161	1.4376 6095	1.4641 0000	4
5	1.4693 2808	1.5036 5669	1.5386 2395	1.5742 3874	1.6105 1000	5
6	1.5868 7432	1.6314 6751	1.6771 0011	1.7237 9142	1.7715 6100	6
7	1.7138 2427	1.7701 4225	1.8280 3912	1.8875 5161	1.9487 1710	7
8	1.8509 3021	1.9206 0434	1.9925 6264	2.0668 6901	2.1435 8881	8
9	1.9990 0463	2.0838 5571	2.1718 9328	2.2632 2156	2.3579 4769	9
10	2.1589 2500	2.2609 8344	2.3673 6367	2.4782 2761	2.5937 4246	10
11	2.3316 3900	2.4531 6703	2.5804 2641	2.7136 5924	2.8531 1671	11
12	2.5181 7012	2.6616 8623	2.8126 6478	2.9714 5686	3.1384 2838	12
13	2.7196 2373	2.8879 2956	3.0658 0461	3.2537 4527	3.4522 7121	13
14	2.9371 9362	3.1334 0357	3.3417 2703	3.5628 5107	3.7974 9834	14
15	3.1721 6911	3.3997 4288	3.6424 8246	3.9013 2192	4.1772 4817	15
16	3.4259 4264	3.6887 2102	3.9703 0588	4.2719 4750	4.5949 7299	16
17	3.7000 1805	4.0022 6231	4.3276 3341	4.6777 8251	5.0544 7028	17
18	3.9960 1950	4.3424 5461	4.7171 2042	5.1221 7185	5.5599 1731	18
19	4.3157 0106	4.7115 6325	5.1416 6125	5.6087 7818	6.1159 0904	19
20	4.6609 5714	5.1120 4612	5.6044 1077	6.1416 1210	6.7274 9995	20
21	5.0338 3372	5.5465 7005	6.1088 0774	6.7250 6525	7.4002 4994	21
22	5.4365 4041	6.0180 2850	6.6586 0043	7.3639 4645	8.1402 7494	22
23	5.8714 6365	6.5295 6092	7.2578 7447	8.0635 2137	8.9543 0243	23
24	6.3411 8074	7.0845 7360	7.9110 8317	8.8295 5590	9.8497 3268	24
25	6.8484 7520	7.6867 6236	8.6230 8066	9.6683 6371	10.8347 0594	25
26	7.3963 5321	8.3401 3716	9.3991 5792	10.5868 5826	11.9181 7654	26
27	7.9880 6147	9.0490 4881	10.2450 8213	11.5926 0979	13.1099 9419	27
28	8.6271 0639	9.8182 1796	11.1671 3952	12.6939 0772	14.4209 9361	28
29	9.3172 7490	10.6527 6649	12.1721 8208	13.8998 2896	15.8630 9297	29
30	10.0626 5689	11.5582 5164	13.2676 7847	15.2203 1271	17.4494 0227	30
31	10.8676 6944	12.5407 0303	14.4617 6953	16.6662 4241	19.1943 4250	31
32	11.7370 8300	13.6066 6279	15.7633 2879	18.2495 3544	21.1137 7675	32
33	12.6760 4964	14.7632 2913	17.1820 2838	19.9832 4131	23.2251 5442	33
34	13.6901 3361	16.0181 0360	18.7284 1093	21.8816 4924	25.5476 6986	34
35	14.7853 4429	17.3796 4241	20.4139 6792	23.9604 0591	28.1024 3685	35
36	15.9681 7184	18.8569 1201	22.2512 2503	26.2366 4448	30.9126 8053	36
37	17.2456 2558	20.4597 4953	24.2538 3528	28.7291 2570	34.0039 4859	37
38	18.6252 7563	22.1988 2824	26.4366 8046	31.4583 9264	37.4043 4344	38
39	20.1152 9768	24.0857 2865	28.8159 8170	34.4469 3994	41.1447 7779	39
40	21.7245 2150	26.1330 1558	31.4094 2005	37.7193 9924	45.2592 5557	40
41	23.4624 8322	28.3543 2190	34.2362 6786	41.3027 4216	49.7851 8112	41
42	25.3394 8187	30.7644 3927	37.3175 3197	45.2265 0267	54.7636 9924	42
43	27.3666 4042	33.3794 1660	40.6761 0984	49.5230 2042	60.2400 6916	43
44	29.5559 7166	36.2166 6702	44.3369 5973	54.2277 0736	66.2640 7608	44
45	31.9204 4939	39.2950 8371	48.3272 8610	59.3793 3956	72.8904 8369	45
46	34.4740 8534	42.6351 6583	52.6767 4185	65.0203 7682	80.1795 3205	46
47	37.2320 1217	46.2591 5492	57.4176 4862	71.1973 1262	88.1974 8526	47
48	40.2105 7314	50.1911 8309	62.5852 3700	77.9610 5732	97.0172 3378	48
49	43.4274 1899	54.4574 3365	68.2179 0833	85.3673 5777	106.7189 5716	49
50	46.9016 1251	59.0863 1551	74.3575 2008	93.4772 5675	117.3908 5288	50
51	50.6537 4151	64.1086 5233	81.0496 9688	102.3575 9614	129.1299 3817	51
52	54.7060 4084	69.5578 8778	88.3441 6960	112.0815 6778	142.0429 3198	52
53	59.0825 2410	75.4703 0824	96.2951 4487	122.7293 1672	156.2472 2518	53
54	63.8091 2603	81.8852 8444	104.9617 0790	134.3886 0181	171.8719 4770	54
55	68.9138 5611	88.8455 3362	114.4082 6162	147.1555 1898	189.0591 4247	55
56	74.4269 6460	96.3974 0398	124.7050 0516	161.1352 9328	207.9650 5672	56
57	80.3811 2177	104.5911 8332	135.9284 5563	176.4431 4614	228.7615 6239	57
58	86.8116 1151	113.4814 3390	148.1620 1663	193.2052 4502	251.6377 1863	58
59	93.7565 4043	123.1273 5578	161.4965 9813	211.5597 4330	276.8014 9049	59
60	101.2570 6367	133.5931 8102	176.0312 9196	231.6579 1892	304.4816 3954	60

TABLE I

N	8	8 1/2	9	9 1/2	10	N
61	109.3576 2876	144.9486 0141	191.8741 0824	253.6654 2121	334.9298 0350	61
62	118.1062 3906	157.2692 3253	209.1427 7798	277.7636 3623	368.4227 8385	62
63	127.5547 3819	170.6371 1729	227.9656 2800	304.1511 8167	405.2650 6223	63
64	137.7591 1724	185.1412 7226	248.4825 3452	333.0455 4393	445.7915 6845	64
65	148.7798 4662	200.8782 8041	270.8459 6262	364.6848 7060	490.3707 2530	65
66	160.6822 3435	217.9529 3424	295.2220 9926	399.3299 3331	539.4077 9783	66
67	173.5368 1310	236.4789 3365	321.7920 8819	437.2662 7697	593.3485 7761	67
68	187.4197 5815	256.5796 4301	350.7533 7613	478.8065 7329	652.6834 3537	68
69	202.4133 3880	278.3889 1267	382.3211 7998	524.2931 9775	717.9517 7891	69
70	218.6064 0590	302.0519 7024	416.7300 8618	574.1010 5153	789.7469 5680	70
71	236.0949 1837	327.7263 8771	454.2357 9393	628.6406 5143	868.7216 5248	71
72	254.9825 1184	355.5831 3067	495.1170 1539	688.3615 1331	955.5938 1773	72
73	275.3811 1279	385.8076 9678	539.6775 4677	753.7558 5708	1051.1531 9950	73
74	297.4116 0181	418.6013 5100	588.2485 2598	825.3626 6350	1156.2685 1945	74
75	321.2045 2996	454.1824 6584	641.1908 9332	903.7721 1653	1271.8953 7140	75
76	346.9008 9236	492.7879 7543	698.8980 7372	989.6304 6761	1399.0849 0853	76
77	374.6529 6374	534.6749 5335	761.7989 0036	1083.6453 6203	1538.9933 9939	77
78	404.6252 0084	580.1223 2438	830.3608 0139	1186.5916 7142	1692.8927 3933	78
79	436.9952 1691	629.4327 2195	905.0932 7351	1299.3178 8021	1862.1820 1326	79
80	471.9548 3426	682.9345 0332	986.5516 6813	1422.7530 7883	2048.4002 1459	80
81	509.7112 2101	740.9839 3610	1075.3413 1826	1557.9146 2131	2253.2402 3604	81
82	550.4881 1869	803.9675 7067	1172.1220 3690	1705.9165 1034	2478.5642 5965	82
83	594.5271 6818	872.3048 1418	1277.6130 2022	1867.9785 7882	2726.4206 8561	83
84	642.0893 4164	946.4507 2338	1392.5981 9204	2045.4365 4381	2999.0627 5417	84
85	693.4564 8897	1026.8990 3487	1517.9320 2933	2239.7530 1547	3298.9690 2959	85
86	748.9330 0808	1114.1854 5283	1654.5459 1197	2452.5295 5194	3628.8659 3255	86
87	808.8476 4873	1208.8912 1633	1803.4550 4404	2685.5198 5938	3991.7525 2581	87
88	873.5554 6063	1311.6469 6971	1965.7659 9801	2940.6442 4602	4390.9277 7839	88
89	943.4398 9748	1423.1369 6214	2142.6849 3783	3220.0054 4939	4830.0205 5623	89
90	1018.9150 8928	1544.1036 0392	2335.5265 8223	3525.9059 6708	5313.0226 1185	90
91	1100.4282 9642	1675.3524 1025	2545.7239 7464	3860.8670 3395	5844.3248 7303	91
92	1188.4625 6013	1817.7573 6512	2774.8391 3235	4227.6494 0218	6428.7573 6034	92
93	1283.5395 6494	1972.2667 4116	3024.5746 5426	4629.2760 9538	7071.6330 9637	93
94	1386.2227 3014	2139.9094 1416	3296.7863 7315	5069.0573 2445	7778.7964 0601	94
95	1497.1205 4855	2321.8017 1436	3593.4971 4673	5550.6177 7027	8556.6760 4661	95
96	1616.8901 9244	2519.1548 6008	3916.9118 8994	6077.9264 5844	9412.3436 5127	96
97	1746.2414 0783	2733.2830 2319	4269.4339 6003	6655.3294 7199	10353.5780 1640	97
98	1885.9407 2046	2965.6120 8016	4653.6830 1643	7287.5857 7183	11388.9358 1803	98
99	2036.8159 7809	3217.6891 0698	5072.5144 8791	7979.9064 2016	12527.8293 9984	99
100	2199.7612 5634	3491.1926 8107	5529.0407 9183	8737.9975 3007	13780.6123 3982	100
101	2375.7421 5685	3787.9440 5896	6026.6544 6309	9568.1072 9543	15158.6735 7380	101
102	2565.8015 2940	4109.9193 0397	6569.0533 6477	10477.0774 8850	16674.5409 3118	102
103	2771.0656 5175	4459.2624 4481	7160.2681 6760	11472.3998 4990	18341.9950 2430	103
104	2992.7509 0389	4838.2997 5262	7804.6923 0268	12562.2778 3564	20176.1945 2673	104
105	3232.1709 7620	5249.5552 3159	8507.1146 0992	13755.6942 3003	22193.8139 7941	105
106	3490.7446 5429	5695.7674 2627	9272.7549 2482	15062.4851 8188	24413.1953 7735	106
107	3770.0042 2664	6179.9076 5751	10107.3028 6805	16493.4212 7416	26854.5149 1508	107
108	4071.6045 6477	6705.1998 0840	11016.9601 2617	18060.2962 9521	29539.9664 0659	108
109	4397.3329 2995	7275.1417 9211	12008.4865 3753	19776.0244 4325	32493.9630 4725	109
110	4749.1195 6435	7893.5288 4444	13089.2503 2591	21654.7467 6536	35743.3593 5197	110
111	5129.0491 2950	8564.4787 9622	14267.2828 5524	23711.9477 0807	39317.6952 8717	111
112	5539.3730 5985	9292.4594 9389	15551.3383 1221	25964.5827 4034	43249.4648 1589	112
113	5982.5229 0464	10082.3185 5088	16950.9587 6031	28431.2181 0067	47574.4112 9748	113
114	6461.1247 3701	10939.3156 2770	18476.5450 4874	31132.1838 2023	52331.8524 2723	114
115	6978.0147 1598	11869.1574 5605	20139.4341 0312	34089.7412 8316	57565.0376 6995	115
116	7536.2558 9325	12878.0358 3982	21951.9831 7240	37328.2667 0506	63321.5414 3694	116
117	8139.1563 6471	13972.6688 8620	23927.6616 5792	40874.4520 4204	69653.6955 8064	117
118	8790.2888 7389	15160.3457 4153	26081.1512 0713	44757.5249 8603	76619.0651 3870	118
119	9493.5119 8380	16448.9751 2956	28428.4548 1577	49009.4898 5970	84280.9716 5257	119
120	10252.9929 4251	17847.1380 1557	30987.0157 4919	53665.3913 9638	92709.0688 1783	120

TABLE I

N	10 1/2	11	11 1/2	12	12 1/2	N
1	1.1050 0000	1.1100 0000	1.1150 0000	1.1200 0000	1.1250 0000	1
2	1.2210 2500	1.2321 0000	1.2432 2500	1.2544 0000	1.2656 2500	2
3	1.3492 3262	1.3676 3100	1.3861 9587	1.4049 2800	1.4238 2812	3
4	1.4909 0205	1.5180 7041	1.5456 0840	1.5735 1936	1.6018 0664	4
5	1.6474 4677	1.6850 5816	1.7233 5337	1.7623 4168	1.8020 3247	5
6	1.8204 2868	1.8704 1455	1.9215 3900	1.9738 2269	2.0272 8653	6
7	2.0115 7369	2.0761 6015	2.1425 1599	2.2106 8141	2.2806 9735	7
8	2.2227 8892	2.3045 3777	2.3889 0533	2.4759 6318	2.5657 8451	8
9	2.4561 8176	2.5580 3692	2.6636 2944	2.7730 7876	2.8865 0758	9
10	2.7140 8085	2.8394 2099	2.9699 4683	3.1058 4821	3.2473 2103	10
11	2.9990 5934	3.1517 5729	3.3114 9071	3.4785 4999	3.6532 3615	11
12	3.3139 6057	3.4984 5060	3.6923 1214	3.8959 7599	4.1098 9067	12
13	3.6619 2643	3.8832 8016	4.1169 2804	4.3634 9311	4.6236 2701	13
14	4.0464 2870	4.3104 4098	4.5903 7476	4.8871 1229	5.2015 8038	14
15	4.4713 0371	4.7845 8949	5.1182 6786	5.4735 6576	5.8517 7793	15
16	4.9407 9060	5.3108 9433	5.7068 6867	6.1303 9365	6.5832 5017	16
17	5.4595 7362	5.8950 9271	6.3631 5856	6.8660 4089	7.4061 5644	17
18	6.0328 2885	6.5435 5291	7.0949 2180	7.6899 6580	8.3319 2600	18
19	6.6662 7588	7.2633 4373	7.9108 3780	8.6127 6169	9.3734 1675	19
20	7.3662 3484	8.0623 1154	8.8205 8415	9.6462 9309	10.5450 9384	20
21	8.1396 8950	8.9491 6581	9.8349 5133	10.8038 4826	11.8632 3057	21
22	8.9943 5690	9.9335 7404	10.9659 7073	12.1003 1006	13.3461 3439	22
23	9.9387 6437	11.0262 6719	12.2270 5737	13.5523 4726	15.0144 0119	23
24	10.9823 3463	12.2391 5658	13.6331 6896	15.1786 2893	16.8912 0134	24
25	12.1354 7977	13.5854 6380	15.2009 8340	17.0000 6441	19.0026 0151	25
26	13.4097 0514	15.0798 6482	16.9490 9649	19.0400 7214	21.3779 2670	26
27	14.8177 2418	16.7386 4995	18.8982 4258	21.3248 8079	24.0501 6754	27
28	16.3735 8522	18.5799 0145	21.0715 4048	23.8838 6649	27.0564 3848	28
29	18.0928 1167	20.6236 9061	23.4947 6763	26.7499 3047	30.4384 9329	29
30	19.9925 5690	22.8922 9657	26.1966 6591	29.9599 2212	34.2433 0495	30
31	22.0917 7537	25.4104 4919	29.2092 8249	33.5551 1278	38.5237 1807	31
32	24.4114 1178	28.2055 9861	32.5683 4998	37.5817 2631	43.3391 8283	32
33	26.9746 1002	31.3082 1445	36.3137 1022	42.0915 3347	48.7565 8068	33
34	29.8069 4407	34.7521 1804	40.4897 8690	47.1425 1748	54.8511 5327	34
35	32.9366 7320	38.5748 5103	45.1461 1239	52.7996 1958	61.7075 4742	35
36	36.3950 2389	42.8180 8464	50.3379 1532	59.1355 7393	69.4209 9085	36
37	40.2165 0140	47.5280 7395	56.1267 7558	66.2318 4280	78.0986 1471	37
38	44.4392 3404	52.7561 6209	62.5813 5477	74.1796 6394	87.8609 4155	38
39	49.1053 5362	58.5593 3991	69.7782 1057	83.0812 2361	98.8435 5924	39
40	54.2614 1575	65.0008 6731	77.8027 0479	93.0509 7044	111.1990 0415	40
41	59.9588 6440	72.1509 6271	86.7500 1584	104.2170 8689	125.0988 7966	41
42	66.2545 4516	80.0875 6861	96.7262 6766	116.7231 3732	140.7362 3962	42
43	73.2112 7240	88.8972 0115	107.8497 8844	130.7299 1380	158.3282 6958	43
44	80.8984 5601	98.6758 9328	120.2525 1411	146.4175 0346	178.1193 0327	44
45	89.3927 9389	109.5302 4154	134.0815 5323	163.9876 0387	200.3842 1618	45
46	98.7790 3724	121.5785 6811	149.5009 3186	183.6661 1634	225.4322 4320	46
47	109.1508 3616	134.9522 1060	166.6935 3902	205.7060 5030	253.6112 7360	47
48	120.6116 7395	149.7969 5377	185.8632 9601	230.3907 7633	285.3126 8280	48
49	133.2758 9972	166.2746 1868	207.2375 7505	258.0376 6949	320.9767 6816	49
50	147.2698 6919	184.5648 2674	231.0698 9618	289.0021 8983	361.0988 6417	50
51	162.7332 0545	204.8669 5768	257.6429 3424	323.6824 5261	406.2362 2220	51
52	179.8201 9202	227.4023 2303	287.2718 7167	362.5243 4692	457.0157 4997	52
53	198.7013 1219	252.4165 7856	320.3081 3692	406.0272 6855	514.1427 1872	53
54	219.5649 4997	280.1824 0220	357.1435 7266	454.7505 4078	578.4105 5856	54
55	242.6192 6971	311.0024 6644	398.2150 8352	509.3206 0567	650.7118 7838	55
56	268.0942 9303	345.2127 3775	444.0098 1812	570.4390 7835	732.0508 6317	56
57	296.2441 9380	383.1861 3890	495.0709 4721	638.8917 6776	823.5572 2107	57
58	327.3498 3415	425.3366 1418	552.0041 0614	715.5587 7989	926.5018 7370	58
59	361.7215 6674	472.1236 4174	615.4845 7834	801.4258 3347	1042.3146 0792	59
60	399.7023 3124	524.0572 4234	686.2653 0485	897.5969 3349	1172.6039 3391	60

TABLE I

N	10 1/2	11	11 1/2	12	12 1/2	N
61	441.6710 7602	581.7035 3899	765.1858 1491	1005.3085 6551	1319.1794 2565	61
62	488.0465 3901	645.6909 2828	853.1821 8362	1125.9455 9337	1484.0768 5385	62
63	539.2914 2560	716.7169 3039	951.2981 3474	1261.0590 6458	1669.5864 6058	63
64	595.9170 2529	795.5557 9274	1060.6974 2023	1412.3861 5232	1878.2847 6816	64
65	658.4883 1295	883.0669 2994	1182.6776 2356	1581.8724 9060	2113.0703 6417	65
66	727.6295 8581	980.2042 9223	1318.6855 5027	1771.6971 8948	2377.2041 5970	66
67	804.0306 9231	1088.0267 6438	1470.3343 8855	1984.3008 5221	2674.3546 7966	67
68	888.4539 1501	1207.7097 0846	1639.4228 4324	2222.4169 5448	3008.6490 1462	68
69	981.7415 7608	1340.5577 7639	1827.9564 7021	2489.1069 8902	3384.7301 4144	69
70	1084.8244 4157	1488.0191 3179	2038.1714 6428	2787.7998 2770	3807.8214 0912	70
71	1198.7310 0794	1651.7012 3629	2272.5611 8267	3122.3358 0702	4283.7990 8526	71
72	1324.5977 6377	1833.3883 7228	2533.9057 1868	3497.0161 0386	4819.2739 7092	72
73	1463.6805 2897	2035.0610 9323	2825.3048 7633	3916.6580 3633	5421.6832 1729	73
74	1617.3669 8451	2258.9178 1349	3150.2149 3711	4386.6570 0069	6099.3936 1945	74
75	1787.1905 1788	2507.3987 7297	3512.4896 5487	4913.0558 4077	6861.8178 2188	75
76	1974.8455 2226	2783.2126 3800	3916.4259 6518	5502.6225 4166	7719.5450 4961	76
77	2182.2043 0210	3089.3660 2818	4366.8149 5118	6162.9372 4666	8684.4881 8082	77
78	2411.3357 5382	3429.1962 9128	4868.9986 7057	6902.4897 1626	9770.0492 0342	78
79	2664.5260 0797	3806.4078 8332	5428.9335 1768	7730.7884 8221	10991.3053 5384	79
80	2944.3012 3880	4225.1127 5048	6053.2608 7222	8658.4831 0008	12365.2185 2308	80
81	3253.4528 6888	4689.8751 5303	6749.3858 7252	9697.5010 7209	13910.8708 3846	81
82	3595.0654 2011	5205.7614 1987	7525.5652 4786	10861.2012 0074	15649.7296 9327	82
83	3972.5472 8922	5778.3951 7605	8391.0052 5136	12164.5453 4483	17605.9459 0493	83
84	4389.6647 5459	6414.0186 4542	9355.9708 5527	13624.2907 8621	19806.6891 4304	84
85	4850.5795 5382	7119.5606 9641	10431.9075 0363	15259.2056 8055	22282.5252 8592	85
86	5359.8904 0697	7902.7123 7302	11631.5768 6654	17090.3103 6222	25067.8409 4666	86
87	5922.6788 9971	8772.0107 3405	12969.2082 0620	19141.1476 0569	28201.3210 6499	87
88	6544.5601 8417	9736.9319 1480	14460.6671 4991	21438.0853 1837	31726.4861 9812	88
89	7231.7390 0351	10807.9944 2542	16123.6438 7215	24010.6555 5657	35692.2969 7288	89
90	7991.0715 9888	11996.8738 1222	17977.8629 1745	26891.9342 2336	40153.8340 9449	90
91	8830.1341 1676	13316.5299 3157	20045.3171 5295	30118.9663 3016	45173.0633 5631	91
92	9757.2981 9902	14781.3482 2404	22350.5286 2554	33733.2422 8978	50819.6962 7584	92
93	10781.8145 0992	16407.2965 2868	24920.8394 1748	37781.2313 6456	57172.1583 1032	93
94	11913.9050 3346	18212.0991 4684	27786.7359 5049	42314.9791 2830	64318.6780 9912	94
95	13164.8650 6198	20215.4300 5299	30982.2105 8480	47392.7766 2370	72358.5128 6150	95
96	14547.1758 9348	22439.1273 5882	34545.1648 0205	53079.9098 1854	81403.3269 6919	96
97	16074.6293 6230	24907.4313 6829	38517.8587 5428	59449.4989 9677	91578.7428 4034	97
98	17762.4654 4534	27647.2488 1880	42947.4125 1103	66583.4388 7638	103026.0856 9538	98
99	19627.5243 1710	30688.4461 8887	47886.3649 4979	74573.4515 4155	115904.3464 0731	99
100	21688.4143 7040	34064.1752 6964	53393.2969 1902	83522.2657 2653	130392.3897 0822	100
101	23965.6978 7929	37811.2345 4930	59533.5260 6471	93544.9376 1372	146691.4384 2175	101
102	26482.0961 5662	41970.4703 4973	66379.8815 6215	104770.3301 2736	165027.8682 2447	102
103	29262.7162 5306	46587.2220 8820	74013.5679 4180	117342.7697 4265	185656.3517 5253	103
104	32335.3014 5963	51711.8165 1790	82525.1282 5510	131423.9021 1177	208863.3957 2159	104
105	35730.5081 1289	57400.1163 3487	92015.5180 0444	147194.7703 6518	234971.3201 8679	105
106	39482.2114 6475	63714.1291 3170	102597.3025 7495	164858.1428 0900	264342.7352 1014	106
107	43627.8436 6855	70722.6833 3619	114395.9923 7107	184641.1199 4608	297385.5771 1141	107
108	48208.7672 5374	78502.1785 0317	127551.5314 9374	206798.0543 3961	334558.7742 5033	108
109	53270.6878 1539	87137.4181 3852	142219.9576 1552	231613.8208 6036	376378.6210 3163	109
110	58864.1100 3600	96722.5341 3376	158575.2527 4131	259407.4793 6360	423425.9486 6058	110
111	65044.8415 8978	107362.0128 8847	176811.4068 0656	290536.3768 8724	476354.1922 4315	111
112	71874.5499 5671	119171.8343 0620	197144.7185 8931	325400.7421 1370	535898.4662 7354	112
113	79421.3777 0217	132280.7360 7989	219816.3612 2708	364448.8311 6735	602885.7745 5774	113
114	87760.6223 6089	146831.6170 4867	245095.2427 6820	408182.6909 0743	678246.4963 7745	114
115	96975.4877 0879	162983.0949 2403	273281.1956 8654	457164.6138 1632	763027.3084 2464	115
116	107157.9139 1821	180911.2353 6567	304708.5331 9049	512024.3674 7428	858405.7219 7772	116
117	118409.4948 7962	200811.4712 5590	339750.0145 0740	573467.2915 7119	965706.4372 2493	117
118	130842.4918 4198	222900.7330 9404	378821.2661 7575	642283.3665 5974	1086419.7418 7805	118
119	144580.9534 8539	247419.8137 3439	422385.7117 8596	719357.3705 4691	1222222.2096 1280	119
120	159761.9536 0136	274635.9932 4517	470960.0686 4134	805680.2550 1253	1374999.9858 1440	120

TABLE II
PRESENT VALUE OF 1 AT COMPOUND INTEREST
$V^n = (1 + i)^{-n}$

TABLE II

N	1/6	5/24	1/4	7/24	1/3	N
1	0.9983 3611	0.9979 2100	0.9975 0623	0.9970 9182	0.9966 7774	1
2	0.9966 7498	0.9958 4632	0.9950 1869	0.9941 9209	0.9933 6652	2
3	0.9950 1662	0.9937 7595	0.9925 3734	0.9913 0079	0.9900 6630	3
4	0.9933 6102	0.9917 0989	0.9900 6219	0.9884 1791	0.9867 7704	4
5	0.9917 0817	0.9896 4812	0.9875 9321	0.9855 4341	0.9834 9871	5
6	0.9900 5808	0.9875 9064	0.9851 3038	0.9826 7727	0.9802 3127	6
7	0.9884 1072	0.9855 3744	0.9826 7370	0.9798 1946	0.9769 7469	7
8	0.9867 6611	0.9834 8850	0.9802 2314	0.9769 6996	0.9737 2893	8
9	0.9851 2424	0.9814 4383	0.9777 7869	0.9741 2875	0.9704 9395	9
10	0.9834 8510	0.9794 0341	0.9753 4034	0.9712 9581	0.9672 6972	10
11	0.9818 4868	0.9773 6722	0.9729 0807	0.9684 7110	0.9640 5620	11
12	0.9802 1499	0.9753 3528	0.9704 8187	0.9656 5461	0.9608 5335	12
13	0.9785 8402	0.9733 0755	0.9680 6171	0.9628 4631	0.9576 6115	13
14	0.9769 5576	0.9712 8404	0.9656 4759	0.9600 4617	0.9544 7955	14
15	0.9753 3021	0.9692 6474	0.9632 3949	0.9572 5418	0.9513 0852	15
16	0.9737 0736	0.9672 4964	0.9608 3740	0.9544 7031	0.9481 4803	16
17	0.9720 8722	0.9652 3872	0.9584 4130	0.9516 9453	0.9449 9803	17
18	0.9704 6977	0.9632 3199	0.9560 5117	0.9489 2683	0.9418 5851	18
19	0.9688 5501	0.9612 2943	0.9536 6700	0.9461 6718	0.9387 2941	19
20	0.9672 4294	0.9592 3103	0.9512 8878	0.9434 1555	0.9356 1071	20
21	0.9656 3355	0.9572 3679	0.9489 1649	0.9406 7192	0.9325 0236	21
22	0.9640 2684	0.9552 4669	0.9465 5011	0.9379 3627	0.9294 0435	22
23	0.9624 2280	0.9532 6073	0.9441 8964	0.9352 0858	0.9263 1663	23
24	0.9608 2143	0.9512 7890	0.9418 3505	0.9324 8882	0.9232 3916	24
25	0.9592 2273	0.9493 0119	0.9394 8634	0.9297 7697	0.9201 7192	25
26	0.9576 2668	0.9473 2759	0.9371 4348	0.9270 7301	0.9171 1487	26
27	0.9560 3329	0.9453 5809	0.9348 0646	0.9243 7691	0.9140 6798	27
28	0.9544 4256	0.9433 9269	0.9324 7527	0.9216 8865	0.9110 3121	28
29	0.9528 5446	0.9414 3138	0.9301 4990	0.9190 0821	0.9080 0453	29
30	0.9512 6902	0.9394 7414	0.9278 3032	0.9163 3557	0.9049 8790	30
31	0.9496 8621	0.9375 2097	0.9255 1653	0.9136 7069	0.9019 8130	31
32	0.9481 0603	0.9355 7186	0.9232 0851	0.9110 1357	0.8989 8468	32
33	0.9465 2848	0.9336 2681	0.9209 0624	0.9083 6417	0.8959 9802	33
34	0.9449 5356	0.9316 8580	0.9186 0972	0.9057 2248	0.8930 2128	34
35	0.9433 8126	0.9297 4882	0.9163 1892	0.9030 8848	0.8900 5444	35
36	0.9418 1157	0.9278 1587	0.9140 3384	0.9004 6213	0.8870 9745	36
37	0.9402 4450	0.9258 8694	0.9117 5445	0.8978 4342	0.8841 5028	37
38	0.9386 8003	0.9239 6202	0.9094 8075	0.8952 3232	0.8812 1290	38
39	0.9371 1817	0.9220 4110	0.9072 1272	0.8926 2882	0.8782 8528	39
40	0.9355 5890	0.9201 2417	0.9049 5034	0.8900 3289	0.8753 6739	40
41	0.9340 0223	0.9182 1123	0.9026 9361	0.8874 4451	0.8724 5920	41
42	0.9324 4815	0.9163 0227	0.9004 4250	0.8848 6366	0.8695 6066	42
43	0.9308 9666	0.9143 9727	0.8981 9701	0.8822 9031	0.8666 7175	43
44	0.9293 4774	0.9124 9624	0.8959 5712	0.8797 2445	0.8637 9245	44
45	0.9278 0141	0.9105 9916	0.8937 2281	0.8771 6605	0.8609 2270	45
46	0.9262 5765	0.9087 0602	0.8914 9407	0.8746 1509	0.8580 6249	46
47	0.9247 1645	0.9068 1682	0.8892 7090	0.8720 7155	0.8552 1179	47
48	0.9231 7782	0.9049 3155	0.8870 5326	0.8695 3540	0.8523 7055	48
49	0.9216 4175	0.9030 5019	0.8848 4116	0.8670 0663	0.8495 3876	49
50	0.9201 0824	0.9011 7275	0.8826 3457	0.8644 8522	0.8467 1637	50
51	0.9185 7728	0.8992 9921	0.8804 3349	0.8619 7114	0.8439 0336	51
52	0.9170 4886	0.8974 2956	0.8782 3790	0.8594 6436	0.8410 9969	52
53	0.9155 2299	0.8955 6381	0.8760 4778	0.8569 6488	0.8383 0534	53
54	0.9139 9966	0.8937 0193	0.8738 6312	0.8544 7267	0.8355 2027	54
55	0.9124 7886	0.8918 4392	0.8716 8391	0.8519 8771	0.8327 4446	55
56	0.9109 6059	0.8899 8977	0.8695 1013	0.8495 0997	0.8299 7787	56
57	0.9094 4485	0.8881 3948	0.8673 4178	0.8470 3944	0.8272 2047	57
58	0.9079 3163	0.8862 9304	0.8651 7883	0.8445 7609	0.8244 7222	58
59	0.9064 2093	0.8844 5043	0.8630 2128	0.8421 1991	0.8217 3311	59
60	0.9049 1274	0.8826 1166	0.8608 6911	0.8396 7087	0.8190 0310	60

TABLE II

N	1/6	5/24	1/4	7/24	1/3	N
61	0.9034 0706	0.8807 7671	0.8587 2230	0.8372 2895	0.8162 8216	61
62	0.9019 0389	0.8789 4557	0.8565 8085	0.8347 9413	0.8135 7026	62
63	0.9004 0322	0.8771 1824	0.8544 4474	0.8323 6640	0.8108 6737	63
64	0.8989 0504	0.8752 9471	0.8523 1395	0.8299 4572	0.8081 7346	64
65	0.8974 0936	0.8734 7497	0.8501 8848	0.8275 3209	0.8054 8850	65
66	0.8959 1617	0.8716 5901	0.8480 6831	0.8251 2547	0.8028 1246	66
67	0.8944 2546	0.8698 4683	0.8459 5343	0.8227 2586	0.8001 4531	67
68	0.8929 3723	0.8680 3842	0.8438 4382	0.8203 3322	0.7974 8702	68
69	0.8914 5148	0.8662 3377	0.8417 3947	0.8179 4754	0.7948 3756	69
70	0.8899 6820	0.8644 3287	0.8396 4037	0.8155 6879	0.7921 9690	70
71	0.8884 8738	0.8626 3571	0.8375 4650	0.8131 9697	0.7895 6502	71
72	0.8870 0903	0.8608 4229	0.8354 5786	0.8108 3204	0.7869 4188	72
73	0.8855 3315	0.8590 5259	0.8333 7442	0.8084 7399	0.7843 2745	73
74	0.8840 5971	0.8572 6662	0.8312 9618	0.8061 2280	0.7817 2171	74
75	0.8825 8873	0.8554 8436	0.8292 2312	0.8037 7845	0.7791 2463	75
76	0.8811 2020	0.8537 0581	0.8271 5523	0.8014 4091	0.7765 3618	76
77	0.8796 5411	0.8519 3095	0.8250 9250	0.7991 1018	0.7739 5632	77
78	0.8781 9046	0.8501 5979	0.8230 3491	0.7967 8622	0.7713 8504	78
79	0.8767 2924	0.8483 9230	0.8209 8246	0.7944 6901	0.7688 2230	79
80	0.8752 7046	0.8466 2849	0.8189 3512	0.7921 5855	0.7662 6807	80
81	0.8738 1410	0.8448 6835	0.8168 9289	0.7898 5481	0.7637 2233	81
82	0.8723 6017	0.8431 1187	0.8148 5575	0.7875 5776	0.7611 8505	82
83	0.8709 0865	0.8413 5904	0.8128 2369	0.7852 6740	0.7586 5619	83
84	0.8694 5955	0.8396 0985	0.8107 9670	0.7829 8370	0.7561 3574	84
85	0.8680 1287	0.8378 6430	0.8087 7476	0.7807 0664	0.7536 2366	85
86	0.8665 6858	0.8361 2238	0.8067 5787	0.7784 3620	0.7511 1993	86
87	0.8651 2671	0.8343 8408	0.8047 4600	0.7761 7236	0.7486 2451	87
88	0.8636 8723	0.8326 4939	0.8027 3915	0.7739 1511	0.7461 3739	88
89	0.8622 5014	0.8309 1831	0.8007 3731	0.7716 6442	0.7436 5853	89
90	0.8608 1545	0.8291 9083	0.7987 4046	0.7694 2028	0.7411 8790	90
91	0.8593 8315	0.8274 6694	0.7967 4859	0.7671 8266	0.7387 2548	91
92	0.8579 5322	0.8257 4663	0.7947 6168	0.7649 5156	0.7362 7125	92
93	0.8565 2568	0.8240 2991	0.7927 7973	0.7627 2694	0.7338 2516	93
94	0.8551 0051	0.8223 1675	0.7908 0273	0.7605 0878	0.7313 8720	94
95	0.8536 7772	0.8206 0715	0.7888 3065	0.7582 9708	0.7289 5735	95
96	0.8522 5729	0.8189 0110	0.7868 6349	0.7560 9182	0.7265 3556	96
97	0.8508 3922	0.8171 9861	0.7849 0124	0.7538 9296	0.7241 2182	97
98	0.8494 2352	0.8154 9965	0.7829 4388	0.7517 0050	0.7217 1610	98
99	0.8480 1017	0.8138 0422	0.7809 9140	0.7495 1442	0.7193 1837	99
100	0.8465 9917	0.8121 1232	0.7790 4379	0.7473 3469	0.7169 2861	100
101	0.8451 9052	0.8104 2394	0.7771 0104	0.7451 6131	0.7145 4679	101
102	0.8437 8421	0.8087 3907	0.7751 6313	0.7429 9424	0.7121 7288	102
103	0.8423 8024	0.8070 5770	0.7732 3006	0.7408 3347	0.7098 0686	103
104	0.8409 7861	0.8053 7982	0.7713 0180	0.7386 7899	0.7074 4869	104
105	0.8395 7931	0.8037 0543	0.7693 7836	0.7365 3078	0.7050 9837	105
106	0.8381 8234	0.8020 3453	0.7674 5971	0.7343 8881	0.7027 5585	106
107	0.8367 8770	0.8003 6710	0.7655 4584	0.7322 5307	0.7004 2111	107
108	0.8353 9537	0.7987 0313	0.7636 3675	0.7301 2355	0.6980 9413	108
109	0.8340 0536	0.7970 4263	0.7617 3242	0.7280 0021	0.6957 7488	109
110	0.8326 1767	0.7953 8557	0.7598 3284	0.7258 8305	0.6934 6333	110
111	0.8312 3228	0.7937 3197	0.7579 3799	0.7237 7205	0.6911 5947	111
112	0.8298 4920	0.7920 8180	0.7560 4787	0.7216 6719	0.6888 6326	112
113	0.8284 6842	0.7904 3506	0.7541 6247	0.7195 6845	0.6865 7468	113
114	0.8270 8993	0.7887 9174	0.7522 8176	0.7174 7581	0.6842 9370	114
115	0.8257 1374	0.7871 5184	0.7504 0575	0.7153 8926	0.6820 2030	115
116	0.8243 3984	0.7855 1535	0.7485 3441	0.7133 0877	0.6797 5445	116
117	0.8229 6823	0.7838 8226	0.7466 6774	0.7112 3434	0.6774 9613	117
118	0.8215 9890	0.7822 5257	0.7448 0573	0.7091 6594	0.6752 4531	118
119	0.8202 3185	0.7806 2626	0.7429 4836	0.7071 0356	0.6730 0197	119
120	0.8188 6707	0.7790 0334	0.7410 9562	0.7050 4717	0.6707 6608	120

TABLE II

N	1/6	5/24	1/4	7/24	1/3	N
121	0.8175 0456	0.7773 8379	0.7392 4750	0.7029 9676	0.6685 3763	121
122	0.8161 4432	0.7757 6761	0.7374 0399	0.7009 5232	0.6663 1657	122
123	0.8147 8634	0.7741 5479	0.7355 6508	0.6989 1382	0.6641 0289	123
124	0.8134 3063	0.7725 4532	0.7337 3075	0.6968 8125	0.6618 9657	124
125	0.8120 7716	0.7709 3919	0.7319 0100	0.6948 5459	0.6596 9758	125
126	0.8107 2595	0.7693 3641	0.7300 7581	0.6928 3382	0.6575 0589	126
127	0.8093 7699	0.7677 3696	0.7282 5517	0.6908 1893	0.6553 2149	127
128	0.8080 3027	0.7661 4083	0.7264 3907	0.6888 0991	0.6531 4434	128
129	0.8066 8580	0.7645 4802	0.7246 2750	0.6868 0672	0.6509 7443	129
130	0.8053 4356	0.7629 5853	0.7228 2045	0.6848 0936	0.6488 1172	130
131	0.8040 0355	0.7613 7233	0.7210 1791	0.6828 1781	0.6466 5620	131
132	0.8026 6578	0.7597 8944	0.7192 1986	0.6808 3205	0.6445 0784	132
133	0.8013 3023	0.7582 0983	0.7174 2629	0.6788 5206	0.6423 6662	133
134	0.7999 9690	0.7566 3351	0.7156 3720	0.6768 7783	0.6402 3251	134
135	0.7986 6579	0.7550 6047	0.7138 5257	0.6749 0935	0.6381 0549	135
136	0.7973 3689	0.7534 9070	0.7120 7239	0.6729 4659	0.6359 8554	136
137	0.7960 1021	0.7519 2419	0.7102 9664	0.6709 8954	0.6338 7263	137
138	0.7946 8573	0.7503 6094	0.7085 2533	0.6690 3817	0.6317 6674	138
139	0.7933 6346	0.7488 0094	0.7067 5843	0.6670 9249	0.6296 6785	139
140	0.7920 4339	0.7472 4418	0.7049 9595	0.6651 5246	0.6275 7593	140
141	0.7907 2551	0.7456 9066	0.7032 3785	0.6632 1807	0.6254 9096	141
142	0.7894 0983	0.7441 4036	0.7014 8414	0.6612 8931	0.6234 1292	142
143	0.7880 9634	0.7425 9329	0.6997 3480	0.6593 6616	0.6213 4178	143
144	0.7867 8503	0.7410 4944	0.6979 8983	0.6574 4860	0.6192 7752	144
145	0.7854 7590	0.7395 0880	0.6962 4921	0.6555 3662	0.6172 2012	145
146	0.7841 6895	0.7379 7136	0.6945 1292	0.6536 3020	0.6151 6955	146
147	0.7828 6418	0.7364 3711	0.6927 8097	0.6517 2932	0.6131 2580	147
148	0.7815 6158	0.7349 0606	0.6910 5334	0.6498 3397	0.6110 8884	148
149	0.7802 6114	0.7333 7819	0.6893 3001	0.6479 4414	0.6090 5864	149
150	0.7789 6287	0.7318 5349	0.6876 1098	0.6460 5980	0.6070 3519	150
151	0.7776 6676	0.7303 3197	0.6858 9624	0.6441 8093	0.6050 1846	151
152	0.7763 7280	0.7288 1361	0.6841 8578	0.6423 0754	0.6030 0843	152
153	0.7750 8100	0.7272 9840	0.6824 7958	0.6404 3959	0.6010 0508	153
154	0.7737 9135	0.7257 8635	0.6807 7764	0.6385 7707	0.5990 0839	154
155	0.7725 0384	0.7242 7744	0.6790 7994	0.6367 1997	0.5970 1833	155
156	0.7712 1848	0.7227 7166	0.6773 8647	0.6348 6827	0.5950 3488	156
157	0.7699 3525	0.7212 6902	0.6756 9723	0.6330 2196	0.5930 5802	157
158	0.7686 5416	0.7197 6950	0.6740 1220	0.6311 8101	0.5910 8773	158
159	0.7673 7521	0.7182 7310	0.6723 3137	0.6293 4542	0.5891 2398	159
160	0.7660 9837	0.7167 7980	0.6706 5473	0.6275 1517	0.5871 6676	160
161	0.7648 2367	0.7152 8962	0.6689 8228	0.6256 9024	0.5852 1604	161
162	0.7635 5108	0.7138 0253	0.6673 1399	0.6238 7062	0.5832 7180	162
163	0.7622 8062	0.7123 1853	0.6656 4987	0.6220 5629	0.5813 3402	163
164	0.7610 1226	0.7108 3762	0.6639 8989	0.6202 4723	0.5794 0268	164
165	0.7597 4602	0.7093 5979	0.6623 3406	0.6184 4344	0.5774 7775	165
166	0.7584 8188	0.7078 8503	0.6606 8235	0.6166 4489	0.5755 5922	166
167	0.7572 1985	0.7064 1333	0.6590 3476	0.6148 5158	0.5736 4706	167
168	0.7559 5992	0.7049 4470	0.6573 9129	0.6130 6347	0.5717 4126	168
169	0.7547 0208	0.7034 7912	0.6557 5191	0.6112 8057	0.5698 4179	169
170	0.7534 4634	0.7020 1658	0.6541 1661	0.6095 0285	0.5679 4862	170
171	0.7521 9268	0.7005 5709	0.6524 8540	0.6077 3031	0.5660 6175	171
172	0.7509 4111	0.6991 0063	0.6508 5826	0.6059 6292	0.5641 8115	172
173	0.7496 9163	0.6976 4720	0.6492 3517	0.6042 0066	0.5623 0679	173
174	0.7484 4422	0.6961 9679	0.6476 1613	0.6024 4354	0.5604 3866	174
175	0.7471 9889	0.6947 4939	0.6460 0112	0.6006 9152	0.5585 7674	175
176	0.7459 5563	0.6933 0501	0.6443 9015	0.5989 4460	0.5567 2100	176
177	0.7447 1444	0.6918 6362	0.6427 8319	0.5972 0276	0.5548 7143	177
178	0.7434 7531	0.6904 2524	0.6411 8024	0.5954 6598	0.5530 2801	178
179	0.7422 3825	0.6889 8984	0.6395 8129	0.5937 3426	0.5511 9070	179
180	0.7410 0324	0.6875 5743	0.6379 8632	0.5920 0757	0.5493 5950	180

TABLE II

N	1/6	5/24	1/4	7/24	1/3	N
181	0.7397 7029	0.6861 2800	0.6363 9533	0.5902 8590	0.5475 3439	181
182	0.7385 3939	0.6847 0154	0.6348 0831	0.5885 6924	0.5457 1534	182
183	0.7373 1054	0.6832 7804	0.6332 2525	0.5868 5757	0.5439 0233	183
184	0.7360 8374	0.6818 5750	0.6316 4613	0.5851 5088	0.5420 9535	184
185	0.7348 5897	0.6804 3992	0.6300 7096	0.5834 4916	0.5402 9437	185
186	0.7336 3624	0.6790 2528	0.6284 9971	0.5817 5238	0.5384 9937	186
187	0.7324 1555	0.6776 1359	0.6269 3238	0.5800 6053	0.5367 1033	187
188	0.7311 9689	0.6762 0483	0.6253 6895	0.5783 7361	0.5349 2724	188
189	0.7299 8026	0.6747 9900	0.6238 0943	0.5766 9159	0.5331 5008	189
190	0.7287 6565	0.6733 9609	0.6222 5380	0.5750 1447	0.5313 7881	190
191	0.7275 5306	0.6719 9610	0.6207 0204	0.5733 4222	0.5296 1343	191
192	0.7263 4249	0.6705 9902	0.6191 5416	0.5716 7484	0.5278 5392	192
193	0.7251 3393	0.6692 0484	0.6176 1013	0.5700 1230	0.5261 0025	193
194	0.7239 2739	0.6678 1356	0.6160 6996	0.5683 5460	0.5243 5241	194
195	0.7227 2285	0.6664 2518	0.6145 3362	0.5667 0172	0.5226 1038	195
196	0.7215 2031	0.6650 3968	0.6130 0112	0.5650 5365	0.5208 7413	196
197	0.7203 1978	0.6636 5706	0.6114 7244	0.5634 1037	0.5191 4365	197
198	0.7191 2125	0.6622 7731	0.6099 4757	0.5617 7186	0.5174 1892	198
199	0.7179 2470	0.6609 0044	0.6084 2650	0.5601 3813	0.5156 9992	199
200	0.7167 3015	0.6595 2642	0.6069 0923	0.5585 0914	0.5139 8663	200
201	0.7155 3759	0.6581 5527	0.6053 9574	0.5568 8490	0.5122 7904	201
202	0.7143 4701	0.6567 8696	0.6038 8602	0.5552 6537	0.5105 7711	202
203	0.7131 5842	0.6554 2150	0.6023 8007	0.5536 5056	0.5088 8084	203
204	0.7119 7180	0.6540 5888	0.6008 7788	0.5520 4044	0.5071 9021	204
205	0.7107 8715	0.6526 9909	0.5993 7943	0.5504 3500	0.5055 0519	205
206	0.7096 0448	0.6513 4212	0.5978 8472	0.5488 3424	0.5038 2577	206
207	0.7084 2377	0.6499 8798	0.5963 9373	0.5472 3813	0.5021 5193	207
208	0.7072 4503	0.6486 3666	0.5949 0647	0.5456 4666	0.5004 8365	208
209	0.7060 6825	0.6472 8814	0.5934 2291	0.5440 5982	0.4988 2092	209
210	0.7048 9343	0.6459 4243	0.5919 4305	0.5424 7759	0.4971 6371	210
211	0.7037 2056	0.6445 9951	0.5904 6689	0.5408 9996	0.4955 1200	211
212	0.7025 4964	0.6432 5939	0.5889 9440	0.5393 2693	0.4938 6578	212
213	0.7013 8067	0.6419 2205	0.5875 2559	0.5377 5847	0.4922 2503	213
214	0.7002 1365	0.6405 8749	0.5860 6044	0.5361 9456	0.4905 8973	214
215	0.6990 4857	0.6392 5571	0.5845 9894	0.5346 3521	0.4889 5986	215
216	0.6978 8543	0.6379 2670	0.5831 4109	0.5330 8039	0.4873 3541	216
217	0.6967 2422	0.6366 0044	0.5816 8687	0.5315 3010	0.4857 1636	217
218	0.6955 6495	0.6352 7695	0.5802 3628	0.5299 8431	0.4841 0268	218
219	0.6944 0760	0.6339 5621	0.5787 8930	0.5284 4302	0.4824 9437	219
220	0.6932 5218	0.6326 3821	0.5773 4594	0.5269 0621	0.4808 9140	220
221	0.6920 9868	0.6313 2296	0.5759 0617	0.5253 7387	0.4792 9375	221
222	0.6909 4710	0.6300 1043	0.5744 7000	0.5238 4598	0.4777 0141	222
223	0.6897 9744	0.6287 0064	0.5730 3741	0.5223 2254	0.4761 1437	223
224	0.6886 4969	0.6273 9357	0.5716 0838	0.5208 0353	0.4745 3259	224
225	0.6875 0385	0.6260 8922	0.5701 8293	0.5192 8894	0.4729 5607	225
226	0.6863 5992	0.6247 8758	0.5687 6102	0.5177 7875	0.4713 8479	226
227	0.6852 1789	0.6234 8864	0.5673 4267	0.5162 7296	0.4698 1872	227
228	0.6840 7776	0.6221 9241	0.5659 2785	0.5147 7154	0.4682 5787	228
229	0.6829 3953	0.6208 9887	0.5645 1656	0.5132 7449	0.4667 0219	229
230	0.6818 0319	0.6196 0802	0.5631 0879	0.5117 8179	0.4651 5169	230
231	0.6806 6874	0.6183 1985	0.5617 0452	0.5102 9344	0.4636 0633	231
232	0.6795 3618	0.6170 3437	0.5603 0376	0.5088 0941	0.4620 6611	232
233	0.6784 0550	0.6157 5155	0.5589 0650	0.5073 2970	0.4605 3101	233
234	0.6772 7671	0.6144 7140	0.5575 1272	0.5058 5429	0.4590 0100	234
235	0.6761 4979	0.6131 9391	0.5561 2241	0.5043 8317	0.4574 7608	235
236	0.6750 2475	0.6119 1908	0.5547 3557	0.5029 1633	0.4559 5623	236
237	0.6739 0158	0.6106 4690	0.5533 5219	0.5014 5376	0.4544 4142	237
238	0.6727 8028	0.6093 7736	0.5519 7226	0.4999 9544	0.4529 3165	238
239	0.6716 6085	0.6081 1047	0.5505 9577	0.4985 4136	0.4514 2690	239
240	0.6705 4328	0.6068 4621	0.5492 2271	0.4970 9151	0.4499 2714	240

TABLE II

N	1/6	5/24	1/4	7/24	1/3	N
241	0.6694 2756	0.6055 8457	0.5478 5308	0.4956 4588	0.4484 3236	241
242	0.6683 1371	0.6043 2556	0.5464 8686	0.4942 0445	0.4469 4256	242
243	0.6672 0170	0.6030 6916	0.5451 2405	0.4927 6721	0.4454 5770	243
244	0.6660 9155	0.6018 1538	0.5437 6464	0.4913 3415	0.4439 7777	244
245	0.6649 8325	0.6005 6421	0.5424 0862	0.4899 0526	0.4425 0276	245
246	0.6638 7678	0.5993 1563	0.5410 5598	0.4884 8052	0.4410 3265	246
247	0.6627 7216	0.5980 6965	0.5397 0671	0.4870 5993	0.4395 6743	247
248	0.6616 6938	0.5968 2627	0.5383 6081	0.4856 4347	0.4381 0707	248
249	0.6605 6843	0.5955 8546	0.5370 1827	0.4842 3113	0.4366 5157	249
250	0.6594 6932	0.5943 4724	0.5356 7907	0.4828 2290	0.4352 0090	250
251	0.6583 7203	0.5931 1159	0.5343 4321	0.4814 1876	0.4337 5505	251
252	0.6572 7657	0.5918 7851	0.5330 1068	0.4800 1871	0.4323 1400	252
253	0.6561 8293	0.5906 4799	0.5316 8148	0.4786 2272	0.4308 7774	253
254	0.6550 9111	0.5894 2004	0.5303 5559	0.4772 3080	0.4294 4625	254
255	0.6540 0111	0.5881 9463	0.5290 3301	0.4758 4292	0.4280 1952	255
256	0.6529 1292	0.5869 7177	0.5277 1372	0.4744 5909	0.4265 9753	256
257	0.6518 2655	0.5857 5146	0.5263 9773	0.4730 7927	0.4251 8026	257
258	0.6507 4198	0.5845 3368	0.5250 8502	0.4717 0347	0.4237 6770	258
259	0.6496 5921	0.5833 1843	0.5237 7558	0.4703 3167	0.4223 5984	259
260	0.6485 7825	0.5821 0571	0.5224 6941	0.4689 6386	0.4209 5665	260
261	0.6474 9908	0.5808 9551	0.5211 6649	0.4676 0002	0.4195 5812	261
262	0.6464 2171	0.5796 8783	0.5198 6682	0.4662 4016	0.4181 6424	262
263	0.6453 4614	0.5784 8266	0.5185 7040	0.4648 8424	0.4167 7499	263
264	0.6442 7235	0.5772 7999	0.5172 7720	0.4635 3228	0.4153 9036	264
265	0.6432 0035	0.5760 7982	0.5159 8723	0.4621 8424	0.4140 1032	265
266	0.6421 3013	0.5748 8215	0.5147 0048	0.4608 4012	0.4126 3487	266
267	0.6410 6170	0.5736 8697	0.5134 1694	0.4594 9991	0.4112 6399	267
268	0.6399 9504	0.5724 9428	0.5121 3660	0.4581 6360	0.4098 9767	268
269	0.6389 3015	0.5713 0406	0.5108 5945	0.4568 3118	0.4085 3588	269
270	0.6378 6704	0.5701 1632	0.5095 8549	0.4555 0263	0.4071 7862	270
271	0.6368 0570	0.5689 3104	0.5083 1470	0.4541 7794	0.4058 2587	271
272	0.6357 4612	0.5677 4823	0.5070 4708	0.4528 5711	0.4044 7761	272
273	0.6346 8831	0.5665 6788	0.5057 8263	0.4515 4012	0.4031 3383	273
274	0.6336 3225	0.5653 8999	0.5045 2132	0.4502 2696	0.4017 9451	274
275	0.6325 7796	0.5642 1454	0.5032 6317	0.4489 1761	0.4004 5965	275
276	0.6315 2542	0.5630 4154	0.5020 0814	0.4476 1208	0.3991 2922	276
277	0.6304 7462	0.5618 7097	0.5007 5625	0.4463 1034	0.3978 0321	277
278	0.6294 2558	0.5607 0284	0.4995 0749	0.4450 1239	0.3964 8160	278
279	0.6283 7828	0.5595 3714	0.4982 6183	0.4437 1821	0.3951 6439	279
280	0.6273 3273	0.5583 7386	0.4970 1928	0.4424 2779	0.3938 5155	280
281	0.6262 8892	0.5572 1300	0.4957 7983	0.4411 4113	0.3925 4307	281
282	0.6252 4684	0.5560 5455	0.4945 4347	0.4398 5821	0.3912 3894	282
283	0.6242 0649	0.5548 9852	0.4933 1020	0.4385 7902	0.3899 3914	283
284	0.6231 6788	0.5537 4488	0.4920 8000	0.4373 0356	0.3886 4366	284
285	0.6221 3099	0.5525 9364	0.4908 5287	0.4360 3180	0.3873 5249	285
286	0.6210 9584	0.5514 4480	0.4896 2879	0.4347 6373	0.3860 6560	286
287	0.6200 6240	0.5502 9835	0.4884 0778	0.4334 9936	0.3847 8299	287
288	0.6190 3068	0.5491 5427	0.4871 8980	0.4322 3867	0.3835 0464	288
289	0.6180 0068	0.5480 1258	0.4859 7486	0.4309 8164	0.3822 3054	289
290	0.6169 7239	0.5468 7326	0.4847 6296	0.4297 2826	0.3809 6067	290
291	0.6159 4582	0.5457 3631	0.4835 5407	0.4284 7853	0.3796 9502	291
292	0.6149 2095	0.5446 0172	0.4823 4820	0.4272 3244	0.3784 3358	292
293	0.6138 9778	0.5434 6950	0.4811 4534	0.4259 8997	0.3771 7632	293
294	0.6128 7632	0.5423 3962	0.4799 4547	0.4247 5111	0.3759 2325	294
295	0.6118 5656	0.5412 1210	0.4787 4860	0.4235 1586	0.3746 7433	295
296	0.6108 3850	0.5400 8692	0.4775 5472	0.4222 8419	0.3734 2957	296
297	0.6098 2213	0.5389 6407	0.4763 6381	0.4210 5611	0.3721 8894	297
298	0.6088 0745	0.5378 4357	0.4751 7587	0.4198 3160	0.3709 5243	298
299	0.6077 9446	0.5367 2539	0.4739 9089	0.4186 1066	0.3697 2003	299
300	0.6067 8315	0.5356 0954	0.4728 0887	0.4173 9326	0.3684 9172	300

TABLE II

N	1/6	5/24	1/4	7/24	1/3	N
301	0.6057 7353	0.5344 9600	0.4716 2979	0.4161 7940	0.3672 6750	301
302	0.6047 6559	0.5333 8478	0.4704 5366	0.4149 6908	0.3660 4734	302
303	0.6037 5932	0.5322 7588	0.4692 8046	0.4137 6227	0.3648 3124	303
304	0.6027 5473	0.5311 6927	0.4681 1018	0.4125 5897	0.3636 1917	304
305	0.6017 5181	0.5300 6497	0.4669 4282	0.4113 5917	0.3624 1114	305
306	0.6007 5056	0.5289 6297	0.4657 7838	0.4101 6287	0.3612 0711	306
307	0.5997 5098	0.5278 6325	0.4646 1684	0.4089 7004	0.3600 0709	307
308	0.5987 5305	0.5267 6582	0.4634 5819	0.4077 8068	0.3588 1105	308
309	0.5977 5679	0.5256 7067	0.4623 0243	0.4065 9478	0.3576 1899	309
310	0.5967 6219	0.5245 7780	0.4611 4956	0.4054 1232	0.3564 3089	310
311	0.5957 6924	0.5234 8721	0.4599 9956	0.4042 3331	0.3552 4673	311
312	0.5947 7794	0.5223 9887	0.4588 5243	0.4030 5772	0.3540 6651	312
313	0.5937 8830	0.5213 1281	0.4577 0816	0.4018 8556	0.3528 9021	313
314	0.5928 0030	0.5202 2900	0.4565 6674	0.4007 1680	0.3517 1781	314
315	0.5918 1394	0.5191 4744	0.4554 2817	0.3995 5144	0.3505 4932	315
316	0.5908 2922	0.5180 6813	0.4542 9244	0.3983 8947	0.3493 8470	316
317	0.5898 4615	0.5169 9107	0.4531 5954	0.3972 3088	0.3482 2395	317
318	0.5888 6471	0.5159 1624	0.4520 2947	0.3960 7566	0.3470 6706	318
319	0.5878 8490	0.5148 4365	0.4509 0221	0.3949 2380	0.3459 1402	319
320	0.5869 0672	0.5137 7329	0.4497 7777	0.3937 7529	0.3447 6480	320
321	0.5859 3017	0.5127 0515	0.4486 5613	0.3926 3012	0.3436 1940	321
322	0.5849 5524	0.5116 3924	0.4475 3729	0.3914 8828	0.3424 7781	322
323	0.5839 8194	0.5105 7554	0.4464 2123	0.3903 4976	0.3413 4001	323
324	0.5830 1026	0.5095 1405	0.4453 0796	0.3892 1455	0.3402 0599	324
325	0.5820 4019	0.5084 5477	0.4441 9747	0.3880 8264	0.3390 7574	325
326	0.5810 7174	0.5073 9769	0.4430 8975	0.3869 5402	0.3379 4924	326
327	0.5801 0490	0.5063 4281	0.4419 8478	0.3858 2869	0.3368 2649	327
328	0.5791 3966	0.5052 9012	0.4408 8258	0.3847 0663	0.3357 0746	328
329	0.5781 7604	0.5042 3962	0.4397 8312	0.3835 8783	0.3345 9215	329
330	0.5772 1401	0.5031 9131	0.4386 8640	0.3824 7229	0.3334 8055	330
331	0.5762 5359	0.5021 4517	0.4375 9242	0.3813 5999	0.3323 7264	331
332	0.5752 9477	0.5011 0121	0.4365 0117	0.3802 5092	0.3312 6842	332
333	0.5743 3754	0.5000 5942	0.4354 1264	0.3791 4508	0.3301 6786	333
334	0.5733 8190	0.4990 1980	0.4343 2682	0.3780 4246	0.3290 7095	334
335	0.5724 2785	0.4979 8233	0.4332 4371	0.3769 4304	0.3279 7769	335
336	0.5714 7539	0.4969 4703	0.4321 6330	0.3758 4682	0.3268 8807	336
337	0.5705 2452	0.4959 1387	0.4310 8559	0.3747 5379	0.3258 0206	337
338	0.5695 7523	0.4948 8287	0.4300 1056	0.3736 6394	0.3247 1966	338
339	0.5686 2752	0.4938 5400	0.4289 3822	0.3725 7725	0.3236 4086	339
340	0.5676 8138	0.4928 2728	0.4278 6855	0.3714 9373	0.3225 6564	340
341	0.5667 3682	0.4918 0269	0.4268 0154	0.3704 1336	0.3214 9399	341
342	0.5657 9383	0.4907 8023	0.4257 3720	0.3693 3613	0.3204 2591	342
343	0.5648 5241	0.4897 5990	0.4246 7551	0.3682 6203	0.3193 6137	343
344	0.5639 1255	0.4887 4169	0.4236 1647	0.3671 9106	0.3183 0037	344
345	0.5629 7426	0.4877 2559	0.4225 6007	0.3661 2320	0.3172 4289	345
346	0.5620 3753	0.4867 1161	0.4215 0630	0.3650 5844	0.3161 8893	346
347	0.5611 0236	0.4856 9974	0.4204 5516	0.3639 9679	0.3151 3847	347
348	0.5601 6875	0.4846 8997	0.4194 0665	0.3629 3822	0.3140 9149	348
349	0.5592 3669	0.4836 8229	0.4183 6075	0.3618 8272	0.3130 4800	349
350	0.5583 0618	0.4826 7672	0.4173 1745	0.3608 3030	0.3120 0797	350
351	0.5573 7722	0.4816 7323	0.4162 7676	0.3597 8094	0.3109 7140	351
352	0.5564 4980	0.4806 7183	0.4152 3866	0.3587 3463	0.3099 3828	352
353	0.5555 2393	0.4796 7251	0.4142 0316	0.3576 9137	0.3089 0858	353
354	0.5545 9959	0.4786 7527	0.4131 7023	0.3566 5113	0.3078 8231	354
355	0.5536 7680	0.4776 8011	0.4121 3988	0.3556 1393	0.3068 5944	355
356	0.5527 5554	0.4766 8701	0.4111 1210	0.3545 7974	0.3058 3997	356
357	0.5518 3581	0.4756 9598	0.4100 8688	0.3535 4855	0.3048 2389	357
358	0.5509 1762	0.4747 0700	0.4090 6422	0.3525 2037	0.3038 1119	358
359	0.5500 0095	0.4737 2009	0.4080 4411	0.3514 9517	0.3028 0185	359
360	0.5490 8581	0.4727 3522	0.4070 2655	0.3504 7296	0.3017 9587	360

TABLE II

N	3/8	5/12	11/24	1/2	13/24	N
1	0.9962 6401	0.9958 5062	0.9954 3758	0.9950 2488	0.9946 1252	1
2	0.9925 4198	0.9917 1846	0.9908 9597	0.9900 7450	0.9892 5406	2
3	0.9888 3385	0.9876 0345	0.9863 7509	0.9851 4876	0.9839 2447	3
4	0.9851 3958	0.9835 0551	0.9818 7483	0.9802 4752	0.9786 2359	4
5	0.9814 5911	0.9794 2457	0.9773 9510	0.9753 7067	0.9733 5127	5
6	0.9777 9238	0.9753 6057	0.9729 3581	0.9705 1808	0.9681 0735	6
7	0.9741 3936	0.9713 1343	0.9684 9687	0.9656 8963	0.9628 9169	7
8	0.9704 9999	0.9672 8308	0.9640 7817	0.9608 8520	0.9577 0413	8
9	0.9668 7421	0.9632 6946	0.9596 7964	0.9561 0468	0.9525 4451	9
10	0.9632 6198	0.9592 7249	0.9553 0118	0.9513 4794	0.9474 1269	10
11	0.9596 6324	0.9552 9211	0.9509 4269	0.9466 1487	0.9423 0852	11
12	0.9560 7795	0.9513 2824	0.9466 0409	0.9419 0534	0.9372 3185	12
13	0.9525 0605	0.9473 8082	0.9422 8528	0.9372 1924	0.9321 8253	13
14	0.9489 4750	0.9434 4978	0.9379 8618	0.9325 5646	0.9271 6041	14
15	0.9454 0224	0.9395 3505	0.9337 0669	0.9279 1688	0.9221 6534	15
16	0.9418 7022	0.9356 3657	0.9294 4672	0.9233 0037	0.9171 9719	16
17	0.9383 5141	0.9317 5426	0.9252 0620	0.9187 0684	0.9122 5581	17
18	0.9348 4573	0.9278 8806	0.9209 8502	0.9141 3616	0.9073 4104	18
19	0.9313 5316	0.9240 3790	0.9167 8309	0.9095 8822	0.9024 5276	19
20	0.9278 7363	0.9202 0372	0.9126 0034	0.9050 6290	0.8975 9081	20
21	0.9244 0711	0.9163 8544	0.9084 3667	0.9005 6010	0.8927 5505	21
22	0.9209 5353	0.9125 8301	0.9042 9200	0.8960 7971	0.8879 4535	22
23	0.9175 1286	0.9087 9636	0.9001 6624	0.8916 2160	0.8831 6155	23
24	0.9140 8504	0.9050 2542	0.8960 5930	0.8871 8567	0.8784 0354	24
25	0.9106 7003	0.9012 7013	0.8919 7110	0.8827 7181	0.8736 7115	25
26	0.9072 6777	0.8975 3042	0.8879 0155	0.8783 7991	0.8689 6426	26
27	0.9038 7823	0.8938 0623	0.8838 5057	0.8740 0986	0.8642 8273	27
28	0.9005 0135	0.8900 9749	0.8798 1807	0.8696 6155	0.8596 2642	28
29	0.8971 3709	0.8864 0414	0.8758 0397	0.8653 3488	0.8549 9520	29
30	0.8937 8539	0.8827 2611	0.8718 0818	0.8610 2973	0.8503 8892	30
31	0.8904 4622	0.8790 6335	0.8678 3062	0.8567 4600	0.8458 0747	31
32	0.8871 1952	0.8754 1578	0.8638 7121	0.8524 8358	0.8412 5069	32
33	0.8838 0525	0.8717 8335	0.8599 2987	0.8482 4237	0.8367 1847	33
34	0.8805 0336	0.8681 6599	0.8560 0651	0.8440 2226	0.8322 1066	34
35	0.8772 1381	0.8645 6365	0.8521 0104	0.8398 2314	0.8277 2714	35
36	0.8739 3655	0.8609 7624	0.8482 1340	0.8356 4492	0.8232 6777	36
37	0.8706 7153	0.8574 0373	0.8443 4349	0.8314 8748	0.8188 3243	37
38	0.8674 1871	0.8538 4604	0.8404 9124	0.8273 5073	0.8144 2098	38
39	0.8641 7804	0.8503 0311	0.8366 5656	0.8232 3455	0.8100 3330	39
40	0.8609 4948	0.8467 7488	0.8328 3938	0.8191 3886	0.8056 6926	40
41	0.8577 3298	0.8432 6129	0.8290 3962	0.8150 6354	0.8013 2873	41
42	0.8545 2850	0.8397 6228	0.8252 5719	0.8110 0850	0.7970 1158	42
43	0.8513 3599	0.8362 7779	0.8214 9202	0.8069 7363	0.7927 1769	43
44	0.8481 5541	0.8328 0776	0.8177 4402	0.8029 5884	0.7884 4694	44
45	0.8449 8671	0.8293 5212	0.8140 1313	0.7989 6402	0.7841 9919	45
46	0.8418 2985	0.8259 1083	0.8102 9926	0.7949 8907	0.7799 7433	46
47	0.8386 8478	0.8224 8381	0.8066 0233	0.7910 3390	0.7757 7223	47
48	0.8355 5146	0.8190 7102	0.8029 2227	0.7870 9841	0.7715 9277	48
49	0.8324 2985	0.8156 7238	0.7992 5900	0.7831 8250	0.7674 3583	49
50	0.8293 1990	0.8122 8785	0.7956 1244	0.7792 8607	0.7633 0128	50
51	0.8262 2157	0.8089 1736	0.7919 8252	0.7754 0902	0.7591 8901	51
52	0.8231 3481	0.8055 6086	0.7883 6916	0.7715 5127	0.7550 9889	52
53	0.8200 5959	0.8022 1828	0.7847 7229	0.7677 1270	0.7510 3080	53
54	0.8169 9585	0.7988 8957	0.7811 9183	0.7638 9324	0.7469 8464	54
55	0.8139 4357	0.7955 7468	0.7776 2770	0.7600 9277	0.7429 6027	55
56	0.8109 0268	0.7922 7354	0.7740 7984	0.7563 1122	0.7389 5758	56
57	0.8078 7316	0.7889 8610	0.7705 4816	0.7525 4847	0.7349 7646	57
58	0.8048 5495	0.7857 1230	0.7670 3259	0.7488 0445	0.7310 1678	58
59	0.8018 4802	0.7824 5208	0.7635 3306	0.7450 7906	0.7270 7844	59
60	0.7988 5232	0.7792 0539	0.7600 4950	0.7413 7220	0.7231 6132	60

TABLE II

N	3/8	5/12	11/24	1/2	13/24	N
61	0.7958 6782	0.7759 7217	0.7565 8184	0.7376 8378	0.7192 6530	61
62	0.7928 9447	0.7727 5237	0.7531 2999	0.7340 1371	0.7153 9027	62
63	0.7899 3222	0.7695 4593	0.7496 9389	0.7303 6190	0.7115 3611	63
64	0.7869 8104	0.7663 5279	0.7462 7347	0.7267 2826	0.7077 0272	64
65	0.7840 4089	0.7631 7291	0.7428 6866	0.7231 1269	0.7038 8999	65
66	0.7811 1172	0.7600 0621	0.7394 7938	0.7195 1512	0.7000 9779	66
67	0.7781 9349	0.7568 5266	0.7361 0556	0.7159 3544	0.6963 2602	67
68	0.7752 8617	0.7537 1219	0.7327 4714	0.7123 7357	0.6925 7458	68
69	0.7723 8971	0.7505 8476	0.7294 0404	0.7088 2943	0.6888 4334	69
70	0.7695 0407	0.7474 7030	0.7260 7619	0.7053 0291	0.6851 3221	70
71	0.7666 2921	0.7443 6876	0.7227 6352	0.7017 9394	0.6814 4107	71
72	0.7637 6509	0.7412 8009	0.7194 6597	0.6983 0243	0.6777 6982	72
73	0.7609 1167	0.7382 0424	0.7161 8346	0.6948 2829	0.6741 1834	73
74	0.7580 6891	0.7351 4115	0.7129 1593	0.6913 7143	0.6704 8654	74
75	0.7552 3677	0.7320 9078	0.7096 6331	0.6879 3177	0.6668 7431	75
76	0.7524 1522	0.7290 5306	0.7064 2552	0.6845 0923	0.6632 8153	76
77	0.7496 0420	0.7260 2794	0.7032 0251	0.6811 0371	0.6597 0811	77
78	0.7468 0369	0.7230 1537	0.6999 9420	0.6777 1513	0.6561 5395	78
79	0.7440 1364	0.7200 1531	0.6968 0053	0.6743 4342	0.6526 1893	79
80	0.7412 3401	0.7170 2770	0.6936 2144	0.6709 8847	0.6491 0295	80
81	0.7384 6477	0.7140 5248	0.6904 5684	0.6676 5022	0.6456 0592	81
82	0.7357 0587	0.7110 8960	0.6873 0669	0.6643 2858	0.6421 2773	82
83	0.7329 5728	0.7081 3902	0.6841 7090	0.6610 2346	0.6386 6827	83
84	0.7302 1896	0.7052 0069	0.6810 4943	0.6577 3479	0.6352 2746	84
85	0.7274 9087	0.7022 7454	0.6779 4219	0.6544 6248	0.6318 0518	85
86	0.7247 7297	0.6993 6054	0.6748 4913	0.6512 0644	0.6284 0134	86
87	0.7220 6522	0.6964 5863	0.6717 7019	0.6479 6661	0.6250 1584	87
88	0.7193 6760	0.6935 6876	0.6687 0529	0.6447 4290	0.6216 4858	88
89	0.7166 8005	0.6906 9088	0.6656 5437	0.6415 3522	0.6182 9945	89
90	0.7140 0254	0.6878 2495	0.6626 1738	0.6383 4350	0.6149 6837	90
91	0.7113 3503	0.6849 7090	0.6595 9424	0.6351 6766	0.6116 5524	91
92	0.7086 7749	0.6821 2870	0.6565 8489	0.6320 0763	0.6083 5996	92
93	0.7060 2988	0.6792 9829	0.6535 8927	0.6288 6331	0.6050 8243	93
94	0.7033 9216	0.6764 7962	0.6506 0732	0.6257 3464	0.6018 2256	94
95	0.7007 6429	0.6736 7265	0.6476 3897	0.6226 2153	0.5985 8025	95
96	0.6981 4624	0.6708 7733	0.6446 8417	0.6195 2391	0.5953 5541	96
97	0.6955 3797	0.6680 9361	0.6417 4285	0.6164 4170	0.5921 4794	97
98	0.6929 3945	0.6653 2143	0.6388 1495	0.6133 7483	0.5889 5775	98
99	0.6903 5064	0.6625 6076	0.6359 0041	0.6103 2321	0.5857 8475	99
100	0.6877 7149	0.6598 1155	0.6329 9916	0.6072 8678	0.5826 2884	100
101	0.6852 0199	0.6570 7374	0.6301 1115	0.6042 6545	0.5794 8994	101
102	0.6826 4208	0.6543 4730	0.6272 3632	0.6012 5915	0.5763 6795	102
103	0.6800 9173	0.6516 3216	0.6243 7460	0.5982 6781	0.5732 6277	103
104	0.6775 5092	0.6489 2829	0.6215 2594	0.5952 9136	0.5701 7433	104
105	0.6750 1959	0.6462 3565	0.6186 9028	0.5923 2971	0.5671 0252	105
106	0.6724 9773	0.6435 5417	0.6158 6755	0.5893 8279	0.5640 4727	106
107	0.6699 8528	0.6408 8382	0.6130 5770	0.5864 5054	0.5610 0847	107
108	0.6674 8223	0.6382 2455	0.6102 6067	0.5835 3288	0.5579 8605	108
109	0.6649 8852	0.6355 7632	0.6074 7641	0.5806 2973	0.5549 7991	109
110	0.6625 0413	0.6329 3907	0.6047 0484	0.5777 4102	0.5519 8996	110
111	0.6600 2902	0.6303 1277	0.6019 4592	0.5748 6669	0.5490 1612	111
112	0.6575 6316	0.6276 9736	0.5991 9959	0.5720 0666	0.5460 5831	112
113	0.6551 0651	0.6250 9281	0.5964 6579	0.5691 6085	0.5431 1643	113
114	0.6526 5904	0.6224 9906	0.5937 4446	0.5663 2921	0.5401 9039	114
115	0.6502 2071	0.6199 1608	0.5910 3555	0.5635 1165	0.5372 8013	115
116	0.6477 9149	0.6173 4381	0.5883 3900	0.5607 0811	0.5343 8554	116
117	0.6453 7135	0.6147 8222	0.5856 5474	0.5579 1852	0.5315 0655	117
118	0.6429 6025	0.6122 3126	0.5829 8274	0.5551 4280	0.5286 4306	118
119	0.6405 5815	0.6096 9088	0.5803 2293	0.5523 8090	0.5257 9501	119
120	0.6381 6504	0.6071 6104	0.5776 7525	0.5496 3273	0.5229 6229	120

TABLE II

N	3/8	5/12	11/24	1/2	13/24	N
121	0.6357 8086	0.6046 4170	0.5750 3965	0.5468 9824	0.5201 4484	121
122	0.6334 0559	0.6021 3281	0.5724 1608	0.5441 7736	0.5173 4257	122
123	0.6310 3919	0.5996 3434	0.5698 0447	0.5414 7001	0.5145 5539	123
124	0.6286 8163	0.5971 4623	0.5672 0478	0.5387 7612	0.5117 8324	124
125	0.6263 3288	0.5946 6844	0.5646 1696	0.5360 9565	0.5090 2601	125
126	0.6239 9291	0.5922 0094	0.5620 4094	0.5334 2850	0.5062 8364	126
127	0.6216 6168	0.5897 4367	0.5594 7667	0.5307 7463	0.5035 5605	127
128	0.6193 3916	0.5872 9660	0.5569 2410	0.5281 3396	0.5008 4315	128
129	0.6170 2531	0.5848 5969	0.5543 8318	0.5255 0643	0.4981 4486	129
130	0.6147 2011	0.5824 3288	0.5518 5385	0.5228 9197	0.4954 6111	130
131	0.6124 2352	0.5800 1615	0.5493 3606	0.5202 9052	0.4927 9182	131
132	0.6101 3552	0.5776 0944	0.5468 2975	0.5177 0201	0.4901 3692	132
133	0.6078 5606	0.5752 1273	0.5443 3488	0.5151 2637	0.4874 9631	133
134	0.6055 8511	0.5728 2595	0.5418 5140	0.5125 6356	0.4848 6993	134
135	0.6033 2265	0.5704 4908	0.5393 7924	0.5100 1349	0.4822 5770	135
136	0.6010 6864	0.5680 8207	0.5369 1837	0.5074 7611	0.4796 5955	136
137	0.5988 2306	0.5657 2488	0.5344 6872	0.5049 5135	0.4770 7539	137
138	0.5965 8586	0.5633 7748	0.5320 3025	0.5024 3916	0.4745 0515	138
139	0.5943 5702	0.5610 3981	0.5296 0290	0.4999 3946	0.4719 4876	139
140	0.5921 3651	0.5587 1185	0.5271 8663	0.4974 5220	0.4694 0615	140
141	0.5899 2429	0.5563 9354	0.5247 8138	0.4949 7731	0.4668 7723	141
142	0.5877 2034	0.5540 8485	0.5223 8711	0.4925 1474	0.4643 6193	142
143	0.5855 2463	0.5517 8574	0.5200 0376	0.4900 6442	0.4618 6019	143
144	0.5833 3711	0.5494 9618	0.5176 3128	0.4876 2628	0.4593 7193	144
145	0.5811 5777	0.5472 1611	0.5152 6963	0.4852 0028	0.4568 9707	145
146	0.5789 8657	0.5449 4550	0.5129 1875	0.4827 8635	0.4544 3554	146
147	0.5768 2348	0.5426 8432	0.5105 7860	0.4803 8443	0.4519 8728	147
148	0.5746 6848	0.5404 3252	0.5082 4912	0.4779 9446	0.4495 5220	148
149	0.5725 2152	0.5381 9006	0.5059 3028	0.4756 1637	0.4471 3025	149
150	0.5703 8258	0.5359 5690	0.5036 2201	0.4732 5012	0.4447 2134	150
151	0.5682 5164	0.5337 3302	0.5013 2427	0.4708 9565	0.4423 2541	151
152	0.5661 2866	0.5315 1836	0.4990 3702	0.4685 5288	0.4399 4239	152
153	0.5640 1361	0.5293 1289	0.4967 6020	0.4662 2177	0.4375 7221	153
154	0.5619 0646	0.5271 1657	0.4944 9377	0.4639 0226	0.4352 1479	154
155	0.5598 0718	0.5249 2936	0.4922 3768	0.4615 9429	0.4328 7008	155
156	0.5577 1575	0.5227 5123	0.4899 9189	0.4592 9780	0.4305 3800	156
157	0.5556 3213	0.5205 8214	0.4877 5634	0.4570 1274	0.4282 1848	157
158	0.5535 5629	0.5184 2205	0.4855 3099	0.4547 3904	0.4259 1146	158
159	0.5514 8821	0.5162 7092	0.4833 1579	0.4524 7666	0.4236 1687	159
160	0.5494 2786	0.5141 2872	0.4811 1070	0.4502 2553	0.4213 3464	160
161	0.5473 7520	0.5119 9540	0.4789 1567	0.4479 8560	0.4190 6471	161
162	0.5453 3021	0.5098 7094	0.4767 3065	0.4457 5682	0.4168 0700	162
163	0.5432 9286	0.5077 5529	0.4745 5561	0.4435 3912	0.4145 6146	163
164	0.5412 6313	0.5056 4842	0.4723 9048	0.4413 3246	0.4123 2802	164
165	0.5392 4097	0.5035 5030	0.4702 3524	0.4391 3678	0.4101 0661	165
166	0.5372 2637	0.5014 6088	0.4680 8983	0.4369 5202	0.4078 9717	166
167	0.5352 1930	0.4993 8013	0.4659 5420	0.4347 7813	0.4056 9963	167
168	0.5332 1973	0.4973 0801	0.4638 2832	0.4326 1505	0.4035 1393	168
169	0.5312 2762	0.4952 4449	0.4617 1214	0.4304 6274	0.4013 4000	169
170	0.5292 4296	0.4931 8954	0.4596 0562	0.4283 2113	0.3991 7779	170
171	0.5272 6572	0.4911 4311	0.4575 0870	0.4261 9018	0.3970 2722	171
172	0.5252 9586	0.4891 0517	0.4554 2135	0.4240 6983	0.3948 8825	172
173	0.5233 3336	0.4870 7569	0.4533 4353	0.4219 6003	0.3927 6079	173
174	0.5213 7819	0.4850 5462	0.4512 7518	0.4198 6073	0.3906 4480	174
175	0.5194 3032	0.4830 4195	0.4492 1628	0.4177 7187	0.3885 4021	175
176	0.5174 8974	0.4810 3763	0.4471 6676	0.4156 9340	0.3864 4695	176
177	0.5155 5640	0.4790 4162	0.4451 2660	0.4136 2528	0.3843 6497	177
178	0.5136 3029	0.4770 5390	0.4430 9574	0.4115 6744	0.3822 9421	178
179	0.5117 1137	0.4750 7442	0.4410 7415	0.4095 1984	0.3802 3461	179
180	0.5097 9962	0.4731 0316	0.4390 6179	0.4074 8243	0.3781 8610	180

TABLE II

N	3/8	5/12	11/24	1/2	13/24	N
181	0.5078 9501	0.4711 4007	0.4370 5860	0.4054 5515	0.3761 4863	181
182	0.5059 9752	0.4691 8513	0.4350 6456	0.4034 3796	0.3741 2214	182
183	0.5041 0712	0.4672 3831	0.4330 7961	0.4014 3081	0.3721 0656	183
184	0.5022 2378	0.4652 9956	0.4311 0372	0.3994 3364	0.3701 0184	184
185	0.5003 4748	0.4633 6886	0.4291 3684	0.3974 4641	0.3681 0792	185
186	0.4984 7819	0.4614 4616	0.4271 7893	0.3954 6906	0.3661 2475	186
187	0.4966 1588	0.4595 3145	0.4252 2996	0.3935 0155	0.3641 5225	187
188	0.4947 6053	0.4576 2468	0.4232 8989	0.3915 4383	0.3621 9039	188
189	0.4929 1211	0.4557 2582	0.4213 5866	0.3895 9586	0.3602 3909	189
190	0.4910 7059	0.4538 3484	0.4194 3624	0.3876 5757	0.3582 9831	190
191	0.4892 3596	0.4519 5171	0.4175 2260	0.3857 2892	0.3563 6799	191
192	0.4874 0817	0.4500 7639	0.4156 1768	0.3838 0987	0.3544 4806	192
193	0.4855 8722	0.4482 0886	0.4137 2146	0.3819 0037	0.3525 3848	193
194	0.4837 7307	0.4463 4907	0.4118 3389	0.3800 0037	0.3506 3918	194
195	0.4819 6570	0.4444 9700	0.4099 5493	0.3781 0982	0.3487 5012	195
196	0.4801 6508	0.4426 5261	0.4080 8454	0.3762 2868	0.3468 7123	196
197	0.4783 7119	0.4408 1588	0.4062 2269	0.3743 5689	0.3450 0247	197
198	0.4765 8400	0.4389 8677	0.4043 6933	0.3724 9442	0.3431 4377	198
199	0.4748 0349	0.4371 6525	0.4025 2442	0.3706 4121	0.3412 9509	199
200	0.4730 2963	0.4353 5128	0.4006 8794	0.3687 9723	0.3394 5637	200
201	0.4712 6239	0.4335 4484	0.3988 5983	0.3669 6242	0.3376 2755	201
202	0.4695 0176	0.4317 4590	0.3970 4006	0.3651 3673	0.3358 0859	202
203	0.4677 4771	0.4299 5443	0.3952 2860	0.3633 2013	0.3339 9943	203
204	0.4660 0021	0.4281 7038	0.3934 2540	0.3615 1257	0.3322 0001	204
205	0.4642 5923	0.4263 9374	0.3916 3042	0.3597 1400	0.3304 1029	205
206	0.4625 2477	0.4246 2447	0.3898 4364	0.3579 2438	0.3286 3021	206
207	0.4607 9678	0.4228 6255	0.3880 6501	0.3561 4366	0.3268 5972	207
208	0.4590 7525	0.4211 0793	0.3862 9449	0.3543 7180	0.3250 9876	208
209	0.4573 6015	0.4193 6059	0.3845 3205	0.3526 0876	0.3233 4730	209
210	0.4556 5145	0.4176 2051	0.3827 7766	0.3508 5448	0.3216 0527	210
211	0.4539 4914	0.4158 8764	0.3810 3126	0.3491 0894	0.3198 7263	211
212	0.4522 5319	0.4141 6197	0.3792 9284	0.3473 7208	0.3181 4932	212
213	0.4505 6358	0.4124 4345	0.3775 6234	0.3456 4386	0.3164 3529	213
214	0.4488 8028	0.4107 3207	0.3758 3975	0.3439 2424	0.3147 3050	214
215	0.4472 0327	0.4090 2779	0.3741 2501	0.3422 1317	0.3130 3490	215
216	0.4455 3252	0.4073 3058	0.3724 1809	0.3405 1062	0.3113 4843	216
217	0.4438 6802	0.4056 4041	0.3707 1896	0.3388 1654	0.3096 7104	217
218	0.4422 0973	0.4039 5725	0.3690 2758	0.3371 3088	0.3080 0270	218
219	0.4405 5764	0.4022 8108	0.3673 4393	0.3354 5361	0.3063 4334	219
220	0.4389 1172	0.4006 1187	0.3656 6795	0.3337 8469	0.3046 9292	220
221	0.4372 7195	0.3989 4958	0.3639 9962	0.3321 2407	0.3030 5139	221
222	0.4356 3831	0.3972 9418	0.3623 3890	0.3304 7171	0.3014 1870	222
223	0.4340 1077	0.3956 4566	0.3606 8575	0.3288 2757	0.2997 9481	223
224	0.4323 8931	0.3940 0398	0.3590 4015	0.3271 9162	0.2981 7967	224
225	0.4307 7390	0.3923 6911	0.3574 0206	0.3255 6380	0.2965 7324	225
226	0.4291 6454	0.3907 4102	0.3557 7144	0.3239 4408	0.2949 7545	226
227	0.4275 6118	0.3891 1969	0.3541 4826	0.3223 3241	0.2933 8628	227
228	0.4259 6382	0.3875 0508	0.3525 3249	0.3207 2877	0.2918 0566	228
229	0.4243 7242	0.3858 9718	0.3509 2408	0.3191 3311	0.2902 3356	229
230	0.4227 8697	0.3842 9594	0.3493 2302	0.3175 4538	0.2886 6994	230
231	0.4212 0744	0.3827 0136	0.3477 2926	0.3159 6555	0.2871 1473	231
232	0.4196 3382	0.3811 1338	0.3461 4277	0.3143 9358	0.2855 6790	232
233	0.4180 6607	0.3795 3200	0.3445 6352	0.3128 2944	0.2840 2941	233
234	0.4165 0418	0.3779 5718	0.3429 9148	0.3112 7307	0.2824 9921	234
235	0.4149 4812	0.3763 8889	0.3414 2661	0.3097 2445	0.2809 7725	235
236	0.4133 9788	0.3748 2711	0.3398 6888	0.3081 8353	0.2794 6349	236
237	0.4118 5343	0.3732 7181	0.3383 1825	0.3066 5028	0.2779 5788	237
238	0.4103 1475	0.3717 2297	0.3367 7470	0.3051 2466	0.2764 6039	238
239	0.4087 8182	0.3701 8055	0.3352 3819	0.3036 0662	0.2749 7096	239
240	0.4072 5461	0.3686 4453	0.3337 0869	0.3020 9614	0.2734 8956	240

TABLE II

N	3/8	5/12	11/24	1/2	13/24	N
241	0.4057 3311	0.3671 1488	0.3321 8617	0.3005 9318	0.2720 1614	241
242	0.4042 1730	0.3655 9159	0.3306 7060	0.2990 9769	0.2705 5066	242
243	0.4027 0715	0.3640 7461	0.3291 6194	0.2976 0964	0.2690 9307	243
244	0.4012 0264	0.3625 6392	0.3276 6016	0.2961 2899	0.2676 4333	244
245	0.3997 0375	0.3610 5951	0.3261 6524	0.2946 5572	0.2662 0141	245
246	0.3982 1046	0.3595 6134	0.3246 7714	0.2931 8977	0.2647 6725	246
247	0.3967 2275	0.3580 6938	0.3231 9582	0.2917 3111	0.2633 4082	247
248	0.3952 4060	0.3565 8362	0.3217 2127	0.2902 7971	0.2619 2208	248
249	0.3937 6398	0.3551 0402	0.3202 5344	0.2888 3553	0.2605 1098	249
250	0.3922 9288	0.3536 3056	0.3187 9231	0.2873 9854	0.2591 0748	250
251	0.3908 2728	0.3521 6321	0.3173 3784	0.2859 6870	0.2577 1154	251
252	0.3893 6715	0.3507 0195	0.3158 9001	0.2845 4597	0.2563 2313	252
253	0.3879 1248	0.3492 4676	0.3144 4879	0.2831 3032	0.2549 4219	253
254	0.3864 6324	0.3477 9760	0.3130 1414	0.2817 2171	0.2535 6869	254
255	0.3850 1942	0.3463 5446	0.3115 8604	0.2803 2011	0.2522 0259	255
256	0.3835 8099	0.3449 1730	0.3101 6445	0.2789 2548	0.2508 4386	256
257	0.3821 4794	0.3434 8611	0.3087 4935	0.2775 3779	0.2494 9244	257
258	0.3807 2024	0.3420 6086	0.3073 4071	0.2761 5701	0.2481 4830	258
259	0.3792 9787	0.3406 4152	0.3059 3849	0.2747 8309	0.2468 1141	259
260	0.3778 8082	0.3392 2807	0.3045 4267	0.2734 1601	0.2454 8172	260
261	0.3764 6906	0.3378 2048	0.3031 5321	0.2720 5573	0.2441 5919	261
262	0.3750 6257	0.3364 1874	0.3017 7010	0.2707 0222	0.2428 4378	262
263	0.3736 6134	0.3350 2281	0.3003 9330	0.2693 5544	0.2415 3547	263
264	0.3722 6535	0.3336 3267	0.2990 2278	0.2680 1537	0.2402 3420	264
265	0.3708 7457	0.3322 4830	0.2976 5851	0.2666 8196	0.2389 3994	265
266	0.3694 8898	0.3308 6968	0.2963 0047	0.2653 5518	0.2376 5265	266
267	0.3681 0858	0.3294 9678	0.2949 4862	0.2640 3501	0.2363 7230	267
268	0.3667 3333	0.3281 2957	0.2936 0294	0.2627 2140	0.2350 9885	268
269	0.3653 6322	0.3267 6804	0.2922 6340	0.2614 1433	0.2338 3226	269
270	0.3639 9822	0.3254 1215	0.2909 2997	0.2601 1376	0.2325 7249	270
271	0.3626 3833	0.3240 6189	0.2896 0262	0.2588 1966	0.2313 1951	271
272	0.3612 8352	0.3227 1724	0.2882 8133	0.2575 3200	0.2300 7328	272
273	0.3599 3376	0.3213 7816	0.2869 6607	0.2562 5075	0.2288 3377	273
274	0.3585 8905	0.3200 4464	0.2856 5681	0.2549 7587	0.2276 0093	274
275	0.3572 4937	0.3187 1666	0.2843 5353	0.2537 0733	0.2263 7473	275
276	0.3559 1469	0.3173 9418	0.2830 5618	0.2524 4511	0.2251 5514	276
277	0.3545 8500	0.3160 7719	0.2817 6476	0.2511 8916	0.2239 4212	277
278	0.3532 6027	0.3147 6567	0.2804 7923	0.2499 3946	0.2227 3564	278
279	0.3519 4049	0.3134 5959	0.2791 9957	0.2486 9598	0.2215 3565	279
280	0.3506 2565	0.3121 5893	0.2779 2574	0.2474 5869	0.2203 4213	280
281	0.3493 1571	0.3108 6366	0.2766 5773	0.2462 2755	0.2191 5504	281
282	0.3480 1067	0.3095 7377	0.2753 9550	0.2450 0254	0.2179 7435	282
283	0.3467 1051	0.3082 8923	0.2741 3903	0.2437 8362	0.2168 0001	283
284	0.3454 1520	0.3070 1002	0.2728 8829	0.2425 7077	0.2156 3201	284
285	0.3441 2473	0.3057 3612	0.2716 4326	0.2413 6395	0.2144 7029	285
286	0.3428 3909	0.3044 6751	0.2704 0391	0.2401 6313	0.2133 1484	286
287	0.3415 5824	0.3032 0416	0.2691 7021	0.2389 6829	0.2121 6561	287
288	0.3402 8219	0.3019 4605	0.2679 4214	0.2377 7939	0.2110 2257	288
289	0.3390 1089	0.3006 9316	0.2667 1968	0.2365 9641	0.2098 8569	289
290	0.3377 4435	0.2994 4547	0.2655 0279	0.2354 1931	0.2087 5493	290
291	0.3364 8254	0.2982 0296	0.2642 9145	0.2342 4807	0.2076 3027	291
292	0.3352 2545	0.2969 6560	0.2630 8564	0.2330 8266	0.2065 1166	292
293	0.3339 7305	0.2957 3338	0.2618 8534	0.2319 2305	0.2053 9908	293
294	0.3327 2533	0.2945 0627	0.2606 9050	0.2307 6920	0.2042 9250	294
295	0.3314 8227	0.2932 8425	0.2595 0112	0.2296 2109	0.2031 9188	295
296	0.3302 4386	0.2920 6731	0.2583 1717	0.2284 7870	0.2020 9718	296
297	0.3290 1007	0.2908 5541	0.2571 3862	0.2273 4199	0.2010 0839	297
298	0.3277 8089	0.2896 4854	0.2559 6544	0.2262 1094	0.1999 2546	298
299	0.3265 5630	0.2884 4668	0.2547 9762	0.2250 8551	0.1988 4836	299
300	0.3253 3629	0.2872 4980	0.2536 3513	0.2239 6568	0.1977 7707	300

TABLE II

N	3/8	5/12	11/24	1/2	13/24	N
301	0.3241 2084	0.2860 5790	0.2524 7794	0.2228 5142	0.1967 1155	301
302	0.3229 0993	0.2848 7093	0.2513 2603	0.2217 4271	0.1956 5177	302
303	0.3217 0354	0.2836 8890	0.2501 7937	0.2206 3951	0.1945 9770	303
304	0.3205 0166	0.2825 1176	0.2490 3795	0.2195 4180	0.1935 4931	304
305	0.3193 0427	0.2813 3952	0.2479 0173	0.2184 4955	0.1925 0656	305
306	0.3181 1135	0.2801 7213	0.2467 7070	0.2173 6274	0.1914 6944	306
307	0.3169 2289	0.2790 0959	0.2456 4483	0.2162 8133	0.1904 3790	307
308	0.3157 3887	0.2778 5188	0.2445 2409	0.2152 0531	0.1894 1192	308
309	0.3145 5927	0.2766 9896	0.2434 0847	0.2141 3463	0.1883 9146	309
310	0.3133 8408	0.2755 5084	0.2422 9794	0.2130 6929	0.1873 7651	310
311	0.3122 1328	0.2744 0747	0.2411 9247	0.2120 0924	0.1863 6702	311
312	0.3110 4685	0.2732 6885	0.2400 9205	0.2109 5447	0.1853 6297	312
313	0.3098 8479	0.2721 3496	0.2389 9665	0.2099 0495	0.1843 6433	313
314	0.3087 2706	0.2710 0576	0.2379 0624	0.2088 6064	0.1833 7107	314
315	0.3075 7366	0.2698 8126	0.2368 2081	0.2078 2153	0.1823 8316	315
316	0.3064 2457	0.2687 6142	0.2357 4034	0.2067 8760	0.1814 0057	316
317	0.3052 7977	0.2676 4623	0.2346 6479	0.2057 5880	0.1804 2328	317
318	0.3041 3925	0.2665 3566	0.2335 9415	0.2047 3513	0.1794 5125	318
319	0.3030 0298	0.2654 2971	0.2325 2840	0.2037 1654	0.1784 8446	319
320	0.3018 7097	0.2643 2834	0.2314 6750	0.2027 0303	0.1775 2288	320
321	0.3007 4318	0.2632 3154	0.2304 1145	0.2016 9456	0.1765 6648	321
322	0.2996 1961	0.2621 3929	0.2293 6022	0.2006 9110	0.1756 1523	322
323	0.2985 0023	0.2610 5158	0.2283 1378	0.1996 9264	0.1746 6911	323
324	0.2973 8504	0.2599 6838	0.2272 7211	0.1986 9914	0.1737 2808	324
325	0.2962 7401	0.2588 8967	0.2262 3520	0.1977 1059	0.1727 9212	325
326	0.2951 6713	0.2578 1544	0.2252 0302	0.1967 2695	0.1718 6121	326
327	0.2940 6439	0.2567 4566	0.2241 7555	0.1957 4821	0.1709 3531	327
328	0.2929 6577	0.2556 8033	0.2231 5277	0.1947 7434	0.1700 1440	328
329	0.2918 7125	0.2546 1941	0.2221 3465	0.1938 0531	0.1690 9845	329
330	0.2907 8083	0.2535 6290	0.2211 2118	0.1928 4111	0.1681 8743	330
331	0.2896 9447	0.2525 1077	0.2201 1233	0.1918 8170	0.1672 8132	331
332	0.2886 1218	0.2514 6301	0.2191 0808	0.1909 2707	0.1663 8010	332
333	0.2875 3392	0.2504 1960	0.2181 0842	0.1899 7718	0.1654 8373	333
334	0.2864 5970	0.2493 8051	0.2171 1332	0.1890 3202	0.1645 9219	334
335	0.2853 8949	0.2483 4574	0.2161 2276	0.1880 9156	0.1637 0545	335
336	0.2843 2328	0.2473 1526	0.2151 3671	0.1871 5578	0.1628 2349	336
337	0.2832 6105	0.2462 8905	0.2141 5517	0.1862 2466	0.1619 4628	337
338	0.2822 0279	0.2452 6711	0.2131 7810	0.1852 9817	0.1610 7380	338
339	0.2811 4848	0.2442 4940	0.2122 0549	0.1843 7629	0.1602 0601	339
340	0.2800 9811	0.2432 3592	0.2112 3732	0.1834 5899	0.1593 4291	340
341	0.2790 5167	0.2422 2664	0.2102 7357	0.1825 4626	0.1584 8445	341
342	0.2780 0913	0.2412 2155	0.2093 1421	0.1816 3807	0.1576 3062	342
343	0.2769 7050	0.2402 2063	0.2083 5923	0.1807 3440	0.1567 8138	343
344	0.2759 3574	0.2392 2387	0.2074 0861	0.1798 3522	0.1559 3673	344
345	0.2749 0484	0.2382 3124	0.2064 6232	0.1789 4052	0.1550 9662	345
346	0.2738 7780	0.2372 4272	0.2055 2036	0.1780 5027	0.1542 6104	346
347	0.2728 5460	0.2362 5831	0.2045 8268	0.1771 6445	0.1534 2996	347
348	0.2718 3521	0.2352 7799	0.2036 4929	0.1762 8303	0.1526 0336	348
349	0.2708 1964	0.2343 0173	0.2027 2016	0.1754 0600	0.1517 8121	349
350	0.2698 0786	0.2333 2953	0.2017 9526	0.1745 3333	0.1509 6349	350
351	0.2687 9986	0.2323 6135	0.2008 7459	0.1736 6501	0.1501 5018	351
352	0.2677 9563	0.2313 9720	0.1999 5811	0.1728 0100	0.1493 4125	352
353	0.2667 9515	0.2304 3704	0.1990 4582	0.1719 4130	0.1485 3667	353
354	0.2657 9840	0.2294 8087	0.1981 3769	0.1710 8587	0.1477 3643	354
355	0.2648 0538	0.2285 2867	0.1972 3370	0.1702 3469	0.1469 4051	355
356	0.2638 1607	0.2275 8042	0.1963 3384	0.1693 8776	0.1461 4887	356
357	0.2628 3046	0.2266 3610	0.1954 3808	0.1685 4503	0.1453 6149	357
358	0.2618 4853	0.2256 9570	0.1945 4641	0.1677 0650	0.1445 7836	358
359	0.2608 7026	0.2247 5921	0.1936 5881	0.1668 7214	0.1437 9944	359
360	0.2598 9565	0.2238 2660	0.1927 7525	0.1660 4193	0.1430 2473	360

TABLE II

N	7/12	5/8	2/3	17/24	3/4	N
1	0.9942 0050	0.9937 8882	0.9933 7748	0.9929 6649	0.9925 5583	1
2	0.9884 3463	0.9876 1622	0.9867 9882	0.9859 8245	0.9851 6708	2
3	0.9827 0220	0.9814 8196	0.9802 6373	0.9790 4753	0.9778 3333	3
4	0.9770 0301	0.9753 8580	0.9737 7192	0.9721 6138	0.9705 5417	4
5	0.9713 3688	0.9693 2750	0.9673 2310	0.9653 2367	0.9633 2920	5
6	0.9657 0361	0.9633 0683	0.9609 1699	0.9585 3406	0.9561 5802	6
7	0.9601 0301	0.9573 2356	0.9545 5330	0.9517 9220	0.9490 4022	7
8	0.9545 3489	0.9513 7745	0.9482 3175	0.9450 9775	0.9419 7540	8
9	0.9489 9906	0.9454 6827	0.9419 5207	0.9384 5040	0.9349 6318	9
10	0.9434 9534	0.9395 9580	0.9357 1398	0.9318 4979	0.9280 0315	10
11	0.9380 2354	0.9337 5980	0.9295 1720	0.9252 9562	0.9210 9494	11
12	0.9325 8347	0.9279 6005	0.9233 6145	0.9187 8754	0.9142 3815	12
13	0.9271 7495	0.9221 9632	0.9172 4648	0.9123 2523	0.9074 3241	13
14	0.9217 9779	0.9164 6840	0.9111 7200	0.9059 0838	0.9006 7733	14
15	0.9164 5182	0.9107 7604	0.9051 3775	0.8995 3666	0.8939 7254	15
16	0.9111 3686	0.9051 1905	0.8991 4346	0.8932 0976	0.8873 1766	16
17	0.9058 5272	0.8994 9719	0.8931 8886	0.8869 2736	0.8807 1231	17
18	0.9005 9922	0.8939 1025	0.8872 7371	0.8806 8915	0.8741 5614	18
19	0.8953 7619	0.8883 5802	0.8813 9772	0.8744 9481	0.8676 4878	19
20	0.8901 8346	0.8828 4027	0.8755 6065	0.8683 4404	0.8611 8985	20
21	0.8850 2084	0.8773 5679	0.8697 6224	0.8622 3653	0.8547 7901	21
22	0.8798 8815	0.8719 0736	0.8640 0222	0.8561 7198	0.8484 1589	22
23	0.8747 8524	0.8664 9179	0.8582 8035	0.8501 5008	0.8421 0014	23
24	0.8697 1192	0.8611 0985	0.8525 9638	0.8441 7054	0.8358 3140	24
25	0.8646 6802	0.8557 6135	0.8469 5004	0.8382 3305	0.8296 0933	25
26	0.8596 5338	0.8504 4606	0.8413 4110	0.8323 3733	0.8234 3358	26
27	0.8546 6782	0.8451 6378	0.8357 6931	0.8264 8308	0.8173 0380	27
28	0.8497 1117	0.8399 1432	0.8302 3441	0.8206 7000	0.8112 1966	28
29	0.8447 8327	0.8346 9746	0.8247 3617	0.8148 9780	0.8051 8080	29
30	0.8398 8394	0.8295 1300	0.8192 7434	0.8091 6621	0.7991 8690	30
31	0.8350 1303	0.8243 6075	0.8138 4868	0.8034 7493	0.7932 3762	31
32	0.8301 7037	0.8192 4050	0.8084 5896	0.7978 2368	0.7873 3262	32
33	0.8253 5580	0.8141 5205	0.8031 0492	0.7922 1218	0.7814 7158	33
34	0.8205 6914	0.8090 9520	0.7977 8635	0.7866 4014	0.7756 5418	34
35	0.8158 1025	0.8040 6976	0.7925 0299	0.7811 0730	0.7698 8008	35
36	0.8110 7896	0.7990 7554	0.7872 5463	0.7756 1337	0.7641 4896	36
37	0.8063 7510	0.7941 1234	0.7820 4102	0.7701 5808	0.7584 6051	37
38	0.8016 9853	0.7891 7997	0.7768 6194	0.7647 4117	0.7528 1440	38
39	0.7970 4907	0.7842 7823	0.7717 1716	0.7593 6235	0.7472 1032	39
40	0.7924 2659	0.7794 0693	0.7666 0645	0.7540 2137	0.7416 4796	40
41	0.7878 3091	0.7745 6590	0.7615 2959	0.7487 1795	0.7361 2701	41
42	0.7832 6188	0.7697 5493	0.7564 8635	0.7434 5183	0.7306 4716	42
43	0.7787 1935	0.7649 7384	0.7514 7650	0.7382 2275	0.7252 0809	43
44	0.7742 0316	0.7602 2245	0.7464 9984	0.7330 3045	0.7198 0952	44
45	0.7697 1317	0.7555 0057	0.7415 5613	0.7278 7467	0.7144 5114	45
46	0.7652 4922	0.7508 0802	0.7366 4516	0.7227 5516	0.7091 3264	46
47	0.7608 1115	0.7461 4462	0.7317 6672	0.7176 7165	0.7038 5374	47
48	0.7563 9883	0.7415 1018	0.7269 2058	0.7126 2390	0.6986 1414	48
49	0.7520 1209	0.7369 0453	0.7221 0654	0.7076 1165	0.6934 1353	49
50	0.7476 5079	0.7323 2748	0.7173 2437	0.7026 3465	0.6882 5165	50
51	0.7433 1479	0.7277 7886	0.7125 7388	0.6976 9266	0.6831 2819	51
52	0.7390 0393	0.7232 5850	0.7078 5485	0.6927 8543	0.6780 4286	52
53	0.7347 1808	0.7187 6621	0.7031 6707	0.6879 1272	0.6729 9540	53
54	0.7304 5708	0.7143 0182	0.6985 1033	0.6830 7428	0.6679 8551	54
55	0.7262 2079	0.7098 6516	0.6938 8444	0.6782 6986	0.6630 1291	55
56	0.7220 0907	0.7054 5606	0.6892 8918	0.6734 9924	0.6580 7733	56
57	0.7178 2178	0.7010 7435	0.6847 2435	0.6687 6218	0.6531 7849	57
58	0.7136 5877	0.6967 1985	0.6801 8975	0.6640 5843	0.6483 1612	58
59	0.7095 1990	0.6923 9240	0.6756 8518	0.6593 8777	0.6434 8995	59
60	0.7054 0504	0.6880 9182	0.6712 1044	0.6547 4996	0.6386 9970	60

TABLE II

N	7/12	5/8	2/3	17/24	3/4	N
61	0.7013 1404	0.6838 1796	0.6667 6534	0.6501 4476	0.6339 4511	61
62	0.6972 4677	0.6795 7065	0.6623 4968	0.6455 7196	0.6292 2592	62
63	0.6932 0308	0.6753 4971	0.6579 6326	0.6410 3132	0.6245 4185	63
64	0.6891 8285	0.6711 5499	0.6536 0588	0.6365 2262	0.6198 9266	64
65	0.6851 8593	0.6669 8633	0.6492 7737	0.6320 4563	0.6152 7807	65
66	0.6812 1219	0.6628 4355	0.6449 7752	0.6276 0013	0.6106 9784	66
67	0.6772 6150	0.6587 2651	0.6407 0614	0.6231 8590	0.6061 5170	67
68	0.6733 3372	0.6546 3504	0.6364 6306	0.6188 0271	0.6016 3940	68
69	0.6694 2872	0.6505 6899	0.6322 4807	0.6144 5036	0.5971 6070	69
70	0.6655 4637	0.6465 2819	0.6280 6100	0.6101 2861	0.5927 1533	70
71	0.6616 8653	0.6425 1248	0.6239 0165	0.6058 3726	0.5883 0306	71
72	0.6578 4908	0.6385 2172	0.6197 6985	0.6015 7610	0.5839 2363	72
73	0.6540 3388	0.6345 5575	0.6156 6542	0.5973 4491	0.5795 7681	73
74	0.6502 4081	0.6306 1441	0.6115 8816	0.5931 4347	0.5752 6234	74
75	0.6464 6973	0.6266 9755	0.6075 3791	0.5889 7159	0.5709 7999	75
76	0.6427 2053	0.6228 0502	0.6035 1448	0.5848 2905	0.5667 2952	76
77	0.6389 9307	0.6189 3666	0.5995 1769	0.5807 1565	0.5625 1069	77
78	0.6352 8723	0.6150 9234	0.5955 4738	0.5766 3118	0.5583 2326	78
79	0.6316 0288	0.6112 7189	0.5916 0336	0.5725 7544	0.5541 6701	79
80	0.6279 3989	0.6074 7517	0.5876 8545	0.5685 4822	0.5500 4170	80
81	0.6242 9816	0.6037 0203	0.5837 9350	0.5645 4933	0.5459 4710	81
82	0.6206 7754	0.5999 5233	0.5799 2731	0.5605 7856	0.5418 8297	82
83	0.6170 7792	0.5962 2592	0.5760 8674	0.5566 3573	0.5378 4911	83
84	0.6134 9917	0.5925 2265	0.5722 7159	0.5527 2062	0.5338 4527	84
85	0.6099 4118	0.5888 4238	0.5684 8171	0.5488 3306	0.5298 7123	85
86	0.6064 0382	0.5851 8498	0.5647 1693	0.5449 7283	0.5259 2678	86
87	0.6028 8698	0.5815 5029	0.5609 7709	0.5411 3976	0.5220 1169	87
88	0.5993 9054	0.5779 3818	0.5572 6201	0.5373 3365	0.5181 2575	88
89	0.5959 1437	0.5743 4850	0.5535 7153	0.5335 5430	0.5142 6873	89
90	0.5924 5836	0.5707 8112	0.5499 0549	0.5298 0154	0.5104 4043	90
91	0.5890 2240	0.5672 3589	0.5462 6374	0.5260 7518	0.5066 4063	91
92	0.5856 0636	0.5637 1269	0.5426 4610	0.5223 7502	0.5028 6911	92
93	0.5822 1014	0.5602 1137	0.5390 5241	0.5187 0089	0.4991 2567	93
94	0.5788 3361	0.5567 3179	0.5354 8253	0.5150 5260	0.4954 1009	94
95	0.5754 7666	0.5532 7383	0.5319 3629	0.5114 2997	0.4917 2217	95
96	0.5721 3918	0.5498 3735	0.5284 1353	0.5078 3282	0.4880 6171	96
97	0.5688 2106	0.5464 2221	0.5249 1410	0.5042 6097	0.4844 2850	97
98	0.5655 2218	0.5430 2828	0.5214 3785	0.5007 1425	0.4808 2233	98
99	0.5622 4243	0.5396 5544	0.5179 8462	0.4971 9247	0.4772 4301	99
100	0.5589 8171	0.5363 0354	0.5145 5426	0.4936 9546	0.4736 9033	100
101	0.5557 3989	0.5329 7246	0.5111 4661	0.4902 2304	0.4701 6410	101
102	0.5525 1688	0.5296 6207	0.5077 6154	0.4867 7505	0.4666 6412	102
103	0.5493 1255	0.5263 7225	0.5043 9888	0.4833 5131	0.4631 9019	103
104	0.5461 2681	0.5231 0285	0.5010 5849	0.4799 5166	0.4597 4213	104
105	0.5429 5955	0.5198 5377	0.4977 4022	0.4765 7591	0.4563 1973	105
106	0.5398 1065	0.5166 2486	0.4944 4393	0.4732 2391	0.4529 2281	106
107	0.5366 8002	0.5134 1601	0.4911 6946	0.4698 9548	0.4495 5117	107
108	0.5335 6754	0.5102 2709	0.4879 1669	0.4665 9047	0.4462 0464	108
109	0.5304 7312	0.5070 5798	0.4846 8545	0.4633 0870	0.4428 8302	109
110	0.5273 9664	0.5039 0855	0.4814 7561	0.4600 5001	0.4395 8612	110
111	0.5243 3800	0.5007 7868	0.4782 8703	0.4568 1424	0.4363 1377	111
112	0.5212 9710	0.4976 6826	0.4751 1957	0.4536 0123	0.4330 6577	112
113	0.5182 7383	0.4945 7715	0.4719 7308	0.4504 1082	0.4298 4196	113
114	0.5152 6810	0.4915 0524	0.4688 4743	0.4472 4285	0.4266 4214	114
115	0.5122 7980	0.4884 5242	0.4657 4248	0.4440 9716	0.4234 6615	115
116	0.5093 0884	0.4854 1855	0.4626 5809	0.4409 7360	0.4203 1379	116
117	0.5063 5510	0.4824 0353	0.4595 9413	0.4378 7201	0.4171 8491	117
118	0.5034 1849	0.4794 0723	0.4565 5046	0.4347 9223	0.4140 7931	118
119	0.5004 9891	0.4764 2955	0.4535 2695	0.4317 3411	0.4109 9683	119
120	0.4975 9627	0.4734 7036	0.4505 2346	0.4286 9751	0.4079 3730	120

TABLE II

N	7/12	5/8	2/3	17/24	3/4	N
121	0.4947 1046	0.4705 2955	0.4475 3986	0.4256 8226	0.4049 0055	121
122	0.4918 4138	0.4676 0700	0.4445 7602	0.4226 8821	0.4018 8640	122
123	0.4889 8895	0.4647 0261	0.4416 3181	0.4197 1523	0.3988 9469	123
124	0.4861 5305	0.4618 1626	0.4387 0710	0.4167 6316	0.3959 2525	124
125	0.4833 3361	0.4589 4784	0.4358 0175	0.4138 3185	0.3929 7792	125
126	0.4805 3051	0.4560 9723	0.4329 1565	0.4109 2116	0.3900 5252	126
127	0.4777 4367	0.4532 6433	0.4300 4866	0.4080 3094	0.3871 4891	127
128	0.4749 7300	0.4504 4902	0.4272 0065	0.4051 6105	0.3842 6691	128
129	0.4722 1839	0.4476 5120	0.4243 7151	0.4023 1134	0.3814 0636	129
130	0.4694 7976	0.4448 7076	0.4215 6110	0.3994 8168	0.3785 6711	130
131	0.4667 5701	0.4421 0759	0.4187 6930	0.3966 7192	0.3757 4899	131
132	0.4640 5005	0.4393 6158	0.4159 9600	0.3938 8193	0.3729 5185	132
133	0.4613 5879	0.4366 3262	0.4132 4106	0.3911 1155	0.3701 7553	133
134	0.4586 8314	0.4339 2062	0.4105 0436	0.3883 6066	0.3674 1988	134
135	0.4560 2301	0.4312 2546	0.4077 8579	0.3856 2912	0.3646 8475	135
136	0.4533 7830	0.4285 4704	0.4050 8522	0.3829 1680	0.3619 6997	136
137	0.4507 4893	0.4258 8526	0.4024 0254	0.3802 2355	0.3592 7541	137
138	0.4481 3481	0.4232 4001	0.3997 3762	0.3775 4924	0.3566 0090	138
139	0.4455 3585	0.4206 1119	0.3970 9035	0.3748 9374	0.3539 4630	139
140	0.4429 5197	0.4179 9870	0.3944 6061	0.3722 5692	0.3513 1147	140
141	0.4403 8306	0.4154 0243	0.3918 4829	0.3696 3865	0.3486 9625	141
142	0.4378 2906	0.4128 2229	0.3892 5327	0.3670 3879	0.3461 0049	142
143	0.4352 8987	0.4102 5818	0.3866 7543	0.3644 5722	0.3435 2406	143
144	0.4327 6541	0.4077 0999	0.3841 1467	0.3618 9380	0.3409 6681	144
145	0.4302 5558	0.4051 7763	0.3815 7086	0.3593 4842	0.3384 2860	145
146	0.4277 6031	0.4026 6100	0.3790 4390	0.3568 2094	0.3359 0928	146
147	0.4252 7952	0.4001 6000	0.3765 3368	0.3543 1123	0.3334 0871	147
148	0.4228 1311	0.3976 7453	0.3740 4008	0.3518 1918	0.3309 2676	148
149	0.4203 6100	0.3952 0451	0.3715 6299	0.3493 4466	0.3284 6329	149
150	0.4179 2312	0.3927 4982	0.3691 0231	0.3468 8754	0.3260 1815	150
151	0.4154 9937	0.3903 1038	0.3666 5792	0.3444 4770	0.3235 9122	151
152	0.4130 8968	0.3878 8609	0.3642 2973	0.3420 2502	0.3211 8235	152
153	0.4106 9396	0.3854 7686	0.3618 1761	0.3396 1938	0.3187 9141	153
154	0.4083 1214	0.3830 8259	0.3594 2147	0.3372 3067	0.3164 1828	154
155	0.4059 4414	0.3807 0320	0.3570 4119	0.3348 5875	0.3140 6280	155
156	0.4035 8986	0.3783 3858	0.3546 7668	0.3325 0352	0.3117 2487	156
157	0.4012 4924	0.3759 8865	0.3523 2783	0.3301 6485	0.3094 0434	157
158	0.3989 2220	0.3736 5332	0.3499 9453	0.3278 4263	0.3071 0108	158
159	0.3966 0864	0.3713 3249	0.3476 7669	0.3255 3675	0.3048 1496	159
160	0.3943 0851	0.3690 2608	0.3453 7419	0.3232 4708	0.3025 4587	160
161	0.3920 2172	0.3667 3399	0.3430 8695	0.3209 7352	0.3002 9367	161
162	0.3897 4819	0.3644 5614	0.3408 1485	0.3187 1594	0.2980 5823	162
163	0.3874 8784	0.3621 9244	0.3385 5779	0.3164 7425	0.2958 3944	163
164	0.3852 4060	0.3599 4280	0.3363 1569	0.3142 4833	0.2936 3716	164
165	0.3830 0640	0.3577 0713	0.3340 8843	0.3120 3806	0.2914 5127	165
166	0.3807 8515	0.3554 8534	0.3318 7593	0.3098 4333	0.2892 8166	166
167	0.3785 7679	0.3532 7736	0.3296 7807	0.3076 6405	0.2871 2820	167
168	0.3763 8123	0.3510 8309	0.3274 9478	0.3055 0009	0.2849 9077	168
169	0.3741 9841	0.3489 0245	0.3253 2594	0.3033 5135	0.2828 6925	169
170	0.3720 2824	0.3467 3535	0.3231 7146	0.3012 1772	0.2807 6352	170
171	0.3698 7066	0.3445 8172	0.3210 3125	0.2990 9910	0.2786 7347	171
172	0.3677 2560	0.3424 4146	0.3189 0522	0.2969 9539	0.2765 9898	172
173	0.3655 9297	0.3403 1449	0.3167 9326	0.2949 0647	0.2745 3993	173
174	0.3634 7272	0.3382 0074	0.3146 9529	0.2928 3224	0.2724 9621	174
175	0.3613 6475	0.3361 0011	0.3126 1122	0.2907 7260	0.2704 6770	175
176	0.3592 6902	0.3340 1254	0.3105 4094	0.2887 2745	0.2684 5429	176
177	0.3571 8544	0.3319 3792	0.3084 8438	0.2866 9668	0.2664 5587	177
178	0.3551 1394	0.3298 7620	0.3064 4144	0.2846 8019	0.2644 7233	178
179	0.3530 5445	0.3278 2728	0.3044 1203	0.2826 7789	0.2625 0355	179
180	0.3510 0691	0.3257 9108	0.3023 9605	0.2806 8967	0.2605 4943	180

TABLE II

N	7/12	5/8	2/3	17/24	3/4	N
181	0.3489 7125	0.3237 6754	0.3003 9343	0.2787 1544	0.2586 0986	181
182	0.3469 4739	0.3217 5656	0.2984 0407	0.2767 5509	0.2566 8472	182
183	0.3449 3527	0.3197 5807	0.2964 2788	0.2748 0853	0.2547 7392	183
184	0.3429 3481	0.3177 7199	0.2944 6478	0.2728 7566	0.2528 7734	184
185	0.3409 4596	0.3157 9825	0.2925 1469	0.2709 5639	0.2509 9488	185
186	0.3389 6864	0.3138 3677	0.2905 7750	0.2690 5061	0.2491 2643	186
187	0.3370 0279	0.3118 8748	0.2886 5315	0.2671 5824	0.2472 7189	187
188	0.3350 4835	0.3099 5029	0.2867 4154	0.2652 7918	0.2454 3116	188
189	0.3331 0523	0.3080 2513	0.2848 4259	0.2634 1333	0.2436 0413	189
190	0.3311 7339	0.3061 1193	0.2829 5621	0.2615 6061	0.2417 9070	190
191	0.3292 5275	0.3042 1062	0.2810 8233	0.2597 2092	0.2399 9077	191
192	0.3273 4324	0.3023 2111	0.2792 2086	0.2578 9417	0.2382 0423	192
193	0.3254 4482	0.3004 4334	0.2773 7171	0.2560 8027	0.2364 3100	193
194	0.3235 5740	0.2985 7723	0.2755 3482	0.2542 7913	0.2346 7097	194
195	0.3216 8093	0.2967 2271	0.2737 1008	0.2524 9065	0.2329 2404	195
196	0.3198 1534	0.2948 7972	0.2718 9743	0.2507 1476	0.2311 9011	196
197	0.3179 6057	0.2930 4816	0.2700 9679	0.2489 5135	0.2294 6909	197
198	0.3161 1655	0.2912 2799	0.2683 0807	0.2472 0035	0.2277 6089	198
199	0.3142 8323	0.2894 1912	0.2665 3119	0.2454 6166	0.2260 6540	199
200	0.3124 6055	0.2876 2149	0.2647 6608	0.2437 3520	0.2243 8253	200
201	0.3106 4843	0.2858 3502	0.2630 1267	0.2420 2089	0.2227 1219	201
202	0.3088 4683	0.2840 5964	0.2612 7086	0.2403 1863	0.2210 5428	202
203	0.3070 5567	0.2822 9530	0.2595 4059	0.2386 2835	0.2194 0871	203
204	0.3052 7490	0.2805 4191	0.2578 2178	0.2369 4995	0.2177 7540	204
205	0.3035 0445	0.2787 9941	0.2561 1435	0.2352 8336	0.2161 5424	205
206	0.3017 4428	0.2770 6774	0.2544 1823	0.2336 2849	0.2145 4515	206
207	0.2999 9431	0.2753 4682	0.2527 3334	0.2319 8526	0.2129 4804	207
208	0.2982 5450	0.2736 3660	0.2510 5961	0.2303 5359	0.2113 6282	208
209	0.2965 2477	0.2719 3699	0.2493 9696	0.2287 3340	0.2097 8940	209
210	0.2948 0507	0.2702 4794	0.2477 4533	0.2271 2460	0.2082 2769	210
211	0.2930 9535	0.2685 6938	0.2461 0463	0.2255 2712	0.2066 7761	211
212	0.2913 9554	0.2669 0125	0.2444 7480	0.2239 4087	0.2051 3907	212
213	0.2897 0559	0.2652 4348	0.2428 5576	0.2223 6578	0.2036 1198	213
214	0.2880 2544	0.2635 9600	0.2412 4744	0.2208 0176	0.2020 9626	214
215	0.2863 5504	0.2619 5876	0.2396 4978	0.2192 4875	0.2005 9182	215
216	0.2846 9432	0.2603 3169	0.2380 6269	0.2177 0666	0.1990 9858	216
217	0.2830 4324	0.2587 1472	0.2364 8612	0.2161 7542	0.1976 1646	217
218	0.2814 0173	0.2571 0780	0.2349 1998	0.2146 5495	0.1961 4537	218
219	0.2797 6974	0.2555 1085	0.2333 6422	0.2131 4517	0.1946 8523	219
220	0.2781 4721	0.2539 2383	0.2318 1876	0.2116 4601	0.1932 3596	220
221	0.2765 3410	0.2523 4666	0.2302 8354	0.2101 5740	0.1917 9748	221
222	0.2749 3033	0.2507 7929	0.2287 5848	0.2086 7925	0.1903 6970	222
223	0.2733 3588	0.2492 2166	0.2272 4353	0.2072 1150	0.1889 5256	223
224	0.2717 5066	0.2476 7370	0.2257 3860	0.2057 5408	0.1875 4596	224
225	0.2701 7464	0.2461 3535	0.2242 4365	0.2043 0690	0.1861 4984	225
226	0.2686 0777	0.2446 0656	0.2227 5859	0.2028 6991	0.1847 6411	226
227	0.2670 4997	0.2430 8726	0.2212 8337	0.2014 4302	0.1833 8869	227
228	0.2655 0122	0.2415 7740	0.2198 1791	0.2000 2617	0.1820 2352	228
229	0.2639 6144	0.2400 7692	0.2183 6217	0.1986 1928	0.1806 6850	229
230	0.2624 3060	0.2385 8576	0.2169 1606	0.1972 2229	0.1793 2358	230
231	0.2609 0863	0.2371 0386	0.2154 7953	0.1958 3513	0.1779 8866	231
232	0.2593 9549	0.2356 3117	0.2140 5251	0.1944 5772	0.1766 6368	232
233	0.2578 9112	0.2341 6762	0.2126 3495	0.1930 9000	0.1753 4857	233
234	0.2563 9548	0.2327 1316	0.2112 2677	0.1917 3190	0.1740 4325	234
235	0.2549 0852	0.2312 6774	0.2098 2791	0.1903 8335	0.1727 4764	235
236	0.2534 3018	0.2298 3129	0.2084 3833	0.1890 4428	0.1714 6168	236
237	0.2519 6041	0.2284 0377	0.2070 5794	0.1877 1464	0.1701 8529	237
238	0.2504 9916	0.2269 8511	0.2056 8669	0.1863 9434	0.1689 1840	238
239	0.2490 4639	0.2255 7527	0.2043 2453	0.1850 8334	0.1676 6094	239
240	0.2476 0205	0.2241 7418	0.2029 7139	0.1837 8155	0.1664 1284	240

TABLE II

N	7/12	5/8	2/3	17/24	3/4	N
241	0.2461 6608	0.2227 8179	0.2016 2721	0.1824 8892	0.1651 7404	241
242	0.2447 3844	0.2213 9806	0.2002 9193	0.1812 0538	0.1639 4446	242
243	0.2433 1907	0.2200 2291	0.1989 6549	0.1799 3087	0.1627 2403	243
244	0.2419 0794	0.2186 5631	0.1976 4784	0.1786 6533	0.1615 1268	244
245	0.2405 0500	0.2172 9820	0.1963 3891	0.1774 0868	0.1603 1035	245
246	0.2391 1019	0.2159 4852	0.1950 3866	0.1761 6088	0.1591 1698	246
247	0.2377 2347	0.2146 0722	0.1937 4701	0.1749 2185	0.1579 3248	247
248	0.2363 4479	0.2132 7426	0.1924 6392	0.1736 9153	0.1567 5681	248
249	0.2349 7411	0.2119 4957	0.1911 8932	0.1724 6987	0.1555 8988	249
250	0.2336 1138	0.2106 3312	0.1899 2317	0.1712 5680	0.1544 3164	250
251	0.2322 5655	0.2093 2484	0.1886 6540	0.1700 5226	0.1532 8203	251
252	0.2309 0957	0.2080 2468	0.1874 1596	0.1688 5620	0.1521 4097	252
253	0.2295 7041	0.2067 3260	0.1861 7479	0.1676 6855	0.1510 0841	253
254	0.2282 3902	0.2054 4855	0.1849 4185	0.1664 8925	0.1498 8428	254
255	0.2269 1535	0.2041 7247	0.1837 1707	0.1653 1824	0.1487 6851	255
256	0.2255 9935	0.2029 0432	0.1825 0040	0.1641 5548	0.1476 6106	256
257	0.2242 9099	0.2016 4405	0.1812 9178	0.1630 0089	0.1465 6184	257
258	0.2229 9021	0.2003 9160	0.1800 9118	0.1618 5442	0.1454 7081	258
259	0.2216 9698	0.1991 4693	0.1788 9852	0.1607 1601	0.1443 8790	259
260	0.2204 1124	0.1979 0999	0.1777 1376	0.1595 8561	0.1433 1305	260
261	0.2191 3297	0.1966 8074	0.1765 3685	0.1584 6317	0.1422 4621	261
262	0.2178 6211	0.1954 5912	0.1753 6773	0.1573 4861	0.1411 8730	262
263	0.2165 9861	0.1942 4509	0.1742 0635	0.1562 4190	0.1401 3628	263
264	0.2153 4245	0.1930 3860	0.1730 5267	0.1551 4297	0.1390 9308	264
265	0.2140 9357	0.1918 3960	0.1719 0663	0.1540 5177	0.1380 5765	265
266	0.2128 5194	0.1906 4805	0.1707 6817	0.1529 6825	0.1370 2992	266
267	0.2116 1750	0.1894 6390	0.1696 3726	0.1518 9234	0.1360 0985	267
268	0.2103 9022	0.1882 8710	0.1685 1383	0.1508 2401	0.1349 9737	268
269	0.2091 7006	0.1871 1762	0.1673 9785	0.1497 6318	0.1339 9243	269
270	0.2079 5698	0.1859 5540	0.1662 8925	0.1487 0982	0.1329 9497	270
271	0.2067 5094	0.1848 0039	0.1651 8800	0.1476 6387	0.1320 0493	271
272	0.2055 5188	0.1836 5257	0.1640 9404	0.1466 2527	0.1310 2226	272
273	0.2043 5978	0.1825 1187	0.1630 0732	0.1455 9398	0.1300 4691	273
274	0.2031 7460	0.1813 7825	0.1619 2780	0.1445 6995	0.1290 7882	274
275	0.2019 9629	0.1802 5168	0.1608 5543	0.1435 5311	0.1281 1793	275
276	0.2008 2481	0.1791 3210	0.1597 9017	0.1425 4343	0.1271 6420	276
277	0.1996 6012	0.1780 1948	0.1587 3195	0.1415 4085	0.1262 1757	277
278	0.1985 0220	0.1769 1377	0.1576 8075	0.1405 4532	0.1252 7799	278
279	0.1973 5098	0.1758 1493	0.1566 3650	0.1395 5679	0.1243 4540	279
280	0.1962 0644	0.1747 2291	0.1555 9918	0.1385 7522	0.1234 1975	280
281	0.1950 6854	0.1736 3767	0.1545 6872	0.1376 0055	0.1225 0099	281
282	0.1939 3724	0.1725 5918	0.1535 4508	0.1366 3273	0.1215 8907	282
283	0.1928 1250	0.1714 8738	0.1525 2823	0.1356 7172	0.1206 8394	283
284	0.1916 9429	0.1704 2224	0.1515 1811	0.1347 1747	0.1197 8555	284
285	0.1905 8256	0.1693 6372	0.1505 1468	0.1337 6994	0.1188 9385	285
286	0.1894 7727	0.1683 1177	0.1495 1789	0.1328 2906	0.1180 0878	286
287	0.1883 7840	0.1672 6636	0.1485 2771	0.1318 9481	0.1171 3030	287
288	0.1872 8590	0.1662 2744	0.1475 4408	0.1309 6713	0.1162 5837	288
289	0.1861 9973	0.1651 9497	0.1465 6697	0.1300 4597	0.1153 9292	289
290	0.1851 1987	0.1641 6891	0.1455 9632	0.1291 3129	0.1145 3391	290
291	0.1840 4626	0.1631 4923	0.1446 3211	0.1282 2304	0.1136 8130	291
292	0.1829 7889	0.1621 3588	0.1436 7428	0.1273 2118	0.1128 3504	292
293	0.1819 1770	0.1611 2883	0.1427 2280	0.1264 2567	0.1119 9508	293
294	0.1808 6267	0.1601 2803	0.1417 7761	0.1255 3645	0.1111 6137	294
295	0.1798 1375	0.1591 3344	0.1408 3869	0.1246 5349	0.1103 3386	295
296	0.1787 7092	0.1581 4503	0.1399 0598	0.1237 7674	0.1095 1252	296
297	0.1777 3414	0.1571 6277	0.1389 7945	0.1229 0615	0.1086 9729	297
298	0.1767 0337	0.1561 8660	0.1380 5906	0.1220 4169	0.1078 8813	298
299	0.1756 7858	0.1552 1650	0.1371 4476	0.1211 8331	0.1070 8499	299
300	0.1746 5973	0.1542 5242	0.1362 3652	0.1203 3096	0.1062 8783	300

TABLE II

N	7/12	5/8	2/3	17/24	3/4	N
301	0.1736 4679	0.1532 9433	0.1353 3429	0.1194 8461	0.1054 9661	301
302	0.1726 3973	0.1523 4219	0.1344 3803	0.1186 4422	0.1047 1127	302
303	0.1716 3850	0.1513 9597	0.1335 4772	0.1178 0973	0.1039 3179	303
304	0.1706 4308	0.1504 5562	0.1326 6329	0.1169 8111	0.1031 5810	304
305	0.1696 5344	0.1495 2111	0.1317 8473	0.1161 5833	0.1023 9017	305
306	0.1686 6953	0.1485 9241	0.1309 1198	0.1153 4133	0.1016 2796	306
307	0.1676 9133	0.1476 6948	0.1300 4502	0.1145 3007	0.1008 7143	307
308	0.1667 1881	0.1467 5227	0.1291 8379	0.1137 2452	0.1001 2052	308
309	0.1657 5192	0.1458 4077	0.1283 2827	0.1129 2464	0.0993 7521	309
310	0.1647 9064	0.1449 3493	0.1274 7841	0.1121 3038	0.0986 3544	310
311	0.1638 3494	0.1440 3471	0.1266 3418	0.1113 4171	0.0979 0119	311
312	0.1628 8478	0.1431 4008	0.1257 9555	0.1105 5859	0.0971 7239	312
313	0.1619 4013	0.1422 5101	0.1249 6246	0.1097 8097	0.0964 4903	313
314	0.1610 0095	0.1413 6747	0.1241 3490	0.1090 0883	0.0957 3104	314
315	0.1600 6723	0.1404 8941	0.1233 1281	0.1082 4211	0.0950 1840	315
316	0.1591 3892	0.1396 1680	0.1224 9617	0.1074 8079	0.0943 1107	316
317	0.1582 1599	0.1387 4962	0.1216 8494	0.1067 2482	0.0936 0900	317
318	0.1572 9842	0.1378 8782	0.1208 7908	0.1059 7417	0.0929 1216	318
319	0.1563 8616	0.1370 3137	0.1200 7855	0.1052 2880	0.0922 2051	319
320	0.1554 7920	0.1361 8025	0.1192 8333	0.1044 8867	0.0915 3400	320
321	0.1545 7750	0.1353 3441	0.1184 9338	0.1037 5375	0.0908 5261	321
322	0.1536 8103	0.1344 9382	0.1177 0865	0.1030 2400	0.0901 7629	322
323	0.1527 8975	0.1336 5846	0.1169 2912	0.1022 9938	0.0895 0500	323
324	0.1519 0365	0.1328 2828	0.1161 5476	0.1015 7985	0.0888 3871	324
325	0.1510 2268	0.1320 0326	0.1153 8552	0.1008 6539	0.0881 7738	325
326	0.1501 4683	0.1311 8336	0.1146 2138	0.1001 5595	0.0875 2097	326
327	0.1492 7605	0.1303 6856	0.1138 6230	0.0994 5150	0.0868 6945	327
328	0.1484 1032	0.1295 5882	0.1131 0824	0.0987 5201	0.0862 2278	328
329	0.1475 4962	0.1287 5410	0.1123 5918	0.0980 5744	0.0855 8092	329
330	0.1466 9390	0.1279 5439	0.1116 1508	0.0973 6775	0.0849 4384	330
331	0.1458 4315	0.1271 5964	0.1108 7591	0.0966 8291	0.0843 1151	331
332	0.1449 9733	0.1263 6983	0.1101 4163	0.0960 0289	0.0836 8388	332
333	0.1441 5642	0.1255 8492	0.1094 1222	0.0953 2765	0.0830 6092	333
334	0.1433 2039	0.1248 0489	0.1086 8763	0.0946 5717	0.0824 4260	334
335	0.1424 8920	0.1240 2971	0.1079 6785	0.0939 9139	0.0818 2889	335
336	0.1416 6283	0.1232 5934	0.1072 5283	0.0933 3030	0.0812 1974	336
337	0.1408 4126	0.1224 9375	0.1065 4254	0.0926 7386	0.0806 1512	337
338	0.1400 2445	0.1217 3292	0.1058 3696	0.0920 2204	0.0800 1501	338
339	0.1392 1238	0.1209 7681	0.1051 3606	0.0913 7480	0.0794 1937	339
340	0.1384 0501	0.1202 2541	0.1044 3979	0.0907 3212	0.0788 2816	340
341	0.1376 0233	0.1194 7866	0.1037 4814	0.0900 9395	0.0782 4135	341
342	0.1368 0431	0.1187 3656	0.1030 6106	0.0894 6027	0.0776 5890	342
343	0.1360 1091	0.1179 9907	0.1023 7854	0.0888 3105	0.0770 8080	343
344	0.1352 2212	0.1172 6615	0.1017 0054	0.0882 0626	0.0765 0699	344
345	0.1344 3789	0.1165 3779	0.1010 2702	0.0875 8586	0.0759 3746	345
346	0.1336 5822	0.1158 1395	0.1003 5797	0.0869 6982	0.0753 7217	346
347	0.1328 8307	0.1150 9461	0.0996 9335	0.0863 5812	0.0748 1109	347
348	0.1321 1241	0.1143 7974	0.0990 3313	0.0857 5072	0.0742 5418	348
349	0.1313 4623	0.1136 6931	0.0983 7728	0.0851 4759	0.0737 0142	349
350	0.1305 8449	0.1129 6329	0.0977 2577	0.0845 4870	0.0731 5278	350
351	0.1298 2716	0.1122 6165	0.0970 7858	0.0839 5403	0.0726 0822	351
352	0.1290 7423	0.1115 6437	0.0964 3568	0.0833 6354	0.0720 6771	352
353	0.1283 2566	0.1108 7143	0.0957 9703	0.0827 7720	0.0715 3122	353
354	0.1275 8144	0.1101 8278	0.0951 6261	0.0821 9499	0.0709 9873	354
355	0.1268 4153	0.1094 9842	0.0945 3240	0.0816 1687	0.0704 7021	355
356	0.1261 0591	0.1088 1831	0.0939 0636	0.0810 4281	0.0699 4561	356
357	0.1253 7456	0.1081 4242	0.0932 8446	0.0804 7280	0.0694 2493	357
358	0.1246 4745	0.1074 7072	0.0926 6668	0.0799 0679	0.0689 0812	358
359	0.1239 2455	0.1068 0320	0.0920 5299	0.0793 4476	0.0683 9515	359
360	0.1232 0585	0.1061 3983	0.0914 4337	0.0787 8669	0.0678 8601	360

TABLE II

N	19/24	5/6	7/8	11/12	23/24	N
1	0.9921 4551	0.9917 3554	0.9913 2590	0.9909 1660	0.9905 0764	1
2	0.9843 5272	0.9835 3938	0.9827 2704	0.9819 1570	0.9811 0538	2
3	0.9766 2114	0.9754 1095	0.9742 0276	0.9729 9657	0.9717 9237	3
4	0.9689 5028	0.9673 4970	0.9657 5243	0.9641 5845	0.9625 6776	4
5	0.9613 3968	0.9593 5508	0.9573 7539	0.9554 0061	0.9534 3071	5
6	0.9537 8885	0.9514 2652	0.9490 7102	0.9467 2232	0.9443 8040	6
7	0.9462 9733	0.9435 6349	0.9408 3868	0.9381 2286	0.9354 1600	7
8	0.9388 6465	0.9357 6545	0.9326 7775	0.9296 0152	0.9265 3669	8
9	0.9314 9035	0.9280 3185	0.9245 8761	0.9211 5757	0.9177 4166	9
10	0.9241 7397	0.9203 6217	0.9165 6765	0.9127 9033	0.9090 3012	10
11	0.9169 1506	0.9127 5587	0.9086 1724	0.9044 9909	0.9004 0128	11
12	0.9097 1317	0.9052 1243	0.9007 3581	0.8962 8316	0.8918 5434	12
13	0.9025 6784	0.8977 3134	0.8929 2273	0.8881 4186	0.8833 8853	13
14	0.8954 7863	0.8903 1207	0.8851 7743	0.8800 7451	0.8750 0309	14
15	0.8884 4511	0.8829 5412	0.8774 9931	0.8720 8044	0.8666 9724	15
16	0.8814 6683	0.8756 5698	0.8698 8779	0.8641 5898	0.8584 7023	16
17	0.8745 4336	0.8684 2014	0.8623 4230	0.8563 0947	0.8503 2132	17
18	0.8676 7427	0.8612 4312	0.8548 6225	0.8485 3127	0.8422 4976	18
19	0.8608 5914	0.8541 2540	0.8474 4709	0.8408 2372	0.8342 5482	19
20	0.8540 9753	0.8470 6652	0.8400 9625	0.8331 8618	0.8263 3577	20
21	0.8473 8904	0.8400 6597	0.8328 0917	0.8256 1802	0.8184 9189	21
22	0.8407 3323	0.8331 2327	0.8255 8530	0.8181 1860	0.8107 2246	22
23	0.8341 2970	0.8262 3796	0.8184 2409	0.8106 8729	0.8030 2679	23
24	0.8275 7804	0.8194 0954	0.8113 2499	0.8033 2350	0.7954 0417	24
25	0.8210 7784	0.8126 3756	0.8042 8748	0.7960 2659	0.7878 5390	25
26	0.8146 2870	0.8059 2155	0.7973 1101	0.7887 9596	0.7803 7530	26
27	0.8082 3021	0.7992 6104	0.7903 9505	0.7816 3101	0.7729 6770	27
28	0.8018 8198	0.7926 5558	0.7835 3908	0.7745 3114	0.7656 3041	28
29	0.7955 8361	0.7861 0471	0.7767 4258	0.7674 9576	0.7583 6276	29
30	0.7893 3471	0.7796 0797	0.7700 0504	0.7605 2429	0.7511 6411	30
31	0.7831 3489	0.7731 6493	0.7633 2594	0.7536 1614	0.7440 3378	31
32	0.7769 8377	0.7667 7514	0.7567 0477	0.7467 7074	0.7369 7114	32
33	0.7708 8096	0.7604 3815	0.7501 4104	0.7399 8752	0.7299 7554	33
34	0.7648 2609	0.7541 5354	0.7436 3424	0.7332 6592	0.7230 4635	34
35	0.7588 1877	0.7479 2087	0.7371 8388	0.7266 0537	0.7161 8293	35
36	0.7528 5864	0.7417 3970	0.7307 8947	0.7200 0532	0.7093 8466	36
37	0.7469 4533	0.7356 0962	0.7244 5053	0.7134 6522	0.7026 5092	37
38	0.7410 7845	0.7295 3020	0.7181 6657	0.7069 8453	0.6959 8110	38
39	0.7352 5766	0.7235 0103	0.7119 3712	0.7005 6270	0.6893 7460	39
40	0.7294 8259	0.7175 2168	0.7057 6171	0.6941 9921	0.6828 3080	40
41	0.7237 5288	0.7115 9175	0.6996 3986	0.6878 9352	0.6763 4912	41
42	0.7180 6818	0.7057 1083	0.6935 7111	0.6816 4511	0.6699 2897	42
43	0.7124 2812	0.6998 7851	0.6875 5500	0.6754 5345	0.6635 6976	43
44	0.7068 3237	0.6940 9439	0.6815 9108	0.6693 1804	0.6572 7091	44
45	0.7012 8056	0.6883 5807	0.6756 7889	0.6632 3835	0.6510 3186	45
46	0.6957 7236	0.6826 6916	0.6698 1798	0.6572 1389	0.6448 5203	46
47	0.6903 0743	0.6770 2727	0.6640 0792	0.6512 4415	0.6387 3085	47
48	0.6848 8542	0.6714 3200	0.6582 4824	0.6453 2864	0.6326 6779	48
49	0.6795 0600	0.6658 8297	0.6525 3853	0.6394 6686	0.6266 6228	49
50	0.6741 6883	0.6603 7981	0.6468 7835	0.6336 5833	0.6207 1377	50
51	0.6688 7358	0.6549 2212	0.6412 6726	0.6279 0255	0.6148 2173	51
52	0.6636 1992	0.6495 0955	0.6357 0484	0.6221 9906	0.6089 8561	52
53	0.6584 0753	0.6441 4170	0.6301 9067	0.6165 4738	0.6032 0490	53
54	0.6532 3608	0.6388 1821	0.6247 2433	0.6109 4703	0.5974 7906	54
55	0.6481 0524	0.6335 3872	0.6193 0541	0.6053 9755	0.5918 0757	55
56	0.6430 1471	0.6283 0287	0.6139 3349	0.5998 9848	0.5861 8992	56
57	0.6379 6416	0.6231 1028	0.6086 0817	0.5944 4936	0.5806 2559	57
58	0.6329 5328	0.6179 6061	0.6033 2904	0.5890 4974	0.5751 1408	58
59	0.6279 8176	0.6128 5350	0.5980 9571	0.5836 9916	0.5696 5489	59
60	0.6230 4928	0.6077 8859	0.5929 0776	0.5783 9719	0.5642 4751	60

TABLE II

N	19/24	5/6	7/8	11/12	23/24	N
61	0.6181 5555	0.6027 6555	0.5877 6482	0.5731 4338	0.5588 9147	61
62	0.6133 0026	0.5977 8401	0.5826 6649	0.5679 3728	0.5535 8627	62
63	0.6084 8310	0.5928 4365	0.5776 1238	0.5627 7848	0.5483 3143	63
64	0.6037 0378	0.5879 4411	0.5726 0211	0.5576 6654	0.5431 2646	64
65	0.5989 6200	0.5830 8507	0.5676 3530	0.5526 0103	0.5379 7091	65
66	0.5942 5746	0.5782 6619	0.5627 1158	0.5475 8153	0.5328 6429	66
67	0.5895 8987	0.5734 8713	0.5578 3056	0.5426 0763	0.5278 0615	67
68	0.5849 5895	0.5687 4756	0.5529 9188	0.5376 7890	0.5227 9602	68
69	0.5803 6440	0.5640 4717	0.5481 9517	0.5327 9495	0.5178 3345	69
70	0.5758 0593	0.5593 8562	0.5434 4007	0.5279 5536	0.5129 1799	70
71	0.5712 8327	0.5547 6260	0.5387 2622	0.5231 5973	0.5080 4918	71
72	0.5667 9614	0.5501 7779	0.5340 5325	0.5184 0766	0.5032 2660	72
73	0.5623 4424	0.5456 3086	0.5294 2082	0.5136 9875	0.4984 4978	73
74	0.5579 2732	0.5411 2152	0.5248 2857	0.5090 3262	0.4937 1832	74
75	0.5535 4509	0.5366 4944	0.5202 7615	0.5044 0887	0.4890 3176	75
76	0.5491 9728	0.5322 1432	0.5157 6322	0.4998 2712	0.4843 8970	76
77	0.5448 8361	0.5278 1585	0.5112 8944	0.4952 8699	0.4797 9169	77
78	0.5406 0383	0.5234 5374	0.5068 5447	0.4907 8810	0.4752 3733	78
79	0.5363 5767	0.5191 2768	0.5024 5796	0.4863 3008	0.4707 2621	79
80	0.5321 4486	0.5148 3736	0.4980 9959	0.4819 1255	0.4662 5790	80
81	0.5279 6513	0.5105 8251	0.4937 7902	0.4775 3514	0.4618 3201	81
82	0.5238 1824	0.5063 6282	0.4894 9593	0.4731 9750	0.4574 4813	82
83	0.5197 0391	0.5021 7800	0.4852 4999	0.4688 9925	0.4531 0587	83
84	0.5156 2191	0.4980 2777	0.4810 4089	0.4646 4005	0.4488 0482	84
85	0.5115 7196	0.4939 1184	0.4768 6829	0.4604 1954	0.4445 4460	85
86	0.5075 5383	0.4898 2992	0.4727 3188	0.4562 3736	0.4403 2483	86
87	0.5035 6725	0.4857 8174	0.4686 3136	0.4520 9318	0.4361 4510	87
88	0.4996 1199	0.4817 6702	0.4645 6640	0.4479 8663	0.4320 0505	88
89	0.4956 8780	0.4777 8547	0.4605 3671	0.4439 1739	0.4279 0430	89
90	0.4917 9443	0.4738 3683	0.4565 4197	0.4398 8511	0.4238 4248	90
91	0.4879 3163	0.4699 2082	0.4525 8187	0.4358 8946	0.4198 1921	91
92	0.4840 9918	0.4660 3718	0.4486 5613	0.4319 3010	0.4158 3413	92
93	0.4802 9683	0.4621 8563	0.4447 6444	0.4280 0670	0.4118 8689	93
94	0.4765 2435	0.4583 6592	0.4409 0651	0.4241 1895	0.4079 7711	94
95	0.4727 8149	0.4545 7777	0.4370 8204	0.4202 6650	0.4041 0444	95
96	0.4690 6804	0.4508 2093	0.4332 9075	0.4164 4905	0.4002 6853	96
97	0.4653 8375	0.4470 9514	0.4295 3234	0.4126 6628	0.3964 6904	97
98	0.4617 2840	0.4434 0014	0.4258 0654	0.4089 1787	0.3927 0561	98
99	0.4581 0176	0.4397 3567	0.4221 1305	0.4052 0350	0.3889 7790	99
100	0.4545 0361	0.4361 0149	0.4184 5159	0.4015 2287	0.3852 8558	100
101	0.4509 3372	0.4324 9735	0.4148 2190	0.3978 7568	0.3816 2831	101
102	0.4473 9186	0.4289 2299	0.4112 2370	0.3942 6161	0.3780 0576	102
103	0.4438 7783	0.4253 7817	0.4076 5670	0.3906 8038	0.3744 1759	103
104	0.4403 9140	0.4218 6265	0.4041 2064	0.3871 3167	0.3708 6348	104
105	0.4369 3235	0.4183 7618	0.4006 1526	0.3836 1520	0.3673 4311	105
106	0.4335 0047	0.4149 1853	0.3971 4028	0.3801 3067	0.3638 5615	106
107	0.4300 9555	0.4114 8945	0.3936 9545	0.3766 7779	0.3604 0230	107
108	0.4267 1737	0.4080 8871	0.3902 8049	0.3732 5627	0.3569 8123	108
109	0.4233 6572	0.4047 1608	0.3868 9516	0.3698 6583	0.3535 9263	109
110	0.4200 4040	0.4013 7131	0.3835 3919	0.3665 0619	0.3502 3620	110
111	0.4167 4120	0.3980 5420	0.3802 1233	0.3631 7707	0.3469 1163	111
112	0.4134 6792	0.3947 6449	0.3769 1433	0.3598 7819	0.3436 1862	112
113	0.4102 2034	0.3915 0198	0.3736 4494	0.3566 0927	0.3403 5687	113
114	0.4069 9827	0.3882 6642	0.3704 0391	0.3533 7004	0.3371 2607	114
115	0.4038 0151	0.3850 5761	0.3671 9099	0.3501 6024	0.3339 2595	115
116	0.4006 2985	0.3818 7531	0.3640 0593	0.3469 7960	0.3307 5620	116
117	0.3974 8311	0.3787 1932	0.3608 4851	0.3438 2784	0.3276 1655	117
118	0.3943 6109	0.3755 8941	0.3577 1847	0.3407 0471	0.3245 0669	118
119	0.3912 6358	0.3724 8536	0.3546 1559	0.3376 0996	0.3214 2635	119
120	0.3881 9041	0.3694 0697	0.3515 3961	0.3345 4331	0.3183 7526	120

TABLE II

N	19/24	5/6	7/8	11/12	23/24	N
121	0.3851 4137	0.3663 5402	0.3484 9032	0.3315 0452	0.3153 5312	121
122	0.3821 1629	0.3633 2630	0.3454 6748	0.3284 9333	0.3123 5968	122
123	0.3791 1496	0.3603 2361	0.3424 7086	0.3255 0949	0.3093 9464	123
124	0.3761 3721	0.3573 4572	0.3395 0024	0.3225 5276	0.3064 5776	124
125	0.3731 8284	0.3543 9245	0.3365 5538	0.3196 2288	0.3035 4875	125
126	0.3702 5168	0.3514 6359	0.3336 3606	0.3167 1962	0.3006 6735	126
127	0.3673 4355	0.3485 5893	0.3307 4207	0.3138 4273	0.2978 1331	127
128	0.3644 5825	0.3456 7828	0.3278 7318	0.3109 9197	0.2949 8636	128
129	0.3615 9562	0.3428 2144	0.3250 2917	0.3081 6710	0.2921 8624	129
130	0.3587 5547	0.3399 8820	0.3222 0984	0.3053 6790	0.2894 1270	130
131	0.3559 3763	0.3371 7838	0.3194 1496	0.3025 9412	0.2866 6549	131
132	0.3531 4193	0.3343 9178	0.3166 4432	0.2998 4553	0.2839 4436	132
133	0.3503 6818	0.3316 2821	0.3138 9771	0.2971 2192	0.2812 4905	133
134	0.3476 1622	0.3288 8749	0.3111 7493	0.2944 2304	0.2785 7933	134
135	0.3448 8587	0.3261 6941	0.3084 7577	0.2917 4867	0.2759 3496	135
136	0.3421 7697	0.3234 7379	0.3058 0002	0.2890 9860	0.2733 1568	136
137	0.3394 8935	0.3208 0045	0.3031 4748	0.2864 7261	0.2707 2127	137
138	0.3368 2283	0.3181 4921	0.3005 1795	0.2838 7046	0.2681 5148	138
139	0.3341 7726	0.3155 1988	0.2979 1122	0.2812 9195	0.2656 0609	139
140	0.3315 5247	0.3129 1228	0.2953 2711	0.2787 3686	0.2630 8486	140
141	0.3289 4830	0.3103 2622	0.2927 6541	0.2762 0498	0.2605 8757	141
142	0.3263 6458	0.3077 6155	0.2902 2594	0.2736 9610	0.2581 1397	142
143	0.3238 0115	0.3052 1806	0.2877 0849	0.2712 1001	0.2556 6386	143
144	0.3212 5786	0.3026 9560	0.2852 1288	0.2687 4650	0.2532 3701	144
145	0.3187 3455	0.3001 9398	0.2827 3891	0.2663 0537	0.2508 3319	145
146	0.3162 3105	0.2977 1304	0.2802 8640	0.2638 8641	0.2484 5219	146
147	0.3137 4722	0.2952 5260	0.2778 5517	0.2614 8942	0.2460 9379	147
148	0.3112 8289	0.2928 1250	0.2754 4503	0.2591 1421	0.2437 5778	148
149	0.3088 3793	0.2903 9256	0.2730 5579	0.2567 6057	0.2414 4394	149
150	0.3064 1216	0.2879 9262	0.2706 8728	0.2544 2831	0.2391 5207	150
151	0.3040 0545	0.2856 1252	0.2683 3931	0.2521 1724	0.2368 8195	151
152	0.3016 1765	0.2832 5208	0.2660 1170	0.2498 2715	0.2346 3338	152
153	0.2992 4860	0.2809 1116	0.2637 0429	0.2475 5787	0.2324 0615	153
154	0.2968 9815	0.2785 8958	0.2614 1689	0.2453 0921	0.2302 0007	154
155	0.2945 6617	0.2762 8718	0.2591 4934	0.2430 8096	0.2280 1492	155
156	0.2922 5251	0.2740 0382	0.2569 0145	0.2408 7296	0.2258 5052	156
157	0.2899 5701	0.2717 3932	0.2546 7306	0.2386 8502	0.2237 0667	157
158	0.2876 7955	0.2694 9354	0.2524 6400	0.2365 1694	0.2215 8316	158
159	0.2854 1997	0.2672 6632	0.2502 7410	0.2343 6857	0.2194 7981	159
160	0.2831 7815	0.2650 5751	0.2481 0320	0.2322 3970	0.2173 9643	160
161	0.2809 5393	0.2628 6695	0.2459 5113	0.2301 3017	0.2153 3283	161
162	0.2787 4718	0.2606 9450	0.2438 1772	0.2280 3981	0.2132 8881	162
163	0.2765 5776	0.2585 4000	0.2417 0282	0.2259 6843	0.2112 6419	163
164	0.2743 8555	0.2564 0331	0.2396 0627	0.2239 1587	0.2092 5880	164
165	0.2722 3039	0.2542 8427	0.2375 2790	0.2218 8195	0.2072 7244	165
166	0.2700 9216	0.2521 8275	0.2354 6756	0.2198 6651	0.2053 0493	166
167	0.2679 7072	0.2500 9859	0.2334 2509	0.2178 6937	0.2033 5610	167
168	0.2658 6595	0.2480 3166	0.2314 0033	0.2158 9038	0.2014 2577	168
169	0.2637 7771	0.2459 8181	0.2293 9314	0.2139 2936	0.1995 1376	169
170	0.2617 0587	0.2439 4891	0.2274 0336	0.2119 8615	0.1976 1991	170
171	0.2596 5031	0.2419 3280	0.2254 3084	0.2100 6060	0.1957 4403	171
172	0.2576 1089	0.2399 3335	0.2234 7543	0.2081 5253	0.1938 8595	172
173	0.2555 8749	0.2379 5043	0.2215 3699	0.2062 6180	0.1920 4552	173
174	0.2535 7998	0.2359 8390	0.2196 1535	0.2043 8824	0.1902 2255	174
175	0.2515 8824	0.2340 3362	0.2177 1039	0.2025 3170	0.1884 1689	175
176	0.2496 1214	0.2320 9946	0.2158 2194	0.2006 9202	0.1866 2837	176
177	0.2476 5157	0.2301 8128	0.2139 4988	0.1988 6906	0.1848 5682	177
178	0.2457 0639	0.2282 7896	0.2120 9406	0.1970 6265	0.1831 0209	178
179	0.2437 7650	0.2263 9235	0.2102 5433	0.1952 7265	0.1813 6402	179
180	0.2418 6176	0.2245 2134	0.2084 3057	0.1934 9891	0.1796 4245	180

TABLE II

N	19/24	5/6	7/8	11/12	23/24	N
181	0.2399 6206	0.2226 6579	0.2066 2262	0.1917 4128	0.1779 3722	181
182	0.2380 7728	0.2208 2558	0.2048 3035	0.1899 9962	0.1762 4817	182
183	0.2362 0730	0.2190 0058	0.2030 5363	0.1882 7378	0.1745 7516	183
184	0.2343 5202	0.2171 9065	0.2012 9233	0.1865 6361	0.1729 1803	184
185	0.2325 1130	0.2153 9569	0.1995 4630	0.1848 6898	0.1712 7663	185
186	0.2306 8505	0.2136 1556	0.1978 1541	0.1831 8974	0.1696 5081	186
187	0.2288 7313	0.2118 5014	0.1960 9954	0.1815 2575	0.1680 4042	187
188	0.2270 7545	0.2100 9932	0.1943 9855	0.1798 7688	0.1664 4532	188
189	0.2252 9189	0.2083 6296	0.1927 1232	0.1782 4299	0.1648 6536	189
190	0.2235 2234	0.2066 4095	0.1910 4071	0.1766 2393	0.1633 0040	190
191	0.2217 6669	0.2049 3317	0.1893 8361	0.1750 1959	0.1617 5029	191
192	0.2200 2482	0.2032 3951	0.1877 4087	0.1734 2981	0.1602 1490	192
193	0.2182 9664	0.2015 5985	0.1861 1239	0.1718 5448	0.1586 9408	193
194	0.2165 8203	0.1998 9406	0.1844 9803	0.1702 9346	0.1571 8770	194
195	0.2148 8089	0.1982 4204	0.1828 9768	0.1687 4661	0.1556 9561	195
196	0.2131 9312	0.1966 0368	0.1813 1121	0.1672 1382	0.1542 1769	196
197	0.2115 1859	0.1949 7886	0.1797 3849	0.1656 9495	0.1527 5380	197
198	0.2098 5722	0.1933 6746	0.1781 7942	0.1641 8988	0.1513 0381	198
199	0.2082 0890	0.1917 6938	0.1766 3388	0.1626 9847	0.1498 6758	199
200	0.2065 7353	0.1901 8451	0.1751 0174	0.1612 2062	0.1484 4498	200
201	0.2049 5100	0.1886 1274	0.1735 8289	0.1597 5619	0.1470 3589	201
202	0.2033 4122	0.1870 5396	0.1720 7721	0.1583 0506	0.1456 4017	202
203	0.2017 4408	0.1855 0806	0.1705 8460	0.1568 6711	0.1442 5770	203
204	0.2001 5948	0.1839 7493	0.1691 0493	0.1554 4222	0.1428 8835	204
205	0.1985 8733	0.1824 5448	0.1676 3809	0.1540 3028	0.1415 3200	205
206	0.1970 2753	0.1809 4659	0.1661 8398	0.1526 3116	0.1401 8853	206
207	0.1954 7998	0.1794 5116	0.1647 4249	0.1512 4475	0.1388 5781	207
208	0.1939 4458	0.1779 6810	0.1633 1349	0.1498 7093	0.1375 3972	208
209	0.1924 2125	0.1764 9728	0.1618 9690	0.1485 0959	0.1362 3414	209
210	0.1909 0988	0.1750 3863	0.1604 9259	0.1471 6062	0.1349 4096	210
211	0.1894 1038	0.1735 9203	0.1591 0046	0.1458 2390	0.1336 6005	211
212	0.1879 2266	0.1721 5738	0.1577 2040	0.1444 9932	0.1323 9130	212
213	0.1864 4662	0.1707 3460	0.1563 5232	0.1431 8678	0.1311 3459	213
214	0.1849 8218	0.1693 2357	0.1549 9611	0.1418 8616	0.1298 8982	214
215	0.1835 2924	0.1679 2420	0.1536 5165	0.1405 9735	0.1286 5685	215
216	0.1820 8771	0.1665 3639	0.1523 1886	0.1393 2024	0.1274 3560	216
217	0.1806 5751	0.1651 6006	0.1509 9763	0.1380 5474	0.1262 2593	217
218	0.1792 3854	0.1637 9510	0.1496 8787	0.1368 0074	0.1250 2775	218
219	0.1778 3071	0.1624 4142	0.1483 8946	0.1355 5812	0.1238 4094	219
220	0.1764 3394	0.1610 9893	0.1471 0231	0.1343 2679	0.1226 6540	220
221	0.1750 4814	0.1597 6754	0.1458 2633	0.1331 0665	0.1215 0101	221
222	0.1736 7323	0.1584 4714	0.1445 6142	0.1318 9759	0.1203 4768	222
223	0.1723 0912	0.1571 3766	0.1433 0748	0.1306 9951	0.1192 0530	223
224	0.1709 5572	0.1558 3900	0.1420 6442	0.1295 1231	0.1180 7376	224
225	0.1696 1295	0.1545 5108	0.1408 3213	0.1283 3590	0.1169 5296	225
226	0.1682 8073	0.1532 7380	0.1396 1054	0.1271 7017	0.1158 4280	226
227	0.1669 5897	0.1520 0707	0.1383 9955	0.1260 1503	0.1147 4317	227
228	0.1656 4759	0.1507 5081	0.1371 9905	0.1248 7039	0.1136 5399	228
229	0.1643 4651	0.1495 0494	0.1360 0898	0.1237 3614	0.1125 7514	229
230	0.1630 5566	0.1482 6936	0.1348 2922	0.1226 1220	0.1115 0654	230
231	0.1617 7494	0.1470 4400	0.1336 5970	0.1214 9846	0.1104 4808	231
232	0.1605 0428	0.1458 2876	0.1325 0032	0.1203 9484	0.1093 9967	232
233	0.1592 4360	0.1446 2356	0.1313 5100	0.1193 0125	0.1083 6120	233
234	0.1579 9282	0.1434 2832	0.1302 1165	0.1182 1758	0.1073 3260	234
235	0.1567 5187	0.1422 4297	0.1290 8218	0.1171 4377	0.1063 1376	235
236	0.1555 2067	0.1410 6740	0.1279 6251	0.1160 7970	0.1053 0459	236
237	0.1542 9913	0.1399 0156	0.1268 5255	0.1150 2530	0.1043 0500	237
238	0.1530 8719	0.1387 4535	0.1257 5221	0.1139 8048	0.1033 1490	238
239	0.1518 8477	0.1375 9869	0.1246 6143	0.1129 4515	0.1023 3420	239
240	0.1506 9179	0.1364 6151	0.1235 8010	0.1119 1923	0.1013 6280	240

TABLE II

N	19/24	5/6	7/8	11/12	23/24	N
241	0.1495 0819	0.1353 3373	0.1225 0815	0.1109 0262	0.1004 0063	241
242	0.1483 3388	0.1342 1527	0.1214 4551	0.1098 9525	0.0994 4759	242
243	0.1471 6879	0.1331 0605	0.1203 9208	0.1088 9702	0.0985 0360	243
244	0.1460 1286	0.1320 0600	0.1193 4778	0.1079 0787	0.0975 6857	244
245	0.1448 6600	0.1309 1504	0.1183 1255	0.1069 2770	0.0966 4241	245
246	0.1437 2815	0.1298 3310	0.1172 8629	0.1059 5643	0.0957 2505	246
247	0.1425 9924	0.1287 6010	0.1162 6894	0.1049 9398	0.0948 1639	247
248	0.1414 7920	0.1276 9597	0.1152 6041	0.1040 4028	0.0939 1636	248
249	0.1403 6795	0.1266 4063	0.1142 6063	0.1030 9524	0.0930 2487	249
250	0.1392 6543	0.1255 9401	0.1132 6952	0.1021 5879	0.0921 4184	250
251	0.1381 7158	0.1245 5604	0.1122 8701	0.1012 3084	0.0912 6720	251
252	0.1370 8631	0.1235 2666	0.1113 1302	0.1003 1132	0.0904 0086	252
253	0.1360 0957	0.1225 0577	0.1103 4748	0.0994 0015	0.0895 4274	253
254	0.1349 4128	0.1214 9333	0.1093 9032	0.0984 9726	0.0886 9277	254
255	0.1338 8139	0.1204 8925	0.1084 4145	0.0976 0257	0.0878 5086	255
256	0.1328 2982	0.1194 9347	0.1075 0082	0.0967 1600	0.0870 1695	256
257	0.1317 8651	0.1185 0592	0.1065 6835	0.0958 3749	0.0861 9095	257
258	0.1307 5139	0.1175 2654	0.1056 4396	0.0949 6696	0.0853 7280	258
259	0.1297 2441	0.1165 5524	0.1047 2760	0.0941 0434	0.0845 6241	259
260	0.1287 0549	0.1155 9198	0.1038 1918	0.0932 4955	0.0837 5971	260
261	0.1276 9457	0.1146 3667	0.1029 1864	0.0924 0253	0.0829 6463	261
262	0.1266 9160	0.1136 8926	0.1020 2591	0.0915 6320	0.0821 7710	262
263	0.1256 9650	0.1127 4968	0.1011 4093	0.0907 3149	0.0813 9705	263
264	0.1247 0922	0.1118 1786	0.1002 6362	0.0899 0734	0.0806 2440	264
265	0.1237 2969	0.1108 9375	0.0993 9393	0.0890 9068	0.0798 5908	265
266	0.1227 5786	0.1099 7727	0.0985 3177	0.0882 8143	0.0791 0103	266
267	0.1217 9366	0.1090 6837	0.0976 7710	0.0874 7954	0.0783 5017	267
268	0.1208 3703	0.1081 6698	0.0968 2984	0.0866 8493	0.0776 0645	268
269	0.1198 8792	0.1072 7304	0.0959 8993	0.0858 9753	0.0768 6978	269
270	0.1189 4626	0.1063 8648	0.0951 5730	0.0851 1729	0.0761 4010	270
271	0.1180 1200	0.1055 0725	0.0943 3190	0.0843 4413	0.0754 1735	271
272	0.1170 8508	0.1046 3529	0.0935 1365	0.0835 7800	0.0747 0146	272
273	0.1161 6544	0.1037 7054	0.0927 0250	0.0828 1883	0.0739 9237	273
274	0.1152 5302	0.1029 1293	0.0918 9839	0.0820 6655	0.0732 9001	274
275	0.1143 4776	0.1020 6241	0.0911 0126	0.0813 2111	0.0725 9431	275
276	0.1134 4962	0.1012 1892	0.0903 1104	0.0805 8244	0.0719 0522	276
277	0.1125 5853	0.1003 8240	0.0895 2767	0.0798 5048	0.0712 2267	277
278	0.1116 7444	0.0995 5279	0.0887 5110	0.0791 2516	0.0705 4660	278
279	0.1107 9730	0.0987 3004	0.0879 8126	0.0784 0644	0.0698 7694	279
280	0.1099 2704	0.0979 1409	0.0872 1810	0.0776 9424	0.0692 1364	280
281	0.1090 6362	0.0971 0489	0.0864 6156	0.0769 8851	0.0685 5664	281
282	0.1082 0698	0.0963 0237	0.0857 1159	0.0762 8919	0.0679 0588	282
283	0.1073 5707	0.0955 0648	0.0849 6812	0.0755 9623	0.0672 6129	283
284	0.1065 1384	0.0947 1717	0.0842 3109	0.0749 0956	0.0666 2282	284
285	0.1056 7723	0.0939 3438	0.0835 0047	0.0742 2912	0.0659 9041	285
286	0.1048 4719	0.0931 5806	0.0827 7617	0.0735 5487	0.0653 6401	286
287	0.1040 2367	0.0923 8816	0.0820 5817	0.0728 8674	0.0647 4355	287
288	0.1032 0661	0.0916 2463	0.0813 4638	0.0722 2468	0.0641 2898	288
289	0.1023 9598	0.0908 6740	0.0806 4078	0.0715 6864	0.0635 2025	289
290	0.1015 9171	0.0901 1643	0.0799 4129	0.0709 1855	0.0629 1729	290
291	0.1007 9376	0.0893 7166	0.0792 4787	0.0702 7437	0.0623 2005	291
292	0.1000 0208	0.0886 3305	0.0785 6047	0.0696 3604	0.0617 2849	292
293	0.0992 1661	0.0879 0055	0.0778 7903	0.0690 0350	0.0611 4254	293
294	0.0984 3732	0.0871 7410	0.0772 0350	0.0683 7672	0.0605 6215	294
295	0.0976 6414	0.0864 5365	0.0765 3383	0.0677 5563	0.0599 8728	295
296	0.0968 9704	0.0857 3916	0.0758 6996	0.0671 4017	0.0594 1785	296
297	0.0961 3596	0.0850 3057	0.0752 1186	0.0665 3031	0.0588 5384	297
298	0.0953 8087	0.0843 2784	0.0745 5946	0.0659 2599	0.0582 9518	298
299	0.0946 3170	0.0836 3091	0.0739 1273	0.0653 2716	0.0577 4182	299
300	0.0938 8841	0.0829 3975	0.0732 7160	0.0647 3377	0.0571 9371	300

TABLE II

N	19/24	5/6	7/8	11/12	23/24	N
301	0.0931 5097	0.0822 5430	0.0726 3604	0.0641 4576	0.0566 5081	301
302	0.0924 1932	0.0815 7451	0.0720 0598	0.0635 6310	0.0561 1306	302
303	0.0916 9341	0.0809 0034	0.0713 8140	0.0629 8573	0.0555 8041	303
304	0.0909 7321	0.0802 3174	0.0707 6223	0.0624 1361	0.0550 5282	304
305	0.0902 5866	0.0795 6867	0.0701 4843	0.0618 4668	0.0545 3024	305
306	0.0895 4972	0.0789 1108	0.0695 3995	0.0612 8490	0.0540 1262	306
307	0.0888 4636	0.0782 5892	0.0689 3676	0.0607 2823	0.0534 9991	307
308	0.0881 4851	0.0776 1215	0.0683 3879	0.0601 7661	0.0529 9207	308
309	0.0874 5615	0.0769 7073	0.0677 4601	0.0596 3000	0.0524 8905	309
310	0.0867 6923	0.0763 3461	0.0671 5838	0.0590 8836	0.0519 9081	310
311	0.0860 8770	0.0757 0374	0.0665 7584	0.0585 5163	0.0514 9729	311
312	0.0854 1153	0.0750 7809	0.0659 9835	0.0580 1978	0.0510 0846	312
313	0.0847 4066	0.0744 5761	0.0654 2588	0.0574 9277	0.0505 2427	313
314	0.0840 7507	0.0738 4226	0.0648 5837	0.0569 7054	0.0500 4467	314
315	0.0834 1470	0.0732 3199	0.0642 9578	0.0564 5305	0.0495 6963	315
316	0.0827 5952	0.0726 2677	0.0637 3807	0.0559 4026	0.0490 9910	316
317	0.0821 0949	0.0720 2655	0.0631 8520	0.0554 3214	0.0486 3303	317
318	0.0814 6456	0.0714 3129	0.0626 3713	0.0549 2862	0.0481 7139	318
319	0.0808 2470	0.0708 4095	0.0620 9381	0.0544 2969	0.0477 1413	319
320	0.0801 8986	0.0702 5548	0.0615 5520	0.0539 3528	0.0472 6121	320
321	0.0795 6001	0.0696 7486	0.0610 2126	0.0534 4536	0.0468 1259	321
322	0.0789 3511	0.0690 9904	0.0604 9196	0.0529 5990	0.0463 6823	322
323	0.0783 1512	0.0685 2797	0.0599 6724	0.0524 7884	0.0459 2808	323
324	0.0776 9999	0.0679 6162	0.0594 4708	0.0520 0215	0.0454 9212	324
325	0.0770 8970	0.0673 9996	0.0589 3143	0.0515 2980	0.0450 6029	325
326	0.0764 8420	0.0668 4293	0.0584 2025	0.0510 6173	0.0446 3256	326
327	0.0758 8345	0.0662 9051	0.0579 1351	0.0505 9792	0.0442 0889	327
328	0.0752 8743	0.0657 4266	0.0574 1116	0.0501 3832	0.0437 8924	328
329	0.0746 9608	0.0651 9933	0.0569 1317	0.0496 8289	0.0433 7358	329
330	0.0741 0938	0.0646 6049	0.0564 1950	0.0492 3160	0.0429 6186	330
331	0.0735 2729	0.0641 2611	0.0559 3011	0.0487 8441	0.0425 5405	331
332	0.0729 4977	0.0635 9614	0.0554 4497	0.0483 4128	0.0421 5011	332
333	0.0723 7679	0.0630 7055	0.0549 6403	0.0479 0218	0.0417 5001	333
334	0.0718 0831	0.0625 4931	0.0544 8727	0.0474 6706	0.0413 5370	334
335	0.0712 4429	0.0620 3237	0.0540 1464	0.0470 3590	0.0409 6116	335
336	0.0706 8470	0.0615 1971	0.0535 4611	0.0466 0866	0.0405 7234	336
337	0.0701 2951	0.0610 1128	0.0530 8165	0.0461 8529	0.0401 8721	337
338	0.0695 7868	0.0605 0705	0.0526 2121	0.0457 6577	0.0398 0574	338
339	0.0690 3218	0.0600 0699	0.0521 6477	0.0453 5006	0.0394 2789	339
340	0.0684 8996	0.0595 1107	0.0517 1229	0.0449 3813	0.0390 5363	340
341	0.0679 5201	0.0590 1924	0.0512 6373	0.0445 2994	0.0386 8292	341
342	0.0674 1828	0.0585 3148	0.0508 1907	0.0441 2545	0.0383 1572	342
343	0.0668 8875	0.0580 4775	0.0503 7826	0.0437 2465	0.0379 5202	343
344	0.0663 6337	0.0575 6801	0.0499 4127	0.0433 2748	0.0375 9176	344
345	0.0658 4212	0.0570 9225	0.0495 0807	0.0429 3392	0.0372 3493	345
346	0.0653 2496	0.0566 2041	0.0490 7864	0.0425 4393	0.0368 8148	346
347	0.0648 1187	0.0561 5247	0.0486 5292	0.0421 5749	0.0365 3139	347
348	0.0643 0281	0.0556 8840	0.0482 3090	0.0417 7455	0.0361 8462	348
349	0.0637 9774	0.0552 2817	0.0478 1254	0.0413 9510	0.0358 4114	349
350	0.0632 9664	0.0547 7174	0.0473 9781	0.0410 1909	0.0355 0092	350
351	0.0627 9948	0.0543 1908	0.0469 8668	0.0406 4650	0.0351 6394	351
352	0.0623 0622	0.0538 7016	0.0465 7911	0.0402 7729	0.0348 3015	352
353	0.0618 1684	0.0534 2495	0.0461 7508	0.0399 1143	0.0344 9953	353
354	0.0613 3130	0.0529 8342	0.0457 7455	0.0395 4890	0.0341 7204	354
355	0.0608 4957	0.0525 4554	0.0453 7750	0.0391 8966	0.0338 4767	355
356	0.0603 7163	0.0521 1128	0.0449 8389	0.0388 3369	0.0335 2638	356
357	0.0598 9744	0.0516 8061	0.0445 9370	0.0384 8095	0.0332 0813	357
358	0.0594 2698	0.0512 5350	0.0442 0688	0.0381 3141	0.0328 9291	358
359	0.0589 6021	0.0508 2992	0.0438 2343	0.0377 8504	0.0325 8068	359
360	0.0584 9711	0.0504 0983	0.0434 4330	0.0374 4183	0.0322 7141	360

TABLE II

N	1	1 1/8	1 1/4	1 3/8	1 1/2	N
1	0.9900 9901	0.9888 7515	0.9876 5432	0.9864 3650	0.9852 2167	1
2	0.9802 9605	0.9778 7407	0.9754 6106	0.9730 5696	0.9706 6175	2
3	0.9705 9015	0.9669 9537	0.9634 1833	0.9598 5890	0.9563 1699	3
4	0.9609 8034	0.9562 3770	0.9515 2428	0.9468 3986	0.9421 8423	4
5	0.9514 6569	0.9455 9970	0.9397 7706	0.9339 9739	0.9282 6033	5
6	0.9420 4524	0.9350 8005	0.9281 7488	0.9213 2912	0.9145 4219	6
7	0.9327 1805	0.9246 7743	0.9167 1593	0.9088 3267	0.9010 2679	7
8	0.9234 8322	0.9143 9054	0.9053 9845	0.8965 0571	0.8877 1112	8
9	0.9143 3982	0.9042 1808	0.8942 2069	0.8843 4596	0.8745 9224	9
10	0.9052 8695	0.8941 5880	0.8831 8093	0.8723 5113	0.8616 6723	10
11	0.8963 2372	0.8842 1142	0.8722 7746	0.8605 1899	0.8489 3323	11
12	0.8874 4923	0.8743 7470	0.8615 0860	0.8488 4734	0.8363 8742	12
13	0.8786 6260	0.8646 4742	0.8508 7269	0.8373 3400	0.8240 2702	13
14	0.8699 6297	0.8550 2835	0.8403 6809	0.8259 7682	0.8118 4928	14
15	0.8613 4947	0.8455 1629	0.8299 9318	0.8147 7368	0.7998 5150	15
16	0.8528 2126	0.8361 1005	0.8197 4635	0.8037 2250	0.7880 3104	16
17	0.8443 7749	0.8268 0846	0.8096 2602	0.7928 2120	0.7763 8526	17
18	0.8360 1731	0.8176 1034	0.7996 3064	0.7820 6777	0.7649 1159	18
19	0.8277 3992	0.8085 1455	0.7897 5866	0.7714 6020	0.7536 0747	19
20	0.8195 4447	0.7995 1995	0.7800 0855	0.7609 9649	0.7424 7042	20
21	0.8114 3017	0.7906 2542	0.7703 7881	0.7506 7472	0.7314 9795	21
22	0.8033 9621	0.7818 2983	0.7608 6796	0.7404 9294	0.7206 8763	22
23	0.7954 4179	0.7731 3210	0.7514 7453	0.7304 4926	0.7100 3708	23
24	0.7875 6613	0.7645 3112	0.7421 9707	0.7205 4181	0.6995 4392	24
25	0.7797 6844	0.7560 2583	0.7330 3414	0.7107 6874	0.6892 0583	25
26	0.7720 4796	0.7476 1516	0.7239 8434	0.7011 2823	0.6790 2052	26
27	0.7644 0392	0.7392 9806	0.7150 4626	0.6916 1847	0.6689 8574	27
28	0.7568 3557	0.7310 7348	0.7062 1853	0.6822 3771	0.6590 9925	28
29	0.7493 4215	0.7229 4040	0.6974 9978	0.6729 8417	0.6493 5887	29
30	0.7419 2292	0.7148 9780	0.6888 8867	0.6638 5615	0.6397 6243	30
31	0.7345 7715	0.7069 4467	0.6803 8387	0.6548 5194	0.6303 0781	31
32	0.7273 0411	0.6990 8002	0.6719 8407	0.6459 6985	0.6209 9292	32
33	0.7201 0307	0.6913 0287	0.6636 8797	0.6372 0824	0.6118 1568	33
34	0.7129 7334	0.6836 1223	0.6554 9429	0.6285 6546	0.6027 7407	34
35	0.7059 1420	0.6760 0715	0.6474 0177	0.6200 3991	0.5938 6608	35
36	0.6989 2495	0.6684 8667	0.6394 0916	0.6116 3000	0.5850 8974	36
37	0.6920 0490	0.6610 4986	0.6315 1522	0.6033 3416	0.5764 4309	37
38	0.6851 5337	0.6536 9578	0.6237 1873	0.5951 5083	0.5679 2423	38
39	0.6783 6967	0.6464 2352	0.6160 1850	0.5870 7850	0.5595 3126	39
40	0.6716 5314	0.6392 3216	0.6084 1334	0.5791 1566	0.5512 6232	40
41	0.6650 0311	0.6321 2080	0.6009 0206	0.5712 6083	0.5431 1559	41
42	0.6584 1892	0.6250 8855	0.5934 8352	0.5635 1253	0.5350 8925	42
43	0.6518 9992	0.6181 3454	0.5861 5656	0.5558 6933	0.5271 8153	43
44	0.6454 4546	0.6112 5789	0.5789 2006	0.5483 2979	0.5193 9067	44
45	0.6390 5492	0.6044 5774	0.5717 7290	0.5408 9252	0.5117 1494	45
46	0.6327 2764	0.5977 3324	0.5647 1397	0.5335 5612	0.5041 5265	46
47	0.6264 6301	0.5910 8355	0.5577 4219	0.5263 1923	0.4967 0212	47
48	0.6202 6041	0.5845 0784	0.5508 5649	0.5191 8050	0.4893 6170	48
49	0.6141 1921	0.5780 0528	0.5440 5579	0.5121 3860	0.4821 2975	49
50	0.6080 3882	0.5715 7506	0.5373 3905	0.5051 9220	0.4750 0468	50
51	0.6020 1864	0.5652 1637	0.5307 0524	0.4983 4003	0.4679 8491	51
52	0.5960 5806	0.5589 2843	0.5241 5332	0.4915 8079	0.4610 6887	52
53	0.5901 5649	0.5527 1044	0.5176 8229	0.4849 1323	0.4542 5505	53
54	0.5843 1336	0.5465 6162	0.5112 9115	0.4783 3611	0.4475 4192	54
55	0.5785 2808	0.5404 8120	0.5049 7892	0.4718 4820	0.4409 2800	55
56	0.5728 0008	0.5344 6843	0.4987 4461	0.4654 4829	0.4344 1182	56
57	0.5671 2879	0.5285 2256	0.4925 8727	0.4591 3518	0.4279 9194	57
58	0.5615 1365	0.5226 4282	0.4865 0594	0.4529 0770	0.4216 6694	58
59	0.5559 5411	0.5168 2850	0.4804 9970	0.4467 6468	0.4154 3541	59
60	0.5504 4962	0.5110 7887	0.4745 6760	0.4407 0499	0.4092 9597	60

TABLE II

N	1	1 1/8	1 1/4	1 3/8	1 1/2	N
61	0.5449 9962	0.5053 9319	0.4687 0874	0.4347 2749	0.4032 4726	61
62	0.5396 0358	0.4997 7077	0.4629 2222	0.4288 3106	0.3972 8794	62
63	0.5342 6097	0.4942 1090	0.4572 0713	0.4230 1461	0.3914 1669	63
64	0.5289 7126	0.4887 1288	0.4515 6259	0.4172 7705	0.3856 3221	64
65	0.5237 3392	0.4832 7602	0.4459 8775	0.4116 1731	0.3799 3321	65
66	0.5185 4844	0.4778 9965	0.4404 8173	0.4060 3434	0.3743 1843	66
67	0.5134 1429	0.4725 8309	0.4350 4368	0.4005 2709	0.3687 8663	67
68	0.5083 3099	0.4673 2568	0.4296 7277	0.3950 9454	0.3633 3658	68
69	0.5032 9801	0.4621 2675	0.4243 6817	0.3897 3568	0.3579 6708	69
70	0.4983 1486	0.4569 8566	0.4191 2905	0.3844 4949	0.3526 7692	70
71	0.4933 8105	0.4519 0177	0.4139 5462	0.3792 3501	0.3474 6495	71
72	0.4884 9609	0.4468 7443	0.4088 4407	0.3740 9126	0.3423 3000	72
73	0.4836 5949	0.4419 0302	0.4037 9661	0.3690 1727	0.3372 7093	73
74	0.4788 7078	0.4369 8692	0.3988 1147	0.3640 1210	0.3322 8663	74
75	0.4741 2949	0.4321 2551	0.3938 8787	0.3590 7483	0.3273 7599	75
76	0.4694 3514	0.4273 1818	0.3890 2506	0.3542 0451	0.3225 3793	76
77	0.4647 8726	0.4225 6433	0.3842 2228	0.3494 0026	0.3177 7136	77
78	0.4601 8541	0.4178 6337	0.3794 7879	0.3446 6117	0.3130 7523	78
79	0.4556 2912	0.4132 1470	0.3747 9387	0.3399 8636	0.3084 4850	79
80	0.4511 1794	0.4086 1775	0.3701 6679	0.3353 7495	0.3038 9015	80
81	0.4466 5142	0.4040 7194	0.3655 9683	0.3308 2609	0.2993 9916	81
82	0.4422 2913	0.3995 7670	0.3610 8329	0.3263 3893	0.2949 7454	82
83	0.4378 5063	0.3951 3148	0.3566 2547	0.3219 1263	0.2906 1531	83
84	0.4335 1547	0.3907 3570	0.3522 2268	0.3175 4637	0.2863 2050	84
85	0.4292 2324	0.3863 8882	0.3478 7426	0.3132 3933	0.2820 8917	85
86	0.4249 7350	0.3820 9031	0.3435 7951	0.3089 9071	0.2779 2036	86
87	0.4207 6585	0.3778 3961	0.3393 3779	0.3047 9971	0.2738 1316	87
88	0.4165 9985	0.3736 3621	0.3351 4843	0.3006 6556	0.2697 6666	88
89	0.4124 7510	0.3694 7956	0.3310 1080	0.2965 8748	0.2657 7996	89
90	0.4083 9119	0.3653 6916	0.3269 2425	0.2925 6472	0.2618 5218	90
91	0.4043 4771	0.3613 0448	0.3228 8814	0.2885 9652	0.2579 8245	91
92	0.4003 4427	0.3572 8503	0.3189 0187	0.2846 8214	0.2541 6990	92
93	0.3963 8046	0.3533 1029	0.3149 6481	0.2808 2085	0.2504 1369	93
94	0.3924 5590	0.3493 7976	0.3110 7636	0.2770 1194	0.2467 1300	94
95	0.3885 7020	0.3454 9297	0.3072 3591	0.2732 5468	0.2430 6699	95
96	0.3847 2297	0.3416 4941	0.3034 4287	0.2695 4839	0.2394 7487	96
97	0.3809 1383	0.3378 4861	0.2996 9666	0.2658 9237	0.2359 3583	97
98	0.3771 4241	0.3340 9010	0.2959 9670	0.2622 8594	0.2324 4909	98
99	0.3734 0832	0.3303 7340	0.2923 4242	0.2587 2843	0.2290 1389	99
100	0.3697 1121	0.3266 9805	0.2887 3326	0.2552 1916	0.2256 2944	100
101	0.3660 5071	0.3230 6358	0.2851 6865	0.2517 5750	0.2222 9502	101
102	0.3624 2644	0.3194 6955	0.2816 4805	0.2483 4278	0.2190 0987	102
103	0.3588 3806	0.3159 1550	0.2781 7091	0.2449 7439	0.2157 7327	103
104	0.3552 8521	0.3124 0099	0.2747 3670	0.2416 5167	0.2125 8450	104
105	0.3517 6753	0.3089 2558	0.2713 4489	0.2383 7403	0.2094 4286	105
106	0.3482 8469	0.3054 8883	0.2679 9496	0.2351 4085	0.2063 4765	106
107	0.3448 3632	0.3020 9031	0.2646 8638	0.2319 5151	0.2032 9817	107
108	0.3414 2210	0.2987 2960	0.2614 1864	0.2288 0544	0.2002 9377	108
109	0.3380 4168	0.2954 0628	0.2581 9125	0.2257 0203	0.1973 3376	109
110	0.3346 9474	0.2921 1993	0.2550 0371	0.2226 4072	0.1944 1750	110
111	0.3313 8093	0.2888 7014	0.2518 5551	0.2196 2094	0.1915 4433	111
112	0.3280 9993	0.2856 5651	0.2487 4618	0.2166 4211	0.1887 1363	112
113	0.3248 5141	0.2824 7862	0.2456 7524	0.2137 0368	0.1859 2476	113
114	0.3216 3506	0.2793 3609	0.2426 4222	0.2108 0511	0.1831 7710	114
115	0.3184 5056	0.2762 2852	0.2396 4663	0.2079 4586	0.1804 7005	115
116	0.3152 9758	0.2731 5552	0.2366 8803	0.2051 2538	0.1778 0301	116
117	0.3121 7582	0.2701 1671	0.2337 6596	0.2023 4316	0.1751 7538	117
118	0.3090 8497	0.2671 1170	0.2308 7996	0.1995 9868	0.1725 8658	118
119	0.3060 2473	0.2641 4013	0.2280 2959	0.1968 9142	0.1700 3604	119
120	0.3029 9478	0.2612 0161	0.2252 1441	0.1942 2089	0.1675 2319	120

TABLE II

N	1	1 1/8	1 1/4	1 3/8	1 1/2	N
121	0.2999 9483	0.2582 9578	0.2224 3398	0.1915 8657	0.1650 4748	121
122	0.2970 2459	0.2554 2228	0.2196 8789	0.1889 8799	0.1626 0835	122
123	0.2940 8375	0.2525 8075	0.2169 7569	0.1864 2465	0.1602 0527	123
124	0.2911 7203	0.2497 7082	0.2142 9698	0.1838 9608	0.1578 3771	124
125	0.2882 8914	0.2469 9216	0.2116 5134	0.1814 0180	0.1555 0513	125
126	0.2854 3479	0.2442 4441	0.2090 3836	0.1789 4136	0.1532 0702	126
127	0.2826 0870	0.2415 2723	0.2064 5764	0.1765 1429	0.1509 4288	127
128	0.2798 1060	0.2388 4028	0.2039 0878	0.1741 2014	0.1487 1220	128
129	0.2770 4019	0.2361 8322	0.2013 9138	0.1717 5846	0.1465 1448	129
130	0.2742 9722	0.2335 5572	0.1989 0507	0.1694 2881	0.1443 4924	130
131	0.2715 8141	0.2309 5744	0.1964 4945	0.1671 3076	0.1422 1600	131
132	0.2688 9248	0.2283 8808	0.1940 2415	0.1648 6388	0.1401 1429	132
133	0.2662 3018	0.2258 4730	0.1916 2879	0.1626 2775	0.1380 4363	133
134	0.2635 9424	0.2233 3478	0.1892 6300	0.1604 2195	0.1360 0358	134
135	0.2609 8439	0.2208 5021	0.1869 2642	0.1582 4607	0.1339 9367	135
136	0.2584 0039	0.2183 9329	0.1846 1869	0.1560 9970	0.1320 1347	136
137	0.2558 4197	0.2159 6370	0.1823 3945	0.1539 8244	0.1300 6253	137
138	0.2533 0888	0.2135 6114	0.1800 8834	0.1518 9390	0.1281 4043	138
139	0.2508 0087	0.2111 8530	0.1778 6503	0.1498 3368	0.1262 4673	139
140	0.2483 1770	0.2088 3590	0.1756 6916	0.1478 0141	0.1243 8101	140
141	0.2458 5911	0.2065 1263	0.1735 0041	0.1457 9671	0.1225 4287	141
142	0.2434 2486	0.2042 1521	0.1713 5843	0.1438 1920	0.1207 3189	142
143	0.2410 1471	0.2019 4335	0.1692 4289	0.1418 6850	0.1189 4768	143
144	0.2386 2843	0.1996 9676	0.1671 5347	0.1399 4427	0.1171 8983	144
145	0.2362 6577	0.1974 7516	0.1650 8985	0.1380 4614	0.1154 5796	145
146	0.2339 2650	0.1952 7828	0.1630 5171	0.1361 7375	0.1137 5168	146
147	0.2316 1040	0.1931 0584	0.1610 3872	0.1343 2675	0.1120 7062	147
148	0.2293 1723	0.1909 5757	0.1590 5059	0.1325 0481	0.1104 1441	148
149	0.2270 4676	0.1888 3320	0.1570 8700	0.1307 0758	0.1087 8267	149
150	0.2247 9877	0.1867 3245	0.1551 4766	0.1289 3473	0.1071 7504	150
151	0.2225 7304	0.1846 5509	0.1532 3225	0.1271 8592	0.1055 9117	151
152	0.2203 6935	0.1826 0083	0.1513 4050	0.1254 6084	0.1040 3071	152
153	0.2181 8747	0.1805 6942	0.1494 7209	0.1237 5915	0.1024 9331	153
154	0.2160 2720	0.1785 6061	0.1476 2676	0.1220 8054	0.1009 7863	154
155	0.2138 8832	0.1765 7415	0.1458 0421	0.1204 2470	0.0994 8634	155
156	0.2117 7061	0.1746 0979	0.1440 0416	0.1187 9132	0.0980 1610	156
157	0.2096 7387	0.1726 6729	0.1422 2633	0.1171 8010	0.0965 6758	157
158	0.2075 9789	0.1707 4639	0.1404 7045	0.1155 9072	0.0951 4048	158
159	0.2055 4247	0.1688 4686	0.1387 3624	0.1140 2291	0.0937 3446	159
160	0.2035 0739	0.1669 6847	0.1370 2345	0.1124 7636	0.0923 4922	160
161	0.2014 9247	0.1651 1097	0.1353 3180	0.1109 5078	0.0909 8445	161
162	0.1994 9750	0.1632 7413	0.1336 6104	0.1094 4590	0.0896 3986	162
163	0.1975 2227	0.1614 5774	0.1320 1090	0.1079 6143	0.0883 1513	163
164	0.1955 6661	0.1596 6154	0.1303 8114	0.1064 9710	0.0870 0998	164
165	0.1936 3030	0.1578 8533	0.1287 7150	0.1050 5263	0.0857 2412	165
166	0.1917 1317	0.1561 2888	0.1271 8172	0.1036 2774	0.0844 5726	166
167	0.1898 1502	0.1543 9197	0.1256 1158	0.1022 2219	0.0832 0912	167
168	0.1879 3566	0.1526 7439	0.1240 6082	0.1008 3570	0.0819 7943	168
169	0.1860 7492	0.1509 7591	0.1225 2920	0.0994 6801	0.0807 6791	169
170	0.1842 3259	0.1492 9632	0.1210 1650	0.0981 1888	0.0795 7430	170
171	0.1824 0850	0.1476 3543	0.1195 2247	0.0967 8804	0.0783 9832	171
172	0.1806 0248	0.1459 9300	0.1180 4688	0.0954 7526	0.0772 3973	172
173	0.1788 1434	0.1443 6885	0.1165 8951	0.0941 8028	0.0760 9825	173
174	0.1770 4390	0.1427 6277	0.1151 5014	0.0929 0286	0.0749 7365	174
175	0.1752 9099	0.1411 7456	0.1137 2853	0.0916 4278	0.0738 6566	175
176	0.1735 5543	0.1396 0401	0.1123 2447	0.0903 9978	0.0727 7405	176
177	0.1718 3706	0.1380 5094	0.1109 3775	0.0891 7364	0.0716 9857	177
178	0.1701 3571	0.1365 1515	0.1095 6815	0.0879 6413	0.0706 3899	178
179	0.1684 5119	0.1349 9644	0.1082 1546	0.0867 7103	0.0695 9506	179
180	0.1667 8336	0.1334 9462	0.1068 7946	0.0855 9411	0.0685 6657	180

TABLE II

N	1	1 1/8	1 1/4	1 3/8	1 1/2	N
181	0.1651 3204	0.1320 0951	0.1055 5996	0.0844 3316	0.0675 5327	181
182	0.1634 9707	0.1305 4093	0.1042 5675	0.0832 8795	0.0665 5494	182
183	0.1618 7829	0.1290 8868	0.1029 6963	0.0821 5827	0.0655 7137	183
184	0.1602 7553	0.1276 5259	0.1016 9840	0.0810 4392	0.0646 0234	184
185	0.1586 8864	0.1262 3247	0.1004 4287	0.0799 4468	0.0636 4762	185
186	0.1571 1747	0.1248 2816	0.0992 0283	0.0788 6035	0.0627 0702	186
187	0.1555 6185	0.1234 3946	0.0979 7811	0.0777 9073	0.0617 8031	187
188	0.1540 2163	0.1220 6622	0.0967 6850	0.0767 3561	0.0608 6730	188
189	0.1524 9667	0.1207 0825	0.0955 7383	0.0756 9481	0.0599 6779	189
190	0.1509 8680	0.1193 6539	0.0943 9390	0.0746 6812	0.0590 8156	190
191	0.1494 9188	0.1180 3747	0.0932 2855	0.0736 5536	0.0582 0844	191
192	0.1480 1176	0.1167 2432	0.0920 7758	0.0726 5634	0.0573 4821	192
193	0.1465 4630	0.1154 2578	0.0909 4082	0.0716 7086	0.0565 0070	193
194	0.1450 9535	0.1141 4169	0.0898 1809	0.0706 9875	0.0556 6572	194
195	0.1436 5876	0.1128 7188	0.0887 0922	0.0697 3983	0.0548 4307	195
196	0.1422 3640	0.1116 1620	0.0876 1405	0.0687 9391	0.0540 3258	196
197	0.1408 2811	0.1103 7448	0.0865 3239	0.0678 6083	0.0532 3407	197
198	0.1394 3378	0.1091 4658	0.0854 6409	0.0669 4040	0.0524 4736	198
199	0.1380 5324	0.1079 3234	0.0844 0898	0.0660 3245	0.0516 7228	199
200	0.1366 8638	0.1067 3161	0.0833 6689	0.0651 3682	0.0509 0865	200
201	0.1353 3305	0.1055 4424	0.0823 3767	0.0642 5334	0.0501 5630	201
202	0.1339 9312	0.1043 7008	0.0813 2116	0.0633 8184	0.0494 1508	202
203	0.1326 6645	0.1032 0898	0.0803 1719	0.0625 2216	0.0486 8480	203
204	0.1313 5293	0.1020 6079	0.0793 2562	0.0616 7414	0.0479 6532	204
205	0.1300 5240	0.1009 2538	0.0783 4629	0.0608 3762	0.0472 5648	205
206	0.1287 6475	0.0998 0260	0.0773 7906	0.0600 1245	0.0465 5811	206
207	0.1274 8985	0.0986 9231	0.0764 2376	0.0591 9847	0.0458 7005	207
208	0.1262 2758	0.0975 9438	0.0754 8026	0.0583 9553	0.0451 9217	208
209	0.1249 7780	0.0965 0866	0.0745 4840	0.0576 0348	0.0445 2431	209
210	0.1237 4040	0.0954 3501	0.0736 2805	0.0568 2218	0.0438 6631	210
211	0.1225 1524	0.0943 7331	0.0727 1906	0.0560 5147	0.0432 1804	211
212	0.1213 0222	0.0933 2342	0.0718 2130	0.0552 9122	0.0425 7935	212
213	0.1201 0121	0.0922 8521	0.0709 3461	0.0545 4127	0.0419 5010	213
214	0.1189 1209	0.0912 5856	0.0700 5888	0.0538 0150	0.0413 3015	214
215	0.1177 3474	0.0902 4332	0.0691 9395	0.0530 7177	0.0407 1936	215
216	0.1165 6905	0.0892 3938	0.0683 3971	0.0523 5193	0.0401 1759	216
217	0.1154 1490	0.0882 4660	0.0674 9601	0.0516 4185	0.0395 2472	217
218	0.1142 7218	0.0872 6487	0.0666 6272	0.0509 4141	0.0389 4061	218
219	0.1131 4077	0.0862 9406	0.0658 3973	0.0502 5046	0.0383 6514	219
220	0.1120 2057	0.0853 3406	0.0650 2689	0.0495 6889	0.0377 9816	220
221	0.1109 1145	0.0843 8473	0.0642 2409	0.0488 9656	0.0372 3957	221
222	0.1098 1332	0.0834 4596	0.0634 3120	0.0482 3336	0.0366 8923	222
223	0.1087 2606	0.0825 1764	0.0626 4810	0.0475 7914	0.0361 4703	223
224	0.1076 4956	0.0815 9964	0.0618 7466	0.0469 3380	0.0356 1283	224
225	0.1065 8373	0.0806 9186	0.0611 1078	0.0462 9722	0.0350 8654	225
226	0.1055 2844	0.0797 9417	0.0603 5633	0.0456 6926	0.0345 6802	226
227	0.1044 8361	0.0789 0647	0.0596 1119	0.0450 4983	0.0340 5716	227
228	0.1034 4911	0.0780 2865	0.0588 7525	0.0444 3879	0.0335 5385	228
229	0.1024 2487	0.0771 6060	0.0581 4839	0.0438 3605	0.0330 5798	229
230	0.1014 1076	0.0763 0220	0.0574 3051	0.0432 4148	0.0325 6944	230
231	0.1004 0669	0.0754 5335	0.0567 2149	0.0426 5497	0.0320 8812	231
232	0.0994 1257	0.0746 1394	0.0560 2123	0.0420 7642	0.0316 1391	232
233	0.0984 2828	0.0737 8387	0.0553 2961	0.0415 0572	0.0311 4671	233
234	0.0974 5375	0.0729 6304	0.0546 4652	0.0409 4276	0.0306 8641	234
235	0.0964 8886	0.0721 5133	0.0539 7188	0.0403 8743	0.0302 3292	235
236	0.0955 3352	0.0713 4866	0.0533 0556	0.0398 3963	0.0297 8613	236
237	0.0945 8765	0.0705 5492	0.0526 4746	0.0392 9927	0.0293 4594	237
238	0.0936 5113	0.0697 7001	0.0519 9749	0.0387 6623	0.0289 1225	238
239	0.0927 2389	0.0689 9383	0.0513 5555	0.0382 4043	0.0284 8498	239
240	0.0918 0584	0.0682 2628	0.0507 2153	0.0377 2175	0.0280 6402	240

TABLE II

N	1	1 1/8	1 1/4	1 3/8	1 1/2	N
241	0.0908 9687	0.0674 6727	0.0500 9534	0.0372 1011	0.0276 4928	241
242	0.0899 9690	0.0667 1671	0.0494 7688	0.0367 0541	0.0272 4067	242
243	0.0891 0584	0.0659 7450	0.0488 6605	0.0362 0756	0.0268 3810	243
244	0.0882 2360	0.0652 4054	0.0482 6277	0.0357 1646	0.0264 4148	244
245	0.0873 5010	0.0645 1475	0.0476 6693	0.0352 3202	0.0260 5072	245
246	0.0864 8525	0.0637 9703	0.0470 7845	0.0347 5415	0.0256 6573	246
247	0.0856 2896	0.0630 8730	0.0464 9723	0.0342 8276	0.0252 8643	247
248	0.0847 8115	0.0623 8546	0.0459 2319	0.0338 1777	0.0249 1274	248
249	0.0839 4173	0.0616 9144	0.0453 5624	0.0333 5908	0.0245 4457	249
250	0.0831 1063	0.0610 0513	0.0447 9629	0.0329 0661	0.0241 8185	250
251	0.0822 8775	0.0603 2646	0.0442 4325	0.0324 6028	0.0238 2448	251
252	0.0814 7302	0.0596 5533	0.0436 9703	0.0320 2001	0.0234 7239	252
253	0.0806 6635	0.0589 9168	0.0431 5756	0.0315 8571	0.0231 2551	253
254	0.0798 6768	0.0583 3540	0.0426 2476	0.0311 5729	0.0227 8375	254
255	0.0790 7691	0.0576 8643	0.0420 9852	0.0307 3469	0.0224 4705	255
256	0.0782 9397	0.0570 4468	0.0415 7879	0.0303 1782	0.0221 1532	256
257	0.0775 1878	0.0564 1007	0.0410 6547	0.0299 0661	0.0217 8849	257
258	0.0767 5127	0.0557 8251	0.0405 5849	0.0295 0097	0.0214 6649	258
259	0.0759 9136	0.0551 6194	0.0400 5777	0.0291 0083	0.0211 4925	259
260	0.0752 3897	0.0545 4827	0.0395 6323	0.0287 0612	0.0208 3670	260
261	0.0744 9403	0.0539 4143	0.0390 7479	0.0283 1677	0.0205 2877	261
262	0.0737 5646	0.0533 4134	0.0385 9239	0.0279 3269	0.0202 2539	262
263	0.0730 2620	0.0527 4793	0.0381 1594	0.0275 5383	0.0199 2649	263
264	0.0723 0317	0.0521 6111	0.0376 4537	0.0271 8010	0.0196 3201	264
265	0.0715 8729	0.0515 8083	0.0371 8061	0.0268 1144	0.0193 4189	265
266	0.0708 7851	0.0510 0700	0.0367 2159	0.0264 4779	0.0190 5604	266
267	0.0701 7674	0.0504 3956	0.0362 6824	0.0260 8906	0.0187 7443	267
268	0.0694 8192	0.0498 7842	0.0358 2048	0.0257 3520	0.0184 9697	268
269	0.0687 9398	0.0493 2353	0.0353 7826	0.0253 8614	0.0182 2362	269
270	0.0681 1285	0.0487 7482	0.0349 4149	0.0250 4182	0.0179 5430	27C
271	0.0674 3847	0.0482 3221	0.0345 1011	0.0247 0216	0.0176 8897	271
272	0.0667 7076	0.0476 9563	0.0340 8406	0.0243 6712	0.0174 2756	272
273	0.0661 0967	0.0471 6502	0.0336 6327	0.0240 3661	0.0171 7001	273
274	0.0654 5511	0.0466 4032	0.0332 4767	0.0237 1059	0.0169 1626	274
275	0.0648 0704	0.0461 2145	0.0328 3721	0.0233 8899	0.0166 6627	275
276	0.0641 6539	0.0456 0836	0.0324 3181	0.0230 7176	0.0164 1997	276
277	0.0635 3009	0.0451 0097	0.0320 3142	0.0227 5882	0.0161 7731	277
278	0.0629 0108	0.0445 9923	0.0316 3597	0.0224 5013	0.0159 3824	278
279	0.0622 7830	0.0441 0307	0.0312 4540	0.0221 4563	0.0157 0270	279
280	0.0616 6168	0.0436 1243	0.0308 5966	0.0218 4526	0.0154 7064	280
281	0.0610 5117	0.0431 2725	0.0304 7867	0.0215 4896	0.0152 4201	281
282	0.0604 4670	0.0426 4747	0.0301 0239	0.0212 5668	0.0150 1675	282
283	0.0598 4822	0.0421 7302	0.0297 3076	0.0209 6837	0.0147 9483	283
284	0.0592 5566	0.0417 0385	0.0293 6371	0.0206 8396	0.0145 7619	284
285	0.0586 6897	0.0412 3990	0.0290 0120	0.0204 0341	0.0143 6078	285
286	0.0580 8809	0.0407 8112	0.0286 4316	0.0201 2667	0.0141 4855	286
287	0.0575 1296	0.0403 2743	0.0282 8954	0.0198 5368	0.0139 3946	287
288	0.0569 4353	0.0398 7880	0.0279 4028	0.0195 8440	0.0137 3346	288
289	0.0563 7973	0.0394 3515	0.0275 9534	0.0193 1877	0.0135 3050	289
290	0.0558 2151	0.0389 9644	0.0272 5466	0.0190 5674	0.0133 3054	290
291	0.0552 6882	0.0385 6261	0.0269 1818	0.0187 9826	0.0131 3354	291
292	0.0547 2161	0.0381 3361	0.0265 8586	0.0185 4329	0.0129 3945	292
293	0.0541 7981	0.0377 0938	0.0262 5764	0.0182 9178	0.0127 4822	293
294	0.0536 4338	0.0372 8987	0.0259 3347	0.0180 4368	0.0125 5982	294
295	0.0531 1225	0.0368 7502	0.0256 1330	0.0177 9894	0.0123 7421	295
296	0.0525 8639	0.0364 6479	0.0252 9709	0.0175 5753	0.0121 9134	296
297	0.0520 6573	0.0360 5913	0.0249 8478	0.0173 1938	0.0120 1117	297
298	0.0515 5023	0.0356 5798	0.0246 7633	0.0170 8447	0.0118 3367	298
299	0.0510 3983	0.0352 6129	0.0243 7168	0.0168 5275	0.0116 5879	299
300	0.0505 3449	0.0348 6901	0.0240 7079	0.0166 2416	0.0114 8649	300

TABLE II

N	1	1 1/8	1 1/4	1 3/8	1 1/2	N
301	0.0500 3415	0.0344 8110	0.0237 7362	0.0163 9868	0.0113 1674	301
302	0.0495 3876	0.0340 9750	0.0234 8012	0.0161 7626	0.0111 4950	302
303	0.0490 4828	0.0337 1817	0.0231 9025	0.0159 5685	0.0109 8473	303
304	0.0485 6265	0.0333 4306	0.0229 0395	0.0157 4042	0.0108 2239	304
305	0.0480 8183	0.0329 7213	0.0226 2118	0.0155 2693	0.0106 6245	305
306	0.0476 0577	0.0326 0532	0.0223 4191	0.0153 1633	0.0105 0488	306
307	0.0471 3443	0.0322 4259	0.0220 6608	0.0151 0858	0.0103 4963	307
308	0.0466 6775	0.0318 8389	0.0217 9366	0.0149 0366	0.0101 9668	308
309	0.0462 0569	0.0315 2919	0.0215 2460	0.0147 0151	0.0100 4599	309
310	0.0457 4821	0.0311 7843	0.0212 5887	0.0145 0211	0.0098 9753	310
311	0.0452 9526	0.0308 3158	0.0209 9641	0.0143 0541	0.0097 5126	311
312	0.0448 4679	0.0304 8858	0.0207 3720	0.0141 1138	0.0096 0716	312
313	0.0444 0276	0.0301 4940	0.0204 8118	0.0139 1998	0.0094 6518	313
314	0.0439 6313	0.0298 1399	0.0202 2833	0.0137 3117	0.0093 2530	314
315	0.0435 2785	0.0294 8232	0.0199 7860	0.0135 4493	0.0091 8749	315
316	0.0430 9689	0.0291 5433	0.0197 3195	0.0133 6122	0.0090 5171	316
317	0.0426 7018	0.0288 2999	0.0194 8834	0.0131 7999	0.0089 1794	317
318	0.0422 4771	0.0285 0926	0.0192 4775	0.0130 0122	0.0087 8615	318
319	0.0418 2941	0.0281 9210	0.0190 1012	0.0128 2488	0.0086 5630	319
320	0.0414 1526	0.0278 7847	0.0187 7543	0.0126 5093	0.0085 2838	320
321	0.0410 0521	0.0275 6833	0.0185 4363	0.0124 7934	0.0084 0234	321
322	0.0405 9922	0.0272 6163	0.0183 1470	0.0123 1008	0.0082 7817	322
323	0.0401 9724	0.0269 5835	0.0180 8859	0.0121 4311	0.0081 5583	323
324	0.0397 9925	0.0266 5844	0.0178 6527	0.0119 7841	0.0080 3530	324
325	0.0394 0520	0.0263 6187	0.0176 4471	0.0118 1594	0.0079 1656	325
326	0.0390 1505	0.0260 6860	0.0174 2688	0.0116 5567	0.0077 9956	326
327	0.0386 2876	0.0257 7859	0.0172 1173	0.0114 9758	0.0076 8430	327
328	0.0382 4630	0.0254 9181	0.0169 9924	0.0113 4163	0.0075 7074	328
329	0.0378 6762	0.0252 0822	0.0167 8937	0.0111 8780	0.0074 5885	329
330	0.0374 9269	0.0249 2778	0.0165 8210	0.0110 3605	0.0073 4862	330
331	0.0371 2148	0.0246 5046	0.0163 7738	0.0108 8637	0.0072 4002	331
332	0.0367 5394	0.0243 7623	0.0161 7519	0.0107 3871	0.0071 3303	332
333	0.0363 9004	0.0241 0505	0.0159 7550	0.0105 9305	0.0070 2761	333
334	0.0360 2974	0.0238 3688	0.0157 7827	0.0104 4938	0.0069 2376	334
335	0.0356 7301	0.0235 7170	0.0155 8348	0.0103 0765	0.0068 2144	335
336	0.0353 1981	0.0233 0947	0.0153 9109	0.0101 6784	0.0067 2063	336
337	0.0349 7011	0.0230 5015	0.0152 0107	0.0100 2993	0.0066 2131	337
338	0.0346 2387	0.0227 9372	0.0150 1341	0.0098 9389	0.0065 2346	338
339	0.0342 8106	0.0225 4015	0.0148 2806	0.0097 5969	0.0064 2705	339
340	0.0339 4165	0.0222 8939	0.0146 4499	0.0096 2731	0.0063 3207	340
341	0.0336 0559	0.0220 4143	0.0144 6419	0.0094 9673	0.0062 3849	341
342	0.0332 7286	0.0217 9622	0.0142 8562	0.0093 6793	0.0061 4630	342
343	0.0329 4343	0.0215 5374	0.0141 0925	0.0092 4086	0.0060 5547	343
344	0.0326 1726	0.0213 1396	0.0139 3507	0.0091 1552	0.0059 6598	344
345	0.0322 9431	0.0210 7684	0.0137 6303	0.0089 9189	0.0058 7781	345
346	0.0319 7457	0.0208 4237	0.0135 9311	0.0088 6992	0.0057 9094	346
347	0.0316 5799	0.0206 1050	0.0134 2530	0.0087 4962	0.0057 0536	347
348	0.0313 4454	0.0203 8121	0.0132 5955	0.0086 3094	0.0056 2105	348
349	0.0310 3420	0.0201 5447	0.0130 9586	0.0085 1388	0.0055 3798	349
350	0.0307 2693	0.0199 3026	0.0129 3418	0.0083 9840	0.0054 5614	350
351	0.0304 2270	0.0197 0854	0.0127 7450	0.0082 8449	0.0053 7550	351
352	0.0301 2149	0.0194 8928	0.0126 1679	0.0081 7212	0.0052 9606	352
353	0.0298 2326	0.0192 7247	0.0124 6102	0.0080 6128	0.0052 1780	353
354	0.0295 2798	0.0190 5806	0.0123 0718	0.0079 5194	0.0051 4069	354
355	0.0292 3562	0.0188 4604	0.0121 5524	0.0078 4408	0.0050 6471	355
356	0.0289 4616	0.0186 3639	0.0120 0518	0.0077 3769	0.0049 8987	356
357	0.0286 5956	0.0184 2906	0.0118 5697	0.0076 3274	0.0049 1613	357
358	0.0283 7580	0.0182 2404	0.0117 1058	0.0075 2921	0.0048 4347	358
359	0.0280 9486	0.0180 2130	0.0115 6601	0.0074 2709	0.0047 7189	359
360	0.0278 1669	0.0178 2081	0.0114 2322	0.0073 2635	0.0047 0137	360

TABLE II

N	1 5/8	1 3/4	1 7/8	2	2 1/8	N
1	0.9840 0984	0.9828 0098	0.9815 9509	0.9803 9216	0.9791 9217	1
2	0.9682 7537	0.9658 9777	0.9635 2892	0.9611 6878	0.9588 1730	2
3	0.9527 9249	0.9492 8528	0.9457 9526	0.9423 2233	0.9388 6639	3
4	0.9375 5718	0.9329 5851	0.9283 8799	0.9238 4543	0.9193 3061	4
5	0.9225 6549	0.9169 1254	0.9113 0109	0.9057 3081	0.9002 0133	5
6	0.9078 1352	0.9011 4254	0.8945 2868	0.8879 7138	0.8814 7009	6
7	0.8932 9744	0.8856 4378	0.8780 6496	0.8705 6018	0.8631 2861	7
8	0.8790 1347	0.8704 1157	0.8619 0426	0.8534 9037	0.8451 6878	8
9	0.8649 5791	0.8554 4135	0.8460 4099	0.8367 5527	0.8275 8264	9
10	0.8511 2709	0.8407 2860	0.8304 6968	0.8203 4830	0.8103 6244	10
11	0.8375 1743	0.8262 6889	0.8151 8496	0.8042 6304	0.7935 0056	11
12	0.8241 2539	0.8120 5788	0.8001 8156	0.7884 9318	0.7769 8953	12
13	0.8109 4750	0.7980 9128	0.7854 5429	0.7730 3253	0.7608 2206	13
14	0.7979 8032	0.7843 6490	0.7709 9808	0.7578 7502	0.7449 9100	14
15	0.7852 2048	0.7708 7459	0.7568 0793	0.7430 1473	0.7294 8935	15
16	0.7726 6468	0.7576 1631	0.7428 7895	0.7284 4581	0.7143 1026	16
17	0.7603 0965	0.7445 8605	0.7292 0633	0.7141 6256	0.6994 4701	17
18	0.7481 5218	0.7317 7990	0.7157 8536	0.7001 5937	0.6848 9303	18
19	0.7361 8911	0.7191 9401	0.7026 1139	0.6864 3076	0.6706 4189	19
20	0.7244 1732	0.7068 2458	0.6896 7989	0.6729 7133	0.6566 8729	20
21	0.7128 3378	0.6946 6789	0.6769 8640	0.6597 7582	0.6430 2305	21
22	0.7014 3545	0.6827 2028	0.6645 2653	0.6468 3904	0.6296 4313	22
23	0.6902 1938	0.6709 7817	0.6522 9598	0.6341 5592	0.6165 4162	23
24	0.6791 8267	0.6594 3800	0.6402 9053	0.6217 2149	0.6037 1273	24
25	0.6683 2243	0.6480 9632	0.6285 0604	0.6095 3087	0.5911 5077	25
26	0.6576 3584	0.6369 4970	0.6169 3845	0.5975 7928	0.5788 5021	26
27	0.6471 2014	0.6259 9479	0.6055 8375	0.5858 6204	0.5668 0559	27
28	0.6367 7259	0.6152 2829	0.5944 3804	0.5743 7455	0.5550 1159	28
29	0.6265 9049	0.6046 4697	0.5834 9746	0.5631 1231	0.5434 6300	29
30	0.6165 7121	0.5942 4764	0.5727 5824	0.5520 7089	0.5321 5471	30
31	0.6067 1214	0.5840 2716	0.5622 1668	0.5412 4597	0.5210 8173	31
32	0.5970 1071	0.5739 8247	0.5518 6913	0.5306 3330	0.5102 3915	32
33	0.5874 6442	0.5641 1053	0.5417 1203	0.5202 2873	0.4996 2217	33
34	0.5780 7077	0.5544 0839	0.5317 4187	0.5100 2817	0.4892 2612	34
35	0.5688 2732	0.5448 7311	0.5219 5521	0.5000 2761	0.4790 4638	35
36	0.5597 3168	0.5355 0183	0.5123 4867	0.4902 2315	0.4690 7847	36
37	0.5507 8148	0.5262 9172	0.5029 1894	0.4806 1093	0.4593 1796	37
38	0.5419 7440	0.5172 4002	0.4936 6277	0.4711 8719	0.4497 6055	38
39	0.5333 0814	0.5083 4400	0.4845 7695	0.4619 4822	0.4404 0201	39
40	0.5247 8046	0.4996 0098	0.4756 5836	0.4528 9042	0.4312 3819	40
41	0.5163 8914	0.4910 0834	0.4669 0391	0.4440 1021	0.4222 6506	41
42	0.5081 3199	0.4825 6348	0.4583 1058	0.4353 0413	0.4134 7864	42
43	0.5000 0688	0.4742 6386	0.4498 7542	0.4267 6875	0.4048 7505	43
44	0.4920 1169	0.4661 0699	0.4415 9550	0.4184 0074	0.3964 5047	44
45	0.4841 4434	0.4580 9040	0.4334 6798	0.4101 9680	0.3882 0120	45
46	0.4764 0280	0.4502 1170	0.4254 9004	0.4021 5373	0.3801 2357	46
47	0.4687 8504	0.4424 6850	0.4176 5894	0.3942 6836	0.3722 1402	47
48	0.4612 8909	0.4348 5848	0.4099 7196	0.3865 3761	0.3644 6906	48
49	0.4539 1301	0.4273 7934	0.4024 2647	0.3789 5844	0.3568 8524	49
50	0.4466 5487	0.4200 2883	0.3950 1984	0.3715 2788	0.3494 5924	50
51	0.4395 1278	0.4128 0475	0.3877 4954	0.3642 4302	0.3421 8775	51
52	0.4324 8490	0.4057 0492	0.3806 1305	0.3571 0100	0.3350 6756	52
53	0.4255 6940	0.3987 2719	0.3736 0790	0.3500 9902	0.3280 9553	53
54	0.4187 6448	0.3918 6947	0.3667 3168	0.3432 3433	0.3212 6857	54
55	0.4120 6837	0.3851 2970	0.3599 8202	0.3365 0425	0.3145 8367	55
56	0.4054 7933	0.3785 0585	0.3533 5658	0.3299 0613	0.3080 3787	56
57	0.3989 9565	0.3719 9592	0.3468 5308	0.3234 3738	0.3016 2827	57
58	0.3926 1564	0.3655 9796	0.3404 6928	0.3170 9547	0.2953 5203	58
59	0.3863 3766	0.3593 1003	0.3342 0298	0.3108 7791	0.2892 0640	59
60	0.3801 6006	0.3531 3025	0.3280 5200	0.3047 8227	0.2831 8864	60

TABLE II

N	1 5/8	1 3/4	1 7/8	2	2 1/8	N
61	0.3740 8124	0.3470 5676	0.3220 1424	0.2988 0614	0.2772 9610	61
62	0.3680 9962	0.3410 8772	0.3160 8759	0.2929 4720	0.2715 2617	62
63	0.3622 1365	0.3352 2135	0.3102 7003	0.2872 0314	0.2658 7630	63
64	0.3564 2179	0.3294 5587	0.3045 5954	0.2815 7170	0.2603 4399	64
65	0.3507 2255	0.3237 8956	0.2989 5415	0.2760 5069	0.2549 2679	65
66	0.3451 1444	0.3182 2069	0.2934 5193	0.2706 3793	0.2496 2232	66
67	0.3395 9601	0.3127 4761	0.2880 5097	0.2653 3130	0.2444 2822	67
68	0.3341 6581	0.3073 6866	0.2827 4942	0.2601 2873	0.2393 4220	68
69	0.3288 2245	0.3020 8222	0.2775 4544	0.2550 2817	0.2343 6200	69
70	0.3235 6452	0.2968 8670	0.2724 3724	0.2500 2761	0.2294 8544	70
71	0.3183 9067	0.2917 8054	0.2674 2306	0.2451 2511	0.2247 1034	71
72	0.3132 9956	0.2867 6221	0.2625 0116	0.2403 1874	0.2200 3461	72
73	0.3082 8985	0.2818 3018	0.2576 6985	0.2356 0661	0.2154 5616	73
74	0.3033 6024	0.2769 8298	0.2529 2746	0.2309 8687	0.2109 7299	74
75	0.2985 0946	0.2722 1914	0.2482 7236	0.2264 5771	0.2065 8310	75
76	0.2937 3625	0.2675 3724	0.2437 0293	0.2220 1737	0.2022 8455	76
77	0.2890 3936	0.2629 3586	0.2392 1760	0.2176 6408	0.1980 7545	77
78	0.2844 1757	0.2584 1362	0.2348 1482	0.2133 9616	0.1939 5393	78
79	0.2798 6969	0.2539 6916	0.2304 9308	0.2092 1192	0.1899 1817	79
80	0.2753 9453	0.2496 0114	0.2262 5087	0.2051 0973	0.1859 6638	80
81	0.2709 9093	0.2453 0825	0.2220 8674	0.2010 8797	0.1820 9682	81
82	0.2666 5774	0.2410 8919	0.2179 9926	0.1971 4507	0.1783 0778	82
83	0.2623 9384	0.2369 4269	0.2139 8700	0.1932 7948	0.1745 9758	83
84	0.2581 9812	0.2328 6751	0.2100 4859	0.1894 8968	0.1709 6459	84
85	0.2540 6949	0.2288 6242	0.2061 8267	0.1857 7420	0.1674 0718	85
86	0.2500 0688	0.2249 2621	0.2023 8789	0.1821 3157	0.1639 2380	86
87	0.2460 0923	0.2210 5770	0.1986 6296	0.1785 6036	0.1605 1290	87
88	0.2420 7550	0.2172 5572	0.1950 0659	0.1750 5918	0.1571 7298	88
89	0.2382 0468	0.2135 1914	0.1914 1751	0.1716 2665	0.1539 0255	89
90	0.2343 9575	0.2098 4682	0.1878 9449	0.1682 6142	0.1507 0017	90
91	0.2306 4772	0.2062 3766	0.1844 3631	0.1649 6217	0.1475 6443	91
92	0.2269 5963	0.2026 9057	0.1810 4178	0.1617 2762	0.1444 9393	92
93	0.2233 3051	0.1992 0450	0.1777 0972	0.1585 5649	0.1414 8732	93
94	0.2197 5942	0.1957 7837	0.1744 3899	0.1554 4754	0.1385 4328	94
95	0.2162 4543	0.1924 1118	0.1712 2845	0.1523 9955	0.1356 6049	95
96	0.2127 8763	0.1891 0190	0.1680 7701	0.1494 1132	0.1328 3769	96
97	0.2093 8512	0.1858 4953	0.1649 8357	0.1464 8169	0.1300 7363	97
98	0.2060 3702	0.1826 5310	0.1619 4706	0.1436 0950	0.1273 6708	98
99	0.2027 4245	0.1795 1165	0.1589 6644	0.1407 9363	0.1247 1684	99
100	0.1995 0057	0.1764 2422	0.1560 4068	0.1380 3297	0.1221 2176	100
101	0.1963 1052	0.1733 8990	0.1531 6876	0.1353 2644	0.1195 8067	101
102	0.1931 7149	0.1704 0776	0.1503 4971	0.1326 7298	0.1170 9245	102
103	0.1900 8264	0.1674 7692	0.1475 8253	0.1300 7155	0.1146 5601	103
104	0.1870 4319	0.1645 9648	0.1448 6629	0.1275 2113	0.1122 7027	104
105	0.1840 5234	0.1617 6558	0.1422 0004	0.1250 2071	0.1099 3417	105
106	0.1811 0932	0.1589 8337	0.1395 8286	0.1225 6932	0.1076 4668	106
107	0.1782 1335	0.1562 4901	0.1370 1385	0.1201 6600	0.1054 0678	107
108	0.1753 6369	0.1535 6168	0.1344 9212	0.1178 0981	0.1032 1350	108
109	0.1725 5959	0.1509 2057	0.1320 1681	0.1154 9981	0.1010 6585	109
110	0.1698 0034	0.1483 2489	0.1295 8705	0.1132 3511	0.0989 6289	110
111	0.1670 8520	0.1457 7385	0.1272 0201	0.1110 1481	0.0969 0368	111
112	0.1644 1349	0.1432 6668	0.1248 6087	0.1088 3805	0.0948 8733	112
113	0.1617 8449	0.1408 0263	0.1225 6282	0.1067 0397	0.0929 1293	113
114	0.1591 9753	0.1383 8097	0.1203 0706	0.1046 1174	0.0909 7961	114
115	0.1566 5193	0.1360 0095	0.1180 9282	0.1025 6053	0.0890 8652	115
116	0.1541 4704	0.1336 6187	0.1159 1933	0.1005 4954	0.0872 3282	116
117	0.1516 8221	0.1313 6301	0.1137 8585	0.0985 7798	0.0854 1770	117
118	0.1492 5679	0.1291 0370	0.1116 9163	0.0966 4508	0.0836 4034	118
119	0.1468 7015	0.1268 8324	0.1096 3596	0.0947 5007	0.0818 9997	119
120	0.1445 2167	0.1247 0098	0.1076 1812	0.0928 9223	0.0801 9581	120

TABLE II

N	1 5/8	1 3/4	1 7/8	2	2 1/8	N
121	0.1422 1074	0.1225 5624	0.1056 3742	0.0910 7081	0.0785 2710	121
122	0.1399 3677	0.1204 4839	0.1036 9317	0.0892 8511	0.0768 9313	122
123	0.1376 9916	0.1183 7680	0.1017 8471	0.0875 3442	0.0752 9315	123
124	0.1354 9733	0.1163 4084	0.0999 1137	0.0858 1806	0.0737 2646	124
125	0.1333 3070	0.1143 3989	0.0980 7251	0.0841 3535	0.0721 9237	125
126	0.1311 9873	0.1123 7335	0.0962 6749	0.0824 8564	0.0706 9020	126
127	0.1291 0084	0.1104 4064	0.0944 9570	0.0808 6828	0.0692 1929	127
128	0.1270 3649	0.1085 4117	0.0927 5651	0.0792 8262	0.0677 7899	128
129	0.1250 0516	0.1066 7437	0.0910 4934	0.0777 2806	0.0663 6866	129
130	0.1230 0631	0.1048 3968	0.0893 7358	0.0762 0398	0.0649 8767	130
131	0.1210 3942	0.1030 3654	0.0877 2867	0.0747 0979	0.0636 3542	131
132	0.1191 0398	0.1012 6441	0.0861 1403	0.0732 4489	0.0623 1130	132
133	0.1171 9949	0.0995 2276	0.0845 2911	0.0718 0872	0.0610 1474	133
134	0.1153 2545	0.0978 1107	0.0829 7336	0.0704 0070	0.0597 4515	134
135	0.1134 8137	0.0961 2881	0.0814 4624	0.0690 2030	0.0585 0199	135
136	0.1116 6679	0.0944 7549	0.0799 4723	0.0676 6696	0.0572 8469	136
137	0.1098 8122	0.0928 5061	0.0784 7581	0.0663 4015	0.0560 9272	137
138	0.1081 2420	0.0912 5367	0.0770 3147	0.0650 3937	0.0549 2555	138
139	0.1063 9528	0.0896 8419	0.0756 1372	0.0637 6408	0.0537 8267	139
140	0.1046 9400	0.0881 4171	0.0742 2205	0.0625 1381	0.0526 6357	140
141	0.1030 1993	0.0866 2576	0.0728 5600	0.0612 8805	0.0515 6775	141
142	0.1013 7262	0.0851 3589	0.0715 1509	0.0600 8632	0.0504 9474	142
143	0.0997 5166	0.0836 7163	0.0701 9886	0.0589 0816	0.0494 4405	143
144	0.0981 5661	0.0822 3256	0.0689 0686	0.0577 5310	0.0484 1523	144
145	0.0965 8707	0.0808 1824	0.0676 3864	0.0566 2068	0.0474 0781	145
146	0.0950 4263	0.0794 2825	0.0663 9375	0.0555 1047	0.0464 2136	146
147	0.0935 2288	0.0780 6216	0.0651 7178	0.0544 2203	0.0454 5543	147
148	0.0920 2744	0.0767 1957	0.0639 7230	0.0533 5493	0.0445 0960	148
149	0.0905 5590	0.0754 0007	0.0627 9490	0.0523 0876	0.0435 8345	149
150	0.0891 0790	0.0741 0326	0.0616 3916	0.0512 8310	0.0426 7658	150
151	0.0876 8305	0.0728 2876	0.0605 0470	0.0502 7755	0.0417 8857	151
152	0.0862 8098	0.0715 7617	0.0593 9112	0.0492 9171	0.0409 1904	152
153	0.0849 0134	0.0703 4513	0.0582 9803	0.0483 2521	0.0400 6760	153
154	0.0835 4375	0.0691 3527	0.0572 2506	0.0473 7765	0.0392 3388	154
155	0.0822 0787	0.0679 4621	0.0561 7184	0.0464 4868	0.0384 1751	155
156	0.0808 9336	0.0667 7760	0.0551 3800	0.0455 3792	0.0376 1813	156
157	0.0795 9986	0.0656 2909	0.0541 2319	0.0446 4502	0.0368 3537	157
158	0.0783 2704	0.0645 0034	0.0531 2706	0.0437 6963	0.0360 6891	158
159	0.0770 7458	0.0633 9099	0.0521 4926	0.0429 1140	0.0353 1839	159
160	0.0758 4215	0.0623 0073	0.0511 8946	0.0420 7000	0.0345 8349	160
161	0.0746 2942	0.0612 2922	0.0502 4732	0.0412 4510	0.0338 6389	161
162	0.0734 3608	0.0601 7614	0.0493 2252	0.0404 3637	0.0331 5925	162
163	0.0722 6183	0.0591 4117	0.0484 1475	0.0396 4350	0.0324 6928	163
164	0.0711 0635	0.0581 2400	0.0475 2368	0.0388 6618	0.0317 9367	164
165	0.0699 6935	0.0571 2432	0.0466 4901	0.0381 0410	0.0311 3211	165
166	0.0688 5053	0.0561 4184	0.0457 9044	0.0373 5696	0.0304 8432	166
167	0.0677 4960	0.0551 7625	0.0449 4767	0.0366 2447	0.0298 5000	167
168	0.0666 6627	0.0542 2728	0.0441 2041	0.0359 0634	0.0292 2889	168
169	0.0656 0027	0.0532 9462	0.0433 0838	0.0352 0229	0.0286 2070	169
170	0.0645 5131	0.0523 7801	0.0425 1129	0.0345 1205	0.0280 2516	170
171	0.0635 1912	0.0514 7716	0.0417 2888	0.0338 3535	0.0274 4202	171
172	0.0625 0344	0.0505 9180	0.0409 6086	0.0331 7191	0.0268 7101	172
173	0.0615 0400	0.0497 2167	0.0402 0698	0.0325 2148	0.0263 1189	173
174	0.0605 2054	0.0488 6651	0.0394 6697	0.0318 8380	0.0257 6439	174
175	0.0595 5281	0.0480 2605	0.0387 4059	0.0312 5863	0.0252 2829	175
176	0.0586 0055	0.0472 0005	0.0380 2757	0.0306 4572	0.0247 0334	176
177	0.0576 6352	0.0463 8825	0.0373 2768	0.0300 4482	0.0241 8932	177
178	0.0567 4147	0.0455 9042	0.0366 4066	0.0294 5571	0.0236 8599	178
179	0.0558 3416	0.0448 0631	0.0359 6630	0.0288 7814	0.0231 9314	179
180	0.0549 4137	0.0440 3569	0.0353 0434	0.0283 1190	0.0227 1054	180

TABLE II

N	1 5/8	1 3/4	1 7/8	2	2 1/8	N
181	0.0540 6284	0.0432 7832	0.0346 5457	0.0277 5677	0.0222 3798	181
182	0.0531 9837	0.0425 3397	0.0340 1675	0.0272 1252	0.0217 7526	182
183	0.0523 4772	0.0418 0243	0.0333 9068	0.0266 7894	0.0213 2216	183
184	0.0515 1067	0.0410 8347	0.0327 7612	0.0261 5582	0.0208 7850	184
185	0.0506 8701	0.0403 7687	0.0321 7288	0.0256 4296	0.0204 4406	185
186	0.0498 7651	0.0396 8243	0.0315 8074	0.0251 4016	0.0200 1866	186
187	0.0490 7898	0.0389 9993	0.0309 9950	0.0246 4722	0.0196 0212	187
188	0.0482 9420	0.0383 2917	0.0304 2896	0.0241 6394	0.0191 9424	188
189	0.0475 2197	0.0376 6995	0.0298 6892	0.0236 9014	0.0187 9485	189
190	0.0467 6208	0.0370 2206	0.0293 1918	0.0232 2562	0.0184 0377	190
191	0.0460 1435	0.0363 8532	0.0287 7957	0.0227 7022	0.0180 2083	191
192	0.0452 7857	0.0357 5953	0.0282 4988	0.0223 2374	0.0176 4585	192
193	0.0445 5456	0.0351 4450	0.0277 2994	0.0218 8602	0.0172 7868	193
194	0.0438 4213	0.0345 4005	0.0272 1958	0.0214 5689	0.0169 1915	194
195	0.0431 4109	0.0339 4599	0.0267 1860	0.0210 3616	0.0165 6710	195
196	0.0424 5125	0.0333 6215	0.0262 2685	0.0206 2369	0.0162 2237	196
197	0.0417 7245	0.0327 8836	0.0257 4415	0.0202 1930	0.0158 8482	197
198	0.0411 0450	0.0322 2443	0.0252 7033	0.0198 2285	0.0155 5429	198
199	0.0404 4723	0.0316 7020	0.0248 0523	0.0194 3416	0.0152 3064	199
200	0.0398 0048	0.0311 2551	0.0243 4869	0.0190 5310	0.0149 1372	200
201	0.0391 6406	0.0305 9018	0.0239 0056	0.0186 7951	0.0146 0340	201
202	0.0385 3782	0.0300 6406	0.0234 6067	0.0183 1324	0.0142 9954	202
203	0.0379 2160	0.0295 4698	0.0230 2888	0.0179 5416	0.0140 0199	203
204	0.0373 1522	0.0290 3881	0.0226 0503	0.0176 0212	0.0137 1064	204
205	0.0367 1855	0.0285 3937	0.0221 8899	0.0172 5698	0.0134 2535	205
206	0.0361 3141	0.0280 4852	0.0217 8060	0.0169 1861	0.0131 4600	206
207	0.0355 5366	0.0275 6611	0.0213 7973	0.0165 8687	0.0128 7246	207
208	0.0349 8516	0.0270 9200	0.0209 8624	0.0162 6164	0.0126 0461	208
209	0.0344 2574	0.0266 2604	0.0205 9999	0.0159 4278	0.0123 4234	209
210	0.0338 7526	0.0261 6810	0.0202 2085	0.0156 3018	0.0120 8552	210
211	0.0333 3359	0.0257 1804	0.0198 4869	0.0153 2370	0.0118 3405	211
212	0.0328 0058	0.0252 7571	0.0194 8337	0.0150 2324	0.0115 8781	212
213	0.0322 7610	0.0248 4100	0.0191 2479	0.0147 2867	0.0113 4669	213
214	0.0317 6000	0.0244 1375	0.0187 7280	0.0144 3987	0.0111 1059	214
215	0.0312 5215	0.0239 9386	0.0184 2728	0.0141 5673	0.0108 7940	215
216	0.0307 5242	0.0235 8119	0.0180 8813	0.0138 7915	0.0106 5303	216
217	0.0302 6069	0.0231 7562	0.0177 5522	0.0136 0701	0.0104 3136	217
218	0.0297 7681	0.0227 7702	0.0174 2844	0.0133 4021	0.0102 1431	218
219	0.0293 0068	0.0223 8528	0.0171 0767	0.0130 7863	0.0100 0177	219
220	0.0288 3216	0.0220 0027	0.0167 9280	0.0128 2219	0.0097 9365	220
221	0.0283 7112	0.0216 2189	0.0164 8373	0.0125 7077	0.0095 8987	221
222	0.0279 1747	0.0212 5001	0.0161 8035	0.0123 2429	0.0093 9032	222
223	0.0274 7106	0.0208 8453	0.0158 8255	0.0120 8264	0.0091 9493	223
224	0.0270 3179	0.0205 2534	0.0155 9024	0.0118 4572	0.0090 0360	224
225	0.0265 9955	0.0201 7233	0.0153 0330	0.0116 1345	0.0088 1626	225
226	0.0261 7422	0.0198 2538	0.0150 2164	0.0113 8574	0.0086 3281	226
227	0.0257 5569	0.0194 8440	0.0147 4517	0.0111 6249	0.0084 5318	227
228	0.0253 4385	0.0191 4929	0.0144 7379	0.0109 4362	0.0082 7729	228
229	0.0249 3860	0.0188 1994	0.0142 0740	0.0107 2904	0.0081 0506	229
230	0.0245 3983	0.0184 9626	0.0139 4591	0.0105 1866	0.0079 3641	230
231	0.0241 4743	0.0181 7814	0.0136 8924	0.0103 1241	0.0077 7127	231
232	0.0237 6131	0.0178 6549	0.0134 3729	0.0101 1021	0.0076 0957	232
233	0.0233 8136	0.0175 5823	0.0131 8998	0.0099 1197	0.0074 5123	233
234	0.0230 0749	0.0172 5624	0.0129 4722	0.0097 1762	0.0072 9618	234
235	0.0226 3960	0.0169 5945	0.0127 0893	0.0095 2708	0.0071 4437	235
236	0.0222 7759	0.0166 6777	0.0124 7502	0.0093 4027	0.0069 9571	236
237	0.0219 2137	0.0163 8110	0.0122 4542	0.0091 5713	0.0068 5014	237
238	0.0215 7084	0.0160 9936	0.0120 2004	0.0089 7758	0.0067 0760	238
239	0.0212 2592	0.0158 2246	0.0117 9882	0.0088 0155	0.0065 6803	239
240	0.0208 8651	0.0155 5033	0.0115 8166	0.0086 2897	0.0064 3137	240

TABLE II

N	1 5/8	1 3/4	1 7/8	2	2 1/8	N
241	0.0205 5253	0.0152 8288	0.0113 6850	0.0084 5977	0.0062 9754	241
242	0.0202 2390	0.0150 2003	0.0111 5926	0.0082 9389	0.0061 6651	242
243	0.0199 0051	0.0147 6170	0.0109 5388	0.0081 3127	0.0060 3819	243
244	0.0195 8230	0.0145 0782	0.0107 5227	0.0079 7183	0.0059 1255	244
245	0.0192 6918	0.0142 5830	0.0105 5438	0.0078 1552	0.0057 8953	245
246	0.0189 6106	0.0140 1307	0.0103 6013	0.0076 6228	0.0056 6906	246
247	0.0186 5787	0.0137 7206	0.0101 6945	0.0075 1203	0.0055 5110	247
248	0.0183 5953	0.0135 3519	0.0099 8228	0.0073 6474	0.0054 3559	248
249	0.0180 6595	0.0133 0240	0.0097 9856	0.0072 2033	0.0053 2249	249
250	0.0177 7708	0.0130 7361	0.0096 1822	0.0070 7876	0.0052 1174	250
251	0.0174 9282	0.0128 4876	0.0094 4119	0.0069 3996	0.0051 0329	251
252	0.0172 1311	0.0126 2777	0.0092 6743	0.0068 0388	0.0049 9711	252
253	0.0169 3787	0.0124 1059	0.0090 9686	0.0066 7047	0.0048 9313	253
254	0.0166 6703	0.0121 9714	0.0089 2944	0.0065 3968	0.0047 9131	254
255	0.0164 0052	0.0119 8736	0.0087 6509	0.0064 1145	0.0046 9161	255
256	0.0161 3827	0.0117 8119	0.0086 0377	0.0062 8573	0.0045 9399	256
257	0.0158 8022	0.0115 7856	0.0084 4542	0.0061 6248	0.0044 9840	257
258	0.0156 2629	0.0113 7942	0.0082 8998	0.0060 4165	0.0044 0480	258
259	0.0153 7642	0.0111 8371	0.0081 3741	0.0059 2319	0.0043 1314	259
260	0.0151 3055	0.0109 9136	0.0079 8764	0.0058 0705	0.0042 2340	260
261	0.0148 8861	0.0108 0232	0.0078 4063	0.0056 9318	0.0041 3552	261
262	0.0146 5054	0.0106 1653	0.0076 9632	0.0055 8155	0.0040 4947	262
263	0.0144 1628	0.0104 3393	0.0075 5467	0.0054 7211	0.0039 6521	263
264	0.0141 8576	0.0102 5448	0.0074 1563	0.0053 6481	0.0038 8270	264
265	0.0139 5892	0.0100 7811	0.0072 7914	0.0052 5962	0.0038 0191	265
266	0.0137 3572	0.0099 0478	0.0071 4517	0.0051 5649	0.0037 2280	266
267	0.0135 1608	0.0097 3443	0.0070 1366	0.0050 5538	0.0036 4533	267
268	0.0132 9996	0.0095 6701	0.0068 8458	0.0049 5626	0.0035 6948	268
269	0.0130 8729	0.0094 0246	0.0067 5787	0.0048 5908	0.0034 9521	269
270	0.0128 7802	0.0092 4075	0.0066 3349	0.0047 6380	0.0034 2248	270
271	0.0126 7210	0.0090 8182	0.0065 1140	0.0046 7039	0.0033 5127	271
272	0.0124 6947	0.0089 2562	0.0063 9156	0.0045 7882	0.0032 8154	272
273	0.0122 7008	0.0087 7211	0.0062 7392	0.0044 8904	0.0032 1325	273
274	0.0120 7388	0.0086 2124	0.0061 5845	0.0044 0102	0.0031 4639	274
275	0.0118 8082	0.0084 7296	0.0060 4511	0.0043 1472	0.0030 8092	275
276	0.0116 9084	0.0083 2723	0.0059 3385	0.0042 3012	0.0030 1682	276
277	0.0115 0390	0.0081 8401	0.0058 2464	0.0041 4718	0.0029 5404	277
278	0.0113 1996	0.0080 4325	0.0057 1743	0.0040 6586	0.0028 9258	278
279	0.0111 3895	0.0079 0492	0.0056 1221	0.0039 8614	0.0028 3239	279
280	0.0109 6083	0.0077 6896	0.0055 0891	0.0039 0798	0.0027 7345	280
281	0.0107 8557	0.0076 3534	0.0054 0752	0.0038 3135	0.0027 1574	281
282	0.0106 1311	0.0075 0402	0.0053 0800	0.0037 5622	0.0026 5923	282
283	0.0104 4340	0.0073 7496	0.0052 1030	0.0036 8257	0.0026 0390	283
284	0.0102 7641	0.0072 4812	0.0051 1441	0.0036 1037	0.0025 4972	284
285	0.0101 1209	0.0071 2346	0.0050 2028	0.0035 3957	0.0024 9666	285
286	0.0099 5039	0.0070 0094	0.0049 2788	0.0034 7017	0.0024 4471	286
287	0.0097 9128	0.0068 8053	0.0048 3718	0.0034 0213	0.0023 9385	287
288	0.0096 3472	0.0067 6219	0.0047 4816	0.0033 3542	0.0023 4403	288
289	0.0094 8066	0.0066 4589	0.0046 6077	0.0032 7002	0.0022 9526	289
290	0.0093 2906	0.0065 3159	0.0045 7499	0.0032 0590	0.0022 4750	290
291	0.0091 7989	0.0064 1925	0.0044 9078	0.0031 4304	0.0022 0074	291
292	0.0090 3310	0.0063 0885	0.0044 0813	0.0030 8141	0.0021 5494	292
293	0.0088 8866	0.0062 0034	0.0043 2700	0.0030 2099	0.0021 1010	293
294	0.0087 4653	0.0060 9370	0.0042 4736	0.0029 6176	0.0020 6620	294
295	0.0086 0667	0.0059 8890	0.0041 6919	0.0029 0368	0.0020 2320	295
296	0.0084 6905	0.0058 8589	0.0040 9246	0.0028 4675	0.0019 8110	296
297	0.0083 3363	0.0057 8466	0.0040 1713	0.0027 9093	0.0019 3988	297
298	0.0082 0037	0.0056 8517	0.0039 4320	0.0027 3621	0.0018 9952	298
299	0.0080 6925	0.0055 8739	0.0038 7062	0.0026 8256	0.0018 5999	299
300	0.0079 4022	0.0054 9129	0.0037 9939	0.0026 2996	0.0018 2129	300

TABLE II

N	1 5/8	1 3/4	1 7/8	2	2 1/8	N
301	0.0078 1325	0.0053 9685	0.0037 2946	0.0025 7839	0.0017 8339	301
302	0.0076 8832	0.0053 0403	0.0036 6082	0.0025 2783	0.0017 4628	302
303	0.0075 6538	0.0052 1280	0.0035 9344	0.0024 7827	0.0017 0995	303
304	0.0074 4441	0.0051 2315	0.0035 2730	0.0024 2967	0.0016 7437	304
305	0.0073 2537	0.0050 3504	0.0034 6239	0.0023 8203	0.0016 3953	305
306	0.0072 0824	0.0049 4844	0.0033 9866	0.0023 3533	0.0016 0541	306
307	0.0070 9298	0.0048 6333	0.0033 3611	0.0022 8953	0.0015 7201	307
308	0.0069 7956	0.0047 7969	0.0032 7471	0.0022 4464	0.0015 3930	308
309	0.0068 6795	0.0046 9748	0.0032 1444	0.0022 0063	0.0015 0727	309
310	0.0067 5813	0.0046 1669	0.0031 5528	0.0021 5748	0.0014 7591	310
311	0.0066 5007	0.0045 3728	0.0030 9720	0.0021 1518	0.0014 4519	311
312	0.0065 4374	0.0044 5925	0.0030 4020	0.0020 7370	0.0014 1512	312
313	0.0064 3910	0.0043 8255	0.0029 8424	0.0020 3304	0.0013 8568	313
314	0.0063 3614	0.0043 0718	0.0029 2932	0.0019 9318	0.0013 5684	314
315	0.0062 3482	0.0042 3310	0.0028 7541	0.0019 5410	0.0013 2861	315
316	0.0061 3513	0.0041 6029	0.0028 2248	0.0019 1578	0.0013 0097	316
317	0.0060 3702	0.0040 8874	0.0027 7054	0.0018 7822	0.0012 7390	317
318	0.0059 4049	0.0040 1842	0.0027 1955	0.0018 4139	0.0012 4739	318
319	0.0058 4550	0.0039 4931	0.0026 6949	0.0018 0528	0.0012 2143	319
320	0.0057 5203	0.0038 8138	0.0026 2036	0.0017 6988	0.0011 9602	320
321	0.0056 6006	0.0038 1463	0.0025 7213	0.0017 3518	0.0011 7113	321
322	0.0055 6955	0.0037 4902	0.0025 2479	0.0017 0116	0.0011 4676	322
323	0.0054 8049	0.0036 8454	0.0024 7832	0.0016 6780	0.0011 2290	323
324	0.0053 9286	0.0036 2117	0.0024 3271	0.0016 3510	0.0010 9954	324
325	0.0053 0663	0.0035 5889	0.0023 8794	0.0016 0304	0.0010 7666	325
326	0.0052 2177	0.0034 9768	0.0023 4399	0.0015 7161	0.0010 5425	326
327	0.0051 3827	0.0034 3752	0.0023 0085	0.0015 4079	0.0010 3232	327
328	0.0050 5611	0.0033 7840	0.0022 5850	0.0015 1058	0.0010 1084	328
329	0.0049 7527	0.0033 2029	0.0022 1693	0.0014 8096	0.0009 8980	329
330	0.0048 9571	0.0032 6319	0.0021 7613	0.0014 5192	0.0009 6921	330
331	0.0048 1743	0.0032 0706	0.0021 3608	0.0014 2345	0.0009 4904	331
332	0.0047 4040	0.0031 5191	0.0020 9676	0.0013 9554	0.0009 2929	332
333	0.0046 6460	0.0030 9770	0.0020 5817	0.0013 6818	0.0009 0996	333
334	0.0045 9001	0.0030 4442	0.0020 2029	0.0013 4135	0.0008 9102	334
335	0.0045 1661	0.0029 9206	0.0019 8311	0.0013 1505	0.0008 7248	335
336	0.0044 4439	0.0029 4060	0.0019 4661	0.0012 8927	0.0008 5433	336
337	0.0043 7332	0.0028 9002	0.0019 1078	0.0012 6399	0.0008 3655	337
338	0.0043 0339	0.0028 4032	0.0018 7562	0.0012 3920	0.0008 1914	338
339	0.0042 3458	0.0027 9147	0.0018 4110	0.0012 1490	0.0008 0210	339
340	0.0041 6687	0.0027 4346	0.0018 0721	0.0011 9108	0.0007 8541	340
341	0.0041 0024	0.0026 9627	0.0017 7395	0.0011 6773	0.0007 6907	341
342	0.0040 3468	0.0026 4990	0.0017 4130	0.0011 4483	0.0007 5306	342
343	0.0039 7016	0.0026 0432	0.0017 0925	0.0011 2238	0.0007 3739	343
344	0.0039 0668	0.0025 5953	0.0016 7779	0.0011 0038	0.0007 2205	344
345	0.0038 4421	0.0025 1551	0.0016 4691	0.0010 7880	0.0007 0703	345
346	0.0037 8274	0.0024 7224	0.0016 1660	0.0010 5765	0.0006 9232	346
347	0.0037 2226	0.0024 2972	0.0015 8685	0.0010 3691	0.0006 7791	347
348	0.0036 6274	0.0023 8794	0.0015 5764	0.0010 1658	0.0006 6380	348
349	0.0036 0417	0.0023 4687	0.0015 2897	0.0009 9664	0.0006 4999	349
350	0.0035 4654	0.0023 0650	0.0015 0083	0.0009 7710	0.0006 3647	350
351	0.0034 8983	0.0022 6683	0.0014 7321	0.0009 5794	0.0006 2322	351
352	0.0034 3402	0.0022 2784	0.0014 4610	0.0009 3916	0.0006 1026	352
353	0.0033 7911	0.0021 8953	0.0014 1948	0.0009 2074	0.0005 9756	353
354	0.0033 2508	0.0021 5187	0.0013 9336	0.0009 0269	0.0005 8512	354
355	0.0032 7191	0.0021 1486	0.0013 6771	0.0008 8499	0.0005 7295	355
356	0.0032 1959	0.0020 7849	0.0013 4254	0.0008 6764	0.0005 6103	356
357	0.0031 6811	0.0020 4274	0.0013 1783	0.0008 5063	0.0005 4935	357
358	0.0031 1745	0.0020 0761	0.0012 9357	0.0008 3395	0.0005 3792	358
359	0.0030 6761	0.0019 7308	0.0012 6977	0.0008 1760	0.0005 2673	359
360	0.0030 1855	0.0019 3914	0.0012 4640	0.0008 0156	0.0005 1577	360

TABLE II

N	2 1/4	2 3/8	2 1/2	2 5/8	2 3/4	N
1	0.9779 9511	0.9768 0098	0.9756 0976	0.9744 2144	0.9732 3601	1
2	0.9564 7444	0.9541 4015	0.9518 1440	0.9494 9714	0.9471 8833	2
3	0.9354 2732	0.9320 0503	0.9285 9941	0.9252 1037	0.9218 3779	3
4	0.9148 4335	0.9103 8342	0.9059 5064	0.9015 4481	0.8971 6573	4
5	0.8947 1232	0.8892 6342	0.8838 5429	0.8784 8459	0.8731 5400	5
6	0.8750 2427	0.8686 3337	0.8622 9687	0.8560 1422	0.8497 8491	6
7	0.8557 6946	0.8484 8193	0.8412 6524	0.8341 1861	0.8270 4128	7
8	0.8369 3835	0.8287 9798	0.8207 4657	0.8127 8305	0.8049 0635	8
9	0.8185 2161	0.8095 7067	0.8007 2836	0.7919 9323	0.7833 6385	9
10	0.8005 1013	0.7907 8942	0.7811 9840	0.7717 3518	0.7623 9791	10
11	0.7828 9499	0.7724 4388	0.7621 4478	0.7519 9530	0.7419 9310	11
12	0.7656 6748	0.7545 2394	0.7435 5589	0.7327 6035	0.7221 3440	12
13	0.7488 1905	0.7370 1972	0.7254 2038	0.7140 1739	0.7028 0720	13
14	0.7323 4137	0.7199 2158	0.7077 2720	0.6957 5385	0.6839 9728	14
15	0.7162 2628	0.7032 2010	0.6904 6556	0.6779 5747	0.6656 9078	15
16	0.7004 6580	0.6869 0609	0.6736 2493	0.6606 1629	0.6478 7424	16
17	0.6850 5212	0.6709 7053	0.6571 9506	0.6437 1867	0.6305 3454	17
18	0.6699 7763	0.6554 0467	0.6411 6591	0.6272 5328	0.6136 5892	18
19	0.6552 3484	0.6401 9993	0.6255 2772	0.6112 0904	0.5972 3496	19
20	0.6408 1647	0.6253 4791	0.6102 7094	0.5955 7519	0.5812 5057	20
21	0.6267 1538	0.6108 4045	0.5953 8629	0.5803 4123	0.5656 9398	21
22	0.6129 2457	0.5966 6955	0.5808 6467	0.5654 9694	0.5505 5375	22
23	0.5994 3724	0.5828 2740	0.5666 9724	0.5510 3234	0.5358 1874	23
24	0.5862 4668	0.5693 0637	0.5528 7535	0.5369 3772	0.5214 7809	24
25	0.5733 4639	0.5560 9902	0.5393 9059	0.5232 0363	0.5075 2126	25
26	0.5607 2997	0.5431 9807	0.5262 3472	0.5098 2083	0.4939 3796	26
27	0.5483 9117	0.5305 9640	0.5133 9973	0.4967 8035	0.4807 1821	27
28	0.5363 2388	0.5182 8708	0.5008 7778	0.4840 7342	0.4678 5227	28
29	0.5245 2213	0.5062 6333	0.4886 6125	0.4716 9152	0.4553 3068	29
30	0.5129 8008	0.4945 1852	0.4767 4269	0.4596 2633	0.4431 4421	30
31	0.5016 9201	0.4830 4617	0.4651 1481	0.4478 6975	0.4312 8391	31
32	0.4906 5233	0.4718 3997	0.4537 7055	0.4364 1388	0.4197 4103	32
33	0.4798 5558	0.4608 9374	0.4427 0298	0.4252 5104	0.4085 0708	33
34	0.4692 9641	0.4502 0146	0.4319 0534	0.4143 7373	0.3975 7380	34
35	0.4589 6960	0.4397 5722	0.4213 7107	0.4037 7465	0.3869 3314	35
36	0.4488 7002	0.4295 5529	0.4110 9372	0.3934 4667	0.3765 7727	36
37	0.4389 9268	0.4195 9002	0.4010 6705	0.3833 8287	0.3664 9856	37
38	0.4293 3270	0.4098 5594	0.3912 8492	0.3735 7649	0.3566 8959	38
39	0.4198 8528	0.4003 4769	0.3817 4139	0.3640 2094	0.3471 4316	39
40	0.4106 4575	0.3910 6001	0.3724 3062	0.3547 0981	0.3378 5222	40
41	0.4016 0954	0.3819 8780	0.3633 4695	0.3456 3684	0.3288 0995	41
42	0.3927 7216	0.3731 2606	0.3544 8483	0.3367 9595	0.3200 0968	42
43	0.3841 2925	0.3644 6990	0.3458 3886	0.3281 8119	0.3114 4495	43
44	0.3756 7653	0.3560 1455	0.3374 0376	0.3197 8679	0.3031 0944	44
45	0.3674 0981	0.3477 5536	0.3291 7440	0.3116 0710	0.2949 9702	45
46	0.3593 2500	0.3396 8778	0.3211 4576	0.3036 3664	0.2871 0172	46
47	0.3514 1809	0.3318 0735	0.3133 1294	0.2958 7005	0.2794 1773	47
48	0.3436 8518	0.3241 0975	0.3056 7116	0.2883 0212	0.2719 3940	48
49	0.3361 2242	0.3165 9072	0.2982 1576	0.2809 2776	0.2646 6122	49
50	0.3287 2608	0.3092 4612	0.2909 4221	0.2737 4204	0.2575 7783	50
51	0.3214 9250	0.3020 7191	0.2838 4606	0.2667 4011	0.2506 8402	51
52	0.3144 1810	0.2950 6414	0.2769 2298	0.2599 1728	0.2439 7471	52
53	0.3074 9936	0.2882 1894	0.2701 6876	0.2532 6897	0.2374 4497	53
54	0.3007 3287	0.2815 3254	0.2635 7928	0.2467 9071	0.2310 9000	54
55	0.2941 1528	0.2750 0126	0.2571 5052	0.2404 7816	0.2249 0511	55
56	0.2876 4330	0.2686 2150	0.2508 7855	0.2343 2708	0.2188 8575	56
57	0.2813 1374	0.2623 8975	0.2447 5956	0.2283 3333	0.2130 2749	57
58	0.2751 2347	0.2563 0256	0.2387 8982	0.2224 9289	0.2073 2603	58
59	0.2690 6940	0.2503 5659	0.2329 6568	0.2168 0184	0.2017 7716	59
60	0.2631 4856	0.2445 4856	0.2272 8359	0.2112 5636	0.1963 7679	60

TABLE II

N	2 1/4	2 3/8	2 1/2	2 5/8	2 3/4	N
61	0.2573 5801	0.2388 7527	0.2217 4009	0.2058 5273	0.1911 2097	61
62	0.2516 9487	0.2333 3360	0.2163 3179	0.2005 8731	0.1860 0581	62
63	0.2461 5635	0.2279 2049	0.2110 5541	0.1954 5657	0.1810 2755	63
64	0.2407 3971	0.2226 3296	0.2059 0771	0.1904 5708	0.1761 8253	64
65	0.2354 4226	0.2174 6809	0.2008 8557	0.1855 8546	0.1714 6718	65
66	0.2302 6138	0.2124 2304	0.1959 8593	0.1808 3845	0.1668 7804	66
67	0.2251 9450	0.2074 9504	0.1912 0578	0.1762 1286	0.1624 1172	67
68	0.2202 3912	0.2026 8135	0.1865 4223	0.1717 0559	0.1580 6493	68
69	0.2153 9278	0.1979 7934	0.1819 9241	0.1673 1361	0.1538 3448	69
70	0.2106 5309	0.1933 8642	0.1775 5358	0.1630 3397	0.1497 1726	70
71	0.2060 1769	0.1889 0004	0.1732 2300	0.1588 6379	0.1457 1023	71
72	0.2014 8429	0.1845 1774	0.1689 9805	0.1548 0028	0.1418 1044	72
73	0.1970 5065	0.1802 3711	0.1648 7615	0.1508 4071	0.1380 1503	73
74	0.1927 1458	0.1760 5579	0.1608 5478	0.1469 8243	0.1343 2119	74
75	0.1884 7391	0.1719 7147	0.1569 3149	0.1432 2283	0.1307 2622	75
76	0.1843 2657	0.1679 8190	0.1531 0389	0.1395 5939	0.1272 2747	76
77	0.1802 7048	0.1640 8488	0.1493 6965	0.1359 8966	0.1238 2235	77
78	0.1763 0365	0.1602 7827	0.1457 2649	0.1325 1124	0.1205 0837	78
79	0.1724 2411	0.1565 5997	0.1421 7218	0.1291 2180	0.1172 8309	79
80	0.1686 2993	0.1529 2793	0.1387 0457	0.1258 1905	0.1141 4412	80
81	0.1649 1925	0.1493 8015	0.1353 2153	0.1226 0078	0.1110 8917	81
82	0.1612 9022	0.1459 1468	0.1320 2101	0.1194 6482	0.1081 1598	82
83	0.1577 4105	0.1425 2960	0.1288 0098	0.1164 0909	0.1052 2237	83
84	0.1542 6997	0.1392 2306	0.1256 5949	0.1134 3151	0.1024 0620	84
85	0.1508 7528	0.1359 9322	0.1225 9463	0.1105 3009	0.0996 6540	85
86	0.1475 5528	0.1328 3831	0.1196 0452	0.1077 0289	0.0969 9795	86
87	0.1443 0835	0.1297 5659	0.1166 8733	0.1049 4801	0.0944 0190	87
88	0.1411 3286	0.1267 4636	0.1138 4130	0.1022 6359	0.0918 7533	88
89	0.1380 2724	0.1238 0597	0.1110 6468	0.0996 4783	0.0894 1638	89
90	0.1349 8997	0.1209 3379	0.1083 5579	0.0970 9898	0.0870 2324	90
91	0.1320 1953	0.1181 2825	0.1057 1296	0.0946 1533	0.0846 9415	91
92	0.1291 1445	0.1153 8779	0.1031 3460	0.0921 9521	0.0824 2740	92
93	0.1262 7331	0.1127 1090	0.1006 1912	0.0898 3699	0.0802 2131	93
94	0.1234 9468	0.1100 9612	0.0981 6500	0.0875 3909	0.0780 7427	94
95	0.1207 7719	0.1075 4200	0.0957 7073	0.0852 9996	0.0759 8469	95
96	0.1181 1950	0.1050 4713	0.0934 3486	0.0831 1811	0.0739 5104	96
97	0.1155 2029	0.1026 1014	0.0911 5596	0.0809 9207	0.0719 7181	97
98	0.1129 7828	0.1002 2968	0.0889 3264	0.0789 2041	0.0700 4556	98
99	0.1104 9221	0.0979 0445	0.0867 6355	0.0769 0174	0.0681 7086	99
100	0.1080 6084	0.0956 3316	0.0846 4737	0.0749 3470	0.0663 4634	100
101	0.1056 8297	0.0934 1457	0.0825 8280	0.0730 1798	0.0645 7064	101
102	0.1033 5743	0.0912 4744	0.0805 6858	0.0711 5029	0.0628 4248	102
103	0.1010 8306	0.0891 3059	0.0786 0350	0.0693 3036	0.0611 6056	103
104	0.0988 5874	0.0870 6285	0.0766 8634	0.0675 5699	0.0595 2366	104
105	0.0966 8336	0.0850 4307	0.0748 1594	0.0658 2898	0.0579 3057	105
106	0.0945 5586	0.0830 7016	0.0729 9116	0.0641 4517	0.0563 8012	106
107	0.0924 7517	0.0811 4301	0.0712 1089	0.0625 0443	0.0548 7116	107
108	0.0904 4026	0.0792 6057	0.0694 7404	0.0609 0566	0.0534 0259	108
109	0.0884 5013	0.0774 2180	0.0677 7955	0.0593 4778	0.0519 7332	109
110	0.0865 0380	0.0756 2569	0.0661 2639	0.0578 2975	0.0505 8231	110
111	0.0846 0029	0.0738 7125	0.0645 1355	0.0563 5054	0.0492 2852	111
112	0.0827 3867	0.0721 5751	0.0629 4005	0.0549 0918	0.0479 1097	112
113	0.0809 1801	0.0704 8353	0.0614 0493	0.0535 0468	0.0466 2868	113
114	0.0791 3742	0.0688 4838	0.0599 0724	0.0521 3611	0.0453 8071	114
115	0.0773 9601	0.0672 5116	0.0584 4609	0.0508 0254	0.0441 6614	115
116	0.0756 9292	0.0656 9100	0.0570 2058	0.0495 0309	0.0429 8408	116
117	0.0740 2731	0.0641 6704	0.0556 2983	0.0482 3687	0.0418 3366	117
118	0.0723 9834	0.0626 7842	0.0542 7301	0.0470 0304	0.0407 1402	118
119	0.0708 0523	0.0612 2434	0.0529 4928	0.0458 0077	0.0396 2435	119
120	0.0692 4717	0.0598 0400	0.0516 5783	0.0446 2925	0.0385 6385	120

TABLE II

N	2 1/4	2 3/8	2 1/2	2 5/8	2 3/4	N
121	0.0677 2339	0.0584 1660	0.0503 9788	0.0434 8770	0.0375 3172	121
122	0.0662 3314	0.0570 6140	0.0491 6867	0.0423 7534	0.0365 2722	122
123	0.0647 7569	0.0557 3763	0.0479 6943	0.0412 9144	0.0355 4961	123
124	0.0633 5031	0.0544 4457	0.0467 9944	0.0402 3527	0.0345 9816	124
125	0.0619 5629	0.0531 8151	0.0456 5799	0.0392 0611	0.0336 7218	125
126	0.0605 9295	0.0519 4775	0.0445 4438	0.0382 0327	0.0327 7097	126
127	0.0592 5961	0.0507 4261	0.0434 5794	0.0372 2609	0.0318 9389	127
128	0.0579 5561	0.0495 6543	0.0423 9799	0.0362 7390	0.0310 4028	128
129	0.0566 8030	0.0484 1556	0.0413 6389	0.0353 4606	0.0302 0952	129
130	0.0554 3306	0.0472 9237	0.0403 5501	0.0344 4196	0.0294 0100	130
131	0.0542 1326	0.0461 9523	0.0393 7075	0.0335 6099	0.0286 1411	131
132	0.0530 2030	0.0451 2355	0.0384 1048	0.0327 0254	0.0278 4828	132
133	0.0518 5360	0.0440 7673	0.0374 7364	0.0318 6606	0.0271 0295	133
134	0.0507 1256	0.0430 5419	0.0365 5965	0.0310 5097	0.0263 7757	134
135	0.0495 9664	0.0420 5537	0.0356 6795	0.0302 5673	0.0256 7160	135
136	0.0485 0527	0.0410 7973	0.0347 9800	0.0294 8281	0.0249 8452	136
137	0.0474 3792	0.0401 2672	0.0339 4927	0.0287 2868	0.0243 1584	137
138	0.0463 9405	0.0391 9582	0.0331 2124	0.0279 9384	0.0236 6505	138
139	0.0453 7316	0.0382 8652	0.0323 1340	0.0272 7780	0.0230 3168	139
140	0.0443 7472	0.0373 9831	0.0315 2527	0.0265 8007	0.0224 1526	140
141	0.0433 9826	0.0365 3070	0.0307 5636	0.0259 0019	0.0218 1534	141
142	0.0424 4329	0.0356 8323	0.0300 0621	0.0252 3770	0.0212 3147	142
143	0.0415 0933	0.0348 5541	0.0292 7435	0.0245 9216	0.0206 6323	143
144	0.0405 9592	0.0340 4680	0.0285 6034	0.0239 6313	0.0201 1020	144
145	0.0397 0261	0.0332 5695	0.0278 6375	0.0233 5019	0.0195 7197	145
146	0.0388 2896	0.0324 8542	0.0271 8414	0.0227 5292	0.0190 4815	146
147	0.0379 7453	0.0317 3179	0.0265 2112	0.0221 7093	0.0185 3834	147
148	0.0371 3891	0.0309 9564	0.0258 7426	0.0216 0383	0.0180 4218	148
149	0.0363 2167	0.0302 7657	0.0252 4318	0.0210 5124	0.0175 5930	149
150	0.0355 2242	0.0295 7418	0.0246 2749	0.0205 1278	0.0170 8935	150
151	0.0347 4075	0.0288 8809	0.0240 2682	0.0199 8809	0.0166 3197	151
152	0.0339 7628	0.0282 1792	0.0234 4080	0.0194 7682	0.0161 8683	152
153	0.0332 2864	0.0275 6329	0.0228 6907	0.0189 7863	0.0157 5360	153
154	0.0324 9745	0.0269 2385	0.0223 1129	0.0184 9319	0.0153 3197	154
155	0.0317 8234	0.0262 9924	0.0217 6711	0.0180 2016	0.0149 2163	155
156	0.0310 8298	0.0256 8912	0.0212 3621	0.0175 5923	0.0145 2227	156
157	0.0303 9900	0.0250 9316	0.0207 1825	0.0171 1009	0.0141 3359	157
158	0.0297 3007	0.0245 1102	0.0202 1293	0.0166 7244	0.0137 5532	158
159	0.0290 7587	0.0239 4239	0.0197 1993	0.0162 4598	0.0133 8718	159
160	0.0284 3605	0.0233 8695	0.0192 3896	0.0158 3043	0.0130 2888	160
161	0.0278 1032	0.0228 4440	0.0187 6971	0.0154 2551	0.0126 8018	161
162	0.0271 9836	0.0223 1443	0.0183 1192	0.0150 3095	0.0123 4080	162
163	0.0265 9986	0.0217 9676	0.0178 6528	0.0146 4648	0.0120 1051	163
164	0.0260 1453	0.0212 9109	0.0174 2955	0.0142 7184	0.0116 8907	164
165	0.0254 4209	0.0207 9716	0.0170 0444	0.0139 0679	0.0113 7622	165
166	0.0248 8224	0.0203 1469	0.0165 8969	0.0135 5108	0.0110 7175	166
167	0.0243 3471	0.0198 4341	0.0161 8507	0.0132 0446	0.0107 7542	167
168	0.0237 9922	0.0193 8306	0.0157 9031	0.0128 6671	0.0104 8703	168
169	0.0232 7552	0.0189 3339	0.0154 0518	0.0125 3760	0.0102 0635	169
170	0.0227 6335	0.0184 9415	0.0150 2944	0.0122 1690	0.0099 3319	170
171	0.0222 6244	0.0180 6511	0.0146 6287	0.0119 0441	0.0096 6734	171
172	0.0217 7256	0.0176 4602	0.0143 0524	0.0115 9991	0.0094 0860	172
173	0.0212 9346	0.0172 3665	0.0139 5633	0.0113 0320	0.0091 5679	173
174	0.0208 2490	0.0168 3677	0.0136 1593	0.0110 1408	0.0089 1172	174
175	0.0203 6665	0.0164 4618	0.0132 8384	0.0107 3236	0.0086 7321	175
176	0.0199 1848	0.0160 6464	0.0129 5984	0.0104 5784	0.0084 4108	176
177	0.0194 8018	0.0156 9196	0.0126 4375	0.0101 9034	0.0082 1516	177
178	0.0190 5152	0.0153 2792	0.0123 3536	0.0099 2969	0.0079 9529	178
179	0.0186 3229	0.0149 7233	0.0120 3450	0.0096 7570	0.0077 8130	179
180	0.0182 2229	0.0146 2498	0.0117 4098	0.0094 2821	0.0075 7304	180

TABLE II

N	2 1/4	2 3/8	2 1/2	2 5/8	2 3/4	N
181	0.0178 2131	0.0142 8570	0.0114 5461	0.0091 8705	0.0073 7036	181
182	0.0174 2916	0.0139 5428	0.0111 7523	0.0089 5206	0.0071 7310	182
183	0.0170 4563	0.0136 3056	0.0109 0266	0.0087 2308	0.0069 8112	183
184	0.0166 7054	0.0133 1434	0.0106 3675	0.0084 9996	0.0067 9428	184
185	0.0163 0371	0.0130 0546	0.0103 7731	0.0082 8254	0.0066 1243	185
186	0.0159 4495	0.0127 0375	0.0101 2421	0.0080 7068	0.0064 3546	186
187	0.0155 9408	0.0124 0903	0.0098 7728	0.0078 6425	0.0062 6322	187
188	0.0152 5093	0.0121 2116	0.0096 3637	0.0076 6309	0.0060 9559	188
189	0.0149 1534	0.0118 3996	0.0094 0133	0.0074 6708	0.0059 3245	189
190	0.0145 8713	0.0115 6528	0.0091 7203	0.0072 7608	0.0057 7367	190
191	0.0142 6614	0.0112 9698	0.0089 4832	0.0070 8997	0.0056 1915	191
192	0.0139 5222	0.0110 3490	0.0087 3007	0.0069 0862	0.0054 6876	192
193	0.0136 4520	0.0107 7890	0.0085 1714	0.0067 3191	0.0053 2239	193
194	0.0133 4494	0.0105 2884	0.0083 0941	0.0065 5972	0.0051 7994	194
195	0.0130 5128	0.0102 8458	0.0081 0674	0.0063 9193	0.0050 4131	195
196	0.0127 6409	0.0100 4599	0.0079 0901	0.0062 2843	0.0049 0638	196
197	0.0124 8322	0.0098 1293	0.0077 1611	0.0060 6912	0.0047 7507	197
198	0.0122 0853	0.0095 8528	0.0075 2791	0.0059 1388	0.0046 4727	198
199	0.0119 3988	0.0093 6291	0.0073 4431	0.0057 6261	0.0045 2289	199
200	0.0116 7714	0.0091 4570	0.0071 6518	0.0056 1521	0.0044 0184	200
201	0.0114 2019	0.0089 3353	0.0069 9042	0.0054 7158	0.0042 8403	201
202	0.0111 6889	0.0087 2628	0.0068 1992	0.0053 3163	0.0041 6937	202
203	0.0109 2312	0.0085 2384	0.0066 5358	0.0051 9525	0.0040 5778	203
204	0.0106 8276	0.0083 2610	0.0064 9130	0.0050 6236	0.0039 4918	204
205	0.0104 4769	0.0081 3294	0.0063 3297	0.0049 3288	0.0038 4348	205
206	0.0102 1779	0.0079 4426	0.0061 7851	0.0048 0670	0.0037 4061	206
207	0.0099 9294	0.0077 5996	0.0060 2781	0.0046 8375	0.0036 4050	207
208	0.0097 7305	0.0075 7994	0.0058 8079	0.0045 6395	0.0035 4307	208
209	0.0095 5800	0.0074 0409	0.0057 3736	0.0044 4721	0.0034 4824	209
210	0.0093 4767	0.0072 3232	0.0055 9742	0.0043 3345	0.0033 5595	210
211	0.0091 4198	0.0070 6454	0.0054 6090	0.0042 2261	0.0032 6613	211
212	0.0089 4081	0.0069 0065	0.0053 2771	0.0041 1460	0.0031 7872	212
213	0.0087 4407	0.0067 4056	0.0051 9777	0.0040 0936	0.0030 9364	213
214	0.0085 5166	0.0065 8419	0.0050 7099	0.0039 0680	0.0030 1084	214
215	0.0083 6348	0.0064 3144	0.0049 4731	0.0038 0687	0.0029 3026	215
216	0.0081 7944	0.0062 8224	0.0048 2664	0.0037 0950	0.0028 5184	216
217	0.0079 9945	0.0061 3650	0.0047 0892	0.0036 1462	0.0027 7551	217
218	0.0078 2343	0.0059 9414	0.0045 9407	0.0035 2216	0.0027 0123	218
219	0.0076 5127	0.0058 5508	0.0044 8202	0.0034 3207	0.0026 2893	219
220	0.0074 8291	0.0057 1925	0.0043 7270	0.0033 4428	0.0025 5857	220
221	0.0073 1825	0.0055 8656	0.0042 6605	0.0032 5874	0.0024 9009	221
222	0.0071 5721	0.0054 5696	0.0041 6200	0.0031 7538	0.0024 2345	222
223	0.0069 9972	0.0053 3037	0.0040 6049	0.0030 9416	0.0023 5859	223
224	0.0068 4569	0.0052 0671	0.0039 6145	0.0030 1502	0.0022 9546	224
225	0.0066 9505	0.0050 8592	0.0038 6483	0.0029 3790	0.0022 3403	225
226	0.0065 4772	0.0049 6793	0.0037 7056	0.0028 6275	0.0021 7423	226
227	0.0064 0364	0.0048 5268	0.0036 7860	0.0027 8953	0.0021 1604	227
228	0.0062 6273	0.0047 4010	0.0035 8888	0.0027 1817	0.0020 5941	228
229	0.0061 2492	0.0046 3013	0.0035 0134	0.0026 4865	0.0020 0429	229
230	0.0059 9014	0.0045 2272	0.0034 1595	0.0025 8090	0.0019 5065	230
231	0.0058 5833	0.0044 1780	0.0033 3263	0.0025 1488	0.0018 9844	231
232	0.0057 2942	0.0043 1531	0.0032 5135	0.0024 5056	0.0018 4763	232
233	0.0056 0334	0.0042 1520	0.0031 7205	0.0023 8787	0.0017 9818	233
234	0.0054 8004	0.0041 1741	0.0030 9468	0.0023 2680	0.0017 5005	234
235	0.0053 5945	0.0040 2189	0.0030 1920	0.0022 6728	0.0017 0322	235
236	0.0052 4152	0.0039 2858	0.0029 4556	0.0022 0929	0.0016 5763	236
237	0.0051 2618	0.0038 3745	0.0028 7372	0.0021 5278	0.0016 1327	237
238	0.0050 1338	0.0037 4842	0.0028 0363	0.0020 9771	0.0015 7009	238
239	0.0049 0306	0.0036 6146	0.0027 3524	0.0020 4405	0.0015 2807	239
240	0.0047 9517	0.0035 7652	0.0026 6853	0.0019 9177	0.0014 8717	240

TABLE II

N	2 1/4	2 3/8	2 1/2	2 5/8	2 3/4	N
241	0.0046 8965	0.0034 9355	0.0026 0345	0.0019 4082	0.0014 4737	241
242	0.0045 8646	0.0034 1250	0.0025 3995	0.0018 9118	0.0014 0863	242
243	0.0044 8553	0.0033 3333	0.0024 7800	0.0018 4281	0.0013 7093	243
244	0.0043 8683	0.0032 5600	0.0024 1756	0.0017 9567	0.0013 3424	244
245	0.0042 9030	0.0031 8047	0.0023 5859	0.0017 4974	0.0012 9853	245
246	0.0041 9589	0.0031 0668	0.0023 0107	0.0017 0498	0.0012 6377	246
247	0.0041 0356	0.0030 3461	0.0022 4494	0.0016 6137	0.0012 2995	247
248	0.0040 1326	0.0029 6421	0.0021 9019	0.0016 1888	0.0011 9703	248
249	0.0039 2495	0.0028 9544	0.0021 3677	0.0015 7747	0.0011 6500	249
250	0.0038 3858	0.0028 2827	0.0020 8465	0.0015 3712	0.0011 3382	250
251	0.0037 5411	0.0027 6266	0.0020 3381	0.0014 9780	0.0011 0347	251
252	0.0036 7151	0.0026 9857	0.0019 8420	0.0014 5949	0.0010 7394	252
253	0.0035 9071	0.0026 3596	0.0019 3581	0.0014 2216	0.0010 4519	253
254	0.0035 1170	0.0025 7481	0.0018 8859	0.0013 8578	0.0010 1722	254
255	0.0034 3443	0.0025 1508	0.0018 4253	0.0013 5034	0.0009 9000	255
256	0.0033 5885	0.0024 5673	0.0017 9759	0.0013 1580	0.0009 6350	256
257	0.0032 8494	0.0023 9974	0.0017 5375	0.0012 8214	0.0009 3771	257
258	0.0032 1266	0.0023 4407	0.0017 1097	0.0012 4934	0.0009 1262	258
259	0.0031 4196	0.0022 8969	0.0016 6924	0.0012 1739	0.0008 8819	259
260	0.0030 7282	0.0022 3657	0.0016 2853	0.0011 8625	0.0008 6442	260
261	0.0030 0521	0.0021 8468	0.0015 8881	0.0011 5591	0.0008 4128	261
262	0.0029 3908	0.0021 3400	0.0015 5006	0.0011 2634	0.0008 1877	262
263	0.0028 7440	0.0020 8449	0.0015 1225	0.0010 9753	0.0007 9685	263
264	0.0028 1115	0.0020 3613	0.0014 7537	0.0010 6946	0.0007 7553	264
265	0.0027 4929	0.0019 8890	0.0014 3938	0.0010 4210	0.0007 5477	265
266	0.0026 8880	0.0019 4276	0.0014 0427	0.0010 1545	0.0007 3457	266
267	0.0026 2963	0.0018 9769	0.0013 7002	0.0009 8947	0.0007 1491	267
268	0.0025 7176	0.0018 5366	0.0013 3661	0.0009 6416	0.0006 9578	268
269	0.0025 1517	0.0018 1066	0.0013 0401	0.0009 3950	0.0006 7715	269
270	0.0024 5983	0.0017 6865	0.0012 7220	0.0009 1547	0.0006 5903	270
271	0.0024 0570	0.0017 2762	0.0012 4117	0.0008 9205	0.0006 4139	271
272	0.0023 5276	0.0016 8754	0.0012 1090	0.0008 6924	0.0006 2423	272
273	0.0023 0099	0.0016 4839	0.0011 8137	0.0008 4700	0.0006 0752	273
274	0.0022 5036	0.0016 1015	0.0011 5255	0.0008 2534	0.0005 9126	274
275	0.0022 0084	0.0015 7280	0.0011 2444	0.0008 0423	0.0005 7544	275
276	0.0021 5241	0.0015 3631	0.0010 9702	0.0007 8366	0.0005 6003	276
277	0.0021 0504	0.0015 0067	0.0010 7026	0.0007 6361	0.0005 4505	277
278	0.0020 5872	0.0014 6586	0.0010 4416	0.0007 4408	0.0005 3046	278
279	0.0020 1342	0.0014 3185	0.0010 1869	0.0007 2505	0.0005 1626	279
280	0.0019 6912	0.0013 9863	0.0009 9384	0.0007 0650	0.0005 0244	280
281	0.0019 2579	0.0013 6619	0.0009 6960	0.0006 8843	0.0004 8900	281
282	0.0018 8341	0.0013 3449	0.0009 4595	0.0006 7082	0.0004 7591	282
283	0.0018 4197	0.0013 0353	0.0009 2288	0.0006 5366	0.0004 6317	283
284	0.0018 0143	0.0012 7329	0.0009 0037	0.0006 3694	0.0004 5078	284
285	0.0017 6179	0.0012 4375	0.0008 7841	0.0006 2065	0.0004 3871	285
286	0.0017 2302	0.0012 1490	0.0008 5699	0.0006 0477	0.0004 2697	286
287	0.0016 8511	0.0011 8672	0.0008 3609	0.0005 8931	0.0004 1554	287
288	0.0016 4803	0.0011 5918	0.0008 1569	0.0005 7423	0.0004 0442	288
289	0.0016 1176	0.0011 3229	0.0007 9580	0.0005 5954	0.0003 9360	289
290	0.0015 7630	0.0011 0602	0.0007 7639	0.0005 4523	0.0003 8306	290
291	0.0015 4161	0.0010 8037	0.0007 5745	0.0005 3128	0.0003 7281	291
292	0.0015 0769	0.0010 5530	0.0007 3898	0.0005 1770	0.0003 6283	292
293	0.0014 7451	0.0010 3082	0.0007 2095	0.0005 0445	0.0003 5312	293
294	0.0014 4207	0.0010 0691	0.0007 0337	0.0004 9155	0.0003 4367	294
295	0.0014 1033	0.0009 8355	0.0006 8621	0.0004 7898	0.0003 3447	295
296	0.0013 7930	0.0009 6073	0.0006 6948	0.0004 6673	0.0003 2552	296
297	0.0013 4895	0.0009 3844	0.0006 5315	0.0004 5479	0.0003 1681	297
298	0.0013 1926	0.0009 1667	0.0006 3722	0.0004 4315	0.0003 0833	298
299	0.0012 9023	0.0008 9540	0.0006 2168	0.0004 3182	0.0003 0008	299
300	0.0012 6184	0.0008 7463	0.0006 0651	0.0004 2077	0.0002 9205	300

TABLE II

N	2 1/4	2 3/8	2 1/2	2 5/8	2 3/4	N
301	0.0012 3408	0.0008 5434	0.0005 9172	0.0004 1001	0.0002 8423	301
302	0.0012 0692	0.0008 3452	0.0005 7729	0.0003 9952	0.0002 7662	302
303	0.0011 8036	0.0008 1516	0.0005 6321	0.0003 8930	0.0002 6922	303
304	0.0011 5439	0.0007 9625	0.0005 4947	0.0003 7935	0.0002 6201	304
305	0.0011 2899	0.0007 7778	0.0005 3607	0.0003 6964	0.0002 5500	305
306	0.0011 0414	0.0007 5973	0.0005 2299	0.0003 6019	0.0002 4818	306
307	0.0010 7985	0.0007 4211	0.0005 1024	0.0003 5098	0.0002 4153	307
308	0.0010 5608	0.0007 2489	0.0004 9779	0.0003 4200	0.0002 3507	308
309	0.0010 3284	0.0007 0808	0.0004 8565	0.0003 3325	0.0002 2878	309
310	0.0010 1012	0.0006 9165	0.0004 7381	0.0003 2473	0.0002 2266	310
311	0.0009 8789	0.0006 7560	0.0004 6225	0.0003 1642	0.0002 1670	311
312	0.0009 6615	0.0006 5993	0.0004 5098	0.0003 0833	0.0002 1090	312
313	0.0009 4489	0.0006 4462	0.0004 3998	0.0003 0044	0.0002 0525	313
314	0.0009 2410	0.0006 2967	0.0004 2925	0.0002 9276	0.0001 9976	314
315	0.0009 0376	0.0006 1506	0.0004 1878	0.0002 8527	0.0001 9441	315
316	0.0008 8388	0.0006 0079	0.0004 0856	0.0002 7797	0.0001 8921	316
317	0.0008 6443	0.0005 8685	0.0003 9860	0.0002 7086	0.0001 8414	317
318	0.0008 4541	0.0005 7324	0.0003 8888	0.0002 6393	0.0001 7922	318
319	0.0008 2680	0.0005 5994	0.0003 7939	0.0002 5718	0.0001 7442	319
320	0.0008 0861	0.0005 4695	0.0003 7014	0.0002 5060	0.0001 6975	320
321	0.0007 9082	0.0005 3426	0.0003 6111	0.0002 4419	0.0001 6521	321
322	0.0007 7341	0.0005 2187	0.0003 5230	0.0002 3795	0.0001 6079	322
323	0.0007 5640	0.0005 0976	0.0003 4371	0.0002 3186	0.0001 5648	323
324	0.0007 3975	0.0004 9793	0.0003 3533	0.0002 2593	0.0001 5230	324
325	0.0007 2347	0.0004 8638	0.0003 2715	0.0002 2015	0.0001 4822	325
326	0.0007 0755	0.0004 7510	0.0003 1917	0.0002 1452	0.0001 4425	326
327	0.0006 9198	0.0004 6408	0.0003 1138	0.0002 0903	0.0001 4039	327
328	0.0006 7676	0.0004 5331	0.0003 0379	0.0002 0369	0.0001 3663	328
329	0.0006 6186	0.0004 4279	0.0002 9638	0.0001 9848	0.0001 3298	329
330	0.0006 4730	0.0004 3252	0.0002 8915	0.0001 9340	0.0001 2942	330
331	0.0006 3306	0.0004 2249	0.0002 8210	0.0001 8845	0.0001 2595	331
332	0.0006 1913	0.0004 1269	0.0002 7522	0.0001 8363	0.0001 2258	332
333	0.0006 0550	0.0004 0311	0.0002 6851	0.0001 7893	0.0001 1930	333
334	0.0005 9218	0.0003 9376	0.0002 6196	0.0001 7436	0.0001 1611	334
335	0.0005 7915	0.0003 8463	0.0002 5557	0.0001 6990	0.0001 1300	335
336	0.0005 6640	0.0003 7570	0.0002 4933	0.0001 6555	0.0001 0998	336
337	0.0005 5394	0.0003 6699	0.0002 4325	0.0001 6132	0.0001 0703	337
338	0.0005 4175	0.0003 5847	0.0002 3732	0.0001 5719	0.0001 0417	338
339	0.0005 2983	0.0003 5016	0.0002 3153	0.0001 5317	0.0001 0138	339
340	0.0005 1817	0.0003 4203	0.0002 2588	0.0001 4925	0.0000 9867	340
341	0.0005 0677	0.0003 3410	0.0002 2037	0.0001 4544	0.0000 9603	341
342	0.0004 9562	0.0003 2635	0.0002 1500	0.0001 4171	0.0000 9346	342
343	0.0004 8471	0.0003 1878	0.0002 0976	0.0001 3809	0.0000 9096	343
344	0.0004 7404	0.0003 1138	0.0002 0464	0.0001 3456	0.0000 8852	344
345	0.0004 6361	0.0003 0416	0.0001 9965	0.0001 3112	0.0000 8615	345
346	0.0004 5341	0.0002 9710	0.0001 9478	0.0001 2776	0.0000 8385	346
347	0.0004 4343	0.0002 9021	0.0001 9003	0.0001 2449	0.0000 8160	347
348	0.0004 3368	0.0002 8348	0.0001 8539	0.0001 2131	0.0000 7942	348
349	0.0004 2413	0.0002 7690	0.0001 8087	0.0001 1821	0.0000 7729	349
350	0.0004 1480	0.0002 7048	0.0001 7646	0.0001 1518	0.0000 7522	350
351	0.0004 0567	0.0002 6420	0.0001 7216	0.0001 1224	0.0000 7321	351
352	0.0003 9675	0.0002 5807	0.0001 6796	0.0001 0937	0.0000 7125	352
353	0.0003 8802	0.0002 5209	0.0001 6386	0.0001 0657	0.0000 6934	353
354	0.0003 7948	0.0002 4624	0.0001 5986	0.0001 0384	0.0000 6749	354
355	0.0003 7113	0.0002 4053	0.0001 5597	0.0001 0119	0.0000 6568	355
356	0.0003 6296	0.0002 3495	0.0001 5216	0.0000 9860	0.0000 6392	356
357	0.0003 5497	0.0002 2949	0.0001 4845	0.0000 9608	0.0000 6221	357
358	0.0003 4716	0.0002 2417	0.0001 4483	0.0000 9362	0.0000 6055	358
359	0.0003 3952	0.0002 1897	0.0001 4130	0.0000 9122	0.0000 5893	359
360	0.0003 3205	0.0002 1389	0.0001 3785	0.0000 8889	0.0000 5735	360

TABLE II

N	3	3 1/2	4	4 1/2	5	N
1	0.9708 7379	0.9661 8357	0.9615 3846	0.9569 3780	0.9523 8095	1
2	0.9425 9591	0.9335 1070	0.9245 5621	0.9157 2995	0.9070 2948	2
3	0.9151 4166	0.9019 4271	0.8889 9636	0.8762 9660	0.8638 3760	3
4	0.8884 8705	0.8714 4223	0.8548 0419	0.8385 6134	0.8227 0247	4
5	0.8626 0878	0.8419 7317	0.8219 2711	0.8024 5105	0.7835 2617	5
6	0.8374 8426	0.8135 0064	0.7903 1453	0.7678 9574	0.7462 1540	6
7	0.8130 9151	0.7859 9096	0.7599 1781	0.7348 2846	0.7106 8133	7
8	0.7894 0923	0.7594 1156	0.7306 9021	0.7031 8513	0.6768 3936	8
9	0.7664 1673	0.7337 3097	0.7025 8674	0.6729 0443	0.6446 0892	9
10	0.7440 9391	0.7089 1881	0.6755 6417	0.6439 2768	0.6139 1325	10
11	0.7224 2128	0.6849 4571	0.6495 8093	0.6161 9874	0.5846 7929	11
12	0.7013 7988	0.6617 8330	0.6245 9705	0.5896 6386	0.5568 3742	12
13	0.6809 5134	0.6394 0415	0.6005 7409	0.5642 7164	0.5303 2135	13
14	0.6611 1781	0.6177 8179	0.5774 7508	0.5399 7286	0.5050 6795	14
15	0.6418 6195	0.5968 9062	0.5552 6450	0.5167 2044	0.4810 1710	15
16	0.6231 6694	0.5767 0591	0.5339 0818	0.4944 6932	0.4581 1152	16
17	0.6050 1645	0.5572 0378	0.5133 7325	0.4731 7639	0.4362 9669	17
18	0.5873 9461	0.5383 6114	0.4936 2812	0.4528 0037	0.4155 2065	18
19	0.5702 8603	0.5201 5569	0.4746 4242	0.4333 0179	0.3957 3396	19
20	0.5536 7575	0.5025 6588	0.4563 8695	0.4146 4286	0.3768 8948	20
21	0.5375 4928	0.4855 7090	0.4388 3360	0.3967 8743	0.3589 4236	21
22	0.5218 9250	0.4691 5063	0.4219 5539	0.3797 0089	0.3418 4987	22
23	0.5066 9175	0.4532 8563	0.4057 2633	0.3633 5013	0.3255 7131	23
24	0.4919 3374	0.4379 5713	0.3901 2147	0.3477 0347	0.3100 6791	24
25	0.4776 0557	0.4231 4699	0.3751 1680	0.3327 3060	0.2953 0277	25
26	0.4636 9473	0.4088 3767	0.3606 8923	0.3184 0248	0.2812 4073	26
27	0.4501 8906	0.3950 1224	0.3468 1657	0.3046 9137	0.2678 4832	27
28	0.4370 7675	0.3816 5434	0.3334 7747	0.2915 7069	0.2550 9364	28
29	0.4243 4636	0.3687 4815	0.3206 5141	0.2790 1502	0.2429 4632	29
30	0.4119 8676	0.3562 7841	0.3083 1867	0.2670 0002	0.2313 7745	30
31	0.3999 8715	0.3442 3035	0.2964 6026	0.2555 0241	0.2203 5947	31
32	0.3883 3703	0.3325 8971	0.2850 5794	0.2444 9991	0.2098 6617	32
33	0.3770 2625	0.3213 4271	0.2740 9417	0.2339 7121	0.1998 7254	33
34	0.3660 4490	0.3104 7605	0.2635 5209	0.2238 9589	0.1903 5480	34
35	0.3553 8340	0.2999 7686	0.2534 1547	0.2142 5444	0.1812 9029	35
36	0.3450 3243	0.2898 3272	0.2436 6872	0.2050 2817	0.1726 5741	36
37	0.3349 8294	0.2800 3161	0.2342 9685	0.1961 9921	0.1644 3563	37
38	0.3252 2615	0.2705 6194	0.2252 8543	0.1877 5044	0.1566 0536	38
39	0.3157 5355	0.2614 1250	0.2166 2061	0.1796 6549	0.1491 4797	39
40	0.3065 5684	0.2525 7247	0.2082 8904	0.1719 2870	0.1420 4568	40
41	0.2976 2800	0.2440 3137	0.2002 7793	0.1645 2507	0.1352 8160	41
42	0.2889 5922	0.2357 7910	0.1925 7493	0.1574 4026	0.1288 3962	42
43	0.2805 4294	0.2278 0590	0.1851 6820	0.1506 6054	0.1227 0440	43
44	0.2723 7178	0.2201 0231	0.1780 4635	0.1441 7276	0.1168 6133	44
45	0.2644 3862	0.2126 5924	0.1711 9841	0.1379 6437	0.1112 9651	45
46	0.2567 3653	0.2054 6787	0.1646 1386	0.1320 2332	0.1059 9668	46
47	0.2492 5876	0.1985 1968	0.1582 8256	0.1263 3810	0.1009 4921	47
48	0.2419 9880	0.1918 0645	0.1521 9476	0.1208 9771	0.0961 4211	48
49	0.2349 5029	0.1853 2024	0.1463 4112	0.1156 9158	0.0915 6391	49
50	0.2281 0708	0.1790 5337	0.1407 1262	0.1107 0965	0.0872 0373	50
51	0.2214 6318	0.1729 9843	0.1353 0059	0.1059 4225	0.0830 5117	51
52	0.2150 1280	0.1671 4824	0.1300 9672	0.1013 8014	0.0790 9635	52
53	0.2087 5029	0.1614 9589	0.1250 9300	0.0970 1449	0.0753 2986	53
54	0.2026 7019	0.1560 3467	0.1202 8173	0.0928 3683	0.0717 4272	54
55	0.1967 6717	0.1507 5814	0.1156 5551	0.0888 3907	0.0683 2640	55
56	0.1910 3609	0.1456 6004	0.1112 0722	0.0850 1347	0.0650 7276	56
57	0.1854 7193	0.1407 3433	0.1069 3002	0.0813 5260	0.0619 7406	57
58	0.1800 6984	0.1359 7520	0.1028 1733	0.0778 4938	0.0590 2291	58
59	0.1748 2508	0.1313 7701	0.0988 6282	0.0744 9701	0.0562 1230	59
60	0.1697 3309	0.1269 3431	0.0950 6040	0.0712 8901	0.0535 3552	60

TABLE II

N	3	3 1/2	4	4 1/2	5	N
61	0.1647 8941	0.1226 4184	0.0914 0423	0.0682 1915	0.0509 8621	61
62	0.1599 8972	0.1184 9453	0.0878 8868	0.0652 8148	0.0485 5830	62
63	0.1553 2982	0.1144 8747	0.0845 0835	0.0624 7032	0.0462 4600	63
64	0.1508 0565	0.1106 1591	0.0812 5803	0.0597 8021	0.0440 4381	64
65	0.1464 1325	0.1068 7528	0.0781 3272	0.0572 0594	0.0419 4648	65
66	0.1421 4879	0.1032 6114	0.0751 2762	0.0547 4253	0.0399 4903	66
67	0.1380 0853	0.0997 6922	0.0722 3809	0.0523 8519	0.0380 4670	67
68	0.1339 8887	0.0963 9538	0.0694 5970	0.0501 2937	0.0362 3495	68
69	0.1300 8628	0.0931 3563	0.0667 8818	0.0479 7069	0.0345 0948	69
70	0.1262 9736	0.0899 8612	0.0642 1940	0.0459 0497	0.0328 6617	70
71	0.1226 1880	0.0869 4311	0.0617 4942	0.0439 2820	0.0313 0111	71
72	0.1190 4737	0.0840 0300	0.0593 7445	0.0420 3655	0.0298 1058	72
73	0.1155 7998	0.0811 6232	0.0570 9081	0.0402 2637	0.0283 9103	73
74	0.1122 1357	0.0784 1770	0.0548 9501	0.0384 9413	0.0270 3908	74
75	0.1089 4521	0.0757 6590	0.0527 8367	0.0368 3649	0.0257 5150	75
76	0.1057 7205	0.0732 0376	0.0507 5353	0.0352 5023	0.0245 2524	76
77	0.1026 9131	0.0707 2827	0.0488 0147	0.0337 3228	0.0233 5737	77
78	0.0997 0030	0.0683 3650	0.0469 2449	0.0322 7969	0.0222 4512	78
79	0.0967 9641	0.0660 2560	0.0451 1970	0.0308 8965	0.0211 8582	79
80	0.0939 7710	0.0637 9285	0.0433 8433	0.0295 5948	0.0201 7698	80
81	0.0912 3990	0.0616 3561	0.0417 1570	0.0282 8658	0.0192 1617	81
82	0.0885 8243	0.0595 5131	0.0401 1125	0.0270 6850	0.0183 0111	82
83	0.0860 0236	0.0575 3750	0.0385 6851	0.0259 0287	0.0174 2963	83
84	0.0834 9743	0.0555 9178	0.0370 8510	0.0247 8744	0.0165 9965	84
85	0.0810 6547	0.0537 1187	0.0356 5875	0.0237 2003	0.0158 0919	85
86	0.0787 0434	0.0518 9553	0.0342 8726	0.0226 9860	0.0150 5637	86
87	0.0764 1198	0.0501 4060	0.0329 6852	0.0217 2115	0.0143 3940	87
88	0.0741 8639	0.0484 4503	0.0317 0050	0.0207 8579	0.0136 5657	88
89	0.0720 2562	0.0468 0679	0.0304 8125	0.0198 9070	0.0130 0626	89
90	0.0699 2779	0.0452 2395	0.0293 0890	0.0190 3417	0.0123 8691	90
91	0.0678 9105	0.0436 9464	0.0281 8163	0.0182 1451	0.0117 9706	91
92	0.0659 1364	0.0422 1704	0.0270 9772	0.0174 3016	0.0112 3530	92
93	0.0639 9383	0.0407 8941	0.0260 5550	0.0166 7958	0.0107 0028	93
94	0.0621 2993	0.0394 1006	0.0250 5337	0.0159 6132	0.0101 9074	94
95	0.0603 2032	0.0380 7735	0.0240 8978	0.0152 7399	0.0097 0547	95
96	0.0585 6342	0.0367 8971	0.0231 6325	0.0146 1626	0.0092 4331	96
97	0.0568 5769	0.0355 4562	0.0222 7235	0.0139 8685	0.0088 0315	97
98	0.0552 0164	0.0343 4359	0.0214 1572	0.0133 8454	0.0083 8395	98
99	0.0535 9383	0.0331 8221	0.0205 9204	0.0128 0817	0.0079 8471	99
100	0.0520 3284	0.0320 6011	0.0198 0004	0.0122 5663	0.0076 0449	100
101	0.0505 1732	0.0309 7595	0.0190 3850	0.0117 2883	0.0072 4237	101
102	0.0490 4594	0.0299 2846	0.0183 0625	0.0112 2376	0.0068 9750	102
103	0.0476 1742	0.0289 1638	0.0176 0216	0.0107 4044	0.0065 6904	103
104	0.0462 3050	0.0279 3853	0.0169 2516	0.0102 7793	0.0062 5623	104
105	0.0448 8398	0.0269 9375	0.0162 7419	0.0098 3534	0.0059 5832	105
106	0.0435 7668	0.0260 8092	0.0156 4826	0.0094 1181	0.0056 7459	106
107	0.0423 0746	0.0251 9896	0.0150 4640	0.0090 0652	0.0054 0437	107
108	0.0410 7520	0.0243 4682	0.0144 6770	0.0086 1868	0.0051 4702	108
109	0.0398 7884	0.0235 2350	0.0139 1125	0.0082 4754	0.0049 0192	109
110	0.0387 1732	0.0227 2802	0.0133 7620	0.0078 9238	0.0046 6850	110
111	0.0375 8963	0.0219 5944	0.0128 6173	0.0075 5252	0.0044 4619	111
112	0.0364 9479	0.0212 1685	0.0123 6705	0.0072 2729	0.0042 3446	112
113	0.0354 3183	0.0204 9937	0.0118 9139	0.0069 1607	0.0040 3282	113
114	0.0343 9984	0.0198 0615	0.0114 3403	0.0066 1825	0.0038 4078	114
115	0.0333 9790	0.0191 3638	0.0109 9426	0.0063 3325	0.0036 5789	115
116	0.0324 2515	0.0184 8926	0.0105 7140	0.0060 6053	0.0034 8370	116
117	0.0314 8072	0.0178 6401	0.0101 6481	0.0057 9955	0.0033 1781	117
118	0.0305 6381	0.0172 5992	0.0097 7386	0.0055 4981	0.0031 5982	118
119	0.0296 7360	0.0166 7625	0.0093 9794	0.0053 1082	0.0030 0935	119
120	0.0288 0932	0.0161 1232	0.0090 3648	0.0050 8212	0.0028 6605	120

TABLE II

N	5 1/2	6	6 1/2	7	7 1/2	N
1	0.9478 6730	0.9433 9623	0.9389 6714	0.9345 7944	0.9302 3256	1
2	0.8984 5242	0.8899 9644	0.8816 5928	0.8734 3873	0.8653 3261	2
3	0.8516 1366	0.8396 1928	0.8278 4909	0.8162 9788	0.8049 6057	3
4	0.8072 1674	0.7920 9366	0.7773 2309	0.7628 9521	0.7488 0053	4
5	0.7651 3435	0.7472 5817	0.7298 8084	0.7129 8618	0.6965 5863	5
6	0.7252 4583	0.7049 6054	0.6853 3412	0.6663 4222	0.6479 6152	6
7	0.6874 3681	0.6650 5711	0.6435 0621	0.6227 4974	0.6027 5490	7
8	0.6515 9887	0.6274 1237	0.6042 3119	0.5820 0910	0.5607 0223	8
9	0.6176 2926	0.5918 9846	0.5673 5323	0.5439 3374	0.5215 8347	9
10	0.5854 3058	0.5583 9478	0.5327 2604	0.5083 4929	0.4851 9393	10
11	0.5549 1050	0.5267 8753	0.5002 1224	0.4750 9280	0.4513 4319	11
12	0.5259 8152	0.4969 6936	0.4696 8285	0.4440 1196	0.4198 5413	12
13	0.4985 6068	0.4688 3902	0.4410 1676	0.4149 6445	0.3905 6198	13
14	0.4725 6937	0.4423 0096	0.4141 0025	0.3878 1724	0.3633 1347	14
15	0.4479 3305	0.4172 6506	0.3888 2652	0.3624 4602	0.3379 6602	15
16	0.4245 8109	0.3936 4628	0.3650 9533	0.3387 3460	0.3143 8699	16
17	0.4024 4653	0.3713 6442	0.3428 1251	0.3165 7439	0.2924 5302	17
18	0.3814 6590	0.3503 4379	0.3218 8969	0.2958 6392	0.2720 4932	18
19	0.3615 7906	0.3305 1301	0.3022 4384	0.2765 0833	0.2530 6913	19
20	0.3427 2896	0.3118 0473	0.2837 9703	0.2584 1900	0.2354 1315	20
21	0.3248 6158	0.2941 5540	0.2664 7608	0.2415 1309	0.2189 8897	21
22	0.3079 2567	0.2775 0510	0.2502 1228	0.2257 1317	0.2037 1067	22
23	0.2918 7267	0.2617 9726	0.2349 4111	0.2109 4688	0.1894 9830	23
24	0.2766 5656	0.2469 7855	0.2206 0198	0.1971 4662	0.1762 7749	24
25	0.2622 3370	0.2329 9863	0.2071 3801	0.1842 4918	0.1639 7906	25
26	0.2485 6275	0.2198 1003	0.1944 9579	0.1721 9549	0.1525 3866	26
27	0.2356 0450	0.2073 6795	0.1826 2515	0.1609 3037	0.1418 9643	27
28	0.2233 2181	0.1956 3014	0.1714 7902	0.1504 0221	0.1319 9668	28
29	0.2116 7944	0.1845 5674	0.1610 1316	0.1405 6282	0.1227 8761	29
30	0.2006 4402	0.1741 1013	0.1511 8607	0.1313 6712	0.1142 2103	30
31	0.1901 8390	0.1642 5484	0.1419 5875	0.1227 7301	0.1062 5212	31
32	0.1802 6910	0.1549 5740	0.1332 9460	0.1147 4113	0.0988 3918	32
33	0.1708 7119	0.1461 8622	0.1251 5925	0.1072 3470	0.0919 4343	33
34	0.1619 6321	0.1379 1153	0.1175 2042	0.1002 1934	0.0855 2877	34
35	0.1535 1963	0.1301 0522	0.1103 4781	0.0936 6294	0.0795 6164	35
36	0.1455 1624	0.1227 4077	0.1036 1297	0.0875 3546	0.0740 1083	36
37	0.1379 3008	0.1157 9318	0.0972 8917	0.0818 0884	0.0688 4729	37
38	0.1307 3941	0.1092 3885	0.0913 5134	0.0764 5686	0.0640 4399	38
39	0.1239 2362	0.1030 5552	0.0857 7590	0.0714 5501	0.0595 7580	39
40	0.1174 6314	0.0972 2219	0.0805 4075	0.0667 8038	0.0554 1935	40
41	0.1113 3947	0.0917 1905	0.0756 2512	0.0624 1157	0.0515 5288	41
42	0.1055 3504	0.0865 2740	0.0710 0950	0.0583 2857	0.0479 5617	42
43	0.1000 3322	0.0816 2962	0.0666 7559	0.0545 1268	0.0446 1039	43
44	0.0948 1822	0.0770 0908	0.0626 0619	0.0509 4643	0.0414 9804	44
45	0.0898 7509	0.0726 5007	0.0587 8515	0.0476 1349	0.0386 0283	45
46	0.0851 8965	0.0685 3781	0.0551 9733	0.0444 9859	0.0359 0961	46
47	0.0807 4849	0.0646 5831	0.0518 2848	0.0415 8747	0.0334 0428	47
48	0.0765 3885	0.0609 9840	0.0486 6524	0.0388 6679	0.0310 7375	48
49	0.0725 4867	0.0575 4566	0.0456 9506	0.0363 2410	0.0289 0582	49
50	0.0687 6652	0.0542 8836	0.0429 0616	0.0339 4776	0.0268 8913	50
51	0.0651 8153	0.0512 1544	0.0402 8747	0.0317 2688	0.0250 1315	51
52	0.0617 8344	0.0483 1645	0.0378 2861	0.0296 5129	0.0232 6804	52
53	0.0585 6250	0.0455 8156	0.0355 1982	0.0277 1148	0.0216 4469	53
54	0.0555 0948	0.0430 0147	0.0333 5195	0.0258 9858	0.0201 3460	54
55	0.0526 1562	0.0405 6742	0.0313 1638	0.0242 0428	0.0187 2986	55
56	0.0498 7263	0.0382 7115	0.0294 0505	0.0226 2083	0.0174 2312	56
57	0.0472 7263	0.0361 0486	0.0276 1038	0.0211 4096	0.0162 0756	57
58	0.0448 0818	0.0340 6119	0.0259 2524	0.0197 5791	0.0150 7680	58
59	0.0424 7221	0.0321 3320	0.0243 4295	0.0184 6533	0.0140 2493	59
60	0.0402 5802	0.0303 1434	0.0228 5723	0.0172 5732	0.0130 4644	60

TABLE II

N	5 1/2	6	6 1/2	7	7 1/2	N
61	0.0381 5926	0.0285 9843	0.0214 6218	0.0161 2834	0.0121 3623	61
62	0.0361 6992	0.0269 7965	0.0201 5229	0.0150 7321	0.0112 8951	62
63	0.0342 8428	0.0254 5250	0.0189 2233	0.0140 8711	0.0105 0187	63
64	0.0324 9695	0.0240 1179	0.0177 6745	0.0131 6553	0.0097 6918	64
65	0.0308 0279	0.0226 5264	0.0166 8305	0.0123 0423	0.0090 8761	65
66	0.0291 9696	0.0213 7041	0.0156 6484	0.0114 9928	0.0084 5359	66
67	0.0276 7485	0.0201 6077	0.0147 0877	0.0107 4699	0.0078 6381	67
68	0.0262 3208	0.0190 1959	0.0138 1105	0.0100 4392	0.0073 1517	68
69	0.0248 6453	0.0179 4301	0.0129 6812	0.0093 8684	0.0068 0481	69
70	0.0235 6828	0.0169 2737	0.0121 7664	0.0087 7275	0.0063 3006	70
71	0.0223 3960	0.0159 6921	0.0114 3346	0.0081 9883	0.0058 8842	71
72	0.0211 7498	0.0150 6530	0.0107 3565	0.0076 6246	0.0054 7760	72
73	0.0200 7107	0.0142 1254	0.0100 8042	0.0071 6117	0.0050 9544	73
74	0.0190 2471	0.0134 0806	0.0094 6518	0.0066 9269	0.0047 3995	74
75	0.0180 3290	0.0126 4911	0.0088 8750	0.0062 5485	0.0044 0925	75
76	0.0170 9279	0.0119 3313	0.0083 4507	0.0058 4565	0.0041 0163	76
77	0.0162 0170	0.0112 5767	0.0078 3574	0.0054 6323	0.0038 1547	77
78	0.0153 5706	0.0106 2044	0.0073 5751	0.0051 0582	0.0035 4928	78
79	0.0145 5646	0.0100 1928	0.0069 0846	0.0047 7179	0.0033 0165	79
80	0.0137 9759	0.0094 5215	0.0064 8681	0.0044 5962	0.0030 7130	80
81	0.0130 7828	0.0089 1713	0.0060 9090	0.0041 6787	0.0028 5703	81
82	0.0123 9648	0.0084 1238	0.0057 1916	0.0038 9520	0.0026 5770	82
83	0.0117 5022	0.0079 3621	0.0053 7010	0.0036 4038	0.0024 7228	83
84	0.0111 3765	0.0074 8699	0.0050 4235	0.0034 0222	0.0022 9979	84
85	0.0105 5701	0.0070 6320	0.0047 3460	0.0031 7965	0.0021 3934	85
86	0.0100 0664	0.0066 6340	0.0044 4563	0.0029 7163	0.0019 9009	86
87	0.0094 8497	0.0062 8622	0.0041 7430	0.0027 7723	0.0018 5124	87
88	0.0089 9049	0.0059 3040	0.0039 1953	0.0025 9554	0.0017 2209	88
89	0.0085 2180	0.0055 9472	0.0036 8031	0.0024 2574	0.0016 0194	89
90	0.0080 7753	0.0052 7803	0.0034 5569	0.0022 6704	0.0014 9018	90
91	0.0076 5643	0.0049 7928	0.0032 4478	0.0021 1873	0.0013 8621	91
92	0.0072 5728	0.0046 9743	0.0030 4674	0.0019 8012	0.0012 8950	92
93	0.0068 7894	0.0044 3154	0.0028 6079	0.0018 5058	0.0011 9953	93
94	0.0065 2032	0.0041 8070	0.0026 8619	0.0017 2952	0.0011 1585	94
95	0.0061 8040	0.0039 4405	0.0025 2224	0.0016 1637	0.0010 3800	95
96	0.0058 5820	0.0037 2081	0.0023 6831	0.0015 1063	0.0009 6558	96
97	0.0055 5279	0.0035 1019	0.0022 2376	0.0014 1180	0.0008 9821	97
98	0.0052 6331	0.0033 1150	0.0020 8804	0.0013 1944	0.0008 3555	98
99	0.0049 8892	0.0031 2406	0.0019 6060	0.0012 3312	0.0007 7725	99
100	0.0047 2883	0.0029 4723	0.0018 4094	0.0011 5245	0.0007 2303	100
101	0.0044 8231	0.0027 8040	0.0017 2858	0.0010 7706	0.0006 7258	101
102	0.0042 4863	0.0026 2302	0.0016 2308	0.0010 0659	0.0006 2566	102
103	0.0040 2714	0.0024 7455	0.0015 2402	0.0009 4074	0.0005 8201	103
104	0.0038 1719	0.0023 3448	0.0014 3100	0.0008 7920	0.0005 4140	104
105	0.0036 1819	0.0022 0234	0.0013 4367	0.0008 2168	0.0005 0363	105
106	0.0034 2957	0.0020 7768	0.0012 6166	0.0007 6793	0.0004 6849	106
107	0.0032 5077	0.0019 6007	0.0011 8466	0.0007 1769	0.0004 3581	107
108	0.0030 8130	0.0018 4913	0.0011 1235	0.0006 7074	0.0004 0540	108
109	0.0029 2067	0.0017 4446	0.0010 4446	0.0006 2686	0.0003 7712	109
110	0.0027 6840	0.0016 4572	0.0009 8072	0.0005 8585	0.0003 5081	110
111	0.0026 2408	0.0015 5256	0.0009 2086	0.0005 4752	0.0003 2633	111
112	0.0024 8728	0.0014 6468	0.0008 6466	0.0005 1170	0.0003 0357	112
113	0.0023 5761	0.0013 8177	0.0008 1188	0.0004 7823	0.0002 8239	113
114	0.0022 3470	0.0013 0356	0.0007 6233	0.0004 4694	0.0002 6268	114
115	0.0021 1820	0.0012 2977	0.0007 1581	0.0004 1770	0.0002 4436	115
116	0.0020 0777	0.0011 6016	0.0006 7212	0.0003 9037	0.0002 2731	116
117	0.0019 0310	0.0010 9449	0.0006 3110	0.0003 6484	0.0002 1145	117
118	0.0018 0389	0.0010 3254	0.0005 9258	0.0003 4097	0.0001 9670	118
119	0.0017 0985	0.0009 7410	0.0005 5641	0.0003 1866	0.0001 8298	119
120	0.0016 2071	0.0009 1896	0.0005 2245	0.0002 9782	0.0001 7021	120

TABLE II

N	8	8 1/2	9	9 1/2	10	N
1	0.9259 2593	0.9216 5899	0.9174 3119	0.9132 4201	0.9090 9091	1
2	0.8573 3882	0.8494 5529	0.8416 7999	0.8340 1097	0.8264 4628	2
3	0.7938 3224	0.7829 0810	0.7721 8348	0.7616 5385	0.7513 1480	3
4	0.7350 2985	0.7215 7428	0.7084 2521	0.6955 7429	0.6830 1346	4
5	0.6805 8320	0.6650 4542	0.6499 3139	0.6352 2767	0.6209 2132	5
6	0.6301 6963	0.6129 4509	0.5962 6733	0.5801 1659	0.5644 7393	6
7	0.5834 9040	0.5649 2635	0.5470 3424	0.5297 8684	0.5131 5812	7
8	0.5402 6888	0.5206 6945	0.5018 6628	0.4838 2360	0.4665 0738	8
9	0.5002 4897	0.4798 7968	0.4604 2778	0.4418 4803	0.4240 9762	9
10	0.4631 9349	0.4422 8542	0.4224 1081	0.4035 1419	0.3855 4329	10
11	0.4288 8286	0.4076 3633	0.3875 3285	0.3685 0611	0.3504 9390	11
12	0.3971 1376	0.3757 0168	0.3555 3473	0.3365 3526	0.3186 3082	12
13	0.3676 9792	0.3462 6883	0.3261 7865	0.3073 3813	0.2896 6438	13
14	0.3404 6104	0.3191 4178	0.2992 4647	0.2806 7410	0.2633 3125	14
15	0.3152 4170	0.2941 3989	0.2745 3804	0.2563 2337	0.2393 9205	15
16	0.2918 9047	0.2710 9667	0.2518 6976	0.2340 8527	0.2176 2914	16
17	0.2702 6895	0.2498 5869	0.2310 7318	0.2137 7651	0.1978 4467	17
18	0.2502 4903	0.2302 8450	0.2119 9374	0.1952 2969	0.1798 5879	18
19	0.2317 1206	0.2122 4378	0.1944 8967	0.1782 9195	0.1635 0799	19
20	0.2145 4821	0.1956 1639	0.1784 3089	0.1628 2370	0.1486 4363	20
21	0.1986 5575	0.1802 9160	0.1636 9806	0.1486 9744	0.1351 3057	21
22	0.1839 4051	0.1661 6738	0.1501 8171	0.1357 9675	0.1228 4597	22
23	0.1703 1528	0.1531 4965	0.1377 8139	0.1240 1530	0.1116 7816	23
24	0.1576 9934	0.1411 5176	0.1264 0494	0.1132 5598	0.1015 2560	24
25	0.1460 1790	0.1300 9378	0.1159 6784	0.1034 3012	0.0922 9600	25
26	0.1352 0176	0.1199 0210	0.1063 9251	0.0944 5673	0.0839 0545	26
27	0.1251 8682	0.1105 0885	0.0976 0781	0.0862 6185	0.0762 7768	27
28	0.1159 1372	0.1018 5148	0.0895 4845	0.0787 7795	0.0693 4335	28
29	0.1073 2752	0.0938 7233	0.0821 5454	0.0719 4333	0.0630 3941	29
30	0.0993 7733	0.0865 1828	0.0753 7114	0.0657 0167	0.0573 0855	30
31	0.0920 1605	0.0797 4035	0.0691 4783	0.0600 0153	0.0520 9868	31
32	0.0852 0005	0.0734 9341	0.0634 3838	0.0547 9592	0.0473 6244	32
33	0.0788 8893	0.0677 3586	0.0582 0035	0.0500 4193	0.0430 5676	33
34	0.0730 4531	0.0624 2936	0.0533 9481	0.0457 0039	0.0391 4251	34
35	0.0676 3454	0.0575 3858	0.0489 8607	0.0417 3552	0.0355 8410	35
36	0.0626 2458	0.0530 3095	0.0449 4135	0.0381 1463	0.0323 4918	36
37	0.0579 8572	0.0488 7645	0.0412 3059	0.0348 0788	0.0294 0835	37
38	0.0536 9048	0.0450 4742	0.0378 2623	0.0317 8802	0.0267 3486	38
39	0.0497 1341	0.0415 1836	0.0347 0296	0.0290 3015	0.0243 0442	39
40	0.0460 3093	0.0382 6577	0.0318 3758	0.0265 1156	0.0220 9493	40
41	0.0426 2123	0.0352 6799	0.0292 0879	0.0242 1147	0.0200 8630	41
42	0.0394 6411	0.0325 0506	0.0267 9706	0.0221 1093	0.0182 6027	42
43	0.0365 4084	0.0299 5858	0.0245 8446	0.0201 9263	0.0166 0025	43
44	0.0338 3411	0.0276 1160	0.0225 5455	0.0184 4076	0.0150 9113	44
45	0.0313 2788	0.0254 4848	0.0206 9224	0.0168 4087	0.0137 1921	45
46	0.0290 0730	0.0234 5482	0.0189 8371	0.0153 7979	0.0124 7201	46
47	0.0268 5861	0.0216 1734	0.0174 1625	0.0140 4547	0.0113 3819	47
48	0.0248 6908	0.0199 2382	0.0159 7821	0.0128 2692	0.0103 0745	48
49	0.0230 2693	0.0183 6297	0.0146 5891	0.0117 1408	0.0093 7041	49
50	0.0213 2123	0.0169 2439	0.0134 4854	0.0106 9779	0.0085 1855	50
51	0.0197 4188	0.0155 9852	0.0123 3811	0.0097 6967	0.0077 4414	51
52	0.0182 7952	0.0143 7651	0.0113 1937	0.0089 2207	0.0070 4013	52
53	0.0169 2548	0.0132 5024	0.0103 8474	0.0081 4801	0.0064 0011	53
54	0.0156 7174	0.0122 1221	0.0095 2728	0.0074 4111	0.0058 1829	54
55	0.0145 1087	0.0112 5549	0.0087 4063	0.0067 9553	0.0052 8935	55
56	0.0134 3599	0.0103 7372	0.0080 1892	0.0062 0597	0.0048 0850	56
57	0.0124 4073	0.0095 6104	0.0073 5681	0.0056 6755	0.0043 7136	57
58	0.0115 1920	0.0088 1201	0.0067 4937	0.0051 7584	0.0039 7397	58
59	0.0106 6592	0.0081 2167	0.0061 9208	0.0047 2680	0.0036 1270	59
60	0.0098 7585	0.0074 8541	0.0056 8081	0.0043 1671	0.0032 8427	60

TABLE II

N	8	8 1/2	9	9 1/2	10	N
61	0.0091 4431	0.0068 9900	0.0052 1175	0.0039 4220	0.0029 8570	61
62	0.0084 6695	0.0063 5852	0.0047 8142	0.0036 0018	0.0027 1427	62
63	0.0078 3977	0.0058 6039	0.0043 8663	0.0032 8784	0.0024 6752	63
64	0.0072 5905	0.0054 0128	0.0040 2443	0.0030 0259	0.0022 4320	64
65	0.0067 2134	0.0049 7814	0.0036 9214	0.0027 4209	0.0020 3927	65
66	0.0062 2346	0.0045 8815	0.0033 8728	0.0025 0419	0.0018 5388	66
67	0.0057 6247	0.0042 2871	0.0031 0760	0.0022 8694	0.0016 8535	67
68	0.0053 3562	0.0038 9743	0.0028 5101	0.0020 8853	0.0015 3214	68
69	0.0049 4039	0.0035 9210	0.0026 1560	0.0019 0733	0.0013 9285	69
70	0.0045 7443	0.0033 1069	0.0023 9963	0.0017 4185	0.0012 6623	70
71	0.0042 3558	0.0030 5133	0.0022 0150	0.0015 9073	0.0011 5112	71
72	0.0039 2184	0.0028 1228	0.0020 1972	0.0014 5273	0.0010 4647	72
73	0.0036 3133	0.0025 9196	0.0018 5296	0.0013 2669	0.0009 5134	73
74	0.0033 6234	0.0023 8891	0.0016 9996	0.0012 1159	0.0008 6485	74
75	0.0031 1328	0.0022 0176	0.0015 5960	0.0011 0647	0.0007 8623	75
76	0.0028 8267	0.0020 2927	0.0014 3082	0.0010 1048	0.0007 1475	76
77	0.0026 6914	0.0018 7030	0.0013 1268	0.0009 2281	0.0006 4978	77
78	0.0024 7142	0.0017 2377	0.0012 0430	0.0008 4275	0.0005 9070	78
79	0.0022 8835	0.0015 8873	0.0011 0486	0.0007 6963	0.0005 3700	79
80	0.0021 1885	0.0014 6427	0.0010 1363	0.0007 0286	0.0004 8819	80
81	0.0019 6190	0.0013 4956	0.0009 2994	0.0006 4188	0.0004 4381	81
82	0.0018 1657	0.0012 4383	0.0008 5315	0.0005 8620	0.0004 0346	82
83	0.0016 8201	0.0011 4639	0.0007 8271	0.0005 3534	0.0003 6678	83
84	0.0015 5742	0.0010 5658	0.0007 1808	0.0004 8889	0.0003 3344	84
85	0.0014 4205	0.0009 7381	0.0006 5879	0.0004 4648	0.0003 0313	85
86	0.0013 3523	0.0008 9752	0.0006 0440	0.0004 0774	0.0002 7557	86
87	0.0012 3633	0.0008 2720	0.0005 5449	0.0003 7237	0.0002 5052	87
88	0.0011 4475	0.0007 6240	0.0005 0871	0.0003 4006	0.0002 2774	88
89	0.0010 5995	0.0007 0267	0.0004 6670	0.0003 1056	0.0002 0704	89
90	0.0009 8144	0.0006 4762	0.0004 2817	0.0002 8362	0.0001 8822	90
91	0.0009 0874	0.0005 9689	0.0003 9282	0.0002 5901	0.0001 7111	91
92	0.0008 4142	0.0005 5013	0.0003 6038	0.0002 3654	0.0001 5555	92
93	0.0007 7910	0.0005 0703	0.0003 3063	0.0002 1602	0.0001 4141	93
94	0.0007 2138	0.0004 6731	0.0003 0333	0.0001 9728	0.0001 2855	94
95	0.0006 6795	0.0004 3070	0.0002 7828	0.0001 8016	0.0001 1687	95
96	0.0006 1847	0.0003 9696	0.0002 5530	0.0001 6453	0.0001 0624	96
97	0.0005 7266	0.0003 6586	0.0002 3422	0.0001 5026	0.0000 9658	97
98	0.0005 3024	0.0003 3720	0.0002 1488	0.0001 3722	0.0000 8780	98
99	0.0004 9096	0.0003 1078	0.0001 9714	0.0001 2531	0.0000 7982	99
100	0.0004 5459	0.0002 8644	0.0001 8086	0.0001 1444	0.0000 7257	100
101	0.0004 2092	0.0002 6400	0.0001 6593	0.0001 0451	0.0000 6597	101
102	0.0003 8974	0.0002 4331	0.0001 5223	0.0000 9545	0.0000 5997	102
103	0.0003 6087	0.0002 2425	0.0001 3966	0.0000 8717	0.0000 5452	103
104	0.0003 3414	0.0002 0668	0.0001 2813	0.0000 7960	0.0000 4956	104
105	0.0003 0939	0.0001 9049	0.0001 1755	0.0000 7270	0.0000 4506	105
106	0.0002 8647	0.0001 7557	0.0001 0784	0.0000 6639	0.0000 4096	106
107	0.0002 6525	0.0001 6181	0.0000 9894	0.0000 6063	0.0000 3724	107
108	0.0002 4560	0.0001 4914	0.0000 9077	0.0000 5537	0.0000 3385	108
109	0.0002 2741	0.0001 3745	0.0000 8327	0.0000 5057	0.0000 3077	109
110	0.0002 1057	0.0001 2669	0.0000 7640	0.0000 4618	0.0000 2798	110
111	0.0001 9497	0.0001 1676	0.0000 7009	0.0000 4217	0.0000 2543	111
112	0.0001 8053	0.0001 0761	0.0000 6430	0.0000 3851	0.0000 2312	112
113	0.0001 6715	0.0000 9918	0.0000 5899	0.0000 3517	0.0000 2102	113
114	0.0001 5477	0.0000 9141	0.0000 5412	0.0000 3212	0.0000 1911	114
115	0.0001 4331	0.0000 8425	0.0000 4965	0.0000 2933	0.0000 1737	115
116	0.0001 3269	0.0000 7765	0.0000 4555	0.0000 2679	0.0000 1579	116
117	0.0001 2286	0.0000 7157	0.0000 4179	0.0000 2447	0.0000 1436	117
118	0.0001 1376	0.0000 6596	0.0000 3834	0.0000 2234	0.0000 1305	118
119	0.0001 0534	0.0000 6079	0.0000 3518	0.0000 2040	0.0000 1187	119
120	0.0000 9753	0.0000 5603	0.0000 3227	0.0000 1863	0.0000 1079	120

TABLE II

N	10 1/2	11	11 1/2	12	12 1/2	N
1	0.9049 7738	0.9009 0090	0.8968 6099	0.8928 5714	0.8888 8889	1
2	0.8189 8405	0.8116 2243	0.8043 5963	0.7971 9388	0.7901 2346	2
3	0.7411 6204	0.7311 9138	0.7213 9877	0.7117 8025	0.7023 3196	3
4	0.6707 3487	0.6587 3097	0.6469 9441	0.6355 1808	0.6242 9508	4
5	0.6069 9989	0.5934 5133	0.5802 6405	0.5674 2686	0.5549 2896	5
6	0.5493 2116	0.5346 4084	0.5204 1619	0.5066 3112	0.4932 7018	6
7	0.4971 2323	0.4816 5841	0.4667 4097	0.4523 4922	0.4384 6239	7
8	0.4498 8527	0.4339 2650	0.4186 0177	0.4038 8323	0.3897 4434	8
9	0.4071 3599	0.3909 2477	0.3754 2760	0.3606 1002	0.3464 3942	9
10	0.3684 4886	0.3521 8448	0.3367 0636	0.3219 7324	0.3079 4615	10
11	0.3334 3788	0.3172 8331	0.3019 7880	0.2874 7610	0.2737 2991	11
12	0.3017 5374	0.2858 4082	0.2708 3301	0.2566 7509	0.2433 1547	12
13	0.2730 8031	0.2575 1426	0.2428 9956	0.2291 7419	0.2162 8042	13
14	0.2471 3150	0.2319 9482	0.2178 4714	0.2046 1981	0.1922 4926	14
15	0.2236 4842	0.2090 0435	0.1953 7860	0.1826 9626	0.1708 8823	15
16	0.2023 9676	0.1882 9220	0.1752 2744	0.1631 2166	0.1519 0065	16
17	0.1831 6449	0.1696 3262	0.1571 5466	0.1456 4434	0.1350 2280	17
18	0.1657 5972	0.1528 2218	0.1409 4588	0.1300 3959	0.1200 2027	18
19	0.1500 0879	0.1376 7764	0.1264 0886	0.1161 0678	0.1066 8468	19
20	0.1357 5456	0.1240 3391	0.1133 7118	0.1036 6677	0.0948 3083	20
21	0.1228 5481	0.1117 4226	0.1016 7818	0.0925 5961	0.0842 9407	21
22	0.1111 8082	0.1006 6870	0.0911 9120	0.0826 4251	0.0749 2806	22
23	0.1006 1613	0.0906 9252	0.0817 8583	0.0737 8796	0.0666 0272	23
24	0.0910 5532	0.0817 0498	0.0733 5052	0.0658 8210	0.0592 0242	24
25	0.0824 0301	0.0736 0809	0.0657 8522	0.0588 2331	0.0526 2437	25
26	0.0745 7286	0.0663 1359	0.0590 0020	0.0525 2081	0.0467 7722	26
27	0.0674 8675	0.0597 4197	0.0529 1497	0.0468 9358	0.0415 7975	27
28	0.0610 7398	0.0538 2160	0.0474 5738	0.0418 6927	0.0369 5978	28
29	0.0552 7057	0.0484 8793	0.0425 6267	0.0373 8327	0.0328 5314	29
30	0.0500 1861	0.0436 8282	0.0381 7280	0.0333 7792	0.0292 0279	30
31	0.0452 6571	0.0393 5389	0.0342 3569	0.0298 0172	0.0259 5803	31
32	0.0409 6445	0.0354 5395	0.0307 0466	0.0266 0868	0.0230 7381	32
33	0.0370 7190	0.0319 4050	0.0275 3781	0.0237 5775	0.0205 1005	33
34	0.0335 4923	0.0287 7522	0.0246 9759	0.0212 1227	0.0182 3116	34
35	0.0303 6129	0.0259 2363	0.0221 5030	0.0189 3953	0.0162 0547	35
36	0.0274 7628	0.0233 5462	0.0198 6574	0.0169 1029	0.0144 0486	36
37	0.0248 6542	0.0210 4020	0.0178 1681	0.0150 9848	0.0128 0432	37
38	0.0225 0264	0.0189 5513	0.0159 7920	0.0134 8078	0.0113 8162	38
39	0.0203 6438	0.0170 7670	0.0143 3112	0.0120 3641	0.0101 1700	39
40	0.0184 2930	0.0153 8441	0.0128 5302	0.0107 4680	0.0089 9289	40
41	0.0166 7810	0.0138 5983	0.0115 2738	0.0095 9536	0.0079 9368	41
42	0.0150 9330	0.0124 8633	0.0103 3845	0.0085 6728	0.0071 0549	42
43	0.0136 5910	0.0112 4895	0.0092 7216	0.0076 4936	0.0063 1599	43
44	0.0123 6118	0.0101 3419	0.0083 1583	0.0068 2978	0.0056 1421	44
45	0.0111 8658	0.0091 2990	0.0074 5815	0.0060 9802	0.0049 9041	45
46	0.0101 2361	0.0082 2513	0.0066 8892	0.0054 4466	0.0044 3592	46
47	0.0091 6163	0.0074 1003	0.0059 9903	0.0048 6131	0.0039 4304	47
48	0.0082 9107	0.0066 7570	0.0053 8030	0.0043 4045	0.0035 0493	48
49	0.0075 0323	0.0060 1415	0.0048 2538	0.0038 7540	0.0031 1549	49
50	0.0067 9026	0.0054 1815	0.0043 2769	0.0034 6018	0.0027 6932	50
51	0.0061 4503	0.0048 8122	0.0038 8134	0.0030 8945	0.0024 6162	51
52	0.0055 6111	0.0043 9749	0.0034 8102	0.0027 5844	0.0021 8811	52
53	0.0050 3268	0.0039 6170	0.0031 2199	0.0024 6289	0.0019 4499	53
54	0.0045 5446	0.0035 6910	0.0027 9999	0.0021 9901	0.0017 2888	54
55	0.0041 2168	0.0032 1541	0.0025 1121	0.0019 6340	0.0015 3678	55
56	0.0037 3003	0.0028 9676	0.0022 5220	0.0017 5304	0.0013 6603	56
57	0.0033 7559	0.0026 0970	0.0020 1991	0.0015 6521	0.0012 1424	57
58	0.0030 5484	0.0023 5108	0.0018 1158	0.0013 9751	0.0010 7933	58
59	0.0027 6456	0.0021 1809	0.0016 2474	0.0012 4778	0.0009 5940	59
60	0.0025 0186	0.0019 0819	0.0014 5716	0.0011 1409	0.0008 5280	60

TABLE II

N	10 1/2	11	11 1/2	12	12 1/2	N
61	0.0022 6413	0.0017 1909	0.0013 0687	0.0009 9472	0.0007 5805	61
62	0.0020 4898	0.0015 4873	0.0011 7208	0.0008 8814	0.0006 7382	62
63	0.0018 5428	0.0013 9525	0.0010 5120	0.0007 9298	0.0005 9895	63
64	0.0016 7809	0.0012 5698	0.0009 4278	0.0007 0802	0.0005 3240	64
65	0.0015 1863	0.0011 3242	0.0008 4554	0.0006 3216	0.0004 7325	65
66	0.0013 7433	0.0010 2020	0.0007 5833	0.0005 6443	0.0004 2066	66
67	0.0012 4373	0.0009 1910	0.0006 8012	0.0005 0396	0.0003 7392	67
68	0.0011 2555	0.0008 2801	0.0006 0997	0.0004 4996	0.0003 3238	68
69	0.0010 1860	0.0007 4596	0.0005 4706	0.0004 0175	0.0002 9544	69
70	0.0009 2181	0.0006 7203	0.0004 9064	0.0003 5871	0.0002 6262	70
71	0.0008 3422	0.0006 0544	0.0004 4003	0.0003 2027	0.0002 3344	71
72	0.0007 5495	0.0005 4544	0.0003 9465	0.0002 8596	0.0002 0750	72
73	0.0006 8321	0.0004 9139	0.0003 5394	0.0002 5532	0.0001 8444	73
74	0.0006 1829	0.0004 4269	0.0003 1744	0.0002 2796	0.0001 6395	74
75	0.0005 5954	0.0003 9882	0.0002 8470	0.0002 0354	0.0001 4573	75
76	0.0005 0637	0.0003 5930	0.0002 5533	0.0001 8173	0.0001 2954	76
77	0.0004 5825	0.0003 2369	0.0002 2900	0.0001 6226	0.0001 1515	77
78	0.0004 1471	0.0002 9161	0.0002 0538	0.0001 4488	0.0001 0235	78
79	0.0003 7530	0.0002 6271	0.0001 8420	0.0001 2935	0.0000 9098	79
80	0.0003 3964	0.0002 3668	0.0001 6520	0.0001 1549	0.0000 8087	80
81	0.0003 0737	0.0002 1323	0.0001 4816	0.0001 0312	0.0000 7189	81
82	0.0002 7816	0.0001 9209	0.0001 3288	0.0000 9207	0.0000 6390	82
83	0.0002 5173	0.0001 7306	0.0001 1918	0.0000 8221	0.0000 5680	83
84	0.0002 2781	0.0001 5591	0.0001 0688	0.0000 7340	0.0000 5049	84
85	0.0002 0616	0.0001 4046	0.0000 9586	0.0000 6553	0.0000 4488	85
86	0.0001 8657	0.0001 2654	0.0000 8597	0.0000 5851	0.0000 3989	86
87	0.0001 6884	0.0001 1400	0.0000 7711	0.0000 5224	0.0000 3546	87
88	0.0001 5280	0.0001 0270	0.0000 6915	0.0000 4665	0.0000 3152	88
89	0.0001 3828	0.0000 9252	0.0000 6202	0.0000 4165	0.0000 2802	89
90	0.0001 2514	0.0000 8336	0.0000 5562	0.0000 3719	0.0000 2490	90
91	0.0001 1325	0.0000 7509	0.0000 4989	0.0000 3320	0.0000 2214	91
92	0.0001 0249	0.0000 6765	0.0000 4474	0.0000 2964	0.0000 1968	92
93	0.0000 9275	0.0000 6095	0.0000 4013	0.0000 2647	0.0000 1749	93
94	0.0000 8394	0.0000 5491	0.0000 3599	0.0000 2363	0.0000 1555	94
95	0.0000 7596	0.0000 4947	0.0000 3228	0.0000 2110	0.0000 1382	95
96	0.0000 6874	0.0000 4457	0.0000 2895	0.0000 1884	0.0000 1228	96
97	0.0000 6221	0.0000 4015	0.0000 2596	0.0000 1682	0.0000 1092	97
98	0.0000 5630	0.0000 3617	0.0000 2328	0.0000 1502	0.0000 0971	98
99	0.0000 5095	0.0000 3259	0.0000 2088	0.0000 1341	0.0000 0863	99
100	0.0000 4611	0.0000 2936	0.0000 1873	0.0000 1197	0.0000 0767	100
101	0.0000 4173	0.0000 2645	0.0000 1680	0.0000 1069	0.0000 0682	101
102	0.0000 3776	0.0000 2383	0.0000 1506	0.0000 0954	0.0000 0606	102
103	0.0000 3417	0.0000 2147	0.0000 1351	0.0000 0852	0.0000 0539	103
104	0.0000 3093	0.0000 1934	0.0000 1212	0.0000 0761	0.0000 0479	104
105	0.0000 2799	0.0000 1742	0.0000 1087	0.0000 0679	0.0000 0426	105
106	0.0000 2533	0.0000 1570	0.0000 0975	0.0000 0607	0.0000 0378	106
107	0.0000 2292	0.0000 1414	0.0000 0874	0.0000 0542	0.0000 0336	107
108	0.0000 2074	0.0000 1274	0.0000 0784	0.0000 0484	0.0000 0299	108
109	0.0000 1877	0.0000 1148	0.0000 0703	0.0000 0432	0.0000 0266	109
110	0.0000 1699	0.0000 1034	0.0000 0631	0.0000 0385	0.0000 0236	110
111	0.0000 1537	0.0000 0931	0.0000 0566	0.0000 0344	0.0000 0210	111
112	0.0000 1391	0.0000 0839	0.0000 0507	0.0000 0307	0.0000 0187	112
113	0.0000 1259	0.0000 0756	0.0000 0455	0.0000 0274	0.0000 0166	113
114	0.0000 1139	0.0000 0681	0.0000 0408	0.0000 0245	0.0000 0147	114
115	0.0000 1031	0.0000 0614	0.0000 0366	0.0000 0219	0.0000 0131	115
116	0.0000 0933	0.0000 0553	0.0000 0328	0.0000 0195	0.0000 0116	116
117	0.0000 0845	0.0000 0498	0.0000 0294	0.0000 0174	0.0000 0104	117
118	0.0000 0764	0.0000 0449	0.0000 0264	0.0000 0156	0.0000 0092	118
119	0.0000 0692	0.0000 0404	0.0000 0237	0.0000 0139	0.0000 0082	119
120	0.0000 0626	0.0000 0364	0.0000 0212	0.0000 0124	0.0000 0073	120

TABLE III
AMOUNT OF ANNUITY OF 1 PER PERIOD

$$s_{\overline{n}|i} = \frac{(1+i)^n - 1}{i}$$

TABLE III

N	1/6	5/24	1/4	7/24	1/3	N
1	1.0000 0000	1.0000 0000	1.0000 0000	1.0000 0000	1.0000 0000	1
2	2.0016 6667	2.0020 8333	2.0025 0000	2.0029 1667	2.0033 3333	2
3	3.0050 0278	3.0062 5434	3.0075 0625	3.0087 5851	3.0100 1111	3
4	4.0100 1112	4.0125 1737	4.0150 2502	4.0175 3405	4.0200 4448	4
5	5.0166 9447	5.0208 7678	5.0250 6258	5.0292 5186	5.0334 4463	5
6	6.0250 5563	6.0313 3694	6.0376 2523	6.0439 2051	6.0502 2278	6
7	7.0350 9738	7.0439 0223	7.0527 1930	7.0615 4861	7.0703 9019	7
8	8.0468 2255	8.0585 7702	8.0703 5110	8.0821 4480	8.0939 5816	8
9	9.0602 3392	9.0753 6573	9.0905 2697	9.1057 1772	9.1209 3802	9
10	10.0753 3431	10.0942 7274	10.1132 5329	10.1322 7606	10.1513 4114	10
11	11.0921 2653	11.1153 0247	11.1385 3642	11.1618 2853	11.1851 7895	11
12	12.1106 1341	12.1384 5935	12.1663 8277	12.1943 8387	12.2224 6288	12
13	13.1307 9776	13.1637 4781	13.1967 9872	13.2299 5082	13.2632 0442	13
14	14.1526 8243	14.1911 7228	14.2297 9072	14.2685 3818	14.3074 1510	14
15	15.1762 7023	15.2207 3723	15.2653 6520	15.3101 5475	15.3551 0648	15
16	16.2015 6402	16.2524 4710	16.3035 2861	16.3548 0936	16.4062 9017	16
17	17.2285 6662	17.2863 0636	17.3442 8743	17.4025 1089	17.4609 7781	17
18	18.2572 8090	18.3223 1950	18.3876 4815	18.4532 6822	18.5191 8107	18
19	19.2877 0970	19.3604 9100	19.4336 1727	19.5070 9025	19.5809 1167	19
20	20.3198 5588	20.4008 2535	20.4822 0131	20.5639 8593	20.6461 8137	20
21	21.3537 2231	21.4433 2707	21.5334 0682	21.6239 6422	21.7150 0198	21
22	22.3893 1185	22.4880 0067	22.5872 4033	22.6870 3412	22.7873 8532	22
23	23.4266 2737	23.5348 5067	23.6437 0843	23.7532 0463	23.8633 4327	23
24	24.4656 7175	24.5838 8161	24.7028 1770	24.8224 8481	24.9428 8775	24
25	25.5064 4787	25.6350 9803	25.7645 7475	25.8948 8373	26.0260 3071	25
26	26.5489 5861	26.6885 0449	26.8289 8619	26.9704 1047	27.1127 8414	26
27	27.5932 0688	27.7441 0554	27.8960 5865	28.0490 7417	28.2031 6009	27
28	28.6391 9555	28.8019 0576	28.9657 9880	29.1308 8397	29.2971 7062	28
29	29.6869 2755	29.8619 0973	30.0382 1330	30.2158 4904	30.3948 2786	29
30	30.7364 0576	30.9241 2204	31.1133 0883	31.3039 7860	31.4961 4395	30
31	31.7876 3310	31.9885 4729	32.1910 9210	32.3952 8188	32.6011 3110	31
32	32.8406 1249	33.0551 9010	33.2715 6983	33.4897 6811	33.7098 0154	32
33	33.8953 4685	34.1240 5508	34.3547 4876	34.5874 4660	34.8221 6754	33
34	34.9518 3909	35.1951 4686	35.4406 3563	35.6883 2666	35.9382 4143	34
35	36.0100 9216	36.2684 7008	36.5292 3722	36.7924 1761	37.0580 3557	35
36	37.0701 0898	37.3440 2940	37.6205 6031	37.8997 2883	38.1815 6236	36
37	38.1318 9249	38.4218 2946	38.7146 1171	39.0102 6970	39.3088 3423	37
38	39.1954 4564	39.5018 7493	39.8113 9824	40.1240 4966	40.4398 6368	38
39	40.2607 7139	40.5841 7051	40.9109 2673	41.2410 7814	41.5746 6322	39
40	41.3278 7267	41.6687 2086	42.0132 0405	42.3613 6461	42.7132 4543	40
41	42.3967 5246	42.7555 3070	43.1182 3706	43.4849 1859	43.8556 2292	41
42	43.4674 1372	43.8446 0472	44.2260 3265	44.6117 4961	45.0018 0833	42
43	44.5398 5940	44.9359 4765	45.3365 9774	45.7418 6721	46.1518 1436	43
44	45.6140 9250	46.0295 6420	46.4499 3923	46.8752 8099	47.3056 5374	44
45	46.6901 1599	47.1254 5913	47.5660 6408	48.0120 0056	48.4633 3925	45
46	47.7679 3285	48.2236 3717	48.6849 7924	49.1520 3556	49.6248 8371	46
47	48.8475 4607	49.3241 0308	49.8066 9169	50.2953 9566	50.7902 9999	47
48	49.9289 5865	50.4268 6163	50.9312 0842	51.4420 9057	51.9596 0099	48
49	51.0121 7358	51.5319 1759	52.0585 3644	52.5921 3000	53.1327 9966	49
50	52.0971 9387	52.6392 7575	53.1886 8278	53.7455 2371	54.3099 0899	50
51	53.1840 2253	53.7489 4091	54.3216 5449	54.9022 8149	55.4909 4202	51
52	54.2726 6256	54.8609 1787	55.4574 5862	56.0624 1314	56.6759 1183	52
53	55.3631 1700	55.9752 1145	56.5961 0227	57.2259 2851	57.8648 3154	53
54	56.4553 8886	57.0918 2647	57.7375 9252	58.3928 3747	59.0577 1431	54
55	57.5494 8118	58.2107 6778	58.8819 3650	59.5631 4991	60.2545 7336	55
56	58.6453 9698	59.3320 4021	60.0291 4135	60.7368 7577	61.4554 2194	56
57	59.7431 3931	60.4556 4863	61.1792 1420	61.9140 2499	62.6602 7334	57
58	60.8427 1121	61.5815 9790	62.3321 6223	63.0946 0756	63.8691 4092	58
59	61.9441 1573	62.7098 9289	63.4879 9264	64.2786 3350	65.0820 3806	59
60	63.0473 5592	63.8405 3850	64.6467 1262	65.4661 1285	66.2989 7818	60

TABLE III

N	1/6	5/24	1/4	7/24	1/3	N
61	64.1524 3485	64.9735 3962	65.8083 2940	66.6570 5568	67.5199 7478	61
62	65.2593 5557	66.1089 0116	66.9728 5023	67.8514 7209	68.7450 4136	62
63	66.3681 2116	67.2466 2804	68.1402 8235	69.0493 7222	69.9741 9150	63
64	67.4787 3470	68.3867 2518	69.3106 3306	70.2507 6622	71.2074 3880	64
65	68.5911 9926	69.5291 9753	70.4839 0964	71.4556 6429	72.4447 9693	65
66	69.7055 1792	70.6740 5002	71.6601 1942	72.6640 7664	73.6862 7959	66
67	70.8216 9378	71.8212 8763	72.8392 6971	73.8760 1353	74.9319 0052	67
68	71.9397 2994	72.9709 1531	74.0213 6789	75.0914 8524	76.1816 7352	68
69	73.0596 2949	74.1229 3805	75.2064 2131	76.3105 0207	77.4356 1243	69
70	74.1813 9554	75.2773 6084	76.3944 3736	77.5330 7437	78.6937 3114	70
71	75.3050 3120	76.4341 8867	77.5854 2345	78.7592 1250	79.9560 4358	71
72	76.4305 3958	77.5934 2657	78.7793 8701	79.9889 2687	81.2225 6372	72
73	77.5579 2382	78.7550 7954	79.9763 3548	81.2222 2791	82.4933 0560	73
74	78.6871 8702	79.9191 5262	81.1762 7632	82.4591 2607	83.7682 8329	74
75	79.8183 3233	81.0856 5085	82.3792 1701	83.6996 3186	85.0475 1090	75
76	80.9513 6289	82.2545 7929	83.5851 6505	84.9437 5578	86.3310 0260	76
77	82.0862 8183	83.4259 4300	84.7941 2797	86.1915 0840	87.6187 7261	77
78	83.2230 9230	84.5997 4705	86.0061 1329	87.4429 0030	88.9108 3519	78
79	84.3617 9745	85.7759 9652	87.2211 2857	88.6979 4210	90.2072 0464	79
80	85.5024 0045	86.9546 9651	88.4391 8139	89.9566 4443	91.5078 9532	80
81	86.6449 0445	88.1358 5213	89.6602 7934	91.2190 1797	92.8129 2164	81
82	87.7893 1262	89.3194 6849	90.8844 3004	92.4850 7344	94.1222 9804	82
83	88.9356 2814	90.5055 5072	92.1116 4112	93.7548 2157	95.4360 3904	83
84	90.0838 5419	91.6941 0395	93.3419 2022	95.0282 7314	96.7541 5917	84
85	91.2339 9395	92.8851 3333	94.5752 7502	96.3054 3893	98.0766 7303	85
86	92.3860 5060	94.0786 4402	95.8117 1321	97.5863 2980	99.4035 9527	86
87	93.5400 2735	95.2746 4120	97.0512 4249	98.8709 5659	100.7349 4059	87
88	94.6959 2740	96.4731 3004	98.2938 7060	100.1593 3022	102.0707 2373	88
89	95.8537 5394	97.6741 1572	99.5396 0527	101.4514 6160	103.4109 5947	89
90	97.0135 1020	98.8776 0346	100.7884 5429	102.7473 6169	104.7556 6267	90
91	98.1751 9938	100.0835 9847	102.0404 2542	104.0470 4150	106.1048 4821	91
92	99.3388 2472	101.2921 0597	103.2955 2649	105.3505 1203	107.4585 3104	92
93	100.5043 8943	102.5031 3119	104.5537 6530	106.6577 8436	108.8167 2614	93
94	101.6718 9674	103.7166 7938	105.8151 4972	107.9688 6957	110.1794 4856	94
95	102.8413 4990	104.9327 5579	107.0796 8759	109.2837 7877	111.5467 1339	95
96	104.0127 5215	106.1513 6570	108.3473 8681	110.6025 2312	112.9185 3577	96
97	105.1861 0674	107.3725 1438	109.6182 5528	111.9251 1382	114.2949 3089	97
98	106.3614 1692	108.5962 0712	110.8923 0091	113.2515 6206	115.6759 1399	98
99	107.5386 8594	109.8224 4922	112.1695 3167	114.5818 7912	117.0615 0037	99
100	108.7179 1709	111.0512 4599	113.4499 5550	115.9160 7627	118.4517 0537	100
101	109.8991 1362	112.2826 0275	114.7335 8038	117.2541 6482	119.8465 4439	101
102	111.0822 7881	113.5165 2484	116.0204 1434	118.5961 5614	121.2460 3287	102
103	112.2674 1594	114.7530 1760	117.3104 6537	119.9420 6159	122.6501 8632	103
104	113.4545 2830	115.9920 8639	118.6037 4153	121.2918 9261	124.0590 2027	104
105	114.6436 1918	117.2337 3656	119.9002 5089	122.6456 6063	125.4725 5034	105
106	115.8346 9188	118.4779 7352	121.2000 0152	124.0033 7714	126.8907 9217	106
107	117.0277 4970	119.7248 0263	122.5030 0152	125.3650 5365	128.3137 6148	107
108	118.2227 9595	120.9742 2930	123.8092 5902	126.7307 0173	129.7414 7402	108
109	119.4198 3394	122.2262 5894	125.1187 8217	128.1003 3294	131.1739 4560	109
110	120.6188 6700	123.4808 9698	126.4315 7913	129.4739 5891	132.6111 9208	110
111	121.8198 9844	124.7381 4885	127.7476 5807	130.8515 9129	134.0532 2939	111
112	123.0229 3160	125.9980 2000	129.0670 2722	132.2332 4177	135.5000 7349	112
113	124.2279 6982	127.2605 1587	130.3896 9479	133.6189 2205	136.9517 4040	113
114	125.4350 1644	128.5256 4195	131.7156 6902	135.0086 4391	138.4082 4620	114
115	126.6440 7480	129.7934 0370	133.0449 5820	136.4024 1912	139.8696 0702	115
116	127.8551 4826	131.0638 0662	134.3775 7059	137.8002 5951	141.3358 3904	116
117	129.0682 4017	132.3368 5622	135.7135 1452	139.2021 7693	142.8069 5851	117
118	130.2833 5391	133.6125 5800	137.0527 9830	140.6081 8328	144.2829 8170	118
119	131.5004 9283	134.8909 1750	138.3954 3030	142.0182 9048	145.7639 2498	119
120	132.7196 6032	136.1719 4025	139.7414 1888	143.4325 1050	147.2498 0473	120

TABLE III

N	1/6	5/24	1/4	7/24	1/3	N
121	133.9408 5975	137.4556 3179	141.0907 7242	144.8508 5532	148.7406 3741	121
122	135.1640 9452	138.7419 9769	142.4434 9935	146.2733 3698	150.2364 3953	122
123	136.3893 6801	140.0310 4352	143.7996 0810	147.6999 6755	151.7372 2766	123
124	137.6166 8362	141.3227 7486	145.1591 0712	149.1307 5912	153.2430 1842	124
125	138.8460 4476	142.6171 9730	146.5220 0489	150.5657 2383	154.7538 2848	125
126	140.0774 5484	143.9143 1647	147.8883 0990	152.0048 7386	156.2696 7458	126
127	141.3109 1726	145.2141 3796	149.2580 3068	153.4482 2141	157.7905 7349	127
128	142.5464 3546	146.5166 6741	150.6311 7575	154.8957 7872	159.3165 4207	128
129	143.7840 1285	147.8219 1047	152.0077 5369	156.3475 5808	160.8475 9721	129
130	145.0236 5287	149.1298 7278	153.3877 7308	157.8035 7179	162.3837 5587	130
131	146.2653 5896	150.4405 6002	154.7712 4251	159.2638 3221	163.9250 3506	131
132	147.5091 3456	151.7539 7785	156.1581 7062	160.7283 5172	165.4714 5184	132
133	148.7549 8311	153.0701 3197	157.5485 6604	162.1971 4274	167.0230 2335	133
134	150.0029 0809	154.3890 2808	158.9424 3746	163.6702 1774	168.5797 6676	134
135	151.2529 1293	155.7106 7189	160.3397 9355	165.1475 8921	170.1416 9931	135
136	152.5050 0112	157.0350 6912	161.7406 4304	166.6292 6968	171.7088 3831	136
137	153.7591 7612	158.3622 2552	163.1449 9464	168.1152 7172	173.2812 0111	137
138	155.0154 4142	159.6921 4682	164.5528 5713	169.6056 0793	174.8588 0511	138
139	156.2738 0049	161.0248 3879	165.9642 3927	171.1002 9095	176.4416 6779	139
140	157.5342 5682	162.3603 0720	167.3791 4987	172.5993 3346	178.0298 0669	140
141	158.7968 1391	163.6985 5784	168.7975 9775	174.1027 4819	179.6232 3937	141
142	160.0614 7527	165.0395 9651	170.2195 9174	175.6105 4787	181.2219 8351	142
143	161.3282 4440	166.3834 2900	171.6451 4072	177.1227 4530	182.8260 5678	143
144	162.5971 2480	167.7300 6114	173.0742 5357	178.6393 5331	184.4354 7697	144
145	163.8681 2001	169.0794 9877	174.5069 3921	180.1603 8475	186.0502 6190	145
146	165.1412 3354	170.4317 4773	175.9432 0655	181.6858 5254	187.6704 2944	146
147	166.4164 6893	171.7868 1387	177.3830 6457	183.2157 6961	189.2959 9753	147
148	167.6938 2972	173.1447 0306	178.8265 2223	184.7501 4894	190.9269 8419	148
149	168.9733 1943	174.5054 2119	180.2735 8854	186.2890 0354	192.5634 0747	149
150	170.2549 4163	175.8689 7416	181.7242 7251	187.8323 4647	194.2052 8550	150
151	171.5386 9987	177.2353 6785	183.1785 8319	189.3801 9081	195.8526 3645	151
152	172.8245 9770	178.6046 0820	184.6365 2965	190.9325 4970	197.5054 7857	152
153	174.1126 3870	179.9767 0114	186.0981 2097	192.4894 3631	199.1638 3017	153
154	175.4028 2643	181.3516 5260	187.5633 6627	194.0508 6383	200.8277 0960	154
155	176.6951 6447	182.7294 6854	189.0322 7469	195.6168 4551	202.4971 3530	155
156	177.9896 5641	184.1101 5493	190.5048 5538	197.1873 9465	204.1721 2575	156
157	179.2863 0584	185.4937 1775	191.9811 1752	198.7625 2455	205.8526 9950	157
158	180.5851 1635	186.8801 6300	193.4610 7031	200.3422 4858	207.5388 7517	158
159	181.8860 9154	188.2694 9667	194.9447 2298	201.9265 8014	209.2306 7142	159
160	183.1892 3503	189.6617 2479	196.4320 8479	203.5155 3266	210.9281 0699	160
161	184.4945 5042	191.0568 5338	197.9231 6500	205.1091 1963	212.6312 0068	161
162	185.8020 4134	192.4548 8850	199.4179 7292	206.7073 5457	214.3399 7135	162
163	187.1117 1141	193.8558 3618	200.9165 1785	208.3102 5102	216.0544 3792	163
164	188.4235 6426	195.2597 0250	202.4188 0914	209.9178 2258	217.7746 1938	164
165	189.7376 0353	196.6664 9355	203.9248 5617	211.5300 8290	219.5005 3478	165
166	191.0538 3287	198.0762 1541	205.4346 6831	213.1470 4564	221.2322 0323	166
167	192.3722 5593	199.4888 7420	206.9482 5498	214.7687 2452	222.9696 4390	167
168	193.6928 7635	200.9044 7602	208.4656 2562	216.3951 3330	224.7128 7605	168
169	195.0156 9781	202.3230 2701	209.9867 8968	218.0262 8577	226.4619 1897	169
170	196.3407 2398	203.7445 3331	211.5117 5665	219.6621 9577	228.2167 9203	170
171	197.6679 5852	205.1690 0109	213.0405 3605	221.3028 7718	229.9775 1467	171
172	198.9974 0511	206.5964 3651	214.5731 3739	222.9483 4390	231.7441 0639	172
173	200.3290 6746	208.0268 4575	216.1095 7023	224.5986 0991	233.5165 8674	173
174	201.6629 4924	209.4602 3502	217.6498 4415	226.2536 8919	235.2949 7537	174
175	202.9990 5415	210.8966 1051	219.1939 6876	227.9135 9578	237.0792 9195	175
176	204.3373 8591	212.3359 7844	220.7419 5369	229.5783 4377	238.8695 5626	176
177	205.6779 4822	213.7783 4507	222.2938 0857	231.2479 4727	240.6657 8811	177
178	207.0207 4480	215.2237 1662	223.8495 4309	232.9224 2045	242.4680 0741	178
179	208.3657 7937	216.6720 9936	225.4091 6695	234.6017 7751	244.2762 3410	179
180	209.7130 5567	218.1234 9957	226.9726 8987	236.2860 3269	246.0904 8821	180

TABLE III

N	1/6	5/24	1/4	7/24	1/3	N
181	211.0625 7743	219.5779 2353	228.5401 2159	237.9752 0029	247.9107 8984	181
182	212.4143 4839	221.0353 7753	230.1114 7190	239.6692 9462	249.7371 5914	182
183	213.7683 7231	222.4958 6790	231.6867 5058	241.3683 3007	251.5696 1634	183
184	215.1246 5293	223.9594 0096	233.2659 6745	243.0723 2103	253.4081 8172	184
185	216.4831 9402	225.4259 8305	234.8491 3237	244.7812 8196	255.2528 7566	185
186	217.8439 9934	226.8956 2051	236.4362 5520	246.4952 2737	257.1037 1858	186
187	219.2070 7267	228.3683 1972	238.0273 4584	248.2141 7178	258.9607 3098	187
188	220.5724 1779	229.8440 8705	239.6224 1420	249.9381 2978	260.8239 3341	188
189	221.9400 3849	231.3229 2890	241.2214 7024	251.6671 1600	262.6933 4652	189
190	223.3099 3855	232.8048 5167	242.8245 2392	253.4011 4508	264.5689 9101	190
191	224.6821 2178	234.2898 6178	244.4315 8523	255.1402 3176	266.4508 8765	191
192	226.0565 9199	235.7779 6566	246.0426 6419	256.8843 9077	268.3390 5727	192
193	227.4333 5297	237.2691 6975	247.6577 7085	258.6336 3691	270.2335 2080	193
194	228.8124 0856	238.7634 8052	249.2769 1528	260.3879 8501	272.1342 9920	194
195	230.1937 6258	240.2609 0444	250.9001 0756	262.1474 4997	274.0414 1353	195
196	231.5774 1885	241.7614 4799	252.5273 5783	263.9120 4670	275.9548 8491	196
197	232.9633 8121	243.2651 1767	254.1586 7623	265.6817 9017	277.8747 3453	197
198	234.3516 5351	244.7719 2000	255.7940 7292	267.4566 9539	279.8009 8364	198
199	235.7422 3960	246.2818 6150	257.4335 5810	269.2367 7742	281.7336 5359	199
200	237.1351 4334	247.7949 4871	259.0771 4200	271.0220 5135	283.6727 6577	200
201	238.5303 6858	249.3111 8819	260.7248 3485	272.8125 3234	285.6183 4165	201
202	239.9279 1919	250.8305 8650	262.3766 4694	274.6082 3556	287.5704 0279	202
203	241.3277 9905	252.3531 5022	264.0325 8855	276.4091 7624	289.5289 7080	203
204	242.7300 1205	253.8788 8595	265.6926 7003	278.2153 6967	291.4940 6737	204
205	244.1345 6207	255.4078 0030	267.3569 0170	280.0268 3117	293.4657 1426	205
206	245.5414 5301	256.9398 9988	269.0252 9396	281.8435 7609	295.4439 3331	206
207	246.9506 8876	258.4751 9134	270.6978 5719	283.6656 1986	297.4287 4642	207
208	248.3622 7325	260.0136 8132	272.3746 0183	285.4929 7791	299.4201 7557	208
209	249.7762 1037	261.5553 7649	274.0555 3834	287.3256 6577	301.4182 4283	209
210	251.1925 0405	263.1002 8352	275.7406 7718	289.1636 9896	303.4229 7030	210
211	252.6111 5823	264.6484 0911	277.4300 2888	291.0070 9308	305.4343 8020	211
212	254.0321 7682	266.1997 5997	279.1236 0395	292.8558 6377	307.4524 9480	212
213	255.4555 6378	267.7543 4280	280.8214 1296	294.7100 2670	309.4773 3645	213
214	256.8813 2306	269.3121 6435	282.5234 6649	296.5695 9761	311.5089 2757	214
215	258.3094 5860	270.8732 3136	284.2297 7516	298.4345 9227	313.5472 9067	215
216	259.7399 7436	272.4375 5059	285.9403 4960	300.3050 2650	315.5924 4830	216
217	261.1728 7432	274.0051 2882	287.6552 0047	302.1809 1616	317.6444 2313	217
218	262.6081 6244	275.5759 7284	289.3743 3847	304.0622 7717	319.7032 3787	218
219	264.0458 4271	277.1500 8945	291.0977 7432	305.9491 2548	321.7689 1533	219
220	265.4859 1912	278.7274 8547	292.8255 1875	307.8414 7709	323.8414 7838	220
221	266.9283 9565	280.3081 6773	294.5575 8255	309.7393 4807	325.9209 4998	221
222	268.3732 7631	281.8921 4308	296.2939 7651	311.6427 5450	328.0073 5315	222
223	269.8205 6510	283.4794 1838	298.0347 1145	313.5517 1253	330.1007 1099	223
224	271.2702 6604	285.0700 0050	299.7797 9823	315.4662 3836	332.2010 4669	224
225	272.7223 8315	286.6638 9633	301.5292 4772	317.3863 4822	334.3083 8351	225
226	274.1769 2046	288.2611 1278	303.2830 7084	319.3120 5841	336.4227 4479	226
227	275.6338 8199	289.8616 5677	305.0412 7852	321.2433 8524	338.5441 5394	227
228	277.0932 7180	291.4655 3522	306.8038 8171	323.1803 4512	340.6726 3446	228
229	278.5550 9392	293.0727 5508	308.5708 9142	325.1229 5446	342.8082 0990	229
230	280.0193 5241	294.6833 2332	310.3423 1865	327.0712 2974	344.9509 0394	230
231	281.4860 5133	296.2972 4691	312.1181 7444	329.0251 8749	347.1007 4028	231
232	282.9551 9474	297.9145 3285	313.8984 6988	330.9848 4429	349.2577 4275	232
233	284.4267 8674	299.5351 8812	315.6832 1605	332.9502 1675	351.4219 3523	233
234	285.9008 3138	301.1592 1976	317.4724 2409	334.9213 2155	353.5933 4168	234
235	287.3773 3277	302.7866 3481	319.2661 0515	336.8981 7541	355.7719 8615	235
236	288.8562 9499	304.4174 4029	321.0642 7042	338.8807 9508	357.9578 9277	236
237	290.3377 2215	306.0516 4329	322.8669 3109	340.8691 9740	360.1510 8575	237
238	291.8216 1835	307.6892 5089	324.6740 9842	342.8633 9923	362.3515 8937	238
239	293.3079 8771	309.3302 7016	326.4857 8367	344.8634 1748	364.5594 2800	239
240	294.7968 3436	310.9747 0822	328.3019 9813	346.8692 6911	366.7746 2609	240

TABLE III

N	1/6	5/24	1/4	7/24	1/3	N
241	296.2881 6242	312.6225 7220	330.1227 5312	348.8809 7115	368.9972 0818	241
242	297.7819 7602	314.2738 6922	331.9480 6000	350.8985 4065	371.2271 9887	242
243	299.2782 7931	315.9286 0645	333.7779 3015	352.9219 9472	373.4646 2287	243
244	300.7770 7645	317.5867 9105	335.6123 7498	354.9513 5054	375.7095 0494	244
245	302.2783 7157	319.2484 3019	337.4514 0592	356.9866 2531	377.9618 6996	245
246	303.7821 6886	320.9135 3109	339.2950 3443	359.0278 3630	380.2217 4286	246
247	305.2884 7247	322.5821 0095	341.1432 7202	361.0750 0083	382.4891 4867	247
248	306.7972 8660	324.2541 4699	342.9961 3020	363.1281 3624	384.7641 1250	248
249	308.3086 1541	325.9296 7646	344.8536 2052	365.1872 5998	387.0466 5954	249
250	309.8224 6310	327.6086 9662	346.7157 5458	367.2523 8948	389.3368 1507	250
251	311.3388 3387	329.2912 1474	348.5825 4396	369.3235 4229	391.6346 0446	251
252	312.8577 3193	330.9772 3810	350.4540 0032	371.4007 3595	393.9400 5314	252
253	314.3791 6148	332.6667 7402	352.3301 3532	373.4839 8810	396.2531 8665	253
254	315.9031 2675	334.3598 2980	354.2109 6066	375.5733 1640	398.5740 3060	254
255	317.4296 3196	336.0564 1277	356.0964 8806	377.6687 3857	400.9026 1070	255
256	318.9586 8135	337.7565 3030	357.9867 2928	379.7702 7239	403.2389 5274	256
257	320.4902 7915	339.4601 8974	359.8816 9611	381.8779 3568	405.5830 8258	257
258	322.0244 2961	341.1673 9847	361.7814 0035	383.9917 4633	407.9350 2619	258
259	323.5611 3700	342.8781 6388	363.6858 5385	386.1117 2226	410.2948 0961	259
260	325.1004 0556	344.5924 9339	365.5950 6848	388.2378 8145	412.6624 5898	260
261	326.6422 3957	346.3103 9442	367.5090 5615	390.3702 4193	415.0380 0051	261
262	328.1866 4330	348.0318 7441	369.4278 2879	392.5088 2181	417.4214 6051	262
263	329.7336 2104	349.7569 4081	371.3513 9837	394.6536 3920	419.8128 6538	263
264	331.2831 7707	351.4856 0110	373.2797 7686	396.8047 1232	422.2122 4160	264
265	332.8353 1570	353.2178 6277	375.2129 7630	398.9620 5940	424.6196 1573	265
266	334.3900 4123	354.9537 3332	377.1510 0874	401.1256 9874	427.0350 1445	266
267	335.9473 5796	356.6932 2027	379.0938 8627	403.2956 4869	429.4584 6450	267
268	337.5072 7023	358.4363 3114	381.0416 2098	405.4719 2767	431.8899 9272	268
269	339.0697 8235	360.1830 7350	382.9942 2503	407.6545 5412	434.3296 2603	269
270	340.6348 9865	361.9334 5490	384.9517 1060	409.8435 4657	436.7773 9145	270
271	342.2026 2348	363.6874 8293	386.9140 8987	412.0389 2358	439.2333 1608	271
272	343.7729 6119	365.4451 6519	388.8813 7510	414.2407 0378	441.6974 2714	272
273	345.3459 1612	367.2065 0928	390.8535 7854	416.4489 0583	444.1697 5189	273
274	346.9214 9265	368.9715 2284	392.8307 1248	418.6635 4847	446.6503 1773	274
275	348.4996 9514	370.7402 1352	394.8127 8926	420.8846 5049	449.1391 5213	275
276	350.0805 2796	372.5125 8896	396.7998 2124	423.1122 3072	451.6362 8263	276
277	351.6639 9551	374.2886 5685	398.7918 2079	425.3463 0806	454.1417 3691	277
278	353.2501 0217	376.0684 2489	400.7888 0034	427.5869 0146	456.6555 4270	278
279	354.8388 5234	377.8519 0077	402.7907 7234	429.8340 2992	459.1777 2784	279
280	356.4302 5042	379.6390 9223	404.7977 4927	432.0877 1251	461.7083 2027	280
281	358.0243 0084	381.4300 0701	406.8097 4365	434.3479 6833	464.2473 4800	281
282	359.6210 0801	383.2246 5286	408.8267 6801	436.6148 1657	466.7948 3916	282
283	361.2203 7636	385.0230 3755	410.8488 3493	438.8882 7646	469.3508 2196	283
284	362.8224 1032	386.8251 6888	412.8759 5701	441.1683 6726	471.9153 2470	284
285	364.4271 1433	388.6310 5465	414.9081 4690	443.4551 0833	474.4883 7578	285
286	366.0344 9286	390.4407 0268	416.9454 1727	445.7485 1907	477.0700 0370	286
287	367.6445 5035	392.2541 2081	418.9877 8082	448.0486 1891	479.6602 3705	287
288	369.2572 9126	394.0713 1689	421.0352 5027	450.3554 2739	482.2591 0450	288
289	370.8727 2008	395.8922 9880	423.0878 3839	452.6689 6405	484.8666 3485	289
290	372.4908 4128	397.7170 7443	425.1455 5799	454.9892 4853	487.4828 5697	290
291	374.1116 5935	399.5456 5167	427.2084 2188	457.3163 0050	490.1077 9982	291
292	375.7351 7878	401.3780 3844	429.2764 4294	459.6501 3971	492.7414 9249	292
293	377.3614 0408	403.2142 4269	431.3496 3405	461.9907 8595	495.3839 6413	293
294	378.9903 3975	405.0542 7236	433.4280 0813	464.3382 5908	498.0352 4401	294
295	380.6219 9032	406.8981 3543	435.5115 7815	466.6925 7900	500.6953 6149	295
296	382.2563 6031	408.7458 3987	437.6003 5710	469.0537 6569	503.3643 4603	296
297	383.8934 5424	410.5973 9371	439.6943 5799	471.4218 3917	506.0422 2718	297
298	385.5332 7666	412.4528 0494	441.7935 9388	473.7968 1954	508.7290 3461	298
299	387.1758 3212	414.3120 8162	443.8980 7787	476.1787 2693	511.4247 9806	299
300	388.8211 2518	416.1752 3179	446.0078 2306	478.5675 8155	514.1295 4738	300

TABLE III

N	1/6	5/24	1/4	7/24	1/3	N
301	390.4691 6039	418.0422 6352	448.1228 4262	480.9634 0366	516.8433 1254	301
302	392.1199 4232	419.9131 8491	450.2431 4973	483.3662 1359	519.5661 2358	302
303	393.7734 7556	421.7880 0404	452.3687 5760	485.7760 3171	522.2980 1066	303
304	395.4297 6468	423.6667 2905	454.4996 7950	488.1928 7847	525.0390 0403	304
305	397.0888 1429	425.5493 6807	456.6359 2870	490.6167 7436	527.7891 3404	305
306	398.7506 2898	427.4359 2925	458.7775 1852	493.0477 3996	530.5484 3116	306
307	400.4152 1336	429.3264 2077	460.9244 6231	495.4857 9587	533.3169 2593	307
308	402.0825 7205	431.2208 5082	463.0767 7347	497.9309 6277	536.0946 4901	308
309	403.7527 0967	433.1192 2759	465.2344 6540	500.3832 6141	538.8816 3118	309
310	405.4256 3085	435.0215 5931	467.3975 5157	502.8427 1259	541.6779 0328	310
311	407.1013 4024	436.9278 5423	469.5660 4545	505.3093 3717	544.4834 9629	311
312	408.7798 4247	438.8381 2059	471.7399 6056	507.7831 5607	547.2984 4128	312
313	410.4611 4221	440.7523 6667	473.9193 1046	510.2641 9027	550.1227 6942	313
314	412.1452 4411	442.6706 0077	476.1041 0874	512.7524 6083	552.9565 1198	314
315	413.8321 5285	444.5928 3119	478.2943 6901	515.2479 8884	555.7997 0036	315
316	415.5218 7311	446.5190 6626	480.4901 0493	517.7507 9547	558.6523 6602	316
317	417.2144 0956	448.4493 1431	482.6913 3019	520.2609 0196	561.5145 4058	317
318	418.9097 6691	450.3835 8371	484.8980 5852	522.7783 2959	564.3862 5571	318
319	420.6079 4986	452.3218 8285	487.1103 0366	525.3030 9972	567.2675 4323	319
320	422.3089 6311	454.2642 2010	489.3280 7942	527.8352 3376	570.1584 3504	320
321	424.0128 1138	456.2106 0390	491.5513 9962	530.3747 5319	573.0589 6316	321
322	425.7194 9940	458.1610 4265	493.7802 7812	532.9216 7956	575.9691 5970	322
323	427.4290 3190	460.1155 4483	496.0147 2882	535.4760 3445	578.8890 5690	323
324	429.1414 1362	462.0741 1888	498.2547 6564	538.0378 3955	581.8186 8709	324
325	430.8566 4931	464.0367 7329	500.5004 0255	540.6071 1659	584.7580 8271	325
326	432.5747 4372	466.0035 1657	502.7516 5356	543.1838 8734	587.7072 7632	326
327	434.2957 0163	467.9743 5723	505.0085 3269	545.7681 7368	590.6663 0058	327
328	436.0195 2780	469.9493 0381	507.2710 5403	548.3599 9752	593.6351 8825	328
329	437.7462 2701	471.9283 6486	509.5392 3166	550.9593 8085	596.6139 7221	329
330	439.4758 0406	473.9115 4895	511.8130 7974	553.5663 4571	599.6026 8545	330
331	441.2082 6373	475.8988 6468	514.0926 1244	556.1809 1422	602.6013 6107	331
332	442.9436 1084	477.8903 2064	516.3778 4397	558.8031 0855	605.6100 3227	332
333	444.6818 5019	479.8859 2548	518.6687 8858	561.4329 5095	608.6287 3238	333
334	446.4229 8660	481.8856 8782	520.9654 6055	564.0704 6372	611.6574 9482	334
335	448.1670 2492	483.8896 1634	523.2678 7420	566.7156 6924	614.6963 5313	335
336	449.9139 6996	485.8977 1971	525.5760 4389	569.3685 8994	617.7453 4098	336
337	451.6638 2657	487.9100 0662	527.8899 8400	572.0292 4833	620.8044 9212	337
338	453.4165 9962	489.9264 8580	530.2097 0896	574.6976 6697	623.8738 4042	338
339	455.1722 9395	491.9471 6598	532.5352 3323	577.3738 6850	626.9534 1989	339
340	456.9309 1444	493.9720 5591	534.8665 7131	580.0578 7562	630.0432 6462	340
341	458.6924 6596	496.0011 6436	537.2037 3774	582.7497 1109	633.1434 0884	341
342	460.4569 5341	498.0345 0012	539.5467 4709	585.4493 9775	636.2538 8687	342
343	462.2243 8166	500.0720 7200	541.8956 1395	588.1569 5849	639.3747 3316	343
344	463.9947 5563	502.1138 8881	544.2503 5299	590.8724 1628	642.5059 8227	344
345	465.7680 8023	504.1599 5941	546.6109 7887	593.5957 9417	645.6476 6888	345
346	467.5443 6036	506.2102 9266	548.9775 0632	596.3271 1523	648.7998 2777	346
347	469.3236 0096	508.2648 9744	551.3499 5008	599.0664 0265	651.9624 9386	347
348	471.1058 0696	510.3237 8264	553.7283 2496	601.8136 7966	655.1357 0218	348
349	472.8909 8331	512.3869 5719	556.1126 4577	604.5689 6956	658.3194 8785	349
350	474.6791 3495	514.4544 3002	558.5029 2739	607.3322 9572	661.5138 8614	350
351	476.4702 6684	516.5262 1008	560.8991 8470	610.1036 8158	664.7189 3243	351
352	478.2643 8395	518.6023 0635	563.3014 3267	612.8831 5065	667.9346 6221	352
353	480.0614 9126	520.6827 2782	565.7096 8625	615.6707 2651	671.1611 1108	353
354	481.8615 9374	522.7674 8351	568.1239 6046	618.4664 3279	674.3983 1478	354
355	483.6646 9640	524.8565 8243	570.5442 7036	621.2702 9322	677.6463 0917	355
356	485.4708 0422	526.9500 3364	572.9706 3104	624.0823 3158	680.9051 3020	356
357	487.2799 2223	529.0478 4621	575.4030 5762	626.9025 7171	684.1748 1396	357
358	489.0920 5543	531.1500 2923	577.8415 6526	629.7310 3755	687.4553 9668	358
359	490.9072 0886	533.2565 9179	580.2861 6918	632.5677 5307	690.7469 1467	359
360	492.7253 8754	535.3675 4302	582.7368 8460	635.4127 4235	694.0494 0438	360

TABLE III

N	3/8	5/12	11/24	1/2	13/24	N
1	1.0000 0000	1.0000 0000	1.0000 0000	1.0000 0000	1.0000 0000	1
2	2.0037 5000	2.0041 6667	2.0045 8333	2.0050 0000	2.0054 1667	2
3	3.0112 6406	3.0125 1736	3.0137 7101	3.0150 2500	3.0162 7934	3
4	4.0225 5630	4.0250 6952	4.0275 8412	4.0301 0012	4.0326 1752	4
5	5.0376 4089	5.0418 4064	5.0460 4388	5.0502 5063	5.0544 6086	5
6	6.0565 3204	6.0628 4831	6.0691 7159	6.0755 0188	6.0818 3919	6
7	7.0792 4404	7.0881 1018	7.0969 8862	7.1058 7939	7.1147 8249	7
8	8.1057 9120	8.1176 4397	8.1295 1649	8.1414 0879	8.1533 2090	8
9	9.1361 8792	9.1514 6749	9.1667 7677	9.1821 1583	9.1974 8472	9
10	10.1704 4862	10.1895 9860	10.2087 9116	10.2280 2641	10.2473 0443	10
11	11.2085 8781	11.2320 5526	11.2555 8146	11.2791 6654	11.3028 1066	11
12	12.2506 2001	12.2788 5549	12.3071 6954	12.3355 6237	12.3640 3422	12
13	13.2965 5984	13.3300 1739	13.3635 7740	13.3972 4018	13.4310 0607	13
14	14.3464 2194	14.3855 5913	14.4248 2713	14.4642 2639	14.5037 5735	14
15	15.4002 2102	15.4454 9896	15.4909 4092	15.5365 4752	15.5823 1937	15
16	16.4579 7185	16.5098 5520	16.5619 4107	16.6142 3026	16.6667 2360	16
17	17.5196 8924	17.5786 4627	17.6378 4996	17.6973 0141	17.7570 0169	17
18	18.5853 8808	18.6518 9063	18.7186 9011	18.7857 8791	18.8531 8544	18
19	19.6550 8328	19.7296 0684	19.8044 8410	19.8797 1685	19.9553 0687	19
20	20.7287 8984	20.8118 1353	20.8952 5466	20.9791 1544	21.0633 9811	20
21	21.8065 2280	21.8985 2942	21.9910 2457	22.0840 1101	22.1774 9152	21
22	22.8882 9727	22.9897 7330	23.0918 1677	23.1944 3107	23.2976 1960	22
23	23.9741 2838	24.0855 6402	24.1976 5426	24.3104 0322	24.4238 1504	23
24	25.0640 3136	25.1859 2053	25.3085 6018	25.4319 5524	25.5561 1070	24
25	26.1580 2148	26.2908 6187	26.4245 5775	26.5591 1502	26.6945 3963	25
26	27.2561 1406	27.4004 0713	27.5456 7030	27.6919 1059	27.8391 3506	26
27	28.3583 2449	28.5145 7549	28.6719 2129	28.8303 7015	28.9899 3037	27
28	29.4646 6820	29.6333 8622	29.8033 3426	29.9745 2200	30.1469 5916	28
29	30.5751 6071	30.7568 5866	30.9399 3288	31.1243 9461	31.3102 5519	29
30	31.6898 1756	31.8850 1224	32.0817 4090	32.2800 1658	32.4798 5241	30
31	32.8086 5438	33.0178 6646	33.2287 8222	33.4414 1666	33.6557 8494	31
32	33.9316 8683	34.1554 4090	34.3810 8080	34.6086 2375	34.8380 8711	32
33	35.0589 3066	35.2977 5524	35.5386 6076	35.7816 6686	36.0267 9341	33
34	36.1904 0165	36.4448 2922	36.7015 4628	36.9605 7520	37.2219 3854	34
35	37.3261 1565	37.5966 8268	37.8697 6171	38.1453 7807	38.4235 5738	35
36	38.4660 8859	38.7533 3552	39.0433 3145	39.3361 0496	39.6316 8498	36
37	39.6103 3642	39.9148 0775	40.2222 8005	40.5327 8549	40.8463 5661	37
38	40.7588 7518	41.0811 1945	41.4066 3217	41.7354 4942	42.0676 0771	38
39	41.9117 2096	42.2522 9078	42.5964 1256	42.9441 2666	43.2954 7391	39
40	43.0688 8992	43.4283 4199	43.7916 4612	44.1588 4730	44.5299 9106	40
41	44.2303 9825	44.6092 9342	44.9923 5783	45.3796 4153	45.7711 9518	41
42	45.3962 6225	45.7951 6547	46.1985 7281	46.6065 3974	47.0191 2249	42
43	46.5664 9823	46.9859 7866	47.4103 1626	47.8395 7244	48.2738 0940	43
44	47.7411 2260	48.1817 5357	48.6276 1355	49.0787 7030	49.5352 9254	44
45	48.9201 5181	49.3825 1088	49.8504 9011	50.3241 6415	50.8036 0871	45
46	50.1036 0238	50.5882 7134	51.0789 7152	51.5757 8497	52.0787 9492	46
47	51.2914 9089	51.7990 5581	52.3130 8347	52.8336 6390	53.3608 8839	47
48	52.4838 3398	53.0148 8521	53.5528 5177	54.0978 3222	54.6499 2654	48
49	53.6806 4836	54.2357 8056	54.7983 0234	55.3683 2138	55.9459 4697	49
50	54.8819 5079	55.4617 6298	56.0494 6123	56.6451 6299	57.2489 8752	50
51	56.0877 5810	56.6928 5366	57.3063 5459	57.9283 8880	58.5590 8620	51
52	57.2980 8720	57.9290 7388	58.5690 0872	59.2180 3075	59.8762 8125	52
53	58.5129 5502	59.1704 4502	59.8374 5001	60.5141 2090	61.2006 1111	53
54	59.7323 7860	60.4169 8854	61.1117 0499	61.8166 9150	62.5321 1442	54
55	60.9563 7502	61.6687 2600	62.3918 0030	63.1257 7496	63.8708 3004	55
56	62.1849 6143	62.9256 7902	63.6777 6272	64.4414 0384	65.2167 9703	56
57	63.4181 5504	64.1878 6935	64.9696 1913	65.7636 1086	66.5700 5469	57
58	64.6559 7312	65.4553 1881	66.2673 9655	67.0924 2891	67.9306 4248	58
59	65.8984 3302	66.7280 4930	67.5711 2212	68.4278 9105	69.2986 0013	59
60	67.1455 5214	68.0060 8284	68.8808 2310	69.7700 3051	70.6739 6755	60

TABLE III

N	3/8	5/12	11/24	1/2	13/24	N
61	68.3973 4796	69.2894 4152	70.1965 2687	71.1188 8066	72.0567 8487	61
62	69.6538 3802	70.5781 4753	71.5182 6095	72.4744 7507	73.4470 9245	62
63	70.9150 3991	71.8722 2314	72.8460 5298	73.8368 4744	74.8449 3087	63
64	72.1809 7131	73.1716 9074	74.1799 3073	75.2060 3168	76.2503 4091	64
65	73.4516 4995	74.4765 7278	75.5199 2207	76.5820 6184	77.6633 6359	65
66	74.7270 9364	75.7868 9183	76.8660 5505	77.9649 7215	79.0840 4015	66
67	76.0073 2024	77.1026 7055	78.2183 5780	79.3547 9701	80.5124 1203	67
68	77.2923 4769	78.4239 3168	79.5768 5861	80.7515 7099	81.9485 2093	68
69	78.5821 9399	79.7506 9806	80.9415 8588	82.1553 2885	83.3924 0875	69
70	79.8768 7722	81.0829 9264	82.3125 6815	83.5661 0549	84.8441 1763	70
71	81.1764 1551	82.4208 3844	83.6898 3408	84.9839 3602	86.3036 8994	71
72	82.4808 2707	83.7642 5860	85.0734 1249	86.4088 5570	87.7711 6826	72
73	83.7901 3017	85.1132 7634	86.4633 3230	87.8408 9998	89.2465 9542	73
74	85.1043 4316	86.4679 1499	87.8596 2257	89.2801 0448	90.7300 1448	74
75	86.4234 8444	87.8281 9797	89.2623 1251	90.7265 0500	92.2214 6872	75
76	87.7475 7251	89.1941 4880	90.6714 3144	92.1801 3752	93.7210 0168	76
77	89.0766 2591	90.5657 9108	92.0870 0883	93.6410 3821	95.2286 5710	77
78	90.4106 6326	91.9431 4855	93.5090 7429	95.1092 4340	96.7444 7900	78
79	91.7497 0324	93.3262 4500	94.9376 5755	96.5847 8962	98.2685 1159	79
80	93.0937 6463	94.7151 0435	96.3727 8848	98.0677 1357	99.8007 9936	80
81	94.4428 6625	96.1097 5062	97.8144 9709	99.5580 5214	101.3413 8702	81
82	95.7970 2700	97.5102 0792	99.2628 1354	101.0558 4240	102.8903 1954	82
83	97.1562 6585	98.9165 0045	100.7177 6810	102.5611 2161	104.4476 4210	83
84	98.5206 0184	100.3286 5253	102.1793 9120	104.0739 2722	106.0134 0016	84
85	99.8900 5410	101.7466 8859	103.6477 1341	105.5942 9685	107.5876 3941	85
86	101.2646 4180	103.1706 3312	105.1227 6543	107.1222 6834	109.1704 0579	86
87	102.6443 8421	104.6005 1076	106.6045 7811	108.6578 7968	110.7617 4549	87
88	104.0293 0065	106.0363 4622	108.0931 8242	110.2011 6908	112.3617 0495	88
89	105.4194 1053	107.4781 6433	109.5886 0951	111.7521 7492	113.9703 3085	89
90	106.8147 3332	108.9259 9002	111.0908 9064	113.3109 3580	115.5876 7014	90
91	108.2152 8857	110.3798 4831	112.6000 5722	114.8774 9048	117.2137 7002	91
92	109.6210 9590	111.8397 6434	114.1161 4081	116.4518 7793	118.8486 7794	92
93	111.0321 7501	113.3057 6336	115.6391 7313	118.0341 3732	120.4924 4161	93
94	112.4485 4567	114.7778 7071	117.1691 8600	119.6243 0800	122.1451 0901	94
95	113.8702 2771	116.2561 1184	118.7062 1144	121.2224 2954	123.8067 2835	95
96	115.2972 4107	117.7405 1230	120.2502 8157	122.8285 4169	125.4773 4812	96
97	116.7296 0572	119.2310 9777	121.8014 2870	124.4426 8440	127.1570 1709	97
98	118.1673 4174	120.7278 9401	123.3596 8525	126.0648 9782	128.8457 8427	98
99	119.6104 6927	122.2309 2690	124.9250 8380	127.6952 2231	130.5436 9893	99
100	121.0590 0853	123.7402 2243	126.4976 5711	129.3336 9842	132.2508 1064	100
101	122.5129 7981	125.2558 0669	128.0774 3803	130.9803 6692	133.9671 6919	101
102	123.9724 0349	126.7777 0589	129.6644 5962	132.6352 6875	135.6928 2469	102
103	125.4373 0000	128.3059 4633	131.2587 5506	134.2984 4509	137.4278 2749	103
104	126.9076 8988	129.8405 5444	132.8603 5769	135.9699 3732	139.1722 2823	104
105	128.3835 9371	131.3815 5675	134.4693 0100	137.6497 8701	140.9260 7780	105
106	129.8650 3219	132.9289 7990	136.0856 1863	139.3380 3594	142.6894 2738	106
107	131.3520 2606	134.4828 5065	137.7093 4438	141.0347 2612	144.4623 2845	107
108	132.8445 9616	136.0431 9586	139.3405 1221	142.7398 9975	146.2448 3273	108
109	134.3427 6339	137.6100 4251	140.9791 5622	144.4535 9925	148.0369 9224	109
110	135.8465 4876	139.1834 1769	142.6253 1069	146.1758 6725	149.8388 5928	110
111	137.3559 7332	140.7633 4859	144.2790 1003	147.9067 4658	151.6504 8644	111
112	138.8710 5822	142.3498 6255	145.9402 8882	149.6462 8032	153.4719 2657	112
113	140.3918 2468	143.9429 8697	147.6091 8182	151.3945 1172	155.3032 3284	113
114	141.9182 9403	145.5427 4942	149.2857 2390	153.1514 8428	157.1444 5868	114
115	143.4504 8763	147.1491 7754	150.9699 5013	154.9172 4170	158.9956 5783	115
116	144.9884 2696	148.7622 9911	152.6618 9574	156.6918 2791	160.8568 8431	116
117	146.5321 3356	150.3821 4203	154.3615 9609	158.4752 8704	162.7281 9244	117
118	148.0816 2906	152.0087 3429	156.0690 8674	160.2676 6348	164.6096 3681	118
119	149.6369 3517	153.6421 0401	157.7844 0339	162.0690 0180	166.5012 7235	119
120	151.1980 7368	155.2822 7945	159.5075 8191	163.8793 4681	168.4031 5424	120

TABLE III

N	3/8	5/12	11/24	1/2	13/24	N
121	152.7650 6645	156.9292 8894	161.2386 5832	165.6987 4354	170.3153 3799	121
122	154.3379 3545	158.5831 6098	162.9776 6884	167.5272 3726	172.2378 7940	122
123	155.9167 0271	160.2439 2415	164.7246 4982	169.3648 7344	174.1708 3458	123
124	157.5013 9034	161.9116 0717	166.4796 3780	171.2116 9781	176.1142 5994	124
125	159.0920 2056	163.5862 3887	168.2426 6947	173.0677 5630	178.0682 1218	125
126	160.6886 1563	165.2678 4819	170.0137 8171	174.9330 9508	180.0327 4833	126
127	162.2911 9794	166.9564 6423	171.7930 1154	176.8077 6056	182.0079 2572	127
128	163.8997 8994	168.6521 1616	173.5803 9618	178.6917 9936	183.9938 0198	128
129	165.5144 1415	170.3548 3331	175.3759 7299	180.5852 5836	185.9904 3507	129
130	167.1350 9320	172.0646 4512	177.1797 7954	182.4881 8465	187.9978 8326	130
131	168.7618 4980	173.7815 8114	178.9918 5353	184.4006 2557	190.0162 0513	131
132	170.3947 0674	175.5056 7106	180.8122 3285	186.3226 2870	192.0454 5958	132
133	172.0336 8689	177.2369 4469	182.6409 5559	188.2542 4184	194.0857 0582	133
134	173.6788 1321	178.9754 3196	184.4780 5997	190.1955 1305	196.1370 0339	134
135	175.3301 0876	180.7211 6293	186.3235 8441	192.1464 9062	198.1994 1216	135
136	176.9875 9667	182.4741 6777	188.1775 6750	194.1072 2307	200.2729 9231	136
137	178.6513 0016	184.2344 7680	190.0400 4802	196.0777 5919	202.3578 0435	137
138	180.3212 4253	186.0021 2046	191.9110 6491	198.0581 4798	204.4539 0912	138
139	181.9974 4719	187.7771 2929	193.7906 5729	200.0484 3872	206.5613 6780	139
140	183.6799 3762	189.5595 3400	195.6788 6447	202.0486 8092	208.6802 4187	140
141	185.3687 3739	191.3493 6539	197.5757 2593	204.0589 2432	210.8105 9318	141
142	187.0638 7015	193.1466 5441	199.4812 8134	206.0792 1894	212.9524 8390	142
143	188.7653 5966	194.9514 3214	201.3955 7055	208.1096 1504	215.1059 7652	143
144	190.4732 2976	196.7637 2977	203.3186 3358	210.1501 6311	217.2711 3389	144
145	192.1875 0437	198.5835 7865	205.2505 1065	212.2009 1393	219.4480 1920	145
146	193.9082 0752	200.4110 1022	207.1912 4216	214.2619 1850	221.6366 9597	146
147	195.6353 6329	202.2460 5610	209.1408 6868	216.3332 2809	223.8372 2807	147
148	197.3689 9591	204.0887 4800	211.0994 3100	218.4148 9423	226.0496 7972	148
149	199.1091 2964	205.9391 1778	213.0669 7006	220.5069 6870	228.2741 1549	149
150	200.8557 8888	207.7971 9744	215.0435 2700	222.6095 0354	230.5106 0028	150
151	202.6089 9809	209.6630 1910	217.0291 4317	224.7225 5106	232.7591 9937	151
152	204.3687 8183	211.5366 1501	219.0238 6008	226.8461 6382	235.0199 7836	152
153	206.1351 6476	213.4180 1757	221.0277 1943	228.9803 9464	237.2930 0325	153
154	207.9081 7163	215.3072 5931	223.0407 6315	231.1252 9661	239.5783 4035	154
155	209.6878 2727	217.2043 7289	225.0630 3331	233.2809 2309	241.8760 5636	155
156	211.4741 5662	219.1093 9111	227.0945 7222	235.4473 2771	244.1862 1833	156
157	213.2671 8471	221.0223 4691	229.1354 2234	237.6245 6435	246.5088 9368	157
158	215.0669 3665	222.9432 7336	231.1856 2636	239.8126 8717	248.8441 5018	158
159	216.8734 3767	224.8722 0366	233.2452 2714	242.0117 5060	251.1920 5600	159
160	218.6867 1306	226.8091 7118	235.3142 6777	244.2218 0936	253.5526 7964	160
161	220.5067 8823	228.7542 0939	237.3927 9150	246.4429 1840	255.9260 8998	161
162	222.3336 8869	230.7073 5193	239.4808 4179	248.6751 3300	258.3123 5630	162
163	224.1674 4002	232.6686 3256	241.5784 6232	250.9185 0866	260.7115 4823	163
164	226.0080 6792	234.6380 8520	243.6856 9693	253.1731 0121	263.1237 3579	164
165	227.8555 9818	236.6157 4389	245.8025 8971	255.4389 6671	265.5489 8936	165
166	229.7100 5667	238.6016 4282	247.9291 8491	257.7161 6154	267.9873 7971	166
167	231.5714 6938	240.5958 1633	250.0655 2701	260.0047 4235	270.4389 7802	167
168	233.4398 6239	242.5982 9890	252.2116 6068	262.3047 6606	272.9038 5582	168
169	235.3152 6188	244.6091 2514	254.3676 3079	264.6162 8989	275.3820 8504	169
170	237.1976 9411	246.6283 2983	256.5334 8243	266.9393 7134	277.8737 3800	170
171	239.0871 8546	248.6559 4787	258.7092 6089	269.2740 6820	280.3788 8741	171
172	240.9837 6241	250.6920 1432	260.8950 1167	271.6204 3854	282.8976 0639	172
173	242.8874 5151	252.7365 6438	263.0907 8047	273.9785 4073	285.4299 6842	173
174	244.7982 7946	254.7896 3340	265.2966 1322	276.3484 3344	287.9760 4742	174
175	246.7162 7301	256.8512 5687	267.5125 5603	278.7301 7561	290.5359 1767	175
176	248.6414 5903	258.9214 7044	269.7386 5524	281.1238 2648	293.1096 5389	176
177	250.5738 6450	261.0003 0990	271.9749 5741	283.5294 4562	295.6973 3119	177
178	252.5135 1649	263.0878 1120	274.2215 0930	285.9470 9284	298.2990 2506	178
179	254.4604 4218	265.1840 1041	276.4783 5789	288.3768 2831	300.9148 1145	179
180	256.4146 6884	267.2889 4379	278.7455 5036	290.8187 1245	303.5447 6668	180

TABLE III

N	3/8	5/12	11/24	1/2	13/24	N
181	258.3762 2385	269.4026 4772	281.0231 3413	293.2728 0601	306.1889 6750	181
182	260.3451 3469	271.5251 5875	283.3111 5683	295.7391 7004	308.8474 9107	182
183	262.3214 2894	273.6565 1358	285.6096 6630	298.2178 6589	311.5204 1498	183
184	264.3051 3430	275.7967 4905	287.9187 1060	300.7089 5522	314.2078 1723	184
185	266.2962 7855	277.9459 0217	290.2383 3803	303.2125 0000	316.9097 7624	185
186	268.2948 8960	280.1040 1010	292.5685 9708	305.7285 6250	319.6263 7086	186
187	270.3009 9543	282.2711 1014	294.9095 3648	308.2572 0531	322.3576 8037	187
188	272.3146 2417	284.4472 3977	297.2612 0519	310.7984 9134	325.1037 8447	188
189	274.3358 0401	286.6324 3660	299.6236 5238	313.3524 8379	327.8647 6330	189
190	276.3645 6327	288.8267 3842	301.9969 2745	315.9192 4621	330.6406 9744	190
191	278.4009 3038	291.0301 8316	304.3810 8004	318.4988 4244	333.4316 6788	191
192	280.4449 3387	293.2428 0892	306.7761 5999	321.0913 3666	336.2377 5608	192
193	282.4966 0237	295.4646 5396	309.1822 1739	323.6967 9334	339.0590 4393	193
194	284.5559 6463	297.6957 5669	311.5993 0255	326.3152 7731	341.8956 1375	194
195	286.6230 4950	299.9361 5567	314.0274 6602	328.9468 5369	344.7475 4832	195
196	288.6978 8594	302.1858 8965	316.4667 5857	331.5915 8796	347.6149 3088	196
197	290.7805 0301	304.4449 9753	318.9172 3122	334.2495 4590	350.4978 4509	197
198	292.8709 2990	306.7135 1835	321.3789 3519	336.9207 9363	353.3963 7508	198
199	294.9691 9588	308.9914 9134	323.8519 2198	339.6053 9760	356.3106 0545	199
200	297.0753 3037	311.2789 5589	326.3362 4329	342.3034 2459	359.2406 2123	200
201	299.1893 6286	313.5759 5154	328.8319 5107	345.0149 4171	362.1865 0792	201
202	301.3113 2297	315.8825 1801	331.3390 9751	347.7400 1642	365.1483 5151	202
203	303.4412 4043	318.1986 9516	333.8577 3504	350.4787 1650	368.1262 3841	203
204	305.5791 4508	320.5245 2306	336.3879 1633	353.2311 1008	371.1202 5554	204
205	307.7250 6687	322.8600 4191	338.9296 9428	355.9972 6563	374.1304 9026	205
206	309.8790 3587	325.2052 9208	341.4831 2204	358.7772 5196	377.1570 3041	206
207	312.0410 8226	327.5603 1413	344.0482 5302	361.5711 3822	380.1999 6433	207
208	314.2112 3632	329.9251 4877	346.6251 4084	364.3789 9391	383.2593 8080	208
209	316.3895 2845	332.2998 3689	349.2138 3941	367.2008 8888	386.3353 6911	209
210	318.5759 8918	334.6844 1955	351.8144 0284	370.0368 9333	389.4280 1903	210
211	320.7706 4914	337.0789 3796	354.4268 8552	372.8870 7779	392.5374 2080	211
212	322.9735 3908	339.4834 3354	357.0513 4208	375.7515 1318	395.6636 6516	212
213	325.1846 8985	341.8979 4784	359.6878 2739	378.6302 7075	398.8068 4335	213
214	327.4041 3244	344.3225 2263	362.3363 9660	381.5234 2210	401.9670 4708	214
215	329.6318 9793	346.7571 9980	364.9971 0509	384.4310 3921	405.1443 6859	215
216	331.8680 1755	349.2020 2147	367.6700 0849	387.3531 9441	408.3389 0058	216
217	334.1125 2262	351.6570 2989	370.3551 6269	390.2899 6038	411.5507 3629	217
218	336.3654 4458	354.1222 6752	373.0526 2385	393.2414 1018	414.7799 6945	218
219	338.6268 1499	356.5977 7696	375.7624 4838	396.2076 1723	418.0266 9428	219
220	340.8966 6555	359.0836 0104	378.4846 9293	399.1886 5532	421.2910 0554	220
221	343.1750 2805	361.5797 8271	381.2194 1444	402.1845 9859	424.5729 9849	221
222	345.4619 3440	364.0863 6513	383.9666 7009	405.1955 2159	427.8727 6890	222
223	347.7574 1665	366.6033 9166	386.7265 1733	408.2214 9920	431.1904 1306	223
224	350.0615 0697	369.1309 0579	389.4990 1387	411.2626 0669	434.5260 2780	224
225	352.3742 3762	371.6689 5123	392.2842 1768	414.3189 1973	437.8797 1045	225
226	354.6956 4101	374.2175 7186	395.0821 8701	417.3905 1432	441.2515 5888	226
227	357.0257 4966	376.7768 1174	397.8929 8037	420.4774 6690	444.6416 7149	227
228	359.3645 9622	379.3467 1512	400.7166 5653	423.5798 5423	448.0501 4722	228
229	361.7122 1346	381.9273 2644	403.5532 7454	426.6977 5350	451.4770 8551	229
230	364.0686 3426	384.5186 9030	406.4028 9371	429.8312 4227	454.9225 8639	230
231	366.4338 9164	387.1208 5151	409.2655 7364	432.9803 9848	458.3867 5040	231
232	368.8080 1873	389.7338 5505	412.1413 7419	436.1453 0047	461.8696 7863	232
233	371.1910 4880	392.3577 4612	415.0303 5549	439.3260 2697	465.3714 7273	233
234	373.5830 1524	394.9925 7006	417.9325 7795	442.5226 5711	468.8922 3487	234
235	375.9839 5154	397.6383 7243	420.8481 0227	445.7352 7039	472.4320 6781	235
236	378.3938 9136	400.2951 9899	423.7769 8940	448.9639 4675	475.9910 7484	236
237	380.8128 6845	402.9630 9565	426.7193 0060	452.2087 6648	479.5693 5983	237
238	383.2409 1671	405.6421 0855	429.6750 9740	455.4698 1031	483.1670 2720	238
239	385.6780 7015	408.3322 8400	432.6444 4159	458.7471 5936	486.7841 8193	239
240	388.1243 6291	411.0336 6852	435.6273 9528	462.0408 9516	490.4209 2958	240

TABLE III

N	3/8	5/12	11/24	1/2	13/24	N
241	390.5798 2927	413.7463 0880	438.6240 2085	465.3510 9964	494.0773 7628	241
242	393.0445 0363	416.4702 5175	441.6343 8094	468.6778 5514	497.7536 2874	242
243	395.5184 2052	419.2055 4447	444.6585 3852	472.0212 4441	501.4497 9423	243
244	398.0016 1460	421.9522 3424	447.6965 5682	475.3813 5063	505.1659 8061	244
245	400.4941 2065	424.7103 6855	450.7484 9938	478.7582 5739	508.9022 9634	245
246	402.9959 7361	427.4799 9508	453.8144 3000	482.1520 4867	512.6588 5044	246
247	405.5072 0851	430.2611 6173	456.8944 1280	485.5628 0892	516.4357 5255	247
248	408.0278 6054	433.0539 1657	459.9885 1219	488.9906 2296	520.2331 1288	248
249	410.5579 6502	435.8583 0789	463.0967 9287	492.4355 7608	524.0510 4224	249
250	413.0975 5738	438.6743 8417	466.2193 1984	495.8977 5396	527.8896 5205	250
251	415.6466 7322	441.5021 9411	469.3561 5839	499.3772 4273	531.7490 5433	251
252	418.2053 4825	444.3417 8658	472.5073 7412	502.8741 2894	535.6293 6171	252
253	420.7736 1830	447.1932 1069	475.6730 3291	506.3884 9958	539.5306 8742	253
254	423.3515 1937	450.0565 1574	478.8532 0098	509.9204 4208	543.4531 4531	254
255	425.9390 8757	452.9317 5122	482.0479 4482	513.4700 4429	547.3968 4985	255
256	428.5363 5915	455.8189 6685	485.2573 3123	517.0373 9451	551.3619 1612	256
257	431.1433 7050	458.7182 1254	488.4814 2734	520.6225 8149	555.3484 5983	257
258	433.7601 5814	461.6295 3843	491.7203 0054	524.2256 9439	559.3565 9732	258
259	436.3867 5873	464.5529 9484	494.9740 1859	527.8468 2287	563.3864 4556	259
260	439.0232 0907	467.4886 3232	498.2426 4951	531.4860 5698	567.4381 2214	260
261	441.6695 4611	470.4365 0162	501.5262 6165	535.1434 8727	571.5117 4530	261
262	444.3258 0691	473.3966 5371	504.8249 2368	538.8192 0470	575.6074 3392	262
263	446.9920 2868	476.3691 3977	508.1387 0458	542.5133 0073	579.7253 0752	263
264	449.6682 4879	479.3540 1118	511.4676 7365	546.2258 6723	583.8654 8627	264
265	452.3545 0472	482.3513 1956	514.8119 0048	549.9569 9657	588.0280 9098	265
266	455.0508 3411	485.3611 1673	518.1714 5503	553.7067 8155	592.2132 4314	266
267	457.7572 7474	488.3834 5471	521.5464 0753	557.4753 1546	596.4210 6488	267
268	460.4738 6452	491.4183 8578	524.9368 2856	561.2626 9203	600.6516 7898	268
269	463.2006 4152	494.4659 6238	528.3427 8903	565.0690 0549	604.9052 0891	269
270	465.9376 4392	497.5262 3723	531.7643 6014	568.8943 5052	609.1817 7879	270
271	468.6849 1009	500.5992 6321	535.2016 1346	572.7388 2227	613.4815 1342	271
272	471.4424 7850	503.6850 9348	538.6546 2086	576.6025 1638	617.8045 3829	272
273	474.2103 8779	506.7837 8137	542.1234 5454	580.4855 2897	622.1509 7954	273
274	476.9886 7675	509.8953 8046	545.6081 8704	584.3879 5661	626.5209 6401	274
275	479.7773 8428	513.0199 4454	549.1088 9123	588.3098 9639	630.9146 1923	275
276	482.5765 4948	516.1575 2764	552.6256 4031	592.2514 4588	635.3320 7342	276
277	485.3862 1154	519.3081 8401	556.1585 0783	596.2127 0311	639.7734 5548	277
278	488.2064 0983	522.4719 6811	559.7075 6766	600.1937 6662	644.2388 9503	278
279	491.0371 8387	525.6489 3464	563.2728 9401	604.1947 3545	648.7285 2238	279
280	493.8785 7331	528.8391 3854	566.8545 6144	608.2157 0913	653.2424 6854	280
281	496.7306 1796	532.0426 3495	570.4526 4485	612.2567 8768	657.7808 6525	281
282	499.5933 5777	535.2594 7926	574.0672 1947	616.3180 7162	662.3438 4494	282
283	502.4668 3286	538.4897 2709	577.6983 6089	620.3996 6197	666.9315 4076	283
284	505.3510 8349	541.7334 3429	581.3461 4504	624.5016 6028	671.5440 8661	284
285	508.2461 5005	544.9906 5693	585.0106 4821	628.6241 6859	676.1816 1708	285
286	511.1520 7311	548.2614 5133	588.6919 4701	632.7672 8943	680.8442 6750	286
287	514.0688 9339	551.5458 7405	592.3901 1844	636.9311 2588	685.5321 7395	287
288	516.9966 5174	554.8439 8186	596.1052 3981	641.1157 8150	690.2454 7323	288
289	519.9353 8918	558.1558 3178	599.8373 8883	645.3213 6041	694.9843 0287	289
290	522.8851 4689	561.4814 8108	603.5866 4353	649.5479 6721	699.7488 0118	290
291	525.8459 6619	564.8209 8725	607.3530 8231	653.7957 0705	704.5391 0719	291
292	528.8178 8857	568.1744 0803	611.1367 8394	658.0646 8559	709.3553 6069	292
293	531.8009 5565	571.5418 0140	614.9378 2753	662.3550 0901	714.1977 0222	293
294	534.7952 0923	574.9232 2557	618.7562 9257	666.6667 8406	719.0662 7311	294
295	537.8006 9127	578.3187 3901	622.5922 5892	671.0001 1798	723.9612 1542	295
296	540.8174 4386	581.7284 0042	626.4458 0677	675.3551 1857	728.8826 7201	296
297	543.8455 0927	585.1522 6876	630.3170 1672	679.7318 9416	733.8307 8648	297
298	546.8849 2993	588.5904 0321	634.2059 6971	684.1305 5363	738.8057 0324	298
299	549.9357 4842	592.0428 6322	638.1127 4707	688.5512 0640	743.8075 6747	299
300	552.9980 0748	595.5097 0849	642.0374 3050	692.9939 6243	748.8365 2512	300

TABLE III

N	3/8	5/12	11/24	1/2	13/24	N
301	556.0717 5000	598.9909 9894	645.9801 0205	697.4589 3224	753.8927 2257	301
302	559.1570 1907	602.4867 9477	649.9408 4419	701.9462 2691	758.9763 0855	302
303	562.2538 5789	605.9971 5641	653.9197 3972	706.4559 5804	764.0874 3022	303
304	565.3623 0986	609.5221 4457	657.9168 7186	710.9882 3783	769.2262 3713	304
305	568.4824 1852	613.0618 2017	661.9323 2419	715.5431 7902	774.3928 7925	305
306	571.6142 2759	616.6162 4442	665.9661 8068	720.1208 9491	779.5875 0735	306
307	574.7577 8094	620.1854 7877	670.0185 2567	724.7214 9939	784.8102 7301	307
308	577.9131 2262	623.7695 8493	674.0894 4391	729.3451 0689	790.0613 2866	308
309	581.0802 9683	627.3686 2487	678.1790 2053	733.9918 3242	795.3408 2752	309
310	584.2593 4794	630.9826 6081	682.2873 4104	738.6617 9158	800.6489 2367	310
311	587.4503 2050	634.6117 5523	686.4144 9136	743.3551 0054	805.9857 7201	311
312	590.6532 5920	638.2559 7087	690.5605 5778	748.0718 7604	811.3515 2827	312
313	593.8682 0892	641.9153 7075	694.7256 2700	752.8122 3542	816.7463 4905	313
314	597.0952 1470	645.5900 1813	698.9097 8612	757.5762 9660	822.1703 9177	314
315	600.3343 2176	649.2799 7654	703.1131 2264	762.3641 7808	827.6238 1473	315
316	603.5855 7547	652.9853 0977	707.3357 2445	767.1759 9897	833.1067 7706	316
317	606.8490 2137	656.7060 8190	711.5776 7986	772.0118 7897	838.6194 3877	317
318	610.1247 0520	660.4423 5724	715.8390 7756	776.8719 3836	844.1619 6073	318
319	613.4126 7285	664.1942 0039	720.1200 0666	781.7562 9806	849.7345 0468	319
320	616.7129 7037	667.9616 7623	724.4205 5669	786.6650 7955	855.3372 3325	320
321	620.0256 4401	671.7448 4988	728.7408 1758	791.5984 0494	860.9703 0993	321
322	623.3507 4018	675.5437 8675	733.0808 7966	796.5563 9697	866.6338 9911	322
323	626.6883 0545	679.3585 5253	737.4408 3369	801.5391 7895	872.3281 6606	323
324	630.0383 8660	683.1892 1317	741.8207 7084	806.5468 7485	878.0532 7696	324
325	633.4010 3055	687.0358 3489	746.2207 8271	811.5796 0922	883.8093 9888	325
326	636.7762 8441	690.8984 8420	750.6409 6130	816.6375 0727	889.5966 9979	326
327	640.1641 9548	694.7772 2789	755.0813 9904	821.7206 9480	895.4153 4858	327
328	643.5648 1121	698.6721 3300	759.5421 8878	826.8292 9828	901.2655 1505	328
329	646.9781 7925	702.5832 6689	764.0234 2382	831.9634 4477	907.1473 6992	329
330	650.4043 4742	706.5106 9717	768.5251 9784	837.1232 6199	913.0610 8485	330
331	653.8433 6373	710.4544 9174	773.0476 0500	842.3088 7830	919.0068 3239	331
332	657.2952 7634	714.4147 1879	777.5907 3985	847.5204 2270	924.9847 8606	332
333	660.7601 3363	718.3914 4678	782.1546 9741	852.7580 2481	930.9951 2032	333
334	664.2379 8413	722.3847 4448	786.7395 7311	858.0218 1493	937.0380 1056	334
335	667.7288 7657	726.3946 8091	791.3454 6282	863.3119 2401	943.1136 3311	335
336	671.2328 5986	730.4213 2542	795.9724 6286	868.6284 8363	949.2221 6529	336
337	674.7499 8308	734.4647 4761	800.6206 6998	873.9716 2605	955.3637 8535	337
338	678.2802 9552	738.5250 1739	805.2901 8138	879.3414 8418	961.5386 7253	338
339	681.8238 4663	742.6022 0496	809.9810 9471	884.7381 9160	967.7470 0700	339
340	685.3806 8605	746.6963 8082	814.6935 0806	890.1618 8256	973.9889 6996	340
341	688.9508 6362	750.8076 1574	819.4275 1998	895.6126 9197	980.2647 4354	341
342	692.5344 2936	754.9359 8080	824.1832 2944	901.0907 5543	986.5745 1090	342
343	696.1314 3347	759.0815 4739	828.9607 3591	906.5962 0920	992.9184 5617	343
344	699.7419 2635	763.2443 8717	833.7601 3928	912.1291 9025	999.2967 6448	344
345	703.3659 5857	767.4245 7211	838.5815 3992	917.6898 3620	1005.7096 2195	345
346	707.0035 8092	771.6221 7450	843.4250 3865	923.2782 8538	1012.1572 1574	346
347	710.6548 4434	775.8372 6689	848.2907 3674	928.8946 7681	1018.6397 3399	347
348	714.3198 0001	780.0699 2217	853.1787 3595	934.5391 5019	1025.1573 6588	348
349	717.9984 9926	784.3202 1351	858.0891 3849	940.2118 4594	1031.7103 0161	349
350	721.6909 9363	788.5882 1440	863.0220 4704	945.9129 0517	1038.2987 3241	350
351	725.3973 3486	792.8739 9863	867.9775 6476	951.6424 6970	1044.9228 5055	351
352	729.1175 7486	797.1776 4029	872.9557 9526	957.4006 8205	1051.5828 4932	352
353	732.8517 6577	801.4992 1379	877.9568 4266	963.1876 8546	1058.2789 2309	353
354	736.5999 5989	805.8387 9385	882.9808 1152	969.0036 2389	1065.0112 6725	354
355	740.3622 0974	810.1964 5549	888.0278 0691	974.8486 4201	1071.7800 7829	355
356	744.1385 6803	814.5722 7406	893.0979 3435	980.7228 8522	1078.5855 5371	356
357	747.9290 8766	818.9663 2520	898.1912 9989	986.6264 9964	1085.4278 9213	357
358	751.7338 2174	823.3786 8489	903.3080 1001	992.5596 3214	1092.3072 9321	358
359	755.5528 2357	827.8094 2941	908.4481 7172	998.5224 3030	1099.2239 5771	359
360	759.3861 4666	832.2586 3536	913.6118 9251	1004.5150 4245	1106.1780 8748	360

TABLE III

N	7/12	5/8	2/3	17/24	3/4	N
1	1.0000 0000	1.0000 0000	1.0000 0000	1.0000 0000	1.0000 0000	1
2	2.0058 3333	2.0062 5000	2.0066 6667	2.0070 8333	2.0075 0000	2
3	3.0175 3403	3.0187 8906	3.0200 4444	3.0213 0017	3.0225 5625	3
4	4.0351 3631	4.0376 5649	4.0401 7807	4.0427 0105	4.0452 2542	4
5	5.0586 7460	5.0628 9185	5.0671 1259	5.0713 3685	5.0755 6461	5
6	6.0881 8354	6.0945 3492	6.1008 9335	6.1072 5882	6.1136 3135	6
7	7.1236 9794	7.1326 2576	7.1415 6597	7.1505 1857	7.1594 8358	7
8	8.1652 5285	8.1772 0468	8.1891 7641	8.2011 6807	8.2131 7971	8
9	9.2128 8349	9.2283 1220	9.2437 7092	9.2592 5968	9.2747 7856	9
10	10.2666 2531	10.2859 8916	10.3053 9606	10.3248 4610	10.3443 3940	10
11	11.3265 1396	11.3502 7659	11.3740 9870	11.3979 8043	11.4219 2194	11
12	12.3925 8529	12.4212 1582	12.4499 2602	12.4787 1613	12.5075 8636	12
13	13.4648 7537	13.4988 4842	13.5329 2553	13.5671 0703	13.6013 9325	13
14	14.5434 2048	14.5832 1622	14.6231 4503	14.6632 0737	14.7034 0370	14
15	15.6282 5710	15.6743 6132	15.7206 3266	15.7670 7176	15.8136 7923	15
16	16.7194 2193	16.7723 2608	16.8254 3688	16.8787 5518	16.9322 8183	16
17	17.8169 5189	17.8771 5312	17.9376 0646	17.9983 1303	18.0592 7394	17
18	18.9208 8411	18.9888 8532	19.0571 9051	19.1258 0108	19.1947 1849	18
19	20.0312 5593	20.1075 6586	20.1842 3844	20.2612 7551	20.3386 7888	19
20	21.1481 0493	21.2332 3814	21.3188 0003	21.4047 9288	21.4912 1897	20
21	22.2714 6887	22.3659 4588	22.4609 2536	22.5564 1016	22.6524 0312	21
22	23.4013 8577	23.5057 3304	23.6106 6487	23.7161 8473	23.8222 9614	22
23	24.5378 9386	24.6526 4387	24.7680 6930	24.8841 7437	25.0009 6336	23
24	25.6810 3157	25.8067 2290	25.9331 8976	26.0604 3727	26.1884 7059	24
25	26.8308 3759	26.9680 1492	27.1060 7769	27.2450 3204	27.3848 8412	25
26	27.9873 5081	28.1365 6501	28.2867 8488	28.4380 1768	28.5902 7075	26
27	29.1506 1036	29.3124 1854	29.4753 6344	29.6394 5364	29.8046 9778	27
28	30.3206 5558	30.4956 2116	30.6718 6587	30.8493 9977	31.0282 3301	28
29	31.4975 2607	31.6862 1879	31.8763 4497	32.0679 1635	32.2609 4476	29
30	32.6812 6164	32.8842 5766	33.0888 5394	33.2950 6409	33.5029 0184	30
31	33.8719 0233	34.0897 8427	34.3094 4630	34.5309 0413	34.7541 7361	31
32	35.0694 8843	35.3028 4542	35.5381 7594	35.7754 9804	36.0148 2991	32
33	36.2740 6045	36.5234 8820	36.7750 9711	37.0289 0781	37.2849 4113	33
34	37.4856 5913	37.7517 6000	38.0202 6443	38.2911 9591	38.5645 7819	34
35	38.7043 2548	38.9877 0850	39.2737 3286	39.5624 2521	39.8538 1253	35
36	39.9301 0071	40.2313 8168	40.5355 5774	40.8426 5906	41.1527 1612	36
37	41.1630 2630	41.4828 2782	41.8057 9479	42.1319 6123	42.4613 6149	37
38	42.4031 4395	42.7420 9549	43.0845 0009	43.4303 9595	43.7798 2170	38
39	43.6504 9562	44.0092 3359	44.3717 3009	44.7380 2792	45.1081 7037	39
40	44.9051 2352	45.2842 9130	45.6675 4163	46.0549 2229	46.4464 8164	40
41	46.1670 7007	46.5673 1812	46.9719 9191	47.3811 4466	47.7948 3026	41
42	47.4363 7798	47.8583 6386	48.2851 3852	48.7167 6110	49.1532 9148	42
43	48.7130 9018	49.1574 7863	49.6070 3944	50.0618 3815	50.5219 4117	43
44	49.9972 4988	50.4647 1287	50.9377 5304	51.4164 4284	51.9008 5573	44
45	51.2889 0050	51.7801 1733	52.2773 3806	52.7806 4264	53.2901 1215	45
46	52.5880 8575	53.1037 4306	53.6258 5365	54.1545 0553	54.6897 8799	46
47	53.8948 4959	54.4356 4146	54.9833 5934	55.5380 9994	56.0999 6140	47
48	55.2092 3621	55.7758 6421	56.3499 1507	56.9314 9482	57.5207 1111	48
49	56.5312 9009	57.1244 6337	57.7255 8117	58.3347 5957	58.9521 1644	49
50	57.8610 5595	58.4814 9126	59.1104 1837	59.7479 6412	60.3942 5732	50
51	59.1985 7877	59.8470 0058	60.5044 8783	61.1711 7887	61.8472 1424	51
52	60.5439 0381	61.2210 4434	61.9078 5108	62.6044 7472	63.3110 6835	52
53	61.8970 7659	62.6036 7586	63.3205 7009	64.0479 2308	64.7859 0136	53
54	63.2581 4287	63.9949 4884	64.7427 0722	65.5015 9587	66.2717 9562	54
55	64.6271 4870	65.3949 1727	66.1743 2527	66.9655 6551	67.7688 3409	55
56	66.0041 4040	66.8036 3550	67.6154 8744	68.4399 0493	69.2771 0035	56
57	67.3891 6455	68.2211 5822	69.0662 5736	69.9246 8759	70.7966 7860	57
58	68.7822 6801	69.6475 4046	70.5266 9907	71.4199 8746	72.3276 5369	58
59	70.1834 9791	71.0828 3759	71.9968 7706	72.9258 7904	73.8701 1109	59
60	71.5929 0165	72.5271 0532	73.4768 5625	74.4424 3735	75.4241 3693	60

TABLE III

N	7/12	5/8	2/3	17/24	3/4	N
61	73.0105 2691	73.9803 9973	74.9667 0195	75.9697 3794	76.9898 1795	61
62	74.4364 2165	75.4427 7723	76.4664 7997	77.5078 5692	78.5672 4159	62
63	75.8706 3411	76.9142 9459	77.9762 5650	79.0568 7091	80.1564 9590	63
64	77.3132 1281	78.3950 0893	79.4960 9821	80.6168 5708	81.7576 6962	64
65	78.7642 0655	79.8849 7774	81.0260 7220	82.1878 9315	83.3708 5214	65
66	80.2236 6442	81.3842 5885	82.5662 4601	83.7700 5739	84.9961 3353	66
67	81.6916 3580	82.8929 1046	84.1166 8765	85.3634 2863	86.6336 0453	67
68	83.1681 7034	84.4109 9115	85.6774 6557	86.9680 8625	88.2833 5657	68
69	84.6533 1800	85.9385 5985	87.2486 4867	88.5841 1019	89.9454 8174	69
70	86.1471 2902	87.4756 7585	88.8303 0633	90.2115 8097	91.6200 7285	70
71	87.6496 5394	89.0223 9882	90.4225 0837	91.8505 7967	93.3072 2340	71
72	89.1609 4359	90.5787 8882	92.0253 2510	93.5011 8795	95.0070 2758	72
73	90.6810 4909	92.1449 0625	93.6388 2726	95.1634 8803	96.7195 8028	73
74	92.2100 2188	93.7208 1191	95.2630 8611	96.8375 6273	98.4449 7714	74
75	93.7479 1367	95.3065 6698	96.8981 7335	98.5234 9547	100.1833 1446	75
76	95.2947 7650	96.9022 3303	98.5441 6118	100.2213 7023	101.9346 8932	76
77	96.8506 6270	98.5078 7198	100.2011 2225	101.9312 7160	103.6991 9949	77
78	98.4156 2490	100.1235 4618	101.8691 2973	103.6532 8478	105.4769 4349	78
79	99.9897 1604	101.7493 1835	103.5482 5726	105.3874 9554	107.2680 2056	79
80	101.5729 8939	103.3852 5159	105.2385 7898	107.1339 9030	109.0725 3072	80
81	103.1654 9849	105.0314 0941	106.9401 6950	108.8928 5607	110.8905 7470	81
82	104.7672 9723	106.6878 5572	108.6531 0397	110.6641 8046	112.7222 5401	82
83	106.3784 3980	108.3546 5482	110.3774 5799	112.4480 5174	114.5676 7091	83
84	107.9989 8070	110.0318 7141	112.1133 0771	114.2445 5878	116.4269 2845	84
85	109.6289 7475	111.7195 7061	113.8607 2977	116.0537 9107	118.3001 3041	85
86	111.2684 7710	113.4178 1792	115.6198 0130	117.8758 3875	120.1873 8139	86
87	112.9175 4322	115.1266 7928	117.3905 9997	119.7107 9261	122.0887 8675	87
88	114.5762 2889	116.8462 2103	119.1732 0397	121.5587 4406	124.0044 5265	88
89	116.2445 9022	118.5765 0991	120.9676 9200	123.4197 8516	125.9344 8604	89
90	117.9226 8367	120.3176 1310	122.7741 4328	125.2940 0864	127.8789 9469	90
91	119.6105 6599	122.0695 9818	124.5926 3757	127.1815 0787	129.8380 8715	91
92	121.3082 9429	123.8325 3317	126.4232 5515	129.0823 7688	131.8118 7280	92
93	123.0159 2601	125.6064 8650	128.2660 7685	130.9967 1039	133.8004 6185	93
94	124.7335 1891	127.3915 2704	130.1211 8403	132.9246 0375	135.8039 6531	94
95	126.4611 3110	129.1877 2408	131.9886 5859	134.8661 5303	137.8224 9505	95
96	128.1988 2103	130.9951 4736	133.8685 8298	136.8214 5495	139.8561 6377	96
97	129.9466 4749	132.8138 6703	135.7610 4020	138.7906 0692	141.9050 8499	97
98	131.7046 6960	134.6439 5370	137.6661 1380	140.7737 0705	143.9693 7313	98
99	133.4729 4684	136.4854 7841	139.5838 8790	142.7708 5414	146.0491 4343	99
100	135.2515 3903	138.3385 1265	141.5144 4715	144.7821 4769	148.1445 1201	100
101	137.0405 0634	140.2031 2836	143.4578 7680	146.8076 8791	150.2555 9585	101
102	138.8399 0929	142.0793 9791	145.4142 6264	148.8475 7569	152.3825 1281	102
103	140.6498 0877	143.9673 9414	147.3836 9106	150.9019 1269	154.5253 8166	103
104	142.4702 6598	145.8671 9036	149.3662 4900	152.9708 0124	156.6843 2202	104
105	144.3013 4253	147.7788 6030	151.3620 2399	155.0543 4441	158.8594 5444	105
106	146.1431 0037	149.7024 7817	153.3711 0415	157.1526 4602	161.0509 0035	106
107	147.9956 0178	151.6381 1866	155.3935 7818	159.2658 1059	163.2587 8210	107
108	149.8589 0946	153.5858 5690	157.4295 3537	161.3939 4342	165.4832 2296	108
109	151.7330 8643	155.5457 6851	159.4790 6560	163.5371 5052	167.7243 4714	109
110	153.6181 9610	157.5179 2956	161.5422 5937	165.6955 3867	169.9822 7974	110
111	155.5143 0225	159.5024 1662	163.6192 0777	167.8692 1540	172.2571 4684	111
112	157.4214 6901	161.4993 0673	165.7100 0249	170.0582 8901	174.5490 7544	112
113	159.3397 6091	163.5086 7739	167.8147 3584	172.2628 6856	176.8581 9351	113
114	161.2692 4285	165.5306 0663	169.9335 0074	174.4830 6388	179.1846 2996	114
115	163.2099 8010	167.5651 7292	172.0663 9075	176.7189 8558	181.5285 1468	115
116	165.1620 3832	169.6124 5525	174.2135 0002	178.9707 4506	183.8899 7854	116
117	167.1254 8354	171.6725 3310	176.3749 2335	181.2384 5450	186.2691 5338	117
118	169.1003 8220	173.7454 8643	178.5507 5618	183.5222 2689	188.6661 7203	118
119	171.0868 0109	175.8313 9572	180.7410 9455	185.8221 7600	191.0811 6832	119
120	173.0848 0743	177.9303 4194	182.9460 3518	188.1384 1641	193.5142 7708	120

TABLE III

N	7/12	5/8	2/3	17/24	3/4	N
121	175.0944 6881	180.0424 0658	185.1656 7542	190.4710 6353	195.9656 3416	121
122	177.1158 5321	182.1676 7162	187.4001 1325	192.8202 3356	198.4353 7642	122
123	179.1490 2902	184.3062 1957	189.6494 4734	195.1860 4355	200.9236 4174	123
124	181.1940 6502	186.4581 3344	191.9137 7699	197.5686 1136	203.4305 6905	124
125	183.2510 3040	188.6234 9677	194.1932 0217	199.9680 5569	205.9562 9832	125
126	185.3199 9475	190.8023 9363	196.4878 2352	202.3844 9608	208.5009 7056	126
127	187.4010 2805	192.9949 0859	198.7977 4234	204.8180 5293	211.0647 2784	127
128	189.4942 0071	195.2011 2677	201.1230 6062	207.2688 4747	213.6477 1330	128
129	191.5995 8355	197.4211 3381	203.4638 8103	209.7370 0181	216.2500 7115	129
130	193.7172 4779	199.6550 1589	205.8203 0690	212.2226 3890	218.8719 4668	130
131	195.8472 6507	201.9028 5974	208.1924 4228	214.7258 8259	221.5134 8628	131
132	197.9897 0745	204.1647 5262	210.5803 9190	217.2468 5760	224.1748 3743	132
133	200.1446 4741	206.4407 8232	212.9842 6117	219.7856 8950	226.8561 4871	133
134	202.3121 5785	208.7310 3721	215.4041 5625	222.3425 0480	229.5575 6982	134
135	204.4923 1210	211.0356 0619	217.8401 8396	224.9174 3088	232.2792 5160	135
136	206.6851 8393	213.3545 7873	220.2924 5185	227.5105 9602	235.0213 4598	136
137	208.8908 4750	215.6880 4485	222.7610 6820	230.1221 2940	237.7840 0608	137
138	211.1093 7744	218.0360 9513	225.2461 4198	232.7521 6115	240.5673 8612	138
139	213.3408 4881	220.3988 2072	227.7477 8293	235.4008 2230	243.3716 4152	139
140	215.5853 3710	222.7763 1335	230.2661 0148	238.0682 4479	246.1969 2883	140
141	217.8429 1823	225.1686 6531	232.8012 0883	240.7545 6152	249.0434 0580	141
142	220.1136 6858	227.5759 6947	235.3532 1689	243.4599 0633	251.9112 3134	142
143	222.3976 6498	229.9983 1928	237.9222 3833	246.1844 1400	254.8005 6558	143
144	224.6949 8470	232.4358 0878	240.5083 8659	248.9282 2027	257.7115 6982	144
145	227.0057 0544	234.8885 3258	243.1117 7583	251.6914 6183	260.6444 0659	145
146	229.3299 0539	237.3565 8591	245.7325 2100	254.4742 7635	263.5992 3964	146
147	231.6676 6317	239.8400 6457	248.3707 3781	257.2768 0247	266.5762 3354	147
148	234.0190 5787	242.3390 6497	251.0265 4273	260.0991 7982	269.5755 5569	148
149	236.3841 6904	244.8536 8413	253.7000 5301	262.9415 4901	272.5973 7236	149
150	238.7630 7670	247.3840 1966	256.3913 8670	265.8040 5165	275.6418 5265	150
151	241.1558 6131	249.9301 6978	259.1006 6261	268.6868 3035	278.7091 6655	151
152	243.5626 0384	252.4922 3334	261.8280 0036	271.5900 2873	281.7994 8530	152
153	245.9833 8569	255.0703 0980	264.5735 2036	274.5137 9144	284.9129 8144	153
154	248.4182 8877	257.6644 9923	267.3373 4383	277.4582 6413	288.0498 2880	154
155	250.8673 9546	260.2749 0235	270.1195 9279	280.4235 9350	291.2102 0251	155
156	253.3307 8860	262.9016 2049	272.9203 9008	283.4099 2729	294.3942 7903	156
157	255.8085 5153	265.5447 5562	275.7398 5935	286.4174 1427	297.6022 3613	157
158	258.3007 6808	268.2044 1035	278.5781 2507	289.4462 0429	300.8342 5290	158
159	260.8075 2256	270.8806 8791	281.4353 1257	292.4964 4823	304.0905 0979	159
160	263.3288 9978	273.5736 9221	284.3115 4799	295.5682 9808	307.3711 8862	160
161	265.8649 8503	276.2835 2779	287.2069 5831	298.6619 0685	310.6764 7253	161
162	268.4158 6411	279.0102 9983	290.1216 7137	301.7774 2869	314.0065 4608	162
163	270.9816 2331	281.7541 1421	293.0558 1584	304.9150 1881	317.3615 9517	163
164	273.5623 4945	284.5150 7742	296.0095 2128	308.0748 3353	320.7418 0714	164
165	276.1581 2982	287.2932 9666	298.9829 1809	311.2570 3027	324.1473 7069	165
166	278.7690 5225	290.0888 7976	301.9761 3754	314.4617 6757	327.5784 7597	166
167	281.3952 0505	292.9019 3526	304.9893 1179	317.6892 0509	331.0353 1454	167
168	284.0366 7708	295.7325 7235	308.0225 7387	320.9395 0362	334.5180 7940	168
169	286.6935 5770	298.5809 0093	311.0760 5770	324.2128 2511	338.0269 6499	169
170	289.3659 3678	301.4470 3156	314.1498 9808	327.5093 3262	341.5621 6723	170
171	292.0539 0475	304.3310 7551	317.2442 3074	330.8291 9039	345.1238 8349	171
172	294.7575 5252	307.2331 4473	320.3591 9228	334.1725 6382	348.7123 1261	172
173	297.4769 7158	310.1533 5189	323.4949 2022	337.5396 1948	352.3276 5496	173
174	300.2122 5392	313.0918 1033	326.6515 5303	340.9305 2512	355.9701 1237	174
175	302.9634 9206	316.0486 3415	329.8292 3005	344.3454 4967	359.6398 8821	175
176	305.7307 7910	319.0239 3811	333.0280 9158	347.7845 6328	363.3371 8737	176
177	308.5142 0864	322.0178 3773	336.2482 7886	351.2480 3727	367.0622 1628	177
178	311.3138 7486	325.0304 4921	339.4899 3405	354.7360 4420	370.8151 8290	178
179	314.1298 7247	328.0618 8952	342.7532 0028	358.2487 5784	374.5962 9677	179
180	316.9622 9672	331.1122 7633	346.0382 2161	361.7863 5321	378.4057 6900	180

TABLE III

N	7/12	5/8	2/3	17/24	3/4	N
181	319.8112 4345	334.1817 2806	349.3451 4309	365.3490 0655	382.2438 1226	181
182	322.6768 0904	337.2703 6386	352.6741 1071	368.9368 9534	386.1106 4086	182
183	325.5590 9043	340.3783 0363	356.0252 7145	372.5501 9835	390.0064 7066	183
184	328.4581 8512	343.5056 6803	359.3987 7326	376.1890 9559	393.9315 1919	184
185	331.3741 9120	346.6525 7845	362.7947 6508	379.8537 6835	397.8860 0559	185
186	334.3072 0731	349.8191 5707	366.2133 9685	383.5443 9921	401.8701 5063	186
187	337.2573 3269	353.0055 2680	369.6548 1949	387.2611 7204	405.8841 7676	187
188	340.2246 6713	356.2118 1134	373.1191 8496	391.0042 7201	409.9283 0808	188
189	343.2093 1102	359.4381 3516	376.6066 4619	394.7738 8560	414.0027 7039	189
190	346.2113 6534	362.6846 2351	380.1173 5716	398.5702 0062	418.1077 9117	190
191	349.2309 3163	365.9514 0241	383.6514 7288	402.3934 0621	422.2435 9961	191
192	352.2681 1207	369.2385 9867	387.2091 4936	406.2436 9284	426.4104 2660	192
193	355.3230 0939	372.5463 3991	390.7905 4369	410.1212 5233	430.6085 0480	193
194	358.3957 2694	375.8747 5454	394.3958 1398	414.0262 7786	434.8380 6859	194
195	361.4863 6868	379.2239 7175	398.0251 1941	417.9589 6400	439.0993 5410	195
196	364.5950 3917	382.5941 2158	401.6786 2021	421.9195 0666	443.3925 9926	196
197	367.7218 4356	385.9853 3484	405.3564 7767	425.9081 0317	447.7180 4375	197
198	370.8668 8765	389.3977 4318	409.0588 5419	429.9249 5223	452.0759 2908	198
199	374.0302 7783	392.8314 7907	412.7859 1322	433.9702 5398	456.4664 9855	199
200	377.2121 2112	396.2866 7582	416.5378 1931	438.0442 0994	460.8899 9729	200
201	380.4125 2516	399.7634 6754	420.3147 3810	442.1470 2310	465.3466 7227	201
202	383.6315 9822	403.2619 8921	424.1168 3636	446.2788 9784	469.8367 7231	202
203	386.8694 4921	406.7823 7665	427.9442 8193	450.4400 4004	474.3605 4810	203
204	390.1261 8766	410.3247 6650	431.7972 4381	454.6306 5699	478.9182 5221	204
205	393.4019 2376	413.8892 9629	435.6758 9210	458.8509 5747	483.5101 3911	205
206	396.6967 6831	417.4761 0439	439.5803 9805	463.1011 5175	488.1364 6515	206
207	400.0108 3280	421.0853 3005	443.5109 3404	467.3814 5158	492.7974 8864	207
208	403.3442 2932	424.7171 1336	447.4676 7360	471.6920 7020	497.4934 6980	208
209	406.6970 7066	428.3715 9532	451.4507 9142	476.0332 2236	502.2246 7083	209
210	410.0694 7024	432.0489 1779	455.4604 6337	480.4051 2435	506.9913 5586	210
211	413.4615 4215	435.7492 2352	459.4968 6646	484.8079 9398	511.7937 9103	211
212	416.8734 0114	439.4726 5617	463.5601 7890	489.2420 5061	516.6322 4446	212
213	420.3051 6265	443.2193 6027	467.6505 8009	493.7075 1513	521.5069 8629	213
214	423.7569 4276	446.9894 8127	471.7682 5062	498.2046 1003	526.4182 8869	214
215	427.2288 5826	450.7831 6553	475.9133 7230	502.7335 5935	531.3664 2585	215
216	430.7210 2660	454.6005 6032	480.0861 2811	507.2945 8873	536.3516 7405	216
217	434.2335 6593	458.4418 1382	484.2867 0230	511.8879 2540	541.3743 1160	217
218	437.7665 9506	462.3070 7515	488.5152 8031	516.5137 9820	546.4346 1894	218
219	441.3202 3353	466.1964 9437	492.7720 4885	521.1724 3761	551.5328 7858	219
220	444.8946 0156	470.1102 2246	497.0571 9584	525.8640 7571	556.6693 7517	220
221	448.4898 2007	474.0484 1135	501.3709 1048	530.5889 4624	561.8443 9549	221
222	452.1060 1069	478.0112 1392	505.7133 8322	535.3472 8461	567.0582 2845	222
223	455.7432 9575	481.9987 8401	510.0848 0577	540.1393 2788	572.3111 6517	223
224	459.4017 9831	486.0112 7641	514.4853 7114	544.9653 1479	577.6034 9890	224
225	463.0816 4213	490.0488 4689	518.9152 7362	549.8254 8577	582.9355 2515	225
226	466.7829 5171	494.1116 5218	523.3747 0878	554.7200 8296	588.3075 4158	226
227	470.5058 5226	498.1998 5001	527.8638 7350	559.6493 5021	593.7198 4815	227
228	474.2504 6973	502.3135 9907	532.3829 6599	564.6135 3311	599.1727 4701	228
229	478.0169 3081	506.4530 5907	536.9321 8576	569.6128 7897	604.6665 4261	229
230	481.8053 6290	510.6183 9068	541.5117 3367	574.6476 3686	610.2015 4168	230
231	485.6158 9419	514.8097 5563	546.1218 1189	579.7180 5762	615.7780 5324	231
232	489.4486 5357	519.0273 1660	550.7626 2397	584.8243 9386	621.3963 8864	232
233	493.3037 7071	523.2712 3733	555.4343 7480	589.9668 9999	627.0568 6156	233
234	497.1813 7604	527.5416 8256	560.1372 7063	595.1458 3219	632.7597 8802	234
235	501.0816 0074	531.8388 1808	564.8715 1910	600.3614 4851	638.5054 8643	235
236	505.0045 7674	536.1628 1069	569.6373 2923	605.6140 0877	644.2942 7758	236
237	508.9504 3677	540.5138 2826	574.4349 1142	610.9037 7466	650.1264 8466	237
238	512.9193 1432	544.8920 3968	579.2644 7750	616.2310 0973	656.0024 3329	238
239	516.9113 4365	549.2976 1493	584.1262 4068	621.5959 7938	661.9224 5154	239
240	520.9266 5983	553.7307 2502	589.0204 1562	626.9989 5090	667.8868 6993	240

TABLE III

N	7/12	5/8	2/3	17/24	3/4	N
241	524.9653 9867	558.1915 4206	593.9472 1839	632.4401 9347	673.8960 2145	241
242	529.0276 9683	562.6802 3919	598.9068 6651	637.9199 7818	679.9502 4162	242
243	533.1136 9173	567.1969 9069	603.8995 7896	643.4385 7802	686.0498 6843	243
244	537.2235 2160	571.7419 7188	608.9255 7615	648.9962 6795	692.1952 4244	244
245	541.3573 2548	576.3153 5921	613.9850 7999	654.5933 2485	698.3867 0676	245
246	545.5152 4321	580.9173 3020	619.0783 1386	660.2300 2757	704.6246 0706	246
247	549.6974 1546	585.5480 6351	624.2055 0262	665.9066 5693	710.9092 9161	247
248	553.9039 8372	590.2077 3891	629.3668 7264	671.6234 9575	717.2411 1130	248
249	558.1350 9029	594.8965 3728	634.5626 5179	677.3808 2884	723.6204 1963	249
250	562.3908 7832	599.6146 4064	639.7930 6946	683.1789 4305	730.0475 7278	250
251	566.6714 9177	604.3622 3214	645.0583 5659	689.0181 2723	736.5229 2958	251
252	570.9770 7547	609.1394 9609	650.3587 4564	694.8986 7229	743.0468 5155	252
253	575.3077 7508	613.9466 1794	655.6944 7061	700.8208 7122	749.6197 0294	253
254	579.6637 3710	618.7837 8430	661.0657 6708	706.7850 1906	756.2418 5071	254
255	584.0451 0890	623.6511 8296	666.4728 7219	712.7914 1295	762.9136 6459	255
256	588.4520 3870	628.5490 0285	671.9160 2468	718.8403 5212	769.6355 1707	256
257	592.8846 7560	633.4774 3412	677.3954 6484	724.9321 3795	776.4077 8345	257
258	597.3431 6954	638.4366 6808	682.9114 3461	731.0670 7393	783.2308 4183	258
259	601.8276 7136	643.4268 9726	688.4641 7750	737.2454 6570	790.1050 7314	259
260	606.3383 3278	648.4483 1536	694.0539 3869	743.4676 2108	797.0308 6119	260
261	610.8753 0638	653.5011 1734	699.6809 6494	749.7338 5006	804.0085 9265	261
262	615.4387 4567	658.5854 9932	705.3455 0471	756.0444 6484	811.0386 5709	262
263	620.0288 0502	663.7016 5869	711.0478 0808	762.3997 7979	818.1214 4702	263
264	624.6456 3972	668.8497 9406	716.7881 2680	768.8001 1157	825.2573 5787	264
265	629.2894 0595	674.0301 0527	722.5667 1431	775.2457 7902	832.4467 8806	265
266	633.9602 6082	679.2427 9343	728.3838 2574	781.7371 0329	839.6901 3897	266
267	638.6583 6234	684.4880 6089	734.2397 1791	788.2744 0777	846.9878 1501	267
268	643.3838 6945	689.7661 1127	740.1346 4936	794.8580 1816	854.3402 2362	268
269	648.1369 4202	695.0771 4946	746.0688 8036	801.4882 6246	861.7477 7530	269
270	652.9177 4085	700.4213 8165	752.0426 7289	808.1654 7098	869.2108 8361	270
271	657.7264 2767	705.7990 1528	758.0562 9071	814.8899 7640	876.7299 6524	271
272	662.5631 6517	711.2102 5913	764.1099 9932	821.6621 1374	884.3054 3998	272
273	667.4281 1697	716.6553 2325	770.2040 6598	828.4822 2038	891.9377 3078	273
274	672.3214 4765	722.1344 1902	776.3387 5975	835.3506 3610	899.6272 6376	274
275	677.2433 2276	727.6477 5914	782.5143 5148	842.2677 0311	907.3744 6824	275
276	682.1939 0881	733.1955 5763	788.7311 1383	849.2337 6601	915.1797 7675	276
277	687.1733 7328	738.7780 2987	794.9893 2125	856.2491 7185	923.0436 2508	277
278	692.1818 8462	744.3953 9255	801.2892 5006	863.3142 7015	930.9664 5227	278
279	697.2196 1228	750.0478 6376	807.6311 7839	870.4294 1290	938.9487 0066	279
280	702.2867 2669	755.7356 6290	814.0153 8625	877.5949 5457	946.9908 1591	280
281	707.3833 9926	761.4590 1080	820.4421 5549	884.8112 5217	955.0932 4703	281
282	712.5098 0242	767.2181 2961	826.9117 6986	892.0786 6520	963.2564 4638	282
283	717.6661 0960	773.0132 4292	833.4245 1499	899.3975 5575	971.4808 6973	283
284	722.8524 9524	778.8445 7569	839.9806 7843	906.7682 8843	979.7669 7626	284
285	728.0691 3480	784.7123 5429	846.5805 4962	914.1912 3048	988.1152 2858	285
286	733.3162 0475	790.6168 0651	853.2244 1995	921.6667 5169	996.5260 9279	286
287	738.5938 8261	796.5581 6155	859.9125 8275	929.1952 2452	1005.0000 3849	287
288	743.9023 4693	802.5366 5006	866.6453 3330	936.7770 2402	1013.5375 3878	288
289	749.2417 7728	808.5525 0412	873.4229 6885	944.4125 2794	1022.1390 7032	289
290	754.6123 5432	814.6059 5727	880.2457 8865	952.1021 1668	1030.8051 1334	290
291	760.0142 5972	820.6972 4450	887.1140 9390	959.8461 7334	1039.5361 5169	291
292	765.4476 7623	826.8266 0228	894.0281 8786	967.6450 8374	1048.3326 7283	292
293	770.9127 8768	832.9942 6854	900.9883 7578	975.4992 3641	1057.1951 6788	293
294	776.4097 7894	839.2004 8272	907.9949 6495	983.4090 2267	1066.1241 3164	294
295	781.9388 3598	845.4454 8574	915.0482 6472	991.3748 3658	1075.1200 6262	295
296	787.5001 4586	851.7295 2003	922.1485 8649	999.3970 7501	1084.1834 6309	296
297	793.0938 9671	858.0528 2953	929.2962 4373	1007.4761 3762	1093.3148 3907	297
298	798.7202 7777	864.4156 5971	936.4915 5202	1015.6124 2693	1102.5147 0036	298
299	804.3794 7939	870.8182 5758	943.7348 2903	1023.8063 4829	1111.7835 6061	299
300	810.0716 9302	877.2608 7169	951.0263 9456	1032.0583 0992	1121.1219 3732	300

TABLE III

N	7/12	5/8	2/3	17/24	3/4	N
301	815.7971 1123	883.7437 5214	958.3665 7052	1040.3687 2295	1130.5303 5185	301
302	821.5559 2771	890.2671 5059	965.7556 8099	1048.7380 0141	1140.0093 2949	302
303	827.3483 3729	896.8313 2028	973.1940 5220	1057.1665 6225	1149.5593 9946	303
304	833.1745 3593	903.4365 1604	980.6820 1255	1065.6548 2540	1159.1810 9495	304
305	839.0347 2072	910.0829 9426	988.2198 9263	1074.2032 1374	1168.8749 5317	305
306	844.9290 8992	916.7710 1298	995.8080 2525	1082.8121 5318	1178.6415 1531	306
307	850.8578 4295	923.5008 3181	1003.4467 4542	1091.4820 7259	1188.4813 2668	307
308	856.8211 8037	930.2727 1200	1011.1363 9039	1100.2134 0394	1198.3949 3663	308
309	862.8193 0392	937.0869 1645	1018.8772 9966	1109.0065 8222	1208.3828 9865	309
310	868.8524 1652	943.9437 0968	1026.6698 1499	1117.8620 4551	1218.4457 7039	310
311	874.9207 2229	950.8433 5787	1034.5142 8042	1126.7802 3500	1228.5841 1367	311
312	881.0244 2650	957.7861 2885	1042.4110 4229	1135.7615 9500	1238.7984 9452	312
313	887.1637 3566	964.7722 9216	1050.3604 4924	1144.8065 7296	1249.0894 8323	313
314	893.3388 5745	971.8021 1899	1058.3628 5224	1153.9156 1952	1259.4576 5436	314
315	899.5500 0078	978.8758 8223	1066.4186 0458	1163.0891 8849	1269.9035 8677	315
316	905.7973 7579	985.9938 5649	1074.5280 6195	1172.3277 3691	1280.4278 6367	316
317	912.0811 9381	993.1563 1810	1082.6915 8236	1181.6317 2505	1291.0310 7264	317
318	918.4016 6744	1000.3635 4509	1090.9095 2624	1191.0016 1643	1301.7138 0569	318
319	924.7590 1050	1007.6158 1724	1099.1822 5642	1200.4378 7788	1312.4766 5923	319
320	931.1534 3806	1014.9134 1610	1107.5101 3813	1209.9409 7952	1323.3202 3418	320
321	937.5851 6645	1022.2566 2495	1115.8935 3905	1219.5113 9479	1334.2451 3593	321
322	944.0544 1326	1029.6457 2886	1124.3328 2931	1229.1496 0050	1345.2519 7445	322
323	950.5613 9733	1037.0810 1466	1132.8283 8150	1238.8560 7684	1356.3413 6426	323
324	957.1063 3882	1044.5627 7100	1141.3805 7071	1248.6313 0738	1367.5139 2449	324
325	963.6894 5913	1052.0912 8832	1149.9897 7452	1258.4757 7914	1378.7702 7893	325
326	970.3109 8097	1059.6668 5887	1158.6563 7302	1268.3899 8258	1390.1110 5602	326
327	976.9711 2836	1067.2897 7674	1167.3807 4884	1278.3744 1162	1401.5368 8894	327
328	983.6701 2661	1074.9603 3785	1176.1632 8716	1288.4295 6370	1413.0484 1560	328
329	990.4082 0235	1082.6788 3996	1185.0043 7574	1298.5559 3978	1424.6462 7872	329
330	997.1855 8353	1090.4455 8271	1193.9044 0491	1308.7540 4435	1436.3311 2581	330
331	1004.0024 9943	1098.2608 6760	1202.8637 6761	1319.0243 8550	1448.1036 0926	331
332	1010.8591 8068	1106.1249 9802	1211.8828 5940	1329.3674 7490	1459.9643 8632	332
333	1017.7558 5923	1114.0382 7926	1220.9620 7846	1339.7838 2785	1471.9141 1922	333
334	1024.6927 6841	1122.0010 1851	1230.1018 2565	1350.2739 6329	1483.9534 7512	334
335	1031.6701 4290	1130.0135 2487	1239.3025 0449	1360.8384 0387	1496.0831 2618	335
336	1038.6882 1873	1138.0761 0940	1248.5645 2118	1371.4776 7589	1508.3037 4963	336
337	1045.7472 3334	1146.1890 8509	1257.8882 8466	1382.1923 0943	1520.6160 2775	337
338	1052.8474 2553	1154.3527 6687	1267.2742 0656	1392.9828 3829	1533.0206 4796	338
339	1059.9890 3552	1162.5674 7166	1276.7227 0127	1403.8498 0006	1545.5183 0282	339
340	1067.1723 0489	1170.8335 1836	1286.2341 8594	1414.7937 3615	1558.1096 9009	340
341	1074.3974 7667	1179.1512 2785	1295.8090 8051	1425.8151 9178	1570.7955 1276	341
342	1081.6647 9528	1187.5209 2302	1305.4478 0772	1436.9147 1605	1583.5764 7911	342
343	1088.9745 0659	1195.9429 2879	1315.1507 9310	1448.0928 6196	1596.4533 0270	343
344	1096.3268 5788	1204.4175 7210	1324.9184 6506	1459.3501 8640	1609.4267 0247	344
345	1103.7220 9788	1212.9451 8192	1334.7512 5482	1470.6872 5022	1622.4974 0274	345
346	1111.1604 7678	1221.5260 8931	1344.6495 9652	1482.1046 1824	1635.6661 3326	346
347	1118.6422 4623	1230.1606 2737	1354.6139 2717	1493.6028 5928	1648.9336 2926	347
348	1126.1676 5934	1238.8491 3129	1364.6446 8668	1505.1825 4620	1662.3006 3148	348
349	1133.7369 7068	1247.5919 3836	1374.7423 1792	1516.8442 5591	1675.7678 8622	349
350	1141.3504 3634	1256.3893 8797	1384.9072 6671	1528.5885 6939	1689.3361 4536	350
351	1149.0083 1389	1265.2418 2165	1395.1399 8182	1540.4160 7175	1703.0061 6645	351
352	1156.7108 6239	1274.1495 8303	1405.4409 1503	1552.3273 5226	1716.7787 1270	352
353	1164.4583 4242	1283.1130 1793	1415.8105 2113	1564.3230 0434	1730.6545 5305	353
354	1172.2510 1608	1292.1324 7429	1426.2492 5794	1576.4036 2562	1744.6344 6219	354
355	1180.0891 4701	1301.2083 0225	1436.7575 8633	1588.5698 1797	1758.7192 2066	355
356	1187.9730 0037	1310.3408 5414	1447.3359 7024	1600.8221 8751	1772.9096 1482	356
357	1195.9028 4287	1319.5304 8448	1457.9848 7671	1613.1613 4467	1787.2064 3693	357
358	1203.8789 4278	1328.7775 5001	1468.7047 7588	1625.5879 0420	1801.6104 8520	358
359	1211.9015 6995	1338.0824 0970	1479.4961 4106	1638.1024 8519	1816.1225 6384	359
360	1219.9709 9578	1347.4454 2476	1490.3594 4866	1650.7057 1112	1830.7434 8307	360

TABLE III

N	19/24	5/6	7/8	11/12	23/24	N
1	1.0000 0000	1.0000 0000	1.0000 0000	1.0000 0000	1.0000 0000	1
2	2.0079 1667	2.0083 3333	2.0087 5000	2.0091 6667	2.0095 8333	2
3	3.0238 1267	3.0250 6944	3.0263 2656	3.0275 8403	3.0288 4184	3
4	4.0477 5119	4.0502 7836	4.0528 0692	4.0553 3688	4.0578 6824	4
5	5.0797 9589	5.0840 3068	5.0882 6898	5.0925 1080	5.0967 5615	5
6	6.1200 1094	6.1263 9760	6.1327 9133	6.1391 9215	6.1456 0006	6
7	7.1684 6102	7.1774 5091	7.1864 5326	7.1954 6808	7.2044 9539	7
8	8.2252 1134	8.2372 6300	8.2493 3472	8.2614 2654	8.2735 3847	8
9	9.2903 2760	9.3059 0686	9.3215 1640	9.3371 5628	9.3528 2655	9
10	10.3638 7602	10.3834 5608	10.4030 7967	10.4227 4688	10.4424 5780	10
11	11.4459 2338	11.4699 8489	11.4941 0662	11.5182 8873	11.5425 3136	11
12	12.5365 3694	12.5655 6809	12.5946 8005	12.6238 7304	12.6531 4728	12
13	13.6357 8452	13.6702 8116	13.7048 8350	13.7395 9188	13.7744 0661	13
14	14.7437 3448	14.7842 0017	14.8248 0123	14.8655 3813	14.9064 1134	14
15	15.8604 5571	15.9074 0184	15.9545 1824	16.0018 0557	16.0492 6445	15
16	16.9860 1765	17.0399 6352	17.0941 2028	17.1484 8879	17.2030 6990	16
17	18.1204 9029	18.1819 6322	18.2436 9383	18.3056 8327	18.3679 3266	17
18	19.2639 4418	19.3334 7958	19.4033 2615	19.4734 8536	19.5439 5868	18
19	20.4164 5040	20.4945 9191	20.5731 0526	20.6519 9231	20.7312 5495	19
20	21.5780 8063	21.6653 8017	21.7531 1993	21.8413 0224	21.9299 2947	20
21	22.7489 0710	22.8459 2501	22.9434 5973	23.0415 1418	23.1400 9130	21
22	23.9290 0262	24.0363 0772	24.1442 1500	24.2527 2806	24.3618 5051	22
23	25.1184 4056	25.2366 1028	25.3554 7688	25.4750 4473	25.5953 1824	23
24	26.3172 9488	26.4469 1537	26.5773 3730	26.7085 6598	26.8406 0671	24
25	27.5256 4013	27.6673 0633	27.8098 8900	27.9533 9450	28.0978 2919	25
26	28.7435 5145	28.8978 6721	29.0532 2553	29.2096 3395	29.3671 0005	26
27	29.9711 0456	30.1386 8277	30.3074 4126	30.4773 8892	30.6485 3476	27
28	31.2083 7581	31.3898 3846	31.5726 3137	31.7567 6499	31.9422 4988	28
29	32.4554 4211	32.6514 2045	32.8488 9189	33.0478 6867	33.2483 6311	29
30	33.7123 8103	33.9235 1562	34.1363 1970	34.3508 0746	34.5669 9326	30
31	34.9792 7071	35.2062 1158	35.4350 1249	35.6656 8987	35.8982 6028	31
32	36.2561 8994	36.4995 9668	36.7450 6885	36.9926 2536	37.2422 8527	32
33	37.5432 1811	37.8037 5999	38.0665 8820	38.3317 2442	38.5991 9051	33
34	38.8404 3525	39.1187 9132	39.3996 7085	39.6830 9856	39.9690 9941	34
35	40.1479 2203	40.4447 8125	40.7444 1797	41.0468 6030	41.3521 3662	35
36	41.4657 5975	41.7818 2109	42.1009 3163	42.4231 2319	42.7484 2793	36
37	42.7940 3035	43.1300 0293	43.4693 1478	43.8120 0182	44.1581 0036	37
38	44.1328 1642	44.4894 1962	44.8496 7128	45.2136 1183	45.5812 8216	38
39	45.4822 0122	45.8601 6479	46.2421 0591	46.6280 6994	47.0181 0278	39
40	46.8422 6864	47.2423 3283	47.6467 2433	48.0554 9391	48.4686 9293	40
41	48.2131 0327	48.6360 1893	49.0636 3317	49.4960 0261	49.9331 8457	41
42	49.5947 9034	50.0413 1909	50.4929 3996	50.9497 1597	51.4117 1092	42
43	50.9874 1576	51.4583 3008	51.9347 5319	52.4167 5503	52.9044 0648	43
44	52.3910 6614	52.8871 4950	53.3891 8228	53.8972 4195	54.4114 0705	44
45	53.8058 2874	54.3278 7575	54.8563 3762	55.3913 0000	55.9328 4970	45
46	55.2317 9155	55.7806 0805	56.3363 3058	56.8990 5358	57.4688 7284	46
47	56.6690 4324	57.2454 4645	57.8292 7347	58.4206 2824	59.0196 1620	47
48	58.1176 7316	58.7224 9183	59.3352 7961	59.9561 5067	60.5852 2086	48
49	59.5777 7141	60.2118 4593	60.8544 6331	61.5057 4872	62.1658 2923	49
50	61.0494 2877	61.7136 1131	62.3869 3986	63.0695 5141	63.7615 8509	50
51	62.5327 3674	63.2278 9141	63.9328 2559	64.6476 8897	65.3726 3361	51
52	64.0277 8758	64.7547 9050	65.4922 3781	66.2402 9278	66.9991 2135	52
53	65.5346 7423	66.2944 1376	67.0652 9489	67.8474 9547	68.6411 9627	53
54	67.0534 9040	67.8468 6721	68.6521 1622	69.4694 3084	70.2990 0773	54
55	68.5843 3053	69.4122 5777	70.2528 2224	71.1062 3396	71.9727 0655	55
56	70.1272 8981	70.9906 9325	71.8675 3443	72.7580 4110	73.6624 4499	56
57	71.6824 6419	72.5822 8236	73.4963 7536	74.4249 8981	75.3683 7676	57
58	73.2499 5037	74.1871 3471	75.1394 6864	76.1072 1889	77.0906 5703	58
59	74.8298 4581	75.8053 6083	76.7969 3900	77.8048 6839	78.8294 4250	59
60	76.4222 4875	77.4370 7217	78.4689 1221	79.5180 7969	80.5848 9132	60

TABLE III

N	19/24	5/6	7/8	11/12	23/24	N
61	78.0272 5822	79.0823 8111	80.1555 1519	81.2469 9542	82.3571 6320	61
62	79.6449 7402	80.7414 0095	81.8568 7595	82.9917 5954	84.1464 1934	62
63	81.2754 9673	82.4142 4596	83.5731 2362	84.7525 1734	85.9528 2253	63
64	82.9189 2774	84.1010 3134	85.3043 8845	86.5294 1541	87.7765 3708	64
65	84.5753 6926	85.8018 7327	87.0508 0185	88.3226 0172	89.6177 2889	65
66	86.2449 2426	87.5168 8888	88.8124 9636	90.1322 2557	91.4765 6546	66
67	87.9276 9658	89.2461 9629	90.5896 0571	91.9584 3764	93.3532 1588	67
68	89.6237 9084	90.9899 1459	92.3822 6476	93.8013 8998	95.2478 5086	68
69	91.3333 1252	92.7481 6388	94.1906 0957	95.6612 3606	97.1606 4277	69
70	93.0563 6791	94.5210 6524	96.0147 7741	97.5381 3072	99.0917 6559	70
71	94.7930 6416	96.3087 4079	97.8549 0671	99.4322 3025	101.0413 9501	71
72	96.5435 0925	98.1113 1363	99.7111 3714	101.3436 9236	103.0097 0838	72
73	98.3078 1203	99.9289 0791	101.5836 0959	103.2726 7621	104.9968 8476	73
74	100.0860 8221	101.7616 4881	103.4724 6618	105.2193 4241	107.0031 0490	74
75	101.8784 3036	103.6096 6255	105.3778 5025	107.1838 5305	109.0285 5132	75
76	103.6849 6793	105.4730 7640	107.2999 0644	109.1663 7170	111.0734 0827	76
77	105.5058 0726	107.3520 1870	109.2387 8063	111.1670 6344	113.1378 6177	77
78	107.3410 6157	109.2466 1886	111.1946 1996	113.1860 9486	115.2220 9961	78
79	109.1908 4497	111.1570 0735	113.1675 7288	115.2236 3406	117.3263 1140	79
80	111.0552 7250	113.0833 1575	115.1577 8914	117.2798 5070	119.4506 8855	80
81	112.9344 6007	115.0256 7671	117.1654 1980	119.3549 1600	121.5954 2432	81
82	114.8285 2455	116.9842 2402	119.1906 1722	121.4490 0273	123.7607 1380	82
83	116.7375 8370	118.9590 9255	121.2335 3512	123.5622 8526	125.9467 5397	83
84	118.6617 5624	120.9504 1832	123.2943 2855	125.6949 3954	128.1537 4370	84
85	120.6011 6181	122.9583 3847	125.3731 5393	127.8471 4315	130.3818 8374	85
86	122.5559 2101	124.9829 9129	127.4701 6903	130.0190 7530	132.6313 7679	86
87	124.5261 5538	127.0245 1622	129.5855 3301	132.2109 1682	134.9024 2749	87
88	126.5119 8744	129.0830 5386	131.7194 0642	134.4228 5022	137.1952 4242	88
89	128.5135 4068	131.1587 4597	133.8719 5123	136.6550 5968	139.5100 3016	89
90	130.5309 3954	133.2517 3552	136.0433 3080	138.9077 3107	141.8470 0128	90
91	132.5643 0948	135.3621 6665	138.2337 0994	141.1810 5193	144.2063 6838	91
92	134.6137 7693	137.4901 8471	140.4432 5491	143.4752 1158	146.5883 4607	92
93	136.6794 6933	139.6359 3625	142.6721 3339	145.7904 0102	148.9931 5106	93
94	138.7615 1513	141.7995 6905	144.9205 1455	148.1268 1302	151.4210 0209	94
95	140.8600 4379	143.9812 3212	147.1885 6906	150.4846 4214	153.8721 2002	95
96	142.9751 8580	146.1810 7572	149.4764 6903	152.8640 8470	156.3467 2784	96
97	145.1070 7269	148.3992 5136	151.7843 8814	155.2653 3881	158.8450 5065	97
98	147.2558 3702	150.6359 1178	154.1125 0153	157.6886 0441	161.3673 1572	98
99	149.4216 1239	152.8912 1105	156.4609 8592	160.1340 8329	163.9137 5249	99
100	151.6045 3349	155.1653 0447	158.8300 1955	162.6019 7905	166.4845 9262	100
101	153.8047 3605	157.4583 4868	161.2197 8222	165.0924 9719	169.0800 6997	101
102	156.0223 5687	159.7705 0158	163.6304 5532	167.6058 4508	171.7004 2064	102
103	158.2575 3387	162.1019 2243	166.0622 2180	170.1422 3200	174.3458 8300	103
104	160.5104 0601	164.4527 7178	168.5152 6624	172.7018 6912	177.0166 9772	104
105	162.7811 1339	166.8232 1155	170.9897 7482	175.2849 6959	179.7131 0773	105
106	165.0697 9720	169.2134 0498	173.4859 3535	177.8917 4848	182.4353 5835	106
107	167.3765 9977	171.6235 1669	176.0039 3728	180.5224 2284	185.1836 9720	107
108	169.7016 6451	174.0537 1266	178.5439 7174	183.1772 1171	187.9583 7430	108
109	172.0451 3602	176.5041 6026	181.1062 3149	185.8563 3615	190.7596 4205	109
110	174.4071 6002	178.9750 2827	183.6909 1101	188.5600 1924	193.5877 5529	110
111	176.7878 8337	181.4664 8684	186.2982 0648	191.2884 8608	196.4429 7128	111
112	179.1874 5411	183.9787 0756	188.9283 1579	194.0419 6387	199.3255 4975	112
113	181.6060 2146	186.5118 6346	191.5814 3855	196.8206 8187	202.2357 5294	113
114	184.0437 3579	189.0661 2898	194.2577 7614	199.6248 7145	205.1738 4557	114
115	186.5007 4870	191.6416 8006	196.9575 3168	202.4547 6611	208.1400 9492	115
116	188.9772 1296	194.2386 9406	199.6809 1009	205.3106 0146	211.1347 7083	116
117	191.4732 8256	196.8573 4984	202.4281 1805	208.1926 1531	214.1581 4572	117
118	193.9891 1272	199.4978 2776	205.1993 6408	211.1010 4762	217.2104 9462	118
119	196.5248 5986	202.1603 0966	207.9948 5852	214.0361 4056	220.2920 9519	119
120	199.0806 8167	204.8449 7890	210.8148 1353	216.9981 3851	223.4032 2777	120

TABLE III

N	19/24	5/6	7/8	11/12	23/24	N
121	201.6567 3706	207.5520 2039	213.6594 4315	219.9872 8811	226.5441 7537	121
122	204.2531 8623	210.2816 2056	216.5289 6328	223.0038 3825	229.7152 2372	122
123	206.8701 9062	213.0339 6740	219.4235 9170	226.0480 4010	232.9166 6128	123
124	209.5079 1297	215.8092 5046	222.3435 4813	229.1201 4714	236.1487 7928	124
125	212.1665 1728	218.6076 6088	225.2890 5418	232.2204 1515	239.4118 7175	125
126	214.8461 6887	221.4293 9139	228.2603 3340	235.3491 0229	242.7062 3552	126
127	217.5470 3438	224.2746 3632	231.2576 1132	238.5064 6906	246.0321 7028	127
128	220.2692 8173	227.1435 9162	234.2811 1542	241.6927 7836	249.3899 7858	128
129	223.0130 8021	230.0364 5489	237.3310 7518	244.9082 9550	252.7799 6587	129
130	225.7786 0043	232.9534 2534	240.4077 2209	248.1532 8821	256.2024 4054	130
131	228.5660 1435	235.8947 0389	243.5112 8965	251.4280 2668	259.6577 1393	131
132	231.3754 9530	238.8604 9309	246.6420 1344	254.7327 8359	263.1461 0036	132
133	234.2072 1797	241.8509 9720	249.8001 3106	258.0678 3411	266.6679 1715	133
134	237.0613 5844	244.8664 2217	252.9858 8220	261.4334 5592	270.2234 8469	134
135	239.9380 9420	247.9069 7569	256.1995 0867	264.8299 2927	273.8131 2642	135
136	242.8376 0411	250.9728 6716	259.4412 5437	268.2575 3695	277.4371 6888	136
137	245.7600 6848	254.0643 0771	262.7113 6535	271.7165 6438	281.0959 4175	137
138	248.7056 6902	257.1815 1028	266.0100 8980	275.2072 9955	284.7897 7786	138
139	251.6745 8890	260.3246 8953	269.3376 7808	278.7300 3313	288.5190 1323	139
140	254.6670 1273	263.4940 6194	272.6943 8276	282.2850 5843	292.2839 8711	140
141	257.6831 2658	266.6898 4579	276.0804 5861	285.8726 7147	296.0850 4198	141
142	260.7231 1800	269.9122 6118	279.4961 6263	289.4931 7096	299.9225 2363	142
143	263.7871 7601	273.1615 3002	282.9417 5405	293.1468 5836	303.7967 8115	143
144	266.8754 9116	276.4378 7610	286.4174 9440	296.8340 3789	307.7081 6697	144
145	269.9882 5546	279.7415 2507	289.9236 4747	300.5550 1657	311.6570 3691	145
146	273.1256 6249	283.0727 0445	293.4604 7939	304.3101 0422	315.6437 5018	146
147	276.2879 0731	286.4316 4365	297.0282 5858	308.0996 1351	319.6686 6945	147
148	279.4751 8658	289.8185 7401	300.6272 5585	311.9238 5997	323.7321 6086	148
149	282.6876 9847	293.2337 2880	304.2577 4433	315.7831 6202	327.8345 9407	149
150	285.9256 4275	296.6773 4320	307.9199 9960	319.6778 4101	331.9763 4226	150
151	289.1892 2076	300.1496 5440	311.6142 9959	323.6082 2121	336.1577 8221	151
152	292.4786 3542	303.6509 0152	315.3409 2472	327.5746 2991	340.3792 9429	152
153	295.7940 9129	307.1813 2570	319.1001 5781	331.5773 9735	344.6412 6253	153
154	299.1357 9451	310.7411 7008	322.8922 8419	335.6168 5683	348.9440 7463	154
155	302.5039 5288	314.3306 7983	326.7175 9167	339.6933 4468	353.2881 2201	155
156	305.8987 7584	317.9501 0216	330.5763 7060	343.8072 0034	357.6737 9985	156
157	309.3204 7448	321.5996 8634	334.4689 1384	347.9587 6634	362.1015 0709	157
158	312.7692 6157	325.2796 8373	338.3955 1684	352.1483 8837	366.5716 4654	158
159	316.2453 5156	328.9903 4776	342.3564 7761	356.3764 1526	371.0846 2482	159
160	319.7489 6059	332.7319 3399	346.3520 9679	360.6431 9907	375.6408 5247	160
161	323.2803 0653	336.5047 0011	350.3826 7764	364.9490 9506	380.2407 4397	161
162	326.8396 0896	340.3089 0594	354.4485 2607	369.2944 6176	384.8847 1777	162
163	330.4270 8920	344.1448 1349	358.5499 5067	373.6796 6100	389.5731 9632	163
164	334.0429 7032	348.0126 8694	362.6872 6274	378.1050 5789	394.3066 0611	164
165	337.6874 7717	351.9127 9266	366.8607 7629	382.5710 2092	399.0853 7775	165
166	341.3608 3636	355.8453 9927	371.0708 0808	387.0779 2194	403.9099 4596	166
167	345.0632 7632	359.8107 7760	375.3176 7765	391.6261 3623	408.7807 4961	167
168	348.7950 2725	363.8092 0074	379.6017 0733	396.2160 4248	413.6982 3179	168
169	352.5563 2122	367.8409 4408	383.9232 2227	400.8480 2287	418.6628 3985	169
170	356.3473 9210	371.9062 8528	388.2825 5046	405.5224 6308	423.6750 2539	170
171	360.1684 7562	376.0055 0433	392.6800 2278	410.2397 5232	428.7352 4439	171
172	364.0198 0938	380.1388 8353	397.1159 7298	415.0002 8338	433.8439 5715	172
173	367.9016 3287	384.3067 0756	401.5907 3774	419.8044 5265	439.0016 2840	173
174	371.8141 8747	388.5092 6345	406.1046 5670	424.6526 6013	444.2087 2734	174
175	375.7577 1645	392.7468 4065	410.6580 7245	429.5453 0952	449.4657 2764	175
176	379.7324 6504	397.0197 3099	415.2513 3058	434.4828 0819	454.7731 0753	176
177	383.7386 8039	401.3282 2875	419.8847 7972	439.4655 6726	460.1313 4982	177
178	387.7766 1161	405.6726 3065	424.5587 7154	444.4940 0163	465.5409 4192	178
179	391.8465 0578	410.0532 3591	429.2736 6080	449.5685 2998	471.0023 7594	179
180	395.9486 2799	414.4703 4621	434.0298 0533	454.6895 7484	476.5161 4871	180

TABLE III

N	19/24	5/6	7/8	11/12	23/24	N
181	400.0832 2129	418.9242 6576	438.8275 6612	459.8575 6260	482.0827 6181	181
182	404.2505 4679	423.4153 0131	443.6673 0733	465.0729 2359	487.7027 2161	182
183	408.4508 6362	427.9437 6215	448.5493 9627	470.3360 9206	493.3765 3935	183
184	412.6844 3296	432.5099 6017	453.4742 0348	475.6475 0624	499.1047 3119	184
185	416.9515 1805	437.1142 0984	458.4421 0276	481.0076 0838	504.8878 1820	185
186	421.2523 8424	441.7568 2825	463.4534 7116	486.4168 4479	510.7263 2646	186
187	425.5872 9895	446.4381 3516	468.5086 8904	491.8756 6587	516.6207 8708	187
188	429.9565 3173	451.1584 5295	473.6081 4007	497.3845 2614	522.5717 3629	188
189	434.3603 5427	455.9181 0672	478.7522 1129	502.9438 8429	528.5797 1543	189
190	438.7990 4041	460.7174 2428	483.9412 9314	508.5542 0323	534.6452 7104	190
191	443.2728 6615	465.5567 3615	489.1757 7946	514.2159 5010	540.7689 5489	191
192	447.7821 0967	470.4363 7562	494.4560 6753	519.9295 9630	546.9513 2404	192
193	452.3270 5137	475.3566 7875	499.7825 5812	525.6956 1760	553.1929 4089	193
194	456.9079 7386	480.3179 8440	505.1556 5550	531.5144 9410	559.4943 7324	194
195	461.5251 6199	485.3206 3427	510.5757 6749	537.3867 1029	565.8561 9432	195
196	466.1789 0285	490.3649 7289	516.0433 0545	543.3127 5514	572.2789 8285	196
197	470.8694 8583	495.4513 4767	521.5586 8437	549.2931 2206	578.7633 2310	197
198	475.5972 0260	500.5801 0890	527.1223 2286	555.3283 0901	585.3098 0495	198
199	480.3623 4712	505.7516 0980	532.7346 4319	561.4188 1851	591.9190 2391	199
200	485.1652 1570	510.9662 0655	538.3960 7131	567.5651 5768	598.5915 8122	200
201	490.0061 0699	516.2242 5827	544.1070 3694	573.7678 3829	605.3280 8388	201
202	494.8853 2200	521.5261 2709	549.8679 7351	580.0273 7681	612.1291 4468	202
203	499.8031 6414	526.8721 7815	555.6793 1828	586.3442 9443	618.9953 8232	203
204	504.7599 3919	532.2627 7964	561.5415 1232	592.7191 1713	625.9274 2140	204
205	509.7559 5537	537.6983 0280	567.4550 0055	599.1523 7571	632.9258 9252	205
206	514.7915 2335	543.1791 2199	573.4202 3180	605.6446 0582	639.9914 3232	206
207	519.8669 5624	548.7056 1467	579.4376 5883	612.1963 4804	647.1246 8355	207
208	524.9825 6965	554.2781 6146	585.5077 3835	618.8081 4789	654.3262 9510	208
209	530.1386 8166	559.8971 4614	591.6309 3106	625.4805 5592	661.5969 2210	209
210	535.3356 1289	565.5629 5569	597.8077 0170	632.2141 2768	668.9372 2593	210
211	540.5736 8649	571.2759 8032	604.0385 1909	639.0094 2385	676.3478 7435	211
212	545.8532 2817	577.0366 1349	610.3238 5613	645.8670 1023	683.8295 4148	212
213	551.1745 6623	582.8452 5194	616.6641 8988	652.7874 5783	691.3829 0792	213
214	556.5380 3155	588.7022 9570	623.0600 0154	659.7713 4286	699.0086 6078	214
215	561.9439 5763	594.6081 4817	629.5117 7655	666.8192 4683	706.7074 9378	215
216	567.3926 8063	600.5632 1607	636.0200 0460	673.9317 5660	714.4801 0726	216
217	572.8845 3935	606.5679 0954	642.5851 7964	681.1094 6437	722.3272 0829	217
218	578.4198 7529	612.6226 4212	649.2077 9996	688.3529 6779	730.2495 1071	218
219	583.9990 3263	618.7278 3080	655.8883 6821	695.6628 6999	738.2477 3518	219
220	589.6223 5831	624.8838 9606	662.6273 9143	703.0397 7963	746.3226 0931	220
221	595.2902 0198	631.0912 6186	669.4253 8110	710.4843 1095	754.4748 6765	221
222	601.0029 1608	637.3503 5571	676.2828 5319	717.9970 8380	762.7052 5180	222
223	606.7608 5583	643.6616 0867	683.2003 2815	725.5787 2373	771.0145 1046	223
224	612.5643 7927	650.0254 5541	690.1783 3103	733.2298 6203	779.4033 9952	224
225	618.4138 4727	656.4423 3420	697.2173 9142	740.9511 3577	787.8726 8210	225
226	624.3096 2356	662.9126 8699	704.3180 4360	748.7431 8785	796.4231 2864	226
227	630.2520 7475	669.4369 5938	711.4808 2648	756.6066 6707	805.0555 1695	227
228	636.2415 7034	676.0156 0071	718.7062 8371	764.5422 2818	813.7706 3232	228
229	642.2784 8277	682.6490 6405	725.9949 6369	772.5505 3194	822.5692 6755	229
230	648.3631 8743	689.3378 0625	733.3474 1963	780.6322 4515	831.4522 2303	230
231	654.4960 6266	696.0822 8797	740.7642 0955	788.7880 4073	840.4203 0683	231
232	660.6774 8983	702.8829 7370	748.2458 9638	797.0185 9777	849.4743 3478	232
233	666.9078 5329	709.7403 3181	755.7930 4797	805.3246 0159	858.6151 3048	233
234	673.1875 4046	716.6548 3458	763.4062 3714	813.7067 4377	867.8435 2548	234
235	679.5169 4182	723.6269 5820	771.0860 4172	822.1657 2225	877.1603 5927	235
236	685.8964 5094	730.6571 8285	778.8330 4458	830.7022 4137	886.5664 7938	236
237	692.3264 6451	737.7459 9271	786.6478 3372	839.3170 1192	896.0627 4147	237
238	698.8073 8236	744.8938 7598	794.5310 0227	848.0107 5119	905.6500 0941	238
239	705.3396 0747	752.1013 2495	802.4831 4854	856.7841 8308	915.3291 5534	239
240	711.9235 4603	759.3688 3599	810.5048 7609	865.6380 3809	925.1010 5974	240

TABLE III

N	19/24	5/6	7/8	11/12	23/24	N
241	718.5596 0743	766.6969 0962	818.5967 9375	874.5730 5344	934.9666 1156	241
242	725.2482 0432	774.0860 5054	826.7595 1570	883.5899 7310	944.9267 0826	242
243	731.9897 5261	781.5367 6762	834.9936 6146	892.6895 4785	954.9822 5588	243
244	738.7846 7148	789.0495 7402	843.2998 5600	901.8725 3537	965.1341 6916	244
245	745.6333 8347	796.6249 8714	851.6787 2974	911.1397 0028	975.3833 7162	245
246	752.5363 1442	804.2635 2870	860.1309 1862	920.4918 1420	985.7307 9560	246
247	759.4938 9357	811.9657 2477	868.6570 6416	929.9296 5583	996.1773 8239	247
248	766.5065 5357	819.7321 0581	877.2578 1347	939.4540 1101	1006.7240 8230	248
249	773.5747 3045	827.5632 0669	885.9338 1934	949.0656 7278	1017.3718 5476	249
250	780.6988 6373	835.4595 6675	894.6857 4026	958.7654 4144	1028.1216 6837	250
251	787.8793 9640	843.4217 2980	903.5142 4049	968.5541 2466	1038.9745 0102	251
252	795.1167 7496	851.4502 4422	912.4199 9009	978.4325 3747	1049.9313 3999	252
253	802.4114 4942	859.5456 6292	921.4036 6501	988.4015 0239	1060.9931 8200	253
254	809.7638 7340	867.7085 4344	930.4659 4707	998.4618 4950	1072.1610 3333	254
255	817.1745 0406	875.9394 4797	939.6075 2411	1008.6144 1645	1083.4359 0989	255
256	824.6438 0222	884.2389 4337	948.8290 8995	1018.8600 4860	1094.8188 3736	256
257	832.1722 3232	892.6076 0123	958.1313 4448	1029.1995 9905	1106.3108 5122	257
258	839.7602 6249	901.0459 9791	967.5149 9375	1039.6339 2870	1117.9129 9688	258
259	847.4083 6457	909.5547 1456	976.9807 4994	1050.1639 0638	1129.6263 2977	259
260	855.1170 1413	918.1343 3718	986.5293 3151	1060.7904 0886	1141.4519 1543	260
261	862.8866 9049	926.7854 5666	996.1614 6316	1071.5143 2094	1153.3908 2962	261
262	870.7178 7679	935.5086 6880	1005.8778 7596	1082.3365 3555	1165.4441 5840	262
263	878.6110 5998	944.3045 7437	1015.6793 0737	1093.2579 5379	1177.6129 9825	263
264	886.5667 3087	953.1737 7916	1025.5665 0131	1104.2794 8504	1189.8984 5615	264
265	894.5853 8416	962.1168 9398	1035.5402 0820	1115.4020 4698	1202.3016 4969	265
266	902.6675 1845	971.1345 3477	1045.6011 8502	1126.6265 6575	1214.8237 0717	266
267	910.8136 3630	980.2273 2256	1055.7501 9539	1137.9539 7593	1227.4657 6769	267
268	919.0242 4426	989.3958 8358	1065.9880 0960	1149.3852 2071	1240.2289 8130	268
269	927.2998 5286	998.6408 4927	1076.3154 0468	1160.9212 5190	1253.1145 0904	269
270	935.6409 7669	1007.9628 5635	1086.7331 6448	1172.5630 3004	1266.1235 2308	270
271	944.0481 3442	1017.3625 4682	1097.2420 7966	1184.3115 2449	1279.2572 0685	271
272	952.5218 4882	1026.8405 6804	1107.8429 4786	1196.1677 1346	1292.5167 5508	272
273	961.0626 4679	1036.3975 7278	1118.5365 7366	1208.1325 8417	1305.9033 7398	273
274	969.6710 5941	1046.0342 1922	1129.3237 6868	1220.2071 3285	1319.4182 8131	274
275	978.3476 2196	1055.7511 7105	1140.2053 5165	1232.3923 6491	1333.0627 0651	275
276	987.0928 7397	1065.5490 9747	1151.1821 4848	1244.6892 9492	1346.8378 9078	276
277	995.9073 5922	1075.4286 7328	1162.2549 9228	1257.0989 4679	1360.7450 8723	277
278	1004.7916 2582	1085.3905 7889	1173.4247 2346	1269.6223 5380	1374.7855 6099	278
279	1013.7462 2619	1095.4355 0038	1184.6921 8979	1282.2605 5871	1388.9605 8928	279
280	1022.7717 1715	1105.5641 2955	1196.0582 4645	1295.0146 1383	1403.2714 6159	280
281	1031.8686 5991	1115.7771 6397	1207.5237 5611	1307.8855 8112	1417.7194 7977	281
282	1041.0376 2013	1126.0753 0700	1219.0895 8897	1320.8745 3228	1432.3059 5811	282
283	1050.2791 6796	1136.4592 6789	1230.7566 2288	1333.9825 4883	1447.0322 2355	283
284	1059.5938 7804	1146.9297 6179	1242.5257 4333	1347.2107 2220	1461.8996 1569	284
285	1068.9823 2957	1157.4875 0981	1254.3978 4358	1360.5601 5382	1476.9094 8701	285
286	1078.4451 0635	1168.1332 3905	1266.3738 2471	1374.0319 5523	1492.0632 0292	286
287	1087.9827 9677	1178.8676 8271	1278.4545 9568	1387.6272 4815	1507.3621 4195	287
288	1097.5959 9391	1189.6915 8007	1290.6410 7339	1401.3471 6459	1522.8076 9581	288
289	1107.2852 9553	1200.6056 7657	1302.9341 8278	1415.1928 4693	1538.4012 6956	289
290	1117.0513 0412	1211.6107 2387	1315.3348 5688	1429.1654 4803	1554.1442 8173	290
291	1126.8946 2695	1222.7074 7991	1327.8440 3688	1443.2661 3130	1570.0381 6443	291
292	1136.8158 7608	1233.8967 0891	1340.4626 7220	1457.4960 7084	1586.0843 6351	292
293	1146.8156 6843	1245.1791 8148	1353.1917 2058	1471.8564 5149	1602.2843 3866	293
294	1156.8946 2580	1256.5556 7466	1366.0321 4814	1486.3484 6896	1618.6395 6357	294
295	1167.0533 7492	1268.0269 7195	1378.9849 2944	1500.9733 2993	1635.1515 2605	295
296	1177.2925 4748	1279.5938 6338	1392.0510 4757	1515.7322 5212	1651.8217 2818	296
297	1187.6127 8014	1291.2571 4558	1405.2314 9423	1530.6264 6443	1668.6516 8641	297
298	1198.0147 1465	1303.0176 2179	1418.5272 6981	1545.6572 0702	1685.6429 3173	298
299	1208.4989 9781	1314.8761 0197	1431.9393 8342	1560.8257 3142	1702.7970 0983	299
300	1219.0662 8154	1326.8334 0282	1445.4688 5302	1576.1333 0062	1720.1154 8117	300

TABLE III

N	19/24	5/6	7/8	11/12	23/24	N
301	1229.7172 2294	1338.8903 4784	1459.1167 0549	1591.5811 8921	1737.5999 2120	301
302	1240.4524 8429	1351.0477 6741	1472.8839 7666	1607.1706 8344	1755.2519 2045	302
303	1251.2727 3312	1363.3064 9880	1486.7717 1146	1622.9030 8138	1773.0730 8468	303
304	1262.1786 4226	1375.6673 8629	1500.7809 6393	1638.7796 9295	1791.0650 3508	304
305	1273.1708 8984	1388.1312 8118	1514.9127 9737	1654.8018 4014	1809.2294 0833	305
306	1284.2501 5939	1400.6990 4186	1529.1682 8434	1670.9708 5701	1827.5678 5683	306
307	1295.4171 3982	1413.3715 3387	1543.5485 0683	1687.2880 8986	1846.0820 4879	307
308	1306.6725 2551	1426.1496 2999	1558.0545 5627	1703.7548 9735	1864.7736 6842	308
309	1318.0170 1633	1439.0342 1024	1572.6875 3363	1720.3726 5058	1883.6444 1608	309
310	1329.4513 1771	1452.0261 6199	1587.4485 4955	1737.1427 3321	1902.6960 0840	310
311	1340.9761 4064	1465.1263 8001	1602.3387 2436	1754.0665 4160	1921.9301 7848	311
312	1352.5922 0176	1478.3357 6651	1617.3591 8820	1771.1454 8490	1941.3486 7602	312
313	1364.3002 2335	1491.6552 3123	1632.5110 8110	1788.3809 8517	1960.9532 6750	313
314	1376.1009 3346	1505.0856 9149	1647.7955 5306	1805.7744 7754	1980.7457 3632	314
315	1387.9950 6585	1518.6280 7225	1663.2137 6415	1823.3274 1025	2000.7278 8296	315
316	1399.9833 6012	1532.2833 0618	1678.7668 8458	1841.0412 4484	2020.9015 2517	316
317	1412.0665 6172	1546.0523 3374	1694.4560 9482	1858.9174 5625	2041.2684 9812	317
318	1424.2454 2200	1559.9361 0318	1710.2825 8565	1876.9575 3294	2061.8306 5456	318
319	1436.5206 9826	1573.9355 7071	1726.2475 5828	1895.1629 7699	2082.5898 6500	319
320	1448.8931 5378	1588.0517 0047	1742.3522 2441	1913.5353 0428	2103.5480 1787	320
321	1461.3635 5792	1602.2854 6464	1758.5978 0638	1932.0760 4457	2124.7070 1971	321
322	1473.9326 8608	1616.6378 4351	1774.9855 3718	1950.7867 4164	2146.0687 9531	322
323	1486.6013 1985	1631.1098 2554	1791.5166 6063	1969.6689 5344	2167.6352 8793	323
324	1499.3702 4696	1645.7024 0742	1808.1924 3141	1988.7242 5218	2189.4084 5944	324
325	1512.2402 6142	1660.4165 9415	1825.0141 1519	2007.9542 2449	2211.3902 9051	325
326	1525.2121 6349	1675.2533 9910	1841.9829 8869	2027.3604 7155	2233.5827 8080	326
327	1538.2867 5978	1690.2138 4409	1859.1003 3985	2046.9446 0921	2255.9879 4911	327
328	1551.4648 6330	1705.2989 5946	1876.3674 6782	2066.7082 6812	2278.6078 3363	328
329	1564.7472 9347	1720.5097 8412	1893.7856 8316	2086.6530 9391	2301.4444 9203	329
330	1578.1348 7621	1735.8473 6565	1911.3563 0789	2106.7807 4728	2324.5000 0175	330
331	1591.6284 4398	1751.3127 6037	1929.0806 7558	2127.0929 0413	2347.7764 6010	331
332	1605.2288 3582	1766.9070 3337	1946.9601 3150	2147.5912 5575	2371.2759 8451	332
333	1618.9368 5744	1782.6312 5865	1964.9960 3265	2168.2775 0892	2395.0007 1269	333
334	1632.7534 8121	1798.4865 1914	1983.1897 4793	2189.1533 8609	2418.9528 0285	334
335	1646.6794 4627	1814.4739 0680	2001.5426 5823	2210.2206 2546	2443.1344 3388	335
336	1660.7156 5856	1830.5945 2269	2020.0561 5649	2231.4809 8120	2467.5478 0554	336
337	1674.8629 9085	1846.8494 7704	2038.7316 4785	2252.9362 2352	2492.1951 3868	337
338	1689.1223 2286	1863.2398 8935	2057.5705 4977	2274.5881 3891	2517.0786 7542	338
339	1703.4945 4125	1879.7668 8843	2076.5742 9208	2296.4385 3018	2542.2006 7939	339
340	1717.9805 3970	1896.4316 1250	2095.7443 1714	2318.4892 1671	2567.5634 3591	340
341	1732.5812 1898	1913.2352 0927	2115.0820 7991	2340.7420 3453	2593.1692 5217	341
342	1747.2974 8696	1930.1788 3601	2134.5890 4811	2363.1988 3651	2619.0204 5750	342
343	1762.1302 5873	1947.2636 5965	2154.2667 0229	2385.8614 9251	2645.1194 0355	343
344	1777.0804 5661	1964.4908 5681	2174.1165 3593	2408.7318 8952	2671.4684 6450	344
345	1792.1490 1023	1981.8616 1395	2194.1400 5562	2431.8119 3185	2698.0700 3729	345
346	1807.3368 5656	1999.3771 2740	2214.3387 8111	2455.1035 4122	2724.9265 4181	346
347	1822.6449 4001	2017.0386 0346	2234.7142 4544	2478.6086 5701	2752.0404 2117	347
348	1838.0742 1245	2034.8472 5849	2255.2679 9509	2502.3292 3637	2779.4141 4187	348
349	1853.6256 3330	2052.8043 1898	2276.0015 9005	2526.2672 5437	2807.0501 9407	349
350	1869.3001 6956	2070.9110 2164	2296.9166 0396	2550.4247 0420	2834.9510 9176	350
351	1885.0987 9590	2089.1686 1348	2318.0146 2424	2574.8035 9732	2863.1193 7305	351
352	1901.0224 9470	2107.5783 5193	2339.2972 5221	2599.4059 6363	2891.5576 0038	352
353	1917.0722 5612	2126.1415 0486	2360.7661 0316	2624.2338 5163	2920.2683 6072	353
354	1933.2490 7815	2144.8593 5074	2382.4228 0656	2649.2893 2861	2949.2542 6584	354
355	1949.5539 6668	2163.7331 7866	2404.2690 0612	2674.5744 8079	2978.5179 5255	355
356	1965.9879 3559	2182.7642 8848	2426.3063 5993	2700.0914 1353	3008.0620 8293	356
357	1982.5520 0674	2201.9539 9089	2448.5365 4058	2725.8422 5148	3037.8893 4456	357
358	1999.2472 1013	2221.3036 0748	2470.9612 3531	2751.8291 3879	3068.0024 5078	358
359	2016.0745 8388	2240.8144 7087	2493.5821 4611	2778.0542 3923	3098.4041 4093	359
360	2033.0351 7433	2260.4879 2480	2516.4009 8989	2804.5197 3642	3129.0971 8062	360

TABLE III

N	1	1 1/8	1 1/4	1 3/8	1 1/2	N
1	1.0000 0000	1.0000 0000	1.0000 0000	1.0000 0000	1.0000 0000	1
2	2.0100 0000	2.0112 5000	2.0125 0000	2.0137 5000	2.0150 0000	2
3	3.0301 0000	3.0338 7656	3.0376 5625	3.0414 3906	3.0452 2500	3
4	4.0604 0100	4.0680 0767	4.0756 2695	4.0832 5885	4.0909 0337	4
5	5.1010 0501	5.1137 7276	5.1265 7229	5.1394 0366	5.1522 6693	5
6	6.1520 1506	6.1713 0270	6.1906 5444	6.2100 7046	6.2295 5093	6
7	7.2135 3521	7.2407 2986	7.2680 3762	7.2954 5893	7.3229 9419	7
8	8.2856 7056	8.3221 8807	8.3588 8809	8.3957 7149	8.4328 3911	8
9	9.3685 2727	9.4158 1269	9.4633 7420	9.5112 1335	9.5593 3169	9
10	10.4622 1254	10.5217 4058	10.5816 6637	10.6419 9253	10.7027 2167	10
11	11.5668 3467	11.6401 1016	11.7139 3720	11.7883 1993	11.8632 6249	11
12	12.6825 0301	12.7710 6140	12.8603 6142	12.9504 0933	13.0412 1143	12
13	13.8093 2804	13.9147 3584	14.0211 1594	14.1284 7745	14.2368 2960	13
14	14.9474 2132	15.0712 7662	15.1963 7988	15.3227 4402	15.4503 8205	14
15	16.0968 9554	16.2408 2848	16.3863 3463	16.5334 3175	16.6821 3778	15
16	17.2578 6449	17.4235 3780	17.5911 6382	17.7607 6644	17.9323 6984	16
17	18.4304 4314	18.6195 5260	18.8110 5336	19.0049 7697	19.2013 5539	17
18	19.6147 4757	19.8290 2257	20.0461 9153	20.2662 9541	20.4893 7572	18
19	20.8108 9504	21.0520 9907	21.2967 6893	21.5449 5697	21.7967 1636	19
20	22.0190 0399	22.2889 3519	22.5629 7854	22.8412 0013	23.1236 6710	20
21	23.2391 9403	23.5396 8571	23.8450 1577	24.1552 6663	24.4705 2211	21
22	24.4715 8598	24.8045 0717	25.1430 7847	25.4874 0155	25.8375 7994	22
23	25.7163 0183	26.0835 5788	26.4573 6695	26.8378 5332	27.2251 4364	23
24	26.9734 6485	27.3769 9790	27.7880 8403	28.2068 7380	28.6335 2080	24
25	28.2431 9950	28.6849 8913	29.1354 3508	29.5947 1832	30.0630 2361	25
26	29.5256 3150	30.0076 9526	30.4996 2802	31.0016 4569	31.5139 6896	26
27	30.8208 8781	31.3452 8183	31.8808 7337	32.4279 1832	32.9866 7850	27
28	32.1290 9669	32.6979 1625	33.2793 8429	33.8738 0220	34.4814 7867	28
29	33.4503 8766	34.0657 6781	34.6953 7659	35.3395 6698	35.9987 0085	29
30	34.7848 9153	35.4490 0769	36.1290 6880	36.8254 8602	37.5386 8137	30
31	36.1327 4045	36.8478 0903	37.5806 8216	38.3318 3646	39.1017 6159	31
32	37.4940 6785	38.2623 4688	39.0504 4069	39.8588 9921	40.6882 8801	32
33	38.8690 0853	39.6927 9829	40.5385 7120	41.4069 5907	42.2986 1233	33
34	40.2576 9862	41.1393 4227	42.0453 0334	42.9763 0476	43.9330 9152	34
35	41.6602 7560	42.6021 5987	43.5708 6963	44.5672 2895	45.5920 8789	35
36	43.0768 7836	44.0814 3417	45.1155 0550	46.1800 2835	47.2759 6921	36
37	44.5076 4714	45.5773 5030	46.6794 4932	47.8150 0374	48.9851 0874	37
38	45.9527 2361	47.0900 9549	48.2629 4243	49.4724 6004	50.7198 8538	38
39	47.4122 5085	48.6198 5906	49.8662 2921	51.1527 0636	52.4806 8366	39
40	48.8863 7336	50.1668 3248	51.4895 5708	52.8560 5608	54.2678 9391	40
41	50.3752 3709	51.7312 0934	53.1331 7654	54.5828 2685	56.0819 1232	41
42	51.8789 8946	53.3131 8545	54.7973 4125	56.3333 4072	57.9231 4100	42
43	53.3977 7936	54.9129 5879	56.4823 0801	58.1079 2415	59.7919 8812	43
44	54.9317 5715	56.5307 2957	58.1883 3687	59.9069 0811	61.6888 6794	44
45	56.4810 7472	58.1667 0028	59.9156 9108	61.7306 2809	63.6142 0096	45
46	58.0458 8547	59.8210 7566	61.6646 3721	63.5794 2423	65.5684 1398	46
47	59.6263 4432	61.4940 6276	63.4354 4518	65.4536 4131	67.5519 4018	47
48	61.2226 0777	63.1858 7097	65.2283 8824	67.3536 2888	69.5652 1929	48
49	62.8348 3385	64.8967 1201	67.0437 4310	69.2797 4128	71.6086 9758	49
50	64.4631 8218	66.6268 0002	68.8817 8989	71.2323 3772	73.6828 2804	50
51	66.1078 1401	68.3763 5152	70.7428 1226	73.2117 8237	75.7880 7046	51
52	67.7688 9215	70.1455 8548	72.6270 9741	75.2184 4437	77.9248 9152	52
53	69.4465 8107	71.9347 2332	74.5349 3613	77.2526 9798	80.0937 6489	53
54	71.1410 4688	73.7439 8895	76.4666 2283	79.3149 2258	82.2951 7136	54
55	72.8524 5735	75.5736 0883	78.4224 5562	81.4055 0277	84.5295 9893	55
56	74.5809 8192	77.4238 1193	80.4027 3631	83.5248 2843	86.7975 4292	56
57	76.3267 9174	79.2948 2981	82.4077 7052	85.6732 9482	89.0995 0606	57
58	78.0900 5966	81.1868 9665	84.4378 6765	87.8513 0262	91.4359 9865	58
59	79.8709 6025	83.1002 4923	86.4933 4099	90.0592 5804	93.8075 3863	59
60	81.6696 6986	85.0351 2704	88.5745 0776	92.2975 7283	96.2146 5171	60

TABLE III

N	1	1 1/8	1 1/4	1 3/8	1 1/2	N
61	83.4863 6655	86.9917 7222	90.6816 8910	94.5666 6446	98.6578 7149	61
62	85.3212 3022	88.9704 2966	92.8152 1022	96.8669 5610	101.1377 3956	62
63	87.1744 4252	90.9713 4699	94.9754 0034	99.1988 7674	103.6548 0565	63
64	89.0461 8695	92.9947 7464	97.1625 9285	101.5628 6130	106.2096 2774	64
65	90.9366 4882	95.0409 6586	99.3771 2526	103.9593 5064	108.8027 7215	65
66	92.8460 1531	97.1101 7672	101.6193 3933	106.3887 9171	111.4348 1374	66
67	94.7744 7546	99.2026 6621	103.8895 8107	108.8516 3760	114.1063 3594	67
68	96.7222 2021	101.3186 9621	106.1882 0083	111.3483 4761	116.8179 3098	68
69	98.6894 4242	103.4585 3154	108.5155 5334	113.8793 8739	119.5701 9995	69
70	100.6763 3684	105.6224 4002	110.8719 9776	116.4452 2897	122.3637 5295	70
71	102.6831 0021	107.8106 9247	113.2578 9773	119.0463 5087	125.1992 0924	71
72	104.7099 3121	110.0235 6276	115.6736 2145	121.6832 3819	128.0771 9738	72
73	106.7570 3052	112.2613 2784	118.1195 4172	124.3563 8272	130.9983 5534	73
74	108.8246 0083	114.5242 6778	120.5960 3599	127.0662 8298	133.9633 3067	74
75	110.9128 4684	116.8126 6579	123.1034 8644	129.8134 4437	136.9727 8063	75
76	113.0219 7530	119.1268 0828	125.6422 8002	132.5983 7923	140.0273 7234	76
77	115.1521 9506	121.4669 8487	128.2128 0852	135.4216 0695	143.1277 8292	77
78	117.3037 1701	123.8334 8845	130.8154 6863	138.2836 5404	146.2746 9967	78
79	119.4767 5418	126.2266 1520	133.4506 6199	141.1850 5429	149.4688 2016	79
80	121.6715 2172	128.6466 6462	136.1187 9526	144.1263 4878	152.7108 5247	80
81	123.8882 3694	131.0939 3960	138.8202 8020	147.1080 8608	156.0015 1525	81
82	126.1271 1931	133.5687 4642	141.5555 3370	150.1308 2226	159.3415 3798	82
83	128.3883 9050	136.0713 9481	144.3249 7787	153.1951 2107	162.7316 6105	83
84	130.6722 7440	138.6021 9801	147.1290 4010	156.3015 5398	166.1726 3597	84
85	132.9789 9715	141.1614 7273	149.9681 5310	159.4507 0035	169.6652 2551	85
86	135.3087 8712	143.7495 3930	152.8427 5501	162.6431 4748	173.2102 0389	86
87	137.6618 7499	146.3667 2162	155.7532 8945	165.8794 9076	176.8083 5695	87
88	140.0384 9374	149.0133 4724	158.7002 0557	169.1603 3375	180.4604 8230	88
89	142.4388 7868	151.6897 4739	161.6839 5814	172.4862 8834	184.1673 8954	89
90	144.8632 6746	154.3962 5705	164.7050 0762	175.8579 7481	187.9299 0038	90
91	147.3119 0014	157.1332 1494	167.7638 2021	179.2760 2196	191.7488 4889	91
92	149.7850 1914	159.9009 6361	170.8608 6796	182.7410 6726	195.6250 8162	92
93	152.2828 6933	162.6998 4945	173.9966 2881	186.2537 5694	199.5594 5784	93
94	154.8056 9803	165.5302 2276	177.1715 8667	189.8147 4610	203.5528 4971	94
95	157.3537 5501	168.3924 3776	180.3862 3151	193.4246 9886	207.6061 4246	95
96	159.9272 9256	171.2868 5269	183.6410 5940	197.0842 8847	211.7202 3459	96
97	162.5265 6548	174.2138 2978	186.9365 7264	200.7941 9743	215.8960 3811	97
98	165.1518 3114	177.1737 3537	190.2732 7980	204.5551 1765	220.1344 7868	98
99	167.8033 4945	180.1669 3989	193.6516 9580	208.3677 5051	224.4364 9586	99
100	170.4813 8294	183.1938 1796	197.0723 4200	212.2328 0708	228.8030 4330	100
101	173.1861 9677	186.2547 4842	200.5357 4627	216.1510 0818	233.2350 8895	101
102	175.9180 5874	189.3501 1434	204.0424 4310	220.1230 8454	237.7336 1529	102
103	178.6772 3933	192.4803 0312	207.5929 7364	224.1497 7696	242.2996 1951	103
104	181.4640 1172	195.6457 0653	211.1878 8581	228.2318 3639	246.9341 1381	104
105	184.2786 5184	198.8467 2073	214.8277 3438	232.3700 2414	251.6381 2551	105
106	187.1214 3836	202.0837 4634	218.5130 8106	236.5651 1197	256.4126 9740	106
107	189.9926 5274	205.3571 8849	222.2444 9457	240.8178 8226	261.2588 8786	107
108	192.8925 7927	208.6674 5686	226.0225 5076	245.1291 2814	266.1777 7118	108
109	195.8215 0506	212.0149 6575	229.8478 3264	249.4996 5365	271.1704 3774	109
110	198.7797 2011	215.4001 3411	233.7209 3055	253.9302 7389	276.2379 9431	110
111	201.7675 1731	218.8233 8562	237.6424 4218	258.4218 1516	281.3815 6422	111
112	204.7851 9248	222.2851 4871	241.6129 7271	262.9751 1512	286.6022 8769	112
113	207.8330 4441	225.7858 5663	245.6331 3487	267.5910 2295	291.9013 2200	113
114	210.9113 7485	229.3259 4752	249.7035 4905	272.2703 9951	297.2798 4183	114
115	214.0204 8860	232.9058 6443	253.8248 4342	277.0141 1751	302.7390 3946	115
116	217.1606 9349	236.5260 5540	257.9976 5396	281.8230 6162	308.2801 2505	116
117	220.3323 0042	240.1869 7352	262.2226 2463	286.6981 2872	313.9043 2693	117
118	223.5356 2343	243.8890 7698	266.5004 0744	291.6402 2799	319.6128 9183	118
119	226.7709 7966	247.6328 2909	270.8316 6253	296.6502 8113	325.4070 8521	119
120	230.0386 8946	251.4186 9842	275.2170 5832	301.7292 2249	331.2881 9149	120

TABLE III

N	1	1 1/8	1 1/4	1 3/8	1 1/2	N
121	233.3390 7635	255.2471 5878	279.6572 7154	306.8779 9930	337.2575 1436	121
122	236.6724 6712	259.1186 8931	284.1529 8744	312.0975 7179	343.3163 7708	122
123	240.0391 9179	263.0337 7457	288.7048 9978	317.3889 1340	349.4661 2273	123
124	243.4395 8370	266.9929 0453	293.3137 1103	322.7530 1096	355.7081 1457	124
125	246.8739 7954	270.9965 7471	297.9801 3242	328.1908 6486	362.0437 3629	125
126	250.3427 1934	275.0452 8617	302.7048 8407	333.7034 8925	368.4743 9234	126
127	253.8461 4653	279.1395 4564	307.4886 9512	339.2919 1223	375.0015 0822	127
128	257.3846 0800	283.2798 6553	312.3323 0381	344.9571 7603	381.6265 3084	128
129	260.9584 5408	287.4667 6402	317.2364 5761	350.7003 3720	388.3509 2881	129
130	264.5680 3862	291.7007 6511	322.2019 1333	356.5224 6683	395.1761 9274	130
131	268.2137 1900	295.9823 9872	327.2294 3725	362.4246 5075	402.1038 3563	131
132	271.8958 5619	300.3122 0071	332.3198 0521	368.4079 8970	409.1353 9316	132
133	275.6148 1475	304.6907 1296	337.4738 0278	374.4735 9956	416.2724 2406	133
134	279.3709 6290	309.1184 8349	342.6922 2531	380.6226 1155	423.5165 1042	134
135	283.1646 7253	313.5960 6642	347.9758 7813	386.8561 7246	430.8692 5808	135
136	286.9963 1926	318.1240 2217	353.3255 7660	393.1754 4483	438.3322 9695	136
137	290.8662 8245	322.7029 1742	358.7421 4631	399.5816 0720	445.9072 8140	137
138	294.7749 4527	327.3333 2524	364.2264 2314	406.0758 5430	453.5958 9063	138
139	298.7226 9473	332.0158 2515	369.7792 5343	412.6593 9729	461.3998 2899	139
140	302.7099 2167	336.7510 0318	375.4014 9410	419.3334 6401	469.3208 2642	140
141	306.7370 2089	341.5394 5197	381.0940 1277	426.0992 9914	477.3606 3882	141
142	310.8043 9110	346.3817 7081	386.8576 8793	432.9581 6450	485.5210 4840	142
143	314.9124 3501	351.2785 6573	392.6934 0903	439.9113 3926	493.8038 6412	143
144	319.0615 5936	356.2304 4959	398.6020 7665	446.9601 2018	502.2109 2209	144
145	323.2521 7495	361.2380 4215	404.5846 0260	454.1058 2183	510.7440 8592	145
146	327.4846 9670	366.3019 7012	410.6419 1014	461.3497 7688	519.4052 4721	146
147	331.7595 4367	371.4228 6729	416.7749 3401	468.6933 3631	528.1963 2591	147
148	336.0771 3911	376.6013 7454	422.9846 2069	476.1378 6968	537.1192 7080	148
149	340.4379 1050	381.8381 4001	429.2719 2845	483.6847 6539	546.1760 5987	149
150	344.8422 8960	387.1338 1908	435.6378 2755	491.3354 3092	555.3687 0076	150
151	349.2907 1250	392.4890 7455	442.0833 0040	499.0912 9309	564.6992 3127	151
152	353.7836 1962	397.9045 7664	448.6093 4165	506.9537 9837	574.1697 1974	152
153	358.3214 5582	403.3810 0312	455.2169 5842	514.9244 1310	583.7822 6554	153
154	362.9046 7038	408.9190 3941	461.9071 7040	523.0046 2378	593.5389 9952	154
155	367.5337 1708	414.5193 7860	468.6810 1003	531.1959 3736	603.4420 8452	155
156	372.2090 5425	420.1827 2161	475.5395 2266	539.4998 8150	613.4937 1578	156
157	376.9311 4480	425.9097 7723	482.4837 6669	547.9180 0487	623.6961 2152	157
158	381.7004 5624	431.7012 6222	489.5148 1378	556.4518 7743	634.0515 6334	158
159	386.5174 6081	437.5579 0142	496.6337 4895	565.1030 9075	644.5623 3679	159
160	391.3826 3541	443.4804 2781	503.8416 7081	573.8732 5825	655.2307 7185	160
161	396.2964 6177	449.4695 8263	511.1396 9169	582.7640 1555	666.0592 3342	161
162	401.2594 2639	455.5261 1543	518.5289 3784	591.7770 2076	677.0501 2192	162
163	406.2720 2065	461.6507 8423	526.0105 4956	600.9139 5480	688.2058 7375	163
164	411.3347 4086	467.8443 5555	533.5856 8143	610.1765 2167	699.5289 6186	164
165	416.4480 8826	474.1076 0455	541.2555 0245	619.5664 4885	711.0218 9629	165
166	421.6125 6915	480.4413 1510	549.0211 9623	629.0854 8752	722.6872 2473	166
167	426.8286 9484	486.8462 7990	556.8839 6118	638.7354 1297	734.5275 3310	167
168	432.0969 8179	493.3233 0055	564.8450 1070	648.5180 2490	746.5454 4610	168
169	437.4179 5161	499.8731 8768	572.9055 7333	658.4351 4774	758.7436 2779	169
170	442.7921 3112	506.4967 6104	581.0668 9300	668.4886 3102	771.1247 8221	170
171	448.2200 5243	513.1948 4960	589.3302 2916	678.6803 4970	783.6916 5394	171
172	453.7022 5296	519.9682 9166	597.6968 5703	689.0122 0451	796.4470 2875	172
173	459.2392 7549	526.8179 3494	606.1680 6774	699.4861 2232	809.3937 3418	173
174	464.8316 6824	533.7446 3671	614.7451 6859	710.1040 5650	822.5346 4019	174
175	470.4799 8492	540.7492 6387	623.4294 8319	720.8679 8728	835.8726 5980	175
176	476.1847 8477	547.8326 9309	632.2223 5173	731.7799 2210	849.4107 4969	176
177	481.9466 3262	554.9958 1089	641.1251 3113	742.8418 9603	863.1519 1094	177
178	487.7660 9895	562.2395 1376	650.1391 9527	754.0559 7210	877.0991 8960	178
179	493.6437 5994	569.5647 0829	659.2659 3521	765.4242 4172	891.2556 7745	179
180	499.5801 9754	576.9723 1126	668.5067 5940	776.9488 2504	905.6245 1261	180

TABLE III

N	1	1 1/8	1 1/4	1 3/8	1 1/2	N
181	505.5759 9951	584.4632 4976	677.8630 9389	788.6318 7139	920.2088 8030	181
182	511.6317 5951	592.0384 6132	687.3363 8257	800.4755 5962	935.0120 1350	182
183	517.7480 7710	599.6988 9401	696.9280 8735	812.4820 9857	950.0371 9370	183
184	523.9255 5787	607.4455 0657	706.6396 8844	824.6537 2742	965.2877 5161	184
185	530.1648 1345	615.2792 6852	716.4726 8455	836.9927 1617	980.7670 6788	185
186	536.4664 6159	623.2011 6029	726.4285 9310	849.5013 6602	996.4785 7390	186
187	542.8311 2620	631.2121 7334	736.5089 5052	862.1820 0980	1012.4257 5251	187
188	549.2594 3746	639.3133 1029	746.7153 1240	875.0370 1244	1028.6121 3880	188
189	555.7520 3184	647.5055 8503	757.0492 5380	888.0687 7136	1045.0413 2088	189
190	562.3095 5216	655.7900 2286	767.5123 6948	901.2797 1696	1061.7169 4069	190
191	568.9326 4768	664.1676 6062	778.1062 7409	914.6723 1307	1078.6426 9480	191
192	575.6219 7415	672.6395 4680	788.8326 0252	928.2490 5738	1095.8223 3523	192
193	582.3781 9390	681.2067 4170	799.6930 1005	942.0124 8192	1113.2596 7026	193
194	589.2019 7584	689.8703 1755	810.6891 7268	955.9651 5354	1130.9585 6531	194
195	596.0939 9559	698.6313 5862	821.8227 8734	970.1096 7440	1148.9229 4379	195
196	603.0549 3555	707.4909 6140	833.0955 7218	984.4486 8243	1167.1567 8795	196
197	610.0854 8490	716.4502 3472	844.5092 6683	998.9848 5181	1185.6641 3976	197
198	617.1863 3975	725.5102 9986	856.0656 3267	1013.7208 9352	1204.4491 0186	198
199	624.3582 0315	734.6722 9073	867.7664 5307	1028.6595 5581	1223.5158 3839	199
200	631.6017 8518	743.9373 5401	879.6135 3374	1043.8036 2470	1242.8685 7597	200
201	638.9178 0303	753.3066 4924	891.6087 0291	1059.1559 2454	1262.5116 0460	201
202	646.3069 8107	762.7813 4904	903.7538 1170	1074.7193 1850	1282.4492 7867	202
203	653.7700 5088	772.3626 3922	916.0507 3434	1090.4967 0913	1302.6860 1785	203
204	661.3077 5138	782.0517 1891	928.5013 6852	1106.4910 3888	1323.2263 0812	204
205	668.9208 2890	791.8498 0075	941.1076 3563	1122.7052 9067	1344.0747 0274	205
206	676.6100 3719	801.7581 1101	953.8714 8107	1139.1424 8841	1365.2358 2328	206
207	684.3761 3756	811.7778 8975	966.7948 7459	1155.8056 9763	1386.7143 6063	207
208	692.2198 9893	821.9103 9101	979.8798 1052	1172.6980 2597	1408.5150 7604	208
209	700.1420 9792	832.1568 8291	993.1283 0815	1189.8226 2383	1430.6428 0218	209
210	708.1435 1890	842.5186 4785	1006.5424 1200	1207.1826 8491	1453.1024 4422	210
211	716.2249 5409	852.9969 8263	1020.1241 9215	1224.7814 4683	1475.8989 8088	211
212	724.3872 0363	863.5931 9869	1033.8757 4455	1242.6221 9172	1499.0374 6559	212
213	732.6310 7567	874.3086 2217	1047.7991 9136	1260.7082 4686	1522.5230 2758	213
214	740.9573 8643	885.1445 9417	1061.8966 8125	1279.0429 8525	1546.3608 7299	214
215	749.3669 6029	896.1024 7086	1076.1703 8977	1297.6298 2630	1570.5562 8609	215
216	757.8606 2989	907.1836 2366	1090.6225 1964	1316.4722 3641	1595.1146 3038	216
217	766.4392 3619	918.3894 3942	1105.2553 0114	1335.5737 2966	1620.0413 4983	217
218	775.1036 2855	929.7213 2061	1120.0709 9240	1354.9378 6844	1645.3419 7008	218
219	783.8546 6484	941.1806 8547	1135.0718 7980	1374.5682 6413	1671.0220 9963	219
220	792.6932 1149	952.7689 6818	1150.2602 7830	1394.4685 7776	1697.0874 3113	220
221	801.6201 4360	964.4876 1908	1165.6385 3178	1414.6425 2071	1723.5437 4259	221
222	810.6363 4504	976.3381 0479	1181.2090 1343	1435.0938 5537	1750.3968 9873	222
223	819.7427 0849	988.3219 0847	1196.9741 2610	1455.8263 9588	1777.6528 5221	223
224	828.9401 3557	1000.4405 2994	1212.9363 0267	1476.8440 0882	1805.3176 4500	224
225	838.2295 3693	1012.6954 8590	1229.0980 0646	1498.1506 1394	1833.3974 0967	225
226	847.6118 3230	1025.0883 1012	1245.4617 3154	1519.7501 8489	1861.8983 7082	226
227	857.0879 5062	1037.6205 5361	1262.0300 0318	1541.6467 4993	1890.8268 4638	227
228	866.6588 3013	1050.2937 8483	1278.8053 7822	1563.8443 9274	1920.1892 4907	228
229	876.3254 1843	1063.1095 8991	1295.7904 4545	1586.3472 5314	1949.9920 8781	229
230	886.0886 7261	1076.0695 7280	1312.9878 2602	1609.1595 2787	1980.2419 6913	230
231	895.9495 5934	1089.1753 5549	1330.4001 7384	1632.2854 7138	2010.9455 9866	231
232	905.9090 5493	1102.4285 7824	1348.0301 7601	1655.7293 9661	2042.1097 8264	232
233	915.9681 4548	1115.8308 9975	1365.8805 5321	1679.4956 7581	2073.7414 2938	233
234	926.1278 2694	1129.3839 9737	1383.9540 6013	1703.5887 4136	2105.8475 5082	234
235	936.3891 0521	1143.0895 6734	1402.2534 8588	1728.0130 8655	2138.4352 6409	235
236	946.7529 9626	1156.9493 2497	1420.7816 5446	1752.7732 6649	2171.5117 9305	236
237	957.2205 2622	1170.9650 0488	1439.5414 2514	1777.8738 9890	2205.0844 6994	237
238	967.7927 3148	1185.1383 6118	1458.5356 9295	1803.3196 6501	2239.1607 3699	238
239	978.4706 5880	1199.4711 6775	1477.7673 8911	1829.1153 1041	2273.7481 4805	239
240	989.2553 6539	1213.9652 1839	1497.2394 8148	1855.2656 4593	2308.8543 7027	240

TABLE III

N	1	1 1/8	1 1/4	1 3/8	1 1/2	N
241	1000.1479 1904	1228.6223 2709	1516.9549 7499	1881.7755 4856	2344.4871 8582	241
242	1011.1493 9823	1243.4443 2827	1536.9169 1218	1908.6499 6235	2380.6544 9361	242
243	1022.2608 9221	1258.4330 7696	1557.1283 7358	1935.8938 9933	2417.3643 1101	243
244	1033.4835 0114	1273.5904 4908	1577.5924 7825	1963.5124 4045	2454.6247 7568	244
245	1044.8183 3615	1288.9183 4163	1598.3123 8423	1991.5107 3650	2492.4441 4731	245
246	1056.2665 1951	1304.4186 7298	1619.2912 8903	2019.8940 0913	2530.8308 0952	246
247	1067.8291 8470	1320.0933 8305	1640.5324 3015	2048.6675 5176	2569.7932 7167	247
248	1079.5074 7655	1335.9444 3361	1662.0390 8552	2077.8367 3059	2609.3401 7074	248
249	1091.3025 5132	1351.9738 0848	1683.8145 7409	2107.4069 8564	2649.4802 7330	249
250	1103.2155 7683	1368.1835 1383	1705.8622 5627	2137.3838 3169	2690.2224 7740	250
251	1115.2477 3260	1384.5755 7836	1728.1855 3447	2167.7728 5938	2731.5758 1456	251
252	1127.4002 0992	1401.1520 5362	1750.7878 5365	2198.5797 3619	2773.5494 5178	252
253	1139.6742 1202	1417.9150 1422	1773.6727 0182	2229.8102 0757	2816.1526 9356	253
254	1152.0709 5414	1434.8665 5813	1796.8436 1060	2261.4700 9792	2859.3949 8396	254
255	1164.5916 6368	1452.0088 0691	1820.3041 5573	2293.5653 1177	2903.2859 0872	255
256	1177.2375 8032	1469.3439 0599	1844.0579 5768	2326.1018 3480	2947.8351 9735	256
257	1190.0099 5612	1486.8740 2493	1868.1086 8215	2359.0857 3503	2993.0527 2531	257
258	1202.9100 5569	1504.6013 5771	1892.4600 4067	2392.5231 6389	3038.9485 1619	258
259	1215.9391 5624	1522.5281 2298	1917.1157 9118	2426.4203 5739	3085.5327 4393	259
260	1229.0985 4781	1540.6565 6437	1942.0797 3857	2460.7836 3731	3132.8157 3509	260
261	1242.3895 3328	1558.9889 5072	1967.3557 3530	2495.6194 1232	3180.8079 7112	261
262	1255.8134 2862	1577.5275 7641	1992.9476 8200	2530.9341 7924	3229.5200 9069	262
263	1269.3715 6290	1596.2747 6165	2018.8595 2802	2566.7345 2420	3278.9628 9205	263
264	1283.0652 7853	1615.2328 5272	2045.0952 7212	2603.0271 2391	3329.1473 3543	264
265	1296.8959 3132	1634.4042 2231	2071.6589 6302	2639.8187 4687	3380.0845 4546	265
266	1310.8648 9063	1653.7912 6981	2098.5547 0006	2677.1162 5463	3431.7858 1364	266
267	1324.9735 3954	1673.3964 2159	2125.7866 3381	2714.9266 0314	3484.2626 0085	267
268	1339.2232 7493	1693.2221 3134	2153.3589 6673	2753.2568 4393	3537.5265 3986	268
269	1353.6155 0768	1713.2708 8032	2181.2759 5382	2792.1141 2553	3591.5894 3796	269
270	1368.1516 6276	1733.5451 7772	2209.5419 0324	2831.5056 9476	3646.4632 7953	270
271	1382.8331 7939	1754.0475 6097	2238.1611 7703	2871.4388 9806	3702.1602 2872	271
272	1397.6615 1118	1774.7805 9603	2267.1381 9174	2911.9211 8291	3758.6926 3215	272
273	1412.6381 2629	1795.7468 7773	2296.4774 1914	2952.9600 9918	3816.0730 2163	273
274	1427.7645 0755	1816.9490 3011	2326.1833 8688	2994.5633 0054	3874.3141 1696	274
275	1443.0421 5263	1838.3897 0670	2356.2606 7922	3036.7385 4592	3933.4288 2871	275
276	1458.4725 7416	1860.0715 9090	2386.7139 3771	3079.4937 0093	3993.4302 6114	276
277	1474.0572 9990	1881.9973 9630	2417.5478 6193	3122.8367 3932	4054.3317 1506	277
278	1489.7978 7290	1904.1698 6700	2448.7672 1020	3166.7757 4448	4116.1466 9078	278
279	1505.6958 5163	1926.5917 7801	2480.3768 0033	3211.3189 1097	4178.8888 9115	279
280	1521.7528 1014	1949.2659 3551	2512.3815 1033	3256.4745 4599	4242.5722 2451	280
281	1537.9703 3824	1972.1951 7728	2544.7862 7921	3302.2510 7100	4307.2108 0788	281
282	1554.3500 4163	1995.3823 7303	2577.5961 0770	3348.6570 2323	4372.8189 7000	282
283	1570.8935 4204	2018.8304 2473	2610.8160 5905	3395.7010 5730	4439.4112 5455	283
284	1587.6024 7746	2042.5422 6700	2644.4512 5979	3443.3919 4683	4507.0024 2337	284
285	1604.4785 0224	2066.5208 6751	2678.5069 0053	3491.7385 8610	4575.6074 5972	285
286	1621.5232 8726	2090.7692 2727	2712.9882 3679	3540.7499 9166	4645.2415 7161	286
287	1638.7385 2013	2115.2903 8107	2747.9005 8975	3590.4353 0405	4715.9201 9519	287
288	1656.1259 0533	2140.0873 9786	2783.2493 4712	3640.8037 8948	4787.6589 9812	288
289	1673.6871 6439	2165.1633 8109	2819.0399 6396	3691.8648 4158	4860.4738 8309	289
290	1691.4240 3603	2190.5214 6912	2855.2779 6351	3743.6279 8316	4934.3809 9133	290
291	1709.3382 7639	2216.1648 3565	2891.9689 3806	3796.1028 6792	5009.3967 0620	291
292	1727.4316 5915	2242.0966 9005	2929.1185 4978	3849.2992 8236	5085.5376 5680	292
293	1745.7059 7575	2268.3202 7782	2966.7325 3165	3903.2271 4749	5162.8207 2165	293
294	1764.1630 3550	2294.8388 8094	3004.8166 8830	3957.8965 2077	5241.2630 3247	294
295	1782.8046 6586	2321.6558 1835	3043.3768 9690	4013.3175 9793	5320.8819 7796	295
296	1801.6327 1252	2348.7744 4631	3082.4191 0811	4069.5007 1490	5401.6952 0763	296
297	1820.6490 3964	2376.1981 5883	3121.9493 4697	4126.4563 4973	5483.7206 3574	297
298	1839.8555 3004	2403.9303 8812	3161.9737 1380	4184.1951 2454	5566.9764 4528	298
299	1859.2540 8534	2431.9746 0498	3202.4983 8523	4242.7278 0750	5651.4810 9196	299
300	1878.8466 2619	2460.3343 1929	3243.5296 1504	4302.0653 1485	5737.2533 0834	300

TABLE III

N	1	1 1/8	1 1/4	1 3/8	1 1/2	N
301	1898.6350 9245	2489.0130 8038	3285.0737 3523	4362.2187 1293	5824.3121 0796	301
302	1918.6214 4338	2518.0144 7754	3327.1371 5692	4423.1992 2024	5912.6767 8958	302
303	1938.8076 5781	2547.3421 4041	3369.7263 7138	4485.0182 0952	6002.3669 4143	303
304	1959.1957 3439	2576.9997 3949	3412.8479 5102	4547.6872 0990	6093.4024 4555	304
305	1979.7876 9173	2606.9909 8656	3456.5085 5041	4611.2179 0903	6185.8034 8223	305
306	2000.5855 6865	2637.3196 3515	3500.7149 0729	4675.6221 5528	6279.5905 3447	306
307	2021.5914 2434	2667.9894 8105	3545.4738 4363	4740.9119 5992	6374.7843 9248	307
308	2042.8073 3858	2699.0043 6271	3590.7922 6668	4807.0994 9937	6471.4061 5837	308
309	2064.2354 1197	2730.3681 6179	3636.6771 7001	4874.1971 1748	6569.4772 5075	309
310	2085.8777 6609	2762.0848 0361	3683.1356 3464	4942.2173 2785	6669.0194 0951	310
311	2107.7365 4375	2794.1582 5765	3730.1748 3007	5011.1728 1610	6770.0547 0065	311
312	2129.8139 0919	2826.5925 3805	3777.8020 1544	5081.0764 4233	6872.6055 2116	312
313	2152.1120 4828	2859.3917 0411	3826.0245 4064	5151.9412 4341	6976.6946 0398	313
314	2174.6331 6876	2892.5598 6078	3874.8498 4740	5223.7804 3550	7082.3450 2304	314
315	2197.3795 0045	2926.1011 5921	3924.2854 7049	5296.6074 1649	7189.5801 9838	315
316	2220.3532 9545	2960.0197 9725	3974.3390 3887	5370.4357 6847	7298.4239 0136	316
317	2243.5568 2841	2994.3200 1997	4025.0182 7686	5445.2792 6029	7408.9002 5988	317
318	2266.9923 9669	3029.0061 2019	4076.3310 0532	5521.1518 5012	7521.0337 6378	318
319	2290.6623 2066	3064.0824 3905	4128.2851 4288	5598.0676 8805	7634.8492 7023	319
320	2314.5689 4386	3099.5533 6649	4180.8887 0717	5676.0411 1877	7750.3720 0929	320
321	2338.7146 3330	3135.4233 4186	4234.1498 1601	5755.0866 8415	7867.6275 8942	321
322	2363.1017 7964	3171.6968 5446	4288.0766 8871	5835.2191 2606	7986.6420 0327	322
323	2387.7327 9743	3208.3784 4407	4342.6776 4732	5916.4533 8904	8107.4416 3332	323
324	2412.6101 2541	3245.4727 0156	4397.9611 1791	5998.8046 2314	8230.0532 5781	324
325	2437.7362 2666	3282.9842 6946	4453.9356 3188	6082.2881 8671	8354.5040 5668	325
326	2463.1135 8893	3320.9178 4249	4510.6098 2728	6166.9196 4927	8480.8216 1753	326
327	2488.7447 2482	3359.2781 6822	4567.9924 5012	6252.7147 9445	8609.0339 4180	327
328	2514.6321 7206	3398.0700 4761	4626.0923 5575	6339.6896 2287	8739.1694 5092	328
329	2540.7784 9379	3437.2983 3564	4684.9185 1020	6427.8603 5519	8871.2569 9269	329
330	2567.1862 7872	3476.9679 4192	4744.4799 9157	6517.2434 3507	9005.3258 4758	330
331	2593.8581 4151	3517.0838 3127	4804.7859 9147	6607.8555 3230	9141.4057 3529	331
332	2620.7967 2293	3557.6510 2437	4865.8458 1636	6699.7135 4587	9279.5268 2132	332
333	2648.0046 9016	3598.6745 9839	4927.6688 8906	6792.8346 0713	9419.7197 2364	333
334	2675.4847 3706	3640.1596 8762	4990.2647 5018	6887.2360 8298	9562.0155 1949	334
335	2703.2395 8443	3682.1114 8411	5053.6430 5956	6982.9355 7912	9706.4457 5229	335
336	2731.2719 8027	3724.5352 3831	5117.8135 9780	7079.9509 4333	9853.0424 3857	336
337	2759.5847 0007	3767.4362 5974	5182.7862 6777	7178.3002 6880	10001.8380 7515	337
338	2788.1805 4707	3810.8199 1766	5248.5710 9612	7278.0018 9750	10152.8656 4628	338
339	2817.0623 5255	3854.6916 4173	5315.1782 3482	7379.0744 2359	10306.1586 3097	339
340	2846.2329 7607	3899.0569 2270	5382.6179 6276	7481.5366 9691	10461.7510 1043	340
341	2875.6953 0583	3943.9213 1308	5450.9006 8729	7585.4078 2650	10619.6772 7559	341
342	2905.4522 5889	3989.2904 2785	5520.0369 4588	7690.7071 8411	10779.9724 3473	342
343	2935.5067 8148	4035.1699 4517	5590.0374 0771	7797.4544 0789	10942.6720 2125	343
344	2965.8618 4929	4081.5656 0705	5660.9128 7530	7905.6694 0600	11107.8121 0156	344
345	2996.5204 6779	4128.4832 2013	5732.6742 8624	8015.3723 6033	11275.4292 8309	345
346	3027.4856 7246	4175.9286 5636	5805.3327 1482	8126.5837 3029	11445.5607 2233	346
347	3058.7605 2919	4223.9078 5374	5878.8993 7376	8239.3242 5658	11618.2441 3317	347
348	3090.3481 3448	4272.4268 1710	5953.3856 1593	8353.6149 6511	11793.5177 9517	348
349	3122.2516 1583	4321.4916 1879	6028.8029 3613	8469.4771 7088	11971.4205 6209	349
350	3154.4741 3198	4371.1083 9950	6105.1629 7283	8586.9324 8198	12151.9918 7053	350
351	3187.0188 7330	4421.2833 6899	6182.4775 0999	8706.0028 0360	12335.2717 4858	351
352	3219.8890 6204	4472.0228 0689	6260.7584 7886	8826.7103 4215	12521.3008 2481	352
353	3253.0879 5266	4523.3330 6347	6340.0179 5985	8949.0776 0936	12710.1203 3718	353
354	3286.6188 3218	4575.2205 6044	6420.2681 8435	9073.1274 2649	12901.7721 4224	354
355	3320.4850 2051	4627.6917 9174	6501.5215 3665	9198.8829 2860	13096.2987 2438	355
356	3354.6898 7071	4680.7533 2440	6583.7905 5586	9326.3675 6887	13293.7432 0524	356
357	3389.2367 6942	4734.4117 9930	6667.0879 3781	9455.6051 2294	13494.1493 5332	357
358	3424.1291 3711	4788.6739 3204	6751.4265 3703	9586.6196 9338	13697.5615 9362	358
359	3459.3704 2848	4843.5465 1378	6836.8193 6874	9719.4357 1417	13904.0250 1752	359
360	3494.9641 3277	4899.0364 1206	6923.2796 1085	9854.0779 5524	14113.5853 9279	360

TABLE III

N	1 5/8	1 3/4	1 7/8	2	2 1/8	N
1	1.0000 0000	1.0000 0000	1.0000 0000	1.0000 0000	1.0000 0000	1
2	2.0162 5000	2.0175 0000	2.0187 5000	2.0200 0000	2.0212 5000	2
3	3.0490 1406	3.0528 0625	3.0566 0156	3.0604 0000	3.0642 0156	3
4	4.0985 6054	4.1062 3036	4.1139 1284	4.1216 0800	4.1293 1585	4
5	5.1651 6215	5.1780 8939	5.1910 4871	5.2040 4016	5.2170 6381	5
6	6.2490 9603	6.2687 0596	6.2883 8087	6.3081 2096	6.3279 2641	6
7	7.3506 4385	7.3784 0831	7.4062 8801	7.4342 8338	7.4623 9485	7
8	8.4700 9181	8.5075 3045	8.5451 5591	8.5829 6905	8.6209 7074	8
9	9.6077 3080	9.6564 1224	9.7053 7759	9.7546 2843	9.8041 6637	9
10	10.7638 5643	10.8253 9945	10.8873 5342	10.9497 2100	11.0125 0490	10
11	11.9387 6909	12.0148 4394	12.0914 9129	12.1687 1542	12.2465 2063	11
12	13.1327 7409	13.2251 0371	13.3182 0675	13.4120 8973	13.5067 5920	12
13	14.3461 8167	14.4565 4303	14.5679 2313	14.6803 3152	14.7937 7783	13
14	15.5793 0712	15.7095 3253	15.8410 7169	15.9739 3815	16.1081 4561	14
15	16.8324 7086	16.9844 4935	17.1380 9178	17.2934 1692	17.4504 4370	15
16	18.1059 9851	18.2816 7721	18.4594 3100	18.6392 8525	18.8212 6563	16
17	19.4002 2099	19.6016 0656	19.8055 4534	20.0120 7096	20.2212 1753	17
18	20.7154 7458	20.9446 3468	21.1768 9931	21.4123 1238	21.6509 1840	18
19	22.0521 0104	22.3111 6578	22.5739 6617	22.8405 5863	23.1110 0041	19
20	23.4104 4768	23.7016 1119	23.9972 2804	24.2973 6980	24.6021 0917	20
21	24.7908 6746	25.1163 8938	25.4471 7606	25.7833 1719	26.1249 0399	21
22	26.1937 1905	26.5559 2620	26.9243 1062	27.2989 8354	27.6800 5820	22
23	27.6193 6699	28.0206 5490	28.4291 4144	28.8449 6321	29.2682 5944	23
24	29.0681 8170	29.5110 1637	29.9621 8784	30.4218 6247	30.8902 0995	24
25	30.5405 3966	31.0274 5915	31.5239 7886	32.0302 9972	32.5466 2691	25
26	32.0368 2343	32.5704 3969	33.1150 5347	33.6709 0572	34.2382 4274	26
27	33.5574 2181	34.1404 2238	34.7359 6072	35.3443 2383	35.9658 0539	27
28	35.1027 2991	35.7378 7977	36.3872 5998	37.0512 1031	37.7300 7876	28
29	36.6731 4927	37.3632 9267	38.0695 2111	38.7922 3451	39.5318 4293	29
30	38.2690 8795	39.0171 5029	39.7833 2463	40.5680 7921	41.3718 9459	30
31	39.8909 6063	40.6999 5042	41.5292 6197	42.3794 4079	43.2510 4735	31
32	41.5391 8874	42.4121 9955	43.3079 3563	44.2270 2961	45.1701 3211	32
33	43.2142 0055	44.1544 1305	45.1199 5942	46.1115 7020	47.1299 9742	33
34	44.9164 3131	45.9271 1527	46.9659 5866	48.0338 0160	49.1315 0986	34
35	46.6463 2332	47.7308 3979	48.8465 7038	49.9944 7763	51.1755 5445	35
36	48.4043 2608	49.5661 2949	50.7624 4358	51.9943 6719	53.2630 3498	36
37	50.1908 9637	51.4335 3675	52.7142 3940	54.0342 5453	55.3948 7447	37
38	52.0064 9844	53.3336 2365	54.7026 3138	56.1149 3962	57.5720 1556	38
39	53.8516 0404	55.2669 6206	56.7283 0572	58.2372 3841	59.7954 2089	39
40	55.7266 9261	57.2341 3390	58.7919 6146	60.4019 8318	62.0660 7358	40
41	57.6322 5136	59.2357 3124	60.8943 1073	62.6100 2284	64.3849 7764	41
42	59.5687 7544	61.2723 5654	63.0360 7906	64.8622 2330	66.7531 5842	42
43	61.5367 6805	63.3446 2278	65.2180 0554	67.1594 6777	69.1716 6304	43
44	63.5367 4053	65.4531 5367	67.4408 4315	69.5026 5712	71.6415 6087	44
45	65.5692 1256	67.5985 8386	69.7053 5895	71.8927 1027	74.1639 4404	45
46	67.6347 1226	69.7815 5908	72.0123 3443	74.3305 6447	76.7399 2785	46
47	69.7337 7634	72.0027 3637	74.3625 6571	76.8171 7576	79.3706 5132	47
48	71.8669 5020	74.2627 8425	76.7568 6381	79.3535 1927	82.0572 7766	48
49	74.0347 8814	76.5623 8298	79.1960 5501	81.9405 8966	84.8009 9481	49
50	76.2378 5345	78.9022 2468	81.6809 8104	84.5794 0145	87.6030 1595	50
51	78.4767 1857	81.2830 1361	84.2124 9943	87.2709 8948	90.4645 8004	51
52	80.7519 6525	83.7054 6635	86.7914 8380	90.0164 0927	93.3869 5237	52
53	83.0641 8468	86.1703 1201	89.4188 2412	92.8167 3746	96.3714 2510	53
54	85.4139 7768	88.6782 9247	92.0954 2707	95.6730 7221	99.4193 1789	54
55	87.8019 5482	91.2301 6259	94.8222 1633	98.5865 3365	102.5319 7839	55
56	90.2287 3659	93.8266 9043	97.6001 3289	101.5582 6432	105.7107 8293	56
57	92.6949 5356	96.4686 5752	100.4301 3538	104.5894 2961	108.9571 3707	57
58	95.2012 4655	99.1568 5902	103.3132 0042	107.6812 1820	112.2724 7623	58
59	97.7482 6681	101.8921 0405	106.2503 2292	110.8348 4257	115.6582 6635	59
60	100.3366 7614	104.6752 1588	109.2425 1648	114.0515 3942	119.1160 0451	60

TABLE III

N	1 5/8	1 3/4	1 7/8	2	2 1/8	N
61	102.9671 4713	107.5070 3215	112.2908 1366	117.3325 7021	122.6472 1961	61
62	105.6403 6327	110.3884 0522	115.3962 6642	120.6792 2161	126.2534 7303	62
63	108.3570 1918	113.3202 0231	118.5599 4641	124.0928 0604	129.9363 5933	63
64	111.1178 2074	116.3033 0585	121.7829 4541	127.5746 6216	133.6975 0696	64
65	113.9234 8532	119.3386 1370	125.0663 7564	131.1261 5541	137.5385 7899	65
66	116.7747 4196	122.4270 3944	128.4113 7018	134.7486 7852	141.4612 7379	66
67	119.6723 3152	125.5695 1263	131.8190 8337	138.4436 5209	145.4673 2586	67
68	122.6170 0690	128.7669 7910	135.2906 9118	142.2125 2513	149.5585 0653	68
69	125.6095 3327	132.0204 0124	138.8273 9164	146.0567 7563	153.7366 2480	69
70	128.6506 8818	135.3307 5826	142.4304 0524	149.9779 1114	158.0035 2807	70
71	131.7412 6186	138.6990 4653	146.1009 7533	153.9774 6937	162.3611 0305	71
72	134.8820 5737	142.1262 7984	149.8403 6862	158.0570 1875	166.8112 7649	72
73	138.0738 9080	145.6134 8974	153.6498 7553	162.2181 5913	171.3560 1611	73
74	141.3175 9153	149.1617 2581	157.5308 1070	166.4625 2231	175.9973 3145	74
75	144.6140 0239	152.7720 5601	161.4845 1340	170.7917 7276	180.7372 7475	75
76	147.9639 7993	156.4455 6699	165.5123 4803	175.2076 0821	185.5779 4183	76
77	151.3683 9460	160.1833 6441	169.6157 0455	179.7117 6038	190.5214 7310	77
78	154.8281 3102	163.9865 7329	173.7959 9901	184.3059 9558	195.5700 5440	78
79	158.3440 8814	167.8563 3832	178.0546 7399	188.9921 1549	200.7259 1806	79
80	161.9171 7958	171.7938 2424	182.3931 9913	193.7719 5780	205.9913 4382	80
81	165.5483 3374	175.8002 1617	186.8130 7162	198.6473 9696	211.3686 5987	81
82	169.2384 9417	179.8767 1995	191.3158 1671	203.6203 4490	216.8602 4390	82
83	172.9886 1970	184.0245 6255	195.9029 8827	208.6927 5180	222.4685 2408	83
84	176.7996 8477	188.2449 9239	200.5761 6930	213.8666 0683	228.1959 8021	84
85	180.6726 7965	192.5392 7976	205.3369 7248	219.1439 3897	234.0451 4479	85
86	184.6086 1069	196.9087 1716	210.1870 4071	224.5268 1775	240.0186 0412	86
87	188.6085 0061	201.3546 1971	215.1280 4772	230.0173 5411	246.1189 9946	87
88	192.6733 8875	205.8783 2555	220.1616 9862	235.6177 0119	252.3490 2820	88
89	196.8043 3132	210.4811 9625	225.2897 3047	241.3300 5521	258.7114 4505	89
90	201.0024 0170	215.1646 1718	230.5139 1291	247.1566 5632	265.2090 6325	90
91	205.2686 9073	219.9299 9798	235.8360 4878	253.0997 8944	271.8447 5585	91
92	209.6043 0695	224.7787 7295	241.2579 7469	259.1617 8523	278.6214 5691	92
93	214.0103 7694	229.7124 0148	246.7815 6172	265.3450 2094	285.5421 6287	93
94	218.4880 4557	234.7323 6850	252.4087 1600	271.6519 2135	292.6099 3383	94
95	223.0384 7631	239.8401 8495	258.1413 7943	278.0849 5978	299.8278 9492	95
96	227.6628 5155	245.0373 8819	263.9815 3029	284.6466 5898	307.1992 3769	96
97	232.3623 7288	250.3255 4248	269.9311 8398	291.3395 9216	314.7272 2149	97
98	237.1382 6144	255.7062 3947	275.9923 9368	298.1663 8400	322.4151 7495	98
99	241.9917 5819	261.1810 9866	282.1672 5107	305.1297 1168	330.2664 9742	99
100	246.9241 2426	266.7517 6789	288.4578 8702	312.2323 0591	338.2846 6049	100
101	251.9366 4128	272.4199 2383	294.8664 7241	319.4769 5203	346.4732 0952	101
102	257.0306 1170	278.1872 7250	301.3952 1876	326.8664 9107	354.8357 6522	102
103	262.2073 5914	284.0555 4976	308.0463 7911	334.4038 2089	363.3760 2524	103
104	267.4682 2873	290.0265 2188	314.8222 4872	342.0918 9731	372.0977 6577	104
105	272.8145 8744	296.1019 8602	321.7251 6589	349.9337 3526	381.0048 4329	105
106	278.2478 2449	302.2837 7077	328.7575 1275	357.9324 0996	390.1011 9621	106
107	283.7693 5164	308.5737 3676	335.9217 1611	366.0910 5816	399.3908 4663	107
108	289.3806 0360	314.9737 7716	343.2202 4829	374.4128 7932	408.8779 0212	108
109	295.0830 3841	321.4858 1826	350.6556 2794	382.9011 3691	418.5665 5754	109
110	300.8781 3779	328.1118 2007	358.2304 2097	391.5591 5965	428.4610 9689	110
111	306.7674 0752	334.8537 7693	365.9472 4136	400.3903 4284	438.5658 9520	111
112	312.7523 7790	341.7137 1802	373.8087 5214	409.3981 4970	448.8854 2047	112
113	318.8346 0404	348.6937 0809	381.8176 6624	418.5861 1269	459.4242 3566	113
114	325.0156 6635	355.7958 4798	389.9767 4748	427.9578 3495	470.1870 0067	114
115	331.2971 7093	363.0222 7532	398.2888 1150	437.5169 9165	481.1784 7443	115
116	337.6807 4996	370.3751 6514	406.7567 2671	447.2673 3148	492.4035 1701	116
117	344.1680 6215	377.8567 3053	415.3834 1534	457.2126 7811	503.8670 9175	117
118	350.7607 9316	385.4692 2331	424.1718 5437	467.3569 3167	515.5742 6745	118
119	357.4606 5604	393.2149 3472	433.1250 7664	477.7040 7030	527.5302 2063	119
120	364.2693 9171	401.0961 9608	442.2461 7183	488.2581 5171	539.7402 3782	120

TABLE III

N	1 5/8	1 3/4	1 7/8	2	2 1/8	N
121	371.1887 6932	409.1153 7951	451.5382 8755	499.0233 1474	552.2097 1788	121
122	378.2205 8682	417.2748 9865	461.0046 3044	510.0037 8104	564.9441 7438	122
123	385.3666 7136	425.5772 0938	470.6484 6727	521.2038 5666	577.9492 3809	123
124	392.6288 7977	434.0248 1054	480.4731 2603	532.6279 3379	591.2306 5939	124
125	400.0090 9906	442.6202 4472	490.4819 9714	544.2804 9247	604.7943 1091	125
126	407.5092 4692	451.3660 9901	500.6785 3459	556.1661 0232	618.6461 9001	126
127	415.1312 7219	460.2650 0574	511.0662 5711	568.2894 2436	632.7924 2155	127
128	422.8771 5536	469.3196 4334	521.6487 4943	580.6552 1285	647.2392 6051	128
129	430.7489 0913	478.5327 3710	532.4296 6348	593.2683 1711	661.9930 9480	129
130	438.7485 7891	487.9070 6000	543.4127 1967	606.1336 8345	677.0604 4806	130
131	446.8782 4331	497.4454 3355	554.6017 0817	619.2563 5712	692.4479 8258	131
132	455.1400 1477	507.1507 2863	566.0004 9019	632.6414 8426	708.1625 0221	132
133	463.5360 4001	517.0258 6639	577.6129 9939	646.2943 1395	724.2109 5538	133
134	472.0685 0066	527.0738 1905	589.4432 4312	660.2202 0023	740.6004 3818	134
135	480.7396 1379	537.2976 1088	601.4953 0393	674.4246 0423	757.3381 9750	135
136	489.5516 3252	547.7003 1907	613.7733 4088	688.9130 9632	774.4316 3419	136
137	498.5068 4655	558.2850 7465	626.2815 9102	703.6913 5824	791.8883 0642	137
138	507.6075 8280	569.0550 6346	639.0243 7085	718.7651 8541	809.7159 3293	138
139	516.8562 0602	580.0135 2707	652.0060 7781	734.1404 8912	827.9223 9651	139
140	526.2551 1937	591.1637 6380	665.2311 9177	749.8232 9890	846.5157 4743	140
141	535.8067 6506	602.5091 2966	678.7042 7661	765.8197 6488	865.5042 0706	141
142	545.5136 2499	614.0530 3943	692.4299 8180	782.1361 6017	884.8961 7146	142
143	555.3782 2140	625.7989 6762	706.4130 4396	798.7788 8338	904.7002 1511	143
144	565.4031 1750	637.7504 4955	720.6582 8853	815.7544 6104	924.9250 9468	144
145	575.5909 1816	649.9110 8242	735.1706 3144	833.0695 5027	945.5797 5294	145
146	585.9442 7058	662.2845 2636	749.9550 8078	850.7309 4127	966.6733 2269	146
147	596.4658 6497	674.8745 0558	765.0167 3855	868.7455 6010	988.2151 3080	147
148	607.1584 3528	687.6848 0942	780.3608 0239	887.1204 7130	1010.2147 0233	148
149	618.0247 5985	700.7192 9359	795.9925 6744	905.8628 8072	1032.6817 6475	149
150	629.0676 6220	713.9818 8123	811.9174 2808	924.9801 3834	1055.6262 5225	150
151	640.2900 1171	727.4765 6415	828.1408 7986	944.4797 4110	1079.0583 1011	151
152	651.6947 2440	741.2074 0402	844.6685 2135	964.3693 3593	1102.9882 9920	152
153	663.2847 6367	755.1785 3359	861.5060 5613	984.6567 2265	1127.4268 0056	153
154	675.0631 4108	769.3941 5793	878.6592 9468	1005.3498 5710	1152.3846 2007	154
155	687.0329 1712	783.8585 5569	896.1341 5646	1026.4568 5424	1177.8727 9325	155
156	699.1972 0203	798.5760 8042	913.9366 7189	1047.9859 9133	1203.9025 9011	156
157	711.5591 5656	813.5511 6182	932.0729 8449	1069.9457 1115	1230.4855 2015	157
158	724.1219 9285	828.7883 0716	950.5493 5295	1092.3446 2537	1257.6333 3745	158
159	736.8889 7524	844.2921 0253	969.3721 5331	1115.1915 1788	1285.3580 4587	159
160	749.8634 2109	860.0672 1433	988.5478 8119	1138.4953 4824	1313.6719 0434	160
161	763.0487 0168	876.1183 9058	1008.0831 5396	1162.2652 5520	1342.5874 3231	161
162	776.4482 4308	892.4504 6241	1027.9847 1310	1186.5105 6031	1372.1174 1525	162
163	790.0655 2703	909.0683 4550	1048.2594 2647	1211.2407 7151	1402.2749 1032	163
164	803.9040 9185	925.9770 4155	1068.9142 9071	1236.4655 8695	1433.0732 5217	164
165	817.9675 3334	943.1816 3978	1089.9564 3367	1262.1948 9868	1464.5260 5878	165
166	832.2595 0575	960.6873 1847	1111.3931 1680	1288.4387 9666	1496.6472 3752	166
167	846.7837 2272	978.4993 4655	1133.2317 3774	1315.2075 7259	1529.4509 9132	167
168	861.5439 5822	996.6230 8511	1155.4798 3282	1342.5117 2404	1562.9518 2489	168
169	876.5440 4754	1015.0639 8910	1178.1450 7968	1370.3619 5852	1597.1645 5117	169
170	891.7878 8831	1033.8276 0891	1201.2352 9993	1398.7691 9769	1632.1042 9788	170
171	907.2794 4150	1052.9195 9207	1224.7584 6180	1427.7445 8165	1667.7865 1421	171
172	923.0227 3242	1072.3456 8493	1248.7226 8296	1457.2994 7328	1704.2269 7764	172
173	939.0218 5182	1092.1117 3441	1273.1362 3327	1487.4454 6275	1741.4418 0091	173
174	955.2809 5691	1112.2236 8976	1298.0075 3764	1518.1943 7200	1779.4474 3918	174
175	971.8042 7246	1132.6876 0434	1323.3451 7897	1549.5582 5944	1818.2606 9726	175
176	988.5960 9189	1153.5096 3741	1349.1579 0108	1581.5494 2463	1857.8987 3708	176
177	1005.6607 7839	1174.6960 5607	1375.4546 1172	1614.1804 1312	1898.3790 8524	177
178	1023.0027 6603	1196.2532 3705	1402.2443 8569	1647.4640 2139	1939.7196 4080	178
179	1040.6265 6098	1218.1876 6870	1429.5364 6792	1681.4133 0181	1981.9386 8317	179
180	1058.5367 4260	1240.5059 5290	1457.3402 7670	1716.0415 6785	2025.0548 8019	180

TABLE III

N	1 5/8	1 3/4	1 7/8	2	2 1/8	N
181	1076.7379 6467	1263.2148 0707	1485.6654 0689	1751.3623 9921	2069.0872 9639	181
182	1095.2349 5659	1286.3210 6620	1514.5216 3326	1787.3896 4719	2114.0554 0144	182
183	1114.0325 2464	1309.8316 8486	1543.9189 1389	1824.1374 4013	2159.9790 7872	183
184	1133.1355 5316	1333.7537 3934	1573.8673 9352	1861.6201 8894	2206.8786 3414	184
185	1152.5490 0590	1358.0944 2978	1604.3774 0715	1899.8525 9272	2254.7748 0512	185
186	1172.2779 2725	1382.8610 8230	1635.4594 8354	1938.8496 4457	2303.6887 6973	186
187	1192.3274 4356	1408.0611 5124	1667.1243 4885	1978.6266 3746	2353.6421 5609	187
188	1212.7027 6452	1433.7022 2139	1699.3829 3039	2019.1991 7021	2404.6570 5190	188
189	1233.4091 8444	1459.7920 1026	1732.2463 6034	2060.5831 5361	2456.7560 1425	189
190	1254.4520 8369	1486.3383 7044	1765.7259 7959	2102.7948 1669	2509.9620 7956	190
191	1275.8369 3005	1513.3492 9192	1799.8333 4171	2145.8507 1302	2564.2987 7375	191
192	1297.5692 8017	1540.8329 0453	1834.5802 1687	2189.7677 2728	2619.7901 2269	192
193	1319.6547 8097	1568.7974 8036	1869.9785 9594	2234.5630 8183	2676.4606 6280	193
194	1342.0991 7116	1597.2514 3627	1906.0406 9461	2280.2543 4346	2734.3354 5188	194
195	1364.9082 8269	1626.2033 3640	1942.7789 5763	2326.8594 3033	2793.4400 8023	195
196	1388.0880 4228	1655.6618 9479	1980.2060 6309	2374.3966 1894	2853.8006 8194	196
197	1411.6444 7297	1685.6359 7795	2018.3349 2677	2422.8845 5132	2915.4439 4643	197
198	1435.5836 9566	1716.1346 0756	2057.1787 0665	2472.3422 4234	2978.3971 3029	198
199	1459.9119 3071	1747.1669 6320	2096.7508 0740	2522.7890 8719	3042.6880 6931	199
200	1484.6354 9959	1778.7423 8505	2137.0648 8504	2574.2448 6894	3108.3451 9078	200
201	1509.7608 2645	1810.8703 7679	2178.1348 5163	2626.7297 6631	3175.3975 2609	201
202	1535.2944 3988	1843.5606 0838	2219.9748 8010	2680.2643 6164	3243.8747 2352	202
203	1561.2429 7453	1876.8229 1903	2262.5994 0910	2734.8696 4887	3313.8070 6139	203
204	1587.6131 7287	1910.6673 2011	2306.0231 4802	2790.5670 4185	3385.2254 6145	204
205	1614.4118 8693	1945.1039 9821	2350.2610 8205	2847.3783 8269	3458.1615 0250	205
206	1641.6460 8009	1980.1433 1818	2395.3284 7734	2905.3259 5034	3532.6474 3443	206
207	1669.3228 2889	2015.7958 2625	2441.2408 8629	2964.4324 6935	3608.7161 9241	207
208	1697.4493 2486	2052.0722 5321	2488.0141 5290	3024.7211 1874	3686.4014 1150	208
209	1726.0328 7639	2088.9835 1764	2535.6644 1827	3086.2155 4111	3765.7374 4150	209
210	1755.0809 1063	2126.5407 2920	2584.2081 2611	3148.9398 5193	3846.7593 6213	210
211	1784.6009 7543	2164.7551 9196	2633.6620 2848	3212.9186 4897	3929.5029 9857	211
212	1814.6007 4128	2203.6384 0782	2684.0431 9151	3278.1770 2195	4014.0049 3729	212
213	1845.0880 0332	2243.2020 7996	2735.3690 0135	3344.7405 6239	4100.3025 4221	213
214	1876.0706 8338	2283.4581 1636	2787.6571 7013	3412.6353 7364	4188.4339 7123	214
215	1907.5568 3198	2324.4186 3339	2840.9257 4207	3481.8880 8111	4278.4381 9312	215
216	1939.5546 3050	2366.0959 5948	2895.1930 9973	3552.5258 4273	4370.3550 0472	216
217	1972.0723 9325	2408.5026 3877	2950.4779 7035	3624.5763 5959	4464.2250 4857	217
218	2005.1185 6964	2451.6514 3495	3006.7994 3230	3698.0678 8678	4560.0898 3086	218
219	2038.7017 4640	2495.5553 3506	3064.1769 2165	3773.0292 4451	4657.9917 3976	219
220	2072.8306 4977	2540.2275 5342	3122.6302 3893	3849.4898 2940	4757.9740 6423	220
221	2107.5141 4783	2585.6815 3561	3182.1795 5591	3927.4796 2599	4860.0810 1310	221
222	2142.7612 5274	2631.9309 6248	3242.8454 2259	4007.0292 1851	4964.3577 3463	222
223	2178.5811 2309	2678.9897 5432	3304.6487 7426	4088.1698 0288	5070.8503 3649	223
224	2214.9830 6634	2726.8720 7502	3367.6109 3878	4170.9331 9894	5179.6059 0614	224
225	2251.9765 4117	2775.5923 3634	3431.7536 4388	4255.3518 6292	5290.6725 3164	225
226	2289.5711 5997	2825.1652 0222	3497.0990 2470	4341.4589 0018	5404.0993 2294	226
227	2327.7766 9131	2875.6055 9326	3563.6696 3141	4429.2880 7818	5519.9364 3355	227
228	2366.6030 6255	2926.9286 9114	3631.4884 3700	4518.8738 3974	5638.2350 8276	228
229	2406.0603 6232	2979.1499 4324	3700.5788 4520	4610.2513 1654	5759.0475 7827	229
230	2446.1588 4320	3032.2850 6725	3770.9646 9854	4703.4563 4287	5882.4273 3931	230
231	2486.9089 2440	3086.3500 5592	3842.6702 8664	4798.5254 6973	6008.4289 2027	231
232	2528.3211 9443	3141.3611 8190	3915.7203 5452	4895.4959 7912	6137.1080 3483	232
233	2570.4064 1384	3197.3350 0259	3990.1401 1116	4994.4058 9870	6268.5215 8057	233
234	2613.1755 1806	3254.2883 6513	4065.9552 3825	5095.2940 1668	6402.7276 6416	234
235	2656.6396 2023	3312.2384 1152	4143.1918 9897	5198.1998 9701	6539.7856 2702	235
236	2700.8100 1406	3371.2025 8372	4221.8767 4707	5303.1638 9495	6679.7560 7159	236
237	2745.6981 7679	3431.1986 2894	4302.0369 3608	5410.2271 7285	6822.7008 8811	237
238	2791.3157 7216	3492.2446 0494	4383.7001 2863	5519.4317 1631	6968.6832 8199	238
239	2837.6746 5346	3554.3588 8553	4466.8945 0604	5630.8203 5063	7117.7678 0173	239
240	2884.7868 6658	3617.5601 6603	4551.6487 7803	5744.4367 5765	7270.0203 6752	240

TABLE III

N	1 5/8	1 3/4	1 7/8	2	2 1/8	N
241	2932.6646 5316	3681.8674 6893	4637.9921 9262	5860.3254 9280	7425.5083 0033	241
242	2981.3204 5377	3747.3001 4964	4725.9545 4623	5978.5320 0266	7584.3003 5171	242
243	3030.7669 1114	3813.8779 0226	4815.5661 9397	6099.1026 4271	7746.4667 3418	243
244	3081.0168 7345	3881.6207 6555	4906.8580 6011	6222.0846 9556	7912.0791 5228	244
245	3132.0833 9764	3950.5491 2894	4999.8616 4874	6347.5263 8947	8081.2108 3427	245
246	3183.9797 5286	4020.6837 3870	5094.6090 5465	6475.4769 1726	8253.9365 6450	246
247	3236.7194 2384	4092.0457 0413	5191.1329 7442	6605.9864 5561	8430.3327 1649	247
248	3290.3161 1448	4164.6565 0395	5289.4667 1769	6739.1061 8472	8610.4772 8672	248
249	3344.7837 5134	4238.5379 9277	5389.6442 1865	6874.8883 0842	8794.4499 2906	249
250	3400.1364 8730	4313.7124 0764	5491.7000 4775	7013.3860 7458	8982.3319 9005	250
251	3456.3887 0522	4390.2023 7478	5595.6694 2365	7154.6537 9608	9174.2065 4484	251
252	3513.5550 2168	4468.0309 1633	5701.5882 2534	7298.7468 7200	9370.1584 3392	252
253	3571.6502 9078	4547.2214 5737	5809.4930 0456	7445.7218 0944	9570.2743 0064	253
254	3630.6896 0800	4627.7978 3287	5919.4209 9840	7595.6362 4563	9774.6426 2953	254
255	3690.6883 1413	4709.7842 9495	6031.4101 4212	7748.5489 7054	9983.3537 8541	255
256	3751.6619 9924	4793.2055 2011	6145.4990 8228	7904.5199 4995	10196.5000 5335	256
257	3813.6265 0673	4878.0866 1671	6261.7271 9008	8063.6103 4895	10414.1756 7948	257
258	3876.5979 3746	4964.4531 3251	6380.1345 7489	8225.8825 5593	10636.4769 1267	258
259	3940.5926 5394	5052.3310 6232	6500.7620 9817	8391.4002 0705	10863.5020 4706	259
260	4005.6272 8457	5141.7468 5592	6623.6513 8751	8560.2282 1119	11095.3514 6556	260
261	4071.7187 2794	5232.7274 2589	6748.8448 5103	8732.4327 7541	11332.1276 8421	261
262	4138.8841 5727	5325.3001 5585	6876.3856 9198	8908.0814 3092	11573.9353 9750	262
263	4207.1410 2483	5419.4929 0857	7006.3179 2371	9087.2430 5954	11820.8815 2469	263
264	4276.5070 6648	5515.3340 3447	7138.6863 8478	9269.9879 2073	12073.0752 5709	264
265	4347.0003 0631	5612.8523 8008	7273.5367 5449	9456.3876 7914	12330.6281 0631	265
266	4418.6390 6129	5712.0772 9673	7410.9155 6864	9646.5154 3273	12593.6539 5356	266
267	4491.4419 4604	5813.0386 4942	7550.8702 3555	9840.4457 4138	12862.2691 0008	267
268	4565.4278 7766	5915.7668 2579	7693.4490 5247	10038.2546 5621	13136.5923 1845	268
269	4640.6160 8067	6020.2927 4524	7838.7012 2220	10240.0197 4933	13416.7449 0522	269
270	4717.0260 9198	6126.6478 6828	7986.6768 7012	10445.8201 4432	13702.8507 3446	270
271	4794.6777 6598	6234.8642 0597	8137.4270 6143	10655.7365 4720	13995.0363 1256	271
272	4873.5912 7967	6344.9743 2958	8291.0038 1883	10869.8512 7815	14293.4308 3421	272
273	4953.7871 3797	6457.0113 8035	8447.4601 4044	11088.2483 0371	14598.1662 3943	273
274	5035.2861 7896	6571.0090 7950	8606.8500 1807	11311.0132 6979	14909.3772 7202	274
275	5118.1095 7937	6687.0017 3839	8769.2284 5591	11538.2335 3518	15227.2015 3905	275
276	5202.2788 6003	6805.0242 6882	8934.6514 8946	11769.9982 0588	15551.7795 7176	276
277	5287.8158 9151	6925.1121 9352	9103.1762 0489	12006.3981 7000	15883.2548 8766	277
278	5374.7428 9975	7047.3016 5691	9274.8607 5873	12247.5261 3340	16221.7740 5402	278
279	5463.0824 7187	7171.6294 3590	9449.7643 9795	12493.4766 5607	16567.4867 5267	279
280	5552.8575 6203	7298.1329 5103	9627.9474 8042	12744.3461 8919	16920.5458 4616	280
281	5644.0914 9742	7426.8502 7767	9809.4714 9567	13000.2331 1298	17281.1074 4539	281
282	5736.8079 8425	7557.8201 5753	9994.3990 8622	13261.2377 7524	17649.3309 7861	282
283	5831.0311 1399	7691.0820 1029	10182.7940 6908	13527.4625 3074	18025.3792 6190	283
284	5926.7853 6960	7826.6759 4547	10374.7214 5788	13799.0117 8135	18409.4185 7122	284
285	6024.0956 3185	7964.6427 7452	10570.2474 8521	14075.9920 1698	18801.6187 1586	285
286	6122.9871 8587	8105.0240 2307	10769.4396 2556	14358.5118 5732	19202.1531 1357	286
287	6223.4857 2764	8247.8619 4347	10972.3666 1854	14646.6820 9447	19611.1988 6723	287
288	6325.6173 7072	8393.1995 2748	11179.0984 9264	14940.6157 3636	20028.9368 4316	288
289	6429.4086 5299	8541.0805 1922	11389.7065 8938	15240.4280 5108	20455.5517 5108	289
290	6534.8865 4360	8691.5494 2830	11604.2635 8793	15546.2366 1211	20891.2322 2579	290
291	6642.0784 4993	8844.6515 4330	11822.8435 3020	15858.1613 4435	21336.1709 1059	291
292	6751.0122 2475	9000.4329 4530	12045.5218 4639	16176.3245 7124	21790.5645 4244	292
293	6861.7161 7340	9158.9405 2185	12272.3753 8101	16500.8510 6266	22254.6140 3896	293
294	6974.2190 6122	9320.2219 8098	12503.4824 1940	16831.8680 8391	22728.5245 8729	294
295	7088.5501 2096	9484.3258 6565	12738.9227 1477	17169.5054 4559	23212.5057 3477	295
296	7204.7390 6043	9651.3015 6830	12978.7775 1567	17513.8955 5450	23706.7714 8163	296
297	7322.8160 7016	9821.1993 4574	13223.1295 9409	17865.1734 6559	24211.5403 7562	297
298	7442.8118 3130	9994.0703 3429	13472.0632 7398	18223.4769 3491	24727.0356 0860	298
299	7564.7575 2356	10169.9665 6514	13725.6644 6037	18588.9464 7360	25253.4851 1528	299
300	7688.6848 3331	10348.9409 8003	13984.0206 6900	18961.7254 0308	25791.1216 7398	300

TABLE III

N	1 5/8	1 3/4	1 7/8	2	2 1/8	N
301	7814.6259 6186	10531.0474 4718	14247.2210 5654	19341.9599 1114	26340.1830 0955	301
302	7942.6136 3374	10716.3407 7751	14515.3564 5135	19729.7991 0936	26900.9118 9851	302
303	8072.6811 0528	10904.8767 4111	14788.5193 8481	20125.3950 9155	27473.5562 7635	303
304	8204.8621 7324	11096.7120 8408	15066.8041 2328	20528.9029 9338	28058.3693 4722	304
305	8339.1911 8356	11291.9045 4556	15350.3067 0059	20940.4810 5325	28655.6096 9585	305
306	8475.7030 4029	11490.5128 7510	15639.1249 5123	21360.2906 7431	29265.5414 0189	306
307	8614.4332 1470	11692.5968 5042	15933.3585 4406	21788.4964 8780	29888.4341 5668	307
308	8755.4177 5444	11898.2172 9530	16233.1090 1676	22225.2664 1755	30524.5633 8251	308
309	8898.6932 9295	12107.4360 9797	16538.4798 1083	22670.7717 4590	31174.2103 5439	309
310	9044.2970 5896	12320.3162 2968	16849.5763 0728	23125.1871 8082	31837.6623 2442	310
311	9192.2668 8616	12536.9217 6370	17166.5058 6304	23588.6909 2444	32515.2126 4881	311
312	9342.6412 2306	12757.3178 9457	17489.3778 4797	24061.4647 4293	33207.1609 1760	312
313	9495.4591 4294	12981.5709 5772	17818.3036 8262	24543.6940 3779	33913.8130 8710	313
314	9650.7603 5401	13209.7484 4948	18153.3968 7667	25035.5679 1854	34635.4816 1520	314
315	9808.5852 0976	13441.9190 4735	18494.7730 6811	25537.2792 7691	35372.4855 9952	315
316	9968.9747 1942	13678.1526 3067	18842.5500 6314	26049.0248 6245	36125.1509 1851	316
317	10131.9705 5861	13918.5203 0171	19196.8478 7682	26571.0053 5970	36893.8103 7553	317
318	10297.6150 8019	14163.0944 0699	19557.7887 7451	27103.4254 6689	37678.8038 4601	318
319	10465.9513 2524	14411.9485 5911	19925.4973 1403	27646.4939 7623	38480.4784 2774	319
320	10637.0230 3428	14665.1576 5890	20300.1003 8867	28200.4238 5576	39299.1885 9433	320
321	10810.8746 5859	14922.7979 1793	20681.7272 7096	28765.4323 3287	40135.2963 5196	321
322	10987.5513 7179	15184.9468 8149	21070.5096 5729	29341.7409 7953	40989.1713 9944	322
323	11167.0990 8158	15451.6834 5192	21466.5817 1336	29929.5757 9912	41861.1912 9167	323
324	11349.5644 4166	15723.0879 1233	21870.0801 2049	30529.1673 1510	42751.7416 0662	324
325	11534.9948 6383	15999.2419 5079	22281.1441 2275	31140.7506 6140	43661.2161 1576	325
326	11723.4385 3037	16280.2286 8493	22699.9155 7505	31764.5656 7463	44590.0169 5822	326
327	11914.9444 0649	16566.1326 8692	23126.5389 9208	32400.8569 8812	45538.5548 1858	327
328	12109.5622 5309	16857.0400 0894	23561.1615 9819	33049.8741 2789	46507.2491 0848	328
329	12307.3426 3971	17153.0382 0910	24003.9333 7815	33711.8716 1044	47496.5281 5203	329
330	12508.3369 5760	17454.2163 7776	24455.0071 2899	34387.1090 4265	48506.8293 7526	330
331	12712.5974 3316	17760.6651 6437	24914.5385 1266	35075.8512 2351	49538.5994 9949	331
332	12920.1771 4145	18072.4768 0474	25382.6861 0977	35778.3682 4798	50592.2947 3885	332
333	13131.1300 2000	18389.7451 4883	25859.6114 7433	36494.9356 1294	51668.3810 0205	333
334	13345.5108 8283	18712.5656 8893	26345.4791 8947	37225.8343 2519	52767.3340 9835	334
335	13563.3754 3467	19041.0355 8849	26840.4569 2428	37971.3510 1170	53889.6399 4794	335
336	13784.7802 8548	19375.2537 1128	27344.7154 9161	38731.7780 3193	55035.7947 9683	336
337	14009.7829 6512	19715.3206 5123	27858.4289 0707	39507.4135 9257	56206.3054 3626	337
338	14238.4419 3831	20061.3387 6263	28381.7744 4908	40298.5618 6442	57401.6894 2678	338
339	14470.8166 1980	20413.4121 9097	28914.9327 2000	41105.5331 0171	58622.4753 2710	339
340	14706.9673 8988	20771.6469 0432	29458.0877 0850	41928.6437 6374	59869.2029 2780	340
341	14946.9556 0996	21136.1507 2514	30011.4268 5304	42768.2166 3902	61142.4234 9002	341
342	15190.8436 3862	21507.0333 6283	30575.1411 0653	43624.5809 7180	62442.6999 8918	342
343	15438.6948 4775	21884.4064 4668	31149.4250 0228	44498.0725 9124	63770.6073 6395	343
344	15690.5736 3903	22268.3835 5950	31734.4767 2107	45389.0340 4306	65126.7327 7044	344
345	15946.5454 6066	22659.0802 7179	32330.4981 5959	46297.8147 2392	66511.6758 4181	345
346	16206.6768 2440	23056.6141 7655	32937.6950 0008	47224.7710 1840	67926.0489 5345	346
347	16471.0353 2279	23461.1049 2464	33556.2767 8134	48170.2664 3877	69370.4774 9371	347
348	16739.6896 4679	23872.6742 6082	34186.4569 7099	49134.6717 6754	70845.6001 4045	348
349	17012.7096 0355	24291.4460 6038	34828.4530 3919	50118.3652 0289	72352.0691 4343	349
350	17290.1661 3461	24717.5463 6644	35482.4865 3368	51121.7325 0695	73890.5506 1273	350
351	17572.1313 3429	25151.1034 2785	36148.7831 5618	52145.1671 5709	75461.7248 1325	351
352	17858.6784 6848	25592.2477 3784	36827.5728 4036	53189.0705 0023	77066.2864 6553	352
353	18149.8819 9359	26041.1120 7325	37519.0898 3112	54253.8519 1024	78704.9450 5293	353
354	18445.8175 7599	26497.8315 3453	38223.5727 6545	55339.9289 4844	80378.4251 3530	354
355	18746.5621 1160	26962.5435 8639	38941.2647 5480	56447.7275 2741	82087.4666 6943	355
356	19052.1937 4591	27435.3880 9915	39672.4134 6896	57577.6820 7796	83832.8253 3615	356
357	19362.7918 9428	27916.5073 9088	40417.2712 2150	58730.2357 1952	85615.2728 7455	357
358	19678.4372 6256	28406.0462 7022	41176.0950 5690	59905.8404 3391	87435.5974 2313	358
359	19999.2118 6808	28904.1520 7995	41949.1468 3922	61104.9572 4259	89294.6038 6837	359
360	20325.1990 6093	29410.9747 4135	42736.6933 4245	62328.0563 8744	91193.1142 0057	360

TABLE III

N	2 1/4	2 3/8	2 1/2	2 5/8	2 3/4	N
1	1.0000 0000	1.0000 0000	1.0000 0000	1.0000 0000	1.0000 0000	1
2	2.0225 0000	2.0237 5000	2.0250 0000	2.0262 5000	2.0275 0000	2
3	3.0680 0625	3.0718 1406	3.0756 2500	3.0794 3906	3.0832 5625	3
4	4.1370 3639	4.1447 6965	4.1525 1562	4.1602 7434	4.1680 4580	4
5	5.2301 1971	5.2432 0793	5.2563 2852	5.2694 8154	5.2826 6706	5
6	6.3477 9740	6.3677 3411	6.3877 3673	6.4078 0543	6.4279 4040	6
7	7.4906 2284	7.5189 6780	7.5474 3015	7.5760 1032	7.6047 0876	7
8	8.6591 6186	8.6975 4328	8.7361 1590	8.7748 8059	8.8138 3825	8
9	9.8539 9300	9.9041 0994	9.9545 1880	10.0052 2121	10.0562 1880	9
10	11.0757 0784	11.1393 3255	11.2033 8177	11.2678 5827	11.3327 6482	10
11	12.3249 1127	12.4038 9170	12.4834 6631	12.5636 3954	12.6444 1585	11
12	13.6022 2177	13.6984 8412	13.7955 5297	13.8934 3508	13.9921 3729	12
13	14.9082 7176	15.0238 2312	15.1404 4179	15.2581 3775	15.3769 2107	13
14	16.2437 0788	16.3806 3892	16.5189 5284	16.6586 6387	16.7997 8639	14
15	17.6091 9130	17.7696 7910	17.9319 2666	18.0959 5380	18.2617 8052	15
16	19.0053 9811	19.1917 0897	19.3802 2483	19.5709 7258	19.7639 7948	16
17	20.4330 1957	20.6475 1206	20.8647 3045	21.0847 1061	21.3074 8892	17
18	21.8927 6251	22.1378 9047	22.3863 4871	22.6381 8427	22.8934 4487	18
19	23.3853 4966	23.6636 6537	23.9460 0743	24.2324 3660	24.5230 1460	19
20	24.9115 2003	25.2256 7743	25.5446 5761	25.8685 3807	26.1973 9750	20
21	26.4720 2923	26.8247 8726	27.1832 7405	27.5475 8719	27.9178 2593	21
22	28.0676 4989	28.4618 7596	28.8628 5590	29.2707 1135	29.6855 6615	22
23	29.6991 7201	30.1378 4552	30.5844 2730	31.0390 6753	31.5019 1921	23
24	31.3674 0338	31.8536 1935	32.3490 3798	32.8538 4305	33.3682 2199	24
25	33.0731 6996	33.6101 4281	34.1577 6393	34.7162 5643	35.2858 4810	25
26	34.8173 1628	35.4083 8370	36.0117 0803	36.6275 5816	37.2562 0892	26
27	36.6007 0590	37.2493 3281	37.9120 0073	38.5890 3156	39.2807 5467	27
28	38.4242 2178	39.1340 0446	39.8598 0075	40.6019 9364	41.3609 7542	28
29	40.2887 6677	41.0634 3707	41.8562 9577	42.6677 9597	43.4984 0224	29
30	42.1952 6402	43.0386 9370	43.9027 0316	44.7878 2562	45.6946 0831	30
31	44.1446 5746	45.0608 6268	46.0002 7074	46.9635 0604	47.9512 1003	31
32	46.1379 1226	47.1310 5817	48.1502 7751	49.1962 9807	50.2698 6831	32
33	48.1760 1528	49.2504 2080	50.3540 3445	51.4877 0090	52.6522 8969	33
34	50.2599 7563	51.4201 1829	52.6128 8531	53.8392 5305	55.1002 2765	34
35	52.3908 2508	53.6413 4610	54.9282 0744	56.2525 3344	57.6154 8391	35
36	54.5696 1864	55.9153 2807	57.3014 1263	58.7291 6244	60.1999 0972	36
37	56.7974 3506	58.2433 1711	59.7339 4794	61.2708 0296	62.8554 0724	37
38	59.0753 7735	60.6265 9589	62.2272 9664	63.8791 6153	65.5839 3094	38
39	61.4045 7334	63.0664 7755	64.7829 7906	66.5559 8952	68.3874 8904	39
40	63.7861 7624	65.5643 0639	67.4025 5354	69.3030 8425	71.2681 4499	40
41	66.2213 6521	68.1214 5866	70.0876 1737	72.1222 9021	74.2280 1898	41
42	68.7113 4592	70.7393 4331	72.8398 0781	75.0155 0033	77.2692 8950	42
43	71.2573 5121	73.4194 0271	75.6608 0300	77.9846 5721	80.3941 9496	43
44	73.8606 4161	76.1631 1352	78.5523 2308	81.0317 5446	83.6050 3532	44
45	76.5225 0605	78.9719 8747	81.5161 3116	84.1588 3802	86.9041 7379	45
46	79.2442 6243	81.8475 7217	84.5540 3443	87.3680 0752	90.2940 3857	46
47	82.0272 5834	84.7914 5201	87.6678 8530	90.6614 1771	93.7771 2463	47
48	84.8728 7165	87.8052 4900	90.8595 8243	94.0412 7993	97.3559 9556	48
49	87.7825 1126	90.8906 2366	94.1310 7199	97.5098 6353	101.0332 8544	49
50	90.7576 1776	94.0492 7597	97.4843 4879	101.0694 9745	104.8117 0079	50
51	93.7996 6416	97.2829 4628	100.9214 5751	104.7225 7175	108.6940 2256	51
52	96.9101 5661	100.5934 1625	104.4444 9395	108.4715 3926	112.6831 0818	52
53	100.0906 3513	103.9825 0989	108.0556 0629	112.3189 1717	116.7818 9365	53
54	103.3426 7442	107.4520 9450	111.7569 9645	116.2672 8874	120.9933 9573	54
55	106.6678 8460	111.0040 8174	115.5509 2136	120.3193 0507	125.3207 1411	55
56	110.0679 1200	114.6404 2868	119.4396 9440	124.4776 8683	129.7670 3375	56
57	113.5444 4002	118.3631 3886	123.4256 8676	128.7452 2611	134.3356 2718	57
58	117.0991 8992	122.1742 6341	127.5113 2893	133.1247 8830	139.0298 5692	58
59	120.7339 2169	126.0759 0217	131.6991 1215	137.6193 1399	143.8531 7799	59
60	124.4504 3493	130.0702 0485	135.9915 8995	142.2318 2098	148.8091 4038	60

TABLE III

N	2 1/4	2 3/8	2 1/2	2 5/8	2 3/4	N
61	128.2505 6972	134.1593 7221	140.3913 7970	146.9654 0628	153.9013 9174	61
62	132.1362 0754	138.3456 5730	144.9011 6419	151.8232 4820	159.1336 8002	62
63	136.1092 7221	142.6313 6666	149.5236 9330	156.8086 0846	164.5098 5622	63
64	140.1717 3083	147.0188 6162	154.2617 8563	161.9248 3443	170.0338 7726	64
65	144.3255 9477	151.5105 5958	159.1183 3027	167.1753 6134	175.7098 0889	65
66	148.5729 2066	156.1089 3537	164.0962 8853	172.5637 1457	181.5418 2863	66
67	152.9158 1137	160.8165 2259	169.1986 9574	178.0935 1208	187.5342 2892	67
68	157.3564 1713	165.6359 1500	174.4286 6314	183.7684 6677	193.6914 2022	68
69	161.8969 3651	170.5697 6798	179.7893 7971	189.5923 8902	200.0179 3427	69
70	166.5396 1758	175.6207 9997	185.2841 1421	195.5691 8924	206.5184 2746	70
71	171.2867 5898	180.7917 9397	190.9162 1706	201.7028 8045	213.1976 8422	71
72	176.1407 1106	186.0855 9908	196.6891 2249	207.9975 8107	220.0606 2054	72
73	181.1038 7705	191.5051 3205	202.6063 5055	214.4575 1757	227.1122 8760	73
74	186.1787 1429	197.0533 7894	208.6715 0931	221.0870 2740	234.3578 7551	74
75	191.3677 3536	202.7333 9669	214.8882 9705	227.8905 6187	241.8027 1709	75
76	196.6735 0941	208.5483 1486	221.2605 0447	234.8726 8912	249.4522 9181	76
77	202.0986 6337	214.5013 3734	227.7920 1709	242.0380 9721	257.3122 2983	77
78	207.6458 8329	220.5957 4410	234.4868 1751	249.3915 9726	265.3883 1615	78
79	213.3179 1567	226.8348 9302	241.3489 8795	256.9381 2669	273.6864 9485	79
80	219.1175 6877	233.2222 2173	248.3827 1265	264.6827 5252	282.2128 7345	80
81	225.0477 1407	239.7612 4950	255.5922 8047	272.6306 7477	290.9737 2747	81
82	231.1112 8763	246.4555 7918	262.9820 8748	280.7872 2998	299.9755 0498	82
83	237.3112 9160	253.3088 9918	270.5566 3966	289.1578 9477	309.2248 3137	83
84	243.6507 9567	260.3249 8554	278.3205 5566	297.7482 8951	318.7285 1423	84
85	250.1329 3857	267.5077 0394	286.2785 6955	306.5641 8211	328.4935 4837	85
86	256.7609 2969	274.8610 1191	294.4355 3379	315.6114 9189	338.5271 2095	86
87	263.5380 5060	282.3889 6094	302.7964 2213	324.8962 9355	348.8366 1678	87
88	270.4676 5674	290.0956 9877	311.3663 3268	334.4248 2126	359.4296 2374	88
89	277.5531 7902	297.9854 7161	320.1504 9100	344.2034 7282	370.3139 3839	89
90	284.7981 2555	306.0626 2656	329.1542 5328	354.2388 1398	381.4975 7170	90
91	292.2060 8337	314.3316 1394	338.3831 0961	364.5375 8284	392.9887 5492	91
92	299.7807 2025	322.7969 8978	347.8426 8735	375.1066 9439	404.7959 4568	92
93	307.5257 8645	331.4634 1828	357.5387 5453	385.9532 4512	416.9278 3418	93
94	315.4451 1665	340.3356 7447	367.4772 2339	397.0845 1781	429.3933 4962	94
95	323.5426 3177	349.4186 4674	377.6641 5398	408.5079 8640	442.2016 6674	95
96	331.8223 4099	358.7173 3960	388.1057 5783	420.2313 2104	455.3622 1257	96
97	340.2883 4366	368.2368 7641	398.8084 0177	432.2623 9322	468.8846 7342	97
98	348.9448 3139	377.9825 0223	409.7786 1182	444.6092 8104	482.7790 0194	98
99	357.7960 9010	387.9595 8665	421.0230 7711	457.2802 7467	497.0554 2449	99
100	366.8465 0213	398.1736 2684	432.5486 5404	470.2838 8188	511.7244 4867	100
101	376.1005 4842	408.6302 5047	444.3623 7039	483.6288 3378	526.7968 7100	101
102	385.5628 1076	419.3352 1892	456.4714 2965	497.3240 9066	542.2837 8496	102
103	395.2379 7401	430.2944 3037	468.8832 1539	511.3788 4804	558.1965 8904	103
104	405.1308 2842	441.5139 2309	481.6052 9578	525.8025 4280	574.5469 9524	104
105	415.2462 7206	452.9998 7877	494.6454 2817	540.6048 5955	591.3470 3761	105
106	425.5893 1318	464.7586 2589	508.0115 6388	555.7957 3712	608.6090 8114	106
107	436.1650 7273	476.7966 4325	521.7118 5298	571.3853 7522	626.3458 3088	107
108	446.9787 8687	489.1205 6353	535.7546 4930	587.3842 4132	644.5703 4123	108
109	458.0358 0957	501.7371 7691	550.1485 1553	603.8030 7765	663.2960 2561	109
110	469.3416 1529	514.6534 3486	564.9022 2842	620.6529 0844	682.5366 6631	110
111	480.9018 0163	527.8764 5394	580.0247 8413	637.9450 4728	702.3064 2464	111
112	492.7220 9217	541.4135 1972	595.5254 0373	655.6911 0478	722.6198 5131	112
113	504.8083 3924	555.2720 9082	611.4135 3883	673.9029 9628	743.4918 9723	113
114	517.1665 2687	569.4598 0297	627.6988 7730	692.5929 4993	764.9379 2440	114
115	529.8027 7373	583.9844 7329	644.3913 4923	711.7735 1486	786.9737 1732	115
116	542.7233 3614	598.8541 0454	661.5011 3296	731.4575 6963	809.6154 9455	116
117	555.9346 1120	614.0768 8952	679.0386 6129	751.6583 3083	832.8799 2065	117
118	569.4431 3995	629.6612 1564	697.0146 2782	772.3893 6202	856.7841 1846	118
119	583.2556 1060	645.6156 6952	715.4399 9351	793.6645 8277	881.3456 8172	119
120	597.3788 6184	661.9490 4167	734.3259 9335	815.4982 7807	906.5826 8797	120

TABLE III

N	2 1/4	2 3/8	2 1/2	2 5/8	2 3/4	N
121	611.8198 8623	678.6703 3141	753.6841 4318	837.9051 0787	932.5137 1189	121
122	626.5858 3367	695.7887 5178	773.5262 4676	860.9001 1695	959.1578 3897	122
123	641.6840 1493	713.3137 3463	793.8644 0293	884.4987 4502	986.5346 7954	123
124	657.1219 0526	731.2549 3583	814.7110 1301	908.7168 3707	1014.6643 8322	124
125	672.9071 4813	749.6222 4056	836.0787 8833	933.5706 5405	1043.5676 5376	125
126	689.0475 5896	768.4257 6877	857.9807 5804	959.0768 8372	1073.2657 6424	126
127	705.5511 2904	787.6758 8078	880.4302 7699	985.2526 5191	1103.7805 7276	127
128	722.4260 2944	807.3831 8295	903.4410 3392	1012.1155 3403	1135.1345 3851	128
129	739.6806 1511	827.5585 3354	927.0270 5976	1039.6835 6679	1167.3507 3832	129
130	757.3234 2895	848.2130 4871	951.2027 3626	1067.9752 6042	1200.4528 8362	130
131	775.3632 0610	869.3581 0862	975.9828 0466	1097.0096 1101	1234.4653 3792	131
132	793.8088 7824	891.0053 6370	1001.3823 7478	1126.8061 1330	1269.4131 3471	132
133	812.6695 7800	913.1667 4109	1027.4169 3415	1157.3847 7377	1305.3219 9592	133
134	831.9546 4350	935.8544 5119	1054.1023 5750	1188.7661 2408	1342.2183 5081	134
135	851.6736 2298	959.0809 9440	1081.4549 1644	1220.9712 3484	1380.1293 5545	135
136	871.8362 7950	982.8591 6802	1109.4912 8935	1254.0217 2976	1419.0829 1273	136
137	892.4525 9579	1007.2020 7326	1138.2285 7159	1287.9398 0016	1459.1076 9283	137
138	913.5327 7919	1032.1231 2250	1167.6842 8588	1322.7482 1992	1500.2331 5438	138
139	935.0872 6672	1057.6360 4666	1197.8763 9302	1358.4703 6069	1542.4895 6613	139
140	957.1267 3022	1083.7549 0277	1228.8233 0285	1395.1302 0766	1585.9080 2920	140
141	979.6620 8165	1110.4940 8171	1260.5438 8542	1432.7523 7561	1630.5205 0000	141
142	1002.7044 7849	1137.8683 1615	1293.0574 8256	1471.3621 2547	1676.3598 1375	142
143	1026.2653 2926	1165.8926 8866	1326.3839 1962	1510.9853 8126	1723.4597 0863	143
144	1050.3562 9917	1194.5826 4001	1360.5435 1761	1551.6487 4752	1771.8548 5061	144
145	1074.9893 1590	1223.9539 7771	1395.5571 0555	1593.3795 2714	1821.5808 5901	145
146	1100.1765 7550	1254.0228 8468	1431.4460 3319	1636.2057 3973	1872.6743 3263	146
147	1125.9305 4845	1284.8059 2820	1468.2321 8402	1680.1561 4040	1925.1728 7678	147
148	1152.2639 8579	1316.3200 6899	1505.9379 8862	1725.2602 3908	1979.1151 3089	148
149	1179.1899 2547	1348.5826 7063	1544.5864 3834	1771.5483 2036	2034.5407 9699	149
150	1206.7216 9880	1381.6115 0906	1584.2010 9929	1819.0514 6377	2091.4906 6890	150
151	1234.8729 3702	1415.4247 8240	1624.8061 2678	1867.8015 6469	2150.0066 6230	151
152	1263.6575 7810	1450.0411 2098	1666.4262 7995	1917.8313 5576	2210.1318 4551	152
153	1293.0898 7361	1485.4795 9760	1709.0869 3694	1969.1744 2885	2271.9104 7126	153
154	1323.1843 9577	1521.7597 3805	1752.8141 1037	2021.8652 5761	2335.3880 0922	154
155	1353.9560 4467	1558.9015 3182	1797.6344 6313	2075.9392 2062	2400.6111 7948	155
156	1385.4200 5568	1596.9254 4320	1843.5753 2470	2131.4326 2516	2467.6279 8691	156
157	1417.5920 0693	1635.8524 2248	1890.6647 0782	2188.3827 3157	2536.4877 5655	157
158	1450.4878 2708	1675.7039 1751	1938.9313 2552	2246.8277 7828	2607.2411 6986	158
159	1484.1238 0319	1716.5018 8556	1988.4046 0866	2306.8070 0746	2679.9403 0203	159
160	1518.5165 8877	1758.2688 0534	2039.1147 2387	2368.3606 9140	2754.6386 6033	160
161	1553.6832 1201	1801.0276 8946	2091.0925 9197	2431.5301 5955	2831.3912 2349	161
162	1589.6410 8428	1844.8020 9709	2144.3699 0677	2496.3578 2624	2910.2544 8214	162
163	1626.4080 0868	1889.6161 4689	2198.9791 5444	2562.8872 1918	2991.2864 8040	163
164	1664.0021 8887	1935.4945 3038	2254.9536 3330	2631.1630 0868	3074.5468 5861	164
165	1702.4422 3812	1982.4625 2548	2312.3274 7413	2701.2310 3766	3160.0968 9722	165
166	1741.7471 8848	2030.5460 1046	2371.1356 6098	2773.1383 5240	3247.9995 6189	166
167	1781.9365 0022	2079.7714 7821	2431.4140 5251	2846.9332 3415	3338.3195 4985	167
168	1823.0300 7148	2130.1660 5082	2493.1994 0382	2922.6652 3155	3431.1233 3747	168
169	1865.0482 4809	2181.7574 9452	2556.5293 8892	3000.3851 9388	3526.4792 2925	169
170	1908.0118 3367	2234.5742 3502	2621.4426 2364	3080.1453 0521	3624.4574 0805	170
171	1951.9420 9993	2288.6453 7310	2687.9786 8923	3161.9991 1948	3725.1299 8677	171
172	1996.8607 9717	2344.0007 0071	2756.1781 5646	3246.0015 9636	3828.5710 6141	172
173	2042.7901 6511	2400.6707 1735	2826.0826 1037	3332.2091 3827	3934.8567 6560	173
174	2089.7529 4383	2458.6866 4689	2897.7346 7563	3420.6796 2815	4044.0653 2665	174
175	2137.7723 8506	2518.0804 5475	2971.1780 4252	3511.4724 6839	4156.2771 2313	175
176	2186.8722 6373	2578.8848 6555	3046.4574 9359	3604.6486 2068	4271.5747 4402	176
177	2237.0768 8966	2641.1333 8111	3123.6189 3093	3700.2706 4697	4390.0430 4948	177
178	2288.4111 1968	2704.8602 9891	3202.7094 0420	3798.4027 5146	4511.7692 3334	178
179	2340.9003 6987	2770.1007 3101	3283.7771 3930	3899.1108 2368	4636.8428 8726	179
180	2394.5706 2819	2836.8906 2337	3366.8715 6779	4002.4624 8280	4765.3560 6666	180

TABLE III

N	2 1/4	2 3/8	2 1/2	2 5/8	2 3/4	N
181	2449.4484 6733	2905.2667 7568	3452.0433 5698	4108.5271 2298	4897.4033 5849	181
182	2505.5610 5784	2975.2668 6160	3539.3444 4091	4217.3759 5996	5033.0819 5085	182
183	2562.9361 8164	3046.9294 4956	3628.8280 5193	4329.0820 7890	5172.4917 0450	183
184	2621.6022 4573	3120.2940 2399	3720.5487 5323	4443.7204 8348	5315.7352 2637	184
185	2681.5882 9626	3195.4010 0706	3814.5624 7206	4561.3681 4617	5462.9179 4510	185
186	2742.9240 3292	3272.2917 8098	3910.9265 3386	4682.1040 6000	5614.1481 8859	186
187	2805.6398 2366	3351.0087 1078	4009.6996 9721	4806.0092 9158	5769.5372 6377	187
188	2869.7667 1970	3431.5951 6766	4110.9421 8964	4933.1670 3548	5929.1995 3853	188
189	2935.3364 7089	3514.0955 5289	4214.7157 4438	5063.6626 7016	6093.2525 2584	189
190	3002.3815 4148	3598.5553 2227	4321.0836 3799	5197.5838 1526	6261.8169 7030	190
191	3070.9351 2617	3685.0210 1117	4430.1107 2894	5335.0203 9041	6435.0169 3698	191
192	3141.0311 6651	3773.5402 6019	4541.8634 9716	5476.0646 7565	6612.9799 0275	192
193	3212.7043 6775	3864.1618 4137	4656.4100 8459	5620.8113 7339	6795.8368 5007	193
194	3285.9902 1603	3956.9356 8510	4773.8203 3670	5769.3576 7194	6983.7223 6345	194
195	3360.9249 9589	4051.9129 0762	4894.1658 4512	5921.8033 1083	7176.7747 2845	195
196	3437.5458 0830	4149.1458 3918	5017.5199 9125	6078.2506 4774	7375.1360 3348	196
197	3515.8905 8898	4248.6880 5286	5143.9579 9103	6238.8047 2724	7578.9522 7440	197
198	3595.9981 2723	4350.5943 9411	5273.5569 4081	6403.5733 5133	7788.3734 6194	198
199	3677.9080 8510	4454.9210 1097	5406.3958 6433	6572.6671 5181	8003.5537 3215	199
200	3761.6610 1701	4561.7253 8498	5542.5557 6093	6746.1996 6454	8224.6514 5978	200
201	3847.2983 8990	4671.0663 6288	5682.1196 5496	6924.2874 0573	8451.8293 7493	201
202	3934.8626 0367	4783.0041 8900	5825.1726 4633	7107.0499 5013	8685.2546 8274	202
203	4024.3970 1225	4897.6005 3849	5971.8019 6249	7294.6100 1133	8925.0991 8651	203
204	4115.9459 4503	5014.9185 5127	6122.0970 1155	7487.0935 2412	9171.5394 1414	204
205	4209.5547 2879	5135.0228 6687	6276.1494 3684	7684.6297 2913	9424.7567 4803	205
206	4305.2697 1019	5257.9796 5996	6434.0531 7276	7887.3512 5952	9684.9375 5860	206
207	4403.1382 7867	5383.8566 7688	6595.9045 0208	8095.3942 3008	9952.2733 4146	207
208	4503.2088 8994	5512.7232 7296	6761.8021 1463	8308.8983 2862	10226.9608 5835	208
209	4605.5310 8996	5644.6504 5069	6931.8471 6750	8528.0069 0975	10509.2022 8196	209
210	4710.1555 3948	5779.7108 9889	7106.1433 4669	8752.8670 9113	10799.2053 4471	210
211	4817.1340 3912	5917.9790 3274	7284.7969 3035	8983.6298 5227	11097.1834 9169	211
212	4926.5195 5500	6059.5310 3477	7467.9168 5361	9220.4501 3589	11403.3560 3771	212
213	5038.3662 4499	6204.4448 9684	7655.6147 7495	9463.4869 5196	11717.9483 2875	213
214	5152.7294 8550	6352.8004 6314	7848.0051 4433	9712.9034 8445	12041.1919 0779	214
215	5269.6658 9893	6504.6794 7414	8045.2052 7293	9968.8672 0092	12373.3246 8525	215
216	5389.2333 8165	6660.1656 1165	8247.3354 0476	10231.5499 6494	12714.5911 1410	216
217	5511.4911 3274	6819.3445 4493	8454.5187 8988	10501.1281 5152	13065.2423 6974	217
218	5636.4996 8323	6982.3039 7787	8666.8817 5962	10777.7827 6550	13425.5365 3490	218
219	5764.3209 2610	7149.1336 9735	8884.5538 0361	11061.6995 6309	13795.7387 8961	219
220	5895.0181 4694	7319.9256 2266	9107.6676 4870	11353.0691 7662	14176.1216 0633	220
221	6028.6560 5524	7494.7738 5620	9336.3593 3992	11652.0872 4251	14566.9649 5050	221
222	6165.3008 1648	7673.7747 3528	9570.7683 2342	11958.9545 3263	14968.5564 8664	222
223	6305.0200 8486	7857.0268 8525	9811.0375 3151	12273.8770 8911	15381.1917 9002	223
224	6447.8830 3676	8044.6312 7377	10057.3134 6979	12597.0663 6270	15805.1745 6425	224
225	6593.9604 0509	8236.6912 6652	10309.7463 0654	12928.7393 5472	16240.8168 6477	225
226	6743.3245 1421	8433.3126 8410	10568.4899 6420	13269.1187 6278	16688.4393 2855	226
227	6896.0493 1578	8634.6038 6035	10833.7022 1331	13618.4331 3030	17148.3714 1008	227
228	7052.2104 2538	8840.6757 0203	11105.5447 6864	13976.9169 9997	17620.9516 2386	228
229	7211.8851 5995	9051.6417 4996	11384.1833 8786	14344.8110 7122	18106.5277 9351	229
230	7375.1525 7605	9267.6182 4152	11669.7879 7255	14722.3623 6184	18605.4573 0784	230
231	7542.0935 0901	9488.7241 7475	11962.5326 7187	15109.8243 7384	19118.1073 8380	231
232	7712.7906 1296	9715.0813 7390	12262.5959 8866	15507.4572 6365	19644.8553 3686	232
233	7887.3284 0176	9946.8145 5653	12570.1608 8838	15915.5280 1682	20186.0888 5862	233
234	8065.7932 9080	10184.0514 0225	12885.4149 1059	16334.3106 2727	20742.2063 0223	234
235	8248.2736 3984	10426.9226 2306	13208.5502 8335	16764.0862 8123	21313.6169 7554	235
236	8434.8597 9674	10675.5620 3535	13539.7640 4044	17205.1435 4611	21900.7414 4237	236
237	8625.6441 4216	10930.1066 3369	13879.2581 4145	17657.7785 6420	22504.0118 3204	237
238	8820.7211 3536	11190.6966 6624	14227.2395 9498	18122.2952 5151	23123.8721 5742	238
239	9020.1873 6091	11457.4757 1207	14583.9205 8486	18599.0055 0186	23760.7786 4175	239
240	9224.1415 7653	11730.5907 6023	14949.5185 9948	19088.2293 9629	24415.2000 5439	240

TABLE III

N	2 1/4	2 3/8	2 1/2	2 5/8	2 3/4	N
241	9432.6847 6200	12010.1922 9078	15324.2565 6447	19590.2954 1794	25087.6180 5589	241
242	9645.9201 6914	12296.4343 5769	15708.3629 7858	20105.5406 7266	25778.5275 5243	242
243	9863.9533 7295	12589.4746 7368	16102.0720 5304	20634.3111 1532	26488.4370 6012	243
244	10086.8923 2384	12889.4746 9718	16505.6238 5437	21176.9617 8209	27217.8690 7927	244
245	10314.8474 0113	13196.5997 2124	16919.2644 5073	21733.8570 2887	27967.3604 7895	245
246	10547.9314 6765	13511.0189 6462	17343.2460 6200	22305.3707 7588	28737.4628 9212	246
247	10786.2599 2567	13832.9056 6503	17777.8272 1355	22891.8867 5875	29528.7431 2166	247
248	11029.9507 7400	14162.4371 7458	18223.2728 9388	23493.7987 8617	30341.7835 5750	248
249	11279.1246 6642	14499.7950 5747	18679.8547 1623	24111.5110 0430	31177.1826 0533	249
250	11533.9049 7141	14845.1651 9009	19147.8510 8414	24745.4381 6817	32035.5551 2698	250
251	11794.4178 3327	15198.7378 6335	19627.5473 6124	25396.0059 2008	32917.5328 9297	251
252	12060.7922 3452	15560.7078 8761	20119.2360 4527	26063.6510 7548	33823.7650 4753	252
253	12333.1600 5979	15931.2746 9994	20623.2169 4640	26748.8219 1621	34754.9185 8633	253
254	12611.6561 6114	16310.6424 7406	21139.7973 7006	27451.9784 9151	35711.6788 4746	254
255	12896.4184 2476	16699.0202 3282	21669.2923 0432	28173.5929 2692	36694.7500 1576	255
256	13187.5878 3932	17096.6219 6335	22212.0246 1192	28914.1497 4125	37704.8556 4120	256
257	13485.3085 6571	17503.6667 3498	22768.3252 2722	29674.1461 7196	38742.7391 7133	257
258	13789.7280 0843	17920.3788 1993	23338.5333 5790	30454.0925 0897	39809.1644 9854	258
259	14100.9968 8862	18346.9878 1691	23922.9966 9185	31254.5124 3733	40904.9165 2225	259
260	14419.2693 1862	18783.7287 7756	24522.0716 0915	32075.9433 8881	42030.8017 2661	260
261	14744.7028 7829	19230.8423 3603	25136.1233 9937	32918.9369 0277	43187.6487 7410	261
262	15077.4586 9305	19688.5748 4151	25765.5264 8436	33784.0589 9646	44376.3091 1538	262
263	15417.7015 1364	20157.1784 9399	26410.6646 4647	34671.8905 4512	45597.6576 1606	263
264	15765.5997 9770	20636.9114 8322	27071.9312 6263	35583.0276 7193	46852.5932 0050	264
265	16121.3257 9315	21128.0381 3095	27749.7295 4420	36518.0821 4832	48142.0395 1351	265
266	16485.0556 2349	21630.8290 3656	28444.4727 8280	37477.6818 0471	49466.9456 0013	266
267	16856.9693 7502	22145.5612 2618	29156.5846 0237	38462.4709 5209	50828.2866 0414	267
268	17237.2511 8596	22672.5183 0530	29886.4992 1743	39473.1108 1458	52227.0644 8575	268
269	17626.0893 3764	23211.9906 1505	30634.6616 9787	40510.2799 7346	53664.3087 5911	269
270	18023.6763 4774	23764.2753 9216	31401.5282 4031	41574.6748 2276	55141.0772 4998	270
271	18430.2090 6557	24329.6769 3272	32187.5664 4632	42667.0100 3686	56658.4568 7436	271
272	18845.8887 6954	24908.5067 5988	32993.2556 0748	43788.0190 5033	58217.5644 3840	272
273	19270.9212 6685	25501.0837 9542	33819.0869 9766	44938.4545 5040	59819.5474 6046	273
274	19705.5169 9536	26107.7345 3556	34665.5641 7261	46119.0889 8235	61465.5850 1562	274
275	20149.8911 2775	26728.7932 3078	35533.2032 7692	47330.7150 6814	63156.8886 0355	275
276	20604.2636 7813	27364.6020 7001	36422.5333 5884	48574.1463 3867	64894.7030 4015	276
277	21068.8596 1089	28015.5113 6918	37334.0966 9282	49850.2176 8006	66680.3073 7375	277
278	21543.9089 5213	28681.8797 6420	38268.4491 1014	51159.7858 9417	68515.0158 2653	278
279	22029.6469 0356	29364.0744 0860	39226.1603 3789	52503.7302 7389	70400.1787 6176	279
280	22526.3139 5889	30062.4711 7580	40207.8143 4634	53882.9531 9358	72337.1836 7771	280
281	23034.1560 2296	30777.4548 6622	41214.0097 0499	55298.3807 1491	74327.4562 2885	281
282	23553.4245 3348	31509.4194 1930	42245.3599 4762	56750.9632 0867	76372.4612 7514	282
283	24084.3765 8548	32258.7681 3051	43302.4939 4631	58241.6759 9290	78473.7039 6021	283
284	24627.2750 5865	33025.9138 7361	44386.0562 9497	59771.5199 8772	80632.7308 1911	284
285	25182.3887 4747	33811.2793 2810	45496.7077 0234	61341.5223 8739	82851.1309 1664	285
286	25749.9924 9429	34615.2972 1215	46635.1253 9490	62952.7373 5006	85130.5370 1685	286
287	26330.3673 2541	35438.4105 2093	47802.0035 2977	64606.2467 0550	87472.6267 8481	287
288	26923.8005 9023	36281.0727 7081	48998.0536 1802	66303.1606 8152	89879.1240 2139	288
289	27530.5861 0351	37143.7482 4911	50224.0049 5847	68044.6186 4941	92351.7999 3198	289
290	28151.0242 9084	38026.9122 7003	51480.6050 8243	69831.7898 8896	94892.4744 3011	290
291	28785.4223 3739	38931.0514 3644	52768.6202 0949	71665.8743 7354	97503.0174 7694	291
292	29434.0943 3998	39856.6639 0806	54088.8357 1473	73548.1035 7585	100185.3504 5755	292
293	30097.3614 6263	40804.2596 7587	55442.0566 0760	75479.7412 9472	102941.4475 9514	293
294	30775.5520 9554	41774.3608 4318	56829.1080 2279	77462.0845 0370	105773.3374 0400	294
295	31469.0020 1769	42767.5019 1320	58250.8357 2336	79496.4642 2192	108683.1041 8261	295
296	32178.0545 6309	43784.2300 8364	59708.1066 1644	81584.2464 0775	111672.8895 4763	296
297	32903.0607 9075	44825.1055 4813	61201.8092 8185	83726.8328 7595	114744.8940 1019	297
298	33644.3796 5855	45890.7018 0490	62732.8545 1390	85925.6622 3895	117901.3785 9547	298
299	34402.3782 0086	46981.6059 7276	64302.1758 7674	88182.2108 7272	121144.6665 0685	299
300	35177.4317 1038	48098.4191 1461	65910.7302 7366	90497.9939 0813	124477.1448 3579	300

TABLE III

N	2 1/4	2 3/8	2 1/2	2 5/8	2 3/4	N
301	35969.9239 2387	49241.7565 6859	67559.4985 3050	92874.5662 4822	127901.2663 1877	301
302	36780.2472 1215	50412.2482 8709	69249.4859 9377	95313.5236 1223	131419.5511 4254	302
303	37608.8027 7443	51610.5391 8391	70981.7231 4361	97816.5036 0705	135034.5887 9896	303
304	38456.0008 3685	52837.2894 8953	72757.2662 2220	100385.1868 2674	138749.0399 9093	304
305	39322.2608 5568	54093.1751 1490	74577.1978 7776	103021.2979 8094	142565.6385 9068	305
306	40208.0117 2493	55378.8880 2388	76442.6278 2470	105726.6070 5294	146487.1936 5192	306
307	41113.6919 8874	56695.1366 1445	78354.6935 2032	108502.9304 8808	150516.5914 7735	307
308	42039.7500 5849	58042.6461 0904	80314.5608 5832	111352.1324 1339	154656.7977 4298	308
309	42986.6444 3481	59422.1589 5413	82323.4248 7978	114276.1258 8924	158910.8596 8091	309
310	43954.8439 3459	60834.4352 2929	84382.5105 0178	117276.8741 9383	163281.9083 2213	310
311	44944.8279 2312	62280.2530 6599	86493.0732 6432	120356.3921 4142	167773.1608 0099	311
312	45957.0865 5139	63760.4090 7631	88656.4000 9593	123516.7474 3513	172387.9227 2302	312
313	46992.1209 9880	65275.7187 9187	90873.8100 9833	126760.0620 5531	177129.5905 9790	313
314	48050.4437 2127	66827.0171 1318	93146.6553 5079	130088.5136 8426	182001.6543 3935	314
315	49132.5787 0500	68415.1587 6961	95476.3217 3456	133504.3371 6847	187007.6998 3368	315
316	50239.0617 2586	70041.0187 9039	97864.2297 7792	137009.8260 1914	192151.4115 7910	316
317	51370.4406 1469	71705.4929 8666	100311.8355 2237	140607.3339 5215	197436.5753 9753	317
318	52527.2755 2852	73409.4984 4510	102820.6314 1043	144299.2764 6839	202867.0812 2096	318
319	53710.1392 2791	75153.9740 3317	105392.1471 9569	148088.1324 7568	208446.9259 5454	319
320	54919.6173 6054	76939.8809 1645	108027.9508 7558	151976.4459 5317	214180.2164 1829	320
321	56156.3087 5115	78768.2030 8822	110729.6496 4747	155966.8276 5944	220071.1723 6979	321
322	57420.8256 9805	80639.9479 1157	113498.8908 8866	160061.9568 8550	226124.1296 0996	322
323	58713.7942 7626	82556.1466 7447	116337.3631 6087	164264.5832 5375	232343.5431 7423	323
324	60035.8546 4748	84517.8551 5798	119246.7972 3989	168577.5285 6416	238733.9906 1152	324
325	61387.6613 7705	86526.1542 1799	122228.9671 7089	173003.6886 8897	245300.1753 5334	325
326	62769.8837 5803	88582.1503 8066	125285.6913 5016	177546.0355 1705	252046.9301 7556	326
327	64183.2061 4258	90686.9764 5220	128418.8336 3392	182207.6189 4937	258979.2207 5539	327
328	65628.3282 8079	92841.7921 4294	131630.3044 7477	186991.5689 4680	266102.1493 2616	328
329	67105.9656 6711	95047.7847 0634	134922.0620 8664	191901.0976 3165	273420.9584 3263	329
330	68616.8498 9462	97306.1695 9311	138296.1136 3880	196939.5014 4448	280941.0347 8953	330
331	70161.7290 1725	99618.1911 2095	141754.5164 7977	202110.1633 5740	288667.9132 4624	331
332	71741.3679 2014	101985.1231 6007	145299.3793 9177	207416.5551 4553	296607.2808 6051	332
333	73356.5486 9834	104408.2698 3513	148932.8638 7656	212862.2397 1810	304764.9810 8417	333
334	75008.0710 4405	106888.9662 4371	152657.1854 7347	218450.8735 1070	313147.0180 6399	334
335	76696.7526 4254	109428.5791 9200	156474.6151 1031	224186.2089 4036	321759.5610 6075	335
336	78423.4295 7700	112028.5079 4781	160387.4804 8807	230072.0969 2504	330608.9489 8992	336
337	80188.9567 4248	114690.1850 1157	164398.1675 0027	236112.4894 6932	339701.6950 8714	337
338	81994.2082 6919	117415.0769 0559	168509.1216 8778	242311.4423 1789	349044.4917 0204	338
339	83840.0779 5525	120204.6849 8210	172722.8497 2997	248673.1176 7874	358644.2152 2384	339
340	85727.4797 0924	123060.5462 5043	177041.9209 7322	255201.7870 1780	368507.9311 4250	340
341	87657.3480 0270	125984.2342 2387	181468.9689 9755	261901.8339 2702	378642.8992 4892	341
342	89630.6383 3276	128977.3597 8669	186006.6932 2249	268777.7570 6760	389056.5789 7826	342
343	91648.3276 9525	132041.5720 8162	190657.8605 5305	275834.1731 9063	399756.6349 0016	343
344	93711.4150 6839	135178.5594 1856	195425.3070 6688	283075.8202 3688	410750.9423 5992	344
345	95820.9219 0743	138390.0502 0475	200311.9397 4355	290507.5605 1810	422047.5932 7482	345
346	97977.8926 5034	141677.8138 9712	205320.7382 3714	298134.3839 8170	433654.9020 8987	346
347	100183.3952 3498	145043.6619 7717	210454.7566 9307	305961.4115 6122	445581.4118 9734	347
348	102438.5216 2776	148489.4489 4913	215717.1256 1039	313993.8986 1470	457835.9007 2452	348
349	104744.3883 6439	152017.0733 6167	221111.0537 5065	322237.2384 5334	470427.3879 9445	349
350	107102.1371 0259	155628.4788 5401	226639.8300 9442	330696.9659 6274	483365.1411 6429	350
351	109512.9351 8740	159325.6552 2679	232306.8258 4678	339378.7613 1926	496658.6825 4631	351
352	111977.9762 2911	163110.6395 3843	238115.4964 9295	348288.4538 0389	510317.7963 1633	352
353	114498.4806 9427	166985.5172 2747	244069.3839 0527	357432.0257 1624	524352.5357 1503	353
354	117075.6965 0989	170952.4232 6162	250172.1185 0290	366815.6163 9129	538773.2304 4720	354
355	119710.8996 8136	175013.5433 1408	256427.4214 6548	376445.5263 2157	553590.4942 8450	355
356	122405.3949 2419	179171.1149 6779	262839.1070 0211	386328.2213 8751	568815.2328 7732	356
357	125160.5163 0998	183427.4289 4828	269411.0846 7717	396470.3371 9893	584458.6517 8144	357
358	127977.6279 2696	187784.8303 8580	276147.3617 9410	406878.6835 5040	600532.2647 0543	358
359	130858.1245 5532	192245.7201 0746	283052.0458 3895	417560.2489 9360	617047.9019 8483	359
360	133803.4323 5781	196812.5559 6002	290129.3469 8492	428522.2055 2968	634017.7192 8942	360

TABLE III

N	3	3 1/2	4	4 1/2	5	N
1	1.0000 0000	1.0000 0000	1.0000 0000	1.0000 0000	1.0000 0000	1
2	2.0300 0000	2.0350 0000	2.0400 0000	2.0450 0000	2.0500 0000	2
3	3.0909 0000	3.1062 2500	3.1216 0000	3.1370 2500	3.1525 0000	3
4	4.1836 2700	4.2149 4287	4.2464 6400	4.2781 9112	4.3101 2500	4
5	5.3091 3581	5.3624 6588	5.4163 2256	5.4707 0973	5.5256 3125	5
6	6.4684 0988	6.5501 5218	6.6329 7546	6.7168 9166	6.8019 1281	6
7	7.6624 6218	7.7794 0751	7.8982 9448	8.0191 5179	8.1420 0845	7
8	8.8923 3605	9.0516 8677	9.2142 2626	9.3800 1362	9.5491 0888	8
9	10.1591 0613	10.3684 9581	10.5827 9531	10.8021 1423	11.0265 6432	9
10	11.4638 7931	11.7313 9316	12.0061 0712	12.2882 0937	12.5778 9254	10
11	12.8077 9569	13.1419 9192	13.4863 5141	13.8411 7879	14.2067 8716	11
12	14.1920 2956	14.6019 6164	15.0258 0546	15.4640 3184	15.9171 2652	12
13	15.6177 9045	16.1130 3030	16.6268 3768	17.1599 1327	17.7129 8285	13
14	17.0863 2416	17.6769 8636	18.2919 1119	18.9321 0937	19.5986 3199	14
15	18.5989 1389	19.2956 8088	20.0235 8764	20.7840 5429	21.5785 6359	15
16	20.1568 8130	20.9710 2971	21.8245 3114	22.7193 3673	23.6574 9177	16
17	21.7615 8774	22.7050 1575	23.6975 1239	24.7417 0689	25.8403 6636	17
18	23.4144 3537	24.4996 9130	25.6454 1288	26.8550 8370	28.1323 8467	18
19	25.1168 6844	26.3571 8050	27.6712 2940	29.0635 6246	30.5390 0391	19
20	26.8703 7449	28.2796 8181	29.7780 7858	31.3714 2277	33.0659 5410	20
21	28.6764 8572	30.2694 7068	31.9692 0172	33.7831 3680	35.7192 5181	21
22	30.5367 8030	32.3289 0215	34.2479 6979	36.3033 7795	38.5052 1440	22
23	32.4528 8370	34.4604 1373	36.6178 8858	38.9370 2996	41.4304 7512	23
24	34.4264 7022	36.6665 2821	39.0826 0412	41.6891 9631	44.5019 9887	24
25	36.4592 6432	38.9498 5669	41.6459 0829	44.5652 1015	47.7270 9882	25
26	38.5530 4225	41.3131 0168	44.3117 4462	47.5706 4460	51.1134 5376	26
27	40.7096 3352	43.7590 6024	47.0842 1440	50.7113 2361	54.6691 2645	27
28	42.9309 2252	46.2906 2734	49.9675 8298	53.9933 3317	58.4025 8277	28
29	45.2188 5020	48.9107 9930	52.9662 8630	57.4230 3316	62.3227 1191	29
30	47.5754 1571	51.6226 7728	56.0849 3775	61.0070 6966	66.4388 4750	30
31	50.0026 7818	54.4294 7098	59.3283 3526	64.7523 8779	70.7607 8988	31
32	52.5027 5852	57.3345 0247	62.7014 6867	68.6662 4524	75.2988 2937	32
33	55.0778 4128	60.3412 1005	66.2095 2742	72.7562 2628	80.0637 7084	33
34	57.7301 7652	63.4531 5240	69.8579 0851	77.0302 5646	85.0669 5938	34
35	60.4620 8181	66.6740 1274	73.6522 2486	81.4966 1800	90.3203 0735	35
36	63.2759 4427	70.0076 0318	77.5983 1385	86.1639 6581	95.8363 2272	36
37	66.1742 2259	73.4578 6930	81.7022 4640	91.0413 4427	101.6281 3886	37
38	69.1594 4927	77.0288 9472	85.9703 3626	96.1382 0476	107.7095 4580	38
39	72.2342 3275	80.7249 0604	90.4091 4971	101.4644 2398	114.0950 2309	39
40	75.4012 5973	84.5502 7775	95.0255 1570	107.0303 2306	120.7997 7424	40
41	78.6632 9753	88.5095 3747	99.8265 3633	112.8466 8760	127.8397 6295	41
42	82.0231 9645	92.6073 7128	104.8195 9778	118.9247 8854	135.2317 5110	42
43	85.4838 9234	96.8486 2928	110.0123 8169	125.2764 0402	142.9933 3866	43
44	89.0484 0911	101.2383 3130	115.4128 7696	131.9138 4220	151.1430 0559	44
45	92.7198 6139	105.7816 7290	121.0293 9204	138.8499 6510	159.7001 5587	45
46	96.5014 5723	110.4840 3145	126.8705 6772	146.0982 1353	168.6851 6366	46
47	100.3965 0095	115.3509 7255	132.9453 9043	153.6726 3314	178.1194 2185	47
48	104.4083 9598	120.3882 5659	139.2632 0604	161.5879 0163	188.0253 9294	48
49	108.5406 4785	125.6018 4557	145.8337 3429	169.8593 5720	198.4266 6259	49
50	112.7968 6729	130.9979 1016	152.6670 8366	178.5030 2828	209.3479 9572	50
51	117.1807 7331	136.5828 3702	159.7737 6700	187.5356 6455	220.8153 9550	51
52	121.6961 9651	142.3632 3631	167.1647 1768	196.9747 6946	232.8561 6528	52
53	126.3470 8240	148.3459 4958	174.8513 0639	206.8386 3408	245.4989 7354	53
54	131.1374 9488	154.5380 5782	182.8453 5865	217.1463 7262	258.7739 2222	54
55	136.0716 1972	160.9468 8984	191.1591 7299	227.9179 5938	272.7126 1833	55
56	141.1537 6831	167.5800 3099	199.8055 3991	239.1742 6756	287.3482 4924	56
57	146.3883 8136	174.4453 3207	208.7977 6151	250.9371 0960	302.7156 6171	57
58	151.7800 3280	181.5509 1869	218.1496 7197	263.2292 7953	318.8514 4479	58
59	157.3334 3379	188.9052 0085	227.8756 5885	276.0745 9711	335.7940 1703	59
60	163.0534 3680	196.5168 8288	237.9906 8520	289.4979 5398	353.5837 1788	60

TABLE III

N	3	3 1/2	4	4 1/2	5	N
61	168.9450 3991	204.3949 7378	248.5103 1261	303.5253 6190	372.2629 0378	61
62	175.0133 9110	212.5487 9786	259.4507 2511	318.1840 0319	391.8760 4897	62
63	181.2637 9284	220.9880 0579	270.8287 5412	333.5022 8333	412.4698 5141	63
64	187.7017 0662	229.7225 8599	282.6619 0428	349.5098 8608	434.0933 4398	64
65	194.3327 5782	238.7628 7650	294.9683 8045	366.2378 3096	456.7980 1118	65
66	201.1627 4055	248.1195 7718	307.7671 1567	383.7185 3335	480.6379 1174	66
67	208.1976 2277	257.8037 6238	321.0778 0030	401.9858 6735	505.6698 0733	67
68	215.4435 5145	267.8268 9406	334.9209 1231	421.0752 3138	531.9532 9770	68
69	222.9068 5800	278.2008 3535	349.3177 4880	441.0236 1679	559.5509 6258	69
70	230.5940 6374	288.9378 6459	364.2904 5876	461.8696 7955	588.5285 1071	70
71	238.5118 8565	300.0506 8985	379.8620 7711	483.6538 1513	618.9549 3625	71
72	246.6672 4222	311.5524 6400	396.0565 6019	506.4182 3681	650.9026 8306	72
73	255.0672 5949	323.4568 0024	412.8988 2260	530.2070 5747	684.4478 1721	73
74	263.7192 7727	335.7777 8824	430.4147 7550	555.0663 7505	719.6702 0807	74
75	272.6308 5559	348.5300 1083	448.6313 6652	581.0443 6193	756.6537 1848	75
76	281.8097 8126	361.7285 6121	467.5766 2118	608.1913 5822	795.4864 0440	76
77	291.2640 7469	375.3890 6085	487.2796 8603	636.5599 6934	836.2607 2462	77
78	301.0019 9693	389.5276 7798	507.7708 7347	666.2051 6796	879.0737 6085	78
79	311.0320 5684	404.1611 4671	529.0817 0841	697.1844 0052	924.0274 4889	79
80	321.3630 1855	419.3067 8685	551.2449 7675	729.5576 9854	971.2288 2134	80
81	332.0039 0910	434.9825 2439	574.2947 7582	763.3877 9497	1020.7902 6240	81
82	342.9640 2638	451.2069 1274	598.2665 6685	798.7402 4575	1072.8297 7552	82
83	354.2529 4717	467.9991 5469	623.1972 2952	835.6835 5680	1127.4712 6430	83
84	365.8805 3558	485.3791 2510	649.1251 1870	874.2893 1686	1184.8448 2752	84
85	377.8569 5165	503.3673 9448	676.0901 2345	914.6323 3612	1245.0870 6889	85
86	390.1926 6020	521.9852 5329	704.1337 2839	956.7907 9125	1308.3414 2234	86
87	402.8984 4001	541.2547 3715	733.2990 7753	1000.8463 7685	1374.7584 9345	87
88	415.9853 9321	561.1986 5295	763.6310 4063	1046.8844 6381	1444.4964 1812	88
89	429.4649 5500	581.8406 0581	795.1762 8225	1094.9942 6468	1517.7212 3903	89
90	443.3489 0365	603.2050 2701	827.9833 3354	1145.2690 0659	1594.6073 0098	90
91	457.6493 7076	625.3172 0295	862.1026 6688	1197.8061 1189	1675.3376 6603	91
92	472.3788 5189	648.2033 0506	897.5867 7356	1252.7073 8692	1760.1045 4933	92
93	487.5502 1744	671.8904 2074	934.4902 4450	1310.0792 1933	1849.1097 7680	93
94	503.1767 2397	696.4065 8546	972.8698 5428	1370.0327 8420	1942.5652 6564	94
95	519.2720 2568	721.7808 1595	1012.7846 4845	1432.6842 5949	2040.6935 2892	95
96	535.8501 8645	748.0431 4451	1054.2960 3439	1498.1550 5117	2143.7282 0537	96
97	552.9256 9205	775.2246 5457	1097.4678 7577	1566.5720 2847	2251.9146 1564	97
98	570.5134 6281	803.3575 1748	1142.3665 9080	1638.0677 6976	2365.5103 4642	98
99	588.6288 6669	832.4750 3059	1189.0612 5443	1712.7808 1939	2484.7858 6374	99
100	607.2877 3270	862.6116 5666	1237.6237 0461	1790.8559 5627	2610.0251 5693	100
101	626.5063 6468	893.8030 6464	1288.1286 5279	1872.4444 7430	2741.5264 1477	101
102	646.3015 5562	926.0861 7191	1340.6537 9890	1957.7044 7564	2879.6027 3551	102
103	666.6906 0228	959.4991 8792	1395.2799 5086	2046.8011 7705	3024.5828 7229	103
104	687.6913 2035	994.0816 5950	1452.0911 4889	2139.9072 3001	3176.8120 1590	104
105	709.3220 5996	1029.8745 1758	1511.1747 9485	2237.2030 5536	3336.6526 1670	105
106	731.6017 2176	1066.9201 2570	1572.6217 8664	2338.8771 9286	3504.4852 4753	106
107	754.5497 7342	1105.2623 3010	1636.5266 5811	2445.1266 6653	3680.7095 0991	107
108	778.1862 6662	1144.9465 1165	1702.9877 2443	2556.1573 6653	3865.7449 8540	108
109	802.5318 5462	1186.0196 3956	1772.1072 3341	2672.1844 4802	4060.0322 3467	109
110	827.6078 1026	1228.5303 2694	1843.9915 2275	2793.4327 4818	4264.0338 4641	110
111	853.4360 4456	1272.5288 8839	1918.7511 8366	2920.1372 2185	4478.2355 3873	111
112	880.0391 2590	1318.0673 9948	1996.5012 3100	3052.5433 9683	4703.1473 1566	112
113	907.4402 9968	1365.1997 5846	2077.3612 8024	3190.9078 4969	4939.3046 8145	113
114	935.6635 0867	1413.9817 5001	2161.4557 3145	3335.4987 0293	5187.2699 1552	114
115	964.7334 1393	1464.4711 1126	2248.9139 6071	3486.5961 4456	5447.6334 1129	115
116	994.6754 1634	1516.7276 0015	2339.8705 1914	3644.4929 7106	5721.0150 8186	116
117	1025.5156 7884	1570.8130 6616	2434.4653 3990	3809.4951 5476	6008.0658 3595	117
118	1057.2811 4920	1626.7915 2347	2532.8439 5350	3981.9224 3673	6309.4691 2775	118
119	1089.9995 8368	1684.7292 2679	2635.1577 1164	4162.1089 4638	6625.9425 8414	119
120	1123.6995 7119	1744.6947 4973	2741.5640 2011	4350.4038 4897	6958.2397 1334	120

TABLE III

N	5 1/2	6	6 1/2	7	7 1/2	N
1	1.0000 0000	1.0000 0000	1.0000 0000	1.0000 0000	1.0000 0000	1
2	2.0550 0000	2.0600 0000	2.0650 0000	2.0700 0000	2.0750 0000	2
3	3.1680 2500	3.1836 0000	3.1992 2500	3.2149 0000	3.2306 2500	3
4	4.3422 6637	4.3746 1600	4.4071 7462	4.4399 4300	4.4729 2187	4
5	5.5810 9103	5.6370 9296	5.6936 4098	5.7507 3901	5.8083 9102	5
6	6.8880 5103	6.9753 1854	7.0637 2764	7.1532 9074	7.2440 2034	6
7	8.2668 9384	8.3938 3765	8.5228 6994	8.6540 2109	8.7873 2187	7
8	9.7215 7300	9.8974 6791	10.0768 5648	10.2598 0257	10.4463 7101	8
9	11.2562 5951	11.4913 1598	11.7318 5215	11.9779 8875	12.2298 4883	9
10	12.8753 5379	13.1807 9494	13.4944 2254	13.8164 4796	14.1470 8750	10
11	14.5834 9825	14.9716 4264	15.3715 6001	15.7835 9932	16.2081 1906	11
12	16.3855 9065	16.8699 4120	17.3707 1141	17.8884 5127	18.4237 2799	12
13	18.2867 9814	18.8821 3767	19.4998 0765	20.1406 4286	20.8055 0759	13
14	20.2925 7203	21.0150 6593	21.7672 9515	22.5504 8786	23.3659 2066	14
15	22.4086 6350	23.2759 6988	24.1821 6933	25.1290 2201	26.1183 6470	15
16	24.6411 3999	25.6725 2808	26.7540 1034	27.8880 5355	29.0772 4206	16
17	26.9964 0269	28.2128 7976	29.4930 2101	30.8402 1730	32.2580 3521	17
18	29.4812 0483	30.9056 5255	32.4100 6738	33.9990 3251	35.6773 8785	18
19	32.1026 7110	33.7599 9170	35.5167 2176	37.3789 6479	39.3531 9194	19
20	34.8683 1801	36.7855 9120	38.8253 0867	40.9954 9232	43.3046 8134	20
21	37.7860 7550	39.9927 2668	42.3489 5373	44.8651 7678	47.5525 3244	21
22	40.8643 0965	43.3922 9028	46.1016 3573	49.0057 3916	52.1189 7237	22
23	44.1118 4669	46.9958 2769	50.0982 4205	53.4361 4090	57.0278 9530	23
24	47.5379 9825	50.8155 7735	54.3546 2778	58.1766 7076	62.3049 8744	24
25	51.1525 8816	54.8645 1200	58.8876 7859	63.2490 3772	67.9778 6150	25
26	54.9659 8051	59.1563 8272	63.7153 7769	68.6764 7036	74.0762 0112	26
27	58.9891 0943	63.7057 6568	68.8568 7725	74.4838 2328	80.6319 1620	27
28	63.2335 1045	68.5281 1162	74.3325 7427	80.6976 9091	87.6793 0991	28
29	67.7113 5353	73.6397 9832	80.1641 9159	87.3465 2927	95.2552 5816	29
30	72.4354 7797	79.0581 8622	86.3748 6405	94.4607 8632	103.3994 0252	30
31	77.4194 2926	84.8016 7739	92.9892 3021	102.0730 4137	112.1543 5771	31
32	82.6774 9787	90.8897 7803	100.0335 3017	110.2181 5426	121.5659 3454	32
33	88.2247 6025	97.3431 6471	107.5357 0963	118.9334 2506	131.6833 7963	33
34	94.0771 2207	104.1837 5460	115.5255 3076	128.2587 6481	142.5596 3310	34
35	100.2513 6378	111.4347 7987	124.0346 9026	138.2368 7835	154.2516 0558	35
36	106.7651 8879	119.1208 6666	133.0969 4513	148.9134 5984	166.8204 7600	36
37	113.6372 7417	127.2681 1866	142.7482 4656	160.3374 0202	180.3320 1170	37
38	120.8873 2425	135.9042 0578	153.0268 8259	172.5610 2017	194.8569 1258	38
39	128.5361 2708	145.0584 5813	163.9736 2996	185.6402 9158	210.4711 8102	39
40	136.6056 1407	154.7619 6562	175.6319 1590	199.6351 1199	227.2565 1960	40
41	145.1189 2285	165.0476 8356	188.0479 9044	214.6095 6983	245.3007 5857	41
42	154.1004 6360	175.9505 4457	201.2711 0981	230.6322 3972	264.6983 1546	42
43	163.5759 8910	187.5075 7724	215.3537 3195	247.7764 9650	285.5506 8912	43
44	173.5726 6850	199.7580 3188	230.3517 2453	266.1208 5125	307.9669 9080	44
45	184.1191 6527	212.7435 1379	246.3245 8662	285.7493 1084	332.0645 1511	45
46	195.2457 1936	226.5081 2462	263.3356 8475	306.7517 6260	357.9693 5375	46
47	206.9842 3392	241.0986 1210	281.4525 0426	329.2243 8598	385.8170 5528	47
48	219.3683 6679	256.5645 2882	300.7469 1704	353.2700 9300	415.7533 3442	48
49	232.4336 2696	272.9584 0055	321.2954 6665	378.9989 9951	447.9348 3451	49
50	246.2174 7645	290.3359 0458	343.1796 7198	406.5289 2947	482.5299 4709	50
51	260.7594 3765	308.7560 5886	366.4863 5066	435.9859 5454	519.7196 9313	51
52	276.1012 0672	328.2814 2239	391.3079 6345	467.5049 7135	559.6986 7011	52
53	292.2867 7309	348.9783 0773	417.7429 8108	501.2303 1935	602.6760 7037	53
54	309.3625 4561	370.9170 0620	445.8962 7485	537.3164 4170	648.8767 7565	54
55	327.3774 8562	394.1720 2657	475.8795 3271	575.9285 9262	698.5425 3382	55
56	346.3832 4733	418.8223 4816	507.8117 0234	617.2435 9410	751.9332 2386	56
57	366.4343 2593	444.9516 8905	541.8194 6299	661.4506 4569	809.3282 1564	57
58	387.5882 1386	472.6487 9040	578.0377 2808	708.7521 9089	871.0278 3182	58
59	409.9055 6562	502.0077 1782	616.6101 8041	759.3648 4425	937.3549 1920	59
60	433.4503 7173	533.1281 8089	657.6898 4214	813.5203 8335	1008.6565 3814	60

TABLE III

N	5 1/2	6	6 1/2	7	7 1/2	N
61	458.2901 4217	566.1158 7174	701.4396 8187	871.4668 1019	1085.3057 7851	61
62	484.4960 9999	601.0828 2405	748.0332 6120	933.4694 8690	1167.7037 1189	62
63	512.1433 8549	638.1477 9349	797.6554 2317	999.8123 5098	1256.2814 9029	63
64	541.3112 7170	677.4366 6110	850.5030 2568	1070.7992 1555	1351.5026 0206	64
65	572.0833 9164	719.0828 6076	906.7857 2235	1146.7551 6064	1453.8652 9721	65
66	604.5479 7818	763.2278 3241	966.7267 9430	1228.0280 2188	1563.9051 9450	66
67	638.7981 1698	810.0215 0236	1030.5640 3593	1314.9899 8341	1682.1980 8409	67
68	674.9320 1341	859.6227 9250	1098.5506 9827	1408.0392 8225	1809.3629 4040	68
69	713.0532 7415	912.2001 6005	1170.9564 9365	1507.6020 3201	1946.0651 6093	69
70	753.2712 0423	967.9321 6965	1248.0686 6574	1614.1341 7425	2093.0200 4800	70
71	795.7011 2046	1027.0080 9983	1330.1931 2901	1728.1235 6645	2250.9965 5160	71
72	840.4646 8209	1089.6285 8582	1417.6556 8240	1850.0922 1610	2420.8212 9296	72
73	887.6902 3960	1156.0063 0097	1510.8033 0176	1980.5986 7123	2603.3828 8994	73
74	937.5132 0278	1226.3666 7903	1610.0055 1637	2120.2405 7821	2799.6366 0668	74
75	990.0764 2893	1300.9486 7977	1715.6558 7493	2269.6574 1869	3010.6093 5218	75
76	1045.5306 3252	1380.0056 0055	1828.1735 0681	2429.5334 3800	3237.4050 5360	76
77	1104.0348 1731	1463.8059 3659	1948.0047 8475	2600.6007 7866	3481.2104 3262	77
78	1165.7567 3226	1552.6342 9278	2075.6250 9576	2783.6428 3316	3743.3012 1506	78
79	1230.8733 5254	1646.7923 5035	2211.5407 2698	2979.4978 3148	4025.0488 0619	79
80	1299.5713 8693	1746.5998 9137	2356.2908 7423	3189.0626 7969	4327.9274 6666	80
81	1372.0478 1321	1852.3958 8485	2510.4497 8106	3413.2970 6727	4653.5220 2666	81
82	1448.5104 4294	1964.5396 3794	2674.6290 1683	3653.2278 6198	5003.5361 7866	82
83	1529.1785 1730	2083.4120 1622	2849.4799 0292	3909.9538 1231	5379.8013 9206	83
84	1614.2833 3575	2209.4167 3719	3035.6960 9661	4184.6505 7918	5784.2864 9646	84
85	1704.0689 1921	2342.9817 4142	3234.0163 4289	4478.5761 1972	6219.1079 8369	85
86	1798.7927 0977	2484.5606 4591	3445.2274 0518	4793.0764 4810	6686.5410 8247	86
87	1898.7263 0881	2634.6342 8466	3670.1671 8652	5129.5917 9946	7189.0316 6366	87
88	2004.1562 5579	2793.7123 4174	3909.7280 5364	5489.6632 2543	7729.2090 3843	88
89	2115.3848 4986	2962.3350 8225	4164.8603 7713	5874.9396 5121	8309.8997 1631	89
90	2232.7310 1660	3141.0751 8718	4436.5763 0164	6287.1854 2679	8934.1421 9504	90
91	2356.5312 2252	3330.5396 9841	4725.9537 6125	6728.2884 0667	9605.2028 5966	91
92	2487.1404 3976	3531.3720 8032	5034.1407 5573	7200.2685 9513	10326.5930 7414	92
93	2624.9331 6394	3744.2544 0514	5362.3599 0485	7705.2873 9679	11102.0875 5470	93
94	2770.3044 8796	3969.9096 6944	5711.9132 9867	8245.6575 1457	11935.7441 2130	94
95	2923.6712 3480	4209.1042 4961	6084.1876 6308	8823.8535 4059	12831.9249 3040	95
96	3085.4731 5271	4462.6505 0459	6480.6598 6118	9442.5232 8843	13795.3193 0018	96
97	3256.1741 7611	4731.4095 3486	6902.9027 5216	10104.4999 1862	14830.9682 4769	97
98	3436.2637 5580	5016.2941 0696	7352.5914 3105	10812.8149 1292	15944.2908 6627	98
99	3626.2582 6237	5318.2717 5337	7831.5098 7406	11570.7119 5683	17141.1126 8124	99
100	3826.7024 6680	5638.3680 5857	8341.5580 1588	12381.6617 9381	18427.6961 3233	100
101	4038.1711 0247	5977.6701 4209	8884.7592 8691	13249.3781 1937	19810.7733 4226	101
102	4261.2705 1311	6337.3303 5061	9463.2686 4056	14177.8345 8773	21297.5813 4293	102
103	4496.6403 9133	6718.5701 7165	10079.3811 0220	15171.2830 0887	22895.8999 4365	103
104	4744.9556 1285	7122.6843 8195	10735.5408 7384	16234.2728 1949	24614.0924 3942	104
105	5006.9281 7156	7551.0454 4487	11434.3510 3064	17371.6719 1685	26461.1493 7238	105
106	5283.3092 2099	8005.1081 7156	12178.5838 4763	18588.6889 5103	28446.7355 7531	106
107	5574.8912 2815	8486.4146 6185	12971.1917 9773	19890.8971 7761	30581.2407 4346	107
108	5882.5102 4569	8996.5995 4156	13815.3192 6458	21284.2599 8004	32875.8337 9921	108
109	6207.0483 0921	9537.3955 1406	14714.3150 1678	22775.1581 7864	35342.5213 3416	109
110	6549.4359 6621	10110.6392 4490	15671.7454 9287	24370.4192 5115	37994.2104 3422	110
111	6910.6549 4436	10718.2775 9960	16691.4089 4990	26077.3485 9873	40844.7762 1678	111
112	7291.7409 6630	11362.3742 5557	17777.3505 3165	27903.7630 0064	43909.1344 3304	112
113	7693.7867 1944	12045.1167 1091	18933.8783 1620	29858.0264 1068	47203.3195 1552	113
114	8117.9449 8901	12768.8237 1356	20165.5804 0676	31949.0882 5943	50744.5684 7918	114
115	8565.4319 6341	13535.9531 3637	21477.3431 3320	34186.5244 3759	54551.4111 1512	115
116	9037.5307 2139	14349.1103 2456	22874.3704 3685	36580.5811 4822	58643.7669 4876	116
117	9535.5949 1107	15211.0569 4403	24362.2045 1525	39142.2218 2860	63043.0494 6991	117
118	10061.0526 3118	16124.7203 6067	25946.7478 0874	41883.1773 5660	67772.2781 8016	118
119	10615.4105 2589	17093.2035 8231	27634.2864 1631	44815.9997 7156	72856.1990 4367	119
120	11200.2581 0482	18119.7957 9725	29431.5150 3337	47954.1197 5557	78321.4139 7194	120

TABLE III

N	8	8 1/2	9	9 1/2	10	N
1	1.0000 0000	1.0000 0000	1.0000 0000	1.0000 0000	1.0000 0000	1
2	2.0800 0000	2.0850 0000	2.0900 0000	2.0950 0000	2.1000 0000	2
3	3.2464 0000	3.2622 2500	3.2781 0000	3.2940 2500	3.3100 0000	3
4	4.5061 1200	4.5395 1412	4.5731 2900	4.6069 5737	4.6410 0000	4
5	5.8666 0096	5.9253 7283	5.9847 1061	6.0446 1833	6.1051 0000	5
6	7.3359 2904	7.4290 2952	7.5233 3456	7.6188 5707	7.7156 1000	6
7	8.9228 0336	9.0604 9702	9.2004 3468	9.3426 4849	9.4871 7100	7
8	10.6366 2763	10.8306 3927	11.0284 7380	11.2302 0009	11.4358 8810	8
9	12.4875 5784	12.7512 4361	13.0210 3644	13.2970 6910	13.5794 7691	9
10	14.4865 6247	14.8350 9932	15.1929 2972	15.5602 9067	15.9374 2460	10
11	16.6454 8746	17.0960 8276	17.5602 9339	18.0385 1828	18.5311 6706	11
12	18.9771 2646	19.5492 4979	20.1407 1980	20.7521 7752	21.3842 8377	12
13	21.4952 9658	22.2109 3603	22.9533 8458	23.7236 3438	24.5227 1214	13
14	24.2149 2030	25.0988 6559	26.0191 8919	26.9773 7965	27.9749 8336	14
15	27.1521 1393	28.2322 6916	29.3609 1622	30.5402 3072	31.7724 8169	15
16	30.3242 8304	31.6320 1204	33.0033 9868	34.4415 5263	35.9497 2986	16
17	33.7502 2569	35.3207 3306	36.9737 0456	38.7135 0013	40.5447 0285	17
18	37.4502 4374	39.3229 9538	41.3013 3797	43.3912 8265	45.5991 7313	18
19	41.4462 6324	43.6654 4998	46.0184 5839	48.5134 5450	51.1590 9045	19
20	45.7619 6430	48.3770 1323	51.1601 1964	54.1222 3267	57.2749 9949	20
21	50.4229 2144	53.4890 5936	56.7645 3041	60.2638 4478	64.0024 9944	21
22	55.4567 5516	59.0356 2940	62.8733 3815	66.9889 1003	71.4027 4939	22
23	60.8932 9557	65.0536 5790	69.5319 3858	74.3528 5649	79.5430 2433	23
24	66.7647 5922	71.5832 1882	76.7898 1305	82.4163 7785	88.4973 2676	24
25	73.1059 3995	78.6677 9242	84.7008 9623	91.2459 3375	98.3470 5943	25
26	79.9544 1515	86.3545 5478	93.3239 7689	100.9142 9745	109.1817 6538	26
27	87.3507 6836	94.6946 9193	102.7231 3481	111.5011 5571	121.0999 4191	27
28	95.3388 2983	103.7437 4075	112.9682 1694	123.0937 6551	134.2099 3611	28
29	103.9659 3622	113.5619 5871	124.1353 5646	135.7876 7323	148.6309 2972	29
30	113.2832 1111	124.2147 2520	136.3075 3855	149.6875 0218	164.4940 2269	30
31	123.3458 6800	135.7729 7684	149.5752 1702	164.9078 1489	181.9434 2496	31
32	134.2135 3744	148.3136 7987	164.0369 8655	181.5740 5731	201.1377 6745	32
33	145.9506 2044	161.9203 4266	179.8003 1534	199.8235 9275	222.2515 4420	33
34	158.6266 7007	176.6835 7179	196.9823 4372	219.8068 3406	245.4766 9862	34
35	172.3168 0368	192.7016 7539	215.7107 5465	241.6884 8330	271.0243 6848	35
36	187.1021 4797	210.0813 1780	236.1247 2257	265.6488 8921	299.1268 0533	36
37	203.0703 1981	228.9382 2981	258.3759 4760	291.8855 3369	330.0394 8586	37
38	220.3159 4540	249.3979 7935	282.6297 8288	320.6146 5939	364.0434 3445	38
39	238.9412 2103	271.5968 0759	309.0664 6334	352.0730 5203	401.4477 7789	39
40	259.0565 1871	295.6825 3624	337.8824 4504	386.5199 9197	442.5925 5568	40
41	280.7810 4021	321.8155 5182	369.2918 6510	424.2393 9121	487.8518 1125	41
42	304.2435 2342	350.1698 7372	403.5281 3296	465.5421 3337	537.6369 9237	42
43	329.5830 0530	380.9343 1299	440.8456 6492	510.7686 3604	592.4006 9161	43
44	356.9496 4572	414.3137 2959	481.5217 7477	560.2916 5647	652.6407 6077	44
45	386.5056 1738	450.5303 9661	525.8587 3450	614.5193 6383	718.9048 3685	45
46	418.4260 6677	489.8254 8032	574.1860 2060	673.8987 0340	791.7953 2054	46
47	452.9001 5211	532.4606 4615	626.8627 6245	738.9190 8022	871.9748 5259	47
48	490.1321 6428	578.7198 0107	684.2804 1107	810.1163 9284	960.1723 3785	48
49	530.3427 3742	628.9109 8416	746.8656 4807	888.0774 5016	1057.1895 7163	49
50	573.7701 5642	683.3684 1782	815.0835 5640	973.4448 0793	1163.9085 2880	50
51	620.6717 6893	742.4547 3333	889.4410 7647	1066.9220 6468	1281.2993 8168	51
52	671.3255 1044	806.5633 8566	970.4907 7336	1169.2796 6082	1410.4293 1984	52
53	726.0315 5128	876.1212 7345	1058.8349 4296	1281.3612 2860	1552.4722 5183	53
54	785.1140 7538	951.5915 8169	1155.1300 8782	1404.0905 4532	1708.7194 7701	54
55	848.9232 0141	1033.4768 6613	1260.0917 9573	1538.4791 4713	1880.5914 2471	55
56	917.8370 5752	1122.3223 9975	1374.5000 5734	1685.6346 6610	2069.6505 6718	56
57	992.2640 2213	1218.7198 0373	1499.2050 6251	1846.7699 5938	2277.6156 2390	57
58	1072.6451 4390	1323.3109 8705	1635.1335 1813	2023.2131 0552	2506.3771 8629	58
59	1159.4567 5541	1436.7924 2095	1783.2955 3476	2216.4183 5055	2758.0149 0492	59
60	1253.2132 9584	1559.9197 7673	1944.7921 3289	2427.9780 9385	3034.8163 9541	60

TABLE III

N	8	8 1/2	9	9 1/2	10	N
61	1354.4703 5951	1693.5129 5775	2120.8234 2485	2659.6360 1277	3339.2980 3496	61
62	1463.8279 8827	1838.4615 5916	2312.6975 3309	2913.3014 3398	3674.2278 3845	62
63	1581.9342 2733	1995.7307 9169	2521.8403 1107	3191.0650 7021	4042.6506 2230	63
64	1709.4889 6552	2166.3679 0898	2749.8059 3906	3495.2162 5188	4447.9156 8453	64
65	1847.2480 8276	2351.5091 8125	2998.2884 7358	3828.2617 9580	4893.7072 5298	65
66	1996.0279 2938	2552.3874 6165	3269.1344 3620	4192.9466 6641	5384.0779 7828	66
67	2156.7101 6373	2770.3403 9589	3564.3565 3546	4592.2765 9971	5923.4857 7610	67
68	2330.2469 7683	3006.8193 2954	3886.1486 2365	5029.5428 7669	6516.8343 5371	68
69	2517.6667 3497	3263.3989 7255	4236.9019 9978	5508.3494 4997	7169.5177 8909	69
70	2720.0800 7377	3541.7878 8522	4619.2231 7976	6032.6426 4772	7887.4695 6799	70
71	2938.6864 7967	3843.8398 5546	5035.9532 6594	6606.7436 9925	8677.2165 2479	71
72	3174.7813 9805	4171.5662 4318	5490.1890 5987	7235.3843 5068	9545.9381 7727	72
73	3429.7639 0989	4527.1493 7385	5985.3060 7526	7923.7458 6400	10501.5319 9500	73
74	3705.1450 2268	4912.9570 7063	6524.9836 2203	8677.5017 2108	11552.6851 9450	74
75	4002.5566 2449	5331.5584 2163	7113.2321 4801	9502.8643 8458	12708.9537 1395	75
76	4323.7611 5445	5785.7408 8747	7754.4230 4134	10406.6365 0111	13980.8490 8535	76
77	4670.6620 4681	6278.5288 6290	8453.3211 1506	11396.2669 6872	15379.9339 9388	77
78	5045.3150 1056	6813.2038 1625	9215.1200 1541	12479.9123 3075	16918.9273 9327	78
79	5449.9402 1140	7393.3261 4063	10045.4808 1680	13666.5040 0217	18611.8201 3259	79
80	5886.9354 2831	8022.7588 6259	10950.5740 9031	14965.8218 8238	20474.0021 4585	80
81	6358.8902 6258	8705.6933 6591	11937.1257 5844	16388.5749 6120	22522.4023 6044	81
82	6868.6014 8358	9446.6773 0201	13012.4670 7670	17946.4895 8251	24775.6425 9648	82
83	7419.0896 0227	10250.6448 7268	14184.5891 1360	19652.4060 9285	27254.2068 5613	83
84	8013.6167 7045	11122.9496 8686	15462.2021 3382	21520.3846 7167	29980.6275 4175	84
85	8655.7061 1209	12069.4004 1024	16854.8003 2587	23565.8212 1548	32979.6902 9592	85
86	9349.1626 0105	13096.2994 4511	18372.7323 5520	25805.5742 3096	36278.6593 2551	86
87	10098.0956 0914	14210.4848 9794	20027.2782 6716	28258.1037 8290	39907.5252 5806	87
88	10906.9432 5787	15419.3761 1427	21830.7333 1121	30943.6236 4227	43899.2777 8387	88
89	11780.4987 1850	16731.0230 8398	23796.4993 0922	33884.2678 8829	48290.2055 6226	89
90	12723.9386 1598	18154.1600 4612	25939.1842 4705	37104.2733 3767	53120.2261 1848	90
91	13742.8537 0526	19698.2636 5004	28274.7108 2928	40630.1793 0475	58433.2487 3033	91
92	14843.2820 0168	21373.6160 6029	30820.4348 0392	44491.0463 3870	64277.5736 0336	92
93	16031.7445 6181	23191.3734 2542	33595.2739 3627	48718.6957 4088	70706.3309 6370	93
94	17315.2841 2676	25163.6401 6658	36619.8485 9053	53347.9718 3626	77777.9640 6007	94
95	18701.5068 5690	27303.5495 8074	39916.6349 6368	58417.0291 6071	85556.7604 6608	95
96	20198.6274 0545	29625.3512 9510	43510.1321 1041	63967.6469 3098	94113.4365 1268	96
97	21815.5175 9788	32144.5061 5518	47427.0440 0035	70045.5733 8942	103525.7801 6395	97
98	23561.7590 0571	34877.7891 7837	51696.4779 6038	76700.9028 6142	113879.3581 8035	98
99	25447.6997 2617	37843.4012 5853	56350.1609 7682	83988.4886 3325	125268.2939 9838	99
100	27484.5157 0427	41061.0903 6551	61422.6754 6473	91968.3950 5341	137796.1233 9822	100
101	29684.2769 6061	44552.2830 4658	66951.7162 5656	100706.3925 8348	151576.7357 3804	101
102	32060.0191 1746	48340.2271 0554	72978.3707 1965	110274.4998 7891	166735.4093 1185	102
103	34625.8206 4685	52450.1464 0951	79547.4240 8442	120751.5773 6741	183409.9502 4303	103
104	37396.8862 9860	56909.4088 5432	86707.6922 5201	132223.9772 1731	201751.9452 6733	104
105	40389.6372 0249	61747.7086 0693	94512.3845 5469	144786.2550 5296	221928.1397 9407	105
106	43621.8081 7869	66997.2638 3852	103019.4991 6462	158541.9492 8299	244121.9537 7347	106
107	47112.5528 3298	72693.0312 6480	112292.2540 8943	173604.4344 6487	268535.1491 5082	107
108	50882.5570 5962	78872.9389 2230	122399.5569 5748	190097.8557 3904	295389.6640 6590	108
109	54954.1616 2439	85578.1387 3070	133416.5170 8365	208158.1520 3425	324929.6304 7250	109
110	59351.4945 5434	92853.2805 2281	145425.0036 2118	227934.1764 7750	357423.5935 1974	110
111	64100.6141 1869	100746.8093 6725	158514.2539 4709	249588.9232 4286	393166.9528 7172	111
112	69229.6632 4818	109311.2881 6346	172781.5368 0233	273300.8709 5093	432484.6481 5889	112
113	74769.0363 0804	118603.7476 5736	188332.8751 1454	299265.4536 9127	475734.1129 7478	113
114	80751.5592 1268	128686.0662 0823	205283.8338 7484	327696.6717 9194	523308.5242 7226	114
115	87212.6839 4970	139625.3818 3593	223760.3789 2358	358828.8556 1218	575640.3766 9948	115
116	94190.6986 6567	151494.5392 9199	243899.8130 2670	392918.5968 9533	633205.4143 6943	116
117	101726.9545 5893	164372.5751 3181	265851.7961 9911	430246.8636 0039	696526.9558 0637	117
118	109866.1109 2364	178345.2440 1801	289779.4578 5702	471121.3156 4243	766180.6513 8701	118
119	118656.3997 9753	193505.5897 5954	315860.6090 6416	515878.8406 2846	842799.7165 2571	119
120	128149.9117 8133	209954.5648 8910	344289.0638 7993	564888.3304 8816	927080.6881 7828	120

TABLE III

N	10 1/2	11	11 1/2	12	12 1/2	N
1	1.0000 0000	1.0000 0000	1.0000 0000	1.0000 0000	1.0000 0000	1
2	2.1050 0000	2.1100 0000	2.1150 0000	2.1200 0000	2.1250 0000	2
3	3.3260 2500	3.3421 0000	3.3582 2500	3.3744 0000	3.3906 2500	3
4	4.6752 5762	4.7097 3100	4.7444 2087	4.7793 2800	4.8144 5312	4
5	6.1661 5968	6.2278 0141	6.2900 2928	6.3528 4736	6.4162 5977	5
6	7.8136 0644	7.9128 5957	8.0133 8264	8.1151 8904	8.2182 9224	6
7	9.6340 3512	9.7832 7412	9.9349 2165	10.0890 1173	10.2455 7877	7
8	11.6456 0881	11.8594 3427	12.0774 3764	12.2996 9314	12.5262 7611	8
9	13.8683 9773	14.1639 7204	14.4663 4296	14.7756 5631	15.0920 6063	9
10	16.3245 7949	16.7220 0896	17.1299 7240	17.5487 3507	17.9785 6820	10
11	19.0386 6034	19.5614 2995	20.0999 1923	20.6545 8328	21.2258 8923	11
12	22.0377 1967	22.7131 8724	23.4114 0994	24.1331 3327	24.8791 2538	12
13	25.3516 8024	26.2116 3784	27.1037 2209	28.0291 0926	28.9890 1606	13
14	29.0136 0666	30.0949 1800	31.2206 5013	32.3926 0238	33.6126 4306	14
15	33.0600 3536	34.4053 5898	35.8110 2489	37.2797 1466	38.8142 2345	15
16	37.5313 3908	39.1899 4847	40.9292 9275	42.7532 8042	44.6660 0138	16
17	42.4721 2968	44.5008 4281	46.6361 6142	48.8836 7407	51.2492 5155	17
18	47.9317 0330	50.3959 3551	52.9993 1998	55.7497 1496	58.6554 0799	18
19	53.9645 3214	56.9394 8842	60.0942 4178	63.4396 8075	66.9873 3399	19
20	60.6308 0802	64.2028 3215	68.0050 7958	72.0524 4244	76.3607 5074	20
21	67.9970 4286	72.2651 4368	76.8256 6374	81.6987 3554	86.9058 4458	21
22	76.1367 3236	81.2143 0949	86.6606 1507	92.5025 8380	98.7690 7515	22
23	85.1310 8926	91.1478 8353	97.6265 8580	104.6028 9386	112.1152 0955	23
24	95.0698 5363	102.1741 5072	109.8536 4317	118.1552 4112	127.1296 1074	24
25	106.0521 8826	114.4133 0730	123.4868 1213	133.3338 7006	144.0208 1209	25
26	118.1876 6803	127.9987 7110	138.6877 9553	150.3339 3446	163.0234 1360	26
27	131.5973 7317	143.0786 3592	155.6368 9201	169.3740 0660	184.4013 4030	27
28	146.4150 9736	159.8172 8587	174.5351 3459	190.6988 8739	208.4515 0783	28
29	162.7886 8258	178.3971 8732	195.6066 7507	214.5827 5388	235.5079 4631	29
30	180.8814 9425	199.0208 7793	219.1014 4270	241.3326 8434	265.9464 3960	30
31	200.8740 5114	221.9131 7450	245.2981 0861	271.2926 0646	300.1897 4455	31
32	222.9658 2651	247.3236 2369	274.5073 9111	304.8477 1924	338.7134 6262	32
33	247.3772 3830	275.5292 2230	307.0757 4108	342.4294 4555	382.0526 4545	33
34	274.3518 4832	306.8374 3675	343.3894 5131	384.5209 7901	430.8092 2613	34
35	304.1587 9239	341.5895 5480	383.8792 3821	431.6634 9649	485.6603 7939	35
36	337.0954 6560	380.1644 0582	429.0253 5060	484.4631 1607	547.3679 2682	36
37	373.4904 8948	422.9824 9046	479.3632 6592	543.5986 9000	616.7889 1767	37
38	413.7069 5088	470.5105 6441	535.4900 4150	609.8305 3280	694.8875 3238	38
39	458.1462 2492	523.2667 2650	598.0713 9627	684.0101 9674	782.7484 7393	39
40	507.2515 7854	581.8260 6641	667.8496 0685	767.0914 2034	881.5920 3317	40
41	561.5129 9428	646.8269 3372	745.6523 1163	860.1423 9079	992.7910 3731	41
42	621.4718 5868	718.9778 9643	832.4023 2747	964.3594 7768	1117.8899 1698	42
43	687.7264 0385	799.0654 6504	929.1285 9513	1081.0826 1500	1258.6261 5660	43
44	760.9376 7625	887.9626 6619	1036.9783 8357	1211.8125 2880	1416.9544 2618	44
45	841.8361 3225	986.6385 5947	1157.2308 9768	1358.2300 3226	1595.0737 2945	45
46	931.2289 2614	1096.1688 0101	1291.3124 5091	1522.2176 3613	1795.4579 4563	46
47	1030.0079 6339	1217.7473 6912	1440.8133 8277	1705.8837 5247	2020.8901 8883	47
48	1139.1587 9954	1352.6995 7973	1607.5069 2179	1911.5898 0276	2274.5014 6244	48
49	1259.7704 7349	1502.4965 3350	1793.3702 1779	2141.9805 7909	2559.8141 4524	49
50	1393.0463 7321	1668.7711 5218	2000.6077 9284	2400.0182 4858	2880.7909 1340	50
51	1540.3162 4240	1853.3359 7892	2231.6776 8902	2689.0204 3841	3241.8897 7757	51
52	1703.0494 4785	2058.2029 3661	2489.3206 2325	3012.7028 9102	3648.1259 9977	52
53	1882.8696 3987	2285.6052 5963	2776.5924 9493	3375.2272 3795	4105.1417 4974	53
54	2081.5709 5206	2538.0218 3819	3096.9006 3184	3781.2545 0650	4619.2844 6846	54
55	2301.1359 0203	2818.2042 4039	3454.0442 0450	4236.0050 4728	5197.6950 2701	55
56	2543.7551 7174	3129.2067 0684	3852.2592 8802	4745.3256 5295	5848.4069 0539	56
57	2811.8494 6477	3474.4194 4459	4296.2691 0615	5315.7647 3131	6580.4577 6856	57
58	3108.0936 5857	3857.6055 8349	4791.3400 5335	5954.6564 9906	7404.0149 8963	58
59	3435.4434 9272	4282.9421 9768	5343.3441 5949	6670.2152 7895	8330.5168 6334	59
60	3797.1650 5946	4755.0658 3942	5958.8287 3783	7471.6411 1243	9372.8314 7126	60

TABLE III

N	10 1/2	11	11 1/2	12	12 1/2	N
61	4196.8673 9070	5279.1230 8176	6645.0940 4268	8369.2380 4592	10545.4354 0516	61
62	4638.5384 6673	5860.8266 2075	7410.2798 5759	9374.5466 1143	11864.6148 3081	62
63	5126.5850 0573	6506.5175 4903	8263.4620 4121	10500.4922 0480	13348.6916 8466	63
64	5665.8764 3134	7223.2344 7943	9214.7601 7595	11761.5512 6937	15018.2781 4524	64
65	6261.7934 5663	8018.7902 7216	10275.4575 9618	13173.9374 2170	16896.5629 1340	65
66	6920.2817 6957	8901.8572 0210	11458.1352 1974	14755.8099 1230	19009.6332 7757	66
67	7647.9113 5538	9882.0614 9433	12776.8207 7002	16527.5071 0178	21386.8374 3727	67
68	8451.9420 4769	10970.0882 5871	14247.1551 5857	18511.8079 5399	24061.1921 1693	68
69	9340.3959 6270	12177.7979 6717	15886.5780 0180	20734.2249 0847	27069.8411 3154	69
70	10322.1375 3878	13518.3557 4356	17714.5344 7201	23223.3318 9749	30454.5712 7299	70
71	11406.9619 8035	15006.3748 7535	19752.7059 3629	26011.1317 2519	34262.3926 8211	71
72	12605.6929 8829	16658.0761 1164	22025.2671 1896	29133.4675 3221	38546.1917 6738	72
73	13930.2907 5206	18491.4644 8392	24559.1728 3764	32630.4836 3607	43365.4657 3830	73
74	15393.9712 8103	20526.5255 7715	27384.4777 1397	36547.1416 7240	48787.1489 5558	74
75	17011.3382 6554	22785.4433 9063	30534.6926 5108	40933.7986 7309	54886.5425 7503	75
76	18798.5287 8342	25292.8421 6360	34047.1823 0596	45846.8545 1386	61748.3603 9691	76
77	20773.3743 0568	28076.0548 0160	37963.6082 7114	51349.4770 5552	69467.9054 4653	77
78	22955.5786 0777	31165.4208 2978	42330.4232 2232	57512.4143 0219	78152.3936 2734	78
79	25366.9143 6159	34594.6171 2105	47199.4218 9289	64414.9040 1845	87922.4428 3076	79
80	28031.4403 6956	38401.0250 0437	52628.3554 1057	72145.6925 0066	98913.7481 8460	80
81	30975.7416 0836	42626.1377 5485	58681.6162 8279	80804.1756 0074	111278.9667 0768	81
82	34229.1944 7724	47316.0129 0788	65431.0021 5531	90501.6766 7283	125189.8375 4614	82
83	37824.2598 9735	52521.7743 2775	72956.5674 0317	101362.8778 7357	140839.5672 3941	83
84	41796.8071 8657	58300.1695 0380	81347.5726 5453	113527.4232 1840	158445.5131 4433	84
85	46186.4719 4116	64714.1881 4922	90703.5435 0980	127151.7140 0461	178252.2022 8737	85
86	51037.0514 9498	71833.7488 4563	101135.4510 1343	142410.9196 8516	200534.7275 7330	86
87	56396.9419 0196	79736.4612 1865	112767.0278 7997	159501.2300 4738	225602.5685 1996	87
88	62319.6208 0166	88508.4719 5270	125736.2360 8617	178642.3776 5306	253803.8895 8495	88
89	68864.1809 8584	98245.4038 6750	140196.9032 3608	200080.4629 7143	285530.3757 8307	89
90	76095.9199 8935	109053.3982 9292	156320.5471 0823	224091.1185 2800	321222.6727 5595	90
91	84086.9915 8823	121050.2721 0514	174298.4100 2568	250983.0527 5136	361376.5068 5045	91
92	92917.1257 0499	134366.8020 3671	194343.7271 7863	281102.0190 8153	406549.5702 0675	92
93	102674.4239 0402	149148.1502 6075	216694.2558 0417	314835.2613 7131	457369.2664 8260	93
94	113456.2384 1394	165555.4467 8943	241615.0952 2165	352616.4927 3587	514541.4247 9292	94
95	125370.1434 4740	183767.5459 3627	269401.8311 7214	394931.4718 6417	578860.1028 9204	95
96	138535.0085 0938	203982.9759 8926	300384.0417 5694	442324.2484 8787	651218.6157 5354	96
97	153082.1844 0287	226422.1033 4808	334929.2065 5898	495404.1583 0642	732621.9427 2274	97
98	169156.8137 6517	251329.5347 1636	373447.0653 1327	554853.6573 0319	824200.6855 6308	98
99	186919.2792 1051	278976.7835 3516	416394.4778 2429	621437.0961 7957	927226.7712 5846	99
100	206546.8035 2761	309665.2297 2403	464280.8427 7408	696010.5477 2112	1043131.1176 6577	100
101	228235.2178 9801	343729.4049 9368	517674.1396 9310	779532.8134 4765	1173523.5073 7399	101
102	252200.9157 7730	381540.6395 4298	577207.6657 5781	873077.7510 6137	1320214.9457 9574	102
103	278683.0119 3392	423511.1098 9271	643587.5473 1996	977848.0811 8873	1485242.8140 2021	103
104	307945.7281 8698	470098.3319 8091	717601.1152 6176	1095190.8509 3138	1670899.1657 7274	104
105	340281.0296 4661	521810.1484 9881	800126.2435 1686	1226614.7530 4314	1879762.5614 9433	105
106	376011.5377 5951	579210.2648 3367	892141.7615 2130	1373809.5234 0832	2114733.8816 8112	106
107	415493.7492 2426	642924.3939 6538	994739.0640 9624	1538667.6662 1732	2379076.6168 9126	107
108	459121.5928 9280	713647.0773 0157	1109135.0564 6731	1723308.7861 6340	2676462.1940 0267	108
109	507330.3601 4655	792149.2558 0474	1236686.5879 6105	1930106.8405 0301	3011020.9682 5300	109
110	560601.0479 6194	879286.6739 4326	1378906.5455 7657	2161720.6613 6337	3387399.5892 8463	110
111	619465.1579 9794	976009.2080 7702	1537481.7983 1788	2421128.1407 2697	3810825.5379 4521	111
112	684509.9995 8772	1083371.2209 6550	1714293.2051 2444	2711664.5176 1421	4287179.7301 8836	112
113	756384.5495 4443	1202543.0552 7170	1911437.9237 1375	3037065.2597 2791	4823078.1964 6190	113
114	835805.9272 4660	1334823.7913 5159	2131254.2849 4083	3401514.0908 9526	5425963.9710 1964	114
115	923566.5496 0749	1481655.4084 0026	2376349.5277 0902	3809696.7818 0269	6104210.4673 9709	115
116	1020542.0373 1628	1644638.5033 2429	2649630.7233 9556	4266861.3956 1901	6867237.7758 2173	116
117	1127699.9512 3449	1825549.7386 8996	2954339.2565 8605	4778885.7630 9329	7725643.4977 9944	117
118	1246109.4461 1411	2026361.2099 4586	3294089.2710 9344	5352353.0546 6449	8691349.9350 2437	118
119	1376951.9379 5609	2249261.9430 3990	3672910.5372 6919	5994636.4212 2422	9777769.6769 0242	119
120	1521532.8914 4148	2496681.7567 7429	4095296.2490 5515	6713993.7917 7113	10999991.8865 1522	120

TABLE IV
PRESENT VALUE OF ANNUITY OF 1 PER PERIOD

$$a_{\overline{n}|i} = 1 - \frac{(1+i)^{-n}}{i}$$

TABLE IV

N	1/6	5/24	1/4	7/24	1/3	N
1	0.9983 3611	0.9979 2100	0.9975 0623	0.9970 9182	0.9966 7774	1
2	1.9950 1109	1.9937 6732	1.9925 2492	1.9912 8390	1.9900 4426	2
3	2.9900 2771	2.9875 4327	2.9850 6227	2.9825 8470	2.9801 1056	3
4	3.9833 8873	3.9792 5316	3.9751 2446	3.9710 0261	3.9668 8760	4
5	4.9750 9690	4.9689 0128	4.9627 1766	4.9565 4602	4.9503 8631	5
6	5.9651 5497	5.9564 9192	5.9478 4804	5.9392 2328	5.9306 1759	6
7	6.9535 6570	6.9420 2936	6.9305 2174	6.9190 4274	6.9075 9228	7
8	7.9403 3181	7.9255 1786	7.9107 4487	7.8960 1270	7.8813 2121	8
9	8.9254 5605	8.9069 6169	8.8885 2357	8.8701 4146	8.8518 1516	9
10	9.9089 4115	9.8863 6510	9.8638 6391	9.8414 3726	9.8190 8487	10
11	10.8907 8983	10.8637 3232	10.8367 7198	10.8099 0837	10.7831 4107	11
12	11.8710 0483	11.8390 6760	11.8072 5384	11.7755 6297	11.7439 9442	12
13	12.8495 8884	12.8123 7515	12.7753 1555	12.7384 0928	12.7016 5557	13
14	13.8265 4460	13.7836 5920	13.7409 6314	13.6984 5545	13.6561 3512	14
15	14.8018 7481	14.7529 2394	14.7042 0264	14.6557 0963	14.6074 4364	15
16	15.7755 8217	15.7201 7358	15.6650 4004	15.6101 7994	15.5555 9167	16
17	16.7476 6939	16.6854 1230	16.6234 8133	16.5618 7447	16.5005 8970	17
18	17.7181 3916	17.6486 4429	17.5795 3250	17.5108 0130	17.4424 4821	18
19	18.6869 9417	18.6098 7372	18.5331 9950	18.4569 6848	18.3811 7762	19
20	19.6542 3711	19.5691 0475	19.4844 8828	19.4003 8402	19.3167 8832	20
21	20.6198 7066	20.5263 4154	20.4334 0477	20.3410 5594	20.2492 9069	21
22	21.5838 9749	21.4815 8823	21.3799 5488	21.2789 9222	21.1786 9504	22
23	22.5463 2029	22.4348 4896	22.3241 4452	22.2142 0080	22.1050 1167	23
24	23.5071 4172	23.3861 2786	23.2659 7957	23.1466 8962	23.0282 5083	24
25	24.4663 6445	24.3354 2905	24.2054 6591	24.0764 6659	23.9484 2275	25
26	25.4239 9113	25.2827 5664	25.1426 0939	25.0035 3960	24.8655 3763	26
27	26.3800 2442	26.2281 1474	26.0774 1585	25.9279 1651	25.7796 0561	27
28	27.3344 6698	27.1715 0743	27.0098 9112	26.8496 0516	26.6906 3682	28
29	28.2873 2144	28.1129 3881	27.9400 4102	27.7686 1337	27.5986 4135	29
30	29.2385 9046	29.0524 1295	28.8678 7134	28.6849 4894	28.5036 2925	30
31	30.1882 7667	29.9899 3392	29.7933 8787	29.5986 1963	29.4056 1055	31
32	31.1363 8269	30.9255 0578	30.7165 9638	30.5096 3320	30.3045 9523	32
33	32.0829 1118	31.8591 3259	31.6375 0262	31.4179 9738	31.2005 9325	33
34	33.0278 6473	32.7908 1838	32.5561 1234	32.3237 1986	32.0936 1454	34
35	33.9712 4599	33.7205 6720	33.4724 3126	33.2268 0834	32.9836 6898	35
36	34.9130 5756	34.6483 8307	34.3864 6510	34.1272 7046	33.8707 6642	36
37	35.8533 0206	35.5742 7001	35.2982 1955	35.0251 1388	34.7549 1670	37
38	36.7919 8209	36.4982 3202	36.2077 0030	35.9203 4621	35.6361 2960	38
39	37.7291 0025	37.4202 7312	37.1149 1302	36.8129 7503	36.5144 1488	39
40	38.6646 5916	38.3403 9729	38.0198 6336	37.7030 0792	37.3897 8228	40
41	39.5986 6139	39.2586 0853	38.9225 5697	38.5904 5244	38.2622 4147	41
42	40.5311 0954	40.1749 1080	39.8229 9947	39.4753 1610	39.1318 0213	42
43	41.4620 0619	41.0893 0807	40.7211 9648	40.3576 0641	39.9984 7389	43
44	42.3913 5394	42.0018 0431	41.6171 5359	41.2373 3086	40.8622 6633	44
45	43.3191 5535	42.9124 0347	42.5108 7640	42.1144 9691	41.7231 8903	45
46	44.2454 1299	43.8211 0949	43.4023 7047	42.9891 1200	42.5812 5153	46
47	45.1701 2944	44.7279 2631	44.2916 4137	43.8611 8355	43.4364 6332	47
48	46.0933 0726	45.6328 5786	45.1786 9463	44.7307 1895	44.2888 3387	48
49	47.0149 4901	46.5359 0805	46.0635 3580	45.5977 2559	45.1383 7263	49
50	47.9350 5725	47.4370 8080	46.9461 7037	46.4622 1081	45.9850 8900	50
51	48.8536 3453	48.3363 8001	47.8266 0386	47.3241 8194	46.8289 9236	51
52	49.7706 8339	49.2338 0957	48.7048 4176	48.1836 4631	47.6700 9205	52
53	50.6862 0638	50.1293 7338	49.5808 8953	49.0406 1119	48.5083 9739	53
54	51.6002 0603	51.0230 7530	50.4547 5265	49.8950 8386	49.3439 1767	54
55	52.5126 8489	51.9149 1922	51.3264 3656	50.7470 7157	50.1766 6213	55
56	53.4236 4548	52.8049 0899	52.1959 4669	51.5965 8154	51.0066 3999	56
57	54.3330 9033	53.6930 4848	53.0632 8847	52.4436 2098	51.8338 6046	57
58	55.2410 2196	54.5793 4152	53.9284 6730	53.2881 9707	52.6583 3268	58
59	56.1474 4289	55.4637 9195	54.7914 8858	54.1303 1698	53.4800 6580	59
60	57.0523 5563	56.3464 0361	55.6523 5769	54.9699 8785	54.2990 6890	60

TABLE IV

N	1/6	5/24	1/4	7/24	1/3	N
61	57.9557 6269	57.2271 8032	56.5110 7999	55.8072 1680	55.1153 5106	61
62	58.8576 6658	58.1061 2589	57.3676 6083	56.6420 1094	55.9289 2133	62
63	59.7580 6980	58.9832 4413	58.2221 0557	57.4743 7734	56.7397 8870	63
64	60.6569 7484	59.8585 3884	59.0744 1952	58.3043 2306	57.5479 6216	64
65	61.5543 8420	60.7320 1381	59.9246 0800	59.1318 5515	58.3534 5065	65
66	62.4503 0037	61.6036 7283	60.7726 7631	59.9569 8062	59.1562 6311	66
67	63.3447 2583	62.4735 1966	61.6186 2974	60.7797 0648	59.9564 0842	67
68	64.2376 6305	63.3415 5808	62.4624 7355	61.6000 3970	60.7538 9543	68
69	65.1291 1453	64.2077 9185	63.3042 1302	62.4179 8723	61.5487 3299	69
70	66.0190 8272	65.0722 2471	64.1438 5339	63.2335 5603	62.3409 2989	70
71	66.9075 7011	65.9348 6042	64.9813 9989	64.0467 5300	63.1304 9491	71
72	67.7945 7914	66.7957 0271	65.8168 5774	64.8575 8504	63.9174 3678	72
73	68.6801 1229	67.6547 5530	66.6502 3216	65.6660 5904	64.7017 6424	73
74	69.5641 7200	68.5120 2192	67.4815 2834	66.4721 8184	65.4834 8595	74
75	70.4467 6073	69.3675 0628	68.3107 5146	67.2759 6029	66.2626 1058	75
76	71.3278 8093	70.2212 1209	69.1379 0670	68.0774 0120	67.0391 4676	76
77	72.2075 3504	71.0731 4304	69.9629 9920	68.8765 1138	67.8131 0308	77
78	73.0857 2550	71.9233 0283	70.7860 3411	69.6732 9759	68.5844 8812	78
79	73.9624 5474	72.7716 9513	71.6070 1657	70.4677 6661	69.3533 1042	79
80	74.8377 2520	73.6183 2362	72.4259 5169	71.2599 2516	70.1195 7849	80
81	75.7115 3930	74.4631 9197	73.2428 4458	72.0497 7997	70.8833 0082	81
82	76.5838 9947	75.3063 0384	74.0577 0033	72.8373 3773	71.6444 8587	82
83	77.4548 0812	76.1476 6287	74.8705 2402	73.6226 0513	72.4031 4206	83
84	78.3242 6767	76.9872 7272	75.6813 2072	74.4055 8883	73.1592 7780	84
85	79.1922 8054	77.8251 3702	76.4900 9548	75.1862 9547	73.9129 0146	85
86	80.0588 4912	78.6612 5940	77.2968 5335	75.9647 3167	74.6640 2139	86
87	80.9239 7583	79.4956 4347	78.1015 9935	76.7409 0403	75.4126 4591	87
88	81.7876 6306	80.3282 9286	78.9043 3850	77.5148 1914	76.1587 8330	88
89	82.6499 1320	81.1592 1117	79.7050 7581	78.2864 8357	76.9024 4182	89
90	83.5107 2866	81.9884 0200	80.5038 1627	79.0559 0385	77.6436 2972	90
91	84.3701 1180	82.8158 6894	81.3005 6486	79.8230 8651	78.3823 5521	91
92	85.2280 6503	83.6416 1558	82.0953 2654	80.5880 3807	79.1186 2645	92
93	86.0845 9071	84.4656 4548	82.8881 0628	81.3507 6500	79.8524 5161	93
94	86.9396 9123	85.2879 6223	83.6789 0900	82.1112 7379	80.5838 3882	94
95	87.7933 6894	86.1085 6937	84.4677 3966	82.8695 7087	81.3127 9616	95
96	88.6456 2623	86.9274 7048	85.2546 0315	83.6256 6269	82.0393 3172	96
97	89.4964 6546	87.7446 6908	86.0395 0439	84.3795 5565	82.7634 5355	97
98	90.3458 8898	88.5601 6873	86.8224 4827	85.1312 5616	83.4851 6965	98
99	91.1938 9914	89.3739 7295	87.6034 3967	85.8807 7057	84.2044 8802	99
100	92.0404 9831	90.1860 8528	88.3824 8346	86.6281 0527	84.9214 1663	100
101	92.8856 8883	90.9965 0922	89.1595 8450	87.3732 6657	85.6359 6342	101
102	93.7294 7304	91.8052 4828	89.9347 4763	88.1162 6081	86.3481 3630	102
103	94.5718 5329	92.6123 0598	90.7079 7768	88.8570 9429	87.0579 4315	103
104	95.4128 3190	93.4176 8580	91.4792 7948	89.5957 7328	87.7653 9185	104
105	96.2524 1122	94.2213 9123	92.2486 5784	90.3323 0406	88.4704 9021	105
106	97.0905 9356	95.0234 2576	93.0161 1755	91.0666 9287	89.1732 4606	106
107	97.9273 8126	95.8237 9286	93.7816 6339	91.7989 4595	89.8736 6717	107
108	98.7627 7663	96.6224 9600	94.5453 0014	92.5290 6950	90.5717 6130	108
109	99.5967 8199	97.4195 3862	95.3070 3256	93.2570 6971	91.2675 3618	109
110	100.4293 9966	98.2149 2420	96.0668 6539	93.9829 5276	91.9609 9951	110
111	101.2606 3194	99.0086 5616	96.8248 0338	94.7067 2482	92.6521 5898	111
112	102.0904 8114	99.8007 3796	97.5808 5126	95.4283 9201	93.3410 2224	112
113	102.9189 4956	100.5911 7302	98.3350 1372	96.1479 6046	94.0275 9692	113
114	103.7460 3949	101.3799 6476	99.0872 9548	96.8654 3627	94.7118 9062	114
115	104.5717 5324	102.1671 1660	99.8377 0123	97.5808 2553	95.3939 1091	115
116	105.3960 9308	102.9526 3195	100.5862 3564	98.2941 3430	96.0736 6536	116
117	106.2190 6131	103.7365 1421	101.3329 0338	99.0053 6864	96.7511 6149	117
118	107.0406 6021	104.5187 6678	102.0777 0911	99.7145 3458	97.4264 0680	118
119	107.8608 9206	105.2993 9304	102.8206 5747	100.4216 3814	98.0994 0877	119
120	108.6797 5913	106.0783 9638	103.5617 5308	101.1266 8531	98.7701 7486	120

TABLE IV

N	1/6	5/24	1/4	7/24	1/3	N
121	109.4972 6369	106.8557 8017	104.3010 0058	101.8296 8207	99.4387 1248	121
122	110.3134 0801	107.6315 4778	105.0384 0457	102.5306 3438	100.1050 2905	122
123	111.1281 9435	108.4057 0257	105.7739 6965	103.2295 4820	100.7691 3195	123
124	111.9416 2497	109.1782 4789	106.5077 0040	103.9264 2945	101.4310 2852	124
125	112.7537 0214	109.9491 8708	107.2396 0139	104.6212 8404	102.0907 2610	125
126	113.5644 2809	110.7185 2349	107.9696 7720	105.3141 1786	102.7482 3199	126
127	114.3738 0508	111.4862 6045	108.6979 3237	106.0049 3679	103.4035 5348	127
128	115.1818 3536	112.2524 0128	109.4243 7144	106.6937 4670	104.0566 9782	128
129	115.9885 2116	113.0169 4930	110.1489 9894	107.3805 5342	104.7076 7225	129
130	116.7938 6471	113.7799 0783	110.8718 1939	108.0653 6278	105.3564 8397	130
131	117.5978 6827	114.5412 8016	111.5928 3730	108.7481 8058	106.0031 4016	131
132	118.4005 3404	115.3010 6960	112.3120 5716	109.4290 1263	106.6476 4800	132
133	119.2018 6427	116.0592 7943	113.0294 8345	110.1078 6469	107.2900 1462	133
134	120.0018 6117	116.8159 1295	113.7451 2065	110.7847 4253	107.9302 4713	134
135	120.8005 2696	117.5709 7342	114.4589 7321	111.4596 5187	108.5683 5262	135
136	121.5978 6385	118.3244 6412	115.1710 4560	112.1325 9846	109.2043 3816	136
137	122.3938 7406	119.0763 8831	115.8813 4224	112.8035 8800	109.8382 1079	137
138	123.1885 5979	119.8267 4925	116.5898 6758	113.4726 2617	110.4699 7754	138
139	123.9819 2325	120.5755 5019	117.2966 2601	114.1397 1866	111.0996 4538	139
140	124.7739 6664	121.3227 9436	118.0016 2196	114.8048 7112	111.7272 2131	140
141	125.5646 9216	122.0684 8502	118.7048 5981	115.4680 8919	112.3527 1227	141
142	126.3541 0199	122.8126 2538	119.4063 4395	116.1293 7850	112.9761 2519	142
143	127.1421 9832	123.5552 1868	120.1060 7875	116.7887 4466	113.5974 6696	143
144	127.9289 8335	124.2962 6812	120.8040 6858	117.4461 9327	114.2167 4448	144
145	128.7144 5925	125.0357 7692	121.5003 1778	118.1017 2989	114.8339 6460	145
146	129.4986 2820	125.7737 4828	122.1948 3071	118.7553 6009	115.4491 3415	146
147	130.2814 9238	126.5101 8539	122.8876 1168	119.4070 8941	116.0622 5995	147
148	131.0630 5396	127.2450 9145	123.5786 6501	120.0569 2338	116.6733 4879	148
149	131.8433 1510	127.9784 6964	124.2679 9503	120.7048 6752	117.2824 0743	149
150	132.6222 7797	128.7103 2313	124.9556 0601	121.3509 2732	117.8894 4262	150
151	133.3999 4473	129.4406 5510	125.6415 0226	121.9951 0825	118.4944 6109	151
152	134.1763 1754	130.1694 6871	126.3256 8804	122.6374 1579	119.0974 6952	152
153	134.9513 9854	130.8967 6711	127.0081 6762	123.2778 5538	119.6984 7461	153
154	135.7251 8989	131.6225 5345	127.6889 4525	123.9164 3245	120.2974 8300	154
155	136.4976 9373	132.3468 3089	128.3680 2519	124.5531 5242	120.8945 0133	155
156	137.2689 1221	133.0696 0255	129.0454 1166	125.1880 2069	121.4895 3621	156
157	138.0388 4747	133.7908 7157	129.7211 0889	125.8210 4265	122.0825 9422	157
158	138.8075 0163	134.5106 4107	130.3951 2109	126.4522 2367	122.6736 8195	158
159	139.5748 7683	135.2289 1416	131.0674 5246	127.0815 6909	123.2628 0593	159
160	140.3409 7521	135.9456 9397	131.7381 0719	127.7090 8426	123.8499 7269	160
161	141.1057 9888	136.6609 8358	132.4070 8946	128.3347 7450	124.4351 8873	161
162	141.8693 4996	137.3747 8611	133.0744 0346	128.9586 4512	125.0184 6053	162
163	142.6316 3058	138.0871 0465	133.7400 5332	129.5807 0141	125.5997 9454	163
164	143.3926 4284	138.7979 4227	134.4040 4321	130.2009 4864	126.1791 9722	164
165	144.1523 8886	139.5073 0205	135.0663 7727	130.8193 9208	126.7566 7497	165
166	144.9108 7074	140.2151 8708	135.7270 5962	131.4360 3697	127.3322 3419	166
167	145.6680 9059	140.9216 0041	136.3860 9439	132.0508 8855	127.9058 8125	167
168	146.4240 5050	141.6265 4511	137.0434 8567	132.6639 5202	128.4776 2251	168
169	147.1787 5258	142.3300 2423	137.6992 3758	133.2752 3259	129.0474 6430	169
170	147.9321 9892	143.0320 4081	138.3533 5419	133.8847 3545	129.6154 1292	170
171	148.6843 9160	143.7325 9790	139.0058 3959	134.4924 6576	130.1814 7467	171
172	149.4353 3271	144.4316 9852	139.6566 9785	135.0984 2867	130.7456 5582	172
173	150.1850 2434	145.1293 4572	140.3059 3302	135.7026 2934	131.3079 6261	173
174	150.9334 6856	145.8255 4251	140.9535 4914	136.3050 7287	131.8684 0127	174
175	151.6806 6744	146.5202 9190	141.5995 5027	136.9057 6439	132.4269 7801	175
176	152.4266 2307	147.2135 9690	142.2439 4042	137.5047 0899	132.9836 9901	176
177	153.1713 3751	147.9054 6053	142.8867 2361	138.1019 1175	133.5385 7045	177
178	153.9148 1282	148.5958 8577	143.5279 0385	138.6973 7773	134.0915 9845	178
179	154.6570 5107	149.2848 7561	144.1674 8514	139.2911 1199	134.6427 8915	179
180	155.3980 5431	149.9724 3304	144.8054 7146	139.8831 1956	135.1921 4866	180

TABLE IV

N	1/6	5/24	1/4	7/24	1/3	N
181	156.1378 2461	150.6585 6104	145.4418 6679	140.4734 0546	135.7396 8305	181
182	156.8763 6400	151.3432 6257	146.0766 7510	141.0619 7470	136.2853 9839	182
183	157.6136 7454	152.0265 4061	146.7099 0035	141.6488 3227	136.8293 0072	183
184	158.3497 5828	152.7083 9812	147.3415 4649	142.2339 8315	137.3713 9606	184
185	159.0846 1725	153.3888 3804	147.9716 1744	142.8174 3231	137.9116 9043	185
186	159.8182 5349	154.0678 6332	148.6001 1715	143.3991 8469	138.4501 8980	186
187	160.5506 6904	154.7454 7691	149.2270 4952	143.9792 4522	138.9869 0013	187
188	161.2818 6593	155.4216 8174	149.8524 1848	144.5576 1883	139.5218 2737	188
189	162.0118 4619	156.0964 8074	150.4762 2791	145.1343 1043	140.0549 7745	189
190	162.7406 1184	156.7698 7683	151.0984 8170	145.7093 2490	140.5863 5626	190
191	163.4681 6490	157.4418 7293	151.7191 8375	146.2826 6712	141.1159 6969	191
192	164.1945 0738	158.1124 7195	152.3383 3790	146.8543 4195	141.6438 2362	192
193	164.9196 4131	158.7816 7679	152.9559 4803	147.4243 5425	142.1699 2387	193
194	165.6435 6870	159.4494 9035	153.5720 1799	147.9927 0885	142.6942 7628	194
195	166.3662 9155	160.1159 1552	154.1865 5161	148.5594 1057	143.2168 8666	195
196	167.0878 1186	160.7809 5520	154.7995 5272	149.1244 6422	143.7377 6079	196
197	167.8081 3164	161.4446 1226	155.4110 2516	149.6878 7458	144.2569 0444	197
198	168.5272 5289	162.1068 8957	156.0209 7273	150.2496 4645	144.7743 2336	198
199	169.2451 7759	162.7677 9001	156.6293 9923	150.8097 8458	145.2900 2329	199
200	169.9619 0774	163.4273 1643	157.2363 0846	151.3682 9372	145.8040 0992	200
201	170.6774 4534	164.0854 7170	157.8417 0420	151.9251 7862	146.3162 8896	201
202	171.3917 9235	164.7422 5866	158.4455 9022	152.4804 4399	146.8268 6607	202
203	172.1049 5076	165.3976 8016	159.0479 7030	153.0340 9455	147.3357 4691	203
204	172.8169 2256	166.0517 3904	159.6488 4818	153.5861 3499	147.8429 3712	204
205	173.5277 0971	166.7044 3813	160.2482 2761	154.1365 6999	148.3484 4232	205
206	174.2373 1419	167.3557 8025	160.8461 1233	154.6854 0423	148.8522 6809	206
207	174.9457 3796	168.0057 6823	161.4425 0606	155.2326 4235	149.3544 2002	207
208	175.6529 8299	168.6544 0489	162.0374 1253	155.7782 8901	149.8549 0368	208
209	176.3590 5123	169.3016 9303	162.6308 3544	156.3223 4883	150.3537 2459	209
210	177.0639 4466	169.9476 3546	163.2227 7850	156.8648 2642	150.8508 8830	210
211	177.7676 6522	170.5922 3497	163.8132 4538	157.4057 2638	151.3464 0030	211
212	178.4702 1486	171.2354 9435	164.4022 3978	157.9450 5331	151.8402 6608	212
213	179.1715 9553	171.8774 1640	164.9897 6537	158.4828 1177	152.3324 9111	213
214	179.8718 0918	172.5180 0389	165.5758 2581	159.0190 0634	152.8230 8084	214
215	180.5708 5775	173.1572 5960	166.1604 2474	159.5536 4155	153.3120 4070	215
216	181.2687 4318	173.7951 8630	166.7435 6583	160.0867 2195	153.7993 7612	216
217	181.9654 6740	174.4317 8674	167.3252 5270	160.6182 5204	154.2850 9247	217
218	182.6610 3235	175.0670 6369	167.9054 8898	161.1482 3635	154.7691 9516	218
219	183.3554 3995	175.7010 1990	168.4842 7828	161.6766 7937	155.2516 8953	219
220	184.0486 9213	176.3336 5811	169.0616 2422	162.2035 8558	155.7325 8092	220
221	184.7407 9081	176.9649 8107	169.6375 3039	162.7289 5945	156.2118 7467	221
222	185.4317 3791	177.5949 9150	170.2120 0039	163.2528 0543	156.6895 7609	222
223	186.1215 3536	178.2236 9215	170.7850 3780	163.7751 2798	157.1656 9045	223
224	186.8101 8505	178.8510 8572	171.3566 4618	164.2959 3151	157.6402 2304	224
225	187.4976 8890	179.4771 7494	171.9268 2911	164.8152 2045	158.1131 7911	225
226	188.1840 4882	180.1019 6251	172.4955 9013	165.3329 9920	158.5845 6390	226
227	188.8692 6671	180.7254 5116	173.0629 3280	165.8492 7216	159.0543 8262	227
228	189.5533 4447	181.3476 4357	173.6288 6065	166.3640 4370	159.5226 4049	228
229	190.2362 8399	181.9685 4244	174.1933 7721	166.8773 1819	159.9893 4268	229
230	190.9180 8718	182.5881 5046	174.7564 8599	167.3890 9998	160.4544 9436	230
231	191.5987 5592	183.2064 7031	175.3181 9052	167.8993 9341	160.9181 0070	231
232	192.2782 9210	183.8235 0468	175.8784 9428	168.4082 0282	161.3801 6681	232
233	192.9566 9760	184.4392 5623	176.4374 0078	168.9155 3252	161.8406 9781	233
234	193.6339 7431	185.0537 2763	176.9949 1350	169.4213 8681	162.2996 9882	234
235	194.3101 2411	185.6669 2154	177.5510 3591	169.9257 6998	162.7571 7490	235
236	194.9851 4886	186.2788 4062	178.1057 7148	170.4286 8631	163.2131 3113	236
237	195.6590 5044	186.8894 8752	178.6591 2367	170.9301 4007	163.6675 7256	237
238	196.3318 3072	187.4988 6489	179.2110 9593	171.4301 3551	164.1205 0421	238
239	197.0034 9157	188.1069 7536	179.7616 9170	171.9286 7687	164.5719 3110	239
240	197.6740 3485	188.7138 2156	180.3109 1441	172.4257 6838	165.0218 5824	240

TABLE IV

N	1/6	5/24	1/4	7/24	1/3	N
241	198.3434 6241	189.3194 0613	180.8587 6749	172.9214 1425	165.4702 9061	241
242	199.0117 7612	189.9237 3169	181.4052 5436	173.4156 1870	165.9172 3316	242
243	199.6789 7782	190.5268 0085	181.9503 7841	173.9083 8590	166.3626 9086	243
244	200.3450 6937	191.1286 1624	182.4941 4305	174.3997 2005	166.8066 6863	244
245	201.0100 5262	191.7291 8045	183.0365 5167	174.8896 2531	167.2491 7139	245
246	201.6739 2940	192.3284 9608	183.5776 0766	175.3781 0584	167.6902 0405	246
247	202.3367 0156	192.9265 6573	184.1173 1437	175.8651 6577	168.1297 7148	247
248	202.9983 7095	193.5233 9200	184.6556 7518	176.3508 0924	168.5678 7855	248
249	203.6589 3938	194.1189 7746	185.1926 9345	176.8350 4038	169.0045 3011	249
250	204.3184 0870	194.7133 2470	185.7283 7252	177.3178 6327	169.4397 3101	250
251	204.9767 8073	195.3064 3629	186.2627 1573	177.7992 8204	169.8734 8606	251
252	205.6340 5730	195.8983 1481	186.7957 2641	178.2793 0074	170.3058 0006	252
253	206.2902 4024	196.4889 6280	187.3274 0789	178.7579 2347	170.7366 7780	253
254	206.9453 3135	197.0783 8284	187.8577 6348	179.2351 5427	171.1661 2405	254
255	207.5993 3246	197.6665 7747	188.3867 9649	179.7109 9719	171.5941 4357	255
256	208.2522 4539	198.2535 4924	188.9145 1022	180.1854 5628	172.0207 4110	256
257	208.9040 7193	198.8393 0069	189.4409 0795	180.6585 3555	172.4459 2136	257
258	209.5548 1391	199.4238 3437	189.9659 9296	181.1302 3902	172.8696 8907	258
259	210.2044 7312	200.0071 5280	190.4897 6854	181.6005 7069	173.2920 4890	259
260	210.8530 5137	200.5892 5852	191.0122 3795	182.0695 3454	173.7130 0555	260
261	211.5005 5045	201.1701 5403	191.5334 0444	182.5371 3457	174.1325 6367	261
262	212.1469 7217	201.7498 4186	192.0532 7126	183.0033 7472	174.5507 2791	262
263	212.7923 1830	202.3283 2452	192.5718 4165	183.4682 5897	174.9675 0290	263
264	213.4365 9065	202.9056 0451	193.0891 1886	183.9317 9124	175.3828 9326	264
265	214.0797 9100	203.4816 8433	193.6051 0609	184.3939 7548	175.7969 0358	265
266	214.7219 2113	204.0565 6648	194.1198 0658	184.8548 1560	176.2095 3845	266
267	215.3629 8283	204.6302 5346	194.6332 2352	185.3143 1552	176.6208 0244	267
268	216.0029 7786	205.2027 4773	195.1453 6012	185.7724 7912	177.0307 0011	268
269	216.6419 0802	205.7740 5179	195.6562 1957	186.2293 1030	177.4392 3599	269
270	217.2797 7506	206.3441 6811	196.1658 0506	186.6848 1293	177.8464 1461	270
271	217.9165 8076	206.9130 9915	196.6741 1976	187.1389 9087	178.2522 4047	271
272	218.5523 2688	207.4808 4738	197.1811 6684	187.5918 4798	178.6567 1808	272
273	219.1870 1519	208.0474 1527	197.6869 4947	188.0433 8810	179.0598 5191	273
274	219.8206 4744	208.6128 0526	198.1914 7079	188.4936 1505	179.4616 4642	274
275	220.4532 2540	209.1770 1980	198.6947 3395	188.9425 3267	179.8621 0607	275
276	221.0847 5081	209.7400 6134	199.1967 4210	189.3901 4475	180.2612 3528	276
277	221.7152 2544	210.3019 3231	199.6974 9835	189.8364 5508	180.6590 3849	277
278	222.3446 5102	210.8626 3516	200.1970 0584	190.2814 6747	181.0555 2009	278
279	222.9730 2930	211.4221 7230	200.6952 6767	190.7251 8568	181.4506 8447	279
280	223.6003 6203	211.9805 4616	201.1922 8695	191.1676 1347	181.8445 3602	280
281	224.2266 5095	212.5377 5916	201.6880 6678	191.6087 5461	182.2370 7909	281
282	224.8518 9779	213.0938 1372	202.1826 1026	192.0486 1282	182.6283 1803	282
283	225.4761 0428	213.6487 1223	202.6759 2046	192.4871 9184	183.0182 5717	283
284	226.0992 7216	214.2024 5711	203.1680 0046	192.9244 9540	183.4069 0083	284
285	226.7214 0315	214.7550 5076	203.6588 5332	193.3605 2719	183.7942 5332	285
286	227.3424 9899	215.3064 9556	204.1484 8212	193.7952 9093	184.1803 1893	286
287	227.9625 6139	215.8567 9391	204.6368 8989	194.2287 9029	184.5651 0192	287
288	228.5815 9207	216.4059 4818	205.1240 7969	194.6610 2896	184.9486 0657	288
289	229.1995 9274	216.9539 6076	205.6100 5456	195.0920 1059	185.3308 3711	289
290	229.8165 6514	217.5008 3402	206.0948 1751	195.5217 3885	185.7117 9778	290
291	230.4325 1095	218.0465 7034	206.5783 7158	195.9502 1739	186.0914 9281	291
292	231.0474 3190	218.5911 7206	207.0607 1978	196.3774 4982	186.4699 2638	292
293	231.6613 2968	219.1346 4156	207.5418 6512	196.8034 3979	186.8471 0271	293
294	232.2742 0600	219.6769 8118	208.0218 1060	197.2281 9090	187.2230 2596	294
295	232.8860 6257	220.2181 9328	208.5005 5920	197.6517 0676	187.5977 0029	295
296	233.4969 0107	220.7582 8019	208.9781 1391	198.0739 9095	187.9711 2986	296
297	234.1067 2319	221.2972 4427	209.4544 7772	198.4950 4706	188.3433 1879	297
298	234.7155 3064	221.8350 8783	209.9296 5358	198.9148 7867	188.7142 7122	298
299	235.3233 2510	222.3718 1322	210.4036 4447	199.3334 8932	189.0839 9125	299
300	235.9301 0825	222.9074 2276	210.8764 5334	199.7508 8258	189.4524 8297	300

TABLE IV

N	1/6	5/24	1/4	7/24	1/3	N
301	236.5358 8178	223.4419 1876	211.3480 8313	200.1670 6198	189.8197 5047	301
302	237.1406 4737	223.9753 0355	211.8185 3679	200.5820 3106	190.1857 9781	302
303	237.7444 0669	224.5075 7942	212.2878 1725	200.9957 9333	190.5506 2905	303
304	238.3471 6142	225.0387 4870	212.7559 2743	201.4083 5230	190.9142 4822	304
305	238.9489 1324	225.5688 1367	213.2228 7025	201.8197 1148	191.2766 5936	305
306	239.5496 6380	226.0977 7663	213.6886 4863	202.2298 7434	191.6378 6647	306
307	240.1494 1477	226.6256 3988	214.1532 6547	202.6388 4438	191.9978 7356	307
308	240.7481 6783	227.1524 0571	214.6167 2366	203.0466 2506	192.3566 8461	308
309	241.3459 2462	227.6780 7638	215.0790 2609	203.4532 1983	192.7143 0360	309
310	241.9426 8681	228.2026 5418	215.5401 7565	203.8586 3216	193.0707 3448	310
311	242.5384 5605	228.7261 4139	216.0001 7522	204.2628 6546	193.4259 8121	311
312	243.1332 3399	229.2485 4026	216.4590 2765	204.6659 2319	193.7800 4772	312
313	243.7270 2229	229.7698 5307	216.9167 3581	205.0678 0875	194.1329 3793	313
314	244.3198 2258	230.2900 8206	217.3733 0255	205.4685 2555	194.4846 5574	314
315	244.9116 3652	230.8092 2950	217.8287 3072	205.8680 7699	194.8352 0506	315
316	245.5024 6574	231.3272 9763	218.2830 2317	206.2664 6646	195.1845 8976	316
317	246.0923 1189	231.8442 8870	218.7361 8271	206.6636 9734	195.5328 1371	317
318	246.6811 7660	232.3602 0494	219.1882 1218	207.0597 7301	195.8798 8078	318
319	247.2690 6149	232.8750 4859	219.6391 1439	207.4546 9681	196.2257 9479	319
320	247.8559 6821	233.3888 2187	220.0888 9216	207.8484 7210	196.5705 5960	320
321	248.4418 9838	233.9015 2703	220.5375 4829	208.2411 0222	196.9141 7900	321
322	249.0268 5363	234.4131 6626	220.9850 8558	208.6325 9049	197.2566 5681	322
323	249.6108 3557	234.9237 4180	221.4315 0681	209.0229 4025	197.5979 9682	323
324	250.1938 4582	235.4332 5585	221.8768 1477	209.4121 5480	197.9382 0281	324
325	250.7758 8601	235.9417 1062	222.3210 1224	209.8002 3744	198.2772 7855	325
326	251.3569 5775	236.4491 0831	222.7641 0199	210.1871 9146	198.6152 2779	326
327	251.9370 6265	236.9554 5112	223.2060 8677	210.5730 2016	198.9520 5427	327
328	252.5162 0231	237.4607 4125	223.6469 6935	210.9577 2679	199.2877 6174	328
329	253.0943 7835	237.9649 8087	224.0867 5247	211.3413 1462	199.6223 5389	329
330	253.6715 9236	238.4681 7218	224.5254 3887	211.7237 8691	199.9558 3444	330
331	254.2478 4595	238.9703 1735	224.9630 3129	212.1051 4690	200.2882 0708	331
332	254.8231 4071	239.4714 1856	225.3995 3246	212.4853 9782	200.6194 7550	332
333	255.3974 7825	239.9714 7798	225.8349 4510	212.8645 4290	200.9496 4335	333
334	255.9708 6015	240.4704 9778	226.2692 7192	213.2425 8536	201.2787 1431	334
335	256.5432 8800	240.9684 8011	226.7025 1563	213.6195 2840	201.6066 9200	335
336	257.1147 6340	241.4654 2714	227.1346 7893	213.9953 7523	201.9335 8007	336
337	257.6852 8792	241.9613 4101	227.5657 6452	214.3701 2902	202.2593 8213	337
338	258.2548 6315	242.4562 2388	227.9957 7508	214.7437 9295	202.5841 0179	338
339	258.8234 9066	242.9500 7788	228.4247 1330	215.1163 7021	202.9077 4265	339
340	259.3911 7204	243.4429 0516	228.8525 8184	215.4878 6394	203.2303 0828	340
341	259.9579 0886	243.9347 0785	229.2793 8339	215.8582 7729	203.5518 0228	341
342	260.5237 0269	244.4254 8809	229.7051 2058	216.2276 1342	203.8722 2818	342
343	261.0885 5510	244.9152 4799	230.1297 9609	216.5958 7545	204.1915 8955	343
344	261.6524 6765	245.4039 8968	230.5534 1256	216.9630 6651	204.5098 8992	344
345	262.2154 4192	245.8917 1527	230.9759 7263	217.3291 8970	204.8271 3281	345
346	262.7774 7945	246.3784 2688	231.3974 7893	217.6942 4815	205.1433 2174	346
347	263.3385 8181	246.8641 2662	231.8179 3410	218.0582 4493	205.4584 6020	347
348	263.8987 5056	247.3488 1658	232.2373 4075	218.4211 8315	205.7725 5170	348
349	264.4579 8725	247.8324 9887	232.6557 0149	218.7830 6587	206.0855 9970	349
350	265.0162 9343	248.3151 7559	233.0730 1895	219.1438 9618	206.3976 0767	350
351	265.5736 7064	248.7968 4882	233.4892 9571	219.5036 7712	206.7085 7907	351
352	266.1301 2044	249.2775 2066	233.9045 3437	219.8624 1175	207.0185 1735	352
353	266.6856 4437	249.7571 9317	234.3187 3753	220.2201 0312	207.3274 2593	353
354	267.2402 4396	250.2358 6844	234.7319 0776	220.5767 5425	207.6353 0824	354
355	267.7939 2076	250.7135 4855	235.1440 4764	220.9323 6818	207.9421 6768	355
356	268.3466 7630	251.1902 3556	235.5551 5974	221.2869 4791	208.2480 0765	356
357	268.8985 1211	251.6659 3154	235.9652 4662	221.6404 9646	208.5528 3155	357
358	269.4494 2973	252.1406 3854	236.3743 1085	221.9930 1683	208.8566 4274	358
359	269.9994 3068	252.6143 5863	236.7823 5496	222.3445 1200	209.1594 4459	359
360	270.5485 1649	253.0870 9385	237.1893 8150	222.6949 8496	209.4612 4045	360

TABLE IV

N	3/8	5/12	11/24	1/2	13/24	N
1	0.9962 6401	0.9958 5062	0.9954 3758	0.9950 2488	0.9946 1252	1
2	1.9888 0599	1.9875 6908	1.9863 3355	1.9850 9938	1.9838 6657	2
3	2.9776 3984	2.9751 7253	2.9727 0863	2.9702 4814	2.9677 9104	3
4	3.9627 7942	3.9586 7804	3.9545 8346	3.9504 9566	3.9464 1462	4
5	4.9442 3852	4.9381 0261	4.9319 7856	4.9258 6633	4.9197 6589	5
6	5.9220 3090	5.9134 6318	5.9049 1437	5.8963 8441	5.8878 7325	6
7	6.8961 7027	6.8847 7661	6.8734 1123	6.8620 7404	6.8507 6494	7
8	7.8666 7025	7.8520 5970	7.8374 8941	7.8229 5924	7.8084 6906	8
9	8.8335 4446	8.8153 2916	8.7971 6905	8.7790 6392	8.7610 1357	9
10	9.7968 0644	9.7746 0165	9.7524 7023	9.7304 1186	9.7084 2626	10
11	10.7564 6968	10.7298 9376	10.7034 1292	10.6770 2673	10.6507 3478	11
12	11.7125 4762	11.6812 2200	11.6500 1701	11.6189 3207	11.5879 6663	12
13	12.6650 5367	12.6286 0283	12.5923 0229	12.5561 5131	12.5201 4916	13
14	13.6140 0117	13.5720 5261	13.5302 8846	13.4887 0777	13.4473 0956	14
15	14.5594 0340	14.5115 8766	14.4639 9515	14.4166 2465	14.3694 7491	15
16	15.5012 7363	15.4472 2422	15.3934 4188	15.3399 2502	15.2866 7210	16
17	16.4396 2503	16.3789 7848	16.3186 4807	16.2586 3186	16.1989 2791	17
18	17.3744 7077	17.3068 6654	17.2396 3309	17.1727 6802	17.1062 6895	18
19	18.3058 2393	18.2309 0443	18.1564 1618	18.0823 5624	18.0087 2171	19
20	19.2336 9756	19.1511 0815	19.0690 1652	18.9874 1915	18.9063 1251	20
21	20.1581 0467	20.0674 9359	19.9774 5320	19.8879 7925	19.7990 6756	21
22	21.0790 5820	20.9800 7661	20.8817 4520	20.7840 5896	20.6870 1291	22
23	21.9965 7106	21.8888 7297	21.7819 1144	21.6756 8055	21.5701 7447	23
24	22.9106 5610	22.7938 9839	22.6779 7074	22.5628 6622	22.4485 7800	24
25	23.8213 2613	23.6951 6853	23.5699 4184	23.4456 3803	23.3222 4915	25
26	24.7285 9390	24.5926 9895	24.4578 4339	24.3240 1794	24.1912 1341	26
27	25.6324 7213	25.4865 0517	25.3416 9396	25.1980 2780	25.0554 9614	27
28	26.5329 7348	26.3766 0266	26.2215 1203	26.0676 8936	25.9151 2256	28
29	27.4301 1056	27.2630 0680	27.0973 1600	26.9330 2423	26.7701 1776	29
30	28.3238 9595	28.1457 3291	27.9691 2418	27.7940 5397	27.6205 0668	30
31	29.2143 4217	29.0247 9626	28.8369 5480	28.6507 9997	28.4663 1414	31
32	30.1014 6169	29.9002 1205	29.7008 2601	29.5032 8355	29.3075 6483	32
33	30.9852 6694	30.7719 9540	30.5607 5588	30.3515 2592	30.1442 8330	33
34	31.8657 7030	31.6401 6139	31.4167 6239	31.1955 4818	30.9764 9396	34
35	32.7429 8411	32.5047 2504	32.2688 6343	32.0353 7132	31.8042 2109	35
36	33.6169 2066	33.3657 0128	33.1170 7683	32.8710 1624	32.6274 8886	36
37	34.4875 9219	34.2231 0501	33.9614 2032	33.7025 0372	33.4463 2129	37
38	35.3550 1090	35.0769 5105	34.8019 1156	34.5298 5445	34.2607 4227	38
39	36.2191 8894	35.9272 5416	35.6385 6812	35.3530 8900	35.0707 7557	39
40	37.0801 3842	36.7740 2904	36.4714 0750	36.1722 2786	35.8764 4482	40
41	37.9378 7140	37.6172 9033	37.3004 4712	36.9872 9141	36.6777 7355	41
42	38.7923 9990	38.4570 5261	38.1257 0431	37.7982 9991	37.4747 8513	42
43	39.6437 3589	39.2933 3040	38.9471 9633	38.6052 7354	38.2675 0282	43
44	40.4918 9130	40.1261 3816	39.7649 4035	39.4082 3238	39.0559 4976	44
45	41.3368 7801	40.9554 9028	40.5789 5348	40.2071 9640	39.8401 4896	45
46	42.1787 0785	41.7814 0111	41.3892 5274	41.0021 8547	40.6201 2329	46
47	43.0173 9263	42.6038 8492	42.1958 5507	41.7932 1937	41.3958 9552	47
48	43.8529 4409	43.4229 5594	42.9987 7734	42.5803 1778	42.1674 8829	48
49	44.6853 7394	44.2386 2832	43.7980 3634	43.3635 0028	42.9349 2412	49
50	45.5146 9384	45.0509 1617	44.5936 4878	44.1427 8635	43.6982 2540	50
51	46.3409 1540	45.8598 3353	45.3856 3131	44.9181 9537	44.4574 1441	51
52	47.1640 5021	46.6653 9439	46.1740 0047	45.6897 4664	45.2125 1329	52
53	47.9841 0980	47.4676 1267	46.9587 7276	46.4574 5934	45.9635 4409	53
54	48.8011 0566	48.2665 0224	47.7399 6459	47.2213 5258	46.7105 2873	54
55	49.6150 4922	49.0620 7692	48.5175 9229	47.9814 4535	47.4534 8900	55
56	50.4259 5190	49.8543 5046	49.2916 7213	48.7377 5657	48.1924 4658	56
57	51.2338 2506	50.6433 3656	50.0622 2029	49.4903 0505	48.9274 2304	57
58	52.0386 8001	51.4290 4885	50.8292 5288	50.2391 0950	49.6584 3982	58
59	52.8405 2803	52.2115 0093	51.5927 8594	50.9841 8855	50.3855 1826	59
60	53.6393 8035	52.9907 0632	52.3528 3545	51.7255 6075	51.1086 7958	60

TABLE IV

N	3/8	5/12	11/24	1/2	13/24	N
61	54.4352 4817	53.7666 7850	53.1094 1728	52.4632 4453	51.8279 4488	61
62	55.2281 4264	54.5394 3087	53.8625 4727	53.1972 5824	52.5433 3515	62
63	56.0180 7486	55.3089 7680	54.6122 4117	53.9276 2014	53.2548 7126	63
64	56.8050 5590	56.0753 2959	55.3585 1464	54.6543 4839	53.9625 7399	64
65	57.5890 9678	56.8385 0250	56.1013 8330	55.3774 6109	54.6664 6398	65
66	58.3702 0850	57.5985 0871	56.8408 6268	56.0969 7621	55.3665 6177	66
67	59.1484 0199	58.3553 6137	57.5769 6825	56.8129 1165	56.0628 8779	67
68	59.9236 8816	59.1090 7357	58.3097 1538	57.5252 8522	56.7554 6237	68
69	60.6960 7787	59.8596 5832	59.0391 1942	58.2341 1465	57.4443 0571	69
70	61.4655 8194	60.6071 2862	59.7651 9561	58.9394 1756	58.1294 3792	70
71	62.2322 1115	61.3514 9738	60.4879 5913	59.6412 1151	58.8108 7900	71
72	62.9959 7624	62.0927 7748	61.2074 2509	60.3395 1394	59.4886 4882	72
73	63.7568 8791	62.8309 8172	61.9236 0856	61.0343 4222	60.1627 6716	73
74	64.5149 5682	63.5661 2287	62.6365 2449	61.7257 1366	60.8332 5370	74
75	65.2701 9359	64.2982 1365	63.3461 8779	62.4136 4543	61.5001 2801	75
76	66.0226 0881	65.0272 6670	64.0526 1331	63.0981 5466	62.1634 0954	76
77	66.7722 1301	65.7532 9464	64.7558 1582	63.7792 5836	62.8231 1765	77
78	67.5190 1670	66.4763 1002	65.4558 1003	64.4569 7350	63.4792 7160	78
79	68.2630 3033	67.1963 2533	66.1526 1056	65.1313 1691	64.1318 9053	79
80	69.0042 6434	67.9133 5303	66.8462 3200	65.8023 0538	64.7809 9348	80
81	69.7427 2911	68.6274 0550	67.5366 8884	66.4699 5561	65.4265 9940	81
82	70.4784 3498	69.3384 9511	68.2239 9553	67.1342 8419	66.0687 2713	82
83	71.2113 9226	70.0466 3413	68.9081 6643	67.7953 0765	66.7073 9540	83
84	71.9416 1121	70.7518 3482	69.5892 1586	68.4530 4244	67.3426 2286	84
85	72.6691 0208	71.4541 0936	70.2671 5805	69.1075 0491	67.9744 2804	85
86	73.3938 7505	72.1534 6991	70.9420 0719	69.7587 1135	68.6028 2938	86
87	74.1159 4027	72.8499 2854	71.6137 7737	70.4066 7796	69.2278 4522	87
88	74.8353 0787	73.5434 9730	72.2824 8266	71.0514 2086	69.8494 9380	88
89	75.5519 8792	74.2341 8818	72.9481 3703	71.6929 5608	70.4677 9325	89
90	76.2659 9045	74.9220 1313	73.6107 5441	72.3312 9958	71.0827 6162	90
91	76.9773 2548	75.6069 8403	74.2703 4864	72.9664 6725	71.6944 1687	91
92	77.6860 0297	76.2891 1272	74.9269 3353	73.5984 7487	72.3027 7682	92
93	78.3920 3285	76.9684 1101	75.5805 2280	74.2273 3818	72.9078 5925	93
94	79.0954 2500	77.6448 9063	76.2311 3012	74.8530 7282	73.5096 8181	94
95	79.7961 8929	78.3185 6329	76.8787 6910	75.4756 9434	74.1082 6206	95
96	80.4943 3553	78.9894 4062	77.5234 5327	76.0952 1825	74.7036 1746	96
97	81.1898 7351	79.6575 3422	78.1651 9612	76.7116 5995	75.2957 6540	97
98	81.8828 1296	80.3228 5566	78.8040 1107	77.3250 3478	75.8847 2315	98
99	82.5731 6360	80.9854 1642	79.4399 1148	77.9353 5799	76.4705 0790	99
100	83.2609 3509	81.6452 2797	80.0729 1064	78.5426 4477	77.0531 3674	100
101	83.9461 3708	82.3023 0172	80.7030 2179	79.1469 1021	77.6326 2668	101
102	84.6287 7915	82.9566 4901	81.3302 5810	79.7481 6937	78.2089 9463	102
103	85.3088 7089	83.6082 8117	81.9546 3270	80.3464 3718	78.7822 5740	103
104	85.9864 2181	84.2572 0947	82.5761 5864	80.9417 2854	79.3524 3173	104
105	86.6614 4140	84.9034 4511	83.1948 4892	81.5340 5825	79.9195 3425	105
106	87.3339 3913	85.5469 9928	83.8107 1647	82.1234 4104	80.4835 8152	106
107	88.0039 2441	86.1878 8310	84.4237 7417	82.7098 9158	81.0445 8999	107
108	88.6714 0664	86.8261 0765	85.0340 3484	83.2934 2446	81.6025 7603	108
109	89.3363 9516	87.4616 8397	85.6415 1125	83.8740 5419	82.1575 5594	109
110	89.9988 9928	88.0946 2304	86.2462 1609	84.4517 9522	82.7095 4590	110
111	90.6589 2830	88.7249 3581	86.8481 6202	85.0266 6191	83.2585 6202	111
112	91.3164 9146	89.3526 3317	87.4473 6161	85.5986 6856	83.8046 2033	112
113	91.9715 9797	89.9777 2598	88.0438 2740	86.1678 2942	84.3477 3675	113
114	92.6242 5700	90.6002 2504	88.6375 7186	86.7341 5862	84.8879 2715	114
115	93.2744 7771	91.2201 4112	89.2286 0741	87.2976 7027	85.4252 0728	115
116	93.9222 6920	91.8374 8493	89.8169 4641	87.8583 7838	85.9595 9281	116
117	94.5676 4055	92.4522 6715	90.4026 0115	88.4162 9690	86.4910 9936	117
118	95.2106 0080	93.0644 9841	90.9855 8389	88.9714 3970	87.0197 4242	118
119	95.8511 5895	93.6741 8929	91.5659 0682	89.5238 2059	87.5455 3743	119
120	96.4893 2399	94.2813 5033	92.1435 8207	90.0734 5333	88.0684 9972	120

TABLE IV

N	3/8	5/12	11/24	1/2	13/24	N
121	97.1251 0484	94.8859 9203	92.7186 2172	90.6203 5157	88.5886 4456	121
122	97.7585 1043	95.4881 2484	93.2910 3780	91.1645 2892	89.1059 8713	122
123	98.3895 4962	96.0877 5918	93.8608 4227	91.7059 9893	89.6205 4253	123
124	99.0182 3125	96.6849 0541	94.4280 4705	92.2447 7505	90.1323 2576	124
125	99.6445 6414	97.2795 7385	94.9926 6401	92.7808 7070	90.6413 5177	125
126	100.2685 5705	97.8717 7479	95.5547 0495	93.3142 9921	91.1476 3541	126
127	100.8902 1873	98.4615 1846	96.1141 8161	93.8450 7384	91.6511 9146	127
128	101.5095 5788	99.0488 1506	96.6711 0571	94.3732 0780	92.1520 3461	128
129	102.1265 8320	99.6336 7475	97.2254 8889	94.8987 1423	92.6501 7947	129
130	102.7413 0331	100.2161 0764	97.7773 4273	95.4216 0619	93.1456 4058	130
131	103.3537 2683	100.7961 2379	98.3266 7879	95.9418 9671	93.6384 3241	131
132	103.9638 6235	101.3737 3323	98.8735 0854	96.4595 9872	94.1285 6932	132
133	104.5717 1841	101.9489 4596	99.4178 4343	96.9747 2509	94.6160 6563	133
134	105.1773 0352	102.5217 7191	99.9596 9483	97.4872 8865	95.1009 3557	134
135	105.7806 2617	103.0922 2099	100.4990 7407	97.9973 0214	95.5831 9327	135
136	106.3816 9481	103.6603 0306	101.0359 9244	98.5047 7825	96.0628 5282	136
137	106.9805 1787	104.2260 2794	101.5704 6116	99.0097 2960	96.5399 2820	137
138	107.5771 0373	104.7894 0542	102.1024 9141	99.5121 6876	97.0144 3336	138
139	108.1714 6076	105.3504 4523	102.6320 9431	100.0121 0821	97.4863 8212	139
140	108.7635 9727	105.9091 5708	103.1592 8094	100.5095 6041	97.9557 8827	140
141	109.3535 2156	106.4655 5061	103.6840 6232	101.0045 3772	98.4226 6550	141
142	109.9412 4190	107.0196 3547	104.2064 4942	101.4970 5246	98.8870 2743	142
143	110.5267 6653	107.5714 2121	104.7264 5318	101.9871 1688	99.3488 8762	143
144	111.1101 0364	108.1209 1739	105.2440 8446	102.4747 4316	99.8082 5955	144
145	111.6912 6141	108.6681 3350	105.7593 5409	102.9599 4344	100.2651 5662	145
146	112.2702 4798	109.2130 7900	106.2722 7284	103.4427 2979	100.7195 9216	146
147	112.8470 7146	109.7557 6332	106.7828 5143	103.9231 1422	101.1715 7944	147
148	113.4217 3994	110.2961 9584	107.2911 0056	104.4011 0868	101.6211 3164	148
149	113.9942 6146	110.8343 8590	107.7970 3083	104.8767 2506	102.0682 6189	149
150	114.5646 4404	111.3703 4280	108.3006 5284	105.3499 7518	102.5129 8323	150
151	115.1328 9568	111.9040 7582	108.8019 7711	105.8208 7083	102.9553 0864	151
152	115.6990 2434	112.4355 9418	109.3010 1413	106.2894 2371	103.3952 5103	152
153	116.2630 3795	112.9649 0707	109.7977 7433	106.7556 4548	103.8328 2324	153
154	116.8249 4441	113.4920 2364	110.2922 6810	107.2195 4774	104.2680 3804	154
155	117.3847 5159	114.0169 5300	110.7845 0578	107.6811 4203	104.7009 0812	155
156	117.9424 6734	114.5397 0423	111.2744 9767	108.1404 3983	105.1314 4612	156
157	118.4980 9946	115.0602 8637	111.7622 5400	108.5974 5257	105.5596 6460	157
158	119.0516 5575	115.5787 0842	112.2477 8499	109.0521 9161	105.9855 7606	158
159	119.6031 4396	116.0949 7934	112.7311 0078	109.5046 6827	106.4091 9293	159
160	120.1525 7182	116.6091 0805	113.2122 1148	109.9548 9380	106.8305 2758	160
161	120.6999 4702	117.1211 0346	113.6911 2714	110.4028 7940	107.2495 9229	161
162	121.2452 7723	117.6309 7440	114.1678 5779	110.8486 3622	107.6663 9929	162
163	121.7885 7009	118.1387 2969	114.6424 1340	111.2921 7535	108.0809 6075	163
164	122.3298 3322	118.6443 7811	115.1148 0388	111.7335 0781	108.4932 8877	164
165	122.8690 7419	119.1479 2841	115.5850 3912	112.1726 4458	108.9033 9538	165
166	123.4063 0056	119.6493 8929	116.0531 2895	112.6095 9660	109.3112 9254	166
167	123.9415 1986	120.1487 6942	116.5190 8315	113.0443 7473	109.7169 9217	167
168	124.4747 3959	120.6460 7743	116.9829 1147	113.4769 8978	110.1205 0610	168
169	125.0059 6721	121.1413 2192	117.4446 2361	113.9074 5252	110.5218 4610	169
170	125.5352 1017	121.6345 1146	117.9042 2923	114.3357 7365	110.9210 2388	170
171	126.0624 7589	122.1256 5456	118.3617 3793	114.7619 6383	111.3180 5111	171
172	126.5877 7174	122.6147 5973	118.8171 5928	115.1860 3366	111.7129 3935	172
173	127.1111 0510	123.1018 3542	119.2705 0281	115.6079 9369	112.1057 0014	173
174	127.6324 8329	123.5868 9004	119.7217 7799	116.0278 5442	112.4963 4494	174
175	128.1519 1361	124.0699 3199	120.1709 9427	116.4456 2629	112.8848 8515	175
176	128.6694 0335	124.5509 6962	120.6181 6103	116.8613 1969	113.2713 3210	176
177	129.1849 5975	125.0300 1124	121.0632 8763	117.2749 4496	113.6556 9707	177
178	129.6985 9004	125.5070 6513	121.5063 8337	117.6865 1240	114.0379 9129	178
179	130.2103 0141	125.9821 3955	121.9474 5753	118.0960 3224	114.4182 2589	179
180	130.7201 0103	126.4552 4271	122.3865 1931	118.5035 1467	114.7964 1200	180

TABLE IV

N	3/8	5/12	11/24	1/2	13/24	N
181	131.2279 9604	126.9263 8278	122.8235 7792	118.9089 6982	115.1725 6063	181
182	131.7339 9357	127.3955 6791	123.2586 4247	119.3124 0778	115.5466 8276	182
183	132.2381 0069	127.8628 0622	123.6917 2208	119.7138 3859	115.9187 8932	183
184	132.7403 2447	128.3281 0578	124.1228 2579	120.1132 7223	116.2888 9116	184
185	133.2406 7195	128.7914 7463	124.5519 6263	120.5107 1863	116.6569 9908	185
186	133.7391 5014	129.2529 2080	124.9791 4157	120.9061 8769	117.0231 2383	186
187	134.2357 6602	129.7124 5225	125.4043 7153	121.2996 8925	117.3872 7608	187
188	134.7305 2654	130.1700 7693	125.8276 6141	121.6912 3308	117.7494 6647	188
189	135.2234 3865	130.6258 0275	126.2490 2007	122.0808 2894	118.1097 0557	189
190	135.7145 0924	131.0796 3759	126.6684 5631	122.4684 8651	118.4680 0388	190
191	136.2037 4519	131.5315 8930	127.0859 7891	122.8542 1543	118.8243 7186	191
192	136.6911 5337	131.9816 6570	127.5015 9659	123.2380 2530	119.1788 1992	192
193	137.1767 4059	132.4298 7455	127.9153 1805	123.6199 2567	119.5313 5840	193
194	137.6605 1367	132.8762 2362	128.3271 5194	123.9999 2604	119.8819 9758	194
195	138.1424 7937	133.3207 2062	128.7371 0687	124.3780 3586	120.2307 4769	195
196	138.6226 4445	133.7633 7323	129.1451 9141	124.7542 6454	120.5776 1893	196
197	139.1010 1564	134.2041 8911	129.5514 1409	125.1286 2143	120.9226 2139	197
198	139.5775 9964	134.6431 7587	129.9557 8342	125.5011 1585	121.2657 6516	198
199	140.0524 0313	135.0803 4112	130.3583 0784	125.8717 5707	121.6070 6026	199
200	140.5254 3276	135.5156 9240	130.7589 9577	126.2405 5430	121.9465 1662	200
201	140.9966 9515	135.9492 3725	131.1578 5560	126.6075 1671	122.2841 4418	201
202	141.4661 9691	136.3809 8315	131.5548 9566	126.9726 5345	122.6199 5277	202
203	141.9339 4462	136.8109 3758	131.9501 2426	127.3359 7358	122.9539 5219	203
204	142.3999 4483	137.2391 0796	132.3435 4966	127.6974 8615	123.2861 5220	204
205	142.8642 0406	137.6655 0170	132.7351 8008	128.0572 0015	123.6165 6249	205
206	143.3267 2883	138.0901 2618	133.1250 2373	128.4151 2452	123.9451 9269	206
207	143.7875 2561	138.5129 8872	133.5130 8874	128.7712 6818	124.2720 5241	207
208	144.2466 0086	138.9340 9665	133.8993 8323	129.1256 3998	124.5971 5117	208
209	144.7039 6100	139.3534 5725	134.2839 1528	129.4782 4874	124.9204 9847	209
210	145.1596 1246	139.7710 7776	134.6666 9294	129.8291 0322	125.2421 0374	210
211	145.6135 6160	140.1869 6540	135.0477 2421	130.1782 1216	125.5619 7637	211
212	146.0658 1479	140.6011 2737	135.4270 1704	130.5255 8424	125.8801 2569	212
213	146.5163 7838	141.0135 7083	135.8045 7939	130.8712 2810	126.1965 6099	213
214	146.9652 5866	141.4243 0290	136.1804 1913	131.2151 5234	126.5112 9149	214
215	147.4124 6192	141.8333 3069	136.5545 4414	131.5573 6551	126.8243 2639	215
216	147.8579 9444	142.2406 6127	136.9269 6223	131.8978 7613	127.1356 7482	216
217	148.3018 6246	142.6463 0167	137.2976 8119	132.2366 9267	127.4453 4586	217
218	148.7440 7219	143.0502 5893	137.6667 0878	132.5738 2355	127.7533 4856	218
219	149.1846 2983	143.4525 4001	138.0340 5270	132.9092 7716	128.0596 9189	219
220	149.6235 4155	143.8531 5188	138.3997 2065	133.2430 6186	128.3643 8481	220
221	150.0608 1350	144.2521 0146	138.7637 2026	133.5751 8593	128.6674 3619	221
222	150.4964 5180	144.6493 9564	139.1260 5916	133.9056 5764	128.9688 5490	222
223	150.9304 6257	145.0450 4130	139.4867 4491	134.2344 8521	129.2686 4971	223
224	151.3628 5187	145.4390 4528	139.8457 8506	134.5616 7683	129.5668 2939	224
225	151.7936 2578	145.8314 1439	140.2031 8712	134.8872 4062	129.8634 0262	225
226	152.2227 9031	146.2221 5541	140.5589 5856	135.2111 8470	130.1583 7807	226
227	152.6503 5149	146.6112 7509	140.9131 0682	135.5335 1712	130.4517 6435	227
228	153.0763 1531	146.9987 8018	141.2656 3931	135.8542 4589	130.7435 7001	228
229	153.5006 8773	147.3846 7735	141.6165 6339	136.1733 7899	131.0338 0358	229
230	153.9234 7470	147.7689 7330	141.9658 8641	136.4909 2437	131.3224 7351	230
231	154.3446 8214	148.1516 7465	142.3136 1568	136.8068 8992	131.6095 8824	231
232	154.7643 1596	148.5327 8804	142.6597 5845	137.1212 8350	131.8951 5615	232
233	155.1823 8203	148.9123 2004	143.0043 2197	137.4341 1294	132.1791 8556	233
234	155.5988 8620	149.2902 7722	143.3473 1345	137.7453 8601	132.4616 8476	234
235	156.0138 3432	149.6666 6611	143.6887 4006	138.0551 1045	132.7426 6201	235
236	156.4272 3220	150.0414 9322	144.0286 0894	138.3632 9398	133.0221 2550	236
237	156.8390 8563	150.4147 6503	144.3669 2719	138.6699 4426	133.3000 8338	237
238	157.2494 0038	150.7864 8800	144.7037 0189	138.9750 6892	133.5765 4377	238
239	157.6581 8220	151.1566 6855	145.0389 4008	139.2786 7554	133.8515 1473	239
240	158.0654 3681	151.5253 1307	145.3726 4877	139.5807 7168	134.1250 0429	240

TABLE IV

N	3/8	5/12	11/24	1/2	13/24	N
241	158.4711 6992	151.8924 2796	145.7048 3494	139.8813 6486	134.3970 2043	241
242	158.8753 8722	152.2580 1954	146.0355 0554	140.1804 6255	134.6675 7109	242
243	159.2780 9437	152.6220 9415	146.3646 6749	140.4780 7218	134.9366 6416	243
244	159.6792 9700	152.9846 5808	146.6923 2765	140.7742 0118	135.2043 0749	244
245	160.0790 0075	153.3457 1759	147.0184 9289	141.0688 5689	135.4705 0890	245
246	160.4772 1121	153.7052 7892	147.3431 7003	141.3620 4666	135.7352 7615	246
247	160.8739 3396	154.0633 4831	147.6663 6585	141.6537 7777	135.9986 1698	247
248	161.2691 7455	154.4199 3192	147.9880 8712	141.9440 5749	136.2605 3906	248
249	161.6629 3853	154.7750 3594	148.3083 4056	142.2328 9302	136.5210 5004	249
250	162.0552 3141	155.1286 6650	148.6271 3287	142.5202 9156	136.7801 5752	250
251	162.4460 5869	155.4808 2971	148.9444 7071	142.8062 6026	137.0378 6906	251
252	162.8354 2585	155.8315 3166	149.2603 6072	143.0908 0623	137.2941 9219	252
253	163.2233 3833	156.1807 7841	149.5748 0951	143.3739 3655	137.5491 3438	253
254	163.6098 0157	156.5285 7601	149.8878 2365	143.6556 5826	137.8027 0307	254
255	163.9948 2099	156.8749 3047	150.1994 0969	143.9359 7836	138.0549 0566	255
256	164.3784 0199	157.2198 4777	150.5095 7414	144.2149 0384	138.3057 4952	256
257	164.7605 4992	157.5633 3388	150.8183 2349	144.4924 4164	138.5552 4196	257
258	165.1412 7016	157.9053 9473	151.1256 6420	144.7685 9864	138.8033 9026	258
259	165.5205 6803	158.2460 3625	151.4316 0269	145.0433 8173	139.0502 0167	259
260	165.8984 4885	158.5852 6432	151.7361 4536	145.3167 9775	139.2956 8338	260
261	166.2749 1791	158.9230 8480	152.0392 9857	145.5888 5348	139.5398 4257	261
262	166.6499 8048	159.2595 0353	152.3410 6867	145.8595 5570	139.7826 8635	262
263	167.0236 4182	159.5945 2634	152.6414 6197	146.1289 1114	140.0242 2182	263
264	167.3959 0717	159.9281 5901	152.9404 8475	146.3969 2651	140.2644 5601	264
265	167.7667 8174	160.2604 0731	153.2381 4326	146.6636 0847	140.5033 9595	265
266	168.1362 7072	160.5912 7699	153.5344 4373	146.9289 6365	140.7410 4861	266
267	168.5043 7930	160.9207 7377	153.8293 9234	147.1929 9866	140.9774 2091	267
268	168.8711 1263	161.2489 0334	154.1229 9528	147.4557 2006	141.2125 1976	268
269	169.2364 7584	161.5756 7137	154.4152 5868	147.7171 3439	141.4463 5202	269
270	169.6004 7407	161.9010 8352	154.7061 8865	147.9772 4814	141.6789 2451	270
271	169.9631 1240	162.2251 4542	154.9957 9127	148.2360 6781	141.9102 4402	271
272	170.3243 9591	162.5478 6266	155.2840 7261	148.4935 9981	142.1403 1730	272
273	170.6843 2967	162.8692 4082	155.5710 3868	148.7498 5055	142.3691 5107	273
274	171.0429 1873	163.1892 8546	155.8566 9549	149.0048 2642	142.5967 5200	274
275	171.4001 6810	163.5080 0212	156.1410 4902	149.2585 3375	142.8231 2673	275
276	171.7560 8279	163.8253 9630	156.4241 0520	149.5109 7886	143.0482 8187	276
277	172.1106 6778	164.1414 7350	156.7058 6996	149.7621 6802	143.2722 2399	277
278	172.4639 2805	164.4562 3917	156.9863 4920	150.0121 0748	143.4949 5962	278
279	172.8158 6855	164.7696 9876	157.2655 4876	150.2608 0346	143.7164 9527	279
280	173.1664 9419	165.0818 5768	157.5434 7451	150.5082 6215	143.9368 3740	280
281	173.5158 0991	165.3927 2134	157.8201 3223	150.7544 8970	144.1559 9244	281
282	173.8638 2058	165.7022 9511	158.0955 2773	150.9994 9224	144.3739 6679	282
283	174.2105 3109	166.0105 8435	158.3696 6676	151.2432 7586	144.5907 6680	283
284	174.5559 4629	166.3175 9437	158.6425 5505	151.4858 4663	144.8063 9881	284
285	174.9000 7102	166.6233 3049	158.9141 9831	151.7272 1058	145.0208 6910	285
286	175.2429 1011	166.9277 9800	159.1846 0221	151.9673 7371	145.2341 8394	286
287	175.5844 6835	167.2310 0216	159.4537 7242	152.2063 4200	145.4463 4955	287
288	175.9247 5054	167.5329 4821	159.7217 1456	152.4441 2139	145.6573 7211	288
289	176.2637 6143	167.8336 4137	159.9884 3424	152.6807 1780	145.8672 5780	289
290	176.6015 0579	168.1330 8684	160.2539 3703	152.9161 3712	146.0760 1273	290
291	176.9379 8833	168.4312 8980	160.5182 2848	153.1503 8519	146.2836 4300	291
292	177.2732 1378	168.7282 5540	160.7813 1413	153.3834 6785	146.4901 5466	292
293	177.6071 8683	169.0239 8878	161.0431 9946	153.6153 9090	146.6955 5375	293
294	177.9399 1216	169.3184 9505	161.3038 8997	153.8461 6010	146.8998 4624	294
295	178.2713 9443	169.6117 7931	161.5633 9109	154.0757 8119	147.1030 3812	295
296	178.6016 3829	169.9038 4661	161.8217 0826	154.3042 5989	147.3051 3531	296
297	178.9306 4835	170.1947 0202	162.0788 4688	154.5316 0188	147.5061 4369	297
298	179.2584 2924	170.4843 5056	162.3348 1232	154.7578 1282	147.7060 6915	298
299	179.5849 8555	170.7727 9724	162.5896 0994	154.9828 9833	147.9049 1752	299
300	179.9103 2184	171.0600 4704	162.8432 4507	155.2068 6401	148.1026 9459	300

TABLE IV

N	3/8	5/12	11/24	1/2	13/24	N
301	180.2344 4268	171.3461 0494	163.0957 2301	155.4297 1543	148.2994 0614	301
302	180.5573 5261	171.6309 7587	163.3470 4903	155.6514 5814	148.4950 5791	302
303	180.8790 5615	171.9146 6477	163.5972 2840	155.8720 9765	148.6896 5561	303
304	181.1995 5781	172.1971 7653	163.8462 6635	156.0916 3945	148.8832 0491	304
305	181.5188 6207	172.4785 1605	164.0941 6808	156.3100 8901	149.0757 1148	305
306	181.8369 7342	172.7586 8818	164.3409 3877	156.5274 5175	149.2671 8051	306
307	182.1538 9631	173.0376 9777	164.5865 8360	156.7437 3308	149.4576 1881	307
308	182.4696 3518	173.3155 4965	164.8311 0769	156.9589 3839	149.6470 3073	308
309	182.7841 9445	173.5922 4861	165.0745 1616	157.1730 7303	149.8354 2219	309
310	183.0975 7853	173.8677 9945	165.3168 1409	157.3861 4232	150.0227 9870	310
311	183.4097 9181	174.1422 0692	165.5580 0656	157.5981 5156	150.2091 6572	311
312	183.7208 3867	174.4154 7577	165.7980 9861	157.8091 0603	150.3945 2869	312
313	184.0307 2345	174.6876 1073	166.0370 9526	158.0190 1097	150.5788 9302	313
314	184.3394 5052	174.9586 1649	166.2750 0150	158.2278 7162	150.7622 6408	314
315	184.6470 2417	175.2284 9775	166.5118 2231	158.4356 9315	150.9446 4725	315
316	184.9534 4874	175.4972 5917	166.7475 6265	158.6424 8075	151.1260 4782	316
317	185.2587 2851	175.7649 0540	166.9822 2744	158.8482 3955	151.3064 7110	317
318	185.5628 6776	176.0314 4106	167.2158 2159	159.0529 7467	151.4859 2236	318
319	185.8658 7074	176.2968 7077	167.4483 4999	159.2566 9122	151.6644 0682	319
320	186.1677 4171	176.5611 9910	167.6798 1749	159.4593 9425	151.8419 2970	320
321	186.4684 8489	176.8244 3064	167.9102 2894	159.6610 8880	152.0184 9618	321
322	186.7681 0450	177.0865 6993	168.1395 8916	159.8617 7990	152.1941 1141	322
323	187.0666 0473	177.3476 2151	168.3679 0294	160.0614 7254	152.3687 8051	323
324	187.3639 8977	177.6075 8989	168.5951 7505	160.2601 7168	152.5425 0859	324
325	187.6602 6378	177.8664 7956	168.8214 1026	160.4578 8227	152.7153 0071	325
326	187.9554 3091	178.1242 9499	169.0466 1328	160.6546 0923	152.8871 6192	326
327	188.2494 9531	178.3810 4066	169.2707 8883	160.8503 5744	153.0580 9723	327
328	188.5424 6108	178.6367 2099	169.4939 4160	161.0451 3178	153.2281 1162	328
329	188.8343 3233	178.8913 4040	169.7160 7625	161.2389 3709	153.3972 1007	329
330	189.1251 1316	179.1449 0330	169.9371 9743	161.4317 7820	153.5653 9750	330
331	189.4148 0763	179.3974 1408	170.1573 0976	161.6236 5990	153.7326 7882	331
332	189.7034 1980	179.6488 7709	170.3764 1784	161.8145 8697	153.8990 5892	332
333	189.9909 5373	179.8992 9669	170.5945 2626	162.0045 6415	154.0645 4265	333
334	190.2774 1343	180.1486 7720	170.8116 3958	162.1935 9617	154.2291 3483	334
335	190.5628 0292	180.3970 2294	171.0277 6234	162.3816 8773	154.3928 4028	335
336	190.8471 2619	180.6443 3819	171.2428 9905	162.5688 4351	154.5556 6377	336
337	191.1303 8724	180.8906 2725	171.4570 5422	162.7550 6817	154.7176 1005	337
338	191.4125 9003	181.1358 9435	171.6702 3232	162.9403 6634	154.8786 8384	338
339	191.6937 3851	181.3801 4376	171.8824 3781	163.1247 4262	155.0388 8986	339
340	191.9738 3662	181.6233 7967	172.0936 7514	163.3082 0162	155.1982 3276	340
341	192.2528 8829	181.8656 0631	172.3039 4870	163.4907 4788	155.3567 1721	341
342	192.5308 9743	182.1068 2786	172.5132 6292	163.6723 8595	155.5143 4783	342
343	192.8078 6792	182.3470 4850	172.7216 2215	163.8531 2035	155.6711 2921	343
344	193.0838 0366	182.5862 7236	172.9290 3076	164.0329 5557	155.8270 6594	344
345	193.3587 0850	182.8245 0360	173.1354 9308	164.2118 9609	155.9821 6256	345
346	193.6325 8630	183.0617 4632	173.3410 1343	164.3899 4636	156.1364 2359	346
347	193.9054 4090	183.2980 0463	173.5455 9612	164.5671 1080	156.2898 5355	347
348	194.1772 7611	183.5332 8262	173.7492 4541	164.7433 9383	156.4424 5691	348
349	194.4480 9575	183.7675 8435	173.9519 6557	164.9187 9983	156.5942 3812	349
350	194.7179 0362	184.0009 1388	174.1537 6083	165.0933 3317	156.7452 0161	350
351	194.9867 0348	184.2332 7523	174.3546 3542	165.2669 9818	156.8953 5179	351
352	195.2544 9911	184.4646 7243	174.5545 9353	165.4397 9918	157.0446 9304	352
353	195.5212 9425	184.6951 0948	174.7536 3935	165.6117 4048	157.1932 2971	353
354	195.7870 9265	184.9245 9035	174.9517 7704	165.7828 2635	157.3409 6614	354
355	196.0518 9804	185.1531 1902	175.1490 1074	165.9530 6104	157.4879 0665	355
356	196.3157 1411	185.3806 9944	175.3453 4458	166.1224 4880	157.6340 5552	356
357	196.5785 4457	185.6073 3554	175.5407 8266	166.2909 9383	157.7794 1701	357
358	196.8403 9309	185.8330 3124	175.7353 2907	166.4587 0033	157.9239 9536	358
359	197.1012 6336	186.0577 9045	175.9289 8787	166.6255 7246	158.0677 9481	359
360	197.3611 5901	186.2816 1705	176.1217 6312	166.7916 1439	158.2108 1954	360

TABLE IV

N	7/12	5/8	2/3	17/24	3/4	N
1	0.9942 0050	0.9937 8882	0.9933 7748	0.9929 6649	0.9925 5583	1
2	1.9826 3513	1.9814 0504	1.9801 7631	1.9789 4893	1.9777 2291	2
3	2.9653 3732	2.9628 8699	2.9604 4004	2.9579 9646	2.9555 5624	3
4	3.9423 4034	3.9382 7279	3.9342 1196	3.9301 5784	3.9261 1041	4
5	4.9136 7722	4.9076 0029	4.9015 3506	4.8954 8151	4.8894 3961	5
6	5.8793 8083	5.8709 0712	5.8624 5205	5.8540 1557	5.8455 9763	6
7	6.8394 8384	6.8282 3068	6.8170 0535	6.8058 0776	6.7946 3785	7
8	7.7940 1874	7.7796 0813	7.7652 3710	7.7509 0552	7.7366 1325	8
9	8.7430 1780	8.7250 7640	8.7071 8917	8.6893 5591	8.6715 7642	9
10	9.6865 1314	9.6646 7220	9.6429 0315	9.6212 0570	9.5995 7958	10
11	10.6245 3667	10.5984 3200	10.5724 2035	10.5465 0132	10.5206 7452	11
12	11.5571 2014	11.5263 9205	11.4957 8180	11.4652 8886	11.4349 1267	12
13	12.4842 9509	12.4485 8837	12.4130 2828	12.3776 1409	12.3423 4508	13
14	13.4060 9288	13.3650 5676	13.3242 0028	13.2835 2247	13.2430 2242	14
15	14.3225 4470	14.2758 3281	14.2293 3802	14.1830 5914	14.1369 9495	15
16	15.2336 8156	15.1809 5186	15.1284 8148	15.0762 6890	15.0243 1261	16
17	16.1395 3427	16.0804 4905	16.0216 7035	15.9631 9626	15.9050 2492	17
18	17.0401 3350	16.9743 5931	16.9089 4405	16.8438 8540	16.7791 8107	18
19	17.9355 0969	17.8627 1733	17.7903 4177	17.7183 8021	17.6468 2984	19
20	18.8256 9315	18.7455 5759	18.6659 0242	18.5867 2425	18.5080 1969	20
21	19.7107 1398	19.6229 1438	19.5356 6466	19.4489 6078	19.3627 9870	21
22	20.5906 0213	20.4948 2174	20.3996 6688	20.3051 3275	20.2112 1459	22
23	21.4653 8738	21.3613 1353	21.2579 4723	21.1552 8283	21.0533 1473	23
24	22.3350 9930	22.2224 2338	22.1105 4361	21.9994 5337	21.8891 4614	24
25	23.1997 6732	23.0781 8473	22.9574 9365	22.8376 8643	22.7187 5547	25
26	24.0594 2070	23.9286 3079	23.7988 3475	23.6700 2376	23.5421 8905	26
27	24.9140 8852	24.7737 9457	24.6346 0406	24.4965 0683	24.3594 9286	27
28	25.7637 9968	25.6137 0889	25.4648 3847	25.3171 7683	25.1707 1251	28
29	26.6085 8295	26.4484 0635	26.2895 7464	26.1320 7464	25.9758 9331	29
30	27.4484 6689	27.2779 1935	27.1088 4898	26.9412 4085	26.7750 8021	30
31	28.2834 7993	28.1022 8010	27.9226 9766	27.7447 1578	27.5683 1783	31
32	29.1136 5030	28.9215 2060	28.7311 5662	28.5425 3946	28.3556 5045	32
33	29.9390 0610	29.7356 7265	29.5342 6154	29.3347 5163	29.1371 2203	33
34	30.7595 7524	30.5447 6785	30.3320 4789	30.1213 9177	29.9127 7621	34
35	31.5753 8549	31.3488 3761	31.1245 5088	30.9024 9907	30.6826 5629	35
36	32.3864 6445	32.1479 1315	31.9118 0551	31.6781 1244	31.4468 0525	36
37	33.1928 3955	32.9420 2550	32.6938 4653	32.4482 7053	32.2052 6576	37
38	33.9945 3808	33.7312 0546	33.4707 0848	33.2130 1169	32.9580 8016	38
39	34.7915 8716	34.5154 8369	34.2424 2564	33.9723 7404	33.7052 9048	39
40	35.5840 1374	35.2948 9062	35.0090 3209	34.7263 9541	34.4469 3844	40
41	36.3718 4465	36.0694 5652	35.7705 6168	35.4751 1336	35.1830 6545	41
42	37.1551 0653	36.8392 1145	36.5270 4803	36.2185 6519	35.9137 1260	42
43	37.9338 2588	37.6041 8529	37.2785 2453	36.9567 8794	36.6389 2070	43
44	38.7080 2904	38.3644 0774	38.0250 2437	37.6898 1839	37.3587 3022	44
45	39.4777 4221	39.1199 0831	38.7665 8050	38.4176 9306	38.0731 8136	45
46	40.2429 9143	39.8707 1634	39.5032 2566	39.1404 4822	38.7823 1401	46
47	41.0038 0258	40.6168 6096	40.2349 9238	39.8581 1987	39.4861 6775	47
48	41.7602 0141	41.3583 7114	40.9619 1296	40.5707 4377	40.1847 8189	48
49	42.5122 1349	42.0952 7566	41.6840 1949	41.2783 5542	40.8781 9542	49
50	43.2598 6428	42.8276 0314	42.4013 4387	41.9809 9008	41.5664 4707	50
51	44.0031 7907	43.5553 8201	43.1139 1775	42.6786 8274	42.2495 7525	51
52	44.7421 8301	44.2786 4050	43.8217 7260	43.3714 6817	42.9276 1812	52
53	45.4769 0108	44.9974 0671	44.5249 3967	44.0593 8089	43.6006 1351	53
54	46.2073 5816	45.7117 0853	45.2234 5000	44.7424 5517	44.2685 9902	54
55	46.9335 7895	46.4215 7370	45.9173 3444	45.4207 2503	44.9316 1193	55
56	47.6555 8802	47.1270 2976	46.6066 2361	46.0942 2428	45.5896 8926	56
57	48.3734 0980	47.8281 0411	47.2913 4796	46.7629 8646	46.2428 6776	57
58	49.0870 6856	48.5248 2396	47.9715 3771	47.4270 4489	46.8911 8388	58
59	49.7965 8846	49.2172 1636	48.6472 2289	48.0864 3266	47.5346 7382	59
60	50.5019 9350	49.9053 0818	49.3184 3334	48.7411 8261	48.1733 7352	60

TABLE IV

N	7/12	5/8	2/3	17/24	3/4	N
61	51.2033 0754	50.5891 2614	49.9851 9868	49.3913 2738	48.8073 1863	61
62	51.9005 5431	51.2686 9679	50.6475 4836	50.0368 9934	49.4365 4455	62
63	52.5937 5739	51.9440 4650	51.3055 1161	50.6779 3067	50.0610 8640	63
64	53.2829 4024	52.6152 0149	51.9591 1749	51.3144 5329	50.6809 7906	64
65	53.9681 2617	53.2821 8781	52.6083 9486	51.9464 9892	51.2962 5713	65
66	54.6493 3836	53.9450 3137	53.2533 7238	52.5740 9905	51.9069 5497	66
67	55.3265 9986	54.6037 5788	53.8940 7852	53.1972 8495	52.5131 0667	67
68	55.9999 3358	55.2583 9293	54.5305 4158	53.8160 8766	53.1147 4607	68
69	56.6693 6230	55.9089 6191	55.1627 8965	54.4305 3802	53.7119 0677	69
70	57.3349 0867	56.5554 9010	55.7908 5064	55.0406 6663	54.3046 2210	70
71	57.9965 9520	57.1980 0259	56.4147 5230	55.6465 0389	54.8929 2516	71
72	58.6544 4427	57.8365 2431	57.0345 2215	56.2480 7999	55.4768 4880	72
73	59.3084 7815	58.4710 8006	57.6501 8756	56.8454 2490	56.0564 2561	73
74	59.9587 1896	59.1016 9447	58.2617 7573	57.4385 6837	56.6316 8795	74
75	60.6051 8869	59.7283 9202	58.8693 1363	58.0275 3997	57.2026 6794	75
76	61.2479 0922	60.3511 9704	59.4728 2811	58.6123 6902	57.7693 9746	76
77	61.8869 0229	60.9701 3370	60.0723 4581	59.1930 8467	58.3319 0815	77
78	62.5221 8952	61.5852 2604	60.6678 9319	59.7697 1585	58.8902 3141	78
79	63.1537 9239	62.1964 9793	61.2594 9654	60.3422 9129	59.4443 9842	79
80	63.7817 3229	62.8039 7309	61.8471 8200	60.9108 3951	59.9944 4012	80
81	64.4060 3044	63.4076 7512	62.4309 7549	61.4753 8884	60.5403 8722	81
82	65.0267 0798	64.0076 2745	63.0109 0281	62.0359 6740	61.0822 7019	82
83	65.6437 8590	64.6038 5337	63.5869 8954	62.5926 0313	61.6201 1930	83
84	66.2572 8507	65.1963 7602	64.1592 6114	63.1453 2375	62.1539 6456	84
85	66.8672 2625	65.7852 1840	64.7277 4285	63.6941 5681	62.6838 3579	85
86	67.4736 3007	66.3704 0338	65.2924 5979	64.2391 2964	63.2097 6257	86
87	68.0765 1706	66.9519 5367	65.8534 3687	64.7802 6940	63.7317 7427	87
88	68.6759 0759	67.5298 9185	66.4106 9888	65.3176 0304	64.2499 0002	88
89	69.2718 2197	68.1042 4035	66.9642 7041	65.8511 5734	64.7641 6875	89
90	69.8642 8033	68.6750 2146	67.5141 7591	66.3809 5889	65.2746 0918	90
91	70.4533 0273	69.2422 5735	68.0604 3964	66.9070 3406	65.7812 4981	91
92	71.0389 0910	69.8059 7004	68.6030 8574	67.4294 0908	66.2841 1892	92
93	71.6211 1923	70.3661 8141	69.1421 3815	67.9481 0997	66.7832 4458	93
94	72.1999 5284	70.9229 1320	69.6776 2068	68.4631 6257	67.2786 5467	94
95	72.7754 2950	71.4761 8703	70.2095 5696	68.9745 9254	67.7703 7685	95
96	73.3475 6869	72.0260 2438	70.7379 7049	69.4824 2536	68.2584 3856	96
97	73.9163 8975	72.5724 4659	71.2628 8460	69.9866 8633	68.7428 6705	97
98	74.4819 1193	73.1154 7487	71.7843 2245	70.4874 0057	69.2236 8938	98
99	75.0441 5436	73.6551 3030	72.3023 0707	70.9845 9304	69.7009 3239	99
100	75.6031 3606	74.1914 3384	72.8168 6133	71.4782 8850	70.1746 2272	100
101	76.1588 7596	74.7244 0630	73.3280 0794	71.9685 1154	70.6447 8682	101
102	76.7113 9283	75.2540 6838	73.8357 6948	72.4552 8659	71.1114 5094	102
103	77.2607 0538	75.7804 4062	74.3401 6835	72.9386 3791	71.5746 4113	103
104	77.8068 3219	76.3035 4348	74.8412 2684	73.4185 8956	72.0343 8325	104
105	78.3497 9174	76.8233 9724	75.3389 6706	73.8951 6548	72.4907 0258	105
106	78.8896 0240	77.3400 2210	75.8334 1099	74.3683 8938	72.9436 2579	106
107	79.4262 8241	77.8534 3812	76.3245 8045	74.8382 8487	73.3931 7696	107
108	79.9598 4996	78.3636 6521	76.8124 9714	75.3048 7533	73.8393 8160	108
109	80.4903 2307	78.8707 2319	77.2971 8259	75.7681 8403	74.2822 6461	109
110	81.0177 1971	79.3746 3174	77.7786 5820	76.2282 3404	74.7218 5073	110
111	81.5420 5770	79.8754 1043	78.2569 4523	76.6850 4828	75.1581 6450	111
112	82.0633 5480	80.3730 7868	78.7320 6480	77.1386 4951	75.5912 3027	112
113	82.5816 2863	80.8676 5583	79.2040 3788	77.5890 6033	76.0210 7223	113
114	83.0968 9674	81.3591 6108	79.6728 8531	78.0363 0319	76.4477 1437	114
115	83.6091 7654	81.8476 1349	80.1386 2779	78.4804 0035	76.8711 8052	115
116	84.1184 8537	82.3330 3204	80.6012 8589	78.9213 7395	77.2914 9431	116
117	84.6248 4047	82.8154 3557	81.0608 8002	79.3592 4596	77.7086 7922	117
118	85.1282 5896	83.2948 4280	81.5174 3048	79.7940 3819	78.1227 5853	118
119	85.6287 5787	83.7712 7235	81.9709 5743	80.2257 7230	78.5337 5536	119
120	86.1263 5414	84.2447 4271	82.4214 8089	80.6544 6981	78.9416 9267	120

TABLE IV

N	7/12	5/8	2/3	17/24	3/4	N
121	86.6210 6460	84.7152 7226	82.8690 2076	81.0801 5206	79.3465 9322	121
122	87.1129 0598	85.1828 7926	83.3135 9678	81.5028 4028	79.7484 7962	122
123	87.6018 9493	85.6475 8188	83.7552 2859	81.9225 5551	80.1473 7432	123
124	88.0880 4798	86.1093 9814	84.1939 3568	82.3393 1867	80.5432 9957	124
125	88.5713 8159	86.5683 4597	84.6297 3743	82.7531 5052	80.9362 7749	125
126	89.0519 1210	87.0244 4320	85.0626 5308	83.1640 7168	81.3263 3001	126
127	89.5296 5577	87.4777 0753	85.4927 0173	83.5721 0262	81.7134 7892	127
128	90.0046 2877	87.9281 5655	85.9199 0238	83.9772 6367	82.0977 4583	128
129	90.4768 4716	88.3758 0776	86.3442 7389	84.3795 7501	82.4791 5219	129
130	90.9463 2692	88.8206 7852	86.7658 3499	84.7790 5669	82.8577 1929	130
131	91.4130 8393	89.2627 8610	87.1846 0430	85.1757 2862	83.2334 6828	131
132	91.8771 3399	89.7021 4768	87.6006 0029	85.5696 1054	83.6064 2013	132
133	92.3384 9278	90.1387 8030	88.0138 4135	85.9607 2209	83.9765 9566	133
134	92.7971 7592	90.5727 0092	88.4243 4571	86.3490 8276	84.3440 1554	134
135	93.2531 9893	91.0039 2638	88.8321 3150	86.7347 1188	84.7087 0029	135
136	93.7065 7722	91.4324 7342	89.2372 1673	87.1176 2868	85.0706 7026	136
137	94.1573 2616	91.8583 5868	89.6396 1926	87.4978 5223	85.4299 4567	137
138	94.6054 6097	92.2815 9869	90.0393 5688	87.8754 0146	85.7865 4657	138
139	95.0509 9682	92.7022 0988	90.4364 4724	88.2502 9521	86.1404 9288	139
140	95.4939 4878	93.1202 0857	90.8309 0785	88.6225 5213	86.4918 0434	140
141	95.9343 3185	93.5356 1100	91.2227 5614	88.9921 9078	86.8405 0059	141
142	96.3721 6091	93.9484 3330	91.6120 0941	89.3592 2957	87.1866 0108	142
143	96.8074 5078	94.3586 9148	91.9986 8485	89.7236 8679	87.5301 2514	143
144	97.2402 1619	94.7664 0147	92.3827 9952	90.0855 8059	87.8710 9195	144
145	97.6704 7177	95.1715 7910	92.7643 7038	90.4449 2901	88.2095 2055	145
146	98.0982 3208	95.5742 4010	93.1434 1429	90.8017 4995	88.5454 2982	146
147	98.5235 1160	95.9744 0010	93.5199 4797	91.1560 6118	88.8788 3854	147
148	98.9463 2470	96.3720 7463	93.8939 8805	91.5078 8036	89.2097 6530	148
149	99.3666 8570	96.7672 7913	94.2655 5104	91.8572 2502	89.5382 2858	149
150	99.7846 0882	97.1600 2895	94.6346 5335	92.2041 1256	89.8642 4673	150
151	100.2001 0819	97.5503 3933	95.0013 1128	92.5485 6025	90.1878 3795	151
152	100.6131 9786	97.9382 2542	95.3655 4100	92.8905 8527	90.5090 2029	152
153	101.0238 9183	98.3237 0228	95.7273 5861	93.2302 0466	90.8278 1171	153
154	101.4322 0397	98.7067 8488	96.0867 8008	93.5674 3532	91.1442 2998	154
155	101.8381 4811	99.0874 8808	96.4438 2127	93.9022 9407	91.4582 9279	155
156	102.2417 3797	99.4658 2666	96.7984 9795	94.2347 9759	91.7700 1765	156
157	102.6429 8721	99.8418 1532	97.1508 2578	94.5649 6244	92.0794 2199	157
158	103.0419 0941	100.2154 6864	97.5008 2031	94.8928 0507	92.3865 2307	158
159	103.4385 1805	100.5868 0113	97.8484 9700	95.2183 4182	92.6913 3803	159
160	103.8328 2656	100.9558 2721	98.1938 7119	95.5415 8890	92.9938 8390	160
161	104.2248 4828	101.3225 6120	98.5369 5813	95.8625 6241	93.2941 7757	161
162	104.6145 9647	101.6870 1734	98.8777 7298	96.1812 7836	93.5922 3580	162
163	105.0020 8431	102.0492 0978	99.2163 3077	96.4977 5261	93.8880 7524	163
164	105.3873 2491	102.4091 5258	99.5526 4647	96.8120 0094	94.1817 1239	164
165	105.7703 3132	102.7668 5971	99.8867 3490	97.1240 3899	94.4731 6367	165
166	106.1511 1647	103.1223 4505	100.2186 1083	97.4338 8233	94.7624 4533	166
167	106.5296 9326	103.4756 2241	100.5482 8890	97.7415 4637	95.0495 7352	167
168	106.9060 7449	103.8267 0550	100.8757 8368	98.0470 4646	95.3345 6429	168
169	107.2802 7290	104.1756 0795	101.2011 0961	98.3503 9781	95.6174 3354	169
170	107.6523 0114	104.5223 4330	101.5242 8107	98.6516 1553	95.8981 9706	170
171	108.0221 7181	104.8669 2502	101.8453 1232	98.9507 1464	96.1768 7053	171
172	108.3898 9741	105.2093 6648	102.1642 1754	99.2477 1003	96.4534 6951	172
173	108.7554 9038	105.5496 8098	102.4810 1080	99.5426 1649	96.7280 0944	173
174	109.1189 6309	105.8878 8172	102.7957 0609	99.8354 4873	97.0005 0565	174
175	109.4803 2785	106.2239 8183	103.1083 1731	100.1262 2133	97.2709 7335	175
176	109.8395 9687	106.5579 9436	103.4188 5826	100.4149 4877	97.5394 2764	176
177	110.1967 8230	106.8899 3229	103.7273 4264	100.7016 4545	97.8058 8352	177
178	110.5518 9624	107.2198 0849	104.0337 8408	100.9863 2565	98.0703 5585	178
179	110.9049 5070	107.5476 3576	104.3381 9610	101.2690 0354	98.3328 5940	179
180	111.2559 5761	107.8734 2684	104.6405 9216	101.5496 9321	98.5934 0884	180

TABLE IV

N	7/12	5/8	2/3	17/24	3/4	N
181	111.6049 2886	108.1971 9438	104.9409 8559	101.8284 0865	98.8520 1869	181
182	111.9518 7625	108.5189 5094	105.2393 8965	102.1051 6374	99.1087 0342	182
183	112.2968 1151	108.8387 0900	105.5358 1754	102.3799 7227	99.3634 7734	183
184	112.6397 4633	109.1564 8100	105.8302 8232	102.6528 4793	99.6163 5468	184
185	112.9806 9229	109.4722 7925	106.1227 9701	102.9238 0432	99.8673 4956	185
186	113.3196 6093	109.7861 1603	106.4133 7451	103.1928 5493	100.1164 7599	186
187	113.6566 6373	110.0980 0351	106.7020 2766	103.4600 1317	100.3637 4788	187
188	113.9917 1207	110.4079 5379	106.9887 6920	103.7252 9235	100.6091 7904	188
189	114.3248 1731	110.7159 7893	107.2736 1179	103.9887 0568	100.8527 8316	189
190	114.6559 9069	111.0220 9086	107.5565 6800	104.2502 6629	101.0945 7386	190
191	114.9852 4344	111.3263 0147	107.8376 5033	104.5099 8722	101.3345 6462	191
192	115.3125 8668	111.6286 2258	108.1168 7119	104.7678 8139	101.5727 6886	192
193	115.6380 3150	111.9290 6592	108.3942 4291	105.0239 6166	101.8091 9986	193
194	115.9615 8890	112.2276 4315	108.6697 7772	105.2782 4079	102.0438 7083	194
195	116.2832 6982	112.5243 6586	108.9434 8780	105.5307 3144	102.2767 9487	195
196	116.6030 8516	112.8192 4558	109.2153 8523	105.7814 4620	102.5079 8498	196
197	116.9210 4573	113.1122 9374	109.4854 8202	106.0303 9755	102.7374 5407	197
198	117.2371 6228	113.4035 2173	109.7537 9009	106.2775 9790	102.9652 1496	198
199	117.5514 4552	113.6929 4085	110.0203 2128	106.5230 5956	103.1912 8036	199
200	117.8639 0606	113.9805 6234	110.2850 8736	106.7667 9476	103.4156 6289	200
201	118.1745 5450	114.2663 9735	110.5481 0003	107.0088 1565	103.6383 7507	201
202	118.4834 0132	114.5504 5700	110.8093 7089	107.2491 3429	103.8594 2935	202
203	118.7904 5699	114.8327 5230	111.0689 1148	107.4877 6263	104.0788 3807	203
204	119.0957 3189	115.1132 9421	111.3267 3326	107.7247 1259	104.2966 1347	204
205	119.3992 3634	115.3920 9362	111.5828 4761	107.9599 9595	104.5127 6771	205
206	119.7009 8062	115.6691 6136	111.8372 6583	108.1936 2444	104.7273 1286	206
207	120.0009 7493	115.9445 0819	112.0899 9917	108.4256 0971	104.9402 6091	207
208	120.2992 2943	116.2181 4478	112.3410 5878	108.6559 6330	105.1516 2373	208
209	120.5957 5420	116.4900 8177	112.5904 5574	108.8846 9670	105.3614 1313	209
210	120.8905 5927	116.7603 2971	112.8382 0107	109.1118 2130	105.5696 4082	210
211	121.1836 5461	117.0288 9909	113.0843 0570	109.3373 4841	105.7763 1843	211
212	121.4750 5016	117.2958 0034	113.3287 8049	109.5612 8928	105.9814 5750	212
213	121.7647 5575	117.5610 4382	113.5716 3625	109.7836 5506	106.1850 6948	213
214	122.0527 8119	117.8246 3982	113.8128 8370	110.0044 5682	106.3871 6574	214
215	122.3391 3623	118.0865 9858	114.0525 3347	110.2237 0557	106.5877 5756	215
216	122.6238 3055	118.3469 3026	114.2905 9616	110.4414 1224	106.7868 5614	216
217	122.9068 7379	118.6056 4498	114.5270 8228	110.6575 8766	106.9844 7259	217
218	123.1882 7551	118.8627 5278	114.7620 0227	110.8722 4261	107.1806 1796	218
219	123.4680 4525	119.1182 6363	114.9953 6649	111.0853 8778	107.3753 0318	219
220	123.7461 9246	119.3721 8746	115.2271 8526	111.2970 3379	107.5685 3914	220
221	124.0227 2655	119.6245 3412	115.4574 6880	111.5071 9118	107.7603 3661	221
222	124.2976 5689	119.8753 1341	115.6862 2728	111.7158 7043	107.9507 0632	222
223	124.5709 9276	120.1245 3507	115.9134 7081	111.9230 8194	108.1396 5888	223
224	124.8427 4343	120.3722 0876	116.1392 0941	112.1288 3601	108.3272 0484	224
225	125.1129 1807	120.6183 4411	116.3634 5306	112.3331 4292	108.5133 5468	225
226	125.3815 2584	120.8629 5067	116.5862 1165	112.5360 1283	108.6981 1879	226
227	125.6485 7581	121.1060 3793	116.8074 9502	112.7374 5585	108.8815 0748	227
228	125.9140 7703	121.3476 1534	117.0273 1293	112.9374 8202	109.0635 3100	228
229	126.1780 3847	121.5876 9226	117.2456 7510	113.1361 0130	109.2441 9950	229
230	126.4404 6907	121.8262 7802	117.4625 9115	113.3333 2359	109.4235 2308	230
231	126.7013 7770	122.0633 8188	117.6780 7068	113.5291 5872	109.6015 1174	231
232	126.9607 7319	122.2990 1305	117.8921 2320	113.7236 1643	109.7781 7543	232
233	127.2186 6431	122.5331 8067	118.1047 5814	113.9167 0643	109.9535 2400	233
234	127.4750 5980	122.7658 9384	118.3159 8491	114.1084 3833	110.1275 6724	234
235	127.7299 6832	122.9971 6158	118.5258 1282	114.2988 2167	110.3003 1488	235
236	127.9833 9849	123.2269 9287	118.7342 5115	114.4878 6595	110.4717 7656	236
237	128.2353 5890	123.4553 9664	118.9413 0909	114.6755 8059	110.6419 6184	237
238	128.4858 5806	123.6823 8176	119.1469 9578	114.8619 7494	110.8108 8024	238
239	128.7349 0445	123.9079 5703	119.3513 2031	115.0470 5827	110.9785 4118	239
240	128.9825 0650	124.1321 3121	119.5542 9170	115.2308 3982	111.1449 5403	240

TABLE IV

N	7/12	5/8	2/3	17/24	3/4	N
241	129.2286 7257	124.3549 1300	119.7559 1891	115.4133 2875	111.3101 2807	241
242	129.4734 1101	124.5763 1105	119.9562 1084	115.5945 3413	111.4740 7252	242
243	129.7167 3008	124.7963 3397	120.1551 7633	115.7744 6500	111.6367 9655	243
244	129.9586 3803	125.0149 9028	120.3528 2417	115.9531 3033	111.7983 0923	244
245	130.1991 4303	125.2322 8848	120.5491 6308	116.1305 3901	111.9586 1958	245
246	130.4382 5322	125.4482 3699	120.7442 0174	116.3066 9989	112.1177 3656	246
247	130.6759 7669	125.6628 4422	120.9379 4874	116.4816 2173	112.2756 6904	247
248	130.9123 2148	125.8761 1848	121.1304 1266	116.6553 1326	112.4324 2585	248
249	131.1472 9559	126.0880 6805	121.3216 0198	116.8277 8313	112.5880 1573	249
250	131.3809 0696	126.2987 0117	121.5115 2515	116.9990 3993	112.7424 4737	250
251	131.6131 6351	126.5080 2601	121.7001 9054	117.1690 9220	112.8957 2940	251
252	131.8440 7308	126.7160 5069	121.8876 0650	117.3379 4840	113.0478 7038	252
253	132.0736 4350	126.9227 8329	122.0737 8129	117.5056 1694	113.1988 7878	253
254	132.3018 8251	127.1282 3185	122.2587 2314	117.6721 0619	113.3487 6306	254
255	132.5287 9786	127.3324 0432	122.4424 4020	117.8374 2443	113.4975 3157	255
256	132.7543 9721	127.5353 0864	122.6249 4060	118.0015 7991	113.6451 9263	256
257	132.9786 8819	127.7369 5269	122.8062 3238	118.1645 8080	113.7917 5447	257
258	133.2016 7840	127.9373 4428	122.9863 2356	118.3264 3521	113.9372 2528	258
259	133.4233 7538	128.1364 9121	123.1652 2208	118.4871 5123	114.0816 1318	259
260	133.6437 8663	128.3344 0121	123.3429 3584	118.6467 3684	114.2249 2624	260
261	133.8629 1959	128.5310 8194	123.5194 7269	118.8052 0001	114.3671 7244	261
262	134.0807 8170	128.7265 4106	123.6948 4042	118.9625 4862	114.5083 5974	262
263	134.2973 8032	128.9207 8615	123.8690 4677	119.1187 9052	114.6484 9602	263
264	134.5127 2277	129.1138 2474	124.0420 9944	119.2739 3349	114.7875 8911	264
265	134.7268 1634	129.3056 6434	124.2140 0607	119.4279 8526	114.9256 4676	265
266	134.9396 6827	129.4963 1239	124.3847 7424	119.5809 5351	115.0626 7668	266
267	135.1512 8577	129.6857 7629	124.5544 1150	119.7328 4585	115.1986 8653	267
268	135.3616 7600	129.8740 6339	124.7229 2533	119.8836 6986	115.3336 8390	268
269	135.5708 4606	130.0611 8101	124.8903 2317	120.0334 3304	115.4676 7633	269
270	135.7788 0304	130.2471 3641	125.0566 1242	120.1821 4286	115.6006 7129	270
271	135.9855 5398	130.4319 3680	125.2218 0042	120.3298 0673	115.7326 7622	271
272	136.1911 0586	130.6155 8937	125.3858 9446	120.4764 3200	115.8636 9848	272
273	136.3954 6564	130.7981 0124	125.5489 0178	120.6220 2598	115.9937 4539	273
274	136.5986 4024	130.9794 7949	125.7108 2958	120.7665 9593	116.1228 2421	274
275	136.8006 3653	131.1597 3117	125.8716 8502	120.9101 4904	116.2509 4215	275
276	137.0014 6134	131.3388 6327	126.0314 7518	121.0526 9247	116.3781 0635	276
277	137.2011 2146	131.5168 8276	126.1902 0713	121.1942 3332	116.5043 2392	277
278	137.3996 2366	131.6937 9653	126.3478 8788	121.3347 7863	116.6296 0191	278
279	137.5969 7464	131.8696 1146	126.5045 2439	121.4743 3543	116.7539 4730	279
280	137.7931 8108	132.0443 3437	126.6601 2356	121.6129 1064	116.8773 6705	280
281	137.9882 4963	132.2179 7204	126.8146 9228	121.7505 1119	116.9998 6804	281
282	138.1821 8687	132.3905 3122	126.9682 3736	121.8871 4392	117.1214 5711	282
283	138.3749 9937	132.5620 1861	127.1207 6559	122.0228 1564	117.2421 4105	283
284	138.5666 9366	132.7324 4085	127.2722 8370	122.1575 3311	117.3619 2660	284
285	138.7572 7622	132.9018 0457	127.4227 9838	122.2913 0305	117.4808 2045	285
286	138.9467 5349	133.0701 1634	127.5723 1627	122.4241 3212	117.5988 2923	286
287	139.1351 3189	133.2373 8270	127.7208 4398	122.5560 2692	117.7159 5953	287
288	139.3224 1778	133.4036 1014	127.8683 8806	122.6869 9405	117.8322 1790	288
289	139.5086 1751	133.5688 0511	128.0149 5502	122.8170 4002	117.9476 1082	289
290	139.6937 3738	133.7329 7402	128.1605 5135	122.9461 7130	118.0621 4473	290
291	139.8777 8364	133.8961 2325	128.3051 8346	123.0743 9434	118.1758 2604	291
292	140.0607 6253	134.0582 5913	128.4488 5774	123.2017 1553	118.2886 6108	292
293	140.2426 8022	134.2193 8796	128.5915 8054	123.3281 4119	118.4006 5616	293
294	140.4235 4289	134.3795 1598	128.7333 5815	123.4536 7764	118.5118 1753	294
295	140.6033 5664	134.5386 4942	128.8741 9684	123.5783 3113	118.6221 5139	295
296	140.7821 2757	134.6967 9446	129.0141 0282	123.7021 0787	118.7316 6391	296
297	140.9598 6171	134.8539 5722	129.1530 8227	123.8250 1402	118.8403 6120	297
298	141.1365 6508	135.0101 4382	129.2911 4133	123.9470 5570	118.9482 4933	298
299	141.3122 4366	135.1653 6032	129.4282 8609	124.0682 3901	119.0553 3432	299
300	141.4869 0339	135.3196 1274	129.5645 2260	124.1885 6997	119.1616 2216	300

TABLE IV

N	7/12	5/8	2/3	17/24	3/4	N
301	141.6605 5018	135.4729 0707	129.6998 5685	124.3080 5459	119.2671 1877	301
302	141.8331 8990	135.6252 4927	129.8342 9492	124.4266 9880	119.3718 3004	302
303	142.0048 2840	135.7766 4523	129.9678 4264	124.5445 0854	119.4757 6183	303
304	142.1754 7149	135.9271 0085	130.1005 0593	124.6614 8965	119.5789 1993	304
305	142.3451 2492	136.0766 2197	130.2322 9066	124.7776 4798	119.6813 1010	305
306	142.5137 9446	136.2252 1438	130.3632 0264	124.8929 8930	119.7829 3807	306
307	142.6814 8579	136.3728 8385	130.4932 4766	125.0075 1937	119.8838 0950	307
308	142.8482 0460	136.5196 3613	130.6224 3145	125.1212 4390	119.9839 3002	308
309	143.0139 5652	136.6654 7690	130.7507 5972	125.2341 6854	120.0833 0523	309
310	143.1787 4716	136.8104 1182	130.8782 3813	125.3462 9892	120.1819 4068	310
311	143.3425 8210	136.9544 4653	131.0048 7232	125.4576 4063	120.2798 4186	311
312	143.5054 6687	137.0975 8661	131.1306 6786	125.5681 9922	120.3770 1426	312
313	143.6674 0700	137.2398 3763	131.2556 3033	125.6779 8019	120.4734 6328	313
314	143.8284 0795	137.3812 0510	131.3797 6523	125.7869 8902	120.5691 9432	314
315	143.9884 7518	137.5216 9451	131.5030 7804	125.8952 3113	120.6642 1273	315
316	144.1476 1410	137.6613 1131	131.6255 7421	126.0027 1192	120.7585 2380	316
317	144.3058 3009	137.8000 6093	131.7472 5915	126.1094 3675	120.8521 3280	317
318	144.4631 2851	137.9379 4875	131.8681 3823	126.2154 1092	120.9450 4497	318
319	144.6195 1467	138.0749 8012	131.9882 1678	126.3206 3972	121.0372 6548	319
320	144.7749 9387	138.2111 6037	132.1075 0012	126.4251 2840	121.1287 9948	320
321	144.9295 7137	138.3464 9478	132.2259 9349	126.5288 8215	121.2196 5209	321
322	145.0832 5240	138.4809 8860	132.3437 0215	126.6319 0615	121.3098 2838	322
323	145.2360 4215	138.6146 4706	132.4606 3127	126.7342 0552	121.3993 3338	323
324	145.3879 4580	138.7474 7534	132.5767 8603	126.8357 8538	121.4881 7209	324
325	145.5389 6849	138.8794 7859	132.6921 7155	126.9366 5077	121.5763 4946	325
326	145.6891 1532	139.0106 6196	132.8067 9293	127.0368 0672	121.6638 7044	326
327	145.8383 9137	139.1410 3052	132.9206 5523	127.1362 5822	121.7507 3989	327
328	145.9868 0169	139.2705 8933	133.0337 6348	127.2350 1024	121.8369 6267	328
329	146.1343 5131	139.3993 4344	133.1461 2266	127.3330 6767	121.9225 4359	329
330	146.2810 4521	139.5272 9783	133.2577 3774	127.4304 3542	122.0074 8743	330
331	146.4268 8836	139.6544 5747	133.3686 1365	127.5271 1833	122.0917 9894	331
332	146.5718 8569	139.7808 2730	133.4787 5528	127.6231 2122	122.1754 8282	332
333	146.7160 4211	139.9064 1222	133.5881 6750	127.7184 4888	122.2585 4374	333
334	146.8593 6250	140.0312 1711	133.6968 5513	127.8131 0604	122.3409 8635	334
335	147.0018 5170	140.1552 4682	133.8048 2298	127.9070 9744	122.4228 1523	335
336	147.1435 1453	140.2785 0616	133.9120 7580	128.0004 2774	122.5040 3497	336
337	147.2843 5579	140.4009 9991	134.0186 1835	128.0931 0160	122.5846 5009	337
338	147.4243 8024	140.5227 3283	134.1244 5531	128.1851 2365	122.6646 6510	338
339	147.5635 9261	140.6437 0964	134.2295 9137	128.2764 9845	122.7440 8447	339
340	147.7019 9763	140.7639 3505	134.3340 3116	128.3672 3056	122.8229 1263	340
341	147.8395 9996	140.8834 1371	134.4377 7930	128.4573 2452	122.9011 5397	341
342	147.9764 0427	141.0021 5027	134.5408 4036	128.5467 8479	122.9788 1288	342
343	148.1124 1518	141.1201 4934	134.6432 1891	128.6356 1584	123.0558 9367	343
344	148.2476 3730	141.2374 1549	134.7449 1944	128.7238 2210	123.1324 0067	344
345	148.3820 7519	141.3539 5328	134.8459 4647	128.8114 0797	123.2083 3813	345
346	148.5157 3341	141.4697 6724	134.9463 0444	128.8983 7779	123.2837 1030	346
347	148.6486 1648	141.5848 6185	135.0459 9778	128.9847 3591	123.3585 2139	347
348	148.7807 2890	141.6992 4159	135.1450 3091	129.0704 8663	123.4327 7558	348
349	148.9120 7513	141.8129 1090	135.2434 0819	129.1556 3422	123.5064 7700	349
350	149.0426 5961	141.9258 7419	135.3411 3396	129.2401 8292	123.5796 2978	350
351	149.1724 8677	142.0381 3584	135.4382 1255	129.3241 3695	123.6522 3799	351
352	149.3015 6100	142.1497 0021	135.5346 4823	129.4075 0049	123.7243 0570	352
353	149.4298 8666	142.2605 7164	135.6304 4526	129.4902 7769	123.7958 3692	353
354	149.5574 6810	142.3707 5442	135.7256 0787	129.5724 7268	123.8668 3565	354
355	149.6843 0962	142.4802 5284	135.8201 4027	129.6540 8954	123.9373 0586	355
356	149.8104 1553	142.5890 7115	135.9140 4663	129.7351 3236	124.0072 5147	356
357	149.9357 9009	142.6972 1356	136.0073 3109	129.8156 0515	124.0766 7640	357
358	150.0604 3754	142.8046 8429	136.0999 9777	129.8955 1194	124.1455 8452	358
359	150.1843 6209	142.9114 8749	136.1920 5076	129.9748 5671	124.2139 7967	359
360	150.3075 6795	143.0176 2732	136.2834 9413	130.0536 4340	124.2818 6568	360

TABLE IV

N	19/24	5/6	7/8	11/12	23/24	N
1	0.9921 4551	0.9917 3554	0.9913 2590	0.9909 1660	0.9905 0764	1
2	1.9764 9824	1.9752 7491	1.9740 5294	1.9728 3230	1.9716 1301	2
3	2.9531 1938	2.9506 8586	2.9482 5570	2.9458 2887	2.9434 0538	3
4	3.9220 6966	3.9180 3557	3.9140 0813	3.9099 8732	3.9059 7313	4
5	4.8834 0933	4.8773 9065	4.8713 8352	4.8653 8793	4.8594 0385	5
6	5.8371 9818	5.8288 1717	5.8204 5454	5.8121 1025	5.8037 8425	6
7	6.7834 9551	6.7723 8066	6.7612 9323	6.7502 3312	6.7392 0024	7
8	7.7223 6016	7.7081 4611	7.6939 7098	7.6798 3463	7.6657 3693	8
9	8.6538 5051	8.6361 7796	8.6185 5859	8.6009 9220	8.5834 7860	9
10	9.5780 2448	9.5565 4013	9.5351 2624	9.5137 8253	9.4925 0872	10
11	10.4949 3954	10.4692 9600	10.4437 4348	10.4182 8162	10.3929 1000	11
12	11.4046 5271	11.3745 0843	11.3444 7929	11.3145 6477	11.2847 6434	12
13	12.3072 2055	12.2722 3976	12.2374 0202	12.2027 0663	12.1681 5288	13
14	13.2026 9918	13.1625 5183	13.1225 7945	13.0827 8113	13.0431 5597	14
15	14.0911 4428	14.0455 0595	14.0000 7876	13.9548 6157	13.9098 5321	15
16	14.9726 1111	14.9211 6292	14.8699 6656	14.8190 2055	14.7683 2344	16
17	15.8471 5447	15.7895 8306	15.7323 0885	15.6753 3002	15.6186 4476	17
18	16.7148 2875	16.6508 2618	16.5871 7111	16.5238 6129	16.4608 9452	18
19	17.5756 8788	17.5049 5158	17.4346 1820	17.3646 8502	17.2951 4934	19
20	18.4297 8542	18.3520 1810	18.2747 1445	18.1978 7120	18.1214 8511	20
21	19.2771 7445	19.1920 8406	19.1075 2361	19.0234 8921	18.9399 7699	21
22	20.1179 0768	20.0252 0734	19.9331 0891	19.8416 0781	19.7506 9946	22
23	20.9520 3739	20.8514 4529	20.7515 3300	20.6522 9510	20.5537 2625	23
24	21.7796 1543	21.6708 5483	21.5628 5799	21.4556 1860	21.3491 3042	24
25	22.6006 9328	22.4834 9240	22.3671 4547	22.2516 4518	22.1369 8432	25
26	23.4153 2198	23.2894 1395	23.1644 5647	23.0404 4114	22.9173 5962	26
27	24.2235 5219	24.0886 7499	23.9548 5152	23.8220 7214	23.6903 2732	27
28	25.0254 3417	24.8813 3057	24.7383 9060	24.5966 0328	24.4559 5772	28
29	25.8210 1778	25.6674 3527	25.5151 3319	25.3640 9904	25.2143 2048	29
30	26.6103 5249	26.4470 4325	26.2851 3823	26.1246 2333	25.9654 8459	30
31	27.3934 8738	27.2202 0818	27.0484 6417	26.8782 3946	26.7095 1837	31
32	28.1704 7115	27.9869 8332	27.8051 6894	27.6250 1020	27.4464 8951	32
33	28.9413 5211	28.7474 2147	28.5553 0998	28.3649 9773	28.1764 6506	33
34	29.7061 7820	29.5015 7501	29.2989 4422	29.0982 6364	28.8995 1141	34
35	30.4649 9697	30.2494 9588	30.0361 2809	29.8248 6901	29.6156 9433	35
36	31.2178 5562	30.9912 3559	30.7669 1757	30.5448 7433	30.3250 7899	36
37	31.9648 0094	31.7268 4521	31.4913 6810	31.2583 3955	31.0277 2992	37
38	32.7058 7940	32.4563 7541	32.2095 3467	31.9653 2408	31.7237 1102	38
39	33.4411 3706	33.1798 7644	32.9214 7179	32.6658 8678	32.4130 8562	39
40	34.1706 1966	33.8973 9813	33.6272 3350	33.3600 8599	33.0959 1642	40
41	34.8943 7254	34.6089 8988	34.3268 7335	34.0479 7952	33.7722 6554	41
42	35.6124 4072	35.3147 0070	35.0204 4446	34.7296 2462	34.4421 9451	42
43	36.3248 6884	36.0145 7921	35.7079 9947	35.4050 7807	35.1057 6427	43
44	37.0317 0121	36.7086 7360	36.3895 9055	36.0743 9611	35.7630 3518	44
45	37.7329 8177	37.3970 3167	37.0652 6944	36.7376 3446	36.4140 6704	45
46	38.4287 5413	38.0797 0083	37.7350 8743	37.3948 4835	37.0589 1906	46
47	39.1190 6156	38.7567 2809	38.3990 9535	38.0460 9250	37.6976 4992	47
48	39.8039 4698	39.4281 6009	39.0573 4359	38.6914 2114	38.3303 1771	48
49	40.4834 5298	40.0940 4307	39.7098 8212	39.3308 8800	38.9569 7998	49
50	41.1576 2180	40.7544 2288	40.3567 6047	39.9645 4633	39.5776 9375	50
51	41.8264 9538	41.4093 4500	40.9980 2772	40.5924 4888	40.1925 1548	51
52	42.4901 1530	42.0588 5455	41.6337 3256	41.2146 4794	40.8015 0109	52
53	43.1485 2283	42.7029 9624	42.2639 2324	41.8311 9532	41.4047 0599	53
54	43.8017 5891	43.3418 1446	42.8886 4757	42.4421 4234	42.0021 8505	54
55	44.4498 6415	43.9753 5318	43.5079 5298	43.0475 3990	42.5939 9262	55
56	45.0928 7886	44.6036 5605	44.1218 8647	43.6474 3838	43.1801 8254	56
57	45.7308 4302	45.2267 6633	44.7304 9465	44.2418 8774	43.7608 0813	57
58	46.3637 9630	45.8447 2694	45.3338 2369	44.8309 3748	44.3359 2221	58
59	46.9917 7805	46.4575 8043	45.9319 1939	45.4146 3664	44.9055 7709	59
60	47.6148 2734	47.0653 6902	46.5248 2716	45.9930 3383	45.4698 2461	60

TABLE IV

N	19/24	5/6	7/8	11/12	23/24	N
61	48.2329 8289	47.6681 3457	47.1125 9198	46.5661 7721	46.0287 1608	61
62	48.8462 8315	48.2659 1858	47.6952 5846	47.1341 1449	46.5823 0235	62
63	49.4547 6625	48.8587 6223	48.2728 7084	47.6968 9297	47.1306 3377	63
64	50.0584 7003	49.4467 0634	48.8454 7296	48.2545 5951	47.6737 6024	64
65	50.6574 3202	50.0297 9141	49.4131 0826	48.8071 6054	48.2117 3115	65
66	51.2516 8948	50.6080 5760	49.9758 1984	49.3547 4207	48.7445 9544	66
67	51.8412 7935	51.1815 4473	50.5336 5039	49.8973 4970	49.2724 0159	67
68	52.4262 3830	51.7502 9229	51.0866 4227	50.4350 2860	49.7951 9762	68
69	53.0066 0269	52.3143 3946	51.6348 3745	50.9678 2355	50.3130 3107	69
70	53.5824 0863	52.8737 2509	52.1782 7752	51.4957 7891	50.8259 4906	70
71	54.1536 9190	53.4284 8769	52.7170 0374	52.0189 3864	51.3339 9824	71
72	54.7204 8804	53.9786 6548	53.2510 5699	52.5373 4630	51.8372 2484	72
73	55.2828 3228	54.5242 9634	53.7804 7781	53.0510 4506	52.3356 7462	73
74	55.8407 5960	55.0654 1786	54.3053 0638	53.5600 7768	52.8293 9294	74
75	56.3943 0469	55.6020 6730	54.8255 8253	54.0644 8655	53.3184 2470	75
76	56.9435 0196	56.1342 8162	55.3413 4575	54.5643 1367	53.8028 1440	76
77	57.4883 8558	56.6620 9747	55.8526 3520	55.0596 0067	54.2826 0609	77
78	58.0289 8941	57.1855 5121	56.3594 8966	55.5503 8877	54.7578 4342	78
79	58.5653 4708	57.7046 7889	56.8619 4762	56.0367 1885	55.2285 6963	79
80	59.0974 9194	58.2195 1625	57.3600 4721	56.5186 3139	55.6948 2753	80
81	59.6254 5707	58.7300 9876	57.8538 2623	56.9961 6653	56.1566 5955	81
82	60.1492 7530	59.2364 6158	58.3433 2216	57.4693 6403	56.6141 0768	82
83	60.6689 7922	59.7386 3959	58.8285 7215	57.9382 6328	57.0672 1355	83
84	61.1846 0113	60.2366 6736	59.3096 1304	58.4029 0334	57.5160 1837	84
85	61.6961 7309	60.7305 7920	59.7864 8133	58.8633 2288	57.9605 6298	85
86	62.2037 2692	61.2204 0912	60.2592 1321	59.3195 6024	58.4008 8780	86
87	62.7072 9417	61.7061 9087	60.7278 4457	59.7716 5342	58.8370 3291	87
88	63.2069 0617	62.1879 5788	61.1924 1097	60.2196 4005	59.2690 3796	88
89	63.7025 9396	62.6657 4336	61.6529 4768	60.6635 5744	59.6969 4226	89
90	64.1943 8839	63.1395 8019	62.1094 8965	61.1034 4255	60.1207 8474	90
91	64.6823 2002	63.6095 0101	62.5620 7152	61.5393 3201	60.5406 0395	91
92	65.1664 1920	64.0755 3819	63.0107 2765	61.9712 6211	60.9564 3809	92
93	65.6467 1603	64.5377 2383	63.4554 9210	62.3992 6881	61.3683 2497	93
94	66.1232 4038	64.9960 8975	63.8963 9861	62.8233 8775	61.7763 0208	94
95	66.5960 2188	65.4506 6752	64.3334 8066	63.2436 5426	62.1804 0652	95
96	67.0650 8991	65.9014 8845	64.7667 7141	63.6601 0331	62.5806 7505	96
97	67.5304 7366	66.3485 8358	65.1963 0375	64.0727 6959	62.9771 4408	97
98	67.9922 0206	66.7919 8372	65.6221 1028	64.4816 8745	63.3698 4969	98
99	68.4503 0383	67.2317 1939	66.0442 2333	64.8868 9095	63.7588 2759	99
100	68.9048 0743	67.6678 2088	66.4626 7492	65.2884 1383	64.1441 1317	100
101	69.3557 4115	68.1003 1823	66.8774 9683	65.6862 8951	64.5257 4149	101
102	69.8031 3301	68.5292 4122	67.2887 2052	66.0805 5112	64.9037 4724	102
103	70.2470 1084	68.9546 1939	67.6963 7722	66.4712 3150	65.2781 6483	103
104	70.6874 0224	69.3764 8204	68.1004 9786	66.8583 6317	65.6490 2831	104
105	71.1243 3459	69.7948 5823	68.5011 1312	67.2419 7837	66.0163 7141	105
106	71.5578 3507	70.2097 7675	68.8982 5341	67.6221 0903	66.3802 2757	106
107	71.9879 3062	70.6212 6620	69.2919 4885	67.9987 8682	66.7406 2986	107
108	72.4146 4799	71.0293 5491	69.6822 2935	68.3720 4309	67.0976 1109	108
109	72.8380 1371	71.4340 7099	70.0691 2451	68.7419 0893	67.4512 0372	109
110	73.2580 5412	71.8354 4230	70.4526 6370	69.1084 1512	67.8014 3992	110
111	73.6747 9532	72.2334 9650	70.8328 7604	69.4715 9219	68.1483 5155	111
112	74.0882 6324	72.6282 6099	71.2097 9037	69.8314 7038	68.4919 7017	112
113	74.4984 8357	73.0197 6296	71.5834 3531	70.1880 7965	68.8323 2704	113
114	74.9054 8184	73.4080 2938	71.9538 3922	70.5414 4970	69.1694 5311	114
115	75.3092 8335	73.7930 8699	72.3210 3020	70.8916 0994	69.5033 7906	115
116	75.7099 1320	74.1749 6231	72.6850 3614	71.2385 8954	69.8341 3527	116
117	76.1073 9632	74.5536 8163	73.0458 8465	71.5824 1738	70.1617 5181	117
118	76.5017 5740	74.9292 7103	73.4036 0312	71.9231 2209	70.4862 5850	118
119	76.8930 2099	75.3017 5640	73.7582 1871	72.2607 3205	70.8076 8486	119
120	77.2812 1140	75.6711 6337	74.1097 5832	72.5952 7536	71.1260 6011	120

TABLE IV

N	19/24	5/6	7/8	11/12	23/24	N
121	77.6663 5277	76.0375 1739	74.4582 4864	72.9267 7987	71.4414 1324	121
122	78.0484 6906	76.4008 4369	74.8037 1613	73.2552 7320	71.7537 7291	122
123	78.4275 8402	76.7611 6730	75.1461 8699	73.5807 8269	72.0631 6756	123
124	78.8037 2122	77.1185 1302	75.4856 8723	73.9033 3545	72.3696 2531	124
125	79.1769 0407	77.4729 0548	75.8222 4261	74.2229 5833	72.6731 7406	125
126	79.5471 5575	77.8243 6907	76.1558 7867	74.5396 7795	72.9738 4142	126
127	79.9144 9930	78.1729 2800	76.4866 2074	74.8535 2068	73.2716 5472	127
128	80.2789 5755	78.5186 0628	76.8144 9391	75.1645 1265	73.5666 4108	128
129	80.6405 5317	78.8614 2772	77.1395 2309	75.4726 7975	73.8588 2732	129
130	80.9993 0864	79.2014 1592	77.4617 3292	75.7780 4765	74.1482 4002	130
131	81.3552 4628	79.5385 9430	77.7811 4788	76.0806 4176	74.4349 0551	131
132	81.7083 8820	79.8729 8608	78.0977 9220	76.3804 8730	74.7188 4986	132
133	82.0587 5638	80.2046 1430	78.4116 8991	76.6776 0921	75.0000 9891	133
134	82.4063 7260	80.5335 0178	78.7228 6484	76.9720 3225	75.2786 7825	134
135	82.7512 5847	80.8596 7119	79.0313 4061	77.2637 8093	75.5546 1321	135
136	83.0934 3544	81.1831 4498	79.3371 4063	77.5528 7953	75.8279 2889	136
137	83.4329 2479	81.5039 4544	79.6402 8811	77.8393 5214	76.0986 5016	137
138	83.7697 4762	81.8220 9465	79.9408 0606	78.1232 2259	76.3668 0164	138
139	84.1039 2488	82.1376 1453	80.2387 1728	78.4045 1454	76.6324 0773	139
140	84.4354 7735	82.4505 2680	80.5340 4440	78.6832 5141	76.8954 9260	140
141	84.7644 2565	82.7608 5303	80.8268 0981	78.9594 5639	77.1560 8016	141
142	85.0907 9022	83.0686 1457	81.1170 3575	79.2331 5249	77.4141 9413	142
143	85.4145 9137	83.3738 3263	81.4047 4423	79.5043 6250	77.6698 5799	143
144	85.7358 4924	83.6765 2823	81.6899 5711	79.7731 0900	77.9230 9500	144
145	86.0545 8378	83.9767 2221	81.9726 9602	80.0394 1437	78.1739 2819	145
146	86.3708 1483	84.2744 3525	82.2529 8242	80.3033 0078	78.4223 8038	146
147	86.6845 6205	84.5696 8786	82.5308 3759	80.5647 9020	78.6684 7417	147
148	86.9958 4494	84.8625 0035	82.8062 8262	80.8239 0441	78.9122 3194	148
149	87.3046 8287	85.1528 9291	83.0793 3841	81.0806 6498	79.1536 7588	149
150	87.6110 9503	85.4408 8553	83.3500 2569	81.3350 9330	79.3928 2795	150
151	87.9151 0049	85.7264 9805	83.6183 6499	81.5872 1053	79.6297 0990	151
152	88.2167 1813	86.0097 5013	83.8843 7670	81.8370 3769	79.8643 4327	152
153	88.5159 6673	86.2906 6129	84.1480 8099	82.0845 9556	80.0967 4942	153
154	88.8128 6488	86.5692 5086	84.4094 9788	82.3299 0477	80.3269 4949	154
155	89.1074 3106	86.8455 3805	84.6686 4722	82.5729 8573	80.5549 6442	155
156	89.3996 8356	87.1195 4186	84.9255 4867	82.8138 5869	80.7808 1494	156
157	89.6896 4057	87.3912 8119	85.1802 2173	83.0525 4371	81.0045 2161	157
158	89.9773 2012	87.6607 7473	85.4326 8573	83.2890 6065	81.2261 0477	158
159	90.2627 4010	87.9280 4106	85.6829 5983	83.5234 2922	81.4455 8458	159
160	90.5459 1824	88.1930 9857	85.9310 6303	83.7556 6892	81.6629 8102	160
161	90.8268 7217	88.4559 6552	86.1770 1415	83.9857 9910	81.8783 1384	161
162	91.1056 1935	88.7166 6002	86.4208 3187	84.2138 3891	82.0916 0265	162
163	91.3821 7712	88.9752 0002	86.6625 3470	84.4398 0734	82.3028 6684	163
164	91.6565 6266	89.2316 0333	86.9021 4096	84.6637 2321	82.5121 2564	164
165	91.9287 9305	89.4858 8760	87.1396 6886	84.8856 0516	82.7193 9807	165
166	92.1988 8521	89.7380 7034	87.3751 3642	85.1054 7167	82.9247 0300	166
167	92.4668 5593	89.9881 6894	87.6085 6150	85.3233 4105	83.1280 5910	167
168	92.7327 2188	90.2362 0060	87.8399 6184	85.5392 3142	83.3294 8487	168
169	92.9964 9960	90.4821 8241	88.0693 5498	85.7531 6078	83.5289 9864	169
170	93.2582 0547	90.7261 3132	88.2967 5835	85.9651 4694	83.7266 1854	170
171	93.5178 5578	90.9680 6412	88.5221 8919	86.1752 0753	83.9223 6257	171
172	93.7754 6667	91.2079 9747	88.7456 6462	86.3833 6007	84.1162 4852	172
173	94.0310 5416	91.4459 4790	88.9672 0161	86.5896 2187	84.3082 9403	173
174	94.2846 3413	91.6819 3181	89.1868 1696	86.7940 1011	84.4985 1658	174
175	94.5362 2237	91.9159 6543	89.4045 2735	86.9965 4181	84.6869 3347	175
176	94.7858 3452	92.1480 6489	89.6203 4929	87.1972 3383	84.8735 6184	176
177	95.0334 8609	92.3782 4617	89.8342 9917	87.3961 0289	85.0584 1866	177
178	95.2791 9248	92.6065 2513	90.0463 9323	87.5931 6554	85.2415 2075	178
179	95.5229 6897	92.8329 1748	90.2566 4757	87.7884 3819	85.4228 8477	179
180	95.7648 3073	93.0574 3882	90.4650 7813	87.9819 3710	85.6025 2722	180

TABLE IV

N	19/24	5/6	7/8	11/12	23/24	N
181	96.0047 9279	93.2801 0462	90.6717 0075	88.1736 7838	85.7804 6444	181
182	96.2428 7007	93.5009 3020	90.8765 3110	88.3636 7800	85.9567 1261	182
183	96.4790 7737	93.7199 3078	91.0795 8474	88.5519 5177	86.1312 8776	183
184	96.7134 2939	93.9371 2143	91.2808 7706	88.7385 1538	86.3042 0579	184
185	96.9459 4069	94.1525 1712	91.4804 2336	88.9233 8436	86.4754 8242	185
186	97.1766 2574	94.3661 3268	91.6782 3877	89.1065 7409	86.6451 3323	186
187	97.4054 9887	94.5779 8283	91.8743 3831	89.2880 9985	86.8131 7365	187
188	97.6325 7432	94.7880 8214	92.0687 3686	89.4679 7673	86.9796 1896	188
189	97.8578 6622	94.9964 4510	92.2614 4918	89.6462 1971	87.1444 8432	189
190	98.0813 8856	95.2030 8605	92.4524 8989	89.8228 4365	87.3077 8472	190
191	98.3031 5525	95.4080 1922	92.6418 7350	89.9978 6323	87.4695 3501	191
192	98.5231 8007	95.6112 5873	92.8296 1438	90.1712 9305	87.6297 4990	192
193	98.7414 7671	95.8128 1858	93.0157 2677	90.3431 4753	87.7884 4398	193
194	98.9580 5875	96.0127 1264	93.2002 2480	90.5134 4098	87.9456 3168	194
195	99.1729 3964	96.2109 5468	93.3831 2248	90.6821 8760	88.1013 2729	195
196	99.3861 3276	96.4075 5836	93.5644 3368	90.8494 0142	88.2555 4499	196
197	99.5976 5135	96.6025 3722	93.7441 7218	91.0150 9637	88.4082 9879	197
198	99.8075 0858	96.7959 0468	93.9223 5160	91.1792 8624	88.5596 0260	198
199	100.0157 1748	96.9876 7406	94.0989 8548	91.3419 8472	88.7094 7018	199
200	100.2222 9101	97.1778 5858	94.2740 8721	91.5032 0534	88.8579 1516	200
201	100.4272 4201	97.3664 7131	94.4476 7010	91.6629 6152	89.0049 5104	201
202	100.6305 8322	97.5535 2527	94.6197 4731	91.8212 6658	89.1505 9121	202
203	100.8323 2730	97.7390 3333	94.7903 3191	91.9781 3369	89.2948 4891	203
204	101.0324 8678	97.9230 0826	94.9594 3684	92.1335 7591	89.4377 3726	204
205	101.2310 7411	98.1054 6273	95.1270 7493	92.2876 0618	89.5792 6926	205
206	101.4281 0164	98.2864 0932	95.2932 5891	92.4402 3734	89.7194 5779	206
207	101.6235 8162	98.4658 6049	95.4580 0140	92.5914 8209	89.8583 1560	207
208	101.8175 2620	98.6438 2858	95.6213 1490	92.7413 5302	89.9958 5532	208
209	102.0099 4745	98.8203 2587	95.7832 1179	92.8898 6261	90.1320 8946	209
210	102.2008 5733	98.9953 6450	95.9437 0438	93.0370 2323	90.2670 3042	210
211	102.3902 6771	99.1689 5652	96.1028 0484	93.1828 4713	90.4006 9047	211
212	102.5781 9037	99.3411 1391	96.2605 2524	93.3273 4646	90.5330 8177	212
213	102.7646 3699	99.5118 4850	96.4168 7756	93.4705 3324	90.6642 1636	213
214	102.9496 1918	99.6811 7207	96.5718 7367	93.6124 1939	90.7941 0618	214
215	103.1331 4842	99.8490 9627	96.7255 2532	93.7530 1674	90.9227 6303	215
216	103.3152 3613	100.0156 3266	96.8778 4419	93.8923 3698	91.0501 9863	216
217	103.4958 9364	100.1807 9272	97.0288 4182	94.0303 9173	91.1764 2456	217
218	103.6751 3218	100.3445 8782	97.1785 2968	94.1671 9246	91.3014 5231	218
219	103.8529 6289	100.5070 2925	97.3269 1914	94.3027 5058	91.4252 9325	219
220	104.0293 9683	100.6681 2818	97.4740 2145	94.4370 7737	91.5479 5865	220
221	104.2044 4497	100.8278 9571	97.6198 4779	94.5701 8402	91.6694 5966	221
222	104.3781 1820	100.9863 4286	97.7644 0921	94.7020 8160	91.7898 0734	222
223	104.5504 2732	101.1434 8052	97.9077 1668	94.8327 8111	91.9090 1263	223
224	104.7213 8304	101.2993 1952	98.0497 8110	94.9622 9342	92.0270 8639	224
225	104.8909 9599	101.4538 7060	98.1906 1323	95.0906 2932	92.1440 3934	225
226	105.0592 7671	101.6071 4440	98.3302 2378	95.2177 9949	92.2598 8214	226
227	105.2262 3568	101.7591 5147	98.4686 2332	95.3438 1452	92.3746 2531	227
228	105.3918 8327	101.9099 0228	98.6058 2238	95.4686 8491	92.4882 7930	228
229	105.5562 2979	102.0594 0722	98.7418 3135	95.5924 2105	92.6008 5445	229
230	105.7192 8544	102.2076 7659	98.8766 6057	95.7150 3325	92.7123 6099	230
231	105.8810 6038	102.3547 2058	99.0103 2027	95.8365 3171	92.8228 0907	231
232	106.0415 6466	102.5005 4934	99.1428 2059	95.9569 2655	92.9322 0874	232
233	106.2008 0826	102.6451 7290	99.2741 7159	96.0762 2779	93.0405 6994	233
234	106.3588 0109	102.7886 0122	99.4043 8323	96.1944 4538	93.1479 0254	234
235	106.5155 5296	102.9308 4418	99.5334 6541	96.3115 8914	93.2542 1630	235
236	106.6710 7363	103.0719 1159	99.6614 2792	96.4276 6884	93.3595 2089	236
237	106.8253 7276	103.2118 1314	99.7882 8046	96.5426 9415	93.4638 2590	237
238	106.9784 5995	103.3505 5849	99.9140 3268	96.6566 7463	93.5671 4080	238
239	107.1303 4472	103.4881 5718	100.0386 9410	96.7696 1978	93.6694 7499	239
240	107.2810 3652	103.6246 1869	100.1622 7421	96.8815 3901	93.7708 3780	240

TABLE IV

N	19/24	5/6	7/8	11/12	23/24	N
241	107.4305 4470	103.7599 5242	100.2847 8236	96.9924 4163	93.8712 3843	241
242	107.5788 7858	103.8941 6769	100.4062 2787	97.1023 3687	93.9706 8602	242
243	107.7260 4737	104.0272 7374	100.5266 1994	97.2112 3389	94.0691 8962	243
244	107.8720 6023	104.1592 7975	100.6459 6772	97.3191 4176	94.1667 5819	244
245	108.0169 2623	104.2901 9479	100.7642 8027	97.4260 6946	94.2634 0060	245
246	108.1606 5438	104.4200 2789	100.8815 6656	97.5320 2589	94.3591 2565	246
247	108.3032 5363	104.5487 8799	100.9978 3550	97.6370 1987	94.4539 4203	247
248	108.4447 3282	104.6764 8396	101.1130 9591	97.7410 6015	94.5478 5839	248
249	108.5851 0078	104.8031 2458	101.2273 5654	97.8441 5540	94.6408 8326	249
250	108.7243 6621	104.9287 1860	101.3406 2607	97.9463 1418	94.7330 2510	250
251	108.8625 3779	105.0532 7464	101.4529 1308	98.0475 4502	94.8242 9230	251
252	108.9996 2410	105.1768 0130	101.5642 2610	98.1478 5634	94.9146 9316	252
253	109.1356 3366	105.2993 0707	101.6745 7358	98.2472 5649	95.0042 3590	253
254	109.2705 7494	105.4208 0040	101.7839 6390	98.3457 5374	95.0929 2867	254
255	109.4044 5633	105.5412 8965	101.8924 0535	98.4433 5631	95.1807 7953	255
256	109.5372 8615	105.6607 8313	101.9999 0617	98.5400 7231	95.2677 9648	256
257	109.6690 7266	105.7792 8905	102.1064 7452	98.6359 0981	95.3539 8743	257
258	109.7998 2405	105.8968 1559	102.2121 1848	98.7308 7677	95.4393 6023	258
259	109.9295 4846	106.0133 7083	102.3168 4608	98.8249 8111	95.5239 2264	259
260	110.0582 5395	106.1289 6281	102.4206 6526	98.9182 3066	95.6076 8235	260
261	110.1859 4852	106.2435 9948	102.5235 8390	99.0106 3319	95.6906 4698	261
262	110.3126 4012	106.3572 8874	102.6256 0981	99.1021 9639	95.7728 2408	262
263	110.4383 3662	106.4700 3842	102.7267 5074	99.1929 2789	95.8542 2113	263
264	110.5630 4584	106.5818 5628	102.8270 1437	99.2828 3523	95.9348 4553	264
265	110.6867 7554	106.6927 5003	102.9264 0829	99.3719 2591	96.0147 0461	265
266	110.8095 3340	106.8027 2731	103.0249 4007	99.4602 0734	96.0938 0564	266
267	110.9313 2706	106.9117 9568	103.1226 1717	99.5476 8688	96.1721 5581	267
268	111.0521 6409	107.0199 6265	103.2194 4701	99.6343 7180	96.2497 6226	268
269	111.1720 5201	107.1272 3569	103.3154 3693	99.7202 6933	96.3266 3203	269
270	111.2909 9828	107.2336 2217	103.4105 9423	99.8053 8662	96.4027 7213	270
271	111.4090 1028	107.3391 2943	103.5049 2613	99.8897 3076	96.4781 8949	271
272	111.5260 9536	107.4437 6472	103.5984 3978	99.9733 0876	96.5528 9095	272
273	111.6422 6079	107.5475 3526	103.6911 4229	100.0561 2759	96.6268 8332	273
274	111.7575 1381	107.6504 4819	103.7830 4068	100.1381 9415	96.7001 7332	274
275	111.8718 6157	107.7525 1060	103.8741 4194	100.2195 1526	96.7727 6763	275
276	111.9853 1119	107.8537 2952	103.9644 5298	100.3000 9769	96.8446 7285	276
277	112.0978 6972	107.9541 1193	104.0539 8065	100.3799 4817	96.9158 9552	277
278	112.2095 4417	108.0536 6472	104.1427 3174	100.4590 7333	96.9864 4211	278
279	112.3203 4146	108.1523 9476	104.2307 1300	100.5374 7977	97.0563 1906	279
280	112.4302 6850	108.2503 0886	104.3179 3111	100.6151 7400	97.1255 3270	280
281	112.5393 3212	108.3474 1374	104.4043 9267	100.6921 6251	97.1940 8935	281
282	112.6475 3911	108.4437 1611	104.4901 0426	100.7684 5171	97.2619 9522	282
283	112.7548 9618	108.5392 2259	104.5750 7238	100.8440 4793	97.3292 5652	283
284	112.8614 1002	108.6339 3975	104.6593 0347	100.9189 5749	97.3958 7934	284
285	112.9670 8724	108.7278 7414	104.7428 0394	100.9931 8661	97.4618 6975	285
286	113.0719 3443	108.8210 3220	104.8255 8011	101.0667 4148	97.5272 3376	286
287	113.1759 5809	108.9134 2036	104.9076 3828	101.1396 2822	97.5919 7731	287
288	113.2791 6470	109.0050 4499	104.9889 8466	101.2118 5291	97.6561 0630	288
289	113.3815 6068	109.0959 1239	105.0696 2544	101.2834 2154	97.7196 2654	289
290	113.4831 5239	109.1860 2881	105.1495 6673	101.3543 4009	97.7825 4383	290
291	113.5839 4615	109.2754 0048	105.2288 1460	101.4246 1446	97.8448 6388	291
292	113.6839 4823	109.3640 3353	105.3073 7507	101.4942 5050	97.9065 9237	292
293	113.7831 6484	109.4519 3408	105.3852 5410	101.5632 5400	97.9677 3491	293
294	113.8816 0216	109.5391 0818	105.4624 5759	101.6316 3072	98.0282 9707	294
295	113.9792 6630	109.6255 6183	105.5389 9142	101.6993 8634	98.0882 8434	295
296	114.0761 6334	109.7113 0099	105.6148 6138	101.7665 2652	98.1477 0220	296
297	114.1722 9930	109.7963 3156	105.6900 7324	101.8330 5683	98.2065 5603	297
298	114.2676 8017	109.8806 5940	105.7646 3270	101.8989 8282	98.2648 5121	298
299	114.3623 1187	109.9642 9031	105.8385 4543	101.9643 0998	98.3225 9303	299
300	114.4562 0028	110.0472 3006	105.9118 1703	102.0290 4375	98.3797 8674	300

TABLE IV

N	19/24	5/6	7/8	11/12	23/24	N
301	114.5493 5125	110.1294 8436	105.9844 5307	102.0931 8951	98.4364 3754	301
302	114.6417 7057	110.2110 5887	106.0564 5905	102.1567 5261	98.4925 5060	302
303	114.7334 6398	110.2919 5921	106.1278 4045	102.2197 3834	98.5481 3101	303
304	114.8244 3718	110.3721 9095	106.1986 0267	102.2821 5195	98.6031 8383	304
305	114.9146 9584	110.4517 5962	106.2687 5110	102.3439 9863	98.6577 1407	305
306	115.0042 4556	110.5306 7070	106.3382 9105	102.4052 8353	98.7117 2669	306
307	115.0930 9192	110.6089 2962	106.4072 2781	102.4660 1175	98.7652 2661	307
308	115.1812 4043	110.6865 4177	106.4755 6660	102.5261 8836	98.8182 1868	308
309	115.2686 9658	110.7635 1250	106.5433 1262	102.5858 1836	98.8707 0773	309
310	115.3554 6581	110.8398 4710	106.6104 7100	102.6449 0671	98.9226 9853	310
311	115.4415 5351	110.9155 5085	106.6770 4684	102.7034 5835	98.9741 9582	311
312	115.5269 6504	110.9906 2894	106.7430 4519	102.7614 7813	99.0252 0428	312
313	115.6117 0570	111.0650 8655	106.8084 7107	102.8189 7090	99.0757 2855	313
314	115.6957 8077	111.1389 2881	106.8733 2944	102.8759 4143	99.1257 7322	314
315	115.7791 9547	111.2121 6080	106.9376 2522	102.9323 9448	99.1753 4285	315
316	115.8619 5500	111.2847 8757	107.0013 6329	102.9883 3475	99.2244 4195	316
317	115.9440 6449	111.3568 1412	107.0645 4849	103.0437 6689	99.2730 7498	317
318	116.0255 2905	111.4282 4541	107.1271 8561	103.0986 9551	99.3212 4637	318
319	116.1063 5375	111.4990 8636	107.1892 7942	103.1531 2520	99.3689 6050	319
320	116.1865 4361	111.5693 4184	107.2508 3462	103.2070 6047	99.4162 2171	320
321	116.2661 0362	111.6390 1670	107.3118 5588	103.2605 0584	99.4630 3430	321
322	116.3450 3873	111.7081 1574	107.3723 4783	103.3134 6574	99.5094 0252	322
323	116.4233 5385	111.7766 4371	107.4323 1508	103.3659 4458	99.5553 3060	323
324	116.5010 5384	111.8446 0533	107.4917 6216	103.4179 4673	99.6008 2272	324
325	116.5781 4354	111.9120 0529	107.5506 9359	103.4694 7653	99.6458 8301	325
326	116.6546 2773	111.9788 4822	107.6091 1384	103.5205 3826	99.6905 1557	326
327	116.7305 1119	112.0451 3873	107.6670 2735	103.5711 3618	99.7347 2446	327
328	116.8057 9862	112.1108 8138	107.7244 3852	103.6212 7450	99.7785 1370	328
329	116.8804 9470	112.1760 8071	107.7813 5169	103.6709 5739	99.8218 8728	329
330	116.9546 0408	112.2407 4120	107.8377 7119	103.7201 8899	99.8648 4914	330
331	117.0281 3138	112.3048 6731	107.8937 0130	103.7689 7340	99.9074 0320	331
332	117.1010 8115	112.3684 6345	107.9491 4627	103.8173 1468	99.9495 5331	332
333	117.1734 5794	112.4315 3400	108.0041 1031	103.8652 1686	99.9913 0332	333
334	117.2452 6625	112.4940 8330	108.0585 9758	103.9126 8393	100.0326 5702	334
335	117.3165 1054	112.5561 1567	108.1126 1222	103.9597 1983	100.0736 1818	335
336	117.3871 9525	112.6176 3538	108.1661 5834	104.0063 2848	100.1141 9052	336
337	117.4573 2476	112.6786 4665	108.2192 3999	104.0525 1377	100.1543 7774	337
338	117.5269 0344	112.7391 5371	108.2718 6120	104.0982 7954	100.1941 8348	338
339	117.5959 3562	112.7991 6070	108.3240 2598	104.1436 2961	100.2336 1137	339
340	117.6644 2558	112.8586 7177	108.3757 3827	104.1885 6773	100.2726 6500	340
341	117.7323 7759	112.9176 9101	108.4270 0200	104.2330 9767	100.3113 4791	341
342	117.7997 9587	112.9762 2249	108.4778 2106	104.2772 2313	100.3496 6364	342
343	117.8666 8462	113.0342 7024	108.5281 9932	104.3209 4777	100.3876 1565	343
344	117.9330 4799	113.0918 3825	108.5781 4059	104.3642 7525	100.4252 0742	344
345	117.9988 9011	113.1489 3050	108.6276 4866	104.4072 0917	100.4624 4234	345
346	118.0642 1507	113.2055 5091	108.6767 2730	104.4497 5310	100.4993 2382	346
347	118.1290 2694	113.2617 0338	108.7253 8022	104.4919 1058	100.5358 5521	347
348	118.1933 2975	113.3173 9178	108.7736 1113	104.5336 8513	100.5720 3983	348
349	118.2571 2749	113.3726 1995	108.8214 2367	104.5750 8023	100.6078 8097	349
350	118.3204 2413	113.4273 9168	108.8688 2148	104.6160 9932	100.6433 8189	350
351	118.3832 2361	113.4817 1076	108.9158 0816	104.6567 4582	100.6785 4583	351
352	118.4455 2984	113.5355 8092	108.9623 8727	104.6970 2311	100.7133 7598	352
353	118.5073 4667	113.5890 0587	109.0085 6235	104.7369 3454	100.7478 7550	353
354	118.5686 7797	113.6419 8929	109.0543 3690	104.7764 8344	100.7820 4755	354
355	118.6295 2755	113.6945 3484	109.0997 1440	104.8156 7311	100.8158 9522	355
356	118.6898 9918	113.7466 4612	109.1446 9829	104.8545 0679	100.8494 2159	356
357	118.7497 9662	113.7983 2673	109.1892 9199	104.8929 8774	100.8826 2973	357
358	118.8092 2360	113.8495 8023	109.2334 9887	104.9311 1915	100.9155 2263	358
359	118.8681 8381	113.9004 1014	109.2773 2230	104.9689 0419	100.9481 0331	359
360	118.9266 8092	113.9508 1998	109.3207 6560	105.0063 4602	100.9803 7472	360

TABLE IV

N	1	1 1/8	1 1/4	1 3/8	1 1/2	N
1	0.9900 9901	0.9888 7515	0.9876 5432	0.9864 3650	0.9852 2167	1
2	1.9703 9506	1.9667 4923	1.9631 1538	1.9594 9346	1.9558 8342	2
3	2.9409 8521	2.9337 4460	2.9265 3371	2.9193 5237	2.9122 0042	3
4	3.9019 6555	3.8899 8230	3.8780 5798	3.8661 9222	3.8543 8465	4
5	4.8534 3124	4.8355 8200	4.8178 3504	4.8001 8962	4.7826 4497	5
6	5.7954 7647	5.7706 6205	5.7460 0992	5.7215 1874	5.6971 8717	6
7	6.7281 9453	6.6953 3948	6.6627 2585	6.6303 5140	6.5982 1396	7
8	7.6516 7775	7.6097 3002	7.5681 2429	7.5268 5712	7.4859 2508	8
9	8.5660 1758	8.5139 4810	8.4623 4498	8.4112 0308	8.3605 1732	9
10	9.4713 0453	9.4081 0690	9.3455 2591	9.2835 5421	9.2221 8455	10
11	10.3676 2825	10.2923 1832	10.2178 0337	10.1440 7320	10.0711 1779	11
12	11.2550 7747	11.1666 9302	11.0793 1197	10.9929 2054	10.9075 0521	12
13	12.1337 4007	12.0313 4044	11.9301 8466	11.8302 5454	11.7315 3222	13
14	13.0037 0304	12.8863 6880	12.7705 5275	12.6562 3136	12.5433 8150	14
15	13.8650 5252	13.7318 8509	13.6005 4592	13.4710 0504	13.3432 3301	15
16	14.7178 7378	14.5679 9514	14.4202 9227	14.2747 2754	14.1312 6405	16
17	15.5622 5127	15.3948 0360	15.2299 1829	15.0675 4874	14.9076 4931	17
18	16.3982 6858	16.2124 1395	16.0295 4893	15.8496 1651	15.6725 6089	18
19	17.2260 0850	17.0209 2850	16.8193 0759	16.6210 7671	16.4261 6837	19
20	18.0455 5297	17.8204 4845	17.5993 1613	17.3820 7320	17.1686 3879	20
21	18.8569 8313	18.6110 7387	18.3696 9495	18.1327 4792	17.9001 3673	21
22	19.6603 7934	19.3929 0371	19.1305 6291	18.8732 4086	18.6208 2437	22
23	20.4558 2113	20.1660 3580	19.8820 3744	19.6036 9012	19.3308 6145	23
24	21.2433 8726	20.9305 6693	20.6242 3451	20.3242 3193	20.0304 0537	24
25	22.0231 5570	21.6865 9276	21.3572 6865	21.0350 0067	20.7196 1120	25
26	22.7952 0366	22.4342 0792	22.0812 5299	21.7361 2890	21.3986 3172	26
27	23.5596 0759	23.1735 0598	22.7962 9925	22.4277 4737	22.0676 1746	27
28	24.3164 4316	23.9045 7946	23.5025 1778	23.1099 8508	22.7267 1671	28
29	25.0657 8530	24.6275 1986	24.2000 1756	23.7829 6925	23.3760 7558	29
30	25.8077 0822	25.3424 1766	24.8889 0623	24.4468 2540	24.0158 3801	30
31	26.5422 8537	26.0493 6233	25.5692 9010	25.1016 7734	24.6461 4582	31
32	27.2695 8947	26.7484 4236	26.2412 7418	25.7476 4719	25.2671 3874	32
33	27.9896 9255	27.4397 4522	26.9049 6215	26.3848 5543	25.8789 5442	33
34	28.7026 6589	28.1233 5745	27.5604 5644	27.0134 2089	26.4817 2849	34
35	29.4085 8009	28.7993 6460	28.2078 5822	27.6334 6080	27.0755 9458	35
36	30.1075 0504	29.4678 5127	28.8472 6737	28.2450 9080	27.6606 8431	36
37	30.7995 0994	30.1289 0114	29.4787 8259	28.8484 2496	28.2371 2740	37
38	31.4846 6330	30.7825 9692	30.1025 0133	29.4435 7579	28.8050 5163	38
39	32.1630 3298	31.4290 2044	30.7185 1983	30.0306 5430	29.3645 8288	39
40	32.8346 8611	32.0682 5260	31.3269 3316	30.6097 6996	29.9158 4520	40
41	33.4996 8922	32.7003 7340	31.9278 3522	31.1810 3079	30.4589 6079	41
42	34.1581 0814	33.3254 6195	32.5213 1874	31.7445 4332	30.9940 5004	42
43	34.8100 0806	33.9435 9649	33.1074 7530	32.3004 1264	31.5212 3157	43
44	35.4554 5352	34.5548 5438	33.6863 9536	32.8487 4243	32.0406 2223	44
45	36.0945 0844	35.1593 1212	34.2581 6825	33.3896 3495	32.5523 3718	45
46	36.7272 3608	35.7570 4536	34.8228 8222	33.9231 9108	33.0564 8983	46
47	37.3536 9909	36.3481 2891	35.3806 2442	34.4495 1031	33.5531 9195	47
48	37.9739 5949	36.9326 3674	35.9314 8091	34.9686 9081	34.0425 5365	48
49	38.5880 7871	37.5106 4202	36.4755 3670	35.4808 2941	34.5246 8339	49
50	39.1961 1753	38.0822 1708	37.0128 7575	35.9860 2161	34.9996 8807	50
51	39.7981 3617	38.6474 3345	37.5435 8099	36.4843 6164	35.4676 7298	51
52	40.3941 9423	39.2063 6188	38.0677 3431	36.9759 4243	35.9287 4185	52
53	40.9843 5072	39.7590 7232	38.5854 1660	37.4608 5566	36.3829 9690	53
54	41.5686 6408	40.3056 3394	39.0967 0776	37.9391 9178	36.8305 3882	54
55	42.1471 9216	40.8461 1514	39.6016 8667	38.4110 3998	37.2714 6681	55
56	42.7199 9224	41.3805 8358	40.1004 3128	38.8764 8826	37.7058 7863	56
57	43.2871 2102	41.9091 0613	40.5930 1855	39.3356 2344	38.1338 7058	57
58	43.8486 3468	42.4317 4896	41.0795 2449	39.7885 3114	38.5555 3751	58
59	44.4045 8879	42.9485 7746	41.5600 2419	40.2352 9582	38.9709 7292	59
60	44.9550 3841	43.4596 5633	42.0345 9179	40.6760 0081	39.3802 6889	60

TABLE IV

N	1	1 1/8	1 1/4	1 3/8	1 1/2	N
61	45.5000 3803	43.9650 4952	42.5033 0054	41.1107 2829	39.7835 1614	61
62	46.0396 4161	44.4648 2029	42.9662 2275	41.5395 5935	40.1808 0408	62
63	46.5739 0258	44.9590 3119	43.4234 2988	41.9625 7396	40.5722 2077	63
64	47.1028 7385	45.4477 4407	43.8749 9247	42.3798 5101	40.9578 5298	64
65	47.6266 0777	45.9310 2009	44.3209 8022	42.7914 6832	41.3377 8618	65
66	48.1451 5621	46.4089 1975	44.7614 6195	43.1975 0266	41.7121 0461	66
67	48.6585 7050	46.8815 0284	45.1965 0563	43.5980 2975	42.0808 9125	67
68	49.1669 0149	47.3488 2852	45.6261 7840	43.9931 2429	42.4442 2783	68
69	49.6701 9949	47.8109 5527	46.0505 4656	44.3828 5997	42.8021 9490	69
70	50.1685 1435	48.2679 4094	46.4696 7562	44.7673 0946	43.1548 7183	70
71	50.6618 9539	48.7198 4270	46.8836 3024	45.1465 4448	43.5023 3678	71
72	51.1503 9148	49.1667 1714	47.2924 7431	45.5206 3573	43.8446 6677	72
73	51.6340 5097	49.6086 2016	47.6962 7093	45.8896 5300	44.1819 3771	73
74	52.1129 2175	50.0456 0708	48.0950 8240	46.2536 6511	44.5142 2434	74
75	52.5870 5124	50.4777 3259	48.4889 7027	46.6127 3994	44.8416 0034	75
76	53.0564 8638	50.9050 5077	48.8779 9533	46.9669 4445	45.1641 3826	76
77	53.5212 7364	51.3276 1510	49.2622 1761	47.3163 4471	45.4819 0962	77
78	53.9814 5905	51.7454 7847	49.6416 9640	47.6610 0588	45.7949 8485	78
79	54.4370 8817	52.1586 9317	50.0164 9027	48.0009 9224	46.1034 3335	79
80	54.8882 0611	52.5673 1092	50.3866 5706	48.3363 6719	46.4073 2349	80
81	55.3348 5753	52.9713 8286	50.7522 5389	48.6671 9328	46.7067 2265	81
82	55.7770 8666	53.3709 5957	51.1133 3717	48.9935 3221	47.0016 9720	82
83	56.2149 3729	53.7660 9104	51.4699 6264	49.3154 4484	47.2923 1251	83
84	56.6484 5276	54.1568 2674	51.8221 8532	49.6329 9122	47.5786 3301	84
85	57.0776 7600	54.5432 1557	52.1700 5958	49.9462 3055	47.8607 2218	85
86	57.5026 4951	54.9253 0588	52.5136 3909	50.2552 2125	48.1386 4254	86
87	57.9234 1535	55.3031 4549	52.8529 7688	50.5600 2096	48.4124 5571	87
88	58.3400 1520	55.6767 8169	53.1881 2531	50.8606 8653	48.6822 2237	88
89	58.7524 9030	56.0462 6126	53.5191 3611	51.1572 7401	48.9480 0234	89
90	59.1608 8148	56.4116 3041	53.8460 6036	51.4498 3873	49.2098 5452	90
91	59.5652 2919	56.7729 3490	54.1689 4850	51.7384 3524	49.4678 3696	91
92	59.9655 7346	57.1302 1992	54.4878 5037	52.0231 1738	49.7220 0686	92
93	60.3619 5392	57.4835 3021	54.8028 1518	52.3039 3823	49.9724 2055	93
94	60.7544 0982	57.8329 0997	55.1138 9154	52.5809 5016	50.2191 3355	94
95	61.1429 8002	58.1784 0294	55.4211 2744	52.8542 0484	50.4622 0054	95
96	61.5277 0299	58.5200 5235	55.7245 7031	53.1237 5324	50.7016 7541	96
97	61.9086 1682	58.8579 0096	56.0242 6698	53.3896 4561	50.9376 1124	97
98	62.2857 5923	59.1919 9106	56.3202 6368	53.6519 3155	51.1700 6034	98
99	62.6591 6755	59.5223 6446	56.6126 0610	53.9106 5998	51.3990 7422	99
100	63.0288 7877	59.8490 6251	56.9013 3936	54.1658 7914	51.6247 0367	100
101	63.3949 2947	60.1721 2609	57.1865 0801	54.4176 3664	51.8469 9869	101
102	63.7573 5591	60.4915 9564	57.4681 5606	54.6659 7942	52.0660 0856	102
103	64.1161 9397	60.8075 1114	57.7463 2697	54.9109 5380	52.2817 8183	103
104	64.4714 7918	61.1199 1213	58.0210 6368	55.1526 0548	52.4943 6634	104
105	64.8232 4671	61.4288 3770	58.2924 0857	55.3909 7951	52.7038 0920	105
106	65.1715 3140	61.7343 2653	58.5604 0353	55.6261 2035	52.9101 5685	106
107	65.5163 6772	62.0364 1684	58.8250 8990	55.8580 7187	53.1134 5502	107
108	65.8577 8983	62.3351 4644	59.0865 0855	56.0868 7730	53.3137 4879	108
109	66.1958 3151	62.6305 5273	59.3446 9980	56.3125 7934	53.5110 8255	109
110	66.5305 2625	62.9226 7266	59.5997 0350	56.5352 2006	53.7055 0005	110
111	66.8619 0718	63.2115 4280	59.8515 5902	56.7548 4100	53.8970 4438	111
112	67.1900 0710	63.4971 9931	60.1003 0520	56.9714 8311	54.0857 5801	112
113	67.5148 5852	63.7796 7793	60.3459 8045	57.1851 8679	54.2716 8277	113
114	67.8364 9358	64.0590 1402	60.5886 2266	57.3959 9190	54.4548 5987	114
115	68.1549 4414	64.3352 4255	60.8282 6930	57.6039 3775	54.6353 2993	115
116	68.4702 4172	64.6083 9807	61.0649 5733	57.8090 6314	54.8131 3293	116
117	68.7824 1755	64.8785 1478	61.2987 2329	58.0114 0630	54.9883 0831	117
118	69.0915 0252	65.1456 2648	61.5296 0325	58.2110 0498	55.1608 9488	118
119	69.3975 2725	65.4097 6660	61.7576 3284	58.4078 9641	55.3309 3092	119
120	69.7005 2203	65.6709 6821	61.9828 4725	58.6021 1729	55.4984 5411	120

TABLE IV

N	1	1 1/8	1 1/4	1 3/8	1 1/2	N
121	70.0005 1686	65.9292 6399	62.2052 8123	58.7937 0386	55.6635 0158	121
122	70.2975 4145	66.1846 8627	62.4249 6912	58.9826 9185	55.8261 0994	122
123	70.5916 2520	66.4372 6702	62.6419 4481	59.1691 1650	55.9863 1521	123
124	70.8827 9722	66.6870 3784	62.8562 4179	59.3530 1258	56.1441 5291	124
125	71.1710 8636	66.9340 3000	63.0678 9312	59.5344 1438	56.2996 5804	125
126	71.4565 2115	67.1782 7442	63.2769 3148	59.7133 5574	56.4528 6507	126
127	71.7391 2985	67.4198 0165	63.4833 8911	59.8898 7003	56.6038 0795	127
128	72.0189 4045	67.6586 4193	63.6872 9789	60.0639 9016	56.7525 2015	128
129	72.2959 8064	67.8948 2514	63.8886 8927	60.2357 4862	56.8990 3463	129
130	72.5702 7786	68.1283 8086	64.0875 9435	60.4051 7743	57.0433 8387	130
131	72.8418 5927	68.3593 3830	64.2840 4380	60.5723 0819	57.1855 9987	131
132	73.1107 5175	68.5877 2638	64.4780 6795	60.7371 7207	57.3257 1416	132
133	73.3769 8193	68.8135 7368	64.6696 9674	60.8997 9983	57.4637 5779	133
134	73.6405 7617	69.0369 0846	64.8589 5974	61.0602 2178	57.5997 6137	134
135	73.9015 6056	69.2577 5867	65.0458 8617	61.2184 6784	57.7337 5504	135
136	74.1599 6095	69.4761 5196	65.2305 0485	61.3745 6754	57.8657 6852	136
137	74.4158 0293	69.6921 1566	65.4128 4430	61.5285 4998	57.9958 3105	137
138	74.6691 1181	69.9056 7680	65.5929 3264	61.6804 4387	58.1239 7148	138
139	74.9199 1268	70.1168 6210	65.7707 9767	61.8302 7756	58.2502 1821	139
140	75.1682 3038	70.3256 9800	65.9464 6684	61.9780 7897	58.3745 9922	140
141	75.4140 8948	70.5322 1063	66.1199 6725	62.1238 7568	58.4971 4209	141
142	75.6575 1434	70.7364 2584	66.2913 2568	62.2676 9488	58.6178 7398	142
143	75.8985 2905	70.9383 6918	66.4605 6857	62.4095 6338	58.7368 2165	143
144	76.1371 5747	71.1380 6594	66.6277 2204	62.5495 0765	58.8540 1148	144
145	76.3734 2324	71.3355 4110	66.7928 1189	62.6875 5379	58.9694 6944	145
146	76.6073 4974	71.5308 1939	66.9558 6360	62.8237 2753	59.0832 2112	146
147	76.8389 6014	71.7239 2523	67.1169 0232	62.9580 5429	59.1952 9175	147
148	77.0682 7737	71.9148 8280	67.2759 5291	63.0905 5910	59.3057 0615	148
149	77.2953 2413	72.1037 1599	67.4330 3991	63.2212 6668	59.4144 8882	149
150	77.5201 2290	72.2904 4845	67.5881 8756	63.3502 0141	59.5216 6386	150
151	77.7426 9594	72.4751 0353	67.7414 1982	63.4773 8734	59.6272 5504	151
152	77.9630 6529	72.6577 0436	67.8927 6031	63.6028 4817	59.7312 8575	152
153	78.1812 5276	72.8382 7378	68.0422 3241	63.7266 0732	59.8337 7906	153
154	78.3972 7996	73.0168 3439	68.1898 5917	63.8486 8786	59.9347 5770	154
155	78.6111 6828	73.1934 0854	68.3356 6338	63.9691 1257	60.0342 4404	155
156	78.8229 3889	73.3680 1834	68.4796 6753	64.0879 0389	60.1322 6014	156
157	79.0326 1276	73.5406 8562	68.6218 9386	64.2050 8398	60.2288 2772	157
158	79.2402 1065	73.7114 3201	68.7623 6431	64.3206 7471	60.3239 6820	158
159	79.4457 5312	73.8802 7888	68.9011 0055	64.4346 9761	60.4177 0266	159
160	79.6492 6052	74.0472 4734	69.0381 2400	64.5471 7397	60.5100 5188	160
161	79.8507 5299	74.2123 5831	69.1734 5580	64.6581 2476	60.6010 3633	161
162	80.0502 5048	74.3756 3245	69.3071 1684	64.7675 7066	60.6906 7619	162
163	80.2477 7275	74.5370 9018	69.4391 2774	64.8755 3209	60.7789 9132	163
164	80.4433 3936	74.6967 5173	69.5695 0888	64.9820 2919	60.8660 0130	164
165	80.6369 6966	74.8546 3706	69.6982 8038	65.0870 8182	60.9517 2542	165
166	80.8286 8284	75.0107 6594	69.8254 6210	65.1907 0956	61.0361 8268	166
167	81.0184 9786	75.1651 5792	69.9510 7368	65.2929 3175	61.1193 9180	167
168	81.2064 3352	75.3178 3230	70.0751 3450	65.3937 6745	61.2013 7124	168
169	81.3925 0844	75.4688 0821	70.1976 6370	65.4932 3546	61.2821 3915	169
170	81.5767 4103	75.6181 0453	70.3186 8020	65.5913 5434	61.3617 1345	170
171	81.7591 4953	75.7657 3996	70.4382 0267	65.6881 4238	61.4401 1177	171
172	81.9397 5201	75.9117 3296	70.5562 4955	65.7836 1764	61.5173 5150	172
173	82.1185 6635	76.0561 0182	70.6728 3906	65.8777 9792	61.5934 4975	173
174	82.2956 1025	76.1988 6459	70.7879 8919	65.9707 0078	61.6684 2340	174
175	82.4709 0123	76.3400 3915	70.9017 1772	66.0623 4356	61.7422 8906	175
176	82.6444 5667	76.4796 4317	71.0140 4220	66.1527 4334	61.8150 6312	176
177	82.8162 9373	76.6176 9411	71.1249 7995	66.2419 1698	61.8867 6169	177
178	82.9864 2944	76.7542 0925	71.2345 4810	66.3298 8111	61.9574 0068	178
179	83.1548 8063	76.8892 0569	71.3427 6355	66.4166 5214	62.0269 9575	179
180	83.3216 6399	77.0227 0031	71.4496 4301	66.5022 4626	62.0955 6231	180

TABLE IV

N	1	1 1/8	1 1/4	1 3/8	1 1/2	N
181	83.4867 9603	77.1547 0983	71.5552 0298	66.5866 7942	62.1631 1558	181
182	83.6502 9310	77.2852 5075	71.6594 5973	66.6699 6737	62.2296 7052	182
183	83.8121 7138	77.4143 3944	71.7624 2936	66.7521 2564	62.2952 4189	183
184	83.9724 4691	77.5419 9203	71.8641 2777	66.8331 6956	62.3598 4423	184
185	84.1311 3556	77.6682 2450	71.9645 7063	66.9131 1424	62.4234 9185	185
186	84.2882 5303	77.7930 5266	72.0637 7346	66.9919 7459	62.4861 9887	186
187	84.4438 1488	77.9164 9212	72.1617 5157	67.0697 6531	62.5479 7918	187
188	84.5978 3651	78.0385 5834	72.2585 2007	67.1465 0092	62.6088 4648	188
189	84.7503 3318	78.1592 6659	72.3540 9389	67.2221 9573	62.6688 1427	189
190	84.9013 1998	78.2786 3198	72.4484 8780	67.2968 6386	62.7278 9583	190
191	85.0508 1186	78.3966 6945	72.5417 1634	67.3705 1922	62.7861 0427	191
192	85.1988 2363	78.5133 9377	72.6337 9392	67.4431 7555	62.8434 5248	192
193	85.3453 6993	78.6288 1955	72.7247 3473	67.5148 4641	62.8999 5318	193
194	85.4904 6528	78.7429 6124	72.8145 5282	67.5855 4517	62.9556 1890	194
195	85.6341 2404	78.8558 3311	72.9032 6205	67.6552 8500	63.0104 6197	195
196	85.7763 6043	78.9674 4931	72.9908 7610	67.7240 7891	63.0644 9455	196
197	85.9171 8855	79.0778 2379	73.0774 0849	67.7919 3974	63.1177 2862	197
198	86.0566 2232	79.1869 7037	73.1628 7258	67.8588 8014	63.1701 7598	198
199	86.1946 7557	79.2949 0272	73.2472 8156	67.9249 1259	63.2218 4826	199
200	86.3313 6195	79.4016 3433	73.3306 4846	67.9900 4941	63.2727 5690	200
201	86.4666 9500	79.5071 7857	73.4129 8613	68.0543 0275	63.3229 1321	201
202	86.6006 8812	79.6115 4865	73.4943 0729	68.1176 8459	63.3723 2828	202
203	86.7333 5457	79.7147 5763	73.5746 2449	68.1802 0674	63.4210 1309	203
204	86.8647 0750	79.8168 1842	73.6539 5011	68.2418 8088	63.4689 7841	204
205	86.9947 5990	79.9177 4380	73.7322 9640	68.3027 1850	63.5162 3489	205
206	87.1235 2465	80.0175 4641	73.8096 7546	68.3627 3095	63.5627 9299	206
207	87.2510 1451	80.1162 3872	73.8860 9922	68.4219 2942	63.6086 6305	207
208	87.3772 4208	80.2138 3310	73.9615 7948	68.4803 2495	63.6538 5522	208
209	87.5022 1989	80.3103 4175	74.0361 2788	68.5379 2844	63.6983 7952	209
210	87.6259 6028	80.4057 7676	74.1097 5593	68.5947 5062	63.7422 4584	210
211	87.7484 7553	80.5001 5008	74.1824 7499	68.6508 0209	63.7854 6388	211
212	87.8697 7775	80.5934 7350	74.2542 9629	68.7060 9331	63.8280 4323	212
213	87.9898 7896	80.6857 5871	74.3252 3090	68.7606 3458	63.8699 9333	213
214	88.1087 9105	80.7770 1727	74.3952 8978	68.8144 3608	63.9113 2348	214
215	88.2265 2579	80.8672 6059	74.4644 8373	68.8675 0785	63.9520 4284	215
216	88.3430 9484	80.9564 9996	74.5328 2344	68.9198 5978	63.9921 6043	216
217	88.4585 0975	81.0447 4656	74.6003 1945	68.9715 0163	64.0316 8515	217
218	88.5727 8193	81.1320 1144	74.6669 8217	69.0224 4304	64.0706 2577	218
219	88.6859 2270	81.2183 0550	74.7328 2190	69.0726 9350	64.1089 9090	219
220	88.7979 4327	81.3036 3955	74.7978 4879	69.1222 6240	64.1467 8907	220
221	88.9088 5472	81.3880 2428	74.8620 7288	69.1711 5896	64.1840 2864	221
222	89.0186 6804	81.4714 7024	74.9255 0407	69.2193 9232	64.2207 1787	222
223	89.1273 9410	81.5539 8788	74.9881 5217	69.2669 7146	64.2568 6489	223
224	89.2350 4366	81.6355 8752	75.0500 2684	69.3139 0526	64.2924 7773	224
225	89.3416 2739	81.7162 7937	75.1111 3762	69.3602 0248	64.3275 6426	225
226	89.4471 5583	81.7960 7355	75.1714 9394	69.4058 7174	64.3621 3228	226
227	89.5516 3944	81.8749 8002	75.2311 0513	69.4509 2157	64.3961 8944	227
228	89.6550 8855	81.9530 0867	75.2899 8037	69.4953 6036	64.4297 4329	228
229	89.7575 1342	82.0301 6927	75.3481 2876	69.5391 9641	64.4628 0127	229
230	89.8589 2417	82.1064 7147	75.4055 5927	69.5824 3789	64.4953 7071	230
231	89.9593 3087	82.1819 2481	75.4622 8076	69.6250 9287	64.5274 5883	231
232	90.0587 4343	82.2565 3875	75.5183 0199	69.6671 6929	64.5590 7274	232
233	90.1571 7171	82.3303 2262	75.5736 3159	69.7086 7501	64.5902 1944	233
234	90.2546 2546	82.4032 8566	75.6282 7812	69.7496 1776	64.6209 0586	234
235	90.3511 1432	82.4754 3699	75.6822 4999	69.7900 0519	64.6511 3878	235
236	90.4466 4784	82.5467 8565	75.7355 5555	69.8298 4482	64.6809 2490	236
237	90.5412 3548	82.6173 4057	75.7882 0301	69.8691 4409	64.7102 7084	237
238	90.6348 8662	82.6871 1058	75.8402 0050	69.9079 1033	64.7391 8309	238
239	90.7276 1051	82.7561 0440	75.8915 5605	69.9461 5075	64.7676 6807	239
240	90.8194 1635	82.8243 3068	75.9422 7758	69.9838 7251	64.7957 3209	240

TABLE IV

N	1	1 1/8	1 1/4	1 3/8	1 1/2	N
241	90.9103 1322	82.8917 9796	75.9923 7292	70.0210 8262	64.8233 8137	241
242	91.0003 1011	82.9585 1467	76.0418 4980	70.0577 8804	64.8506 2204	242
243	91.0894 1596	83.0244 8916	76.0907 1585	70.0939 9560	64.8774 6014	243
244	91.1776 3956	83.0897 2970	76.1389 7862	70.1297 1205	64.9039 0161	244
245	91.2649 8966	83.1542 4445	76.1866 4555	70.1649 4407	64.9299 5233	245
246	91.3514 7491	83.2180 4149	76.2337 2400	70.1996 9822	64.9556 1806	246
247	91.4371 0388	83.2811 2879	76.2802 2123	70.2339 8098	64.9809 0449	247
248	91.5218 8503	83.3435 1425	76.3261 4443	70.2677 9875	65.0058 1723	248
249	91.6058 2676	83.4052 0569	76.3715 0067	70.3011 5783	65.0303 6180	249
250	91.6889 3738	83.4662 1082	76.4162 9696	70.3340 6445	65.0545 4365	250
251	91.7712 2513	83.5265 3727	76.4605 4021	70.3665 2473	65.0783 6813	251
252	91.8526 9815	83.5861 9261	76.5042 3724	70.3985 4474	65.1018 4052	252
253	91.9333 6451	83.6451 8428	76.5473 9481	70.4301 3045	65.1249 6603	253
254	92.0132 3218	83.7035 1969	76.5900 1956	70.4612 8774	65.1477 4978	254
255	92.0923 0909	83.7612 0612	76.6321 1808	70.4920 2243	65.1701 9683	255
256	92.1706 0306	83.8182 5080	76.6736 9687	70.5223 4025	65.1923 1215	256
257	92.2481 2184	83.8746 6086	76.7147 6234	70.5522 4686	65.2141 0064	257
258	92.3248 7311	83.9304 4337	76.7553 2083	70.5817 4783	65.2355 6713	258
259	92.4008 6447	83.9856 0531	76.7953 7860	70.6108 4866	65.2567 1639	259
260	92.4761 0343	84.0401 5359	76.8349 4183	70.6395 5478	65.2775 5309	260
261	92.5505 9746	84.0940 9502	76.8740 1662	70.6678 7155	65.2980 8186	261
262	92.6243 5392	84.1474 3636	76.9126 0901	70.6958 0424	65.3183 0725	262
263	92.6973 8012	84.2001 8428	76.9507 2495	70.7233 5806	65.3382 3375	263
264	92.7696 8329	84.2523 4540	76.9883 7032	70.7505 3816	65.3578 6576	264
265	92.8412 7058	84.3039 2623	77.0255 5093	70.7773 4961	65.3772 0765	265
266	92.9121 4909	84.3549 3323	77.0622 7252	70.8037 9739	65.3962 6369	266
267	92.9823 2583	84.4053 7279	77.0985 4076	70.8298 8645	65.4150 3812	267
268	93.0518 0775	84.4552 5121	77.1343 6125	70.8556 2166	65.4335 3509	268
269	93.1206 0174	84.5045 7474	77.1697 3951	70.8810 0780	65.4517 5871	269
270	93.1887 1459	84.5533 4956	77.2046 8099	70.9060 4962	65.4697 1302	270
271	93.2561 5306	84.6015 8177	77.2391 9110	70.9307 5178	65.4874 0199	271
272	93.3229 2382	84.6492 7740	77.2732 7516	70.9551 1890	65.5048 2954	272
273	93.3890 3349	84.6964 4242	77.3069 3843	70.9791 5551	65.5219 9955	273
274	93.4544 8860	84.7430 8274	77.3401 8611	71.0028 6610	65.5389 1581	274
275	93.5192 9564	84.7892 0419	77.3730 2332	71.0262 5509	65.5555 8208	275
276	93.5834 6103	84.8348 1255	77.4054 5513	71.0493 2685	65.5720 0205	276
277	93.6469 9112	84.8799 1352	77.4374 8655	71.0720 8567	65.5881 7936	277
278	93.7098 9220	84.9245 1275	77.4691 2251	71.0945 3580	65.6041 1760	278
279	93.7721 7050	84.9686 1583	77.5003 6791	71.1166 8143	65.6198 2029	279
280	93.8338 3217	85.0122 2826	77.5312 2757	71.1385 2669	65.6352 9093	280
281	93.8948 8334	85.0553 5551	77.5617 0624	71.1600 7565	65.6505 3293	281
282	93.9553 3004	85.0980 0297	77.5918 0863	71.1813 3233	65.6655 4969	282
283	94.0151 7826	85.1401 7599	77.6215 3939	71.2023 0070	65.6803 4452	283
284	94.0744 3392	85.1818 7985	77.6509 0310	71.2229 8466	65.6949 2071	284
285	94.1331 0289	85.2231 1975	77.6799 0430	71.2433 8807	65.7092 8149	285
286	94.1911 9098	85.2639 0086	77.7085 4746	71.2635 1474	65.7234 3004	286
287	94.2487 0394	85.3042 2830	77.7368 3699	71.2833 6843	65.7373 6949	287
288	94.3056 4747	85.3441 0709	77.7647 7728	71.3029 5283	65.7511 0295	288
289	94.3620 2719	85.3835 4224	77.7923 7262	71.3222 7159	65.7646 3345	289
290	94.4178 4871	85.4225 3868	77.8196 2728	71.3413 2833	65.7779 6399	290
291	94.4731 1753	85.4611 0129	77.8465 4546	71.3601 2659	65.7910 9753	291
292	94.5278 3914	85.4992 3490	77.8731 3132	71.3786 6988	65.8040 3697	292
293	94.5820 1895	85.5369 4428	77.8993 8896	71.3969 6165	65.8167 8519	293
294	94.6356 6233	85.5742 3414	77.9253 2243	71.4150 0533	65.8293 4502	294
295	94.6887 7458	85.6111 0916	77.9509 3573	71.4328 0427	65.8417 1923	295
296	94.7413 6097	85.6475 7396	77.9762 3282	71.4503 6180	65.8539 1057	296
297	94.7934 2670	85.6836 3308	78.0012 1760	71.4676 8118	65.8659 2175	297
298	94.8449 7694	85.7192 9106	78.0258 9393	71.4847 6565	65.8777 5541	298
299	94.8960 1677	85.7545 5235	78.0502 6561	71.5016 1840	65.8894 1420	299
300	94.9465 5125	85.7894 2136	78.0743 3640	71.5182 4256	65.9009 0069	300

TABLE IV

N	1	1 1/8	1 1/4	1 3/8	1 1/2	N
301	94.9965 8540	85.8239 0245	78.0981 1003	71.5346 4125	65.9122 1743	301
302	95.0461 2416	85.8579 9995	78.1215 9015	71.5508 1751	65.9233 6693	302
303	95.0951 7243	85.8917 1812	78.1447 8039	71.5667 7436	65.9343 5165	303
304	95.1437 3508	85.9250 6119	78.1676 8434	71.5825 1478	65.9451 7404	304
305	95.1918 1691	85.9580 3331	78.1903 0552	71.5980 4171	65.9558 3649	305
306	95.2394 2269	85.9906 3863	78.2126 4743	71.6133 5803	65.9663 4137	306
307	95.2865 5712	86.0228 8121	78.2347 1351	71.6284 6662	65.9766 9101	307
308	95.3332 2487	86.0547 6511	78.2565 0717	71.6433 7028	65.9868 8769	308
309	95.3794 3056	86.0862 9430	78.2780 3177	71.6580 7179	65.9969 3369	309
310	95.4251 7877	86.1174 7273	78.2992 9064	71.6725 7390	66.0068 3122	310
311	95.4704 7403	86.1483 0430	78.3202 8705	71.6868 7931	66.0165 8248	311
312	95.5153 2083	86.1787 9288	78.3410 2425	71.7009 9069	66.0261 8964	312
313	95.5597 2359	86.2089 4228	78.3615 0543	71.7149 1066	66.0356 5481	313
314	95.6036 8672	86.2387 5628	78.3817 3376	71.7286 4184	66.0449 8011	314
315	95.6472 1458	86.2682 3859	78.4017 1235	71.7421 8677	66.0541 6760	315
316	95.6903 1146	86.2973 9292	78.4214 4430	71.7555 4799	66.0632 1931	316
317	95.7329 8165	86.3262 2291	78.4409 3264	71.7687 2798	66.0721 3725	317
318	95.7752 2935	86.3547 3218	78.4601 8039	71.7817 2920	66.0809 2340	318
319	95.8170 5877	86.3829 2428	78.4791 9051	71.7945 5408	66.0895 7970	319
320	95.8584 7402	86.4108 0275	78.4979 6593	71.8072 0501	66.0981 0808	320
321	95.8994 7923	86.4383 7107	78.5165 0956	71.8196 8435	66.1065 1043	321
322	95.9400 7845	86.4656 3270	78.5348 2426	71.8319 9443	66.1147 8860	322
323	95.9802 7569	86.4925 9105	78.5529 1285	71.8441 3754	66.1229 4443	323
324	96.0200 7494	86.5192 4950	78.5707 7812	71.8561 1594	66.1309 7973	324
325	96.0594 8014	86.5456 1137	78.5884 2284	71.8679 3188	66.1388 9629	325
326	96.0984 9519	86.5716 7997	78.6058 4971	71.8795 8755	66.1466 9585	326
327	96.1371 2395	86.5974 5856	78.6230 6145	71.8910 8513	66.1543 8015	327
328	96.1753 7025	86.6229 5037	78.6400 6069	71.9024 2676	66.1619 5089	328
329	96.2132 3787	86.6481 5859	78.6568 5006	71.9136 1456	66.1694 0974	329
330	96.2507 3056	86.6730 8636	78.6734 3216	71.9246 5062	66.1767 5837	330
331	96.2878 5204	86.6977 3683	78.6898 0954	71.9355 3698	66.1839 9839	331
332	96.3246 0598	86.7221 1305	78.7059 8473	71.9462 7569	66.1911 3142	332
333	96.3609 9602	86.7462 1810	78.7219 6023	71.9568 6875	66.1981 5903	333
334	96.3970 2576	86.7700 5498	78.7377 3850	71.9673 1812	66.2050 8279	334
335	96.4326 9878	86.7936 2668	78.7533 2197	71.9776 2577	66.2119 0423	335
336	96.4680 1859	86.8169 3615	78.7687 1306	71.9877 9361	66.2186 2485	336
337	96.5029 8870	86.8399 8630	78.7839 1413	71.9978 2353	66.2252 4616	337
338	96.5376 1258	86.8627 8003	78.7989 2754	72.0077 1742	66.2317 6962	338
339	96.5718 9364	86.8853 2018	78.8137 5559	72.0174 7711	66.2381 9667	339
340	96.6058 3529	86.9076 0957	78.8284 0059	72.0271 0442	66.2445 2874	340
341	96.6394 4088	86.9296 5099	78.8428 6478	72.0366 0116	66.2507 6723	341
342	96.6727 1374	86.9514 4721	78.8571 5040	72.0459 6908	66.2569 1353	342
343	96.7056 5717	86.9730 0095	78.8712 5965	72.0552 0994	66.2629 6899	343
344	96.7382 7443	86.9943 1491	78.8851 9472	72.0643 2547	66.2689 3497	344
345	96.7705 6874	87.0153 9175	78.8989 5775	72.0733 1736	66.2748 1277	345
346	96.8025 4331	87.0362 3412	78.9125 5086	72.0821 8728	66.2806 0372	346
347	96.8342 0129	87.0568 4462	78.9259 7616	72.0909 3690	66.2863 0908	347
348	96.8655 4583	87.0772 2583	78.9392 3571	72.0995 6784	66.2919 3013	348
349	96.8965 8003	87.0973 8030	78.9523 3157	72.1080 8172	66.2974 6811	349
350	96.9273 0696	87.1173 1055	78.9652 6575	72.1164 8012	66.3029 2425	350
351	96.9577 2967	87.1370 1909	78.9780 4024	72.1247 6460	66.3082 9975	351
352	96.9878 5116	87.1565 0837	78.9906 5703	72.1329 3672	66.3135 9581	352
353	97.0176 7441	87.1757 8084	79.0031 1805	72.1409 9800	66.3188 1361	353
354	97.0472 0239	87.1948 3890	79.0154 2524	72.1489 4994	66.3239 5429	354
355	97.0764 3801	87.2136 8494	79.0275 8048	72.1567 9402	66.3290 1901	355
356	97.1053 8417	87.2323 2133	79.0395 8566	72.1645 3171	66.3340 0887	356
357	97.1340 4373	87.2507 5039	79.0514 4263	72.1721 6445	66.3389 2500	357
358	97.1624 1953	87.2689 7442	79.0631 5321	72.1796 9366	66.3437 6847	358
359	97.1905 1439	87.2869 9572	79.0747 1922	72.1871 2075	66.3485 4037	359
360	97.2183 3108	87.3048 1654	79.0861 4244	72.1944 4710	66.3532 4174	360

TABLE IV

N	1 5/8	1 3/4	1 7/8	2	2 1/8	N
1	0.9840 0984	0.9828 0098	0.9815 9509	0.9803 9216	0.9791 9217	1
2	1.9522 8521	1.9486 9875	1.9451 2402	1.9415 6094	1.9380 0947	2
3	2.9050 7769	2.8979 8403	2.8909 1928	2.8838 8327	2.8768 7585	3
4	3.8426 3488	3.8309 4254	3.8193 0727	3.8077 2870	3.7962 0647	4
5	4.7652 0037	4.7478 5508	4.7306 0836	4.7134 5951	4.6964 0780	5
6	5.6730 1389	5.6489 9762	5.6251 3704	5.6014 3089	5.5778 7790	6
7	6.5663 1134	6.5346 4139	6.5032 0200	6.4719 9107	6.4410 0651	7
8	7.4453 2481	7.4050 5297	7.3651 0626	7.3254 8144	7.2861 7528	8
9	8.3102 8271	8.2604 9432	8.2111 4725	8.1622 3671	8.1137 5793	9
10	9.1614 0980	9.1012 2291	9.0416 1693	8.9825 8501	8.9241 2037	10
11	9.9989 2724	9.9274 9181	9.8568 0190	9.7868 4805	9.7176 2092	11
12	10.8230 5263	10.7395 4969	10.6569 8346	10.5753 4122	10.4946 1045	12
13	11.6340 0013	11.5376 4097	11.4424 3775	11.3483 7375	11.2554 3251	13
14	12.4319 8045	12.3220 0587	12.2134 3583	12.1062 4877	12.0004 2351	14
15	13.2172 0093	13.0928 8046	12.9702 4376	12.8492 6350	12.7299 1286	15
16	13.9898 6562	13.8504 9677	13.7131 2271	13.5777 0931	13.4442 2312	16
17	14.7501 7527	14.5950 8282	14.4423 2904	14.2918 7188	14.1436 7013	17
18	15.4983 2745	15.3268 6272	15.1581 1439	14.9920 3125	14.8285 6316	18
19	16.2345 1655	16.0460 5673	15.8607 2578	15.6784 6201	15.4992 0506	19
20	16.9589 3388	16.7528 8130	16.5504 0568	16.3514 3334	16.1558 9234	20
21	17.6717 6765	17.4475 4919	17.2273 9208	17.0112 0916	16.7989 1539	21
22	18.3732 0310	18.1302 6948	17.8919 1860	17.6580 4820	17.4285 5852	22
23	19.0634 2249	18.8012 4764	18.5442 1458	18.2922 0412	18.0451 0015	23
24	19.7426 0515	19.4606 8565	19.1845 0511	18.9139 2560	18.6488 1287	24
25	20.4109 2758	20.1087 8196	19.8130 1115	19.5234 5647	19.2399 6364	25
26	21.0685 6342	20.7457 3166	20.4299 4960	20.1210 3576	19.8188 1385	26
27	21.7156 8357	21.3717 2644	21.0355 3334	20.7068 9780	20.3856 1944	27
28	22.3524 5615	21.9869 5474	21.6299 7138	21.2812 7236	20.9406 3103	28
29	22.9790 4665	22.5916 0171	22.2134 6884	21.8443 8466	21.4840 9403	29
30	23.5956 1786	23.1858 4934	22.7862 2708	22.3964 5555	22.0162 4874	30
31	24.2023 2999	23.7698 7650	23.3484 4376	22.9377 0152	22.5373 3047	31
32	24.7993 4071	24.3438 5897	23.9003 1290	23.4683 3482	23.0475 6962	32
33	25.3868 0512	24.9079 6951	24.4420 2493	23.9885 6355	23.5471 9179	33
34	25.9648 7589	25.4623 7789	24.9737 6680	24.4985 9172	24.0364 1791	34
35	26.5337 0321	26.0072 5100	25.4957 2201	24.9986 1933	24.5154 6429	35
36	27.0934 3490	26.5427 5283	26.0080 7069	25.4888 4248	24.9845 4276	36
37	27.6442 1638	27.0690 4455	26.5109 8963	25.9694 5341	25.4438 6072	37
38	28.1861 9078	27.5862 8457	27.0046 5240	26.4406 4060	25.8936 2127	38
39	28.7194 9892	28.0946 2857	27.4892 2935	26.9025 8883	26.3340 2327	39
40	29.2442 7938	28.5942 2955	27.9648 8770	27.3554 7924	26.7652 6147	40
41	29.7606 6852	29.0852 3789	28.4317 9161	27.7994 8945	27.1875 2653	41
42	30.2688 0051	29.5678 0136	28.8901 0220	28.2347 9358	27.6010 0517	42
43	30.7688 0739	30.0420 6522	29.3399 7762	28.6615 6233	28.0058 8021	43
44	31.2608 1908	30.5081 7221	29.7815 7312	29.0799 6307	28.4023 3069	44
45	31.7449 6342	30.9662 6261	30.2150 4110	29.4901 5987	28.7905 3188	45
46	32.2213 6622	31.4164 7431	30.6405 3114	29.8923 1360	29.1706 5546	46
47	32.6901 5127	31.8589 4281	31.0581 9008	30.2865 8196	29.5428 6948	47
48	33.1514 4036	32.2938 0129	31.4681 6204	30.6731 1957	29.9073 3854	48
49	33.6053 5337	32.7211 8063	31.8705 8850	31.0520 7801	30.2642 2378	49
50	34.0520 0823	33.1412 0946	32.2656 0835	31.4236 0589	30.6136 8302	50
51	34.4915 2102	33.5540 1421	32.6533 5789	31.7878 4892	30.9558 7076	51
52	34.9240 0592	33.9597 1913	33.0339 7093	32.1449 4992	31.2909 3832	52
53	35.3495 7532	34.3584 4632	33.4075 7883	32.4950 4894	31.6190 3385	53
54	35.7683 3980	34.7503 1579	33.7743 1051	32.8382 8327	31.9403 0243	54
55	36.1804 0817	35.1354 4550	34.1342 9252	33.1747 8752	32.2548 8610	55
56	36.5858 8750	35.5139 5135	34.4876 4910	33.5046 9365	32.5629 2396	56
57	36.9848 8314	35.8859 4727	34.8345 0219	33.8281 3103	32.8645 5223	57
58	37.3774 9879	36.2515 4523	35.1749 7147	34.1452 2650	33.1599 0426	58
59	37.7638 3645	36.6108 5526	35.5091 7445	34.4561 0441	33.4491 1066	59
60	38.1439 9650	36.9639 8552	35.8372 2645	34.7608 8668	33.7322 9930	60

TABLE IV

N	1 5/8	1 3/4	1 7/8	2	2 1/8	N
61	38.5180 7774	37.3110 4228	36.1592 4069	35.0596 9282	34.0095 9540	61
62	38.8861 7736	37.6521 3000	36.4753 2828	35.3526 4002	34.2811 2157	62
63	39.2483 9100	37.9873 5135	36.7855 9832	35.6398 4316	34.5469 9786	63
64	39.6048 1280	38.3168 0723	37.0901 5786	35.9214 1486	34.8073 4185	64
65	39.9555 3535	38.6405 9678	37.3891 1201	36.1974 6555	35.0622 6864	65
66	40.3006 4979	38.9588 1748	37.6825 6393	36.4681 0348	35.3118 9096	66
67	40.6402 4579	39.2715 6509	37.9706 1490	36.7334 3478	35.5563 1917	67
68	40.9744 1161	39.5789 3375	38.2533 6432	36.9935 6351	35.7956 6137	68
69	41.3032 3405	39.8810 1597	38.5309 0976	37.2485 9168	36.0300 2337	69
70	41.6267 9858	40.1779 0267	38.8033 4701	37.4986 1929	36.2595 0881	70
71	41.9451 8925	40.4696 8321	39.0707 7007	37.7437 4441	36.4842 1915	71
72	42.2584 8881	40.7564 4542	39.3332 7123	37.9840 6314	36.7042 5376	72
73	42.5667 7865	41.0382 7560	39.5909 4109	38.2196 6975	36.9197 0993	73
74	42.8701 3890	41.3152 5857	39.8438 6855	38.4506 5662	37.1306 8291	74
75	43.1686 4836	41.5874 7771	40.0921 4091	38.6771 1433	37.3372 6601	75
76	43.4623 8461	41.8550 1495	40.3358 4384	38.8991 3170	37.5395 5056	76
77	43.7514 2397	42.1179 5081	40.5750 6144	39.1167 9578	37.7376 2601	77
78	44.0358 4155	42.3763 6443	40.8098 7626	39.3301 9194	37.9315 7993	78
79	44.3157 1124	42.6303 3359	41.0403 6933	39.5394 0386	38.1214 9810	79
80	44.5911 0577	42.8799 3474	41.2666 2020	39.7445 1359	38.3074 6448	80
81	44.8620 9670	43.1252 4298	41.4887 0695	39.9456 0156	38.4895 6130	81
82	45.1287 5444	43.3663 3217	41.7067 0621	40.1427 4663	38.6678 6908	82
83	45.3911 4828	43.6032 7486	41.9206 9321	40.3360 2611	38.8424 6667	83
84	45.6493 4640	43.8361 4237	42.1307 4180	40.5255 1579	39.0134 3125	84
85	45.9034 1589	44.0650 0479	42.3369 2447	40.7112 8999	39.1808 3844	85
86	46.1534 2277	44.2899 3099	42.5393 1236	40.8934 2156	39.3447 6224	86
87	46.3994 3200	44.5109 8869	42.7379 7532	41.0719 8192	39.5052 7514	87
88	46.6415 0750	44.7282 4441	42.9329 8191	41.2470 4110	39.6624 4812	88
89	46.8797 1218	44.9417 6355	43.1243 9942	41.4186 6774	39.8163 5067	89
90	47.1141 0793	45.1516 1037	43.3122 9391	41.5869 2916	39.9670 5084	90
91	47.3447 5565	45.3578 4803	43.4967 3022	41.7518 9133	40.1146 1526	91
92	47.5717 1528	45.5605 3860	43.6777 7199	41.9136 1895	40.2591 0919	92
93	47.7950 4578	45.7597 4310	43.8554 8171	42.0721 7545	40.4005 9652	93
94	48.0148 0520	45.9555 2147	44.0299 2070	42.2276 2299	40.5391 3980	94
95	48.2310 5062	46.1479 3265	44.2011 4915	42.3800 2254	40.6748 0029	95
96	48.4438 3825	46.3370 3455	44.3692 2616	42.5294 3386	40.8076 3798	96
97	48.6532 2337	46.5228 8408	44.5342 0973	42.6759 1555	40.9377 1161	97
98	48.8592 6039	46.7055 3718	44.6961 5679	42.8195 2505	41.0650 7869	98
99	49.0620 0285	46.8850 4882	44.8551 2323	42.9603 1867	41.1897 9553	99
100	49.2615 0341	47.0614 7304	45.0111 6391	43.0983 5164	41.3119 1729	100
101	49.4578 1394	47.2348 6294	45.1643 3267	43.2336 7808	41.4314 9796	101
102	49.6509 8543	47.4052 7071	45.3146 8237	43.3663 5106	41.5485 9041	102
103	49.8410 6807	47.5727 4762	45.4622 6491	43.4964 2261	41.6632 4643	103
104	50.0281 1126	47.7373 4410	45.6071 3120	43.6239 4373	41.7755 1670	104
105	50.2121 6360	47.8991 0968	45.7493 3124	43.7489 6444	41.8854 5087	105
106	50.3932 7292	48.0580 9305	45.8889 1410	43.8715 3377	41.9930 9754	106
107	50.5714 8627	48.2143 4207	46.0259 2795	43.9916 9977	42.0985 0433	107
108	50.7468 4995	48.3679 0375	46.1604 2007	44.1095 0958	42.2017 1782	108
109	50.9194 0955	48.5188 2432	46.2924 3688	44.2250 0939	42.3027 8367	109
110	51.0892 0989	48.6671 4921	46.4220 2393	44.3382 4450	42.4017 4656	110
111	51.2562 9509	48.8129 2306	46.5492 2595	44.4492 5932	42.4986 5024	111
112	51.4207 0858	48.9561 8974	46.6740 8682	44.5580 9737	42.5935 3756	112
113	51.5824 9307	49.0969 9237	46.7966 4964	44.6648 0134	42.6864 5049	113
114	51.7416 9059	49.2353 7334	46.9169 5670	44.7694 1308	42.7774 3010	114
115	51.8983 4253	49.3713 7429	47.0350 4952	44.8719 7361	42.8665 1662	115
116	52.0524 8957	49.5050 3616	47.1509 6885	44.9725 2314	42.9537 4945	116
117	52.2041 7178	49.6363 9917	47.2647 5470	45.0711 0112	43.0391 6715	117
118	52.3534 2857	49.7655 0287	47.3764 4633	45.1677 4620	43.1228 0749	118
119	52.5002 9871	49.8923 8611	47.4860 8229	45.2624 9627	43.2047 0745	119
120	52.6448 2038	50.0170 8709	47.5937 0041	45.3553 8850	43.2849 0326	120

TABLE IV

N	1 5/8	1 3/4	1 7/8	2	2 1/8	N
121	52.7870 3113	50.1396 4333	47.6993 3782	45.4464 5932	43.3634 3036	121
122	52.9269 6790	50.2600 9173	47.8030 3099	45.5357 4443	43.4403 2349	122
123	53.0646 6706	50.3784 6853	47.9048 1570	45.6232 7885	43.5156 1664	123
124	53.2001 6439	50.4948 0936	48.0047 2707	45.7090 9691	43.5893 4310	124
125	53.3334 9509	50.6091 4925	48.1027 9957	45.7932 3227	43.6615 3547	125
126	53.4646 9382	50.7215 2261	48.1990 6707	45.8757 1791	43.7322 2567	126
127	53.5937 9465	50.8319 6325	48.2935 6277	45.9565 8619	43.8014 4497	127
128	53.7208 3115	50.9405 0442	48.3863 1928	46.0358 6881	43.8692 2396	128
129	53.8458 3631	51.0471 7879	48.4773 6862	46.1135 9687	43.9355 9261	129
130	53.9688 4261	51.1520 1847	48.5667 4220	46.1898 0085	44.0005 8028	130
131	54.0898 8203	51.2550 5501	48.6544 7087	46.2645 1064	44.0642 1570	131
132	54.2089 8601	51.3563 1942	48.7405 8491	46.3377 5553	44.1265 2700	132
133	54.3261 8550	51.4558 4218	48.8251 1402	46.4095 6425	44.1875 4174	133
134	54.4415 1094	51.5536 5325	48.9080 8738	46.4799 6495	44.2472 8689	134
135	54.5549 9232	51.6497 8206	48.9895 3362	46.5489 8524	44.3057 8888	135
136	54.6666 5911	51.7442 5755	49.0694 8086	46.6166 5220	44.3630 7357	136
137	54.7765 4033	51.8371 0816	49.1479 5667	46.6829 9235	44.4191 6628	137
138	54.8846 6453	51.9283 6183	49.2249 8814	46.7480 3172	44.4740 9183	138
139	54.9910 5981	52.0180 4602	49.3006 0186	46.8117 9580	44.5278 7450	139
140	55.0957 5381	52.1061 8774	49.3748 2391	46.8743 0961	44.5805 3806	140
141	55.1987 7373	52.1928 1350	49.4476 7991	46.9355 9766	44.6321 0581	141
142	55.3001 4636	52.2779 4939	49.5191 9500	46.9956 8398	44.6826 0055	142
143	55.3998 9801	52.3616 2102	49.5893 9387	47.0545 9213	44.7320 4461	143
144	55.4980 5462	52.4438 5358	49.6583 0073	47.1123 4523	44.7804 5983	144
145	55.5946 4170	52.5246 7183	49.7259 3937	47.1689 6591	44.8278 6765	145
146	55.6896 8433	52.6041 0007	49.7923 3312	47.2244 7638	44.8742 8900	146
147	55.7832 0721	52.6821 6223	49.8575 0490	47.2788 9841	44.9197 4444	147
148	55.8752 3465	52.7588 8180	49.9214 7721	47.3322 5335	44.9642 5404	148
149	55.9657 9055	52.8342 8187	49.9842 7211	47.3845 6211	45.0078 3749	149
150	56.0548 9845	52.9083 8513	50.0459 1127	47.4358 4520	45.0505 1407	150
151	56.1425 8150	52.9812 1389	50.1064 1597	47.4861 2275	45.0923 0264	151
152	56.2288 6249	53.0527 9006	50.1658 0709	47.5354 1446	45.1332 2168	152
153	56.3137 6382	53.1231 3520	50.2241 0512	47.5837 3966	45.1732 8928	153
154	56.3973 0758	53.1922 7046	50.2813 3017	47.6311 1732	45.2125 2316	154
155	56.4795 1545	53.2602 1667	50.3375 0201	47.6775 6600	45.2509 4067	155
156	56.5604 0881	53.3269 9427	50.3926 4001	47.7231 0392	45.2885 5880	156
157	56.6400 0867	53.3926 2336	50.4467 6320	47.7677 4894	45.3253 9417	157
158	56.7183 3571	53.4571 2370	50.4998 9026	47.8115 1857	45.3614 6308	158
159	56.7954 1029	53.5205 1469	50.5520 3952	47.8544 2997	45.3967 8147	159
160	56.8712 5244	53.5828 1542	50.6032 2898	47.8964 9997	45.4313 6497	160
161	56.9458 8186	53.6440 4464	50.6534 7629	47.9377 4507	45.4652 2886	161
162	57.0193 1794	53.7042 2078	50.7027 9882	47.9781 8144	45.4983 8811	162
163	57.0915 7977	53.7633 6194	50.7512 1356	48.0178 2494	45.5308 5739	163
164	57.1626 8612	53.8214 8594	50.7987 3724	48.0566 9112	45.5626 5105	164
165	57.2326 5547	53.8786 1026	50.8453 8625	48.0947 9521	45.5937 8316	165
166	57.3015 0600	53.9347 5210	50.8911 7668	48.1321 5217	45.6242 6748	166
167	57.3692 5560	53.9899 2835	50.9361 2435	48.1687 7664	45.6541 1748	167
168	57.4359 2187	54.0441 5563	50.9802 4476	48.2046 8298	45.6833 4637	168
169	57.5015 2213	54.0974 5025	51.0235 5314	48.2398 8527	45.7119 6707	169
170	57.5660 7344	54.1498 2825	51.0660 6443	48.2743 9733	45.7399 9224	170
171	57.6295 9256	54.2013 0541	51.1077 9331	48.3082 3267	45.7674 3426	171
172	57.6920 9600	54.2518 9721	51.1487 5417	48.3414 0458	45.7943 0527	172
173	57.7536 0000	54.3016 1888	51.1889 6115	48.3739 2606	45.8206 1716	173
174	57.8141 2054	54.3504 8538	51.2284 2812	48.4058 0986	45.8463 8155	174
175	57.8736 7335	54.3985 1143	51.2671 6871	48.4370 6849	45.8716 0984	175
176	57.9322 7390	54.4457 1148	51.3051 9628	48.4677 1421	45.8963 1318	176
177	57.9899 3741	54.4920 9974	51.3425 2395	48.4977 5903	45.9205 0251	177
178	58.0466 7888	54.5376 9016	51.3791 6462	48.5272 1473	45.9441 8850	178
179	58.1025 1305	54.5824 9647	51.4151 3091	48.5560 9288	45.9673 8164	179
180	58.1574 5441	54.6265 3216	51.4504 3525	48.5844 0478	45.9900 9218	180

TABLE IV

N	1 5/8	1 3/4	1 7/8	2	2 1/8	N
181	58.2115 1726	54.6698 1047	51.4850 8982	48.6121 6155	46.0123 3017	181
182	58.2647 1563	54.7123 4445	51.5191 0657	48.6393 7407	46.0341 0543	182
183	58.3170 6335	54.7541 4688	51.5524 9724	48.6660 5301	46.0554 2759	183
184	58.3685 7402	54.7952 3035	51.5852 7337	48.6922 0883	46.0763 0608	184
185	58.4192 6103	54.8356 0722	51.6174 4625	48.7178 5180	46.0967 5014	185
186	58.4691 3754	54.8752 8965	51.6490 2700	48.7429 9196	46.1167 6881	186
187	58.5182 1652	54.9142 8958	51.6800 2650	48.7676 3917	46.1363 7092	187
188	58.5665 1072	54.9526 1875	51.7104 5546	48.7918 0311	46.1555 6516	188
189	58.6140 3269	54.9902 8870	51.7403 2438	48.8154 9325	46.1743 6001	189
190	58.6607 9478	55.0273 1076	51.7696 4356	48.8387 1887	46.1927 6378	190
191	58.7068 0913	55.0636 9608	51.7984 2313	48.8614 8909	46.2107 8461	191
192	58.7520 8770	55.0994 5561	51.8266 7301	48.8838 1283	46.2284 3046	192
193	58.7966 4227	55.1346 0011	51.8544 0295	48.9056 9885	46.2457 0914	193
194	58.8404 8440	55.1691 4015	51.8816 2253	48.9271 5574	46.2626 2829	194
195	58.8836 2548	55.2030 8615	51.9083 4113	48.9481 9190	46.2791 9539	195
196	58.9260 7674	55.2364 4830	51.9345 6798	48.9688 1559	46.2954 1776	196
197	58.9678 4919	55.2692 3666	51.9603 1213	48.9890 3489	46.3113 0258	197
198	59.0089 5369	55.3014 6109	51.9855 8246	49.0088 5774	46.3268 5688	198
199	59.0494 0092	55.3331 3129	52.0103 8769	49.0282 9190	46.3420 8752	199
200	59.0892 0140	55.3642 5680	52.0347 3638	49.0473 4500	46.3570 0124	200
201	59.1283 6546	55.3948 4698	52.0586 3694	49.0660 2451	46.3716 0464	201
202	59.1669 0328	55.4249 1103	52.0820 9761	49.0843 3775	46.3859 0418	202
203	59.2048 2488	55.4544 5802	52.1051 2649	49.1022 9191	46.3999 0617	203
204	59.2421 4010	55.4834 9682	52.1277 3152	49.1198 9403	46.4136 1681	204
205	59.2788 5865	55.5120 3619	52.1499 2051	49.1371 5101	46.4270 4217	205
206	59.3149 9006	55.5400 8471	52.1717 0112	49.1540 6962	46.4401 8817	206
207	59.3505 4373	55.5676 5082	52.1930 8085	49.1706 5649	46.4530 6063	207
208	59.3855 2888	55.5947 4282	52.2140 6709	49.1869 1813	46.4656 6524	208
209	59.4199 5462	55.6213 6886	52.2346 6709	49.2028 6091	46.4780 0758	209
210	59.4538 2988	55.6475 3697	52.2548 8794	49.2184 9109	46.4900 9310	210
211	59.4871 6348	55.6732 5501	52.2747 3663	49.2338 1479	46.5019 2715	211
212	59.5199 6406	55.6985 3072	52.2942 2000	49.2488 3803	46.5135 1496	212
213	59.5522 4016	55.7233 7171	52.3133 4479	49.2635 6670	46.5248 6165	213
214	59.5840 0016	55.7477 8547	52.3321 1758	49.2780 0657	46.5359 7224	214
215	59.6152 5231	55.7717 7933	52.3505 4486	49.2921 6330	46.5468 5164	215
216	59.6460 0473	55.7953 6052	52.3686 3300	49.3060 4245	46.5575 0467	216
217	59.6762 6542	55.8185 3614	52.3863 8822	49.3196 4946	46.5679 3603	217
218	59.7060 4223	55.8413 1316	52.4038 1665	49.3329 8967	46.5781 5033	218
219	59.7353 4291	55.8636 9843	52.4209 2432	49.3460 6830	46.5881 5210	219
220	59.7641 7506	55.8856 9871	52.4377 1713	49.3588 9049	46.5979 4575	220
221	59.7925 4619	55.9073 2060	52.4542 0086	49.3714 6127	46.6075 3562	221
222	59.8204 6365	55.9285 7061	52.4703 8121	49.3837 8556	46.6169 2594	222
223	59.8479 3471	55.9494 5515	52.4862 6377	49.3958 6819	46.6261 2088	223
224	59.8749 6651	55.9699 8049	52.5018 5401	49.4077 1391	46.6351 2448	224
225	59.9015 6606	55.9901 5281	52.5171 5731	49.4193 2737	46.6439 4074	225
226	59.9277 4028	56.0099 7819	52.5321 7895	49.4307 1311	46.6525 7355	226
227	59.9534 9597	56.0294 6260	52.5469 2412	49.4418 7559	46.6610 2673	227
228	59.9788 3982	56.0486 1189	52.5613 9791	49.4528 1921	46.6693 0402	228
229	60.0037 7842	56.0674 3183	52.5756 0531	49.4635 4824	46.6774 0908	229
230	60.0283 1825	56.0859 2809	52.5895 5123	49.4740 6691	46.6853 4549	230
231	60.0524 6568	56.1041 0623	52.6032 4047	49.4843 7932	46.6931 1676	231
232	60.0762 2700	56.1219 7173	52.6166 7776	49.4944 8953	46.7007 2632	232
233	60.0996 0836	56.1395 2995	52.6298 6774	49.5044 0150	46.7081 7755	233
234	60.1226 1585	56.1567 8620	52.6428 1496	49.5141 1912	46.7154 7373	234
235	60.1452 5545	56.1737 4565	52.6555 2389	49.5236 4619	46.7226 1810	235
236	60.1675 3304	56.1904 1341	52.6679 9891	49.5329 8646	46.7296 1381	236
237	60.1894 5441	56.2067 9451	52.6802 4433	49.5421 4359	46.7364 6395	237
238	60.2110 2525	56.2228 9387	52.6922 6437	49.5511 2117	46.7431 7155	238
239	60.2322 5116	56.2387 1633	52.7040 6318	49.5599 2271	46.7497 3959	239
240	60.2531 3768	56.2542 6666	52.7156 4484	49.5685 5168	46.7561 7095	240

TABLE IV

N	1 5/8	1 3/4	1 7/8	2	2 1/8	N
241	60.2736 9021	56.2695 4955	52.7270 1334	49.5770 1145	46.7624 6850	241
242	60.2939 1411	56.2845 6958	52.7381 7261	49.5853 0534	46.7686 3500	242
243	60.3138 1462	56.2993 3128	52.7491 2649	49.5934 3661	46.7746 7320	243
244	60.3333 9692	56.3138 3910	52.7598 7876	49.6014 0844	46.7805 8575	244
245	60.3526 6610	56.3280 9739	52.7704 3314	49.6092 2396	46.7863 7528	245
246	60.3716 2715	56.3421 1046	52.7807 9326	49.6168 8624	46.7920 4433	246
247	60.3902 8502	56.3558 8252	52.7909 6271	49.6243 9827	46.7975 9543	247
248	60.4086 4455	56.3694 1771	52.8009 4499	49.6317 6301	46.8030 3102	248
249	60.4267 1050	56.3827 2010	52.8107 4355	49.6389 8335	46.8083 5351	249
250	60.4444 8758	56.3957 9371	52.8203 6177	49.6460 6210	46.8135 6525	250
251	60.4619 8040	56.4086 4247	52.8298 0296	49.6530 0206	46.8186 6854	251
252	60.4791 9350	56.4212 7024	52.8390 7039	49.6598 0594	46.8236 6565	252
253	60.4961 3137	56.4336 8083	52.8481 6726	49.6664 7642	46.8285 5877	253
254	60.5127 9839	56.4458 7796	52.8570 9670	49.6730 1609	46.8333 5008	254
255	60.5291 9891	56.4578 6532	52.8658 6179	49.6794 2754	46.8380 4170	255
256	60.5453 3718	56.4696 4651	52.8744 6556	49.6857 1328	46.8426 3569	256
257	60.5612 1740	56.4812 2507	52.8829 1098	49.6918 7576	46.8471 3409	257
258	60.5768 4369	56.4926 0449	52.8912 0096	49.6979 1741	46.8515 3889	258
259	60.5922 2011	56.5037 8819	52.8993 3836	49.7038 4060	46.8558 5203	259
260	60.6073 5067	56.5147 7955	52.9073 2600	49.7096 4765	46.8600 7543	260
261	60.6222 3928	56.5255 8187	52.9151 6663	49.7153 4083	46.8642 1095	261
262	60.6368 8982	56.5361 9840	52.9228 6295	49.7209 2239	46.8682 6041	262
263	60.6513 0609	56.5466 3233	52.9304 1762	49.7263 9450	46.8722 2562	263
264	60.6654 9185	56.5568 8681	52.9378 3324	49.7317 5931	46.8761 0832	264
265	60.6794 5078	56.5669 6493	52.9451 1239	49.7370 1893	46.8799 1022	265
266	60.6931 8650	56.5768 6971	52.9522 5756	49.7421 7542	46.8836 3302	266
267	60.7067 0258	56.5866 0413	52.9592 7122	49.7472 3081	46.8872 7836	267
268	60.7200 0254	56.5961 7114	52.9661 5580	49.7521 8706	46.8908 4784	268
269	60.7330 8983	56.6055 7360	52.9729 1367	49.7570 4614	46.8943 4305	269
270	60.7459 6785	56.6148 1435	52.9795 4716	49.7618 0994	46.8977 6553	270
271	60.7586 3995	56.6238 9617	52.9860 5856	49.7664 8034	46.9011 1680	271
272	60.7711 0942	56.6328 2179	52.9924 5012	49.7710 5915	46.9043 9834	272
273	60.7833 7951	56.6415 9389	52.9987 2405	49.7755 4819	46.9076 1159	273
274	60.7954 5339	56.6502 1513	53.0048 8250	49.7799 4921	46.9107 5798	274
275	60.8073 3421	56.6586 8809	53.0109 2761	49.7842 6393	46.9138 3891	275
276	60.8190 2505	56.6670 1532	53.0168 6145	49.7884 9405	46.9168 5572	276
277	60.8305 2895	56.6751 9933	53.0226 8609	49.7926 4122	46.9198 0977	277
278	60.8418 4891	56.6832 4259	53.0284 0352	49.7967 0708	46.9227 0234	278
279	60.8529 8786	56.6911 4750	53.0340 1573	49.8006 9322	46.9255 3473	279
280	60.8639 4869	56.6989 1647	53.0395 2464	49.8046 0119	46.9283 0818	280
281	60.8747 3426	56.7065 5181	53.0449 3216	49.8084 3254	46.9310 2392	281
282	60.8853 4736	56.7140 5583	53.0502 4016	49.8121 8877	46.9336 8315	282
283	60.8957 9076	56.7214 3079	53.0554 5046	49.8158 7134	46.9362 8705	283
284	60.9060 6717	56.7286 7891	53.0605 6487	49.8194 8170	46.9388 3677	284
285	60.9161 7926	56.7358 0237	53.0655 8515	49.8230 2128	46.9413 3344	285
286	60.9261 2965	56.7428 0331	53.0705 1303	49.8264 9145	46.9437 7815	286
287	60.9359 2094	56.7496 8385	53.0753 5022	49.8298 9358	46.9461 7200	287
288	60.9455 5566	56.7564 4604	53.0800 9837	49.8332 2900	46.9485 1603	288
289	60.9550 3632	56.7630 9193	53.0847 5914	49.8364 9902	46.9508 1129	289
290	60.9643 6538	56.7696 2352	53.0893 3412	49.8397 0492	46.9530 5879	290
291	60.9735 4527	56.7760 4277	53.0938 2491	49.8428 4796	46.9552 5953	291
292	60.9825 7837	56.7823 5162	53.0982 3304	49.8459 2937	46.9574 1447	292
293	60.9914 6703	56.7885 5196	53.1025 6004	49.8489 5037	46.9595 2457	293
294	61.0002 1356	56.7946 4566	53.1068 0740	49.8519 1212	46.9615 9077	294
295	61.0088 2023	56.8006 3455	53.1109 7659	49.8548 1581	46.9636 1397	295
296	61.0172 8928	56.8065 2045	53.1150 6904	49.8576 6256	46.9655 9508	296
297	61.0256 2291	56.8123 0511	53.1190 8618	49.8604 5349	46.9675 3496	297
298	61.0338 2328	56.8179 9028	53.1230 2938	49.8631 8969	46.9694 3448	298
299	61.0418 9253	56.8235 7767	53.1269 0000	49.8658 7225	46.9712 9447	299
300	61.0498 3275	56.8290 6896	53.1306 9939	49.8685 0220	46.9731 1576	300

TABLE IV

N	1 5/8	1 3/4	1 7/8	2	2 1/8	N
301	61.0576 4600	56.8344 6581	53.1344 2885	49.8710 8059	46.9748 9915	301
302	61.0653 3432	56.8397 6984	53.1380 8966	49.8736 0842	46.9766 4544	302
303	61.0728 9970	56.8449 8264	53.1416 8311	49.8760 8669	46.9783 5538	303
304	61.0803 4410	56.8501 0579	53.1452 1041	49.8785 1636	46.9800 2975	304
305	61.0876 6948	56.8551 4083	53.1486 7280	49.8808 9839	46.9816 6928	305
306	61.0948 7771	56.8600 8926	53.1520 7146	49.8832 3372	46.9832 7469	306
307	61.1019 7069	56.8649 5259	53.1554 0756	49.8855 2325	46.9848 4670	307
308	61.1089 5025	56.8697 3228	53.1586 8227	49.8877 6790	46.9863 8600	308
309	61.1158 1820	56.8744 2976	53.1618 9671	49.8899 6853	46.9878 9327	309
310	61.1225 7634	56.8790 4644	53.1650 5198	49.8921 2601	46.9893 6917	310
311	61.1292 2641	56.8835 8373	53.1681 4919	49.8942 4118	46.9908 1437	311
312	61.1357 7014	56.8880 4298	53.1711 8939	49.8963 1488	46.9922 2949	312
313	61.1422 0924	56.8924 2553	53.1741 7363	49.8983 4793	46.9936 1517	313
314	61.1485 4538	56.8967 3271	53.1771 0295	49.9003 4110	46.9949 7201	314
315	61.1547 8020	56.9009 6581	53.1799 7836	49.9022 9520	46.9963 0062	315
316	61.1609 1533	56.9051 2610	53.1828 0084	49.9042 1098	46.9976 0159	316
317	61.1669 5235	56.9092 1484	53.1855 7138	49.9060 8920	46.9988 7548	317
318	61.1728 9284	56.9132 3326	53.1882 9092	49.9079 3058	47.0001 2287	318
319	61.1787 3834	56.9171 8256	53.1909 6041	49.9097 3587	47.0013 4431	319
320	61.1844 9038	56.9210 6394	53.1935 8077	49.9115 0575	47.0025 4033	320
321	61.1901 5043	56.9248 7857	53.1961 5291	49.9132 4093	47.0037 1146	321
322	61.1957 1998	56.9286 2759	53.1986 7770	49.9149 4209	47.0048 5822	322
323	61.2012 0047	56.9323 1212	53.2011 5603	49.9166 0989	47.0059 8112	323
324	61.2065 9333	56.9359 3329	53.2035 8874	49.9182 4499	47.0070 8066	324
325	61.2118 9996	56.9394 9218	53.2059 7667	49.9198 4803	47.0081 5731	325
326	61.2171 2173	56.9429 8986	53.2083 2066	49.9214 1964	47.0092 1157	326
327	61.2222 6000	56.9464 2738	53.2106 2151	49.9229 6043	47.0102 4389	327
328	61.2273 1612	56.9498 0578	53.2128 8001	49.9244 7101	47.0112 5472	328
329	61.2322 9138	56.9531 2607	53.2150 9694	49.9259 5197	47.0122 4453	329
330	61.2371 8709	56.9563 8926	53.2172 7307	49.9274 0389	47.0132 1373	330
331	61.2420 0452	56.9595 9632	53.2194 0915	49.9288 2735	47.0141 6278	331
332	61.2467 4491	56.9627 4823	53.2215 0591	49.9302 2289	47.0150 9207	332
333	61.2514 0951	56.9658 4592	53.2235 6409	49.9315 9107	47.0160 0203	333
334	61.2559 9952	56.9688 9034	53.2255 8438	49.9329 3242	47.0168 9305	334
335	61.2605 1613	56.9718 8240	53.2275 6749	49.9342 4747	47.0177 6553	335
336	61.2649 6052	56.9748 2300	53.2295 1410	49.9355 3674	47.0186 1986	336
337	61.2693 3385	56.9777 1302	53.2314 2488	49.9368 0072	47.0194 5641	337
338	61.2736 3724	56.9805 5334	53.2333 0050	49.9380 3992	47.0202 7556	338
339	61.2778 7182	56.9833 4480	53.2351 4159	49.9392 5483	47.0210 7765	339
340	61.2820 3870	56.9860 8826	53.2369 4880	49.9404 4591	47.0218 6306	340
341	61.2861 3894	56.9887 8453	53.2387 2275	49.9416 1364	47.0226 3213	341
342	61.2901 7362	56.9914 3443	53.2404 6405	49.9427 5847	47.0233 8520	342
343	61.2941 4378	56.9940 3875	53.2421 7330	49.9438 8085	47.0241 2259	343
344	61.2980 5046	56.9965 9828	53.2438 5109	49.9449 8122	47.0248 4464	344
345	61.3018 9467	56.9991 1379	53.2454 9801	49.9460 6002	47.0255 5167	345
346	61.3056 7741	57.0015 8603	53.2471 1461	49.9471 1767	47.0262 4399	346
347	61.3093 9967	57.0040 1576	53.2487 0145	49.9481 5458	47.0269 2189	347
348	61.3130 6241	57.0064 0369	53.2502 5910	49.9491 7116	47.0275 8570	348
349	61.3166 6657	57.0087 5056	53.2517 8807	49.9501 6780	47.0282 3569	349
350	61.3202 1311	57.0110 5706	53.2532 8890	49.9511 4490	47.0288 7216	350
351	61.3237 0294	57.0133 2389	53.2547 6211	49.9521 0285	47.0294 9538	351
352	61.3271 3696	57.0155 5174	53.2562 0821	49.9530 4201	47.0301 0564	352
353	61.3305 1608	57.0177 4126	53.2576 2769	49.9539 6275	47.0307 0319	353
354	61.3338 4116	57.0198 9313	53.2590 2105	49.9548 6544	47.0312 8832	354
355	61.3371 1307	57.0220 0799	53.2603 8876	49.9557 5043	47.0318 6126	355
356	61.3403 3266	57.0240 8648	53.2617 3130	49.9566 1807	47.0324 2229	356
357	61.3435 0078	57.0261 2922	53.2630 4912	49.9574 6870	47.0329 7164	357
358	61.3466 1823	57.0281 3682	53.2643 4270	49.9583 0264	47.0335 0956	358
359	61.3496 8584	57.0301 0990	53.2656 1246	49.9591 2024	47.0340 3629	359
360	61.3527 0439	57.0320 4904	53.2668 5886	49.9599 2180	47.0345 5206	360

TABLE IV

N	2 1/4	2 3/8	2 1/2	2 5/8	2 3/4	N
1	0.9779 9511	0.9768 0098	0.9756 0976	0.9744 2144	0.9732 3601	1
2	1.9344 6955	1.9309 4113	1.9274 2415	1.9239 1857	1.9204 2434	2
3	2.8698 9687	2.8629 4615	2.8560 2356	2.8491 2894	2.8422 6213	3
4	3.7847 4021	3.7733 2958	3.7619 7421	3.7506 7375	3.7394 2787	4
5	4.6794 5253	4.6625 9299	4.6458 2850	4.6291 5835	4.6125 8186	5
6	5.5544 7680	5.5312 2637	5.5081 2536	5.4851 7257	5.4623 6678	6
7	6.4102 4626	6.3797 0829	6.3493 9060	6.3192 9117	6.2894 0806	7
8	7.2471 8461	7.2085 0627	7.1701 3717	7.1320 7423	7.0943 1441	8
9	8.0657 0622	8.0180 7694	7.9708 6553	7.9240 6746	7.8776 7826	9
10	8.8662 1635	8.8088 6637	8.7520 6393	8.6958 0264	8.6400 7616	10
11	9.6491 1134	9.5813 1025	9.5142 0871	9.4477 9794	9.3820 6926	11
12	10.4147 7882	10.3358 3419	10.2577 6460	10.1805 5828	10.1042 0366	12
13	11.1635 9787	11.0728 5391	10.9831 8497	10.8945 7567	10.8070 1086	13
14	11.8959 3924	11.7927 7549	11.6909 1217	11.5903 2952	11.4910 0814	14
15	12.6121 6551	12.4959 9559	12.3813 7773	12.2682 8699	12.1566 9892	15
16	13.3126 3131	13.1829 0168	13.0550 0266	12.9289 0328	12.8045 7315	16
17	13.9976 8343	13.8538 7221	13.7121 9772	13.5726 2195	13.4351 0769	17
18	14.6676 6106	14.5092 7689	14.3533 6363	14.1998 7523	14.0487 6661	18
19	15.3228 9590	15.1494 7681	14.9788 9134	14.8110 8427	14.6460 0157	19
20	15.9637 1237	15.7748 2473	15.5891 6229	15.4066 5946	15.2272 5213	20
21	16.5904 2775	16.3856 6518	16.1845 4857	15.9870 0069	15.7929 4612	21
22	17.2033 5232	16.9823 3473	16.7654 1324	16.5524 9762	16.3434 9987	22
23	17.8027 8955	17.5651 6213	17.3321 1048	17.1035 2996	16.8793 1861	23
24	18.3890 3624	18.1344 6850	17.8849 8583	17.6404 6769	17.4007 9670	24
25	18.9623 8263	18.6905 6752	18.4243 7642	18.1636 7131	17.9083 1795	25
26	19.5231 1260	19.2337 6559	18.9506 1114	18.6734 9215	18.4022 5592	26
27	20.0715 0376	19.7643 6199	19.4640 1087	19.1702 7249	18.8829 7413	27
28	20.6078 2764	20.2826 4908	19.9648 8866	19.6543 4591	19.3508 2640	28
29	21.1323 4977	20.7889 1241	20.4535 4991	20.1260 3743	19.8061 5708	29
30	21.6453 2985	21.2834 3092	20.9302 9259	20.5856 6376	20.2493 0130	30
31	22.1470 2186	21.7664 7709	21.3954 0741	21.0335 3350	20.6805 8520	31
32	22.6376 7419	22.2383 1706	21.8491 7796	21.4699 4738	21.1003 2623	32
33	23.1175 2977	22.6992 1080	22.2918 8094	21.8951 9842	21.5088 3332	33
34	23.5868 2618	23.1494 1226	22.7237 8628	22.3095 7216	21.9064 0712	34
35	24.0457 9577	23.5891 6949	23.1451 5734	22.7133 4680	22.2933 4026	35
36	24.4946 6579	24.0187 2477	23.5562 5107	23.1067 9347	22.6699 1753	36
37	24.9336 5848	24.4383 1480	23.9573 1812	23.4901 7634	23.0364 1609	37
38	25.3629 9118	24.8481 7074	24.3486 0304	23.8637 5283	23.3931 0568	38
39	25.7828 7646	25.2485 1843	24.7303 4443	24.2277 7377	23.7402 4884	39
40	26.1935 2221	25.6395 7844	25.1027 7505	24.5824 8358	24.0781 0106	40
41	26.5951 3174	26.0215 6624	25.4661 2200	24.9281 2042	24.4069 1101	41
42	26.9879 0390	26.3946 9230	25.8206 0683	25.2649 1636	24.7269 2069	42
43	27.3720 3316	26.7591 6220	26.1664 4569	25.5930 9755	25.0383 6563	43
44	27.7477 0969	27.1151 7675	26.5038 4945	25.9128 8434	25.3414 7507	44
45	28.1151 1950	27.4629 3211	26.8330 2386	26.2244 9144	25.6364 7209	45
46	28.4744 4450	27.8026 1989	27.1541 6962	26.5281 2807	25.9235 7381	46
47	28.8258 6259	28.1344 2724	27.4674 8255	26.8239 9812	26.2029 9154	47
48	29.1695 4777	28.4585 3699	27.7731 5371	27.1123 0024	26.4749 3094	48
49	29.5056 7019	28.7751 2771	28.0713 6947	27.3932 2801	26.7395 9215	49
50	29.8343 9627	29.0843 7383	28.3623 1168	27.6669 7004	26.9971 6998	50
51	30.1558 8877	29.3864 4574	28.6461 5774	27.9337 1015	27.2478 5400	51
52	30.4703 0687	29.6815 0988	28.9230 8072	28.1936 2743	27.4918 2871	52
53	30.7778 0623	29.9697 2882	29.1932 4948	28.4468 9640	27.7292 7368	53
54	31.0785 3910	30.2512 6137	29.4568 2876	28.6936 8711	27.9603 6368	54
55	31.3726 5438	30.5262 6263	29.7139 7928	28.9341 6528	28.1852 6879	55
56	31.6602 9768	30.7948 8413	29.9648 5784	29.1684 9235	28.4041 5454	56
57	31.9416 1142	31.0572 7388	30.2096 1740	29.3968 2568	28.6171 8203	57
58	32.2167 3489	31.3135 7644	30.4484 0722	29.6193 1857	28.8245 0806	58
59	32.4858 0429	31.5639 3303	30.6813 7290	29.8361 2041	29.0262 8522	59
60	32.7489 5285	31.8084 8159	30.9086 5649	30.0473 7676	29.2226 6201	60

TABLE IV

N	2 1/4	2 3/8	2 1/2	2 5/8	2 3/4	N
61	33.0063 1086	32.0473 5686	31.1303 9657	30.2532 2949	29.4137 8298	61
62	33.2580 0573	32.2806 9046	31.3467 2836	30.4538 1680	29.5997 8879	62
63	33.5041 6208	32.5086 1095	31.5577 8377	30.6492 7337	29.7808 1634	63
64	33.7449 0179	32.7312 4391	31.7636 9148	30.8397 3045	29.9569 9887	64
65	33.9803 4405	32.9487 1200	31.9645 7705	31.0253 1591	30.1284 6605	65
66	34.2106 0543	33.1611 3504	32.1605 6298	31.2061 5436	30.2953 4409	66
67	34.4357 9993	33.3686 3008	32.3517 6876	31.3823 6722	30.4577 5581	67
68	34.6560 3905	33.5713 1143	32.5383 1099	31.5540 7280	30.6158 2074	68
69	34.8714 3183	33.7692 9078	32.7203 0340	31.7213 8641	30.7696 5522	69
70	35.0820 8492	33.9626 7719	32.8978 5698	31.8844 2038	30.9193 7247	70
71	35.2881 0261	34.1515 7723	33.0710 7998	32.0432 8417	31.0650 8270	71
72	35.4895 8691	34.3360 9498	33.2400 7803	32.1980 8445	31.2068 9314	72
73	35.6866 3756	34.5163 3209	33.4049 5417	32.3489 2516	31.3449 0816	73
74	35.8793 5214	34.6923 8788	33.5658 0895	32.4959 0759	31.4792 2936	74
75	36.0678 2605	34.8643 5935	33.7227 4044	32.6391 3042	31.6099 5558	75
76	36.2521 5262	35.0323 4124	33.8758 4433	32.7786 8981	31.7371 8304	76
77	36.4324 2310	35.1964 2612	34.0252 1398	32.9146 7947	31.8610 0540	77
78	36.6087 2675	35.3567 0439	34.1709 4047	33.0471 9072	31.9815 1377	78
79	36.7811 5085	35.5132 6436	34.3131 1265	33.1763 1251	32.0987 9685	79
80	36.9497 8079	35.6661 9230	34.4518 1722	33.3021 3156	32.2129 4098	80
81	37.1147 0004	35.8155 7245	34.5871 3875	33.4247 3234	32.3240 3015	81
82	37.2759 9026	35.9614 8713	34.7191 5976	33.5441 9716	32.4321 4613	82
83	37.4337 3130	36.1040 1673	34.8479 6074	33.6606 0625	32.5373 6850	83
84	37.5880 0127	36.2432 3979	34.9736 2023	33.7740 3776	32.6397 7469	84
85	37.7388 7655	36.3792 3300	35.0962 1486	33.8845 6785	32.7394 4009	85
86	37.8864 3183	36.5120 7131	35.2158 1938	33.9922 7074	32.8364 3804	86
87	38.0307 4018	36.6418 2790	35.3325 0671	34.0972 1875	32.9308 3994	87
88	38.1718 7304	36.7685 7426	35.4463 4801	34.1994 8234	33.0227 1527	88
89	38.3099 0028	36.8923 8023	35.5574 1269	34.2991 3017	33.1121 3165	89
90	38.4448 9025	37.0133 1402	35.6657 6848	34.3962 2916	33.1991 5489	90
91	38.5769 0978	37.1314 4227	35.7714 8144	34.4908 4449	33.2838 4905	91
92	38.7060 2423	37.2468 3005	35.8746 1604	34.5830 3970	33.3662 7644	92
93	38.8322 9754	37.3595 4096	35.9752 3516	34.6728 7668	33.4464 9776	93
94	38.9557 9221	37.4696 3708	36.0734 0016	34.7604 1577	33.5245 7202	94
95	39.0765 6940	37.5771 7907	36.1691 7089	34.8457 1573	33.6005 5671	95
96	39.1946 8890	37.6822 2620	36.2626 0574	34.9288 3384	33.6745 0775	96
97	39.3102 0920	37.7848 3634	36.3537 6170	35.0098 2591	33.7464 7956	97
98	39.4231 8748	37.8850 6602	36.4426 9434	35.0887 4632	33.8165 2512	98
99	39.5336 7968	37.9829 7047	36.5294 5790	35.1656 4806	33.8846 9598	99
100	39.6417 4052	38.0786 0363	36.6141 0526	35.2405 8276	33.9510 4232	100
101	39.7474 2349	38.1720 1820	36.6966 8806	35.3136 0074	34.0156 1296	101
102	39.8507 8092	38.2632 6564	36.7772 5665	35.3847 5103	34.0784 5544	102
103	39.9518 6398	38.3523 9623	36.8558 6014	35.4540 8139	34.1396 1600	103
104	40.0507 2272	38.4394 5908	36.9325 4648	35.5216 3838	34.1991 3966	104
105	40.1474 0609	38.5245 0215	37.0073 6242	35.5874 6737	34.2570 7023	105
106	40.2419 6194	38.6075 7231	37.0803 5358	35.6516 1254	34.3134 5034	106
107	40.3344 3711	38.6887 1532	37.1515 6447	35.7141 1697	34.3683 2150	107
108	40.4248 7737	38.7679 7589	37.2210 3851	35.7750 2262	34.4217 2409	108
109	40.5133 2750	38.8453 9770	37.2888 1806	35.8343 7040	34.4736 9741	109
110	40.5998 3129	38.9210 2339	37.3549 4444	35.8922 0015	34.5242 7972	110
111	40.6844 3158	38.9948 9465	37.4194 5799	35.9485 5069	34.5735 0824	111
112	40.7671 7025	39.0670 5216	37.4823 9804	36.0034 5987	34.6214 1921	112
113	40.8480 8827	39.1375 3568	37.5438 0297	36.0569 6455	34.6680 4790	113
114	40.9272 2569	39.2063 8406	37.6037 1021	36.1091 0066	34.7134 2861	114
115	41.0046 2170	39.2736 3523	37.6621 5631	36.1599 0320	34.7575 9475	115
116	41.0803 1462	39.3393 2623	37.7191 7688	36.2094 0628	34.8005 7884	116
117	41.1543 4193	39.4034 9326	37.7748 0672	36.2576 4315	34.8424 1249	117
118	41.2267 4027	39.4661 7169	37.8290 7972	36.3046 4619	34.8831 2651	118
119	41.2975 4550	39.5273 9603	37.8820 2900	36.3504 4696	34.9227 5086	119
120	41.3667 9266	39.5872 0003	37.9336 8683	36.3950 7621	34.9613 1471	120

TABLE IV

N	2 1/4	2 3/8	2 1/2	2 5/8	2 3/4	N
121	41.4345 1605	39.6456 1663	37.9840 8471	36.4385 6390	34.9988 4643	121
122	41.5007 4919	39.7026 7803	38.0332 5338	36.4809 3925	35.0353 7366	122
123	41.5655 2489	39.7584 1566	38.0812 2281	36.5222 3069	35.0709 2327	123
124	41.6288 7519	39.8128 6023	38.1280 2225	36.5624 6596	35.1055 2143	124
125	41.6908 3148	39.8660 4174	38.1736 8024	36.6016 7207	35.1391 9360	125
126	41.7514 2443	39.9179 8949	38.2182 2463	36.6398 7534	35.1719 6458	126
127	41.8106 8404	39.9687 3210	38.2616 8256	36.6771 0143	35.2038 5847	127
128	41.8686 3965	40.0182 9753	38.3040 8055	36.7133 7533	35.2348 9875	128
129	41.9253 1995	40.0667 1310	38.3454 4444	36.7487 2139	35.2651 0828	129
130	41.9807 5301	40.1140 0547	38.3857 9945	36.7831 6335	35.2945 0927	130
131	42.0349 6627	40.1602 0070	38.4251 7020	36.8167 2434	35.3231 2338	131
132	42.0879 8657	40.2053 2425	38.4635 8068	36.8494 2688	35.3509 7166	132
133	42.1398 4017	40.2494 0098	38.5010 5432	36.8812 9294	35.3780 7461	133
134	42.1905 5273	40.2924 5517	38.5376 1397	36.9123 4391	35.4044 5217	134
135	42.2401 4937	40.3345 1054	38.5732 8192	36.9426 0065	35.4301 2377	135
136	42.2886 5464	40.3755 9027	38.6080 7993	36.9720 8346	35.4551 0829	136
137	42.3360 9256	40.4157 1699	38.6420 2920	37.0008 1214	35.4794 2413	137
138	42.3824 8661	40.4549 1281	38.6751 5044	37.0288 0598	35.5030 8917	138
139	42.4278 5976	40.4931 9933	38.7074 6384	37.0560 8378	35.5261 2085	139
140	42.4722 3449	40.5305 9764	38.7389 8911	37.0826 6386	35.5485 3611	140
141	42.5156 3275	40.5671 2834	38.7697 4547	37.1085 6405	35.5703 5144	141
142	42.5580 7604	40.6028 1156	38.7997 5168	37.1338 0175	35.5915 8291	142
143	42.5995 8537	40.6376 6697	38.8290 2603	37.1583 9391	35.6122 4614	143
144	42.6401 8129	40.6717 1377	38.8575 8637	37.1823 5704	35.6323 5634	144
145	42.6798 8390	40.7049 7072	38.8854 5012	37.2057 0723	35.6519 2832	145
146	42.7187 1286	40.7374 5613	38.9126 3426	37.2284 6015	35.6709 7646	146
147	42.7566 8740	40.7691 8792	38.9391 5538	37.2506 3108	35.6895 1481	147
148	42.7938 2631	40.8001 8356	38.9650 2964	37.2722 3492	35.7075 5699	148
149	42.8301 4798	40.8304 6013	38.9902 7282	37.2932 8615	35.7251 1629	149
150	42.8656 7039	40.8600 3432	39.0149 0031	37.3137 9893	35.7422 0564	150
151	42.9004 1114	40.8889 2241	39.0389 2713	37.3337 8702	35.7588 3760	151
152	42.9343 8742	40.9171 4033	39.0623 6793	37.3532 6385	35.7750 2443	152
153	42.9676 1606	40.9447 0362	39.0852 3701	37.3722 4248	35.7907 7803	153
154	43.0001 1351	40.9716 2746	39.1075 4830	37.3907 3567	35.8061 1001	154
155	43.0318 9585	40.9979 2670	39.1293 1541	37.4087 5583	35.8210 3164	155
156	43.0629 7883	41.0236 1583	39.1505 5162	37.4263 1506	35.8355 5391	156
157	43.0933 7783	41.0487 0899	39.1712 6988	37.4434 2515	35.8496 8750	157
158	43.1231 0790	41.0732 2002	39.1914 8281	37.4600 9759	35.8634 4282	158
159	43.1521 8377	41.0971 6241	39.2112 0274	37.4763 4357	35.8768 3000	159
160	43.1806 1982	41.1205 4936	39.2304 4170	37.4921 7400	35.8898 5888	160
161	43.2084 3014	41.1433 9376	39.2492 1141	37.5075 9951	35.9025 3905	161
162	43.2356 2850	41.1657 0819	39.2675 2333	37.5226 3046	35.9148 7986	162
163	43.2622 2836	41.1875 0495	39.2853 8861	37.5372 7694	35.9268 9037	163
164	43.2882 4290	41.2087 9604	39.3028 1816	37.5515 4879	35.9385 7944	164
165	43.3136 8498	41.2295 9320	39.3198 2259	37.5654 5558	35.9499 5566	165
166	43.3385 6722	41.2499 0789	39.3364 1229	37.5790 0665	35.9610 2740	166
167	43.3629 0193	41.2697 5130	39.3525 9735	37.5922 1111	35.9718 0283	167
168	43.3867 0115	41.2891 3436	39.3683 8766	37.6050 7782	35.9822 8986	168
169	43.4099 7668	41.3080 6775	39.3837 9284	37.6176 1542	35.9924 9621	169
170	43.4327 4003	41.3265 6190	39.3988 2228	37.6298 3232	36.0024 2940	170
171	43.4550 0247	41.3446 2701	39.4134 8515	37.6417 3673	36.0120 9674	171
172	43.4767 7503	41.3622 7303	39.4277 9039	37.6533 3664	36.0215 0534	172
173	43.4980 6849	41.3795 0967	39.4417 4673	37.6646 3985	36.0306 6214	173
174	43.5188 9339	41.3963 4644	39.4553 6266	37.6756 5393	36.0395 7385	174
175	43.5392 6004	41.4127 9262	39.4686 4650	37.6863 8629	36.0482 4706	175
176	43.5591 7852	41.4288 5726	39.4816 0634	37.6968 4413	36.0566 8814	176
177	43.5786 5870	41.4445 4921	39.4942 5009	37.7070 3448	36.0649 0330	177
178	43.5977 1022	41.4598 7713	39.5065 8545	37.7169 6417	36.0728 9858	178
179	43.6163 4252	41.4748 4946	39.5186 1995	37.7266 3987	36.0806 7989	179
180	43.6345 6481	41.4894 7444	39.5303 6093	37.7360 6808	36.0882 5293	180

TABLE IV

N	2 1/4	2 3/8	2 1/2	2 5/8	2 3/4	N
181	43.6523 8612	41.5037 6014	39.5418 1554	37.7452 5514	36.0956 2329	181
182	43.6698 1528	41.5177 1442	39.5529 9077	37.7542 0720	36.1027 9639	182
183	43.6868 6091	41.5313 4498	39.5638 9343	37.7629 3028	36.1097 7751	183
184	43.7035 3145	41.5446 5932	39.5745 3018	37.7714 3023	36.1165 7179	184
185	43.7198 3516	41.5576 6478	39.5849 0749	37.7797 1277	36.1231 8422	185
186	43.7357 8010	41.5703 6853	39.5950 3170	37.7877 8346	36.1296 1968	186
187	43.7513 7419	41.5827 7756	39.6049 0898	37.7956 4771	36.1358 8290	187
188	43.7666 2512	41.5948 9871	39.6145 4534	37.8033 1080	36.1419 7849	188
189	43.7815 4046	41.6067 3867	39.6239 4668	37.8107 7788	36.1479 1094	189
190	43.7961 2759	41.6183 0395	39.6331 1871	37.8180 5396	36.1536 8461	190
191	43.8103 9373	41.6296 0093	39.6420 6703	37.8251 4393	36.1593 0376	191
192	43.8243 4595	41.6406 3583	39.6507 9710	37.8320 5255	36.1647 7251	192
193	43.8379 9115	41.6514 1473	39.6593 1425	37.8387 8446	36.1700 9490	193
194	43.8513 3608	41.6619 4357	39.6676 2366	37.8453 4418	36.1752 7485	194
195	43.8643 8737	41.6722 2815	39.6757 3040	37.8517 3610	36.1803 1615	195
196	43.8771 5146	41.6822 7414	39.6836 3941	37.8579 6453	36.1852 2253	196
197	43.8896 3468	41.6920 8707	39.6913 5552	37.8640 3365	36.1899 9760	197
198	43.9018 4321	41.7016 7235	39.6988 8344	37.8699 4753	36.1946 4486	198
199	43.9137 8309	41.7110 3527	39.7062 2774	37.8757 1014	36.1991 6775	199
200	43.9254 6023	41.7201 8097	39.7133 9292	37.8813 2535	36.2035 6959	200
201	43.9368 8042	41.7291 1450	39.7203 8334	37.8867 9693	36.2078 5361	201
202	43.9480 4931	41.7378 4078	39.7272 0326	37.8921 2855	36.2120 2298	202
203	43.9589 7243	41.7463 6462	39.7338 5684	37.8973 2380	36.2160 8076	203
204	43.9696 5519	41.7546 9072	39.7403 4813	37.9023 8617	36.2200 2994	204
205	43.9801 0288	41.7628 2365	39.7466 8110	37.9073 1904	36.2238 7342	205
206	43.9903 2066	41.7707 6792	39.7528 5961	37.9121 2574	36.2276 1403	206
207	44.0003 1361	41.7785 2788	39.7588 8743	37.9168 0949	36.2312 5453	207
208	44.0100 8666	41.7861 0782	39.7647 6822	37.9213 7344	36.2347 9760	208
209	44.0196 4465	41.7935 1191	39.7705 0558	37.9258 2065	36.2382 4584	209
210	44.0289 9232	41.8007 4424	39.7761 0301	37.9301 5410	36.2416 0179	210
211	44.0381 3430	41.8078 0878	39.7815 6391	37.9343 7671	36.2448 6792	211
212	44.0470 7511	41.8147 0943	39.7868 9162	37.9384 9132	36.2480 4664	212
213	44.0558 1918	41.8214 4999	39.7920 8939	37.9425 0067	36.2511 4028	213
214	44.0643 7084	41.8280 3418	39.7971 6038	37.9464 0748	36.2541 5113	214
215	44.0727 3432	41.8344 6562	39.8021 0768	37.9502 1435	36.2570 8139	215
216	44.0809 1376	41.8407 4786	39.8069 3433	37.9539 2385	36.2599 3322	216
217	44.0889 1321	41.8468 8436	39.8116 4324	37.9575 3846	36.2627 0873	217
218	44.0967 3663	41.8528 7849	39.8162 3731	37.9610 6062	36.2654 0996	218
219	44.1043 8791	41.8587 3357	39.8207 1933	37.9644 9269	36.2680 3889	219
220	44.1118 7081	41.8644 5281	39.8250 9203	37.9678 3697	36.2705 9746	220
221	44.1191 8906	41.8700 3938	39.8293 5808	37.9710 9571	36.2730 8755	221
222	44.1263 4627	41.8754 9634	39.8335 2007	37.9742 7109	36.2755 1100	222
223	44.1333 4598	41.8808 2671	39.8375 8056	37.9773 6525	36.2778 6959	223
224	44.1401 9167	41.8860 3341	39.8415 4201	37.9803 8027	36.2801 6505	224
225	44.1468 8672	41.8911 1933	39.8454 0684	37.9833 1817	36.2823 9907	225
226	44.1534 3444	41.8960 8726	39.8491 7740	37.9861 8092	36.2845 7331	226
227	44.1598 3809	41.9009 3993	39.8528 5600	37.9889 7045	36.2866 8935	227
228	44.1661 0082	41.9056 8003	39.8564 4488	37.9916 8862	36.2887 4876	228
229	44.1722 2574	41.9103 1017	39.8599 4623	37.9943 3727	36.2907 5305	229
230	44.1782 1588	41.9148 3289	39.8633 6217	37.9969 1816	36.2927 0370	230
231	44.1840 7421	41.9192 5068	39.8666 9480	37.9994 3305	36.2946 0214	231
232	44.1898 0363	41.9235 6599	39.8699 4615	38.0018 8360	36.2964 4977	232
233	44.1954 0697	41.9277 8119	39.8731 1819	38.0042 7148	36.2982 4795	233
234	44.2008 8702	41.9318 9859	39.8762 1287	38.0065 9827	36.2999 9801	234
235	44.2062 4647	41.9359 2048	39.8792 3207	38.0088 6555	36.3017 0122	235
236	44.2114 8799	41.9398 4907	39.8821 7763	38.0110 7484	36.3033 5885	236
237	44.2166 1417	41.9436 8651	39.8850 5135	38.0132 2761	36.3049 7212	237
238	44.2216 2755	41.9474 3493	39.8878 5497	38.0153 2532	36.3065 4221	238
239	44.2265 3061	41.9510 9639	39.8905 9022	38.0173 6938	36.3080 7028	239
240	44.2313 2578	41.9546 7291	39.8932 5875	38.0193 6115	36.3095 5745	240

TABLE IV

N	2 1/4	2 3/8	2 1/2	2 5/8	2 3/4	N
241	44.2360 1544	41.9581 6646	39.8958 6219	38.0213 0197	36.3110 0482	241
242	44.2406 0189	41.9615 7896	39.8984 0214	38.0231 9315	36.3124 1345	242
243	44.2450 8743	41.9649 1229	39.9008 8014	38.0250 3596	36.3137 8438	243
244	44.2494 7426	41.9681 6829	39.9032 9769	38.0268 3163	36.3151 1861	244
245	44.2537 6455	41.9713 4876	39.9056 5629	38.0285 8136	36.3164 1714	245
246	44.2579 6044	41.9744 5544	39.9079 5735	38.0302 8635	36.3176 8092	246
247	44.2620 6400	41.9774 9006	39.9102 0229	38.0319 4772	36.3189 1087	247
248	44.2660 7726	41.9804 5427	39.9123 9248	38.0335 6660	36.3201 0790	248
249	44.2700 0221	41.9833 4971	39.9145 2925	38.0351 4407	36.3212 7290	249
250	44.2738 4080	41.9861 7798	39.9166 1390	38.0366 8118	36.3224 0671	250
251	44.2775 9491	41.9889 4064	39.9186 4771	38.0381 7899	36.3235 1018	251
252	44.2812 6642	41.9916 3921	39.9206 3191	38.0396 3848	36.3245 8412	252
253	44.2848 5713	41.9942 7518	39.9225 6772	38.0410 6063	36.3256 2931	253
254	44.2883 6883	41.9968 4999	39.9244 5631	38.0424 4642	36.3266 4653	254
255	44.2918 0326	41.9993 6507	39.9262 9884	38.0437 9675	36.3276 3653	255
256	44.2951 6211	42.0018 2180	39.9280 9643	38.0451 1255	36.3286 0003	256
257	44.2984 4705	42.0042 2154	39.9298 5018	38.0463 9469	36.3295 3774	257
258	44.3016 5971	42.0065 6561	39.9315 6115	38.0476 4403	36.3304 5035	258
259	44.3048 0167	42.0088 5529	39.9332 3039	38.0488 6142	36.3313 3854	259
260	44.3078 7450	42.0110 9186	39.9348 5891	38.0500 4767	36.3322 0296	260
261	44.3108 7970	42.0132 7654	39.9364 4772	38.0512 0357	36.3330 4425	261
262	44.3138 1878	42.0154 1054	39.9379 9778	38.0523 2991	36.3338 6301	262
263	44.3166 9318	42.0174 9504	39.9395 1003	38.0534 2744	36.3346 5987	263
264	44.3195 0434	42.0195 3117	39.9409 8539	38.0544 9690	36.3354 3539	264
265	44.3222 5363	42.0215 2007	39.9424 2477	38.0555 3900	36.3361 9016	265
266	44.3249 4242	42.0234 6283	39.9438 2905	38.0565 5445	36.3369 2473	266
267	44.3275 7205	42.0253 6052	39.9451 9907	38.0575 4392	36.3376 3964	267
268	44.3301 4382	42.0272 1418	39.9465 3568	38.0585 0808	36.3383 3542	268
269	44.3326 5899	42.0290 2484	39.9478 3969	38.0594 4758	36.3390 1257	269
270	44.3351 1882	42.0307 9349	39.9491 1189	38.0603 6305	36.3396 7161	270
271	44.3375 2452	42.0325 2112	39.9503 5306	38.0612 5511	36.3403 1300	271
272	44.3398 7728	42.0342 0866	39.9515 6396	38.0621 2434	36.3409 3722	272
273	44.3421 7827	42.0358 5706	39.9527 4533	38.0629 7134	36.3415 4474	273
274	44.3444 2862	42.0374 6721	39.9538 9788	38.0637 9668	36.3421 3600	274
275	44.3466 2946	42.0390 4001	39.9550 2232	38.0646 0091	36.3427 1144	275
276	44.3487 8187	42.0405 7632	39.9561 1934	38.0653 8456	36.3432 7147	276
277	44.3508 8691	42.0420 7699	39.9571 8960	38.0661 4817	36.3438 1652	277
278	44.3529 4563	42.0435 4285	39.9582 3376	38.0668 9225	36.3443 4698	278
279	44.3549 5906	42.0449 7470	39.9592 5245	38.0676 1730	36.3448 6324	279
280	44.3569 2817	42.0463 7333	39.9602 4629	38.0683 2380	36.3453 6568	280
281	44.3588 5396	42.0477 3952	39.9612 1589	38.0690 1223	36.3458 5468	281
282	44.3607 3737	42.0490 7401	39.9621 6185	38.0696 8305	36.3463 3059	282
283	44.3625 7933	42.0503 7755	39.9630 8473	38.0703 3671	36.3467 9376	283
284	44.3643 8076	42.0516 5084	39.9639 8510	38.0709 7365	36.3472 4453	284
285	44.3661 4256	42.0528 9459	39.9648 6351	38.0715 9430	36.3476 8324	285
286	44.3678 6558	42.0541 0949	39.9657 2050	38.0721 9907	36.3481 1021	286
287	44.3695 5069	42.0552 9621	39.9665 5658	38.0727 8838	36.3485 2576	287
288	44.3711 9872	42.0564 5539	39.9673 7228	38.0733 6261	36.3489 3018	288
289	44.3728 1048	42.0575 8768	39.9681 6808	38.0739 2215	36.3493 2377	289
290	44.3743 8678	42.0586 9371	39.9689 4446	38.0744 6738	36.3497 0683	290
291	44.3759 2839	42.0597 7407	39.9697 0192	38.0749 9867	36.3500 7964	291
292	44.3774 3608	42.0608 2938	39.9704 4089	38.0755 1636	36.3504 4248	292
293	44.3789 1059	42.0618 6020	39.9711 6185	38.0760 2082	36.3507 9560	293
294	44.3803 5266	42.0628 6710	39.9718 6522	38.0765 1237	36.3511 3927	294
295	44.3817 6299	42.0638 5065	39.9725 5143	38.0769 9135	36.3514 7374	295
296	44.3831 4229	42.0648 1138	39.9732 2091	38.0774 5807	36.3517 9926	296
297	44.3844 9124	42.0657 4982	39.9738 7406	38.0779 1286	36.3521 1607	297
298	44.3858 1050	42.0666 6649	39.9745 1128	38.0783 5601	36.3524 2440	298
299	44.3871 0073	42.0675 6190	39.9751 3295	38.0787 8783	36.3527 2447	299
300	44.3883 6258	42.0684 3653	39.9757 3947	38.0792 0861	36.3530 1652	300

TABLE IV

N	2 1/4	2 3/8	2 1/2	2 5/8	2 3/4	N
301	44.3895 9665	42.0692 9087	39.9763 3119	38.0796 1862	36.3533 0075	301
302	44.3908 0357	42.0701 2539	39.9769 0847	38.0800 1814	36.3535 7737	302
303	44.3919 8393	42.0709 4056	39.9774 7168	38.0804 0745	36.3538 4659	303
304	44.3931 3832	42.0717 3681	39.9780 2115	38.0807 8679	36.3541 0860	304
305	44.3942 6731	42.0725 1458	39.9785 5722	38.0811 5644	36.3543 6360	305
306	44.3953 7145	42.0732 7432	39.9790 8022	38.0815 1663	36.3546 1178	306
307	44.3964 5129	42.0740 1643	39.9795 9046	38.0818 6760	36.3548 5331	307
308	44.3975 0738	42.0747 4132	39.9800 8825	38.0822 0960	36.3550 8838	308
309	44.3985 4022	42.0754 4940	39.9805 7390	38.0825 4285	36.3553 1716	309
310	44.3995 5034	42.0761 4105	39.9810 4771	38.0828 6758	36.3555 3982	310
311	44.4005 3823	42.0768 1665	39.9815 0996	38.0831 8400	36.3557 5651	311
312	44.4015 0438	42.0774 7659	39.9819 6094	38.0834 9232	36.3559 6741	312
313	44.4024 4927	42.0781 2121	39.9824 0091	38.0837 9276	36.3561 7266	313
314	44.4033 7337	42.0787 5087	39.9828 3016	38.0840 8552	36.3563 7242	314
315	44.4042 7714	42.0793 6593	39.9832 4894	38.0843 7078	36.3565 6683	315
316	44.4051 6101	42.0799 6672	39.9836 5750	38.0846 4875	36.3567 5604	316
317	44.4060 2544	42.0805 5358	39.9840 5610	38.0849 1961	36.3569 4019	317
318	44.4068 7085	42.0811 2681	39.9844 4497	38.0851 8355	36.3571 1940	318
319	44.4076 9765	42.0816 8675	39.9848 2436	38.0854 4073	36.3572 9382	319
320	44.4085 0626	42.0822 3370	39.9851 9450	38.0856 9133	36.3574 6357	320
321	44.4092 9707	42.0827 6796	39.9855 5561	38.0859 3552	36.3576 2878	321
322	44.4100 7049	42.0832 8983	39.9859 0791	38.0861 7347	36.3577 8957	322
323	44.4108 2688	42.0837 9959	39.9862 5162	38.0864 0533	36.3579 4605	323
324	44.4115 6663	42.0842 9752	39.9865 8695	38.0866 3126	36.3580 9835	324
325	44.4122 9011	42.0847 8391	39.9869 1410	38.0868 5141	36.3582 4657	325
326	44.4129 9766	42.0852 5900	39.9872 3326	38.0870 6593	36.3583 9082	326
327	44.4136 8964	42.0857 2308	39.9875 4465	38.0872 7496	36.3585 3121	327
328	44.4143 6640	42.0861 7639	39.9878 4844	38.0874 7865	36.3586 6785	328
329	44.4150 2826	42.0866 1919	39.9881 4482	38.0876 7712	36.3588 0082	329
330	44.4156 7556	42.0870 5171	39.9884 3397	38.0878 7052	36.3589 3024	330
331	44.4163 0862	42.0874 7420	39.9887 1607	38.0880 5897	36.3590 5620	331
332	44.4169 2774	42.0878 8688	39.9889 9128	38.0882 4260	36.3591 7878	332
333	44.4175 3325	42.0882 9000	39.9892 5979	38.0884 2154	36.3592 9808	333
334	44.4181 2542	42.0886 8376	39.9895 2175	38.0885 9590	36.3594 1419	334
335	44.4187 0457	42.0890 6838	39.9897 7731	38.0887 6579	36.3595 2719	335
336	44.4192 7097	42.0894 4409	39.9900 2665	38.0889 3135	36.3596 3717	336
337	44.4198 2491	42.0898 1107	39.9902 6990	38.0890 9266	36.3597 4421	337
338	44.4203 6666	42.0901 6955	39.9905 0722	38.0892 4986	36.3598 4838	338
339	44.4208 9649	42.0905 1970	39.9907 3875	38.0894 0303	36.3599 4976	339
340	44.4214 1466	42.0908 6174	39.9909 6463	38.0895 5228	36.3600 4843	340
341	44.4219 2143	42.0911 9584	39.9911 8501	38.0896 9771	36.3601 4445	341
342	44.4224 1705	42.0915 2218	39.9914 0001	38.0898 3943	36.3602 3791	342
343	44.4229 0176	42.0918 4096	39.9916 0976	38.0899 7752	36.3603 2887	343
344	44.4233 7580	42.0921 5234	39.9918 1440	38.0901 1208	36.3604 1739	344
345	44.4238 3942	42.0924 5650	39.9920 1405	38.0902 4319	36.3605 0354	345
346	44.4242 9283	42.0927 5360	39.9922 0883	38.0903 7096	36.3605 8739	346
347	44.4247 3626	42.0930 4381	39.9923 9886	38.0904 9545	36.3606 6899	347
348	44.4251 6994	42.0933 2729	39.9925 8425	38.0906 1676	36.3607 4841	348
349	44.4255 9407	42.0936 0419	39.9927 6513	38.0907 3497	36.3608 2570	349
350	44.4260 0887	42.0938 7467	39.9929 4159	38.0908 5015	36.3609 0093	350
351	44.4264 1454	42.0941 3887	39.9931 1374	38.0909 6239	36.3609 7414	351
352	44.4268 1129	42.0943 9694	39.9932 8170	38.0910 7175	36.3610 4539	352
353	44.4271 9931	42.0946 4903	39.9934 4556	38.0911 7832	36.3611 1474	353
354	44.4275 7878	42.0948 9526	39.9936 0543	38.0912 8217	36.3611 8222	354
355	44.4279 4991	42.0951 3579	39.9937 6139	38.0913 8335	36.3612 4791	355
356	44.4283 1287	42.0953 7073	39.9939 1355	38.0914 8195	36.3613 1183	356
357	44.4286 6784	42.0956 0023	39.9940 6200	38.0915 7803	36.3613 7404	357
358	44.4290 1501	42.0958 2440	39.9942 0683	38.0916 7165	36.3614 3459	358
359	44.4293 5453	42.0960 4337	39.9943 4813	38.0917 6287	36.3614 9352	359
360	44.4296 8658	42.0962 5726	39.9944 8598	38.0918 5176	36.3615 5087	360

TABLE IV

N	3	3 1/2	4	4 1/2	5	N
1	0.9708 7379	0.9661 8357	0.9615 3846	0.9569 3780	0.9523 8095	1
2	1.9134 6970	1.8996 9428	1.8860 9467	1.8726 6775	1.8594 1043	2
3	2.8286 1135	2.8016 3698	2.7750 9103	2.7489 6435	2.7232 4803	3
4	3.7170 9840	3.6730 7921	3.6298 9522	3.5875 2570	3.5459 5050	4
5	4.5797 0719	4.5150 5238	4.4518 2233	4.3899 7674	4.3294 7667	5
6	5.4171 9144	5.3285 5302	5.2421 3686	5.1578 7248	5.0756 9207	6
7	6.2302 8296	6.1145 4398	6.0020 5467	5.8927 0094	5.7863 7340	7
8	7.0196 9219	6.8739 5554	6.7327 4487	6.5958 8607	6.4632 1276	8
9	7.7861 0892	7.6076 8651	7.4353 3161	7.2687 9050	7.1078 2168	9
10	8.5302 0284	8.3166 0532	8.1108 9578	7.9127 1818	7.7217 3493	10
11	9.2526 2411	9.0015 5104	8.7604 7671	8.5289 1692	8.3064 1422	11
12	9.9540 0399	9.6633 3433	9.3850 7376	9.1185 8078	8.8632 5164	12
13	10.6349 5533	10.3027 3849	9.9856 4785	9.6828 5242	9.3935 7299	13
14	11.2960 7314	10.9205 2028	10.5631 2293	10.2228 2528	9.8986 4094	14
15	11.9379 3509	11.5174 1090	11.1183 8743	10.7395 4573	10.3796 5804	15
16	12.5611 0203	12.0941 1681	11.6522 9561	11.2340 1505	10.8377 6956	16
17	13.1661 1847	12.6513 2059	12.1656 6885	11.7071 9143	11.2740 6625	17
18	13.7535 1308	13.1896 8173	12.6592 9697	12.1599 9180	11.6895 8690	18
19	14.3237 9911	13.7098 3742	13.1339 3940	12.5932 9359	12.0853 2086	19
20	14.8774 7486	14.2124 0330	13.5903 2634	13.0079 3645	12.4622 1034	20
21	15.4150 2414	14.6979 7420	14.0291 5995	13.4047 2388	12.8211 5271	21
22	15.9369 1664	15.1671 2484	14.4511 1533	13.7844 2476	13.1630 0258	22
23	16.4436 0839	15.6204 1047	14.8568 4167	14.1477 7489	13.4885 7388	23
24	16.9355 4212	16.0583 6760	15.2469 6314	14.4954 7837	13.7986 4179	24
25	17.4131 4769	16.4815 1459	15.6220 7994	14.8282 0896	14.0939 4457	25
26	17.8768 4242	16.8903 5226	15.9827 6918	15.1466 1145	14.3751 8530	26
27	18.3270 3147	17.2853 6451	16.3295 8575	15.4513 0282	14.6430 3362	27
28	18.7641 0823	17.6670 1885	16.6630 6322	15.7428 7351	14.8981 2726	28
29	19.1884 5459	18.0357 6700	16.9837 1463	16.0218 8853	15.1410 7358	29
30	19.6004 4135	18.3920 4541	17.2920 3330	16.2888 8854	15.3724 5103	30
31	20.0004 2849	18.7362 7576	17.5884 9356	16.5443 9095	15.5928 1050	31
32	20.3887 6553	19.0688 6547	17.8735 5150	16.7888 9086	15.8026 7667	32
33	20.7657 9178	19.3902 0818	18.1476 4567	17.0228 6207	16.0025 4921	33
34	21.1318 3668	19.7006 8423	18.4111 9776	17.2467 5796	16.1929 0401	34
35	21.4872 2007	20.0006 6110	18.6646 1323	17.4610 1240	16.3741 9429	35
36	21.8322 5250	20.2904 9381	18.9082 8195	17.6660 4058	16.5468 5171	36
37	22.1672 3544	20.5705 2542	19.1425 7880	17.8622 3979	16.7112 8734	37
38	22.4924 6159	20.8410 8736	19.3678 6423	18.0499 9023	16.8678 9271	38
39	22.8082 1513	21.1024 9987	19.5844 8484	18.2296 5572	17.0170 4067	39
40	23.1147 7197	21.3550 7234	19.7927 7388	18.4015 8442	17.1590 8635	40
41	23.4123 9997	21.5991 0371	19.9930 5181	18.5661 0949	17.2943 6796	41
42	23.7013 5920	21.8348 8281	20.1856 2674	18.7235 4975	17.4232 0758	42
43	23.9819 0213	22.0626 8870	20.3707 9494	18.8742 1029	17.5459 1198	43
44	24.2542 7392	22.2827 9102	20.5488 4129	19.0183 8305	17.6627 7331	44
45	24.5187 1254	22.4954 5026	20.7200 3970	19.1563 4742	17.7740 6982	45
46	24.7754 4907	22.7009 1813	20.8846 5356	19.2883 7074	17.8800 6650	46
47	25.0247 0783	22.8994 3780	21.0429 3612	19.4147 0884	17.9810 1571	47
48	25.2667 0664	23.0912 4425	21.1951 3088	19.5356 0654	18.0771 5782	48
49	25.5016 5693	23.2765 6450	21.3414 7200	19.6512 9813	18.1687 2173	49
50	25.7297 6401	23.4556 1787	21.4821 8462	19.7620 0778	18.2559 2546	50
51	25.9512 2719	23.6286 1630	21.6174 8521	19.8679 5003	18.3389 7663	51
52	26.1662 3999	23.7957 6454	21.7475 8193	19.9693 3017	18.4180 7298	52
53	26.3749 9028	23.9572 6043	21.8726 7493	20.0663 4466	18.4934 0284	53
54	26.5776 6047	24.1132 9510	21.9929 5667	20.1591 8149	18.5651 4556	54
55	26.7744 2764	24.2640 5323	22.1086 1218	20.2480 2057	18.6334 7196	55
56	26.9654 6373	24.4097 1327	22.2198 1940	20.3330 3404	18.6985 4473	56
57	27.1509 3566	24.5504 4760	22.3267 4943	20.4143 8664	18.7605 1879	57
58	27.3310 0549	24.6864 2281	22.4295 6676	20.4922 3602	18.8195 4170	58
59	27.5058 3058	24.8177 9981	22.5284 2957	20.5667 3303	18.8757 5400	59
60	27.6755 6367	24.9447 3412	22.6234 8997	20.6380 2204	18.9292 8953	60

TABLE IV

N	3	3 1/2	4	4 1/2	5	N
61	27.8403 5307	25.0673 7596	22.7148 9421	20.7062 4118	18.9802 7574	61
62	28.0003 4279	25.1858 7049	22.8027 8289	20.7715 2266	19.0288 3404	62
63	28.1556 7261	25.3003 5796	22.8872 9124	20.8339 9298	19.0750 8003	63
64	28.3064 7826	25.4109 7388	22.9685 4927	20.8937 7319	19.1191 2384	64
65	28.4528 9152	25.5178 4916	23.0466 8199	20.9509 7913	19.1610 7033	65
66	28.5950 4031	25.6211 1030	23.1218 0961	21.0057 2165	19.2010 1936	66
67	28.7330 4884	25.7208 7951	23.1940 4770	21.0581 0684	19.2390 6606	67
68	28.8670 3771	25.8172 7489	23.2635 0740	21.1082 3621	19.2753 0101	68
69	28.9971 2399	25.9104 1052	23.3302 9558	21.1562 0690	19.3098 1048	69
70	29.1234 2135	26.0003 9664	23.3945 1498	21.2021 1187	19.3426 7665	70
71	29.2460 4015	26.0873 3975	23.4562 6440	21.2460 4007	19.3739 7776	71
72	29.3650 8752	26.1713 4275	23.5156 3885	21.2880 7662	19.4037 8834	72
73	29.4806 6750	26.2525 0508	23.5727 2966	21.3283 0298	19.4321 7937	73
74	29.5928 8107	26.3309 2278	23.6276 2468	21.3667 9711	19.4592 1845	74
75	29.7018 2628	26.4066 8868	23.6804 0834	21.4036 3360	19.4849 6995	75
76	29.8075 9833	26.4798 9244	23.7311 6187	21.4388 8383	19.5094 9519	76
77	29.9102 8964	26.5506 2072	23.7799 6333	21.4726 1611	19.5328 5257	77
78	30.0099 8994	26.6189 5721	23.8268 8782	21.5048 9579	19.5550 9768	78
79	30.1067 8635	26.6849 8281	23.8720 0752	21.5357 8545	19.5762 8351	79
80	30.2007 6345	26.7487 7567	23.9153 9185	21.5653 4493	19.5964 6048	80
81	30.2920 0335	26.8104 1127	23.9571 0755	21.5936 3151	19.6156 7665	81
82	30.3805 8577	26.8699 6258	23.9972 1879	21.6207 0001	19.6339 7776	82
83	30.4665 8813	26.9275 0008	24.0357 8730	21.6466 0288	19.6514 0739	83
84	30.5500 8556	26.9830 9186	24.0728 7241	21.6713 9032	19.6680 0704	84
85	30.6311 5103	27.0368 0373	24.1085 3116	21.6951 1035	19.6838 1623	85
86	30.7098 5537	27.0886 9926	24.1428 1842	21.7178 0895	19.6988 7260	86
87	30.7862 6735	27.1388 3986	24.1757 8694	21.7395 3009	19.7132 1200	87
88	30.8604 5374	27.1872 8489	24.2074 8745	21.7603 1588	19.7268 6857	88
89	30.9324 7936	27.2340 9168	24.2379 6870	21.7802 0658	19.7398 7483	89
90	31.0024 0714	27.2793 1564	24.2672 7759	21.7992 4075	19.7522 6174	90
91	31.0702 9820	27.3230 1028	24.2954 5923	21.8174 5526	19.7640 5880	91
92	31.1362 1184	27.3652 2732	24.3225 5695	21.8348 8542	19.7752 9410	92
93	31.2002 0567	27.4060 1673	24.3486 1245	21.8515 6499	19.7859 9438	93
94	31.2623 3560	27.4454 2680	24.3736 6582	21.8675 2631	19.7961 8512	94
95	31.3226 5592	27.4835 0415	24.3977 5559	21.8828 0030	19.8058 9059	95
96	31.3812 1934	27.5202 9387	24.4209 1884	21.8974 1655	19.8151 3390	96
97	31.4380 7703	27.5558 3948	24.4431 9119	21.9114 0340	19.8239 3705	97
98	31.4932 7867	27.5901 8308	24.4646 0692	21.9247 8794	19.8323 2100	98
99	31.5468 7250	27.6233 6529	24.4851 9896	21.9375 9612	19.8403 0571	99
100	31.5989 0534	27.6554 2540	24.5049 9900	21.9498 5274	19.8479 1020	100
101	31.6494 2266	27.6864 0135	24.5240 3750	21.9615 8157	19.8551 5257	101
102	31.6984 6860	27.7163 2981	24.5423 4375	21.9728 0533	19.8620 5007	102
103	31.7460 8602	27.7452 4619	24.5599 4591	21.9835 4577	19.8686 1911	103
104	31.7923 1652	27.7731 8473	24.5768 7107	21.9938 2371	19.8748 7535	104
105	31.8372 0051	27.8001 7848	24.5931 4526	22.0036 5905	19.8808 3366	105
106	31.8807 7719	27.8262 5940	24.6087 9352	22.0130 7086	19.8865 0825	106
107	31.9230 8465	27.8514 5836	24.6238 3992	22.0220 7738	19.8919 1262	107
108	31.9641 5986	27.8758 0518	24.6383 0762	22.0306 9605	19.8970 5964	108
109	32.0040 3870	27.8993 2868	24.6522 1886	22.0389 4359	19.9019 6156	109
110	32.0427 5602	27.9220 5669	24.6655 9506	22.0468 3597	19.9066 3006	110
111	32.0803 4565	27.9440 1613	24.6784 5679	22.0543 8849	19.9110 7624	111
112	32.1168 4043	27.9652 3297	24.6908 2383	22.0616 1578	19.9153 1071	112
113	32.1522 7227	27.9857 3234	24.7027 1523	22.0685 3185	19.9193 4353	113
114	32.1866 7210	28.0055 3849	24.7141 4925	22.0751 5009	19.9231 8432	114
115	32.2200 7000	28.0246 7487	24.7251 4351	22.0814 8334	19.9268 4221	115
116	32.2524 9515	28.0431 6413	24.7357 1492	22.0875 4387	19.9303 2591	116
117	32.2839 7587	28.0610 2814	24.7458 7973	22.0933 4342	19.9336 4372	117
118	32.3145 3968	28.0782 8806	24.7556 5359	22.0988 9322	19.9368 0355	118
119	32.3442 1328	28.0949 6431	24.7650 5152	22.1042 0404	19.9398 1290	119
120	32.3730 2261	28.1110 7663	24.7740 8800	22.1092 8616	19.9426 7895	120

TABLE IV

N	5 1/2	6	6 1/2	7	7 1/2	N
1	0.9478 6730	0.9433 9623	0.9389 6714	0.9345 7944	0.9302 3256	1
2	1.8463 1971	1.8333 9267	1.8206 2642	1.8080 1817	1.7955 6517	2
3	2.6979 3338	2.6730 1195	2.6484 7551	2.6243 1604	2.6005 2574	3
4	3.5051 5012	3.4651 0561	3.4257 9860	3.3872 1126	3.3493 2627	4
5	4.2702 8448	4.2123 6379	4.1556 7944	4.1001 9744	4.0458 8490	5
6	4.9955 3031	4.9173 2433	4.8410 1356	4.7665 3966	4.6938 4642	6
7	5.6829 6712	5.5823 8144	5.4845 1977	5.3892 8940	5.2966 0132	7
8	6.3345 6599	6.2097 9381	6.0887 5096	5.9712 9851	5.8573 0355	8
9	6.9521 9525	6.8016 9227	6.6561 0419	6.5152 3225	6.3788 8703	9
10	7.5376 2583	7.3600 8705	7.1888 3022	7.0235 8154	6.8640 8096	10
11	8.0925 3633	7.8868 7458	7.6890 4246	7.4986 7434	7.3154 2415	11
12	8.6185 1785	8.3838 4394	8.1587 2532	7.9426 8630	7.7352 7827	12
13	9.1170 7853	8.8526 8296	8.5997 4208	8.3576 5074	8.1258 4026	13
14	9.5896 4790	9.2949 8393	9.0138 4233	8.7454 6799	8.4891 5373	14
15	10.0375 8094	9.7122 4899	9.4026 6885	9.1079 1401	8.8271 1975	15
16	10.4621 6203	10.1058 9527	9.7677 6418	9.4466 4860	9.1415 0674	16
17	10.8646 0856	10.4772 5969	10.1105 7670	9.7632 2299	9.4339 5976	17
18	11.2460 7447	10.8276 0348	10.4324 6638	10.0590 8691	9.7060 0908	18
19	11.6076 5352	11.1581 1649	10.7347 1022	10.3355 9524	9.9590 7821	19
20	11.9503 8248	11.4699 2122	11.0185 0725	10.5940 1425	10.1944 9136	20
21	12.2752 4406	11.7640 7662	11.2849 8333	10.8355 2733	10.4134 8033	21
22	12.5831 6973	12.0415 8172	11.5351 9562	11.0612 4050	10.6171 9101	22
23	12.8750 4239	12.3033 7898	11.7701 3673	11.2721 8738	10.8066 8931	23
24	13.1516 9895	12.5503 5753	11.9907 3871	11.4693 3400	10.9829 6680	24
25	13.4139 3266	12.7833 5616	12.1978 7673	11.6535 8318	11.1469 4586	25
26	13.6624 9541	13.0031 6619	12.3923 7251	11.8257 7867	11.2994 8452	26
27	13.8980 9991	13.2105 3414	12.5749 9766	11.9867 0904	11.4413 8095	27
28	14.1214 2172	13.4061 6428	12.7464 7668	12.1371 1125	11.5733 7763	28
29	14.3331 0116	13.5907 2102	12.9074 8984	12.2776 7407	11.6961 6524	29
30	14.5337 4517	13.7648 3115	13.0586 7591	12.4090 4118	11.8103 8627	30
31	14.7239 2907	13.9290 8599	13.2006 3465	12.5318 1419	11.9166 3839	31
32	14.9041 9817	14.0840 4339	13.3339 2925	12.6465 5532	12.0154 7757	32
33	15.0750 6936	14.2302 2961	13.4590 8850	12.7537 9002	12.1074 2099	33
34	15.2370 3257	14.3681 4114	13.5766 0892	12.8540 0936	12.1929 4976	34
35	15.3905 5220	14.4982 4636	13.6869 5673	12.9476 7230	12.2725 1141	35
36	15.5360 6843	14.6209 8713	13.7905 6970	13.0352 0776	12.3465 2224	36
37	15.6739 9851	14.7367 8031	13.8878 5887	13.1170 1660	12.4153 6952	37
38	15.8047 3793	14.8460 1916	13.9792 1021	13.1934 7345	12.4794 1351	38
39	15.9286 6154	14.9490 7468	14.0649 8611	13.2649 2846	12.5389 8931	39
40	16.0461 2469	15.0462 9687	14.1455 2687	13.3317 0884	12.5944 0866	40
41	16.1574 6416	15.1380 1592	14.2211 5199	13.3941 2041	12.6459 6155	41
42	16.2629 9920	15.2245 4332	14.2921 6149	13.4524 4898	12.6939 1772	42
43	16.3630 3242	15.3061 7294	14.3588 3708	13.5069 6167	12.7385 2811	43
44	16.4578 5063	15.3831 8202	14.4214 4327	13.5579 0810	12.7800 2615	44
45	16.5477 2572	15.4558 3209	14.4802 2842	13.6055 2159	12.8186 2898	45
46	16.6329 1537	15.5243 6990	14.5354 2575	13.6500 2018	12.8545 3858	46
47	16.7136 6386	15.5890 2821	14.5872 5422	13.6916 0764	12.8879 4287	47
48	16.7902 0271	15.6500 2661	14.6359 1946	13.7304 7443	12.9190 1662	48
49	16.8627 5139	15.7075 7227	14.6816 1451	13.7667 9853	12.9479 2244	49
50	16.9315 1790	15.7618 6064	14.7245 2067	13.8007 4629	12.9748 1157	50
51	16.9966 9943	15.8130 7607	14.7648 0814	13.8324 7317	12.9998 2472	51
52	17.0584 8287	15.8613 9252	14.8026 3675	13.8621 2446	13.0230 9276	52
53	17.1170 4538	15.9069 7408	14.8381 5658	13.8898 3594	13.0447 3745	53
54	17.1725 5486	15.9499 7554	14.8715 0852	13.9157 3453	13.0648 7205	54
55	17.2251 7048	15.9905 4297	14.9028 2490	13.9399 3881	13.0836 0190	55
56	17.2750 4311	16.0288 1412	14.9322 2996	13.9625 5964	13.1010 2503	56
57	17.3223 1575	16.0649 1898	14.9598 4033	13.9837 0059	13.1172 3258	57
58	17.3671 2393	16.0989 8017	14.9857 6557	14.0034 5850	13.1323 0938	58
59	17.4095 9614	16.1311 1337	15.0101 0852	14.0219 2383	13.1463 3431	59
60	17.4498 5416	16.1614 2771	15.0329 6574	14.0391 8115	13.1593 8075	60

TABLE IV

N	5 1/2	6	6 1/2	7	7 1/2	N
61	17.4880 1343	16.1900 2614	15.0544 2793	14.0553 0949	13.1715 1698	61
62	17.5241 8334	16.2170 0579	15.0745 8022	14.0703 8270	13.1828 0649	62
63	17.5584 6762	16.2424 5829	15.0935 0255	14.0844 6981	13.1933 0836	63
64	17.5909 6457	16.2664 7009	15.1112 7000	14.0976 3534	13.2030 7755	64
65	17.6217 6737	16.2891 2272	15.1279 5305	14.1099 3957	13.2121 6516	65
66	17.6509 6433	16.3104 9314	15.1436 1789	14.1214 3885	13.2206 1875	66
67	17.6786 3917	16.3306 5390	15.1583 2666	14.1321 8584	13.2284 8256	67
68	17.7048 7125	16.3496 7349	15.1721 3771	14.1422 2976	13.2357 9773	68
69	17.7297 3579	16.3676 1650	15.1851 0583	14.1516 1659	13.2426 0254	69
70	17.7533 0406	16.3845 4387	15.1972 8247	14.1603 8934	13.2489 3260	70
71	17.7756 4366	16.4005 1308	15.2087 1593	14.1685 8817	13.2548 2102	71
72	17.7968 1864	16.4155 7838	15.2194 5158	14.1762 5063	13.2602 9862	72
73	17.8168 8970	16.4297 9093	15.2295 3200	14.1834 1180	13.2653 9407	73
74	17.8359 1441	16.4431 9899	15.2389 9718	14.1901 0449	13.2701 3402	74
75	17.8539 4731	16.4558 4810	15.2478 8468	14.1963 5933	13.2745 4327	75
76	17.8710 4010	16.4677 8123	15.2562 2974	14.2022 0498	13.2786 4490	76
77	17.8872 4180	16.4790 3889	15.2640 6549	14.2076 6821	13.2824 6038	77
78	17.9025 9887	16.4896 5933	15.2714 2299	14.2127 7403	13.2860 0965	78
79	17.9171 5532	16.4996 7862	15.2783 3145	14.2175 4582	13.2893 1130	79
80	17.9309 5291	16.5091 3077	15.2848 1826	14.2220 0544	13.2923 8261	80
81	17.9440 3120	16.5180 4790	15.2909 0917	14.2261 7331	13.2952 3964	81
82	17.9564 2767	16.5264 6028	15.2966 2832	14.2300 6851	13.2978 9734	82
83	17.9681 7789	16.5343 9649	15.3019 9843	14.2337 0889	13.3003 6961	83
84	17.9793 1554	16.5418 8348	15.3070 4078	14.2371 1111	13.3026 6941	84
85	17.9898 7255	16.5489 4668	15.3117 7538	14.2402 9076	13.3048 0875	85
86	17.9998 7919	16.5556 1008	15.3162 2101	14.2432 6239	13.3067 9884	86
87	18.0093 6416	16.5618 9630	15.3203 9532	14.2460 3962	13.3086 5008	87
88	18.0183 5466	16.5678 2670	15.3243 1485	14.2486 3516	13.3103 7217	88
89	18.0268 7645	16.5734 2141	15.3279 9516	14.2510 6089	13.3119 7411	89
90	18.0349 5398	16.5786 9944	15.3314 5086	14.2533 2794	13.3134 6429	90
91	18.0426 1041	16.5836 7872	15.3346 9564	14.2554 4667	13.3148 5050	91
92	18.0498 6769	16.5883 7615	15.3377 4239	14.2574 2680	13.3161 4000	92
93	18.0567 4662	16.5928 0769	15.3406 0318	14.2592 7738	13.3173 3954	93
94	18.0632 6694	16.5969 8839	15.3432 8937	14.2610 0690	13.3184 5538	94
95	18.0694 4734	16.6009 3244	15.3458 1162	14.2626 2327	13.3194 9338	95
96	18.0753 0553	16.6046 5325	15.3481 7992	14.2641 3390	13.3204 5896	96
97	18.0808 5832	16.6081 6344	15.3504 0368	14.2655 4570	13.3213 5717	97
98	18.0861 2164	16.6114 7494	15.3524 9172	14.2668 6514	13.3221 9272	98
99	18.0911 1055	16.6145 9900	15.3544 5232	14.2680 9826	13.3229 6997	99
100	18.0958 3939	16.6175 4623	15.3562 9326	14.2692 5071	13.3236 9299	100
101	18.1003 2169	16.6203 2663	15.3580 2184	14.2703 2777	13.3243 6558	101
102	18.1045 7033	16.6229 4965	15.3596 4492	14.2713 3436	13.3249 9123	102
103	18.1085 5747	16.6254 2420	15.3611 6894	14.2722 7510	13.3255 7324	103
104	18.1124 1466	16.6277 5868	15.3625 9994	14.2731 5430	13.3261 1464	104
105	18.1160 3285	16.6299 6102	15.3639 4361	14.2739 7598	13.3266 1827	105
106	18.1194 6242	16.6320 3870	15.3652 0526	14.2747 4391	13.3270 8676	106
107	18.1227 1319	16.6339 9877	15.3663 8992	14.2754 6160	13.3275 2257	107
108	18.1257 9450	16.6358 4790	15.3675 0227	14.2761 3233	13.3279 2797	108
109	18.1287 1516	16.6375 9236	15.3685 4673	14.2767 5919	13.3283 0509	109
110	18.1314 8357	16.6392 3807	15.3695 2745	14.2773 4504	13.3286 5590	110
111	18.1341 0765	16.6407 9063	15.3704 4831	14.2778 9256	13.3289 8223	111
112	18.1365 9493	16.6422 5531	15.3713 1297	14.2784 0426	13.3292 8580	112
113	18.1389 5254	16.6436 3709	15.3721 2485	14.2788 8249	13.3295 6818	113
114	18.1411 8724	16.6449 4065	15.3728 8718	14.2793 2943	13.3298 3087	114
115	18.1433 0544	16.6461 7042	15.3736 0299	14.2797 4713	13.3300 7523	115
116	18.1453 1321	16.6473 3059	15.3742 7511	14.2801 3750	13.3303 0254	116
117	18.1472 1631	16.6484 2508	15.3749 0621	14.2805 0234	13.3305 1399	117
118	18.1490 2020	16.6494 5763	15.3754 9878	14.2808 4331	13.3307 1069	118
119	18.1507 3005	16.6504 3172	15.3760 5520	14.2811 6197	13.3308 9366	119
120	18.1523 5076	16.6513 5068	15.3765 7765	14.2814 5978	13.3310 6387	120

TABLE IV

N	8	8 1/2	9	9 1/2	10	N
1	0.9259 2593	0.9216 5899	0.9174 3119	0.9132 4201	0.9090 9091	1
2	1.7832 6475	1.7711 1427	1.7591 1119	1.7472 5298	1.7355 3719	2
3	2.5770 9699	2.5540 2237	2.5312 9467	2.5089 0683	2.4868 5199	3
4	3.3121 2684	3.2755 9666	3.2397 1988	3.2044 8112	3.1698 6545	4
5	3.9927 1004	3.9406 4208	3.8896 5126	3.8397 0879	3.7907 8677	5
6	4.6228 7966	4.5535 8717	4.4859 1859	4.4198 2538	4.3552 6070	6
7	5.2063 7006	5.1185 1352	5.0329 5284	4.9496 1222	4.8684 1882	7
8	5.7466 3894	5.6391 8297	5.5348 1911	5.4334 3581	5.3349 2620	8
9	6.2468 8791	6.1190 6264	5.9952 4689	5.8752 8385	5.7590 2382	9
10	6.7100 8140	6.5613 4806	6.4176 5770	6.2787 9803	6.1445 6711	10
11	7.1389 6426	6.9689 8439	6.8051 9055	6.6473 0414	6.4950 6101	11
12	7.5360 7802	7.3446 8607	7.1607 2528	6.9838 3940	6.8136 9182	12
13	7.9037 7594	7.6909 5490	7.4869 0392	7.2911 7753	7.1033 5620	13
14	8.2442 3698	8.0100 9668	7.7861 5039	7.5718 5163	7.3666 8746	14
15	8.5594 7869	8.3042 3658	8.0606 8843	7.8281 7500	7.6060 7951	15
16	8.8513 6916	8.5753 3325	8.3125 5819	8.0622 6028	7.8237 0864	16
17	9.1216 3811	8.8251 9194	8.5436 3137	8.2760 3678	8.0215 5331	17
18	9.3718 8714	9.0554 7644	8.7556 2511	8.4712 6647	8.2014 1210	18
19	9.6035 9920	9.2677 2022	8.9501 1478	8.6495 5842	8.3649 2009	19
20	9.8181 4741	9.4633 3661	9.1285 4567	8.8123 8212	8.5135 6372	20
21	10.0168 0316	9.6436 2821	9.2922 4373	8.9610 7956	8.6486 9429	21
22	10.2007 4366	9.8097 9559	9.4424 2544	9.0968 7631	8.7715 4026	22
23	10.3710 5895	9.9629 4524	9.5802 0683	9.2208 9161	8.8832 1842	23
24	10.5287 5828	10.1040 9700	9.7066 1177	9.3341 4759	8.9847 4402	24
25	10.6747 7619	10.2341 9078	9.8225 7960	9.4375 7770	9.0770 4002	25
26	10.8099 7795	10.3540 9288	9.9289 7211	9.5320 3443	9.1609 4547	26
27	10.9351 6477	10.4646 0174	10.0265 7992	9.6182 9629	9.2372 2316	27
28	11.0510 7849	10.5664 5321	10.1161 2837	9.6970 7423	9.3065 6651	28
29	11.1584 0601	10.6603 2554	10.1982 8291	9.7690 1756	9.3696 0591	29
30	11.2577 8334	10.7468 4382	10.2736 5404	9.8347 1924	9.4269 1447	30
31	11.3497 9939	10.8265 8416	10.3428 0187	9.8947 2076	9.4790 1315	31
32	11.4349 9944	10.9000 7757	10.4062 4025	9.9495 1668	9.5263 7559	32
33	11.5138 8837	10.9678 1343	10.4644 4060	9.9995 5861	9.5694 3236	33
34	11.5869 3367	11.0302 4279	10.5178 3541	10.0452 5901	9.6085 7487	34
35	11.6545 6822	11.0877 8137	10.5668 2148	10.0869 9453	9.6441 5897	35
36	11.7171 9279	11.1408 1233	10.6117 6282	10.1251 0916	9.6765 0816	36
37	11.7751 7851	11.1896 8878	10.6529 9342	10.1599 1704	9.7059 1651	37
38	11.8288 6899	11.2347 3620	10.6908 1965	10.1917 0506	9.7326 5137	38
39	11.8785 8240	11.2762 5457	10.7255 2261	10.2207 3521	9.7569 5579	39
40	11.9246 1333	11.3145 2034	10.7573 6020	10.2472 4677	9.7790 5072	40
41	11.9672 3457	11.3497 8833	10.7865 6899	10.2714 5824	9.7991 3702	41
42	12.0066 9867	11.3822 9339	10.8133 6604	10.2935 6917	9.8173 9729	42
43	12.0432 3951	11.4122 5197	10.8379 5050	10.3137 6180	9.8339 9753	43
44	12.0770 7362	11.4398 6357	10.8605 0504	10.3322 0255	9.8490 8867	44
45	12.1084 0150	11.4653 1205	10.8811 9729	10.3490 4343	9.8628 0788	45
46	12.1374 0880	11.4887 6686	10.9001 8100	10.3644 2322	9.8752 7989	46
47	12.1642 6741	11.5103 8420	10.9175 9725	10.3784 6870	9.8866 1808	47
48	12.1891 3649	11.5303 0802	10.9335 7546	10.3912 9561	9.8969 2553	48
49	12.2121 6341	11.5486 7099	10.9482 3436	10.4030 0969	9.9062 9594	49
50	12.2334 8464	11.5655 9538	10.9616 8290	10.4137 0748	9.9148 1449	50
51	12.2532 2652	11.5811 9390	10.9740 2101	10.4234 7715	9.9225 5862	51
52	12.2715 0604	11.5955 7041	10.9853 4038	10.4323 9922	9.9295 9875	52
53	12.2884 3152	11.6088 2066	10.9957 2512	10.4405 4724	9.9359 9886	53
54	12.3041 0326	11.6210 3287	11.0052 5240	10.4479 8834	9.9418 1715	54
55	12.3186 1413	11.6322 8835	11.0139 9303	10.4547 8388	9.9471 0650	55
56	12.3320 5012	11.6426 6208	11.0220 1195	10.4609 8984	9.9519 1500	56
57	12.3444 9085	11.6522 2311	11.0293 6876	10.4666 5739	9.9562 8636	57
58	12.3560 1005	11.6610 3513	11.0361 1813	10.4718 3323	9.9602 6033	58
59	12.3666 7597	11.6691 5680	11.0423 1021	10.4765 6003	9.9638 7303	59
60	12.3765 5182	11.6766 4221	11.0479 9102	10.4808 7674	9.9671 5730	60

TABLE IV

N	8	8 1/2	9	9 1/2	10	N
61	12.3856 9613	11.6835 4121	11.0532 0277	10.4848 1894	9.9701 4300	61
62	12.3941 6308	11.6898 9973	11.0579 8419	10.4884 1912	9.9728 5727	62
63	12.4020 0286	11.6957 6012	11.0623 7082	10.4917 0696	9.9753 2479	63
64	12.4092 6190	11.7011 6140	11.0663 9525	10.4947 0955	9.9775 6799	64
65	12.4159 8324	11.7061 3954	11.0700 8738	10.4974 5165	9.9796 0727	65
66	12.4222 0671	11.7107 2769	11.0734 7466	10.4999 5584	9.9814 6115	66
67	12.4279 6917	11.7149 5639	11.0765 8226	10.5022 4278	9.9831 4650	67
68	12.4333 0479	11.7188 5382	11.0794 3327	10.5043 3130	9.9846 7864	68
69	12.4382 4518	11.7224 4592	11.0820 4887	10.5062 3863	9.9860 7149	69
70	12.4428 1961	11.7257 5661	11.0844 4850	10.5079 8049	9.9873 3772	70
71	12.4470 5519	11.7288 0793	11.0866 5000	10.5095 7122	9.9884 8883	71
72	12.4509 7703	11.7316 2021	11.0886 6973	10.5110 2395	9.9895 3530	72
73	12.4546 0836	11.7342 1218	11.0905 2269	10.5123 5064	9.9904 8664	73
74	12.4579 7070	11.7366 0109	11.0922 2265	10.5135 6223	9.9913 5149	74
75	12.4610 8399	11.7388 0284	11.0937 8225	10.5146 6870	9.9921 3772	75
76	12.4639 6665	11.7408 3211	11.0952 1307	10.5156 7918	9.9928 5247	76
77	12.4666 3579	11.7427 0241	11.0965 2575	10.5166 0199	9.9935 0225	77
78	12.4691 0721	11.7444 2618	11.0977 3005	10.5174 4474	9.9940 9295	78
79	12.4713 9557	11.7460 1492	11.0988 3491	10.5182 1437	9.9946 2996	79
80	12.4735 1441	11.7474 7919	11.0998 4854	10.5189 1724	9.9951 1814	80
81	12.4754 7631	11.7488 2874	11.1007 7847	10.5195 5912	9.9955 6195	81
82	12.4772 9288	11.7500 7257	11.1016 3163	10.5201 4531	9.9959 6541	82
83	12.4789 7489	11.7512 1896	11.1024 1434	10.5206 8065	9.9963 3219	83
84	12.4805 3230	11.7522 7554	11.1031 3242	10.5211 6955	9.9966 6562	84
85	12.4819 7436	11.7532 4935	11.1037 9121	10.5216 1602	9.9969 6875	85
86	12.4833 0959	11.7541 4686	11.1043 9561	10.5220 2377	9.9972 4432	86
87	12.4845 4592	11.7549 7407	11.1049 5010	10.5223 9613	9.9974 9483	87
88	12.4856 9066	11.7557 3647	11.1054 5881	10.5227 3619	9.9977 2258	88
89	12.4867 5061	11.7564 3914	11.1059 2551	10.5230 4675	9.9979 2962	89
90	12.4877 3205	11.7570 8677	11.1063 5368	10.5233 3037	9.9981 1783	90
91	12.4886 4079	11.7576 8365	11.1067 4649	10.5235 8938	9.9982 8894	91
92	12.4894 8221	11.7582 3378	11.1071 0687	10.5238 2592	9.9984 4449	92
93	12.4902 6131	11.7587 4081	11.1074 3750	10.5240 4193	9.9985 8590	93
94	12.4909 8269	11.7592 0812	11.1077 4083	10.5242 3921	9.9987 1445	94
95	12.4916 5064	11.7596 3882	11.1080 1911	10.5244 1937	9.9988 3132	95
96	12.4922 6911	11.7600 3578	11.1082 7441	10.5245 8390	9.9989 3757	96
97	12.4928 4177	11.7604 0164	11.1085 0863	10.5247 3415	9.9990 3415	97
98	12.4933 7201	11.7607 3884	11.1087 2352	10.5248 7137	9.9991 2195	98
99	12.4938 6297	11.7610 4962	11.1089 2066	10.5249 9669	9.9992 0178	99
100	12.4943 1757	11.7613 3606	11.1091 0152	10.5251 1113	9.9992 7434	100
101	12.4947 3849	11.7616 0005	11.1092 6745	10.5252 1564	9.9993 4031	101
102	12.4951 2823	11.7618 4337	11.1094 1968	10.5253 1109	9.9994 0028	102
103	12.4954 8910	11.7620 6762	11.1095 5934	10.5253 9826	9.9994 5480	103
104	12.4958 2324	11.7622 7430	11.1096 8747	10.5254 7786	9.9995 0437	104
105	12.4961 3263	11.7624 6480	11.1098 0501	10.5255 5056	9.9995 4942	105
106	12.4964 1910	11.7626 4037	11.1099 1286	10.5256 1695	9.9995 9039	106
107	12.4966 8435	11.7628 0218	11.1100 1180	10.5256 7758	9.9996 2762	107
108	12.4969 2996	11.7629 5132	11.1101 0257	10.5257 3295	9.9996 6148	108
109	12.4971 5737	11.7630 8877	11.1101 8584	10.5257 8351	9.9996 9225	109
110	12.4973 6793	11.7632 1546	11.1102 6224	10.5258 2969	9.9997 2023	110
111	12.4975 6290	11.7633 3222	11.1103 3233	10.5258 7186	9.9997 4566	111
112	12.4977 4343	11.7634 3983	11.1103 9663	10.5259 1038	9.9997 6878	112
113	12.4979 1058	11.7635 3902	11.1104 5563	10.5259 4555	9.9997 8980	113
114	12.4980 6535	11.7636 3043	11.1105 0975	10.5259 7767	9.9998 0891	114
115	12.4982 0866	11.7637 1468	11.1105 5940	10.5260 0701	9.9998 2628	115
116	12.4983 4135	11.7637 9233	11.1106 0496	10.5260 3380	9.9998 4208	116
117	12.4984 6421	11.7638 6390	11.1106 4675	10.5260 5826	9.9998 5643	117
118	12.4985 7798	11.7639 2986	11.1106 8509	10.5260 8060	9.9998 6948	118
119	12.4986 8331	11.7639 9066	11.1107 2027	10.5261 0101	9.9998 8135	119
120	12.4987 8084	11.7640 4669	11.1107 5254	10.5261 1964	9.9998 9214	120

TABLE IV

N	10 1/2	11	11 1/2	12	12 1/2	N
1	0.9049 7738	0.9009 0090	0.8968 6099	0.8928 5714	0.8888 8889	1
2	1.7239 6143	1.7125 2333	1.7012 2062	1.6900 5102	1.6790 1235	2
3	2.4651 2346	2.4437 1472	2.4226 1939	2.4018 3127	2.3813 4431	3
4	3.1358 5834	3.1024 4569	3.0696 1380	3.0373 4935	3.0056 3938	4
5	3.7428 5822	3.6958 9702	3.6498 7785	3.6047 7620	3.5605 6834	5
6	4.2921 7939	4.2305 3785	4.1702 9403	4.1114 0732	4.0538 3853	6
7	4.7893 0261	4.7121 9626	4.6370 3501	4.5637 5654	4.4923 0091	7
8	5.2391 8789	5.1461 2276	5.0556 3678	4.9676 3977	4.8820 4525	8
9	5.6463 2388	5.5370 4753	5.4310 6437	5.3282 4979	5.2284 8467	9
10	6.0147 7274	5.8892 3201	5.7677 7074	5.6502 2303	5.5364 3082	10
11	6.3482 1062	6.2065 1533	6.0697 4954	5.9376 9913	5.8101 6073	11
12	6.6499 6437	6.4923 5615	6.3405 8255	6.1943 7423	6.0534 7620	12
13	6.9230 4468	6.7498 7040	6.5834 8211	6.4235 4842	6.2697 5662	13
14	7.1701 7618	6.9818 6523	6.8013 2924	6.6281 6823	6.4620 0589	14
15	7.3938 2459	7.1908 6958	6.9967 0784	6.8108 6449	6.6328 9412	15
16	7.5962 2135	7.3791 6178	7.1719 3528	6.9739 8615	6.7847 9478	16
17	7.7793 8584	7.5487 9440	7.3290 8994	7.1196 3049	6.9198 1758	17
18	7.9451 4556	7.7016 1657	7.4700 3582	7.2496 7008	7.0398 3785	18
19	8.0951 5435	7.8392 9421	7.5964 4468	7.3657 7686	7.1465 2253	19
20	8.2309 0891	7.9633 2812	7.7098 1586	7.4694 4362	7.2413 5336	20
21	8.3537 6372	8.0750 7038	7.8114 9404	7.5620 0324	7.3256 4743	21
22	8.4649 4455	8.1757 3908	7.9026 8524	7.6446 4575	7.4005 7550	22
23	8.5655 6067	8.2664 3160	7.9844 7107	7.7184 3370	7.4671 7822	23
24	8.6566 1599	8.3481 3658	8.0578 2159	7.7843 1581	7.5263 8064	24
25	8.7390 1900	8.4217 4466	8.1236 0680	7.8431 3911	7.5790 0501	25
26	8.8135 9186	8.4880 5826	8.1826 0700	7.8956 5992	7.6257 8223	26
27	8.8810 7860	8.5478 0023	8.2355 2197	7.9425 5350	7.6673 6198	27
28	8.9421 5258	8.6016 2183	8.2829 7935	7.9844 2277	7.7043 2176	28
29	8.9974 2315	8.6501 0976	8.3255 4202	8.0218 0604	7.7371 7490	29
30	9.0474 4176	8.6937 9257	8.3637 1481	8.0551 8397	7.7663 7769	30
31	9.0927 0748	8.7331 4646	8.3979 5050	8.0849 8569	7.7923 3572	31
32	9.1336 7193	8.7686 0042	8.4286 5516	8.1115 9436	7.8154 0953	32
33	9.1707 4383	8.8005 4092	8.4561 9297	8.1353 5211	7.8359 1958	33
34	9.2042 9305	8.8293 1614	8.4808 9056	8.1565 6438	7.8541 5074	34
35	9.2346 5435	8.8552 3977	8.5030 4086	8.1755 0391	7.8703 5622	35
36	9.2621 3063	8.8785 9438	8.5229 0660	8.1924 1421	7.8847 6108	36
37	9.2869 9605	8.8996 3458	8.5407 2341	8.2075 1269	7.8975 6540	37
38	9.3094 9868	8.9185 8971	8.5567 0261	8.2209 9347	7.9089 4703	38
39	9.3298 6306	8.9356 6641	8.5710 3373	8.2330 2988	7.9190 6402	39
40	9.3482 9237	8.9510 5082	8.5838 8675	8.2437 7668	7.9280 5691	40
41	9.3649 7047	8.9649 1065	8.5954 1413	8.2533 7204	7.9360 5059	41
42	9.3800 6377	8.9773 9698	8.6057 5258	8.2619 3932	7.9431 5608	42
43	9.3937 2287	8.9886 4593	8.6150 2474	8.2695 8868	7.9494 7207	43
44	9.4060 8404	8.9987 8011	8.6233 4057	8.2764 1846	7.9550 8628	44
45	9.4172 7063	9.0079 1001	8.6307 9872	8.2825 1648	7.9600 7670	45
46	9.4273 9423	9.0161 3515	8.6374 8764	8.2879 6115	7.9645 1262	46
47	9.4365 5587	9.0235 4518	8.6434 8667	8.2928 2245	7.9684 5566	47
48	9.4448 4694	9.0302 2088	8.6488 6697	8.2971 6290	7.9719 6059	48
49	9.4523 5017	9.0362 3503	8.6536 9235	8.3010 3831	7.9750 7608	49
50	9.4591 4043	9.0416 5318	8.6580 2004	8.3044 9849	7.9778 4540	50
51	9.4652 8545	9.0465 3439	8.6619 0139	8.3075 8794	7.9803 0702	51
52	9.4708 4656	9.0509 3189	8.6653 8241	8.3103 4637	7.9824 9513	52
53	9.4758 7924	9.0548 9359	8.6685 0440	8.3128 0926	7.9844 4012	53
54	9.4804 3370	9.0584 6270	8.6713 0440	8.3150 0827	7.9861 6899	54
55	9.4845 5539	9.0616 7810	8.6738 1560	8.3169 7167	7.9877 0577	55
56	9.4882 8542	9.0645 7487	8.6760 6780	8.3187 2470	7.9890 7180	56
57	9.4916 6101	9.0671 8457	8.6780 8772	8.3202 8991	7.9902 8604	57
58	9.4947 1585	9.0695 3565	8.6798 9930	8.3216 8742	7.9913 6537	58
59	9.4974 8041	9.0716 5373	8.6815 2403	8.3229 3520	7.9923 2477	59
60	9.4999 8227	9.0735 6192	8.6829 8120	8.3240 4928	7.9931 7758	60

TABLE IV

N	10 1/2	11	11 1/2	12	12 1/2	N
61	9.5022 4640	9.0752 8101	8.6842 8807	8.3250 4400	7.9939 3562	61
62	9.5042 9538	9.0768 2974	8.6854 6015	8.3259 3215	7.9946 0944	62
63	9.5061 4967	9.0782 2499	8.6865 1135	8.3267 2513	7.9952 0839	63
64	9.5078 2775	9.0794 8197	8.6874 5412	8.3274 3315	7.9957 4079	64
65	9.5093 4638	9.0806 1439	8.6882 9966	8.3280 6531	7.9962 1404	65
66	9.5107 2071	9.0816 3459	8.6890 5799	8.3286 2975	7.9966 3470	66
67	9.5119 6444	9.0825 5368	8.6897 3811	8.3291 3370	7.9970 0862	67
68	9.5130 8999	9.0833 8170	8.6903 4808	8.3295 8366	7.9973 4100	68
69	9.5141 0859	9.0841 2765	8.6908 9514	8.3299 8541	7.9976 3644	69
70	9.5150 3040	9.0847 9969	8.6913 8578	8.3303 4412	7.9978 9906	70
71	9.5158 6461	9.0854 0512	8.6918 2581	8.3306 6439	7.9981 3250	71
72	9.5166 1956	9.0859 5056	8.6922 2046	8.3309 5035	7.9983 4000	72
73	9.5173 0277	9.0864 4195	8.6925 7440	8.3312 0567	7.9985 2444	73
74	9.5179 2106	9.0868 8464	8.6928 9184	8.3314 3363	7.9986 8839	74
75	9.5184 8060	9.0872 8346	8.6931 7654	8.3316 3717	7.9988 3413	75
76	9.5189 8696	9.0876 4275	8.6934 3187	8.3318 1890	7.9989 6367	76
77	9.5194 4522	9.0879 6645	8.6936 6087	8.3319 8116	7.9990 7882	77
78	9.5198 5992	9.0882 5806	8.6938 6625	8.3321 2604	7.9991 8117	78
79	9.5202 3523	9.0885 2077	8.6940 5045	8.3322 5539	7.9992 7215	79
80	9.5205 7487	9.0887 5745	8.6942 1565	8.3323 7089	7.9993 5302	80
81	9.5208 8223	9.0889 7068	8.6943 6381	8.3324 7401	7.9994 2491	81
82	9.5211 6039	9.0891 6277	8.6944 9669	8.3325 6608	7.9994 8881	82
83	9.5214 1212	9.0893 3583	8.6946 1587	8.3326 4828	7.9995 4561	83
84	9.5216 3993	9.0894 9174	8.6947 2275	8.3327 2168	7.9995 9610	84
85	9.5218 4609	9.0896 3220	8.6948 1861	8.3327 8721	7.9996 4097	85
86	9.5220 3266	9.0897 5874	8.6949 0458	8.3328 4573	7.9996 8087	86
87	9.5222 0150	9.0898 7274	8.6949 8169	8.3328 9797	7.9997 1633	87
88	9.5223 5430	9.0899 7544	8.6950 5084	8.3329 4462	7.9997 4784	88
89	9.5224 9258	9.0900 6796	8.6951 1286	8.3329 8627	7.9997 7586	89
90	9.5226 1772	9.0901 5132	8.6951 6849	8.3330 2345	7.9998 0077	90
91	9.5227 3097	9.0902 2641	8.6952 1837	8.3330 5665	7.9998 2290	91
92	9.5228 3345	9.0902 9407	8.6952 6312	8.3330 8630	7.9998 4258	92
93	9.5229 2620	9.0903 5501	8.6953 0324	8.3331 1277	7.9998 6007	93
94	9.5230 1014	9.0904 0992	8.6953 3923	8.3331 3640	7.9998 7562	94
95	9.5230 8610	9.0904 5939	8.6953 7151	8.3331 5750	7.9998 8944	95
96	9.5231 5484	9.0905 0395	8.6954 0046	8.3331 7634	7.9999 0172	96
97	9.5232 1705	9.0905 4410	8.6954 2642	8.3331 9316	7.9999 1264	97
98	9.5232 7335	9.0905 8027	8.6954 4970	8.3332 0818	7.9999 2235	98
99	9.5233 2430	9.0906 1286	8.6954 7058	8.3332 2159	7.9999 3098	99
100	9.5233 7040	9.0906 4221	8.6954 8931	8.3332 3356	7.9999 3865	100
101	9.5234 1213	9.0906 6866	8.6955 0611	8.3332 4425	7.9999 4546	101
102	9.5234 4989	9.0906 9249	8.6955 2118	8.3332 5379	7.9999 5152	102
103	9.5234 8406	9.0907 1395	8.6955 3469	8.3332 6232	7.9999 5691	103
104	9.5235 1499	9.0907 3329	8.6955 4680	8.3332 6993	7.9999 6170	104
105	9.5235 4298	9.0907 5071	8.6955 5767	8.3332 7672	7.9999 6595	105
106	9.5235 6831	9.0907 6641	8.6955 6742	8.3332 8278	7.9999 6974	106
107	9.5235 9123	9.0907 8055	8.6955 7616	8.3332 8820	7.9999 7310	107
108	9.5236 1197	9.0907 9329	8.6955 8400	8.3332 9304	7.9999 7609	108
109	9.5236 3074	9.0908 0476	8.6955 9103	8.3332 9735	7.9999 7874	109
110	9.5236 4773	9.0908 1510	8.6955 9734	8.3333 0121	7.9999 8111	110
111	9.5236 6310	9.0908 2442	8.6956 0299	8.3333 0465	7.9999 8321	111
112	9.5236 7702	9.0908 3281	8.6956 0807	8.3333 0772	7.9999 8507	112
113	9.5236 8961	9.0908 4037	8.6956 1262	8.3333 1047	7.9999 8673	113
114	9.5237 0100	9.0908 4718	8.6956 1670	8.3333 1292	7.9999 8820	114
115	9.5237 1132	9.0908 5331	8.6956 2035	8.3333 1511	7.9999 8952	115
116	9.5237 2065	9.0908 5884	8.6956 2364	8.3333 1706	7.9999 9068	116
117	9.5237 2909	9.0908 6382	8.6956 2658	8.3333 1880	7.9999 9172	117
118	9.5237 3674	9.0908 6831	8.6956 2922	8.3333 2036	7.9999 9264	118
119	9.5237 4365	9.0908 7235	8.6956 3159	8.3333 2175	7.9999 9345	119
120	9.5237 4991	9.0908 7599	8.6956 3371	8.3333 2299	7.9999 9418	120

TABLE V
PERIODIC RENT OF ANNUITY WHOSE PRESENT VALUE IS 1

$$\frac{1}{s_{\overline{n}|i}} = \frac{1}{a_{\overline{n}|i}} - i \qquad R = \frac{1}{a_{\overline{n}|i}} \qquad i = \frac{1}{a_{\overline{n}|i}} - \frac{1}{s_{\overline{n}|i}}$$

TABLE V

N	1/6	5/24	1/4	7/24	1/3	N
1	1.0016 6667	1.0020 8333	1.0025 0000	1.0029 1667	1.0033 3333	1
2	0.5012 5035	0.5015 6304	0.5018 7578	0.5021 8856	0.5025 0139	2
3	0.3344 4506	0.3347 2319	0.3350 0139	0.3352 7967	0.3355 5802	3
4	0.2510 4253	0.2513 0344	0.2515 6445	0.2518 2557	0.2520 8680	4
5	0.2010 0111	0.2012 5173	0.2015 0250	0.2017 5340	0.2020 0444	5
6	0.1676 4024	0.1678 8405	0.1681 2803	0.1683 7218	0.1686 1650	6
7	0.1438 1111	0.1440 5010	0.1442 8928	0.1445 2866	0.1447 6824	7
8	0.1259 3932	0.1261 7472	0.1264 1035	0.1266 4620	0.1268 8228	8
9	0.1120 3909	0.1122 7173	0.1125 0462	0.1127 3777	0.1129 7118	9
10	0.1009 1896	0.1011 4941	0.1013 8015	0.1016 1117	0.1018 4248	10
11	0.0918 2070	0.0920 4940	0.0922 7840	0.0925 0772	0.0927 3736	11
12	0.0842 3887	0.0844 6611	0.0846 9370	0.0849 2163	0.0851 4990	12
13	0.0778 2350	0.0780 4954	0.0782 7595	0.0785 0274	0.0787 2989	13
14	0.0723 2465	0.0725 4968	0.0727 7510	0.0730 0093	0.0732 2716	14
15	0.0675 5901	0.0677 8317	0.0680 0777	0.0682 3279	0.0684 5825	15
16	0.0633 8910	0.0636 1253	0.0638 3642	0.0640 6076	0.0642 8557	16
17	0.0597 0980	0.0599 3259	0.0601 5587	0.0603 7964	0.0606 0389	17
18	0.0564 3934	0.0566 6158	0.0568 8433	0.0571 0761	0.0573 3140	18
19	0.0535 1315	0.0537 3492	0.0539 5722	0.0541 8008	0.0544 0348	19
20	0.0508 7961	0.0511 0096	0.0513 2288	0.0515 4537	0.0517 6844	20
21	0.0484 9691	0.0487 1789	0.0489 3947	0.0491 6166	0.0493 8445	21
22	0.0463 3084	0.0465 5149	0.0467 7278	0.0469 9471	0.0472 1726	22
23	0.0443 5314	0.0445 7351	0.0447 9455	0.0450 1625	0.0452 3861	23
24	0.0425 4026	0.0427 6039	0.0429 8121	0.0432 0272	0.0434 2492	24
25	0.0408 7244	0.0410 9235	0.0413 1298	0.0415 3433	0.0417 5640	25
26	0.0393 3293	0.0395 5265	0.0397 7312	0.0399 9434	0.0402 1630	26
27	0.0379 0747	0.0381 2703	0.0383 4736	0.0385 6847	0.0387 9035	27
28	0.0365 8385	0.0368 0326	0.0370 2347	0.0372 4450	0.0374 6632	28
29	0.0353 5153	0.0355 7081	0.0357 9093	0.0360 1188	0.0362 3367	29
30	0.0342 0138	0.0344 2055	0.0346 4059	0.0348 6149	0.0350 8325	30
31	0.0331 2544	0.0333 4452	0.0335 6449	0.0337 8536	0.0340 0712	31
32	0.0321 1677	0.0323 3577	0.0325 5569	0.0327 7653	0.0329 9830	32
33	0.0311 6924	0.0313 8817	0.0316 0806	0.0318 2889	0.0320 5067	33
34	0.0302 7746	0.0304 9634	0.0307 1620	0.0309 3703	0.0311 5885	34
35	0.0294 3666	0.0296 5549	0.0298 7533	0.0300 9618	0.0303 1803	35
36	0.0286 4258	0.0288 6138	0.0290 8121	0.0293 0208	0.0295 2399	36
37	0.0278 9143	0.0281 1020	0.0283 3004	0.0285 5094	0.0287 7291	37
38	0.0271 7983	0.0273 9859	0.0276 1843	0.0278 3938	0.0280 6141	38
39	0.0265 0474	0.0267 2348	0.0269 4335	0.0271 6434	0.0273 8644	39
40	0.0258 6341	0.0260 8215	0.0263 0204	0.0265 2308	0.0267 4527	40
41	0.0252 5338	0.0254 7212	0.0256 9204	0.0259 1315	0.0261 3543	41
42	0.0246 7241	0.0248 9116	0.0251 1112	0.0253 3229	0.0255 5466	42
43	0.0241 1847	0.0243 3723	0.0245 5724	0.0247 7848	0.0250 0095	43
44	0.0235 8972	0.0238 0850	0.0240 2855	0.0242 4987	0.0244 7246	44
45	0.0230 8448	0.0233 0329	0.0235 2339	0.0237 4479	0.0239 6749	45
46	0.0226 0121	0.0228 2005	0.0230 4022	0.0232 6170	0.0234 8451	46
47	0.0221 3852	0.0223 5740	0.0225 7762	0.0227 9920	0.0230 2213	47
48	0.0216 9512	0.0219 1403	0.0221 3433	0.0223 5600	0.0225 7905	48
49	0.0212 6983	0.0214 8878	0.0217 0915	0.0219 3092	0.0221 5410	49
50	0.0208 6156	0.0210 8056	0.0213 0099	0.0215 2287	0.0217 4618	50
51	0.0204 6931	0.0206 8835	0.0209 0886	0.0211 3085	0.0213 5429	51
52	0.0200 9215	0.0203 1125	0.0205 3184	0.0207 5393	0.0209 7751	52
53	0.0197 2923	0.0199 4838	0.0201 6906	0.0203 9126	0.0206 1499	53
54	0.0193 7977	0.0195 9898	0.0198 1974	0.0200 4205	0.0202 6592	54
55	0.0190 4302	0.0192 6229	0.0194 8314	0.0197 0557	0.0199 2958	55
56	0.0187 1830	0.0189 3763	0.0191 5858	0.0193 8113	0.0196 0529	56
57	0.0184 0499	0.0186 2438	0.0188 4542	0.0190 6810	0.0192 9241	57
58	0.0181 0249	0.0183 2195	0.0185 4308	0.0187 6588	0.0189 9035	58
59	0.0178 1025	0.0180 2978	0.0182 5101	0.0184 7394	0.0186 9856	59
60	0.0175 2776	0.0177 4736	0.0179 6869	0.0181 9174	0.0184 1652	60

TABLE V

N	1/6	5/24	1/4	7/24	1/3	N
61	0.0172 5454	0.0174 7421	0.0176 9564	0.0179 1883	0.0181 4377	61
62	0.0169 9014	0.0172 0989	0.0174 3142	0.0176 5474	0.0178 7984	62
63	0.0167 3414	0.0169 5397	0.0171 7561	0.0173 9906	0.0176 2432	63
64	0.0164 8615	0.0167 0605	0.0169 2780	0.0171 5139	0.0173 7681	64
65	0.0162 4580	0.0164 6578	0.0166 8764	0.0169 1136	0.0171 3695	65
66	0.0160 1273	0.0162 3280	0.0164 5476	0.0166 7863	0.0169 0438	66
67	0.0157 8663	0.0160 0678	0.0162 2886	0.0164 5286	0.0166 7878	67
68	0.0155 6719	0.0157 8742	0.0160 0961	0.0162 3376	0.0164 5985	68
69	0.0153 5412	0.0155 7443	0.0157 9674	0.0160 2102	0.0162 4729	69
70	0.0151 4714	0.0153 6754	0.0155 8996	0.0158 1439	0.0160 4083	70
71	0.0149 4599	0.0151 6648	0.0153 8902	0.0156 1359	0.0158 4021	71
72	0.0147 5044	0.0149 7102	0.0151 9368	0.0154 1840	0.0156 4518	72
73	0.0145 6026	0.0147 8093	0.0150 0370	0.0152 2857	0.0154 5553	73
74	0.0143 7522	0.0145 9598	0.0148 1887	0.0150 4389	0.0152 7103	74
75	0.0141 9512	0.0144 1597	0.0146 3898	0.0148 6415	0.0150 9147	75
76	0.0140 1976	0.0142 4071	0.0144 6385	0.0146 8916	0.0149 1666	76
77	0.0138 4897	0.0140 7001	0.0142 9327	0.0145 1874	0.0147 4641	77
78	0.0136 8256	0.0139 0370	0.0141 2708	0.0143 5270	0.0145 8056	78
79	0.0135 2037	0.0137 4161	0.0139 6511	0.0141 9089	0.0144 1892	79
80	0.0133 6224	0.0135 8357	0.0138 0721	0.0140 3313	0.0142 6135	80
81	0.0132 0803	0.0134 2945	0.0136 5321	0.0138 7929	0.0141 0770	81
82	0.0130 5757	0.0132 7910	0.0135 0298	0.0137 2922	0.0139 5781	82
83	0.0129 1075	0.0131 3238	0.0133 5639	0.0135 8278	0.0138 1156	83
84	0.0127 6744	0.0129 8916	0.0132 1330	0.0134 3985	0.0136 6881	84
85	0.0126 2749	0.0128 4932	0.0130 7359	0.0133 0030	0.0135 2944	85
86	0.0124 9081	0.0127 1274	0.0129 3714	0.0131 6400	0.0133 9333	86
87	0.0123 5728	0.0125 7931	0.0128 0384	0.0130 3086	0.0132 6038	87
88	0.0122 2678	0.0124 4891	0.0126 7357	0.0129 0076	0.0131 3046	88
89	0.0120 9923	0.0123 2146	0.0125 4625	0.0127 7360	0.0130 0349	89
90	0.0119 7451	0.0121 9685	0.0124 2177	0.0126 4928	0.0128 7936	90
91	0.0118 5254	0.0120 7498	0.0123 0004	0.0125 2770	0.0127 5797	91
92	0.0117 3322	0.0119 5577	0.0121 8096	0.0124 0879	0.0126 3925	92
93	0.0116 1648	0.0118 3913	0.0120 6446	0.0122 9245	0.0125 2310	93
94	0.0115 0223	0.0117 2498	0.0119 5044	0.0121 7860	0.0124 0944	94
95	0.0113 9038	0.0116 1325	0.0118 3884	0.0120 6716	0.0122 9819	95
96	0.0112 8087	0.0115 0384	0.0117 2957	0.0119 5805	0.0121 8928	96
97	0.0111 7363	0.0113 9670	0.0116 2257	0.0118 5121	0.0120 8263	97
98	0.0110 6857	0.0112 9176	0.0115 1776	0.0117 4657	0.0119 7818	98
99	0.0109 6565	0.0111 8894	0.0114 1508	0.0116 4405	0.0118 7585	99
100	0.0108 6478	0.0110 8819	0.0113 1446	0.0115 4360	0.0117 7559	100
101	0.0107 6592	0.0109 8943	0.0112 1584	0.0114 4515	0.0116 7734	101
102	0.0106 6900	0.0108 9262	0.0111 1917	0.0113 4864	0.0115 8103	102
103	0.0105 7397	0.0107 9770	0.0110 2439	0.0112 5403	0.0114 8660	103
104	0.0104 8077	0.0107 0461	0.0109 3144	0.0111 6124	0.0113 9401	104
105	0.0103 8935	0.0106 1330	0.0108 4027	0.0110 7024	0.0113 0320	105
106	0.0102 9966	0.0105 2372	0.0107 5082	0.0109 8096	0.0112 1413	106
107	0.0102 1165	0.0104 3582	0.0106 6307	0.0108 9337	0.0111 2673	107
108	0.0101 2527	0.0103 4956	0.0105 7694	0.0108 0741	0.0110 4097	108
109	0.0100 4049	0.0102 6488	0.0104 9241	0.0107 2305	0.0109 5680	109
110	0.0099 5724	0.0101 8175	0.0104 0942	0.0106 4023	0.0108 7417	110
111	0.0098 7551	0.0101 0013	0.0103 2793	0.0105 5891	0.0107 9306	111
112	0.0097 9523	0.0100 1997	0.0102 4791	0.0104 7906	0.0107 1340	112
113	0.0097 1638	0.0099 4123	0.0101 6932	0.0104 0064	0.0106 3518	113
114	0.0096 3892	0.0098 6388	0.0100 9211	0.0103 2360	0.0105 5834	114
115	0.0095 6281	0.0097 8789	0.0100 1626	0.0102 4791	0.0104 8285	115
116	0.0094 8802	0.0097 1320	0.0099 4172	0.0101 7355	0.0104 0868	116
117	0.0094 1451	0.0096 3981	0.0098 6846	0.0101 0046	0.0103 3579	117
118	0.0093 4224	0.0095 6766	0.0097 9646	0.0100 2863	0.0102 6416	118
119	0.0092 7120	0.0094 9673	0.0097 2567	0.0099 5801	0.0101 9374	119
120	0.0092 0135	0.0094 2699	0.0096 5607	0.0098 8859	0.0101 2451	120

TABLE V

N	1/6	5/24	1/4	7/24	1/3	N
121	0.0091 3265	0.0093 5841	0.0095 8764	0.0098 2032	0.0100 5645	121
122	0.0090 6508	0.0092 9096	0.0095 2033	0.0097 5318	0.0099 8951	122
123	0.0089 9862	0.0092 2461	0.0094 5412	0.0096 8715	0.0099 2367	123
124	0.0089 3323	0.0091 5933	0.0093 8899	0.0096 2219	0.0098 5892	124
125	0.0088 6889	0.0090 9511	0.0093 2491	0.0095 5828	0.0097 9521	125
126	0.0088 0557	0.0090 3191	0.0092 6186	0.0094 9540	0.0097 3253	126
127	0.0087 4326	0.0089 6972	0.0091 9981	0.0094 3352	0.0096 7085	127
128	0.0086 8192	0.0089 0850	0.0091 3873	0.0093 7262	0.0096 1015	128
129	0.0086 2154	0.0088 4823	0.0090 7861	0.0093 1267	0.0095 5040	129
130	0.0085 6209	0.0087 8890	0.0090 1942	0.0092 5366	0.0094 9158	130
131	0.0085 0356	0.0087 3048	0.0089 6115	0.0091 9556	0.0094 3368	131
132	0.0084 4591	0.0086 7295	0.0089 0376	0.0091 3834	0.0093 7667	132
133	0.0083 8913	0.0086 1629	0.0088 4725	0.0090 8200	0.0093 2053	133
134	0.0083 3320	0.0085 6048	0.0087 9159	0.0090 2651	0.0092 6524	134
135	0.0082 7811	0.0085 0550	0.0087 3675	0.0089 7186	0.0092 1079	135
136	0.0082 2383	0.0084 5134	0.0086 8274	0.0089 1801	0.0091 5715	136
137	0.0081 7034	0.0083 9797	0.0086 2952	0.0088 6497	0.0091 0430	137
138	0.0081 1764	0.0083 4538	0.0085 7707	0.0088 1270	0.0090 5223	138
139	0.0080 6569	0.0082 9356	0.0085 2539	0.0087 6119	0.0090 0093	139
140	0.0080 1449	0.0082 4247	0.0084 7446	0.0087 1043	0.0089 5037	140
141	0.0079 6402	0.0081 9212	0.0084 2425	0.0086 6040	0.0089 0054	141
142	0.0079 1427	0.0081 4249	0.0083 7476	0.0086 1109	0.0088 5143	142
143	0.0078 6521	0.0080 9355	0.0083 2597	0.0085 6247	0.0088 0301	143
144	0.0078 1684	0.0080 4529	0.0082 7787	0.0085 1454	0.0087 5528	144
145	0.0077 6913	0.0079 9771	0.0082 3043	0.0084 6728	0.0087 0822	145
146	0.0077 2209	0.0079 5078	0.0081 8365	0.0084 2067	0.0086 6182	146
147	0.0076 7569	0.0079 0450	0.0081 3752	0.0083 7471	0.0086 1607	147
148	0.0076 2992	0.0078 5885	0.0080 9201	0.0083 2938	0.0085 7094	148
149	0.0075 8476	0.0078 1381	0.0080 4712	0.0082 8467	0.0085 2643	149
150	0.0075 4021	0.0077 6938	0.0080 0284	0.0082 4056	0.0084 8252	150
151	0.0074 9625	0.0077 2555	0.0079 5915	0.0081 9705	0.0084 3921	151
152	0.0074 5288	0.0076 8229	0.0079 1605	0.0081 5412	0.0083 9648	152
153	0.0074 1008	0.0076 3961	0.0078 7351	0.0081 1176	0.0083 5433	153
154	0.0073 6783	0.0075 9748	0.0078 3153	0.0080 6995	0.0083 1273	154
155	0.0073 2613	0.0075 5590	0.0077 9010	0.0080 2870	0.0082 7167	155
156	0.0072 8497	0.0075 1486	0.0077 4921	0.0079 8798	0.0082 3116	156
157	0.0072 4434	0.0074 7435	0.0077 0885	0.0079 4780	0.0081 9118	157
158	0.0072 0422	0.0074 3436	0.0076 6900	0.0079 0813	0.0081 5171	158
159	0.0071 6461	0.0073 9487	0.0076 2966	0.0078 6896	0.0081 1275	159
160	0.0071 2550	0.0073 5588	0.0075 9082	0.0078 3030	0.0080 7429	160
161	0.0070 8688	0.0073 1738	0.0075 5247	0.0077 9212	0.0080 3631	161
162	0.0070 4874	0.0072 7936	0.0075 1459	0.0077 5442	0.0079 9882	162
163	0.0070 1107	0.0072 4181	0.0074 7719	0.0077 1720	0.0079 6180	163
164	0.0069 7386	0.0072 0472	0.0074 4025	0.0076 8044	0.0079 2524	164
165	0.0069 3710	0.0071 6808	0.0074 0377	0.0076 4413	0.0078 8913	165
166	0.0069 0079	0.0071 3190	0.0073 6773	0.0076 0826	0.0078 5347	166
167	0.0068 6492	0.0070 9614	0.0073 3213	0.0075 7284	0.0078 1825	167
168	0.0068 2948	0.0070 6082	0.0072 9695	0.0075 3784	0.0077 8346	168
169	0.0067 9446	0.0070 2592	0.0072 6220	0.0075 0327	0.0077 4909	169
170	0.0067 5985	0.0069 9144	0.0072 2787	0.0074 6911	0.0077 1513	170
171	0.0067 2566	0.0069 5736	0.0071 9394	0.0074 3536	0.0076 8158	171
172	0.0066 9186	0.0069 2369	0.0071 6042	0.0074 0201	0.0076 4844	172
173	0.0066 5845	0.0068 9041	0.0071 2728	0.0073 6905	0.0076 1568	173
174	0.0066 2544	0.0068 5751	0.0070 9454	0.0073 3648	0.0075 8332	174
175	0.0065 9280	0.0068 2499	0.0070 6217	0.0073 0429	0.0075 5133	175
176	0.0065 6053	0.0067 9285	0.0070 3018	0.0072 7248	0.0075 1972	176
177	0.0065 2864	0.0067 6108	0.0069 9855	0.0072 4103	0.0074 8847	177
178	0.0064 9710	0.0067 2966	0.0069 6729	0.0072 0994	0.0074 5759	178
179	0.0064 6592	0.0066 9860	0.0069 3638	0.0071 7921	0.0074 2706	179
180	0.0064 3509	0.0066 6789	0.0069 0582	0.0071 4883	0.0073 9688	180

TABLE V

N	1/6	5/24	1/4	7/24	1/3	N
181	0.0064 0460	0.0066 3753	0.0068 7560	0.0071 1879	0.0073 6704	181
182	0.0063 7445	0.0066 0750	0.0068 4572	0.0070 8908	0.0073 3754	182
183	0.0063 4463	0.0065 7780	0.0068 1617	0.0070 5971	0.0073 0838	183
184	0.0063 1513	0.0065 4843	0.0067 8695	0.0070 3067	0.0072 7954	184
185	0.0062 8596	0.0065 1938	0.0067 5805	0.0070 0195	0.0072 5102	185
186	0.0062 5711	0.0064 9065	0.0067 2947	0.0069 7354	0.0072 2281	186
187	0.0062 2856	0.0064 6222	0.0067 0120	0.0069 4545	0.0071 9492	187
188	0.0062 0033	0.0064 3411	0.0066 7323	0.0069 1766	0.0071 6734	188
189	0.0061 7239	0.0064 0629	0.0066 4557	0.0068 9017	0.0071 4005	189
190	0.0061 4475	0.0063 7878	0.0066 1820	0.0068 6298	0.0071 1307	190
191	0.0061 1740	0.0063 5155	0.0065 9112	0.0068 3608	0.0070 8637	191
192	0.0060 9034	0.0063 2461	0.0065 6434	0.0068 0947	0.0070 5996	192
193	0.0060 6356	0.0062 9796	0.0065 3783	0.0067 8314	0.0070 3384	193
194	0.0060 3706	0.0062 7158	0.0065 1160	0.0067 5709	0.0070 0799	194
195	0.0060 1083	0.0062 4548	0.0064 8565	0.0067 3131	0.0069 8242	195
196	0.0059 8488	0.0062 1964	0.0064 5997	0.0067 0581	0.0069 5711	196
197	0.0059 5919	0.0061 9407	0.0064 3455	0.0066 8057	0.0069 3208	197
198	0.0059 3376	0.0061 6877	0.0064 0939	0.0066 5559	0.0069 0730	198
199	0.0059 0859	0.0061 4372	0.0063 8450	0.0066 3087	0.0068 8279	199
200	0.0058 8367	0.0061 1893	0.0063 5985	0.0066 0640	0.0068 5852	200
201	0.0058 5900	0.0060 9438	0.0063 3546	0.0065 8219	0.0068 3451	201
202	0.0058 3459	0.0060 7009	0.0063 1131	0.0065 5822	0.0068 1074	202
203	0.0058 1041	0.0060 4603	0.0062 8741	0.0065 3449	0.0067 8722	203
204	0.0057 8647	0.0060 2222	0.0062 6375	0.0065 1100	0.0067 6393	204
205	0.0057 6277	0.0059 9864	0.0062 4032	0.0064 8775	0.0067 4089	205
206	0.0057 3930	0.0059 7529	0.0062 1712	0.0064 6473	0.0067 1807	206
207	0.0057 1606	0.0059 5218	0.0061 9416	0.0064 4194	0.0066 9548	207
208	0.0056 9304	0.0059 2928	0.0061 7141	0.0064 1938	0.0066 7312	208
209	0.0056 7025	0.0059 0662	0.0061 4890	0.0063 9704	0.0066 5098	209
210	0.0056 4768	0.0058 8417	0.0061 2660	0.0063 7492	0.0066 2906	210
211	0.0056 2532	0.0058 6193	0.0061 0451	0.0063 5301	0.0066 0736	211
212	0.0056 0318	0.0058 3991	0.0060 8264	0.0063 3132	0.0065 8587	212
213	0.0055 8124	0.0058 1810	0.0060 6098	0.0063 0983	0.0065 6459	213
214	0.0055 5951	0.0057 9650	0.0060 3953	0.0062 8856	0.0065 4351	214
215	0.0055 3799	0.0057 7510	0.0060 1828	0.0062 6748	0.0065 2264	215
216	0.0055 1667	0.0057 5390	0.0059 9723	0.0062 4661	0.0065 0198	216
217	0.0054 9555	0.0057 3290	0.0059 7638	0.0062 2594	0.0064 8151	217
218	0.0054 7462	0.0057 1210	0.0059 5573	0.0062 0547	0.0064 6123	218
219	0.0054 5389	0.0056 9149	0.0059 3527	0.0061 8518	0.0064 4115	219
220	0.0054 3334	0.0056 7107	0.0059 1500	0.0061 6509	0.0064 2126	220
221	0.0054 1299	0.0056 5084	0.0058 9492	0.0061 4519	0.0064 0156	221
222	0.0053 9282	0.0056 3079	0.0058 7503	0.0061 2547	0.0063 8205	222
223	0.0053 7283	0.0056 1093	0.0058 5531	0.0061 0593	0.0063 6271	223
224	0.0053 5303	0.0055 9124	0.0058 3578	0.0060 8658	0.0063 4356	224
225	0.0053 3340	0.0055 7174	0.0058 1643	0.0060 6740	0.0063 2458	225
226	0.0053 1395	0.0055 5241	0.0057 9725	0.0060 4840	0.0063 0578	226
227	0.0052 9467	0.0055 3325	0.0057 7824	0.0060 2957	0.0062 8716	227
228	0.0052 7556	0.0055 1427	0.0057 5941	0.0060 1091	0.0062 6870	228
229	0.0052 5662	0.0054 9546	0.0057 4075	0.0059 9243	0.0062 5042	229
230	0.0052 3785	0.0054 7681	0.0057 2225	0.0059 7410	0.0062 3230	230
231	0.0052 1924	0.0054 5832	0.0057 0391	0.0059 5595	0.0062 1434	231
232	0.0052 0080	0.0054 4000	0.0056 8574	0.0059 3795	0.0061 9655	232
233	0.0051 8251	0.0054 2184	0.0056 6773	0.0059 2012	0.0061 7892	233
234	0.0051 6438	0.0054 0384	0.0056 4988	0.0059 0244	0.0061 6144	234
235	0.0051 4641	0.0053 8599	0.0056 3218	0.0058 8492	0.0061 4412	235
236	0.0051 2860	0.0053 6830	0.0056 1464	0.0058 6756	0.0061 2696	236
237	0.0051 1093	0.0053 5076	0.0055 9725	0.0058 5034	0.0061 0995	237
238	0.0050 9342	0.0053 3337	0.0055 8001	0.0058 3328	0.0060 9308	238
239	0.0050 7605	0.0053 1612	0.0055 6292	0.0058 1637	0.0060 7637	239
240	0.0050 5883	0.0052 9903	0.0055 4598	0.0057 9960	0.0060 5980	240

TABLE V

N	1/6	5/24	1/4	7/24	1/3	N
241	0.0050 4176	0.0052 8208	0.0055 2918	0.0057 8297	0.0060 4338	241
242	0.0050 2483	0.0052 6527	0.0055 1252	0.0057 6649	0.0060 2710	242
243	0.0050 0804	0.0052 4861	0.0054 9600	0.0057 5015	0.0060 1096	243
244	0.0049 9139	0.0052 3208	0.0054 7963	0.0057 3395	0.0059 9496	244
245	0.0049 7488	0.0052 1569	0.0054 6339	0.0057 1789	0.0059 7910	245
246	0.0049 5850	0.0051 9944	0.0054 4729	0.0057 0197	0.0059 6338	246
247	0.0049 4226	0.0051 8332	0.0054 3132	0.0056 8617	0.0059 4779	247
248	0.0049 2615	0.0051 6733	0.0054 1548	0.0056 7052	0.0059 3233	248
249	0.0049 1017	0.0051 5148	0.0053 9978	0.0056 5499	0.0059 1700	249
250	0.0048 9432	0.0051 3576	0.0053 8421	0.0056 3959	0.0059 0180	250
251	0.0048 7860	0.0051 2016	0.0053 6876	0.0056 2432	0.0058 8673	251
252	0.0048 6301	0.0051 0469	0.0053 5344	0.0056 0918	0.0058 7179	252
253	0.0048 4754	0.0050 8934	0.0053 3825	0.0055 9416	0.0058 5697	253
254	0.0048 3219	0.0050 7412	0.0053 2318	0.0055 7926	0.0058 4228	254
255	0.0048 1697	0.0050 5902	0.0053 0823	0.0055 6449	0.0058 2770	255
256	0.0048 0187	0.0050 4405	0.0052 9340	0.0055 4984	0.0058 1325	256
257	0.0047 8689	0.0050 2919	0.0052 7869	0.0055 3530	0.0057 9892	257
258	0.0047 7202	0.0050 1445	0.0052 6410	0.0055 2089	0.0057 8470	258
259	0.0047 5727	0.0049 9982	0.0052 4963	0.0055 0659	0.0057 7061	259
260	0.0047 4264	0.0049 8531	0.0052 3527	0.0054 9241	0.0057 5662	260
261	0.0047 2812	0.0049 7092	0.0052 2102	0.0054 7834	0.0057 4275	261
262	0.0047 1371	0.0049 5663	0.0052 0689	0.0054 6438	0.0057 2899	262
263	0.0046 9942	0.0049 4246	0.0051 9287	0.0054 5053	0.0057 1535	263
264	0.0046 8523	0.0049 2840	0.0051 7896	0.0054 3680	0.0057 0181	264
265	0.0046 7116	0.0049 1445	0.0051 6515	0.0054 2317	0.0056 8838	265
266	0.0046 5719	0.0049 0060	0.0051 5146	0.0054 0965	0.0056 7506	266
267	0.0046 4332	0.0048 8686	0.0051 3787	0.0053 9624	0.0056 6185	267
268	0.0046 2957	0.0048 7323	0.0051 2439	0.0053 8293	0.0056 4874	268
269	0.0046 1591	0.0048 5970	0.0051 1101	0.0053 6972	0.0056 3573	269
270	0.0046 0236	0.0048 4627	0.0050 9773	0.0053 5662	0.0056 2283	270
271	0.0045 8891	0.0048 3295	0.0050 8455	0.0053 4362	0.0056 1003	271
272	0.0045 7556	0.0048 1972	0.0050 7148	0.0053 3072	0.0055 9733	272
273	0.0045 6231	0.0048 0660	0.0050 5850	0.0053 1792	0.0055 8472	273
274	0.0045 4916	0.0047 9357	0.0050 4563	0.0053 0522	0.0055 7222	274
275	0.0045 3611	0.0047 8064	0.0050 3285	0.0052 9261	0.0055 5981	275
276	0.0045 2315	0.0047 6781	0.0050 2016	0.0052 8011	0.0055 4750	276
277	0.0045 1029	0.0047 5507	0.0050 0757	0.0052 6769	0.0055 3529	277
278	0.0044 9752	0.0047 4242	0.0049 9508	0.0052 5537	0.0055 2317	278
279	0.0044 8485	0.0047 2987	0.0049 8268	0.0052 4315	0.0055 1114	279
280	0.0044 7226	0.0047 1741	0.0049 7037	0.0052 3101	0.0054 9920	280
281	0.0044 5977	0.0047 0505	0.0049 5815	0.0052 1897	0.0054 8736	281
282	0.0044 4737	0.0046 9277	0.0049 4602	0.0052 0701	0.0054 7560	282
283	0.0044 3506	0.0046 8058	0.0049 3399	0.0051 9515	0.0054 6394	283
284	0.0044 2284	0.0046 6848	0.0049 2203	0.0051 8337	0.0054 5236	284
285	0.0044 1070	0.0046 5647	0.0049 1017	0.0051 7169	0.0054 4087	285
286	0.0043 9865	0.0046 4454	0.0048 9840	0.0051 6008	0.0054 2946	286
287	0.0043 8669	0.0046 3270	0.0048 8670	0.0051 4857	0.0054 1814	287
288	0.0043 7481	0.0046 2095	0.0048 7510	0.0051 3714	0.0054 0691	288
289	0.0043 6301	0.0046 0927	0.0048 6358	0.0051 2579	0.0053 9576	289
290	0.0043 5130	0.0045 9768	0.0048 5214	0.0051 1452	0.0053 8469	290
291	0.0043 3967	0.0045 8618	0.0048 4078	0.0051 0334	0.0053 7370	291
292	0.0043 2812	0.0045 7475	0.0048 2950	0.0050 9223	0.0053 6280	292
293	0.0043 1665	0.0045 6340	0.0048 1830	0.0050 8121	0.0053 5197	293
294	0.0043 0526	0.0045 5214	0.0048 0719	0.0050 7027	0.0053 4122	294
295	0.0042 9395	0.0045 4095	0.0047 9615	0.0050 5940	0.0053 3056	295
296	0.0042 8271	0.0045 2984	0.0047 8519	0.0050 4862	0.0053 1997	296
297	0.0042 7156	0.0045 1881	0.0047 7431	0.0050 3791	0.0053 0945	297
298	0.0042 6048	0.0045 0785	0.0047 6350	0.0050 2728	0.0052 9902	298
299	0.0042 4947	0.0044 9697	0.0047 5277	0.0050 1672	0.0052 8866	299
300	0.0042 3854	0.0044 8617	0.0047 4211	0.0050 0624	0.0052 7837	300

TABLE V

N	1/6	5/24	1/4	7/24	1/3	N
301	0.0042 2769	0.0044 7544	0.0047 3153	0.0049 9583	0.0052 6816	301
302	0.0042 1691	0.0044 6478	0.0047 2102	0.0049 8549	0.0052 5802	302
303	0.0042 0620	0.0044 5419	0.0047 1059	0.0049 7523	0.0052 4795	303
304	0.0041 9556	0.0044 4368	0.0047 0022	0.0049 6504	0.0052 3795	304
305	0.0041 8499	0.0044 3324	0.0046 8993	0.0049 5492	0.0052 2803	305
306	0.0041 7450	0.0044 2287	0.0046 7971	0.0049 4487	0.0052 1818	306
307	0.0041 6407	0.0044 1256	0.0046 6955	0.0049 3489	0.0052 0839	307
308	0.0041 5372	0.0044 0233	0.0046 5947	0.0049 2498	0.0051 9868	308
309	0.0041 4343	0.0043 9217	0.0046 4945	0.0049 1513	0.0051 8903	309
310	0.0041 3321	0.0043 8207	0.0046 3951	0.0049 0536	0.0051 7945	310
311	0.0041 2306	0.0043 7204	0.0046 2963	0.0048 9565	0.0051 6994	311
312	0.0041 1297	0.0043 6208	0.0046 1981	0.0048 8601	0.0051 6049	312
313	0.0041 0295	0.0043 5218	0.0046 1006	0.0048 7644	0.0051 5111	313
314	0.0040 9300	0.0043 4235	0.0046 0038	0.0048 6693	0.0051 4179	314
315	0.0040 8311	0.0043 3258	0.0045 9076	0.0048 5748	0.0051 3254	315
316	0.0040 7328	0.0043 2288	0.0045 8121	0.0048 4810	0.0051 2336	316
317	0.0040 6352	0.0043 1324	0.0045 7172	0.0048 3878	0.0051 1423	317
318	0.0040 5382	0.0043 0366	0.0045 6229	0.0048 2952	0.0051 0517	318
319	0.0040 4418	0.0042 9415	0.0045 5292	0.0048 2033	0.0050 9617	319
320	0.0040 3460	0.0042 8470	0.0045 4362	0.0048 1120	0.0050 8723	320
321	0.0040 2509	0.0042 7530	0.0045 3438	0.0048 0213	0.0050 7835	321
322	0.0040 1563	0.0042 6597	0.0045 2519	0.0047 9312	0.0050 6954	322
323	0.0040 0624	0.0042 5670	0.0045 1607	0.0047 8416	0.0050 6078	323
324	0.0039 9690	0.0042 4749	0.0045 0701	0.0047 7527	0.0050 5208	324
325	0.0039 8762	0.0042 3833	0.0044 9800	0.0047 6644	0.0050 4344	325
326	0.0039 7841	0.0042 2924	0.0044 8905	0.0047 5766	0.0050 3486	326
327	0.0039 6925	0.0042 2020	0.0044 8016	0.0047 4895	0.0050 2634	327
328	0.0039 6014	0.0042 1122	0.0044 7133	0.0047 4029	0.0050 1787	328
329	0.0039 5110	0.0042 0230	0.0044 6256	0.0047 3168	0.0050 0946	329
330	0.0039 4210	0.0041 9343	0.0044 5384	0.0047 2313	0.0050 0110	330
331	0.0039 3317	0.0041 8462	0.0044 4517	0.0047 1464	0.0049 9281	331
332	0.0039 2429	0.0041 7586	0.0044 3657	0.0047 0621	0.0049 8456	332
333	0.0039 1547	0.0041 6716	0.0044 2801	0.0046 9782	0.0049 7637	333
334	0.0039 0669	0.0041 5851	0.0044 1951	0.0046 8949	0.0049 6824	334
335	0.0038 9798	0.0041 4992	0.0044 1107	0.0046 8122	0.0049 6015	335
336	0.0038 8931	0.0041 4138	0.0044 0267	0.0046 7300	0.0049 5212	336
337	0.0038 8070	0.0041 3289	0.0043 9433	0.0046 6483	0.0049 4415	337
338	0.0038 7214	0.0041 2446	0.0043 8605	0.0046 5671	0.0049 3622	338
339	0.0038 6364	0.0041 1607	0.0043 7781	0.0046 4865	0.0049 2835	339
340	0.0038 5518	0.0041 0774	0.0043 6963	0.0046 4063	0.0049 2053	340
341	0.0038 4678	0.0040 9946	0.0043 6149	0.0046 3267	0.0049 1275	341
342	0.0038 3842	0.0040 9123	0.0043 5341	0.0046 2476	0.0049 0503	342
343	0.0038 3012	0.0040 8305	0.0043 4537	0.0046 1689	0.0048 9736	343
344	0.0038 2186	0.0040 7491	0.0043 3739	0.0046 0908	0.0048 8974	344
345	0.0038 1366	0.0040 6683	0.0043 2945	0.0046 0131	0.0048 8217	345
346	0.0038 0550	0.0040 5880	0.0043 2157	0.0045 9360	0.0048 7464	346
347	0.0037 9739	0.0040 5081	0.0043 1373	0.0045 8593	0.0048 6716	347
348	0.0037 8933	0.0040 4287	0.0043 0594	0.0045 7831	0.0048 5973	348
349	0.0037 8132	0.0040 3498	0.0042 9820	0.0045 7074	0.0048 5235	349
350	0.0037 7335	0.0040 2714	0.0042 9050	0.0045 6321	0.0048 4502	350
351	0.0037 6543	0.0040 1934	0.0042 8285	0.0045 5573	0.0048 3773	351
352	0.0037 5756	0.0040 1159	0.0042 7525	0.0045 4830	0.0048 3049	352
353	0.0037 4973	0.0040 0389	0.0042 6769	0.0045 4091	0.0048 2329	353
354	0.0037 4195	0.0039 9623	0.0042 6018	0.0045 3357	0.0048 1614	354
355	0.0037 3421	0.0039 8862	0.0042 5271	0.0045 2627	0.0048 0903	355
356	0.0037 2652	0.0039 8105	0.0042 4529	0.0045 1902	0.0048 0197	356
357	0.0037 1888	0.0039 7352	0.0042 3791	0.0045 1181	0.0047 9495	357
358	0.0037 1127	0.0039 6604	0.0042 3058	0.0045 0465	0.0047 8797	358
359	0.0037 0371	0.0039 5860	0.0042 2329	0.0044 9752	0.0047 8104	359
360	0.0036 9619	0.0039 5121	0.0042 1604	0.0044 9045	0.0047 7415	360

TABLE V

N	3/8	5/12	11/24	1/2	13/24	N
1	1.0037 5000	1.0041 6667	1.0045 8333	1.0050 0000	1.0054 1667	1
2	0.5028 1425	0.5031 2717	0.5034 4012	0.5037 5312	0.5040 6616	2
3	0.3358 3645	0.3361 1496	0.3363 9355	0.3366 7221	0.3369 5095	3
4	0.2523 4814	0.2526 0958	0.2528 7113	0.2531 3279	0.2533 9456	4
5	0.2022 5561	0.2025 0693	0.2027 5838	0.2030 0997	0.2032 6170	5
6	0.1688 6099	0.1691 0564	0.1693 5047	0.1695 9546	0.1698 4061	6
7	0.1450 0802	0.1452 4800	0.1454 8817	0.1457 2854	0.1459 6910	7
8	0.1271 1859	0.1273 5512	0.1275 9188	0.1278 2886	0.1280 6608	8
9	0.1132 0484	0.1134 3876	0.1136 7293	0.1139 0736	0.1141 4204	9
10	0.1020 7408	0.1023 0596	0.1025 3812	0.1027 7057	0.1030 0331	10
11	0.0929 6731	0.0931 9757	0.0934 2814	0.0936 5903	0.0938 9024	11
12	0.0853 7852	0.0856 0748	0.0858 3678	0.0860 6643	0.0862 9642	12
13	0.0789 5742	0.0791 8532	0.0794 1360	0.0796 4224	0.0798 7125	13
14	0.0734 5379	0.0736 8082	0.0739 0825	0.0741 3609	0.0743 6432	14
15	0.0686 8413	0.0689 1045	0.0691 3719	0.0693 6436	0.0695 9197	15
16	0.0645 1083	0.0647 3655	0.0649 6273	0.0651 8937	0.0654 1646	16
17	0.0608 2864	0.0610 5387	0.0612 7959	0.0615 0579	0.0617 3248	17
18	0.0575 5571	0.0577 8053	0.0580 0587	0.0582 3173	0.0584 5810	18
19	0.0546 2742	0.0548 5191	0.0550 7695	0.0553 0253	0.0555 2865	19
20	0.0519 9208	0.0522 1630	0.0524 4109	0.0526 6645	0.0528 9239	20
21	0.0496 0784	0.0498 3183	0.0500 5643	0.0502 8163	0.0505 0743	21
22	0.0474 4045	0.0476 6427	0.0478 8872	0.0481 1380	0.0483 3951	22
23	0.0454 6163	0.0456 8531	0.0459 0965	0.0461 3465	0.0463 6031	23
24	0.0436 4781	0.0438 7139	0.0440 9566	0.0443 2061	0.0445 4625	24
25	0.0419 7919	0.0422 0270	0.0424 2692	0.0426 5186	0.0428 7751	25
26	0.0404 3902	0.0406 6247	0.0408 8668	0.0411 1163	0.0413 3732	26
27	0.0390 1301	0.0392 3645	0.0394 6066	0.0396 8565	0.0399 1140	27
28	0.0376 8895	0.0379 1239	0.0381 3663	0.0383 6167	0.0385 8751	28
29	0.0364 5629	0.0366 7974	0.0369 0402	0.0371 2914	0.0373 5508	29
30	0.0353 0588	0.0355 2936	0.0357 5371	0.0359 7892	0.0362 0498	30
31	0.0342 2976	0.0344 5330	0.0346 7773	0.0349 0304	0.0351 2924	31
32	0.0332 2098	0.0334 4458	0.0336 6910	0.0338 9453	0.0341 2088	32
33	0.0322 7340	0.0324 9708	0.0327 2170	0.0329 4727	0.0331 7379	33
34	0.0313 8164	0.0316 0540	0.0318 3014	0.0320 5586	0.0322 8254	34
35	0.0305 4089	0.0307 6476	0.0309 8963	0.0312 1550	0.0314 4237	35
36	0.0297 4692	0.0299 7090	0.0301 9590	0.0304 2194	0.0306 4900	36
37	0.0289 9594	0.0292 2003	0.0294 4518	0.0296 7139	0.0298 9865	37
38	0.0282 8453	0.0285 0875	0.0287 3405	0.0289 6045	0.0291 8793	38
39	0.0276 0967	0.0278 3402	0.0280 5949	0.0282 8607	0.0285 1377	39
40	0.0269 6862	0.0271 9310	0.0274 1874	0.0276 4552	0.0278 7344	40
41	0.0263 5889	0.0265 8352	0.0268 0933	0.0270 3631	0.0272 6447	41
42	0.0257 7825	0.0260 0303	0.0262 2902	0.0264 5622	0.0266 8461	42
43	0.0252 2467	0.0254 4961	0.0256 7579	0.0259 0320	0.0261 3183	43
44	0.0246 9630	0.0249 2141	0.0251 4778	0.0253 7541	0.0256 0429	44
45	0.0241 9147	0.0244 1675	0.0246 4332	0.0248 7117	0.0251 0031	45
46	0.0237 0864	0.0239 3409	0.0241 6086	0.0243 8894	0.0246 1834	46
47	0.0232 4641	0.0234 7204	0.0236 9901	0.0239 2733	0.0241 5698	47
48	0.0228 0349	0.0230 2929	0.0232 5648	0.0234 8503	0.0237 1495	48
49	0.0223 7869	0.0226 0468	0.0228 3207	0.0230 6087	0.0232 9106	49
50	0.0219 7093	0.0221 9711	0.0224 2472	0.0226 5376	0.0228 8422	50
51	0.0215 7920	0.0218 0557	0.0220 3341	0.0222 6269	0.0224 9344	51
52	0.0212 0259	0.0214 2916	0.0216 5721	0.0218 8675	0.0221 1777	52
53	0.0208 4023	0.0210 6700	0.0212 9528	0.0215 2507	0.0217 5637	53
54	0.0204 9134	0.0207 1830	0.0209 4681	0.0211 7686	0.0214 0845	54
55	0.0201 5518	0.0203 8234	0.0206 1108	0.0208 4139	0.0210 7327	55
56	0.0198 3106	0.0200 5843	0.0202 8740	0.0205 1797	0.0207 5014	56
57	0.0195 1836	0.0197 4593	0.0199 7514	0.0202 0598	0.0204 3844	57
58	0.0192 1648	0.0194 4426	0.0196 7371	0.0199 0481	0.0201 3756	58
59	0.0189 2487	0.0191 5287	0.0193 8255	0.0196 1392	0.0198 4697	59
60	0.0186 4302	0.0188 7123	0.0191 0116	0.0193 3280	0.0195 6615	60

TABLE V

N	3/8	5/12	11/24	1/2	13/24	N
61	0.0183 7045	0.0185 9888	0.0188 2905	0.0190 6096	0.0192 9461	61
62	0.0181 0671	0.0183 3536	0.0185 6578	0.0187 9796	0.0190 3191	62
63	0.0178 5138	0.0180 8025	0.0183 1091	0.0185 4337	0.0187 7762	63
64	0.0176 0407	0.0178 3315	0.0180 6407	0.0182 9681	0.0185 3136	64
65	0.0173 6440	0.0175 9371	0.0178 2487	0.0180 5789	0.0182 9275	65
66	0.0171 3203	0.0173 6156	0.0175 9298	0.0178 2627	0.0180 6144	66
67	0.0169 0663	0.0171 3639	0.0173 6806	0.0176 0163	0.0178 3711	67
68	0.0166 8789	0.0169 1788	0.0171 4980	0.0173 8366	0.0176 1945	68
69	0.0164 7553	0.0167 0574	0.0169 3792	0.0171 7206	0.0174 0817	69
70	0.0162 6927	0.0164 9971	0.0167 3215	0.0169 6657	0.0172 0299	70
71	0.0160 6885	0.0162 9952	0.0165 3222	0.0167 6693	0.0170 0366	71
72	0.0158 7403	0.0161 0493	0.0163 3789	0.0165 7289	0.0168 0993	72
73	0.0156 8458	0.0159 1572	0.0161 4893	0.0163 8422	0.0166 2158	73
74	0.0155 0028	0.0157 3165	0.0159 6513	0.0162 0070	0.0164 3838	74
75	0.0153 2093	0.0155 5253	0.0157 8627	0.0160 2214	0.0162 6013	75
76	0.0151 4633	0.0153 7816	0.0156 1217	0.0158 4832	0.0160 8663	76
77	0.0149 7629	0.0152 0836	0.0154 4263	0.0156 7908	0.0159 1771	77
78	0.0148 1064	0.0150 4295	0.0152 7748	0.0155 1423	0.0157 5317	78
79	0.0146 4922	0.0148 8177	0.0151 1656	0.0153 5360	0.0155 9287	79
80	0.0144 9186	0.0147 2464	0.0149 5971	0.0151 9704	0.0154 3663	80
81	0.0143 3841	0.0145 7144	0.0148 0677	0.0150 4439	0.0152 8430	81
82	0.0141 8874	0.0144 2200	0.0146 5760	0.0148 9552	0.0151 3575	82
83	0.0140 4270	0.0142 7620	0.0145 1207	0.0147 5028	0.0149 9084	83
84	0.0139 0016	0.0141 3391	0.0143 7004	0.0146 0855	0.0148 4944	84
85	0.0137 6101	0.0139 9500	0.0142 3140	0.0144 7021	0.0147 1141	85
86	0.0136 2512	0.0138 5935	0.0140 9602	0.0143 3513	0.0145 7666	86
87	0.0134 9237	0.0137 2685	0.0139 6379	0.0142 0320	0.0144 4505	87
88	0.0133 6268	0.0135 9740	0.0138 3461	0.0140 7431	0.0143 1650	88
89	0.0132 3592	0.0134 7088	0.0137 0837	0.0139 4837	0.0141 9088	89
90	0.0131 1200	0.0133 4721	0.0135 8497	0.0138 2527	0.0140 6811	90
91	0.0129 9084	0.0132 2629	0.0134 6432	0.0137 0493	0.0139 4809	91
92	0.0128 7233	0.0131 0803	0.0133 4634	0.0135 8724	0.0138 3073	92
93	0.0127 5640	0.0129 9234	0.0132 3092	0.0134 7213	0.0137 1594	93
94	0.0126 4296	0.0128 7915	0.0131 1800	0.0133 5950	0.0136 0365	94
95	0.0125 3193	0.0127 6836	0.0130 0749	0.0132 4930	0.0134 9377	95
96	0.0124 2323	0.0126 5992	0.0128 9932	0.0131 4143	0.0133 8623	96
97	0.0123 1681	0.0125 5374	0.0127 9342	0.0130 3583	0.0132 8096	97
98	0.0122 1258	0.0124 4976	0.0126 8971	0.0129 3242	0.0131 7788	98
99	0.0121 1047	0.0123 4790	0.0125 8813	0.0128 3115	0.0130 7694	99
100	0.0120 1043	0.0122 4811	0.0124 8862	0.0127 3194	0.0129 7806	100
101	0.0119 1240	0.0121 5033	0.0123 9111	0.0126 3473	0.0128 8118	101
102	0.0118 1631	0.0120 5449	0.0122 9555	0.0125 3947	0.0127 8625	102
103	0.0117 2211	0.0119 6054	0.0122 0187	0.0124 4610	0.0126 9321	103
104	0.0116 2974	0.0118 6842	0.0121 1003	0.0123 5457	0.0126 0201	104
105	0.0115 3916	0.0117 7809	0.0120 1997	0.0122 6481	0.0125 1259	105
106	0.0114 5030	0.0116 8948	0.0119 3165	0.0121 7679	0.0124 2489	106
107	0.0113 6313	0.0116 0256	0.0118 4500	0.0120 9045	0.0123 3889	107
108	0.0112 7759	0.0115 1727	0.0117 6000	0.0120 0575	0.0122 5452	108
109	0.0111 9365	0.0114 3358	0.0116 7658	0.0119 2264	0.0121 7174	109
110	0.0111 1125	0.0113 5143	0.0115 9471	0.0118 4107	0.0120 9050	110
111	0.0110 3035	0.0112 7079	0.0115 1435	0.0117 6102	0.0120 1078	111
112	0.0109 5092	0.0111 9161	0.0114 3545	0.0116 8242	0.0119 3252	112
113	0.0108 7292	0.0111 1386	0.0113 5798	0.0116 0526	0.0118 5568	113
114	0.0107 9631	0.0110 3750	0.0112 8190	0.0115 2948	0.0117 8024	114
115	0.0107 2105	0.0109 6249	0.0112 0717	0.0114 5506	0.0117 0615	115
116	0.0106 4710	0.0108 8880	0.0111 3376	0.0113 8195	0.0116 3337	116
117	0.0105 7444	0.0108 1639	0.0110 6163	0.0113 1013	0.0115 6188	117
118	0.0105 0303	0.0107 4524	0.0109 9075	0.0112 3956	0.0114 9165	118
119	0.0104 3284	0.0106 7530	0.0109 2110	0.0111 7021	0.0114 2263	119
120	0.0103 6384	0.0106 0655	0.0108 5263	0.0111 0205	0.0113 5480	120

TABLE V

N	3/8	5/12	11/24	1/2	13/24	N
121	0.0102 9600	0.0105 3896	0.0107 8532	0.0110 3505	0.0112 8813	121
122	0.0102 2929	0.0104 7251	0.0107 1914	0.0109 6918	0.0112 2259	122
123	0.0101 6368	0.0104 0715	0.0106 5407	0.0109 0441	0.0111 5816	123
124	0.0100 9915	0.0103 4288	0.0105 9007	0.0108 4072	0.0110 9480	124
125	0.0100 3567	0.0102 7965	0.0105 2713	0.0107 7808	0.0110 3249	125
126	0.0099 7322	0.0102 1745	0.0104 6521	0.0107 1647	0.0109 7121	126
127	0.0099 1176	0.0101 5625	0.0104 0429	0.0106 5586	0.0109 1093	127
128	0.0098 5129	0.0100 9603	0.0103 4435	0.0105 9623	0.0108 5163	128
129	0.0097 9177	0.0100 3677	0.0102 8537	0.0105 3755	0.0107 9329	129
130	0.0097 3318	0.0099 7844	0.0102 2732	0.0104 7981	0.0107 3588	130
131	0.0096 7551	0.0099 2102	0.0101 7018	0.0104 2298	0.0106 7938	131
132	0.0096 1873	0.0098 6449	0.0101 1393	0.0103 6703	0.0106 2377	132
133	0.0095 6282	0.0098 0883	0.0100 5856	0.0103 1197	0.0105 6903	133
134	0.0095 0775	0.0097 5403	0.0100 0403	0.0102 5775	0.0105 1514	134
135	0.0094 5353	0.0097 0005	0.0099 5034	0.0102 0436	0.0104 6209	135
136	0.0094 0011	0.0096 4689	0.0098 9746	0.0101 5179	0.0104 0985	136
137	0.0093 4750	0.0095 9453	0.0098 4538	0.0101 0002	0.0103 5841	137
138	0.0092 9566	0.0095 4295	0.0097 9408	0.0100 4902	0.0103 0774	138
139	0.0092 4458	0.0094 9213	0.0097 4354	0.0099 9879	0.0102 5784	139
140	0.0091 9425	0.0094 4205	0.0096 9375	0.0099 4930	0.0102 0869	140
141	0.0091 4465	0.0093 9271	0.0096 4468	0.0099 0055	0.0101 6026	141
142	0.0090 9577	0.0093 4408	0.0095 9634	0.0098 5250	0.0101 1255	142
143	0.0090 4758	0.0092 9615	0.0095 4869	0.0098 0516	0.0100 6554	143
144	0.0090 0008	0.0092 4890	0.0095 0172	0.0097 5850	0.0100 1921	144
145	0.0089 5325	0.0092 0233	0.0094 5543	0.0097 1252	0.0099 7355	145
146	0.0089 0708	0.0091 5641	0.0094 0979	0.0096 6718	0.0099 2855	146
147	0.0088 6155	0.0091 1114	0.0093 6480	0.0096 2250	0.0098 8420	147
148	0.0088 1665	0.0090 6650	0.0093 2044	0.0095 7844	0.0098 4047	148
149	0.0087 7237	0.0090 2247	0.0092 7669	0.0095 3500	0.0097 9736	149
150	0.0087 2870	0.0089 7905	0.0092 3355	0.0094 9217	0.0097 5486	150
151	0.0086 8561	0.0089 3623	0.0091 9101	0.0094 4993	0.0097 1295	151
152	0.0086 4312	0.0088 9398	0.0091 4905	0.0094 0827	0.0096 7162	152
153	0.0086 0119	0.0088 5231	0.0091 0765	0.0093 6719	0.0096 3087	153
154	0.0085 5982	0.0088 1119	0.0090 6682	0.0093 2666	0.0095 9067	154
155	0.0085 1899	0.0087 7063	0.0090 2653	0.0092 8668	0.0095 5102	155
156	0.0084 7871	0.0087 3060	0.0089 8679	0.0092 4723	0.0095 1190	156
157	0.0084 3895	0.0086 9110	0.0089 4756	0.0092 0832	0.0094 7332	157
158	0.0083 9972	0.0086 5211	0.0089 0886	0.0091 6992	0.0094 3525	158
159	0.0083 6098	0.0086 1364	0.0088 7067	0.0091 3203	0.0093 9768	159
160	0.0083 2275	0.0085 7566	0.0088 3297	0.0090 9464	0.0093 6062	160
161	0.0082 8501	0.0085 3817	0.0087 9576	0.0090 5773	0.0093 2404	161
162	0.0082 4774	0.0085 0116	0.0087 5903	0.0090 2131	0.0092 8795	162
163	0.0082 1095	0.0084 6462	0.0087 2278	0.0089 8536	0.0092 5232	163
164	0.0081 7462	0.0084 2855	0.0086 8698	0.0089 4987	0.0092 1716	164
165	0.0081 3874	0.0083 9293	0.0086 5164	0.0089 1483	0.0091 8245	165
166	0.0081 0331	0.0083 5775	0.0086 1674	0.0088 8024	0.0091 4819	166
167	0.0080 6832	0.0083 2301	0.0085 8229	0.0088 4608	0.0091 1436	167
168	0.0080 3376	0.0082 8871	0.0085 4826	0.0088 1236	0.0090 8096	168
169	0.0079 9962	0.0082 5482	0.0085 1465	0.0087 7906	0.0090 4798	169
170	0.0079 6589	0.0082 2135	0.0084 8146	0.0087 4617	0.0090 1542	170
171	0.0079 3257	0.0081 8829	0.0084 4868	0.0087 1369	0.0089 8327	171
172	0.0078 9966	0.0081 5563	0.0084 1629	0.0086 8161	0.0089 5151	172
173	0.0078 6713	0.0081 2336	0.0083 8430	0.0086 4992	0.0089 2015	173
174	0.0078 3500	0.0080 9147	0.0083 5270	0.0086 1862	0.0088 8918	174
175	0.0078 0324	0.0080 5997	0.0083 2148	0.0085 8770	0.0088 5858	175
176	0.0077 7186	0.0080 2884	0.0082 9063	0.0085 5715	0.0088 2836	176
177	0.0077 4084	0.0079 9808	0.0082 6014	0.0085 2697	0.0087 9850	177
178	0.0077 1018	0.0079 6768	0.0082 3002	0.0084 9715	0.0087 6901	178
179	0.0076 7988	0.0079 3763	0.0082 0025	0.0084 6768	0.0087 3987	179
180	0.0076 4993	0.0079 0794	0.0081 7083	0.0084 3857	0.0087 1107	180

TABLE V

N	3/8	5/12	11/24	1/2	13/24	N
181	0.0076 2033	0.0078 7858	0.0081 4176	0.0084 0979	0.0086 8262	181
182	0.0075 9106	0.0078 4957	0.0081 1302	0.0083 8136	0.0086 5451	182
183	0.0075 6212	0.0078 2088	0.0080 8462	0.0083 5325	0.0086 2673	183
184	0.0075 3351	0.0077 9253	0.0080 5654	0.0083 2547	0.0085 9927	184
185	0.0075 0522	0.0077 6449	0.0080 2878	0.0082 9802	0.0085 7214	185
186	0.0074 7724	0.0077 3677	0.0080 0134	0.0082 7088	0.0085 4532	186
187	0.0074 4958	0.0077 0936	0.0079 7420	0.0082 4404	0.0085 1881	187
188	0.0074 2222	0.0076 8226	0.0079 4738	0.0082 1752	0.0084 9261	188
189	0.0073 9517	0.0076 5546	0.0079 2085	0.0081 9129	0.0084 6670	189
190	0.0073 6841	0.0076 2895	0.0078 9463	0.0081 6537	0.0084 4110	190
191	0.0073 4194	0.0076 0274	0.0078 6869	0.0081 3973	0.0084 1578	191
192	0.0073 1576	0.0075 7681	0.0078 4304	0.0081 1438	0.0083 9075	192
193	0.0072 8987	0.0075 5117	0.0078 1767	0.0080 8931	0.0083 6601	193
194	0.0072 6425	0.0075 2580	0.0077 9258	0.0080 6452	0.0083 4154	194
195	0.0072 3890	0.0075 0071	0.0077 6777	0.0080 4000	0.0083 1734	195
196	0.0072 1383	0.0074 7589	0.0077 4322	0.0080 1576	0.0082 9341	196
197	0.0071 8902	0.0074 5133	0.0077 1894	0.0079 9178	0.0082 6975	197
198	0.0071 6447	0.0074 2704	0.0076 9492	0.0079 6806	0.0082 4635	198
199	0.0071 4018	0.0074 0300	0.0076 7116	0.0079 4459	0.0082 2321	199
200	0.0071 1615	0.0073 7922	0.0076 4766	0.0079 2138	0.0082 0032	200
201	0.0070 9236	0.0073 5569	0.0076 2440	0.0078 9843	0.0081 7768	201
202	0.0070 6883	0.0073 3240	0.0076 0139	0.0078 7571	0.0081 5528	202
203	0.0070 4553	0.0073 0936	0.0075 7862	0.0078 5324	0.0081 3313	203
204	0.0070 2247	0.0072 8655	0.0075 5609	0.0078 3101	0.0081 1121	204
205	0.0069 9965	0.0072 6398	0.0075 3380	0.0078 0901	0.0080 8953	205
206	0.0069 7707	0.0072 4165	0.0075 1174	0.0077 8724	0.0080 6808	206
207	0.0069 5471	0.0072 1954	0.0074 8990	0.0077 6571	0.0080 4686	207
208	0.0069 3257	0.0071 9766	0.0074 6829	0.0077 4440	0.0080 2587	208
209	0.0069 1066	0.0071 7600	0.0074 4691	0.0077 2330	0.0080 0509	209
210	0.0068 8897	0.0071 5456	0.0074 2574	0.0077 0243	0.0079 8454	210
211	0.0068 6749	0.0071 3333	0.0074 0479	0.0076 8178	0.0079 6419	211
212	0.0068 4623	0.0071 1232	0.0073 8405	0.0076 6133	0.0079 4407	212
213	0.0068 2518	0.0070 9152	0.0073 6352	0.0076 4110	0.0079 2415	213
214	0.0068 0433	0.0070 7092	0.0073 4320	0.0076 2107	0.0079 0443	214
215	0.0067 8369	0.0070 5053	0.0073 2308	0.0076 0125	0.0078 8492	215
216	0.0067 6325	0.0070 3034	0.0073 0316	0.0075 8162	0.0078 6561	216
217	0.0067 4300	0.0070 1035	0.0072 8344	0.0075 6220	0.0078 4650	217
218	0.0067 2296	0.0069 9055	0.0072 6392	0.0075 4297	0.0078 2758	218
219	0.0067 0310	0.0069 7095	0.0072 4459	0.0075 2393	0.0078 0886	219
220	0.0066 8344	0.0069 5153	0.0072 2545	0.0075 0508	0.0077 9032	220
221	0.0066 6396	0.0069 3231	0.0072 0649	0.0074 8642	0.0077 7197	221
222	0.0066 4467	0.0069 1327	0.0071 8773	0.0074 6794	0.0077 5381	222
223	0.0066 2557	0.0068 9441	0.0071 6914	0.0074 4965	0.0077 3583	223
224	0.0066 0664	0.0068 7573	0.0071 5073	0.0074 3154	0.0077 1802	224
225	0.0065 8789	0.0068 5723	0.0071 3251	0.0074 1360	0.0077 0040	225
226	0.0065 6932	0.0068 3891	0.0071 1445	0.0073 9584	0.0076 8295	226
227	0.0065 5092	0.0068 2076	0.0070 9657	0.0073 7825	0.0076 6567	227
228	0.0065 3269	0.0068 0278	0.0070 7886	0.0073 6083	0.0076 4856	228
229	0.0065 1463	0.0067 8497	0.0070 6132	0.0073 4358	0.0076 3162	229
230	0.0064 9673	0.0067 6732	0.0070 4395	0.0073 2649	0.0076 1484	230
231	0.0064 7901	0.0067 4984	0.0070 2673	0.0073 0957	0.0075 9823	231
232	0.0064 6144	0.0067 3252	0.0070 0969	0.0072 9281	0.0075 8178	232
233	0.0064 4403	0.0067 1536	0.0069 9280	0.0072 7621	0.0075 6549	233
234	0.0064 2678	0.0066 9836	0.0069 7606	0.0072 5977	0.0075 4935	234
235	0.0064 0969	0.0066 8151	0.0069 5949	0.0072 4348	0.0075 3337	235
236	0.0063 9275	0.0066 6482	0.0069 4307	0.0072 2735	0.0075 1755	236
237	0.0063 7596	0.0066 4828	0.0069 2679	0.0072 1137	0.0075 0187	237
238	0.0063 5932	0.0066 3189	0.0069 1067	0.0071 9554	0.0074 8634	238
239	0.0063 4284	0.0066 1565	0.0068 9470	0.0071 7985	0.0074 7097	239
240	0.0063 2649	0.0065 9956	0.0068 7887	0.0071 6431	0.0074 5573	240

TABLE V

N	3/8	5/12	11/24	1/2	13/24	N
241	0.0063 1030	0.0065 8361	0.0068 6319	0.0071 4892	0.0074 4064	241
242	0.0062 9424	0.0065 6780	0.0068 4765	0.0071 3366	0.0074 2569	242
243	0.0062 7833	0.0065 5213	0.0068 3225	0.0071 1855	0.0074 1088	243
244	0.0062 6255	0.0065 3660	0.0068 1699	0.0071 0357	0.0073 9621	244
245	0.0062 4692	0.0065 2121	0.0068 0187	0.0070 8874	0.0073 8168	245
246	0.0062 3141	0.0065 0596	0.0067 8688	0.0070 7403	0.0073 6728	246
247	0.0062 1605	0.0064 9084	0.0067 7202	0.0070 5947	0.0073 5302	247
248	0.0062 0081	0.0064 7585	0.0067 5730	0.0070 4503	0.0073 3888	248
249	0.0061 8571	0.0064 6099	0.0067 4271	0.0070 3072	0.0073 2488	249
250	0.0061 7074	0.0064 4626	0.0067 2825	0.0070 1654	0.0073 1100	250
251	0.0061 5589	0.0064 3166	0.0067 1391	0.0070 0249	0.0072 9725	251
252	0.0061 4117	0.0064 1719	0.0066 9970	0.0069 8857	0.0072 8363	252
253	0.0061 2657	0.0064 0284	0.0066 8562	0.0069 7477	0.0072 7013	253
254	0.0061 1210	0.0063 8861	0.0066 7166	0.0069 6109	0.0072 5675	254
255	0.0060 9775	0.0063 7450	0.0066 5782	0.0069 4753	0.0072 4349	255
256	0.0060 8352	0.0063 6052	0.0066 4410	0.0069 3410	0.0072 3036	256
257	0.0060 6941	0.0063 4665	0.0066 3049	0.0069 2078	0.0072 1734	257
258	0.0060 5542	0.0063 3291	0.0066 1701	0.0069 0758	0.0072 0443	258
259	0.0060 4155	0.0063 1927	0.0066 0364	0.0068 9449	0.0071 9165	259
260	0.0060 2778	0.0063 0576	0.0065 9039	0.0068 8152	0.0071 7897	260
261	0.0060 1414	0.0062 9235	0.0065 7725	0.0068 6866	0.0071 6641	261
262	0.0060 0060	0.0062 7906	0.0065 6422	0.0068 5591	0.0071 5396	262
263	0.0059 8718	0.0062 6588	0.0065 5130	0.0068 4327	0.0071 4162	263
264	0.0059 7386	0.0062 5281	0.0065 3849	0.0068 3074	0.0071 2939	264
265	0.0059 6066	0.0062 3984	0.0065 2579	0.0068 1832	0.0071 1727	265
266	0.0059 4756	0.0062 2699	0.0065 1320	0.0068 0601	0.0071 0525	266
267	0.0059 3456	0.0062 1424	0.0065 0071	0.0067 9380	0.0070 9333	267
268	0.0059 2168	0.0062 0159	0.0064 8832	0.0067 8170	0.0070 8153	268
269	0.0059 0889	0.0061 8905	0.0064 7604	0.0067 6970	0.0070 6982	269
270	0.0058 9621	0.0061 7661	0.0064 6387	0.0067 5780	0.0070 5821	270
271	0.0058 8363	0.0061 6427	0.0064 5179	0.0067 4600	0.0070 4671	271
272	0.0058 7115	0.0061 5203	0.0064 3981	0.0067 3430	0.0070 3530	272
273	0.0058 5877	0.0061 3989	0.0064 2793	0.0067 2270	0.0070 2399	273
274	0.0058 4649	0.0061 2785	0.0064 1615	0.0067 1119	0.0070 1278	274
275	0.0058 3430	0.0061 1591	0.0064 0447	0.0066 9978	0.0070 0167	275
276	0.0058 2221	0.0061 0406	0.0063 9288	0.0066 8847	0.0069 9065	276
277	0.0058 1022	0.0060 9231	0.0063 8138	0.0066 7725	0.0069 7972	277
278	0.0057 9831	0.0060 8064	0.0063 6998	0.0066 6613	0.0069 6889	278
279	0.0057 8651	0.0060 6908	0.0063 5867	0.0066 5510	0.0069 5814	279
280	0.0057 7479	0.0060 5760	0.0063 4745	0.0066 4415	0.0069 4749	280
281	0.0057 6316	0.0060 4622	0.0063 3633	0.0066 3330	0.0069 3693	281
282	0.0057 5163	0.0060 3492	0.0063 2529	0.0066 2254	0.0069 2646	282
283	0.0057 4018	0.0060 2371	0.0063 1434	0.0066 1186	0.0069 1607	283
284	0.0057 2882	0.0060 1259	0.0063 0348	0.0066 0128	0.0069 0577	284
285	0.0057 1755	0.0060 0156	0.0062 9270	0.0065 9078	0.0068 9556	285
286	0.0057 0636	0.0059 9061	0.0062 8201	0.0065 8036	0.0068 8543	286
287	0.0056 9526	0.0059 7975	0.0062 7141	0.0065 7003	0.0068 7539	287
288	0.0056 8425	0.0059 6898	0.0062 6089	0.0065 5978	0.0068 6543	288
289	0.0056 7332	0.0059 5828	0.0062 5045	0.0065 4962	0.0068 5555	289
290	0.0056 6247	0.0059 4767	0.0062 4010	0.0065 3953	0.0068 4575	290
291	0.0056 5170	0.0059 3714	0.0062 2982	0.0065 2953	0.0068 3603	291
292	0.0056 4101	0.0059 2669	0.0062 1963	0.0065 1961	0.0068 2640	292
293	0.0056 3040	0.0059 1632	0.0062 0951	0.0065 0976	0.0068 1684	293
294	0.0056 1987	0.0059 0603	0.0061 9948	0.0065 0000	0.0068 0736	294
295	0.0056 0942	0.0058 9582	0.0061 8952	0.0064 9031	0.0067 9796	295
296	0.0055 9905	0.0058 8568	0.0061 7964	0.0064 8070	0.0067 8863	296
297	0.0055 8876	0.0058 7562	0.0061 6984	0.0064 7117	0.0067 7938	297
298	0.0055 7854	0.0058 6564	0.0061 6011	0.0064 6171	0.0067 7020	298
299	0.0055 6839	0.0058 5573	0.0061 5045	0.0064 5232	0.0067 6110	299
300	0.0055 5832	0.0058 4590	0.0061 4087	0.0064 4301	0.0067 5207	300

TABLE V

N	3/8	5/12	11/24	1/2	13/24	N
301	0.0055 4833	0.0058 3614	0.0061 3137	0.0064 3378	0.0067 4312	301
302	0.0055 3841	0.0058 2645	0.0061 2193	0.0064 2461	0.0067 3423	302
303	0.0055 2856	0.0058 1684	0.0061 1257	0.0064 1552	0.0067 2542	303
304	0.0055 1878	0.0058 0730	0.0061 0328	0.0064 0649	0.0067 1667	304
305	0.0055 0907	0.0057 9782	0.0060 9406	0.0063 9754	0.0067 0800	305
306	0.0054 9943	0.0057 8842	0.0060 8491	0.0063 8866	0.0066 9940	306
307	0.0054 8986	0.0057 7909	0.0060 7583	0.0063 7984	0.0066 9086	307
308	0.0054 8036	0.0057 6982	0.0060 6682	0.0063 7109	0.0066 8239	308
309	0.0054 7093	0.0057 6063	0.0060 5787	0.0063 6241	0.0066 7399	309
310	0.0054 6157	0.0057 5150	0.0060 4899	0.0063 5380	0.0066 6565	310
311	0.0054 5227	0.0057 4243	0.0060 4018	0.0063 4525	0.0066 5738	311
312	0.0054 4304	0.0057 3344	0.0060 3143	0.0063 3677	0.0066 4918	312
313	0.0054 3388	0.0057 2450	0.0060 2275	0.0063 2835	0.0066 4104	313
314	0.0054 2477	0.0057 1564	0.0060 1413	0.0063 2000	0.0066 3296	314
315	0.0054 1574	0.0057 0683	0.0060 0558	0.0063 1171	0.0066 2495	315
316	0.0054 0677	0.0056 9809	0.0059 9709	0.0063 0348	0.0066 1699	316
317	0.0053 9786	0.0056 8942	0.0059 8866	0.0062 9532	0.0066 0910	317
318	0.0053 8901	0.0056 8080	0.0059 8030	0.0062 8721	0.0066 0127	318
319	0.0053 8022	0.0056 7225	0.0059 7199	0.0062 7917	0.0065 9350	319
320	0.0053 7150	0.0056 6376	0.0059 6375	0.0062 7119	0.0065 8580	320
321	0.0053 6284	0.0056 5533	0.0059 5556	0.0062 6327	0.0065 7815	321
322	0.0053 5423	0.0056 4696	0.0059 4744	0.0062 5540	0.0065 7056	322
323	0.0053 4569	0.0056 3864	0.0059 3937	0.0062 4760	0.0065 6302	323
324	0.0053 3720	0.0056 3039	0.0059 3137	0.0062 3985	0.0065 5555	324
325	0.0053 2878	0.0056 2219	0.0059 2342	0.0062 3217	0.0065 4813	325
326	0.0053 2041	0.0056 1406	0.0059 1553	0.0062 2453	0.0065 4077	326
327	0.0053 1210	0.0056 0598	0.0059 0769	0.0062 1696	0.0065 3347	327
328	0.0053 0385	0.0055 9795	0.0058 9992	0.0062 0944	0.0065 2622	328
329	0.0052 9565	0.0055 8999	0.0058 9219	0.0062 0198	0.0065 1902	329
330	0.0052 8751	0.0055 8207	0.0058 8453	0.0061 9457	0.0065 1188	330
331	0.0052 7942	0.0055 7422	0.0058 7691	0.0061 8721	0.0065 0480	331
332	0.0052 7139	0.0055 6641	0.0058 6936	0.0061 7991	0.0064 9777	332
333	0.0052 6341	0.0055 5867	0.0058 6185	0.0061 7267	0.0064 9079	333
334	0.0052 5548	0.0055 5097	0.0058 5440	0.0061 6547	0.0064 8386	334
335	0.0052 4761	0.0055 4333	0.0058 4700	0.0061 5833	0.0064 7698	335
336	0.0052 3980	0.0055 3574	0.0058 3966	0.0061 5124	0.0064 7016	336
337	0.0052 3203	0.0055 2820	0.0058 3236	0.0061 4420	0.0064 6339	337
338	0.0052 2432	0.0055 2072	0.0058 2512	0.0061 3721	0.0064 5667	338
339	0.0052 1665	0.0055 1328	0.0058 1793	0.0061 3028	0.0064 4999	339
340	0.0052 0904	0.0055 0590	0.0058 1079	0.0061 2339	0.0064 4337	340
341	0.0052 0148	0.0054 9857	0.0058 0370	0.0061 1655	0.0064 3680	341
342	0.0051 9397	0.0054 9128	0.0057 9666	0.0061 0977	0.0064 3027	342
343	0.0051 8651	0.0054 8405	0.0057 8966	0.0061 0303	0.0064 2380	343
344	0.0051 7910	0.0054 7686	0.0057 8272	0.0060 9634	0.0064 1737	344
345	0.0051 7173	0.0054 6973	0.0057 7582	0.0060 8969	0.0064 1099	345
346	0.0051 6442	0.0054 6264	0.0057 6898	0.0060 8310	0.0064 0466	346
347	0.0051 5715	0.0054 5560	0.0057 6217	0.0060 7655	0.0063 9837	347
348	0.0051 4993	0.0054 4860	0.0057 5542	0.0060 7005	0.0063 9213	348
349	0.0051 4276	0.0054 4166	0.0057 4871	0.0060 6359	0.0063 8593	349
350	0.0051 3563	0.0054 3476	0.0057 4205	0.0060 5718	0.0063 7978	350
351	0.0051 2855	0.0054 2790	0.0057 3544	0.0060 5081	0.0063 7368	351
352	0.0051 2152	0.0054 2109	0.0057 2887	0.0060 4449	0.0063 6761	352
353	0.0051 1453	0.0054 1433	0.0057 2234	0.0060 3822	0.0063 6160	353
354	0.0051 0759	0.0054 0761	0.0057 1586	0.0060 3199	0.0063 5562	354
355	0.0051 0069	0.0054 0094	0.0057 0942	0.0060 2580	0.0063 4969	355
356	0.0050 9384	0.0053 9430	0.0057 0303	0.0060 1966	0.0063 4381	356
357	0.0050 8703	0.0053 8772	0.0056 9668	0.0060 1355	0.0063 3796	357
358	0.0050 8026	0.0053 8117	0.0056 9038	0.0060 0750	0.0063 3216	358
359	0.0050 7353	0.0053 7467	0.0056 8411	0.0060 0148	0.0063 2640	359
360	0.0050 6685	0.0053 6822	0.0056 7789	0.0059 9551	0.0063 2068	360

TABLE V

N	7/12	5/8	2/3	17/24	3/4	N
1	1.0058 3333	1.0062 5000	1.0066 6667	1.0070 8333	1.0075 0000	1
2	0.5043 7924	0.5046 9237	0.5050 0554	0.5053 1875	0.5056 3200	2
3	0.3372 2976	0.3375 0865	0.3377 8762	0.3380 6667	0.3383 4579	3
4	0.2536 5644	0.2539 1842	0.2541 8051	0.2544 4271	0.2547 0501	4
5	0.2035 1357	0.2037 6558	0.2040 1772	0.2042 7000	0.2045 2242	5
6	0.1700 8594	0.1703 3143	0.1705 7709	0.1708 2291	0.1710 6891	6
7	0.1462 0986	0.1464 5082	0.1466 9198	0.1469 3333	0.1471 7488	7
8	0.1283 0352	0.1285 4118	0.1287 7907	0.1290 1718	0.1292 5552	8
9	0.1143 7698	0.1146 1218	0.1148 4763	0.1150 8333	0.1153 1929	9
10	0.1032 3632	0.1034 6962	0.1037 0321	0.1039 3708	0.1041 7123	10
11	0.0941 2175	0.0943 5358	0.0945 8572	0.0948 1817	0.0950 5094	11
12	0.0865 2675	0.0867 5742	0.0869 8843	0.0872 1978	0.0874 5148	12
13	0.0801 0064	0.0803 3039	0.0805 6052	0.0807 9101	0.0810 2188	13
14	0.0745 9295	0.0748 2198	0.0750 5141	0.0752 8124	0.0755 1146	14
15	0.0698 2000	0.0700 4845	0.0702 7734	0.0705 0665	0.0707 3639	15
16	0.0656 4401	0.0658 7202	0.0661 0049	0.0663 2941	0.0665 5879	16
17	0.0619 5966	0.0621 8732	0.0624 1546	0.0626 4410	0.0628 7321	17
18	0.0586 8499	0.0589 1239	0.0591 4030	0.0593 6872	0.0595 9766	18
19	0.0557 5532	0.0559 8252	0.0562 1027	0.0564 3857	0.0566 6740	19
20	0.0531 1889	0.0533 4597	0.0535 7362	0.0538 0184	0.0540 3063	20
21	0.0507 3383	0.0509 6083	0.0511 8843	0.0514 1663	0.0516 4543	21
22	0.0485 6585	0.0487 9281	0.0490 2041	0.0492 4863	0.0494 7748	22
23	0.0465 8663	0.0468 1360	0.0470 4123	0.0472 6952	0.0474 9846	23
24	0.0447 7258	0.0449 9959	0.0452 2729	0.0454 5567	0.0456 8474	24
25	0.0431 0388	0.0433 3096	0.0435 5876	0.0437 8727	0.0440 1650	25
26	0.0415 6376	0.0417 9094	0.0420 1886	0.0422 4753	0.0424 7693	26
27	0.0401 3793	0.0403 6523	0.0405 9331	0.0408 2215	0.0410 5176	27
28	0.0388 1415	0.0390 4159	0.0392 6983	0.0394 9887	0.0397 2871	28
29	0.0375 8186	0.0378 0946	0.0380 3789	0.0382 6715	0.0384 9723	29
30	0.0364 3191	0.0366 5969	0.0368 8832	0.0371 1782	0.0373 4816	30
31	0.0353 5633	0.0355 8430	0.0358 1316	0.0360 4290	0.0362 7352	31
32	0.0343 4815	0.0345 7633	0.0348 0542	0.0350 3542	0.0352 6634	32
33	0.0334 0124	0.0336 2964	0.0338 5898	0.0340 8926	0.0343 2048	33
34	0.0325 1020	0.0327 3883	0.0329 6843	0.0331 9900	0.0334 3053	34
35	0.0316 7024	0.0318 9911	0.0321 2898	0.0323 5984	0.0325 9170	35
36	0.0308 7710	0.0311 0622	0.0313 3637	0.0315 6754	0.0317 9973	36
37	0.0301 2698	0.0303 5636	0.0305 8680	0.0308 1828	0.0310 5082	37
38	0.0294 1649	0.0296 4614	0.0298 7687	0.0301 0868	0.0303 4157	38
39	0.0287 4258	0.0289 7250	0.0292 0354	0.0294 3568	0.0296 6893	39
40	0.0281 0251	0.0283 3271	0.0285 6406	0.0287 9654	0.0290 3016	40
41	0.0274 9379	0.0277 2429	0.0279 5595	0.0281 8878	0.0284 2276	41
42	0.0269 1420	0.0271 4499	0.0273 7697	0.0276 1015	0.0278 4452	42
43	0.0263 6170	0.0265 9278	0.0268 2510	0.0270 5863	0.0272 9338	43
44	0.0258 3443	0.0260 6583	0.0262 9847	0.0265 3236	0.0267 6751	44
45	0.0253 3073	0.0255 6243	0.0257 9541	0.0260 2967	0.0262 6521	45
46	0.0248 4905	0.0250 8106	0.0253 1439	0.0255 4902	0.0257 8495	46
47	0.0243 8798	0.0246 2032	0.0248 5399	0.0250 8899	0.0253 2532	47
48	0.0239 4624	0.0241 7890	0.0244 1292	0.0246 4830	0.0248 8504	48
49	0.0235 2265	0.0237 5563	0.0239 9001	0.0242 2577	0.0244 6292	49
50	0.0231 1612	0.0233 4943	0.0235 8416	0.0238 2031	0.0240 5787	50
51	0.0227 2563	0.0229 5928	0.0231 9437	0.0234 3090	0.0236 6888	51
52	0.0223 5027	0.0225 8425	0.0228 1971	0.0230 5663	0.0232 9503	52
53	0.0219 8919	0.0222 2350	0.0224 5932	0.0226 9664	0.0229 3546	53
54	0.0216 4157	0.0218 7623	0.0221 1242	0.0223 5014	0.0225 8938	54
55	0.0213 0671	0.0215 4171	0.0217 7827	0.0220 1638	0.0222 5605	55
56	0.0209 8390	0.0212 1925	0.0214 5618	0.0216 9469	0.0219 3478	56
57	0.0206 7251	0.0209 0821	0.0211 4552	0.0213 8443	0.0216 2496	57
58	0.0203 7196	0.0206 0801	0.0208 4569	0.0210 8502	0.0213 2597	58
59	0.0200 8170	0.0203 1809	0.0205 5616	0.0207 9589	0.0210 3727	59
60	0.0198 0120	0.0200 3795	0.0202 7639	0.0205 1653	0.0207 5836	60

TABLE V

N	7/12	5/8	2/3	17/24	3/4	N
61	0.0195 2999	0.0197 6709	0.0200 0592	0.0202 4647	0.0204 8873	61
62	0.0192 6762	0.0195 0508	0.0197 4429	0.0199 8525	0.0202 2795	62
63	0.0190 1366	0.0192 5148	0.0194 9108	0.0197 3246	0.0199 7560	63
64	0.0187 6773	0.0190 0591	0.0192 4590	0.0194 8769	0.0197 3127	64
65	0.0185 2946	0.0187 6800	0.0190 0837	0.0192 5058	0.0194 9460	65
66	0.0182 9848	0.0185 3739	0.0187 7815	0.0190 2077	0.0192 6524	66
67	0.0180 7449	0.0183 1376	0.0185 5491	0.0187 9795	0.0190 4286	67
68	0.0178 5716	0.0180 9680	0.0183 3835	0.0185 8180	0.0188 2716	68
69	0.0176 4622	0.0178 8622	0.0181 2816	0.0183 7204	0.0186 1785	69
70	0.0174 4138	0.0176 8175	0.0179 2409	0.0181 6838	0.0184 1464	70
71	0.0172 4239	0.0174 8313	0.0177 2586	0.0179 7058	0.0182 1728	71
72	0.0170 4901	0.0172 9011	0.0175 3324	0.0177 7838	0.0180 2554	72
73	0.0168 6100	0.0171 0247	0.0173 4600	0.0175 9157	0.0178 3917	73
74	0.0166 7814	0.0169 1999	0.0171 6391	0.0174 0990	0.0176 5796	74
75	0.0165 0024	0.0167 4246	0.0169 8678	0.0172 3320	0.0174 8170	75
76	0.0163 2709	0.0165 6968	0.0168 1440	0.0170 6125	0.0173 1020	76
77	0.0161 5851	0.0164 0147	0.0166 4659	0.0168 9387	0.0171 4328	77
78	0.0159 9432	0.0162 3766	0.0164 8318	0.0167 3088	0.0169 8074	78
79	0.0158 3436	0.0160 7808	0.0163 2400	0.0165 7213	0.0168 2244	79
80	0.0156 7847	0.0159 2256	0.0161 6889	0.0164 1744	0.0166 6821	80
81	0.0155 2650	0.0157 7096	0.0160 1769	0.0162 6667	0.0165 1790	81
82	0.0153 7830	0.0156 2314	0.0158 7027	0.0161 1968	0.0163 7136	82
83	0.0152 3373	0.0154 7895	0.0157 2649	0.0159 7633	0.0162 2847	83
84	0.0150 9268	0.0153 3828	0.0155 8621	0.0158 3649	0.0160 8908	84
85	0.0149 5501	0.0152 0098	0.0154 4933	0.0157 0003	0.0159 5308	85
86	0.0148 2060	0.0150 6696	0.0153 1570	0.0155 6684	0.0158 2034	86
87	0.0146 8935	0.0149 3608	0.0151 8524	0.0154 3680	0.0156 9076	87
88	0.0145 6115	0.0148 0826	0.0150 5781	0.0153 0981	0.0155 6423	88
89	0.0144 3588	0.0146 8337	0.0149 3334	0.0151 8576	0.0154 4064	89
90	0.0143 1347	0.0145 6134	0.0148 1170	0.0150 6456	0.0153 1989	90
91	0.0141 9380	0.0144 4205	0.0146 9282	0.0149 4611	0.0152 0190	91
92	0.0140 7679	0.0143 2542	0.0145 7660	0.0148 3032	0.0150 8657	92
93	0.0139 6236	0.0142 1137	0.0144 6296	0.0147 1711	0.0149 7382	93
94	0.0138 5042	0.0140 9982	0.0143 5181	0.0146 0640	0.0148 6356	94
95	0.0137 4090	0.0139 9067	0.0142 4308	0.0144 9809	0.0147 5571	95
96	0.0136 3372	0.0138 8387	0.0141 3668	0.0143 9213	0.0146 5020	96
97	0.0135 2880	0.0137 7933	0.0140 3255	0.0142 8843	0.0145 4696	97
98	0.0134 2608	0.0136 7700	0.0139 3062	0.0141 8693	0.0144 4592	98
99	0.0133 2549	0.0135 7679	0.0138 3082	0.0140 8756	0.0143 4701	99
100	0.0132 2696	0.0134 7865	0.0137 3308	0.0139 9026	0.0142 5017	100
101	0.0131 3045	0.0133 8251	0.0136 3735	0.0138 9497	0.0141 5533	101
102	0.0130 3587	0.0132 8832	0.0135 4357	0.0138 0162	0.0140 6243	102
103	0.0129 4319	0.0131 9602	0.0134 5168	0.0137 1015	0.0139 7143	103
104	0.0128 5234	0.0131 0555	0.0133 6162	0.0136 2053	0.0138 8226	104
105	0.0127 6328	0.0130 1687	0.0132 7334	0.0135 3269	0.0137 9487	105
106	0.0126 7594	0.0129 2992	0.0131 8680	0.0134 4657	0.0137 0922	106
107	0.0125 9029	0.0128 4465	0.0131 0194	0.0133 6214	0.0136 2524	107
108	0.0125 0628	0.0127 6102	0.0130 1871	0.0132 7935	0.0135 4291	108
109	0.0124 2385	0.0126 7898	0.0129 3708	0.0131 9815	0.0134 6216	109
110	0.0123 4298	0.0125 9848	0.0128 5700	0.0131 1850	0.0133 8297	110
111	0.0122 6361	0.0125 1950	0.0127 7842	0.0130 4035	0.0133 0527	111
112	0.0121 8571	0.0124 4198	0.0127 0131	0.0129 6367	0.0132 2905	112
113	0.0121 0923	0.0123 6588	0.0126 2562	0.0128 8841	0.0131 5425	113
114	0.0120 3414	0.0122 9118	0.0125 5132	0.0128 1455	0.0130 8084	114
115	0.0119 6041	0.0122 1783	0.0124 7838	0.0127 4203	0.0130 0878	115
116	0.0118 8799	0.0121 4579	0.0124 0675	0.0126 7084	0.0129 3803	116
117	0.0118 1686	0.0120 7504	0.0123 3641	0.0126 0093	0.0128 6858	117
118	0.0117 4698	0.0120 0555	0.0122 6732	0.0125 3226	0.0128 0037	118
119	0.0116 7832	0.0119 3727	0.0121 9944	0.0124 6482	0.0127 3338	119
120	0.0116 1085	0.0118 7018	0.0121 3276	0.0123 9857	0.0126 6758	120

TABLE V

N	7/12	5/8	2/3	17/24	3/4	N
121	0.0115 4454	0.0118 0425	0.0120 6724	0.0123 3347	0.0126 0294	121
122	0.0114 7936	0.0117 3945	0.0120 0284	0.0122 6951	0.0125 3942	122
123	0.0114 1528	0.0116 7575	0.0119 3955	0.0122 0665	0.0124 7702	123
124	0.0113 5228	0.0116 1313	0.0118 7734	0.0121 4487	0.0124 1568	124
125	0.0112 9033	0.0115 5157	0.0118 1618	0.0120 8413	0.0123 5540	125
126	0.0112 2941	0.0114 9102	0.0117 5604	0.0120 2442	0.0122 9614	126
127	0.0111 6948	0.0114 3148	0.0116 9690	0.0119 6572	0.0122 3788	127
128	0.0111 1054	0.0113 7292	0.0116 3875	0.0119 0799	0.0121 8060	128
129	0.0110 5255	0.0113 1531	0.0115 8154	0.0118 5121	0.0121 2428	129
130	0.0109 9550	0.0112 5864	0.0115 2527	0.0117 9537	0.0120 6888	130
131	0.0109 3935	0.0112 0288	0.0114 6991	0.0117 4043	0.0120 1440	131
132	0.0108 8410	0.0111 4801	0.0114 1545	0.0116 8639	0.0119 6080	132
133	0.0108 2972	0.0110 9400	0.0113 6185	0.0116 3322	0.0119 0808	133
134	0.0107 7619	0.0110 4085	0.0113 0910	0.0115 8090	0.0118 5621	134
135	0.0107 2349	0.0109 8854	0.0112 5719	0.0115 2941	0.0118 0516	135
136	0.0106 7161	0.0109 3703	0.0112 0609	0.0114 7873	0.0117 5493	136
137	0.0106 2052	0.0108 8633	0.0111 5578	0.0114 2885	0.0117 0550	137
138	0.0105 7021	0.0108 3640	0.0111 0625	0.0113 7975	0.0116 5684	138
139	0.0105 2067	0.0107 8723	0.0110 5749	0.0113 3141	0.0116 0894	139
140	0.0104 7187	0.0107 3881	0.0110 0947	0.0112 8381	0.0115 6179	140
141	0.0104 2380	0.0106 9112	0.0109 6218	0.0112 3694	0.0115 1536	141
142	0.0103 7644	0.0106 4414	0.0109 1560	0.0111 9079	0.0114 6965	142
143	0.0103 2978	0.0105 9786	0.0108 6972	0.0111 4533	0.0114 2464	143
144	0.0102 8381	0.0105 5226	0.0108 2453	0.0111 0056	0.0113 8031	144
145	0.0102 3851	0.0105 0734	0.0107 8000	0.0110 5645	0.0113 3664	145
146	0.0101 9386	0.0104 6307	0.0107 3613	0.0110 1300	0.0112 9364	146
147	0.0101 4986	0.0104 1945	0.0106 9291	0.0109 7020	0.0112 5127	147
148	0.0101 0649	0.0103 7645	0.0106 5031	0.0109 2802	0.0112 0954	148
149	0.0100 6374	0.0103 3407	0.0106 0833	0.0108 8646	0.0111 6841	149
150	0.0100 2159	0.0102 9230	0.0105 6695	0.0108 4550	0.0111 2790	150
151	0.0099 8003	0.0102 5112	0.0105 2617	0.0108 0514	0.0110 8797	151
152	0.0099 3905	0.0102 1052	0.0104 8597	0.0107 6535	0.0110 4862	152
153	0.0098 9865	0.0101 7049	0.0104 4633	0.0107 2614	0.0110 0984	153
154	0.0098 5880	0.0101 3102	0.0104 0726	0.0106 8748	0.0109 7162	154
155	0.0098 1950	0.0100 9209	0.0103 6873	0.0106 4937	0.0109 3395	155
156	0.0097 8074	0.0100 5370	0.0103 3074	0.0106 1179	0.0108 9681	156
157	0.0097 4251	0.0100 1584	0.0102 9327	0.0105 7474	0.0108 6019	157
158	0.0097 0479	0.0099 7850	0.0102 5632	0.0105 3821	0.0108 2409	158
159	0.0096 6758	0.0099 4166	0.0102 1988	0.0105 0218	0.0107 8849	159
160	0.0096 3087	0.0099 0532	0.0101 8393	0.0104 6665	0.0107 5340	160
161	0.0095 9464	0.0098 6947	0.0101 4848	0.0104 3160	0.0107 1878	161
162	0.0095 5890	0.0098 3410	0.0101 1350	0.0103 9703	0.0106 8465	162
163	0.0095 2362	0.0097 9919	0.0100 7899	0.0103 6294	0.0106 5098	163
164	0.0094 8881	0.0097 6475	0.0100 4494	0.0103 2930	0.0106 1777	164
165	0.0094 5445	0.0097 3076	0.0100 1134	0.0102 9611	0.0105 8502	165
166	0.0094 2053	0.0096 9722	0.0099 7819	0.0102 6337	0.0105 5270	166
167	0.0093 8705	0.0096 6411	0.0099 4547	0.0102 3106	0.0105 2083	167
168	0.0093 5401	0.0096 3143	0.0099 1318	0.0101 9919	0.0104 8938	168
169	0.0093 2138	0.0095 9918	0.0098 8131	0.0101 6773	0.0104 5834	169
170	0.0092 8917	0.0095 6733	0.0098 4986	0.0101 3668	0.0104 2772	170
171	0.0092 5736	0.0095 3590	0.0098 1881	0.0101 0604	0.0103 9751	171
172	0.0092 2595	0.0095 0486	0.0097 8816	0.0100 7580	0.0103 6769	172
173	0.0091 9494	0.0094 7421	0.0097 5791	0.0100 4595	0.0103 3827	173
174	0.0091 6431	0.0094 4395	0.0097 2803	0.0100 1648	0.0103 0922	174
175	0.0091 3406	0.0094 1407	0.0096 9854	0.0099 8739	0.0102 8056	175
176	0.0091 0418	0.0093 8456	0.0096 6942	0.0099 5868	0.0102 5226	176
177	0.0090 7468	0.0093 5542	0.0096 4066	0.0099 3032	0.0102 2433	177
178	0.0090 4553	0.0093 2663	0.0096 1226	0.0099 0233	0.0101 9676	178
179	0.0090 1673	0.0092 9821	0.0095 8422	0.0098 7469	0.0101 6954	179
180	0.0089 8828	0.0092 7012	0.0095 5652	0.0098 4740	0.0101 4267	180

TABLE V

N	7/12	5/8	2/3	17/24	3/4	N
181	0.0089 6018	0.0092 4238	0.0095 2917	0.0098 2044	0.0101 1613	181
182	0.0089 3241	0.0092 1498	0.0095 0215	0.0097 9382	0.0100 8993	182
183	0.0089 0497	0.0091 8791	0.0094 7546	0.0097 6754	0.0100 6406	183
184	0.0088 7786	0.0091 6116	0.0094 4909	0.0097 4157	0.0100 3851	184
185	0.0088 5107	0.0091 3473	0.0094 2305	0.0097 1593	0.0100 1328	185
186	0.0088 2459	0.0091 0862	0.0093 9731	0.0096 9059	0.0099 8837	186
187	0.0087 9843	0.0090 8282	0.0093 7189	0.0096 6557	0.0099 6376	187
188	0.0087 7257	0.0090 5732	0.0093 4678	0.0096 4085	0.0099 3945	188
189	0.0087 4701	0.0090 3212	0.0093 2196	0.0096 1643	0.0099 1544	189
190	0.0087 2174	0.0090 0722	0.0092 9743	0.0095 9230	0.0098 9173	190
191	0.0086 9677	0.0089 8260	0.0092 7320	0.0095 6846	0.0098 6830	191
192	0.0086 7208	0.0089 5828	0.0092 4925	0.0095 4491	0.0098 4516	192
193	0.0086 4767	0.0089 3423	0.0092 2558	0.0095 2164	0.0098 2230	193
194	0.0086 2355	0.0089 1046	0.0092 0219	0.0094 9864	0.0097 9971	194
195	0.0085 9969	0.0088 8696	0.0091 7907	0.0094 7591	0.0097 7739	195
196	0.0085 7610	0.0088 6374	0.0091 5622	0.0094 5345	0.0097 5534	196
197	0.0085 5278	0.0088 4077	0.0091 3363	0.0094 3126	0.0097 3355	197
198	0.0085 2972	0.0088 1807	0.0091 1130	0.0094 0932	0.0097 1202	198
199	0.0085 0691	0.0087 9562	0.0090 8923	0.0093 8764	0.0096 9074	199
200	0.0084 8436	0.0087 7343	0.0090 6741	0.0093 6621	0.0096 6972	200
201	0.0084 6206	0.0087 5148	0.0090 4584	0.0093 4502	0.0096 4894	201
202	0.0084 4000	0.0087 2978	0.0090 2451	0.0093 2408	0.0096 2840	202
203	0.0084 1818	0.0087 0832	0.0090 0342	0.0093 0338	0.0096 0810	203
204	0.0083 9661	0.0086 8709	0.0089 8257	0.0092 8292	0.0095 8804	204
205	0.0083 7526	0.0086 6611	0.0089 6195	0.0092 6269	0.0095 6821	205
206	0.0083 5415	0.0086 4535	0.0089 4156	0.0092 4269	0.0095 4861	206
207	0.0083 3327	0.0086 2482	0.0089 2140	0.0092 2291	0.0095 2923	207
208	0.0083 1261	0.0086 0451	0.0089 0146	0.0092 0336	0.0095 1008	208
209	0.0082 9217	0.0085 8442	0.0088 8175	0.0091 8403	0.0094 9114	209
210	0.0082 7194	0.0085 6455	0.0088 6225	0.0091 6491	0.0094 7242	210
211	0.0082 5194	0.0085 4490	0.0088 4296	0.0091 4601	0.0094 5391	211
212	0.0082 3214	0.0085 2545	0.0088 2388	0.0091 2731	0.0094 3561	212
213	0.0082 1256	0.0085 0622	0.0088 0502	0.0091 0882	0.0094 1752	213
214	0.0081 9318	0.0084 8719	0.0087 8635	0.0090 9054	0.0093 9963	214
215	0.0081 7400	0.0084 6836	0.0087 6789	0.0090 7246	0.0093 8194	215
216	0.0081 5502	0.0084 4973	0.0087 4963	0.0090 5457	0.0093 6445	216
217	0.0081 3624	0.0084 3130	0.0087 3156	0.0090 3689	0.0093 4715	217
218	0.0081 1766	0.0084 1306	0.0087 1369	0.0090 1939	0.0093 3005	218
219	0.0080 9926	0.0083 9502	0.0086 9600	0.0090 0208	0.0093 1313	219
220	0.0080 8106	0.0083 7716	0.0086 7851	0.0089 8497	0.0092 9640	220
221	0.0080 6304	0.0083 5949	0.0086 6120	0.0089 6803	0.0092 7985	221
222	0.0080 4520	0.0083 4200	0.0086 4407	0.0089 5128	0.0092 6349	222
223	0.0080 2755	0.0083 2469	0.0086 2712	0.0089 3471	0.0092 4730	223
224	0.0080 1008	0.0083 0757	0.0086 1036	0.0089 1831	0.0092 3129	224
225	0.0079 9278	0.0082 9061	0.0085 9376	0.0089 0209	0.0092 1546	225
226	0.0079 7566	0.0082 7383	0.0085 7734	0.0088 8604	0.0091 9979	226
227	0.0079 5871	0.0082 5723	0.0085 6109	0.0088 7017	0.0091 8430	227
228	0.0079 4192	0.0082 4079	0.0085 4501	0.0088 5446	0.0091 6897	228
229	0.0079 2531	0.0082 2452	0.0085 2910	0.0088 3891	0.0091 5380	229
230	0.0079 0886	0.0082 0841	0.0085 1335	0.0088 2353	0.0091 3880	230
231	0.0078 9257	0.0081 9247	0.0084 9776	0.0088 0831	0.0091 2396	231
232	0.0078 7645	0.0081 7668	0.0084 8233	0.0087 9325	0.0091 0928	232
233	0.0078 6048	0.0081 6105	0.0084 6706	0.0087 7834	0.0090 9475	233
234	0.0078 4467	0.0081 4558	0.0084 5194	0.0087 6359	0.0090 8038	234
235	0.0078 2902	0.0081 3027	0.0084 3698	0.0087 4900	0.0090 6616	235
236	0.0078 1351	0.0081 1511	0.0084 2217	0.0087 3455	0.0090 5209	236
237	0.0077 9816	0.0081 0009	0.0084 0751	0.0087 2025	0.0090 3816	237
238	0.0077 8296	0.0080 8523	0.0083 9299	0.0087 0610	0.0090 2438	238
239	0.0077 6790	0.0080 7051	0.0083 7863	0.0086 9210	0.0090 1075	239
240	0.0077 5299	0.0080 5593	0.0083 6440	0.0086 7823	0.0089 9726	240

TABLE V

N	7/12	5/8	2/3	17/24	3/4	N
241	0.0077 3822	0.0080 4150	0.0083 5032	0.0086 6451	0.0089 8391	241
242	0.0077 2359	0.0080 2721	0.0083 3638	0.0086 5093	0.0089 7070	242
243	0.0077 0911	0.0080 1306	0.0083 2257	0.0086 3748	0.0089 5762	243
244	0.0076 9476	0.0079 9904	0.0083 0890	0.0086 2417	0.0089 4468	244
245	0.0076 8054	0.0079 8516	0.0082 9537	0.0086 1100	0.0089 3187	245
246	0.0076 6646	0.0079 7142	0.0082 8197	0.0085 9796	0.0089 1920	246
247	0.0076 5252	0.0079 5780	0.0082 6870	0.0085 8505	0.0089 0665	247
248	0.0076 3870	0.0079 4432	0.0082 5557	0.0085 7226	0.0088 9423	248
249	0.0076 2501	0.0079 3096	0.0082 4256	0.0085 5961	0.0088 8194	249
250	0.0076 1146	0.0079 1774	0.0082 2967	0.0085 4708	0.0088 6977	250
251	0.0075 9802	0.0079 0464	0.0082 1691	0.0085 3467	0.0088 5773	251
252	0.0075 8472	0.0078 9166	0.0082 0428	0.0085 2239	0.0088 4581	252
253	0.0075 7153	0.0078 7881	0.0081 9177	0.0085 1023	0.0088 3401	253
254	0.0075 5847	0.0078 6607	0.0081 7938	0.0084 9819	0.0088 2233	254
255	0.0075 4553	0.0078 5346	0.0081 6710	0.0084 8627	0.0088 1076	255
256	0.0075 3271	0.0078 4097	0.0081 5495	0.0084 7446	0.0087 9932	256
257	0.0075 2000	0.0078 2859	0.0081 4291	0.0084 6277	0.0087 8798	257
258	0.0075 0741	0.0078 1633	0.0081 3099	0.0084 5120	0.0087 7676	258
259	0.0074 9494	0.0078 0418	0.0081 1918	0.0084 3973	0.0087 6565	259
260	0.0074 8258	0.0077 9214	0.0081 0748	0.0084 2838	0.0087 5466	260
261	0.0074 7033	0.0077 8022	0.0080 9589	0.0084 1714	0.0087 4377	261
262	0.0074 5819	0.0077 6841	0.0080 8441	0.0084 0601	0.0087 3299	262
263	0.0074 4616	0.0077 5670	0.0080 7304	0.0083 9498	0.0087 2231	263
264	0.0074 3424	0.0077 4510	0.0080 6178	0.0083 8406	0.0087 1174	264
265	0.0074 2243	0.0077 3361	0.0080 5062	0.0083 7325	0.0087 0128	265
266	0.0074 1072	0.0077 2223	0.0080 3957	0.0083 6254	0.0086 9092	266
267	0.0073 9912	0.0077 1095	0.0080 2862	0.0083 5193	0.0086 8065	267
268	0.0073 8762	0.0076 9977	0.0080 1777	0.0083 4142	0.0086 7049	268
269	0.0073 7622	0.0076 8869	0.0080 0703	0.0083 3101	0.0086 6043	269
270	0.0073 6492	0.0076 7771	0.0079 9638	0.0083 2070	0.0086 5047	270
271	0.0073 5372	0.0076 6683	0.0079 8583	0.0083 1049	0.0086 4060	271
272	0.0073 4262	0.0076 5605	0.0079 7538	0.0083 0038	0.0086 3083	272
273	0.0073 3162	0.0076 4537	0.0079 6502	0.0082 9036	0.0086 2115	273
274	0.0073 2072	0.0076 3478	0.0079 5476	0.0082 8044	0.0086 1157	274
275	0.0073 0991	0.0076 2429	0.0079 4460	0.0082 7060	0.0086 0208	275
276	0.0072 9919	0.0076 1389	0.0079 3453	0.0082 6087	0.0085 9268	276
277	0.0072 8857	0.0076 0359	0.0079 2455	0.0082 5122	0.0085 8337	277
278	0.0072 7804	0.0075 9337	0.0079 1466	0.0082 4166	0.0085 7415	278
279	0.0072 6760	0.0075 8325	0.0079 0486	0.0082 3219	0.0085 6502	279
280	0.0072 5725	0.0075 7321	0.0078 9514	0.0082 2281	0.0085 5598	280
281	0.0072 4699	0.0075 6327	0.0078 8552	0.0082 1352	0.0085 4702	281
282	0.0072 3682	0.0075 5341	0.0078 7599	0.0082 0431	0.0085 3815	282
283	0.0072 2674	0.0075 4364	0.0078 6654	0.0081 9519	0.0085 2936	283
284	0.0072 1674	0.0075 3395	0.0078 5717	0.0081 8615	0.0085 2065	284
285	0.0072 0683	0.0075 2435	0.0078 4789	0.0081 7720	0.0085 1203	285
286	0.0071 9700	0.0075 1484	0.0078 3869	0.0081 6832	0.0085 0349	286
287	0.0071 8726	0.0075 0540	0.0078 2958	0.0081 5953	0.0084 9502	287
288	0.0071 7760	0.0074 9605	0.0078 2054	0.0081 5082	0.0084 8664	288
289	0.0071 6802	0.0074 8678	0.0078 1159	0.0081 4219	0.0084 7834	289
290	0.0071 5852	0.0074 7759	0.0078 0271	0.0081 3364	0.0084 7012	290
291	0.0071 4910	0.0074 6848	0.0077 9392	0.0081 2517	0.0084 6197	291
292	0.0071 3976	0.0074 5944	0.0077 8520	0.0081 1677	0.0084 5390	292
293	0.0071 3050	0.0074 5049	0.0077 7656	0.0081 0845	0.0084 4590	293
294	0.0071 2131	0.0074 4161	0.0077 6799	0.0081 0020	0.0084 3798	294
295	0.0071 1221	0.0074 3281	0.0077 5951	0.0080 9203	0.0084 3013	295
296	0.0071 0317	0.0074 2408	0.0077 5109	0.0080 8394	0.0084 2235	296
297	0.0070 9422	0.0074 1543	0.0077 4275	0.0080 7591	0.0084 1465	297
298	0.0070 8534	0.0074 0685	0.0077 3448	0.0080 6796	0.0084 0702	298
299	0.0070 7653	0.0073 9835	0.0077 2629	0.0080 6008	0.0083 9946	299
300	0.0070 6779	0.0073 8991	0.0077 1816	0.0080 5227	0.0083 9196	300

TABLE V

N	7/12	5/8	2/3	17/24	3/4	N
301	0.0070 5913	0.0073 8155	0.0077 1011	0.0080 4453	0.0083 8454	301
302	0.0070 5054	0.0073 7326	0.0077 0213	0.0080 3686	0.0083 7719	302
303	0.0070 4201	0.0073 6504	0.0076 9421	0.0080 2926	0.0083 6990	303
304	0.0070 3356	0.0073 5688	0.0076 8637	0.0080 2172	0.0083 6268	304
305	0.0070 2518	0.0073 4880	0.0076 7859	0.0080 1426	0.0083 5552	305
306	0.0070 1686	0.0073 4078	0.0076 7088	0.0080 0685	0.0083 4843	306
307	0.0070 0862	0.0073 3284	0.0076 6323	0.0079 9952	0.0083 4141	307
308	0.0070 0044	0.0073 2495	0.0076 5565	0.0079 9225	0.0083 3445	308
309	0.0069 9232	0.0073 1714	0.0076 4814	0.0079 8504	0.0083 2755	309
310	0.0069 8428	0.0073 0939	0.0076 4069	0.0079 7790	0.0083 2072	310
311	0.0069 7629	0.0073 0170	0.0076 3330	0.0079 7082	0.0083 1395	311
312	0.0069 6838	0.0072 9407	0.0076 2598	0.0079 6380	0.0083 0723	312
313	0.0069 6052	0.0072 8651	0.0076 1872	0.0079 5684	0.0083 0058	313
314	0.0069 5273	0.0072 7902	0.0076 1152	0.0079 4995	0.0082 9399	314
315	0.0069 4500	0.0072 7158	0.0076 0438	0.0079 4311	0.0082 8746	315
316	0.0069 3733	0.0072 6421	0.0075 9731	0.0079 3634	0.0082 8099	316
317	0.0069 2973	0.0072 5689	0.0075 9029	0.0079 2962	0.0082 7457	317
318	0.0069 2218	0.0072 4964	0.0075 8333	0.0079 2296	0.0082 6822	318
319	0.0069 1470	0.0072 4244	0.0075 7643	0.0079 1636	0.0082 6192	319
320	0.0069 0727	0.0072 3531	0.0075 6959	0.0079 0982	0.0082 5567	320
321	0.0068 9990	0.0072 2823	0.0075 6281	0.0079 0333	0.0082 4949	321
322	0.0068 9259	0.0072 2121	0.0075 5608	0.0078 9690	0.0082 4336	322
323	0.0068 8534	0.0072 1424	0.0075 4941	0.0078 9053	0.0082 3728	323
324	0.0068 7815	0.0072 0734	0.0075 4280	0.0078 8421	0.0082 3125	324
325	0.0068 7101	0.0072 0049	0.0075 3624	0.0078 7795	0.0082 2528	325
326	0.0068 6393	0.0071 9369	0.0075 2974	0.0078 7173	0.0082 1937	326
327	0.0068 5691	0.0071 8695	0.0075 2329	0.0078 6558	0.0082 1350	327
328	0.0068 4993	0.0071 8027	0.0075 1689	0.0078 5947	0.0082 0769	328
329	0.0068 4302	0.0071 7363	0.0075 1055	0.0078 5342	0.0082 0193	329
330	0.0068 3616	0.0071 6706	0.0075 0425	0.0078 4742	0.0081 9622	330
331	0.0068 2935	0.0071 6053	0.0074 9802	0.0078 4147	0.0081 9056	331
332	0.0068 2259	0.0071 5406	0.0074 9183	0.0078 3557	0.0081 8495	332
333	0.0068 1589	0.0071 4764	0.0074 8569	0.0078 2972	0.0081 7939	333
334	0.0068 0924	0.0071 4126	0.0074 7961	0.0078 2392	0.0081 7388	334
335	0.0068 0264	0.0071 3495	0.0074 7357	0.0078 1817	0.0081 6841	335
336	0.0067 9609	0.0071 2868	0.0074 6759	0.0078 1247	0.0081 6300	336
337	0.0067 8959	0.0071 2246	0.0074 6165	0.0078 0682	0.0081 5763	337
338	0.0067 8314	0.0071 1629	0.0074 5576	0.0078 0122	0.0081 5231	338
339	0.0067 7674	0.0071 1017	0.0074 4992	0.0077 9566	0.0081 4703	339
340	0.0067 7039	0.0071 0409	0.0074 4413	0.0077 9015	0.0081 4180	340
341	0.0067 6409	0.0070 9807	0.0074 3839	0.0077 8469	0.0081 3662	341
342	0.0067 5783	0.0070 9209	0.0074 3269	0.0077 7927	0.0081 3148	342
343	0.0067 5163	0.0070 8616	0.0074 2704	0.0077 7390	0.0081 2639	343
344	0.0067 4547	0.0070 8028	0.0074 2143	0.0077 6857	0.0081 2134	344
345	0.0067 3936	0.0070 7444	0.0074 1587	0.0077 6329	0.0081 1633	345
346	0.0067 3329	0.0070 6865	0.0074 1035	0.0077 5805	0.0081 1137	346
347	0.0067 2727	0.0070 6290	0.0074 0488	0.0077 5286	0.0081 0645	347
348	0.0067 2130	0.0070 5720	0.0073 9946	0.0077 4770	0.0081 0158	348
349	0.0067 1537	0.0070 5154	0.0073 9408	0.0077 4260	0.0080 9674	349
350	0.0067 0949	0.0070 4593	0.0073 8874	0.0077 3753	0.0080 9195	350
351	0.0067 0365	0.0070 4036	0.0073 8344	0.0077 3251	0.0080 8720	351
352	0.0066 9785	0.0070 3484	0.0073 7819	0.0077 2753	0.0080 8249	352
353	0.0066 9210	0.0070 2935	0.0073 7298	0.0077 2259	0.0080 7782	353
354	0.0066 8639	0.0070 2391	0.0073 6781	0.0077 1769	0.0080 7319	354
355	0.0066 8073	0.0070 1852	0.0073 6268	0.0077 1283	0.0080 6860	355
356	0.0066 7510	0.0070 1316	0.0073 5759	0.0077 0801	0.0080 6404	356
357	0.0066 6952	0.0070 0785	0.0073 5254	0.0077 0323	0.0080 5953	357
358	0.0066 6398	0.0070 0257	0.0073 4754	0.0076 9850	0.0080 5506	358
359	0.0066 5848	0.0069 9734	0.0073 4257	0.0076 9380	0.0080 5062	359
360	0.0066 5302	0.0069 9215	0.0073 3765	0.0076 8913	0.0080 4623	360

TABLE V

N	19/24	5/6	7/8	11/12	23/24	N
1	1.0079 1667	1.0083 3333	1.0087 5000	1.0091 6667	1.0095 8333	1
2	0.5059 4530	0.5062 5864	0.5065 7203	0.5068 8546	0.5071 9893	2
3	0.3386 2498	0.3389 0426	0.3391 8361	0.3394 6303	0.3397 4253	3
4	0.2549 6742	0.2552 2994	0.2554 9257	0.2557 5531	0.2560 1815	4
5	0.2047 7497	0.2050 2766	0.2052 8049	0.2055 3346	0.2057 8656	5
6	0.1713 1507	0.1715 6139	0.1718 0789	0.1720 5455	0.1723 0137	6
7	0.1474 1662	0.1476 5856	0.1479 0070	0.1481 4303	0.1483 8556	7
8	0.1294 9409	0.1297 3288	0.1299 7190	0.1302 1114	0.1304 5060	8
9	0.1155 5550	0.1157 9196	0.1160 2868	0.1162 6566	0.1165 0288	9
10	0.1044 0566	0.1046 4038	0.1048 7538	0.1051 1066	0.1053 4623	10
11	0.0952 8402	0.0955 1741	0.0957 5111	0.0959 8512	0.0962 1944	11
12	0.0876 8351	0.0879 1589	0.0881 4860	0.0883 8166	0.0886 1505	12
13	0.0812 5311	0.0814 8472	0.0817 1669	0.0819 4903	0.0821 8174	13
14	0.0757 4209	0.0759 7311	0.0762 0453	0.0764 3635	0.0766 6856	14
15	0.0709 6656	0.0711 9715	0.0714 2817	0.0716 5961	0.0718 9148	15
16	0.0667 8862	0.0670 1890	0.0672 4965	0.0674 8084	0.0677 1249	16
17	0.0631 0281	0.0633 3289	0.0635 6346	0.0637 9451	0.0640 2604	17
18	0.0598 2712	0.0600 5708	0.0602 8756	0.0605 1854	0.0607 5004	18
19	0.0568 9678	0.0571 2669	0.0573 5715	0.0575 8815	0.0578 1968	19
20	0.0542 5999	0.0544 8992	0.0547 2042	0.0549 5148	0.0551 8312	20
21	0.0518 7482	0.0521 0482	0.0523 3541	0.0525 6659	0.0527 9837	21
22	0.0497 0696	0.0499 3706	0.0501 6779	0.0503 9914	0.0506 3112	22
23	0.0477 2806	0.0479 5831	0.0481 8921	0.0484 2077	0.0486 5298	23
24	0.0459 1449	0.0461 4493	0.0463 7604	0.0466 0784	0.0468 4032	24
25	0.0442 4643	0.0444 7708	0.0447 0843	0.0449 4050	0.0451 7327	25
26	0.0427 0708	0.0429 3796	0.0431 6959	0.0434 0195	0.0436 3504	26
27	0.0412 8214	0.0415 1328	0.0417 4520	0.0419 7788	0.0422 1132	27
28	0.0399 5935	0.0401 9078	0.0404 2300	0.0406 5602	0.0408 8983	28
29	0.0387 2814	0.0389 5987	0.0391 9243	0.0394 2580	0.0396 6000	29
30	0.0375 7936	0.0378 1141	0.0380 4431	0.0382 7806	0.0385 1266	30
31	0.0365 0503	0.0367 3741	0.0369 7068	0.0372 0482	0.0374 3984	31
32	0.0354 9816	0.0357 3090	0.0359 6454	0.0361 9908	0.0364 3453	32
33	0.0345 5264	0.0347 8573	0.0350 1976	0.0352 5472	0.0354 9061	33
34	0.0336 6303	0.0338 9650	0.0341 3092	0.0343 6631	0.0346 0266	34
35	0.0328 2456	0.0330 5840	0.0332 9324	0.0335 2907	0.0337 6588	35
36	0.0320 3295	0.0322 6719	0.0325 0244	0.0327 3872	0.0329 7601	36
37	0.0312 8441	0.0315 1905	0.0317 5473	0.0319 9146	0.0322 2924	37
38	0.0305 7554	0.0308 1059	0.0310 4671	0.0312 8390	0.0315 2216	38
39	0.0299 0329	0.0301 3875	0.0303 7531	0.0306 1298	0.0308 5174	39
40	0.0292 6491	0.0295 0079	0.0297 3780	0.0299 7594	0.0302 1521	40
41	0.0286 5792	0.0288 9423	0.0291 3169	0.0293 7032	0.0296 1010	41
42	0.0280 8007	0.0283 1682	0.0285 5475	0.0287 9386	0.0290 3415	42
43	0.0275 2935	0.0277 6653	0.0280 0493	0.0282 4454	0.0284 8535	43
44	0.0270 0389	0.0272 4152	0.0274 8039	0.0277 2049	0.0279 6183	44
45	0.0265 0201	0.0267 4009	0.0269 7943	0.0272 2004	0.0274 6191	45
46	0.0260 2218	0.0262 6071	0.0265 0053	0.0267 4165	0.0269 8406	46
47	0.0255 6299	0.0258 0197	0.0260 4228	0.0262 8391	0.0265 2685	47
48	0.0251 2314	0.0253 6258	0.0256 0338	0.0258 4552	0.0260 8901	48
49	0.0247 0145	0.0249 4136	0.0251 8265	0.0254 2531	0.0256 6934	49
50	0.0242 9684	0.0245 3721	0.0247 7900	0.0250 2218	0.0252 6676	50
51	0.0239 0829	0.0241 4914	0.0243 9142	0.0246 3512	0.0248 8025	51
52	0.0235 3489	0.0237 7621	0.0240 1899	0.0242 6322	0.0245 0890	52
53	0.0231 7576	0.0234 1756	0.0236 6084	0.0239 0560	0.0241 5184	53
54	0.0228 3013	0.0230 7241	0.0233 1619	0.0235 6149	0.0238 0829	54
55	0.0224 9726	0.0227 4001	0.0229 8430	0.0232 3013	0.0234 7749	55
56	0.0221 7645	0.0224 1969	0.0226 6449	0.0229 1085	0.0231 5877	56
57	0.0218 6708	0.0221 1080	0.0223 5611	0.0226 0301	0.0228 5150	57
58	0.0215 6855	0.0218 1276	0.0220 5858	0.0223 0602	0.0225 5507	58
59	0.0212 8032	0.0215 2501	0.0217 7135	0.0220 1933	0.0222 6895	59
60	0.0210 0186	0.0212 4704	0.0214 9390	0.0217 4242	0.0219 9261	60

TABLE V

N	19/24	5/6	7/8	11/12	23/24	N
61	0.0207 3270	0.0209 7837	0.0212 2575	0.0214 7481	0.0217 2557	61
62	0.0204 7239	0.0207 1855	0.0209 6644	0.0212 1606	0.0214 6738	62
63	0.0202 2050	0.0204 6716	0.0207 1557	0.0209 6573	0.0212 1762	63
64	0.0199 7664	0.0202 2379	0.0204 7273	0.0207 2343	0.0209 7590	64
65	0.0197 4044	0.0199 8809	0.0202 3754	0.0204 8880	0.0207 4184	65
66	0.0195 1155	0.0197 5970	0.0200 0968	0.0202 6148	0.0205 1509	66
67	0.0192 8965	0.0195 3829	0.0197 8879	0.0200 4114	0.0202 9534	67
68	0.0190 7442	0.0193 2356	0.0195 7459	0.0198 2749	0.0200 8226	68
69	0.0188 6557	0.0191 1522	0.0193 6677	0.0196 2022	0.0198 7557	69
70	0.0186 6284	0.0189 1299	0.0191 6506	0.0194 1907	0.0196 7499	70
71	0.0184 6596	0.0187 1661	0.0189 6921	0.0192 2377	0.0194 8027	71
72	0.0182 7469	0.0185 2584	0.0187 7897	0.0190 3408	0.0192 9116	72
73	0.0180 8880	0.0183 4045	0.0185 9411	0.0188 4977	0.0191 0743	73
74	0.0179 0807	0.0181 6022	0.0184 1441	0.0186 7062	0.0189 2886	74
75	0.0177 3229	0.0179 8494	0.0182 3966	0.0184 9643	0.0187 5524	75
76	0.0175 6127	0.0178 1443	0.0180 6967	0.0183 2700	0.0185 8639	76
77	0.0173 9482	0.0176 4848	0.0179 0426	0.0181 6214	0.0184 2211	77
78	0.0172 3277	0.0174 8693	0.0177 4324	0.0180 0167	0.0182 6222	78
79	0.0170 7494	0.0173 2962	0.0175 8645	0.0178 4544	0.0181 0657	79
80	0.0169 2119	0.0171 7637	0.0174 3374	0.0176 9328	0.0179 5499	80
81	0.0167 7136	0.0170 2704	0.0172 8494	0.0175 4504	0.0178 0733	81
82	0.0166 2530	0.0168 8149	0.0171 3992	0.0174 0058	0.0176 6344	82
83	0.0164 8289	0.0167 3958	0.0169 9854	0.0172 5975	0.0175 2320	83
84	0.0163 4398	0.0166 0118	0.0168 6067	0.0171 2244	0.0173 8646	84
85	0.0162 0846	0.0164 6617	0.0167 2619	0.0169 8851	0.0172 5311	85
86	0.0160 7621	0.0163 3442	0.0165 9497	0.0168 5785	0.0171 2303	86
87	0.0159 4711	0.0162 0583	0.0164 6691	0.0167 3034	0.0169 9610	87
88	0.0158 2106	0.0160 8028	0.0163 4190	0.0166 0588	0.0168 7222	88
89	0.0156 9795	0.0159 5768	0.0162 1982	0.0164 8436	0.0167 5128	89
90	0.0155 7769	0.0158 3793	0.0161 0060	0.0163 6569	0.0166 3318	90
91	0.0154 6018	0.0157 2092	0.0159 8413	0.0162 4977	0.0165 1784	91
92	0.0153 4533	0.0156 0658	0.0158 7031	0.0161 3651	0.0164 0516	92
93	0.0152 3305	0.0154 9481	0.0157 5908	0.0160 2583	0.0162 9505	93
94	0.0151 2328	0.0153 8554	0.0156 5033	0.0159 1764	0.0161 8744	94
95	0.0150 1591	0.0152 7868	0.0155 4401	0.0158 1186	0.0160 8224	95
96	0.0149 1089	0.0151 7416	0.0154 4002	0.0157 0843	0.0159 7937	96
97	0.0148 0813	0.0150 7191	0.0153 3829	0.0156 0725	0.0158 7878	97
98	0.0147 0757	0.0149 7186	0.0152 3877	0.0155 0828	0.0157 8038	98
99	0.0146 0914	0.0148 7393	0.0151 4137	0.0154 1143	0.0156 8410	99
100	0.0145 1278	0.0147 7807	0.0150 4604	0.0153 1665	0.0155 8990	100
101	0.0144 1842	0.0146 8422	0.0149 5271	0.0152 2388	0.0154 9769	101
102	0.0143 2600	0.0145 9231	0.0148 6133	0.0151 3305	0.0154 0743	102
103	0.0142 3548	0.0145 0229	0.0147 7184	0.0150 4410	0.0153 1906	103
104	0.0141 4679	0.0144 1411	0.0146 8418	0.0149 5699	0.0152 3252	104
105	0.0140 5989	0.0143 2770	0.0145 9830	0.0148 7166	0.0151 4776	105
106	0.0139 7471	0.0142 4303	0.0145 1416	0.0147 8806	0.0150 6473	106
107	0.0138 9122	0.0141 6004	0.0144 3169	0.0147 0614	0.0149 8338	107
108	0.0138 0936	0.0140 7869	0.0143 5086	0.0146 2586	0.0149 0366	108
109	0.0137 2909	0.0139 9892	0.0142 7162	0.0145 4717	0.0148 2553	109
110	0.0136 5038	0.0139 2070	0.0141 9393	0.0144 7002	0.0147 4895	110
111	0.0135 7316	0.0138 4399	0.0141 1774	0.0143 9437	0.0146 7387	111
112	0.0134 9741	0.0137 6874	0.0140 4301	0.0143 2019	0.0146 0025	112
113	0.0134 2309	0.0136 9492	0.0139 6971	0.0142 4743	0.0145 2806	113
114	0.0133 5016	0.0136 2249	0.0138 9780	0.0141 7606	0.0144 5725	114
115	0.0132 7858	0.0135 5140	0.0138 2724	0.0141 0604	0.0143 8779	115
116	0.0132 0831	0.0134 8164	0.0137 5799	0.0140 3734	0.0143 1964	116
117	0.0131 3933	0.0134 1315	0.0136 9003	0.0139 6991	0.0142 5278	117
118	0.0130 7160	0.0133 4592	0.0136 2331	0.0139 0373	0.0141 8716	118
119	0.0130 0508	0.0132 7990	0.0135 5781	0.0138 3877	0.0141 2276	119
120	0.0129 3976	0.0132 1507	0.0134 9350	0.0137 7500	0.0140 5954	120

TABLE V

N	19/24	5/6	7/8	11/12	23/24	N
121	0.0128 7559	0.0131 5140	0.0134 3035	0.0137 1238	0.0139 9748	121
122	0.0128 1255	0.0130 8886	0.0133 6832	0.0136 5089	0.0139 3655	122
123	0.0127 5062	0.0130 2742	0.0133 0740	0.0135 9051	0.0138 7671	123
124	0.0126 8976	0.0129 6706	0.0132 4754	0.0135 3119	0.0138 1795	124
125	0.0126 2995	0.0129 0774	0.0131 8874	0.0134 7292	0.0137 6024	125
126	0.0125 7116	0.0128 4945	0.0131 3096	0.0134 1567	0.0137 0354	126
127	0.0125 1337	0.0127 9215	0.0130 7418	0.0133 5943	0.0136 4784	127
128	0.0124 5656	0.0127 3583	0.0130 1838	0.0133 0415	0.0135 9312	128
129	0.0124 0071	0.0126 8047	0.0129 6352	0.0132 4983	0.0135 3934	129
130	0.0123 4578	0.0126 2604	0.0129 0960	0.0131 9643	0.0134 8650	130
131	0.0122 9177	0.0125 7251	0.0128 5659	0.0131 4395	0.0134 3456	131
132	0.0122 3865	0.0125 1988	0.0128 0446	0.0130 9235	0.0133 8350	132
133	0.0121 8639	0.0124 6811	0.0127 5320	0.0130 4162	0.0133 3332	133
134	0.0121 3498	0.0124 1719	0.0127 0279	0.0129 9173	0.0132 8397	134
135	0.0120 8441	0.0123 6710	0.0126 5321	0.0129 4267	0.0132 3546	135
136	0.0120 3465	0.0123 1783	0.0126 0444	0.0128 9443	0.0131 8775	136
137	0.0119 8568	0.0122 6934	0.0125 5646	0.0128 4697	0.0131 4084	137
138	0.0119 3748	0.0122 2164	0.0125 0926	0.0128 0029	0.0130 9470	138
139	0.0118 9005	0.0121 7469	0.0124 6281	0.0127 5437	0.0130 4931	139
140	0.0118 4336	0.0121 2849	0.0124 1711	0.0127 0919	0.0130 0466	140
141	0.0117 9740	0.0120 8301	0.0123 7213	0.0126 6473	0.0129 6074	141
142	0.0117 5215	0.0120 3824	0.0123 2787	0.0126 2098	0.0129 1753	142
143	0.0117 0760	0.0119 9417	0.0122 8430	0.0125 7793	0.0128 7501	143
144	0.0116 6373	0.0119 5078	0.0122 4141	0.0125 3555	0.0128 3317	144
145	0.0116 2053	0.0119 0806	0.0121 9918	0.0124 9384	0.0127 9199	145
146	0.0115 7799	0.0118 6599	0.0121 5761	0.0124 5279	0.0127 5146	146
147	0.0115 3608	0.0118 2457	0.0121 1668	0.0124 1237	0.0127 1157	147
148	0.0114 9480	0.0117 8377	0.0120 7638	0.0123 7258	0.0126 7231	148
149	0.0114 5414	0.0117 4358	0.0120 3669	0.0123 3340	0.0126 3365	149
150	0.0114 1408	0.0117 0400	0.0119 9760	0.0122 9482	0.0125 9560	150
151	0.0113 7461	0.0116 6500	0.0119 5910	0.0122 5682	0.0125 5813	151
152	0.0113 3572	0.0116 2659	0.0119 2117	0.0122 1941	0.0125 2123	152
153	0.0112 9740	0.0115 8874	0.0118 8381	0.0121 8255	0.0124 8490	153
154	0.0112 5963	0.0115 5145	0.0118 4701	0.0121 4625	0.0124 4912	154
155	0.0112 2241	0.0115 1470	0.0118 1075	0.0121 1050	0.0124 1388	155
156	0.0111 8572	0.0114 7848	0.0117 7502	0.0120 7527	0.0123 7918	156
157	0.0111 4956	0.0114 4279	0.0117 3981	0.0120 4057	0.0123 4499	157
158	0.0111 1391	0.0114 0761	0.0117 0512	0.0120 0638	0.0123 1131	158
159	0.0110 7877	0.0113 7294	0.0116 7093	0.0119 7269	0.0122 7814	159
160	0.0110 4412	0.0113 3876	0.0116 3724	0.0119 3949	0.0122 4545	160
161	0.0110 0996	0.0113 0506	0.0116 0402	0.0119 0677	0.0122 1325	161
162	0.0109 7627	0.0112 7184	0.0115 7128	0.0118 7453	0.0121 8151	162
163	0.0109 4305	0.0112 3909	0.0115 3901	0.0118 4276	0.0121 5025	163
164	0.0109 1029	0.0112 0679	0.0115 0720	0.0118 1143	0.0121 1943	164
165	0.0108 7798	0.0111 7495	0.0114 7583	0.0117 8056	0.0120 8906	165
166	0.0108 4612	0.0111 4354	0.0114 4490	0.0117 5013	0.0120 5913	166
167	0.0108 1469	0.0111 1257	0.0114 1441	0.0117 2012	0.0120 2963	167
168	0.0107 8368	0.0110 8203	0.0113 8434	0.0116 9054	0.0120 0055	168
169	0.0107 5309	0.0110 5190	0.0113 5469	0.0116 6138	0.0119 7189	169
170	0.0107 2292	0.0110 2218	0.0113 2544	0.0116 3262	0.0119 4363	170
171	0.0106 9315	0.0109 9287	0.0112 9660	0.0116 0427	0.0119 1578	171
172	0.0106 6377	0.0109 6395	0.0112 6816	0.0115 7630	0.0118 8831	172
173	0.0106 3478	0.0109 3542	0.0112 4010	0.0115 4873	0.0118 6123	173
174	0.0106 0618	0.0109 0727	0.0112 1242	0.0115 2153	0.0118 3453	174
175	0.0105 7796	0.0108 7950	0.0111 8512	0.0114 9471	0.0118 0820	175
176	0.0105 5010	0.0108 5210	0.0111 5818	0.0114 6825	0.0117 8223	176
177	0.0105 2261	0.0108 2506	0.0111 3161	0.0114 4216	0.0117 5663	177
178	0.0104 9547	0.0107 9838	0.0111 0539	0.0114 1642	0.0117 3137	178
179	0.0104 6869	0.0107 7204	0.0110 7952	0.0113 9102	0.0117 0646	179
180	0.0104 4225	0.0107 4605	0.0110 5399	0.0113 6597	0.0116 8190	180

TABLE V

N	19/24	5/6	7/8	11/12	23/24	N
181	0.0104 1615	0.0107 2040	0.0110 2880	0.0113 4125	0.0116 5767	181
182	0.0103 9038	0.0106 9508	0.0110 0394	0.0113 1687	0.0116 3376	182
183	0.0103 6494	0.0106 7009	0.0109 7941	0.0112 9281	0.0116 1018	183
184	0.0103 3983	0.0106 4542	0.0109 5520	0.0112 6906	0.0115 8692	184
185	0.0103 1503	0.0106 2106	0.0109 3130	0.0112 4564	0.0115 6397	185
186	0.0102 9054	0.0105 9702	0.0109 0771	0.0112 2252	0.0115 4133	186
187	0.0102 6636	0.0105 7329	0.0108 8443	0.0111 9970	0.0115 1899	187
188	0.0102 4248	0.0105 4985	0.0108 6145	0.0111 7718	0.0114 9695	188
189	0.0102 1890	0.0105 2671	0.0108 3876	0.0111 5496	0.0114 7520	189
190	0.0101 9561	0.0105 0386	0.0108 1637	0.0111 3303	0.0114 5373	190
191	0.0101 7261	0.0104 8130	0.0107 9425	0.0111 1137	0.0114 3255	191
192	0.0101 4990	0.0104 5902	0.0107 7242	0.0110 9000	0.0114 1165	192
193	0.0101 2746	0.0104 3702	0.0107 5087	0.0110 6891	0.0113 9102	193
194	0.0101 0529	0.0104 1529	0.0107 2959	0.0110 4808	0.0113 7066	194
195	0.0100 8340	0.0103 9383	0.0107 0857	0.0110 2752	0.0113 5057	195
196	0.0100 6177	0.0103 7263	0.0106 8782	0.0110 0723	0.0113 3073	196
197	0.0100 4040	0.0103 5169	0.0106 6733	0.0109 8719	0.0113 1116	197
198	0.0100 1929	0.0103 3102	0.0106 4709	0.0109 6740	0.0112 9183	198
199	0.0099 9843	0.0103 1059	0.0106 2711	0.0109 4787	0.0112 7275	199
200	0.0099 7782	0.0102 9041	0.0106 0737	0.0109 2858	0.0112 5392	200
201	0.0099 5746	0.0102 7048	0.0105 8787	0.0109 0953	0.0112 3533	201
202	0.0099 3734	0.0102 5078	0.0105 6862	0.0108 9072	0.0112 1698	202
203	0.0099 1745	0.0102 3133	0.0105 4960	0.0108 7215	0.0111 9885	203
204	0.0098 9781	0.0102 1210	0.0105 3081	0.0108 5381	0.0111 8096	204
205	0.0098 7839	0.0101 9311	0.0105 1225	0.0108 3569	0.0111 6330	205
206	0.0098 5920	0.0101 7435	0.0104 9392	0.0108 1780	0.0111 4585	206
207	0.0098 4024	0.0101 5580	0.0104 7581	0.0108 0013	0.0111 2863	207
208	0.0098 2149	0.0101 3748	0.0104 5792	0.0107 8268	0.0111 1162	208
209	0.0098 0297	0.0101 1938	0.0104 4024	0.0107 6544	0.0110 9483	209
210	0.0097 8465	0.0101 0148	0.0104 2278	0.0107 4841	0.0110 7824	210
211	0.0097 6655	0.0100 8380	0.0104 0552	0.0107 3159	0.0110 6186	211
212	0.0097 4866	0.0100 6633	0.0103 8847	0.0107 1497	0.0110 4569	212
213	0.0097 3097	0.0100 4905	0.0103 7163	0.0106 9856	0.0110 2971	213
214	0.0097 1349	0.0100 3198	0.0103 5498	0.0106 8234	0.0110 1393	214
215	0.0096 9620	0.0100 1511	0.0103 3853	0.0106 6632	0.0109 9835	215
216	0.0096 7911	0.0099 9844	0.0103 2228	0.0106 5050	0.0109 8295	216
217	0.0096 6222	0.0099 8195	0.0103 0621	0.0106 3486	0.0109 6775	217
218	0.0096 4551	0.0099 6566	0.0102 9034	0.0106 1941	0.0109 5273	218
219	0.0096 2900	0.0099 4955	0.0102 7465	0.0106 0414	0.0109 3789	219
220	0.0096 1267	0.0099 3363	0.0102 5914	0.0105 8906	0.0109 2324	220
221	0.0095 9652	0.0099 1789	0.0102 4382	0.0105 7416	0.0109 0876	221
222	0.0095 8055	0.0099 0233	0.0102 2867	0.0105 5943	0.0108 9446	222
223	0.0095 6476	0.0098 8694	0.0102 1370	0.0105 4488	0.0108 8033	223
224	0.0095 4915	0.0098 7173	0.0101 9890	0.0105 3050	0.0108 6637	224
225	0.0095 3371	0.0098 5670	0.0101 8427	0.0105 1628	0.0108 5257	225
226	0.0095 1844	0.0098 4183	0.0101 6981	0.0105 0224	0.0108 3895	226
227	0.0095 0333	0.0098 2713	0.0101 5552	0.0104 8836	0.0108 2548	227
228	0.0094 8840	0.0098 1259	0.0101 4139	0.0104 7464	0.0108 1218	228
229	0.0094 7362	0.0097 9821	0.0101 2742	0.0104 6108	0.0107 9904	229
230	0.0094 5901	0.0097 8400	0.0101 1361	0.0104 4768	0.0107 8605	230
231	0.0094 4456	0.0097 6995	0.0100 9996	0.0104 3443	0.0107 7321	231
232	0.0094 3026	0.0097 5605	0.0100 8646	0.0104 2134	0.0107 6053	232
233	0.0094 1612	0.0097 4230	0.0100 7311	0.0104 0840	0.0107 4800	233
234	0.0094 0214	0.0097 2871	0.0100 5992	0.0103 9561	0.0107 3561	234
235	0.0093 8830	0.0097 1526	0.0100 4687	0.0103 8297	0.0107 2338	235
236	0.0093 7461	0.0097 0196	0.0100 3397	0.0103 7047	0.0107 1128	236
237	0.0093 6107	0.0096 8881	0.0100 2122	0.0103 5811	0.0106 9933	237
238	0.0093 4768	0.0096 7581	0.0100 0860	0.0103 4590	0.0106 8751	238
239	0.0093 3442	0.0096 6294	0.0099 9613	0.0103 3382	0.0106 7584	239
240	0.0093 2131	0.0096 5022	0.0099 8380	0.0103 2188	0.0106 6430	240

TABLE V

N	19/24	5/6	7/8	11/12	23/24	N
241	0.0093 0834	0.0096 3763	0.0099 7160	0.0103 1008	0.0106 5289	241
242	0.0092 9550	0.0096 2518	0.0099 5954	0.0102 9841	0.0106 4162	242
243	0.0092 8281	0.0096 1286	0.0099 4761	0.0102 8688	0.0106 3047	243
244	0.0092 7024	0.0096 0068	0.0099 3582	0.0102 7547	0.0106 1946	244
245	0.0092 5781	0.0095 8863	0.0099 2415	0.0102 6419	0.0106 0857	245
246	0.0092 4551	0.0095 7671	0.0099 1261	0.0102 5304	0.0105 9781	246
247	0.0092 3333	0.0095 6491	0.0099 0120	0.0102 4202	0.0105 8717	247
248	0.0092 2129	0.0095 5324	0.0098 8992	0.0102 3111	0.0105 7665	248
249	0.0092 0937	0.0095 4170	0.0098 7875	0.0102 2033	0.0105 6626	249
250	0.0091 9757	0.0095 3028	0.0098 6771	0.0102 0967	0.0105 5598	250
251	0.0091 8590	0.0095 1898	0.0098 5679	0.0101 9913	0.0105 4582	251
252	0.0091 7434	0.0095 0780	0.0098 4599	0.0101 8871	0.0105 3578	252
253	0.0091 6291	0.0094 9674	0.0098 3530	0.0101 7840	0.0105 2585	253
254	0.0091 5159	0.0094 8579	0.0098 2473	0.0101 6821	0.0105 1603	254
255	0.0091 4040	0.0094 7496	0.0098 1427	0.0101 5813	0.0105 0632	255
256	0.0091 2931	0.0094 6425	0.0098 0393	0.0101 4816	0.0104 9673	256
257	0.0091 1834	0.0094 5365	0.0097 9370	0.0101 3830	0.0104 8724	257
258	0.0091 0748	0.0094 4315	0.0097 8358	0.0101 2854	0.0104 7786	258
259	0.0090 9674	0.0094 3277	0.0097 7356	0.0101 1890	0.0104 6858	259
260	0.0090 8610	0.0094 2250	0.0097 6365	0.0101 0936	0.0104 5941	260
261	0.0090 7557	0.0094 1233	0.0097 5385	0.0100 9993	0.0104 5034	261
262	0.0090 6514	0.0094 0227	0.0097 4416	0.0100 9059	0.0104 4138	262
263	0.0090 5483	0.0093 9231	0.0097 3456	0.0100 8136	0.0104 3251	263
264	0.0090 4461	0.0093 8246	0.0097 2507	0.0100 7223	0.0104 2374	264
265	0.0090 3450	0.0093 7271	0.0097 1568	0.0100 6320	0.0104 1507	265
266	0.0090 2449	0.0093 6306	0.0097 0639	0.0100 5427	0.0104 0650	266
267	0.0090 1459	0.0093 5350	0.0096 9719	0.0100 4544	0.0103 9802	267
268	0.0090 0478	0.0093 4405	0.0096 8810	0.0100 3670	0.0103 8964	268
269	0.0089 9507	0.0093 3469	0.0096 7910	0.0100 2805	0.0103 8135	269
270	0.0089 8545	0.0093 2543	0.0096 7019	0.0100 1950	0.0103 7315	270
271	0.0089 7593	0.0093 1627	0.0096 6138	0.0100 1104	0.0103 6504	271
272	0.0089 6651	0.0093 0719	0.0096 5266	0.0100 0267	0.0103 5702	272
273	0.0089 5718	0.0092 9821	0.0096 4403	0.0099 9439	0.0103 4909	273
274	0.0089 4794	0.0092 8933	0.0096 3549	0.0099 8620	0.0103 4124	274
275	0.0089 3880	0.0092 8053	0.0096 2703	0.0099 7810	0.0103 3349	275
276	0.0089 2974	0.0092 7182	0.0096 1867	0.0099 7008	0.0103 2581	276
277	0.0089 2078	0.0092 6320	0.0096 1040	0.0099 6215	0.0103 1822	277
278	0.0089 1190	0.0092 5466	0.0096 0221	0.0099 5430	0.0103 1072	278
279	0.0089 0311	0.0092 4621	0.0095 9410	0.0099 4654	0.0103 0330	279
280	0.0088 9440	0.0092 3785	0.0095 8608	0.0099 3886	0.0102 9595	280
281	0.0088 8578	0.0092 2957	0.0095 7814	0.0099 3126	0.0102 8869	281
282	0.0088 7725	0.0092 2137	0.0095 7028	0.0099 2374	0.0102 8151	282
283	0.0088 6879	0.0092 1326	0.0095 6251	0.0099 1630	0.0102 7440	283
284	0.0088 6042	0.0092 0523	0.0095 5481	0.0099 0894	0.0102 6737	284
285	0.0088 5214	0.0091 9727	0.0095 4720	0.0099 0166	0.0102 6042	285
286	0.0088 4393	0.0091 8940	0.0095 3966	0.0098 9445	0.0102 5355	286
287	0.0088 3580	0.0091 8160	0.0095 3219	0.0098 8732	0.0102 4674	287
288	0.0088 2775	0.0091 7389	0.0095 2481	0.0098 8027	0.0102 4002	288
289	0.0088 1978	0.0091 6625	0.0095 1750	0.0098 7328	0.0102 3336	289
290	0.0088 1188	0.0091 5868	0.0095 1026	0.0098 6638	0.0102 2677	290
291	0.0088 0406	0.0091 5119	0.0095 0310	0.0098 5954	0.0102 2026	291
292	0.0087 9632	0.0091 4377	0.0094 9601	0.0098 5277	0.0102 1382	292
293	0.0087 8865	0.0091 3643	0.0094 8899	0.0098 4608	0.0102 0744	293
294	0.0087 8105	0.0091 2916	0.0094 8205	0.0098 3946	0.0102 0114	294
295	0.0087 7353	0.0091 2196	0.0094 7517	0.0098 3290	0.0101 9490	295
296	0.0087 6607	0.0091 1483	0.0094 6836	0.0098 2641	0.0101 8873	296
297	0.0087 5869	0.0091 0777	0.0094 6163	0.0098 1999	0.0101 8262	297
298	0.0087 5138	0.0091 0078	0.0094 5496	0.0098 1364	0.0101 7658	298
299	0.0087 4414	0.0090 9386	0.0094 4835	0.0098 0735	0.0101 7060	299
300	0.0087 3697	0.0090 8701	0.0094 4182	0.0098 0113	0.0101 6469	300

TABLE V

N	19/24	5/6	7/8	11/12	23/24	N
301	0.0087 2986	0.0090 8022	0.0094 3535	0.0097 9497	0.0101 5884	301
302	0.0087 2282	0.0090 7350	0.0094 2894	0.0097 8888	0.0101 5305	302
303	0.0087 1585	0.0090 6684	0.0094 2260	0.0097 8285	0.0101 4733	303
304	0.0087 0895	0.0090 6025	0.0094 1632	0.0097 7688	0.0101 4166	304
305	0.0087 0211	0.0090 5373	0.0094 1010	0.0097 7097	0.0101 3605	305
306	0.0086 9533	0.0090 4726	0.0094 0395	0.0097 6512	0.0101 3051	306
307	0.0086 8862	0.0090 4086	0.0093 9786	0.0097 5933	0.0101 2502	307
308	0.0086 8197	0.0090 3452	0.0093 9183	0.0097 5361	0.0101 1959	308
309	0.0086 7538	0.0090 2824	0.0093 8585	0.0097 4794	0.0101 1422	309
310	0.0086 6886	0.0090 2203	0.0093 7994	0.0097 4232	0.0101 0890	310
311	0.0086 6239	0.0090 1587	0.0093 7409	0.0097 3677	0.0101 0364	311
312	0.0086 5599	0.0090 0977	0.0093 6829	0.0097 3127	0.0100 9844	312
313	0.0086 4964	0.0090 0373	0.0093 6255	0.0097 2583	0.0100 9329	313
314	0.0086 4336	0.0089 9775	0.0093 5687	0.0097 2045	0.0100 8819	314
315	0.0086 3713	0.0089 9182	0.0093 5125	0.0097 1511	0.0100 8315	315
316	0.0086 3096	0.0089 8595	0.0093 4568	0.0097 0984	0.0100 7816	316
317	0.0086 2485	0.0089 8014	0.0093 4016	0.0097 0461	0.0100 7322	317
318	0.0086 1879	0.0089 7439	0.0093 3470	0.0096 9944	0.0100 6834	318
319	0.0086 1279	0.0089 6868	0.0093 2929	0.0096 9433	0.0100 6350	319
320	0.0086 0685	0.0089 6304	0.0093 2394	0.0096 8926	0.0100 5872	320
321	0.0086 0096	0.0089 5744	0.0093 1863	0.0096 8424	0.0100 5399	321
322	0.0085 9512	0.0089 5190	0.0093 1338	0.0096 7928	0.0100 4930	322
323	0.0085 8934	0.0089 4641	0.0093 0819	0.0096 7437	0.0100 4467	323
324	0.0085 8361	0.0089 4098	0.0093 0304	0.0096 6950	0.0100 4008	324
325	0.0085 7794	0.0089 3559	0.0092 9794	0.0096 6469	0.0100 3554	325
326	0.0085 7231	0.0089 3026	0.0092 9289	0.0096 5992	0.0100 3104	326
327	0.0085 6674	0.0089 2497	0.0092 8789	0.0096 5520	0.0100 2660	327
328	0.0085 6122	0.0089 1974	0.0092 8294	0.0096 5053	0.0100 2220	328
329	0.0085 5575	0.0089 1456	0.0092 7804	0.0096 4590	0.0100 1784	329
330	0.0085 5033	0.0089 0942	0.0092 7319	0.0096 4132	0.0100 1353	330
331	0.0085 4495	0.0089 0433	0.0092 6838	0.0096 3679	0.0100 0927	331
332	0.0085 3963	0.0088 9929	0.0092 6362	0.0096 3230	0.0100 0505	332
333	0.0085 3436	0.0088 9430	0.0092 5891	0.0096 2786	0.0100 0087	333
334	0.0085 2913	0.0088 8936	0.0092 5424	0.0096 2346	0.0099 9674	334
335	0.0085 2395	0.0088 8446	0.0092 4961	0.0096 1911	0.0099 9264	335
336	0.0085 1882	0.0088 7960	0.0092 4504	0.0096 1480	0.0099 8859	336
337	0.0085 1373	0.0088 7480	0.0092 4050	0.0096 1053	0.0099 8459	337
338	0.0085 0869	0.0088 7003	0.0092 3601	0.0096 0631	0.0099 8062	338
339	0.0085 0370	0.0088 6531	0.0092 3156	0.0096 0212	0.0099 7669	339
340	0.0084 9875	0.0088 6064	0.0092 2716	0.0095 9798	0.0099 7281	340
341	0.0084 9384	0.0088 5601	0.0092 2279	0.0095 9388	0.0099 6896	341
342	0.0084 8898	0.0088 5142	0.0092 1847	0.0095 8982	0.0099 6516	342
343	0.0084 8416	0.0088 4687	0.0092 1420	0.0095 8580	0.0099 6139	343
344	0.0084 7939	0.0088 4237	0.0092 0996	0.0095 8182	0.0099 5766	344
345	0.0084 7466	0.0088 3791	0.0092 0576	0.0095 7788	0.0099 5397	345
346	0.0084 6997	0.0088 3349	0.0092 0160	0.0095 7398	0.0099 5032	346
347	0.0084 6532	0.0088 2911	0.0091 9748	0.0095 7012	0.0099 4670	347
348	0.0084 6071	0.0088 2477	0.0091 9341	0.0095 6629	0.0099 4312	348
349	0.0084 5615	0.0088 2047	0.0091 8937	0.0095 6251	0.0099 3958	349
350	0.0084 5163	0.0088 1621	0.0091 8537	0.0095 5876	0.0099 3607	350
351	0.0084 4714	0.0088 1199	0.0091 8140	0.0095 5505	0.0099 3260	351
352	0.0084 4270	0.0088 0781	0.0091 7748	0.0095 5137	0.0099 2917	352
353	0.0084 3830	0.0088 0367	0.0091 7359	0.0095 4773	0.0099 2577	353
354	0.0084 3393	0.0087 9956	0.0091 6974	0.0095 4413	0.0099 2240	354
355	0.0084 2960	0.0087 9550	0.0091 6593	0.0095 4056	0.0099 1907	355
356	0.0084 2532	0.0087 9147	0.0091 6215	0.0095 3702	0.0099 1577	356
357	0.0084 2107	0.0087 8748	0.0091 5841	0.0095 3353	0.0099 1251	357
358	0.0084 1685	0.0087 8352	0.0091 5470	0.0095 3006	0.0099 0928	358
359	0.0084 1268	0.0087 7960	0.0091 5103	0.0095 2663	0.0099 0608	359
360	0.0084 0854	0.0087 7572	0.0091 4739	0.0095 2323	0.0099 0291	360

TABLE V

N	1	1 1/8	1 1/4	1 3/8	1 1/2	N
1	1.0100 0000	1.0112 5000	1.0125 0000	1.0137 5000	1.0150 0000	1
2	0.5075 1244	0.5084 5323	0.5093 9441	0.5103 3597	0.5112 7792	2
3	0.3400 2211	0.3408 6130	0.3417 0117	0.3425 4173	0.3433 8296	3
4	0.2562 8109	0.2570 7058	0.2578 6102	0.2586 5243	0.2594 4479	4
5	0.2060 3980	0.2068 0034	0.2075 6211	0.2083 2510	0.2090 8932	5
6	0.1725 4837	0.1732 9034	0.1740 3381	0.1747 7877	0.1755 2521	6
7	0.1486 2828	0.1493 5762	0.1500 8872	0.1508 2157	0.1515 5616	7
8	0.1306 9029	0.1314 1071	0.1321 3314	0.1328 5758	0.1335 8402	8
9	0.1167 4036	0.1174 5432	0.1181 7055	0.1188 8906	0.1196 0982	9
10	0.1055 8208	0.1062 9131	0.1070 0307	0.1077 1737	0.1084 3418	10
11	0.0964 5408	0.0971 5984	0.0978 6839	0.0985 7973	0.0992 9384	11
12	0.0888 4879	0.0895 5203	0.0902 5831	0.0909 6764	0.0916 7999	12
13	0.0824 1482	0.0831 1626	0.0838 2100	0.0845 2903	0.0852 4036	13
14	0.0769 0117	0.0776 0138	0.0783 0515	0.0790 1246	0.0797 2332	14
15	0.0721 2378	0.0728 2321	0.0735 2646	0.0742 3351	0.0749 4436	15
16	0.0679 4460	0.0686 4363	0.0693 4672	0.0700 5388	0.0707 6508	16
17	0.0642 5806	0.0649 5698	0.0656 6023	0.0663 6780	0.0670 7966	17
18	0.0609 8205	0.0616 8113	0.0623 8479	0.0630 9301	0.0638 0578	18
19	0.0580 5175	0.0587 5120	0.0594 5548	0.0601 6457	0.0608 7847	19
20	0.0554 1531	0.0561 1531	0.0568 2039	0.0575 3054	0.0582 4574	20
21	0.0530 3075	0.0537 3145	0.0544 3749	0.0551 4884	0.0558 6550	21
22	0.0508 6372	0.0515 6525	0.0522 7238	0.0529 8507	0.0537 0332	22
23	0.0488 8584	0.0495 8833	0.0502 9666	0.0510 1080	0.0517 3075	23
24	0.0470 7347	0.0477 7701	0.0484 8665	0.0492 0235	0.0499 2410	24
25	0.0454 0675	0.0461 1144	0.0468 2247	0.0475 3981	0.0482 6345	25
26	0.0438 6888	0.0445 7479	0.0452 8729	0.0460 0635	0.0467 3196	26
27	0.0424 4553	0.0431 5273	0.0438 6677	0.0445 8763	0.0453 1527	27
28	0.0411 2444	0.0418 3299	0.0425 4863	0.0432 7134	0.0440 0108	28
29	0.0398 9502	0.0406 0498	0.0413 2228	0.0420 4689	0.0427 7878	29
30	0.0387 4811	0.0394 5953	0.0401 7854	0.0409 0511	0.0416 3919	30
31	0.0376 7573	0.0383 8866	0.0391 0942	0.0398 3798	0.0405 7430	31
32	0.0366 7089	0.0373 8535	0.0381 0791	0.0388 3850	0.0395 7710	32
33	0.0357 2744	0.0364 4349	0.0371 6786	0.0379 0053	0.0386 4144	33
34	0.0348 3997	0.0355 5763	0.0362 8387	0.0370 1864	0.0377 6189	34
35	0.0340 0368	0.0347 2299	0.0354 5111	0.0361 8801	0.0369 3363	35
36	0.0332 1431	0.0339 3529	0.0346 6533	0.0354 0438	0.0361 5240	36
37	0.0324 6805	0.0331 9072	0.0339 2270	0.0346 6394	0.0354 1437	37
38	0.0317 6150	0.0324 8589	0.0332 1983	0.0339 6327	0.0347 1613	38
39	0.0310 9160	0.0318 1773	0.0325 5365	0.0332 9931	0.0340 5463	39
40	0.0304 5560	0.0311 8349	0.0319 2141	0.0326 6931	0.0334 2710	40
41	0.0298 5102	0.0305 8069	0.0313 2063	0.0320 7078	0.0328 3106	41
42	0.0292 7563	0.0300 0709	0.0307 4906	0.0315 0148	0.0322 6426	42
43	0.0287 2737	0.0294 6064	0.0302 0466	0.0309 5936	0.0317 2465	43
44	0.0282 0441	0.0289 3949	0.0296 8557	0.0304 4257	0.0312 1038	44
45	0.0277 0505	0.0284 4197	0.0291 9012	0.0299 4941	0.0307 1976	45
46	0.0272 2775	0.0279 6652	0.0287 1675	0.0294 7836	0.0302 5125	46
47	0.0267 7111	0.0275 1173	0.0282 6406	0.0290 2799	0.0298 0342	47
48	0.0263 3384	0.0270 7632	0.0278 3075	0.0285 9701	0.0293 7500	48
49	0.0259 1474	0.0266 5910	0.0274 1563	0.0281 8423	0.0289 6478	49
50	0.0255 1273	0.0262 5898	0.0270 1763	0.0277 8857	0.0285 7168	50
51	0.0251 2680	0.0258 7494	0.0266 3571	0.0274 0900	0.0281 9469	51
52	0.0247 5603	0.0255 0606	0.0262 6897	0.0270 4461	0.0278 3287	52
53	0.0243 9956	0.0251 5149	0.0259 1653	0.0266 9453	0.0274 8537	53
54	0.0240 5658	0.0248 1043	0.0255 7760	0.0263 5797	0.0271 5138	54
55	0.0237 2637	0.0244 8213	0.0252 5145	0.0260 3418	0.0268 3018	55
56	0.0234 0824	0.0241 6592	0.0249 3739	0.0257 2249	0.0265 2106	56
57	0.0231 0156	0.0238 6116	0.0246 3478	0.0254 2225	0.0262 2341	57
58	0.0228 0573	0.0235 6726	0.0243 4303	0.0251 3287	0.0259 3661	58
59	0.0225 2020	0.0232 8366	0.0240 6158	0.0248 5380	0.0256 6012	59
60	0.0222 4445	0.0230 0985	0.0237 8993	0.0245 8452	0.0253 9343	60

TABLE V

N	1	1 1/8	1 1/4	1 3/8	1 1/2	N
61	0.0219 7800	0.0227 4534	0.0235 2758	0.0243 2455	0.0251 3604	61
62	0.0217 2041	0.0224 8969	0.0232 7410	0.0240 7344	0.0248 8751	62
63	0.0214 7125	0.0222 4247	0.0230 2904	0.0238 3076	0.0246 4741	63
64	0.0212 3013	0.0220 0329	0.0227 9203	0.0235 9612	0.0244 1534	64
65	0.0209 9667	0.0217 7178	0.0225 6268	0.0233 6914	0.0241 9094	65
66	0.0207 7052	0.0215 4758	0.0223 4065	0.0231 4949	0.0239 7386	66
67	0.0205 5136	0.0213 3037	0.0221 2560	0.0229 3682	0.0237 6376	67
68	0.0203 3889	0.0211 1985	0.0219 1724	0.0227 3082	0.0235 6033	68
69	0.0201 3280	0.0209 1571	0.0217 1527	0.0225 3122	0.0233 6329	69
70	0.0199 3282	0.0207 1769	0.0215 1941	0.0223 3773	0.0231 7235	70
71	0.0197 3870	0.0205 2552	0.0213 2941	0.0221 5009	0.0229 8727	71
72	0.0195 5019	0.0203 3896	0.0211 4501	0.0219 6806	0.0228 0779	72
73	0.0193 6706	0.0201 5779	0.0209 6600	0.0217 9140	0.0226 3368	73
74	0.0191 8910	0.0199 8177	0.0207 9215	0.0216 1991	0.0224 6473	74
75	0.0190 1609	0.0198 1072	0.0206 2325	0.0214 5336	0.0223 0072	75
76	0.0188 4784	0.0196 4442	0.0204 5910	0.0212 9157	0.0221 4146	76
77	0.0186 8416	0.0194 8269	0.0202 9953	0.0211 3435	0.0219 8676	77
78	0.0185 2488	0.0193 2536	0.0201 4436	0.0209 8151	0.0218 3645	78
79	0.0183 6983	0.0191 7226	0.0199 9341	0.0208 3290	0.0216 9036	79
80	0.0182 1885	0.0190 2323	0.0198 4652	0.0206 8836	0.0215 4832	80
81	0.0180 7179	0.0188 7812	0.0197 0356	0.0205 4772	0.0214 1019	81
82	0.0179 2851	0.0187 3678	0.0195 6437	0.0204 1086	0.0212 7583	82
83	0.0177 8887	0.0185 9908	0.0194 2881	0.0202 7762	0.0211 4509	83
84	0.0176 5273	0.0184 6489	0.0192 9675	0.0201 4789	0.0210 1784	84
85	0.0175 1998	0.0183 3409	0.0191 6808	0.0200 2153	0.0208 9396	85
86	0.0173 9050	0.0182 0654	0.0190 4267	0.0198 9843	0.0207 7333	86
87	0.0172 6418	0.0180 8215	0.0189 2041	0.0197 7847	0.0206 5584	87
88	0.0171 4089	0.0179 6081	0.0188 0119	0.0196 6155	0.0205 4138	88
89	0.0170 2056	0.0178 4240	0.0186 8491	0.0195 4756	0.0204 2984	89
90	0.0169 0306	0.0177 2684	0.0185 7146	0.0194 3641	0.0203 2113	90
91	0.0167 8832	0.0176 1403	0.0184 6076	0.0193 2799	0.0202 1516	91
92	0.0166 7624	0.0175 0387	0.0183 5272	0.0192 2222	0.0201 1182	92
93	0.0165 6673	0.0173 9629	0.0182 4724	0.0191 1902	0.0200 1104	93
94	0.0164 5971	0.0172 9119	0.0181 4425	0.0190 1829	0.0199 1273	94
95	0.0163 5511	0.0171 8851	0.0180 4366	0.0189 1997	0.0198 1681	95
96	0.0162 5284	0.0170 8816	0.0179 4541	0.0188 2397	0.0197 2321	96
97	0.0161 5284	0.0169 9007	0.0178 4941	0.0187 3022	0.0196 3186	97
98	0.0160 5503	0.0168 9418	0.0177 5560	0.0186 3866	0.0195 4268	98
99	0.0159 5936	0.0168 0041	0.0176 6391	0.0185 4921	0.0194 5560	99
100	0.0158 6574	0.0167 0870	0.0175 7428	0.0184 6181	0.0193 7057	100
101	0.0157 7413	0.0166 1899	0.0174 8664	0.0183 7640	0.0192 8752	101
102	0.0156 8446	0.0165 3122	0.0174 0094	0.0182 9291	0.0192 0639	102
103	0.0155 9668	0.0164 4534	0.0173 1712	0.0182 1130	0.0191 2712	103
104	0.0155 1073	0.0163 6128	0.0172 3512	0.0181 3151	0.0190 4966	104
105	0.0154 2656	0.0162 7900	0.0171 5489	0.0180 5348	0.0189 7396	105
106	0.0153 4412	0.0161 9844	0.0170 7639	0.0179 7717	0.0188 9996	106
107	0.0152 6336	0.0161 1956	0.0169 9955	0.0179 0252	0.0188 2762	107
108	0.0151 8423	0.0160 4231	0.0169 2434	0.0178 2948	0.0187 5689	108
109	0.0151 0669	0.0159 6665	0.0168 5070	0.0177 5802	0.0186 8772	109
110	0.0150 3069	0.0158 9252	0.0167 7861	0.0176 8809	0.0186 2007	110
111	0.0149 5620	0.0158 1990	0.0167 0800	0.0176 1964	0.0185 5389	111
112	0.0148 8317	0.0157 4873	0.0166 3885	0.0175 5264	0.0184 8916	112
113	0.0148 1155	0.0156 7898	0.0165 7111	0.0174 8705	0.0184 2582	113
114	0.0147 4133	0.0156 1061	0.0165 0475	0.0174 2282	0.0183 6383	114
115	0.0146 7245	0.0155 4358	0.0164 3972	0.0173 5992	0.0183 0317	115
116	0.0146 0488	0.0154 7786	0.0163 7600	0.0172 9833	0.0182 4380	116
117	0.0145 3860	0.0154 1342	0.0163 1355	0.0172 3799	0.0181 8568	117
118	0.0144 7356	0.0153 5022	0.0162 5234	0.0171 7888	0.0181 2878	118
119	0.0144 0974	0.0152 8824	0.0161 9233	0.0171 2097	0.0180 7307	119
120	0.0143 4709	0.0152 2743	0.0161 3350	0.0170 6423	0.0180 1852	120

TABLE V

N	1	1 1/8	1 1/4	1 3/8	1 1/2	N
121	0.0142 8561	0.0151 6777	0.0160 7581	0.0170 0862	0.0179 6509	121
122	0.0142 2525	0.0151 0924	0.0160 1923	0.0169 5413	0.0179 1277	122
123	0.0141 6599	0.0150 5179	0.0159 6374	0.0169 0071	0.0178 6151	123
124	0.0141 0780	0.0149 9542	0.0159 0932	0.0168 4834	0.0178 1129	124
125	0.0140 5065	0.0149 4008	0.0158 5593	0.0167 9701	0.0177 6210	125
126	0.0139 9452	0.0148 8576	0.0158 0355	0.0167 4667	0.0177 1389	126
127	0.0139 3939	0.0148 3244	0.0157 5215	0.0166 9731	0.0176 6666	127
128	0.0138 8524	0.0147 8008	0.0157 0172	0.0166 4891	0.0176 2036	128
129	0.0138 3203	0.0147 2866	0.0156 5222	0.0166 0144	0.0175 7499	129
130	0.0137 7975	0.0146 7817	0.0156 0364	0.0165 5487	0.0175 3052	130
131	0.0137 2837	0.0146 2858	0.0155 5596	0.0165 0919	0.0174 8692	131
132	0.0136 7788	0.0145 7987	0.0155 0915	0.0164 6438	0.0174 4418	132
133	0.0136 2825	0.0145 3202	0.0154 6319	0.0164 2042	0.0174 0227	133
134	0.0135 7947	0.0144 8501	0.0154 1807	0.0163 7727	0.0173 6118	134
135	0.0135 3151	0.0144 3882	0.0153 7376	0.0163 3494	0.0173 2089	135
136	0.0134 8437	0.0143 9343	0.0153 3025	0.0162 9339	0.0172 8137	136
137	0.0134 3801	0.0143 4883	0.0152 8752	0.0162 5262	0.0172 4262	137
138	0.0133 9242	0.0143 0499	0.0152 4554	0.0162 1259	0.0172 0461	138
139	0.0133 4759	0.0142 6190	0.0152 0432	0.0161 7331	0.0171 6732	139
140	0.0133 0349	0.0142 1955	0.0151 6381	0.0161 3474	0.0171 3074	140
141	0.0132 6012	0.0141 7792	0.0151 2402	0.0160 9687	0.0170 9485	141
142	0.0132 1746	0.0141 3699	0.0150 8493	0.0160 5969	0.0170 5964	142
143	0.0131 7549	0.0140 9674	0.0150 4652	0.0160 2319	0.0170 2510	143
144	0.0131 3419	0.0140 5717	0.0150 0877	0.0159 8734	0.0169 9120	144
145	0.0130 9356	0.0140 1826	0.0149 7167	0.0159 5213	0.0169 5793	145
146	0.0130 5358	0.0139 7999	0.0149 3521	0.0159 1755	0.0169 2528	146
147	0.0130 1423	0.0139 4235	0.0148 9938	0.0158 8359	0.0168 9324	147
148	0.0129 7551	0.0139 0533	0.0148 6415	0.0158 5023	0.0168 6178	148
149	0.0129 3739	0.0138 6891	0.0148 2953	0.0158 1746	0.0168 3091	149
150	0.0128 9988	0.0138 3309	0.0147 9548	0.0157 8527	0.0168 0061	150
151	0.0128 6294	0.0137 9784	0.0147 6202	0.0157 5364	0.0167 7085	151
152	0.0128 2659	0.0137 6317	0.0147 2911	0.0157 2257	0.0167 4165	152
153	0.0127 9079	0.0137 2905	0.0146 9675	0.0156 9203	0.0167 1297	153
154	0.0127 5554	0.0136 9547	0.0146 6494	0.0156 6203	0.0166 8481	154
155	0.0127 2084	0.0136 6243	0.0146 3365	0.0156 3254	0.0166 5716	155
156	0.0126 8666	0.0136 2992	0.0146 0287	0.0156 0357	0.0166 3001	156
157	0.0126 5300	0.0135 9792	0.0145 7261	0.0155 7509	0.0166 0334	157
158	0.0126 1986	0.0135 6642	0.0145 4284	0.0155 4710	0.0165 7716	158
159	0.0125 8721	0.0135 3541	0.0145 1356	0.0155 1959	0.0165 5144	159
160	0.0125 5504	0.0135 0489	0.0144 8475	0.0154 9255	0.0165 2618	160
161	0.0125 2336	0.0134 7484	0.0144 5641	0.0154 6596	0.0165 0137	161
162	0.0124 9215	0.0134 4526	0.0144 2853	0.0154 3983	0.0164 7700	162
163	0.0124 6141	0.0134 1614	0.0144 0110	0.0154 1413	0.0164 5305	163
164	0.0124 3111	0.0133 8746	0.0143 7411	0.0153 8887	0.0164 2953	164
165	0.0124 0126	0.0133 5923	0.0143 4756	0.0153 6403	0.0164 0643	165
166	0.0123 7185	0.0133 3142	0.0143 2142	0.0153 3961	0.0163 8372	166
167	0.0123 4286	0.0133 0404	0.0142 9571	0.0153 1559	0.0163 6142	167
168	0.0123 1430	0.0132 7707	0.0142 7040	0.0152 9198	0.0163 3950	168
169	0.0122 8614	0.0132 5051	0.0142 4549	0.0152 6875	0.0163 1797	169
170	0.0122 5840	0.0132 2435	0.0142 2097	0.0152 4591	0.0162 9681	170
171	0.0122 3105	0.0131 9858	0.0141 9684	0.0152 2345	0.0162 7601	171
172	0.0122 0409	0.0131 7319	0.0141 7309	0.0152 0135	0.0162 5558	172
173	0.0121 7751	0.0131 4819	0.0141 4971	0.0151 7962	0.0162 3549	173
174	0.0121 5132	0.0131 2356	0.0141 2669	0.0151 5824	0.0162 1575	174
175	0.0121 2549	0.0130 9929	0.0141 0403	0.0151 3722	0.0161 9635	175
176	0.0121 0003	0.0130 7537	0.0140 8172	0.0151 1653	0.0161 7729	176
177	0.0120 7492	0.0130 5182	0.0140 5976	0.0150 9618	0.0161 5854	177
178	0.0120 5016	0.0130 2860	0.0140 3813	0.0150 7616	0.0161 4012	178
179	0.0120 2575	0.0130 0573	0.0140 1684	0.0150 5647	0.0161 2201	179
180	0.0120 0168	0.0129 8319	0.0139 9587	0.0150 3709	0.0161 0421	180

TABLE V

N	1	1 1/8	1 1/4	1 3/8	1 1/2	N
181	0.0119 7794	0.0129 6097	0.0139 7522	0.0150 1802	0.0160 8671	181
182	0.0119 5453	0.0129 3908	0.0139 5489	0.0149 9926	0.0160 6950	182
183	0.0119 3144	0.0129 1750	0.0139 3487	0.0149 8080	0.0160 5259	183
184	0.0119 0867	0.0128 9624	0.0139 1515	0.0149 6263	0.0160 3596	184
185	0.0118 8621	0.0128 7528	0.0138 9573	0.0149 4475	0.0160 1961	185
186	0.0118 6405	0.0128 5462	0.0138 7660	0.0149 2716	0.0160 0353	186
187	0.0118 4219	0.0128 3425	0.0138 5776	0.0149 0985	0.0159 8773	187
188	0.0118 2063	0.0128 1418	0.0138 3920	0.0148 9281	0.0159 7218	188
189	0.0117 9936	0.0127 9439	0.0138 2092	0.0148 7604	0.0159 5690	189
190	0.0117 7838	0.0127 7488	0.0138 0291	0.0148 5953	0.0159 4187	190
191	0.0117 5768	0.0127 5564	0.0137 8517	0.0148 4329	0.0159 2709	191
192	0.0117 3725	0.0127 3668	0.0137 6770	0.0148 2730	0.0159 1256	192
193	0.0117 1710	0.0127 1798	0.0137 5048	0.0148 1156	0.0158 9826	193
194	0.0116 9721	0.0126 9955	0.0137 3352	0.0147 9606	0.0158 8421	194
195	0.0116 7759	0.0126 8137	0.0137 1681	0.0147 8081	0.0158 7038	195
196	0.0116 5822	0.0126 6345	0.0137 0034	0.0147 6580	0.0158 5678	196
197	0.0116 3911	0.0126 4577	0.0136 8412	0.0147 5102	0.0158 4341	197
198	0.0116 2026	0.0126 2834	0.0136 6813	0.0147 3646	0.0158 3026	198
199	0.0116 0164	0.0126 1115	0.0136 5238	0.0147 2214	0.0158 1732	199
200	0.0115 8328	0.0125 9420	0.0136 3686	0.0147 0803	0.0158 0459	200
201	0.0115 6515	0.0125 7748	0.0136 2157	0.0146 9415	0.0157 9207	201
202	0.0115 4725	0.0125 6099	0.0136 0650	0.0146 8048	0.0157 7976	202
203	0.0115 2959	0.0125 4473	0.0135 9164	0.0146 6701	0.0157 6764	203
204	0.0115 1216	0.0125 2869	0.0135 7700	0.0146 5376	0.0157 5573	204
205	0.0114 9495	0.0125 1287	0.0135 6258	0.0146 4071	0.0157 4401	205
206	0.0114 7796	0.0124 9726	0.0135 4836	0.0146 2785	0.0157 3247	206
207	0.0114 6118	0.0124 8186	0.0135 3435	0.0146 1520	0.0157 2113	207
208	0.0114 4463	0.0124 6668	0.0135 2053	0.0146 0273	0.0157 0997	208
209	0.0114 2828	0.0124 5170	0.0135 0692	0.0145 9046	0.0156 9899	209
210	0.0114 1214	0.0124 3692	0.0134 9350	0.0145 7838	0.0156 8818	210
211	0.0113 9621	0.0124 2234	0.0134 8027	0.0145 6647	0.0156 7755	211
212	0.0113 8048	0.0124 0795	0.0134 6723	0.0145 5475	0.0156 6709	212
213	0.0113 6494	0.0123 9376	0.0134 5438	0.0145 4320	0.0156 5680	213
214	0.0113 4961	0.0123 7976	0.0134 4171	0.0145 3183	0.0156 4668	214
215	0.0113 3446	0.0123 6594	0.0134 2922	0.0145 2064	0.0156 3672	215
216	0.0113 1950	0.0123 5231	0.0134 1691	0.0145 0961	0.0156 2691	216
217	0.0113 0473	0.0123 3886	0.0134 0477	0.0144 9874	0.0156 1727	217
218	0.0112 9015	0.0123 2559	0.0133 9280	0.0144 8804	0.0156 0778	218
219	0.0112 7575	0.0123 1250	0.0133 8100	0.0144 7750	0.0155 9844	219
220	0.0112 6152	0.0122 9957	0.0133 6937	0.0144 6712	0.0155 8924	220
221	0.0112 4747	0.0122 8682	0.0133 5790	0.0144 5689	0.0155 8020	221
222	0.0112 3360	0.0122 7424	0.0133 4659	0.0144 4682	0.0155 7130	222
223	0.0112 1989	0.0122 6182	0.0133 3544	0.0144 3690	0.0155 6254	223
224	0.0112 0636	0.0122 4956	0.0133 2445	0.0144 2712	0.0155 5392	224
225	0.0111 9299	0.0122 3746	0.0133 1360	0.0144 1749	0.0155 4544	225
226	0.0111 7979	0.0122 2553	0.0133 0292	0.0144 0800	0.0155 3709	226
227	0.0111 6674	0.0122 1374	0.0132 9237	0.0143 9866	0.0155 2887	227
228	0.0111 5386	0.0122 0211	0.0132 8198	0.0143 8945	0.0155 2078	228
229	0.0111 4113	0.0121 9064	0.0132 7173	0.0143 8038	0.0155 1282	229
230	0.0111 2856	0.0121 7931	0.0132 6162	0.0143 7144	0.0155 0499	230
231	0.0111 1613	0.0121 6813	0.0132 5165	0.0143 6264	0.0154 9728	231
232	0.0111 0386	0.0121 5709	0.0132 4182	0.0143 5396	0.0154 8969	232
233	0.0110 9174	0.0121 4619	0.0132 3213	0.0143 4542	0.0154 8222	233
234	0.0110 7976	0.0121 3544	0.0132 2257	0.0143 3700	0.0154 7487	234
235	0.0110 6793	0.0121 2482	0.0132 1314	0.0143 2870	0.0154 6763	235
236	0.0110 5624	0.0121 1434	0.0132 0384	0.0143 2052	0.0154 6051	236
237	0.0110 4469	0.0121 0400	0.0131 9467	0.0143 1247	0.0154 5350	237
238	0.0110 3328	0.0120 9378	0.0131 8562	0.0143 0453	0.0154 4660	238
239	0.0110 2200	0.0120 8370	0.0131 7670	0.0142 9671	0.0154 3980	239
240	0.0110 1086	0.0120 7375	0.0131 6790	0.0142 8901	0.0154 3312	240

TABLE V

N	1	1 1/8	1 1/4	1 3/8	1 1/2	N
241	0.0109 9985	0.0120 6392	0.0131 5922	0.0142 8141	0.0154 2653	241
242	0.0109 8897	0.0120 5422	0.0131 5065	0.0142 7393	0.0154 2005	242
243	0.0109 7822	0.0120 4464	0.0131 4221	0.0142 6656	0.0154 1367	243
244	0.0109 6760	0.0120 3518	0.0131 3388	0.0142 5929	0.0154 0739	244
245	0.0109 5710	0.0120 2584	0.0131 2566	0.0142 5213	0.0154 0121	245
246	0.0109 4673	0.0120 1663	0.0131 1755	0.0142 4508	0.0153 9513	246
247	0.0109 3648	0.0120 0752	0.0131 0956	0.0142 3812	0.0153 8914	247
248	0.0109 2635	0.0119 9853	0.0131 0167	0.0142 3127	0.0153 8324	248
249	0.0109 1634	0.0119 8966	0.0130 9389	0.0142 2452	0.0153 7743	249
250	0.0109 0644	0.0119 8090	0.0130 8621	0.0142 1786	0.0153 7172	250
251	0.0108 9666	0.0119 7224	0.0130 7864	0.0142 1130	0.0153 6609	251
252	0.0108 8700	0.0119 6370	0.0130 7117	0.0142 0484	0.0153 6055	252
253	0.0108 7744	0.0119 5526	0.0130 6380	0.0141 9847	0.0153 5509	253
254	0.0108 6800	0.0119 4693	0.0130 5653	0.0141 9219	0.0153 4972	254
255	0.0108 5867	0.0119 3870	0.0130 4936	0.0141 8600	0.0153 4444	255
256	0.0108 4945	0.0119 3058	0.0130 4228	0.0141 7990	0.0153 3923	256
257	0.0108 4033	0.0119 2255	0.0130 3530	0.0141 7389	0.0153 3411	257
258	0.0108 3132	0.0119 1463	0.0130 2841	0.0141 6797	0.0153 2906	258
259	0.0108 2241	0.0119 0680	0.0130 2162	0.0141 6213	0.0153 2409	259
260	0.0108 1360	0.0118 9907	0.0130 1491	0.0141 5637	0.0153 1920	260
261	0.0108 0490	0.0118 9144	0.0130 0830	0.0141 5070	0.0153 1439	261
262	0.0107 9630	0.0118 8390	0.0130 0177	0.0141 4511	0.0153 0964	262
263	0.0107 8779	0.0118 7646	0.0129 9533	0.0141 3960	0.0153 0497	263
264	0.0107 7938	0.0118 6911	0.0129 8897	0.0141 3417	0.0153 0038	264
265	0.0107 7107	0.0118 6184	0.0129 8270	0.0141 2881	0.0152 9585	265
266	0.0107 6286	0.0118 5467	0.0129 7652	0.0141 2354	0.0152 9139	266
267	0.0107 5473	0.0118 4759	0.0129 7041	0.0141 1833	0.0152 8700	267
268	0.0107 4670	0.0118 4059	0.0129 6439	0.0141 1321	0.0152 8268	268
269	0.0107 3876	0.0118 3368	0.0129 5845	0.0141 0815	0.0152 7843	269
270	0.0107 3091	0.0118 2685	0.0129 5258	0.0141 0317	0.0152 7424	270
271	0.0107 2315	0.0118 2011	0.0129 4680	0.0140 9826	0.0152 7011	271
272	0.0107 1548	0.0118 1345	0.0129 4108	0.0140 9342	0.0152 6605	272
273	0.0107 0790	0.0118 0687	0.0129 3545	0.0140 8864	0.0152 6205	273
274	0.0107 0040	0.0118 0037	0.0129 2989	0.0140 8394	0.0152 5811	274
275	0.0106 9298	0.0117 9395	0.0129 2440	0.0140 7930	0.0152 5423	275
276	0.0106 8565	0.0117 8761	0.0129 1899	0.0140 7473	0.0152 5041	276
277	0.0106 7840	0.0117 8135	0.0129 1364	0.0140 7022	0.0152 4665	277
278	0.0106 7123	0.0117 7516	0.0129 0837	0.0140 6578	0.0152 4295	278
279	0.0106 6414	0.0117 6905	0.0129 0316	0.0140 6140	0.0152 3930	279
280	0.0106 5714	0.0117 6301	0.0128 9803	0.0140 5708	0.0152 3571	280
281	0.0106 5021	0.0117 5705	0.0128 9296	0.0140 5282	0.0152 3217	281
282	0.0106 4336	0.0117 5116	0.0128 8796	0.0140 4863	0.0152 2869	282
283	0.0106 3658	0.0117 4534	0.0128 8302	0.0140 4449	0.0152 2526	283
284	0.0106 2988	0.0117 3959	0.0128 7815	0.0140 4041	0.0152 2188	284
285	0.0106 2326	0.0117 3391	0.0128 7334	0.0140 3639	0.0152 1855	285
286	0.0106 1670	0.0117 2829	0.0128 6860	0.0140 3243	0.0152 1527	286
287	0.0106 1023	0.0117 2275	0.0128 6391	0.0140 2852	0.0152 1205	287
288	0.0106 0382	0.0117 1727	0.0128 5929	0.0140 2466	0.0152 0887	288
289	0.0105 9748	0.0117 1186	0.0128 5473	0.0140 2087	0.0152 0574	289
290	0.0105 9122	0.0117 0651	0.0128 5023	0.0140 1712	0.0152 0266	290
291	0.0105 8502	0.0117 0123	0.0128 4579	0.0140 1343	0.0151 9962	291
292	0.0105 7889	0.0116 9601	0.0128 4140	0.0140 0979	0.0151 9664	292
293	0.0105 7283	0.0116 9085	0.0128 3707	0.0140 0620	0.0151 9369	293
294	0.0105 6684	0.0116 8576	0.0128 3280	0.0140 0266	0.0151 9079	294
295	0.0105 6091	0.0116 8073	0.0128 2858	0.0139 9917	0.0151 8794	295
296	0.0105 5505	0.0116 7575	0.0128 2442	0.0139 9573	0.0151 8513	296
297	0.0105 4925	0.0116 7084	0.0128 2031	0.0139 9234	0.0151 8236	297
298	0.0105 4352	0.0116 6599	0.0128 1626	0.0139 8899	0.0151 7963	298
299	0.0105 3785	0.0116 6119	0.0128 1226	0.0139 8570	0.0151 7694	299
300	0.0105 3224	0.0116 5645	0.0128 0831	0.0139 8245	0.0151 7430	300

TABLE V

N	1	1 1/8	1 1/4	1 3/8	1 1/2	N
301	0.0105 2669	0.0116 5177	0.0128 0441	0.0139 7924	0.0151 7169	301
302	0.0105 2121	0.0116 4714	0.0128 0056	0.0139 7608	0.0151 6913	302
303	0.0105 1578	0.0116 4257	0.0127 9676	0.0139 7296	0.0151 6660	303
304	0.0105 1041	0.0116 3805	0.0127 9301	0.0139 6989	0.0151 6411	304
305	0.0105 0510	0.0116 3358	0.0127 8931	0.0139 6686	0.0151 6166	305
306	0.0104 9985	0.0116 2917	0.0127 8566	0.0139 6388	0.0151 5925	306
307	0.0104 9466	0.0116 2481	0.0127 8205	0.0139 6093	0.0151 5687	307
308	0.0104 8952	0.0116 2051	0.0127 7849	0.0139 5803	0.0151 5453	308
309	0.0104 8444	0.0116 1625	0.0127 7498	0.0139 5516	0.0151 5222	309
310	0.0104 7941	0.0116 1205	0.0127 7151	0.0139 5234	0.0151 4995	310
311	0.0104 7444	0.0116 0789	0.0127 6808	0.0139 4955	0.0151 4771	311
312	0.0104 6952	0.0116 0378	0.0127 6470	0.0139 4681	0.0151 4551	312
313	0.0104 6466	0.0115 9972	0.0127 6137	0.0139 4410	0.0151 4333	313
314	0.0104 5985	0.0115 9571	0.0127 5807	0.0139 4143	0.0151 4120	314
315	0.0104 5509	0.0115 9175	0.0127 5482	0.0139 3880	0.0151 3909	315
316	0.0104 5038	0.0115 8784	0.0127 5161	0.0139 3620	0.0151 3702	316
317	0.0104 4572	0.0115 8397	0.0127 4845	0.0139 3365	0.0151 3497	317
318	0.0104 4111	0.0115 8014	0.0127 4532	0.0139 3112	0.0151 3296	318
319	0.0104 3655	0.0115 7636	0.0127 4223	0.0139 2863	0.0151 3098	319
320	0.0104 3205	0.0115 7263	0.0127 3918	0.0139 2618	0.0151 2903	320
321	0.0104 2759	0.0115 6894	0.0127 3617	0.0139 2376	0.0151 2710	321
322	0.0104 2317	0.0115 6529	0.0127 3320	0.0139 2137	0.0151 2521	322
323	0.0104 1881	0.0115 6168	0.0127 3027	0.0139 1902	0.0151 2334	323
324	0.0104 1449	0.0115 5812	0.0127 2738	0.0139 1670	0.0151 2151	324
325	0.0104 1022	0.0115 5460	0.0127 2452	0.0139 1441	0.0151 1970	325
326	0.0104 0599	0.0115 5112	0.0127 2170	0.0139 1216	0.0151 1791	326
327	0.0104 0181	0.0115 4768	0.0127 1891	0.0139 0993	0.0151 1616	327
328	0.0103 9767	0.0115 4428	0.0127 1617	0.0139 0774	0.0151 1443	328
329	0.0103 9358	0.0115 4093	0.0127 1345	0.0139 0557	0.0151 1272	329
330	0.0103 8953	0.0115 3761	0.0127 1077	0.0139 0344	0.0151 1105	330
331	0.0103 8553	0.0115 3433	0.0127 0813	0.0139 0134	0.0151 0939	331
332	0.0103 8156	0.0115 3108	0.0127 0551	0.0138 9926	0.0151 0776	332
333	0.0103 7764	0.0115 2788	0.0127 0294	0.0138 9721	0.0151 0616	333
334	0.0103 7376	0.0115 2471	0.0127 0039	0.0138 9520	0.0151 0458	334
335	0.0103 6993	0.0115 2158	0.0126 9788	0.0138 9321	0.0151 0302	335
336	0.0103 6613	0.0115 1849	0.0126 9540	0.0138 9124	0.0151 0149	336
337	0.0103 6237	0.0115 1543	0.0126 9295	0.0138 8931	0.0150 9998	337
338	0.0103 5866	0.0115 1241	0.0126 9053	0.0138 8740	0.0150 9849	338
339	0.0103 5498	0.0115 0942	0.0126 8814	0.0138 8552	0.0150 9703	339
340	0.0103 5134	0.0115 0647	0.0126 8578	0.0138 8366	0.0150 9559	340
341	0.0103 4774	0.0115 0355	0.0126 8346	0.0138 8183	0.0150 9416	341
342	0.0103 4418	0.0115 0067	0.0126 8116	0.0138 8003	0.0150 9276	342
343	0.0103 4066	0.0114 9782	0.0126 7889	0.0138 7825	0.0150 9139	343
344	0.0103 3717	0.0114 9500	0.0126 7665	0.0138 7649	0.0150 9003	344
345	0.0103 3372	0.0114 9222	0.0126 7444	0.0138 7476	0.0150 8869	345
346	0.0103 3031	0.0114 8947	0.0126 7226	0.0138 7305	0.0150 8737	346
347	0.0103 2693	0.0114 8675	0.0126 7010	0.0138 7137	0.0150 8607	347
348	0.0103 2359	0.0114 8406	0.0126 6797	0.0138 6971	0.0150 8479	348
349	0.0103 2028	0.0114 8140	0.0126 6587	0.0138 6807	0.0150 8353	349
350	0.0103 1701	0.0114 7877	0.0126 6380	0.0138 6646	0.0150 8229	350
351	0.0103 1377	0.0114 7618	0.0126 6175	0.0138 6486	0.0150 8107	351
352	0.0103 1057	0.0114 7361	0.0126 5973	0.0138 6329	0.0150 7986	352
353	0.0103 0740	0.0114 7108	0.0126 5773	0.0138 6174	0.0150 7868	353
354	0.0103 0426	0.0114 6857	0.0126 5576	0.0138 6022	0.0150 7751	354
355	0.0103 0116	0.0114 6609	0.0126 5381	0.0138 5871	0.0150 7636	355
356	0.0102 9809	0.0114 6364	0.0126 5189	0.0138 5722	0.0150 7522	356
357	0.0102 9505	0.0114 6122	0.0126 4999	0.0138 5576	0.0150 7411	357
358	0.0102 9205	0.0114 5883	0.0126 4812	0.0138 5431	0.0150 7301	358
359	0.0102 8907	0.0114 5646	0.0126 4627	0.0138 5289	0.0150 7192	359
360	0.0102 8613	0.0114 5412	0.0126 4444	0.0138 5148	0.0150 7085	360

TABLE V

N	1 5/8	1 3/4	1 7/8	2	2 1/8	N
1	1.0162 5000	1.0175 0000	1.0187 5000	1.0200 0000	1.0212 5000	1
2	0.5122 2024	0.5131 6295	0.5141 0604	0.5150 4950	0.5159 9335	2
3	0.3442 2487	0.3450 6746	0.3459 1073	0.3467 5467	0.3475 9929	3
4	0.2602 3810	0.2610 3237	0.2618 2759	0.2626 2375	0.2634 2087	4
5	0.2098 5476	0.2106 2142	0.2113 8930	0.2121 5839	0.2129 2870	5
6	0.1762 7314	0.1770 2256	0.1777 7345	0.1785 2581	0.1792 7965	6
7	0.1522 9250	0.1530 3059	0.1537 7040	0.1545 1196	0.1552 5524	7
8	0.1343 1247	0.1350 4292	0.1357 7537	0.1365 0980	0.1372 4622	8
9	0.1203 3285	0.1210 5813	0.1217 8566	0.1225 1544	0.1232 4745	9
10	0.1091 5351	0.1098 7534	0.1105 9969	0.1113 2653	0.1120 5586	10
11	0.1000 1073	0.1007 3038	0.1014 5278	0.1021 7794	0.1029 0585	11
12	0.0923 9537	0.0931 1377	0.0938 3518	0.0945 5960	0.0952 8701	12
13	0.0859 5496	0.0866 7283	0.0873 9396	0.0881 1835	0.0888 4599	13
14	0.0804 3771	0.0811 5562	0.0818 7704	0.0826 0197	0.0833 3039	14
15	0.0756 5898	0.0763 7739	0.0770 9955	0.0778 2547	0.0785 5513	15
16	0.0714 8031	0.0721 9958	0.0729 2285	0.0736 5013	0.0743 8139	16
17	0.0677 9580	0.0685 1623	0.0692 4091	0.0699 6984	0.0707 0301	17
18	0.0645 2309	0.0652 4492	0.0659 7127	0.0667 0210	0.0674 3742	18
19	0.0615 9715	0.0623 2061	0.0630 4882	0.0637 8177	0.0645 1944	19
20	0.0589 6597	0.0596 9122	0.0604 2148	0.0611 5672	0.0618 9692	20
21	0.0565 8743	0.0573 1464	0.0580 4709	0.0587 8477	0.0595 2765	21
22	0.0544 2709	0.0551 5638	0.0558 9116	0.0566 3140	0.0573 7709	22
23	0.0524 5648	0.0531 8796	0.0539 2517	0.0546 6810	0.0554 1671	23
24	0.0506 5188	0.0513 8565	0.0521 2540	0.0528 7110	0.0536 2272	24
25	0.0489 9336	0.0497 2952	0.0504 7188	0.0512 2044	0.0519 7515	25
26	0.0474 6408	0.0482 0269	0.0489 4775	0.0496 9923	0.0504 5711	26
27	0.0460 4967	0.0467 9079	0.0475 3861	0.0482 9309	0.0490 5419	27
28	0.0447 3781	0.0454 8151	0.0462 3215	0.0469 8967	0.0477 5405	28
29	0.0435 1791	0.0442 6424	0.0450 1773	0.0457 7836	0.0465 4606	29
30	0.0423 8075	0.0431 2975	0.0438 8616	0.0446 4992	0.0454 2100	30
31	0.0413 1834	0.0420 7005	0.0428 2941	0.0435 9635	0.0443 7083	31
32	0.0403 2365	0.0410 7812	0.0418 4046	0.0426 1061	0.0433 8852	32
33	0.0393 9054	0.0401 4779	0.0409 1314	0.0416 8653	0.0424 6791	33
34	0.0385 1357	0.0392 7363	0.0400 4202	0.0408 1867	0.0416 0354	34
35	0.0376 8792	0.0384 5082	0.0392 2227	0.0400 0221	0.0407 9058	35
36	0.0369 0931	0.0376 7507	0.0384 4960	0.0392 3285	0.0400 2475	36
37	0.0361 7393	0.0369 4257	0.0377 2021	0.0385 0678	0.0393 0221	37
38	0.0354 7837	0.0362 4990	0.0370 3066	0.0378 2057	0.0386 1955	38
39	0.0348 1955	0.0355 9399	0.0363 7788	0.0371 7114	0.0379 7369	39
40	0.0341 9472	0.0349 7209	0.0357 5913	0.0365 5575	0.0373 6186	40
41	0.0336 0140	0.0343 8170	0.0351 7190	0.0359 7188	0.0367 8157	41
42	0.0330 3732	0.0338 2057	0.0346 1393	0.0354 1729	0.0362 3056	42
43	0.0325 0045	0.0332 8666	0.0340 8319	0.0348 8993	0.0357 0679	43
44	0.0319 8893	0.0327 7810	0.0335 7781	0.0343 8794	0.0352 0838	44
45	0.0315 0106	0.0322 9321	0.0330 9610	0.0339 0962	0.0347 3364	45
46	0.0310 3531	0.0318 3043	0.0326 3651	0.0334 5342	0.0342 8103	46
47	0.0305 9025	0.0313 8836	0.0321 9763	0.0330 1792	0.0338 4912	47
48	0.0301 6460	0.0309 6569	0.0317 7815	0.0326 0184	0.0334 3661	48
49	0.0297 5716	0.0305 6124	0.0313 7689	0.0322 0396	0.0330 4231	49
50	0.0293 6684	0.0301 7391	0.0309 9275	0.0318 2321	0.0326 6513	50
51	0.0289 9263	0.0298 0269	0.0306 2472	0.0314 5856	0.0323 0405	51
52	0.0286 3360	0.0294 4665	0.0302 7187	0.0311 0909	0.0319 5813	52
53	0.0282 8888	0.0291 0492	0.0299 3333	0.0307 7392	0.0316 2652	53
54	0.0279 5769	0.0287 7672	0.0296 0830	0.0304 5226	0.0313 0841	54
55	0.0276 3927	0.0284 6129	0.0292 9605	0.0301 4337	0.0310 0305	55
56	0.0273 3294	0.0281 5795	0.0289 9589	0.0298 4656	0.0307 0977	56
57	0.0270 3807	0.0278 6606	0.0287 0717	0.0295 6120	0.0304 2792	57
58	0.0267 5406	0.0275 8503	0.0284 2931	0.0292 8667	0.0301 5690	58
59	0.0264 8036	0.0273 1430	0.0281 6174	0.0290 2243	0.0298 9616	59
60	0.0262 1645	0.0270 5336	0.0279 0395	0.0287 6797	0.0296 4518	60

TABLE V

N	1 5/8	1 3/4	1 7/8	2	2 1/8	N
61	0.0259 6184	0.0268 0172	0.0276 5545	0.0285 2278	0.0294 0347	61
62	0.0257 1608	0.0265 5892	0.0274 1579	0.0282 8643	0.0291 7057	62
63	0.0254 7875	0.0263 2455	0.0271 8455	0.0280 5848	0.0289 4608	63
64	0.0252 4946	0.0260 9821	0.0269 6133	0.0278 3855	0.0287 2957	64
65	0.0250 2782	0.0258 7952	0.0267 4575	0.0276 2624	0.0285 2069	65
66	0.0248 1350	0.0256 6813	0.0265 3747	0.0274 2122	0.0283 1907	66
67	0.0246 0615	0.0254 6372	0.0263 3616	0.0272 2316	0.0281 2440	67
68	0.0244 0548	0.0252 6597	0.0261 4149	0.0270 3173	0.0279 3635	68
69	0.0242 1118	0.0250 7459	0.0259 5319	0.0268 4665	0.0277 5463	69
70	0.0240 2299	0.0248 8930	0.0257 7097	0.0266 6765	0.0275 7897	70
71	0.0238 4064	0.0247 0985	0.0255 9458	0.0264 9446	0.0274 0911	71
72	0.0236 6388	0.0245 3600	0.0254 2377	0.0263 2683	0.0272 4480	72
73	0.0234 9250	0.0243 6750	0.0252 5830	0.0261 6454	0.0270 8580	73
74	0.0233 2626	0.0242 0413	0.0250 9796	0.0260 0736	0.0269 3190	74
75	0.0231 6496	0.0240 4570	0.0249 4254	0.0258 5508	0.0267 8289	75
76	0.0230 0840	0.0238 9200	0.0247 9185	0.0257 0751	0.0266 3857	76
77	0.0228 5640	0.0237 4285	0.0246 4568	0.0255 6447	0.0264 9875	77
78	0.0227 0877	0.0235 9806	0.0245 0387	0.0254 2576	0.0263 6326	78
79	0.0225 6536	0.0234 5748	0.0243 6625	0.0252 9123	0.0262 3192	79
80	0.0224 2600	0.0233 2093	0.0242 3266	0.0251 6071	0.0261 0457	80
81	0.0222 9053	0.0231 8828	0.0241 0294	0.0250 3405	0.0259 8107	81
82	0.0221 5882	0.0230 5936	0.0239 7696	0.0249 1110	0.0258 6126	82
83	0.0220 3073	0.0229 3406	0.0238 5457	0.0247 9173	0.0257 4502	83
84	0.0219 0612	0.0228 1223	0.0237 3564	0.0246 7581	0.0256 3220	84
85	0.0217 8487	0.0226 9375	0.0236 2004	0.0245 6321	0.0255 2268	85
86	0.0216 6687	0.0225 7850	0.0235 0767	0.0244 5381	0.0254 1634	86
87	0.0215 5199	0.0224 6636	0.0233 9839	0.0243 4750	0.0253 1308	87
88	0.0214 4013	0.0223 5724	0.0232 9212	0.0242 4416	0.0252 1277	88
89	0.0213 3119	0.0222 5102	0.0231 8873	0.0241 4370	0.0251 1531	89
90	0.0212 2506	0.0221 4760	0.0230 8813	0.0240 4602	0.0250 2061	90
91	0.0211 2166	0.0220 4690	0.0229 9023	0.0239 5101	0.0249 2857	91
92	0.0210 2089	0.0219 4882	0.0228 9494	0.0238 5859	0.0248 3910	92
93	0.0209 2267	0.0218 5327	0.0228 0217	0.0237 6868	0.0247 5211	93
94	0.0208 2691	0.0217 6017	0.0227 1183	0.0236 8118	0.0246 6752	94
95	0.0207 3353	0.0216 6944	0.0226 2385	0.0235 9602	0.0245 8525	95
96	0.0206 4246	0.0215 8101	0.0225 3814	0.0235 1313	0.0245 0522	96
97	0.0205 5362	0.0214 9480	0.0224 5465	0.0234 3242	0.0244 2735	97
98	0.0204 6695	0.0214 1074	0.0223 7329	0.0233 5383	0.0243 5159	98
99	0.0203 8237	0.0213 2876	0.0222 9400	0.0232 7729	0.0242 7786	99
100	0.0202 9983	0.0212 4880	0.0222 1671	0.0232 0274	0.0242 0609	100
101	0.0202 1925	0.0211 7080	0.0221 4137	0.0231 3012	0.0241 3623	101
102	0.0201 4059	0.0210 9470	0.0220 6790	0.0230 5935	0.0240 6821	102
103	0.0200 6378	0.0210 2044	0.0219 9626	0.0229 9040	0.0240 0197	103
104	0.0199 8876	0.0209 4796	0.0219 2640	0.0229 2319	0.0239 3747	104
105	0.0199 1549	0.0208 7721	0.0218 5824	0.0228 5768	0.0238 7464	105
106	0.0198 4392	0.0208 0815	0.0217 9176	0.0227 9382	0.0238 1344	106
107	0.0197 7399	0.0207 4072	0.0217 2688	0.0227 3156	0.0237 5381	107
108	0.0197 0566	0.0206 7487	0.0216 6358	0.0226 7085	0.0236 9572	108
109	0.0196 3888	0.0206 1056	0.0216 0180	0.0226 1164	0.0236 3911	109
110	0.0195 7360	0.0205 4774	0.0215 4150	0.0225 5389	0.0235 8393	110
111	0.0195 0980	0.0204 8638	0.0214 8263	0.0224 9756	0.0235 3016	111
112	0.0194 4742	0.0204 2643	0.0214 2516	0.0224 4261	0.0234 7774	112
113	0.0193 8642	0.0203 6785	0.0213 6905	0.0223 8899	0.0234 2664	113
114	0.0193 2677	0.0203 1060	0.0213 1426	0.0223 3668	0.0233 7681	114
115	0.0192 6844	0.0202 5465	0.0212 6074	0.0222 8563	0.0233 2823	115
116	0.0192 1138	0.0201 9997	0.0212 0847	0.0222 3580	0.0232 8085	116
117	0.0191 5556	0.0201 4651	0.0211 5741	0.0221 8717	0.0232 3465	117
118	0.0191 0095	0.0200 9424	0.0211 0754	0.0221 3969	0.0231 8958	118
119	0.0190 4751	0.0200 4314	0.0210 5880	0.0220 9335	0.0231 4563	119
120	0.0189 9522	0.0199 9317	0.0210 1118	0.0220 4810	0.0231 0274	120

TABLE V

N	1 5/8	1 3/4	1 7/8	2	2 1/8	N
121	0.0189 4405	0.0199 4430	0.0209 6465	0.0220 0391	0.0230 6091	121
122	0.0188 9396	0.0198 9650	0.0209 1918	0.0219 6077	0.0230 2009	122
123	0.0188 4493	0.0198 4975	0.0208 7473	0.0219 1864	0.0229 8026	123
124	0.0187 9693	0.0198 0402	0.0208 3128	0.0218 7748	0.0229 4139	124
125	0.0187 4994	0.0197 5927	0.0207 8881	0.0218 3729	0.0229 0345	125
126	0.0187 0393	0.0197 1550	0.0207 4729	0.0217 9802	0.0228 6643	126
127	0.0186 5888	0.0196 7266	0.0207 0669	0.0217 5967	0.0228 3030	127
128	0.0186 1475	0.0196 3074	0.0206 6700	0.0217 2219	0.0227 9502	128
129	0.0185 7154	0.0195 8972	0.0206 2818	0.0216 8558	0.0227 6059	129
130	0.0185 2921	0.0195 4957	0.0205 9022	0.0216 4980	0.0227 2697	130
131	0.0184 8775	0.0195 1027	0.0205 5310	0.0216 1484	0.0226 9415	131
132	0.0184 4713	0.0194 7180	0.0205 1678	0.0215 8067	0.0226 6211	132
133	0.0184 0733	0.0194 3414	0.0204 8126	0.0215 4728	0.0226 3081	133
134	0.0183 6834	0.0193 9727	0.0204 4652	0.0215 1465	0.0226 0026	134
135	0.0183 3013	0.0193 6117	0.0204 1252	0.0214 8275	0.0225 7041	135
136	0.0182 9269	0.0193 2582	0.0203 7927	0.0214 5156	0.0225 4127	136
137	0.0182 5599	0.0192 9120	0.0203 4673	0.0214 2108	0.0225 1280	137
138	0.0182 2003	0.0192 5730	0.0203 1489	0.0213 9127	0.0224 8500	138
139	0.0181 8477	0.0192 2410	0.0202 8373	0.0213 6214	0.0224 5784	139
140	0.0181 5022	0.0191 9158	0.0202 5324	0.0213 3365	0.0224 3131	140
141	0.0181 1634	0.0191 5973	0.0202 2340	0.0213 0579	0.0224 0540	141
142	0.0180 8313	0.0191 2852	0.0201 9419	0.0212 7855	0.0223 8008	142
143	0.0180 5057	0.0190 9796	0.0201 6560	0.0212 5191	0.0223 5534	143
144	0.0180 1865	0.0190 6801	0.0201 3762	0.0212 2586	0.0223 3117	144
145	0.0179 8734	0.0190 3867	0.0201 1023	0.0212 0038	0.0223 0755	145
146	0.0179 5665	0.0190 0993	0.0200 8341	0.0211 7546	0.0222 8448	146
147	0.0179 2654	0.0189 8176	0.0200 5716	0.0211 5109	0.0222 6193	147
148	0.0178 9702	0.0189 5415	0.0200 3146	0.0211 2724	0.0222 3989	148
149	0.0178 6806	0.0189 2710	0.0200 0629	0.0211 0392	0.0222 1835	149
150	0.0178 3965	0.0189 0060	0.0199 8165	0.0210 8110	0.0221 9730	150
151	0.0178 1179	0.0188 7461	0.0199 5752	0.0210 5878	0.0221 7673	151
152	0.0177 8446	0.0188 4915	0.0199 3390	0.0210 3695	0.0221 5663	152
153	0.0177 5765	0.0188 2419	0.0199 1076	0.0210 1558	0.0221 3698	153
154	0.0177 3134	0.0187 9972	0.0198 8810	0.0209 9468	0.0221 1777	154
155	0.0177 0553	0.0187 7574	0.0198 6590	0.0209 7423	0.0220 9899	155
156	0.0176 8021	0.0187 5223	0.0198 4417	0.0209 5421	0.0220 8063	156
157	0.0176 5536	0.0187 2918	0.0198 2288	0.0209 3463	0.0220 6269	157
158	0.0176 3098	0.0187 0658	0.0198 0202	0.0209 1546	0.0220 4514	158
159	0.0176 0706	0.0186 8442	0.0197 8160	0.0208 9671	0.0220 2799	159
160	0.0175 8358	0.0186 6270	0.0197 6158	0.0208 7835	0.0220 1123	160
161	0.0175 6053	0.0186 4140	0.0197 4198	0.0208 6039	0.0219 9483	161
162	0.0175 3792	0.0186 2051	0.0197 2278	0.0208 4281	0.0219 7880	162
163	0.0175 1572	0.0186 0003	0.0197 0396	0.0208 2560	0.0219 6313	163
164	0.0174 9393	0.0185 7994	0.0196 8553	0.0208 0876	0.0219 4780	164
165	0.0174 7254	0.0185 6024	0.0196 6747	0.0207 9227	0.0219 3281	165
166	0.0174 5155	0.0185 4092	0.0196 4977	0.0207 7613	0.0219 1816	166
167	0.0174 3094	0.0185 2197	0.0196 3243	0.0207 6034	0.0219 0383	167
168	0.0174 1071	0.0185 0339	0.0196 1544	0.0207 4487	0.0218 8981	168
169	0.0173 9084	0.0184 8516	0.0195 9879	0.0207 2973	0.0218 7611	169
170	0.0173 7134	0.0184 6728	0.0195 8248	0.0207 1491	0.0218 6271	170
171	0.0173 5220	0.0184 4974	0.0195 6649	0.0207 0041	0.0218 4960	171
172	0.0173 3340	0.0184 3254	0.0195 5082	0.0206 8620	0.0218 3678	172
173	0.0173 1494	0.0184 1566	0.0195 3546	0.0206 7229	0.0218 2424	173
174	0.0172 9681	0.0183 9910	0.0195 2041	0.0206 5868	0.0218 1197	174
175	0.0172 7901	0.0183 8286	0.0195 0566	0.0206 4535	0.0217 9998	175
176	0.0172 6154	0.0183 6692	0.0194 9120	0.0206 3229	0.0217 8824	176
177	0.0172 4437	0.0183 5128	0.0194 7703	0.0206 1951	0.0217 7677	177
178	0.0172 2751	0.0183 3594	0.0194 6314	0.0206 0699	0.0217 6554	178
179	0.0172 1096	0.0183 2089	0.0194 4953	0.0205 9474	0.0217 5456	179
180	0.0171 9470	0.0183 0612	0.0194 3618	0.0205 8274	0.0217 4381	180

TABLE V

N	1 5/8	1 3/4	1 7/8	2	2 1/8	N
181	0.0171 7873	0.0182 9163	0.0194 2310	0.0205 7098	0.0217 3330	181
182	0.0171 6305	0.0182 7741	0.0194 1027	0.0205 5948	0.0217 2302	182
183	0.0171 4764	0.0182 6346	0.0193 9770	0.0205 4820	0.0217 1297	183
184	0.0171 3251	0.0182 4976	0.0193 8538	0.0205 3717	0.0217 0313	184
185	0.0171 1764	0.0182 3633	0.0193 7329	0.0205 2636	0.0216 9350	185
186	0.0171 0304	0.0182 2314	0.0193 6145	0.0205 1577	0.0216 8409	186
187	0.0170 8870	0.0182 1020	0.0193 4984	0.0205 0540	0.0216 7487	187
188	0.0170 7460	0.0181 9749	0.0193 3845	0.0204 9525	0.0216 6586	188
189	0.0170 6076	0.0181 8503	0.0193 2729	0.0204 8530	0.0216 5704	189
190	0.0170 4716	0.0181 7279	0.0193 1634	0.0204 7556	0.0216 4841	190
191	0.0170 3380	0.0181 6079	0.0193 0561	0.0204 6602	0.0216 3997	191
192	0.0170 2067	0.0181 4900	0.0192 9508	0.0204 5667	0.0216 3171	192
193	0.0170 0777	0.0181 3743	0.0192 8477	0.0204 4751	0.0216 2363	193
194	0.0169 9510	0.0181 2608	0.0192 7465	0.0204 3855	0.0216 1572	194
195	0.0169 8265	0.0181 1493	0.0192 6473	0.0204 2976	0.0216 0798	195
196	0.0169 7042	0.0181 0399	0.0192 5500	0.0204 2116	0.0216 0041	196
197	0.0169 5839	0.0180 9325	0.0192 4546	0.0204 1273	0.0215 9300	197
198	0.0169 4658	0.0180 8270	0.0192 3610	0.0204 0447	0.0215 8575	198
199	0.0169 3497	0.0180 7236	0.0192 2693	0.0203 9639	0.0215 7866	199
200	0.0169 2357	0.0180 6219	0.0192 1793	0.0203 8846	0.0215 7171	200
201	0.0169 1236	0.0180 5222	0.0192 0911	0.0203 8070	0.0215 6492	201
202	0.0169 0134	0.0180 4243	0.0192 0046	0.0203 7310	0.0215 5827	202
203	0.0168 9052	0.0180 3282	0.0191 9197	0.0203 6565	0.0215 5177	203
204	0.0168 7988	0.0180 2338	0.0191 8365	0.0203 5835	0.0215 4540	204
205	0.0168 6942	0.0180 1411	0.0191 7548	0.0203 5120	0.0215 3917	205
206	0.0168 5914	0.0180 0501	0.0191 6748	0.0203 4420	0.0215 3307	206
207	0.0168 4905	0.0179 9608	0.0191 5963	0.0203 3733	0.0215 2711	207
208	0.0168 3912	0.0179 8731	0.0191 5193	0.0203 3061	0.0215 2127	208
209	0.0168 2936	0.0179 7870	0.0191 4437	0.0203 2402	0.0215 1555	209
210	0.0168 1977	0.0179 7025	0.0191 3697	0.0203 1757	0.0215 0996	210
211	0.0168 1035	0.0179 6195	0.0191 2970	0.0203 1124	0.0215 0449	211
212	0.0168 0109	0.0179 5379	0.0191 2257	0.0203 0505	0.0214 9913	212
213	0.0167 9198	0.0179 4579	0.0191 1558	0.0202 9898	0.0214 9388	213
214	0.0167 8303	0.0179 3793	0.0191 0872	0.0202 9303	0.0214 8875	214
215	0.0167 7423	0.0179 3022	0.0191 0200	0.0202 8720	0.0214 8373	215
216	0.0167 6558	0.0179 2264	0.0190 9540	0.0202 8149	0.0214 7881	216
217	0.0167 5708	0.0179 1520	0.0190 8893	0.0202 7589	0.0214 7400	217
218	0.0167 4872	0.0179 0789	0.0190 8258	0.0202 7041	0.0214 6929	218
219	0.0167 4051	0.0179 0071	0.0190 7635	0.0202 6504	0.0214 6468	219
220	0.0167 3243	0.0178 9367	0.0190 7024	0.0202 5977	0.0214 6017	220
221	0.0167 2449	0.0178 8675	0.0190 6425	0.0202 5462	0.0214 5576	221
222	0.0167 1669	0.0178 7995	0.0190 5837	0.0202 4956	0.0214 5144	222
223	0.0167 0901	0.0178 7328	0.0190 5260	0.0202 4461	0.0214 4721	223
224	0.0167 0147	0.0178 6672	0.0190 4695	0.0202 3975	0.0214 4306	224
225	0.0166 9405	0.0178 6028	0.0190 4140	0.0202 3500	0.0214 3901	225
226	0.0166 8676	0.0178 5396	0.0190 3595	0.0202 3034	0.0214 3504	226
227	0.0166 7959	0.0178 4775	0.0190 3061	0.0202 2577	0.0214 3116	227
228	0.0166 7255	0.0178 4166	0.0190 2537	0.0202 2129	0.0214 2736	228
229	0.0166 6562	0.0178 3567	0.0190 2023	0.0202 1691	0.0214 2364	229
230	0.0166 5880	0.0178 2978	0.0190 1518	0.0202 1261	0.0214 2000	230
231	0.0166 5211	0.0178 2401	0.0190 1024	0.0202 0840	0.0214 1643	231
232	0.0166 4552	0.0178 1833	0.0190 0538	0.0202 0427	0.0214 1294	232
233	0.0166 3904	0.0178 1276	0.0190 0062	0.0202 0022	0.0214 0953	233
234	0.0166 3268	0.0178 0729	0.0189 9594	0.0201 9626	0.0214 0618	234
235	0.0166 2642	0.0178 0191	0.0189 9136	0.0201 9237	0.0214 0291	235
236	0.0166 2026	0.0177 9663	0.0189 8686	0.0201 8857	0.0213 9971	236
237	0.0166 1421	0.0177 9144	0.0189 8245	0.0201 8484	0.0213 9657	237
238	0.0166 0825	0.0177 8635	0.0189 7812	0.0201 8118	0.0213 9350	238
239	0.0166 0240	0.0177 8134	0.0189 7387	0.0201 7759	0.0213 9049	239
240	0.0165 9665	0.0177 7643	0.0189 6970	0.0201 7408	0.0213 8755	240

TABLE V

N	1 5/8	1 3/4	1 7/8	2	2 1/8	N
241	0.0165 9099	0.0177 7160	0.0189 6561	0.0201 7064	0.0213 8467	241
242	0.0165 8542	0.0177 6686	0.0189 6160	0.0201 6727	0.0213 8185	242
243	0.0165 7995	0.0177 6220	0.0189 5766	0.0201 6396	0.0213 7909	243
244	0.0165 7457	0.0177 5762	0.0189 5380	0.0201 6072	0.0213 7639	244
245	0.0165 6928	0.0177 5313	0.0189 5001	0.0201 5754	0.0213 7374	245
246	0.0165 6407	0.0177 4871	0.0189 4629	0.0201 5443	0.0213 7115	246
247	0.0165 5895	0.0177 4438	0.0189 4264	0.0201 5138	0.0213 6862	247
248	0.0165 5392	0.0177 4012	0.0189 3905	0.0201 4839	0.0213 6614	248
249	0.0165 4897	0.0177 3593	0.0189 3554	0.0201 4546	0.0213 6371	249
250	0.0165 4411	0.0177 3182	0.0189 3209	0.0201 4258	0.0213 6133	250
251	0.0165 3932	0.0177 2778	0.0189 2871	0.0201 3977	0.0213 5900	251
252	0.0165 3461	0.0177 2381	0.0189 2539	0.0201 3701	0.0213 5672	252
253	0.0165 2998	0.0177 1991	0.0189 2213	0.0201 3431	0.0213 5449	253
254	0.0165 2543	0.0177 1609	0.0189 1894	0.0201 3165	0.0213 5231	254
255	0.0165 2095	0.0177 1232	0.0189 1580	0.0201 2906	0.0213 5017	255
256	0.0165 1655	0.0177 0863	0.0189 1272	0.0201 2651	0.0213 4807	256
257	0.0165 1222	0.0177 0500	0.0189 0970	0.0201 2401	0.0213 4602	257
258	0.0165 0796	0.0177 0143	0.0189 0674	0.0201 2157	0.0213 4402	258
259	0.0165 0377	0.0176 9793	0.0189 0383	0.0201 1917	0.0213 4205	259
260	0.0164 9965	0.0176 9449	0.0189 0097	0.0201 1682	0.0213 4013	260
261	0.0164 9560	0.0176 9110	0.0188 9817	0.0201 1452	0.0213 3824	261
262	0.0164 9161	0.0176 8778	0.0188 9543	0.0201 1226	0.0213 3640	262
263	0.0164 8769	0.0176 8452	0.0188 9273	0.0201 1004	0.0213 3460	263
264	0.0164 8384	0.0176 8131	0.0188 9008	0.0201 0788	0.0213 3283	264
265	0.0164 8004	0.0176 7816	0.0188 8748	0.0201 0575	0.0213 3110	265
266	0.0164 7631	0.0176 7507	0.0188 8494	0.0201 0366	0.0213 2941	266
267	0.0164 7265	0.0176 7203	0.0188 8244	0.0201 0162	0.0213 2775	267
268	0.0164 6904	0.0176 6904	0.0188 7998	0.0200 9962	0.0213 2612	268
269	0.0164 6549	0.0176 6610	0.0188 7757	0.0200 9766	0.0213 2453	269
270	0.0164 6200	0.0176 6322	0.0188 7521	0.0200 9573	0.0213 2298	270
271	0.0164 5856	0.0176 6039	0.0188 7289	0.0200 9385	0.0213 2145	271
272	0.0164 5519	0.0176 5761	0.0188 7061	0.0200 9200	0.0213 1996	272
273	0.0164 5187	0.0176 5487	0.0188 6838	0.0200 9019	0.0213 1850	273
274	0.0164 4860	0.0176 5218	0.0188 6619	0.0200 8841	0.0213 1707	274
275	0.0164 4538	0.0176 4954	0.0188 6404	0.0200 8667	0.0213 1567	275
276	0.0164 4222	0.0176 4695	0.0188 6192	0.0200 8496	0.0213 1430	276
277	0.0164 3911	0.0176 4440	0.0188 5985	0.0200 8329	0.0213 1296	277
278	0.0164 3606	0.0176 4190	0.0188 5782	0.0200 8165	0.0213 1165	278
279	0.0164 3305	0.0176 3944	0.0188 5582	0.0200 8004	0.0213 1036	279
280	0.0164 3009	0.0176 3702	0.0188 5386	0.0200 7847	0.0213 0910	280
281	0.0164 2718	0.0176 3465	0.0188 5194	0.0200 7692	0.0213 0787	281
282	0.0164 2431	0.0176 3231	0.0188 5006	0.0200 7541	0.0213 0666	282
283	0.0164 2150	0.0176 3002	0.0188 4820	0.0200 7392	0.0213 0548	283
284	0.0164 1873	0.0176 2777	0.0188 4639	0.0200 7247	0.0213 0432	284
285	0.0164 1600	0.0176 2555	0.0188 4461	0.0200 7104	0.0213 0319	285
286	0.0164 1332	0.0176 2338	0.0188 4286	0.0200 6965	0.0213 0208	286
287	0.0164 1068	0.0176 2124	0.0188 4114	0.0200 6827	0.0213 0099	287
288	0.0164 0809	0.0176 1914	0.0188 3945	0.0200 6693	0.0212 9993	288
289	0.0164 0554	0.0176 1708	0.0188 3780	0.0200 6561	0.0212 9889	289
290	0.0164 0302	0.0176 1505	0.0188 3618	0.0200 6432	0.0212 9787	290
291	0.0164 0056	0.0176 1306	0.0188 3458	0.0200 6306	0.0212 9687	291
292	0.0163 9813	0.0176 1111	0.0188 3302	0.0200 6182	0.0212 9589	292
293	0.0163 9574	0.0176 0918	0.0188 3148	0.0200 6060	0.0212 9493	293
294	0.0163 9339	0.0176 0729	0.0188 2998	0.0200 5941	0.0212 9400	294
295	0.0163 9107	0.0176 0544	0.0188 2850	0.0200 5824	0.0212 9308	295
296	0.0163 8880	0.0176 0361	0.0188 2705	0.0200 5710	0.0212 9218	296
297	0.0163 8656	0.0176 0182	0.0188 2563	0.0200 5597	0.0212 9130	297
298	0.0163 8436	0.0176 0006	0.0188 2423	0.0200 5487	0.0212 9044	298
299	0.0163 8219	0.0175 9833	0.0188 2286	0.0200 5380	0.0212 8960	299
300	0.0163 8006	0.0175 9663	0.0188 2151	0.0200 5274	0.0212 8877	300

TABLE V

N	1 5/8	1 3/4	1 7/8	2	2 1/8	N
301	0.0163 7797	0.0175 9496	0.0188 2019	0.0200 5170	0.0212 8796	301
302	0.0163 7590	0.0175 9332	0.0188 1889	0.0200 5068	0.0212 8717	302
303	0.0163 7387	0.0175 9170	0.0188 1762	0.0200 4969	0.0212 8640	303
304	0.0163 7188	0.0175 9012	0.0188 1637	0.0200 4871	0.0212 8564	304
305	0.0163 6992	0.0175 8856	0.0188 1515	0.0200 4775	0.0212 8490	305
306	0.0163 6798	0.0175 8703	0.0188 1394	0.0200 4682	0.0212 8417	306
307	0.0163 6608	0.0175 8552	0.0188 1276	0.0200 4590	0.0212 8346	307
308	0.0163 6421	0.0175 8405	0.0188 1160	0.0200 4499	0.0212 8276	308
309	0.0163 6238	0.0175 8259	0.0188 1047	0.0200 4411	0.0212 8208	309
310	0.0163 6057	0.0175 8117	0.0188 0935	0.0200 4324	0.0212 8141	310
311	0.0163 5879	0.0175 7976	0.0188 0825	0.0200 4239	0.0212 8075	311
312	0.0163 5704	0.0175 7839	0.0188 0718	0.0200 4156	0.0212 8011	312
313	0.0163 5531	0.0175 7703	0.0188 0612	0.0200 4074	0.0212 7949	313
314	0.0163 5362	0.0175 7570	0.0188 0509	0.0200 3994	0.0212 7887	314
315	0.0163 5195	0.0175 7439	0.0188 0407	0.0200 3916	0.0212 7827	315
316	0.0163 5031	0.0175 7311	0.0188 0307	0.0200 3839	0.0212 7768	316
317	0.0163 4870	0.0175 7185	0.0188 0209	0.0200 3764	0.0212 7710	317
318	0.0163 4711	0.0175 7061	0.0188 0113	0.0200 3690	0.0212 7654	318
319	0.0163 4555	0.0175 6939	0.0188 0019	0.0200 3617	0.0212 7599	319
320	0.0163 4401	0.0175 6819	0.0187 9926	0.0200 3546	0.0212 7545	320
321	0.0163 4250	0.0175 6701	0.0187 9835	0.0200 3476	0.0212 7492	321
322	0.0163 4101	0.0175 6585	0.0187 9746	0.0200 3408	0.0212 7440	322
323	0.0163 3955	0.0175 6472	0.0187 9658	0.0200 3341	0.0212 7389	323
324	0.0163 3811	0.0175 6360	0.0187 9572	0.0200 3276	0.0212 7339	324
325	0.0163 3669	0.0175 6250	0.0187 9488	0.0200 3211	0.0212 7290	325
326	0.0163 3530	0.0175 6142	0.0187 9405	0.0200 3148	0.0212 7243	326
327	0.0163 3393	0.0175 6036	0.0187 9324	0.0200 3086	0.0212 7196	327
328	0.0163 3258	0.0175 5932	0.0187 9244	0.0200 3026	0.0212 7150	328
329	0.0163 3125	0.0175 5830	0.0187 9166	0.0200 2966	0.0212 7105	329
330	0.0163 2995	0.0175 5729	0.0187 9089	0.0200 2908	0.0212 7062	330
331	0.0163 2866	0.0175 5630	0.0187 9014	0.0200 2851	0.0212 7019	331
332	0.0163 2740	0.0175 5533	0.0187 8940	0.0200 2795	0.0212 6977	332
333	0.0163 2615	0.0175 5438	0.0187 8867	0.0200 2740	0.0212 6935	333
334	0.0163 2493	0.0175 5344	0.0187 8796	0.0200 2686	0.0212 6895	334
335	0.0163 2373	0.0175 5252	0.0187 8726	0.0200 2634	0.0212 6856	335
336	0.0163 2254	0.0175 5161	0.0187 8657	0.0200 2582	0.0212 6817	336
337	0.0163 2138	0.0175 5072	0.0187 8590	0.0200 2531	0.0212 6779	337
338	0.0163 2023	0.0175 4985	0.0187 8523	0.0200 2481	0.0212 6742	338
339	0.0163 1910	0.0175 4899	0.0187 8458	0.0200 2433	0.0212 6706	339
340	0.0163 1799	0.0175 4814	0.0187 8395	0.0200 2385	0.0212 6670	340
341	0.0163 1690	0.0175 4731	0.0187 8332	0.0200 2338	0.0212 6636	341
342	0.0163 1583	0.0175 4650	0.0187 8271	0.0200 2292	0.0212 6601	342
343	0.0163 1477	0.0175 4569	0.0187 8210	0.0200 2247	0.0212 6568	343
344	0.0163 1373	0.0175 4491	0.0187 8151	0.0200 2203	0.0212 6535	344
345	0.0163 1271	0.0175 4413	0.0187 8093	0.0200 2160	0.0212 6503	345
346	0.0163 1170	0.0175 4337	0.0187 8036	0.0200 2118	0.0212 6472	346
347	0.0163 1071	0.0175 4262	0.0187 7980	0.0200 2076	0.0212 6442	347
348	0.0163 0974	0.0175 4189	0.0187 7925	0.0200 2035	0.0212 6412	348
349	0.0163 0878	0.0175 4117	0.0187 7871	0.0200 1995	0.0212 6382	349
350	0.0163 0784	0.0175 4046	0.0187 7818	0.0200 1956	0.0212 6353	350
351	0.0163 0691	0.0175 3976	0.0187 7766	0.0200 1918	0.0212 6325	351
352	0.0163 0600	0.0175 3907	0.0187 7715	0.0200 1880	0.0212 6298	352
353	0.0163 0510	0.0175 3840	0.0187 7665	0.0200 1843	0.0212 6271	353
354	0.0163 0421	0.0175 3774	0.0187 7616	0.0200 1807	0.0212 6244	354
355	0.0163 0334	0.0175 3709	0.0187 7568	0.0200 1772	0.0212 6218	355
356	0.0163 0249	0.0175 3645	0.0187 7521	0.0200 1737	0.0212 6193	356
357	0.0163 0165	0.0175 3582	0.0187 7474	0.0200 1703	0.0212 6168	357
358	0.0163 0082	0.0175 3520	0.0187 7429	0.0200 1669	0.0212 6144	358
359	0.0163 0000	0.0175 3460	0.0187 7384	0.0200 1637	0.0212 6120	359
360	0.0162 9920	0.0175 3400	0.0187 7340	0.0200 1604	0.0212 6097	360

TABLE V

N	2 1/4	2 3/8	2 1/2	2 5/8	2 3/4	N
1	1.0225 0000	1.0237 5000	1.0250 0000	1.0262 5000	1.0275 0000	1
2	0.5169 3758	0.5178 8218	0.5188 2716	0.5197 7252	0.5207 1825	2
3	0.3484 4458	0.3492 9054	0.3501 3717	0.3509 8447	0.3518 3243	3
4	0.2642 1893	0.2650 1793	0.2658 1788	0.2666 1876	0.2674 2059	4
5	0.2137 0021	0.2144 7293	0.2152 4686	0.2160 2199	0.2167 9832	5
6	0.1800 3496	0.1807 9173	0.1815 4997	0.1823 0967	0.1830 7083	6
7	0.1560 0025	0.1567 4698	0.1574 9543	0.1582 4560	0.1589 9747	7
8	0.1379 8462	0.1387 2500	0.1394 6735	0.1402 1166	0.1409 5795	8
9	0.1239 8170	0.1247 1818	0.1254 5689	0.1261 9782	0.1269 4095	9
10	0.1127 8768	0.1135 2199	0.1142 5876	0.1149 9801	0.1157 3972	10
11	0.1036 3649	0.1043 6986	0.1051 0596	0.1058 4477	0.1065 8629	11
12	0.0960 1740	0.0967 5078	0.0974 8713	0.0982 2644	0.0989 6871	12
13	0.0895 7686	0.0903 1095	0.0910 4827	0.0917 8880	0.0925 3252	13
14	0.0840 6230	0.0847 9768	0.0855 3652	0.0862 7882	0.0870 2457	14
15	0.0792 8852	0.0800 2564	0.0807 6646	0.0815 1097	0.0822 5917	15
16	0.0751 1663	0.0758 5583	0.0765 9899	0.0773 4608	0.0780 9710	16
17	0.0714 4039	0.0721 8199	0.0729 2777	0.0736 7773	0.0744 3186	17
18	0.0681 7720	0.0689 2142	0.0696 7008	0.0704 2315	0.0711 8063	18
19	0.0652 6182	0.0660 0888	0.0667 6062	0.0675 1700	0.0682 7802	19
20	0.0626 4207	0.0633 9215	0.0641 4713	0.0649 0700	0.0656 7173	20
21	0.0602 7572	0.0610 2895	0.0617 8733	0.0625 5082	0.0633 1941	21
22	0.0581 2821	0.0588 8472	0.0596 4661	0.0604 1384	0.0611 8640	22
23	0.0561 7097	0.0569 3087	0.0576 9638	0.0584 6746	0.0592 4410	23
24	0.0543 8023	0.0551 4361	0.0559 1282	0.0566 8784	0.0574 6863	24
25	0.0527 3599	0.0535 0292	0.0542 7592	0.0550 5495	0.0558 3997	25
26	0.0512 2134	0.0519 9190	0.0527 6875	0.0535 5185	0.0543 4116	26
27	0.0498 2188	0.0505 9612	0.0513 7687	0.0521 6410	0.0529 5776	27
28	0.0485 2525	0.0493 0322	0.0500 8793	0.0508 7933	0.0516 7738	28
29	0.0473 2081	0.0481 0256	0.0488 9127	0.0496 8688	0.0504 8935	29
30	0.0461 9934	0.0469 8491	0.0477 7764	0.0485 7750	0.0493 8442	30
31	0.0451 5280	0.0459 4221	0.0467 3900	0.0475 4313	0.0483 5453	31
32	0.0441 7415	0.0449 6743	0.0457 6831	0.0465 7673	0.0473 9263	32
33	0.0432 5722	0.0440 5440	0.0448 5938	0.0456 7211	0.0464 9253	33
34	0.0423 9655	0.0431 9764	0.0440 0675	0.0448 2381	0.0456 4875	34
35	0.0415 8731	0.0423 9234	0.0432 0558	0.0440 2698	0.0448 5645	35
36	0.0408 2522	0.0416 3418	0.0424 5158	0.0432 7732	0.0441 1132	36
37	0.0401 0643	0.0409 1935	0.0417 4090	0.0425 7099	0.0434 0953	37
38	0.0394 2753	0.0402 4441	0.0410 7012	0.0419 0456	0.0427 4764	38
39	0.0387 8543	0.0396 0628	0.0404 3615	0.0412 7494	0.0421 2256	39
40	0.0381 7738	0.0390 0220	0.0398 3623	0.0406 7937	0.0415 3151	40
41	0.0376 0087	0.0384 2966	0.0392 6786	0.0401 1534	0.0409 7200	41
42	0.0370 5364	0.0378 8640	0.0387 2876	0.0395 8058	0.0404 4175	42
43	0.0365 3364	0.0373 7038	0.0382 1688	0.0390 7304	0.0399 3871	43
44	0.0360 3901	0.0368 7972	0.0377 3037	0.0385 9084	0.0394 6100	44
45	0.0355 6805	0.0364 1272	0.0372 6751	0.0381 3229	0.0390 0693	45
46	0.0351 1921	0.0359 6783	0.0368 2676	0.0376 9584	0.0385 7493	46
47	0.0346 9107	0.0355 4364	0.0364 0669	0.0372 8005	0.0381 6358	47
48	0.0342 8233	0.0351 3884	0.0360 0599	0.0368 8363	0.0377 7158	48
49	0.0338 9179	0.0347 5223	0.0356 2348	0.0365 0537	0.0373 9773	49
50	0.0335 1836	0.0343 8272	0.0352 5806	0.0361 4418	0.0370 4092	50
51	0.0331 6102	0.0340 2929	0.0349 0870	0.0357 9904	0.0367 0014	51
52	0.0328 1884	0.0336 9101	0.0345 7446	0.0354 6901	0.0363 7444	52
53	0.0324 9094	0.0333 6700	0.0342 5449	0.0351 5322	0.0360 6297	53
54	0.0321 7654	0.0330 5647	0.0339 4799	0.0348 5087	0.0357 6491	54
55	0.0318 7489	0.0327 5868	0.0336 5419	0.0345 6122	0.0354 7953	55
56	0.0315 8530	0.0324 7293	0.0333 7243	0.0342 8357	0.0352 0612	56
57	0.0313 0712	0.0321 9858	0.0331 0204	0.0340 1728	0.0349 4404	57
58	0.0310 3977	0.0319 3503	0.0328 4244	0.0337 6175	0.0346 9270	58
59	0.0307 8268	0.0316 8173	0.0325 9307	0.0335 1642	0.0344 5153	59
60	0.0305 3533	0.0314 3816	0.0323 5340	0.0332 8078	0.0342 2002	60

TABLE V

N	2 1/4	2 3/8	2 1/2	2 5/8	2 3/4	N
61	0.0302 9724	0.0312 0382	0.0321 2294	0.0330 5432	0.0339 9767	61
62	0.0300 6795	0.0309 7827	0.0319 0126	0.0328 3661	0.0337 8402	62
63	0.0298 4704	0.0307 6108	0.0316 8790	0.0326 2720	0.0335 7866	63
64	0.0296 3411	0.0305 5185	0.0314 8249	0.0324 2570	0.0333 8118	64
65	0.0294 2878	0.0303 5020	0.0312 8463	0.0322 3174	0.0331 9120	65
66	0.0292 3070	0.0301 5578	0.0310 9398	0.0320 4496	0.0330 0837	66
67	0.0290 3955	0.0299 6827	0.0309 1021	0.0318 6503	0.0328 3236	67
68	0.0288 5500	0.0297 8734	0.0307 3300	0.0316 9163	0.0326 6285	68
69	0.0286 7677	0.0296 1270	0.0305 6206	0.0315 2447	0.0324 9955	69
70	0.0285 0458	0.0294 4409	0.0303 9712	0.0313 6328	0.0323 4218	70
71	0.0283 3816	0.0292 8122	0.0302 3790	0.0312 0779	0.0321 9048	71
72	0.0281 7728	0.0291 2387	0.0300 8417	0.0310 5775	0.0320 4420	72
73	0.0280 2169	0.0289 7179	0.0299 3568	0.0309 1293	0.0319 0311	73
74	0.0278 7118	0.0288 2477	0.0297 9222	0.0307 7311	0.0317 6698	74
75	0.0277 2554	0.0286 8259	0.0296 5358	0.0306 3807	0.0316 3560	75
76	0.0275 8457	0.0285 4505	0.0295 1956	0.0305 0763	0.0315 0878	76
77	0.0274 4808	0.0284 1198	0.0293 8997	0.0303 8158	0.0313 8633	77
78	0.0273 1589	0.0282 8318	0.0292 6463	0.0302 5976	0.0312 6806	78
79	0.0271 8784	0.0281 5849	0.0291 4338	0.0301 4199	0.0311 5382	79
80	0.0270 6376	0.0280 3776	0.0290 2605	0.0300 2811	0.0310 4342	80
81	0.0269 4350	0.0279 2082	0.0289 1248	0.0299 1797	0.0309 3674	81
82	0.0268 2692	0.0278 0753	0.0288 0254	0.0298 1142	0.0308 3361	82
83	0.0267 1387	0.0276 9775	0.0286 9608	0.0297 0832	0.0307 3389	83
84	0.0266 0423	0.0275 9135	0.0285 9298	0.0296 0854	0.0306 3747	84
85	0.0264 9787	0.0274 8821	0.0284 9310	0.0295 1196	0.0305 4420	85
86	0.0263 9467	0.0273 8820	0.0283 9633	0.0294 1845	0.0304 5397	86
87	0.0262 9452	0.0272 9121	0.0283 0255	0.0293 2791	0.0303 6667	87
88	0.0261 9730	0.0271 9714	0.0282 1165	0.0292 4021	0.0302 8219	88
89	0.0261 0291	0.0271 0587	0.0281 2353	0.0291 5526	0.0302 0041	89
90	0.0260 1126	0.0270 1731	0.0280 3809	0.0290 7295	0.0301 2125	90
91	0.0259 2224	0.0269 3135	0.0279 5523	0.0289 9320	0.0300 4460	91
92	0.0258 3577	0.0268 4792	0.0278 7486	0.0289 1591	0.0299 7038	92
93	0.0257 5176	0.0267 6692	0.0277 9690	0.0288 4099	0.0298 9850	93
94	0.0256 7012	0.0266 8828	0.0277 2126	0.0287 6836	0.0298 2887	94
95	0.0255 9078	0.0266 1190	0.0276 4786	0.0286 9793	0.0297 6141	95
96	0.0255 1366	0.0265 3771	0.0275 7662	0.0286 2964	0.0296 9605	96
97	0.0254 3868	0.0264 6564	0.0275 0747	0.0285 6341	0.0296 3272	97
98	0.0253 6578	0.0263 9563	0.0274 4034	0.0284 9917	0.0295 7134	98
99	0.0252 9489	0.0263 2759	0.0273 7517	0.0284 3684	0.0295 1185	99
100	0.0252 2594	0.0262 6147	0.0273 1188	0.0283 7638	0.0294 5418	100
101	0.0251 5886	0.0261 9720	0.0272 5042	0.0283 1770	0.0293 9826	101
102	0.0250 9361	0.0261 3473	0.0271 9072	0.0282 6076	0.0293 4405	102
103	0.0250 3012	0.0260 7399	0.0271 3273	0.0282 0550	0.0292 9148	103
104	0.0249 6834	0.0260 1493	0.0270 7639	0.0281 5185	0.0292 4050	104
105	0.0249 0821	0.0259 5751	0.0270 2165	0.0280 9978	0.0291 9105	105
106	0.0248 4968	0.0259 0165	0.0269 6846	0.0280 4922	0.0291 4309	106
107	0.0247 9271	0.0258 4733	0.0269 1677	0.0280 0013	0.0290 9656	107
108	0.0247 3724	0.0257 9449	0.0268 6653	0.0279 5246	0.0290 5142	108
109	0.0246 8324	0.0257 4308	0.0268 1769	0.0279 0617	0.0290 0762	109
110	0.0246 3064	0.0256 9306	0.0267 7022	0.0278 6121	0.0289 6512	110
111	0.0245 7943	0.0256 4438	0.0267 2406	0.0278 1753	0.0289 2388	111
112	0.0245 2954	0.0255 9702	0.0266 7919	0.0277 7511	0.0288 8385	112
113	0.0244 8095	0.0255 5092	0.0266 3555	0.0277 3389	0.0288 4500	113
114	0.0244 3361	0.0255 0605	0.0265 9312	0.0276 9385	0.0288 0730	114
115	0.0243 8749	0.0254 6237	0.0265 5185	0.0276 5494	0.0287 7069	115
116	0.0243 4256	0.0254 1986	0.0265 1171	0.0276 1713	0.0287 3515	116
117	0.0242 9877	0.0253 7846	0.0264 7267	0.0275 8039	0.0287 0065	117
118	0.0242 5610	0.0253 3816	0.0264 3469	0.0275 4468	0.0286 6716	118
119	0.0242 1451	0.0252 9891	0.0263 9774	0.0275 0998	0.0286 3463	119
120	0.0241 7398	0.0252 6069	0.0263 6179	0.0274 7624	0.0286 0304	120

TABLE V

N	2 1/4	2 3/8	2 1/2	2 5/8	2 3/4	N
121	0.0241 3447	0.0252 2347	0.0263 2682	0.0274 4345	0.0285 7237	121
122	0.0240 9595	0.0251 8722	0.0262 9278	0.0274 1157	0.0285 4258	122
123	0.0240 5840	0.0251 5191	0.0262 5966	0.0273 8058	0.0285 1365	123
124	0.0240 2179	0.0251 1751	0.0262 2743	0.0273 5045	0.0284 8555	124
125	0.0239 8609	0.0250 8401	0.0261 9606	0.0273 2116	0.0284 5825	125
126	0.0239 5128	0.0250 5136	0.0261 6553	0.0272 9267	0.0284 3174	126
127	0.0239 1733	0.0250 1956	0.0261 3581	0.0272 6497	0.0284 0598	127
128	0.0238 8422	0.0249 8857	0.0261 0688	0.0272 3803	0.0283 8095	128
129	0.0238 5193	0.0249 5837	0.0260 7872	0.0272 1183	0.0283 5664	129
130	0.0238 2044	0.0249 2895	0.0260 5130	0.0271 8635	0.0283 3302	130
131	0.0237 8972	0.0249 0027	0.0260 2461	0.0271 6157	0.0283 1007	131
132	0.0237 5975	0.0248 7233	0.0259 9862	0.0271 3746	0.0282 8777	132
133	0.0237 3051	0.0248 4509	0.0259 7331	0.0271 1402	0.0282 6609	133
134	0.0237 0199	0.0248 1854	0.0259 4867	0.0270 9121	0.0282 4504	134
135	0.0236 7416	0.0247 9266	0.0259 2468	0.0270 6902	0.0282 2457	135
136	0.0236 4700	0.0247 6744	0.0259 0131	0.0270 4743	0.0282 0468	136
137	0.0236 2051	0.0247 4285	0.0258 7856	0.0270 2643	0.0281 8535	137
138	0.0235 9465	0.0247 1888	0.0258 5640	0.0270 0600	0.0281 6656	138
139	0.0235 6942	0.0246 9550	0.0258 3481	0.0269 8612	0.0281 4830	139
140	0.0235 4479	0.0246 7272	0.0258 1379	0.0269 6678	0.0281 3055	140
141	0.0235 2076	0.0246 5050	0.0257 9331	0.0269 4796	0.0281 1330	141
142	0.0234 9730	0.0246 2884	0.0257 7336	0.0269 2964	0.0280 9653	142
143	0.0234 7441	0.0246 0771	0.0257 5393	0.0269 1182	0.0280 8023	143
144	0.0234 5206	0.0245 8711	0.0257 3500	0.0268 9448	0.0280 6438	144
145	0.0234 3024	0.0245 6702	0.0257 1656	0.0268 7760	0.0280 4897	145
146	0.0234 0895	0.0245 4743	0.0256 9859	0.0268 6117	0.0280 3400	146
147	0.0233 8815	0.0245 2833	0.0256 8109	0.0268 4518	0.0280 1943	147
148	0.0233 6786	0.0245 0969	0.0256 6404	0.0268 2962	0.0280 0528	148
149	0.0233 4804	0.0244 9152	0.0256 4742	0.0268 1448	0.0279 9151	149
150	0.0233 2869	0.0244 7379	0.0256 3123	0.0267 9974	0.0279 7813	150
151	0.0233 0980	0.0244 5650	0.0256 1546	0.0267 8539	0.0279 6511	151
152	0.0232 9135	0.0244 3964	0.0256 0009	0.0267 7142	0.0279 5246	152
153	0.0232 7334	0.0244 2318	0.0255 8511	0.0267 5783	0.0279 4016	153
154	0.0232 5575	0.0244 0713	0.0255 7051	0.0267 4459	0.0279 2819	154
155	0.0232 3858	0.0243 9148	0.0255 5629	0.0267 3171	0.0279 1656	155
156	0.0232 2180	0.0243 7620	0.0255 4242	0.0267 1917	0.0279 0525	156
157	0.0232 0542	0.0243 6130	0.0255 2891	0.0267 0696	0.0278 9425	157
158	0.0231 8942	0.0243 4676	0.0255 1575	0.0266 9507	0.0278 8355	158
159	0.0231 7380	0.0243 3258	0.0255 0292	0.0266 8350	0.0278 7314	159
160	0.0231 5854	0.0243 1874	0.0254 9041	0.0266 7223	0.0278 6302	160
161	0.0231 4363	0.0243 0524	0.0254 7822	0.0266 6126	0.0278 5318	161
162	0.0231 2907	0.0242 9206	0.0254 6634	0.0266 5058	0.0278 4361	162
163	0.0231 1485	0.0242 7921	0.0254 5476	0.0266 4018	0.0278 3430	163
164	0.0231 0096	0.0242 6666	0.0254 4347	0.0266 3006	0.0278 2525	164
165	0.0230 8739	0.0242 5442	0.0254 3246	0.0266 2020	0.0278 1645	165
166	0.0230 7414	0.0242 4248	0.0254 2174	0.0266 1060	0.0278 0788	166
167	0.0230 6119	0.0242 3082	0.0254 1128	0.0266 0126	0.0277 9955	167
168	0.0230 4854	0.0242 1945	0.0254 0109	0.0265 9215	0.0277 9145	168
169	0.0230 3618	0.0242 0835	0.0253 9116	0.0265 8329	0.0277 8357	169
170	0.0230 2411	0.0241 9751	0.0253 8147	0.0265 7466	0.0277 7590	170
171	0.0230 1231	0.0241 8694	0.0253 7203	0.0265 6626	0.0277 6845	171
172	0.0230 0079	0.0241 7662	0.0253 6282	0.0265 5807	0.0277 6119	172
173	0.0229 8953	0.0241 6655	0.0253 5385	0.0265 5010	0.0277 5414	173
174	0.0229 7853	0.0241 5672	0.0253 4510	0.0265 4234	0.0277 4728	174
175	0.0229 6778	0.0241 4713	0.0253 3657	0.0265 3478	0.0277 4060	175
176	0.0229 5727	0.0241 3776	0.0253 2825	0.0265 2742	0.0277 3411	176
177	0.0229 4701	0.0241 2863	0.0253 2014	0.0265 2025	0.0277 2779	177
178	0.0229 3698	0.0241 1970	0.0253 1224	0.0265 1327	0.0277 2164	178
179	0.0229 2719	0.0241 1100	0.0253 0453	0.0265 0647	0.0277 1566	179
180	0.0229 1761	0.0241 0250	0.0252 9701	0.0264 9985	0.0277 0985	180

TABLE V

N	2 1/4	2 3/8	2 1/2	2 5/8	2 3/4	N
181	0.0229 0826	0.0240 9420	0.0252 8968	0.0264 9340	0.0277 0419	181
182	0.0228 9911	0.0240 8610	0.0252 8254	0.0264 8711	0.0276 9869	182
183	0.0228 9018	0.0240 7820	0.0252 7557	0.0264 8100	0.0276 9333	183
184	0.0228 8145	0.0240 7048	0.0252 6878	0.0264 7504	0.0276 8812	184
185	0.0228 7291	0.0240 6295	0.0252 6215	0.0264 6923	0.0276 8305	185
186	0.0228 6457	0.0240 5560	0.0252 5569	0.0264 6358	0.0276 7812	186
187	0.0228 5642	0.0240 4842	0.0252 4940	0.0264 5807	0.0276 7332	187
188	0.0228 4846	0.0240 4141	0.0252 4325	0.0264 5271	0.0276 6866	188
189	0.0228 4068	0.0240 3457	0.0252 3726	0.0264 4749	0.0276 6412	189
190	0.0228 3307	0.0240 2789	0.0252 3142	0.0264 4240	0.0276 5970	190
191	0.0228 2563	0.0240 2137	0.0252 2573	0.0264 3744	0.0276 5540	191
192	0.0228 1837	0.0240 1500	0.0252 2017	0.0264 3261	0.0276 5122	192
193	0.0228 1126	0.0240 0879	0.0252 1476	0.0264 2791	0.0276 4715	193
194	0.0228 0432	0.0240 0272	0.0252 0948	0.0264 2333	0.0276 4319	194
195	0.0227 9754	0.0239 9680	0.0252 0432	0.0264 1887	0.0276 3934	195
196	0.0227 9091	0.0239 9101	0.0251 9930	0.0264 1452	0.0276 3559	196
197	0.0227 8442	0.0239 8537	0.0251 9440	0.0264 1029	0.0276 3194	197
198	0.0227 7809	0.0239 7985	0.0251 8963	0.0264 0616	0.0276 2840	198
199	0.0227 7189	0.0239 7447	0.0251 8497	0.0264 0215	0.0276 2494	199
200	0.0227 6584	0.0239 6922	0.0251 8042	0.0263 9823	0.0276 2159	200
201	0.0227 5992	0.0239 6408	0.0251 7599	0.0263 9442	0.0276 1832	201
202	0.0227 5414	0.0239 5907	0.0251 7167	0.0263 9071	0.0276 1514	202
203	0.0227 4848	0.0239 5418	0.0251 6745	0.0263 8709	0.0276 1204	203
204	0.0227 4296	0.0239 4941	0.0251 6334	0.0263 8356	0.0276 0903	204
205	0.0227 3755	0.0239 4474	0.0251 5933	0.0263 8013	0.0276 0610	205
206	0.0227 3227	0.0239 4019	0.0251 5542	0.0263 7679	0.0276 0325	206
207	0.0227 2711	0.0239 3574	0.0251 5161	0.0263 7353	0.0276 0048	207
208	0.0227 2206	0.0239 3140	0.0251 4789	0.0263 7035	0.0275 9778	208
209	0.0227 1713	0.0239 2716	0.0251 4426	0.0263 6726	0.0275 9515	209
210	0.0227 1231	0.0239 2302	0.0251 4072	0.0263 6425	0.0275 9260	210
211	0.0227 0759	0.0239 1898	0.0251 3727	0.0263 6131	0.0275 9011	211
212	0.0227 0298	0.0239 1503	0.0251 3391	0.0263 5845	0.0275 8769	212
213	0.0226 9848	0.0239 1117	0.0251 3062	0.0263 5567	0.0275 8534	213
214	0.0226 9407	0.0239 0741	0.0251 2742	0.0263 5296	0.0275 8305	214
215	0.0226 8977	0.0239 0374	0.0251 2430	0.0263 5031	0.0275 8082	215
216	0.0226 8556	0.0239 0015	0.0251 2125	0.0263 4774	0.0275 7865	216
217	0.0226 8144	0.0238 9664	0.0251 1828	0.0263 4523	0.0275 7654	217
218	0.0226 7742	0.0238 9322	0.0251 1538	0.0263 4278	0.0275 7448	218
219	0.0226 7348	0.0238 8988	0.0251 1255	0.0263 4040	0.0275 7249	219
220	0.0226 6963	0.0238 8661	0.0251 0980	0.0263 3808	0.0275 7054	220
221	0.0226 6587	0.0238 8343	0.0251 0711	0.0263 3582	0.0275 6865	221
222	0.0226 6220	0.0238 8031	0.0251 0448	0.0263 3362	0.0275 6681	222
223	0.0226 5860	0.0238 7727	0.0251 0193	0.0263 3147	0.0275 6501	223
224	0.0226 5509	0.0238 7431	0.0250 9943	0.0263 2938	0.0275 6327	224
225	0.0226 5165	0.0238 7141	0.0250 9700	0.0263 2735	0.0275 6157	225
226	0.0226 4829	0.0238 6858	0.0250 9462	0.0263 2536	0.0275 5992	226
227	0.0226 4501	0.0238 6581	0.0250 9230	0.0263 2343	0.0275 5831	227
228	0.0226 4180	0.0238 6311	0.0250 9005	0.0263 2155	0.0275 5675	228
229	0.0226 3866	0.0238 6048	0.0250 8784	0.0263 1971	0.0275 5523	229
230	0.0226 3559	0.0238 5790	0.0250 8569	0.0263 1792	0.0275 5375	230
231	0.0226 3259	0.0238 5539	0.0250 8359	0.0263 1618	0.0275 5231	231
232	0.0226 2965	0.0238 5293	0.0250 8155	0.0263 1449	0.0275 5090	232
233	0.0226 2679	0.0238 5053	0.0250 7955	0.0263 1283	0.0275 4954	233
234	0.0226 2398	0.0238 4819	0.0250 7761	0.0263 1122	0.0275 4821	234
235	0.0226 2124	0.0238 4591	0.0250 7571	0.0263 0965	0.0275 4692	235
236	0.0226 1856	0.0238 4367	0.0250 7386	0.0263 0812	0.0275 4566	236
237	0.0226 1593	0.0238 4149	0.0250 7205	0.0263 0663	0.0275 4444	237
238	0.0226 1337	0.0238 3936	0.0250 7029	0.0263 0518	0.0275 4325	238
239	0.0226 1086	0.0238 3728	0.0250 6857	0.0263 0377	0.0275 4209	239
240	0.0226 0841	0.0238 3525	0.0250 6689	0.0263 0239	0.0275 4096	240

TABLE V

N	2 1/4	2 3/8	2 1/2	2 5/8	2 3/4	N
241	0.0226 0601	0.0238 3326	0.0250 6526	0.0263 0105	0.0275 3986	241
242	0.0226 0367	0.0238 3132	0.0250 6366	0.0262 9974	0.0275 3879	242
243	0.0226 0138	0.0238 2943	0.0250 6210	0.0262 9846	0.0275 3775	243
244	0.0225 9914	0.0238 2758	0.0250 6059	0.0262 9722	0.0275 3674	244
245	0.0225 9695	0.0238 2578	0.0250 5910	0.0262 9601	0.0275 3576	245
246	0.0225 9481	0.0238 2401	0.0250 5766	0.0262 9483	0.0275 3480	246
247	0.0225 9271	0.0238 2229	0.0250 5625	0.0262 9368	0.0275 3387	247
248	0.0225 9066	0.0238 2061	0.0250 5487	0.0262 9256	0.0275 3296	248
249	0.0225 8866	0.0238 1897	0.0250 5353	0.0262 9147	0.0275 3207	249
250	0.0225 8670	0.0238 1736	0.0250 5223	0.0262 9041	0.0275 3122	250
251	0.0225 8479	0.0238 1579	0.0250 5095	0.0262 8938	0.0275 3038	251
252	0.0225 8291	0.0238 1426	0.0250 4970	0.0262 8837	0.0275 2957	252
253	0.0225 8108	0.0238 1277	0.0250 4849	0.0262 8738	0.0275 2877	253
254	0.0225 7929	0.0238 1131	0.0250 4730	0.0262 8643	0.0275 2800	254
255	0.0225 7754	0.0238 0988	0.0250 4615	0.0262 8549	0.0275 2725	255
256	0.0225 7583	0.0238 0849	0.0250 4502	0.0262 8459	0.0275 2652	256
257	0.0225 7415	0.0238 0713	0.0250 4392	0.0262 8370	0.0275 2581	257
258	0.0225 7252	0.0238 0580	0.0250 4285	0.0262 8284	0.0275 2512	258
259	0.0225 7092	0.0238 0450	0.0250 4180	0.0262 8200	0.0275 2445	259
260	0.0225 6935	0.0238 0324	0.0250 4078	0.0262 8118	0.0275 2379	260
261	0.0225 6782	0.0238 0200	0.0250 3978	0.0262 8038	0.0275 2315	261
262	0.0225 6632	0.0238 0079	0.0250 3881	0.0262 7960	0.0275 2253	262
263	0.0225 6486	0.0237 9961	0.0250 3786	0.0262 7884	0.0275 2193	263
264	0.0225 6343	0.0237 9846	0.0250 3694	0.0262 7810	0.0275 2134	264
265	0.0225 6203	0.0237 9733	0.0250 3604	0.0262 7738	0.0275 2077	265
266	0.0225 6066	0.0237 9623	0.0250 3516	0.0262 7668	0.0275 2022	266
267	0.0225 5932	0.0237 9516	0.0250 3430	0.0262 7600	0.0275 1967	267
268	0.0225 5801	0.0237 9411	0.0250 3346	0.0262 7533	0.0275 1915	268
269	0.0225 5673	0.0237 9308	0.0250 3264	0.0262 7469	0.0275 1863	269
270	0.0225 5548	0.0237 9208	0.0250 3185	0.0262 7405	0.0275 1814	270
271	0.0225 5426	0.0237 9110	0.0250 3107	0.0262 7344	0.0275 1765	271
272	0.0225 5306	0.0237 9015	0.0250 3031	0.0262 7284	0.0275 1718	272
273	0.0225 5189	0.0237 8921	0.0250 2957	0.0262 7225	0.0275 1672	273
274	0.0225 5075	0.0237 8830	0.0250 2885	0.0262 7168	0.0275 1627	274
275	0.0225 4963	0.0237 8741	0.0250 2814	0.0262 7113	0.0275 1583	275
276	0.0225 4853	0.0237 8654	0.0250 2746	0.0262 7059	0.0275 1541	276
277	0.0225 4746	0.0237 8569	0.0250 2679	0.0262 7006	0.0275 1500	277
278	0.0225 4642	0.0237 8487	0.0250 2613	0.0262 6955	0.0275 1460	278
279	0.0225 4539	0.0237 8406	0.0250 2549	0.0262 6905	0.0275 1420	279
280	0.0225 4439	0.0237 8326	0.0250 2487	0.0262 6856	0.0275 1382	280
281	0.0225 4341	0.0237 8249	0.0250 2426	0.0262 6808	0.0275 1345	281
282	0.0225 4246	0.0237 8174	0.0250 2367	0.0262 6762	0.0275 1309	282
283	0.0225 4152	0.0237 8100	0.0250 2309	0.0262 6717	0.0275 1274	283
284	0.0225 4061	0.0237 8028	0.0250 2253	0.0262 6673	0.0275 1240	284
285	0.0225 3971	0.0237 7958	0.0250 2198	0.0262 6630	0.0275 1207	285
286	0.0225 3883	0.0237 7889	0.0250 2144	0.0262 6588	0.0275 1175	286
287	0.0225 3798	0.0237 7822	0.0250 2092	0.0262 6548	0.0275 1143	287
288	0.0225 3714	0.0237 7756	0.0250 2041	0.0262 6508	0.0275 1113	288
289	0.0225 3632	0.0237 7692	0.0250 1991	0.0262 6470	0.0275 1083	289
290	0.0225 3552	0.0237 7630	0.0250 1942	0.0262 6432	0.0275 1054	290
291	0.0225 3474	0.0237 7569	0.0250 1895	0.0262 6395	0.0275 1026	291
292	0.0225 3397	0.0237 7509	0.0250 1849	0.0262 6360	0.0275 0998	292
293	0.0225 3323	0.0237 7451	0.0250 1804	0.0262 6325	0.0275 0971	293
294	0.0225 3249	0.0237 7394	0.0250 1760	0.0262 6291	0.0275 0945	294
295	0.0225 3178	0.0237 7338	0.0250 1717	0.0262 6258	0.0275 0920	295
296	0.0225 3108	0.0237 7284	0.0250 1675	0.0262 6226	0.0275 0895	296
297	0.0225 3039	0.0237 7231	0.0250 1634	0.0262 6194	0.0275 0871	297
298	0.0225 2972	0.0237 7179	0.0250 1594	0.0262 6164	0.0275 0848	298
299	0.0225 2907	0.0237 7128	0.0250 1555	0.0262 6134	0.0275 0825	299
300	0.0225 2843	0.0237 7079	0.0250 1517	0.0262 6105	0.0275 0803	300

TABLE V

N	2 1/4	2 3/8	2 1/2	2 5/8	2 3/4	N
301	0.0225 2780	0.0237 7031	0.0250 1480	0.0262 6077	0.0275 0782	301
302	0.0225 2719	0.0237 6984	0.0250 1444	0.0262 6049	0.0275 0761	302
303	0.0225 2659	0.0237 6938	0.0250 1409	0.0262 6022	0.0275 0741	303
304	0.0225 2600	0.0237 6893	0.0250 1374	0.0262 5996	0.0275 0721	304
305	0.0225 2543	0.0237 6849	0.0250 1341	0.0262 5971	0.0275 0701	305
306	0.0225 2487	0.0237 6806	0.0250 1308	0.0262 5946	0.0275 0683	306
307	0.0225 2432	0.0237 6764	0.0250 1276	0.0262 5922	0.0275 0664	307
308	0.0225 2379	0.0237 6723	0.0250 1245	0.0262 5898	0.0275 0647	308
309	0.0225 2326	0.0237 6683	0.0250 1215	0.0262 5875	0.0275 0629	309
310	0.0225 2275	0.0237 6644	0.0250 1185	0.0262 5853	0.0275 0612	310
311	0.0225 2225	0.0237 6606	0.0250 1156	0.0262 5831	0.0275 0596	311
312	0.0225 2176	0.0237 6568	0.0250 1128	0.0262 5810	0.0275 0580	312
313	0.0225 2128	0.0237 6532	0.0250 1100	0.0262 5789	0.0275 0565	313
314	0.0225 2081	0.0237 6496	0.0250 1074	0.0262 5769	0.0275 0549	314
315	0.0225 2035	0.0237 6462	0.0250 1047	0.0262 5749	0.0275 0535	315
316	0.0225 1990	0.0237 6428	0.0250 1022	0.0262 5730	0.0275 0520	316
317	0.0225 1947	0.0237 6395	0.0250 0997	0.0262 5711	0.0275 0506	317
318	0.0225 1904	0.0237 6362	0.0250 0973	0.0262 5693	0.0275 0493	318
319	0.0225 1862	0.0237 6331	0.0250 0949	0.0262 5675	0.0275 0480	319
320	0.0225 1821	0.0237 6300	0.0250 0926	0.0262 5658	0.0275 0467	320
321	0.0225 1781	0.0237 6270	0.0250 0903	0.0262 5641	0.0275 0454	321
322	0.0225 1742	0.0237 6240	0.0250 0881	0.0262 5625	0.0275 0442	322
323	0.0225 1703	0.0237 6211	0.0250 0860	0.0262 5609	0.0275 0430	323
324	0.0225 1666	0.0237 6183	0.0250 0839	0.0262 5593	0.0275 0419	324
325	0.0225 1629	0.0237 6156	0.0250 0818	0.0262 5578	0.0275 0408	325
326	0.0225 1593	0.0237 6129	0.0250 0798	0.0262 5563	0.0275 0397	326
327	0.0225 1558	0.0237 6103	0.0250 0779	0.0262 5549	0.0275 0386	327
328	0.0225 1524	0.0237 6077	0.0250 0760	0.0262 5535	0.0275 0376	328
329	0.0225 1490	0.0237 6052	0.0250 0741	0.0262 5521	0.0275 0366	329
330	0.0225 1457	0.0237 6028	0.0250 0723	0.0262 5508	0.0275 0356	330
331	0.0225 1425	0.0237 6004	0.0250 0705	0.0262 5495	0.0275 0346	331
332	0.0225 1394	0.0237 5981	0.0250 0688	0.0262 5482	0.0275 0337	332
333	0.0225 1363	0.0237 5958	0.0250 0671	0.0262 5470	0.0275 0328	333
334	0.0225 1333	0.0237 5936	0.0250 0655	0.0262 5458	0.0275 0319	334
335	0.0225 1304	0.0237 5914	0.0250 0639	0.0262 5446	0.0275 0311	335
336	0.0225 1275	0.0237 5893	0.0250 0623	0.0262 5435	0.0275 0302	336
337	0.0225 1247	0.0237 5872	0.0250 0608	0.0262 5424	0.0275 0294	337
338	0.0225 1220	0.0237 5852	0.0250 0593	0.0262 5413	0.0275 0286	338
339	0.0225 1193	0.0237 5832	0.0250 0579	0.0262 5402	0.0275 0279	339
340	0.0225 1166	0.0237 5813	0.0250 0565	0.0262 5392	0.0275 0271	340
341	0.0225 1141	0.0237 5794	0.0250 0551	0.0262 5382	0.0275 0264	341
342	0.0225 1116	0.0237 5775	0.0250 0538	0.0262 5372	0.0275 0257	342
343	0.0225 1091	0.0237 5757	0.0250 0524	0.0262 5363	0.0275 0250	343
344	0.0225 1067	0.0237 5740	0.0250 0512	0.0262 5353	0.0275 0243	344
345	0.0225 1044	0.0237 5723	0.0250 0499	0.0262 5344	0.0275 0237	345
346	0.0225 1021	0.0237 5706	0.0250 0487	0.0262 5335	0.0275 0231	346
347	0.0225 0998	0.0237 5689	0.0250 0475	0.0262 5327	0.0275 0224	347
348	0.0225 0976	0.0237 5673	0.0250 0464	0.0262 5318	0.0275 0218	348
349	0.0225 0955	0.0237 5658	0.0250 0452	0.0262 5310	0.0275 0213	349
350	0.0225 0934	0.0237 5643	0.0250 0441	0.0262 5302	0.0275 0207	350
351	0.0225 0913	0.0237 5628	0.0250 0430	0.0262 5295	0.0275 0201	351
352	0.0225 0893	0.0237 5613	0.0250 0420	0.0262 5287	0.0275 0196	352
353	0.0225 0873	0.0237 5599	0.0250 0410	0.0262 5280	0.0275 0191	353
354	0.0225 0854	0.0237 5585	0.0250 0400	0.0262 5273	0.0275 0186	354
355	0.0225 0835	0.0237 5571	0.0250 0390	0.0262 5266	0.0275 0181	355
356	0.0225 0817	0.0237 5558	0.0250 0380	0.0262 5259	0.0275 0176	356
357	0.0225 0799	0.0237 5545	0.0250 0371	0.0262 5252	0.0275 0171	357
358	0.0225 0781	0.0237 5533	0.0250 0362	0.0262 5246	0.0275 0167	358
359	0.0225 0764	0.0237 5520	0.0250 0353	0.0262 5239	0.0275 0162	359
360	0.0225 0747	0.0237 5508	0.0250 0345	0.0262 5233	0.0275 0158	360

TABLE V

N	3	3 1/2	4	4 1/2	5	N
1	1.0300 0000	1.0350 0000	1.0400 0000	1.0450 0000	1.0500 0000	1
2	0.5226 1084	0.5264 0049	0.5301 9608	0.5339 9756	0.5378 0488	2
3	0.3535 3036	0.3569 3418	0.3603 4854	0.3637 7336	0.3672 0856	3
4	0.2690 2705	0.2722 5114	0.2754 9005	0.2787 4365	0.2820 1183	4
5	0.2183 5457	0.2214 8137	0.2246 2711	0.2277 9164	0.2309 7480	5
6	0.1845 9750	0.1876 6821	0.1907 6190	0.1938 7839	0.1970 1747	6
7	0.1605 0635	0.1635 4449	0.1666 0961	0.1697 0147	0.1728 1982	7
8	0.1424 5639	0.1454 7665	0.1485 2783	0.1516 0965	0.1547 2181	8
9	0.1284 3386	0.1314 4601	0.1344 9299	0.1375 7447	0.1406 9008	9
10	0.1172 3051	0.1202 4137	0.1232 9094	0.1263 7882	0.1295 0457	10
11	0.1080 7745	0.1110 9197	0.1141 4904	0.1172 4818	0.1203 8889	11
12	0.1004 6209	0.1034 8395	0.1065 5217	0.1096 6619	0.1128 2541	12
13	0.0940 2954	0.0970 6157	0.1001 4373	0.1032 7535	0.1064 5577	13
14	0.0885 2634	0.0915 7073	0.0946 6897	0.0978 2032	0.1010 2397	14
15	0.0837 6658	0.0868 2507	0.0899 4110	0.0931 1381	0.0963 4229	15
16	0.0796 1085	0.0826 8483	0.0858 2000	0.0890 1537	0.0922 6991	16
17	0.0759 5253	0.0790 4313	0.0821 9852	0.0854 1758	0.0886 9914	17
18	0.0727 0870	0.0758 1684	0.0789 9333	0.0822 3690	0.0855 4622	18
19	0.0698 1388	0.0729 4033	0.0761 3862	0.0794 0734	0.0827 4501	19
20	0.0672 1571	0.0703 6108	0.0735 8175	0.0768 7614	0.0802 4259	20
21	0.0648 7178	0.0680 3659	0.0712 8011	0.0746 0057	0.0779 9611	21
22	0.0627 4739	0.0659 3207	0.0691 9881	0.0725 4565	0.0759 7051	22
23	0.0608 1390	0.0640 1880	0.0673 0906	0.0706 8249	0.0741 3682	23
24	0.0590 4742	0.0622 7283	0.0655 8683	0.0689 8703	0.0724 7090	24
25	0.0574 2787	0.0606 7404	0.0640 1196	0.0674 3903	0.0709 5246	25
26	0.0559 3829	0.0592 0540	0.0625 6738	0.0660 2137	0.0695 6432	26
27	0.0545 6421	0.0578 5241	0.0612 3854	0.0647 1946	0.0682 9186	27
28	0.0532 9323	0.0566 0265	0.0600 1298	0.0635 2081	0.0671 2253	28
29	0.0521 1467	0.0554 4538	0.0588 7993	0.0624 1461	0.0660 4551	29
30	0.0510 1926	0.0543 7133	0.0578 3010	0.0613 9154	0.0650 5144	30
31	0.0499 9893	0.0533 7240	0.0568 5535	0.0604 4345	0.0641 3212	31
32	0.0490 4662	0.0524 4150	0.0559 4859	0.0595 6320	0.0632 8042	32
33	0.0481 5612	0.0515 7242	0.0551 0357	0.0587 4453	0.0624 9004	33
34	0.0473 2196	0.0507 5966	0.0543 1477	0.0579 8191	0.0617 5545	34
35	0.0465 3929	0.0499 9835	0.0535 7732	0.0572 7045	0.0610 7171	35
36	0.0458 0379	0.0492 8416	0.0528 8688	0.0566 0578	0.0604 3446	36
37	0.0451 1162	0.0486 1325	0.0522 3957	0.0559 8402	0.0598 3979	37
38	0.0444 5934	0.0479 8214	0.0516 3192	0.0554 0169	0.0592 8423	38
39	0.0438 4385	0.0473 8775	0.0510 6083	0.0548 5567	0.0587 6462	39
40	0.0432 6238	0.0468 2728	0.0505 2349	0.0543 4315	0.0582 7816	40
41	0.0427 1241	0.0462 9822	0.0500 1738	0.0538 6158	0.0578 2229	41
42	0.0421 9167	0.0457 9828	0.0495 4020	0.0534 0868	0.0573 9471	42
43	0.0416 9811	0.0453 2539	0.0490 8989	0.0529 8235	0.0569 9333	43
44	0.0412 2985	0.0448 7768	0.0486 6454	0.0525 8071	0.0566 1625	44
45	0.0407 8518	0.0444 5343	0.0482 6246	0.0522 0202	0.0562 6173	45
46	0.0403 6254	0.0440 5108	0.0478 8205	0.0518 4471	0.0559 2820	46
47	0.0399 6051	0.0436 6919	0.0475 2189	0.0515 0734	0.0556 1421	47
48	0.0395 7777	0.0433 0646	0.0471 8065	0.0511 8858	0.0553 1843	48
49	0.0392 1314	0.0429 6167	0.0468 5712	0.0508 8722	0.0550 3965	49
50	0.0388 6549	0.0426 3371	0.0465 5020	0.0506 0215	0.0547 7674	50
51	0.0385 3382	0.0423 2156	0.0462 5885	0.0503 3232	0.0545 2867	51
52	0.0382 1718	0.0420 2429	0.0459 8212	0.0500 7679	0.0542 9450	52
53	0.0379 1471	0.0417 4100	0.0457 1915	0.0498 3469	0.0540 7334	53
54	0.0376 2558	0.0414 7090	0.0454 6910	0.0496 0519	0.0538 6438	54
55	0.0373 4907	0.0412 1323	0.0452 3124	0.0493 8754	0.0536 6686	55
56	0.0370 8447	0.0409 6730	0.0450 0487	0.0491 8105	0.0534 8010	56
57	0.0368 3114	0.0407 3245	0.0447 8932	0.0489 8506	0.0533 0343	57
58	0.0365 8848	0.0405 0810	0.0445 8401	0.0487 9897	0.0531 3626	58
59	0.0363 5593	0.0402 9366	0.0443 8836	0.0486 2221	0.0529 7802	59
60	0.0361 3296	0.0400 8862	0.0442 0185	0.0484 5426	0.0528 2818	60

TABLE V

N	3	3 1/2	4	4 1/2	5	N
61	0.0359 1908	0.0398 9249	0.0440 2398	0.0482 9462	0.0526 8627	61
62	0.0357 1385	0.0397 0480	0.0438 5430	0.0481 4284	0.0525 5183	62
63	0.0355 1682	0.0395 2513	0.0436 9237	0.0479 9848	0.0524 2442	63
64	0.0353 2760	0.0393 5308	0.0435 3780	0.0478 6115	0.0523 0365	64
65	0.0351 4581	0.0391 8826	0.0433 9019	0.0477 3047	0.0521 8915	65
66	0.0349 7110	0.0390 3031	0.0432 4921	0.0476 0608	0.0520 8057	66
67	0.0348 0313	0.0388 7892	0.0431 1451	0.0474 8765	0.0519 7758	67
68	0.0346 4159	0.0387 3375	0.0429 8578	0.0473 7487	0.0518 7986	68
69	0.0344 8618	0.0385 9453	0.0428 6272	0.0472 6745	0.0517 8715	69
70	0.0343 3663	0.0384 6095	0.0427 4506	0.0471 6511	0.0516 9915	70
71	0.0341 9266	0.0383 3277	0.0426 3253	0.0470 6759	0.0516 1563	71
72	0.0340 5404	0.0382 0973	0.0425 2489	0.0469 7465	0.0515 3633	72
73	0.0339 2053	0.0380 9160	0.0424 2190	0.0468 8606	0.0514 6103	73
74	0.0337 9191	0.0379 7816	0.0423 2334	0.0468 0159	0.0513 8953	74
75	0.0336 6796	0.0378 6919	0.0422 2900	0.0467 2104	0.0513 2161	75
76	0.0335 4849	0.0377 6450	0.0421 3869	0.0466 4422	0.0512 5709	76
77	0.0334 3331	0.0376 6390	0.0420 5221	0.0465 7094	0.0511 9580	77
78	0.0333 2224	0.0375 6721	0.0419 6939	0.0465 0104	0.0511 3756	78
79	0.0332 1510	0.0374 7426	0.0418 9007	0.0464 3434	0.0510 8222	79
80	0.0331 1175	0.0373 8489	0.0418 1408	0.0463 7069	0.0510 2962	80
81	0.0330 1201	0.0372 9894	0.0417 4127	0.0463 0995	0.0509 7963	81
82	0.0329 1576	0.0372 1628	0.0416 7150	0.0462 5197	0.0509 3211	82
83	0.0328 2284	0.0371 3676	0.0416 0463	0.0461 9663	0.0508 8694	83
84	0.0327 3313	0.0370 6025	0.0415 4054	0.0461 4379	0.0508 4399	84
85	0.0326 4650	0.0369 8662	0.0414 7909	0.0460 9334	0.0508 0316	85
86	0.0325 6284	0.0369 1576	0.0414 2018	0.0460 4516	0.0507 6433	86
87	0.0324 8202	0.0368 4756	0.0413 6370	0.0459 9915	0.0507 2740	87
88	0.0324 0393	0.0367 8190	0.0413 0953	0.0459 5522	0.0506 9228	88
89	0.0323 2848	0.0367 1868	0.0412 5758	0.0459 1325	0.0506 5888	89
90	0.0322 5556	0.0366 5781	0.0412 0775	0.0458 7316	0.0506 2711	90
91	0.0321 8508	0.0365 9919	0.0411 5995	0.0458 3486	0.0505 9689	91
92	0.0321 1694	0.0365 4273	0.0411 1410	0.0457 9827	0.0505 6815	92
93	0.0320 5107	0.0364 8834	0.0410 7010	0.0457 6331	0.0505 4080	93
94	0.0319 8737	0.0364 3594	0.0410 2789	0.0457 2991	0.0505 1478	94
95	0.0319 2577	0.0363 8546	0.0409 8738	0.0456 9799	0.0504 9003	95
96	0.0318 6619	0.0363 3682	0.0409 4850	0.0456 6749	0.0504 6648	96
97	0.0318 0856	0.0362 8995	0.0409 1119	0.0456 3834	0.0504 4407	97
98	0.0317 5281	0.0362 4478	0.0408 7538	0.0456 1048	0.0504 2274	98
99	0.0316 9886	0.0362 0124	0.0408 4100	0.0455 8385	0.0504 0245	99
100	0.0316 4667	0.0361 5927	0.0408 0800	0.0455 5839	0.0503 8314	100
101	0.0315 9615	0.0361 1881	0.0407 7632	0.0455 3406	0.0503 6476	101
102	0.0315 4727	0.0360 7981	0.0407 4590	0.0455 1080	0.0503 4727	102
103	0.0314 9995	0.0360 4221	0.0407 1670	0.0454 8857	0.0503 3062	103
104	0.0314 5414	0.0360 0595	0.0406 8866	0.0454 6731	0.0503 1478	104
105	0.0314 0980	0.0359 7099	0.0406 6174	0.0454 4699	0.0502 9970	105
106	0.0313 6686	0.0359 3728	0.0406 3588	0.0454 2756	0.0502 8535	106
107	0.0313 2529	0.0359 0476	0.0406 1105	0.0454 0898	0.0502 7169	107
108	0.0312 8504	0.0358 7340	0.0405 8720	0.0453 9121	0.0502 5868	108
109	0.0312 4606	0.0358 4316	0.0405 6430	0.0453 7423	0.0502 4630	109
110	0.0312 0830	0.0358 1398	0.0405 4230	0.0453 5798	0.0502 3452	110
111	0.0311 7173	0.0357 8584	0.0405 2117	0.0453 4245	0.0502 2330	111
112	0.0311 3631	0.0357 5869	0.0405 0088	0.0453 2760	0.0502 1262	112
113	0.0311 0200	0.0357 3249	0.0404 8138	0.0453 1339	0.0502 0246	113
114	0.0310 6876	0.0357 0722	0.0404 6265	0.0452 9981	0.0501 9278	114
115	0.0310 3656	0.0356 8284	0.0404 4466	0.0452 8681	0.0501 8357	115
116	0.0310 0535	0.0356 5931	0.0404 2737	0.0452 7439	0.0501 7479	116
117	0.0309 7512	0.0356 3661	0.0404 1077	0.0452 6250	0.0501 6644	117
118	0.0309 4582	0.0356 1471	0.0403 9481	0.0452 5113	0.0501 5849	118
119	0.0309 1743	0.0355 9357	0.0403 7948	0.0452 4026	0.0501 5092	119
120	0.0308 8992	0.0355 7317	0.0403 6476	0.0452 2986	0.0501 4371	120

TABLE V

N	5 1/2	6	6 1/2	7	7 1/2	N
1	1.0550 0000	1.0600 0000	1.0650 0000	1.0700 0000	1.0750 0000	1
2	0.5416 1800	0.5454 3689	0.5492 6150	0.5530 9179	0.5569 2771	2
3	0.3706 5407	0.3741 0981	0.3775 7570	0.3810 5167	0.3845 3763	3
4	0.2852 9449	0.2885 9149	0.2919 0274	0.2952 2812	0.2985 6751	4
5	0.2341 7644	0.2373 9640	0.2406 3454	0.2438 9069	0.2471 6472	5
6	0.2001 7895	0.2033 6263	0.2065 6831	0.2097 9580	0.2130 4489	6
7	0.1759 6442	0.1791 3502	0.1823 3137	0.1855 5322	0.1888 0032	7
8	0.1578 6401	0.1610 3594	0.1642 3730	0.1674 6776	0.1707 2702	8
9	0.1438 3946	0.1470 2224	0.1502 3803	0.1534 8647	0.1567 6716	9
10	0.1326 6777	0.1358 6796	0.1391 0469	0.1423 7750	0.1456 8593	10
11	0.1235 7065	0.1267 9294	0.1300 5521	0.1333 5690	0.1366 9747	11
12	0.1160 2923	0.1192 7703	0.1225 6817	0.1259 0199	0.1292 7783	12
13	0.1096 8426	0.1129 6011	0.1162 8256	0.1196 5085	0.1230 6420	13
14	0.1042 7912	0.1075 8491	0.1109 4048	0.1143 4494	0.1177 9737	14
15	0.0996 2560	0.1029 6276	0.1063 5278	0.1097 9462	0.1132 8724	15
16	0.0955 8254	0.0989 5214	0.1023 7757	0.1058 5765	0.1093 9116	16
17	0.0920 4197	0.0954 4480	0.0989 0633	0.1024 2519	0.1060 0003	17
18	0.0889 1992	0.0923 5654	0.0958 5461	0.0994 1260	0.1030 2896	18
19	0.0861 5006	0.0896 2086	0.0931 5575	0.0967 5301	0.1004 1090	19
20	0.0836 7933	0.0871 8456	0.0907 5640	0.0943 9293	0.0980 9219	20
21	0.0814 6478	0.0850 0455	0.0886 1333	0.0922 8900	0.0960 2937	21
22	0.0794 7123	0.0830 4557	0.0866 9120	0.0904 0577	0.0941 8687	22
23	0.0776 6965	0.0812 7848	0.0849 6078	0.0887 1393	0.0925 3528	23
24	0.0760 3580	0.0796 7900	0.0833 9770	0.0871 8902	0.0910 5008	24
25	0.0745 4935	0.0782 2672	0.0819 8148	0.0858 1052	0.0897 1067	25
26	0.0731 9307	0.0769 0435	0.0806 9480	0.0845 6103	0.0884 9961	26
27	0.0719 5228	0.0756 9717	0.0795 2288	0.0834 2573	0.0874 0204	27
28	0.0708 1440	0.0745 9255	0.0784 5305	0.0823 9193	0.0864 0520	28
29	0.0697 6857	0.0735 7961	0.0774 7440	0.0814 4865	0.0854 9811	29
30	0.0688 0539	0.0726 4891	0.0765 7744	0.0805 8640	0.0846 7124	30
31	0.0679 1665	0.0717 9222	0.0757 5393	0.0797 9691	0.0839 1628	31
32	0.0670 9519	0.0710 0234	0.0749 9665	0.0790 7292	0.0832 2599	32
33	0.0663 3469	0.0702 7293	0.0742 9924	0.0784 0807	0.0825 9397	33
34	0.0656 2958	0.0695 9843	0.0736 5610	0.0777 9674	0.0820 1461	34
35	0.0649 7493	0.0689 7386	0.0730 6226	0.0772 3396	0.0814 8291	35
36	0.0643 6635	0.0683 9483	0.0725 1332	0.0767 1531	0.0809 9447	36
37	0.0637 9993	0.0678 5743	0.0720 0534	0.0762 3685	0.0805 4533	37
38	0.0632 7217	0.0673 5812	0.0715 3480	0.0757 9505	0.0801 3197	38
39	0.0627 7991	0.0668 9377	0.0710 9854	0.0753 8676	0.0797 5124	39
40	0.0623 2034	0.0664 6154	0.0706 9373	0.0750 0914	0.0794 0031	40
41	0.0618 9090	0.0660 5886	0.0703 1779	0.0746 5962	0.0790 7663	41
42	0.0614 8927	0.0656 8342	0.0699 6842	0.0743 3591	0.0787 7789	42
43	0.0611 1337	0.0653 3312	0.0696 4352	0.0740 3590	0.0785 0201	43
44	0.0607 6128	0.0650 0606	0.0693 4119	0.0737 5769	0.0782 4710	44
45	0.0604 3127	0.0647 0050	0.0690 5968	0.0734 9957	0.0780 1146	45
46	0.0601 2175	0.0644 1485	0.0687 9743	0.0732 5996	0.0777 9354	46
47	0.0598 3129	0.0641 4768	0.0685 5300	0.0730 3744	0.0775 9190	47
48	0.0595 5854	0.0638 9765	0.0683 2505	0.0728 3070	0.0774 0527	48
49	0.0593 0230	0.0636 6356	0.0681 1240	0.0726 3853	0.0772 3247	49
50	0.0590 6145	0.0634 4429	0.0679 1393	0.0724 5985	0.0770 7241	50
51	0.0588 3495	0.0632 3880	0.0677 2861	0.0722 9365	0.0769 2411	51
52	0.0586 2186	0.0630 4617	0.0675 5553	0.0721 3901	0.0767 8668	52
53	0.0584 2130	0.0628 6551	0.0673 9382	0.0719 9509	0.0766 5927	53
54	0.0582 3245	0.0626 9602	0.0672 4267	0.0718 6110	0.0765 4112	54
55	0.0580 5458	0.0625 3696	0.0671 0137	0.0717 3633	0.0764 3155	55
56	0.0578 8698	0.0623 8765	0.0669 6923	0.0716 2011	0.0763 2991	56
57	0.0577 2900	0.0622 4744	0.0668 4563	0.0715 1183	0.0762 3559	57
58	0.0575 8006	0.0621 1574	0.0667 2999	0.0714 1093	0.0761 4807	58
59	0.0574 3959	0.0619 9200	0.0666 2177	0.0713 1689	0.0760 6683	59
60	0.0573 0707	0.0618 7572	0.0665 2047	0.0712 2923	0.0759 9142	60

TABLE V

N	5 1/2	6	6 1/2	7	7 1/2	N
61	0.0571 8202	0.0617 6642	0.0664 2564	0.0711 4749	0.0759 2140	61
62	0.0570 6400	0.0616 6366	0.0663 3684	0.0710 7127	0.0758 5638	62
63	0.0569 5258	0.0615 6704	0.0662 5367	0.0710 0019	0.0757 9600	63
64	0.0568 4737	0.0614 7615	0.0661 7577	0.0709 3388	0.0757 3992	64
65	0.0567 4800	0.0613 9066	0.0661 0280	0.0708 7203	0.0756 8782	65
66	0.0566 5413	0.0613 1022	0.0660 3442	0.0708 1431	0.0756 3942	66
67	0.0565 6544	0.0612 3454	0.0659 7034	0.0707 6046	0.0755 9446	67
68	0.0564 8163	0.0611 6330	0.0659 1029	0.0707 1021	0.0755 5268	68
69	0.0564 0242	0.0610 9625	0.0658 5400	0.0706 6331	0.0755 1386	69
70	0.0563 2754	0.0610 3313	0.0658 0124	0.0706 1953	0.0754 7778	70
71	0.0562 5675	0.0609 7370	0.0657 5177	0.0705 7866	0.0754 4425	71
72	0.0561 8982	0.0609 1774	0.0657 0539	0.0705 4051	0.0754 1308	72
73	0.0561 2652	0.0608 6505	0.0656 6190	0.0705 0490	0.0753 8412	73
74	0.0560 6665	0.0608 1542	0.0656 2112	0.0704 7164	0.0753 5719	74
75	0.0560 1002	0.0607 6867	0.0655 8287	0.0704 4060	0.0753 3216	75
76	0.0559 5645	0.0607 2463	0.0655 4699	0.0704 1160	0.0753 0889	76
77	0.0559 0577	0.0606 8315	0.0655 1335	0.0703 8453	0.0752 8726	77
78	0.0558 5781	0.0606 4407	0.0654 8178	0.0703 5924	0.0752 6714	78
79	0.0558 1243	0.0606 0724	0.0654 5217	0.0703 3563	0.0752 4844	79
80	0.0557 6948	0.0605 7254	0.0654 2440	0.0703 1357	0.0752 3106	80
81	0.0557 2884	0.0605 3984	0.0653 9833	0.0702 9297	0.0752 1489	81
82	0.0556 9036	0.0605 0903	0.0653 7388	0.0702 7373	0.0751 9986	82
83	0.0556 5395	0.0604 7998	0.0653 5094	0.0702 5576	0.0751 8588	83
84	0.0556 1947	0.0604 5261	0.0653 2941	0.0702 3897	0.0751 7288	84
85	0.0555 8683	0.0604 2681	0.0653 0921	0.0702 2329	0.0751 6079	85
86	0.0555 5593	0.0604 0249	0.0652 9026	0.0702 0863	0.0751 4955	86
87	0.0555 2667	0.0603 7956	0.0652 7247	0.0701 9495	0.0751 3910	87
88	0.0554 9896	0.0603 5795	0.0652 5577	0.0701 8216	0.0751 2938	88
89	0.0554 7273	0.0603 3757	0.0652 4010	0.0701 7021	0.0751 2034	89
90	0.0554 4788	0.0603 1836	0.0652 2540	0.0701 5905	0.0751 1193	90
91	0.0554 2435	0.0603 0025	0.0652 1160	0.0701 4863	0.0751 0411	91
92	0.0554 0207	0.0602 8318	0.0651 9864	0.0701 3888	0.0750 9684	92
93	0.0553 8096	0.0602 6708	0.0651 8649	0.0701 2978	0.0750 9007	93
94	0.0553 6097	0.0602 5189	0.0651 7507	0.0701 2128	0.0750 8378	94
95	0.0553 4204	0.0602 3758	0.0651 6436	0.0701 1333	0.0750 7793	95
96	0.0553 2410	0.0602 2408	0.0651 5431	0.0701 0590	0.0750 7249	96
97	0.0553 0711	0.0602 1135	0.0651 4487	0.0700 9897	0.0750 6743	97
98	0.0552 9101	0.0601 9935	0.0651 3601	0.0700 9248	0.0750 6272	98
99	0.0552 7577	0.0601 8803	0.0651 2769	0.0700 8643	0.0750 5834	99
100	0.0552 6132	0.0601 7736	0.0651 1988	0.0700 8076	0.0750 5427	100
101	0.0552 4764	0.0601 6729	0.0651 1255	0.0700 7548	0.0750 5048	101
102	0.0552 3467	0.0601 5780	0.0651 0567	0.0700 7053	0.0750 4695	102
103	0.0552 2239	0.0601 4884	0.0650 9921	0.0700 6591	0.0750 4368	103
104	0.0552 1075	0.0601 4040	0.0650 9315	0.0700 6160	0.0750 4063	104
105	0.0551 9972	0.0601 3243	0.0650 8746	0.0700 5756	0.0750 3779	105
106	0.0551 8928	0.0601 2492	0.0650 8211	0.0700 5380	0.0750 3515	106
107	0.0551 7938	0.0601 1784	0.0650 7709	0.0700 5027	0.0750 3270	107
108	0.0551 7000	0.0601 1115	0.0650 7238	0.0700 4698	0.0750 3042	108
109	0.0551 6111	0.0601 0485	0.0650 6796	0.0700 4391	0.0750 2829	109
110	0.0551 5268	0.0600 9891	0.0650 6381	0.0700 4103	0.0750 2632	110
111	0.0551 4470	0.0600 9330	0.0650 5991	0.0700 3835	0.0750 2448	111
112	0.0551 3714	0.0600 8801	0.0650 5625	0.0700 3584	0.0750 2277	112
113	0.0551 2998	0.0600 8302	0.0650 5282	0.0700 3349	0.0750 2118	113
114	0.0551 2318	0.0600 7832	0.0650 4959	0.0700 3130	0.0750 1971	114
115	0.0551 1675	0.0600 7388	0.0650 4656	0.0700 2925	0.0750 1833	115
116	0.0551 1065	0.0600 6969	0.0650 4372	0.0700 2734	0.0750 1705	116
117	0.0551 0487	0.0600 6574	0.0650 4105	0.0700 2555	0.0750 1586	117
118	0.0550 9939	0.0600 6202	0.0650 3854	0.0700 2388	0.0750 1476	118
119	0.0550 9420	0.0600 5850	0.0650 3619	0.0700 2231	0.0750 1373	119
120	0.0550 8928	0.0600 5519	0.0650 3398	0.0700 2085	0.0750 1277	120

TABLE V

N	8	8 1/2	9	9 1/2	10	N
1	1.0800 0000	1.0850 0000	1.0900 0000	1.0950 0000	1.1000 0000	1
2	0.5607 6923	0.5646 1631	0.5684 6890	0.5723 2697	0.5761 9048	2
3	0.3880 3351	0.3915 3925	0.3950 5476	0.3985 7997	0.4021 1480	3
4	0.3019 2080	0.3052 8789	0.3086 6866	0.3120 6300	0.3154 7080	4
5	0.2504 5645	0.2537 6575	0.2570 9246	0.2604 3642	0.2637 9748	5
6	0.2163 1539	0.2196 0708	0.2229 1978	0.2262 5328	0.2296 0738	6
7	0.1920 7240	0.1953 6922	0.1986 9052	0.2020 3603	0.2054 0550	7
8	0.1740 1476	0.1773 3065	0.1806 7438	0.1840 4561	0.1874 4402	8
9	0.1600 7971	0.1634 2372	0.1667 9880	0.1702 0454	0.1736 4054	9
10	0.1490 2949	0.1524 0771	0.1558 2009	0.1592 6615	0.1627 4539	10
11	0.1400 7634	0.1434 9293	0.1469 4666	0.1504 3693	0.1539 6314	11
12	0.1326 9502	0.1361 5286	0.1396 5066	0.1431 8771	0.1467 6332	12
13	0.1265 2181	0.1300 2287	0.1335 6656	0.1371 5206	0.1407 7852	13
14	0.1212 9685	0.1248 4244	0.1284 3317	0.1320 6809	0.1357 4622	14
15	0.1168 2954	0.1204 2046	0.1240 5888	0.1277 4370	0.1314 7378	15
16	0.1129 7687	0.1166 1354	0.1202 9991	0.1240 3470	0.1278 1662	16
17	0.1096 2943	0.1133 1198	0.1170 4625	0.1208 3078	0.1246 6413	17
18	0.1067 0210	0.1104 3041	0.1142 1229	0.1180 4610	0.1219 3022	18
19	0.1041 2763	0.1079 0140	0.1117 3041	0.1156 1284	0.1195 4687	19
20	0.1018 5221	0.1056 7097	0.1095 4648	0.1134 7670	0.1174 5962	20
21	0.0998 3225	0.1036 9541	0.1076 1663	0.1115 9370	0.1156 2439	21
22	0.0980 3207	0.1019 3892	0.1059 0499	0.1099 2784	0.1140 0506	22
23	0.0964 2217	0.1003 7193	0.1043 8188	0.1084 4938	0.1125 7181	23
24	0.0949 7796	0.0989 6975	0.1030 2256	0.1071 3351	0.1112 9978	24
25	0.0936 7878	0.0977 1168	0.1018 0625	0.1059 5939	0.1101 6807	25
26	0.0925 0713	0.0965 8017	0.1007 1536	0.1049 0940	0.1091 5904	26
27	0.0914 4810	0.0955 6025	0.0997 3491	0.1039 6852	0.1082 5764	27
28	0.0904 8891	0.0946 3914	0.0988 5205	0.1031 2389	0.1074 5101	28
29	0.0896 1854	0.0938 0577	0.0980 5572	0.1023 6444	0.1067 2807	29
30	0.0888 2743	0.0930 5058	0.0973 3635	0.1016 8058	0.1060 7925	30
31	0.0881 0728	0.0923 6524	0.0966 8560	0.1010 6399	0.1054 9621	31
32	0.0874 5081	0.0917 4247	0.0960 9619	0.1005 0739	0.1049 7172	32
33	0.0868 5163	0.0911 7588	0.0955 6173	0.1000 0441	0.1044 9941	33
34	0.0863 0411	0.0906 5984	0.0950 7660	0.0995 4945	0.1040 7371	34
35	0.0858 0326	0.0901 8937	0.0946 3584	0.0991 3756	0.1036 8971	35
36	0.0853 4467	0.0897 6006	0.0942 3505	0.0987 6437	0.1033 4306	36
37	0.0849 2440	0.0893 6799	0.0938 7033	0.0984 2600	0.1030 2994	37
38	0.0845 3894	0.0890 0966	0.0935 3820	0.0981 1901	0.1027 4692	38
39	0.0841 8513	0.0886 8193	0.0932 3555	0.0978 4032	0.1024 9098	39
40	0.0838 6016	0.0883 8201	0.0929 5961	0.0975 8719	0.1022 5941	40
41	0.0835 6149	0.0881 0737	0.0927 0789	0.0973 5716	0.1020 4980	41
42	0.0832 8684	0.0878 5576	0.0924 7814	0.0971 4803	0.1018 5999	42
43	0.0830 3414	0.0876 2512	0.0922 6837	0.0969 5783	0.1016 8805	43
44	0.0828 0152	0.0874 1363	0.0920 7675	0.0967 8478	0.1015 3224	44
45	0.0825 8728	0.0872 1961	0.0919 0165	0.0966 2729	0.1013 9100	45
46	0.0823 8991	0.0870 4154	0.0917 4160	0.0964 8390	0.1012 6295	46
47	0.0822 0799	0.0868 7807	0.0915 9525	0.0963 5333	0.1011 4682	47
48	0.0820 4027	0.0867 2795	0.0914 6139	0.0962 3439	0.1010 4148	48
49	0.0818 8557	0.0865 9005	0.0913 3893	0.0961 2603	0.1009 4590	49
50	0.0817 4286	0.0864 6334	0.0912 2687	0.0960 2728	0.1008 5917	50
51	0.0816 1116	0.0863 4688	0.0911 2430	0.0959 3728	0.1007 8046	51
52	0.0814 8959	0.0862 3983	0.0910 3041	0.0958 5523	0.1007 0900	52
53	0.0813 7735	0.0861 4139	0.0909 4443	0.0957 8042	0.1006 4413	53
54	0.0812 7370	0.0860 5087	0.0908 6570	0.0957 1220	0.1005 8523	54
55	0.0811 7796	0.0859 6761	0.0907 9359	0.0956 4999	0.1005 3175	55
56	0.0810 8952	0.0858 9101	0.0907 2754	0.0955 9325	0.1004 8317	56
57	0.0810 0780	0.0858 2053	0.0906 6702	0.0955 4149	0.1004 3906	57
58	0.0809 3227	0.0857 5568	0.0906 1157	0.0954 9426	0.1003 9898	58
59	0.0808 6247	0.0856 9599	0.0905 6076	0.0954 5118	0.1003 6258	59
60	0.0807 9795	0.0856 4106	0.0905 1419	0.0954 1187	0.1003 2951	60

TABLE V

N	8	8 1/2	9	9 1/2	10	N
61	0.0807 3830	0.0855 9049	0.0904 7151	0.0953 7599	0.1002 9946	61
62	0.0806 8314	0.0855 4393	0.0904 3240	0.0953 4325	0.1002 7217	62
63	0.0806 3214	0.0855 0107	0.0903 9654	0.0953 1337	0.1002 4736	63
64	0.0805 8497	0.0854 6160	0.0903 6366	0.0952 8611	0.1002 2482	64
65	0.0805 4135	0.0854 2526	0.0903 3352	0.0952 6122	0.1002 0434	65
66	0.0805 0099	0.0853 9179	0.0903 0589	0.0952 3850	0.1001 8573	66
67	0.0804 6367	0.0853 6097	0.0902 8056	0.0952 1776	0.1001 6882	67
68	0.0804 2914	0.0853 3258	0.0902 5732	0.0951 9883	0.1001 5345	68
69	0.0803 9719	0.0853 0643	0.0902 3602	0.0951 8154	0.1001 3948	69
70	0.0803 6764	0.0852 8234	0.0902 1649	0.0951 6576	0.1001 2678	70
71	0.0803 4029	0.0852 6016	0.0901 9857	0.0951 5136	0.1001 1524	71
72	0.0803 1498	0.0852 3972	0.0901 8214	0.0951 3821	0.1001 0476	72
73	0.0802 9157	0.0852 2089	0.0901 6708	0.0951 2620	0.1000 9522	73
74	0.0802 6989	0.0852 0354	0.0901 5326	0.0951 1524	0.1000 8656	74
75	0.0802 4984	0.0851 8756	0.0901 4058	0.0951 0523	0.1000 7868	75
76	0.0802 3128	0.0851 7284	0.0901 2896	0.0950 9609	0.1000 7153	76
77	0.0802 1410	0.0851 5927	0.0901 1830	0.0950 8775	0.1000 6502	77
78	0.0801 9820	0.0851 4677	0.0901 0852	0.0950 8013	0.1000 5911	78
79	0.0801 8349	0.0851 3526	0.0900 9955	0.0950 7317	0.1000 5373	79
80	0.0801 6987	0.0851 2465	0.0900 9132	0.0950 6682	0.1000 4884	80
81	0.0801 5726	0.0851 1487	0.0900 8377	0.0950 6102	0.1000 4440	81
82	0.0801 4559	0.0851 0586	0.0900 7685	0.0950 5572	0.1000 4036	82
83	0.0801 3479	0.0850 9755	0.0900 7050	0.0950 5088	0.1000 3669	83
84	0.0801 2479	0.0850 8990	0.0900 6467	0.0950 4647	0.1000 3335	84
85	0.0801 1553	0.0850 8285	0.0900 5933	0.0950 4243	0.1000 3032	85
86	0.0801 0696	0.0850 7636	0.0900 5443	0.0950 3875	0.1000 2756	86
87	0.0800 9903	0.0850 7037	0.0900 4993	0.0950 3539	0.1000 2506	87
88	0.0800 9168	0.0850 6485	0.0900 4581	0.0950 3232	0.1000 2278	88
89	0.0800 8489	0.0850 5977	0.0900 4202	0.0950 2951	0.1000 2071	89
90	0.0800 7859	0.0850 5508	0.0900 3855	0.0950 2695	0.1000 1883	90
91	0.0800 7277	0.0850 5077	0.0900 3537	0.0950 2461	0.1000 1711	91
92	0.0800 6737	0.0850 4679	0.0900 3245	0.0950 2248	0.1000 1556	92
93	0.0800 6238	0.0850 4312	0.0900 2977	0.0950 2053	0.1000 1414	93
94	0.0800 5775	0.0850 3974	0.0900 2731	0.0950 1874	0.1000 1286	94
95	0.0800 5347	0.0850 3663	0.0900 2505	0.0950 1712	0.1000 1169	95
96	0.0800 4951	0.0850 3375	0.0900 2298	0.0950 1563	0.1000 1063	96
97	0.0800 4584	0.0850 3111	0.0900 2109	0.0950 1428	0.1000 0966	97
98	0.0800 4244	0.0850 2867	0.0900 1934	0.0950 1304	0.1000 0878	98
99	0.0800 3930	0.0850 2642	0.0900 1775	0.0950 1191	0.1000 0798	99
100	0.0800 3638	0.0850 2435	0.0900 1628	0.0950 1087	0.1000 0726	100
101	0.0800 3369	0.0850 2245	0.0900 1494	0.0950 0993	0.1000 0660	101
102	0.0800 3119	0.0850 2069	0.0900 1370	0.0950 0907	0.1000 0600	102
103	0.0800 2888	0.0850 1907	0.0900 1257	0.0950 0828	0.1000 0545	103
104	0.0800 2674	0.0850 1757	0.0900 1153	0.0950 0756	0.1000 0496	104
105	0.0800 2476	0.0850 1619	0.0900 1058	0.0950 0691	0.1000 0451	105
106	0.0800 2292	0.0850 1493	0.0900 0971	0.0950 0631	0.1000 0410	106
107	0.0800 2123	0.0850 1376	0.0900 0891	0.0950 0576	0.1000 0372	107
108	0.0800 1965	0.0850 1268	0.0900 0817	0.0950 0526	0.1000 0339	108
109	0.0800 1820	0.0850 1169	0.0900 0750	0.0950 0480	0.1000 0308	109
110	0.0800 1685	0.0850 1077	0.0900 0688	0.0950 0439	0.1000 0280	110
111	0.0800 1560	0.0850 0993	0.0900 0631	0.0950 0401	0.1000 0254	111
112	0.0800 1444	0.0850 0915	0.0900 0579	0.0950 0366	0.1000 0231	112
113	0.0800 1337	0.0850 0843	0.0900 0531	0.0950 0334	0.1000 0210	113
114	0.0800 1238	0.0850 0777	0.0900 0487	0.0950 0305	0.1000 0191	114
115	0.0800 1147	0.0850 0716	0.0900 0447	0.0950 0279	0.1000 0174	115
116	0.0800 1062	0.0850 0660	0.0900 0410	0.0950 0255	0.1000 0158	116
117	0.0800 0983	0.0850 0608	0.0900 0376	0.0950 0232	0.1000 0144	117
118	0.0800 0910	0.0850 0561	0.0900 0345	0.0950 0212	0.1000 0131	118
119	0.0800 0843	0.0850 0517	0.0900 0317	0.0950 0194	0.1000 0119	119
120	0.0800 0780	0.0850 0476	0.0900 0290	0.0950 0177	0.1000 0108	120

TABLE V

N	10 1/2	11	11 1/2	12	12 1/2	N
1	1.1050 0000	1.1100 0000	1.1150 0000	1.1200 0000	1.1250 0000	1
2	0.5800 5938	0.5839 3365	0.5878 1324	0.5916 9811	0.5955 8824	2
3	0.4056 5920	0.4092 1307	0.4127 7636	0.4163 4898	0.4199 3088	3
4	0.3188 9196	0.3223 2635	0.3257 7388	0.3292 3444	0.3327 0791	4
5	0.2671 7550	0.2705 7031	0.2739 8177	0.2774 0973	0.2808 5404	5
6	0.2329 8187	0.2363 7656	0.2397 9125	0.2432 2572	0.2466 7978	6
7	0.2087 9867	0.2122 1527	0.2156 5505	0.2191 1774	0.2226 0308	7
8	0.1908 6928	0.1943 2105	0.1977 9902	0.2013 0284	0.2048 3219	8
9	0.1771 0638	0.1806 0166	0.1841 2597	0.1876 7889	0.1912 6000	9
10	0.1662 5732	0.1698 0143	0.1733 7721	0.1769 8416	0.1806 2178	10
11	0.1575 2470	0.1611 2101	0.1647 5144	0.1684 1540	0.1721 1228	11
12	0.1503 7675	0.1540 2729	0.1577 1422	0.1614 3681	0.1651 9434	12
13	0.1444 4512	0.1481 5099	0.1518 9530	0.1556 7720	0.1594 9582	13
14	0.1394 6659	0.1432 2820	0.1470 3008	0.1508 7125	0.1547 5071	14
15	0.1352 4800	0.1390 6524	0.1429 2436	0.1468 2424	0.1507 6375	15
16	0.1316 4440	0.1355 1675	0.1394 3238	0.1433 9002	0.1473 8839	16
17	0.1285 4485	0.1324 7148	0.1364 4259	0.1404 5673	0.1445 1248	17
18	0.1258 6302	0.1298 4287	0.1338 6817	0.1379 3731	0.1420 4873	18
19	0.1235 3069	0.1275 6250	0.1316 4053	0.1357 6300	0.1399 2820	19
20	0.1214 9327	0.1255 7564	0.1297 0478	0.1338 7878	0.1380 9573	20
21	0.1197 0652	0.1238 3793	0.1280 1648	0.1322 4009	0.1365 0671	21
22	0.1181 3426	0.1223 1310	0.1265 3927	0.1308 1051	0.1351 2463	22
23	0.1167 4659	0.1209 7118	0.1252 4311	0.1295 5996	0.1339 1940	23
24	0.1155 1858	0.1197 8721	0.1241 0302	0.1284 6344	0.1328 6599	24
25	0.1144 2932	0.1187 4024	0.1230 9803	0.1274 9997	0.1319 4344	25
26	0.1134 6112	0.1178 1258	0.1222 1044	0.1266 5186	0.1311 3409	26
27	0.1125 9894	0.1169 8916	0.1214 2521	0.1259 0409	0.1304 2295	27
28	0.1118 2990	0.1162 5715	0.1207 2951	0.1252 4387	0.1297 9728	28
29	0.1111 4293	0.1156 0547	0.1201 1230	0.1246 6021	0.1292 4614	29
30	0.1105 2848	0.1150 2460	0.1195 6410	0.1241 4366	0.1287 6016	30
31	0.1099 7824	0.1145 0627	0.1190 7667	0.1236 8606	0.1283 3123	31
32	0.1094 8499	0.1140 4329	0.1186 4289	0.1232 8033	0.1279 5235	32
33	0.1090 4241	0.1136 2938	0.1182 5653	0.1229 2031	0.1276 1744	33
34	0.1086 4495	0.1132 5905	0.1179 1215	0.1226 0064	0.1273 2121	34
35	0.1082 8776	0.1129 2749	0.1176 0499	0.1223 1662	0.1270 5905	35
36	0.1079 6652	0.1126 3044	0.1173 3086	0.1220 6414	0.1268 2692	36
37	0.1076 7744	0.1123 6416	0.1170 8610	0.1218 3959	0.1266 2130	37
38	0.1074 1717	0.1121 2535	0.1168 6745	0.1216 3980	0.1264 3908	38
39	0.1071 8271	0.1119 1107	0.1166 7204	0.1214 6197	0.1262 7755	39
40	0.1069 7141	0.1117 1873	0.1164 9734	0.1213 0363	0.1261 3431	40
41	0.1067 8090	0.1115 4601	0.1163 4111	0.1211 6260	0.1260 0726	41
42	0.1066 0908	0.1113 9086	0.1162 0134	0.1210 3696	0.1258 9454	42
43	0.1064 5407	0.1112 5146	0.1160 7628	0.1209 2500	0.1257 9452	43
44	0.1063 1417	0.1111 2617	0.1159 6434	0.1208 2521	0.1257 0574	44
45	0.1061 8788	0.1110 1354	0.1158 6413	0.1207 3625	0.1256 2693	45
46	0.1060 7385	0.1109 1227	0.1157 7441	0.1206 5694	0.1255 5696	46
47	0.1059 7087	0.1108 2119	0.1156 9405	0.1205 8621	0.1254 9483	47
48	0.1058 7784	0.1107 3926	0.1156 2208	0.1205 2312	0.1254 3966	48
49	0.1057 9380	0.1106 6556	0.1155 5761	0.1204 6686	0.1253 9065	49
50	0.1057 1785	0.1105 9924	0.1154 9985	0.1204 1666	0.1253 4713	50
51	0.1056 4922	0.1105 3957	0.1154 4809	0.1203 7188	0.1253 0846	51
52	0.1055 8718	0.1104 8586	0.1154 0172	0.1203 3193	0.1252 7411	52
53	0.1055 3110	0.1104 3752	0.1153 6015	0.1202 9628	0.1252 4360	53
54	0.1054 8041	0.1103 9401	0.1153 2290	0.1202 6446	0.1252 1648	54
55	0.1054 3457	0.1103 5484	0.1152 8952	0.1202 3607	0.1251 9239	55
56	0.1053 9312	0.1103 1957	0.1152 5959	0.1202 1073	0.1251 7099	56
57	0.1053 5564	0.1102 8782	0.1152 3276	0.1201 8812	0.1251 5197	57
58	0.1053 2174	0.1102 5923	0.1152 0871	0.1201 6794	0.1251 3506	58
59	0.1052 9108	0.1102 3348	0.1151 8715	0.1201 4992	0.1251 2004	59
60	0.1052 6335	0.1102 1030	0.1151 6782	0.1201 3384	0.1251 0669	60

TABLE V

N	10 1/2	11	11 1/2	12	12 1/2	N
61	0.1052 3827	0.1101 8943	0.1151 5049	0.1201 1949	0.1250 9483	61
62	0.1052 1559	0.1101 7062	0.1151 3495	0.1201 0667	0.1250 8428	62
63	0.1051 9506	0.1101 5369	0.1151 2101	0.1200 9523	0.1250 7491	63
64	0.1051 7650	0.1101 3844	0.1151 0852	0.1200 8502	0.1250 6659	64
65	0.1051 5970	0.1101 2471	0.1150 9732	0.1200 7591	0.1250 5918	65
66	0.1051 4450	0.1101 1234	0.1150 8727	0.1200 6777	0.1250 5260	66
67	0.1051 3075	0.1101 0119	0.1150 7827	0.1200 6051	0.1250 4676	67
68	0.1051 1832	0.1100 9116	0.1150 7019	0.1200 5402	0.1250 4156	68
69	0.1051 0706	0.1100 8212	0.1150 6295	0.1200 4823	0.1250 3694	69
70	0.1050 9688	0.1100 7397	0.1150 5645	0.1200 4306	0.1250 3284	70
71	0.1050 8767	0.1100 6664	0.1150 5063	0.1200 3845	0.1250 2919	71
72	0.1050 7933	0.1100 6003	0.1150 4540	0.1200 3432	0.1250 2594	72
73	0.1050 7179	0.1100 5408	0.1150 4072	0.1200 3065	0.1250 2306	73
74	0.1050 6496	0.1100 4872	0.1150 3652	0.1200 2736	0.1250 2050	74
75	0.1050 5878	0.1100 4389	0.1150 3275	0.1200 2443	0.1250 1822	75
76	0.1050 5320	0.1100 3954	0.1150 2937	0.1200 2181	0.1250 1619	76
77	0.1050 4814	0.1100 3562	0.1150 2634	0.1200 1947	0.1250 1440	77
78	0.1050 4356	0.1100 3209	0.1150 2362	0.1200 1739	0.1250 1280	78
79	0.1050 3942	0.1100 2891	0.1150 2119	0.1200 1552	0.1250 1137	79
80	0.1050 3567	0.1100 2604	0.1150 1900	0.1200 1386	0.1250 1011	80
81	0.1050 3228	0.1100 2346	0.1150 1704	0.1200 1238	0.1250 0899	81
82	0.1050 2921	0.1100 2113	0.1150 1528	0.1200 1105	0.1250 0799	82
83	0.1050 2644	0.1100 1904	0.1150 1371	0.1200 0987	0.1250 0710	83
84	0.1050 2393	0.1100 1715	0.1150 1229	0.1200 0881	0.1250 0631	84
85	0.1050 2165	0.1100 1545	0.1150 1102	0.1200 0786	0.1250 0561	85
86	0.1050 1959	0.1100 1392	0.1150 0989	0.1200 0702	0.1250 0499	86
87	0.1050 1773	0.1100 1254	0.1150 0887	0.1200 0627	0.1250 0443	87
88	0.1050 1605	0.1100 1130	0.1150 0795	0.1200 0560	0.1250 0394	88
89	0.1050 1452	0.1100 1018	0.1150 0713	0.1200 0500	0.1250 0350	89
90	0.1050 1314	0.1100 0917	0.1150 0640	0.1200 0446	0.1250 0311	90
91	0.1050 1189	0.1100 0826	0.1150 0574	0.1200 0398	0.1250 0277	91
92	0.1050 1076	0.1100 0744	0.1150 0515	0.1200 0356	0.1250 0246	92
93	0.1050 0974	0.1100 0670	0.1150 0461	0.1200 0318	0.1250 0219	93
94	0.1050 0881	0.1100 0604	0.1150 0414	0.1200 0284	0.1250 0194	94
95	0.1050 0798	0.1100 0544	0.1150 0371	0.1200 0253	0.1250 0173	95
96	0.1050 0722	0.1100 0490	0.1150 0333	0.1200 0226	0.1250 0154	96
97	0.1050 0653	0.1100 0442	0.1150 0299	0.1200 0202	0.1250 0136	97
98	0.1050 0591	0.1100 0398	0.1150 0268	0.1200 0180	0.1250 0121	98
99	0.1050 0535	0.1100 0358	0.1150 0240	0.1200 0161	0.1250 0108	99
100	0.1050 0484	0.1100 0323	0.1150 0215	0.1200 0144	0.1250 0096	100
101	0.1050 0438	0.1100 0291	0.1150 0193	0.1200 0128	0.1250 0085	101
102	0.1050 0397	0.1100 0262	0.1150 0173	0.1200 0115	0.1250 0076	102
103	0.1050 0359	0.1100 0236	0.1150 0155	0.1200 0102	0.1250 0067	103
104	0.1050 0325	0.1100 0213	0.1150 0139	0.1200 0091	0.1250 0060	104
105	0.1050 0294	0.1100 0192	0.1150 0125	0.1200 0082	0.1250 0053	105
106	0.1050 0266	0.1100 0173	0.1150 0112	0.1200 0073	0.1250 0047	106
107	0.1050 0241	0.1100 0156	0.1150 0101	0.1200 0065	0.1250 0042	107
108	0.1050 0218	0.1100 0140	0.1150 0090	0.1200 0058	0.1250 0037	108
109	0.1050 0197	0.1100 0126	0.1150 0081	0.1200 0052	0.1250 0033	109
110	0.1050 0178	0.1100 0114	0.1150 0073	0.1200 0046	0.1250 0030	110
111	0.1050 0161	0.1100 0102	0.1150 0065	0.1200 0041	0.1250 0026	111
112	0.1050 0146	0.1100 0092	0.1150 0058	0.1200 0037	0.1250 0023	112
113	0.1050 0132	0.1100 0083	0.1150 0052	0.1200 0033	0.1250 0021	113
114	0.1050 0120	0.1100 0075	0.1150 0047	0.1200 0029	0.1250 0018	114
115	0.1050 0108	0.1100 0067	0.1150 0042	0.1200 0026	0.1250 0016	115
116	0.1050 0098	0.1100 0061	0.1150 0038	0.1200 0023	0.1250 0015	116
117	0.1050 0089	0.1100 0055	0.1150 0034	0.1200 0021	0.1250 0013	117
118	0.1050 0080	0.1100 0049	0.1150 0030	0.1200 0019	0.1250 0012	118
119	0.1050 0073	0.1100 0044	0.1150 0027	0.1200 0017	0.1250 0010	119
120	0.1050 0066	0.1100 0040	0.1150 0024	0.1200 0015	0.1250 0009	120

TABLE VI
SIX-PLACE COMMON LOGARITHMS OF NUMBERS FROM 100 TO 999

N.	0	1	2	3	4	5	6	7	8	9	D.
100	000000	000434	000868	001301	001734	002166	002598	003029	003461	003891	432
1	4321	4751	5181	5609	6038	6466	6894	7321	7748	8174	428
2	8600	9026	9451	9876	010300	010724	011147	011570	011993	012415	424
3	012837	013259	013680	014100	4521	4940	5360	5779	6197	6616	420
4	7033	7451	7868	8284	8700	9116	9532	9947	020361	020775	416
105	021189	021603	022016	022428	022841	023252	023664	024075	4486	4896	412
6	5306	5715	6125	6533	6942	7350	7757	8164	8571	8978	408
7	9384	9789	030195	030600	031004	031408	031812	032216	032619	033021	404
8	033424	033826	4227	4628	5029	5430	5830	6230	6629	7028	400
9	7426	7825	8223	8620	9017	9414	9811	040207	040602	040998	397
110	041393	041787	042182	042576	042969	043362	043755	044148	044540	044932	393
1	5323	5714	6105	6495	6885	7275	7664	8053	8442	8830	390
2	9218	9606	9993	050380	050766	051153	051538	051924	052309	052694	386
3	053078	053463	053846	4230	4613	4996	5378	5760	6142	6524	383
4	6905	7286	7666	8046	8426	8805	9185	9563	9942	060320	379
115	060698	061075	061452	061829	062206	062582	062958	063333	063709	4083	376
6	4458	4832	5206	5580	5953	6326	6699	7071	7443	7815	373
7	8186	8557	8928	9298	9668	070038	070407	070776	071145	071514	370
8	071882	072250	072617	072985	073352	3718	4085	4451	4816	5182	366
9	5547	5912	6276	6640	7004	7368	7731	8094	8457	8819	363
120	079181	079543	079904	080266	080626	080987	081347	081707	082067	082426	360
1	082785	083144	083503	3861	4219	4576	4934	5291	5647	6004	357
2	6360	6716	7071	7426	7781	8136	8490	8845	9198	9552	355
3	9905	090258	090611	090963	091315	091667	092018	092370	092721	093071	352
4	093422	3772	4122	4471	4820	5169	5518	5866	6215	6562	349
125	6910	7257	7604	7951	8298	8644	8990	9335	9681	100026	346
6	100371	100715	101059	101403	101747	102091	102434	102777	103119	3462	343
7	3804	4146	4487	4828	5169	5510	5851	6191	6531	6871	341
8	7210	7549	7888	8227	8565	8903	9241	9579	9916	110253	338
9	110590	110926	111263	111599	111934	112270	112605	112940	113275	3609	335
130	113943	114277	114611	114944	115278	115611	115943	116276	116608	116940	333
1	7271	7603	7934	8265	8595	8926	9256	9586	9915	120245	330
2	120574	120903	121231	121560	121888	122216	122544	122871	123198	3525	328
3	3852	4178	4504	4830	5156	5481	5806	6131	6456	6781	325
4	7105	7429	7753	8076	8399	8722	9045	9368	9690	130012	323
135	130334	130655	130977	131298	131619	131939	132260	132580	132900	3219	321
6	3539	3858	4177	4496	4814	5133	5451	5769	6086	6403	318
7	6721	7037	7354	7671	7987	8303	8618	8934	9249	9564	316
8	9879	140194	140508	140822	141136	141450	141763	142076	142389	142702	314
9	143015	3327	3639	3951	4263	4574	4885	5196	5507	5818	311
140	146128	146438	146748	147058	147367	147676	147985	148294	148603	148911	309
1	9219	9527	9835	150142	150449	150756	151063	151370	151676	151982	307
2	152288	152594	152900	3205	3510	3815	4120	4424	4728	5032	305
3	5336	5640	5943	6246	6549	6852	7154	7457	7759	8061	303
4	8362	8664	8965	9266	9567	9868	160168	160469	160769	161068	301
145	161368	161667	161967	162266	162564	162863	3161	3460	3758	4055	299
6	4353	4650	4947	5244	5541	5838	6134	6430	6726	7022	297
7	7317	7613	7908	8203	8497	8792	9086	9380	9674	9968	295
8	170262	170555	170848	171141	171434	171726	172019	172311	172603	172895	293
9	3186	3478	3769	4060	4351	4641	4932	5222	5512	5802	291
150	176091	176381	176670	176959	177248	177536	177825	178113	178401	178689	289
1	8977	9264	9552	9839	180126	180413	180699	180986	181272	181558	287
2	181844	182129	182415	182700	2985	3270	3555	3839	4123	4407	285
3	4691	4975	5259	5542	5825	6108	6391	6674	6956	7239	283
4	7521	7803	8084	8366	8647	8928	9209	9490	9771	190051	281
155	190332	190612	190892	191171	191451	191730	192010	192289	192567	2846	279
6	3125	3403	3681	3959	4237	4514	4792	5069	5346	5623	278
7	5900	6176	6453	6729	7005	7281	7556	7832	8107	8382	276
8	8657	8932	9206	9481	9755	200029	200303	200577	200850	201124	274
9	201397	201670	201943	202216	202488	2761	3033	3305	3577	3848	272
N.	0	1	2	3	4	5	6	7	8	9	D.

N.	0	1	2	3	4	5	6	7	8	9	D.
160	204120	204391	204663	204934	205204	205475	205746	206016	206286	206556	271
1	6826	7096	7365	7634	7904	8173	8441	8710	8979	9247	269
2	9515	9783	210051	210319	210586	210853	211121	211388	211654	211921	267
3	212188	212454	2720	2986	3252	3518	3783	4049	4314	4579	266
4	4844	5109	5373	5638	5902	6166	6430	6694	6957	7221	264
165	7484	7747	8010	8273	8536	8798	9060	9323	9585	9846	262
6	220108	220370	220631	220892	221153	221414	221675	221936	222196	222456	261
7	2716	2976	3236	3496	3755	4015	4274	4533	4792	5051	259
8	5309	5568	5826	6084	6342	6600	6858	7115	7372	7630	258
9	7887	8144	8400	8657	8913	9170	9426	9682	9938	230193	256
170	230449	230704	230960	231215	231470	231724	231979	232234	232488	232742	255
1	2996	3250	3504	3757	4011	4264	4517	4770	5023	5276	253
2	5528	5781	6033	6285	6537	6789	7041	7292	7544	7795	252
3	8046	8297	8548	8799	9049	9299	9550	9800	240050	240300	250
4	240549	240799	241048	241297	241546	241795	242044	242293	2541	2790	249
175	3038	3286	3534	3782	4030	4277	4525	4772	5019	5266	248
6	5513	5759	6006	6252	6499	6745	6991	7237	7482	7728	246
7	7973	8219	8464	8709	8954	9198	9443	9687	9932	250176	245
8	250420	250664	250908	251151	251395	251638	251881	252125	252368	2610	243
9	2853	3096	3338	3580	3822	4064	4306	4548	4790	5031	242
180	255273	255514	255755	255996	256237	256477	256718	256958	257198	257439	241
1	7679	7918	8158	8398	8637	8877	9116	9355	9594	9833	239
2	260071	260310	260548	260787	261025	261263	261501	261739	261976	262214	238
3	2451	2688	2925	3162	3399	3636	3873	4109	4346	4582	237
4	4818	5054	5290	5525	5761	5996	6232	6467	6702	6937	235
185	7172	7406	7641	7875	8110	8344	8578	8812	9046	9279	234
6	9513	9746	9980	270213	270446	270679	270912	271144	271377	271609	233
7	271842	272074	272306	2538	2770	3001	3233	3464	3696	3927	232
8	4158	4389	4620	4850	5081	5311	5542	5772	6002	6232	230
9	6462	6692	6921	7151	7380	7609	7838	8067	8296	8525	229
190	278754	278982	279211	279439	279667	279895	280123	280351	280578	280806	228
1	281033	281261	281488	281715	281942	282169	2396	2622	2849	3075	227
2	3301	3527	3753	3979	4205	4431	4656	4882	5107	5332	226
3	5557	5782	6007	6232	6456	6681	6905	7130	7354	7578	225
4	7802	8026	8249	8473	8696	8920	9143	9366	9589	9812	223
195	290035	290257	290480	290702	290925	291147	291369	291591	291813	292034	222
6	2256	2478	2699	2920	3141	3363	3584	3804	4025	4246	221
7	4466	4687	4907	5127	5347	5567	5787	6007	6226	6446	220
8	6665	6884	7104	7323	7542	7761	7979	8198	8416	8635	219
9	8853	9071	9289	9507	9725	9943	300161	300378	300595	300813	218
200	301030	301247	301464	301681	301898	302114	302331	302547	302764	302980	217
1	3196	3412	3628	3844	4059	4275	4491	4706	4921	5136	216
2	5351	5566	5781	5996	6211	6425	6639	6854	7068	7282	215
3	7496	7710	7924	8137	8351	8564	8778	8991	9204	9417	213
4	9630	9843	310056	310268	310481	310693	310906	311118	311330	311542	212
205	311754	311966	2177	2389	2600	2812	3023	3234	3445	3656	211
6	3867	4078	4289	4499	4710	4920	5130	5340	5551	5760	210
7	5970	6180	6390	6599	6809	7018	7227	7436	7646	7854	209
8	8063	8272	8481	8689	8898	9106	9314	9522	9730	9938	208
9	320146	320354	320562	320769	320977	321184	321391	321598	321805	322012	207
210	322219	322426	322633	322839	323046	323252	323458	323665	323871	324077	206
1	4282	4488	4694	4899	5105	5310	5516	5721	5926	6131	205
2	6336	6541	6745	6950	7155	7359	7563	7767	7972	8176	204
3	8380	8583	8787	8991	9194	9398	9601	9805	330008	330211	203
4	330414	330617	330819	331022	331225	331427	331630	331832	2034	2236	202
215	2438	2640	2842	3044	3246	3447	3649	3850	4051	4253	202
6	4454	4655	4856	5057	5257	5458	5658	5859	6059	6260	201
7	6460	6660	6860	7060	7260	7459	7659	7858	8058	8257	200
8	8456	8656	8855	9054	9253	9451	9650	9849	340047	340246	199
9	340444	340642	340841	341039	341237	341435	341632	341830	2028	2225	198
N.	0	1	2	3	4	5	6	7	8	9	D.

N.	0	1	2	3	4	5	6	7	8	9	D.
220	342423	342620	342817	343014	343212	343409	343606	343802	343999	344196	197
1	4392	4589	4785	4981	5178	5374	5570	5766	5962	6157	196
2	6353	6549	6744	6939	7135	7330	7525	7720	7915	8110	195
3	8305	8500	8694	8889	9083	9278	9472	9666	9860	350054	194
4	350248	350442	350636	350829	351023	351216	351410	351603	351796	1989	193
225	2183	2375	2568	2761	2954	3147	3339	3532	3724	3916	193
6	4108	4301	4493	4685	4876	5068	5260	5452	5643	5834	192
7	6026	6217	6408	6599	6790	6981	7172	7363	7554	7744	191
8	7935	8125	8316	8506	8696	8886	9076	9266	9456	9646	190
9	9835	360025	360215	360404	360593	360783	360972	361161	361350	361539	189
230	361728	361917	362105	362294	362482	362671	362859	363048	363236	363424	188
1	3612	3800	3988	4176	4363	4551	4739	4926	5113	5301	188
2	5488	5675	5862	6049	6236	6423	6610	6796	6983	7169	187
3	7356	7542	7729	7915	8101	8287	8473	8659	8845	9030	186
4	9216	9401	9587	9772	9958	370143	370328	370513	370698	370883	185
235	371068	371253	371437	371622	371806	1991	2175	2360	2544	2728	184
6	2912	3096	3280	3464	3647	3831	4015	4198	4382	4565	184
7	4748	4932	5115	5298	5481	5664	5846	6029	6212	6394	183
8	6577	6759	6942	7124	7306	7488	7670	7852	8034	8216	182
9	8398	8580	8761	8943	9124	9306	9487	9668	9849	380030	181
240	380211	380392	380573	380754	380934	381115	381296	381476	381656	381837	181
1	2017	2197	2377	2557	2737	2917	3097	3277	3456	3636	180
2	3815	3995	4174	4353	4533	4712	4891	5070	5249	5428	179
3	5606	5785	5964	6142	6321	6499	6677	6856	7034	7212	178
4	7390	7568	7746	7923	8101	8279	8456	8634	8811	8989	178
245	9166	9343	9520	9698	9875	390051	390228	390405	390582	390759	177
6	390935	391112	391288	391464	391641	1817	1993	2169	2345	2521	176
7	2697	2873	3048	3224	3400	3575	3751	3926	4101	4277	176
8	4452	4627	4802	4977	5152	5326	5501	5676	5850	6025	175
9	6199	6374	6548	6722	6896	7071	7245	7419	7592	7766	174
250	397940	398114	398287	398461	398634	398808	398981	399154	399328	399501	173
1	9674	9847	400020	400192	400365	400538	400711	400883	401056	401228	173
2	401401	401573	1745	1917	2089	2261	2433	2605	2777	2949	172
3	3121	3292	3464	3635	3807	3978	4149	4320	4492	4663	171
4	4834	5005	5176	5346	5517	5688	5858	6029	6199	6370	171
255	6540	6710	6881	7051	7221	7391	7561	7731	7901	8070	170
6	8240	8410	8579	8749	8918	9087	9257	9426	9595	9764	169
7	9933	410102	410271	410440	410609	410777	410964	411114	411283	411451	169
8	411620	1788	1956	2124	2293	2461	2629	2796	2964	3132	168
9	3300	3467	3635	3803	3970	4137	4305	4472	4639	4806	167
260	414973	415140	415307	415474	415641	415808	415974	416141	416308	416474	167
1	6641	6807	6973	7139	7306	7472	7638	7804	7970	8135	166
2	8301	8467	8633	8798	8964	9129	9295	9460	9625	9791	165
3	9956	420121	420286	420451	420616	420781	420945	421110	421275	421439	165
4	421604	1768	1933	2097	2261	2426	2590	2754	2918	3082	164
265	3246	3410	3574	3737	3901	4065	4228	4392	4555	4718	164
6	4882	5045	5208	5371	5534	5697	5860	6023	6186	6349	163
7	6511	6674	6836	6999	7161	7324	7486	7648	7811	7973	162
8	8135	8297	8459	8621	8783	8944	9106	9268	9429	9591	162
9	9752	9914	430075	430236	430398	430559	430720	430881	431042	431203	161
270	431364	431525	431685	431846	432007	432167	432328	432488	432649	432809	161
1	2969	3130	3290	3450	3610	3770	3930	4090	4249	4409	160
2	4569	4729	4888	5048	5207	5367	5526	5685	5844	6004	159
3	6163	6322	6481	6640	6799	6957	7116	7275	7433	7592	159
4	7751	7909	8067	8226	8384	8542	8701	8859	9017	9175	158
275	9333	9491	9648	9806	9964	440122	440279	440437	440594	440752	158
6	440909	441066	441224	441381	441538	1695	1852	2009	2166	2323	157
7	2480	2637	2793	2950	3106	3263	3419	3576	3732	3889	157
8	4045	4201	4357	4513	4669	4825	4981	5137	5293	5449	156
9	5604	5760	5915	6071	6226	6382	6537	6692	6848	7003	155
N.	0	1	2	3	4	5	6	7	8	9	D.

N.	0	1	2	3	4	5	6	7	8	9	D.
280	447158	447313	447468	447623	447778	447933	448088	448242	448397	448552	155
1	8706	8861	9015	9170	9324	9478	9633	9787	9941	450095	154
2	450249	450403	450557	450711	450865	451018	451172	451326	451479	1633	154
3	1786	1940	2093	2247	2400	2553	2706	2859	3012	3165	153
4	3318	3471	3624	3777	3930	4082	4235	4387	4540	4692	153
285	4845	4997	5150	5302	5454	5606	5758	5910	6062	6214	152
6	6366	6518	6670	6821	6973	7125	7276	7428	7579	7731	152
7	7882	8033	8184	8336	8487	8638	8789	8940	9091	9242	151
8	9392	9543	9694	9845	9995	460146	460296	460447	460597	460748	151
9	460898	461048	461198	461348	461499	1649	1799	1948	2098	2248	150
290	462398	462548	462697	462847	462997	463146	463296	463445	463594	463744	150
1	3893	4042	4191	4340	4490	4639	4788	4936	5085	5234	149
2	5383	5532	5680	5829	5977	6126	6274	6423	6571	6719	149
3	6868	7016	7164	7312	7460	7608	7756	7904	8052	8200	148
4	8347	8495	8643	8790	8938	9085	9233	9380	9527	9675	148
295	9822	9969	470116	470263	470410	470557	470704	470851	470998	471145	147
6	471292	471438	1585	1732	1878	2025	2171	2318	2464	2610	146
7	2756	2903	3049	3195	3341	3487	3633	3779	3925	4071	146
8	4216	4362	4508	4653	4799	4944	5090	5235	5381	5526	146
9	5671	5816	5962	6107	6252	6397	6542	6687	6832	6976	145
300	477121	477266	477411	477555	477700	477844	477989	478133	478278	478422	145
1	8566	8711	8855	8999	9143	9287	9431	9575	9719	9863	144
2	480007	480151	480294	480438	480582	480725	480869	481012	481156	481299	144
3	1443	1586	1729	1872	2016	2159	2302	2445	2588	2731	143
4	2874	3016	3159	3302	3445	3587	3730	3872	4015	4157	143
305	4300	4442	4585	4727	4869	5011	5153	5295	5437	5579	142
6	5721	5863	6005	6147	6289	6430	6572	6714	6855	6997	142
7	7138	7280	7421	7563	7704	7845	7986	8127	8269	8410	141
8	8551	8692	8833	8974	9114	9255	9396	9537	9677	9818	141
9	9958	490099	490239	490380	490520	490661	490801	490941	491081	491222	140
310	491362	491502	491642	491782	491922	492062	492201	492341	492481	492621	140
1	2760	2900	3040	3179	3319	3458	3597	3737	3876	4015	139
2	4155	4294	4433	4572	4711	4850	4989	5128	5267	5406	139
3	5544	5683	5822	5960	6099	6238	6376	6515	6653	6791	139
4	6930	7068	7206	7344	7483	7621	7759	7897	8035	8173	138
315	8311	8448	8586	8724	8862	8999	9137	9275	9412	9550	138
6	9687	9824	9962	500099	500236	500374	500511	500648	500785	500922	137
7	501059	501196	501333	1470	1607	1744	1880	2017	2154	2291	137
8	2427	2564	2700	2837	2973	3109	3246	3382	3518	3655	136
9	3791	3927	4063	4199	4335	4471	4607	4743	4878	5014	136
320	505150	505286	505421	505557	505693	505828	505964	506099	506234	506370	136
1	6505	6640	6776	6911	7046	7181	7316	7451	7586	7721	135
2	7856	7991	8126	8260	8395	8530	8664	8799	8934	9068	135
3	9203	9337	9471	9606	9740	9874	510009	510143	510277	510411	134
4	510545	510679	510813	510947	511081	511215	1349	1482	1616	1750	134
325	1883	2017	2151	2284	2418	2551	2684	2818	2951	3084	133
6	3218	3351	3484	3617	3750	3883	4016	4149	4282	4415	133
7	4548	4681	4813	4946	5079	5211	5344	5476	5609	5741	133
8	5874	6006	6139	6271	6403	6535	6668	6800	6932	7064	132
9	7196	7328	7460	7592	7724	7855	7987	8119	8251	8382	132
330	518514	518646	518777	518909	519040	519171	519303	519434	519566	519697	131
1	9828	9959	520090	520221	520353	520484	520615	520745	520876	521007	131
2	521138	521269	1400	1530	1661	1792	1922	2053	2183	2314	131
3	2444	2575	2705	2835	2966	3096	3226	3356	3486	3616	130
4	3746	3876	4006	4136	4266	4396	4526	4656	4785	4915	130
335	5045	5174	5304	5434	5563	5693	5822	5951	6081	6210	129
6	6339	6469	6598	6727	6856	6985	7114	7243	7372	7501	129
7	7630	7759	7888	8016	8145	8274	8402	8531	8660	8788	129
8	8917	9045	9174	9302	9430	9559	9687	9815	9943	530072	128
9	530200	530328	530456	530584	530712	530840	530968	531096	531223	1351	128
N.	0	1	2	3	4	5	6	7	8	9	D.

N.	0	1	2	3	4	5	6	7	8	9	D.
340	531479	531607	531734	531862	531990	532117	532245	532372	532500	532627	128
1	2754	2882	3009	3136	3264	3391	3518	3645	3772	3899	127
2	4026	4153	4280	4407	4534	4661	4787	4914	5041	5167	127
3	5294	5421	5547	5674	5800	5927	6053	6180	6306	6432	126
4	6558	6685	6811	6937	7063	7189	7315	7441	7567	7693	126
345	7819	7945	8071	8197	8322	8448	8574	8699	8825	8951	126
6	9076	9202	9327	9452	9578	9703	9829	9954	540079	540204	125
7	540329	540455	540580	540705	540830	540955	541080	541205	1330	1454	125
8	1579	1704	1829	1953	2078	2203	2327	2452	2576	2701	125
9	2825	2950	3074	3199	3323	3447	3571	3696	3820	3944	124
350	544068	544192	544316	544440	544564	544688	544812	544936	545060	545183	124
1	5307	5431	5555	5678	5802	5925	6049	6172	6296	6419	124
2	6543	6666	6789	6913	7036	7159	7282	7405	7529	7652	123
3	7775	7898	8021	8144	8267	8389	8512	8635	8758	8881	123
4	9003	9126	9249	9371	9494	9616	9739	9861	9984	550106	123
355	550228	550351	550473	550595	550717	550840	550962	551084	551206	1328	122
6	1450	1572	1694	1816	1938	2060	2181	2303	2425	2547	122
7	2668	2790	2911	3033	3155	3276	3398	3519	3640	3762	121
8	3883	4004	4126	4247	4368	4489	4610	4731	4852	4973	121
9	5094	5215	5336	5457	5578	5699	5820	5940	6061	6182	121
360	556303	556423	556544	556664	556785	556905	557026	557146	557267	557387	120
1	7507	7627	7748	7868	7988	8108	8228	8349	8469	8589	120
2	8709	8829	8948	9068	9188	9308	9428	9548	9667	9787	120
3	9907	560026	560146	560265	560385	560504	560624	560743	560863	560982	119
4	561101	1221	1340	1459	1578	1698	1817	1936	2055	2174	119
365	2293	2412	2531	2650	2769	2887	3006	3125	3244	3362	119
6	3481	3600	3718	3837	3955	4074	4192	4311	4429	4548	119
7	4666	4784	4903	5021	5139	5257	5376	5494	5612	5730	118
8	5848	5966	6084	6202	6320	6437	6555	6673	6791	6909	118
9	7026	7144	7262	7379	7497	7614	7732	7849	7967	8084	118
370	568202	568319	568436	568554	568671	568788	568905	569023	569140	569257	117
1	9374	9491	9608	9725	9842	9959	570076	570193	570309	570426	117
2	570543	570660	570776	570893	571010	571126	1243	1359	1476	1592	117
3	1709	1825	1942	2058	2174	2291	2407	2523	2639	2755	116
4	2872	2988	3104	3220	3336	3452	3568	3684	3800	3915	116
375	4031	4147	4263	4379	4494	4610	4726	4841	4957	5072	116
6	5188	5303	5419	5534	5650	5765	5880	5996	6111	6226	115
7	6341	6457	6572	6687	6802	6917	7032	7147	7262	7377	115
8	7492	7607	7722	7836	7951	8066	8181	8295	8410	8525	115
9	8639	8754	8868	8983	9097	9212	9326	9441	9555	9669	114
380	579784	579898	580012	580126	580241	580355	580469	580583	580697	580811	114
1	580925	581039	1153	1267	1381	1495	1608	1722	1836	1950	114
2	2063	2177	2291	2404	2518	2631	2745	2858	2972	3085	114
3	3199	3312	3426	3539	3652	3765	3879	3992	4105	4218	113
4	4331	4444	4557	4670	4783	4896	5009	5122	5235	5348	113
385	5461	5574	5686	5799	5912	6024	6137	6250	6362	6475	113
6	6587	6700	6812	6925	7037	7149	7262	7374	7486	7599	112
7	7711	7823	7935	8047	8160	8272	8384	8496	8608	8720	112
8	8832	8944	9056	9167	9279	9391	9503	9615	9726	9838	112
9	9950	590061	590173	590284	590396	590507	590619	590730	590842	590953	112
390	591065	591176	591287	591399	591510	591621	591732	591843	591955	592066	111
1	2177	2288	2399	2510	2621	2732	2843	2954	3064	3175	111
2	3286	3397	3508	3618	3729	3840	3950	4061	4171	4282	111
3	4393	4503	4614	4724	4834	4945	5055	5165	5276	5380	110
4	5496	5606	5717	5827	5937	6047	6157	6267	6377	6487	110
395	6597	6707	6817	6927	7037	7146	7256	7366	7476	7586	110
6	7695	7805	7914	8024	8134	8243	8353	8462	8572	8681	110
7	8791	8900	9009	9119	9228	9337	9446	9556	9665	9774	109
8	9883	9992	600101	600210	600319	600428	600537	600646	600755	600864	109
9	600973	601082	1191	1299	1408	1517	1625	1734	1843	1951	109
N.	0	1	2	3	4	5	6	7	8	9	D.

N.	0	1	2	3	4	5	6	7	8	9	D.
400	602060	602169	602277	602386	602494	602603	602711	602819	602928	603036	108
1	3144	3253	3361	3469	3577	3686	3794	3902	4010	4118	108
2	4226	4334	4442	4550	4658	4766	4874	4982	5089	5197	108
3	5305	5413	5521	5628	5736	5844	5951	6059	6166	6274	108
4	6381	6489	6596	6704	6811	6919	7026	7133	7241	7348	107
405	7455	7562	7669	7777	7884	7991	8098	8205	8312	8419	107
6	8526	8633	8740	8847	8954	9061	9167	9274	9381	9488	107
7	9594	9701	9808	9914	610021	610128	610234	610341	610447	610554	107
8	610660	610767	610873	610979	1086	1192	1298	1405	1511	1617	106
9	1723	1829	1936	2042	2148	2254	2360	2466	2572	2678	106
410	612784	612890	612996	613102	613207	613313	613419	613525	613630	613736	106
1	3842	3947	4053	4159	4264	4370	4475	4581	4686	4792	106
2	4897	5003	5108	5213	5319	5424	5529	5634	5740	5845	105
3	5950	6055	6160	6265	6370	6476	6581	6686	6790	6895	105
4	7000	7105	7210	7315	7420	7525	7629	7734	7839	7943	105
415	8048	8153	8257	8362	8466	8571	8676	8780	8884	8989	105
6	9093	9198	9302	9406	9511	9615	9719	9824	9928	620032	104
7	620136	620240	620344	620448	620552	620656	620760	620864	620968	1072	104
8	1176	1280	1384	1488	1592	1695	1799	1903	2007	2110	104
9	2214	2318	2421	2525	2628	2732	2835	2939	3042	3146	104
420	623249	623353	623456	623559	623663	623766	623869	623973	624076	624179	103
1	4282	4385	4488	4591	4695	4798	4901	5004	5107	5210	103
2	5312	5415	5518	5621	5724	5827	5929	6032	6135	6238	103
3	6340	6443	6546	6648	6751	6853	6956	7058	7161	7263	103
4	7366	7468	7571	7673	7775	7878	7980	8082	8185	8287	102
425	8389	8491	8593	8695	8797	8900	9002	9104	9206	9308	102
6	9410	9512	9613	9715	9817	9919	630021	630123	630224	630326	102
7	630428	630530	630631	630733	630835	630936	1038	1139	1241	1342	102
8	1444	1545	1647	1748	1849	1951	2052	2153	2255	2356	101
9	2457	2559	2660	2761	2862	2963	3064	3165	3266	3367	101
430	633468	633569	633670	633771	633872	633973	634074	634175	634276	634376	101
1	4477	4578	4679	4779	4880	4981	5081	5182	5283	5383	101
2	5484	5584	5685	5785	5886	5986	6087	6187	6287	6388	100
3	6488	6588	6688	6789	6889	6989	7089	7189	7290	7390	100
4	7490	7590	7690	7790	7890	7990	8090	8190	8290	8389	100
435	8489	8589	8689	8789	8888	8988	9088	9188	9287	9387	100
6	9486	9586	9686	9785	9889	9984	640084	640183	640283	640382	99
7	640481	640581	640680	640779	640879	640978	1077	1177	1276	1375	99
8	1474	1573	1672	1771	1871	1970	2069	2168	2267	2366	99
9	2465	2563	2662	2761	2860	2959	3058	3156	3255	3354	99
440	643453	643551	643650	643749	643847	643946	644044	644143	644242	644340	98
1	4439	4537	4636	4734	4832	4931	5029	5127	5226	5324	98
2	5422	5521	5619	5717	5815	5913	6011	6110	6208	6306	98
3	6404	6502	6600	6698	6796	6894	6992	7089	7187	7285	98
4	7383	7481	7579	7676	7774	7872	7969	8067	8165	8262	98
445	8360	8458	8555	8653	8750	8848	8945	9043	9140	9237	97
6	9335	9432	9530	9627	9724	9821	9919	650016	650113	650210	97
7	650308	650405	650502	650599	650696	650793	650890	0987	1084	1181	97
8	1278	1375	1472	1569	1666	1762	1859	1956	2053	2150	97
9	2246	2343	2440	2536	2633	2730	2826	2923	3019	3116	97
450	653213	653309	653405	653502	653598	653695	653791	653888	653984	654080	96
1	4177	4273	4369	4465	4562	4658	4754	4850	4946	5042	96
2	5138	5235	5331	5427	5523	5619	5715	5810	5906	6002	96
3	6098	6194	6290	6386	6482	6577	6673	6769	6864	6960	96
4	7056	7152	7247	7343	7438	7534	7629	7725	7820	7916	96
455	8011	8107	8202	8298	8393	8488	8584	8679	8774	8870	95
6	8965	9060	9155	9250	9346	9441	9536	9631	9726	9821	95
7	9916	660011	660106	660201	660296	660391	660486	660581	660676	660771	95
8	660865	0960	1055	1150	1245	1339	1434	1529	1623	1718	95
9	1813	1907	2002	2096	2191	2286	2380	2475	2569	2663	95
N.	0	1	2	3	4	5	6	7	8	9	D.

N.	0	1	2	3	4	5	6	7	8	9	D.
460	662758	662852	662947	663041	663135	663230	663324	663418	663512	663607	94
1	3701	3795	3889	3983	4078	4172	4266	4360	4454	4548	94
2	4642	4736	4830	4924	5018	5112	5206	5299	5393	5487	94
3	5581	5675	5769	5862	5956	6050	6143	6237	6331	6424	94
4	6518	6612	6705	6799	6892	6986	7079	7173	7266	7360	94
465	7453	7546	7640	7733	7826	7920	8013	8106	8199	8293	93
6	8386	8479	8572	8665	8759	8852	8945	9038	9131	9224	93
7	9317	9410	9503	9596	9689	9782	9875	9967	670060	670153	93
8	670246	670339	670431	670524	670617	670710	670802	670895	0988	1080	93
9	1173	1265	1358	1451	1543	1636	1728	1821	1913	2005	93
470	672098	672190	672283	672375	672467	672560	672652	672744	672836	672929	92
1	3021	3113	3205	3297	3390	3482	3574	3666	3758	3850	92
2	3942	4034	4126	4218	4310	4402	4494	4586	4677	4769	92
3	4861	4953	5045	5137	5228	5320	5412	5503	5595	5687	92
4	5778	5870	5962	6053	6145	6236	6328	6419	6511	6602	92
475	6694	6785	6876	6968	7059	7151	7242	7333	7424	7516	91
6	7607	7698	7789	7881	7972	8063	8154	8245	8336	8427	91
7	8518	8609	8700	8791	8882	8973	9064	9155	9246	9337	91
8	9428	9519	9610	9700	9791	9882	9973	680063	680154	680245	91
9	680336	680426	680517	680607	680698	680789	680879	0970	1060	1151	91
480	681241	681332	681422	681513	681603	681693	681784	681874	681964	682055	90
1	2145	2235	2326	2416	2506	2596	2686	2777	2867	2957	90
2	3047	3137	3227	3317	3407	3497	3587	3677	3767	3857	90
3	3947	4037	4127	4217	4307	4396	4486	4576	4666	4756	90
4	4845	4935	5025	5114	5204	5294	5383	5473	5563	5652	90
485	5742	5831	5921	6010	6100	6189	6279	6368	6458	6547	89
6	6636	6726	6815	6904	6994	7083	7172	7261	7351	7440	89
7	7529	7618	7707	7796	7886	7975	8064	8153	8242	8331	89
8	8420	8509	8598	8687	8776	8865	8953	9042	9131	9220	89
9	9309	9398	9486	9575	9664	9753	9841	9930	690019	690107	89
490	690196	690285	690373	690462	690550	690639	690728	690816	690905	690993	89
1	1081	1170	1258	1347	1435	1524	1612	1700	1789	1877	88
2	1965	2053	2142	2230	2318	2406	2494	2583	2671	2759	88
3	2847	2935	3023	3111	3199	3287	3375	3463	3551	3639	88
4	3727	3815	3903	3991	4078	4166	4254	4342	4430	4517	88
495	4605	4693	4781	4868	4956	5044	5131	5219	5307	5394	88
6	5482	5569	5657	5744	5832	5919	6007	6094	6182	6269	87
7	6356	6444	6531	6618	6706	6793	6880	6968	7055	7142	87
8	7229	7317	7404	7491	7578	7665	7752	7839	7926	8014	87
9	8101	8188	8275	8362	8449	8535	8622	8709	8796	8883	87
500	698970	699057	699144	699231	699317	699404	699491	699578	699664	699751	87
1	9838	9924	700011	700098	700184	700271	700358	700444	700531	700617	87
2	700704	700790	0877	0963	1050	1136	1222	1309	1395	1482	86
3	1568	1654	1741	1827	1913	1999	2086	2172	2258	2344	86
4	2431	2517	2603	2689	2775	2861	2947	3033	3119	3205	86
505	3291	3377	3463	3549	3635	3721	3807	3893	3979	4065	86
6	4151	4236	4322	4408	4494	4579	4665	4751	4837	4922	86
7	5008	5094	5179	5265	5350	5436	5522	5607	5693	5778	86
8	5864	5949	6035	6120	6206	6291	6376	6462	6547	6632	85
9	6718	6803	6888	6974	7059	7144	7229	7315	7400	7485	85
510	707570	707655	707740	707826	707911	707996	708081	708166	708251	708336	85
1	8421	8506	8591	8676	8761	8846	8931	9015	9100	9185	85
2	9270	9355	9440	9524	9609	9694	9779	9863	9948	710033	85
3	710117	710202	710287	710371	710456	710540	710625	710710	710794	0879	85
4	0963	1048	1132	1217	1301	1385	1470	1554	1639	1723	84
515	1807	1892	1976	2060	2144	2229	2313	2397	2481	2566	84
6	2650	2734	2818	2902	2986	3070	3154	3238	3323	3407	84
7	3491	3575	3659	3742	3826	3910	3994	4078	4162	4246	84
8	4330	4414	4497	4581	4665	4749	4833	4916	5000	5084	84
9	5167	5251	5335	5418	5502	5586	5669	5753	5836	5920	84
N.	0	1	2	3	4	5	6	7	8	9	D.

N.	0	1	2	3	4	5	6	7	8	9	D.
520	716003	716087	716170	716254	716337	716421	716504	716588	716671	716754	83
1	6838	6921	7004	7088	7171	7254	7338	7421	7504	7587	83
2	7671	7754	7837	7920	8003	8086	8169	8253	8336	8419	83
3	8502	8585	8668	8751	8834	8917	9000	9083	9165	9248	83
4	9331	9414	9497	9580	9663	9745	9828	9911	9994	720077	83
525	720159	720242	720325	720407	720490	720573	720655	720738	720821	0903	83
6	0986	1068	1151	1233	1316	1398	1481	1563	1646	1728	82
7	1811	1893	1975	2058	2140	2222	2305	2387	2469	2552	82
8	2634	2716	2798	2881	2963	3045	3127	3209	3291	3374	82
9	3456	3538	3620	3702	3784	3866	3948	4030	4112	4194	82
530	724276	724358	724440	724522	724604	724685	724767	724849	724931	725013	82
1	5095	5176	5258	5340	5422	5503	5585	5667	5748	5830	82
2	5912	5993	6075	6156	6238	6320	6401	6483	6564	6646	82
3	6727	6809	6890	6972	7053	7134	7216	7297	7379	7460	81
4	7541	7623	7704	7785	7866	7948	8029	8110	8191	8273	81
535	8354	8435	8516	8597	8678	8759	8841	8922	9003	9084	81
6	9165	9246	9327	9408	9489	9570	9651	9732	9813	9893	81
7	9974	730055	730136	730217	730298	730378	730459	730540	730621	730702	81
8	730782	0863	0944	1024	1105	1186	1266	1347	1428	1508	81
9	1589	1669	1750	1830	1911	1991	2072	2152	2233	2313	81
540	732394	732474	732555	732635	732715	732796	732876	732956	733037	733117	80
1	3197	3278	3358	3438	3518	3598	3679	3759	3839	3919	80
2	3999	4079	4160	4240	4320	4400	4480	4560	4640	4720	80
3	4800	4880	4960	5040	5120	5200	5279	5359	5439	5519	80
4	5599	5679	5759	5838	5918	5998	6078	6157	6237	6317	80
545	6397	6476	6556	6635	6715	6795	6874	6954	7034	7113	80
6	7193	7272	7352	7431	7511	7590	7670	7749	7829	7908	79
7	7987	8067	8146	8225	8305	8384	8463	8543	8622	8701	79
8	8781	8860	8939	9018	9097	9177	9256	9335	9414	9493	79
9	9572	9651	9731	9810	9889	9968	740047	740126	740205	740284	79
550	740363	740442	740521	740600	740678	740757	740836	740915	740994	741073	79
1	1152	1230	1309	1388	1467	1546	1624	1703	1782	1860	79
2	1939	2018	2096	2175	2254	2332	2411	2489	2568	2647	79
3	2725	2804	2882	2961	3039	3118	3196	3275	3353	3431	78
4	3510	3588	3667	3745	3823	3902	3980	4058	4136	4215	78
555	4293	4371	4449	4528	4606	4684	4762	4840	4919	4997	78
6	5075	5153	5231	5309	5387	5465	5543	5621	5699	5777	78
7	5855	5933	6011	6089	6167	6245	6323	6401	6479	6556	78
8	6634	6712	6790	6868	6945	7023	7101	7179	7256	7334	78
9	7412	7489	7567	7645	7722	7800	7878	7955	8033	8110	78
560	748188	748266	748343	748421	748498	748576	748653	748731	748808	748885	77
1	8963	9040	9118	9195	9272	9350	9427	9504	9582	9659	77
2	9736	9814	9891	9968	750045	750123	750200	750277	750354	750431	77
3	750508	750586	750663	750740	0817	0894	0971	1048	1125	1202	77
4	1279	1356	1433	1510	1587	1664	1741	1818	1895	1972	77
565	2048	2125	2202	2279	2356	2433	2509	2586	2663	2740	77
6	2816	2893	2970	3047	3123	3200	3277	3353	3430	3506	77
7	3583	3660	3736	3813	3889	3966	4042	4119	4195	4272	77
8	4348	4425	4501	4578	4654	4730	4807	4883	4960	5036	76
9	5112	5189	5265	5341	5417	5494	5570	5646	5722	5799	76
570	755875	755951	756027	756103	756180	756256	756332	756408	756484	756560	76
1	6636	6712	6788	6864	6940	7016	7092	7168	7244	7320	76
2	7396	7472	7548	7624	7700	7775	7851	7927	8003	8079	76
3	8155	8230	8306	8382	8458	8533	8609	8685	8761	8836	76
4	8912	8988	9063	9139	9214	9290	9366	9441	9517	9592	76
575	9668	9743	9819	9894	9970	760045	760121	760196	760272	760347	75
6	760422	760498	760573	760649	760724	0799	0875	0950	1025	1101	75
7	1176	1251	1326	1402	1477	1552	1627	1702	1778	1853	75
8	1928	2003	2078	2153	2228	2303	2378	2453	2529	2604	75
9	2679	2754	2829	2904	2978	3053	3128	3203	3278	3353	75
N.	0	1	2	3	4	5	6	7	8	9	D.

N.	0	1	2	3	4	5	6	7	8	9	D.
580	763428	763503	763578	763653	763727	763802	763877	763952	764027	764101	75
1	4176	4251	4326	4400	4475	4550	4624	4699	4774	4848	75
2	4923	4998	5072	5147	5221	5296	5370	5445	5520	5594	75
3	5669	5743	5818	5892	5966	6041	6115	6190	6264	6338	74
4	6413	6487	6562	6636	6710	6785	6859	6933	7007	7082	74
585	7156	7230	7304	7379	7453	7527	7601	7675	7749	7823	74
6	7898	7972	8046	8120	8194	8268	8342	8416	8490	8564	74
7	8638	8712	8786	8860	8934	9008	9082	9156	9230	9303	74
8	9377	9451	9525	9599	9673	9746	9820	9894	9968	770042	74
9	770115	770189	770263	770336	770410	770484	770557	770631	770705	0778	74
590	770852	770926	770999	771073	771146	771220	771293	771367	771440	771514	74
1	1587	1661	1734	1808	1881	1955	2028	2102	2175	2248	73
2	2322	2395	2468	2542	2615	2688	2762	2835	2908	2981	73
3	3055	3128	3201	3274	3348	3421	3494	3567	3640	3713	73
4	3786	3860	3933	4006	4079	4152	4225	4298	4371	4444	73
595	4517	4590	4663	4736	4809	4882	4955	5028	5100	5173	73
6	5246	5319	5392	5465	5538	5610	5683	5756	5829	5902	73
7	5974	6047	6120	6193	6265	6338	6411	6483	6556	6629	73
8	6701	6774	6846	6919	6992	7064	7137	7209	7282	7354	73
9	7427	7499	7572	7644	7717	7789	7862	7934	8006	8079	72
600	778151	778224	778296	778368	778441	778513	778585	778658	778730	778802	72
1	8874	8947	9019	9091	9163	9236	9308	9380	9452	9524	72
2	9596	9669	9741	9813	9885	9957	780029	780101	780173	780245	72
3	780317	780389	780461	780533	780605	780677	0749	0821	0893	0965	72
4	1037	1109	1181	1253	1324	1396	1468	1540	1612	1684	72
605	1755	1827	1899	1971	2042	2114	2186	2258	2329	2401	72
6	2473	2544	2616	2688	2759	2831	2902	2974	3046	3117	72
7	3189	3260	3332	3403	3475	3546	3618	3689	3761	3832	71
8	3904	3975	4046	4118	4189	4261	4332	4403	4475	4546	71
9	4617	4689	4760	4831	4902	4974	5045	5116	5187	5259	71
610	785330	785401	785472	785543	785615	785686	785757	785828	785899	785970	71
1	6041	6112	6183	6254	6325	6396	6467	6538	6609	6680	71
2	6751	6822	6893	6964	7035	7106	7177	7248	7319	7390	71
3	7460	7531	7602	7673	7744	7815	7885	7956	8027	8098	71
4	8168	8239	8310	8381	8451	8522	8593	8663	8734	8804	71
615	8875	8946	9016	9087	9157	9228	9299	9369	9440	9510	71
6	9581	9651	9722	9792	9863	9933	790004	790074	790144	790215	70
7	790285	790356	790426	790496	790567	790637	0707	0778	0848	0918	70
8	0988	1059	1129	1199	1269	1340	1410	1480	1550	1620	70
9	1691	1761	1831	1901	1971	2041	2111	2181	2252	2322	70
620	792392	792462	792532	792602	792672	792742	792812	792882	792952	793022	70
1	3092	3162	3231	3301	3371	3441	3511	3581	3651	3721	70
2	3790	3860	3930	4000	4070	4139	4209	4279	4349	4418	70
3	4488	4558	4627	4697	4767	4836	4906	4976	5045	5115	70
4	5185	5254	5324	5393	5463	5532	5602	5672	5741	5811	70
625	5880	5949	6019	6088	6158	6227	6297	6366	6436	6505	69
6	6574	6644	6713	6782	6852	6921	6990	7060	7129	7198	69
7	7268	7337	7406	7475	7545	7614	7683	7752	7821	7890	69
8	7960	8029	8098	8167	8236	8305	8374	8443	8513	8582	69
9	8651	8720	8789	8858	8927	8996	9065	9134	9203	9272	69
630	799341	799409	799478	799547	799616	799685	799754	799823	799892	799961	69
1	800029	800098	800167	800236	800305	800373	800442	800511	800580	800648	69
2	0717	0786	0854	0923	0992	1061	1129	1198	1266	1335	69
3	1404	1472	1541	1609	1678	1747	1815	1884	1952	2021	69
4	2089	2158	2226	2295	2363	2432	2500	2568	2637	2705	68
635	2774	2842	2910	2979	3047	3116	3184	3252	3321	3389	68
6	3457	3525	3594	3662	3730	3798	3867	3935	4003	4071	68
7	4139	4208	4276	4344	4412	4480	4548	4616	4685	4753	68
8	4821	4889	4957	5025	5093	5161	5229	5297	5365	5433	68
9	5501	5569	5637	5705	5773	5841	5908	5976	6044	6112	68
N.	0	1	2	3	4	5	6	7	8	9	D.

N.	0	1	2	3	4	5	6	7	8	9	D.
640	806180	806248	806316	806384	806451	806519	806587	806655	806723	806790	68
1	6858	6926	6994	7061	7129	7197	7264	7332	7400	7467	68
2	7535	7603	7670	7738	7806	7873	7941	8008	8076	8143	68
3	8211	8279	8346	8414	8481	8549	8616	8684	8751	8818	67
4	8886	8953	9021	9088	9156	9223	9290	9358	9425	9492	67
645	9560	9627	9694	9762	9829	9896	9964	810031	810098	810165	67
6	810233	810300	810367	810434	810501	810569	810636	0703	0770	0837	67
7	0904	0971	1039	1106	1173	1240	1307	1374	1441	1508	67
8	1575	1642	1709	1776	1843	1910	1977	2044	2111	2178	67
9	2245	2312	2379	2445	2512	2579	2646	2713	2780	2847	67
650	812913	812980	813047	813114	813181	813247	813314	813381	813448	813514	67
1	3581	3648	3714	3781	3848	3914	3981	4048	4114	4181	67
2	4248	4314	4381	4447	4514	4581	4647	4714	4780	4847	67
3	4913	4980	5046	5113	5179	5246	5312	5378	5445	5511	66
4	5578	5644	5711	5777	5843	5910	5976	6042	6109	6175	66
655	6241	6308	6374	6440	6506	6573	6639	6705	6771	6838	66
6	6904	6970	7036	7102	7169	7235	7301	7367	7433	7499	66
7	7565	7631	7698	7764	7830	7896	7962	8028	8094	8160	66
8	8226	8292	8358	8424	8490	8556	8622	8688	8754	8820	66
9	8885	8951	9017	9083	9149	9215	9281	9346	9412	9478	66
660	819544	819610	819676	819741	819807	819873	819939	820004	820070	820136	66
1	820201	820267	820333	820399	820464	820530	820595	0661	0727	0792	66
2	0858	0924	0989	1055	1120	1186	1251	1317	1382	1448	66
3	1514	1579	1645	1710	1775	1841	1906	1972	2037	2103	65
4	2168	2233	2299	2364	2430	2495	2560	2626	2691	2756	65
665	2822	2887	2952	3018	3083	3148	3213	3279	3344	3409	65
6	3474	3539	3605	3670	3735	3800	3865	3930	3996	4061	65
7	4126	4191	4256	4321	4386	4451	4516	4581	4646	4711	65
8	4776	4841	4906	4971	5036	5101	5166	5231	5296	5361	65
9	5426	5491	5556	5621	5686	5751	5815	5880	5945	6010	65
670	826075	826140	826204	826269	826334	826399	826464	826528	826593	826658	65
1	6723	6787	6852	6917	6981	7046	7111	7175	7240	7305	65
2	7369	7434	7499	7563	7628	7692	7757	7821	7886	7951	65
3	8015	8080	8144	8209	8273	8338	8402	8467	8531	8595	64
4	8660	8724	8789	8853	8918	8982	9046	9111	9175	9239	64
675	9304	9368	9432	9497	9561	9625	9690	9754	9818	9882	64
6	9947	830011	830075	830139	830204	830268	830332	830396	830460	830525	64
7	830589	0653	0717	0781	0845	0909	0973	1037	1102	1166	64
8	1230	1294	1358	1422	1486	1550	1614	1678	1742	1806	64
9	1870	1934	1998	2062	2126	2189	2253	2317	2381	2445	64
680	832509	832573	832637	832700	832764	832828	832892	832956	833020	833083	64
1	3147	3211	3275	3338	3402	3466	3530	3593	3657	3721	64
2	3784	3848	3912	3975	4039	4103	4166	4230	4294	4357	64
3	4421	4484	4548	4611	4675	4739	4802	4866	4929	4993	64
4	5056	5120	5183	5247	5310	5373	5437	5500	5564	5627	63
685	5691	5754	5817	5881	5944	6007	6071	6134	6197	6261	63
6	6324	6387	6451	6514	6577	6641	6704	6767	6830	6894	63
7	6957	7020	7083	7146	7210	7273	7336	7399	7462	7525	63
8	7588	7652	7715	7778	7841	7904	7967	8030	8093	8156	63
9	8219	8282	8345	8408	8471	8534	8597	8660	8723	8786	63
690	838849	838912	838975	839038	839101	839164	839227	839289	839352	839415	63
1	9478	9541	9604	9667	9729	9792	9855	9918	9981	840043	63
2	840106	840169	840232	840294	840357	840420	840482	840545	840608	0671	63
3	0733	0796	0859	0921	0984	1046	1109	1172	1234	1297	63
4	1359	1422	1485	1547	1610	1672	1735	1797	1860	1922	63
695	1985	2047	2110	2172	2235	2297	2360	2422	2484	2547	62
6	2609	2672	2734	2796	2859	2921	2983	3046	3108	3170	62
7	3233	3295	3357	3420	3482	3544	3606	3669	3731	3793	62
8	3855	3918	3980	4042	4104	4166	4229	4291	4353	4415	62
9	4477	4539	4601	4664	4726	4788	4850	4912	4974	5036	62
N.	0	1	2	3	4	5	6	7	8	9	D.

N.	0	1	2	3	4	5	6	7	8	9	D.
700	845098	845160	845222	845284	845346	845408	845470	845532	845594	845656	62
1	5718	5780	5842	5904	5966	6028	6090	6151	6213	6275	62
2	6337	6399	6461	6523	6585	6646	6708	6770	6832	6894	62
3	6955	7017	7079	7141	7202	7264	7326	7388	7449	7511	62
4	7573	7634	7696	7758	7819	7881	7943	8004	8066	8128	62
705	8189	8251	8312	8374	8435	8497	8559	8620	8682	8743	62
6	8805	8866	8928	8989	9051	9112	9174	9235	9297	9358	61
7	9419	9481	9542	9604	9665	9726	9788	9849	9911	9972	61
8	850033	850095	850156	850217	850279	850340	850401	850462	850524	850585	61
9	0646	0707	0769	0830	0891	0952	1014	1075	1136	1197	61
710	851258	851320	851381	851442	851503	851564	851625	851686	851747	851809	61
1	1870	1931	1992	2053	2114	2175	2236	2297	2358	2419	61
2	2480	2541	2602	2663	2724	2785	2846	2907	2968	3029	61
3	3090	3150	3211	3272	3333	3394	3455	3516	3577	3637	61
4	3698	3759	3820	3881	3941	4002	4063	4124	4185	4245	61
715	4306	4367	4428	4488	4549	4610	4670	4731	4792	4852	61
6	4913	4974	5034	5095	5156	5216	5277	5337	5398	5459	61
7	5519	5580	5640	5701	5761	5822	5882	5943	6003	6064	61
8	6124	6185	6245	6306	6366	6427	6487	6548	6608	6668	60
9	6729	6789	6850	6910	6970	7031	7091	7152	7212	7272	60
720	857332	857393	857453	857513	857574	857634	857694	857755	857815	857875	60
1	7935	7995	8056	8116	8176	8236	8297	8357	8417	8477	60
2	8537	8597	8657	8718	8778	8838	8898	8958	9018	9078	60
3	9138	9198	9258	9318	9379	9439	9499	9559	9619	9679	60
4	9739	9799	9859	9918	9978	860038	860098	860158	860218	860278	60
725	860338	860398	860458	860518	860578	0637	0697	0757	0817	0877	60
6	0937	0996	1056	1116	1176	1236	1295	1355	1415	1475	60
7	1534	1594	1654	1714	1773	1833	1893	1952	2012	2072	60
8	2131	2191	2251	2310	2370	2430	2489	2549	2608	2668	60
9	2728	2787	2847	2906	2966	3025	3085	3144	3204	3263	60
730	863323	863382	863442	863501	863561	863620	863680	863739	863799	863858	59
1	3917	3977	4036	4096	4155	4214	4274	4333	4392	4452	59
2	4511	4570	4630	4689	4748	4808	4867	4926	4985	5045	59
3	5104	5163	5222	5282	5341	5400	5459	5519	5578	5637	59
4	5696	5755	5814	5874	5933	5992	6051	6110	6169	6228	59
735	6287	6346	6405	6465	6524	6583	6642	6701	6760	6819	59
6	6878	6937	6996	7055	7114	7173	7232	7291	7350	7409	59
7	7467	7526	7585	7644	7703	7762	7821	7880	7939	7998	59
8	8056	8115	8174	8233	8292	8350	8409	8468	8527	8586	59
9	8644	8703	8762	8821	8879	8938	8997	9056	9114	9173	59
740	869232	869290	869349	869408	869466	869525	869584	869642	869701	869760	59
1	9818	9877	9935	9994	870053	870111	870170	870228	870287	870345	59
2	870404	870462	870521	870579	0638	0696	0755	0813	0872	0930	58
3	0989	1047	1106	1164	1223	1281	1339	1398	1456	1515	58
4	1573	1631	1690	1748	1806	1865	1923	1981	2040	2098	58
745	2156	2215	2273	2331	2389	2448	2506	2564	2622	2681	58
6	2739	2797	2855	2913	2972	3030	3088	3146	3204	3262	58
7	3321	3379	3437	3495	3553	3611	3669	3727	3785	3844	58
8	3902	3960	4018	4076	4134	4192	4250	4308	4366	4424	58
9	4482	4540	4598	4656	4714	4772	4830	4888	4945	5003	58
750	875061	875119	875177	875235	875293	875351	875409	875466	875524	875582	58
1	5640	5698	5756	5813	5871	5929	5987	6045	6102	6160	58
2	6218	6276	6333	6391	6449	6507	6564	6622	6680	6737	58
3	6795	6853	6910	6968	7026	7083	7141	7199	7256	7314	58
4	7371	7429	7487	7544	7602	7659	7717	7774	7832	7889	58
755	7947	8004	8062	8119	8177	8234	8292	8349	8407	8464	57
6	8522	8579	8637	8694	8752	8809	8866	8924	8981	9039	57
7	9096	9153	9211	9268	9325	9383	9440	9497	9555	9612	57
8	9669	9726	9784	9841	9898	9956	880013	880070	880127	880185	57
9	880242	880299	880356	880413	880471	880528	0585	0642	0699	0756	57
N.	0	1	2	3	4	5	6	7	8	9	D.

N.	0	1	2	3	4	5	6	7	8	9	D.
760	880814	880871	880928	880985	881042	881099	881156	881213	881271	881328	57
1	1385	1442	1499	1556	1613	1670	1727	1784	1841	1898	57
2	1955	2012	2069	2126	2183	2240	2297	2354	2411	2468	57
3	2525	2581	2638	2695	2752	2809	2866	2923	2980	3037	57
4	3093	3150	3207	3264	3321	3377	3434	3491	3548	3605	57
765	3661	3718	3775	3832	3888	3945	4002	4059	4115	4172	57
6	4229	4285	4342	4399	4455	4512	4569	4625	4682	4739	57
7	4795	4852	4909	4965	5022	5078	5135	5192	5248	5305	57
8	5361	5418	5474	5531	5587	5644	5700	5757	5813	5870	57
9	5926	5983	6039	6096	6152	6209	6265	6321	6378	6434	56
770	886491	886547	886604	886660	886716	886773	886829	886885	886942	886998	56
1	7054	7111	7167	7223	7280	7336	7392	7449	7505	7561	56
2	7617	7674	7730	7786	7842	7898	7955	8011	8067	8123	56
3	8179	8236	8292	8348	8404	8460	8516	8573	8629	8685	56
4	8741	8797	8853	8909	8965	9021	9077	9134	9190	9246	56
775	9302	9358	9414	9470	9526	9582	9638	9694	9750	9806	56
6	9862	9918	9974	890030	890086	890141	890197	890253	890309	890365	56
7	890421	890477	890533	0589	0645	0700	0756	0812	0868	0924	56
8	0980	1035	1091	1147	1203	1259	1314	1370	1426	1482	56
9	1537	1593	1649	1705	1760	1816	1872	1928	1983	2039	56
780	892095	892150	892206	892262	892317	892373	892429	892484	892540	892595	56
1	2651	2707	2762	2818	2873	2929	2985	3040	3096	3151	56
2	3207	3262	3318	3373	3429	3484	3540	3595	3651	3706	56
3	3762	3817	3873	3928	3984	4039	4094	4150	4205	4261	55
4	4316	4371	4427	4482	4538	4593	4648	4704	4759	4814	55
785	4870	4925	4980	5036	5091	5146	5201	5257	5312	5367	55
6	5423	5478	5533	5588	5644	5699	5754	5809	5864	5920	55
7	5975	6030	6085	6140	6195	6251	6306	6361	6416	6471	55
8	6526	6581	6636	6692	6747	6802	6857	6912	6967	7022	55
9	7077	7132	7187	7242	7297	7352	7407	7462	7517	7572	55
790	897627	897682	897737	897792	897847	897902	897957	898012	898067	898122	55
1	8176	8231	8286	8341	8396	8451	8506	8561	8615	8670	55
2	8725	8780	8835	8890	8944	8999	9054	9109	9164	9218	55
3	9273	9328	9383	9437	9492	9547	9602	9656	9711	9766	55
4	9821	9875	9930	9985	900039	900094	900149	900203	900258	900312	55
795	900367	900422	900476	900531	0586	0640	0695	0749	0804	0859	55
6	0913	0968	1022	1077	1131	1186	1240	1295	1349	1404	55
7	1458	1513	1567	1622	1676	1731	1785	1840	1894	1948	54
8	2003	2057	2112	2166	2221	2275	2329	2384	2438	2492	54
9	2547	2601	2655	2710	2764	2818	2873	2927	2981	3036	54
800	903090	903144	903199	903253	903307	903361	903416	903470	903524	903578	54
1	3633	3687	3741	3795	3849	3904	3958	4012	4066	4120	54
2	4174	4229	4283	4337	4391	4445	4499	4553	4607	4661	54
3	4716	4770	4824	4878	4932	4986	5040	5094	5148	5202	54
4	5256	5310	5364	5418	5472	5526	5580	5634	5688	5742	54
805	5796	5850	5904	5958	6012	6066	6119	6173	6227	6281	54
6	6335	6389	6443	6497	6551	6604	6658	6712	6766	6820	54
7	6874	6927	6981	7035	7089	7143	7196	7250	7304	7358	54
8	7411	7465	7519	7573	7626	7680	7734	7787	7841	7895	54
9	7949	8002	8056	8110	8163	8217	8270	8324	8378	8431	54
810	908485	908539	908592	908646	908699	908753	908807	908860	908914	908967	54
1	9021	9074	9128	9181	9235	9289	9342	9396	9449	9503	54
2	9556	9610	9663	9716	9770	9823	9877	9930	9984	910037	53
3	910091	910144	910197	910251	910304	910358	910411	910464	910518	0571	53
4	0624	0678	0731	0784	0838	0891	0944	0998	1051	1104	53
815	1158	1211	1264	1317	1371	1424	1477	1530	1584	1637	53
6	1690	1743	1797	1850	1903	1956	2009	2063	2116	2169	53
7	2222	2275	2328	2381	2435	2488	2541	2594	2647	2700	53
8	2753	2806	2859	2913	2966	3019	3072	3125	3178	3231	53
9	3284	3337	3390	3443	3496	3549	3602	3655	3708	3761	53
N.	0	1	2	3	4	5	6	7	8	9	D.

N.	0	1	2	3	4	5	6	7	8	9	D.
820	913814	913867	913920	913973	914026	914079	914132	914184	914237	914290	53
1	4343	4396	4449	4502	4555	4608	4660	4713	4766	4819	53
2	4872	4925	4977	5030	5083	5136	5189	5241	5294	5347	53
3	5400	5453	5505	5558	5611	5664	5716	5769	5822	5875	53
4	5927	5980	6033	6085	6138	6191	6243	6296	6349	6401	53
825	6454	6507	6559	6612	6664	6717	6770	6822	6875	6927	53
6	6980	7033	7085	7138	7190	7243	7295	7348	7400	7453	53
7	7506	7558	7611	7663	7716	7768	7820	7873	7925	7978	52
8	8030	8083	8135	8188	8240	8293	8345	8397	8450	8502	52
9	8555	8607	8659	8712	8764	8816	8869	8921	8973	9026	52
830	919078	919130	919183	919235	919287	919340	919392	919444	919496	919549	52
1	9601	9653	9706	9758	9810	9862	9914	9967	920019	920071	52
2	920123	920176	920228	920280	920332	920384	920436	920489	0541	0593	52
3	0645	0697	0749	0801	0853	0906	0958	1010	1062	1114	52
4	1166	1218	1270	1322	1374	1426	1478	1530	1582	1634	52
835	1686	1738	1790	1842	1894	1946	1998	2050	2102	2154	52
6	2206	2258	2310	2362	2414	2466	2518	2570	2622	2674	52
7	2725	2777	2829	2881	2933	2985	3037	3089	3140	3192	52
8	3244	3296	3348	3399	3451	3503	3555	3607	3658	3710	52
9	3762	3814	3865	3917	3969	4021	4072	4124	4176	4228	52
840	924279	924331	924383	924434	924486	924538	924589	924641	924693	924744	52
1	4796	4848	4899	4951	5003	5054	5106	5157	5209	5261	52
2	5312	5364	5415	5467	5518	5570	5621	5673	5725	5776	52
3	5828	5879	5931	5982	6034	6085	6137	6188	6240	6291	51
4	6342	6394	6445	6497	6548	6600	6651	6702	6754	6805	51
845	6857	6908	6959	7011	7062	7114	7165	7216	7268	7319	51
6	7370	7422	7473	7524	7576	7627	7678	7730	7781	7832	51
7	7883	7935	7986	8037	8088	8140	8191	8242	8293	8345	51
8	8396	8447	8498	8549	8601	8652	8703	8754	8805	8857	51
9	8908	8959	9010	9061	9112	9163	9215	9266	9317	9368	51
850	929419	929470	929521	929572	929623	929674	929725	929776	929827	929879	51
1	9930	9981	930032	930083	930134	930185	930236	930287	930338	930389	51
2	930440	930491	0542	0592	0643	0694	0745	0796	0847	0898	51
3	0949	1000	1051	1102	1153	1204	1254	1305	1356	1407	51
4	1458	1509	1560	1610	1661	1712	1763	1814	1865	1915	51
855	1966	2017	2068	2118	2169	2220	2271	2322	2372	2423	51
6	2474	2524	2575	2626	2677	2727	2778	2829	2879	2930	51
7	2981	3031	3082	3133	3183	3234	3285	3335	3386	3437	51
8	3487	3538	3589	3639	3690	3740	3791	3841	3892	3943	51
9	3993	4044	4094	4145	4195	4246	4296	4347	4397	4448	51
860	934498	934549	934599	934650	934700	934751	934801	934852	934902	934953	50
1	5003	5054	5104	5154	5205	5255	5306	5356	5406	5457	50
2	5507	5558	5608	5658	5709	5759	5809	5860	5910	5960	50
3	6011	6061	6111	6162	6212	6262	6313	6363	6413	6463	50
4	6514	6564	6614	6665	6715	6765	6815	6865	6916	6966	50
865	7016	7066	7117	7167	7217	7267	7317	7367	7418	7468	50
6	7518	7568	7618	7668	7718	7769	7819	7869	7919	7969	50
7	8019	8069	8119	8169	8219	8269	8320	8370	8420	8470	50
8	8520	8570	8620	8670	8720	8770	8820	8870	8920	8970	50
9	9020	9070	9120	9170	9220	9270	9320	9369	9419	9469	50
870	939519	939569	939619	939669	939719	939769	939819	939869	939918	939968	50
1	940018	940068	940118	940168	940218	940267	940317	940367	940417	940467	50
2	0516	0566	0616	0666	0716	0765	0815	0865	0915	0964	50
3	1014	1064	1114	1163	1213	1263	1313	1362	1412	1462	50
4	1511	1561	1611	1660	1710	1760	1809	1859	1909	1958	50
875	2008	2058	2107	2157	2207	2256	2306	2355	2405	2455	50
6	2504	2554	2603	2653	2702	2752	2801	2851	2901	2950	50
7	3000	3049	3099	3148	3198	3247	3297	3346	3396	3445	49
8	3495	3544	3593	3643	3692	3742	3791	3841	3890	3939	49
9	3989	4038	4088	4137	4186	4236	4285	4335	4384	4433	49
N.	0	1	2	3	4	5	6	7	8	9	D.

N.	0	1	2	3	4	5	6	7	8	9	D.
880	944483	944532	944581	944631	944680	944729	944779	944828	944877	944927	49
1	4976	5025	5074	5124	5173	5222	5272	5321	5370	5419	49
2	5469	5518	5567	5616	5665	5715	5764	5813	5862	5912	49
3	5961	6010	6059	6108	6157	6207	6256	6305	6354	6403	49
4	6452	6501	6551	6600	6649	6698	6747	6796	6845	6894	49
885	6943	6992	7041	7090	7140	7189	7238	7287	7336	7385	49
6	7434	7483	7532	7581	7630	7679	7728	7777	7826	7875	49
7	7924	7973	8022	8070	8119	8168	8217	8266	8315	8364	49
8	8413	8462	8511	8560	8609	8657	8706	8755	8804	8853	49
9	8902	8951	8999	9048	9097	9146	9195	9244	9292	9341	49
890	949390	949439	949488	949536	949585	949634	949683	949731	949780	949829	49
1	9878	9926	9975	950024	950073	950121	950170	950219	950267	950316	49
2	950365	950414	950462	0511	0560	0608	0657	0706	0754	0803	49
3	0851	0900	0949	0997	1046	1095	1143	1192	1240	1289	49
4	1338	1386	1435	1483	1532	1580	1629	1677	1726	1775	49
895	1823	1872	1920	1969	2017	2066	2114	2163	2211	2260	48
6	2308	2356	2405	2453	2502	2550	2599	2647	2696	2744	48
7	2792	2841	2889	2938	2986	3034	3083	3131	3180	3228	48
8	3276	3325	3373	3421	3470	3518	3566	3615	3663	3711	48
9	3760	3808	3856	3905	3953	4001	4049	4098	4146	4194	48
900	954243	954291	954339	954387	954435	954484	954532	954580	954628	954677	48
1	4725	4773	4821	4869	4918	4966	5014	5062	5110	5158	48
2	5207	5255	5303	5351	5399	5447	5495	5543	5592	5640	48
3	5688	5736	5784	5832	5880	5928	5976	6024	6072	6120	48
4	6168	6216	6265	6313	6361	6409	6457	6505	6553	6601	48
905	6649	6697	6745	6793	6840	6888	6936	6984	7032	7080	48
6	7128	7176	7224	7272	7320	7368	7416	7464	7512	7559	48
7	7607	7655	7703	7751	7799	7847	7894	7942	7990	8038	48
8	8086	8134	8181	8229	8277	8325	8373	8421	8468	8516	48
9	8564	8612	8659	8707	8755	8803	8850	8898	8946	8994	48
910	959041	959089	959137	959185	959232	959280	959328	959375	959423	959471	48
1	9518	9566	9614	9661	9709	9757	9804	9852	9900	9947	48
2	9995	960042	960090	960138	960185	960233	960280	960328	960376	960423	48
3	960471	0518	0566	0613	0661	0709	0756	0804	0851	0899	48
4	0946	0994	1041	1089	1136	1184	1231	1279	1326	1374	48
915	1421	1469	1516	1563	1611	1658	1706	1753	1801	1848	47
6	1895	1943	1990	2038	2085	2132	2180	2227	2275	2322	47
7	2369	2417	2464	2511	2559	2606	2653	2701	2748	2795	47
8	2843	2890	2937	2985	3032	3079	3126	3174	3221	3268	47
9	3316	3363	3410	3457	3504	3552	3599	3646	3693	3741	47
920	963788	963835	963882	963929	963977	964024	964071	964118	964165	964212	47
1	4260	4307	4354	4401	4448	4495	4542	4590	4637	4684	47
2	4731	4778	4825	4872	4919	4966	5013	5061	5108	5155	47
3	5202	5249	5296	5343	5390	5437	5484	5531	5578	5625	47
4	5672	5719	5766	5813	5860	5907	5954	6001	6048	6095	47
925	6142	6189	6236	6283	6329	6376	6423	6470	6517	6564	47
6	6611	6658	6705	6752	6799	6845	6892	6939	6986	7033	47
7	7080	7127	7173	7220	7267	7314	7361	7408	7454	7501	47
8	7548	7595	7642	7688	7735	7782	7829	7875	7922	7969	47
9	8016	8062	8109	8156	8203	8249	8296	8343	8390	8436	47
930	968483	968530	968576	968623	968670	968716	968763	968810	968856	968903	47
1	8950	8996	9043	9090	9136	9183	9229	9276	9323	9369	47
2	9416	9463	9509	9556	9602	9649	9695	9742	9789	9835	47
3	9882	9928	9975	970021	970068	970114	970161	970207	970254	970300	47
4	970347	970393	970440	0486	0533	0579	0626	0672	0719	0765	46
935	0812	0858	0904	0951	0997	1044	1090	1137	1183	1229	46
6	1276	1322	1369	1415	1461	1508	1554	1601	1647	1693	46
7	1740	1786	1832	1879	1925	1971	2018	2064	2110	2157	46
8	2203	2249	2295	2342	2388	2434	2481	2527	2573	2619	46
9	2666	2712	2758	2804	2851	2897	2943	2989	3035	3082	46
N.	0	1	2	3	4	5	6	7	8	9	D.

N.	0	1	2	3	4	5	6	7	8	9	D.
940	973128	973174	973220	973266	973313	973359	973405	973451	973497	973543	46
1	3590	3636	3682	3728	3774	3820	3866	3913	3959	4005	46
2	4051	4097	4143	4189	4235	4281	4327	4374	4420	4466	46
3	4512	4558	4604	4650	4696	4742	4788	4834	4880	4926	46
4	4972	5018	5064	5110	5156	5202	5248	5294	5340	5386	46
945	5432	5478	5524	5570	5616	5662	5707	5753	5799	5845	46
6	5891	5937	5983	6029	6075	6121	6167	6212	6258	6304	46
7	6350	6396	6442	6488	6533	6579	6625	6671	6717	6763	46
8	6808	6854	6900	6946	6992	7037	7083	7129	7175	7220	46
9	7266	7312	7358	7403	7449	7495	7541	7586	7632	7678	46
950	977724	977769	977815	977861	977906	977952	977998	978043	978089	978135	46
1	8181	8226	8272	8317	8363	8409	8454	8500	8546	8591	46
2	8637	8683	8728	8774	8819	8865	8911	8956	9002	9047	46
3	9093	9138	9184	9230	9275	9321	9366	9412	9457	9503	46
4	9548	9594	9639	9685	9730	9776	9821	9867	9912	9958	46
955	980003	980049	980094	980140	980185	980231	980276	980322	980367	980412	45
6	0458	0503	0549	0594	0640	0685	0730	0776	0821	0867	45
7	0912	0957	1003	1048	1093	1139	1184	1229	1275	1320	45
8	1366	1411	1456	1501	1547	1592	1637	1683	1728	1773	45
9	1819	1864	1909	1954	2000	2045	2090	2135	2181	2226	45
960	982271	982316	982362	982407	982452	982497	982543	982588	982633	982678	45
1	2723	2769	2814	2859	2904	2949	2994	3040	3085	3130	45
2	3175	3220	3265	3310	3356	3401	3446	3491	3536	3581	45
3	3626	3671	3716	3762	3807	3852	3897	3942	3987	4032	45
4	4077	4122	4167	4212	4257	4302	4347	4392	4437	4482	45
965	4527	4572	4617	4662	4707	4752	4797	4842	4887	4932	45
6	4977	5022	5067	5112	5157	5202	5247	5292	5337	5382	45
7	5426	5471	5516	5561	5606	5651	5696	5741	5786	5830	45
8	5875	5920	5965	6010	6055	6100	6144	6189	6234	6279	45
9	6324	6369	6413	6458	6503	6548	6593	6637	6682	6727	45
970	986772	986817	986861	986906	986951	986996	987040	987085	987130	987175	45
1	7219	7264	7309	7353	7398	7443	7488	7532	7577	7622	45
2	7666	7711	7756	7800	7845	7890	7934	7979	8024	8068	45
3	8113	8157	8202	8247	8291	8336	8381	8425	8470	8514	45
4	8559	8604	8648	8693	8737	8782	8826	8871	8916	8960	45
975	9005	9049	9094	9138	9183	9227	9272	9316	9361	9405	45
6	9450	9494	9539	9583	9628	9672	9717	9761	9806	9850	44
7	9895	9939	9983	990028	990072	990117	990161	990206	990250	990294	44
8	990339	990383	990428	0472	0516	0561	0605	0650	0694	0738	44
9	0783	0827	0871	0916	0960	1004	1049	1093	1137	1182	44
980	991226	991270	991315	991359	991403	991448	991492	991536	991580	991625	44
1	1669	1713	1758	1802	1846	1890	1935	1979	2023	2067	44
2	2111	2156	2200	2244	2288	2333	2377	2421	2465	2509	44
3	2554	2598	2642	2686	2730	2774	2819	2863	2907	2951	44
4	2995	3039	3083	3127	3172	3216	3260	3304	3348	3392	44
985	3436	3480	3524	3568	3613	3657	3701	3745	3789	3833	44
6	3877	3921	3965	4009	4053	4097	4141	4185	4229	4273	44
7	4317	4361	4405	4449	4493	4537	4581	4625	4669	4713	44
8	4757	4801	4845	4889	4933	4977	5021	5065	5108	5152	44
9	5196	5240	5284	5328	5372	5416	5460	5504	5547	5591	44
990	995635	995679	995723	995767	995811	995854	995898	995942	995986	996030	44
1	6074	6117	6161	6205	6249	6293	6337	6380	6424	6468	44
2	6512	6555	6599	6643	6687	6731	6774	6818	6862	6906	44
3	6949	6993	7037	7080	7124	7168	7212	7255	7299	7343	44
4	7386	7430	7474	7517	7561	7605	7648	7692	7736	7779	44
995	7823	7867	7910	7954	7998	8041	8085	8129	8172	8216	44
6	8259	8303	8347	8390	8434	8477	8521	8564	8608	8652	44
7	8695	8739	8782	8826	8869	8913	8956	9000	9043	9087	44
8	9131	9174	9218	9261	9305	9348	9392	9435	9479	9522	44
9	9565	9609	9652	9696	9739	9783	9826	9870	9913	9957	43
N.	0	1	2	3	4	5	6	7	8	9	D.

TABLE VII
SEVEN-PLACE COMMON LOGARITHMS OF NUMBERS FROM 1000 TO 1100

N.	0	1	2	3	4	5	6	7	8	9	D.
1000	000 0000	0434	0869	1303	1737	2171	2605	3039	3473	3907	434
1001	4341	4775	5208	5642	6076	6510	6943	7377	7810	8244	434
1002	8677	9111	9544	9977	*0411	*0844	*1277	*1710	*2143	*2576	433
1003	001 3009	3442	3875	4308	4741	5174	5607	6039	6472	6905	433
1004	7337	7770	8202	8635	9067	9499	9932	*0364	*0796	*1228	432
1005	002 1661	2093	2525	2957	3389	3821	4253	4685	5116	5548	432
1006	5980	6411	6843	7275	7706	8138	8569	9001	9432	9863	431
1007	003 0295	0726	1157	1588	2019	2451	2882	3313	3744	4174	431
1008	4605	5036	5467	5898	6328	6759	7190	7620	8051	8481	431
1009	8912	9342	9772	*0203	*0633	*1063	*1493	*1924	*2354	*2784	430
1010	004 3214	3644	4074	4504	4933	5363	5793	6223	6652	7082	430
1011	7512	7941	8371	8800	9229	9659	*0088	*0517	*0947	*1376	429
1012	005 1805	2234	2663	3092	3521	3950	4379	4808	5237	5666	429
1013	6094	6523	6952	7380	7809	8238	8666	9094	9523	9951	429
1014	006 0380	0808	1236	1664	2092	2521	2949	3377	3805	4233	428
1015	4660	5088	5516	5944	6372	6799	7227	7655	8082	8510	428
1016	8937	9365	9792	*0219	*0647	*1074	*1501	*1928	*2355	*2782	427
1017	007 3210	3637	4064	4490	4917	5344	5771	6198	6624	7051	427
1018	7478	7904	8331	8757	9184	9610	*0037	*0463	*0889	*1316	426
1019	008 1742	2168	2594	3020	3446	3872	4298	4724	5150	5576	426
1020	6002	6427	6853	7279	7704	8130	8556	8981	9407	9832	426
1021	009 0257	0683	1108	1533	1959	2384	2809	3234	3659	4084	425
1022	4509	4934	5359	5784	6208	6633	7058	7483	7907	8332	425
1023	8756	9181	9605	*0030	*0454	*0878	*1303	*1727	*2151	*2575	424
1024	010 3000	3424	3848	4272	4696	5120	5544	5967	6391	6815	424
1025	7239	7662	8086	8510	8933	9357	9780	*0204	*0627	*1050	424
1026	011 1474	1897	2320	2743	3166	3590	4013	4436	4859	5282	423
1027	5704	6127	6550	6973	7396	7818	8241	8664	9086	9509	423
1028	9931	*0354	*0776	*1198	*1621	*2043	*2465	*2887	*3310	*3732	422
1029	012 4154	4576	4998	5420	5842	6264	6685	7107	7529	7951	422
1030	8372	8794	9215	9637	*0059	*0480	*0901	*1323	*1744	*2165	422
1031	013 2587	3008	3429	3850	4271	4692	5113	5534	5955	6376	421
1032	6797	7218	7639	8059	8480	8901	9321	9742	*0162	*0583	421
1033	014 1003	1424	1844	2264	2685	3105	3525	3945	4365	4785	420
1034	5205	5625	6045	6465	6885	7305	7725	8144	8564	8984	420
1035	9403	9823	*0243	*0662	*1082	*1501	*1920	*2340	*2759	*3178	420
1036	015 3598	4017	4436	4855	5274	5693	6112	6531	6950	7369	419
1037	7788	8206	8625	9044	9462	9881	*0300	*0718	*1137	*1555	419
1038	016 1974	2392	2810	3229	3647	4065	4483	4901	5319	5737	418
1039	6155	6573	6991	7409	7827	8245	8663	9080	9498	9916	418
1040	017 0333	0751	1168	1586	2003	2421	2838	3256	3673	4090	417
1041	4507	4924	5342	5759	6176	6593	7010	7427	7844	8260	417
1042	8677	9094	9511	9927	*0344	*0761	*1177	*1594	*2010	*2427	417
1043	018 2843	3259	3676	4092	4508	4925	5341	5757	6173	6589	416
1044	7005	7421	7837	8253	8669	9084	9500	9916	*0332	*0747	416
1045	019 1163	1578	1994	2410	2825	3240	3656	4071	4486	4902	415
1046	5317	5732	6147	6562	6977	7392	7807	8222	8637	9052	415
1047	9467	9882	*0296	*0711	*1126	*1540	*1955	*2369	*2784	*3198	415
1048	020 3613	4027	4442	4856	5270	5684	6099	6513	6927	7341	414
1049	7755	8169	8583	8997	9411	9824	*0238	*0652	*1066	*1479	414
1050	021 1893	2307	2720	3134	3547	3961	4374	4787	5201	5614	413
N.	0	1	2	3	4	5	6	7	8	9	D.

N.	0	1	2	3	4	5	6	7	8	9	D.
1050	021 1893	2307	2720	3134	3547	3961	4374	4787	5201	5614	413
1051	6027	6440	6854	7267	7680	8093	8506	8919	9332	9745	413
1052	022 0157	0570	0983	1396	1808	2221	2634	3046	3459	3871	413
1053	4284	4696	5109	5521	5933	6345	6758	7170	7582	7994	412
1054	8406	8818	9230	9642	*0054	*0466	*0878	*1289	*1701	*2113	412
1055	023 2525	2936	3348	3759	4171	4582	4994	5405	5817	6228	411
1056	6639	7050	7462	7873	8284	8695	9106	9517	9928	*0339	411
1057	024 0750	1161	1572	1982	2393	2804	3214	3625	4036	4446	411
1058	4857	5267	5678	6088	6498	6909	7319	7729	8139	8549	410
1059	8960	9370	9780	*0190	*0600	*1010	*1419	*1829	*2239	*2649	410
1060	025 3059	3468	3878	4288	4697	5107	5516	5926	6335	6744	410
1061	7154	7563	7972	8382	8791	9200	9609	*0018	*0427	*0836	409
1062	026 1245	1654	2063	2472	2881	3289	3698	4107	4515	4924	409
1063	5333	5741	6150	6558	6967	7375	7783	8192	8600	9008	408
1064	9416	9824	*0233	*0641	*1049	*1457	*1865	*2273	*2680	*3088	408
1065	027 3496	3904	4312	4719	5127	5535	5942	6350	6757	7165	408
1066	7572	7979	8387	8794	9201	9609	*0016	*0423	*0830	*1237	407
1067	028 1644	2051	2458	2865	3272	3679	4086	4492	4899	5306	407
1068	5713	6119	6526	6932	7339	7745	8152	8558	8964	9371	406
1069	9777	*0183	*0590	*0996	*1402	*1808	*2214	*2620	*3026	*3432	406
1070	029 3838	4244	4649	5055	5461	5867	6272	6678	7084	7489	406
1071	7895	8300	8706	9111	9516	9922	*0327	*0732	*1138	*1543	405
1072	030 1948	2353	2758	3163	3568	3973	4378	4783	5188	5592	405
1073	5997	6402	6807	7211	7616	8020	8425	8830	9234	9638	405
1074	031 0043	0447	0851	1256	1660	2064	2468	2872	3277	3681	404
1075	4085	4489	4893	5296	5700	6104	6508	6912	7315	7719	404
1076	8123	8526	8930	9333	9737	*0140	*0544	*0947	*1350	*1754	403
1077	032 2157	2560	2963	3367	3770	4173	4576	4979	5382	5785	403
1078	6188	6590	6993	7396	7799	8201	8604	9007	9409	9812	403
1079	033 0214	0617	1019	1422	1824	2226	2629	3031	3433	3835	402
1080	4238	4640	5042	5444	5846	6248	6650	7052	7453	7855	402
1081	8257	8659	9060	9462	9864	*0265	*0667	*1068	*1470	*1871	402
1082	034 2273	2674	3075	3477	3878	4279	4680	5081	5482	5884	401
1083	6285	6686	7087	7487	7888	8289	8690	9091	9491	9892	401
1084	035 0293	0693	1094	1495	1895	2296	2696	3096	3497	3897	400
1085	4297	4698	5098	5498	5898	6298	6698	7098	7498	7898	400
1086	8298	8698	9098	9498	9898	*0297	*0697	*1097	*1496	*1896	400
1087	036 2295	2695	3094	3494	3893	4293	4692	5091	5491	5890	399
1088	6289	6688	7087	7486	7885	8284	8683	9082	9481	9880	399
1089	037 0279	0678	1076	1475	1874	2272	2671	3070	3468	3867	399
1090	4265	4663	5062	5460	5858	6257	6655	7053	7451	7849	398
1091	8248	8646	9044	9442	9839	*0237	*0635	*1033	*1431	*1829	398
1092	038 2226	2624	3022	3419	3817	4214	4612	5009	5407	5804	398
1093	6202	6599	6996	7393	7791	8188	8585	8982	9379	9776	397
1094	039 0173	0570	0967	1364	1761	2158	2554	2951	3348	3745	397
1095	4141	4538	4934	5331	5727	6124	6520	6917	7313	7709	397
1096	8106	8502	8898	9294	9690	*0086	*0482	*0878	*1274	*1670	396
1097	040 2066	2462	2858	3254	3650	4045	4441	4837	5232	5628	396
1098	6023	6419	6814	7210	7605	8001	8396	8791	9187	9582	395
1099	9977	*0372	*0767	*1162	*1557	*1952	*2347	*2742	*3137	*3532	395
1100	041 3927	4322	4716	5111	5506	5900	6295	6690	7084	7479	395
N.	0	1	2	3	4	5	6	7	8	9	D.

TABLE VIII
SUMS OF THE FIRST SIX POWERS OF THE FIRST 50 NATURAL NUMBERS

The following table, giving the sums of the first six powers of the first M natural numbers from $M = 1$ to $M = 50$ will be most frequently used in connection with the fitting of a trend line to time series. For that type of problem, M is the highest value of X used in the computation table. When the X origin has been taken at the center of the X values, it is necessary to multiply the summations shown in this table by two. When the origin has been taken at the first X value in a time series, N as used in the normal equations is $M + 1$; when the origin has been taken at the center of the X values in a time series, N is $2M + 1$.

The sums of the first six powers of the first M natural numbers may be obtained from the following expressions:

$$\sum_1^M X = \frac{M(M+1)}{2} \qquad \sum_1^M X^4 = \left(\frac{3M^2 + 3M - 1}{5}\right) \sum_1^M X^2$$

$$\sum_1^M X^2 = \left(\frac{2M+1}{3}\right) \sum_1^M X \qquad \sum_1^M X^5 = \left(\frac{2M^2 + 2M - 1}{3}\right) \sum_1^M X^3$$

$$\sum_1^M X^3 = \left(\sum_1^M X\right)^2 \qquad \sum_1^M X^6 = \left(\frac{3M^4 + 6M^3 - 3M + 1}{7}\right) \sum_1^M X^2$$

A table of the sums of the first 7 powers of the first 100 natural numbers may be found in E. S. Pearson and H. O. Hartley, *Biometrika Tables for Statisticians,* Volume I, Cambridge University Press, Cambridge, 1954, pp. 224–225, and in Karl Pearson, *Tables for Statisticians and Biometricians,* Part I, Cambridge University Press, Cambridge, 1948 (third edition), pp. 40–41. It appears also on the same pages in earlier editions.

M	$\sum_{1}^{M} X$	$\sum_{1}^{M} X^2$	$\sum_{1}^{M} X^3$	$\sum_{1}^{M} X^4$	$\sum_{1}^{M} X^5$	$\sum_{1}^{M} X^6$
1	1	1	1	1	1	1
2	3	5	9	17	33	65
3	6	14	36	98	276	794
4	10	30	100	354	1 300	4 890
5	15	55	225	979	4 425	20 515
6	21	91	441	2 275	12 201	67 171
7	28	140	784	4 676	29 008	184 820
8	36	204	1 296	8 772	61 776	446 964
9	45	285	2 025	15 333	120 825	978 405
10	55	385	3 025	25 333	220 825	1 978 405
11	66	506	4 356	39 974	381 874	3 749 966
12	78	650	6 084	60 710	630 708	6 735 950
13	91	819	8 281	89 271	1 002 001	11 562 759
14	105	1 015	11 025	127 687	1 539 825	19 092 295
15	120	1 240	14 400	178 312	2 299 200	30 482 920
16	136	1 496	18 496	243 848	3 347 776	47 260 136
17	153	1 785	23 409	327 369	4 767 633	71 397 705
18	171	2 109	29 241	432 345	6 657 201	105 409 929
19	190	2 470	36 100	562 666	9 133 300	152 455 810
20	210	2 870	44 100	722 666	12 333 300	216 455 810
21	231	3 311	53 361	917 147	16 417 401	302 221 931
22	253	3 795	64 009	1 151 403	21 571 033	415 601 835
23	276	4 324	76 176	1 431 244	28 007 376	563 637 724
24	300	4 900	90 000	1 763 020	35 970 000	754 740 700
25	325	5 525	105 625	2 153 645	45 735 625	998 881 325
26	351	6 201	123 201	2 610 621	57 617 001	1 307 797 101
27	378	6 930	142 884	3 142 062	71 965 908	1 695 217 590
28	406	7 714	164 836	3 756 718	89 176 276	2 177 107 894
29	435	8 555	189 225	4 463 999	109 687 425	2 771 931 215
30	465	9 455	216 225	5 273 999	133 987 425	3 500 931 215
31	496	10 416	246 016	6 197 520	162 616 576	4 388 434 896
32	528	11 440	278 784	7 246 096	196 171 008	5 462 176 720
33	561	12 529	314 721	8 432 017	235 306 401	6 753 644 689
34	595	13 685	354 025	9 768 353	280 741 825	8 298 449 105
35	630	14 910	396 900	11 268 978	333 263 700	10 136 714 730
36	666	16 206	443 556	12 948 594	393 729 876	12 313 497 066
37	703	17 575	494 209	14 822 755	463 073 833	14 879 223 475
38	741	19 019	549 081	16 907 891	542 309 001	17 890 159 859
39	780	20 540	608 400	19 221 332	632 533 200	21 408 903 620
40	820	22 140	672 400	21 781 332	734 933 200	25 504 903 620
41	861	23 821	741 321	24 607 093	850 789 401	30 255 007 861
42	903	25 585	815 409	27 718 789	981 480 633	35 744 039 605
43	946	27 434	894 916	31 137 590	1 128 489 076	42 065 402 654
44	990	29 370	980 100	34 885 686	1 293 405 300	49 321 716 510
45	1 035	31 395	1 071 225	38 986 311	1 477 933 425	57 625 482 135
46	1 081	33 511	1 168 561	43 463 767	1 683 896 401	67 099 779 031
47	1 128	35 720	1 272 384	48 343 448	1 913 241 408	77 878 994 360
48	1 176	38 024	1 382 976	53 651 864	2 168 045 376	90 109 584 824
49	1 225	40 425	1 500 625	59 416 665	2 450 520 625	103 950 872 025
50	1 275	42 925	1 625 625	65 666 665	2 763 020 625	119 575 872 025

TABLE IX
SUMS OF THE FIRST SIX POWERS OF THE FIRST 50 ODD NATURAL NUMBERS

This table shows the sums of the first six powers of the first M_o odd natural numbers from $M_o = 1$ to $M_o = 50$. Note that when $M_o = 2$, we have the odd natural numbers 1 and 3; when $M_o = 3$, reference is to 1, 3, and 5; when $M_o = 4$, the numbers 1, 3, 5, and 7 are involved; and so on. For convenience, the table shows both the highest odd natural number and M_o. The sums shown here will be used almost exclusively in connection with the fitting of a trend line to a time series having an even number of years (or other periods) and where the origin is taken between the two center X values. Under these conditions: (1) the largest X value shown in the computation table is the highest odd natural number and M_o = (highest odd natural number + 1) ÷ 2; (2) the sums read from the table must be multiplied by 2; and (3) N as used in the normal equations is $2M_o$. X_o means "odd value of X."

The sums of the first six powers of the first M_o odd natural numbers may be obtained from the following:

$$\sum_1^{M_o} X_o = M_o^2 \qquad \sum_1^{M_o} X_o^4 = \left(\frac{12M_o^2 - 7}{5}\right) \sum_1^{M_o} X_o^2$$

$$\sum_1^{M_o} X_o^2 = \frac{4M_o^3 - M_o}{3} \qquad \sum_1^{M_o} X_o^5 = \left(\frac{16M_o^4 - 20M_o^2 + 7}{3}\right) \sum_1^{M_o} X_o$$

$$\sum_1^{M_o} X_o^3 = (2M_o^2 - 1) \sum_1^{M_o} X_o \qquad \sum_1^{M_o} X_o^6 = \left(\frac{48M_o^4 - 72M_o^2 + 31}{7}\right) \sum_1^{M_o} X_o^2$$

A table of the sums of the first six powers of the first 100 odd natural numbers is given in "Formulae for Facilitating Computations in Time Series Analysis," by Frank A. Ross, *Journal of The American Statistical Association,* March 1925, pp. 75–79.

(Highest odd natural number)	M_o	$\sum_1^{M_o} X_o$	$\sum_1^{M_o} X_o^2$	$\sum_1^{M_o} X_o^3$	$\sum_1^{M_o} X_o^4$	$\sum_1^{M_o} X_o^5$	$\sum_1^{M_o} X_o^6$
1	1	1	1	1	1	1	1
3	2	4	10	28	82	244	730
5	3	9	35	153	707	3 369	16 355
7	4	16	84	496	3 108	20 176	134 004
9	5	25	165	1 225	9 669	79 225	665 445
11	6	36	286	2 556	24 310	240 276	2 437 006
13	7	49	455	4 753	52 871	611 569	7 263 815
15	8	64	680	8 128	103 496	1 370 944	18 654 440
17	9	81	969	13 041	187 017	2 790 801	42 792 009
19	10	100	1 330	19 900	317 338	5 266 900	89 837 890
21	11	121	1 771	29 161	511 819	9 351 001	175 604 011
23	12	144	2 300	41 328	791 660	15 787 344	323 639 900
25	13	169	2 925	56 953	1 182 285	25 552 969	567 780 525
27	14	196	3 654	76 636	1 713 726	39 901 876	955 201 014
29	15	225	4 495	101 025	2 421 007	60 413 025	1 550 024 335
31	16	256	5 456	130 816	3 344 528	89 042 176	2 437 528 016
33	17	289	6 545	166 753	4 530 449	128 177 569	3 728 995 985
35	18	324	7 770	209 628	6 031 074	180 699 444	5 567 261 610
37	19	361	9 139	260 281	7 905 235	250 043 401	8 132 988 019
39	20	400	10 660	319 600	10 218 676	340 267 600	11 651 731 780
41	21	441	12 341	388 521	13 044 437	456 123 801	16 401 836 021
43	22	484	14 190	468 028	16 463 238	603 132 244	22 723 199 070
45	23	529	16 215	559 153	20 563 863	787 660 369	31 026 964 695
47	24	576	18 424	662 976	25 443 544	1 017 005 376	41 806 180 024
49	25	625	20 825	780 625	31 208 345	1 299 480 625	55 647 467 225
51	26	676	23 426	913 276	37 973 546	1 644 505 876	73 243 755 026
53	27	729	26 235	1 062 153	45 864 027	2 062 701 369	95 408 116 155
55	28	784	29 260	1 228 528	55 014 652	2 565 985 744	123 088 756 780
57	29	841	32 509	1 413 721	65 570 653	3 167 677 801	157 385 204 029
59	30	900	35 990	1 619 100	77 688 014	3 882 602 100	199 565 737 670
61	31	961	39 711	1 846 081	91 533 855	4 727 198 401	251 086 112 031
63	32	1 024	43 680	2 096 128	107 286 816	5 719 634 944	313 609 614 240
65	33	1 089	47 905	2 370 753	125 137 441	6 879 925 569	389 028 504 865
67	34	1 156	52 394	2 671 516	145 288 562	8 230 050 676	479 486 887 034
69	35	1 225	57 155	3 000 025	167 955 683	9 794 082 025	587 405 050 115
71	36	1 296	62 196	3 357 936	193 367 364	11 598 311 376	715 505 334 036
73	37	1 369	67 525	3 746 953	221 765 605	13 671 382 969	866 839 560 325
75	38	1 444	73 150	4 168 828	253 406 230	16 044 429 844	1 044 818 075 950
77	39	1 521	79 079	4 625 361	288 559 271	18 751 214 001	1 253 240 456 039
79	40	1 600	85 320	5 118 400	327 509 352	21 828 270 400	1 496 327 911 560
81	41	1 681	91 881	5 649 841	370 556 073	25 315 054 801	1 778 757 448 041
83	42	1 764	98 770	6 221 628	418 014 394	29 254 095 444	2 105 697 821 410
85	43	1 849	105 995	6 835 753	470 215 019	33 691 148 569	2 482 847 337 035
87	44	1 936	113 564	7 494 256	527 504 780	38 675 357 776	2 916 473 538 044
89	45	2 025	121 485	8 199 225	590 247 021	44 259 417 225	3 413 454 829 005
91	46	2 116	129 766	8 952 796	658 821 982	50 499 738 676	3 981 324 081 046
93	47	2 209	138 415	9 757 153	733 627 183	57 456 622 369	4 628 314 264 495
95	48	2 304	147 440	10 614 528	815 077 808	65 194 431 744	5 363 406 155 120
97	49	2 401	156 849	11 527 201	903 607 089	73 781 772 001	6 196 378 160 049
99	50	2 500	166 650	12 497 500	999 666 690	83 291 672 500	7 137 858 309 450

TABLE X
SQUARES, SQUARE ROOTS, AND RECIPROCALS, 1–1000

No.	Square	Square Root	Reciprocal	No.	Square	Square Root	Reciprocal
1	1	1.0000000	1.000000000	51	26 01	7.1414284	.019607843
2	4	1.4142136	0.500000000	52	27 04	7.2111026	.019230769
3	9	1.7320508	.333333333	53	28 09	7.2801099	.018867925
4	16	2.0000000	.250000000	54	29 16	7.3484692	.018518519
5	25	2.2360680	.200000000	55	30 25	7.4161985	.018181818
6	36	2.4494897	.166666667	56	31 36	7.4833148	.017857143
7	49	2.6457513	.142857143	57	32 49	7.5498344	.017543860
8	64	2.8284271	.125000000	58	33 64	7.6157731	.017241379
9	81	3.0000000	.111111111	59	34 81	7.6811457	.016949153
10	1 00	3.1622777	.100000000	60	36 00	7.7459667	.016666667
11	1 21	3.3166248	.090909091	61	37 21	7.8102497	.016393443
12	1 44	3.4641016	.083333333	62	38 44	7.8740079	.016129032
13	1 69	3.6055513	.076923077	63	39 69	7.9372539	.015873016
14	1 96	3.7416574	.071428571	64	40 96	8.0000000	.015625000
15	2 25	3.8729833	.066666667	65	42 25	8.0622577	.015384615
16	2 56	4.0000000	.062500000	66	43 56	8.1240384	.015151515
17	2 89	4.1231056	.058823529	67	44 89	8.1853528	.014925373
18	3 24	4.2426407	.055555556	68	46 24	8.2462113	.014705882
19	3 61	4.3588989	.052631579	69	47 61	8.3066239	.014492754
20	4 00	4.4721360	.050000000	70	49 00	8.3666003	.014285714
21	4 41	4.5825757	.047619048	71	50 41	8.4261498	.014084507
22	4 84	4.6904158	.045454545	72	51 84	8.4852814	.013888889
23	5 29	4.7958315	.043478261	73	53 29	8.5440037	.013698630
24	5 76	4.8989795	.041666667	74	54 76	8.6023253	.013513514
25	6 25	5.0000000	.040000000	75	56 25	8.6602540	.013333333
26	6 76	5.0990195	.038461538	76	57 76	8.7177979	.013157895
27	7 29	5.1961524	.037037037	77	59 29	8.7749644	.012987013
28	7 84	5.2915026	.035714286	78	60 84	8.8317609	.012820513
29	8 41	5.3851648	.034482759	79	62 41	8.8881944	.012658228
30	9 00	5.4772256	.033333333	80	64 00	8.9442719	.012500000
31	9 61	5.5677644	.032258065	81	65 61	9.0000000	.012345679
32	10 24	5.6568542	.031250000	82	67 24	9.0553851	.012195122
33	10 89	5.7445626	.030303030	83	68 89	9.1104336	.012048193
34	11 56	5.8309519	.029411765	84	70 56	9.1651514	.011904762
35	12 25	5.9160798	.028571429	85	72 25	9.2195445	.011764706
36	12 96	6.0000000	.027777778	86	73 96	9.2736185	.011627907
37	13 69	6.0827625	.027027027	87	75 69	9.3273791	.011494253
38	14 44	6.1644140	.026315789	88	77 44	9.3808315	.011363636
39	15 21	6.2449980	.025641026	89	79 21	9.4339811	.011235955
40	16 00	6.3245553	.025000000	90	81 00	9.4868330	.011111111
41	16 81	6.4031242	.024390244	91	82 81	9.5393920	.010989011
42	17 64	6.4807407	.023809524	92	84 64	9.5916630	.010869565
43	18 49	6.5574385	.023255814	93	86 49	9.6436508	010752688
44	19 36	6.6332496	.022727273	94	88 36	9.6953597	.010638298
45	20 25	6.7082039	.022222222	95	90 25	9.7467943	010526316
46	21 16	6.7823300	.021739130	96	92 16	9.7979590	.010416667
47	22 09	6.8556546	.021276596	97	94 09	9.8488578	.010309278
48	23 04	6.9282032	.020833333	98	96 04	9.8994949	.010204082
49	24 01	7.0000000	.020408163	99	98 01	9.9498744	.010101010
50	25 00	7.0710678	.020000000	100	1 00 00	10.0000000	010000000

No.	Square	Square Root	Reciprocal .00
101	1 02 01	10.0498756	9900990
102	1 04 04	10.0995049	9803922
103	1 06 09	10.1488916	9708738
104	1 08 16	10.1980390	9615385
105	1 10 25	10.2469508	9523810
106	1 12 36	10.2956301	9433962
107	1 14 49	10.3440804	9345794
108	1 16 64	10.3923048	9259259
109	1 18 81	10.4403065	9174312
110	1 21 00	10.4880885	9090909
111	1 23 21	10.5356538	9009009
112	1 25 44	10.5830052	8928571
113	1 27 69	10.6301458	8849558
114	1 29 96	10.6770783	8771930
115	1 32 25	10.7238053	8695652
116	1 34 56	10.7703296	8620690
117	1 36 89	10.8166538	8547009
118	1 39 24	10.8627805	8474576
119	1 41 61	10.9087121	8403361
120	1 44 00	10.9544512	8333333
121	1 46 41	11.0000000	8264463
122	1 48 84	11.0453610	8196721
123	1 51 29	11.0905365	8130081
124	1 53 76	11.1355287	8064516
125	1 56 25	11.1803399	8000000
126	1 58 76	11.2249722	7936508
127	1 61 29	11.2694277	7874016
128	1 63 84	11.3137085	7812500
129	1 66 41	11.3578167	7751938
130	1 69 00	11.4017543	7692308
131	1 71 61	11.4455231	7633588
132	1 74 24	11.4891253	7575758
133	1 76 89	11.5325626	7518797
134	1 79 56	11.5758369	7462687
135	1 82 25	11.6189500	7407407
136	1 84 96	11.6619038	7352941
137	1 87 69	11.7046999	7299270
138	1 90 44	11.7473401	7246377
139	1 93 21	11.7898261	7194245
140	1 96 00	11.8321596	7142857
141	1 98 81	11.8743422	7092199
142	2 01 64	11.9163753	7042254
143	2 04 49	11.9582607	6993007
144	2 07 36	12.0000000	6944444
145	2 10 25	12.0415946	6896552
146	2 13 16	12.0830460	6849315
147	2 16 09	12.1243557	6802721
148	2 19 04	12.1655251	6756757
149	2 22 01	12.2065556	6711409
150	2 25 00	12.2474487	6666667
151	2 28 01	12.2882057	6622517
152	2 31 04	12.3288280	6578947
153	2 34 09	12.3693169	6535948
154	2 37 16	12.4096736	6493506
155	2 40 25	12.4498996	6451613
156	2 43 36	12.4899960	6410256
157	2 46 49	12.5299641	6369427
158	2 49 64	12.5698051	6329114
159	2 52 81	12.6095202	6289308
160	2 56 00	12.6491106	6250000
161	2 59 21	12.6885775	6211180
162	2 62 44	12.7279221	6172840
163	2 65 69	12.7671453	6134969
164	2 68 96	12.8062485	6097561
165	2 72 25	12.8452326	6060606
166	2 75 56	12.8840987	6024096
167	2 78 89	12.9228480	5988024
168	2 82 24	12.9614814	5952381
169	2 85 61	13.0000000	5917160
170	2 89 00	13.0384048	5882353
171	2 92 41	13.0766968	5847953
172	2 95 84	13.1148770	5813953
173	2 99 29	13.1529464	5780347
174	3 02 76	13.1909060	5747126
175	3 06 25	13.2287566	5714286
176	3 09 76	13.2664992	5681818
177	3 13 29	13.3041347	5649718
178	3 16 84	13.3416641	5617978
179	3 20 41	13.3790882	5586592
180	3 24 00	13.4164079	5555556
181	3 27 61	13.4536240	5524862
182	3 31 24	13.4907376	5494505
183	3 34 89	13.5277493	5464481
184	3 38 56	13.5646600	5434783
185	3 42 25	13.6014705	5405405
186	3 45 96	13.6381817	5376344
187	3 49 69	13.6747943	5347594
188	3 53 44	13.7113092	5319149
189	3 57 21	13.7477271	5291005
190	3 61 00	13.7840488	5263158
191	3 64 81	13.8202750	5235602
192	3 68 64	13.8564065	5208333
193	3 72 49	13.8924440	5181347
194	3 76 36	13.9283883	5154639
195	3 80 25	13.9642400	5128205
196	3 84 16	14.0000000	5102041
197	3 88 09	14.0356688	5076142
198	3 92 04	14.0712473	5050505
199	3 96 01	14.1067360	5025126
200	4 00 00	14.1421356	5000000

No.	Square	Square Root	Reciprocal .00
201	4 04 01	14.1774469	4975124
202	4 08 04	14.2126704	4950495
203	4 12 09	14.2478068	4926108
204	4 16 16	14.2828569	4901961
205	4 20 25	14.3178211	4878049
206	4 24 36	14.3527001	4854369
207	4 28 49	14.3874946	4830918
208	4 32 64	14.4222051	4807692
209	4 36 81	14.4568323	4784689
210	4 41 00	14.4913767	4761905
211	4 45 21	14.5258390	4739336
212	4 49 44	14.5602198	4716981
213	4 53 69	14.5945195	4694836
214	4 57 96	14.6287388	4672897
215	4 62 25	14.6628783	4651163
216	4 66 56	14.6969385	4629630
217	4 70 89	14.7309199	4608295
218	4 75 24	14.7648231	4587156
219	4 79 61	14.7986486	4566210
220	4 84 00	14.8323970	4545455
221	4 88 41	14.8660687	4524887
222	4 92 84	14.8996644	4504505
223	4 97 29	14.9331845	4484305
224	5 01 76	14.9666295	4464286
225	5 06 25	15.0000000	4444444
226	5 10 76	15.0332964	4424779
227	5 15 29	15.0665192	4405286
228	5 19 84	15.0996689	4385965
229	5 24 41	15.1327460	4366812
230	5 29 00	15.1657509	4347826
231	5 33 61	15.1986842	4329004
232	5 38 24	15.2315462	4310345
233	5 42 89	15.2643375	4291845
234	5 47 56	15.2970585	4273504
235	5 52 25	15.3297097	4255319
236	5 56 96	15.3622915	4237288
237	5 61 69	15.3948043	4219409
238	5 66 44	15.4272486	4201681
239	5 71 21	15.4596248	4184100
240	5 76 00	15.4919334	4166667
241	5 80 81	15.5241747	4149378
242	5 85 64	15.5563492	4132231
243	5 90 49	15.5884573	4115226
244	5 95 36	15.6204994	4098361
245	6 00 25	15.6524758	4081633
246	6 05 16	15.6843871	4065041
247	6 10 09	15.7162336	4048583
248	6 15 04	15.7480157	4032258
249	6 20 01	15.7797338	4016064
250	6 25 00	15.8113883	4000000
251	6 30 01	15.8429795	3984064
252	6 35 04	15.8745079	3968254
253	6 40 09	15.9059737	3952569
254	6 45 16	15.9373775	3937008
255	6 50 25	15.9687194	3921569
256	6 55 36	16.0000000	3906250
257	6 60 49	16.0312195	3891051
258	6 65 64	16.0623784	3875969
259	6 70 81	16.0934769	3861004
260	6 76 00	16.1245155	3846154
261	6 81 21	16.1554944	3831418
262	6 86 44	16.1864141	3816794
263	6 91 69	16.2172747	3802281
264	6 96 96	16.2480768	3787879
265	7 02 25	16.2788206	3773585
266	7 07 56	16.3095064	3759398
267	7 12 89	16.3401346	3745318
268	7 18 24	16.3707055	3731343
269	7 23 61	16.4012195	3717472
270	7 29 00	16.4316767	3703704
271	7 34 41	16.4620776	3690037
272	7 39 84	16.4924225	3676471
273	7 45 29	16.5227116	3663004
274	7 50 76	16.5529454	3649635
275	7 56 25	16.5831240	3636364
276	7 61 76	16.6132477	3623188
277	7 67 29	16.6433170	3610108
278	7 72 84	16.6733320	3597122
279	7 78 41	16.7032931	3584229
280	7 84 00	16.7332005	3571429
281	7 89 61	16.7630546	3558719
282	7 95 24	16.7928556	3546099
283	8 00 89	16.8226038	3533569
284	8 06 56	16.8522995	3521127
285	8 12 25	16.8819430	3508772
286	8 17 96	16.9115345	3496503
287	8 23 69	16.9410743	3484321
288	8 29 44	16.9705627	3472222
289	8 35 21	17.0000000	3460208
290	8 41 00	17.0293864	3448276
291	8 46 81	17.0587221	3436426
292	8 52 64	17.0880075	3424658
293	8 58 49	17.1172428	3412969
294	8 64 36	17.1464282	3401361
295	8 70 25	17.1755640	3389831
296	8 76 16	17.2046505	3378378
297	8 82 09	17.2336879	3367003
298	8 88 04	17.2626765	3355705
299	8 94 01	17.2916165	3344482
300	9 00 00	17.3205081	3333333

No.	Square	Square Root	Reciprocal .00	No.	Square	Square Root	Reciprocal .00
301	9 06 01	17.3493516	3322259	351	12 32 01	18.7349940	2849003
302	9 12 04	17.3781472	3311258	352	12 39 04	18.7616630	2840909
303	9 18 09	17.4068952	3300330	353	12 46 09	18.7882942	2832861
304	9 24 16	17.4355958	3289474	354	12 53 16	18.8148877	2824859
305	9 30 25	17.4642492	3278689	355	12 60 25	18.8414437	2816901
306	9 36 36	17.4928557	3267974	356	12 67 36	18.8679623	2808989
307	9 42 49	17.5214155	3257329	357	12 74 49	18.8944436	2801120
308	9 48 64	17.5499288	3246753	358	12 81 64	18.9208879	2793296
309	9 54 81	17.5783958	3236246	359	12 88 81	18.9472953	2785515
310	9 61 00	17.6068169	3225806	360	12 96 00	18.9736660	2777778
311	9 67 21	17.6351921	3215434	361	13 03 21	19.0000000	2770083
312	9 73 44	17.6635217	3205128	362	13 10 44	19.0262976	2762431
313	9 79 69	17.6918060	3194888	363	13 17 69	19.0525589	2754821
314	9 85 96	17.7200451	3184713	364	13 24 96	19.0787840	2747253
315	9 92 25	17.7482393	3174603	365	13 32 25	19.1049732	2739726
316	9 98 56	17.7763888	3164557	366	13 39 56	19.1311265	2732240
317	10 04 89	17.8044938	3154574	367	13 46 89	19.1572441	2724796
318	10 11 24	17.8325545	3144654	368	13 54 24	19.1833261	2717391
319	10 17 61	17.8605711	3134796	369	13 61 61	19.2093727	2710027
320	10 24 00	17.8885438	3125000	370	13 69 00	19.2353841	2702703
321	10 30 41	17.9164729	3115265	371	13 76 41	19.2613603	2695418
322	10 36 84	17.9443584	3105590	372	13 83 84	19.2873015	2688172
323	10 43 29	17.9722008	3095975	373	13 91 29	19.3132079	2680965
324	10 49 76	18.0000000	3086420	374	13 98 76	19.3390796	2673797
325	10 56 25	18.0277564	3076923	375	14 06 25	19.3649167	2666667
326	10 62 76	18.0554701	3067485	376	14 13 76	19.3907194	2659574
327	10 69 29	18.0831413	3058104	377	14 21 29	19.4164878	2652520
328	10 75 84	18.1107703	3048780	378	14 28 84	19.4422221	2645503
329	10 82 41	18.1383571	3039514	379	14 36 41	19.4679223	2638522
330	10 89 00	18.1659021	3030303	380	14 44 00	19.4935887	2631579
331	10 95 61	18.1934054	3021148	381	14 51 61	19.5192213	2624672
332	11 02 24	18.2208672	3012048	382	14 59 24	19.5448203	2617801
333	11 08 89	18.2482876	3003003	383	14 66 89	19.5703858	2610966
334	11 15 56	18.2756669	2994012	384	14 74 56	19.5959179	2604167
335	11 22 25	18.3030052	2985075	385	14 82 25	19.6214169	2597403
336	11 28 96	18.3303028	2976190	386	14 89 96	19.6468827	2590674
337	11 35 69	18.3575598	2967359	387	14 97 69	19.6723156	2583979
338	11 42 44	18.3847763	2958580	388	15 05 44	19.6977156	2577320
339	11 49 21	18.4119526	2949853	389	15 13 21	19.7230829	2570694
340	11 56 00	18.4390889	2941176	390	15 21 00	19.7484177	2564103
341	11 62 81	18.4661853	2932551	391	15 28 81	19.7737199	2557545
342	11 69 64	18.4932420	2923977	392	15 36 64	19.7989899	2551020
343	11 76 49	18.5202592	2915452	393	15 44 49	19.8242276	2544529
344	11 83 36	18.5472370	2906977	394	15 52 36	19.8494332	2538071
345	11 90 25	18.5741756	2898551	395	15 60 25	19.8746069	2531646
346	11 97 16	18.6010752	2890173	396	15 68 16	19.8997487	2525253
347	12 04 09	18.6279360	2881844	397	15 76 09	19.9248588	2518892
348	12 11 04	18.6547581	2873563	398	15 84 04	19.9499373	2512563
349	12 18 01	18.6815417	2865330	399	15 92 01	19.9749844	2506266
350	12 25 00	18.7082869	2857143	400	16 00 00	20.0000000	2500000

No.	Square	Square Root	Reciprocal .00
401	16 08 01	20.0249844	2493766
402	16 16 04	20.0499377	2487562
403	16 24 09	20.0748599	2481390
404	16 32 16	20.0997512	2475248
405	16 40 25	20.1246118	2469136
406	16 48 36	20.1494417	2463054
407	16 56 49	20.1742410	2457002
408	16 64 64	20.1990099	2450980
409	16 72 81	20.2237484	2444988
410	16 81 00	20.2484567	2439024
411	16 89 21	20.2731349	2433090
412	16 97 44	20.2977831	2427184
413	17 05 69	20.3224014	2421308
414	17 13 96	20.3469899	2415459
415	17 22 25	20.3715488	2409639
416	17 30 56	20.3960781	2403846
417	17 38 89	20.4205779	2398082
418	17 47 24	20.4450483	2392344
419	17 55 61	20.4694895	2386635
420	17 64 00	20.4939015	2380952
421	17 72 41	20.5182845	2375297
422	17 80 84	20.5426386	2369668
423	17 89 29	20.5669638	2364066
424	17 97 76	20.5912603	2358491
425	18 06 25	20.6155281	2352941
426	18 14 76	20.6397674	2347418
427	18 23 29	20.6639783	2341920
428	18 31 84	20.6881609	2336449
429	18 40 41	20.7123152	2331002
430	18 49 00	20.7364414	2325581
431	18 57 61	20.7605395	2320186
432	18 66 24	20.7846097	2314815
433	18 74 89	20.8086520	2309469
434	18 83 56	20.8326667	2304147
435	18 92 25	20.8566536	2298851
436	19 00 96	20.8806130	2293578
437	19 09 69	20.9045450	2288330
438	19 18 44	20.9284495	2283105
439	19 27 21	20.9523268	2277904
440	19 36 00	20.9761770	2272727
441	19 44 81	21.0000000	2267574
442	19 53 64	21.0237960	2262443
443	19 62 49	21.0475652	2257336
444	19 71 36	21.0713075	2252252
445	19 80 25	21.0950231	2247191
446	19 89 16	21.1187121	2242152
447	19 98 09	21.1423745	2237136
448	20 07 04	21.1660105	2232143
449	20 16 01	21.1896201	2227171
450	20 25 00	21.2132034	2222222

No	Square	Square Root	Reciprocal .00
451	20 34 01	21.2367606	2217295
452	20 43 04	21.2602916	2212389
453	20 52 09	21.2837967	2207506
454	20 61 16	21.3072758	2202643
455	20 70 25	21.3307290	2197802
456	20 79 36	21.3541565	2192982
457	20 88 49	21.3775583	2188184
458	20 97 64	21.4009346	2183406
459	21 06 81	21.4242853	2178649
460	21 16 00	21.4476106	2173913
461	21 25 21	21.4709106	2169197
462	21 34 44	21.4941853	2164502
463	21 43 69	21.5174348	2159827
464	21 52 96	21.5406592	2155172
465	21 62 25	21.5638587	2150538
466	21 71 56	21.5870331	2145923
467	21 80 89	21.6101828	2141328
468	21 90 24	21.6333077	2136752
469	21 99 61	21.6564078	2132196
470	22 09 00	21.6794834	2127660
471	22 18 41	21.7025344	2123142
472	22 27 84	21.7255610	2118644
473	22 37 29	21.7485632	2114165
474	22 46 76	21.7715411	2109705
475	22 56 25	21.7944947	2105263
476	22 65 76	21.8174242	2100840
477	22 75 29	21.8403297	2096436
478	22 84 84	21.8632111	2092050
479	22 94 41	21.8860686	2087683
480	23 04 00	21.9089023	2083333
481	23 13 61	21.9317122	2079002
482	23 23 24	21.9544984	2074689
483	23 32 89	21.9772610	2070393
484	23 42 56	22.0000000	2066116
485	23 52 25	22.0227155	2061856
486	23 61 96	22.0454077	2057613
487	23 71 69	22.0680765	2053388
488	23 81 44	22.0907220	2049180
489	23 91 21	22.1133444	2044990
490	24 01 00	22.1359436	2040816
491	24 10 81	22.1585198	2036660
492	24 20 64	22.1810730	2032520
493	24 30 49	22.2036033	2028398
494	24 40 36	22.2261108	2024291
495	24 50 25	22.2485955	2020202
496	24 60 16	22.2710575	2016129
497	24 70 09	22.2934968	2012072
498	24 80 04	22.3159136	2008032
499	24 90 01	22.3383079	2004008
500	25 00 00	22.3606798	2000000

No.	Square	Square Root	Reciprocal .00
501	25 10 01	22.3830293	1996008
502	25 20 04	22.4053565	1992032
503	25 30 09	22.4276615	1988072
504	25 40 16	22.4499443	1984127
505	25 50 25	22.4722051	1980198
506	25 60 36	22.4944438	1976285
507	25 70 49	22.5166605	1972387
508	25 80 64	22.5388553	1968504
509	25 90 81	22.5610283	1964637
510	26 01 00	22.5831796	1960784
511	26 11 21	22.6053091	1956947
512	26 21 44	22.6274170	1953125
513	26 31 69	22.6495033	1949318
514	26 41 96	22.6715681	1945525
515	26 52 25	22.6936114	1941748
516	26 62 56	22.7156334	1937984
517	26 72 89	22.7376340	1934236
518	26 83 24	22.7596134	1930502
519	26 93 61	22.7815715	1926782
520	27 04 00	22.8035085	1923077
521	27 14 41	22.8254244	1919386
522	27 24 84	22.8473193	1915709
523	27 35 29	22.8691933	1912046
524	27 45 76	22.8910463	1908397
525	27 56 25	22.9128785	1904762
526	27 66 76	22.9346899	1901141
527	27 77 29	22.9564806	1897533
528	27 87 84	22.9782506	1893939
529	27 98 41	23.0000000	1890359
530	28 09 00	23.0217289	1886792
531	28 19 61	23.0434372	1883239
532	28 30 24	23.0651252	1879699
533	28 40 89	23.0867928	1876173
534	28 51 56	23.1084400	1872659
535	28 62 25	23.1300670	1869159
536	28 72 96	23.1516738	1865672
537	28 83 69	23.1732605	1862197
538	28 94 44	23.1948270	1858736
539	29 05 21	23.2163735	1855288
540	29 16 00	23.2379001	1851852
541	29 26 81	23.2594067	1848429
542	29 37 64	23.2808935	1845018
543	29 48 49	23.3023604	1841621
544	29 59 36	23.3238076	1838235
545	29 70 25	23.3452351	1834862
546	29 81 16	23.3666429	1831502
547	29 92 09	23.3880311	1828154
548	30 03 04	23.4093998	1824818
549	30 14 01	23.4307490	1821494
550	30 25 00	23.4520788	1818182
551	30 36 01	23.4733892	1814882
552	30 47 04	23 4946802	1811594
553	30 58 09	23 5159520	1808318
554	30 69 16	23.5372046	1805054
555	30 80 25	23.5584380	1801802
556	30 91 36	23.5796522	1798561
557	31 02 49	23.6008474	1795332
558	31 13 64	23.6220236	1792115
559	31 24 81	23 6431808	1788909
560	31 36 00	23.6643191	1785714
561	31 47 21	23.6854386	1782531
562	31 58 44	23.7065392	1779359
563	31 69 69	23.7276210	1776199
564	31 80 96	23.7486842	1773050
565	31 92 25	23.7697286	1769912
566	32 03 56	23.7907545	1766784
567	32 14 89	23.8117618	1763668
568	32 26 24	23.8327506	1760563
569	32 37 61	23.8537209	1757469
570	32 49 00	23.8746728	1754386
571	32 60 41	23.8956063	1751313
572	32 71 84	23.9165215	1748252
573	32 83 29	23.9374184	1745201
574	32 94 76	23.9582971	1742160
575	33 06 25	23.9791576	1739130
576	33 17 76	24.0000000	1736111
577	33 29 29	24.0208243	1733102
578	33 40 84	24.0416306	1730104
579	33 52 41	24.0624188	1727116
580	33 64 00	24.0831891	1724138
581	33 75 61	24.1039416	1721170
582	33 87 24	24.1246762	1718213
583	33 98 89	24.1453929	1715266
584	34 10 56	24.1660919	1712329
585	34 22 25	24.1867732	1709402
586	34 33 96	24.2074369	1706485
587	34 45 69	24.2280829	1703578
588	34 57 44	24.2487113	1700680
589	34 69 21	24.2693222	1697793
590	34 81 00	24.2899156	1694915
591	34 92 81	24.3104916	1692047
592	35 04 64	24.3310501	1689189
593	35 16 49	24.3515913	1686341
594	35 28 36	24.3721152	1683502
595	35 40 25	24.3926218	1680672
596	35 52 16	24.4131112	1677852
597	35 64 09	24.4335834	1675042
598	35 76 04	24.4540385	1672241
599	35 88 01	24.4744765	1669449
600	36 00 00	24.4948974	1666667

No.	Square	Square Root	Reciprocal .00
601	36 12 01	24.5153013	1663894
602	36 24 04	24.5356883	1661130
603	36 36 09	24.5560583	1658375
604	36 48 16	24.5764115	1655629
605	36 60 25	24.5967478	1652893
606	36 72 36	24.6170673	1650165
607	36 84 49	24.6373700	1647446
608	36 96 64	24.6576560	1644737
609	37 08 81	24.6779254	1642036
610	37 21 00	24.6981781	1639344
611	37 33 21	24.7184142	1636661
612	37 45 44	24.7386338	1633987
613	37 57 69	24.7588368	1631321
614	37 69 96	24.7790234	1628664
615	37 82 25	24.7991935	1626016
616	37 94 56	24.8193473	1623377
617	38 06 89	24.8394847	1620746
618	38 19 24	24.8596058	1618123
619	38 31 61	24.8797106	1615509
620	38 44 00	24.8997992	1612903
621	38 56 41	24.9198716	1610306
622	38 68 84	24.9399278	1607717
623	38 81 29	24.9599679	1605136
624	38 93 76	24.9799920	1602564
625	39 06 25	25.0000000	1600000
626	39 18 76	25.0199920	1597444
627	39 31 29	25.0399681	1594896
628	39 43 84	25.0599282	1592357
629	39 56 41	25.0798724	1589825
630	39 69 00	25.0998008	1587302
631	39 81 61	25.1197134	1584786
632	39 94 24	25.1396102	1582278
633	40 06 89	25.1594913	1579779
634	40 19 56	25.1793566	1577287
635	40 32 25	25.1992063	1574803
636	40 44 96	25.2190404	1572327
637	40 57 69	25.2388589	1569859
638	40 70 44	25.2586619	1567398
639	40 83 21	25.2784493	1564945
640	40 96 00	25.2982213	1562500
641	41 08 81	25.3179778	1560062
642	41 21 64	25 3377189	1557632
643	41 34 49	25.3574447	1555210
644	41 47 36	25.3771551	1552795
645	41 60 25	25.3968502	1550388
646	41 73 16	25.4165301	1547988
647	41 86 09	25.4361947	1545595
648	41 99 04	25.4558441	1543210
649	42 12 01	25.4754784	1540832
650	42 25 00	25.4950976	1538462

No.	Square	Square Root	Reciprocal .00
651	42 38 01	25.5147016	1536098
652	42 51 04	25.5342907	1533742
653	42 64 09	25.5538647	1531394
654	42 77 16	25.5734237	1529052
655	42 90 25	25.5929678	1526718
656	43 03 36	25.6124969	1524390
657	43 16 49	25.6320112	1522070
658	43 29 64	25.6515107	1519757
659	43 42 81	25.6709953	1517451
660	43 56 00	25.6904652	1515152
661	43 69 21	25.7099203	1512859
662	43 82 44	25.7293607	1510574
663	43 95 69	25.7487864	1508296
664	44 08 96	25.7681975	1506024
665	44 22 25	25.7875939	1503759
666	44 35 56	25.8069758	1501502
667	44 48 89	25.8263431	1499250
668	44 62 24	25.8456960	1497006
669	44 75 61	25.8650343	1494768
670	44 89 00	25.8843582	1492537
671	45 02 41	25.9036677	1490313
672	45 15 84	25.9229628	1488095
673	45 29 29	25.9422435	1485884
674	45 42 76	25.9615100	1483680
675	45 56 25	25.9807621	1481481
676	45 69 76	26.0000000	1479290
677	45 83 29	26.0192237	1477105
678	45 96 84	26.0384331	1474926
679	46 10 41	26.0576284	1472754
680	46 24 00	26.0768096	1470588
681	46 37 61	26.0959767	1468429
682	46 51 24	26.1151297	1466276
683	46 64 89	26.1342687	1464129
684	46 78 56	26.1533937	1461988
685	46 92 25	26.1725047	1459854
686	47 05 96	26.1916017	1457726
687	47 19 69	26.2106848	1455604
688	47 33 44	26.2297541	1453488
689	47 47 21	26.2488095	1451379
690	47 61 00	26.2678511	1449275
691	47 74 81	26.2868789	1447178
692	47 88 64	26.3058929	1445087
693	48 02 49	26.3248932	1443001
694	48 16 36	26.3438797	1440922
695	48 30 25	26.3628527	1438849
696	48 44 16	26.3818119	1436782
697	48 58 09	26.4007576	1434720
698	48 72 04	26.4196896	1432665
699	48 86 01	26.4386081	1430615
700	49 00 00	26.4575131	1428571

No.	Square	Square Root	Reciprocal .00
701	49 14 01	26.4764046	1426534
702	49 28 04	26.4952826	1424501
703	49 42 09	26.5141472	1422475
704	49 56 16	26.5329983	1420455
705	49 70 25	26.5518361	1418440
706	49 84 36	26.5706605	1416431
707	49 98 49	26.5894716	1414427
708	50 12 64	26.6082694	1412429
709	50 26 81	26.6270539	1410437
710	50 41 00	26.6458252	1408451
711	50 55 21	26.6645833	1406470
712	50 69 44	26.6833281	1404494
713	50 83 69	26.7020598	1402525
714	50 97 96	26.7207784	1400560
715	51 12 25	26.7394839	1398601
716	51 26 56	26.7581763	1396648
717	51 40 89	26.7768557	1394700
718	51 55 24	26.7955220	1392758
719	51 69 61	26.8141754	1390821
720	51 84 00	26.8328157	1388889
721	51 98 41	26.8514432	1386963
722	52 12 84	26.8700577	1385042
723	52 27 29	26.8886593	1383126
724	52 41 76	26.9072481	1381215
725	52 56 25	26.9258240	1379310
726	52 70 76	26.9443872	1377410
727	52 85 29	26.9629375	1375516
728	52 99 84	26.9814751	1373626
729	53 14 41	27.0000000	1371742
730	53 29 00	27.0185122	1369863
731	53 43 61	27.0370117	1367989
732	53 58 24	27.0554985	1366120
733	53 72 89	27.0739727	1364256
734	53 87 56	27.0924344	1362398
735	54 02 25	27.1108834	1360544
736	54 16 96	27.1293199	1358696
737	54 31 69	27.1477439	1356852
738	54 46 44	27.1661554	1355014
739	54 61 21	27.1845544	1353180
740	54 76 00	27.2029410	1351351
741	54 90 81	27.2213152	1349528
742	55 05 64	27.2396769	1347709
743	55 20 49	27.2580263	1345895
744	55 35 36	27.2763634	1344086
745	55 50 25	27.2946881	1342282
746	55 65 16	27.3130006	1340483
747	55 80 09	27.3313007	1338688
748	55 95 04	27.3495887	1336898
749	56 10 01	27.3678644	1335113
750	56 25 00	27.3861279	1333333

No.	Square	Square Root	Reciprocal .00
751	56 40 01	27.4043792	1331558
752	56 55 04	27.4226184	1329787
753	56 70 09	27.4408455	1328021
754	56 85 16	27.4590604	1326260
755	57 00 25	27.4772633	1324503
756	57 15 36	27.4954542	1322751
757	57 30 49	27.5136330	1321004
758	57 45 64	27.5317998	1319261
759	57 60 81	27.5499546	1317523
760	57 76 00	27.5680975	1315789
761	57 91 21	27.5862284	1314060
762	58 06 44	27.6043475	1312336
763	58 21 69	27.6224546	1310616
764	58 36 96	27.6405499	1308901
765	58 52 25	27.6586334	1307190
766	58 67 56	27.6767050	1305483
767	58 82 89	27.6947648	1303781
768	58 98 24	27.7128129	1302083
769	59 13 61	27.7308492	1300390
770	59 29 00	27.7488739	1298701
771	59 44 41	27.7668868	1297017
772	59 59 84	27.7848880	1295337
773	59 75 29	27.8028775	1293661
774	59 90 76	27.8208555	1291990
775	60 06 25	27.8388218	1290323
776	60 21 76	27.8567766	1288660
777	60 37 29	27.8747197	1287001
778	60 52 84	27.8926514	1285347
779	60 68 41	27.9105715	1283697
780	60 84 00	27.9284801	1282051
781	60 99 61	27.9463772	1280410
782	61 15 24	27.9642629	1278772
783	61 30 89	27.9821372	1277139
784	61 46 56	28.0000000	1275510
785	61 62 25	28.0178515	1273885
786	61 77 96	28.0356915	1272265
787	61 93 69	28.0535203	1270648
788	62 09 44	28.0713377	1269036
789	62 25 21	28.0891438	1267427
790	62 41 00	28.1069386	1265823
791	62 56 81	28.1247222	1264223
792	62 72 64	28.1424946	1262626
793	62 88 49	28.1602557	1261034
794	63 04 36	28.1780056	1259446
795	63 20 25	28.1957444	1257862
796	63 36 16	28.2134720	1256281
797	63 52 09	28.2311884	1254705
798	63 68 04	28.2488938	1253133
799	63 84 01	28.2665881	1251564
800	64 00 00	28.2842712	1250000

No.	Square	Square Root	Reciprocal .00
801	64 16 01	28:3019434	1248439
802	64 32 04	28.3196045	1246883
803	64 48 09	28.3372546	1245330
804	64 64 16	28.3548938	1243781
805	64 80 25	28.3725219	1242236
806	64 96 36	28.3901391	1240695
807	65 12 49	28.4077454	1239157
808	65 28 64	28.4253408	1237624
809	65 44 81	28.4429253	1236094
810	65 61 00	28.4604989	1234568
811	65 77 21	28.4780617	1233046
812	65 93 44	28.4956137	1231527
813	66 09 69	28.5131549	1230012
814	66 25 96	28.5306852	1228501
815	66 42 25	28.5482048	1226994
816	66 58 56	28.5657137	1225490
817	66 74 89	28.5832119	1223990
818	66 91 24	28.6006993	1222494
819	67 07 61	28.6181760	1221001
820	67 24 00	28.6356421	1219512
821	67 40 41	28.6530976	1218027
822	67 56 84	28.6705424	1216545
823	67 73 29	28.6879766	1215067
824	67 89 76	28.7054002	1213592
825	68 06 25	28:7228132	1212121
826	68 22 76	28.7402157	1210654
827	68 39 29	28.7576077	1209190
828	68 55 84	28.7749891	1207729
829	68 72 41	28.7923601	1206273
830	68 89 00	28.8097206	1204819
831	69 05 61	28.8270706	1203369
832	69 22 24	28.8444102	1201923
833	69 38 89	28.8617394	1200480
834	69 55 56	28.8790582	1199041
835	69 72 25	28.8963666	1197605
836	69 88 96	28.9136646	1196172
837	70 05 69	28.9309523	1194743
838	70 22 44	28.9482297	1193317
839	70 39 21	28.9654967	1191895
840	70 56 00	28.9827535	1190476
841	70 72 81	29.0000000	1189061
842	70 89 64	29.0172363	1187648
843	71 06 49	29.0344623	1186240
844	71 23 36	29.0516781	1184834
845	71 40 25	29.0688837	1183432
846	71 57 16	29.0860791	1182033
847	71 74 09	29.1032644	1180638
848	71 91 04	29.1204396	1179245
849	72 08 01	29.1376046	1177856
850	72 25 00	29.1547595	1176471

No.	Square	Square Root	Reciprocal 00
851	72 42 01	29.1719043	1175088
852	72 59 04	29.1890390	1173709
853	72 76 09	29.2061637	1172333
854	72 93 16	29.2232784	1170960
855	73 10 25	29 2403830	1169591
856	73 27 36	29.2574777	1168224
857	73 44 49	29.2745623	1166861
858	73 61 64	29.2916370	1165501
859	73 78 81	29.3087018	1164144
860	73 96 00	29.3257566	1162791
861	74 13 21	29.3428015	1161440
862	74 30 44	29.3598365	1160093
863	74 47 69	29.3768616	1158749
864	74 64 96	29.3938769	1157407
865	74 82 25	29.4108823	1156069
866	74 99 56	29.4278779	1154734
867	75 16 89	29.4448637	1153403
868	75 34 24	29.4618397	1152074
869	75 51 61	29.4788059	1150748
870	75 69 00	29.4957624	1149425
871	75 86 41	29.5127091	1148106
872	76 03 84	29.5296461	1146789
873	76 21 29	29.5465734	1145475
874	76 38 76	29.5634910	1144165
875	76 56 25	29.5803989	1142857
876	76 73 76	29.5972972	1141553
877	76 91 29	29.6141858	1140251
878	77 08 84	29.6310648	1138952
879	77 26 41	29.6479342	1137656
880	77 44 00	29.6647939	1136364
881	77 61 61	29.6816442	1135074
882	77 79 24	29.6984848	1133787
883	77 96 89	29.7153159	1132503
884	78 14 56	29.7321375	1131222
885	78 32 25	29.7489496	1129944
886	78 49 96	29.7657521	1128668
887	78 67 69	29.7825452	1127396
888	78 85 44	29.7993289	1126126
889	79 03 21	29.8161030	1124859
890	79 21 00	29.8328678	1123596
891	79 38 81	29.8496231	1122334
892	79 56 64	29.8663690	1121076
893	79 74 49	29.8831056	1119821
894	79 92 36	29.8998328	1118568
895	80 10 25	29.9165506	1117318
896	80 28 16	29.9332591	1116071
897	80 46 09	29.9499583	1114827
898	80 64 04	29.9666481	1113586
899	80 82 01	29.9833287	1112347
900	81 00 00	30.0000000	1111111

No.	Square	Square Root	Reciprocal .00
901	81 18 01	30.0166620	1109878
902	81 36 04	30.0333148	1108647
903	81 54 09	30.0499584	1107420
904	81 72 16	30.0665928	1106195
905	81 90 25	30.0832179	1104972
906	82 08 36	30.0998339	1103753
907	82 26 49	30.1164407	1102536
908	82 44 64	30.1330383	1101322
909	82 62 81	30.1496269	1100110
910	82 81 00	30.1662063	1098901
911	82 99 21	30.1827765	1097695
912	83 17 44	30.1993377	1096491
913	83 35 69	30.2158899	1095290
914	83 53 96	30.2324329	1094092
915	83 72 25	30.2489669	1092896
916	83 90 56	30.2654919	1091703
917	84 08 89	30.2820079	1090513
918	84 27 24	30.2985148	1089325
919	84 45 61	30.3150128	1088139
920	84 64 00	30.3315018	1086957
921	84 82 41	30.3479818	1085776
922	85 00 84	30.3644529	1084599
923	85 19 29	30.3809151	1083424
924	85 37 76	30.3973683	1082251
925	85 56 25	30.4138127	1081081
926	85 74 76	30.4302481	1079914
927	85 93 29	30.4466747	1078749
928	86 11 84	30.4630924	1077586
929	86 30 41	30.4795013	1076426
930	86 49 00	30.4959014	1075269
931	86 67 61	30.5122926	1074114
932	86 86 24	30.5286750	1072961
933	87 04 89	30.5450487	1071811
934	87 23 56	30.5614136	1070664
935	87 42 25	30.5777697	1069519
936	87 60 96	30.5941171	1068376
937	87 79 69	30.6104557	1067236
938	87 98 44	30.6267857	1066098
939	88 17 21	30.6431069	1064963
940	88 36 00	30.6594194	1063830
941	88 54 81	30.6757233	1062699
942	88 73 64	30.6920185	1061571
943	88 92 49	30.7083051	1060445
944	89 11 36	30.7245830	1059322
945	89 30 25	30.7408523	1058201
946	89 49 16	30.7571130	1057082
947	89 68 09	30.7733651	1055966
948	89 87 04	30.7896086	1054852
949	90 06 01	30.8058436	1053741
950	90 25 00	30.8220700	1052632

No.	Square	Square Root	Reciprocal .00
951	90 44 01	30.8382879	1051525
952	90 63 04	30.8544972	1050420
953	90 82 09	30.8706981	1049318
954	91 01 16	30.8868904	1048218
955	91 20 25	30.9030743	1047120
956	91 39 36	30.9192497	1046025
957	91 58 49	30.9354166	1044932
958	91 77 64	30.9515751	1043841
959	91 96 81	30.9677251	1042753
960	92 16 00	30.9838668	1041667
961	92 35 21	31.0000000	1040583
962	92 54 44	31.0161248	1039501
963	92 73 69	31.0322413	1038422
964	92 92 96	31.0483494	1037344
965	93 12 25	31.0644491	1036269
966	93 31 56	31.0805405	1035197
967	93 50 89	31.0966236	1034126
968	93 70 24	31.1126984	1033058
969	93 89 61	31.1287648	1031992
970	94 09 00	31.1448230	1030928
971	94 28 41	31.1608729	1029866
972	94 47 84	31.1769145	1028807
973	94 67 29	31.1929479	1027749
974	94 86 76	31.2089731	1026694
975	95 06 25	31.2249900	1025641
976	95 25 76	31.2409987	1024590
977	95 45 29	31.2569992	1023541
978	95 64 84	31.2729915	1022495
979	95 84 41	31.2889757	1021450
980	96 04 00	31.3049517	1020408
981	96 23 61	31.3209195	1019368
982	96 43 24	31.3368792	1018330
983	96 62 89	31.3528308	1017294
984	96 82 56	31.3687743	1016260
985	97 02 25	31.3847097	1015228
986	97 21 96	31.4006369	1014199
987	97 41 69	31.4165561	1013171
988	97 61 44	31.4324673	1012146
989	97 81 21	31.4483704	1011122
990	98 01 00	31.4642654	1010101
991	98 20 81	31.4801525	1009082
992	98 40 64	31.4960315	1008065
993	98 60 49	31.5119025	1007049
994	98 80 36	31.5277655	1006036
995	99 00 25	31.5436206	1005025
996	99 20 16	31.5594677	1004016
997	99 40 09	31.5753068	1003009
998	99 60 04	31.5911380	1002004
999	99 80 01	31.6069613	1001001
1000	1 00 00 00	31.6227766	1000000

TABLE XI
AREAS UNDER THE NORMAL CURVE

From the Arithmetic Mean to Distances* $\frac{x}{s}$ or $\frac{x}{\sigma}$ from the Arithmetic Mean, Expressed as Decimal Fractions of the Total Area 1.0000

This table shows the black area:

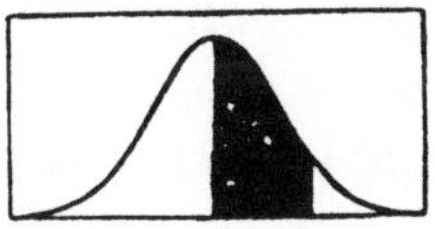

$\frac{x}{s}$ or $\frac{x}{\sigma}$	.00	.01	.02	.03	.04	.05	.06	.07	.08	.09
0.0	.0000	.0040	.0080	.0120	.0160	.0199	.0239	.0279	.0319	.0359
0.1	.0398	.0438	.0478	.0517	.0557	.0596	.0636	.0675	.0714	.0753
0.2	.0793	.0832	.0871	.0910	.0948	.0987	.1026	.1064	.1103	.1141
0.3	.1179	.1217	.1255	.1293	.1331	.1368	.1406	.1443	.1480	.1517
0.4	.1554	.1591	.1628	.1664	.1700	.1736	.1772	.1808	.1844	.1879
0.5	.1915	.1950	.1985	.2019	.2054	.2088	.2123	.2157	.2190	.2224
0.6	.2257	.2291	.2324	.2357	.2389	.2422	.2454	.2486	.2518	.2549
0.7	.2580	.2612	.2642	.2673	.2704	.2734	.2764	.2794	.2823	.2852
0.8	.2881	.2910	.2939	.2967	.2995	.3023	.3051	.3078	.3106	.3133
0.9	.3159	.3186	.3212	.3238	.3264	.3289	.3315	.3340	.3365	.3389
1.0	.3413	.3438	.3461	.3485	.3508	.3531	.3554	.3577	.3599	.3621
1.1	.3643	.3665	.3686	.3708	.3729	.3749	.3770	.3790	.3810	.3830
1.2	.3849	.3869	.3888	.3907	.3925	.3944	.3962	.3980	.3997	.4015
1.3	.4032	.4049	.4066	.4082	.4099	.4115	.4131	.4147	.4162	.4177
1.4	.4192	.4207	.4222	.4236	.4251	.4265	.4279	.4292	.4306	.4319
1.5	.4332	.4345	.4357	.4370	.4382	.4394	.4406	.4418	.4429	.4441
1.6	.4452	.4463	.4474	.4484	.4495	.4505	.4515	.4525	.4535	.4545
1.7	.4554	.4564	.4573	.4582	.4591	.4599	.4608	.4616	.4625	.4633
1.8	.4641	.4649	.4656	.4664	.4671	.4678	.4686	.4693	.4699	.4706
1.9	.4713	.4719	.4726	.4732	.4738	.4744	.4750	.4756	.4761	.4767
2.0	.4772	.4778	.4783	.4788	.4793	.4798	.4803	.4808	.4812	.4817
2.1	.4821	.4826	.4830	.4834	.4838	.4842	.4846	.4850	.4854	.4857
2.2	.4861	.4864	.4868	.4871	.4875	.4878	.4881	.4884	.4887	.4890
2.3	.4893	.4896	.4898	.4901	.4904	.4906	.4909	.4911	.4913	.4916
2.4	.4918	.4920	.4922	.4925	.4927	.4929	.4931	.4932	.4934	.4936
2.5	.4938	.4940	.4941	.4943	.4945	.4946	.4948	.4949	.4951	.4952
2.6	.4953	.4955	.4956	.4957	.4959	.4960	.4961	.4962	.4963	.4964
2.7	.4965	.4966	.4967	.4968	.4969	.4970	.4971	.4972	.4973	.4974
2.8	.4974	.4975	.4976	.4977	.4977	.4978	.4979	.4979	.4980	.4981
2.9	.4981	.4982	.4982	.4983	.4984	.4984	.4985	.4985	.4986	.4986
3.0	.49865	.4987	.4987	.4988	.4988	.4989	.4989	.4989	.4990	.4990
3.1	.49903	.4991	.4991	.4991	.4992	.4992	.4992	.4992	.4993	.4993
3.2	.4993129									
3.3	.4995166									
3.4	.4996631									
3.5	.4997674									
3.6	.4998409									
3.7	.4998922									
3.8	.4999277									
3.9	.4999519									
4.0	.4999683									
4.5	.4999966									
5.0	.4999997133									

* The expression $\frac{x}{s}$ is used when fitting a normal curve (pp. 590–607); $\frac{x}{\sigma}$ is employed when making a test of significance involving the standard deviation of the population and the normal curve (pp. 635–642, 663–666, 670–671, 673–675, 679–680, and 723–725).

Largely from Rugg's *Statistical Methods Applied to Education* (with corrections), by arrangement with the publishers, Houghton Mifflin Company. A more detailed table of normal-curve areas, but in two directions from the arithmetic mean, is given in Federal Works Agency, Work Projects Administration for the City of New York, *Tables of Probability Functions*, National Bureau of Standards, New York, 1942, Vol. II, pp. 2–338.

TABLE XII
ORDINATES OF THE NORMAL CURVE

Erected at Distances $\frac{x}{s}$ from $\overline{X}$, Expressed as Decimal Fractions of the Maximum Ordinate Y_0

The maximum ordinate is computed from the expression $Y_o = \frac{Ni}{s\sqrt{2\pi}} = \frac{Ni}{2.5066s}$. The values tabled below result from solving the expression $e^{\frac{-x^2}{2s^2}}$.

The proportional height of an ordinate to be erected at any given value on the X axis can be read from the table by determining x (the deviation of the given value from the mean) and computing $\frac{x}{s}$. Thus, if $\overline{X} = \$25$, $s = \$4$, $Y_o = 1950$, and it is desired to ascertain the height of an ordinate to be erected at \$23; $x = \$2$ and $\frac{x}{s} = \frac{\$2}{\$4} = 0.50$. From the table the ordinate is found to be 0.88250 of the maximum ordinate Y_o, or $0.88250 \times 1950 = 1721$.

TABLE XII—Continued
ORDINATES OF THE NORMAL CURVE

$\frac{x}{s}$	0	.01	.02	.03	.04	.05	.06	.07	.08	.09
0.0	1.00000	.99995	.99980	.99955	.99920	.99875	.99820	.99755	.99685	.99596
0.1	.99501	.99396	.99283	.99158	.99025	.98881	.98728	.98565	.98393	.98211
0.2	.98020	.97819	.97609	.97390	.97161	.96923	.96676	.96420	.96156	.95882
0.3	.95600	.95309	.95010	.94702	.94387	.94055	.93723	.93382	.93024	.92677
0.4	.92312	.91939	.91558	.91169	.90774	.90371	.89961	.89543	.89119	.88688
0.5	.88250	.87805	.87353	.86896	.86432	.85962	.85488	.85006	.84519	.84060
0.6	.83527	.83023	.82514	.82010	.81481	.80957	.80429	.79896	.79359	.78817
0.7	.78270	.77721	.77167	.76610	.76048	.75484	.74916	.74342	.73769	.73193
0.8	.72615	.72033	.71448	.70861	.70272	.69681	.69087	.68493	.67896	.67298
0.9	.66689	.66097	.65494	.64891	.64287	.63683	.63077	.62472	.61865	.61259
1.0	.60653	.60047	.59440	.58834	.58228	.57623	.57017	.56414	.55810	.55209
1.1	.54607	.54007	.53409	.52812	.52214	.51620	.51027	.50437	.49848	.49260
1.2	.48675	.48092	.47511	.46933	.46357	.45783	.45212	.44644	.44078	.43516
1.3	.42956	.42399	.41845	.41294	.40747	.40202	.39661	.39123	.38569	.38058
1.4	.37531	.37007	.36487	.35971	.35459	.34950	.34445	.33944	.33447	.32954
1.5	.32465	.31980	.31500	.31023	.30550	.30082	.29618	.29158	.28702	.28251
1.6	.27804	.27361	.26923	.26489	.26059	.25634	.25213	.24797	.24385	.23978
1.7	.23575	.23176	.22782	.22392	.22008	.21627	.21251	.20879	.20511	.20148
1.8	.19790	.19436	.19086	.18741	.18400	.18064	.17732	.17404	.17081	.16762
1.9	.16448	.16137	.15831	.15530	.15232	.14939	.14650	.14364	.14083	.13806
2.0	.13534	.13265	.13000	.12740	.12483	.12230	.11981	.11737	.11496	.11259
2.1	.11025	.10795	.10570	.10347	.10129	.09914	.09702	.09495	.09290	.09090
2.2	.08892	.08698	.08507	.08320	.08136	.07956	.07778	.07604	.07433	.07265
2.3	.07100	.06939	.06780	.06624	.06471	.06321	.06174	.06029	.05888	.05750
2.4	.05614	.05481	.05350	.05222	.05096	.04973	.04852	.04734	.04618	.04505
2.5	.04394	.04285	.04179	.04074	.03972	.03873	.03775	.03680	.03586	.03494
2.6	.03405	.03317	.03232	.03148	.03066	.02986	.02908	.02831	.02757	.02684
2.7	.02612	.02542	.02474	.02408	.02343	.02280	.02218	.02157	.02098	.02040
2.8	.01984	.01929	.01876	.01823	.01772	.01723	.01674	.01627	.01581	.01536
2.9	.01492	.01449	.01408	.01367	.01328	.01288	.01252	.01215	.01179	.01145

$\frac{x}{s}$	0	.1	.2	.3	.4	.5	.6	.7	.8	.9
3.	.01111	.00819	.00598	.00432	.00309	.00219	.00153	.00106	.00073	.00050
4.	.00034	.00022	.00015	.00010	.00006	.00004	.00003	.00002	.00001	.00001
5.	.00000									

Largely from Rugg's *Statistical Methods Applied to Education*, by arrangement with the publishers, Houghton Mifflin Company. More detailed tables of normal-curve ordinates may be found in E. S. Pearson and H. O. Hartley, *Biometrika Tables for Statisticians*, Volume I, Cambridge University Press, Cambridge, 1954, pp. 104–110; in Karl Pearson, *Tables for Statisticians and Biometricians, Part I*, The University Press, Cambridge, England, 1948 (third edition), pp. 2–8; and in Federal Works Agency, Work Projects Administration for the City of New York, *Tables of Probability Functions*, National Bureau of Standards, New York, 1942, Vol. II, pp. 2–238. The values shown in these tables should be multiplied by $\sqrt{2\pi} = 2.5066$ to agree with those shown above.

TABLE XIII
VALUES OF *t*

This table shows:

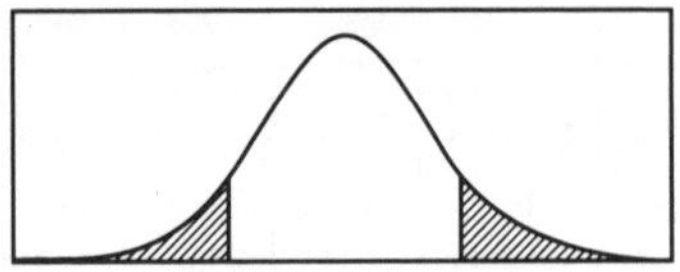

n	Level of Significance (*P*) .9	.8	.7	.6	.5	.4	.3	.2	.1	.05	.02	.01	.001
1	.158	.325	.510	.727	1.000	1.376	1.963	3.078	6.314	12.706	31.821	63.657	636.619
2	.142	.289	.445	.617	.816	1.061	1.386	1.886	2.920	4.303	6.965	9.925	31.598
3	.137	.277	.424	.584	.765	.978	1.250	1.638	2.353	3.182	4.541	5.841	12.941
4	.134	.271	.414	.569	.741	.941	1.190	1.533	2.132	2.776	3.747	4.604	8.610
5	.132	.267	.408	.559	.727	.920	1.156	1.476	2.015	2.571	3.365	4.032	6.859
6	.131	.265	.404	.553	.718	.906	1.134	1.440	1.943	2.447	3.143	3.707	5.959
7	.130	.263	.402	.549	.711	.896	1.119	1.415	1.895	2.365	2.998	3.499	5.405
8	.130	.262	.399	.546	.706	.889	1.108	1.397	1.860	2.306	2.896	3.355	5.041
9	.129	.261	.398	.543	.703	.883	1.100	1.383	1.833	2.262	2.821	3.250	4.781
10	.129	.260	.397	.542	.700	.879	1.093	1.372	1.812	2.228	2.764	3.169	4.587
11	.129	.260	.396	.540	.697	.876	1.088	1.363	1.796	2.201	2.718	3.106	4.437
12	.128	.259	.395	.539	.695	.873	1.083	1.356	1.782	2.179	2.681	3.055	4.318
13	.128	.259	.394	.538	.694	.870	1.079	1.350	1.771	2.160	2.650	3.012	4.221
14	.128	.258	.393	.537	.692	.868	1.076	1.345	1.761	2.145	2.624	2.977	4.140
15	.128	.258	.393	.536	.691	.866	1.074	1.341	1.753	2.131	2.602	2.947	4.073
16	.128	.258	.392	.535	.690	.865	1.071	1.337	1.746	2.120	2.583	2.921	4.015
17	.128	.257	.392	.534	.689	.863	1.069	1.333	1.740	2.110	2.567	2.898	3.965
18	.127	.257	.392	.534	.688	.862	1.067	1.330	1.734	2.101	2.552	2.878	3.922
19	.127	.257	.391	.533	.688	.861	1.066	1.328	1.729	2.093	2.539	2.861	3.883
20	.127	.257	.391	.533	.687	.860	1.064	1.325	1.725	2.086	2.528	2.845	3.850
21	.127	.257	.391	.532	.686	.859	1.063	1.323	1.721	2.080	2.518	2.831	3.819
22	.127	.256	.390	.532	.686	.858	1.061	1.321	1.717	2.074	2.508	2.819	3.792
23	.127	.256	.390	.532	.685	.858	1.060	1.319	1.714	2.069	2.500	2.807	3.767
24	.127	.256	.390	.531	.685	.857	1.059	1.318	1.711	2.064	2.492	2.797	3.745
25	.127	.256	.390	.531	.684	.856	1.058	1.316	1.708	2.060	2.485	2.787	3.725
26	.127	.256	.390	.531	.684	.856	1.058	1.315	1.706	2.056	2.479	2.779	3.707
27	.127	.256	.389	.531	.684	.855	1.057	1.314	1.703	2.052	2.473	2.771	3.690
28	.127	.256	.389	.530	.683	.855	1.056	1.313	1.701	2.048	2.467	2.763	3.674
29	.127	.256	.389	.530	.683	.854	1.055	1.311	1.699	2.045	2.462	2.756	3.659
30	.127	.256	.389	.530	.683	.854	1.055	1.310	1.697	2.042	2.457	2.750	3.646
40	.126	.255	.388	.529	.681	.851	1.050	1.303	1.684	2.021	2.423	2.704	3.551
60	.126	.254	.387	.527	.679	.848	1.046	1.296	1.671	2.000	2.390	2.660	3.460
120	.126	.254	.386	.526	.677	.845	1.041	1.289	1.658	1.980	2.358	2.617	3.373
∞	.126	.253	.385	.524	.674	.842	1.036	1.282	1.645	1.960	2.326	2.576	3.291

At Selected Levels of Significance (*P*) for Given Degrees of Freedom (*n*)

In the use of this table, it is to be remembered that a level of significance refers to both tails of the distribution. Thus, the 0.2 level ($P = 0.2$) includes .01 of the area of the curve in each tail. The "*t*" table, shown *n* (degrees of freedom) in the stub, *t* in the body, and *P* (the level of significance) in the caption. The last row of the "*t*" table, for $N = \infty$, is equal to the values as obtained from the normal curve.

TABLE XIV
SAMPLE SIZE

$\frac{\sigma}{E}$ or $\frac{\sqrt{\pi(1-\pi)}}{E}$

Z	10.0	9.5	9.0	8.5	8.0	7.5	7.0	6.5	6.0	5.5	5.0	4.5	4.0	3.5	3.0	2.5	2.0	1.5	1.0
1.28	164	149	132	119	104	92	80	69	59	50	41	33	26	20	15	10	7	4	
1.31	172	154	139	123	110	97	84	73	62	52	43	35	27	21	15	11	7	4	2
1.34	180	161	146	130	114	102	88	76	65	54	45	36	29	22	16	11	7	4	2
1.37	188	169	151	135	121	106	92	79	68	57	47	38	30	23	17	12	8	4	2
1.41	199	180	161	144	128	112	97	84	72	60	50	40	32	24	18	12	8	4	2
1.44	207	188	169	149	132	117	102	87	75	63	52	42	33	25	19	13	8	5	2
1.48	219	199	177	159	139	123	108	93	79	66	55	44	35	27	20	14	9	5	2
1.51	228	204	185	164	146	128	112	96	82	69	57	46	36	28	21	14	9	5	2
1.56	243	219	196	177	156	137	119	102	88	74	61	49	39	30	22	15	10	5	2
1.60	256	231	207	185	164	144	125	108	92	77	64	52	41	31	23	16	10	6	3
1.65	272	246	222	196	174	154	135	114	98	82	68	55	44	33	25	17	11	6	3
1.70	289	262	234	210	185	164	142	123	104	87	72	59	46	35	26	18	12	7	3
1.75	306	276	250	222	196	171	151	130	110	93	77	62	49	38	28	19	12	7	3
1.81	328	296	266	237	210	185	161	139	119	99	82	66	52	40	29	21	13	7	3
1.88	353	320	286	256	225	199	174	149	128	106	88	72	57	43	32	22	14	8	4
1.96	384	346	310	279	246	216	188	161	139	117	96	78	61	47	35	24	15	9	4
2.05	420	380	342	303	269	237	207	177	151	128	106	85	67	52	38	26	17	9	4
2.17	471	424	380	339	303	266	231	199	169	142	119	95	75	58	42	29	19	10	5
2.33	543	488	441	392	346	305	266	228	196	164	137	110	87	67	49	34	22	12	5
2.58	666	600	538	480	424	376	328	282	240	201	166	135	106	82	60	42	27	15	7
2.61	681	615	552	493	437	384	335	289	246	207	172	137	108	84	61	43	27	15	7
2.65	702	635	571	506	449	396	346	296	253	213	177	142	112	86	63	44	28	16	7
2.70	729	660	590	529	467	412	357	310	262	222	182	149	117	89	66	46	29	16	7
2.75	756	681	615	548	484	424	372	320	272	228	190	154	121	93	68	47	30	17	8
2.81	790	713	640	571	506	445	388	331	286	240	199	159	125	97	71	49	32	18	8
2.88	829	751	671	600	529	467	408	350	299	250	207	169	132	102	75	52	33	19	8
2.96	876	790	708	635	562	493	428	367	317	266	219	177	139	108	79	55	35	20	9
3.08	949	858	767	686	605	534	467	400	342	286	237	193	151	117	85	59	38	21	9

TABLE XV
DISCOVERY SAMPLING
SAMPLE SIZE—95% CONFIDENCE

(95% confidence that at least 1 discrepancy will be found in the sample items tested, given universe size, assumed number discrepancies per 1000 in universe, and sample size)

	Assumed	Number Discrepancies per 1000 in Universe				
	10	8	6	4	2	1
Universe Size	Sample Base Number	Sample Size = Sample Base Number Plus Number Below				
100	100					
200	155	14	29	40	45	45
300	189	25	54	86	109	111
400	211	32	74	127	180	189
500	225	39	91	163	250	274
600	236	43	103	192	315	360
700	244	46	113	216	374	446
800	250	49	121	236	427	531
900	255	51	128	253	475	613
1000	259	53	134	268	517	691
2000	278	63	164	347	776	1275
3000	285	67	175	378	894	1610
4000	289	68	180	394	960	1820
5000	291	70	184	405	1003	1963
6000	292	71	187	412	1034	2066
7000	293	72	189	417	1055	2144
8000	294	72	190	421	1072	2205
9000	295	72	191	424	1085	2253
10000	295	73	192	427	1096	2294
12000	296	73	193	430	1114	2343
14000	296	73	194	433	1126	2394
16000	297	73	195	434	1134	2433
18000	297	74	195	435	1141	2454
20000	297	74	196	436	1146	2479
22000	297	74	196	436	1151	2500
24000	297	74	196	437	1155	2519
26000	298	74	197	437	1158	2534
28000	298	74	197	438	1160	2546
30000	298	74	197	439	1161	2552
32000	298	74	197	440	1162	2562
34000	298	74	198	441	1163	2567

TABLE XVI
DISCOVERY SAMPLING
SAMPLE SIZE—99% CONFIDENCE

(99% confidence that at least 1 discrepancy will be found in the sample items tested, given universe size, assumed number discrepancies per 1000 in universe, and sample size)

	Assumed	Number Discrepancies per 1000 in Universe				
	10	8	6	4	2	1
Universe Size	Sample Base Number	Sample Size = Sample Base Number Plus Number Below				
100	100					
200	180	16	19	19	20	20
300	235	21	42	59	65	65
400	274	31	67	104	125	126
500	301	41	91	149	199	199
600	322	48	111	190	265	280
700	337	55	129	238	337	362
800	350	60	144	260	405	447
900	360	65	156	290	470	535
1000	369	69	167	315	531	621
2000	411	89	226	464	957	1389
3000	427	97	250	529	1181	1927
4000	435	101	263	565	1316	2300
5000	440	104	272	588	1405	2569
6000	443	106	277	605	1469	2772
7000	446	107	281	616	1516	2928
8000	448	107	284	624	1553	3053
9000	449	109	287	632	1583	3156
10000	450	109	289	637	1607	3240
12000	451	110	291	642	1629	3364
14000	452	110	293	647	1652	3462
16000	453	111	293	652	1676	3540
18000	454	111	297	658	1698	3609
20000	455	112	298	664	1720	3658
22000	455	112	299	666	1728	3696
24000	456	112	299	667	1735	3730
26000	456	112	300	669	1741	3765
28000	457	112	300	670	1750	3793
30000	457	113	301	672	1759	3812
32000	458	113	301	673	1766	3832
34000	458	113	302	675	1774	3842

TABLE XVII
RANDOM DECIMAL DIGITS

Line	Column (1)	(2)	(3)	(4)	(5)	(6)
1	10480	15011	01536	02011	81647	91646
2	22368	46573	25595	85393	30995	89198
3	24130	48360	22527	97265	76393	64809
4	42167	93093	06243	61680	07856	16376
5	37570	39975	81837	16656	06121	91782
6	77921	06907	11008	42751	27756	53498
7	99562	72905	56420	69994	98872	31016
8	96301	91977	05463	07972	18876	20922
9	89579	14342	63661	10281	17453	18103
10	85475	36857	53342	53988	53060	59533
11	28918	69578	88231	33276	70997	79936
12	63553	40961	48235	03427	49626	69445
13	09429	93969	52636	92737	88974	33488
14	10365	61129	87529	85689	48237	52267
15	07119	97336	71048	08178	77233	13916
16	51085	12765	51821	51259	77452	16308
17	02368	21382	52404	60268	89368	19885
18	01011	54092	33362	94904	31273	04146
19	52162	53916	46369	58586	23216	14513
20	07056	97628	33787	09998	42698	06691
21	48663	91245	85828	14346	09172	30168
22	54164	58492	22421	74103	47070	25306
23	32639	32363	05597	24200	13363	38005
24	29334	27001	87637	87308	58731	00256
25	02488	33062	28834	07351	19731	92420
26	81525	72295	04839	96423	24878	82651
27	29676	20591	68086	26432	46901	20849
28	00742	57392	39064	66432	84673	40027
29	05366	04213	25669	26422	44407	44048
30	91921	26418	64117	94305	26766	25940
31	00582	04711	87917	77341	42206	35126
32	00725	69884	62797	56170	86324	88072
33	69011	65795	95876	55293	18988	27354
34	25976	57948	29888	88604	67917	48708
35	09763	83473	73577	12908	30883	18317
36	91567	42595	27958	30134	04024	86385
37	17955	56349	90999	49127	20044	59931
38	46503	18584	18845	49618	02304	51038
39	92157	89634	94824	78171	84610	82834
40	14577	62765	35605	48263	39667	47358
41	98427	07523	33362	64270	01638	92477
42	34914	63976	88720	82765	34476	17032
43	70060	28277	39475	46473	23219	53416
44	53976	54914	06990	67245	68350	82948
45	76072	29515	40980	07391	58745	25774
46	90725	52210	83974	29992	65831	38857
47	64364	67412	33339	31926	14883	24413
48	08962	00358	31662	25388	61642	34072
49	95012	68379	93526	70765	10592	04542
50	15664	10493	20492	38391	91132	21999

Column							
(7)	(8)	(9)	(10)	(11)	(12)	(13)	(14)
69179	14194	62590	36207	20969	99570	91291	90700
27982	53402	93965	34095	52666	19174	39615	99505
15179	24830	49340	32081	30680	19655	63348	58629
39440	53537	71341	57004	00849	74917	97758	16379
60468	81305	49684	60672	14110	06927	01263	54613
18602	70659	90655	15053	21916	81825	44394	42880
71194	18738	44013	48840	63213	21069	10634	12952
94595	56869	69014	60045	18425	84903	42508	32307
57740	84378	25331	12566	58678	44947	05585	56941
38867	62300	08158	17983	16439	11458	18593	64952
56865	05859	90106	31595	01547	85590	91610	78188
18663	72695	52180	20847	12234	90511	33703	90322
36320	17617	30015	08272	84115	27156	30613	74952
67689	93394	01511	26358	85104	20285	29975	89868
47564	81056	97735	85977	29372	74461	28551	90707
60756	92144	49442	53900	70960	63990	75601	40719
55322	44819	01188	65255	64835	44919	05944	55157
18594	29852	71585	85030	51132	01915	92747	64951
83149	98736	23495	64350	94738	17752	35156	35749
76988	13602	51851	46104	88916	19509	25625	58104
90229	04734	59193	22178	30421	61666	99904	32812
76468	26384	58151	06646	21524	15227	96909	44592
94342	28728	35806	06912	17012	64161	18296	22851
45834	15398	46557	41135	10367	07684	36188	18510
60952	61280	50001	67658	32586	86679	50720	94953
66566	14778	76797	14780	13300	87074	79666	95725
89768	81536	86645	12659	92259	57102	80428	25280
32832	61362	98947	96067	64760	64584	96096	98253
37937	63904	45766	66134	75470	66520	34693	90449
39972	22209	71500	64568	91402	42416	07844	69618
74087	99547	81817	42607	43808	76655	62028	76630
76222	36086	84637	93161	76038	65855	77919	88006
26575	08625	40801	59920	29841	80150	12777	48501
18912	82271	65424	69774	33611	54262	85963	03547
28290	35797	05998	41688	34952	37888	38917	88050
29880	99730	55536	84855	29080	09250	79656	73211
06115	20542	18059	02008	73708	83517	36103	42791
20655	58727	28168	15475	56942	53389	20562	87338
09922	25417	44137	48413	25555	21246	35509	20468
56873	56307	61607	49518	89636	20103	77490	18062
66969	98420	04880	45585	46565	04102	46880	45709
87589	40836	32427	70002	70663	88863	77775	69348
94970	25832	69975	94884	19661	72828	00102	66794
11398	42878	80287	88267	47363	46634	06541	97809
22987	80059	39911	96189	41151	14222	60697	59583
50490	83765	55657	14361	31720	57375	56228	41546
59744	92351	97473	89286	35931	04110	23726	51900
81249	35648	56891	69352	48373	45578	78547	81788
76463	54328	02349	17247	28865	14777	62730	92277
59516	81652	27195	48223	46751	22923	32261	85653

Line	Column (1)	(2)	(3)	(4)	(5)	(6)
51	16408	81899	04153	53381	79401	21438
52	18629	81953	05520	91962	04739	13092
53	73115	35101	47498	87637	99016	71060
54	57491	16703	23167	49323	45021	33132
55	30405	83946	23792	14422	15059	45799
56	16631	35006	85900	98275	32388	52390
57	96773	20206	42559	78985	05300	22164
58	38935	64202	14349	82674	66523	44133
59	31624	76384	17403	53363	44167	64486
60	78919	19474	23632	27889	47914	02584
61	03931	33309	57047	74211	63445	17361
62	74426	33278	43972	10119	89917	15665
63	09066	00903	20795	95452	92648	45454
64	42238	12426	87025	14267	20979	04508
65	16153	08002	26504	41744	81959	65642
66	21457	40742	29820	96783	29400	21840
67	21581	57802	02050	89728	17937	37621
68	55612	78095	83197	33732	05810	24813
69	44657	66999	99324	51281	84463	60563
70	91340	84979	46949	81973	37949	61023
71	91227	21199	31935	27022	84067	05462
72	50001	38140	66321	19924	72163	09538
73	65390	05224	72958	28609	81406	39147
74	27504	96131	83944	41575	10573	08619
75	37169	94851	39117	89632	00959	16487
76	11508	70225	51111	38351	19444	66499
77	37449	30362	06694	54690	04052	53115
78	46515	70331	85922	38329	57015	15765
79	30986	81223	42416	58353	21532	30502
80	63798	64995	46583	09785	44160	78128
81	82486	84846	99254	67632	43218	50076
82	21885	32906	92431	09060	64297	51674
83	60336	98782	07408	53458	13564	59089
84	43937	46891	24010	25560	86355	33941
85	97656	63175	89303	16275	07100	92063
86	03299	01221	05418	38982	55758	92237
87	79626	06486	03574	17668	07785	76020
88	85636	68335	47539	03129	65651	11977
89	18039	14367	61337	06177	12143	46609
90	08362	15656	60627	36478	65648	16764
91	79556	29068	04142	16268	15387	12856
92	92608	82674	27072	32534	17075	27698
93	23982	25835	40055	67006	12293	02753
94	09915	96306	05908	97901	28395	14186
95	59037	33300	26695	62247	69927	76123
96	42488	78077	69882	61657	34136	79180
97	46764	86273	63003	93017	31204	36692
98	03237	45430	55417	63282	90816	17349
99	86591	81482	52667	61582	14972	90053
100	38534	01715	94964	87288	65680	43772

Column (7)	(8)	(9)	(10)	(11)	(12)	(13)	(14)
83035	92350	36693	31238	59649	91754	72772	02338
97662	24822	94730	06496	35090	04822	86774	98289
88824	71013	18735	20286	23153	72924	35165	43040
12544	41035	80780	45393	44812	12515	98931	91202
22716	19792	09983	74353	68668	30429	70735	25499
16815	69298	82732	38480	73817	32523	41961	44437
24369	54224	35083	19687	11052	91491	60383	19746
00697	35552	35970	19124	63318	29686	03387	59846
64758	75366	76554	31601	12614	33072	60332	92325
37680	20801	72152	39339	34806	08930	85001	87820
62825	39908	05607	91284	68833	25570	38818	46920
52872	73823	73144	88662	88970	74492	51805	99378
09552	88815	16553	51125	79375	97596	16296	66092
64535	31355	86064	29472	47689	05974	52468	16834
74240	56302	00033	67107	77510	70625	28725	34191
15035	34537	33310	06116	95240	15957	16572	06004
47075	42080	97403	48626	68995	43805	33386	21597
86902	60397	16489	03264	88525	42786	05269	92532
79312	93454	68876	25471	93911	25650	12682	73572
43997	15263	80644	43942	89203	71795	99533	50501
35216	14486	29891	68607	41867	14951	91696	85065
12151	06878	91903	18749	34405	56087	82790	70925
25549	48542	42627	45233	57202	94617	23772	07896
64482	73923	36152	05184	94142	25299	84387	34925
65536	49071	39782	17095	02330	74301	00275	48280
71945	05422	13442	78675	84081	66938	93654	59894
62757	95348	78662	11163	18651	50245	34971	52924
97161	17869	45349	61796	66345	81073	49106	79860
32305	86482	05174	07901	54339	58861	74818	46942
83991	42865	92520	83531	80377	35909	81250	54238
21361	64816	51202	88124	41870	52689	51275	83556
64126	62570	26123	05155	59194	52799	28225	85762
26445	29789	85205	41001	12535	12133	14645	23541
25786	54990	71899	15475	95434	98227	21824	19585
21942	18611	47348	20203	18534	03862	78095	50136
26759	86367	21216	98442	08303	56613	91511	75928
79924	25651	83325	88428	85076	72811	22717	50585
02510	26113	99447	68645	34327	15152	55230	93448
32989	74014	64708	00533	35398	58408	13261	47908
53412	09013	07832	41574	17639	82163	60859	75567
66227	38358	22478	73373	88732	09443	82558	05250
98204	63863	11951	34648	88022	56148	34925	57031
14827	23235	35071	99704	37543	11601	35503	85171
00821	80703	70426	75647	76310	88717	37890	40129
50842	43834	86654	70959	79725	93872	28117	19233
97526	43092	04098	73571	80799	76536	71255	64239
40202	35275	87306	55543	53203	18098	47625	88684
88298	90183	36600	78406	06216	95787	42579	90730
89534	76036	49199	43716	97548	04379	46370	28672
39560	12918	86537	62738	19636	51132	25739	56947

Line	Column (1)	(2)	(3)	(4)	(5)	(6)
101	13284	16834	74151	92027	24670	36665
102	21224	00370	30420	03883	94648	89428
103	99052	47887	81085	64933	66279	80432
104	00199	50993	98603	38452	87890	94624
105	60578	06483	28733	37867	07936	98710
106	91240	18312	17441	01929	18163	69201
107	97458	14229	12063	59611	32249	90466
108	35249	38646	34475	72417	60514	69257
109	38980	46600	11759	11900	46743	27860
110	10750	52745	38749	87365	58959	53731
111	36247	27850	73958	20673	37800	63835
112	70994	66986	99744	72438	01174	42159
113	99638	94702	11463	18148	81386	80431
114	72055	15774	43857	99805	10419	76939
115	24038	65541	85788	55835	38835	59399
116	74976	14631	35908	28221	39470	91548
117	35553	71628	70189	26436	63407	91178
118	35676	12797	51434	82976	42010	26344
119	74815	67523	72985	23183	02446	63594
120	45246	88048	65173	50989	91060	89894
121	76509	47069	86378	41797	11910	49672
122	19689	90332	04315	21358	97248	11188
123	42751	35318	97513	61537	54955	08159
124	11946	22681	45045	13964	57517	59419
125	96518	48688	20996	11090	48396	57177
126	35726	58643	76869	84622	39098	36083
127	39737	42750	48968	70536	84864	64952
128	97025	66492	56177	04049	80312	48028
129	62814	08075	09788	56350	76787	51591
130	25578	22950	15227	83291	41737	79599
131	68763	69576	88991	49662	46704	63362
132	17900	00813	64361	60725	88974	61005
133	71944	60227	63551	71109	05624	43836
134	54684	93691	85132	64399	29182	44324
135	25946	27623	11258	65204	52832	50880
136	01353	39318	44961	44972	91766	90262
137	99083	88191	27662	99113	57174	35571
138	52021	45406	37945	75234	24327	86978
139	78755	47744	43776	83098	03225	14281
140	25282	69106	59180	16257	22810	43609
141	11959	94202	02743	86847	79725	51811
142	11644	13792	98190	01424	30078	28197
143	06307	97912	68110	59812	95448	43244
144	76285	75714	89585	99296	52640	46518
145	55322	07598	39600	60866	63007	20007
146	78017	90928	90220	92503	83375	26986
147	44768	43342	20696	26331	43140	69744
148	25100	19336	14605	86603	51680	97678
149	83612	46623	62876	85197	07824	91392
150	41347	81666	82961	60413	71020	83658

Column (7)	(8)	(9)	(10)	(11)	(12)	(13)	(14)
00770	22878	02179	51602	07270	76517	97275	45960
41583	17564	27395	63904	41548	49197	82277	24120
65793	83287	34142	13241	30590	97760	35848	91983
69721	57484	67501	77638	44331	11257	71131	11059
98539	27186	31237	80612	44488	97819	70401	95419
31211	54288	39296	37318	65724	90401	79017	62077
33216	19358	02591	54263	88449	01912	07436	50813
12489	51924	86871	92446	36607	11458	30440	52639
77940	39298	97838	95145	32378	68038	89351	37005
89295	59062	39404	13198	59960	70408	29812	83126
71051	84724	52492	22342	78071	17456	96104	18327
11392	20724	54322	36923	70009	23233	65438	59685
90628	52506	02016	85151	88598	47821	00265	82525
25993	03544	21560	83471	43989	90770	22965	44247
13790	35112	01324	39520	76210	22467	83275	32286
12854	30166	09073	75887	36782	00268	97121	57676
90348	55359	80392	41012	36270	77786	89578	21059
92920	92155	58807	54644	58581	95331	78629	73344
98924	20633	58842	85961	07648	70164	34994	67662
36036	32819	68559	99221	49475	50558	34698	71800
88575	97966	32466	10083	54728	81972	58975	30761
39062	63312	52496	07349	79178	33692	57352	72862
00337	80778	27507	95478	21252	12746	37554	97775
58045	44067	58716	58840	45557	96345	33271	53464
83867	86464	14342	21545	46717	72364	86954	55580
72505	92265	23107	60278	05822	46760	44294	07672
38404	94317	65402	13589	01055	79044	19308	83623
26408	43591	75528	65341	49044	95495	81256	53214
54509	49295	85830	59860	30883	89660	96142	18354
96191	71845	86899	70694	24290	01551	80092	82118
56625	00481	73323	91427	15264	06969	57048	54149
99709	30666	26451	11528	44323	34778	60342	60388
58254	26160	32116	63403	35404	57146	10909	07346
14491	55226	78793	34107	30374	48429	51376	09559
22273	05554	99521	73791	85744	29276	70326	60251
56073	06606	51826	18893	83448	31915	97764	75091
99884	13951	71057	53961	61448	74909	07322	80960
22644	87779	23753	99926	63898	54886	18051	96314
83637	55984	13300	52212	58781	14905	46502	04472
12224	25643	89884	31149	85423	32581	34374	70873
12998	76844	05320	54236	53891	70226	38632	84776
55583	05197	47714	68440	22016	79204	06862	94451
31262	88880	13040	16458	43813	89416	42482	33939
55486	90754	88932	19937	57119	23251	55619	23679
66819	84164	61131	81429	60676	42807	78286	29015
74399	30885	88567	29169	72816	53357	15428	86932
82928	24988	94237	46138	77426	39039	55596	12655
24261	02464	86563	74812	60069	71674	15478	47642
58317	37726	84628	42221	10268	20692	15699	29167
0241-	33322	66036	98712	46795	16308	28413	05417

Line	Column (1)	(2)	(3)	(4)	(5)	(6)
151	38128	51178	75096	13609	16110	73533
152	60950	00455	73254	96067	50717	13878
153	90524	17320	29832	96118	75792	25326
154	49897	18278	67160	39408	97056	43517
155	18494	99209	81060	19488	65596	59787
156	65373	72984	30171	37741	70203	94094
157	40653	12843	04213	70925	95360	55774
158	51638	22238	56344	44587	83231	50317
159	69742	99303	62578	83575	30337	07488
160	58012	74072	67488	74580	47992	69482
161	18348	19855	42887	08279	43206	47077
162	59614	09193	58064	29086	44385	45740
163	75688	28630	39210	52897	62748	72658
164	13941	77802	69101	70061	35460	34576
165	96656	86420	96475	86458	54463	96419
166	03363	82042	15942	14549	38324	87094
167	70366	08390	69155	25496	13240	57407
168	47870	36605	12927	16043	53257	93796
169	79504	77606	22761	30518	28373	73898
170	46967	74841	50923	15339	37755	98995
171	14558	50769	35444	59030	87516	48193
172	12440	25057	01132	38611	28135	68089
173	32293	29938	68653	10497	98919	46587
174	10640	21875	72462	77981	56550	55999
175	47615	23169	39571	56972	20628	21788
176	16948	11128	71624	72754	49084	96303
177	21258	61092	66634	70335	92448	17354
178	15072	48853	15178	30730	47481	48490
179	99154	57412	09858	65671	70655	71479
180	08759	61089	23706	32994	35426	36666
181	67323	57839	61114	62192	47547	58023
182	09255	13986	84834	20764	72206	89393
183	36304	74712	00374	10107	85061	69228
184	15884	67429	86612	47367	10242	44880
185	18745	32031	35303	08134	33925	03004
186	72934	40086	88292	65728	38300	42323
187	17626	02944	20910	57662	80181	38579
188	27117	61399	50967	41399	81636	16663
189	93995	18678	90012	63645	85701	85269
190	67392	89421	09623	80725	62620	84162
191	04910	12261	37566	80016	21245	69377
192	81453	20283	79929	59839	23875	13245
193	19480	75790	48539	23703	15537	48885
194	21456	13162	74608	81011	55512	07481
195	89406	20912	46189	76376	25538	87212
196	09866	07414	55977	16419	01101	69343
197	86541	24681	23421	13521	28000	94917
198	10414	96941	06205	72222	57167	83902
199	49942	06683	41479	58982	56288	42853
200	23995	68882	42291	23374	24299	27024

Column							
(7)	(8)	(9)	(10)	(11)	(12)	(13)	(14)
42564	59870	29399	67834	91055	89917	51096	89011
03216	78274	65863	37011	91283	33914	91303	49326
22940	24904	80523	38928	91374	55597	97567	38914
84426	59650	20247	19293	02019	14790	02852	05819
47939	91225	98768	43688	00438	05548	09443	82897
87261	30056	58124	70133	18936	02138	59372	09075
76439	61768	52817	81151	52188	31940	54273	49032
74541	07719	25472	41602	77318	15145	57515	07633
51941	84316	42067	49692	28616	29101	03013	73449
58624	17106	47538	13452	22620	24260	40155	74716
42637	45606	00011	20662	14642	49984	94509	56380
70752	05663	49081	26960	57454	99264	24142	74648
98059	67202	72789	01869	13496	14663	87645	89713
15412	81304	58757	35498	94830	75521	00603	97701
55417	41375	76886	19008	66877	35934	59801	00497
19069	67590	11087	68570	22591	65232	85915	91499
91407	49160	07379	34444	94567	66035	38918	65708
52721	73120	48025	76074	95605	67422	41646	14557
30550	76684	77366	32276	04690	61667	64798	66276
40162	89561	69199	42257	11647	47603	48779	97907
02945	00922	48189	04724	21263	20892	92955	90251
10954	10097	54243	06460	50856	65435	79377	53890
77701	99119	93165	67788	17638	23097	21468	36992
87310	69643	45124	00349	25748	00844	96831	30651
51736	33133	72696	32605	41569	76148	91544	21121
27830	45817	67867	18062	87453	17226	72904	71474
83432	49608	66520	06442	59664	20420	39201	69549
41436	25015	49932	20474	53821	51015	79841	32405
63520	31357	56968	06729	34465	70685	04184	25250
63988	98844	37533	08269	27021	45886	22835	78451
64630	34886	98777	75442	95592	06141	45096	73117
34548	93438	88730	61805	78955	18952	46436	58740
81969	92216	03568	39630	81869	52824	50937	27954
12060	44309	46629	55105	66793	93173	00480	13311
59929	95418	04917	57596	24878	61733	92834	64454
64068	98373	48971	09049	59943	36538	05976	82118
24580	90529	52303	50436	29401	57824	86039	81062
15634	79717	94696	59240	25543	97989	63306	90946
62263	68331	00389	72571	15210	20769	44686	96176
87368	29560	00519	84545	08004	24526	41252	14521
50420	85658	55263	68667	78770	04533	14513	18099
46808	74124	74703	35769	95588	21014	37078	39170
02861	86587	74539	65227	90799	58789	96257	02708
93551	72189	76261	91206	89941	15132	37738	59284
20748	12831	57166	35026	16817	79121	18929	40628
13305	94302	80703	57910	36933	57771	42546	03003
07423	57523	97234	63951	42876	46829	09781	58160
07460	69507	10600	08858	07685	44472	64220	27040
92196	20632	62045	78812	35895	51851	83534	10689
67460	94783	40937	16961	26053	78749	46704	21983

Line	Column (1)	(2)	(3)	(4)	(5)	(6)
201	78994	36244	02673	25475	84953	61793
202	04909	58485	70686	93930	34880	73059
203	46582	73570	33004	51795	86477	46736
204	29242	89792	88634	60285	07190	07795
205	68104	81339	97090	20601	78940	20228
206	17156	02182	82504	19880	93747	80910
207	50711	94789	07171	02103	99057	98775
208	39449	52409	75095	77720	39729	03205
209	75629	82729	76916	72657	58992	32756
210	01020	55151	36132	51971	32155	60735
211	08337	89989	24260	08618	66798	25889
212	76829	47229	19706	30094	69430	92399
213	39708	30641	21267	56501	95182	72442
214	89836	55817	56747	75195	06818	83043
215	25903	61370	66081	54076	67442	52964
216	71345	03422	01015	68025	19703	77313
217	61454	92263	14647	08473	34124	10740
218	80376	08909	30470	40200	46558	61742
219	45144	54373	05505	90074	24783	86299
220	12191	88527	58852	51175	11534	87218
221	62936	59120	73957	35969	21598	47287
222	31588	96798	43668	12611	01714	77266
223	20787	96048	84726	17512	39450	43618
224	45603	00745	84635	43079	52724	14262
225	31606	64782	34027	56734	09365	20008
226	10452	33074	76718	99556	16026	00013
227	37016	64633	67301	50949	91298	74968
228	66725	97865	25409	37498	00816	99262
229	07380	74438	82120	17890	40963	55757
230	71621	57688	58256	47702	74724	89419
231	03466	13263	23917	20417	11315	52805
232	12692	32931	97387	34822	53775	91674
233	52192	30941	44998	17833	94563	23062
234	56691	72529	66063	73570	86860	68125
235	74952	43041	58869	15677	78598	43520
236	18752	43693	32867	53017	22661	39610
237	61691	04944	43111	28325	82319	65589
238	49197	63948	38947	60207	70667	39843
239	19436	87291	71684	74859	76501	93456
240	39143	64893	14606	13543	09621	68301
241	82244	67549	76491	09761	74494	91307
242	55847	56155	42878	23708	97999	40131
243	94095	95970	07826	25991	37584	56966
244	11751	69469	25521	44097	07511	88976
245	69902	08995	27821	11758	64989	61902
246	21850	25352	25556	92161	23592	43294
247	75850	46992	25165	55906	62339	88958
248	29648	22086	42581	85677	20251	39641
249	82740	28443	42734	25518	82827	35825
250	36842	42092	52075	83926	42875	71500

Column (7)	(8)	(9)	(10)	(11)	(12)	(13)	(14)
50243	63423	69309	80308	49977	18075	43227	08266
06823	80257	44193	08337	47655	75932	29209	41954
60460	70345	37322	19987	67143	41129	89514	46892
27011	85941	01852	43096	31173	43730	48505	17958
22803	96070	10251	62711	66200	74330	13820	18966
78260	25136	62018	62919	73801	57195	83457	70597
37997	18325	88281	61091	97889	79977	04544	72963
09313	43545	43786	70443	41350	73369	42405	80516
01154	84890	04107	17469	59346	68651	97433	89491
64867	35424	25257	93844	39928	52519	34368	02114
52860	57375	52815	43539	18072	44270	27309	56535
98749	22081	52564	90431	35208	40323	87505	10227
21445	17276	90344	33199	02522	97883	09515	65930
47403	58266	52630	75573	91088	41118	27195	40650
23823	02718	28786	06121	29680	55295	67086	57574
04555	83425	46763	95315	23150	15116	18017	42730
40839	05620	62418	73374	92577	06755	21856	56272
11643	92121	22294	26648	69676	46198	00331	85186
20900	15144	26506	53770	76431	23861	71208	80694
04876	85584	78465	82182	03412	13217	14313	70593
39394	08778	38036	30140	89117	32054	44603	61849
55079	24690	84716	77732	35363	85525	17015	56344
30629	24356	05294	34236	65299	36922	46995	65765
05750	89373	79088	38088	65082	92504	80545	03090
93559	78384	99219	61747	96111	86965	33233	29812
78411	95107	10786	44886	44612	06830	27848	87597
73631	57397	08632	04762	69328	34926	07403	60916
14471	10232	19035	21695	07540	96447	20743	92472
13492	68294	87170	49468	40164	13374	23021	17006
08025	68519	95188	54788	32999	34374	05780	17506
33072	07723	87876	75258	22709	99869	11609	46666
76549	37635	91118	31062	89441	31839	88614	78168
95725	38463	03665	49189	46359	37401	73407	61817
40436	31303	79330	59083	34862	00540	21734	75535
97521	83248	52173	17636	77106	01044	22990	74874
03796	02622	78267	24503	73518	76545	99088	08369
66048	98498	46941	81427	44447	70357	18864	15525
60607	15328	09528	17277	84278	04463	12188	35359
95714	92518	10683	75617	78841	25315	74041	71554
69817	52140	03976	48795	60266	99592	68334	18790
64222	66592	67270	38593	18094	95095	08649	25047
52360	90390	73108	40475	80487	07787	35238	50990
68623	83454	49461	97707	12479	25041	40565	18313
30122	67542	54825	03274	02765	67162	40312	76127
32121	28165	21326	97375	44801	66977	08232	06807
10479	37879	21825	11453	29584	70067	09471	16319
91717	15756	78817	35541	01177	06869	10543	57652
65786	80689	49066	14456	91681	69371	18292	39377
90288	32911	79666	52959	01475	83321	24991	80102
69216	01350	92846	84792	87455	06842	22422	77379

Line	Column (1)	(2)	(3)	(4)	(5)	(6)
251	89429	26726	15563	94972	78739	04419
252	43427	25412	25587	21276	44426	17369
253	58575	81958	51846	02676	67781	95137
254	61888	71246	24246	23487	78639	92006
255	73891	47025	40937	71907	26827	98865
256	40938	73894	40854	15997	55293	95033
257	98053	43567	17292	86908	71364	06089
258	59774	29138	46993	39836	99596	59050
259	09765	07548	63043	59782	81449	13652
260	38991	64502	24770	29209	82909	66610
261	25622	27100	56128	62145	82388	45197
262	31864	74120	66231	82306	91784	33177
263	81171	75639	60863	49562	28846	81581
264	69874	52803	28544	51569	56090	44558
265	27848	51107	05761	02159	53911	01952
266	69407	69736	75375	31488	67528	84234
267	29418	03091	06364	13151	40663	43633
268	38222	31231	79415	44558	62490	26936
269	94720	83796	93251	03568	62484	29140
270	45275	16852	02284	41361	73733	61486
271	97260	09352	82626	42915	45847	87401
272	01990	65259	60684	78175	43825	45211
273	24633	42314	81192	50253	67516	59076
274	98071	52677	74920	74461	52266	26967
275	34101	79442	28403	48541	13010	16596
276	77186	93967	25918	66403	73837	73445
277	23114	05481	42335	51396	60823	22680
278	59988	49944	41038	99977	16348	41119
279	11852	42254	82304	05588	75165	20179
280	59992	87922	56299	01700	07003	97507
281	42116	86593	22828	41422	18176	03250
282	39663	61401	21471	42702	70588	53144
283	53542	72009	96296	68908	58657	87117
284	25996	76108	98476	36397	89457	19577
285	91106	26450	14451	50328	29084	32332
286	37133	88924	27845	13024	90687	23726
287	13982	25736	10087	16762	02564	27250
288	26663	36187	81688	25005	46677	75851
289	62572	08275	16313	24936	81680	53829
290	65925	95455	08383	24643	72962	08172
291	97978	74676	08942	48919	51592	71196
292	01914	42524	67820	47985	91773	10383
293	68565	44811	39238	70394	78555	33539
294	54370	31672	03893	32423	54092	69375
295	79954	89601	23881	46951	69084	33477
296	55479	01069	44229	56975	06785	80930
297	38114	70330	42157	86699	46212	74692
298	29766	83452	66202	02488	72704	97821
299	31771	70640	34779	41831	33456	53194
300	77522	87188	83577	99067	83235	48662

Column (7)	(8)	(9)	(10)	(11)	(12)	(13)	(14)
60523	31022	23728	37647	16476	11170	68376	56874
29010	45337	90245	92053	41447	14897	18753	68291
88430	78260	66962	31812	12759	06427	40337	50115
63846	92263	33212	26516	93662	72399	88244	33922
38882	25757	26662	91441	89357	87803	61521	80600
31736	75068	91314	75293	04895	39355	54837	57203
92394	73691	57883	09983	35643	79309	53449	95334
25419	04130	54632	17223	94604	22973	97731	99476
94420	74460	46707	94303	85523	95244	70995	10742
84418	66214	26001	78685	69117	72446	79783	22305
97609	83942	01120	71717	32858	58679	97165	02810
17681	18963	07216	49288	43185	62797	00735	27085
10249	23190	53440	32357	16472	99013	24328	93670
42095	92311	57915	13368	13719	15833	38744	56065
59273	32250	39647	29908	49075	23061	07795	95047
76462	13628	21286	13736	67478	45218	27867	93049
87954	69800	24773	62596	52476	60631	50503	94116
49682	16307	98535	44822	99574	58487	85020	68881
14152	37044	90398	92042	35099	31640	99753	44409
33189	08907	41159	08147	15472	33250	17361	79961
13339	53850	34931	00602	75307	99708	77863	04924
86287	78190	02431	66251	74970	50246	23975	80697
92006	65676	87343	89231	15760	73706	69426	01979
68284	31612	40335	28865	98949	64492	96905	29184
72001	38546	76305	22119	82668	84017	44111	40302
86663	15929	08237	05647	15785	70444	58670	95967
50459	05429	35227	92559	24136	13126	22099	52388
51548	19511	90142	65604	16147	63445	60525	10480
94198	25700	33473	59554	30974	69973	57629	38550
69260	53349	86947	27517	80159	01899	46890	53850
06079	85467	32052	56922	96804	51060	33157	83948
27087	05591	57759	51394	98873	45625	61069	78783
21483	28879	20480	57309	95552	09826	79928	17141
65877	04802	61938	25032	09190	74932	36925	82686
08635	25192	31337	20249	95073	93800	70022	99968
11212	30414	42185	49224	46560	80447	24334	74866
79316	83848	38684	20552	44402	85153	94526	41256
73938	73044	05132	61204	90354	90296	03182	36672
40412	01479	24241	58488	65341	93414	07135	43446
37824	87587	40698	34964	50166	74756	77033	41501
48534	16955	25759	95645	03148	10646	15660	86520
89514	07557	02084	16736	39198	69697	62485	61938
56310	40809	63204	14479	19635	97299	66947	58010
63308	08016	28407	98287	22874	57545	72695	01604
87968	15639	82409	34125	36864	52112	27102	87334
26443	44892	77561	51123	34495	31376	06238	15973
92603	91306	58558	57280	50639	80563	71370	81487
70614	53616	39050	30355	15340	97298	41795	35185
19602	74194	61154	51774	76822	73794	54182	45264
31503	54829	54723	13177	15307	26073	68915	88415

Line	Column (1)	(2)	(3)	(4)	(5)	(6)
301	64670	10396	82981	58320	71478	08143
302	25771	02205	73984	28436	88192	11470
303	27551	13537	54984	89406	88326	33993
304	91224	22417	44820	26189	57541	87558
305	75179	64320	71523	67868	38883	09674
306	64654	91085	65818	03313	39273	46384
307	98059	81123	67832	04102	66188	78200
308	38765	63585	18810	95805	11414	58096
309	01921	03564	71754	10213	80383	13473
310	16211	93671	27704	66778	96307	06732
311	70232	86076	61527	56123	48514	53935
312	22332	94265	67627	85815	00394	75271
313	81333	45965	64171	84367	15052	37965
314	39333	47453	66174	04546	10594	64271
315	29195	20825	50878	80273	26285	90070
316	74420	64037	06960	25109	08821	60143
317	22763	16508	24866	13177	07464	51730
318	72919	54618	40616	33287	51274	78491
319	92385	42402	15922	90033	21555	31647
320	85431	19857	97246	46118	71222	82744
321	40778	12451	14921	51464	45331	75822
322	88903	46592	60637	65231	08778	86813
323	29830	34899	85457	19548	83355	52479
324	22832	47422	08073	10107	46772	92299
325	75159	14809	11930	83531	51239	86298
326	99390	08217	56276	09263	82685	30451
327	68622	80897	08902	10867	91379	30068
328	92393	95901	41179	72129	72502	91097
329	53122	66033	38229	51879	29925	45574
330	43251	11941	86631	93264	53433	70281
331	16613	24901	34866	75002	55163	68308
332	12010	60852	92603	70393	17989	95755
333	85528	97879	27814	08219	02908	71582
334	32590	55079	33556	83169	92087	77939
335	92934	30650	16449	15805	61551	38689
336	80614	10150	09389	61892	79477	14522
337	62398	12034	90764	52872	22285	50592
338	02222	46811	05145	67916	15184	02636
339	08690	31785	61664	61322	24149	21471
340	61187	73897	66168	12885	73191	89432
341	12324	61149	85643	64999	63738	46671
342	47635	42279	98620	70677	52386	50904
343	70965	00390	08878	15373	70276	71889
344	58764	15262	96814	54548	00042	19721
345	07429	05609	31207	50254	68389	07714
346	15665	28659	54952	53217	76898	88931
347	64208	53232	99459	43605	04553	48451
348	17952	73276	52567	48489	64264	24220
349	60531	43217	39999	38615	97195	76928
350	76692	39999	43254	68110	88053	88727

Column (7)	(8)	(9)	(10)	(11)	(12)	(13)	(14)
48294	42631	45464	58092	14187	12271	98179	87812
11775	67385	66360	59884	93873	29948	66302	82227
92324	13249	35271	60400	70762	08343	76456	90068
45835	28461	54835	92411	44369	47512	49508	02841
27645	76240	47587	01677	38342	85598	12482	30749
66677	14148	87552	38383	67435	21072	63866	74644
67466	46043	65406	22834	08620	17509	51424	25187
00295	82626	42683	44518	12209	83245	53771	95469
94128	62199	59411	46782	62871	51149	87146	40129
63750	04191	40003	51653	54228	14916	05361	08884
86784	42351	67586	07432	61499	01773	97463	58815
98385	53697	56378	50592	77441	88505	89791	16331
03122	81914	69381	70034	92563	61804	58326	97895
61026	39471	55981	18628	67943	35599	37209	34061
79586	12449	77293	36577	59192	03658	90056	83145
34485	19257	29417	72713	72326	41572	41553	46946
65802	95718	28560	11332	74272	59189	53167	13133
53604	66742	97777	64468	98224	45485	17257	31561
22288	75692	20592	84620	58679	24587	83517	55327
67892	77155	10785	00344	19641	98279	18716	13895
46859	66829	35803	27645	76095	41535	25508	53066
47819	19218	46837	89671	77661	08518	85216	62664
77801	01596	48890	56104	68733	40830	58611	59181
42975	86376	27869	52954	07900	75918	51398	87598
72661	63015	98804	98491	99565	42801	71816	84000
25742	41105	74711	42007	02082	93025	86641	28952
84289	45020	92459	03831	08531	63496	98230	42884
09488	84896	37720	68104	73817	67626	16221	63527
53938	72801	64067	76328	28941	43645	37181	95329
55000	24550	74751	32855	25399	95743	85393	20261
20070	36953	39378	71191	84510	47599	93608	24379
14672	58786	41996	02893	94163	36156	54203	94138
31439	00360	72264	87245	65903	42298	28061	81889
53792	78795	58159	86394	41749	91623	26973	81474
59179	85485	18537	70496	98694	19796	76804	03673
40270	45744	29582	29717	39590	10223	43049	78775
42505	80560	38213	18917	10015	03887	62589	15851
59078	57773	21259	86090	56705	65556	04487	95954
23328	03093	31266	14840	30703	01640	07874	16630
65414	41886	75911	35708	43208	59193	04727	31037
25408	69313	54455	04917	35047	09951	72776	84697
97403	03931	42090	28179	98028	47728	45696	74176
86953	37931	23286	20508	40100	22486	37323	35429
78869	85937	36639	29135	12633	67225	69588	74178
92268	64698	32823	60122	46213	05646	54742	98304
25786	55912	85269	29212	84976	08888	94332	58528
68154	49436	49891	65524	65133	55163	76765	26006
55498	97548	98437	26033	39026	17377	43519	27425
87688	99010	90189	12522	00675	01995	82781	95130
14187	98623	84225	78440	67082	37425	40559	16838

Line	Column (1)	(2)	(3)	(4)	(5)	(6)
351	06433	80674	24520	18222	10610	05794
352	39298	47829	72648	37414	75755	04717
353	89884	59651	67533	68123	17730	95862
354	61512	32155	51906	61662	64130	16688
355	99653	47635	12506	88535	36553	23757
356	95913	11085	13772	76638	48423	25018
357	55864	44004	13122	44115	01601	50541
358	35334	82410	91601	40617	72876	33967
359	57729	88646	76487	11622	96297	24160
360	86648	89317	63677	70119	94739	25875
361	30574	06039	07967	32422	76791	39725
362	81307	13114	83580	79974	45929	85113
363	02410	96385	79007	54939	21410	86980
364	18969	87444	52233	62319	08598	09066
365	87863	80514	66860	62297	80198	19347
366	68397	10538	15438	62311	72844	60203
367	28529	45247	58729	10854	99058	18260
368	44285	09452	15867	70418	57012	72122
369	86299	22510	33571	23309	57040	29285
370	84842	05748	90894	61658	15001	94055
371	56970	10799	52098	04184	54967	72938
372	83125	85077	60490	44369	66130	72936
373	55503	21383	02464	26141	68779	66388
374	47019	06683	33203	29608	54553	25971
375	84828	61152	79526	29554	84580	37859
376	68921	31331	79227	05748	51276	57143
377	36458	28285	30424	98420	72925	40729
378	95752	96065	36847	87729	81679	59126
379	26768	02513	58454	56958	20575	76746
380	42613	72456	43636	58085	06766	60227
381	95457	12176	65482	25596	02678	54592
382	95276	67524	63564	95958	39750	64379
383	66954	53574	64776	92345	95110	59448
384	17457	44151	14113	62462	02798	54977
385	03704	23322	83214	59337	01695	60666
386	21538	16997	33210	60337	27976	70661
387	57178	16739	98310	70348	11317	71623
388	31048	40058	94953	55866	96283	46620
389	69799	83300	16498	80733	96422	58078
390	90595	65017	59231	17772	67831	33317
391	33570	34761	98939	78784	09977	29398
392	15340	82760	57477	13898	48431	72936
393	64079	07733	36512	56186	99098	48850
394	63491	84886	67118	62063	74958	20946
395	92003	76568	41034	28260	79708	00770
396	52360	46658	66511	04172	73085	11795
397	74622	12142	68355	65635	21828	39539
398	04157	50079	61343	64315	70836	82857
399	86003	60070	66241	32836	27573	11479
400	41268	80187	20351	09636	84668	42486

Column (7)	(8)	(9)	(10)	(11)	(12)	(13)	(14)
37515	48619	62866	33963	14045	79451	04934	45576
29899	78817	03509	78673	73181	29973	18664	04555
08034	19473	63971	37271	31445	49019	49405	46925
37275	51262	11569	08697	91120	64156	40365	74297
34209	55803	96275	26130	47949	14877	69594	83041
99041	77529	81360	18180	97421	55541	90275	18213
00147	77685	58788	33016	61173	93049	04694	43534
73830	15405	96554	88265	34537	38526	67924	40474
09903	14047	22917	60718	66487	46346	30949	03173
38829	68377	43918	77653	04127	69930	43283	35766
53711	93385	13421	67957	20384	58731	53396	59723
72268	09858	52104	32014	53115	03727	98624	84616
91772	93307	34116	49516	42148	57740	31198	70336
95288	04794	01534	92058	03157	91758	80611	45357
73234	86265	49096	97021	92582	61422	75890	86442
46412	65943	79232	45702	67055	39024	57383	44424
38765	90038	94209	04055	27393	61517	23002	96560
36634	97283	95943	78363	36498	40662	94188	18202
67870	21913	72958	75637	99936	58715	07943	23748
36308	41161	37341	81838	19389	80336	46346	91895
56834	23777	98392	31417	98547	92058	02277	50315
69848	59973	08144	61070	73094	27059	69181	55623
75242	82690	74099	77885	23813	10054	11900	44653
69573	83854	24715	48866	65745	31131	47636	45137
28504	61980	34997	41825	11623	07320	15003	56774
31926	99915	45821	97702	87125	44488	77613	56823
22337	48293	86847	43186	42951	37804	85129	28993
59437	33225	31280	41232	34750	91097	60752	69783
49878	06846	32828	24425	30249	78801	26977	92074
96414	32671	45587	79620	84831	38156	74211	82752
63607	82096	21913	75544	55228	89796	05694	91552
46059	51666	10433	10945	55306	78562	89630	41230
77249	54044	67942	24145	42294	27427	84875	37022
48349	66738	60184	75679	38120	17640	36242	99357
97410	55064	17427	89180	74018	44865	53197	74810
08250	69599	60264	84549	78007	88450	06488	72274
55510	64756	87759	92354	78694	63638	80939	98644
52087	80817	74533	68407	55862	32476	19326	95558
99643	39847	96884	84657	33697	39578	90197	80532
00520	90401	41700	95510	61166	33757	23279	85523
93896	78227	90110	81378	96659	37008	04050	04228
78160	87240	52716	87697	79433	16336	52862	69149
72527	08486	10951	26832	39763	02485	71688	90936
28147	39338	32169	03713	93510	61244	73774	01245
88643	21188	01850	69629	49426	49128	14660	14143
52594	13287	22531	04388	64693	11934	35051	68576
18988	53609	04001	19648	14053	49623	10840	31915
35335	87900	36194	31567	53506	34304	39910	79630
94114	81641	00496	36058	75899	46620	70024	88753
71303	19512	50277	71508	20116	79520	06269	74173

Line	Column (1)	(2)	(3)	(4)	(5)	(6)
401	05073	90103	85167	53900	19720	41488
402	93320	80269	56684	39192	53220	74539
403	18806	70257	96424	13606	14356	76599
404	22253	45923	29815	18578	23316	30896
405	93640	45982	40011	74142	29106	45729
406	47630	45980	76619	57138	57492	00030
407	01781	55061	07455	47083	71870	90597
408	69694	45054	33587	03664	95007	31567
409	51236	05052	26503	94651	29874	73492
410	89445	51039	73837	26720	38650	47322
411	40867	96834	02162	41517	88937	26099
412	92946	56944	93407	05010	54896	33173
413	75898	02275	90768	31902	52114	36634
414	22729	21695	90824	80500	09332	54667
415	28733	62663	23644	16416	47135	39137
416	51323	37770	42114	79742	59905	38480
417	69325	65551	49927	68073	56979	49454
418	11333	60801	36992	76128	27959	41306
419	86347	03703	36778	72501	95229	65735
420	73452	36179	82893	92262	43850	31888
421	75483	74009	73699	05870	36804	89338
422	73302	84917	75128	34085	86208	98399
423	42785	24350	05933	65282	12832	75382
424	40429	33209	58622	09308	38098	55947
425	92876	58271	99325	12301	72957	22690
426	32951	39844	99126	94838	48715	36586
427	09772	28139	48130	73301	35915	90923
428	78459	91322	50072	77941	65046	78363
429	14419	96517	99075	43664	81119	63487
430	97769	50967	24427	21011	92226	44380
431	09175	37545	39088	06879	21277	05153
432	52062	95519	54087	14072	50953	63477
433	70558	85169	01086	97202	10390	01819
434	22553	61317	08968	67521	16627	48855
435	95216	75263	60351	02643	00063	20824
436	49087	61399	47781	32173	96672	04528
437	24808	79068	70787	43106	97133	37236
438	89879	79942	43781	05069	80143	59176
439	61178	79295	58926	21977	28435	32631
440	37444	56047	23208	34710	12147	28558
441	99633	00363	16853	20789	87674	03938
442	87363	59239	42023	78056	51254	95644
443	23923	87269	85277	34727	78036	74471
444	45610	26370	13094	34500	36750	54517
445	44166	80095	08286	38126	48834	73423
446	81875	27486	53925	22330	37168	97954
447	79400	83852	52174	42577	18553	14023
448	42799	46647	36718	49704	17150	07935
449	09302	36408	64569	93033	95645	56791
450	88078	81456	17242	84590	93660	34619

Column							
(7)	(8)	(9)	(10)	(11)	(12)	(13)	(14)
57476	39458	16621	69774	47953	35039	39283	21573
26393	00787	94490	23386	38454	33466	32159	77439
25390	63236	04513	16358	30504	10551	32498	18685
64771	11220	86218	75956	22399	36234	61644	80682
43406	21457	04301	39651	76025	73819	11462	97385
77897	76236	64990	35985	57748	11606	72081	18359
10151	59606	96919	31174	99872	15843	99173	79512
25334	26433	75002	67607	33135	07076	82984	82675
88941	08488	09418	08173	63380	82067	58143	64983
68474	95047	20404	41577	46865	39849	78735	99192
56047	49164	35127	64916	75451	79160	14014	00445
30548	23667	43171	47849	40449	91072	91092	17613
46803	97970	92216	55398	75320	70475	82931	20172
46696	38166	02005	24615	85613	25948	75389	25765
62190	31032	58702	03805	67252	23712	92697	19071
25293	32993	36946	62701	51198	72941	52215	85257
79451	60753	70872	07422	06399	75240	80847	78231
93543	15926	99159	27102	98684	80175	98732	45405
14269	50220	77270	68604	05677	23347	43686	31584
71151	40682	49775	63628	45415	96270	31735	01509
73891	40740	98753	74566	74733	34777	05786	38294
79433	61960	01720	87458	24023	89971	09532	68155
29826	33197	81781	53542	63985	57022	22712	61343
12001	73526	23170	13721	37856	86502	74299	01346
62705	73892	01974	77759	92733	11331	08323	86196
42076	15283	19280	29166	24522	73131	83401	38920
19255	75242	84655	30163	75510	83315	98529	93805
21951	42319	46472	67617	34134	05905	61251	51040
95589	51785	07398	23245	10086	49097	46173	00507
23422	10654	43617	80504	90663	60751	79728	41132
81855	84043	35307	59465	75395	74758	09427	84460
64635	34552	75243	70222	75023	81454	70606	31861
88167	21851	87837	85287	69883	08289	74968	46947
97263	94242	93354	72446	28840	88195	82751	94352
67468	89441	84055	47035	29741	47972	61914	66864
15881	46764	20115	03226	79308	31970	49804	85150
77888	48451	20788	44648	70350	54965	57715	94826
47392	70372	26899	16228	71205	14564	97087	95690
23062	31822	70462	05965	22312	33013	74612	23733
58817	98807	56775	08129	08794	23646	92846	61706
36077	41012	08813	51168	78822	37353	61281	31172
90527	41398	74996	94977	22149	96616	54435	52469
12157	11655	25194	47557	26181	67825	80224	41490
85011	26567	01021	32485	58903	43529	24191	91832
13617	08853	16286	16023	77901	39118	14288	39385
11967	03309	97096	64221	11318	98720	01100	13651
69629	61913	41050	69689	57284	38160	57756	16762
62372	39933	20838	27652	54801	41067	08240	35163
14830	81699	45057	85796	63756	93944	60649	84847
51965	85618	36558	54410	68456	98504	83011	19393

Line	Column (1)	(2)	(3)	(4)	(5)	(6)
451	85018	23508	91507	76455	54941	72711
452	11904	73678	08272	62941	02349	71389
453	75344	98489	86268	73652	98210	44546
454	65566	65614	01443	07607	11826	91326
455	51872	72294	95432	53555	96810	17100
456	03805	37913	98633	81009	81060	33449
457	21055	78685	71250	10329	56135	80647
458	48977	36794	56054	59243	57361	65304
459	93077	72941	92779	23581	24548	56415
460	84533	26564	91583	83411	66504	02036
461	11338	12903	14514	27585	45068	05520
462	23853	68500	92274	87026	99717	01542
463	94096	74920	25822	98026	05394	61840
464	83160	82362	09350	98536	38155	42661
465	97425	47335	69709	01386	74319	04318
466	83951	11954	24317	20345	18134	90062
467	93085	35203	05740	03206	92012	42710
468	33762	83193	58045	89880	78101	44392
469	49665	85397	85137	30496	23469	42846
470	37541	82627	80051	72521	35342	56119
471	22145	85304	35348	82854	55846	18076
472	27153	08662	61078	52433	22184	33998
473	00301	49425	66682	25442	83668	66236
474	43815	43272	73778	63469	50083	70696
475	14689	86482	74157	46012	97765	27552
476	16680	55936	82453	19532	49988	13176
477	86938	60429	01137	86168	78257	86249
478	33944	29219	73161	46061	30946	22210
479	16045	67736	18608	18198	19468	76358
480	37044	52523	25627	63107	30806	80857
481	61471	45322	35340	35132	42163	69332
482	47422	21296	16785	66393	39249	51463
483	24133	39719	14484	58613	88717	29289
484	67253	67064	10748	16006	16767	57345
485	62382	76941	01635	35829	77516	98468
486	98011	16503	09201	03523	87192	66483
487	37366	24386	20654	85117	74078	64120
488	73587	83993	54176	05221	94119	20108
489	33583	68291	50547	96085	62180	27453
490	02878	33223	39199	49536	56199	05993
491	91498	41673	17195	33175	04994	09879
492	91127	19815	30219	55591	21725	43827
493	12997	55013	18662	81724	24305	37661
494	96098	13651	15393	69995	14762	69734
495	97627	17837	10472	18983	28387	99781
496	40064	47981	31484	76603	54088	91095
497	16239	68743	71374	55863	22672	91609
498	58354	24913	20435	30965	17453	65623
499	52567	65085	60220	84641	18273	49604
500	06236	29052	91392	07551	83532	68130

Column (7)	(8)	(9)	(10)	(11)	(12)	(13)	(14)
39406	94620	27963	96478	21559	19246	88097	44926
45605	60947	60775	73181	43264	56895	04232	59604
27174	27499	53523	63110	57106	20865	91683	80688
29664	01603	23156	89223	43429	95353	44662	59433
35066	00815	01552	06392	31437	70385	45863	75971
68055	83844	90942	74857	52419	68723	47830	63010
51404	06626	10042	93629	37609	57215	08409	81906
93258	56760	63348	24949	11859	29793	37457	59377
61927	64416	29934	00755	09418	14230	62887	92683
02922	63569	17906	38076	32135	19096	96970	75917
56321	22693	35089	07694	04252	23791	60249	83010
72990	43413	59744	44595	71326	91382	45114	20245
83089	09224	78530	33996	49965	04851	18280	14039
02363	67625	34683	95372	74733	63558	09665	22610
99387	86874	12549	38369	54952	91579	26023	81076
10761	54548	49505	52685	63903	13193	33905	66936
34650	73236	66167	21788	03581	40699	10396	81827
53767	15220	66319	72953	14071	59148	95154	72852
94810	16151	08029	50554	03891	38313	34016	18671
97190	43635	84249	61254	80993	55431	90793	62603
12415	30193	42776	85611	57635	51362	79907	77364
87436	37430	45246	11400	20986	43996	73122	88474
79655	88312	93047	12088	86937	70794	01041	74867
13558	98995	58159	04700	90443	13168	31553	67891
49617	51734	20849	70198	67906	00880	82899	66065
94219	88698	41755	56216	66852	17748	04963	54859
46134	51865	09836	73966	65711	41699	11732	17173
79302	40300	08852	27528	84648	79589	95295	72895
69203	02760	28625	70476	76410	32988	10194	94917
84383	78450	26245	91763	73117	33047	03577	62599
98851	50252	56911	62693	73817	98693	18728	94741
95963	07929	66728	47761	81472	44806	15592	71357
77360	09030	39605	87507	85446	51257	89555	75520
42285	56670	88445	85799	76200	21795	38894	58070
51686	48140	13583	94911	13318	64741	64336	95103
55649	36764	86132	12463	28385	94242	32063	45233
04643	14351	71381	28133	68269	65145	28152	39087
78101	81276	00835	63835	87174	42446	08882	27067
18567	55524	86088	00069	59254	24654	77371	26409
71201	78852	65889	32719	13758	23937	90740	16866
70337	11861	69032	51915	23510	32050	52052	24004
78862	67699	01009	07050	73324	06732	27510	33761
18956	50064	39500	17450	18030	63124	48061	59412
89150	93126	17700	94400	76075	08317	27324	72723
52977	01657	92602	41043	05686	15650	29970	95877
00010	13800	76690	75133	60456	28491	03845	11507
51514	98135	42870	48578	29036	69876	86563	61729
93058	08313	99293	00990	13595	77457	79969	11339
47418	90974	83965	62732	85161	54330	22406	86253
56970	33273	61993	88407	69399	17301	70975	99129

Line \ Col.	(1)	(2)	(3)	(4)	(5)	(6)
501	88188	99345	94118	40373	50387	24802
502	05200	50533	59428	02797	16833	10038
503	82828	41316	92617	31346	89263	06589
504	71006	99318	19269	35233	79183	78538
505	05937	00875	32264	82808	00229	03868
506	06021	04370	93070	90737	05354	68427
507	54789	10960	44023	57857	56556	83993
508	90400	05707	29128	14859	84117	72206
509	51424	01651	99970	73521	82356	03297
510	79743	88757	43370	86536	07166	06401
511	77418	00322	98854	51507	00565	33066
512	17580	49302	16408	05678	75532	46218
513	15489	45559	28548	64330	42126	43145
514	56342	66773	18536	32600	73958	75993
515	20202	19216	23762	47856	04623	70728
516	84877	51708	69357	67914	55372	97225
517	01647	00311	44989	21900	96079	15793
518	45652	89311	45302	14539	32045	86727
519	79975	06153	08932	59185	71386	19070
520	49744	54713	37053	77467	15348	03383
521	40922	94903	29638	46870	14108	84391
522	53319	48020	77444	51447	07916	99506
523	76682	10559	85446	56236	85919	76388
524	48869	97229	69581	84581	71728	45150
525	95961	19279	38078	17473	43945	21562
526	16521	25945	94076	91281	92272	41233
527	78282	26332	44072	55104	16895	98311
528	43473	39179	53174	43498	72674	13087
529	06513	31352	09177	21367	64725	23784
530	48734	39737	03448	99009	98136	34562
531	54832	70111	48339	75270	11652	41697
532	55844	69515	22658	75438	83086	41325
533	42829	54398	93338	90705	00626	97752
534	81128	63461	10925	44382	73365	98875
535	62885	26354	10368	78026	00186	46783
536	19525	10375	27010	42791	49471	90607
537	26570	99202	73924	59888	01827	93314
538	04772	17749	01537	96036	02102	02622
539	49129	12491	62552	64323	44856	29045
540	19937	75104	57780	95871	94547	53541
541	52571	67962	72775	28480	87411	12075
542	54943	80723	81195	84069	28144	48106
543	16375	88048	29625	08111	92924	53335
544	38745	91458	30363	95005	55854	38628
545	09937	17776	86425	88916	80594	28347
546	30097	47192	27960	15937	42080	61048
547	02410	60124	62825	42947	74590	89730
548	44804	80165	19442	72194	76910	40274
549	37352	79142	51032	58844	03167	57351
550	60640	14199	48263	71533	94235	42431

(7)	(8)	(9)	(10)	(11)	(12)	(13)	(14)
81352	61640	56614	71506	75541	37818	88047	94144
18901	40743	99449	49825	44637	72724	42649	67052
07121	07151	23905	98435	50453	12983	04738	76421
06326	62715	28701	52809	56581	05925	85210	17745
71072	11519	44876	34508	07859	62424	54319	32842
25554	11165	00123	80338	03876	85648	24978	01687
70787	28193	65872	33723	00125	99818	85571	69509
53740	00464	51853	78852	83593	82926	48985	64355
36288	93531	69269	84798	78962	06336	95618	89718
14413	23643	21527	91902	91384	31444	54783	38760
65791	47857	32483	38493	52606	91078	13631	67863
74359	77556	82242	00134	70154	09027	79459	18730
81287	73884	69312	03395	06879	49662	40000	61598
84250	19254	06677	54192	53422	58200	74464	73949
86657	70801	53719	25214	65635	07565	49977	45525
52837	46723	00256	96221	26641	00309	36009	48392
13148	01433	78721	02647	25454	53913	97554	41578
40595	55953	93448	07805	53622	27330	18749	57867
87098	19392	13899	56096	83645	45871	35950	52272
96086	93295	12413	55774	97318	66402	11209	52495
87313	65969	43349	85142	25650	01896	48680	51236
83504	22290	63835	45589	04884	92760	70462	00538
59850	03262	60347	31077	07165	26588	31296	56112
16901	88717	62688	24828	89469	35483	76532	30256
90937	52140	73771	56084	08775	94820	78139	25987
58614	18912	58454	34011	85969	83621	92099	19131
56005	23331	21939	03463	53828	78930	30987	40988
54261	01844	45738	93150	13240	16694	59155	67589
18125	74873	83971	92678	96950	69821	41119	43312
30339	93143	07350	94289	76144	47238	08110	00037
43277	58089	70520	96997	71007	87803	52458	06637
04694	40359	28351	53492	73134	02370	72313	53039
93482	27726	51835	23966	50279	26329	25754	43530
77605	27351	49177	36914	50258	62361	38229	89608
02059	98892	98061	15330	31705	71923	29266	72716
98103	31752	04842	13693	84292	48485	76178	41716
63949	35394	12989	05867	11568	45056	16609	20470
06007	52239	61201	57415	35609	38761	19589	24238
76871	80449	81351	73642	48643	23848	48390	56829
77723	54114	90290	62627	65151	15687	81062	06729
45177	08796	99297	48807	88310	75454	45456	85394
04169	16575	62665	97861	71650	56981	61794	94285
09525	88290	17679	08945	25816	11848	95106	22031
13599	73065	40870	82576	37089	86738	16284	44725
08092	64255	55604	78635	13197	72213	95102	36723
14358	44508	72683	51088	55368	85587	27046	11198
16073	28184	30078	92578	83789	08044	76238	47599
93861	06568	92482	70037	66779	63312	00619	94053
51850	92810	35331	78995	44221	41532	51606	26430
44114	90993	41149	06159	39242	11163	14764	19246

Line \ Col.	(1)	(2)	(3)	(4)	(5)	(6)
551	31630	67734	78201	94545	80152	62327
552	25101	98983	36993	40028	58036	14075
553	86207	09805	46240	70644	76012	37000
554	31611	47643	28795	48115	17223	63161
555	10649	89132	59781	12373	35999	30832
556	68210	16228	34801	40972	22887	89759
557	32367	69587	66162	44358	69844	73042
558	14684	42446	01751	37459	31945	03627
559	64260	04661	39957	01200	84800	27930
560	66035	77943	70861	32037	96699	56314
561	20966	71492	32323	11867	47523	24094
562	20498	68176	02027	22358	15907	13247
563	56320	79875	60634	17556	52153	63549
564	50559	90270	33571	88091	34749	56784
565	49366	90095	73459	12225	28483	35358
566	29022	19268	03003	96622	30239	20482
567	77212	76531	68842	37777	20085	38703
568	41121	90499	83459	71424	27596	74645
569	06613	95412	94751	60763	56611	73508
570	66430	95324	60108	42377	56350	67861
571	39380	09648	47285	62864	03421	34292
572	27595	63289	75149	03348	91237	28372
573	43525	45549	58819	48478	14007	11384
574	60024	79858	72015	01236	27444	47010
575	35914	73076	05158	40190	41294	72776
576	58253	32995	54370	34437	98365	17630
577	85887	54618	23532	73821	80904	05950
578	88988	60426	34636	40601	57718	93925
579	65381	17333	32358	49608	36893	43453
580	20214	88406	06098	07770	51679	64857
581	04970	56425	74303	94793	55055	44762
582	87556	31521	19669	16311	01767	67301
583	34615	85796	30299	56090	41453	82886
584	95769	07371	49569	42262	74097	44317
585	57338	58325	53918	08075	69395	08189
586	08882	30762	14602	54767	67683	57818
587	62644	32814	31337	06011	80623	36021
588	55358	48010	24440	51092	89263	82352
589	02254	43319	79888	86311	57615	69666
590	61023	48494	57279	47133	89534	37085
591	41900	90881	96080	35258	70734	59465
592	94500	19764	94752	73077	74726	86176
593	66375	34653	37125	84780	92759	09781
594	27141	20959	02318	57546	45467	06653
595	25670	88933	19316	57014	52797	83779
596	06590	67256	21117	69351	98168	81043
597	36429	99750	38004	64992	25021	45680
598	52011	93461	06334	23801	34422	13728
599	09443	77694	26882	15663	45983	29425
600	25862	81855	15254	28462	95680	42433

(7)	(8)	(9)	(10)	(11)	(12)	(13)	(14)
83165	31035	82295	11824	06765	29501	62849	50419
05980	57094	45527	18766	77741	12985	14112	65058
98321	97197	30645	56169	09363	44394	29087	96569
29677	69820	77159	20762	94296	94528	82984	71418
02508	93055	57173	79848	25439	18861	26742	54970
09095	00587	03998	13659	64179	98567	69313	84637
88091	07288	74971	47066	36927	53520	58309	58605
47690	97813	45272	42789	99315	26662	15833	37246
98937	76108	11043	29101	01767	78894	92922	66537
75755	68667	04730	15256	13957	52743	42306	87515
23334	78839	81588	67374	43855	24512	81956	75721
44784	82957	53009	73379	44093	58405	38515	85531
03661	78290	96447	04192	30157	63198	75932	02367
98486	06018	27447	00884	29564	51522	35571	69208
99941	63054	54358	80748	54049	85937	64718	21466
50028	16632	57708	78559	70241	47977	78645	48550
31753	18608	52524	08585	91711	63572	57007	11379
68790	66478	78885	53799	02026	24596	88692	55936
88479	86151	78563	31633	92321	23304	77153	86639
47478	11961	78516	95316	64393	52020	44994	88205
36084	39604	89838	03635	30064	72710	26327	65521
65330	00966	73904	17477	34953	08975	83142	48425
19576	68138	30774	51898	24711	72537	18360	95682
80938	15828	86484	92753	04322	27171	41828	79025
38528	22272	34709	34561	65554	53461	61776	03585
42196	49736	39619	16731	71792	38047	85559	56700
63441	86109	79900	14063	03152	39235	74289	42342
67763	67671	21739	87534	83385	91492	45796	04621
38580	27639	52832	01522	11108	59992	23168	04414
36998	95796	46745	36780	56791	34690	61634	85411
22800	02663	91182	13102	07408	50545	21312	11365
63016	01227	29273	79256	50368	88653	23329	86500
33077	99791	86553	64640	61529	88660	66941	15936
40304	05346	90342	73324	81555	82769	23559	55238
66668	11663	84852	93146	27182	34936	97267	63996
98756	49119	91258	71916	65948	24841	38607	39412
81846	71868	98242	72307	25917	56240	73499	45106
95072	68828	28001	48991	19201	90963	34192	63336
60651	49084	39681	66415	10201	53931	44245	42850
28495	39162	89121	52021	23143	14829	55792	84641
49227	01431	90694	96186	57811	54512	30108	01261
31623	14569	89225	09606	73432	95276	21237	36807
06912	96802	92502	97497	67702	49763	25950	49924
99212	60612	26046	53553	59757	70491	69632	46009
56495	33104	26858	07662	41253	97688	76883	29444
26682	00063	96223	30436	21987	15450	56574	45011
46501	92943	99165	20707	43410	53746	54716	17090
35016	80605	86628	21689	34082	26035	11928	41817
12085	96233	29036	91135	28258	27709	90674	09705
70311	09702	71615	72688	85922	58369	89734	08750

Line \ Col.	(1)	(2)	(3)	(4)	(5)	(6)
601	60359	07603	81594	66235	48154	61257
602	34992	97880	79115	47587	76167	47086
603	04887	64208	71842	97885	32616	23280
604	09332	86232	88199	66094	72594	30100
605	42326	62962	06485	04978	96639	96214
606	49187	42836	17042	35179	31880	48444
607	09228	57404	42180	07949	98750	31506
608	69720	73477	91252	48009	81393	76401
609	82222	13787	98611	95257	34753	36674
610	30703	00513	54586	05623	43999	55387
611	86369	62151	70713	41166	79321	52215
612	83331	99035	68506	96734	91074	24356
613	43053	60600	98921	43720	77342	26186
614	57104	49148	18487	01775	71782	04679
615	33177	11409	13925	18130	54242	13460
616	05424	76714	05732	29415	01183	45054
617	92950	58665	41191	69259	50244	55322
618	54925	20502	71767	82737	64847	04496
619	41980	43710	55304	57526	29616	92314
620	83825	70977	67987	61545	92066	71215
621	84047	83627	37763	07081	33048	57895
622	12776	69127	67921	57611	85876	30744
623	81419	55440	69506	09115	45032	48343
624	59844	03603	96297	58028	93069	35674
625	18350	74940	07044	11210	53622	00779
626	79960	18784	13376	03415	84450	78874
627	45420	24157	16374	22384	56892	84941
628	13945	09559	68152	56960	39453	51654
629	91206	33871	60730	96821	95808	29763
630	24847	08724	81499	72905	95102	63004
631	94303	08209	27804	49372	66392	50578
632	22732	95331	60954	93333	71142	38827
633	82809	24004	65983	01091	70431	91145
634	62700	79965	09610	97213	48579	43574
635	89870	73755	48525	32765	50818	71468
636	81493	24124	67928	12735	41249	24180
637	43630	32189	08532	43055	08080	84208
638	60234	18992	13283	96334	39746	07272
639	00107	21861	60367	48999	71634	34053
640	09657	36088	05976	88267	62683	57675
641	93948	38350	63464	08008	96607	73505
642	42746	29761	72298	48186	88584	90141
643	12939	04181	27698	48297	20574	30169
644	71032	55283	94804	00202	12254	22920
645	09188	78876	95736	70659	32725	23024
646	79236	54729	47052	49717	22312	06735
647	41337	52635	48056	43317	11599	26382
648	73732	99966	30485	45994	30195	40239
649	92113	55625	03726	76886	64237	33300
650	63797	22667	74860	99731	06975	63055

(7)	(8)	(9)	(10)	(11)	(12)	(13)	(14)
27978	64695	63165	44593	08210	16863	09655	00855
57064	16730	74172	60317	83215	38133	06303	05466
11783	19852	64266	24446	14189	77419	30991	92130
23673	68705	66989	42666	81857	34651	36167	24221
91478	12408	21457	19862	99102	91426	10181	51762
89877	50915	37426	21556	25999	84256	82314	18813
78442	45809	12725	49774	11276	46371	81681	00623
48168	25967	33372	84414	21506	46131	46046	12354
44326	66070	61131	70620	42865	89251	54844	04013
67189	95058	91174	13121	27557	16512	77963	40635
94358	28962	35868	22796	87221	40014	68875	71420
03035	66926	32197	54944	76781	86722	11769	27368
64554	46226	64244	10703	49564	69737	32948	43060
64369	06208	71669	63046	10470	54194	96709	86502
39174	63528	22670	31810	04313	50669	20653	31779
13493	44006	61641	80304	96504	52181	05359	72203
75137	90193	31989	17381	43795	26981	15326	02303
35921	42670	08584	54090	52907	75331	09155	54187
85883	21584	55045	81997	62277	58884	01590	13532
93967	63071	69928	98917	05699	35957	04679	58769
42182	73279	08032	19165	01701	35656	03328	81785
40886	68396	79787	76434	71221	86769	15104	19062
78352	39075	31689	76469	64918	15149	88457	97144
38479	54639	54455	10300	73946	94827	53164	07458
36027	51496	01694	57895	84570	18271	54461	42210
22050	19730	92598	54291	60658	73188	03446	49864
97157	99656	33978	81436	10955	98991	10456	35727
10617	55628	47933	85161	52998	75414	59552	03546
39678	73104	43398	38181	44314	58343	28884	94613
22223	19808	90777	54986	97234	18458	22889	83960
02966	90907	33164	83044	97985	78526	00983	29271
48222	21779	35598	95957	58844	82319	19780	08330
88207	52216	94846	75303	85105	89486	08182	56504
37652	12447	80233	42473	94585	84840	99926	74778
37876	28334	07762	16180	45346	78324	20422	85784
54740	44290	58903	38681	04066	69393	84595	42173
06295	07813	24068	67549	43051	78581	02095	03471
25295	07871	34201	49620	52178	07290	89767	63890
28265	02064	06290	10620	17941	81086	51759	57028
85265	10856	06525	37911	52332	55752	25054	30436
75513	91238	11042	40972	62837	30260	84002	99947
72879	54531	99127	60063	22374	76895	63812	94877
45545	04462	91067	43847	62739	31141	30385	30098
73225	51484	73943	08431	45681	32663	67097	15644
04656	48102	15904	19019	09882	87431	16879	61253
58347	04402	03838	97049	35378	38579	24489	86899
41305	04589	92877	52732	53130	45275	30183	15962
52751	64124	67778	60982	12167	63134	10730	11350
48004	37440	76329	80441	74766	70630	97855	88039
72287	81976	43983	97018	25559	96618	93350	67143

Line \ Col.	(1)	(2)	(3)	(4)	(5)	(6)
651	98707	41348	74106	43550	16638	72858
652	65496	87176	71726	09722	85667	37498
653	17617	18337	83583	73510	52998	02570
654	85006	32658	83348	38599	77549	70275
655	77279	66357	38044	75041	06698	16798
656	84133	32224	55350	73251	64120	86718
657	86535	01806	18470	94806	18228	71262
658	58459	99005	64939	57060	34609	06739
659	38783	61870	02744	23773	74163	30029
660	49454	76832	17745	75922	40087	51566
661	71219	82115	51031	28586	91328	59635
662	57770	63699	49430	82846	13285	69178
663	94539	92056	65825	27167	69783	48976
664	94992	45377	75471	45547	34348	61707
665	60717	63093	60684	08910	30296	12345
666	28040	08603	43675	64665	40567	76211
667	69841	63836	53186	49970	05485	65171
668	80931	69365	75077	19929	67852	63937
669	94000	24074	95072	32602	89373	78009
670	70609	17467	26861	51035	44534	49774
671	24016	76531	77282	21820	61170	37198
672	36008	76472	60324	45386	67266	98846
673	65769	02131	95850	61875	52572	82826
674	71033	43026	99601	18102	33654	29885
675	25152	11755	33527	05149	71696	63492
676	81251	78313	53908	66912	84868	51859
677	37401	18809	83908	01638	72548	80521
678	01383	28893	13771	99613	39531	20895
679	03921	79304	91058	03175	33155	58344
680	19882	28056	10093	45334	89019	23914
681	55339	29655	37282	26504	70059	91780
682	01725	18314	40197	00964	44112	60484
683	45073	49109	77778	46092	30928	16111
684	60861	39467	17392	05446	26083	65352
685	88775	27006	69664	22246	77064	40312
686	20497	65297	17965	97094	26451	47473
687	76692	21880	39663	77289	36681	47935
688	00528	63679	57762	88094	26402	25925
689	57718	09889	94003	43899	32989	87707
690	85652	55278	23342	30372	47987	19936
691	16543	93477	41421	34710	59498	55069
692	50315	17150	14006	10453	96007	41512
693	73876	27245	79551	56241	53843	66714
694	26749	07215	99485	51013	50210	69934
695	89438	39457	58255	75693	72570	17885
696	24388	81801	22581	26331	47945	11717
697	19688	39199	20531	96205	50355	14725
698	07943	07018	03516	05747	94259	73583
699	90391	97135	97952	83722	35578	82905
700	61564	65108	76451	71430	08671	84975

(7)	(8)	(9)	(10)	(11)	(12)	(13)	(14)
32375	50634	80903	43867	54215	65017	70776	09596
03926	72585	15193	45615	67073	65110	42404	28419
37334	82042	07261	97361	93327	81104	17979	15192
85147	08030	20980	86223	58024	56948	10793	81858
83023	84686	53539	86491	70402	31779	09591	22398
61061	66146	36275	48583	74783	85824	87328	39207
39195	99049	75632	67645	26117	89606	83976	53307
40489	08146	74014	24803	50699	05588	73658	24352
64988	67851	68279	53341	88122	03631	97916	27003
38620	92988	84531	99883	40785	53456	03864	20593
15746	09832	53937	07006	00272	00914	31619	73222
66391	44979	69923	02920	98234	68478	52861	04824
07466	76421	71439	98358	21989	77098	86413	62724
77657	29541	67815	56777	91185	00390	17361	18119
22178	71824	11973	61293	25937	61542	76603	48032
18715	62133	75336	98118	88984	44341	11202	34471
40135	67168	42593	37922	55146	40354	32803	63430
67390	94560	76131	58351	72302	68973	72689	28187
38009	60982	27122	29283	08881	91436	80644	09688
88833	15577	80076	68625	42230	94087	97450	13569
16941	14009	97386	61256	11687	70360	18405	85586
17763	98235	53433	01295	74947	71106	33976	55405
09571	61125	81326	72388	40377	93419	38458	13301
48692	09691	95837	77697	69896	47214	85897	59723
32871	48386	37657	82062	02643	34598	36128	42411
15959	31119	92964	94054	57594	61310	42452	76262
02945	29410	37736	96301	32848	16332	63069	35975
92322	01032	66104	86756	84812	10692	73677	58045
13242	02686	57998	84750	88695	99642	86560	79808
12549	69492	09859	46366	22224	63308	95897	20408
59955	01729	92886	28616	52061	47284	02989	20385
07486	10883	23106	18254	23711	26458	09878	12981
15372	76016	15402	98293	24495	79618	69649	19768
24501	20502	13346	11151	37472	05548	35893	47964
14388	70861	47198	24261	69913	07368	78156	07858
07292	03191	47612	36599	67827	74007	48783	12329
76260	96157	44019	73403	83985	84210	58091	88097
10598	09606	41596	90916	25311	91501	63286	87423
46639	53512	25509	92751	60744	24239	13608	90176
89623	38221	45073	67291	57082	13194	39749	75753
70504	08544	80118	77512	88070	03943	84969	02116
36027	60557	57141	50554	80556	47441	56506	62857
24050	26354	14915	62391	75724	57468	34621	22325
73613	95543	94599	13955	29586	62507	90618	52247
07259	10273	25229	52788	55762	14772	50200	55909
42187	06031	02488	09199	74752	65757	27989	81532
38656	79167	44771	43966	73425	79632	77181	84817
43619	99509	02102	08279	57372	53487	10885	95017
41761	66670	43482	34931	94438	93341	60927	31368
36182	70787	79442	29461	01209	20022	93055	28312

Line \ Col.	(1)	(2)	(3)	(4)	(5)	(6)
701	79681	63467	02907	86515	71330	04490
702	30305	20743	10302	71391	18138	23412
703	32763	33847	58250	64362	87550	94978
704	59166	21978	40556	13084	31782	00518
705	55843	94845	30006	51045	17428	50657
706	33537	82468	52422	32155	54419	61661
707	13533	29605	31430	07663	95274	11484
708	24626	54219	12284	06890	05239	42846
709	48002	32024	17230	37523	47488	31080
710	03742	00004	98249	12256	94253	95378
711	17749	89193	37944	53702	49918	65397
712	34837	36219	22048	97047	68804	09633
713	99451	37922	90191	39229	07564	41077
714	74045	00036	53137	15250	19646	20451
715	98998	98774	98159	00032	97323	81490
716	61513	02266	36871	85993	23028	67082
717	67056	19960	53863	63917	68283	31123
718	83036	04625	93284	14368	10979	95800
719	71901	25497	76987	74388	41605	39295
720	46484	77860	02062	92917	70275	40593
721	18312	05137	64361	86541	17794	32313
722	63093	94089	17729	19607	19340	19022
723	38109	69439	62094	49578	37728	17809
724	41421	22003	36770	32741	10325	30892
725	92320	12828	57972	83551	63054	95028
726	42226	72413	67949	96906	17848	21446
727	01094	08525	21349	41981	55232	76652
728	75760	51119	37218	16828	89127	42801
729	62568	56665	42394	67135	03069	93275
730	77151	67677	85258	46925	92504	87860
731	71920	39074	15464	36753	86550	24330
732	99411	04216	66076	90718	67214	03688
733	05654	88507	03119	93043	06951	35126
734	65937	81013	09884	97787	85851	00011
735	87649	70531	88258	21822	97418	67341
736	57827	19642	95661	23788	19164	78112
737	78911	81376	22392	42570	33512	17996
738	91302	54963	94112	60597	31843	40120
739	82950	87509	65702	14385	86299	23769
740	21888	66504	85577	67163	46317	92073
741	73799	60026	87226	26744	12037	98558
742	48237	10339	99550	86134	30229	39131
743	24293	69496	20243	17738	55798	96178
744	18748	01580	73315	84924	81621	67021
745	94470	36824	89203	23689	37016	18462
746	87639	11791	63380	25952	20838	13638
747	65676	78482	33343	65797	56005	15782
748	94357	62236	54083	37960	43467	79372
749	06595	83512	74524	10051	97759	64738
750	34033	69035	18588	88893	83679	27789

(7)	(8)	(9)	(10)	(11)	(12)	(13)	(14)
47372	68791	27576	02044	03784	94581	60105	75131
11858	47818	22324	52031	10600	49892	34101	71430
22888	78355	34651	41604	51892	89533	81610	72641
18621	60508	93095	74017	17416	76900	25261	63227
68237	02969	30500	43569	28051	22505	07159	78162
64835	06496	16377	92607	86248	89492	49306	95414
42579	15718	54485	08857	93691	02973	26687	90437
24773	15025	15161	51340	54739	99433	54328	47800
29352	61444	04011	56275	19259	72475	53451	43397
88918	98167	46646	19727	24181	83358	28999	11769
72597	63520	77429	68355	21003	00657	02157	68031
28689	80484	59331	77577	30376	10021	78267	78049
91554	46657	74652	84677	49671	94805	82406	99797
46677	53620	74712	17246	96626	28587	33618	46845
21552	35001	10913	48910	91005	62408	83253	19770
93486	45110	86288	34493	66710	04268	04955	49074
17443	32019	19695	85622	46808	03535	91566	36785
72182	77004	07320	79516	00915	53209	00884	65464
75622	41203	87987	09672	81312	08728	49867	95245
93265	92722	39193	47099	39046	85989	24607	72287
52847	08862	36752	32624	11035	92500	35016	18519
50080	21998	49864	07107	64287	41647	75264	09230
11563	10073	17299	69238	88068	04754	51698	11641
14112	34880	92387	45169	96668	89183	10099	44382
50857	40315	04962	36431	54964	33961	89397	70359
35722	10376	84226	16403	14642	23253	07162	57664
00857	77173	63362	64936	96601	95816	14729	35398
01084	78402	28359	41533	83339	69672	64909	55192
11662	23607	00878	53800	14840	28975	51693	97620
85299	45952	76388	72989	12170	03449	28315	95994
17873	20798	15221	80763	69974	95552	66857	85097
71088	92479	27623	97466	27560	63689	35799	28078
26154	26820	68861	37807	17485	58902	92005	57597
66801	02686	73801	19522	67200	80477	73121	88815
54342	80836	46142	04718	08348	75316	53030	90533
07304	32337	12845	12588	70054	12267	96360	43459
29406	47329	66928	89312	16994	87633	71914	52038
00386	35486	27379	02873	69868	03803	29671	74165
87183	66267	13819	58266	16843	06546	00521	50286
68325	46664	03841	58572	46048	04635	78350	53233
66640	32882	11415	64686	78236	05844	76840	80802
76976	56296	89453	79556	48059	70552	45852	06593
86022	42073	16407	53031	48671	82154	04054	90741
99065	43590	82522	71919	25097	49536	03140	63610
59404	27230	78689	88837	41119	95462	94394	13374
32782	23841	16936	91384	20472	81876	85484	35003
27311	64066	28230	36207	06446	09976	09463	56698
26370	08273	18180	84100	30757	33315	28583	53434
10370	07874	28301	08201	07624	63508	82486	82993
22340	12208	00381	06023	77844	28666	24220	19220

Line \ Col.	(1)	(2)	(3)	(4)	(5)	(6)
751	03548	52011	53722	62927	01693	90948
752	05066	74263	11659	84658	52063	42299
753	19814	89956	36256	19896	56654	69424
754	44928	11206	21377	35086	62233	93761
755	52158	08923	94812	04443	32028	96465
756	53211	58616	05135	52204	51079	11341
757	27334	43976	14685	38119	29486	57290
758	66166	06709	69495	42150	38018	43875
759	01837	16750	96491	33095	30383	48804
760	38295	51093	63495	13203	93562	94132
761	72510	80830	39948	94133	00780	14167
762	16354	00336	06494	30078	46134	62486
763	45168	70700	04592	35281	47737	28881
764	68137	13619	84666	78104	83546	72551
765	31848	95753	76858	89517	91138	62356
766	17216	37292	05495	50885	98994	32966
767	73211	42922	57386	95490	56100	08977
768	29217	56753	90171	87554	57421	35839
769	66780	34571	71684	28798	47123	25232
770	55780	48081	93674	70837	92534	65892
771	05788	64237	58140	63279	60170	17229
772	21911	51065	51525	65122	52608	52836
773	32645	38561	25181	18042	31903	46525
774	72304	15382	01151	63162	23656	69649
775	27637	04122	86132	22538	98976	90718
776	66305	85906	87925	50081	37585	63674
777	53470	40332	81044	00558	50403	48029
778	01355	77096	64828	02445	94511	09503
779	66954	04728	86153	10933	86557	10877
780	53734	15628	08080	24011	04187	65722
781	23114	08743	07186	23825	04298	72839
782	16803	91335	64192	13631	20332	74852
783	57233	99034	38028	32038	81270	77809
784	83203	59665	72314	67942	01320	24467
785	79299	97340	04568	65386	04876	31514
786	99442	63865	14360	83898	98873	17471
787	77773	19621	81557	84629	18808	89056
788	18581	12572	15185	57989	87644	88902
789	80978	13327	19682	53353	96223	04775
790	96884	95522	04791	93463	20316	84054
791	61113	82511	44196	73740	16111	73200
792	01272	75657	28365	17431	93603	32457
793	82357	77572	75628	93073	38281	72103
794	20434	70899	44243	19741	59954	73617
795	38580	10399	44894	25476	04984	64543
796	20211	12980	45261	82527	87534	39405
797	98954	03124	09433	19894	01380	18962
798	99749	02140	46641	56354	78746	89410
799	47167	24716	84417	40097	46608	11667
800	65812	77947	27864	98144	01818	28214

(7)	(8)	(9)	(10)	(11)	(12)	(13)	(14)
75340	16660	00939	77148	52778	20615	97851	58353
94340	20391	00080	43359	44231	06891	86588	88565
84446	95294	00919	60267	34349	64353	92469	01606
56000	42066	35898	48944	32352	33177	16239	76624
94430	42834	22836	88818	44467	18329	30144	31536
20366	86248	35160	31485	92436	69726	12722	52722
34141	18058	91299	58001	17944	00296	13949	94904
44534	48712	98089	76889	55720	09038	95667	57007
21228	10863	08350	25610	80866	00115	27666	94607
54810	11410	73776	55752	36138	52297	31528	77790
83322	32747	97291	66126	64996	21354	64615	64234
70923	17400	28797	83599	78655	67488	09715	69232
57221	79935	99756	61564	36936	55668	87148	95939
40848	52138	36343	93975	09556	58888	08125	80961
66405	98171	66239	49761	88800	29069	30175	31267
83496	54614	75214	34959	15500	32107	81638	46696
78499	53540	41745	09805	67110	53329	92776	32312
60961	87828	24777	19688	42464	35569	84904	13130
67995	39562	35855	61645	64448	65170	46792	77081
32422	02887	03170	05372	48068	65758	62376	94055
69038	02500	21071	26294	95005	47815	87991	93358
86157	19943	63173	34921	11943	36931	74722	06193
96290	24323	68269	45841	73918	13720	52336	48416
54580	33479	62899	33716	53668	86735	36746	21939
81840	33461	28526	96231	28082	89710	16038	26648
65144	75814	87596	04642	07590	82276	59336	84262
07719	83340	20258	49737	45499	72241	90103	96141
12283	15264	32845	55594	03668	05664	67999	06001
97049	40124	87071	03864	29526	42888	09057	82966
82863	59616	60664	76761	84417	72560	77869	42603
43963	52136	60923	88568	55458	87335	81939	67361
67813	68131	56695	93253	71650	81735	13302	30319
99813	67091	56997	62005	95516	34011	52035	79500
27813	74783	56696	84101	93852	12016	20869	57009
78813	77887	66697	51048	28395	62626	42911	99130
01813	81541	66913	52874	10563	59450	16885	16009
48194	65899	26244	74431	24232	33299	58332	18314
49946	76235	92633	10232	84241	66467	86018	92272
05590	55237	21695	31870	48893	94058	88943	77040
68980	56907	77188	54803	67622	57968	78532	66688
65980	66320	77327	14715	24759	08145	28077	32303
57980	66157	27797	55887	57788	29337	73409	35682
39980	71150	87282	01585	25850	46138	21777	97555
11661	81574	05903	25909	38638	32196	41345	22152
14141	97911	89418	97980	49571	60483	94714	51753
03701	94321	23777	61546	21541	69603	61768	40328
40701	05185	23280	04945	49801	98051	77848	62320
35701	00250	23508	51246	09460	02313	71279	74223
40701	06155	23784	68961	34289	04531	12752	08516
83701	10257	33945	08795	30976	14017	59161	31388

Line \ Col.	(1)	(2)	(3)	(4)	(5)	(6)
801	33993	51249	78123	16507	57399	77922
802	39041	05779	74278	75301	01779	60768
803	56011	26839	38501	03321	43259	73148
804	07397	95853	45764	43803	76659	57736
805	74998	53337	13860	89430	95825	65893
806	59572	95893	69765	43597	90570	60909
807	74645	13920	28640	00127	04261	17650
808	42765	23855	38451	11462	32671	52126
809	66561	56130	30356	54034	53996	98874
810	50670	13172	31460	20224	34193	59458
811	53971	08701	38356	36149	10891	05178
812	47177	03085	37432	94053	87057	61859
813	41494	89270	48063	12253	00383	96010
814	07409	32874	03514	84943	74421	86708
815	03097	12212	43093	46224	14431	15065
816	34722	88896	59205	18004	96431	41366
817	48117	83879	52509	29339	87735	97499
818	14628	89161	66972	19180	40852	91738
819	61512	79376	88184	29415	50716	93393
820	99954	55656	01946	57035	64418	29700
821	61455	28229	82511	11622	60786	18442
822	10398	50239	70191	37585	98373	04651
823	59075	81492	40669	16391	12148	38538
824	91497	76797	82557	55301	61570	69577
825	74619	62316	80041	53053	81252	32739
826	12536	80792	44581	12616	49740	86946
827	10246	49556	07610	59950	34387	70013
828	92506	24397	19145	24185	24479	70118
829	65745	27223	22831	39446	65808	95534
830	01707	04494	48168	58480	74983	63091
831	66959	80109	88908	38759	80716	36340
832	79278	02746	50718	90196	28394	82035
833	11343	22312	41379	22297	71703	78729
834	40415	10553	65932	34938	43977	39262
835	72774	25480	30264	08291	93796	22281
836	75886	86543	47020	14493	38363	64238
837	64628	20234	07967	46676	42907	60909
838	45905	77701	98976	70056	80502	68650
839	77691	00408	64191	11006	39212	26862
840	39172	12824	43379	57590	45307	72206
841	67120	01558	99762	79752	17139	52265
842	88264	85390	92841	63811	64423	50910
843	78097	59495	45090	74592	47474	56157
844	41888	69798	82296	09312	04150	07616
845	46618	07254	28714	18244	53214	39560
846	29213	42101	25089	11881	77558	72738
847	38601	25735	04726	36544	67842	93937
848	92207	10011	64210	77096	00011	79218
849	30610	13236	33241	68731	30955	40587
850	74544	72806	62226	65685	37996	00377

(7)	(8)	(9)	(10)	(11)	(12)	(13)	(14)
38198	63494	00278	30782	33119	64943	17239	69020
22023	07510	67883	55288	67391	54188	31913	29733
43615	49093	91641	77179	50837	48734	85187	41210
44801	45623	23714	69657	87971	24757	94493	78723
96572	73975	19577	87947	23962	78235	64839	73456
06478	77692	30911	08272	81887	57749	02952	51524
34050	78788	57948	36189	88382	72324	59253	30258
23800	02691	57034	34532	19711	71567	90495	55980
78001	29707	91938	72016	16429	69726	41990	33673
24410	01366	68825	22798	52873	18370	15577	63271
55653	31553	20037	39346	28591	13505	04446	92130
97943	81113	62161	11369	54419	58886	89956	12857
41457	54657	46881	75255	29242	07537	53186	95083
34267	66071	62262	99391	61245	95839	75203	93984
18267	60039	62089	38572	70988	17279	05469	28591
50982	92400	59369	43605	26404	04176	05106	08366
42848	81449	80024	81312	59469	91169	70851	90165
23920	75518	32041	13411	61334	52386	33582	72143
96220	82277	64510	43374	09107	28813	41848	08813
99242	42586	11583	82768	44966	39192	82144	05810
36508	98936	19050	57242	33045	54278	21720	87812
67804	84062	27380	75486	63171	24529	60070	66939
73873	68596	25538	83646	61066	45210	24182	18687
23301	31921	09862	73089	69329	41916	41165	34503
65201	92165	93792	30912	59105	76944	70998	00317
41819	85104	25705	92481	95287	61769	29390	05764
64460	96719	43056	24268	23303	19863	43644	76986
42708	54311	95989	08402	77608	98356	47034	01635
03348	11435	24166	62726	99878	59302	81164	08010
81027	72579	67249	48089	34219	71727	86665	94975
30082	43295	37551	18531	43903	94975	31049	19033
03255	39574	41483	12450	32494	65192	54772	97431
65082	57759	79579	41516	46248	37348	34631	88164
95828	98617	27401	50226	17322	44024	23133	57899
51434	66771	20118	00502	07738	31841	90200	46348
16322	45503	90723	35607	43715	85751	15888	80645
73293	38588	31035	12226	37746	45008	43271	32015
24469	15574	40018	90057	96540	47174	03943	37553
99863	58155	66052	96864	61790	11064	49308	94510
53283	75882	93451	44830	06300	45456	49567	51673
97997	66806	55559	62043	51324	32423	88325	99634
38189	88183	56625	22910	52250	70491	71111	37202
88287	47032	66341	38328	70538	91105	12056	36125
34572	83202	58691	27354	37015	11278	49697	65667
68753	16825	48639	38228	95166	53649	05071	26894
57234	28458	74313	29665	97366	94714	48704	07033
68745	62979	97750	28293	75851	08362	71546	17993
52123	29841	76145	82364	55774	15462	44555	26844
45206	11949	28295	12666	98479	82498	49195	46254
59917	91100	07993	15046	51303	19515	25055	56386

Line \ Col.	(1)	(2)	(3)	(4)	(5)	(6)
851	76385	05431	82252	79850	31192	86315
852	08059	15958	10514	86124	29817	19044
853	30636	03463	50326	69684	38422	59826
854	23794	51463	67574	48953	73512	46239
855	01117	60216	29314	65537	84029	00741
856	29527	19577	01414	35290	70174	37019
857	64236	24229	17970	92022	64164	17873
858	92331	30325	61918	71623	38040	51375
859	93454	37190	23790	40058	03758	01774
860	17101	42181	45798	68745	24190	16539
861	30742	93358	95730	52535	34404	76057
862	02472	01280	67106	47893	93551	76697
863	80718	72187	67178	77179	06212	37409
864	85406	73687	02116	57637	94701	46754
865	00563	67156	88141	13491	92592	35746
866	89190	58965	55213	24337	58807	36123
867	01438	81590	83758	45361	76209	65081
868	79127	53282	50510	80129	23960	78423
869	33952	92823	32840	94420	51193	69652
870	57146	14126	71734	56942	83371	31526
871	33158	61761	73207	01764	81696	55137
872	63615	69083	00118	47991	99521	88655
873	89010	46915	70186	55657	76955	25430
874	32547	43398	30909	62599	53105	27460
875	61992	28258	27359	61002	16882	44018
876	78326	74541	22198	48380	45919	76160
877	35493	53008	78622	38329	27611	12327
878	19130	59917	28850	76593	02389	80759
879	00317	05769	03497	42174	32653	23663
880	84122	36454	70776	17000	83017	07027
881	76320	32120	91585	39640	23470	86000
882	09234	36233	94404	42812	39210	25967
883	16206	70598	95378	70573	42636	53862
884	04071	51662	67884	73911	08708	66287
885	97545	87732	23795	38027	90239	80044
886	53253	56120	42720	25660	36921	30891
887	66817	18439	53188	35155	24309	88284
888	28077	26409	11443	22200	23129	32407
889	18889	00291	13701	12401	26466	67700
890	10598	64974	66296	33329	30560	73380
891	18656	81152	45498	14400	92435	67664
892	79044	10440	25777	05486	65659	22183
893	74042	20365	42672	34850	60670	56980
894	87249	06640	09090	03242	68467	85678
895	82839	52537	00518	60559	43669	44297
896	07749	62249	01611	43795	17129	44447
897	37171	34598	87234	28324	85927	23465
898	55432	45030	85336	49128	40487	63959
899	43658	35437	83506	11209	24770	87123
900	59536	79475	04874	50831	16996	04750

(7)	(8)	(9)	(10)	(11)	(12)	(13)	(14)
75612	59985	76421	39300	64976	27951	17855	02220
03555	80725	67857	31395	68780	16560	79952	41739
47858	90601	50834	88109	43882	15687	06212	19886
10953	04622	60650	35048	34705	90502	31011	81004
40851	96344	13861	43421	57107	60813	06877	52161
80223	62206	22928	63414	03940	02188	20345	13183
41189	28240	60697	26495	87634	75899	09741	84939
91127	93903	83715	93244	04366	57679	70829	90088
90696	81674	53791	15559	42798	46892	57960	06575
32330	21732	65547	94356	38651	35102	16327	17886
21325	87526	93020	94861	83865	61393	89645	00773
56598	67982	77376	33312	58893	69370	59118	95277
48788	68930	21672	88783	59304	82369	19410	93050
54019	96344	93343	47764	57490	21321	29075	40086
72117	37593	72780	78271	75915	85972	58615	71755
09235	95541	96979	03336	34380	66288	98659	46572
34785	68423	04408	73827	78494	02765	46174	83192
31988	78571	79458	95043	23997	97528	21631	63898
04332	81675	64644	68673	33718	02256	34414	87710
13444	11912	03152	66411	42853	08437	35667	26251
41834	81860	81310	14711	36599	78042	62086	41752
94451	67445	99377	75528	40794	30140	82298	85868
91951	56473	34225	68103	25353	89595	04715	20102
56734	41954	47696	82113	38508	88941	49983	36899
85376	66756	14395	66865	67036	78374	43612	44134
10974	03127	58980	18350	22089	54977	94019	84739
52541	00861	62380	65890	79729	99710	64836	43706
18481	02724	57578	35705	89265	25033	13767	95888
29569	36342	85908	29572	60063	41170	59957	14755
98058	41274	22476	27436	30798	62287	21235	00249
68204	23980	17625	53197	35128	76385	02848	61680
12232	38195	16649	96739	64610	96067	89561	15772
81334	65439	28858	97619	59608	61460	00581	43226
89261	73451	81146	77733	70162	42449	44755	56401
64677	47912	82144	85918	93508	05816	57549	74831
42042	80370	97880	62507	01218	19202	22323	81363
74644	25454	19606	61460	52684	36568	68108	45653
52401	78416	63693	35633	77724	86835	89829	81383
55805	63818	16067	95185	97241	66126	16774	39342
94905	04959	80213	14228	97242	94826	64276	37466
86229	74358	76537	87066	42293	91743	49462	42808
82080	04351	19530	49941	29181	34667	28910	70927
88333	75288	64996	26913	62379	55068	91239	85752
23411	53443	19526	03205	29261	36061	34325	03761
75071	17146	35492	60718	38106	06409	75657	66013
95197	25088	22150	54427	11578	77560	26460	55002
80833	62872	40826	10066	64858	33605	24848	30881
25879	60415	26744	38584	51543	17333	47300	13834
21494	85056	56630	75919	26005	90077	50380	09261
02246	08846	82410	50997	45824	55547	08168	16679

Line \ Col.	(1)	(2)	(3)	(4)	(5)	(6)
901	77583	63193	14378	66314	92154	31173
902	41435	82033	40363	74800	79198	03991
903	17163	74517	11281	83105	16146	27577
904	47909	53647	99896	13016	53708	18549
905	88024	64045	70954	56434	73860	50310
906	51540	26148	65528	66246	74154	47254
907	29122	04072	85663	33914	63587	20151
908	34873	53537	85834	11394	44898	92403
909	26132	07856	14223	02824	66094	88093
910	26892	74387	97124	32851	83465	51300
911	73485	32215	29894	87362	47818	52494
912	45678	13831	93961	93558	34050	42936
913	71687	79185	46096	22818	19051	39123
914	11833	28572	61695	36928	50851	98599
915	90529	59895	55565	57955	75623	55721
916	31697	92763	05134	45963	15725	39771
917	47212	92010	40601	23364	72705	15989
918	56686	61285	36139	18867	12877	89109
919	50669	06740	74638	62054	53083	22790
920	16821	64195	64269	62235	41829	93374
921	30608	94750	38092	42230	85443	34743
922	83211	45796	33370	31291	76074	40065
923	51774	53905	66945	65882	70352	38447
924	89095	90943	76279	78323	37210	77141
925	54047	41638	45626	98549	20648	89365
926	81549	98773	68979	28308	53686	57192
927	72335	08233	56777	99798	57340	54203
928	02540	14032	90858	26020	28174	91563
929	09226	10658	79614	84200	53035	16839
930	18050	79976	70461	19890	08214	77015
931	44378	42627	16636	69923	89122	92792
932	92101	13475	15373	53642	77422	26662
933	27926	69613	88880	95537	08518	66627
934	06900	75222	25385	63569	03483	90973
935	08717	31244	56529	97336	17309	32629
936	79966	02658	18012	59422	86272	69447
937	85668	03060	61274	14020	16594	72642
938	29530	85435	54205	01781	88806	28369
939	69284	91923	11744	13051	69350	55403
940	41503	48684	36452	06825	80218	76395
941	47063	45686	78929	82808	67899	16936
942	90503	44995	53753	88362	99077	14510
943	08367	68828	82856	56380	26969	16987
944	05207	94071	56234	12584	21319	90050
945	15445	53683	92875	02502	48973	00564
946	99603	19507	68314	12524	57700	39240
947	82736	02198	84682	18512	42010	69026
948	04925	66489	08883	69176	95712	25057
949	48692	63679	55426	75873	21338	78242
950	23766	44510	30176	02784	65111	89090

(7)	(8)	(9)	(10)	(11)	(12)	(13)	(14)
75223	92947	81041	91385	89091	83989	34982	66565
01635	43666	02630	46039	53273	86262	91450	79883
33565	39621	27321	06387	51838	37591	54290	54527
75241	22312	53261	80185	69888	12646	64464	98505
29601	52204	93295	05735	15486	39857	83584	59587
65546	75309	90415	17346	20559	29568	30124	11974
36720	25827	13447	17082	74817	92523	81519	65724
01979	22785	94354	33271	44579	40756	70108	30514
35794	69015	67498	97087	25936	52239	07472	74585
58546	12579	43451	48661	79351	58231	11824	77723
27684	83573	91237	03585	13266	63905	94600	43823
00860	66594	36783	56939	47057	55257	16555	65642
08793	18798	79528	05621	12131	88365	51154	46175
76466	73848	76675	68072	50077	27709	60895	55306
43773	98277	38842	05069	31590	31482	38040	71541
54430	76890	52975	52037	06071	14710	84160	05126
02965	78394	53956	48542	35568	09897	20287	54478
48963	58636	18825	47664	74509	53250	61778	43202
82404	85132	17634	35664	26876	54191	61412	08062
74377	17728	84164	32762	18275	91425	96275	97711
00348	36016	74853	00499	03387	07739	96416	28578
50006	74244	44355	96978	79518	51941	26627	39503
50881	25003	88424	98825	47209	16332	48104	50130
50200	95786	00463	82949	55660	93650	41134	43309
10934	10799	37862	71684	98288	94592	70961	51028
65423	47225	27490	78045	57512	11431	50502	11301
12334	16800	91872	82213	79086	33896	31707	48739
65006	14401	58189	32658	13812	72382	19169	24151
83058	55540	32716	03834	05299	58331	90479	34808
86657	29965	21658	72049	74959	95217	71503	74950
95380	20397	06649	02752	46279	99681	05154	56400
58069	86649	38783	30050	20087	26681	05859	41218
61173	27188	55705	29607	24361	83286	00052	41181
86572	53485	23353	18345	24553	43494	84651	48483
34184	47240	07490	86150	78423	82309	01762	33463
45731	19344	49685	95236	60922	09665	50176	98674
59596	70634	58195	78404	80798	60696	00686	75274
69095	26496	77711	62699	92045	74777	97537	69768
75969	64260	42303	54467	61374	22426	70625	96732
85109	67756	71072	04047	38520	31872	00118	84181
94990	90513	44712	51443	78685	61446	11529	64531
95018	53155	71938	99420	15408	44461	27981	90368
20563	11277	42307	32736	99532	65361	64300	76678
20768	27895	83856	69778	39159	68796	17739	30795
70805	92775	34093	00317	34349	79168	87667	98240
96194	11150	67555	95582	47540	91542	35023	35235
15920	14305	46477	35022	30006	35516	48513	09493
80789	87303	24848	46375	92999	26747	77435	49786
14907	30788	79299	34428	88050	39956	35155	55514
99467	74257	98806	10498	63125	99067	24489	32313

Line \ Col.	(1)	(2)	(3)	(4)	(5)	(6)
951	17222	24847	14225	43238	39943	20269
952	51117	86027	85128	33442	59152	67511
953	98122	85707	47835	60583	81100	24151
954	07079	03751	09486	74453	95050	28861
955	91827	97079	74080	85168	67841	92785
956	63924	46330	97808	84837	61032	98609
957	27527	61690	11334	66616	74361	26430
958	62640	79415	84174	76251	22673	44026
959	24485	14761	49553	21948	82300	95215
960	31163	12555	57763	73074	54090	95819
961	75829	90951	85627	98027	69242	44145
962	50265	07807	43138	62890	82977	38769
963	71200	80801	81289	44767	02901	61530
964	88107	27970	99234	22295	36871	14761
965	61197	02791	14924	93662	36173	00145
966	83405	26615	87854	03164	98061	64144
967	02276	39832	64484	17204	96556	46324
968	13020	23251	09546	06687	39893	85402
969	50766	20504	47573	87991	62684	10921
970	74813	19126	38598	77307	59250	62431
971	34150	68179	87177	64247	40979	62952
972	95035	52598	27655	90383	76468	08022
973	76846	66076	01650	77548	03009	48350
974	24146	49880	75124	54340	74297	31307
975	27427	83596	07262	58388	43212	81674
976	62277	00386	94965	57568	04965	52742
977	26218	09494	96963	28005	15942	13443
978	95828	98777	58855	21092	97414	28481
979	06052	32502	47874	51676	13316	43804
980	79103	19996	36294	42929	95081	45359
981	69040	75170	31286	93852	19394	43743
982	02688	26065	29875	54689	12247	67229
983	59669	62317	56242	90656	43992	64306
984	03409	78084	23818	21489	87944	11732
985	05188	62591	48883	62080	49460	32772
986	91857	24665	14441	83430	90899	23068
987	78853	88643	78621	02377	02253	06181
988	57803	03002	43966	52273	88993	47814
989	20414	62347	23572	02107	86764	95612
990	76748	64133	70898	44429	28121	56265
991	98506	47155	93726	32281	64505	56978
992	54242	81976	67665	70890	07185	20131
993	81990	00775	05836	34512	64536	69060
994	44250	04275	16365	24813	43750	62646
995	27942	19415	30541	10707	42525	84144
996	64300	38752	56657	85280	28224	84314
997	14653	08589	09404	81557	16276	63464
998	95087	67947	29851	06124	04054	73563
999	08774	32723	44960	29042	94665	36955
1000	37039	97547	64673	31546	99314	66854

(7)	(8)	(9)	(10)	(11)	(12)	(13)	(14)
52593	99929	69993	66806	16035	74175	04974	75631
36916	93946	25402	53934	83623	18774	21413	37540
58693	46274	83783	68899	42100	14798	30325	01988
19001	56932	51925	60421	43291	13854	87524	26618
85584	97685	18369	02716	04330	45215	67343	98098
67177	96231	44689	05224	72408	37347	30369	45386
06353	29841	87500	03627	42526	26924	64139	45052
59218	78743	90058	54715	88307	88689	51172	47812
58519	81521	21773	21559	07775	96603	12156	58338
02558	92149	15685	15315	84154	89401	53301	70641
74974	58554	71020	36095	41778	51657	99796	93408
11754	81428	56568	40473	43510	66127	10806	57208
67617	50078	88909	40539	31521	68964	47991	59963
74494	02770	94610	89209	52688	92319	56341	04119
81019	63834	09891	16660	20541	48016	48620	66704
81948	49844	07816	04927	68917	11008	96965	74719
12068	68780	30396	01443	36666	76408	18082	19438
96369	71504	04242	80485	66151	39141	52873	13346
29624	44384	82938	30828	72266	20455	32794	18715
25603	49204	72792	87154	34140	45891	44767	55879
88828	81184	83310	49826	78268	84810	34755	76708
90814	78356	95077	65538	77477	12978	72000	34428
61844	17850	10898	75323	23270	74928	29066	50899
87627	14922	55793	78307	61406	73263	29927	21784
09745	74206	19310	11767	88334	52762	50280	77990
85423	87258	25805	97116	03662	40715	26670	51038
96330	50222	50856	27308	78353	83501	28171	69667
39244	80530	45700	78547	36536	86420	71140	25607
85364	25972	77144	32777	81828	16275	99252	28637
82772	10679	34236	27171	90309	42230	97146	91977
79837	38978	99397	91989	25596	24940	91964	97249
69268	72790	59095	68115	52432	03486	47945	00001
01038	22952	49953	72014	05599	06801	92765	39212
69494	98213	41356	65383	25792	96224	57038	19936
09094	13547	94514	38094	93755	39313	56688	30338
39436	65648	90795	04028	44670	88737	54796	80249
15150	41361	65890	86631	08289	15996	31647	89466
41363	97015	32977	09224	77829	77519	42395	21926
22638	02471	49752	86400	21017	92299	36523	28074
53054	85704	25631	56706	54899	25569	71394	48333
48469	71323	70581	72004	67535	79545	88388	46777
73487	53010	31677	34437	88622	03580	41811	40951
23223	57511	61764	85828	21119	66098	83996	70640
97455	01174	23358	71401	28580	92308	62973	72123
17237	38447	76318	03660	59959	76447	37567	66990
58118	97734	35701	06593	03690	50302	97271	97034
79223	12993	51056	57233	75099	31082	01867	25094
67625	44199	40748	52598	76137	26030	34138	76445
46376	14300	13280	88986	81039	34211	38168	67630
97855	99965	26373	61701	24760	52014	96547	65403

Line \ Col.	(1)	(2)	(3)	(4)	(5)	(6)
1001	25145	84834	23009	51584	66754	77785
1002	98433	54725	18864	65866	76918	78825
1003	97965	68548	81545	82933	93545	85959
1004	78049	67830	14624	17563	25697	07734
1005	50203	25658	91478	08509	23308	48130
1006	40059	67825	18934	64998	49807	71126
1007	84350	67241	54031	34535	04093	35062
1008	30954	51637	91500	48722	60988	60029
1009	86723	36464	98305	08009	00866	29255
1010	50188	22554	86160	92250	14021	63859
1011	50014	00463	13906	35936	71761	95755
1012	66023	21428	14742	94674	23308	58533
1013	04458	61862	63119	09541	01715	87901
1014	57510	36314	30458	09712	37714	95482
1015	43373	58939	95848	28288	60341	52174
1016	40704	48823	65963	39359	12717	56201
1017	07318	44623	00843	33299	59872	86774
1018	94550	23299	45557	07923	75126	00808
1019	34348	81191	21027	77087	10909	03676
1020	92277	57115	50789	68111	75305	58289
1021	61500	12763	64433	02268	57905	72347
1022	78938	71312	99705	71546	42274	23915
1023	64287	93218	35793	43671	64055	88729
1024	35314	29631	06937	54546	04470	75463
1025	96864	11554	70445	24841	04779	76774
1026	96093	58302	52236	64756	50273	61566
1027	16623	17849	96701	94971	94758	08845
1028	50848	93982	66451	32143	05441	10399
1029	48006	58200	98367	66577	68583	21108
1030	56640	27890	28825	96509	21363	53657
1031	01554	40592	26557	79189	81099	03951
1032	63799	48415	28087	17196	42784	58377
1033	77654	05943	43283	63181	72300	50360
1034	51058	95654	72648	60349	59563	59021
1035	14982	68789	41999	84797	17743	18775
1036	22305	50900	77277	32383	41723	35868
1037	51375	62050	18718	88109	36767	27440
1038	14590	70151	63862	02246	33710	46456
1039	60312	56009	52588	65722	46072	26273
1040	48513	62172	46711	56744	52250	95301
1041	19052	03511	71346	50933	10108	19747
1042	11246	92882	40354	14700	66716	93470
1043	34268	97508	69711	07165	69844	07591
1044	22931	31857	95595	48438	78029	07045
1045	11476	16553	10297	23643	06192	72478
1046	57005	88551	02117	87827	00151	39027
1047	76056	48776	41451	27779	86241	63562
1048	11961	67214	64606	51982	87588	67464
1049	28009	20616	02614	15759	65618	92266
1050	09194	83950	36645	00734	74652	87328

(7)	(8)	(9)	(10)	(11)	(12)	(13)	(14)
52357	25532	46346	39806	70361	41836	33098	03790
58210	76835	72248	43023	85884	08785	41152	11830
63282	61454	27337	10560	76390	36976	62785	77529
48243	94318	85992	15716	48891	74601	90030	82376
65047	77873	02912	52675	62971	40993	79767	19178
77818	56893	06714	25147	69782	56399	55494	29547
58168	14205	87257	59443	29927	30667	99040	61060
60873	37423	62206	78386	10008	03027	69882	99663
18514	49158	93679	84854	27953	73627	45315	94563
16237	72296	86715	17588	24327	69905	43592	52283
87002	71667	21899	50605	44017	48019	01348	33230
26507	11208	85354	34288	33031	06081	45402	54274
91260	03079	17350	91991	46955	16951	42276	18627
30507	68475	49167	54279	89734	24807	23802	60439
11879	18115	91925	93506	10331	52809	06032	98707
22811	24863	62130	86396	12606	40352	44181	56860
06926	12672	23096	62738	48877	98889	77375	72317
01312	46689	56900	74653	65614	94333	44775	42054
97723	34469	08852	51465	38544	25247	00105	14825
39751	45760	76922	62810	47392	47765	69009	41520
49498	21871	80128	71588	34936	93724	47479	30366
38906	18779	96970	81430	77457	90793	53509	79535
11168	60260	97668	29687	78958	71480	75638	32812
77112	77126	46942	35873	21104	70323	07091	25408
96129	73594	67259	08958	45986	91442	28529	91358
61962	93280	54750	91572	22825	35238	34955	77692
32280	59823	97638	63913	81772	20605	13104	86762
17775	74169	04324	00195	97321	71104	70286	44675
41361	20732	39538	95746	91363	37416	08833	72639
60119	75385	83475	94949	94360	64076	24305	66042
60438	94263	21708	82714	33487	15713	24149	90641
02026	79893	28219	95848	29099	68424	97854	87967
38411	08823	83158	85734	18917	92697	20102	13956
18616	93244	67666	36344	60506	10937	69837	92511
61437	55258	36401	21686	20416	77429	99664	16803
61829	75281	73850	09094	10748	87175	35537	42489
73438	87774	65688	13701	38111	44531	10728	25248
50225	35742	46423	27373	95388	90238	81178	95956
32049	89647	81900	49167	81910	98790	66208	92721
20401	96558	22600	59000	44669	97303	25080	61986
84712	35431	27652	36130	67396	98295	58395	54493
48587	12514	20234	20769	86575	53071	84995	46531
64588	58016	26532	17957	59119	70048	14130	72848
04453	46783	97341	34526	02731	34808	65028	61054
75968	23807	70533	73805	64118	60682	17286	45369
66060	38915	55240	10473	52382	74523	13452	18918
98013	21109	57835	56161	76084	85338	65491	85719
54389	52910	37447	71173	85880	06581	73833	62987
13545	39578	36021	09262	71240	16627	28570	44003
53507	71924	47057	83163	16248	76396	17886	46311

Index

A

B

C

D

M

N

P

R

S

T

U

V

W

Z